Public Finance and Public Policy

Responsibilities and Limitations of Government: Second Edition

This book is the second edition of *Public Finance and Public Policy* (2003). The second edition retains the first edition's themes of investigation of responsibilities and limitations of government but has been rewritten and restructured. Public-choice and political-economy concepts and political and bureaucratic principal–agent problems that are the sources of limitations on government are introduced at the beginning for application to later topics. Concepts of behavioral economics and experimental results are integrated throughout this edition. Asymmetric information is a recurring theme. The book begins with the efficiency case for the competitive market and the minimal responsibility of government to ensure the rule of law. Subsequent chapters address questions concerning institutions and governance, public goods, taxation and bond financing of public spending, market corrections (externalities and paternalist public policies), voting, social justice, entitlements, and choice of the structure of taxation and the tax base. The final chapter summarizes evidence on and reasons for the growth of government and considers how trust or social capital affects the need for government. The purpose of the book is to provide an accessible introduction to the choice between relying only on personal decisions in markets and the use of public finance and public policy by governments to improve on market outcomes.

Arye L. Hillman is William Gittes Professor of Economics at Bar-Ilan University in Israel. He has taught at Princeton University, the University of California in Los Angeles, and Australian National University and has been an invited lecturer at universities in various countries. Professor Hillman received his Ph.D. in economics from the University of Pennsylvania. His professional research includes studies under the auspices of the International Monetary Fund and the World Bank. He is a former president of the European Public Choice Society. Professor Hillman was jointly awarded the Max Planck Prize in Economics for his contributions to political economy.

ADDITIONAL PRAISE FOR *PUBLIC FINANCE AND PUBLIC POLICY, Second Edition*

"This book provides a comprehensive and accessible account of the core issues in public finance and public policy. Although designed as a textbook, the book is also an organizing guide for practitioners and policymakers, who will find particularly useful the application of concepts to issues in income support and work incentives, education, health care, and the choice between tax financing and user prices."

– Sanjeev Gupta, *Fiscal Affairs Department, International Monetary Fund, Washington, DC*

"This fascinating book provides a clear account of the role of government through public finance and public policy. It gives a balanced and insightful analysis of the scope and limits of what government can and should do. Students will like the clear exposition, and researchers will benefit from the book as a reference volume."

– Kai Konrad, *Max Planck Institute for Intellectual Property, Competition and Tax Law, Munich*

"This book is a gem. It brings alive the topics of public finance. The book is an extraordinary piece of work that enables students to achieve a balanced overview of market failures and government failures and thereby gain mature insight into desirable interactions between the market and the state. Teachers and students will benefit from this major achievement for years to come, making this book a classic."

– Dennis Snower, *Kiel Institute for the World Economy and Christian-Albrechts University, Kiel*

Public Finance and Public Policy

Responsibilities and Limitations of Government: Second Edition

Arye L. Hillman

Bar-Ilan University, Israel

CAMBRIDGE UNIVERSITY PRESS
Cambridge, New York, Melbourne, Madrid, Cape Town, Singapore, São Paulo, Delhi

Cambridge University Press
32 Avenue of the Americas, New York, NY 10013-2473, USA

www.cambridge.org
Information on this title: www.cambridge.org/9780521738057

First published 2009

Printed in the United States of America

A catalog record for this publication is available from the British Library.

Library of Congress Cataloging in Publication data

Hillman, Arye L.
Public finance and public policy : responsibilities and limitations of government /
Arye L. Hillman. – 2nd ed.
p. cm.
Includes bibliographical references and index.
ISBN 978-0-521-49426-7 (hardback) – ISBN 978-0-521-73805-7 (pbk.)
1. Finance, Public. 2. Economic policy. 3. Taxation. I. Title.
HJ141.H53 2009
336–dc22 2008044166

ISBN 978-0-521-49426-7 hardback
ISBN 978-0-521-73805-7 paperback

For Jeannette

Tamara and Yitzi; Ilana and Hovav; Nachman Eliyahu and Galit, Benjamin and Yael

Dafna, Yishai, Mayan, Ya'ara, Dov, Ze'ev, Shani, Lior, Hallel, Harel, Raphael, Michal, Eyal, Ronni, Eliashiv, Eitan, and Libbi, and the others

In memory of my parents, for whom good government allowed a new beginning.
In memory of my brothers and my sister and all the other children.

From *Sayings of the Fathers*

The Individual and Social Justice

If I am not for myself, then who will be for me?
And if I am only for myself, then what am I?
And if not now, when?

*Hillel, 110 BCE – 20 CE**

The Individual and the Dilemma of Government

Pray for the peace of the government; for, except for the fear of that, we should have swallowed each other alive.

R. Hanina, born around the year 20 CE

Be cautious with the government, for they do not make advances to a man except for their own need. They seem like friends in the hour of their advantage, but they do not stand by a man in his hour of adversity.

Rabban Gamliel, around the year 230 CE

* *BCE and CE* are universal ways of indicating dates. *BCE* indicates before the Common Era of counting and *CE* indicates the Common Era.

Contents

Preface to the Second Edition

This book, a treatise on markets and governments, is presented as a text on public finance and public policy. The exposition incorporates concepts of public choice and political economy (which are, in large part, equivalent), as well as concepts and evidence from behavioral economics. Elements of moral philosophy are present, beginning with Adam Smith's description of virtue through personal behavior in markets and how perceptions of human nature affect views on the need for government. The book covers the basic topics of a course in public finance or public economics, or a course in the political economy of markets and governments.

The focus of the book is the achievement, whether through markets or the public finance and public policy of governments, of the social objectives of efficiency and social justice. There are objective criteria for efficiency. Social justice can be defined in different ways, as the natural right of possession, equality of opportunity, or ex-post equality of incomes after redistribution. Ideology can influence choice of the definition of social justice.

The book describes feasible policies. In particular, governments do not use lump-sum taxes. From the outset societies are shown to confront choices between the objectives of efficiency and equality.

This second edition retains the themes of the first edition. Although the themes are the same, the book has been rewritten and restructured. The objective retained from the first edition is to make ideas accessible. Economics can explain and enlighten. Yet, it is a curiosity of contemporary academic economic writings that an idea is often given more applause when the presentation is made arcane and inaccessible. This book presents in an accessible way the topics that arise when governments are called on to improve market outcomes. The book is the product of an ongoing inquiry – proceeding beyond the first edition – into the political economy of markets and government. The line of inquiry in this book has origins in my previous investigations focusing on the political economy of protection: the investigation of why governments prevent free trade is a beginning for the broader questions about markets and governments that are the topics of this book.

A course in intermediate microeconomics or price theory is a helpful prerequisite for using this book as a text, although an introductory course in economics is sufficient for many of the topics. A course in macroeconomics is not required. Questions to motivate discussion of the topics in each chapter are provided at the end of the book. For graduate students and professional readers, a guide to elaboration and more technical exposition of topics in the literature is provided at the end of each chapter.

Other than in setting out the historical perspective on the growth of government, the book does not present data on the composition of government budgets or the sources of government revenue. Such data differ, of course, among countries and also among states, cities, and localities that in fiscal-federal systems levy taxes, engage in public spending, and decide on public policies. The data, which change over time, are readily available from official sources. Issues involving data on government spending and sources of government revenue have been placed inside the topics for discussion. The topics may involve comparisons between government jurisdictions or may ask for contemporary descriptions of taxation, public spending, or public policy. The focus of the book is on ideas and concepts that will outlive the data applicable for any time – or for any place.

I thank Scott Parris of Cambridge University Press in New York for his confidence that a treatise on the need for and consequences of government could be an accessible textbook covering traditional topics of public finance and public policy.

I am thankful to the professors and instructors who chose the first edition of this book as the means for introducing students to the choice between markets and governments and for the support that took the first edition into three printings. The first edition was translated into Chinese by Wang Guohua and into Russian by Mark Levin. Toshihiro Ihori headed the team that translated the first edition into Japanese and provided insights that were incorporated into the second edition. Michael Brooks, Gene Gotwalt, and Heinrich Ursprung read the manuscript of the second edition and provided helpful suggestions. In preparing the second edition, I also benefited from helpful comments from Joel Guttman, Wolfgang Mayer, and Warren Young.

1

MARKETS AND GOVERNMENTS

The most important question in the study of economics is:

When should a society forgo the economic freedom of markets and rely on the public finance and public policy of government?

This is a *normative question.* A normative question asks what ideally *should* be done or what ideally *should* happen. Normative questions are distinct from *positive questions*, the answers to which are predictions and explanations. The primary positive question that we shall ask is:

> *What do we predict will be the outcome when voters and taxpayers delegate responsibilities to governments through public finance and public policy?*

These normative and positive questions, asked in different circumstances, are the focus of this book. We shall take care to distinguish between normative and positive questions. A clear distinction is required because we do not wish to confuse what governments ideally ought to do with what governments actually do. The two can coincide but need not.

We shall not study any one particular government – federal or central, state or provincial, or local. Descriptions of a particular government's budget and public policies become outdated when the government and the policies change. Today's government budget is not necessarily tomorrow's, nor are today's public policies necessarily the policies that will be appropriate or in place in the future. Studying the details of a particular government's budget and public policies, therefore, does not provide useful, long-lasting knowledge. Lasting knowledge requires identification of general principles that remain applicable anywhere at any time. We shall seek to identify such general principles. Our quest is for general principles that apply to societies and governments in high-income democracies; however, occasionally comparisons will be made with other types of societies and governments.

Whether through outcomes in markets or the decisions of government, we shall seek the two objectives of efficiency and social justice. These are *social objectives.* A social objective is an objective that in principle is expected to be sought by consensus. Efficiency as a first approximation requires maximizing the total income of a society. Social justice is multifaceted and involves redistribution of income, equality of opportunity, and protection of rights to life and property.

There are three social objectives sought through public finance and public policy. After efficiency and social justice, the third social objective is macroeconomic stability, expressed in avoiding inflation and unemployment and maintaining stability of the banking and financial system. We shall not study macroeconomics.

Our scope will extend beyond the narrow definition of economics as choice when resources are limited. We shall encounter *political economy*, which is the interface between economics and politics and studies the economic consequences of political decisions. We shall draw extensively on concepts of the school of *public choice*, which is the source of political economy in the modern economics literature; a characteristic of the public-choice approach to economic analysis is that all individuals, whether making decisions outside of or within government, are viewed as seeking their self-interest. We shall study outcomes of collective decisions made by voting. We shall also encounter the influence of ideology on social objectives; an ideology may give preeminence either to efficiency or social justice. The emotions and feelings that underlie views on fairness and social justice will take us to the intersection between economics and psychology known as *behavioral economics*. We also encounter *moral philosophy* and *ethics* – which is where we now begin.

1.1 The Prima Facie Case for the Market

If the social objectives of efficiency and social justice cannot be achieved through markets, governments can be asked to use public finance and public policy to attempt to improve on market outcomes. Before we consider responsibilities for governments, however, we look at outcomes of markets alone. Market outcomes provide the benchmark on which we ask governments to improve.

A. Self-interest with virtue

In markets, buyers and sellers pursue personal self-interest. Buyers maximize utility (or personal benefit) and sellers maximize profits. The decisions of buyers and sellers in markets are personal (rather than collective) and voluntary (rather than coerced). Individuals cannot lose from a personal voluntary market decision; people who perceive that they will not benefit simply can decide not to buy or sell. Buyers and sellers both gain from their personal voluntary decisions: Does the mutual benefit to buyers and sellers then imply that personal decisions in markets achieve the two social objectives of efficiency and social justice?

Adam Smith (1723–90), who is regarded as the founder of modern economics, proposed that when people seek personal benefit in markets, the ensuing market outcomes benefit society at large. Adam Smith first studied at Glasgow University in Scotland and then at Oxford University in England. After leaving Oxford (he did not receive a degree because he had been found to have read the then-banned author, David Hume), he returned to Glasgow University, where he was first a professor of logic and then subsequently a professor of moral philosophy.

It is significant that Adam Smith was a professor of moral philosophy. Moral philosophy studies ethical behavior. In his writings, Adam Smith referred to an *invisible hand* that is the source of social benefit in markets. The invisible hand transforms the quest for private benefit in markets into social benefit.[1]

[1] The "invisible hand" appeared in the books *The Theory of Moral Sentiments* published in 1759 and *An Enquiry into the Causes of the Wealth of Nations* first published in 1776.

People do not intend that their personal market decisions result in social benefit. The social benefit is unintentional: people intend only to benefit themselves. Nonetheless, the invisible hand ensures that personally decided self-interested outcomes are for the good of society.

The invisible hand thereby reconciles self-interest and virtue. People need not have guilt feelings about pursuing their own self-interest in markets and not altruistically caring about consequences of their market decisions for others.

The invisible hand also eliminates hypocrisy from market behavior. There is no reason for people to claim that they are seeking social benefit by doing favors in markets. Adam Smith observed, "I have never known much good done by those who affected to trade for the public good" (1776/1937, p. 423).[2]

B. Efficiency and competitive markets

Adam Smith viewed the invisible hand as maximizing total income for a society. Maximized total income is associated with the social objective of efficiency. The invisible hand is, of course, a metaphor. In the time that has passed since Adam Smith's writings, the need for the metaphor has been surpassed and formal proofs have confirmed that markets – in particular, competitive markets – achieve efficiency. The formal proofs differ in complexity and scope. The simplest proof, with which we now proceed, considers a single competitive market.

Social benefit and efficiency

We first define *social benefit*. With B indicating total benefit and C indicating total cost, social benefit is:

$$W = (B - C). \tag{1.1}$$

The benefit W is social because the personal benefits and costs of everyone in society are included in evaluating B and C. Next we define efficiency.

An outcome is efficient when social benefit $W = (B - C)$ is maximized.

Achieving efficiency thus requires that marginal benefit be equal to marginal cost:[3]

$$MB = MC. \tag{1.2}$$

Efficiency does not depend on who in a population benefits and incurs costs. Questions about the distribution of benefits and costs among people involve

[2] The saying "do not look a gift horse in the mouth" suggests that we should not examine too closely the quality of a gift (the teeth reveal the age and health of the horse). The invisible hand suggests, however, that we should be wary of favors offered in markets.

[3] Expression (1.2) is the first-order condition for maximum W. The second-order condition for a maximum requires that:

$$\frac{\partial MB}{\partial Q} < \frac{\partial MC}{\partial Q}.$$

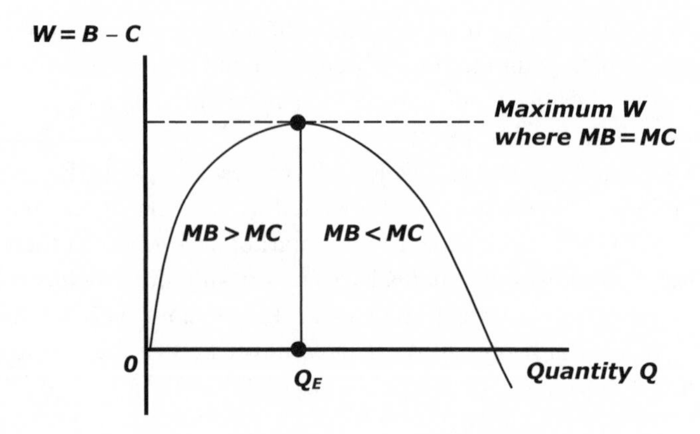

Figure 1.1. The efficient quantity that maximizes $W = (B - C)$ is Q_E.

social justice. Efficiency requires only the largest possible social benefit, independently of how benefits and costs are distributed among a population.

The definitions of *social benefit* and *efficiency* in general apply to any source of benefit or cost. We are in particular interested in benefits and costs associated with markets. When W refers to social benefit provided through a market, B is the total benefit of all buyers in the market and C is the total cost of all sellers.

Figure 1.1 shows social benefit W as depending on the total quantity of output Q supplied in a market. The efficient quantity that maximizes W is Q_E, determined in accord with expression (1.2) where $MB = MC$.[4]

Proof of the efficiency of a competitive market

In a competitive market, individual buyers and sellers do not influence price and are free to enter and leave the market. A proof of the efficiency of a competitive market has three components. The proof requires showing that:

(1) The market assigns goods among different buyers to achieve maximized total benefit, which we denote as B^{max}.
(2) The market assigns supply among different sellers to achieve minimized total costs, which we denote as C^{min}.
(3) With B^{max} and C^{min} achieved, the market also chooses a quantity such as Q_E in figure 1.1 that maximizes $W = B^{max} - C^{min}$.

We begin with buyers.

Buyers

Competitive markets have many buyers. Figure 1.2a shows two representative buyers with personal marginal benefits MB_1 and MB_2 from consumption. The

[4] In figure 1.1, the second-order condition also is satisfied at output Q_E. When $Q = 0$, also $W = 0$. When Q is sufficiently great, $W = B - C$ becomes negative because total costs exceed total benefits.

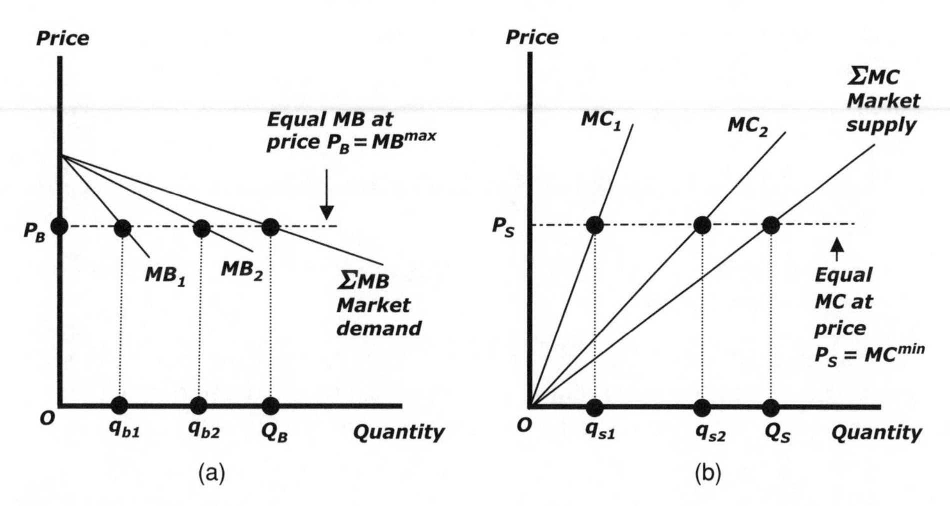

Figure 1.2. (a) B^{max} achieved through self-interested buyers' decisions. (b) C^{min} achieved through self-interested sellers' decisions.

MB functions indicate individual demands, expressed as marginal willingness to pay for additional output. Marginal willingness to pay is an amount of money. MB is therefore measured in terms of money – which can therefore be compared with marginal cost MC, which is also measured in terms of money.[5]

We now regard benefit from consumption as exclusively private or personal for each buyer. Only the buyer benefits and no one else. We shall presently define public goods from which a number of people can benefit simultaneously. In figure 1.2a, MB_1 and MB_2 decline with the quantity consumed, thereby indicating diminishing marginal benefit (or utility) from consumption.[6]

Total benefit of buyers is

$$B = B_1 + B_2, \tag{1.3}$$

which is maximized when

$$MB_1 = MB_2. \tag{1.4}$$

Expression (1.4) is a technical requirement (the first-order condition) for attaining maximal total benefit B^{max}. To prove that the market outcome for buyers is efficient, we need to show that self-interested market behavior of buyers replicates the technical requirement (1.4).

In figure 1.2a, total market demand at the price P_B confronting buyers is $Q_B = (q_{b1} + q_{b2})$. The personal quantities, q_{b1} and q_{b2}, are determined by buyers maximizing utility according to:

$$P_B = MB_1, \quad P_B = MB_2. \tag{1.5}$$

[5] Marginal utility is not measured in money but rather in terms of utility. Utility is ordinal and expresses rankings of outcomes according to preferences. Marginal willingness to pay expressed in MB is cardinally measurable in money terms. We shall refer to utility in some circumstances; for example, we describe people as making decisions to maximize utility. In general, we shall use the terms benefit and utility interchangeably.

[6] Linearity of marginal benefit is only for exposition.

It follows from expression (1.5) that self-interested utility-maximizing behavior of buyers results in:

$$MB_1 = P_B = MB_2. \tag{1.6}$$

The competitive market outcome (1.6) thus replicates the condition for efficiency (1.4). Therefore:

> *A competitive market efficiently assigns goods among buyers to maximize buyers' total benefit.*

The "assignment" of goods among buyers in a competitive market is self-assignment through personal choice. In figure 1.2a, buyers voluntarily choose the personal quantities q_{b1} and q_{b2} that maximize buyers' total benefit.

Sellers

A proof similar to that of the case of buyers shows that self-interested profit-maximizing behavior of sellers minimizes total cost of market supply. In figure 1.2b, MC_1 and MC_2 are marginal costs of two among many competitive sellers. The total cost of supply of the two sellers is

$$C = C_1 + C_2, \tag{1.7}$$

which is minimized when

$$MC_1 = MC_2. \tag{1.8}$$

Expression (1.8) is the technical requirement for achieving minimum total cost C^{min}. We now look at self-interested market behavior of sellers. In figure 1.2b, total market supply offered at price P_S confronting sellers is $Q_S = (q_{s1} + q_{s2})$. Individual sellers' profits are maximized when the sellers supply the quantities q_{s1} and q_{s2}, determined by

$$P_S = MC_1, \quad P_S = MC_2. \tag{1.9}$$

Therefore, self-interested market behavior of sellers results in:

$$MC_1 = P_S = MC_2. \tag{1.10}$$

The technical requirement (the first-order condition) for achieving minimized total cost of supply C^{min} as given by expression (1.8) is equivalent to expression (1.10), which is the consequence of self-interested market behavior of sellers. Therefore:

> *A competitive market efficiently assigns supply of goods among sellers to achieve minimized total cost.*

The assignment of supply to individual sellers is again through voluntary market decisions. That is, the assignment of supply is *self-assignment* through decisions freely made in response to the market selling price.

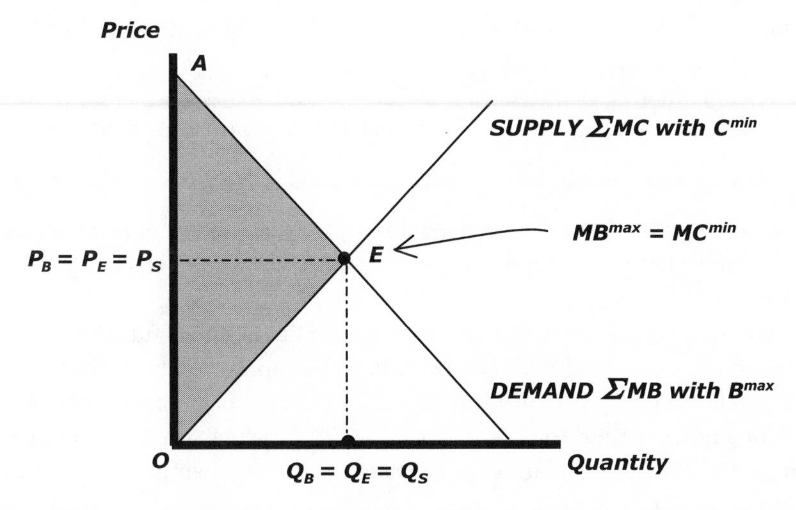

Figure 1.3. The maximum value of $W = B^{max} - C^{min}$ is indicated by the shaded area *AEO*.

The market equilibrium

The third and final condition for efficiency of market outcomes is satisfied if a competitive market maximizes:

$$W = B^{max} - C^{min}. \tag{1.11}$$

The technical requirement is:

$$MB^{max} = MC^{min}. \tag{1.12}$$

In the market shown in figure 1.3, the technical requirement (1.12) is satisfied at point *E*. We now need to show that self-interested market decisions replicate the technical requirement for efficiency (1.12).

The initial two steps of our proof of the efficiency of a competitive market indicated that, respectively, total benefit from consumption is maximized for any total quantity of output Q_B on a market demand function, while total cost of supply is minimized for any quantity of output Q_S on a market supply function. We therefore associate quantities on a market demand function with maximized total benefit to buyers B^{max} and quantities on a market supply function with minimized total cost of suppliers C^{min}. Correspondingly, as in figure 1.3, the market demand function indicates marginal benefit MB^{max} from additional consumption and the market supply function indicates marginal cost MC^{min} of additional supply.

Returning to figure 1.2a, we see that for buyers:

$$P_B = MB_1 = MB_2 \equiv \{MB^{max}\}. \tag{1.13}$$

Similarly, figure 1.2b shows that for sellers:

$$P_S = MC_1 = MC_2 \equiv \{MC^{min}\}. \tag{1.14}$$

In figure 1.3, the output supplied at point E is Q_E and the price is P_E, where:

$$Q_B = Q_E = Q_S, \quad P_B = P_E = P_S. \tag{1.15}$$

Combining expressions (1.13), (1.14), and (1.15) shows that, at point E:

$$MB^{max} = P_E = MC^{min}. \tag{1.16}$$

The outcome of self-interested behavior of buyers and sellers as described by expression (1.16) thus replicates the technical requirement (1.12) for maximized W.

At any quantity in figure 1.3, the area under the demand function measures maximized total benefit B^{max}. The area under the supply function measures minimized total cost C^{min}. The difference between the areas under the demand and supply functions is therefore $W = (B^{max} - C^{min})$, which we have indicated is maximized at point E. The maximized value of W is shown in figure 1.3 by the shaded area AEO.[7]

The competitive market-adjustment mechanism

Although we have shown that the market outcome at point E in figure 1.3 is efficient, the question remains:

How do we know that a competitive market will be at the efficient point E?

A competitive market-adjustment mechanism ensures that the market will be at point E. The point E is indeed the *equilibrium* of a competitive market.

At the quantity $Q_1 < Q_E$ in figure 1.4:

$$P_S = MC < P_B. \tag{1.17}$$

Sellers thus know that buyers' willingness to pay for additional output, given by P_B, exceeds the MC of supply. Sellers therefore increase supply beyond Q_1. At the efficient quantity Q_E at point E, buyers' willingness to pay P_B is precisely equal to suppliers' MC. Suppliers therefore no longer have an incentive to expand output.[8]

Alternatively, at a quantity such as $Q_2 > Q_E$:

$$P_S = MC > P_B. \tag{1.18}$$

[7] The shaded area above the price P_E is known as consumer surplus. The shaded area below the price P_E is known as producer surplus. In using MB to represent demand and using the area under the demand function to represent total benefit B, we rely on the substitution effect of relative price changes. There is also an income effect. For any one good, the income effect is, in general, small and the substitution effect is therefore the basis for a good approximation to total benefit (see Willig, 1976). Income effects will be introduced and explained where income effects have consequences that we wish to emphasize. When income effects are introduced, all goods will be regarded as normal goods (for which demand increases when income increases).

[8] In general, after we proceed beyond the proof of the efficiency of competitive markets, we shall use MB and MC without adding the respective superscripts *max* and *min*. We then take for granted that MB refers to the equal marginal benefit of buyers that has maximized total benefit B and that MC indicates the equal marginal cost of suppliers that has minimized total cost C.

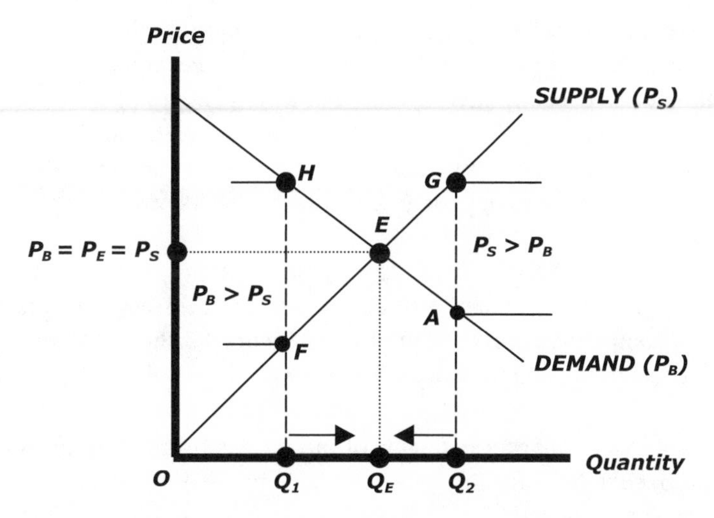

Figure 1.4. The competitive market-adjustment mechanism.

Buyers are therefore willing to pay less than sellers' *MC* of supply and the output supplied falls. The fall in output again ceases at the efficient quantity Q_E at point *E*.

If quantity Q_1 were supplied in figure 1.4, there would be an efficiency loss equal to the area *HEF*. If the quantity Q_2 were supplied, the efficiency loss would be *GEA*.[9] The competitive market-adjustment mechanism does not allow such efficiency losses to persist because the market will not remain at inefficient *disequilibrium* outputs such as Q_1 or Q_2 but will move to the efficient, stable *equilibrium* output Q_E.

We therefore conclude:

> *A competitive market-adjustment mechanism ensures that the market moves to and remains at the efficient market equilibrium.*

How do prices in competitive markets change?

If individual buyers and sellers cannot influence the market price, how do prices in a competitive market change? The inability of individual buyers and sellers to influence price in a competitive market applies only at the equilibrium output Q_E. In figure 1.4, at $Q_1 < Q_E$, sellers are approached by buyers who offer to pay $P_B > P_S = MC$. Sellers therefore can increase the price P_S at which they sell, knowing that buyers will pay. As the price P_S increases, so does the quantity supplied, until the equilibrium quantity Q_E is reached. At Q_E, because $P_S = P_B$, a seller cannot increase price and find buyers willing to buy. Alternatively, at

[9] In figure 1.4, the area HEQ_EQ_1 is the total benefit from supply of the additional output $(Q_E - Q_1)$ that is required to reach the equilibrium output Q_E. The area FEQ_EQ_1 is the total cost of supplying this additional output. The difference is *HEF*, which therefore is the net gain from supply of the efficient output Q_E rather than Q_1. By similar reasoning, *EGA* is the net gain from supply of Q_E rather than Q_2.

$Q_2 > Q_E$ in figure 1.4, sellers approach buyers and offer to sell at $P_S = MC > P_B$. However, the selling price is too high for buyers to be prepared to buy. That is, the selling price exceeds buyers' marginal willingness to pay. To find buyers, sellers need to reduce their selling price P_S. The reduction in the selling price takes place and the output supplied falls until the equilibrium price P_E is attained where buyers are willing to pay the price at which sellers offer to supply.

Confirmation of the social benefit of the invisible hand

We have now confirmed that the three conditions necessary for efficiency are satisfied in a competitive market equilibrium. Figure 1.5 shows the simultaneous fulfillment of the following three conditions.

(1) Self-interested market behavior of buyers has resulted in maximized total benefit B^{max} for any quantity Q demanded in the market. The slope of B^{max} is MB^{max}.

(2) Self-interested market behavior of sellers has resulted in minimized total cost C^{min} for any quantity Q supplied. The slope of C^{min} is MC^{min}.

(3) $W = B^{max} - C^{min}$ is maximized at the equilibrium market quantity Q_E, where $Q_B = Q_S$. At the equilibrium market quantity Q_E, buyers and sellers face the common equilibrium price P_E. We see that $P_E = MB^{max}$ and $P_E = MC^{min}$ and, therefore, that W is maximized because $MB^{max} = MC^{min}$.[10]

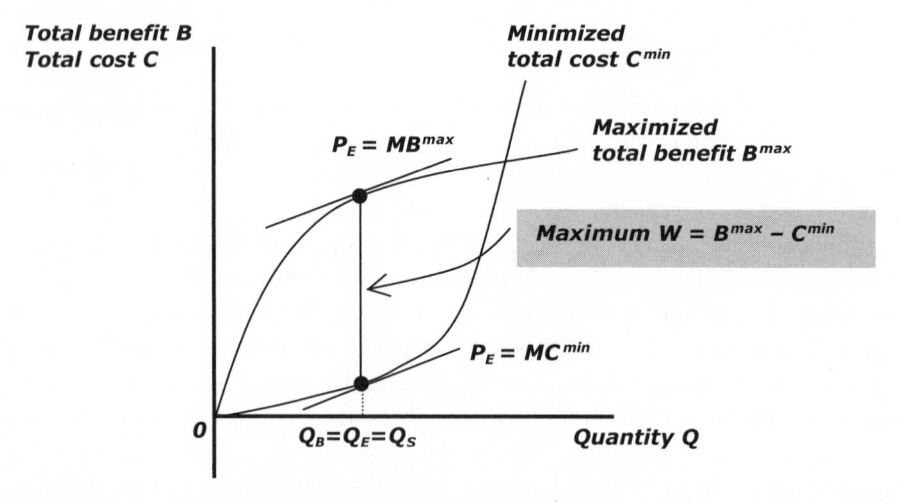

Figure 1.5. A competitive market achieves B^{max} and C^{min} and maximizes $W = B^{max} - C^{min}$.

[10] In figure 1.5, MB (the slope of B^{max}) is declining and MC (the slope of C^{min}) is increasing, indicating that the second-order condition for a maximum of W is satisfied.

We conclude that, as Adam Smith predicted using the metaphor of the invisible hand:

> *Buyers and sellers making self-interested decisions in a competitive market achieve efficiency.*

Normative and positive questions about competitive markets

We have asked and answered a normative and a positive question about competitive markets. The normative question has been:

> *Is the equilibrium outcome of a competitive market efficient?*

The positive question has been:

> *Can we predict that a competitive market will be at the efficient outcome?*

We have affirmative answers to both questions.

Supplement S1A: Market efficiency in general equilibrium

Our proof of market efficiency is based on a single competitive market. A view of a single market is called *partial-equilibrium analysis* because of the partial single-market picture of economic activity. *General-equilibrium analysis*, in contrast, includes all markets in an economy as well as international trade. Supplement S1A presents a general-equilibrium picture of an economy and demonstrates the efficiency of a competitive market economy – and shows that efficiency also requires free international trade. A general-equilibrium proof of the efficiency of a competitive market economy requires a supplementary definition of efficiency (*Pareto efficiency*), which will be introduced presently.

The concepts of supply and demand

Adam Smith used the metaphor of the invisible hand and did not express his ideas in terms of the demand and supply functions of a market. Demand and supply functions were introduced later by Alfred Marshall (1842–1924), who was professor of political economy at Cambridge University in England. Marshall ended a debate about whether the value of a good is *caused* by the cost of production or is *caused* by the willingness of buyers to pay. The water–diamond paradox (which Adam Smith had also noted) is that although it is impossible to survive without water, nonetheless water generally has a low market value (a low price), whereas diamonds, which are unnecessary for life, have a high market value. William Stanley Jevons (1835–82) resolved the water–diamond paradox by observing that people's valuations of goods are determined by marginal benefit, not total benefit. The total benefit from having water exceeds the total benefit from having diamonds. Diamonds, however, are usually more highly valued than water, in that the *MB* of an additional diamond is high relative to the usual *MB* of additional water. Marshall proceeded beyond Jevons' observations in pointing out that neither *MC* on the supply side of the market nor *MB* on the demand side alone *causes* value. Rather, value is expressed in the market price, which is determined *simultaneously* by supply and demand (or by *MB* and *MC*) at the market equilibrium.

Supplement S1B: The competitive market-adjustment mechanism

Alfred Marshall described the competitive market-adjustment mechanism that we have used. Supplement S1B compares Marshall's competitive market-adjustment mechanism with an alternative market-adjustment mechanism associated with the French economist, Léon Walras (1834–1910).

Markets and the benefits of specialization

In showing the social benefit of competitive markets, we did not include the gains from specialization in production, which Adam Smith called "division of labor." Specialization reduces average costs of production through *scale economies*; average costs also decline over time in the course of learning and increased familiarity with processes of production (called *learning by doing*). Benefits from specialization do not require scale economies. With constant costs of production, the market provides gains by leading people to specialize according to *comparative advantage*. We can view comparative advantage in terms of ability or competence in different tasks. A person better suited to be an economist can be an economist and a person better suited to be a physicist can be a physicist. Without markets, benefits from specialization either through scale economies or comparative advantage could not be present because people or households would have to produce for themselves the entire range of goods consumed.[11]

The study of economics

Choice under conditions of scarcity, which is the focus of the study of economics, becomes important when there is a middle class. In an agricultural society in

[11] David Ricardo (1772–1823) introduced the concept of comparative advantage in 1817 in his book *Principles of Political Economy and Taxation*. Comparative advantage stems from people having different opportunity costs of producing different goods and services. If person 1 can produce either two units of good 1 in an hour or one unit of good 2, and person 2 can produce either two units of good 2 or one unit or good 1, more of both goods is available and society and both people personally clearly gain, when person 1 specializes to producing good 1 and person 2 specializes to producing good 2, providing there is demand for the goods produced at the relative market price of the two goods. On relative market prices, see supplement S1A. Comparative advantage is studied in detail in a course in international economics, where the concept is used – as in Ricardo's original exposition – to demonstrate the gains from exchange between countries. Comparative advantage however applies at core to people. People are guided to specialize according to comparative advantage by the prices determined in competitive markets.

which a few people own the land and are rich and the majority of people are poor, questions of choice are not at the forefront of people's minds. The rich do not face the need to choose, and the many people who are poor have little from which to choose. The questions raised in the study of economics about choice from among alternatives become important when a middle class begins emerging, which was the case at the time of Adam Smith.

Multiple and unstable market equilibria

Demand and supply (or *MB* and *MC*) functions have been shown as linear for exposition. However, linearity (with decreasing *MB* and increasing *MC*) also ensures a unique market equilibrium in figures 1.3 and 1.4. Figure 1.6 shows a case in which market demand and supply functions are not linear and market equilibrium is not unique. There are two market equilibria, at points *E1* and *E2*. The supply function in figure 1.6 has a negative slope, indicating decreasing costs.[12]

Because the market in figure 1.6 is competitive, total maximal benefit of buyers B^{max} is achieved for any quantity on the demand function, and total minimized cost of sellers C^{min} is achieved for any quantity on the supply function. The change to a downward-sloping supply function in figure 1.6 in particular does not alter the conclusion that assignment of supply among sellers in a competitive market minimizes total cost of supply.

The equilibrium at point *E2*, where the quantity Q_{E2} is supplied, maximizes *W* and so is efficient. The equilibrium at point *E1*, where Q_{E1} is supplied,

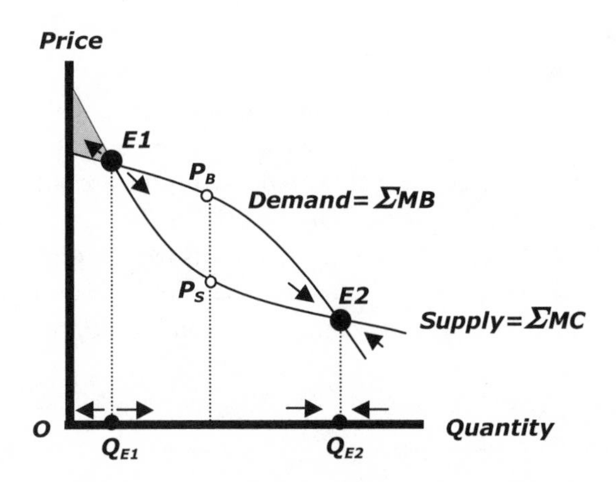

Figure 1.6. A market with a stable and unstable equilibrium.

[12] Decreasing costs can occur at the level of the individual producer or can be due to decreasing industry costs. Scale economies reduce costs for individual producers. Industry marginal costs decline with increased availability of skilled employees and supportive service industries.

minimizes W.[13] The shaded area shows the social loss from existence of the market if the quantity Q_{E1} at point $E1$ were supplied.

Through the competitive market-adjustment mechanism, quantity increases if $P_B > P_S$ and decreases if $P_S > P_B$. At output greater than Q_{E1}, the market therefore moves away from point $E1$ to the efficient stable equilibrium at point $E2$. If output is less than Q_{E1}, the competitive market-adjustment mechanism closes down the market by taking supply to zero. The market is thus attracted to point $E2$ and away from point $E1$.

> *An efficient market equilibrium is stable and an inefficient equilibrium is unstable.*

Had economic analysis at his time included the concepts of market supply and demand, Adam Smith would have been able to attribute to the invisible hand the wisdom of being attracted to efficient market equilibria while escaping from inefficient market equilibria.

C. Reasons why markets fail to achieve efficiency

Although we have confirmed Adam Smith's case for the merit of the invisible hand and have demonstrated the efficiency of competitive market outcomes, markets can nonetheless fail to achieve efficiency. The reason for the failure to achieve efficiency can be that a market is not competitive. However, a market that is competitive also can fail to achieve efficiency. The "market failures" in achieving efficiency introduce the possibility of benefit through governments' use of public finance and public policy.

Non-competitive markets

Competitive markets allow free entry and exit of buyers and sellers. In a monopolized market, artificial barriers prevent entry of potential competitors. Figure 1.7 shows a monopolized market. Monopoly profits are maximized at point F, where the quantity supplied is Q_M and the price is P_M. The efficiency loss due to monopoly is HEF.[14] Even if all monopoly profits were returned to buyers, the efficiency loss HEF would persist.[15] In a competitive market, Q_M could not be an equilibrium output because the competitive market-adjustment mechanism

[13] The second-order condition for a maximum

$$\frac{\partial MB}{\partial Q} < \frac{\partial MC}{\partial Q}$$

is satisfied at point $E2$ but not at point $E1$.

[14] Benefit HEQ_EQ_M is lost when the quantity supplied is Q_M rather than efficient competitive supply Q_E. The cost of producing $(Q_E - Q_M)$ is FEQ_EQ_M. HEF is the difference between benefit from and cost of producing $(Q_E - Q_M)$ and therefore is the efficiency loss due to monopoly.

[15] Total revenue R of the monopolist is the area under the MR function up to quantity Q_M. Total cost C is the area under the MC function up to quantity Q_M. Monopoly profits VFO are the difference between R and C.

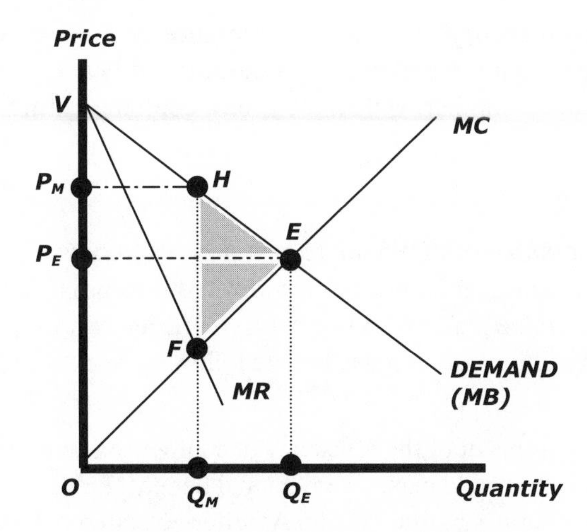

Figure 1.7. The inefficiency of monopoly.

would move the market to the efficient output Q_E. A monopolist's ability to choose price overrides the competitive market-adjustment mechanism.[16]

Monopoly and the compromise of economic freedom

Inefficiency is not the only undesirable aspect of monopoly. A monopolist can also compromise economic freedom. As sole seller, a monopolist can refuse to sell; a monopsonist (or sole buyer) similarly can refuse to buy.

> *Anonymity in competitive markets ensures economic freedom to buy and sell.*

Supplement S1C: Monopoly profits and social justice

When monopoly exists, replacing monopoly by competition eliminates monopolistic inefficiency and ensures personal freedom to buy and sell. However, questions about social justice arise because of asset markets. Supplement S1C addresses these questions.

Competitive markets as a responsibility of government

The adverse effects of monopoly on efficiency and economic freedom are the basis for a role for government:

> *An anti-monopoly or anti-trust agency of government should ensure that markets are competitive.*

[16] Markets can be non-competitive because of oligopoly, a cartel or other form of collusion, monopsony (a sole buyer), and imperfect competition with goods differentiated by sellers. Ability to influence price and so override the competitive market-adjustment mechanism is characteristic of all non-competitive markets.

The anti-monopoly agency identifies the presence of monopoly and collusive practices and investigates whether proposed mergers between firms, or acquisitions of one firm by another, will result in new combined firms with monopoly power.[17]

Why might competitive markets fail to result in efficiency?

We shall at times encounter monopoly. However, our focus is on roles for government when *competitive* markets fail to achieve efficiency. Competitive markets can fail to achieve efficient outcomes for the following reasons.

Public goods: Our proof of the efficiency of competitive markets was based on private goods that yield exclusive personal benefit. Public goods can benefit a number of people simultaneously. A better educated population, a public-health program that eliminates contagious and infectious diseases, use of a highway, personal and national security, and creation and dissemination of knowledge are cases in which many people simultaneously benefit from public goods. When people are not (or cannot be) excluded from the benefits of public goods, there are opportunities to benefit if someone else pays. The prospect of benefit without personally paying underlies an incentive to "free-ride" by letting others pay. If no one pays in anticipation that others will pay, there is no supply of a public good. We can anticipate that because of the incentive to free-ride on payments of others, voluntary payments in

[17] The tasks of an anti-monopoly agency are topics in a course on industrial organization or competition policy. We can, however, summarize. An anti-monopoly agency first needs to decide on the definition of the "market" and rules for designating a market as not competitive. Outright monopoly in a market is uncommon: legal definitions of monopoly are based on measures of market concentration of sellers or the combined market shares of combinations of sellers. If there is a single seller in a market, the market nonetheless may be contestable (markets are contestable when potential competitors can sell in a market if they so wish; therefore, contestable markets provide the benefits of competition through the discipline of potential competition). An anti-monopoly agency needs to make allowance for technological competition through improved quality of goods and changes in the technology of production that reduce costs: an anti-monopoly agency that penalizes success in technological competition creates disincentives for further technological advance (patent protection creates temporary legal monopolies and recognizes the need for incentives to sustain technological competition through invention and innovation). The anti-monopoly agency needs to identify cartels, which is difficult if there is tacit collusion. For example, there is tacit collusion on price when there is agreement that if one seller raises price, other sellers will follow and also increase price. Other subtle forms of collusive practices include an offer by a seller to match the lowest price available elsewhere: competing sellers then have no incentive to decrease price. Setting of retail prices by producers can also be anti-competitive: if retailers are not permitted to reduce prices below prices set by producers, producers do not have the means of increasing market share by offering discounts to retail sellers because the retail sellers cannot pass the discounts onto consumers through reduced retail prices. Another anti-competitive practice called "bundling" occurs when a seller refuses to sell one type of commodity if buyers do not at the same time also purchase other commodities that buyers may not necessarily want or that other sellers can provide more cheaply or with higher quality.

competitive markets fail to result in efficient supply of public goods. Public goods are therefore a source of "market failure."

Externalities: Achieving efficient outcomes in competitive markets requires buyers and sellers to internalize (or take account of) all benefits B and all costs C that stem from their market decisions. Externalities are present when some costs and benefits are not *internalized* in personal market decisions. Failure to internalize costs occurs, for example, when buyers or sellers harm the environment through their market decisions. Failure to internalize benefits occurs when people under-invest in education because they do not consider the benefits to others from having better educated companions and fellow citizens. There are externalities in health care: people who are immunized against diseases provide beneficial externalities (because they cannot infect others) and people who are not immunized are the source of adverse externalities.

Natural monopoly: Monopoly is "natural" if competing suppliers would wastefully duplicate *fixed costs*. It is efficient to *share* fixed costs of infrastructure, for example, for delivering electricity, water, and cable Internet and television to households. Natural monopoly will also be important for our investigation of the role of government because all noncongested public goods are natural monopolies. A case often used to illustrate a public good is a lighthouse. A lighthouse is a natural monopoly because it would be wasteful duplication of fixed costs to build two lighthouses side by side guiding ships to a port.

Asymmetric information: In demonstrating the efficiency of competitive markets, we did not make allowance for asymmetric information. Information is asymmetric when buyers or sellers have private information about themselves that others cannot know. Asymmetric information will arise when we study public goods, externalities, and natural monopoly. We shall also encounter asymmetric information when, in the context of social justice, we study insurance markets. People who face uncertainty about personal income would want insurance against having low future income. When personal effort at self-reliance is an individual's private information that is unobservable to others, insurance companies are unwilling to sell insurance against having low income because it will be impossible to know whether future low personal income will have been due to bad luck or to lack of personal effort at being self-reliant. Because of asymmetric information, insurance markets for personal income then may not exist. There is a social loss because of the benefits that the absent or "missing" markets would have provided, if the markets were to exist.

The prima facie case for the competitive market

We shall consider in detail the reasons why competitive markets can fail to achieve efficiency and why the public finance and public policy of government might therefore be required. Our starting point in each instance of "market failure" is however the *prima facie* case for the market. We shall begin with the supposition that:

Competitive markets are efficient unless proven otherwise.

From this beginning, the burden of proof will be on showing that governments improve on market outcomes.

D. Information and spontaneous order

We now set aside, for the time being, the reasons for market failure and proceed with our investigation of the case for competitive markets.

We have shown that, with reasons for market failure absent, a competitive market equilibrium is efficient. However, we have not shown that market decisions are the *only* means of achieving efficiency. An alternative to a market is a government agency that replaces *decentralized* market decisions of buyers and sellers with *centralized* decisions made on behalf of the population. When a government agency makes centralized decisions, the economic freedom to make personal voluntary market decisions has been lost. With economic freedom forgone, can a centralized government agency nonetheless replicate the efficiency of a market that the agency has replaced? A case based on information suggests that a government agency making centralized decisions cannot achieve the efficiency of the personal, decentralized decisions of a competitive market.

Information

Markets aggregate information. The aggregated information is the sum of the dispersed information that is revealed when individual buyers and sellers make personal market decisions. The aggregated information is expressed in the market demand and supply functions that determine market prices. With market prices determined and observable, people need to know only their own *MBs* as buyers or own *MCs* as sellers to make the personal decisions that result in market efficiency.

Efficiency through decentralized market choice is demonstrated in figure 1.8a, which shows a given quantity of output Q_B and the willingness to pay expressed in MB of two buyers. MB_1 is measured from the O_1 origin and MB_2 from the O_2 origin. The buyers observe the common buying price P_B and they know their own marginal benefits. To maximize utility or personal benefit, each buyer sets the observed market price facing buyers P_B equal to personal MB. Total benefit of the two buyers $B = (B_1 + B_2)$ is maximized by individual decentralized decisions that result in:

$$MB_1 = P_B = MB_2. \qquad (1.19)$$

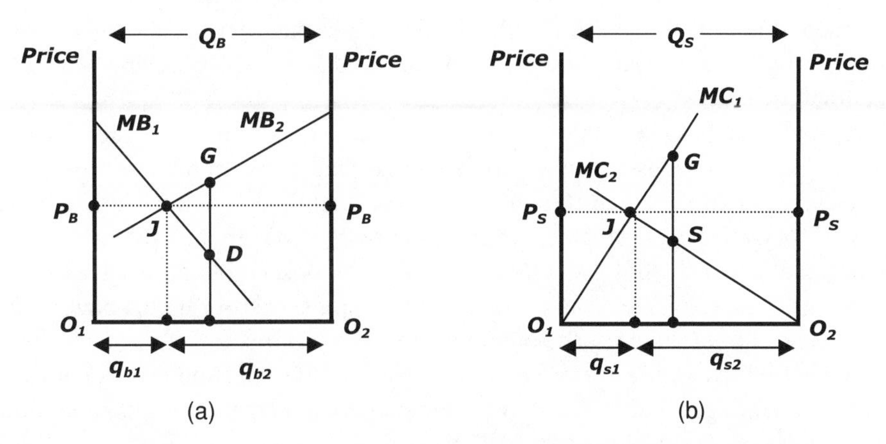

Figure 1.8. (a) Information about *MB*. (b) Information about *MC*.

The efficient division of Q_B at point J in figure 1.8a is thus achieved by decentralized market decisions, with person 1 voluntarily purchasing the quantity q_{b1} and person 2 voluntarily purchasing the quantity q_{b2}.

To replicate the efficient division of output at point J that results from buyers' voluntary decentralized market decisions, a government agency would need to know the location of the personal marginal benefit functions MB_1 and MB_2. However, personal *MB* is private information of buyers. When a government agency seeks to replace a market, we therefore have a case of asymmetric information. Individuals know their *MBs*. The government agency does not. Asymmetric information is not a problem for achieving efficiency through market outcomes. The private information about personal *MB* is revealed spontaneously through personal market decisions when buyers set *MB* equal to the market price. Because an individual's *MB* is private information, a government agency that has replaced the market could only guess at the efficient division of the quantity Q_B in figure 1.8a. For example, a guess by the government agency that efficiency requires an equal division of the quantity Q_B between persons 1 and 2 results in a loss equal to the area *GDJ*.[18]

A government agency that sets out to choose efficient supply assignments among producers is at a similar informational disadvantage compared to a competitive market. Figure 1.8b shows the marginal costs of two suppliers, with O_1 the origin for MC_1 of supplier 1 and O_2 the origin for MC_2 of supplier 2. In a market, the two suppliers observe the common market selling price P_S and maximize profits by setting P_S equal to their personal *MC*. The suppliers know their own marginal costs and choose their respective quantities to supply such that:

$$MC_1 = P_S = MC_2. \qquad (1.20)$$

[18] When there is equal division, MB_2 at point G, exceeds MB_1 at point D. The gain from moving from equal to efficient division is *GDJ*.

Efficient supply is thus achieved through decentralized market decisions, with supplier 1 choosing to supply the quantity q_{s1} and supplier 2 choosing to supply the quantity q_{s2}.

A government agency that has been set the task of replicating the efficient market outcome needs to know suppliers' marginal costs. Information on costs may be easier to find than the information on marginal benefits because costs may be objectively observable, whereas benefits of buyers are subjective and unobservable. Costs, however, include costs of unobservable effort. If government agencies also have replaced markets for inputs, costs of inputs have to be computed without the presence of market valuations. Government agencies cannot be expected to know precise marginal costs of different suppliers. A guess by a government agency of equal division of supply assignments results in an efficiency loss equal to the area *GSJ* in figure 1.8b.

Efficient assignment of goods among consumers or users to achieve maximum total benefit B^{max} and efficient assignment of supply among suppliers to achieve minimum total cost C^{min} are two of the three requirements for efficiency. The third requirement is choice of an efficient quantity Q_E that maximizes $W = (B^{max} - C^{min})$. A government agency that lacks information to achieve B^{max} or C^{min} cannot, of course, compute $W = (B^{max} - C^{min})$. The third requirement for efficiency is then also beyond the information capabilities of the government agency.

A government agency may look diligently for ways to measure personal benefits and costs and use procedures that we shall study known as cost-benefit analysis. However, the information that is sought cannot be found if the information does not exist outside of the market that the government agency has replaced – or is seeking to replace.

With markets not in existence to reveal information, the information that a government agency requires to achieve efficiency may not exist to be found.

Political decision makers

Although government agencies are at an informational disadvantage compared to markets, political decision makers may prefer centralized government decisions because:

Through centralized decisions, political allocation replaces market allocation.

Political allocation provides political decision makers with the means to control the distribution of benefits and costs among a population. Through centralized decisions, political decision makers can take personal credit for providing benefits to constituencies or political supporters. Political decision makers may also be able to decide on which supplier receives a government contract for supply and the price of supply may allow for profits that a supplier would not earn in a competitive market.

Ideology and imposed order

A preference for centralized decisions can be due to ideology rather than self-interested political behavior. An ideology associated with the "left" in economics and politics proposes that centralized government decisions avoid the "anarchy" of markets by imposing "order" on economic activity. The ideology associates market decisions with "anarchy" because of the uncoordinated, decentralized decisions independently made in markets by buyers and sellers. The ideology is therefore in direct contradiction to the invisible hand of Adam Smith according to which markets do not result in anarchy but rather achieve efficiency spontaneously through the economic freedom to make voluntary personal decisions.

A rudimentary example of *spontaneous order* is a farmers' market. Farmers arrive at the market with produce for sale, having independently made supply decisions for the produce that they bring to the market. No centralized directives have been issued about the types of products and the quantities that should be brought to the market. Buyers also arrive at the market to make their purchases. At the end of the day, the farmers leave, to return the next day with new supplies. Buyers also return. Spontaneous order is present, with every buyer and seller knowing "what to do" without centralized instructions. Moreover, centralized instructions could not duplicate the efficiency of the decentralized market decisions because the information required for efficiency is not available without the existence of a market in which the information is revealed through the personal decisions of buyers and sellers.

Information and spontaneous order: Normative and positive conclusions

We now have a normative and a positive conclusion about information and spontaneous order. The normative conclusion extends the prima facie case for the market beyond efficiency and personal freedom:

> *Markets are informationally efficient.*

The positive conclusion is that we cannot predict that markets will necessarily be chosen in preference to centralized decisions of government because:

> *Political decision makers may prefer centralized decisions.*
>
> *Ideology may favor centralized decisions.*

There is a link:

> *Political decision makers may prefer an ideology that favors centralized decisions.*

1.2 Efficiency and Social Justice

A prima facie case for the market has been made based on efficiency, economic freedom, and information. The case for government will be made against this background of attributes of outcomes in competitive markets. Our next step is to investigate criteria for efficiency and social justice. We begin by supplementing our definition of efficiency, by introducing the concept of Pareto efficiency.

A. Pareto efficiency and compensation

Efficiency can be defined in terms of change. The concept of Pareto-improving *change* is named after Vilfredo Pareto.[19]

Change is Pareto-improving when someone gains and no one loses.

A related concept is Pareto efficiency:

An outcome is Pareto-efficient when Pareto-improving change cannot take place (when no one can be made better off without making someone else worse off).

Competitive market outcomes are Pareto-efficient. No one loses from voluntary personal market decisions. After buyers and sellers have made their voluntary market decisions (and have gained), no further Pareto-improving change can take place. Supplement S1A elaborates on the Pareto efficiency of competitive markets.

Cost-benefit analysis

Decisions made by government require investigation to determine if consequences are Pareto-improving. No one person may be willing to build a free-access road. Beneficiaries of the road can ask a government to levy taxes and build the road. However, with efficiency as a social objective, it needs to be determined whether building the road is justified as efficient public spending. The decision whether to build the road is made by applying cost-benefit analysis. The cost-benefit criterion is that change is justified as efficient if:

$$\Delta W = \Delta B - \Delta C > 0. \tag{1.21}$$

The cost-benefit criterion does not necessarily seek efficiency through finding precise efficient public spending that maximizes $W = B - C$. The question can be justification: to decide whether a public spending (and taxation) proposal is justified, ΔB and ΔC are computed to determine whether $\Delta B > \Delta C$.

[19] Vilfredo Pareto (1848–1923) taught at the University of Florence in Italy and the University of Lausanne in Switzerland.

In evaluating whether for a public spending or public policy proposal $\Delta B > \Delta C$, the government requires information. For example, in the case of a road, the government needs to know benefits from the road due to reduced travel time, which requires knowing the values of time of the different users of the road. The government also needs to value benefits from fewer injuries or from lives saved because of reduced likelihood of accidents (or perhaps the likelihood of accidents increases). The government also needs to be able to value costs due to environmental damage or reduced biodiversity. Markets do not exist to reveal such benefits and costs (the benefits and costs are "externalities" associated with the proposed road). The road is also a public good because of simultaneous use by many people. Cost-benefit analysis is the procedure whereby governments indirectly seek to compute costs and benefits that are not revealed in markets – where markets do not exist because of externalities and public goods.

Compensation and Pareto improvement

Building a road may require demolishing some people's houses. The houses have market values; therefore, there is no information problem regarding costs incurred due to demolition of the houses. Cost-benefit evaluations determine whether public-spending proposals are efficient and not whether there is social justice. The distribution of benefits and costs among people in a population therefore does not affect the cost-benefit comparison. Therefore, if $\Delta B > \Delta C$, the cost-benefit criterion justifies building the road on efficiency grounds, even if the owners of the houses lose because their houses are demolished to make way for the road.

The project to construct the road is, however, not Pareto-improving if the owners of the demolished houses are not compensated. The supplementary Pareto criterion blocks the construction of the road if compensation is not provided because without compensation the owners of the demolished houses will be worse off.

However, if cost-benefit calculations reveal that $\Delta B > \Delta C$, the gainers from the road can compensate the losers and still be better off.

Compensation is part of the definition of *efficiency*.

> *If change (a new road) is efficient by the cost-benefit rule $\Delta B > \Delta C$, gainers can compensate the losers and still gain.*

Compensation and social justice

Efficient change therefore allows in principle for Pareto-improving change. A different question is about social justice:

> *Does social justice require that actual compensation take place?*

Property rights to a house are well defined and a house has an objective market value. The value of compensation to losers when houses are demolished to make way for a road can be readily determined and compensation can be paid. When the government demolishes a house to make way for a road, the government is exercising the right of eminent domain, which is the right to override private possession if it is judged to be in the public interest. Social justice requires that when a government exercises the right of eminent domain, compensation be paid to the people who lose.

Compensation for income losses

Do people with specialized skills or human capital have rights to compensation similar to owners of property? In principle, there is no difference between compensation for loss of a house and loss associated with human capital or skills. In the 19th century, steam technology replaced sails for ships. Society as a whole gained, but people who had skills associated with furling and unfurling sails lost. The market introduced the innovation of steam technology without compensating the losers. Similarly, there were gainers and losers in the 20th century when the personal computer was introduced. Before the advent of the personal computer, typing was a specialized skill and few people did their own typing. The introduction of personal computers resulted in losses for typists. Compensating the furlers of sails or the typists would have required certifying that particular people indeed had lost income because of the new technology and determining how much each person lost. Some of the losses would have been subjective. People displaced from their job can have feelings of diminished self-worth. Self-esteem is also diminished when the people who are offered compensatory payments have been guided in life by the principle of a work ethic and have only accepted money that they have productively earned.[20]

How is compensation to be implemented?

To implement compensation, gainers do not need to pay losers directly. Governments can act as mediators. A government can directly compensate owners of houses from general tax revenue. In the case of furlers of sails, taxes could have been levied on owners and users of steamships. Taxes on sales of computers could have financed compensation to typists. The taxes would have been levied on the beneficiaries of efficient change.

Infeasibility of compensation

Compensation may not be feasible. It may not be possible to identify losers. People who lose may not be able to prove the magnitude of their losses.

Compensation and the status quo

As a condition for departing from the status quo and allowing efficient public spending for which the cost-benefit criterion $\Delta B > \Delta C$ is satisfied, a society

[20] If subjective losses are incurred that cannot be objectively measured, we may wonder, of course, how a government might base conclusions on cost-benefit analysis. Cost-benefit analysis is a last resort when market valuations are absent.

might insist on accompanying Pareto improvement through compensation to ensure that no one has lost. When compensation is not feasible, such insistence on compensation blocks efficient change.[21] There are also consequences for social justice: potential losers do not lose but potential gainers from the efficient change that has been blocked do not gain.

> *Insistence on compensation protects potential losers from change but does not protect the gainers from the losses incurred because of efficient change that did not take place.*

A society that does not insist on compensation for allowing efficient change is taking the view that over the course of time, all people will come to benefit from different instances of efficient change, even though on some occasions some people lose. Still, people who lose and are not compensated may never – over the course of their life – gain sufficiently from other instances of efficient change to make up for their own personal losses.

The compensation dilemma

Compensation poses a dilemma. Compensation for losers from efficient change as might be due to a public finance or public policy decision is socially just. However, there is a cost to insistence on the social justice of protecting losers by requiring Pareto improvement through actual accompanying compensation. Efficient change is blocked when compensation is not feasible. There is also injustice because of the benefits forgone by the potential gainers. There is no escape from the dilemma. If losers cannot be compensated, a society has no choice but to decide nonetheless whether to allow efficient change justified by the cost-benefit criterion. The decision whether to insist on actual accompanying compensation influences a society's wealth. Societies that allow efficient change without insisting on compensation will have greater wealth than societies that block efficient change if compensation cannot take place to ensure Pareto improvement. We have identified here a conflict that can arise between efficiency and social justice. Ideology affects choices that societies (or political parties) make regarding insistence on actual compensation as a condition for allowing efficient change.

B. Are competitive markets socially just?

We return now to the market. Our prima facie case with origins in the invisible hand is that competitive markets are efficient. What of social justice? Are outcomes in competitive markets socially just?

[21] The efficiency losses can be substantial. A country may have the technology to produce typewriters but not computers. Competition from imports of personal computers would result in closure of the typewriter factories. Protectionist international-trade policies could sustain local typewriter production by preventing imports of computers. The gains from freedom to trade (see supplement S1A) are then lost, along with the benefits of the new technology of personal computers.

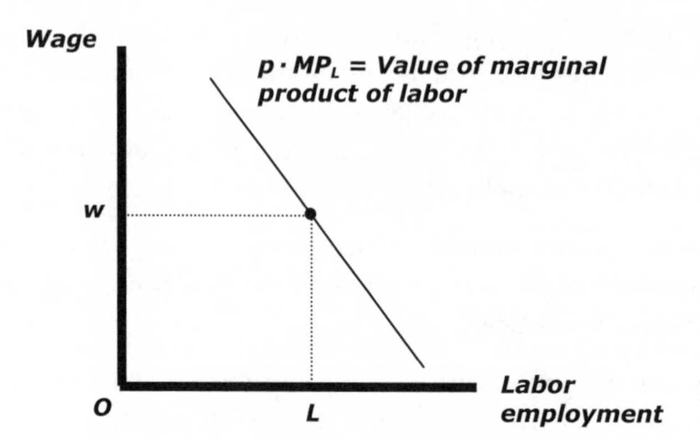

Figure 1.9. Income in a competitive market.

Social justice as the natural right of possession

A definition of social justice is:

> *An outcome is socially just if the natural right of possession is honored.*

Based on the natural right of possession, it is socially just that individuals be rewarded according to the value of their personal productive contributions. This is the outcome in competitive markets. Figure 1.9 shows a competitive market wage w at which employers can hire labor. The wage w is the MC of labor for an employer. The MB to the employer from hiring labor is the value of the marginal product of labor. As indicated in figure 1.9, employers choose to hire labor such that the wage or MC of labor equals the value of marginal product or MB of hiring labor. Workers thus receive as payment the value of their marginal contribution to the value of production.[22]

[22] In competitive markets, employers face market-determined prices for outputs and inputs. We use the following notation: p indicates the competitive market-determined price of output; w is the competitively determined wage paid to labor; L is labor employed; V represents other inputs (taken as having been already chosen); and $q = f(L,V)$ is the output produced using L and other inputs V, where output q increases with labor employment L and the marginal product of labor MP_L is declining (because of diminishing returns to labor given quantities of other inputs V that are fixed). As shown in figure 1.9, the value of the marginal product of labor $p \cdot MP_L$ is declining. Profits of a competitive firm are:

$$\pi = p \cdot q - wL = p \cdot f(L, V) - wL.$$

Profits from employing labor are maximized when:

$$\frac{\partial \pi}{\partial L} = p \cdot MP_L - w = 0.$$

That is, as in figure 1.9, in a competitive labor market, the value of the marginal product of labor equals the wage:

$$w = p \cdot \frac{\partial q}{\partial L} \equiv p \cdot MP_L.$$

If we accept the definition of social justice as personal reward equal to the value of personal productive contribution, we can conclude:

> *Competitive markets achieve social objectives of both efficiency and social justice.*

The right to compensation and the natural right of possession

We have now encountered views of social justice as (1) the right to compensation, and (2) the natural right of possession. The two views of social justice are related. If a house that is to be demolished belongs to a person by the natural right of possession, social justice requires compensation for the loss.

Reservations about the natural right of possession

The natural right of possession might not be acceptable as a definition of social justice. No allowance is made for the advantages of good luck or innate ability, family, and personal connections that affect incomes. Nor is allowance made for personal disadvantages when people are incapacitated, have health problems, or have obligations to care for others. Unequal educational opportunities affect incomes. Or, as in the cases of the furlers of sails and the typists, once-valuable knowledge and skills may no longer be much valued by markets. There can therefore be reservations about defining social justice as reward according to personal contribution. Nonetheless, there is social justice in the natural entitlement of people to their own production.[23]

> *The principle of the natural right of possession recognizes that people are naturally entitled to the products of their own effort.*

If people are not entitled to the consequences of their own productive effort, we might wonder how incentives for a productive society can be provided. Why should people be motivated to apply initiative and personal effort without regard for personal reward? Altruists contribute for the benefit of others: however, if people begin as altruists, will altruism persist over time, or will feelings of exasperation and exploitation come to replace the initial feeling of personal satisfaction from contributing and exerting productive effort so that others can benefit?

We shall adopt the natural right of possession as a possible definition of social justice. However, there are also other possible definitions.

[23] The English political economist, John Stuart Mill (1806–73), in his book *Principles of Political Economy* first published in 1848, described the natural right of possession in the following way: "The institution of property, when limited to its essential elements, consists in the recognition, in each person, of a right to the exclusive disposal of what he or she have produced by their own exertions, or received either by gift or by fair agreement, without force or fraud, from those who produced it" (Book II, Chapter II).

C. Social justice as equality

Social justice is often regarded as requiring *equality*, which is of two types:

- *Ex-ante equality* requires equal opportunity for everyone expressed as equal chances for improvement in life.
- *Ex-post equality* requires that everyone end up equally, as in a race in which everyone is constrained to cross the finish line at the same time.

Ex-ante equality

Ex-ante equality requires that there be no privileged beginnings in life. Yet, we may ask, is that possible? It is not if the definition of privilege includes having high intelligence and ability and having patience to study. People differ also in motivation to succeed. People have different propensities for good health. Family circumstances differ in being supportive of or inimical to personal success. Governments may seek to provide ex-ante equality through equal access to educational opportunities and health care – and perhaps through attempts to stress that deferring a good time and investing by studying will bring greater than compensating benefits in the future when incomes are earned and relationships are formed. In seeking to stress the benefits of education, governments may have to countervail culturally transmitted norms from parents to children. Retained personal traits appear often to be acquired at young ages before children start kindergarten or first grade. By the time children are capable of understanding the message that investment in education is worthwhile through opportunities that are provided, it may be too late to influence attitudes to patience and investment in personal success.

> *As much as we want ex-ante equality, with all good intentions of society and government, ex-ante equality may be an elusive objective that at best takes time to achieve.*

Ex-post equality

The objective of sharing to attain ex-post equality is instinctive in humans. People wandering in early hunter–gatherer groups shared food because failing to share would have resulted in deprivation or death when others who had been successful in finding food reciprocated by also not sharing.

In general, ex-post equality is inconsistent with Pareto improvement. Three people each may have equal incomes of $1,000. After the government spends $600 on education financed by a $200 tax paid by each person, the incomes of all three people increase but unequally. The new incomes after payment of the tax are {$1,400, $1,600, and $2,000}. ΔB is $2,000 (the sum of the increases in incomes) and ΔC is $600 (the additional tax-financed public spending on education). Because $\Delta W = (\Delta B - \Delta C) = 1{,}400 > 0$, the increased public spending on education is justified as efficient by the cost-benefit criterion. The public spending is also at the same time Pareto-improving because all three people are better off (and no one is worse off). Yet, the Pareto-improving change has resulted in departure from the initial conditions of ex-post equality.

> *In general, insisting on ex-post equality prevents Pareto-improving change.*

D. The choice between efficiency and equality

The choice between Pareto efficiency and ex-post equality is illustrated by two travelers in a desert who have only enough water between them for one person to survive. One person owns the water. The ethical and normative question is whether the person who owns the water should share the water with the other traveler. Sharing the water (in any way, not necessarily equally) results in ex-post equality but the equal outcome is that neither person survives. If the person in possession of the water keeps all the water, the outcome is a Pareto improvement compared to division of the water because one person alive is preferable to no one alive. One person benefiting from the water is Pareto-efficient.

The circumstances of the water in the desert are described in the Talmud, in which two opinions are given. A commentator named Ben-Petura proposed that the water should be shared because *it is better that both should drink and die than that one should witness the death of his fellow*. R. Akiva (c. 50–135) proposed that *your life takes precedence over your fellow's life*, so if you have the water and the water can save only one life, you are obliged to use the water to save yourself.[24] The ethical question is:

> *Should the person in possession of the water share the water, when sharing makes no one better off and makes one person worse off, and the only purpose of sharing is to satisfy a principle of ex-post equality?*

Ben-Petura proposed ex-post equality through sharing – even though both people die. Akiva chose Pareto efficiency (albeit some 2,000 years before Pareto).

Efficiency and ex-ante equality

A lottery could assign the water with equal probabilities and thereby provide social justice in the form of ex-ante equality. After the outcome of the lottery is known, one person has all the water, which is Pareto-efficient. The lottery presupposes that neither person owns the water. If a person owns the water, an obligation to offer the water as the prize in a lottery contradicts rights of

[24] Compilation of the Jerusalem Talmud was completed around 1,600 years ago and the Talmud Bavli was completed some 100 years later. In the Talmud, opinions of people who did not live at the same time are often compared, which appears to be the case here.

ownership or natural right of possession. A lottery, therefore, is a socially just way of providing ex-ante equality only if there is no pre-identified owner of the water.[25]

Efficiency and the natural right of possession

Some 3,000 years ago, Solomon, king of Israel in Jerusalem, confronted two women who both claimed to be the mother of the same baby. The two women had given birth around the same time but only one baby had survived. Evidence could support neither woman's claim. Solomon faced a problem of asymmetric information. He did not know the identity of the true mother, although each of the two women knew who the true mother was. The same type of *indivisibility* was present as in the case of the water in the desert: as with the water, dividing the baby was not efficient. The king nonetheless decreed that unless one of the two women renounced her claim, the baby would be cut in half and divided between the claimants. One claimant was satisfied with the offer of ex-post equality and declared: "Neither mine nor yours will he be." The other woman renounced her claim. The king thereupon decreed that the baby should be given to the woman who had renounced her claim, because she was the true mother.[26] The outcome was efficient. When the criterion for social justice is the natural right of possession, the outcome was also just – as would be the case with the water in the desert when the owner of the water is judged to have the right to benefit from the water.

> *Quite evidently, whether an outcome is socially just depends on the definition of social justice.*

The natural right of possession is a conservative criterion for social justice that justifies the status quo of possession. However, when we apply the criterion of the natural right of possession to define social justice, we care about how possession was achieved.

The baby is the natural possession of the true mother. On the other hand, had we lived in a time and a place where we were ruled by a repressive king who claimed natural right of possession of everything in the kingdom through the divine right of kings to rule, and who took what he pleased, we would not have accepted the king's claim to natural right of possession. We would have joined a revolution to overthrow the king because the king was denying the natural

[25] The lottery provides equal opportunity through equal expected utility. If utility from having the water is 100 and the utility from not having the water is zero, and there is a probability of one-half of each outcome, expected utility is $(\frac{1}{2}100 + \frac{1}{2}0) = 50$. Before the outcome of the lottery is known, both persons therefore have the same expected utility of 50 and there is ex-ante equality.

[26] Had the false claimant renounced her claim, the king would have confronted a more difficult problem.

right of possession of people to the property and wealth that they personally created.

The natural right of possession depends on how possession was obtained.

The popular bias against efficiency

To make judgments about social justice, choice of a criterion is required that specifies the meaning of social justice. The choice of ex-post equality as the criterion (or definition) requires in turn a choice between achieving social justice or efficiency. The latter choice may reflect attitudes toward the market, which we have seen presumptively provides efficiency. When confronted with the need to choose, people often reject allocation through markets. After a severe snowstorm, people were asked whether the market price of snow shovels should be permitted to increase to equate demand for the shovels with the limited available supply. Most people viewed market allocation of the shovels as unjust. In a further situation reminiscent of the water in the desert, people were asked how water bottles at a mountain top should be assigned when more people will climb the mountain than the number of water bottles available. The alternatives offered were (1) assignment according to the order of arrival, (2) random assignment as through a lottery, (3) assignment by a government agency, and (4) market assignment through willingness to pay. The majority rejected the market and chose assignment according to the order of arrival.[27]

Evidence from experiments reveals that economists – and students of economics – tend to favor the market and efficiency more than the public, which favors "fair" allocations in the sense of ex-post equality.[28] Economists seem to believe that people who work hard to achieve personal advancement should benefit from their efforts and that people who value something more should be allowed to pay more and thereby obtain what they value.

As has been observed, the origin of the preference for ex-post equality over efficiency – and over the natural right of possession – may be in hunter–gatherer societies in which individuals in small groups shared food as insurance. On any one day, an individual might bring back to the group more food than he or she needs. On another day, an individual may not find enough food for personal needs. Sharing that results in ex-post equality is beneficial because of the insurance that sharing provides in ensuring that a person will have enough food.

Envy

Envy is one of the basic human emotions. In general, envy is not admirably regarded. Envy was present in the case judged by Solomon. The envious woman

[27] Random assignment of water bottles maximizes expected utility by giving everyone an equal chance of obtaining a water bottle. Assignment according to order of arrival also maximizes expected utility if there is equal probability of arriving when water bottles still remain.

[28] The two above cases were reported by Daniel Kahneman, Jack Knetsch, and Richard Thaler (1986) and by Bruno Frey and Werner Pommerehne (1993). Kahneman received the Nobel Prize in 2002 for his research on the interface between economics and psychology.

sought ex-post equality through the other woman (the true mother) also having no child. In the case of the water in the desert, envy is similarly the only reason why the person without the water would insist on sharing and ex-post equality. Sharing the water does not change the fate of the person without the water but ensures the same unfortunate fate for the person who has the water.

Envy affects utility. Through envy, the utility of the person without the water increases if the water is shared and neither person survives – just as the utility of the false claimant to the baby would increase if the true mother were also to be denied a child.

Akiva's answer to the question whether the water in the desert should be shared is akin to the ethical position of Adam Smith regarding behavior in markets. Adam Smith declared that people should not feel guilty about seeking their self-interest in markets. Akiva proposed that a person in possession of the water should not feel guilty about wishing to survive.[29]

In another example of envy, two poor farmers look at the well-kept cow of a neighbor. Both are envious of their neighbor's cow. One farmer thinks: "I wish that I had a beautiful cow like that; I shall work hard, and soon I shall also be able to afford to buy such a cow." The other farmer looks at the well-fed cow of his neighbor and thinks: "I wish that the cow would die." The objective of both envious farmers is ex-post equality. The first farmer seeks ex-post equality together with Pareto improvement (because he will have a cow and the neighbor will be no worse off). The second farmer would achieve ex-post equality with Pareto inefficiency (because he seeks the demise of the neighbor's cow). This example shows that:

> *The response to envy can be productive and result in Pareto improvement or can alternatively be unproductive or destructive and thereby result in a poorer society.*

In chapter 2 where we shall study "institutions," we shall see that the institutions of a society influence which of the two responses can be expected to occur.

Aversion to inequality

People may experience disutility due to guilt feelings about having more than others. They may declare to a person who has less, "I agree that we should be more equal in what we have and I feel uncomfortable in having more than you." They may volunteer their time or give money to charitable causes that help people in need. People may also express aversion to inequality by voting in favor of taxes and income redistribution to increase ex-post equality.

[29] The question is not whether all the water should be given to the other person, which also results in a Pareto-efficient outcome. Whether all the water should be given to the other person is quite a different question than whether the water should be shared.

Voting

Voting introduces the question of why people bother to vote. There is a personal cost to voting in the time taken to vote. However, the likelihood that one person's vote will be decisive in determining a voting outcome in a large population of voters is effectively zero. For anyone whose time is at all valuable, a personal cost-benefit calculation should thus reveal that the personal cost of voting exceeds the expected benefit from voting. A decision to vote, therefore, is not based on a rational economic cost-benefit calculation.

People may vote because of a feeling of civic duty. Voting can also be expressive. By voting expressively, people express their self-identity and identify with principles that they favor. Individuals can in particular confirm or demonstrate their humane nature by visibly expressing political support for political parties and candidates that favor greater ex-post equality. The alternative of voting for conservative political candidates can result in less satisfying feelings. Conservative political parties tend to emphasize the benefits of efficiency through productive incentives and the natural right of possession, and to view social justice as served by providing equal opportunity and allowing people to advance in life on merit. Visible support for a conservative party may be regarded by an individual's friends and peers as evidence of insensitivity and lack of a social conscience.

The emotional and personal-popularity benefits of expressive voting can result in insincere voting – meaning that voters may not want the candidates for whom they vote to actually win the election. When voting, individual voters know that in any event, they cannot influence the voting outcome. If they vote expressively, however, they obtain the utility from expressive voting. Because a single vote is not decisive in influencing the outcome of voting, each voter reasons that he or she can safely vote expressively. In seeking personal satisfaction and social approval through voting, a sufficiently large number of expressive voters may, however, achieve high-tax redistributive outcomes that they do not want.

Political decision makers and a political party that has won the election with the support of the expressive voters may understand the behavior of the expressive-voter constituency and be aware that actually implementing policies of high taxation and extensive redistribution will result in a loss of political support. The policy declarations of a socially aware party when the party is in office can therefore also be expressive.

We saw that feelings and emotions are involved in Adam Smith's invisible hand. The invisible hand avoids guilt feelings about self-interested personal behavior in markets. The invisible hand also avoids the hypocrisy in markets that would be expressed by sellers declaring that they are doing favors for buyers in offering to sell or by buyers declaring favors in offering to buy.

We can therefore compare market and voting behavior and conclude:

> *When people buy and sell in markets, there are no personal benefits from being insincere in deviating from true personal preferences, whereas voting can be expressive and not necessarily sincere.*

Efficiency, equality, and social justice

Summarizing our conclusions regarding efficiency, equality, and social justice, we have seen that:

(1) When social justice is defined as ex-post equality, Pareto efficiency is, in general, inconsistent with social justice. However, efficiency and social justice are consistent objectives when social justice is defined as ex-ante equality or as the natural right of possession.
(2) Ex-post equality is an instinctive objective based on sharing that is also related to envy. The response to envy of those who are envious can be efficient or inefficient.
(3) The response to envy to those being envied can be expressive behavior through voting. While expressive voting can be insincere, there are no benefits from refraining from expressing preferences sincerely in market decisions.

1.3 The Rule of Law

We now turn to the rule of law.

Without the rule of law, neither efficiency nor social justice is attainable.

If the rule of law is absent, there is no point to our studying the choice between markets and the public finance and public policy of government. Markets cannot exist without the rule of law. The rule of law also has consequences for the behavior of governments. Governments have a legal monopoly on coercion. Without the protection of the rule of law, governments can use their monopoly on legal coercion in intrusive and harmful ways.

A. Benefits of the rule of law

The rule of law protects us in many ways. Our right to our possessions is protected as well as the right not to be kidnapped, enslaved, or raped – and the right to life itself. The rule of law includes requisites for a civil society such as provisions for legal enforcement of contracts and for resolution of disputes, and bankruptcy codes that protect rights of debtors and creditors. The rule of law, in principle, should provide equality before the law. Social status or wealth should not determine how the rule of law is applied. For example, the two women between whom Solomon adjudicated were harlots with low social status. In receiving the harlots and judging their case, the king demonstrated the principle of equality before the law. Equality before the law requires that the rule of law not be applied selectively: when the rule of law is applied selectively, people are unsure about whether the rule of law applies to them.

The rule of law is inconsistent with laws and regulations that are retroactive. It is a contradiction of the rule of law for people to be able to be accused today of crimes committed yesterday that were not designated as crimes yesterday. If laws can be retroactive, *anything* that people did in the past can be arbitrarily made illegal and used against them. By disallowing retroactive laws, the rule of law ensures that property that belonged to someone yesterday belongs to the same person today, unless the property was voluntarily sold or given away.

The rule of law is not the same as the rule of government. Without the protection of the rule of law, arbitrary and whimsical men and women who control government can subvert the law so that the "law" becomes the instrument of appropriation and repression. We rely on government to implement the rule of law; however, the rule of law also protects us from government.

The rule of law is not present when honest people cannot abide by laws. Tax rates may be set so high that people who pay taxes honestly cannot survive at a reasonable standard of living. With tax evasion then pervasive, accusations of tax evasion can be used selectively to silence any critic of a government.

Private property rights and markets

The rule of law certifies (or confirms) and protects private property rights. A nomadic hunter–gatherer population roaming where land and game are plentiful does not require private property rights. Private property rights become valuable when there is competition for land and natural resources. Private property rights likewise become personally valuable when crops are planted or when a house is built. Private property rights provide the incentives to plant the crops and build the house.

Certified and protected property rights allow the different types of markets in a society to exist. In *product* and *asset* markets, property rights allow buyers to know that sellers have the right to sell and that new ownership will be defined after payment to sellers has been made. In *labor* markets, people are assured that the output that they produce belongs to them, so there are incentives to be productive. The rule of law allows *capital* markets to function: in the absence of the protection of property rights provided by the rule of law, there is no incentive to invest because there is no assurance that returns from an investment will belong to the people who have made the investment. Without property rights ensured through the rule of law, there also is no assurance that an asset created through an investment will continue to belong to the investor. If property rights are not certified and not protected through the rule of law, assets cannot be traded and diversification to spread risk cannot take place. A house cannot be sold without certified property rights. If people live in the house that they have built but

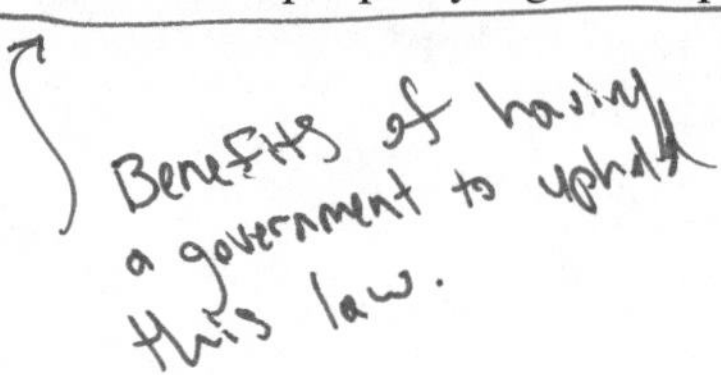

for which the right of possession cannot be legally certified, a mortgage could not have been used to finance construction of the house. The house cannot be insured against damage if the house does not have legally defined owners who can enter into an insurance contract. Without legally certified property rights, collateral (or security for loans) cannot be provided and credit markets therefore are limited. Without defined property rights, *stock* markets cannot exist because a firm cannot be owned by different shareholders who diversify assets and spread risk through ownership of different types of stocks.

Property rights and avoidance of anarchy

If there were no markets, people could still be self-sufficient and not trade. Without the rule of law, however, there is anarchy – true anarchy and not the "anarchy" in markets perceived by people who favor imposed order over the spontaneous order of the market. When there is anarchy, the right of natural possession is not protected. Appropriation, extortion, and theft are means of acquiring the property and goods of others. Without the rule of law, a person can then have only as much property as he or she is capable of defending. There is a social loss through socially unproductive use of time and resources. Activities of appropriation, extortion, theft, and defense use resources and personal time and initiative in socially unproductive ways. There is inefficiency because resources and time could have been used productively to add to available output.

Efficiency and social justice

The rule of law thus allows a society to obtain the benefits of efficiency in two ways:

- The rule of law allows markets to exist.

Without markets, there are nonetheless benefits from the rule of law:

- The rule of law provides incentives to use resources productively rather than to appropriate other people's property.

The rule of law is also the basis for social justice:

- The rule of law protects the natural right of possession and also people's lives.

Ethical behavior

Because of the legal monopoly of government on coercion, the rule of law is a responsibility of government. Still, without the rule of law imposed through government, there would be a civil society if people were to behave according to ethical precepts and respected the property and lives of others.

Anarchy and the prisoners' dilemma

When the rule of law is absent and people do not behave ethically, there is anarchy. Anarchy can give rise to circumstances described in table 1.1 where two identical people face a situation known as the *prisoners' dilemma* (we shall presently see why the dilemma is named after prisoners). The two people in table 1.1 face the same binary choice between using all personal resources productively and using some resources unproductively to take the other person's property. In our description, resources are not used in defense, although, in general, resources also are used to defend property and possessions.[30]

TABLE 1.1. THE PRISONERS' DILEMMA OF ANARCHY

	Person 2 only produces	Person 2 steals
Person 1 only produces	3, 3	1, 4
Person 1 steals	4, 1	2, 2

In table 1.1, four possible outcomes depend on the combinations of decisions that the individuals make. The two numbers in a cell in the table indicate the individuals' personal benefits from an outcome, with the first number indicating the benefit to person 1 and the second number the benefit to person 2. The numbers also indicate rankings of outcomes for each person, with higher values indicating more preferred personal outcomes.

When both individuals use all their resources productively, the outcome is (3, 3). When they both use resources to take from one another, output is lost and the outcome is (2, 2). The outcomes (3, 3) and (2, 2) are symmetric. Benefits for the outcomes (4, 1) and (1, 4) are, in contrast, asymmetric. The highest possible benefit 4 is obtained by taking the property of a person who does not reciprocally steal. The lowest benefit 1 is obtained by not reciprocally stealing when the other person steals.

With the two persons' individual benefits indicated by B_1 and B_2, an outcome is efficient when social (or total) benefit $W = (B_1 + B_2)$ is maximized. The outcome (3, 3) achieves maximal total benefit 6 and is therefore efficient. The question that we shall now consider is: Will independent voluntary decisions result in the efficient outcome (3, 3)?

Table 1.1 describes a *game* in which people interact strategically, with the outcome for each person depending on the person's own decision as well as on the decision made by the other person. Both individuals have full information about the decisions each can make and about the personal benefits available to each in the different possible outcomes. Each person independently makes a decision based on personal self-interest. There is no cooperation or coordination in making decisions.

[30] We shall consider defense when we study public goods.

The Nash equilibrium

We are looking for an *equilibrium* outcome of the two persons' decisions. The definition that we shall use to describe equilibrium is called the Nash equilibrium.[31]

> *In the Nash equilibrium, no person can gain by changing his or her decision, given the decisions that others have made.*

Dominant strategies

In the prisoners' dilemma, each person has a *dominant* strategy. *Strategy* here is another word for *decision*.

> *A dominant strategy exists when a person's best decision does not depend on the other person's decision.*

With both people confronting the same benefits (also known as *payoffs*) and having the same possible strategies, a dominant strategy for one person is also a dominant strategy for the other person. We can readily determine that:

> *The dominant strategy is to steal.*[32]

The dominant strategy guides us to the Nash equilibrium:

> *The Nash equilibrium is at the outcome (2, 2) where both individuals choose the dominant strategy and so each person wastefully uses resources to steal from the other.*

Can agreement to cooperate achieve efficiency?

A move from the Nash equilibrium at (2, 2) to (3, 3) is a Pareto improvement – both people are made better off. It is clearly worthwhile for both people to find a way to implement the move from (2, 2) to (3, 3). The two people could simply agree to move to (3, 3) from (2, 2) by promising not to steal from one other. A legally enforceable contract not to steal is impossible because there is anarchy rather than the rule of law required for contract enforcement. Cooperation not to steal and thereby to attain (3, 3) would require a self-enforcing contract.

> *A self-enforcing contract is self-sustainable through self-interest without external enforcement.*

[31] Nash equilibrium (Nash, 1951) is named after John Nash, who received the Nobel Prize in economics in 1995. The equilibrium is also called Cournot–Nash, to acknowledge the 19th-century French economist and engineer, Augustin Cournot (1801–77), who formulated a similar idea (Cournot, 1838).

[32] Stealing is the best decision *whether or not* the other person decides to steal. Consider person 1. *If person 2 does not steal*, person 1's best response is to steal because 4 > 3. *If person 2 steals*, the best response of person 1 is again to steal because 2 > 1. Stealing is therefore person 1's dominant strategy. Because of symmetry, stealing is likewise the dominant strategy of person 2.

A self-enforcing contract to sustain the efficient outcome (3, 3) is not possible because each person has an interest in departing from the conditions of the contract. The contract requires not stealing. However, compared to the outcome at (3, 3), each person is better off stealing, given that the other person is not stealing. That is, (3, 3) is not sustainable because (3, 3) is not a Nash equilibrium.[33] Promises to remain at (3, 3) are therefore not credible.[34]

Sequential decisions

We have described decisions as made simultaneously – or each person has made a decision without knowing the decision that the other has made. If decisions are made *sequentially* (where one person decides first and then the other), the outcome is again the Nash equilibrium (2, 2). Because the dominant strategy is to steal, the first person to decide steals and the second person's subsequent best response also is to steal.

Figure 1.10 shows the prisoners' dilemma with sequential decisions. The information in figure 1.10 is the same as in table 1.1. We see the four possible outcomes of the game at the end of the "game tree." Person 1 is arbitrarily chosen to decide first. The decision is whether to cooperate and not steal (YES) or to steal (NO to cooperation). Person 1 ideally would like to reach the outcome (4, 1). The path to (4, 1) requires that person 1 begin by declaring non-cooperation (NO). However, person 2 (whose utility and ranking of outcomes are given by the second number) would then respond by also choosing to steal (or NO to cooperation). The outcome is then (2, 2), which we identified as the Nash equilibrium. Choosing not to cooperate (NO) and ending in the Nash equilibrium

[33] Each person has an incentive to depart from (3, 3) to seek the better outcome of 4, which can be obtained by stealing, given that the other person is not stealing.

[34] We can now note the origins of the name "prisoners' dilemma." The police have evidence to convict two prisoners of a *minor* crime but believe that the prisoners have also committed a major crime for which there is no evidence. The prisoners know that the police have no evidence regarding the suspected major crime. The prisoners also know that they can be convicted of the major crime only if one of them confesses and implicates the other. The police take the prisoners to separate rooms and present each prisoner with the following alternatives: (1) if neither prisoner confesses to the major crime, they will both be convicted of the minor crime, for which the sentence is light (e.g., two years in jail); (2) if one of them confesses to the major crime and the other does not, the prisoner who confesses will receive a relatively lenient sentence (e.g., one year in jail), whereas the prisoner who did not confess will receive a very harsh sentence (e.g., ten years in jail); and (3) if both prisoners confess, they each receive quite a severe sentence (e.g., seven years in jail) but less severe than the sentence of the prisoner who does not confess when the other does (which is ten years). The prisoners confront a dilemma. If neither confesses, there is no evidence regarding the major crime. However, the dominant strategy is to confess to the major crime. Each prisoner reasons: "If my partner confesses, my best decision is also to confess (seven years in jail is better than ten). If my partner does not confess, again my best decision is to confess (one year in jail is better than two)." Hence, whatever the decision the other makes, each prisoner's personal best response is to confess to the major crime, which is the dominant strategy. We can observe a potential injustice. In the Nash equilibrium, the two prisoners confess to the major crime whether or not they have committed this crime.

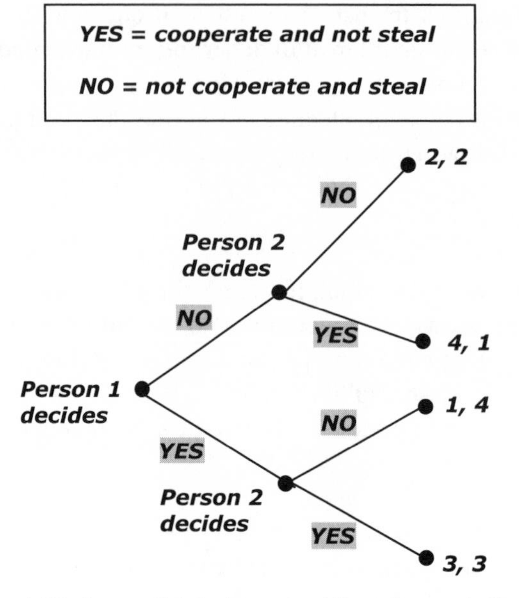

Figure 1.10. Sequential decisions and the prisoners' dilemma.

(2, 2) is the best decision that person 1 can make. Should person 1 choose to cooperate (YES), person 2 would maximize utility by choosing not to cooperate (NO), and the outcome then would be (1, 4).[35]

The inefficiency of independent self-interested decisions

In a competitive market equilibrium, efficiency is achieved through independent self-interested individual decisions. In the circumstances of the prisoners' dilemma, people are also making independent self-interested decisions. Each person is maximizing utility given the decision that the other has made. The outcome, however, is the inefficient Nash equilibrium.

In anarchy without the rule of law, the invisible hand is no longer effective in guiding self-interested decisions to efficient outcomes.

Repeated encounters and the value of reputation

We have described a single encounter of the prisoners' dilemma. Might the efficient outcome (3, 3) be achieved in repeated encounters – or in a repeated game? If the same two people play the prisoners' dilemma daily, they might cooperate to establish a reputation for cooperating. Such reputation will influence the behavior of the other person in the next round of interaction. If person 1 knows

[35] The game as set out in figure 1.10 is in extensive form. The figure is called a "game tree." More complex cases of extensive-form games require attention to subgame perfection (Reinhard Selten 1975; Nobel Prize in economics, 1994).

(or believes) that person 2 cooperates and does not steal, person 1 also can decide not to steal. With both people establishing a reputation for cooperating and not stealing, the efficient outcome (3, 3) is achieved, provided that interactions are known to continue indefinitely or for long but uncertain periods, because then there is always a tomorrow (or the chance of a tomorrow), and a reputation for cooperating therefore has value. Cooperation also requires gains in the future to be valued sufficiently by both people.[36]

Reputation for cooperating is of no value if there are to be no future encounters for which reputation can be of use. It follows that:

> *There is no incentive for cooperation in any round of a repeated prisoners' dilemma if the number of interactions is known to be finite.*[37]

Personal reputation only has value when people know one another – for example, within a family or among friends. In large anonymous populations, personal reputation for cooperating has no value. In societies with large numbers of anonymous people, we therefore cannot rely on personal reputation to provide an incentive for cooperation.

Experiments reveal that anonymous people nonetheless may cooperate in finite repeated encounters – especially if they are not economics students who have studied the prisoners' dilemma. By cooperating, people attribute *empathy* to one another rather than *strict rationality*. It is "natural" to cooperate. As with sharing, cooperation is instinctive, with the instinct dating to small hunter–gatherer groups.

When people cooperate in prisoners'-dilemma experiments, they also can be behaving expressively. By cooperating, people obtain utility from their self-confirmation of their identity as pleasant and cooperative. The highest utility may be obtained by cooperating when the other person does not. The cooperative person may feel socially superior to a person who has displayed self-interested uncooperative behavior. In that case, we are, however, departing from the payoffs of the prisoners' dilemma, which stipulate lowest utility when one person does not steal and the other does. When people feel good about themselves for having cooperated even though materially they lose because the other person in

[36] That is, for a person to have an incentive to cooperate and not steal, the person's discount rate must be sufficiently low to make waiting for future benefits worthwhile. If the discount rate is so high that present benefits from not cooperating are valued more than the stream of future benefits from establishing a reputation for cooperating, there is no incentive to cooperate today.

[37] If it is known that there are to be 20 encounters, reputation has no value in the final 20th encounter. Cooperation will therefore not take place in the final 20th encounter and the outcome will be the Nash equilibrium (2, 2) of the single-encounter game. There is then no point to cooperating in the 19th encounter because reputation in the 20th encounter is known to have no value. That is, the only reason for cooperating in the 19th encounter is to persuade the other player to cooperate in the 20th encounter. Because there is no value to reputation in the 19th encounter, there is no reason to cooperate in the 18th encounter. Nor then does reputation have value in the 17th encounter – nor in any encounter. Cooperation rationally will not take place.

the game has not reciprocated cooperation, the experiments also correspondingly depart from the payoffs of the prisoners' dilemma.

The paradox of gain from coercion

With the payoffs of the prisoners' dilemma, inability to rely on voluntary cooperation is the basis for calling on government to enforce the efficient outcome at (3, 3) through the rule of law. Calling on government introduces the paradox of gain from coercion. In the prisoners' dilemma, people *wish to be coerced* to move from (2, 2) to (3, 3).

TABLE 1.2. THE PRISONERS' DILEMMA AND THE RULE OF LAW

	Person 2 only produces	Person 2 steals
Person 1 only produces	3, 3	$1, 2 = \{4 - 2\}$
Person 1 steals	$\{4 - 2\} = 2, 1$	$0 = \{2 - 2\}, 0 = \{2 - 2\}$

A government can declare a legal penalty for stealing. In table 1.2, a penalty of 2 is imposed for theft. The penalty is subtracted from personal benefit whenever a person steals. The penalty changes the dominant strategy to "not to steal."[38]

The legal penalty achieves the efficient outcome (3, 3) without the penalty being imposed. The penalty is a deterrent, not ever an actual punishment. *Rational behavior* – given the punishment for stealing – is not to steal.

However, to be effective, the threat of punishment through the penalty must be credible. Credibility is costly. The police are required, even if the police never have anyone to apprehend.

Private deterrence

Private deterrence is a possible response to the threat of theft. Personal bodyguards can be hired or a private security force. Personal resources then determine the effectiveness of private deterrence. When people differ in personal resources, protection through private deterrence is unequal. Private deterrence therefore violates the principle of the rule of law that there should be equality before the law. Because of dependence of outcomes on personal resources:

> *Deterrence through personal resources is more akin to anarchy than to the rule of law.*

[38] A person who steals when the other does not receives *(4 – 2)* = *2*. When both steal, each receives *(2 – 2)* = *0*. If person 2 does not steal, person 1's best response also is not to steal because 3 > 2. If person 2 decides to steal, person 1's best response still is not to steal because 1 > 0. The dominant strategy of person 1, therefore, is not to steal, as is likewise the dominant strategy of person 2.

Private deterrence requires resources to be used by individuals for personal protection. The rule of law protects everybody simultaneously by changing incentives as in table 1.2. The rule of law is a public good for the entire population.

Because everybody benefits from the rule of law, the rule of law is a public good.

B. Anarchy with strong and weak

The prisoners' dilemma describes anarchy when people have symmetric capabilities. A population, however, in general consists of people who are strong and others who are weak. If ethics do not restrain the strong from taking advantage of the weak, only the rule of law can protect the weak.

The German philosopher, Friedrich Nietzsche (1846–1900), predicted that in a state of anarchy or "nature" where there are neither ethical nor legal bounds on behavior, the strong exert their will on the weak. The prediction was a positive statement, not a normative statement about what should happen. Nietzsche proposed that ethics and conscience had been introduced into the world by people who were weak as means of protection against the strong. Thus, lambs who are victims of lions would proclaim that it is unethical for lions to eat lambs because lambs are gentle and do not threaten lions. Nietzsche predicted that the lions being strong and the lambs being weak, the lions will eat the lambs in any event.[39]

Nietzsche's theories can be applied to anarchy. Table 1.3a describes circumstances facing the weak and the strong in anarchy.

TABLE 1.3a. NIETZSCHEAN RELATIONS BETWEEN STRONG AND WEAK

	Potential output	Cost of appropriation	Amount taken	Net gain from appropriation	Utility of the weak from leisure
Weak	10				4
Strong	20	3	10	7	

The weak, if they use all their resources and time productively, can produce 10. The strong can produce 20 if they likewise use all their resources productively. The values 10 and 20 are also the respective utilities or benefits of the weak and the strong when they each use resources productively.

The strong can choose to use some of their resources to attempt to appropriate the output of the weak. We can envisage the strong coming to the fields of the weak seeking to take the produce that the weak have produced. The strong incur a cost of appropriation of 3 in traveling to the fields of the weak. If the weak have

[39] Nietzsche died demented, believing that he was the devil.

worked, the strong take the output of 10 that the weak have produced. The net gain to the strong from appropriation is therefore 7.

However, when the strong decide whether to travel to the fields of the weak, they do not know whether the weak have chosen to work. Therefore, the strong do not know whether there will be anything to appropriate from the fields of the weak. If the weak have not worked, the strong incur a net loss of 3 from the unsuccessful attempt at appropriation.

The weak decide whether to work not knowing whether the strong will attempt to appropriate. If the weak decide to work and the strong arrive to take their output, the weak are left with nothing. If the weak decide not to work, they have utility of 4 from leisure. Utility from leisure cannot be appropriated and is therefore independent of whether or not the strong arrive.[40]

The sources of inefficiency

There are two potential sources of inefficiency. There is a loss of 3 in resources and time unproductively used if the strong set out to appropriate. The weak produce 10 if they work but only have utility of 4 if they do not work; hence there is a loss of 6 if the weak do not work.

The equilibrium

The one-time game between the strong and the weak is shown in table 1.3b, which is based on the data in figure 1.3a. The first number in table 1.3b is the benefit for the weak and the second number is the benefit for the strong. The strong and the weak have complete information about the game. They know, in particular, that decisions are made simultaneously – or without one side knowing the decision of the other. We are looking for a Nash equilibrium. We used the presence of dominant strategies to find the Nash equilibrium in the prisoners' dilemma. Our first step in seeking an equilibrium is again to look for dominant strategies.

TABLE 1.3b. ANARCHY WITH WEAK AND STRONG

	The strong seek to appropriate	The strong do *not* seek to appropriate
The weak are productive	0, <u>27</u>	<u>10</u>, 20
The weak are *not* productive	<u>4</u>, 17	4, <u>20</u>

[40] We shall not consider slavery or forced labor whereby the weak are forced to work; nor in our presentation do the strong harm or kill the weak out of frustration if the strong arrive at the fields of the weak and find that the weak have chosen not to work.

In table 1.3b neither the strong nor the weak have a dominant strategy. If the weak choose to work, the best response of the strong is to appropriate; however, if the weak do not work, the best response of the strong is not to use resources in appropriation. If the strong set out to appropriate, the best response of the weak is not to work; however, if the strong do not set out to appropriate, the best response of the weak is to work.

Nash equilibria can exist when there are no dominant strategies. We therefore need to examine the four possible outcomes in table 1.3b to determine whether we can find a Nash equilibrium. We shall, however, not find a Nash equilibrium: in each of the four possible outcomes, either the weak or the strong can do better by changing their decision.

At (0, 27), the weak work and the strong appropriate. The weak have nothing. The strong use 3 to take the output of the weak and have $\{20 + 10 - 3\} = 27$. The outcome at (0, 27) is not a Nash equilibrium because the weak can do better by not working, which moves the outcome to (4, 17).

At (4, 17), the weak have a benefit of 4 from leisure. The strong have 17 because they have lost 3 of their potential output of 20 in the unsuccessful attempt at appropriation. With the weak having produced nothing, the strong can do better by not using resources in attempting to appropriate, which moves the outcome to (4, 20).

At (4, 20), the weak have utility 4 from leisure and the strong, who are now not attempting to appropriate, have 20. Because the strong are not attempting to appropriate, the weak can do better by working, which moves the outcome to (10, 20).

At (10, 20), the outcome is efficient because all resources are being used productively.[41] However, the weak are working and therefore the strong can do better by appropriating, which returns the outcome to (0, 27) – which is where we began.

We have therefore not found a Nash equilibrium. However, we need to qualify what we mean by not having found a Nash equilibrium. To be precise, we have not found a Nash equilibrium in *pure* strategies.

> *A Nash equilibrium in pure strategies is one in which decisions are made with certainty.*

When there is no Nash equilibrium in pure strategies, we look for a Nash equilibrium in mixed strategies.

> *A mixed strategy is a decision based on randomizing behavior.*[42]

[41] The sum $(12 + 20) = 32$ is greater than the total available in any other outcome.

[42] Formally, every finite strategic game has a mixed-strategy equilibrium, and a pure-strategy equilibrium is a special case in which the probabilities of making two decisions are (1, 0); that is, one decision is made with probability 1.

In a mixed-strategy Nash equilibrium, no one has an incentive to change randomizing behavior, given the choice of randomizing behavior of others.[43]

If the strong knew with certainty that the weak will choose to be productive, they would choose to appropriate with certainty. Because the strong do not know the decision of the weak, they can randomize or mix their decisions.

Similarly, if the weak knew with certainty that the strong have predatory intentions, they would not work with certainty. They would work with certainty if they knew with certainty that the strong did not intend to appropriate their output. Because the weak do not know whether the strong have predatory intentions, they too can randomize or mix their decisions.

In table 1.3b, the mixed-strategy equilibrium is that the weak work with 30 percent probability (and do not work with 70 percent probability), whereas the strong set out to appropriate with 60 percent probability (and use all their resources productively with 40 percent probability). How are these probabilities derived?

To find a mixed-strategy equilibrium, we look for probabilities of making decisions that result in decision makers being indifferent between their alternative choices.

We look first at the decision of the strong. Table 1.3b shows that the strong can always achieve 20 *with certainty* by not attempting appropriation. The strong will never choose appropriation if doing so leaves them, *on average* (because of the uncertainty about the behavior of the weak), with less than the 20 that they can obtain with certainty by using all of their resources productively. The strong have 27 if they set out to appropriate and find that the weak have worked, and they have 17 if they arrive at the fields of the weak to find that the weak have not worked. We denote by P_W the probability that the weak work. The expected benefit to the strong from choosing to set out to appropriate is therefore:

$$27 \cdot P_W + 17 \cdot (1 - P_W).$$

The strong, therefore, are indifferent between their alternative actions when:

$$20 = 27 \cdot P_W + 17 \cdot (1 - P_W).$$

The solution to this equation is $P_W = 0.3$. That is, the weak work with a probability of 30 percent.

[43] An example of mixing strategies is when we are presented with a choice between two identical closed boxes, one containing $100 and the other $20, each with probability one-half. In the absence of further information, we can do no better than randomize our decision by flipping a coin to decide. Our decision rule of flipping a coin gives each box a 50 percent chance of being chosen. This is our mixed strategy. We have mixed the strategies (decisions) by assigning a 50 percent probability to choosing either box. More generally, randomizing behavior does not require assigning probabilities of 50 percent to different decisions.

We denote by P_S the probability that the strong set out to appropriate. If the weak have worked and the strong arrive, the weak are left with nothing. If the strong do not arrive to appropriate and the weak have worked, the weak retain their output of 10. The expected benefit of the weak *when they work* is therefore:

$$\{0\} \cdot P_S + 10 \cdot (1 - P_S) = 10 \cdot (1 - P_S).$$

The weak can choose to have 4 with certainty by *not working*. The weak are therefore indifferent between their alternatives of working and not working when:

$$10 \cdot (1 - P_S) = 4.$$

The solution to this equation is $P_S = 0.6$. The strong, therefore, set out to appropriate with a probability of 60 percent.

TABLE 1.3c. PROBABILITIES OF OUTCOMES WITH WEAK AND STRONG

The weak are productive with probability $P_W = 0.3$		The weak are not productive with probability $(1 - P_W) = 0.7$	
The strong do not attempt to appropriate with probability $(1 - P_S) = 0.4$	The strong come to appropriate with probability $P_S = 0.6$	The strong do not attempt to appropriate with probability $(1 - P_S) = 0.4$	The strong come to appropriate with probability $P_S = 0.6$
12%	18%	28%	42%

Table 1.3c shows the likelihoods of the four possible outcomes. To determine the likelihood of an outcome, we compute the *joint probabilities* of the weak and strong making the decisions that result in the outcome.

The probabilities of the four possible outcomes, of course, sum to 1. The efficient outcome, in which the weak work and the strong do not use resources in appropriation, arises with a probability of 12 percent. All other outcomes are inefficient because either the strong use resources unproductively in setting out to appropriate or the weak do not work, or both. The most likely outcome with 42 percent probability is that the weak do not work and the strong unproductively use resources to attempt to appropriate and find that there is nothing to take.[44]

The burden of inefficiency

We do not know with certainty which outcome will arise. We know only the probabilities for each outcome as shown in table 1.3c. However, we do know that the mixed-strategy Nash equilibrium gives the strong, on average, 20 and the weak,

[44] If we changed the values in table 1.3b, we would, of course, obtain different probabilities of the weak and the strong taking their respective actions, and thereby different probabilities of outcomes in table 1.3c.

on average, 4. Total equilibrium benefit for the strong and the weak combined is therefore, on average, $24 = (20 + 4)$.[45]

If the rule of law were present to prevent appropriation by the strong, both the strong and the weak would use their resources productively with certainty, and total social benefit would be $30 = (10 + 20)$. The efficiency loss from the absence of the rule of law is therefore $6 = (30 - 24)$.

In the mixed-strategy Nash equilibrium, the weak have, on average, 4 instead of the 10 they could have from productive use of their resources. The social loss of 6 is imposed on the weak. Thus:

> *The entire burden of inefficiency falls on the weak.*

We would not expect otherwise. The strong would not choose behavior (including randomizing behavior) that is disadvantageous for them.

Credibility

Before decisions are made, if the strong were to declare that they do not intend to appropriate the output of the weak and if the declaration were believed by the weak, the weak would work. However, the promise by the strong not to appropriate is not credible. The weak (and the strong) know that if the weak work, the strong can do better by appropriating.

Laziness and incentives

The weak are not "lazy" because they do not always work. Rather:

> *In not consistently working, the weak respond rationally to predatory behavior of the strong.*

The weak also have an incentive to make the strong believe that, when they work, the weak are not productive.

Roving and stationary bandits

If we refer to the strong as "bandits," we can distinguish between roving and stationary bandits. A *roving bandit* is a predator who encounters the same weak population only once and will be elsewhere afterwards. Roving bandits are extremely dangerous. They have no need for the weak after the single encounter. The case of the roving bandit is the single-encounter game that has been described.[46]

A *stationary bandit* repeatedly encounters the same weak persons over time. A *repeated game* therefore takes place. In the repeated game, both the strong and

[45] The strong can always obtain 20 by being productive and the weak can always obtain 4 by not working, which determine the benefits of each in the mixed-strategy Nash equilibrium.

[46] The distinction between roving and stationary bandits is from Mancur Olson (1932–98), who was a professor at the University of Maryland. See, for example, Olson (2000).

the weak can be better off than in the equilibrium of the single-encounter game. In the repeated game with stationary-bandit behavior, the strong appropriate in each period and still bear the cost of appropriation. However, the strong can provide an incentive for the weak to work consistently and be productive in each period.

The weak have 4 if they do not work. They likewise have an expected return of 4 in the mixed-strategy roving-bandit Nash equilibrium in which they bear the entire burden of inefficiency. If the weak were to work consistently and produce 10, there would be a surplus of $(10 - 4) = 6$, which could be shared between the weak and the strong. Many Pareto-improving divisions of the surplus benefit of 6 are possible.[47]

The strong could bargain with the weak over the division of the surplus. The weak have bargaining power. It is the output of the weak when they work that provides the surplus to be shared that can make both the strong and the weak better off. With the surplus of 6 divided *in any way* that makes both the strong and the weak better off, there is Pareto improvement. Because of the Pareto improvement, stationary-bandit behavior by the strong is sustainable as a *self-enforcing contract* that both the strong and the weak have an incentive to sustain. The self-enforcing contract is based on reputation. The strong, at any time, could choose to appropriate all the output 10 produced by the weak and leave the weak with nothing. The weak would then understandably no longer trust the strong and would revert to the randomizing behavior of the mixed-strategy equilibrium in which they work with 30 percent probability. The strong would then lose – as would the weak. Hence:

> *The strong as stationary bandits have an interest in incentives that lead the weak to be consistently productive, which requires that the strong maintain their reputation for behaving as stationary and not roving bandits.*

Why does the prospect of Pareto improvement not lead all bandits to behave as stationary bandits? Bandits with short time horizons act as the more predatory roving bandits, as do bandits with high discount rates, which reduce (or discount) the value of the future benefits from providing incentives for the weak to be productive. In the absence of the rule of law, the strong today also may fear that they may not retain their dominance tomorrow; therefore, they take what they can today.

Who is a bandit? We have been describing anarchy without the rule of law and without government. However, we have observed that the rule of law and the rule of government are not equivalent. In nondemocratic societies, "government" can be the bandit, by not implementing the rule of law but rather by providing the

[47] We have encountered here an application of the "folk theorem" for infinitely repeated games. This theorem states that when people who meet in repeated encounters care sufficiently about the future, there are infinitely many solutions for repeated games. The conclusion is known as a folk theorem because the theorem was known before the formal analysis was published.

means through the authority of government for the strong to take from the weak. In such a case, the weak can only hope that the behavior of government is at least that of the stationary and not the roving bandit.[48]

Consequences of the rule of law

Stationary bandits are predatory but less so out of self-interest than roving bandits. The rule of law ends both stationary- and roving-bandit predatory behavior. Efficiency is achieved because resources are not used in appropriation and because the weak have incentives to be consistently productive. There is social justice defined as the natural right of possession because the weak retain the product of their own efforts.

C. Anarchy and ethics

The rule of law imposed through a formal legal system would not be required if all people behaved ethically and respected the natural right of possession of others. Without a formal legal system, if the strong nonetheless behaved ethically, they would not appropriate the output of the weak.

The Nietzschean game between strong and weak involves no ethics. Nor does the prisoners' dilemma. The maximal personal benefit in the prisoners' dilemma is achieved by stealing from a person who respects the property rights of others.

We now introduce an honest person. The honest person has utility from ethical behavior. Table 1.4a shows the honest person's personal benefits and costs.

TABLE 1.4a. BENEFITS AND COSTS FOR AN HONEST PERSON

Utility from ethical behavior	Potential output	Cost of stealing	Amount stolen	Net gain from stealing
20	30	3	10	7

The honest person has subjective utility of 20 from personal ethical behavior. Additional utility of 30 is obtainable from using personal resources productively. Should the honest person appropriate or steal, the cost in terms of resources used is 3 and the amount taken or stolen is 10, leaving a net gain of 7. Table 1.4b shows the symmetric game between two representative honest people.

[48] Bandits also can be organized groups in anarchic neighborhoods. The weak in the neighborhood confront the threat of appropriation by the strong, who may behave as the more dangerous roving bandits or as stationary bandits. Because being strong or weak is all that matters, there are incentives to join coalitions or gangs.

TABLE 1.4b. A POPULATION THAT FOLLOWS ETHICAL RULES OF CONDUCT

	Ethical person 2 only produces	Ethical person 2 steals
Ethical person 1 only produces	50, 50	40, 37
Ethical person 1 steals	37, 40	27, 27

The outcomes in table 1.4b arise as follows:

- At (50, 50), both people have maximal personal benefit of (20 + 30), comprised of the utility of 20 from ethical behavior and the utility of 30 from productive activity.
- (27, 27) is the outcome if both people steal from one other. Both lose utility of 20 because of unethical behavior. Each loses 10 through theft by the other and has a net gain of 7 from his or her own theft. Each person, therefore, has *(30 − 10 + 7) = 27.*
- In the asymmetric outcomes (37, 40) and (40, 37), one person is stealing and the other is not. The person stealing loses the utility of 20 because of unethical behavior and adds the net gain of 7 from theft to his or her own output of 30 to obtain in total 37. The person not stealing has the utility of 20 from ethical behavior and is left with output of 20 after the other person has stolen 10, resulting in a benefit of 40.

The dominant strategy in table 1.4b is not to steal, and the Nash equilibrium is the efficient outcome (50, 50).

A mixed population of honest and dishonest people

In a mixed population of honest and dishonest people, an honest person with the personal benefits and costs in table 1.4a can encounter a dishonest person. Table 1.4c shows the benefits and costs for a dishonest person, whose preferences over outcomes are as in the prisoners' dilemma. A dishonest person obtains no utility from ethical behavior.

Table 1.4d shows the game between person 1 who is honest and person 2 who is dishonest, or predatory.

TABLE 1.4c. BENEFITS AND COSTS FOR A DISHONEST PERSON

Utility from ethical behavior	Potential output	Cost of stealing	Amount stolen	Net gain from stealing
–	30	3	10	7

TABLE 1.4d. AN ETHICAL PERSON FACING A PREDATOR

	Predatory person 2 is productive	Predatory person 2 steals
Ethical person 1 is productive	50, 30	40, 37
Ethical person 1 steals	37, 20	27, 27

The outcomes in table 1.4d arise as follows:

- The outcome (50, 30) is obtained when both people use all of their resources productively. This is the efficient outcome. No resources are being used in appropriation and person 1 is deriving utility from ethical behavior. Total benefit is maximized, with $(50 + 30) = 80$.
- The outcome (40, 37) occurs when person 2 steals from honest person 1 who does not steal. Person 1 has a benefit of 40 because person 2 steals 10. Person 2 has 37, obtained through using resources of value 3 to steal 10 from person 1. If utilities were comparable, we could conclude that the honest person has higher utility (40) than the person stealing (37). However, the utilities here are not comparable. Otherwise the predatory person would choose to become honest and thereby have greater utility. The predatory person does not choose to become honest because, unlike the honest person, he obtains no utility from ethical behavior.
- At (37, 20), person 1 loses the utility of 20 because she is stealing. She obtains a net gain of 7 from stealing, giving benefit of $(50 - 20 + 7) = 37$. Person 2 loses 10 from the theft and has $(30 - 10) = 20$.
- At (27, 27), the two people steal from one another. They each have a net gain of 7 from theft. Both have the same benefit of 27 but for different reasons. Person 1 has lost utility because of having behaved unethically and also has lost in having been the victim of theft by person 2. Person 2 has lost because of the theft by person 1 but incurs no loss of utility from having stolen.

The dominant strategy of person 1 is not to steal, the dominant strategy of person 2 is to steal, and the Nash equilibrium is at (40, 37). We therefore conclude:

> *When one person is honest and the other is predatory, the inefficient Nash equilibrium results in the victimization of the honest person.*

The efficient outcome, in which there is also no victimization, can be achieved through the rule of law. A sufficiently high penalty for stealing changes the dominant strategy of person 2 to not stealing. The Nash equilibrium then becomes the efficient outcome at (50, 30).[49]

[49] For example, if the penalty for stealing is 20, person 2 obtains 17 from stealing when person 1 does not steal (and would obtain 7 from stealing if person 1 did steal). The dominant strategy of person 2 becomes not to steal.

D. Imperfections in the rule of law

In general, governments are only imperfectly able to enforce the rule of law. Deterrence through penalties is not always effective. The study of criminology explains why there are people in prison and why people return to prison (known as *recidivism*). Imperfections also arise in the rule of law if the rule of law does not protect people from improper use of the authority of government.

Private protection

A response to the ineffectiveness of government in enforcing the rule of law is private protection through private security firms, bodyguards, and private surveillance systems. We have observed, however, that private solutions based on personal resources violate the principle of equality before the law, because protection through personal resources is akin to the conditions of anarchy. The personal resources determine who is strong and who is weak. The desirability of avoiding reliance on personal resources for protection is the source of the case for responsibility of government to ensure the rule of law.

Insurance

Another response to ineffective enforcement of the rule of law is insurance. Through insurance, the inevitability of loss of property is accepted and people pool or share risk. The people who incur personal losses are compensated by others who have avoided losses.

Insurance provides personal protection when adverse outcomes randomly affect relatively few people in a population. Risks that confront a society at large cannot be spread through insurance. Insurance is thus ineffective when the threat of loss is not through appropriation or theft but from adversaries who seek to inflict maximal harm on as many people as possible. When a large part of a population is simultaneously at risk, risk cannot be spread through insurance; then, only the government can protect.

Crime and suing the government

In principle, people who have been victims of crime should be able to sue a government for compensation for personal losses. After all, people pay taxes to a government so that the government can fulfill responsibilities of providing protection against criminals. In general, a government cannot be sued for personal losses that are due to ineffective enforcement of the rule of law.

Response to breach of contract by the government

Citizens and firms may have claims against a government for breach of contract. A government agency may not have paid for goods or services provided by private suppliers, or a private construction firm may have incurred costs in preparing to undertake a contractually agreed-on project for a government, but then the government neither proceeds with the project nor offers compensation.

> *A test for the presence of the rule of law is whether a private individual or firm that sues a government in a court of law has an objectively reasonable chance of being successful.*

Governments are strong in general (and have a legal monopoly on coercion) and individuals are weak. When government is subject to the rule of law, outcomes are possible in which the courts decide against the government. If a government is immune to legal claims of citizens, the rule of law is not present.

The type of legal system

There are different types of legal systems. A defining attribute of a legal system is in who determines whether a person is innocent or guilty. The decision may be made by a jury of fellow citizens or by judges. A king or government may intend to take someone's property and the owner of the property appeals to the court for protection. A jury of citizens will tend to make an independent decision that provides protection under the rule of law. Judges whose salaries are paid by a king or by government can have incentives to make decisions contrary to the principles of the rule of law.[50]

Supplement S1

Supplement S1A: Market efficiency in general equilibrium

A *partial-equilibrium* description of efficiency looks at a single market. A *general-equilibrium* picture describes the many markets of a competitive economy. A simplified general-equilibrium picture describes an economy populated by two people, with two factors of production used to produce two final consumption goods. The simplified picture suffices to show that in an economy with competitive markets, the following three objectives of efficient allocation are achieved:

- Factors of production (or resources) are efficiently allocated to production of different goods.
- The combination of goods produced in the economy maximizes the value of output.
- Goods produced are allocated efficiently for consumption among the population.

[50] Judges who are democratically elected are accountable to citizens. The mechanisms of tyranny often involve government-appointed judges.

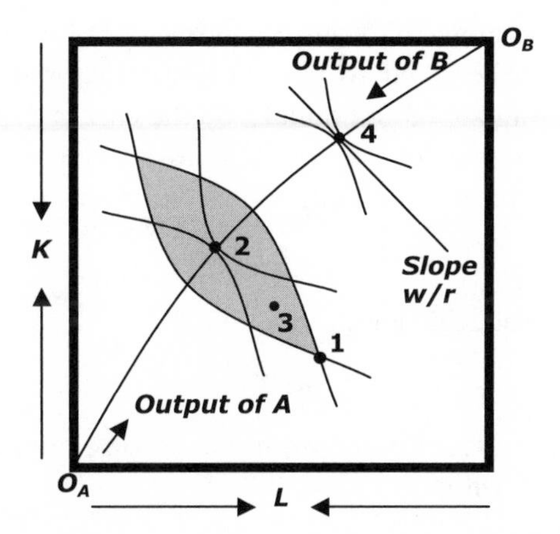

Figure S1.1. Allocation of factors of production.

These objectives are similar to the objectives we posed when considering the efficiency of a single market. The difference now is that we include factor markets and allocation across markets. It remains the case – and we shall not show again – that within any one competitive market, goods are assigned to buyers to maximize total benefit B of buyers, supply is assigned to sellers to minimize the total cost C of supply, and the quantity supplied in a market equilibrium to buyers maximizes $W = B - C$.

Efficient allocation of resources

Figure S1.1 shows an economy with two factors of production, which we identify as labor L and capital K. A point in the box defines an allocation of capital and labor between production of goods A and B.[51] Pareto-efficient allocations lie along the *contract curve* $O_A O_B$, defined by points where *isoquants* of the two goods are tangential.[52] Point 2 on the contract curve is a Pareto-efficient allocation; that is, no move is possible away from point 2 to obtain more of one good without giving up a quantity of the other.[53] Point 1 is an inefficient allocation. From any Pareto-inefficient point such as 1, the allocation can be changed to a point such as 3, which is Pareto-superior in providing more of both goods. From any point such as 3, the allocation can be further changed to a point such as 2, which is Pareto-efficient (and Pareto-superior to point 3).

[51] The box is named after Francis Y. Edgeworth (1845–1926) and Arthur L. Bowley (1869–1957). However, the box was first used by Pareto in 1906.

[52] An *isoquant*, as the name implies, defines a constant *quantity*, available through different combinations of capital and labor. Along an isoquant, output remains constant as substitution of factors used in production takes place.

[53] Moving away from point 2 up the contract curve increases the quantity of good A but decreases the quantity of good B. Moving down the contract curve from point 2 increases the quantity of good B and reduces the quantity of good A. Moving off the contract curve from point 2 decreases the supply of both goods or increases the supply of one good while decreasing the supply of the other.

In a competitive economy, all firms obtain factors of production in the same competitive factor markets and so pay the same factor prices. Let w be the market-determined wage of labor and let r be the cost of capital (r is the return that firms are obliged to pay for investment funds). The production technologies expressed in the substitution possibilities along isoquants in figure S1.1 are:

$$q_i = F^i(K_i, L_i) \quad i = A, B. \tag{S1.1}$$

Profits of a firm j producing good A are:

$$\pi_A^j = P_A F^A(K_A, L_A) - wL_A^j - rK_A^j. \tag{S1.2}$$

A firm producing good A chooses profit-maximizing employment of labor and use of capital in accord with:

$$\frac{\partial \pi_A^j}{\partial L_A^j} = P_A \frac{\partial F^A}{\partial L_A^j} - w = 0, \quad \frac{\partial \pi_A^j}{\partial K_A^j} = P_A \frac{\partial F^A}{\partial K_A^j} - r = 0. \tag{S1.3}$$

Therefore:

$$w = P_A \frac{\partial F^A}{\partial L_A^j} \equiv P_A MP_L^A, \quad r = P_A \frac{\partial F^A}{\partial K_A^j} \equiv P_A MP_K^A. \tag{S1.4a}$$

The same relationships apply to firms producing good B, for which we have:

$$w = P_B \frac{\partial F^B}{\partial L_B^j} \equiv P_B MP_L^B, \quad r = P_B \frac{\partial F^B}{\partial K_B^j} \equiv P_B MP_K^B. \tag{S1.4b}$$

The slope of an isoquant is defined as:

$$\frac{MP_L^i}{MP_K^i} \quad i = A, B. \tag{S1.5}$$

On the contract curve, because slopes of isoquants are equal:

$$\frac{MP_L^A}{MP_K^A} = \frac{MP_L^B}{MP_K^B}. \tag{S1.6}$$

However, competitive factor markets result in:

$$\frac{MP_L^A}{MP_K^A} = \frac{w}{r} = \frac{MP_L^B}{MP_K^B}. \tag{S1.7}$$

At points on the contract curve such as point 4 in figure S1.1, condition (S1.7) is satisfied. Hence:

Competitive-factor markets ensure efficient allocation of an economy's productive resources.

Choice of the combination of goods to produce

The information in figure S1.1 allows derivation of the economy's production-possibility frontier in figure S1.2. Points 1 and 3 in figure S1.2 are inside the

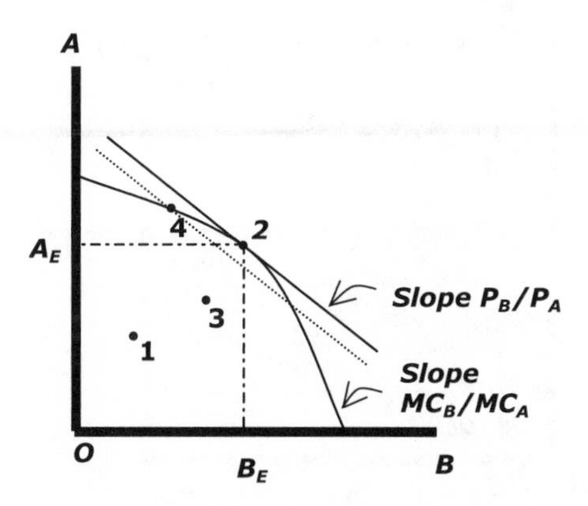

Figure S1.2. Combination of outputs.

production-possibility frontier because of the Pareto inefficiency of such factor allocations. The Pareto-efficient allocations 2 and 4 are on the production-possibility frontier. The value of the economy's national output (or national income), which is:

$$Y = P_A A_E + P_B B_E, \tag{S1.8}$$

is maximized at point 2 where the quantities A_E and B_E are produced and the relative price of the goods is P_B/P_A. At point 4, for example, the value of national output is lower than at point 2. The slope of the production-possibility frontier is defined by:

$$\frac{MC_B}{MC_A} \equiv MRT_{BA}, \tag{S1.9}$$

where MRT_{BA} indicates the marginal rate of transformation between goods B and A, given by the opportunity cost at the margin of transforming one good into the other. In competitive output markets, firms maximize profits by setting:

$$P_A = MC_A, \; P_B = MC_B. \tag{S1.10}$$

Therefore, when output markets are competitive:

$$\frac{P_B}{P_A} = \frac{MC_B}{MC_A} \equiv MRT_{BA}. \tag{S1.11}$$

Accordingly:

Competitive-product markets result in maximized value of national output.

Efficient distribution of goods among buyers

The last objective is efficient distribution of goods among buyers. In figure S1.3, the dimensions of the box indicate the quantities of goods produced at point 2 in figure S1.2, which are the quantities of two goods available for distribution to

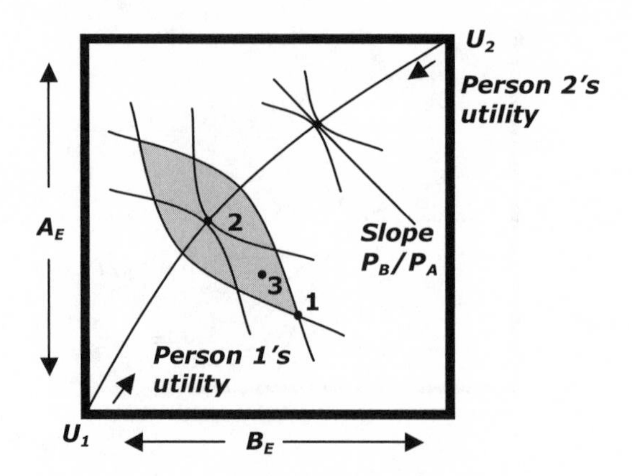

Figure S1.3. Allocation of goods for consumption.

the population. The indifference curves indicate consumption preferences of two consumers, person 1 and person 2.

Figure S1.3 differs from figure S1.1 only in that outputs rather than inputs are being allocated. The allocation of goods at point 1 in figure S1.3 is Pareto-inefficient; point 3 is Pareto-superior to point 1; and point 2 is Pareto-superior to point 3 and is Pareto-efficient. The slope of an indifference curve indicates the marginal rate of substitution between the goods (that is, the substitution between goods at the margin that maintains equal utility):

$$MRS_{AB}^{person\ i} \equiv \frac{MB_B^i}{MB_A^i}, \quad i = 1, 2 \text{ buyers.} \tag{S1.12}$$

Along the contract curve,

$$MRS_{AB}^{person1} = MRS_{AB}^{person2}. \tag{S1.13}$$

An allocation of goods is Pareto-efficient when condition (S1.13) is satisfied. Individuals choose quantities of goods to buy according to:

$$P_A = MB_A^i, \quad P_B = MB_B^i, \quad i = 1, 2 \text{ buyers.} \tag{S1.14}$$

For competitive market outcomes, therefore:

$$MRS_{AB}^{person1} = \frac{P_B}{P_A} = MRS_{AB}^{person2}. \tag{S1.15}$$

Expression (S1.15) is equivalent to (S1.13). Therefore:

Competitive market allocations of goods among buyers are Pareto-efficient.

Simultaneity

We have described (1) how inputs are allocated in production, (2) how the combination of goods to produce is determined, and (3) how goods are allocated among buyers. The description has been sequential. However, the decisions are made

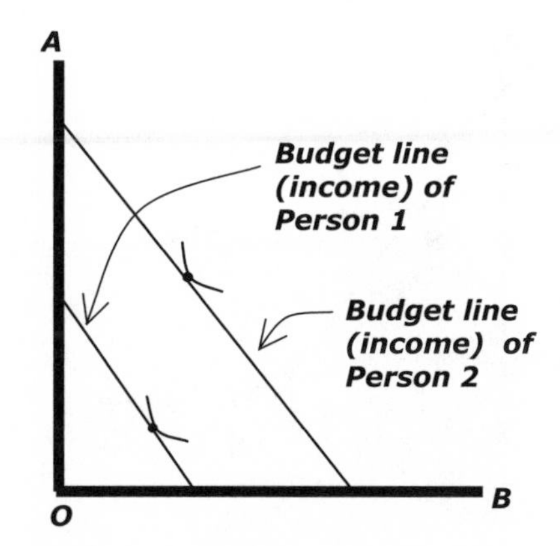

Figure S1.4. Income distribution and efficiency.

simultaneously. Formally, market equilibria are obtained by simultaneously solving demand and supply equations in all markets, to account for the linkages among the markets. Because simultaneous equations can have more than one solution or no solution, economists study whether the general equilibrium of an economy is unique or exists at all.

Incentives and factor supplies

The quantities of factors of production supplied in figure S1.1 depend on incentives through factor prices and are therefore *endogenous* rather than predetermined. Equilibrium factor supplies determine production possibilities in figure S1.2 and, therefore consumption possibilities in figure S1.3.

Income distribution

With equilibrium incomes determined by equilibrium factor prices, figure S1.4 shows two individuals with different incomes and different preferences in consumption. As long as the two individuals confront the same market prices when making buying decisions, the allocation determined through competitive markets is on the contract curve in figure S1.3 and therefore is Pareto-efficient. Income distribution determines where on the contract curve the efficient allocation will be.

International trade

Figure S1.5 shows an economy's production-possibilities frontier supplemented by opportunities for international trade at the terms of trade or relative price P_B/P_A. When the economy is closed to international trade, consumption and production possibilities coincide and both are given by the economy's production-possibilities frontier. Free trade expands consumption possibilities to the country's free-trade budget line *outside* of the domestic production-possibilities

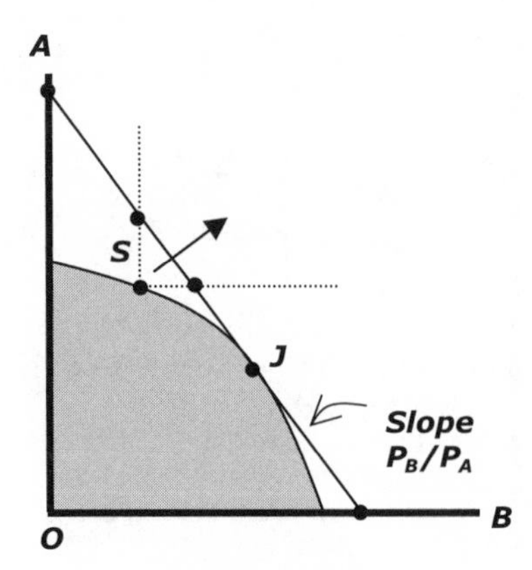

Figure S1.5. The efficiency of international trade.

frontier. For any closed-economy consumption outcome on the production-possibilities frontier such as point *S*, there are Pareto-superior consumption points on the free-trade budget line; the sole exception is the point of tangency *J* of the free-trade budget line with the production-possibilities frontier, where free trade offers no gains but also results in no losses. If the closed-economy consumption point is anywhere but at point *J*, there are thus gains from trade for the economy; if the closed-economy consumption is at point *J*, there are no losses. Therefore:

The case for the efficiency of the market includes international markets.

Although free trade provides aggregate consumption possibilities for an economy that are Pareto-superior to a closed economy, almost inevitably some people, in particular those earning incomes from factors of production specific to import-competing industries, lose from free trade. Because of the Pareto-superiority of free trade compared to a closed economy, the gainers from free trade, in principle, can compensate the losers and still be better off. However, for reasons that we noted when considering Pareto efficiency and compensation, compensation may not be feasible.[54]

Supplement S1B: The competitive market-adjustment mechanism

To show that competitive markets achieve efficient outcomes, we used the Marshallian market-adjustment mechanism associated with Alfred Marshall (1842–1924).[55] An alternative market-adjustment mechanism is associated with the French economist, Léon Walras (1834–1910) and is known as Walrasian.

[54] The reasons for gainers and losers from free trade are studied in a course on international trade or international economics. If compensation to losers from free trade were always feasible, there would always be free trade, given that free trade offers the potential for Pareto improvement.

[55] We recall that Marshall formulated the idea of market equilibrium.

The Marshallian market-adjustment mechanism is based on quantity adjustment. Quantity supplied to the market adjusts in response to the difference $(P_B - P_S)$ between buyers' willingness to pay for additional output and sellers' willingness to supply (because $P_B = MB$ and $P_S = MC$).

The Walrasian market-adjustment mechanism describes price adjustment. There is excess demand in a market if $(Q_B - Q_S) > 0$ and excess supply if $(Q_B - Q_S) < 0$. Price increases in response to excess demand and decreases in response to excess supply. The market equilibrium is attained when price does not change (or is stable), which is where $(Q_B = Q_E = Q_S)$.

In a case such as figure 1.4, where demand and supply functions have the usual negative and positive slopes, both the Marshallian and the Walrasian market-adjustment mechanisms bring the competitive market to the efficient unique equilibrium.

In figure 1.6, where the supply function is downward-sloping, the Marshallian quantity-adjustment mechanism moves the market toward the efficient equilibrium at point *E2* and away from the inefficient equilibrium at point *E1*. The Walrasian price-adjustment mechanism does the opposite. For this reason, the description of the Walrasian price adjustment is often accompanied by the fiction of a market coordinator who calls out prices, compares total demand and total supply in response to a price, and increases price if there is excess demand and decreases price if there is excess supply.

Supplement S1C: Monopoly profits and social justice

Monopoly is inefficient and also is presumptively socially unjust because buyers pay prices in excess of the prices at which competitive firms would offer to supply. When monopoly profits are capitalized into the value of market assets, people who buy shares in a firm earning monopoly profits buy claims to the capitalized monopoly profits; however, they nonetheless receive only a risk-adjusted competitive rate of return from their investment. The return on the financial asset is not determined in the monopolized product market but rather in the competitive asset market in which the stock of the monopoly firm trades.

Ownership of shares in a monopoly, therefore, yields no greater rate of return than ownership of shares in firms selling in competitive product markets. If monopoly in the product market is replaced by competition, the owners of the stock in the monopoly firm incur a capital loss – if the asset market had not anticipated the end of monopoly.

The taxicab market is another example of capitalized monopoly profits. The price of a taxicab license reflects the value of capitalized profits from restriction of entry into the taxicab market, and buying a taxicab license provides only a risk-adjusted competitive rate of return. A person might buy a taxicab license and then find in the future that restrictions on entry have been abolished, in which case the value of the taxicab license falls to zero.

Ending monopoly is another example in the theme of potential conflict between the social objectives of efficiency and social justice. Efficiency justifies replacing monopoly with competition in *product* markets; however, the end of monopoly profits is not necessarily socially just because of distributional consequences in *asset* markets.

Summary

This introductory chapter has provided background for our study of the choice between markets and governments. Section 1 set out the prima facie case for competitive markets. Outcome of competitive markets are the benchmarks that we shall use to judge whether public finance and public policy provide social improvement.

1A. We began with the case for the market based on the metaphor of Adam Smith's invisible hand. Adam Smith was a moral philosopher who used the invisible hand to justify allowing people to do the best for themselves in markets without guilt feelings.

1B. We considered a formal proof of the efficiency of a competitive market and described the competitive market-adjustment mechanism. Supplement S1A confirmed the efficiency of markets in a general-equilibrium (or economy-wide) setting that includes the efficiency of free trade. Supplement S1B described an alternative market-adjustment mechanism.

1C. We noted that market efficiency rests on competitive markets and observed the inefficiency of a monopolized market in which ability to set price overrides the competitive market-adjustment mechanism. We noted that monopoly can also compromise economic freedom. Our first identified responsibility for government was therefore public policy to ensure competitive markets. We also identified cases where competitive markets can fail to result in efficiency. The different instances of market failure provide the topics for subsequent chapters in which roles of government will be investigated in detail.

1D. The decentralized decisions of markets were compared with the centralized decisions of government agencies. Because a government agency, in general, requires information that is not available if markets do not exist to reveal the information, government agencies are at an informational disadvantage compared to markets. We contrasted economic freedom through the spontaneous order of decentralized market decisions with the imposed order of centralized decisions of government agencies. We observed that the informational superiority of markets may not deter political decision makers from preferring imposed order to the spontaneous order of the market. An ideological preference for imposed order is consistent with a preference by political decision makers for centralized decisions.

Section 2 considered the criteria for efficiency and social justice:

2A. We introduced the conception of cost-benefit analysis as means of seeking efficient public finance and public policy, and extended the definition of efficiency to Pareto-efficiency and to the associated concept of Pareto-improvement. We noted the two aspects of compensation, as part of the definition of Pareto efficiency and as part of a criterion for social justice. Compensation based on social justice introduces a social dilemma because of possible conflict between seeking efficiency and seeking social justice. This was our first instance where objectives of efficiency and social justice could be inconsistent. The choice is ideological and reflects the weight that a society wishes to place on efficiency compared to social justice.

2B. We asked whether outcomes in competitive markets might be consistent with social justice. Competitive market outcomes are socially just if the natural right of possession is accepted as the criterion for social justice.

2C. We noted that criteria for social justice often focus on equality and distinguished ex-ante and ex-post equality. We noted the impediments that could delay or forestall ex-ante equality. We observed that a goal of ex-post equality is, in general, inconsistent with Pareto-improvement.

2D. The circumstances of the water in the desert provided an illustration of the conflict between ex-post equality and Pareto improvement. We also considered ex-ante equality and the natural right of possession in the case of the water in the desert. The judgment of Solomon demonstrated in the same circumstances of indivisibility how efficiency and social justice are simultaneously achievable when social justice is defined as the natural right of possession. We noted the popular bias revealed in experiments against the efficiency achievable through markets. Economists are more attuned to the benefits of efficiency than the public at large. The popular preference for ex-post equality and for rules of nonmarket allocation appear to have origins in instincts that emanated from hunter–gatherer societies. We observed a relation between envy and ex-post equality as the criterion for social justice. In the cases of the water in the desert and the judgment of Solomon, only envy by the person without water and likewise envy by the false claimant to the child can explain the wish to have an outcome of ex-post equality (where the water would save no one and the child would die). The example of the farmers illustrated efficient and inefficient responses to envy. Envy and also guilt feelings led us into a comparison between voting and market decisions. Because a single vote is not decisive in elections, the reason why voters choose to vote is not because they believe that they personally will influence the outcome. Voting can be expressive. Market decisions are not expressive. The invisible hand absolves people from guilt feelings about seeking their own good in markets. A counterpart to the invisible hand is not present when people who have been more successful than others vote expressively.

Section 3 introduced the rule of law, without which neither markets nor governments can achieve efficiency or social justice:

3A. Without the rule of law to specify property rights, markets cannot exist. There are also disincentives to be productive if personal possessions and output produced are not safe. A responsibility of government, therefore, is to ensure the rule of law. The rule of law is not the same as the rule of government. Government ideally oversees but does not determine the principles of the rule of law. We used the prisoners' dilemma to describe inefficiency in the absence of the rule of law. The rule of law is implemented through penalties that change dominant strategies and thereby rationally deter unproductive appropriative behavior.

3B. We next considered anarchy in the context of asymmetry between strong and weak where, in the absence of ethical restraint, the strong do as they wish to the weak. The strong can choose to use resources in socially unproductive appropriation while the predatory intent of the strong inhibits the weak from consistently working. In not working consistently, the weak are not lazy but rather respond rationally to the absence of the rule of law. The weak have an incentive to convince the strong that they are lazy and (if working) unproductive. The strong can act as either roving bandits or more efficient stationary bandits. In either case, the rule of law ends the predatory behavior of the strong and provides incentives for efficient productive use of resources. Social justice is achieved through the natural right of possession of the weak to their output.

3C. A population in which everyone behaves ethically in respecting the right of possession does not require a government to impose the rule of law. When a population contains both honest and dishonest people, the Nash equilibrium – as in the case of the strong and weak – is both inefficient and unjust. The rule of law then provides incentives for efficiency and also protects honest people.

3D. Enforcement of the rule of law by governments is usually imperfect. However, people cannot, in general, sue governments for failures in ensuring the rule of law. We noted that private deterrence is inconsistent with equality before the law. Reliance on private protection is also similar to anarchy because personal outcomes depend on personal resources. Insurance is a collective response when governments fail to ensure the rule of law. However, insurance is ineffective if risk cannot be spread because predators simultaneously threaten too many people. The presence of the rule of law is confirmed when private individuals or firms can sue governments for breach of contract and have objectively reasonable chances of success. In some legal systems, innocence or guilt is determined by juries; in other legal systems, by judges. A jury system protects people from government-appointed judges.

Literature notes

1.1 The prima facie case for the market

On the distinction between normative and positive questions, see:

Friedman, M., 1953. The methodology of positive economics. In *Essays in Positive Economics*. University of Chicago Press, Chicago. Reprinted in D. M. Hausman (Ed.), 1994. *The Philosophy of Economics*. Cambridge University Press, New York, pp. 180–213.

Writings on Adam Smith's ideas (1759, 1776) include Reisman (1975) and Evensky (2005). The "invisible hand" has become part of the folklore of economics. Our description of the invisible hand has relied on this folklore. Grampp (2000) provides a qualified account of the meaning of the invisible hand.

Grampp, W. D., 2000. What did Smith mean by the invisible hand? *Journal of Political Economy* 108:441–65.
Evensky, J., 2005. *Adam Smith's Moral Philosophy: A Historical and Contemporary Perspective on Markets, Law, Ethics and Culture*. Cambridge University Press, New York.
Reisman, D. A., 1975. *Adam Smith's Sociological Economics*. Croon Helm, London; Barnes & Noble, New York.
Smith, A., 1759/1976. *The Theory of Moral Sentiments*. Oxford University Press, Oxford.
Smith, A., 1776/1937. *An Enquiry into the Nature and Causes of the Wealth of Nations*. E. Cannan (Ed.), Modern Library Edition. Random House, New York.

The role of marginal benefit in valuation and the solution to the water–diamond paradox were set out by Jevons (1871).

Jevons, W. S., 1871/1957. *The Theory of Political Economy* (5th edition). Kelley and Millman, New York.

The measurement of total benefit that we have used is also called *consumer surplus* and was introduced by Dupuit (1844/1969); see Houghton (1958). On the accuracy of consumer surplus as a measure of benefit, see Willig (1976). For elaboration, see Mishan and Quah (2007).

Dupuit, J., 1844/1969. On the measurement of the utility of public works. In K. J. Arrow and T. Scitovsky (Eds.), *Readings in Welfare Economics*. Irwin, Homewood IL, pp. 255–83.
Houghton, R. W., 1958. A note on the early history of consumer surplus. *Economica* 25:49–57.
Mishan, E. J. and E. Quah, 2007. *Cost-Benefit Analysis*. Routledge, Abington U.K., and New York.
Willig, R. D., 1976. Consumer's surplus without apology. *American Economic Review* 66:589–97.

On market inefficiency and monopoly, see:

Harberger, A. C., 1954. Monopoly and resource allocation. *American Economic Review* 44:77–87.

On the definition and attributes of barriers to entry, see:

Demsetz, H., 1982. Barriers to entry. *American Economic Review* 72:47–57.

1.2 Efficiency and social justice

On Pareto efficiency and compensation, see Kaldor (1939) and Hicks (1939). Kemp and Pezanis-Christou (1999) described Pareto's view of compensation: Pareto (1894) viewed a government agency as compensating losers from change and distributing surplus benefits among the population.

Hicks, J. R., 1939. The foundations of welfare economics. *Economic Journal* 49:696–712.
Kaldor, N., 1939. Welfare propositions of economics and interpersonal comparisons of utility. *Economic Journal* 49:549–52.
Kemp, M. C. and P. Pezanis-Christou, 1999. Pareto's compensation principle. *Social Choice and Welfare* 16:441–4.
Pareto, V., 1894. Il massimo di utilità dato dalla libera concorrenza. *Giornale degli Economisti* 9:48–66.

The quote on the natural right of possession by John Stuart Mill (1806–73) was from:

Mill, J. S., 1848/1909. *Principles of Political Economy* (7th edition). W. J. Ashley (Ed.). Longmans, Green, and Co., London.

Results reported of the experiments showing public preference for avoiding reliance on markets are from Kahneman, Knetsch, and Thaler (1986) and Frey and Pommerehne (1993). Kirchgässner (2005) reviewed evidence comparing views of the public at large and economists on efficiency and social justice.

Frey, B. S. and W. W. Pommerehne, 1993. On the fairness of pricing: An empirical survey among the general population. *Journal of Economic Behavior and Organization* 20:295–307.
Kahneman, D., J. L. Knetsch, and R. Thaler, 1986. Fairness as a constraint on profit seeking. *American Economic Review* 76:728–41.
Kirchgässner, G., 2005. (Why) are economists different? *European Journal of Political Economy* 21:543–62.

Mui (1995) described how envy affects preferences and economic behavior. Konrad (2004) described the symbiotic relationship between envious people and altruists.

Konrad, K. A., 2004. Altruism and envy in contests: An evolutionarily stable symbiosis. *Social Choice and Welfare* 22:479–90.
Mui, V.-L., 1995. The economics of envy. *Journal of Economic Behavior and Organization* 26:311–36.

On expressive voting, see:

Brennan, G. and J. M. Buchanan, 1984. Voter choice: Evaluating political alternatives. *American Behavioral Scientist* 28:185–201.
Brennan, G. and A. Hamlin, 2000. *Democratic Devices and Desires*. Cambridge University Press, Cambridge U.K.
Glazer, A., 2008. Voting to anger and to please others. *Public Choice* 134:247–54.

On market behavior and voting, see:

Buchanan, J. M., 1954. Individual choice in voting and the market. *Journal of Political Economy* 62:334–43.

1.3 The rule of law

Demsetz (1967) described the emergence of property rights. The role of property rights in facilitating financial and insurance markets was emphasized by de Soto (2000). Frey and Buhofer (1988) described property rights to prisoners.

de Soto, H., 2000. *The Mystery of Capital: Why Capitalism Triumphs in the West and Fails Everywhere Else*. Basic Books, New York.
Demsetz, H., 1967. Toward a theory of property rights. *American Economic Review* 57:347–59.
Frey, B. S. and H. Buhofer, 1988. Prisoners and property rights. *Journal of Law and Economics* 31:19–46.

The idea of Nash equilibrium appeared in Cournot (1838) and Nash (1951). On subgame perfection in extensive form games, see Selten (1975).

Cournot, A., 1838. *Recherches sur les principes mathematiques de la theorie des richesses*. English edition: N. Bacon (Ed.), 1897. *Researches into the Mathematical Principles of the Theory of Wealth*. Macmillan, London.
Nash, J. F., 1951. Non-cooperative games. *Annals of Mathematics* 54:286–95.
Selten, R., 1975. Re-examination of the perfectness concept for equilibrium points in extensive games. *International Journal of Game Theory* 4:25–55.

Nietzsche's writings include Nietzsche (1886/1997). The game describing interaction between the weak and the strong in the absence of the rule of law is based on Hillman (2004). The distinction between stationary and roving bandits was made by Olson; see, for example, Olson (2000). Dixit (2004) described the role of the law in economic activity. Moselle and Polak (2001) described the use of government for predation.

Dixit, A. K., 2004. *Lawlessness and Economics: Alternative Modes of Governance*. Princeton University Press, Princeton NJ.
Hillman, A. L., 2004. Nietzschean development failures. *Public Choice* 119:263–80.
Moselle, B. and B. Polak, 2001. A model of a predatory state. *Journal of Law, Economics, and Organization* 17:1–33.
Nietzsche, F., 1886/1997. *Beyond Good and Evil: Prelude to a Philosophy of the Future*. Dover Publications, New York.
Olson, M., 2000. *Power and Prosperity*. Basic Books, New York.

Feld and Voigt (2003) provided evidence on economic consequences of judicial systems.

Feld, L. and S. Voigt, 2003. Economic growth and judicial independence: Cross-country evidence using a new set of indicators. *European Journal of Political Economy* 19:497–527.

Supplement S1A: Market efficiency in general equilibrium

An extensive literature presents proofs of the efficiency of competitive markets. Questions studied include whether equilibrium exists and how preferred equilibrium is to be identified when there are multiple equilibria. The efficiency gains from international trade through comparative advantage were noted by Ricardo (1817/1951). On Pareto efficiency of free trade, see Samuelson (1939). On compensation and the gains from trade, see Kemp (1962). On political economy of departure from free trade, see Hillman (1989/2001).

Hillman, A. L., 1989. *The Political Economy of Protection*. Harwood Academic Publishers, Chur, Switzerland. Reprinted 2001, Routledge, Abington U.K., and New York.
Kemp, M. C., 1962. The gains from international trade. *Economic Journal* 72:803–19.
Ricardo, D., 1817. *Principles of Political Economy and Taxation*. Reprinted as volume I in P. Straffa (Ed.), 1951. *The Works and Correspondence of David Ricardo*. Cambridge University Press, Cambridge U.K.
Samuelson, P. A., 1939. The gains from international trade. *Canadian Journal of Economics and Political Science* 5:195–205.

Supplement S1B: The competitive market-adjustment mechanism

The Marshallian and Walrasian competitive market-adjustment mechanisms were described by Marshall (1938 and previous editions) and Walras (1896 and previous editions, and 1954). See also Samuelson (1947) on market stability and the efficiency of market equilibria.

Marshall, A., 1938. *The Principles of Economics* (8th edition). Macmillan, London.
Samuelson, P. A., 1947. *Foundations of Economic Analysis*. Harvard University Press, Cambridge MA.
Walras, L., 1877, 1889, 1896. *Elements d'economie politique pure, ou Theorie de la richesse sociale*. Corbaz, Lausanne (1877, second edition); Rouge, Lausanne (1889 and 1896, third and fourth editions). In English, 1954. *Theory of Pure Economics*. Translated by W. Jaffe. Allen and Unwin, London.

Supplement S1C: Monopoly profits and social justice

On capitalization of monopoly profits, see:

Tullock, G., 1975. The transitional gains trap. *Bell Journal of Economics* 6:671–78. Reprinted in J. M. Buchanan, R. Tollison, and G. Tullock (Eds.), 1980. *Toward a Theory of the Rent-Seeking Society*. Texas A&M University Press, College Station, pp. 211–21.

2

INSTITUTIONS AND GOVERNANCE

A society's "institutions" determine norms and incentives of personal conduct. Legal institutions determine how or whether the rule of law is provided. Political institutions determine political behavior and how voters' collective decisions are made and implemented. Social institutions determine whether people make long-term commitments to one another. The market is an institution. Private property is an institution, as is collective property.

Institutions persist independently of the identity of individuals: congress or parliament is independent of the identity of incumbent political representatives; a government bureaucracy is independent of the identity of incumbent bureaucrats; and a judiciary or court system is independent of who the judges happen to be at any time. When incumbent judges, political representatives, or bureaucrats depart, the institutions remain. The market is independent of who buys and who sells, and the institution of private property is independent of who owns the property.

Governance is the activity of governing and exercising the authority of government. When taxpayer and voter interests are well served by governments, governance is described as good. Conversely, governance is inadequate or bad when the authority of government is exercised in ways that benefit the people in government, their family, and their friends rather than the taxpayers and voters.

Through consequences for the quality of governance, institutions determine whether public finance and public policy can improve on market outcomes when societies seek efficiency and social justice. We therefore study the *positive* questions about how institutions determine the effectiveness of government before we proceed – in chapters that follow – to consider the *normative* questions about how societies can benefit from ideally designed and implemented public finance and public policy.

Section 1 of this chapter describes how institutions affect public finance and public policy through behavior of political decision makers. Section 2 describes government bureaucracy. Section 3 describes outcomes when the institutions of markets and private property are absent and all decisions are political or bureaucratic.

2.1 The Political Principal–Agent Problem

Adam Smith's "invisible hand" directs self-interested personal market decisions toward the social benefit of efficiency. Self-interested decisions by people in government need not, however, be socially beneficial. Rather, control over decisions of public finance and public policy might be used for the personal benefit of political decision makers.

> *Social benefit from pursuit of self-interest through the invisible hand applies to markets but not necessarily to decisions of political decision makers.*

From a normative perspective, people in government should not seek their own self-interest but should be faithful agents of taxpayers and voters by exclusively serving the public interest. This is the normative ideal for a society. How political decision makers in fact behave depends on institutions and a political principal–agent problem.

> *A political principal–agent problem is present when principals (taxpayers and voters) cannot ensure that agents (political decision makers) will act in the best interests of the principals.*

A principal–agent problem inverts the principal–agent relationship: the agent becomes the principal and the principal becomes the agent. Nonetheless, we shall continue to refer to political decision makers as agents and to taxpayers and voters as principals.

A. Asymmetric information

Democratic institutions are, in principle, intended to ensure that political decision makers are accountable to voters. As political *representatives*, political decision makers are agents of voters and have an obligation to act in the public interest. We define the *public interest* in terms of social objectives:

> *The public interest is the pursuit of social objectives of efficiency or social justice.*

Conversely:

> *It is not in the public interest when political decision makers choose policies that provide special privileges for groups that have narrow self-interested objectives contrary to the best interests of voters and society at large.*

A producer interest group, for example, may wish to forestall environmental policies that would increase costs of production. Protectionist policies may be sought that benefit owners of capital in import-competing industries. Agricultural and other producers may seek subsidies from the government budget. Because of fear of the consequences of increased competition, school administrators and teachers in government schools may seek assurances that private schools will not receive government subsidies and that parental choice among government schools will not be allowed. Medical practitioners may seek limits on compensation payments for malpractice. Lawyers may seek unlimited rights to propose class-action cases and no limitations on damages that courts can assign. Transportation companies may seek increased public spending on highways. Logging companies may want rights to log public land. Various organizations may seek tax-exempt status. Groups may seek public spending in the locations where they reside and where local contractors have advantages in bidding for public contracts. At the local-government level, rezoning of land from agricultural to more valuable commercial and residential use may be sought. Financial advisors and banks may seek avoidance of regulation in financial markets. The political decisions sought by special interests provide privilege but impose costs on taxpayers.

Some interest groups seek *socially beneficial* responses from political decision makers. For example, interest groups seek protection of the environment and of biodiversity. Some interest groups call for greater public attention to road safety. The activities of public-interest groups seeking socially beneficial policies would not be necessary if political decision makers focused on the public interest.

Limits on voters' information

Principal–agent problems exist because of asymmetric information. Agents (the political decision makers) would behave in the manner consistent with the best interests of the principals (voters and taxpayers) if the actions of the agents were observable and thereby known to the principals. If taxpayers and voters knew that political decision makers were acting contrary to the public interest, the institutions of democracy would allow electoral disciplining and replacement of the political decision makers who deviate from the public interest. Political decision makers would not deviate from the public interest in the first place if they knew that their behavior was being observed and that they would be held accountable by voters. The scope or possibility of political behavior that deviates from the public interest therefore depends on the information about political decisions that voters have.

A government budget

Political decisions about public finance and public policy are shown in a government budget. Table 2.1 is a stylized portrayal of a government budget.

The expenditure side of the budget shows public spending on public goods (or public investment), spending on income transfers (or welfare payments), and spending by government on itself (or government consumption). Part of public spending is for interest payments and repayment of government borrowing. Tax revenue also may be transferred to other levels of governments.

The revenue side of the government budget shows the sources of finance for public spending. Taxes and sales of government bonds provide revenue. Another source of revenue is fees and user prices, such as for passports and drivers' licenses and for tolls paid for use of roads and bridges. Transfers of income may be received from other levels of government. Lotteries and inflationary financing also provide revenue.[1]

[1] The income transfers among levels of governments take place in fiscal-federal systems where different levels of government levy taxes and spend government revenue. We shall study fiscal federalism. We shall also study in detail the different means of financing available to governments.

TABLE 2.1. THE COMPONENTS OF A GOVERNMENT BUDGET

Expenditure	Revenue
Public goods and other public investment	Taxes of different types
Income transfers (welfare payments)	Borrowing from the public through sale of government bonds
Government spending on itself (wages and salaries of the bureaucracy and other expenses of the branches of government)	Fees and user prices
Payment of interest on government bonds	Transfers from other governments
Repayment of past borrowing	Other revenue sources such as lotteries
Transfers to other governments	Inflationary financing (not shown in the budget)

Government budgets provide information in greater detail than shown in table 2.1. Availability of information to voters and taxpayers through the government budget is nonetheless limited by aggregation of data. Data on the composition of public spending are too aggregated for individual voters and taxpayers to be able to determine in detail how tax revenue is spent. The government budget also does not provide information on the reasons for political decisions about taxation and public spending. Nor is information provided about the structure of taxes or on tax exemptions and subsidies.

Information provided to taxpayers and voters through the government budget is incomplete.

Information as a public good

We do not expect taxpayers to attempt personally to acquire information about all political decisions that affect their well being. Acquiring information about political behavior and acting on the information is a public good because the benefits from acquiring and using the information to monitor political behavior extend to all taxpayers and voters.

Individual taxpayers and voters confront the incentive to free-ride on information acquisition and political monitoring.

Rational ignorance

Voters also may choose to remain *rationally ignorant*. There is a personal cost to acquiring information. The personal cost may exceed the personal benefit from having the information.

Rational ignorance describes the personal disincentive to invest in acquiring information when personal costs of acquiring information exceed personal benefits.

The sources of asymmetric information for voters or taxpayers

The asymmetric information that underlies the principal–agent problem is due, therefore, to:

- the inability of voters and taxpayers to know the details of political decisions because the information is not provided
- disincentives of voters and taxpayers to acquire information because information is a public good
- rational ignorance by voters and taxpayers.

B. Political support and public policy

A politician's overriding personal objective is to win elections. One cannot be a successful politician or, indeed, perhaps not be a politician at all, without electoral success. The preeminent objective of political parties is likewise to form governments by winning elections. Asymmetric information allows political decision makers flexibility in means of obtaining political support when pursuing objectives of winning elections. To enhance election prospects, politicians need money for political expenses, including political advertising. Politicians and political parties, therefore, may accept financial contributions from special-interest groups. Because of the need for money for campaign expenses, politicians and political parties may see themselves as *compelled* to accept special-interest money. A politician, therefore, may stress the distinction between personal corruption as occurs when money is taken for private benefit and accepting campaign contributions to be used for political expenses.

Principled political candidates prefer not to accept campaign contributions from special interests. However, the candidates confront the prisoners' dilemma set out in table 2.2. Each candidate faces the decision whether to accept or reject special-interest campaign contributions. The dominant strategy is to accept the

TABLE 2.2. THE PRISONERS' DILEMMA FACING PRINCIPLED POLITICAL CANDIDATES

	Politician 2 refuses to accept special-interest contributions	Politician 2 accepts special-interest contributions
Politician 1 refuses to accept special-interest contributions	3, 3	1, 4
Politician 1 accepts special-interest contributions	4, 1	2, 2

contributions; in the Nash equilibrium at (2, 2), the special-interest contributions are accepted.[2]

Politicians who have accepted special-interest money find it difficult to renege on promises to support policies that provide special-interest benefits. Political credibility requires that a winning candidate deliver on promises to special interests. In the future, elections will take place again and campaign contributions will be required again. Political candidates who accept special-interest money have thus entered into a self-enforcing implicit contract.

Politicians who do not seek reelection are sometimes referred to as "lame ducks" (because they will not "fly" again). Incumbent politicians may decide not to seek reelection or term limits may disallow reelection. Evidence from the U.S. Congress (where there are no term limits) confirms that lame ducks are more likely to vote in the public interest than political incumbents seeking reelection, as we expect, because political decision makers who do not require political campaign contributions can vote according to principle.

Public finance for political expenses

Can public finance for political expenses solve the prisoners' dilemma in table 2.2? Furthermore, if political expenses are financed from public funds, which form of public financing would we expect political decision makers to choose?

Public finance in accord with political representation

In a political system in which the political party is more important than the individual politician, we might expect a policy to be chosen that bases public finance for political expenses on the number of political representatives that a party has. Such a policy decision, determined by the majority, would give the majority party the most public money.

Matching public finance as a subsidy for political contributions

Matching public finance can be provided as a subsidy for private political contributions. This public-financing rule benefits special interests, whose political contributions are now subsidized by public money.

Politicians seek political support from voters and through campaign contributions from special interests. Political decisions about policies to support are thus trade-offs between serving the public interest to obtain voter support and catering to special interests to obtain campaign contributions.

[2] Politicians and political parties are usually legally restricted in permissible amounts of campaign contributions from any one donor. Money is, however, fungible and can be transferred through other donors or can be funneled through committees and support organizations. Money can also be given surreptitiously in cash and spent in cash, which may be illegal; however, for the political candidate, winning may be the overriding objective. Political contributions that can be given surreptitiously reinforce the incentives of the Nash equilibrium to accept contributions from special-interest groups: if political contributions are not observable, agreements to cooperate to achieve (3, 3) cannot be verified.

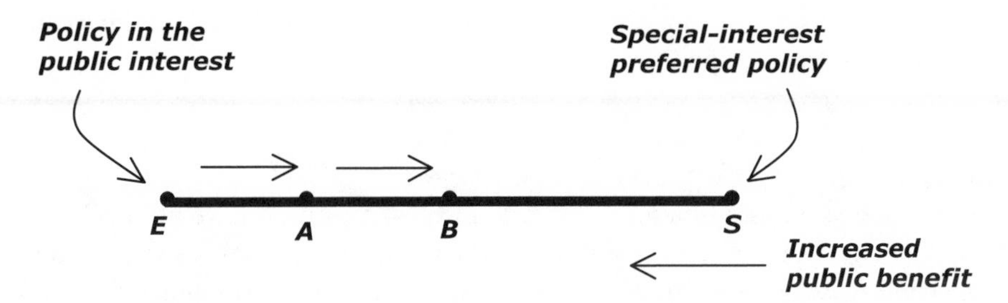

Figure 2.1. Matching public finance for private political contributions.

In figure 2.1, point E is the public-interest policy and point S is the preferred policy of a special-interest group. The scale in figure 2.1 measures the value of benefits to the special-interest group. Special-interest benefits are zero at point E and maximal at point S. In the absence of campaign contributions from special interests, candidates care only about votes and maximize political support by choosing the policy in the public interest at point E.

When special interests provide campaign contributions, candidates increase political support by deviating from the public interest at point E in the direction of the special-interest policy at point S. The policy chosen by the political candidate is indicated at point A, where the marginal political benefit from moving in the direction of point S by catering to special interests is equal to the marginal political loss from deviating from the public interest at point E.

A public policy of providing matching publicly financed political contributions subsidizes special-interest contributions, thereby increasing the political incentive to deviate from the public-interest position at point E in the direction of the special-interest policy at point S. The matching publicly financed contributions move the policy chosen to point B, which is more favorable for special interests than the policy at point A.

Because special interests have a comparative advantage in providing money and voters have a comparative advantage in providing votes:

> *Matching public finance for privately given campaign contributions benefits special-interest groups relative to voters.*

Why vote?

We have noted that rational cost-benefit calculation provides no incentive to vote because the cost of taking time to vote is positive whereas the likelihood that a voter will be decisive in determining the outcome of voting is effectively zero. Although people may vote "out of civic duty," they may also vote expressively to confirm their identity through support for a candidate's policies. People may also vote to personally protest the policies of candidates. They may, in particular, vote to protest against politicians who have been observed to depart from the public interest by catering to special interests.

The advantages of interest groups over voters

Voters' lack of information allows special-interest groups to have political influence. Matching publicly financed grants for political expenses also advantages special interests by subsidizing special-interest campaign contributions. There are other reasons as well why special-interest groups have advantages over voters, even though voters determine the outcomes of voting.

Group size and collective political action

Both voters and interest groups are engaged in collective political action. The collective objective in each case is the public-good benefit of *increasing the probability of a favorable decision from political decision makers*. The small size of an interest group compared to the population of voters allows interest groups to be successful in overcoming coordination and monitoring problems of collective political action.

Voters' coordination problems

Voters also face coordination problems. One vote is of no value but many votes together affect election outcomes. If voting could be coordinated on the principle that "we all vote together," the political principal–agent problem would be diminished. Coordination takes the form of voters agreeing to vote provided that others also agree to vote. The question would then no longer be whether a single vote is decisive in influencing the electoral outcome but rather whether a bloc of votes is decisive. However, unless voting is compulsory, often large parts of the electorate do not bother to vote.

Table 2.3 shows the coordination problem confronting two voters who have the same preferences regarding a voting outcome. If they both vote, they affect the voting outcome and each has a benefit of 2. A voter who does not vote has a benefit of 1. A voter who votes when the other does not has a benefit of zero. There is no dominant strategy because a voter's best decision depends on the decision of the other voter.

TABLE 2.3. THE VOTER-COORDINATION GAME

	Voter 2 votes	Voter 2 does not vote
Voter 1 votes	2, 2	0, 1
Voter 1 does not vote	1, 0	1, 1

The symmetric outcomes at (2, 2) and (1, 1), where both voters make the same decision, are Nash equilibria (no voter can do better by changing his or her decision). The best outcome for the voters is (2, 2), where they both vote and influence the electoral outcome. Thus:

> *Compulsory voting diminishes the advantages of special-interest groups by solving the voter-coordination problem.*

Salient policy issues

Under representative democracy, voters do not vote on issues directly but rather choose representatives to vote on their behalf. There are usually more policy issues in an election than political candidates. Not all issues, therefore, can be decided by voters. Salient policy issues become the focus of voter and media attention, leaving other issues to be decided by political discretion, including decisions that benefit special-interest groups. Direct democracy (in which voters vote directly on each policy question) overcomes the problem that under representative democracy there are more issues to be decided than political candidates.

Stakes in outcomes of political decisions

Members of interest groups have high stakes in the outcome of political decisions. Their personal income or personal wealth is at stake. Individual voters personally have small stakes in whether any one particular interest group succeeds in obtaining privileged benefits from political decisions.

> *Interest groups have an advantage over voters through the size of the stakes from successful political influence.*

Interest groups are thus focused on one issue in collective political action, whereas voters' interests are dispersed over many issues. The dispersion of voters' interests over many issues diminishes voters' capabilities of influencing any one political decision.

The paradox of political spending and advantages of special interests

There is a paradox when political advertising influences the voting decisions of voters.

> *Voters determine the outcome of elections but special interests provide money that political candidates use to persuade voters how to vote.*

The media and the principal–agent problem

In seeking to sell newspapers or offer attractive television viewing, or to attract people to their Web site, the media can report indiscretions and opportunistic behavior of politicians. Objective and informative news media assist voters in monitoring political representatives, thereby helping to overcome the problem of asymmetric information that underlies the political principal–agent problem.

The socially valuable task of providing information to the public is not performed when the media are subservient to a particular political viewpoint and when the media have a prejudicial view of some politicians and some groups of voters. When bias is evident, voters know that they cannot rely on the media for information that will assist them in making informed voting decisions. Special-interest groups benefit when the selective reporting of a biased media exposes the political opportunism of one political party and not another.

> *By not reporting or by downplaying ties between special-interest groups to a preferred political party, biased media facilitate special-interest influence over public policy.*

Regulation of campaign contributions

Buying votes directly from voters is illegal. Because money indirectly buys votes through political advertising to persuade voters how to vote, limits are often placed on the amount of money that an individual can contribute to a political candidate. There are, however, impediments to effective regulation of campaign contributions.

Legal entities as funnels for personal campaign contributions

Because legal entities independent of individual contributors can be used to funnel money to political causes and political candidates, advantages are provided in political influence to people who can buy the legal advice on how to circumvent the limitations on individual political donations. Regulation of political contributions, then, does not achieve the objective of limiting disproportionate political influence of wealthy people who seek electoral outcomes consistent with their own political preferences or interests.

> *Personal wealth can be used to pay for legal manipulability that allows political influence through large personal political contributions that regulation of political spending was intended to prevent.*

The monetary value of endorsements

When personal monetary contributions to political parties and candidates are regulated, consistency requires that non-monetary political contributions likewise be regulated. Political endorsements from owners of newspapers, television, and radio stations, and endorsements that are implicitly expressed in articles and news presentations that mix fact with opinion, all have monetary value. Celebrity endorsements from film stars, singers, hosts of popular programs, and people known to the public because of successful careers in sports also have monetary value. Often the value of an endorsement from a celebrity can be expected to exceed the limit on legally allowable individual campaign monetary contributions.

> *Regulation of the value of individual political contributions that excludes the monetary value of endorsements is inconsistent with the objective of limiting an individual's personal influence on election outcomes.*

Political bias in endorsements

If there is political bias in endorsements from the media and celebrities, regulation that excludes the value of endorsements provides political advantage to political parties and candidates that the media and entertainers support. Thus:

> *Regulation of political contributions that excludes the monetary value of endorsements can be a source of political bias.*

Term limits and the political principal–agent problem

Term limits set bounds on the time a politician can spend in office. The longer a political representative remains in office, the more intimate and deeper the relationships that may develop with special interests. Term limits are intended to ameliorate the political principal–agent problem by preempting entrenched political power of political incumbents.

An alternative interpretation views term limits as socially undesirable. According to this interpretation, politicians benefit from a reputation with voters for honesty and diligence, but term limits make the investment in reputation not worthwhile. Therefore, politicians who would otherwise be socially benevolent are led to act in self-interested ways because of short political time horizons imposed by term limits.

The two interpretations of consequences of term limits are based on different perceptions of sources of political support. The first view of term limits as socially beneficial is based on the premise that political decision makers maximize utility and reelection prospects by seeking special-interest support. The political principal–agent problem is recognized to be present. The second interpretation perceives politicians as basing political support on voters, with whom they require a reputation for socially responsible voting behavior for extended political careers – which term limits disallow. There would, according to this view, be no principal–agent problem if term limits did not distract politicians from catering to voters interests. Which view is correct depends on the institutions that underlie and determine political behavior.

Term limits introduce conflicts among voters in different constituencies. It is beneficial for voters in a constituency to have a political representative who – over the course of time – has become adept at channeling public spending to constituents. The benefits to a constituency of voters are greatest when all political representatives are newly elected other than the voters' own well-entrenched representative. The preferred outcome for society is that term limits are enacted so that public spending that is due to political privilege provided by entrenched representatives does not take place. However, at any point in time, voters in constituencies with entrenched political incumbents have an interest in opposing term limits that would deprive them of their long-tenured representatives.

C. Rent seeking

Two farmers own similar land. One farmer enjoys leisure and does not work all that long or hard. The other farmer works diligently and builds a farmhouse and is successful in growing crops. By the principle of the natural right of possession, the farmhouse and the crops belong to the diligent farmer. The leisure-enjoying farmer, however, may spend time to convince the government that he is more deserving of the diligent farmer's farmhouse and crops. If political decision makers have the discretion to change ownership and are known to be influenced by such lobbying, the diligent and productive farmer – anticipating inability to protect property rights – will have had no incentive to exert effort and be productive in the first place.

The farmer asking the government to change property rights is engaged in the activity of *rent seeking*. Instead of using time and effort productively, the rent-seeking farmer spends time and effort unproductively to seek the transfer of private property from the rightful owner. More generally:

> *A benefit obtained not productively but through influencing the decisions of others is a rent.*

If the rent-seeking farmer obtains the diligent farmer's possessions the entire benefit received is a *rent*. The rent-seeking farmer was successful in changing the distribution of wealth through political persuasion and did nothing productive to obtain the rent.

Alternatively, a political appointee working in a government job may receive an income that exceeds the competitively determined market wage that is available to this individual if working in the private sector. If y is the income received in the government job and w is the competitively determined wage available in the private sector (equal to the value of the individual's marginal product of labor), the government job provides the individual with a rent R given by:

$$R = y - w. \tag{2.1}$$

As long as $R > 0$ and therefore $y > w$, the political appointee prefers the government job.

> *A rent can be taken away without changing economic decisions or behavior.*

Subtracting more than the rent R from the income in the government job results in:

$$w > y. \tag{2.2}$$

The private-sector job is now preferred.

Competitive markets provide no rents because people are paid the value of their marginal contribution to production.

> *A rent is a personal benefit that would not be obtained in a competitive market.*
>
> *A rent is a personal benefit for which there is no corresponding counterpart value of personal productive contribution.*

Rents are obtained through government in forms other than incomes from government jobs. Rents can be provided through privileged benefits from public spending and the privilege of paying no or low taxes. Public policies also confer rents – for example, through lax environmental regulation. A straightforward way to obtain a rent is to have government not enforce anti-monopoly laws, which allows rents to be obtained in the form of monopoly profits. A monopoly profit is a rent because the monopoly profit is not necessary for supply to take place: a competitive market would supply output without the monopoly rent – and would indeed supply more than the monopolistic output at the lower competitive price.

Rent seekers do not ask, "How can I productively earn income today?" Rather, they ask themselves, "How can I convince someone to do something for me today?" Rents can be provided by family and friends as well as by governments.

> *Rents are obtained through seeking and benefiting from favors and privilege.*

Rent seeking as the cause of inefficiency

Favor and privilege are generally inconsistent with the objective of social justice. However, rent seeking is also a cause of inefficiency. Rents obtained through the political decisions of governments are often *contestable*. That is, different people can seek to benefit from the politically assigned rents. In the contests to become the beneficiary of rents, resources are used unproductively that could otherwise have been used productively to add to output. The resources used in rent seeking do not create new wealth but rather are used to contest distribution of income and wealth that already exists.

> *Because of unproductive use of resources, society incurs efficiency losses when rents are contested.*

If the source of rents is other people's income or property, there is an additional source of efficiency loss through adverse effects on productive incentives. As in the previous example of the farmer, if people know that a government will permit their property to be contested by others, there will be little or no output or wealth available to be contested.

We see the link between rent-seeking incentives and the rule of law.

Where the rule of law protects property rights, there is no incentive for rent seeking based on contesting other people's private possessions.

For the most part, rent seeking usually involves not seeking to obtain other people's private property or possessions but rather seeking favor and privilege through the public-finance and public-policy decisions of government.

There would be no incentives for rent seeking to obtain favors and privileges through government if there were no political discretion regarding public finance and public policy.

Political decision makers are not constrained by predetermined rules about public finance and public policy. Rather, the institutions of democratic governance allow political discretion. Institutions differ, however, among societies in permitting political receptivity to rent seeking.

A society's institutions determine the scope and thereby the extent of efficiency loss from rent seeking.

Rent seeking as a prisoners' dilemma

Although rent seeking is socially inefficient because of resources and time unproductively used, it is personally rational to take part in a rent-seeking contest. The personal rationality of participation in rent seeking can be expressed as a prisoners' dilemma. In table 2.4, the choice is between participating in rent seeking and not participating. If neither person engages in rent seeking, expected benefits are (3, 3), obtained through a lottery that gives each person an equal chance of obtaining the rent.

Use of personal time and other resources in rent seeking increases the personal likelihood of a favorable outcome of the political decision that assigns the rent. The Nash-equilibrium outcome (2, 2) in table 2.4 arises when both people engage in socially unproductive rent seeking. After two identical people have used identical resources and time in rent seeking, they again have an equal chance of obtaining the rent.

A person who refrains from rent seeking when the other person engages in rent seeking obtains 1, whereas the rent seeker obtains 4.

TABLE 2.4. THE PRISONERS' DILEMMA AND RENT SEEKING

	Person 2 does not rent seek	Person 1 engages in rent seeking
Person 1 does not rent seek	3, 3	1, 4
Person 1 engages in rent seeking	4, 1	2, 2

In the efficient outcome at (3, 3), no resources are used in rent seeking and the probability of obtaining the rent is one half for each person. In the Nash equilibrium at (2, 2), resources are unproductively used in rent seeking and the probability of obtaining the rent is also one half for each person. Both people, therefore, are drawn by a prisoners' dilemma into rent seeking that is neither personally nor socially advantageous. Nonetheless, participation in rent seeking is personally rational because not participating ensures that the advantage in obtaining the rent is with a person who does engage in rent seeking.

A promise not to engage in rent seeking is not credible because (3, 3) is not a Nash equilibrium. Nor in general could an agreement to refrain from rent seeking be monitored because rent seeking to influence political decisions is usually a furtive, unobservable activity.

In the case described here in terms of the prisoners' dilemma, rent-seeking activity is both privately and socially undesirable. The social loss is the inefficiency because resources are used unproductively. The private loss is that, after resources have been used, the personal likelihood of obtaining the rent remains unchanged. However, we shall presently see that depending on the nature of a rent-seeking contest, there can be expected personal benefits for rent seekers. There is always a social loss from rent seeking because of the unproductive use of resources in contesting the rent.

Lobbyists and asymmetries in rent seeking

The rent-seeking prisoners' dilemma describes two people with equal access to rent-seeking opportunities. Often, access to rent seeking is unequal or asymmetric. Some people are better positioned to be rent seekers than others. Political decision makers would not want everyone to be able to participate in rent seeking because political amenability to persuasion through rent seeking then would be public knowledge and the political decision makers might lose votes when elections take place. Only insiders who have invested in building relationships of trust with political decision makers are therefore usually able to participate in rent-seeking contests. Outsiders hoping to influence political decisions might engage in preliminary contests to be successful insiders who then can compete directly for rents. Rent seekers might delegate rent seeking to professional lobbyists who are insiders and have earned the trust of political decision makers. The lobbyists can be trusted to be discrete because they earn their income from the persistence of rent seeking. The social cost of the lobbyists' delegated rent-seeking activities is the lobbyists' time and initiative that could have been used productively but is used in persuasion of politicians.

Political benefit and rent creation

Rents, if they are to be assigned, need to be created. Why do political decision makers create rents to be assigned through rent seeking? Political decision makers benefit from rent creation and rent assignment either personally (which can involve corruption) or through advantage gained for their political party. Political decision makers cannot directly use public finance or public policy for personal

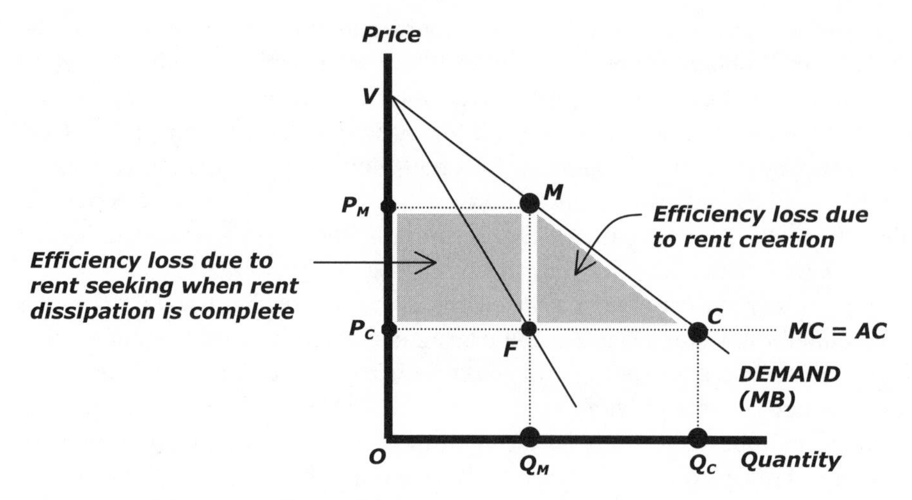

Figure 2.2. The inefficiency of rent creation and rent seeking.

or political benefit. However, by using public finance and public policy to create and assign rents, political decision makers can exchange political favors or public money for personal money or for political contributions.

Social losses due to rent creation and rent seeking

Figure 2.2 shows the efficiency loss *MCF* due to creation of a monopoly rent.[3] Monopoly rents or profits in figure 2.2 are given by the rectangle $P_M P_C FM$. This rectangle is *a transfer of income* from buyers to the monopolist. Rent seeking takes place if being the beneficiary of the monopoly profits can be contested. When rent seeking takes place, the social cost of monopoly consists of the triangle *MCF* plus the value of the resources used to seek or retain the monopoly rents $P_M P_C FM$. The triangle *MCF* is the social cost (or efficiency loss) because of rent creation through monopoly. The rectangle $P_M P_C FM$ indicates the value of the rent that attracts socially unproductive rent seeking.

> *The social cost of a public policy that allows monopoly has two parts: (1) the efficiency loss due to rent creation, and (2) the additional efficiency loss due to resources used in seeking to become the beneficiary of the rent.*

Evaluating the social loss from rent seeking

The size of the triangle *MCF* can be measured to determine the efficiency loss due to rent creation. We also can measure the size of the rectangle $P_M P_C FM$ that

[3] In figure 2.2, there are constant per-unit costs of production expressed as $MC = AC$. The competitive market equilibrium is at point *C* where output is Q_C and the price is P_C. The profit-maximizing output Q_M and price P_M chosen by the monopolist are determined at point *F*, where $MC = MR$.

indicates the magnitude of the monopoly rent. However, how do we obtain information on the value of the resources used in rent seeking to contest the monopoly rent? The question is quite general and pertains to any rent and rent seeking. The information on values of resources used in rent seeking is not published and is not otherwise available because rent seeking takes place out of public sight. No one wants to be seen being a rent seeker and no political decision maker wants to be known as catering to rent seekers. Everyone involved has an interest in denying that the rent seeking ever took place. In general, successful rent seekers propose that their benefits have been obtained on merit and are not the consequence of rent-seeking success.

The social loss from rent seeking includes the resources used in rent seeking by unsuccessful rent seekers. For example, ten thieves perceive the opportunity to perpetrate a theft. Each thief invests time and initiative to plan the theft, but only one thief is ultimately successful in perpetrating the theft. Before the theft takes place, each thief – whether ultimately successful or not – will have used resources in planning to perpetrate the theft. The thieves are rent seekers. Evaluating the social cost of rent seeking thus requires knowing the value of the resources used in rent seeking by the thieves who are unsuccessful rent seekers.

The example of the thieves makes clear that:

> *The social cost of rent seeking is incurred before the identity of the successful rent seeker is known.*

Although rent seeking cannot usually be directly observed, the value of the rent may be visible, as in figure 2.2 where we observe the value of the monopoly rent. Can the value of resources used in rent seeking be inferred from the observed value of a rent?

The use of resources in competing for a rent is known as *rent dissipation*. When resources of value R are used to contest a rent of value V, rent dissipation is defined as:

$$D \equiv \frac{R}{V}. \tag{2.3}$$

Rent dissipation is complete when $D = 1$.

> *When rent dissipation is complete, the observed value of a rent also measures the social loss due to nonobservable rent seeking.*

If rent dissipation could be presumed always to be complete, the information problem that arises because rent-seeking activities are not observable would be resolved. The observed value of a rent could be used as a measure of the social loss due to rent seeking.

In general, we do not know whether rent dissipation is complete. However, the study of outcomes of rent-seeking contests allows inferences about rent dissipation to be made. We need, however, to know the characteristics of rent-seeking contests to be able to infer the extent of rent dissipation. Again, there are informational limitations because the contests are not observed. Nonetheless, what do theoretical analyses of rent-seeking contests indicate about rent dissipation?

Competitive rent seeking

Competitive rent seeking requires free entry into rent seeking and large numbers of rent seekers competing for a rent. This is, of course, inconsistent with furtive rent seeking. If rent seeking were competitive, rent dissipation would, however, be complete if the behavior of rent seekers is not affected by risk. That is, if each of n rent seekers spends an amount x in seeking a rent of value V, then:

$$\lim_{n\to\infty} D \equiv \frac{nx}{V} = 1. \tag{2.4}$$

Therefore:

Competitive rent seeking results in complete rent dissipation.[4]

We do not expect rent-seeking contests to be competitive; political decision makers cannot allow open access to rent seekers but rather generally rely on approaches through the mediation of trusted lobbyists. In addition, not everybody wants to participate in rent seeking. Ethical considerations can deter people from participating in rent seeking. Whereas some people have a comparative advantage in rent seeking, other people have a comparative advantage in (or ethically limit themselves to) being productive and advancing through merit rather than seeking rents through political persuasion.

Rent-seeking contests with small numbers of participants

When rent-seeking contests have small numbers of participants, behavior is strategic, as in the prisoners' dilemma: the resources used in rent seeking by one rent seeker depend on the resources that others use. The Nash equilibrium of a rent-seeking contest depends on the rule or "contest-success function" that identifies the winner of the contest. Two basic rules are (1) resources used determine the probability of winning, and (2) the rent seeker assigning the most resources to the contest wins with certainty. In the first case, investing in rent seeking is viewed as buying lottery tickets with a rent seeker's probability of winning increasing with the number of lottery tickets bought. In the second case, the rent-seeking contest is viewed as equivalent to an auction in which all contenders lose their bids whether or not they win the auction (which is known as an *all-pay auction*).

The probabilistic contest-success function

In the lottery format, the probability of winning a rent increases with the resources used (or the amount spent), given the decisions of other contenders

[4] The formal proof is in Hillman and Katz (1984). The conclusion of complete dissipation is based on risk neutrality of rent seekers. When rent seekers are risk-averse, competitive rent seeking results in less than complete dissipation of a rent. Rent seeking, in general, is a risky venture because resources are invested and lost when a rent seeker is unsuccessful in obtaining the rent.

for the rent. The lottery rule for identifying the winner of a rent-seeking contest is called *non-discriminating* because there is insufficient information to discriminate among the rent-seeking or expenditures to allow the winner of the contest to be identified with certainty. The lottery-type contests are also called *Tullock contests*, after Gordon Tullock, who first noted the social costs of rent seeking.[5] With two contenders making political investments of x_1 and x_2, the probability of rent seeker i winning a Tullock contest is:

$$\rho_i(x_1, x_2) = \frac{x_i}{x_1 + x_2}, \quad i = 1, 2. \tag{2.5}$$

Each rent seeker chooses a political investment x_i to maximize expected benefit, which is given by:

$$EB_i = \rho_i(x_1, x_2)\, V - x_i = \left(\frac{x_i}{x_1 + x_2}\right) V - x_i, \quad i = 1, 2. \tag{2.6}$$

The political investment x_i is lost whether or not a rent seeker wins the rent-seeking contest. Therefore, in expression (2.6), x_i is subtracted from the expected value of the rent. The rent-seeking game is symmetric, between identical people with identical chances of winning. Because of symmetry, rent seekers choose the same equilibrium value of x as the political investment. We are interested in measuring rent dissipation. In the Tullock contest, with total resources used in rent seeking given by $R = nx$, rent dissipation can be shown (see supplement S2A) to be given by:

$$D \equiv \frac{R}{V} = \left(\frac{n-1}{n}\right). \tag{2.7}$$

Rent dissipation in the Tullock contest therefore increases as n increases. In the limit, as n becomes very large, rent dissipation approaches $D = 1$ and we have another proof that competitive rent dissipation is complete. However, for small numbers of competing rent seekers, rent dissipation is incomplete. For example, we see from expression (2.7) that if the contest is between two rent seekers ($n = 2$), half of the rent is dissipated. In that case, it would be inappropriate to base an estimate of the value of resources R used in rent seeking on the value V of an observed rent.

Rent-seeking contests as all-pay auctions

A rent seeker might invite a politician to attend a symposium in pleasant company at a luxury hotel. Making the political investment, however, does not ensure a favorable political response for the rent seeker, given that others are also making political investments in the same political decision maker. The rent seeker incurs the cost of the political investment whether or not he or she is ultimately successful in obtaining the rent that the political decision maker can offer. In this case, the political decision maker may precisely observe different rent seekers' political investments and have the information required to be discriminatory in

[5] See Tullock (1967) and (1980).

assigning the rent to the rent seeker who has spent the most (or in the terminology of auctions, the highest bidder obtains the rent).[6]

Such rent-seeking contests that are all-pay auctions do not have a Nash equilibrium in pure strategies. As do the strong and the weak in the game describing anarchy, randomized decisions are made in a mixed-strategy Nash equilibrium.[7] The outcome is that with n rent seekers in a contest, rent dissipation is given by:

$$D \equiv \frac{nEx}{V} = 1 \quad \text{for all values of } n \geq 2, \tag{2.8}$$

where (because of randomization) Ex is the expected (or average) value of the resources used in rent seeking by individual rent seekers (see supplement 2A). Expression (2.8) shows that rent dissipation is, on average, complete for any number of rent seekers.[8] Therefore:

> *In rent-seeking contests in which the highest bidder wins, the observed value of a rent is a proxy for the unobserved value of resources used in the rent-seeking contest.*

We thus have a justification for a supposition of complete rent dissipation in small-number rent-seeking contests as well as in competitive contests. However, we do not know that the rule for winning a rent-seeking contest is necessarily that the highest bidder wins. The alternative Tullock lottery format for identifying successful rent seekers in small-number contests is also possible.

[6] For example, the policy issue may be the length of time for which patent protection applies to pharmaceuticals: the firms with patents want patents to last a long time and generic drug firms want shorter periods during which patent protection applies.

[7] We can consider two rent seekers choosing their political investments x_1 and x_2 in their quest for a rent of value V. Choice of the same political investment ($x_1 = x_2$) is not a Nash equilibrium because one of the rent seekers can do better and can win the contest by bidding a little more. Choice of different positive political investments (for example, $x_1 > x_2 > 0$) cannot be a Nash equilibrium because the second rent seeker will not choose a bid of x_2 when x_2 loses. If one rent seeker bids V to obtain the rent of V, the second rent seeker will bid zero; however, if the second rent seeker bids zero, there is no point to the first rent seeker bidding V because the contest can be won with a small bid above zero. There is therefore no Nash equilibrium in pure strategies.

[8] The formal proof is in Hillman and Samet (1987). See also supplement S2A. The mixed-strategy equilibrium indicates the probability distribution from which rent seekers draw their choice of political investment x. With $V = 100$ and two rent seekers, the solution is that each rent seeker randomly chooses a value of x between zero and 100 from the uniform distribution and $E(x) = 50$ where $E(x)$ is the expected value of a rent seeker's bid. That is, on average, each rent seeker bids 50 and the bids sum to 100, which is the value of the rent-seeking prize V. When a third rent seeker enters the contest, the chance of any rent seeker winning falls from one-half to one-third (the rent seekers have, in the equilibrium, equal chances of winning). In the new mixed-strategy equilibrium, the solution of a uniform distribution is replaced by a probability distribution that places greater weight on lower bids to compensate for the lower probability of winning because of the presence of the additional third participant in the contest. As the number of contenders n increases, the chance of any particular rent seeker winning further declines and the probability distribution from which the bid x is drawn compensates by placing increasingly greater weight on smaller bids. As n increases, $E(x)$ declines but the increase in n and the decrease in $E(x)$ remain precisely balanced to maintain complete rent dissipation – on average.

Rents that endure over time

Figure 2.2 described a rent at a point in time. Rents usually endure over time. Monopoly privileges last; in general, subsidies provided through the government budget or tax concessions endure; and public policies such as for example set environmental standards and thereby determine costs of compliance with the standards remain in place over time. A policy of protection from import competition likewise provides enduring benefits to import-competing industry interests. Similarly, the benefits of privileged public spending obtained in response to rent seeking endure over time, as do the benefits of privilege obtained through tax laws.

> *How does the persistence of rents over time affect rent dissipation and thereby the social cost of rent-seeking activity?*

If the previous conditions are present to ensure complete dissipation for a rent available at a point in time, we need change none of our prior conclusions about rent dissipation when rents endure or are repeated over time.

The total value of a rent that endures over time is not obtained immediately. Parts of the rent will be available only in the future. If future claims to the rent are secure, a winner of a rent-seeking contest knows that, over the course of time, he or she will obtain the entire rent with certainty. Resources equal to the present value of the stream of future rents are attracted to the rent-seeking contest when the rent is contested and rent dissipation is complete.

A successful rent seeker may, however, not be assured of benefiting from future rents. Rents will need to be re-contested in the future if future political decision makers do not recognize favors provided by past politicians. The re-contesting of rents will attract future resources to rent seeking. The prospect of needing to re-contest a rent – or the prospect that the rent will altogether disappear – reduces the expected present value of a rent and so reduces the value of the resources attracted to contesting the rent. Each time that the enduring rent is contested, resources equal to the expected present value of the rent are, however, used in rent seeking. Again rent dissipation is complete. An incumbent monopolist in figure 2.2 may, for example, need to re-contest the right to benefit from the monopoly rent in the future. We may have information that V is the present value of the monopoly profits in the market in figure 2.2 (although we do not know the identity of the future successful rent seekers who will share V over time by winning future rent-seeking contests). Since rent dissipation will be complete over the course of time, we can use the information about V to infer the social cost of the rent seeking that will take place over time because of the persisting re-contested rent. Thus, for rents that endure:

> *When future resources used in re-contesting rents are taken into account, rent dissipation is complete.*[9]

[9] The need to re-contest rents in the future or the possibility that rents will be eliminated leads rent seekers to discount the present value of a rent beyond discounting because of a positive interest rate.

Supplement S2A: Rent seeking and rent dissipation

Supplement S2A considers in more detail rent dissipation implied by theoretical models of rent-seeking contests. Evaluating the social cost of rent seeking through dissipation of rents requires knowing whether individuals or groups compete for rents; whether rents are shared or provide collective benefit; how individual rent seekers in groups are rewarded for their efforts; whether rent seekers are risk-averse; the number of rent seekers in a contest; the number of stages in a contest; and more. The answers determine whether rent dissipation can be reasonably judged to be complete and thereby whether the observed value of a rent is a close approximation to the value of resources used in contesting the rent.

Measurement and information limitations

Often lacking information on resources used in rent seeking and not knowing the contest-success function and other attributes of rent-seeking contests, economic researchers have observed the values of rents and have presumed complete rent dissipation. We cannot, unfortunately, be sure about the extent of rent dissipation. Theoretical analysis of contests provides insights. However, the social costs of rent seeking are difficult to quantify because of the hidden nature of rent seeking. Certainly, political decision makers and rent seekers will not provide information about rent seeking. There is, of course, no point in looking for information about rent seeking in government documents and statistics.

Political trade-offs as impediments to rent creation

In figure 2.2, monopoly rents were shown as maximized. The monopoly, as a special interest, thus received its most preferred outcome. However, political decision makers can be expected to use political discretion to maximize political support from both special interests and voters. Because of the political trade-off between catering to special interests and choosing public policies in the interest of voters, special interests may not be able to obtain their preferred outcome.

In figure 2.3, the political trade-off between catering to special interests and choosing public policies in the interest of voters is expressed in the equal political-support contours S_1, S_2, and S_3. Along a political-support contour, political support is constant. For example, in a move from point 1 to point 2 along the equal

The need to re-contest the rights to a rent in the future reduces the present value of the recurring rents to αR, where $0 < \alpha < 1$. When the rent is contested today, αR is dissipated and $(1-\alpha)R$ remains undissipated. In the future, when rights to the rent are re-contested, again a share α of the present value of the rent will be dissipated. That is, the amount dissipated will be $\alpha(1-\alpha)R$. In the course of time, by continuation of the process, rent dissipation becomes complete. For a formal proof, see Aidt and Hillman (2008).

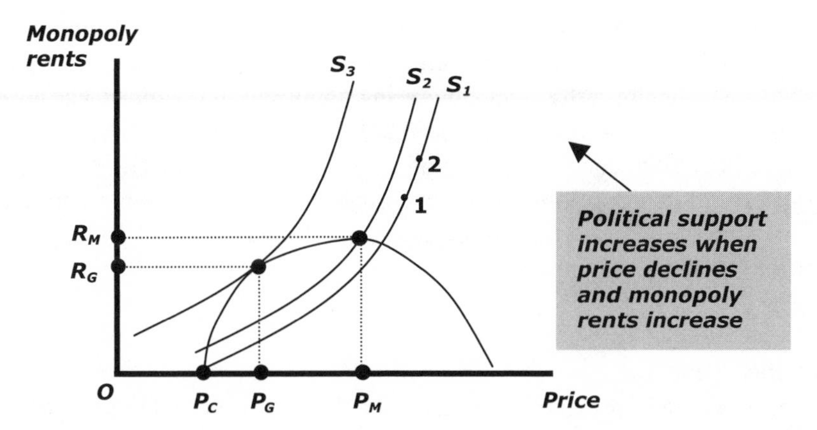

Figure 2.3. The political trade-off in choice of public policy.

political-support contour S_1, industry interests gain through increased monopoly rents and voters as consumers lose because of higher prices.

Figure 2.3 also shows the industry profit function. At the competitive price P_C, voters would obtain their preferred outcome of monopoly rents of zero and political support would be S_1. At the price P_M, special interests would obtain their preferred outcome of maximized monopoly rents R_M and political support would be S_2.

In figure 2.3, the difference in political support is small between political decision makers' providing voters with their preferred outcome at the competitive price P_C and providing industry interests with their preferred outcome at the profit-maximizing price P_M. Political support is maximized when political decision makers choose as public policy the regulated market price P_G, at which monopoly rents are R_G.

Although we have illustrated the political choice of market price using the example of a monopolized market, a politically determined domestic price could be similarly chosen for a competitive import-competing industry through choice of protectionist policy. We shall also observe the political trade-off between the public-interest policy sought by voters and the public policy sought by political interests when we study political influences on choice of environmental policy.

In each case, political decision makers maximize political support by choosing a public policy that is a compromise between the outcomes sought by voters and industry interests. Thus:

Public policies balance voter against special-interest support.

In figure 2.3, if voters had no political influence on political behavior, the rent to be contested would be R_M. The political trade-off reduces the rent to R_G.

Voter dissatisfaction restrains political rent creation.

The question in any instance of political discretion regarding public finance and public policy is, given the political principal–agent problem, how influential is voter dissatisfaction in restraining influencing political rent creation? The answer depends on the different considerations that have been described as affecting the relative political influence of voters and special interests. Indeed, it is because voters' political influence is limited – even though voters determine voting outcomes – that the political choice in figure 2.3 is a compromise of the public interest.

Rules and discretion

Political culture describes norms of political behavior. Rent seeking is influenced by people's perceptions of norms of political behavior.

> *Rent seeking takes place because of the perception that political decision makers can be influenced to create and assign rents.*

That is, rent-seeking incentives are present if political decision makers are perceived as responsive to rent seeking. Rent-seeking incentives, on the contrary, are absent when it is known that political decisions about public finance and public policy are determined according to objective criteria of efficiency and social justice.

> *Rent seeking is deterred when it is known that political decisions are based on predetermined rules rather than political discretion.*

A rent-seeking society

A culture of rent seeking can pervade an entire society and thereby include behavior outside of political activity. In such rent-seeking societies, people mainly spend their time on networking and seeking (and giving) favors rather than on productive activity. Personal success depends on who you know, what other people can give you, and what you have to offer to give them in return. Personal privilege through successful rent seeking replaces achievement by merit.

A rent-seeking society can be quite venal. Admission to university or college can be a rent-seeking contest rather than determined by merit. Students can also find that professors are open to persuasion through personal favors when assigning grades for courses. Complaining to the dean about a professor's behavior is ineffective in a rent-seeking society because the dean will not be concerned that the behavior of the professors is unethical but will also be seeking rents. Ethics do not influence behavior in a rent-seeking society.

There is a loss to society when students respond to rent-seeking incentives and are distracted from studying. Students may come to presume that all achievement in life is necessarily through favors and privilege rather than merit – in a rent-seeking culture, the presumption is correct.

When reward is by merit (as in a competitive market where people earn the value of their marginal product), matching of people to jobs is through personal comparative advantage. The best students, for example, become the professors of the next generation. The abilities of professors at any time determine the quality of the students who will be the professors in the following generations. In a rent-seeking culture, students were not admitted to university on personal merit; as well, the professors who teach the students, in their day as students, were not admitted to study on personal merit. The same disregard for personal merit and ability affects the quality of surgeons and dentists and others in professions on which people rely for specialized skills and knowledge.

> *In a rent-seeking society, because assignment to professions and jobs is not through personal merit, individuals can achieve positions and have jobs contrary to personal comparative advantage.*

Ambiguities in behavior

Rent seeking can be an excessively cynical concept that requires caution when applied to personal relationships. Someone may offer to buy you a cup of coffee or a drink or to pay for dinner because the person regards you as pleasant company. Applying the concept of rent seeking suggests that the offer to pay for your drink or dinner is necessarily a prepayment in anticipation of a request for a return favor or benefit. Adam Smith suggested that we should have a distrusting attitude to personal favors offered in markets. Awareness that rent seeking may be taking place imparts a distrusting attitude to personal favors offered outside of markets.

Yet, when some people are observed systematically to benefit from privileged favors, rent seeking points to a hidden side of an exchange. Awareness of rent seeking brings to the fore the question of why some people benefit from privileged favors whereas others do not.

Adam Smith and rent seeking

A case in favor is also a case against something else. Adam Smith's case for the market was a case against a rent-seeking ideology known as *mercantilism*. Under mercantilism, the monarch (or government) accumulates wealth in the form of gold and silver (or foreign exchange). The country is viewed as one large profit-maximizing firm, with the king or queen (or government) extracting shares of the rents created through legally authorized domestic- and foreign-trade monopolies. Adam Smith pointed out that the "wealth of nations" is not achieved by accumulating gold and silver and through creation of rents but rather through benefit to buyers and sellers from voluntary decisions in competitive markets. As we have observed, competitive markets do not provide rents. The benefits of competitive markets are to society at large. Competitive markets were not favored by the mercantilists and are not favored by political rent extractors of contemporary times. As we also observed previously, political decision makers may prefer their own imposed order to the spontaneous order of competitive markets.

Two types of competition

We have identified two types of competition. Competition in markets provides incentives to be productive, and Adam Smith's "invisible hand" ensures that in doing the best for themselves in markets, people need neither give nor seek favors. In the competition for rents, behavior is unproductive and favors are sought and given.

Rent seeking and anarchy

We study rent seeking to evaluate efficiency losses of political discretion. Rent seeking also has consequences for social justice. The assignment of privilege through successful rent seeking can be expected to be unjust by any criterion of social justice that we might propose. Rent seeking affects efficiency and social justice in a manner similar to the relationship between the strong and the weak in anarchy. Outcomes when the strong impose their will on the weak were seen to be inefficient and also are socially unjust. Rent seeking and anarchy have in common the unproductive use of resources. The difference is in the role of government. In anarchy, resources are used unproductively because of absence of institutions that provide the rule of law. Resources are used unproductively in rent seeking because institutions of governance permit political decision makers to create and assign rents.

Lobbyists and lawyers

The presence of lobbyists is an indication that rent seeking is taking place. The more lobbyists there are, the greater we can surmise is rent-seeking activity. The proportion of lawyers in a population has been proposed as a proxy measure for rent-seeking activity. We have noted that if private property rights were perfectly protected, contestability of property could not occur. Thus, for example, with perfectly protected property rights, a farmer who wants the government to give him his neighbor's field or cow has a wish that will not be fulfilled. If transfer of ownership from rightful owners is possible, good lawyers may be necessary to achieve the result. Of course, lawyers do more than engage in the contestability of rent seeking. Nonetheless, lawyers are instruments of contestability and a large number of lawyers in a population suggests a rent-seeking society.

D. Rent extraction and corruption

Political decision makers provide personal benefits for themselves through rent extraction. Often rent extraction is associated with corruption.

Rent extraction

Rent extraction occurs, for example, when legislation is proposed that, if passed by the legislature, would be disadvantageous to particular interest groups. When the legislation is proposed or hinted at, interest groups begin their activities of warding off the threatened policies. Political contributions are made to legislators to preempt the threatened policies.[10]

Monopoly can be used to demonstrate rent extraction. After monopoly rights have been assigned, a political decision maker in the future – as we observed in the description of rent dissipation when rents endure over time – can reopen the monopoly rent to contestability. Alternatively, the political decision maker can *threaten* to open the monopoly rent to contestability and thereby extract a rent from the incumbent monopolist for deciding not to make the monopoly rent contestable after all.

Corruption

Rent creation and rent seeking in democracies are not illegal – nor necessarily is rent extraction. Illegality involves corruption.

> *Corruption is the illegal use of the authority of government for direct personal benefit.*

To find extensive corruption, we need to look at autocratic low-income societies. Arrival in a low-income country may be accompanied by the need to pay a bribe for confirmation that a valid entry visa is, indeed, valid. A bribe may be required to retrieve baggage. The bribes, which are means of rent extraction, can continue when police officers or government officials are encountered and may be required in any aspect of economic activity.[11]

There is no efficiency loss when a bribe is paid. The bribe alone is transfer of income (as when a thief steals our money). However, the job or position of the

[10] In the United States, political extortion has been associated with the terminology "milker bills." Such bills provide incentives for political payments and campaign contributions to ensure that the bills are not passed. See McChesney (1997).

[11] A question studied in economic development concerns the nexus between low incomes and corruption. Do low-income countries have low incomes (rich elites excluded) because of corruption or is corruption prevalent because of low incomes? That is, does corruption cause low incomes or do low incomes cause corruption? There may be simultaneity – just as demand and supply together determine market price.

government official who has received a bribe may be contestable. If so, a bribe becomes a rent that attracts resources into a rent-seeking contest. The prize in the contest is the job or government position that allows the bribes to received. Perhaps a way to replace an incumbent official benefiting from bribes is to pay a bribe to the incumbent's superior in the government hierarchy. In that case, a transfer of income is again made, and the income transfer through the bribe to the higher official is the stimulus for rent seeking if the position of the senior official receiving the bribe is also contestable.

> *Bribes are income transfers that give rise to rent-seeking contests when the jobs or positions of the persons receiving the bribes are contestable.*

Reasons for wishing to be a politician differ among countries. In rent-seeking societies, political office is sought for self-enrichment through rent extraction. The political decision maker obtains personal income from bribes and from applying the authority of government to create and sometimes personally own monopolies. The personal account of the president may be where the government's tax revenue is deposited. The government officials and minister responsible for international trade can earn income from smuggling. In high-income democracies, institutions are inconsistent with endemic rent-extracting corruption and political office is not sought for personal material self-enrichment. The term *ego-rents* has been used to describe the emotional or psychic benefits from being an elected politician in a democratic high-income society. In high-income democracies, bribes are therefore aberrations and, in general, are neither sought nor paid. Nor, in general, are political decision makers corrupt in using public finance and public policy to extract rents for the personal benefit of themselves, family, or friends. Rent extraction is usually limited to political favors exchanged for political support. Occasionally, personally corrupt politicians do emerge in high-income democratic societies: the prerogatives of government and perceived opportunities for creating and personally extracting rents can be too great a personal temptation.

A society is not corrupt when the activities of corrupt politicians are revealed in the media and when the corrupt politicians are tried in courts of law. In a corrupt society, a corrupt president, government minister, or judge, in general, will not be accused of corruption. Arrests for corruption will take place only if political decision makers or judges have fallen out of favor with the ruler. Corruption is indeed a means of governing in low-income autocratic countries. The ruler allows everybody to be corrupt so that everyone is vulnerable and beholden to the ruler, who has a pretext for dismissing or imprisoning anyone at will.

We continue now in our investigation of the consequences of institutions and governance for public finance and public policy with high-income democracies. We turn now to the principal–agent problem between taxpayers or voters and the government bureaucracy.

2.2

Government Bureaucracy

The tax administration (the Internal Revenue Service in the United States and the Treasury in other countries) collects taxes. Other government bureaucracies implement and administer public spending. Government bureaucracies also have regulatory tasks such as ensuring competitive markets and implementing environmental protection laws. The judicial branch of government has the responsibility to ensure the rule of law. Bureaucracy is therefore an essential component of government.

A. Incentives and behavior in a bureaucracy

In general, government bureaucracies are monopolies. Government departments verify citizenship and issue passports for foreign travel, manage public-health programs, handle tenders for road construction, manage welfare programs, and provide for defense. Regulatory bureaucracies and the legal system are also monopolies.[12] In the private sector, a monopoly rent consists of excess profits that would not be available if there were competition. In government bureaucracies, rents take the form of low effort and low stress and other benefits associated with on-the-job quality of life. Government bureaucracies cannot become bankrupt, with incomes of government bureaucrats assured from tax revenue.

Owners of a private monopoly have incentives to minimize costs of production to increase profits. Incentives in a government bureaucracy can be precisely the opposite – to maximize costs – because costs include bureaucrats' salaries. Bureaucrats' benefits also increase with the size of the budgets that they control. There is asymmetric information because taxpayers and voters do not know precisely what is happening inside bureaucracies. The asymmetric information is the basis for a principal–agent problem between taxpayers or voters and government bureaucrats.

Still, bureaucrats could be faithful public servants with no principal–agent problem. A vision of circumstances in which bureaucratic rents and asymmetric information do not influence incentives and behavior of bureaucrats was set out by Max Weber. Weber (1864–1920) described career bureaucrats as serving only the public interest; thus, he presented a normative vision of how bureaucrats ideally should behave.

Departure from Weber's normative vision takes place if civil servants maximize utility or do their personal best for themselves. Careers and incomes of civil servants are often advanced by control of larger government budgets: in general, the larger the budget that a bureaucrat manages, also the

[12] However, private binding arbitration is a substitute for the judicial system for civil cases.

greater is the bureaucrat's prestige and power. A larger and more extensive bureaucratic hierarchy increases prospects for promotion opportunities, and incomes and power are greater for officials who preside over a more extensive bureaucracy. Budget maximization and expanded bureaucracies are contrary to the interests of taxpayers, who want an efficient bureaucracy that achieves designated objectives with minimal spending. With taxpayers subject to asymmetric information about bureaucratic behavior and bureaucrats having objectives that differ from those of taxpayers, there is a principal–agent problem.

A taxpayer who wants to overcome the asymmetric-information problem and assert rights of accountability could stand outside a government building at the end of the working day and ask government officials leaving the building how they have passed their day and how their activities have contributed to taxpayer benefit. Government bureaucrats as the agents would then be being asked to provide accounts of their contributions to the welfare of society by the taxpayer, who is the principal whose taxes finance the bureaucrats' salaries. A government employee who replies that the question is an intrusion into his or her privacy is acting contrary to principles of accountability. A government employee who asserts "I cannot be accountable to every taxpayer" in all likelihood is prepared to be accountable to no taxpayer. A government employee might name a superior in the bureaucratic hierarchy and reply, "Why not ask my boss?" The next step in the experiment is to make an appointment to meet with the bureaucratic superior in the hierarchy and to again seek accountability, the question now posed with respect to the day of the superior bureaucrat as well as his or her subordinates. Rational ignorance through a comparison of personal benefits and costs would, in general, deter taxpayers from undertaking such an experiment in seeking information about behavior in government bureaucracies. Personal costs are incurred and there would be little personal benefit from the attempt at satisfying curiosity about how the government bureaucrats spend their time. Government officials or bureaucrats (we shall use the terms interchangeably) being questioned may also regard the behavior of a taxpayer seeking accountability as unusual. Accountability is, however, a requisite for solving the principal–agent problem.

B. Demand creation by bureaucracies

Because bureaucrats benefit from larger budgets, the bureaucrats have incentives to create demand for their services. Government officials who are responsible for administering an unemployment compensation program, for example, have a personal interest in sustained unemployment. Government social workers have a personal interest in the persistence of adversity in the population to preserve the client base that justifies their job. To create demand for their services, officials in the Department of State or the Foreign Service have an interest in justifying the need for embassies and consulates in foreign locations. If the officials have invested in learning a foreign language, they particularly will want increased diplomatic representation in countries where the language that they have learned is spoken. The officials also have an interest in biasing foreign policy so as to remain on good terms with countries whose language they speak. Taxpayers lack means of knowing whether proposed increased public spending on foreign representation is justified as being in the public interest. Rational ignorance also deters taxpayers from seeking information that might be available, as does the information free-rider problem.

C. Measurement of bureaucratic output

The inability to measure accurately bureaucratic output compounds the problem of asymmetric information. Ambiguities regarding measurement of output arise in firms in the private sector. However, private profit motives and private ownership provide incentives for private monitoring and evaluation of the worth of employees' activities. Management in private firms is rewarded for the ability to be accurate when making judgments about imperfectly measurable outputs of employees. The accuracy of the judgment is revealed in profits. The same rewards for accuracy in judgment do not apply in government agencies and departments. Profitability is not a criterion for evaluating bureaucratic efficiency because the output of government agencies and departments is generally not valued in markets. The inability to measure accurately bureaucratic output can lead employees in bureaucracies to focus their efforts on activities that are unproductive but visible. Paperwork and forms, multiplicity of network messages that are not informative, expansion of data files, and unnecessary meetings can become part of bureaucratic activity because these activities are observable and the bureaucrats' inputs can be measured in terms of time.

D. Solutions to the bureaucratic principal–agent problem

Principal–agent problems are present in the private sector: shareholders as owners of a firm want profits or long-term market value to be maximized, whereas executives and managers of firms may have other personal objectives. For example, by expanding the scope of activities of a firm beyond core competencies, management benefits from the spreading of risk among different activities; managers' jobs are thereby protected in the event that any one activity incurs losses. Shareholders lose when the firm expands beyond core competencies; to spread their own risk, shareholders do not require diversification of the firm because shareholders can diversify and spread risk by buying stock in different firms. As in government bureaucracies, managers in the private sector can have unnecessary personal assistants or can assign themselves excessive travel and entertainment budgets. The private sector, however, has monitoring and incentive mechanisms to resolve principal–agent problems. Stock-option schemes tie managers' incomes and wealth to the value of a company's shares.[13] Management in private firms is monitored by private owners who can replace inadequately performing managers. In large corporations in which no one shareholder owns a significant share of the company, auditing firms, financial analysts in investment banks and brokerages monitor managerial performance.[14] The responsibility of rating firms is to judge and report the level of risk associated with different firms. In principle also, a board of directors monitors management. The performance incentives and monitoring in the private sector are imperfect. Auditors, financial analysts, and rating firms can even have a personal financial interest in misreporting; if the misreporting is sufficiently extensive, financial crises can occur as assets recommended or valued as low risk turn out to be high risk. Malfeasance can therefore take place in the private sector. However, behavior in the private sector is eventually revealed through accountability in financial markets. The imperfect monitoring mechanisms of the private sector cannot be applied to government departments and agencies because private owners do not exist in the public sector and assets of government agencies are not subject to market valuation.[15] Government departments and agencies do not confront the discipline of ultimately facing a cash constraint or of reporting profits and losses, and stock prices do not exist to fall to indicate insolvency due to indiscretion or incompetence. The government departments and agencies are funded from tax revenue and face a soft-budget constraint.[16]

Contracts

Although incentives associated with asset markets are impossible, could a contract provide incentives for a bureaucracy to make decisions that are in the interest of taxpayers? Output of the bureaucracy may not be measurable but, with costs of inputs including bureaucrats' salaries known, the contract could specify that the head of the bureaucracy will personally receive a share of any cost savings. A sufficiently large personal reward for reducing spending on inputs can counter management benefits from an excessive bureaucracy and can make

[13] Stock-option schemes can also be used to the disadvantage of shareholders in offering excessive rewards to management.

[14] If the performance of management is revealed to be inadequate, financial analysts downgrade the firm in their stock-market evaluations, and the share price of the company falls. This is a market signal for the dismissal of management. New owners might buy the company's stock at the depressed prices and install replacement management.

[15] Governments, however, are disciplined through financial markets. When policies are considered inappropriate, the value of bonds issued by governments falls and governments are obliged to pay higher interest rates for borrowing. Of course, it is not governments that are paying the higher interest rates but the public, whose taxes finance the interest-rate payments.

[16] A "hard" budget constraint is binding and credible. A "soft" budget does not bind on spending. An example of a soft budget is when a child, who has been given lunch money on a Monday for the entire week, announces in midweek that he or she has no money left to buy lunch the next day. Because parents will not normally allow a child to go hungry, the budget constraint confronting the child is soft. The child, knowing the budget constraint is soft, can safely spend the lunch money by midweek.

the self-interest of career bureaucrats consistent with the interest of taxpayers. However, whatever the cost savings, the impediments to measuring bureaucratic output hinder determination of whether there have been net benefits from the reduced spending. The cost-saving contract would need to ensure that the incentive of the managers is not to close down the government department or agency, when closure is an exaggerated response to the principal–agent problem. Cost-saving incentive contracts are rarely if ever used in government bureaucracies.

Political monitoring

Taxpayers can seek to rely on elected political representatives to monitor government bureaucracies. The monitoring is delegated to high-level political appointees who head government bureaucracies or committees of elected representatives who have oversight roles. There are impediments to the effectiveness of political monitoring if career bureaucrats have longer job tenure than elected politicians. The longer job tenure allows career bureaucrats to become better informed than politicians and political appointees about the inner workings of government bureaucracies. Because of career bureaucrats' informational advantages, political appointees who head a bureaucracy can come to rely on the career bureaucracy for information, including information about the resource needs of the bureaucracy. When asymmetric information prevents political representatives from effectively monitoring bureaucrats, a principal–agent problem arises between the elected political representatives and bureaucrats. There are then two principal–agent problems involving government bureaucracy, that between taxpayers and the bureaucracy and that between political representatives and the bureaucracy. In the background is the further political principal–agent problem between taxpayers or voters and politicians.

Criteria for political success and for advancement in a government bureaucracy usually differ. A senior career bureaucrat responsible for economic issues often requires formal qualifications. The same educational attainments may not be necessary for political appointees who oversee government bureaucracies. A political appointment may be a reward for political loyalty rather than competence or expertise in the field of responsibility of a government department. The effectiveness of monitoring of career bureaucrats by political appointees is further diminished if a political appointee is personally focused on political advancement to higher level positions.[17]

[17] The type of political system influences the control exercised by elected politicians over bureaucracy. Although career bureaucrats tend to outlast politicians who rotate among ministries or who go in and out of elected office, in the United States, for example, where political seniority determines appointments to congressional oversight committees and the oversight committees, in turn, control budgets of the bureaucracies, career bureaucrats have incentives to comply with objectives designated by political representatives. The principal–agent problem between political representatives and career bureaucrats is then ameliorated, subject to asymmetric information – when the political representatives who have oversight over the government bureaucracy have the same objectives as taxpayers.

Incentives through efficiency wages

Incentives for behavior in the public interest could be sought by paying "efficiency wages" in government bureaucracies. Efficiency wages are intended to solve the principal–agent problem between employers and employees when there is low probability of detection of an employee's shirking behavior. Wages are set sufficiently high so that it is not worthwhile for employees to shirk (or not exert effort). The high wages provide a financial incentive for employees to exert effort and thereby not to lose their jobs by being caught shirking. We shall return to efficiency wages when we consider reasons for unemployment and the consequences of payment of unemployment insurance. Applied to the principal–agent problem of government bureaucracy, efficiency wages are intended to provide incentives for government bureaucrats to seek the efficiency sought by taxpayers and voters. In high-income countries, government bureaucrats are often paid salaries seemingly greater than alternative private-sector wages; hence, the presence of the bureaucratic rents. According to the theory of efficiency wages, the rents to bureaucrats are inevitable, given the cost of – or impossibility of – direct forms of monitoring of bureaucrats' behavior. Are efficiency wages a solution to the bureaucratic principal–agent problem? We could repeat our experiment of attempting to question government bureaucrats leaving (or entering) a government building. Would efficiency wages ensure transparency and accountability in answers received? We might only know with certainty that we are questioning well-paid bureaucrats.

The Thomas-à-Becket effect

A principal–agent problem between taxpayers and government bureaucracy, of course, would not be present if the bureaucracy were to consist of the benevolent altruistic public servants described by Max Weber. To behave as Weber described, employees in the government bureaucracies would need to have transformed their behavior from the pursuit of self-interest when making decisions in markets outside of government to the altruistic quest for the public interest when making decisions inside the government bureaucracy. How can the required transformation of behavior be achieved?

An example illustrating the required personal transformation is the principled behavior of Thomas-à-Becket, after whom the *Thomas-à-Becket effect* is named. Thomas-à-Becket (1118–70) was a close friend of the English king, Henry II, who in 1162 appointed him to the position of Archbishop of Canterbury. The king had expected that his friend would be a compliant cleric who would support him in disagreements with the church in Rome. Upon becoming archbishop, however, Thomas-à-Becket took the side of the church that he now headed in England. The king is said to have proclaimed: "Who will rid me of this meddlesome priest?" Not asking whether the king's question was intended as rhetorical, four of the king's knights proceeded to Canterbury, where they murdered Thomas-à-Becket on December 29, 1170. The king was rid of the "meddlesome" principled priest.

Thomas-à-Becket went to his death rather than betray the trust of the public office to which he had been appointed. Appeals to the Thomas-à-Becket effect look for the same type of fortitude from government officials.

The Thomas-à-Becket effect requires that bureaucrats realize that the private self-interest that guides behavior of private individuals in markets is inappropriate for behavior of government officials, for the invisible hand is present in markets but not in government bureaucracies. The hope is that, as did Thomas-à-Becket, government bureaucrats will detach themselves from personal self-interest and devote themselves to serving the interests of the public.

Supplement S2B: Institutions and natural monopoly

Principal–agent problems arise when there is natural monopoly. Supplement S2B describes how institutions and principal–agent problems affect outcomes under natural monopoly.

2.3 Life without Markets and Private Property

Political and bureaucratic principal–agent problems are pervasive when government is maximal. A form of maximal government exists when private property is disallowed or limited and property is instead communal or collective, as under communism. In most of the world, communism ceased to exist after around 1990. Nonetheless, it is interesting to look briefly at communist societies because of the comparisons provided in the limit between relying on markets and designating responsibilities to government.

Communism abolishes private property. The justification is that private property is the source of social and economic inequality. With private property absent, markets cannot exist because without private ownership, people do not have the right to buy and sell. With markets then not present, political decision makers set economic objectives for the society. Bureaucrats in government-planning agencies implement plans that are intended to achieve the objectives.

There are also no markets in raw materials and intermediate goods. The planners have the responsibility to ensure that shipments of raw materials and intermediate goods to and between factories are consistent with the political decision makers' plans. Goods for final consumption are not literally delivered to people's doors; there are markets that allow consumers to buy goods for final consumption. The planners and not markets, however, determine prices of goods for final consumption. Prices are not intended to be equilibrium market prices that equate supply and demand but are set according to "social need." There is therefore no necessary relationship between prices and costs of production. All goods are produced in government-owned factories and sold for final consumption in stores also owned by the government. The government has a monopoly on all economic activity. "Costs" are unknown because there are no markets that could reveal costs through the value of the inputs used in production. With prices set low because of social need, there were systematic "shortages" of goods. The communist economy was therefore known as a "shortage economy." Goods were allocated not by how much people were willing to pay but by rationing and waiting in line. With allocation not by markets but through decisions of other people, individuals could advance themselves in a queue or reduce waiting time by rent seeking and by privilege obtained through personal exchanges.[18]

We are purposefully discussing goods rather than "goods and services" because communist ideology regarded only "goods" as production; "services" did not count. Thus, in communist societies, it could be difficult, for example, to find coffee shops and restaurants where people "served" others.

Communist principles were set out by the 19th-century writers, Karl Marx (1818–83) and Frederick Engels (1820–95), who wrote the *Communist Manifesto*, which was published in 1848. Communism as a form of social organization for an entire economy was introduced through the Russian Revolution of October 1917, which displaced the ruling hereditary monarch.[19] Communism subsequently spread, in general, through imposition rather than the choice of voters.

Under communism, control over people was exercised through a hierarchical structure of leaders and committees at the workplace and in the buildings where people lived. People who voiced doubts about the virtues of communism could be certified as insane and committed to an asylum, or be declared "enemies of the state" and exiled to forced-labor camps where life was often cut short by extreme weather and inadequate food. Once in the hands of the secret police, people might disappear, never to be seen again.

Communism had laws but not the rule of law. Lavrentiy Pavlovich Beria (1899–1953) is accredited with the remark when he was in charge of the communist secret police, "Show me a person and I can find the crime." Children were encouraged to report expressions of dissent by their parents and neighbors were

[18] Having a partner who was prepared to wait in line was an advantage. A senior professor of economics in Russia claimed that he and his first wife divorced because of disagreement over who should queue for produce. Both declared that their time was too valuable for them to wait in lines to do the shopping. In the second marriage, the professor chose a woman whose time was less valuable. This example demonstrates aspects of life and personal considerations that are absent in societies based on institutions of markets and market-clearing prices.

[19] Russian monarchs, in general, had been tyrannical. Had we lived in Russia at the time and had we not been members of the royal family or the hereditary nobility, we would have in all likelihood supported overthrowing the czar (as the emperor of Russia was called).

encouraged to monitor one another. People lived in fear of fabricated – if not actual – reports of disloyalty to the principles of communism.

Around 1990, wherever the opportunity presented itself, communism was abolished in democratic elections and private property and markets were made legal.[20]

We are interested in communism because of the display of the attributes of a society with maximal government and no markets.

A. Incentives and human nature

Communist ideology proposed an ideal society in which all individuals would contribute to society according to ability and not be influenced by the incentives of personal rewards. Having contributed according to ability, people would receive according to need. In principle, everyone's needs were expected to be the same because everyone in society was equal. There was no role for natural right of possession to the product of one's own efforts. Everything that a person produced was to be shared altruistically with everyone else.

People were thus being asked to view work as a value in itself and not as a means of earning personal income. Work was to be a means of personal expression of self-worth and self-identity. Human nature was an impediment to the implementation of the ideology. To exert effort to be productive, individuals generally require personal incentives in the form of personal rewards.

The communist solution to the incentive problem was to change human nature through social re-engineering and education so that personal incentives and rewards would no longer matter. Through social re-engineering and education, personal greed was to end and everyone was to become an altruist who contributes for the benefit of society at large and not for personal gain.

Hayek and the fatal conceit

Friedrich von Hayek (1899–1992), who received the Nobel Prize in economics in 1974, predicted that the attempts to change human nature would be unsuccessful

[20] The end of the communist regimes came about because of the end of communism in the Soviet Union, which dismembered into Russia and 14 other independent states. Other countries in Europe had been part of a Soviet empire and could choose to free themselves from communism. The last Soviet leader, Mikhail Gorbachev, believed that he could introduce economic liberalization and allow access to information without political liberalization. Communism relied on disinformation. People were told how well off they were, compared to the "oppressed masses" of private-property societies. The new "openness" and economic freedom made the disinformation difficult to sustain. Communists opposed to the liberalization staged a revolt on August 19, 1991, and placed Gorbachev under house arrest. The revolt collapsed two days later. During the course of the following month, countries that had been part of the communist U.S.S.R. (Union of Soviet Socialist Republics) declared independence. Russia re-emerged as a separate country and democratic elections were held. During the 1990s, a process known as "the transition" took place in the former communist countries, as markets replaced planners and private property replaced communal property.

and described the idea that human nature could be changed through social re-engineering as the "fatal conceit" (Hayek, 1988). He proposed an evolutionary argument for the failure of communism (which had not yet collapsed when Hayek made his predictions). The evolutionary argument, which predicts survival of the fittest, was applied to social and economic organization. Hayek observed that economic prosperity for a broad population (as opposed to wealth and power for elites) has invariably required the institutions of markets and private property. Because only these institutions have ever been successful in providing broad economic benefit, attempts to change the human nature consistent with private property and markets showed disregard for the evolution of successful institutions over time.

Why did communism win hearts and minds?

In general, people care more about fairness than efficiency – as is revealed in the outcomes of the experiments that offered people alternatives of market and non-market assignment. The objective of communism is social equality. A syllogism is as follows:

- Social equality (ex-post and ex-ante) is a desirable objective that takes precedent over other objectives.
- The objective of communism is fairness through equality.
- Therefore, we should support communism.

The argument won the hearts and minds of many people, not only in the parts of the world ruled by communism. Professors of economists could also be convinced. Hayek's prediction that communism would fail made him unpopular with many "mainstream" economists of his time. Hayek was accused of being uncaring in undermining through his writings the belief in the possibility of an egalitarian society in which circumstances at birth and personal ability would no longer matter for outcomes in life.[21]

Of course, Hayek's writings in themselves were not the true problem for the people whose hearts and minds had been won by communism. The problems were the impediments to which Hayek pointed. Silencing Hayek would not have saved communism.

B. Information and efficiency

When disadvantages of communism have been discussed, economists have often focused on information and efficiency. Communism could not achieve efficiency because the information spontaneously revealed in markets was unavailable.[22]

[21] On the criticisms of Hayek, see Caldwell (1988).

[22] There were proposals, most prominently by Lange (1938), about how efficiency might be achieved through computation of "shadow prices," which are the prices that would have existed if markets had existed to reveal the prices. The shadow prices could not be accurately computed because the information needed to compute the shadow prices was not available.

The information limitations made change risky for communist government bureaucrats. Changes might be for the better – or not. If suggestions for innovation and improvement were successful, the innovators would receive no private reward – the benefits belonged to society. If the suggestions for change were unsuccessful, the innovators would suffer undesirable personal consequences. Not wishing to take risks, government agencies simply replicated the past, thereby at least hoping to ensure that everything remained as it had been. With the present and the future consisting of a repetition of past instructions about what and how to produce, technological innovation could not take place.[23]

Supplement S2C: Labor self-management

Supplement 2C describes the institutions of labor self-management, under which property is also collective and equality is sought as a preeminent objective. Workers make employment decisions. Unlike communism, there is, in principle, no centralized control over the economy.

C. Equality and envy

The purpose of communal property is equality. If not efficiency, did communism provide equality?

Theft and social justice

An impediment to equality under institutions of communism was unequal opportunities for theft. Theft at the government factories was rampant. Private property ethically deters theft because the theft is of other people's property. Collective property belongs to everybody and, therefore, to no one in particular. Theft is then more easily personally justifiable. In the government factories, workers might view their output as theirs – justified through the natural right of possession because their effort produced the output. Although formally illegal, workers might barter the output they had produced for output produced in other government factories. The injustice is that opportunities for theft depend on what people produced. School teachers or college professors have little opportunity for theft of output (which is education of students). Openness to rent seeking and bribes could substitute for opportunities for theft. There were then injustices because of unequal means of seeking bribes in return for providing favors.

[23] A source of inefficiency was the hoarding of inputs by government factories. The hoarding protected the factory against unforeseen contingencies that might otherwise prevent supply of the quantities required by the planning bureaucrats. Inability to supply was a violation of the law.

Women

Women had been predicted to gain from communal property. In 1884, Frederick Engels, in his book, *The Origin of the Family, Private Property and the State,* had proposed that private property and the family are capitalist institutions designed to allow men to subjugate women. Engels declared that in hunter–gatherer societies prior to the institutions of private property and the family, women had the personal freedom to choose anyone in the clan as a partner. Any ensuing children were cared for communally. Engels proposed that the institution of communal property liberated women from being the property of men. At the time that Engels wrote, in many societies the rights of women indeed were subjugated to the rights of men. Women subsequently achieved equal rights in capitalist societies, through the right to vote and through security of rights to property, including after a divorce the right of retention of property brought into a marriage and the right to shares of family property.

Envy

The theory was that collective property would end envy; there should be no reason to be envious of others if no one personally owns anything. Yet, when all benefits are personally assigned through government, people know that if someone else has received more than they have, privilege in all likelihood was involved. Envy persisted under communism and was present to a greater degree than when personal benefit is due to personal merit and effort and the incentives of markets. People become cynical when personal outcomes depend on privilege. Social justice is not served for men or women when a person's most valuable asset is the personal ability to please others who hand out favors. With decisions about a person's "needs" made by others, the quest for privilege through rent seeking becomes overriding; all personal benefits have become rents, and personal effort and ability are directed at rent seeking through networking and establishing and maintaining personal relationships. The costs to society through unproductive activity are high when people are exclusively focused on securing privileges for themselves through rent seeking and exchange of favors.

D. Personal freedom

Hayek observed in his book *The Fatal Conceit* (1988, p. 108) that:

> *Imagining that all order is the result of design, socialists conclude that order must be improvable by better design of some superior mind.*

Hayek was pointing to the perception that designed or imposed order is necessary for economic and social progress. The "superior mind" to which Hayek referred was that of the political decision makers and bureaucrats in government agencies. Before Hayek, Adam Smith had remarked:

> *The statesman who would attempt to direct private people in what manner they ought employ their capitals, would... assume an authority which could be safely trusted, not only to no single person, but to no council or senate whatever, and which would nowhere be so dangerous as in the hands of a man who had folly and presumption enough to fancy himself fit to exercise it.* (Smith, 1776/1937, p. 423)

Like Hayek, Adam Smith was remarking on the vanity and the dangers to society of men and women who believe that they can make society better off by imposing "order" rather than allowing people to decide for themselves.

Writing in 1944 in the book, *The Road to Serfdom*, Hayek pointed out that communal property results in enslavement because a ruler who controls communal property controls the entire society. Hayek noted the link between communal property and megalomania:

> *... collectivists must create power – power over men wielded by other men – and their success will depend on the extent to which they achieve such power.* (1944/1972, p. 144)

The institutions of markets and private property limit the scope of power of any one person over others. Hayek observed that where there are markets and private property, political power is "never power over the whole life of a person." A ruler's personal control over communal property, however, "creates a degree of dependence scarcely distinguishable from slavery."[24] To illustrate the loss of personal freedom under communism, Hayek quoted the communist Leon Trotsky (1879–1940),[25] who had noted that:

> *"Where the sole employer is the State, opposition means death by slow starvation. The old principle: he who does not work shall not eat, has been replaced by a new one: who does not obey does not eat."*[26]

We shall not return to institutions of imposed order and collective property. Our study of public finance and public policy will be based on the institutions of markets and private property. Our point of departure for evaluation of the responsibilities of government is minimal government, defined as government that ensures competitive markets and the rule of law.

[24] Adam Smith had observed that markets dissipate personal political power. He noted that in societies without opportunities for exchange in markets, people use their wealth to expand their personal power by hiring private armies to take property by force and enslave others.

[25] Leon Trotsky fled Russia in 1929 seeking safety from the communist dictator, Stalin, with whom he had fallen out of favor. Trotsky made his way to Mexico, where in 1940 he was assassinated. Hayek also fled his land of birth, leaving Austria in 1938 when Austria united with Germany, for the London School of Economics and thereafter the University of Chicago.

[26] Cited by Hayek, 1944, p. 119.

When we consider roles for government, indications of the limitations of government that have appeared in the description of maximal government will nonetheless at times appear. The economic freedom of a society based on markets and private property is the antithesis of the lack of economic freedom when private property is disallowed and "order" is imposed. Still, in economies with markets and private property, the taxes required for public finance create gaps between the value of personal productive contributions (the value of the marginal product of labor) and personal rewards. Attempting to ensure that people are productive under conditions of high taxation is similar to asking people to contribute according to ability without regard for personal reward. Government bureaucracies in market economies lack information when decisions are made and there are also bureaucratic principal–agent problems, and political decision makers can have considerable discretion in deciding who benefits from public finance and public policy. Government tax revenue, until assigned through public spending, is collective property.

Supplement S2

Supplement S2A: Rent seeking and rent dissipation

Rent dissipation is the measure of social loss due to rent seeking. An individual with initial wealth A who spends x in the quest to acquire a rent V in a contest with n identical contenders participates in a contest only if:

$$EU = \left(\frac{n-1}{n}\right) U(A-x) + \left(\frac{1}{n}\right) U[A-x+V] > U(A). \qquad \text{(S2.1)}$$

With risk-neutral rent seekers, we obtain (Hillman & Katz, 1984):

$$\lim_{n\to\infty} D \equiv \frac{nx}{V} = 1. \qquad \text{(S2.2)}$$

In the all-pay auction (Hillman & Samet, 1987):

$$D \equiv \frac{nEx}{V} = 1 \quad \text{for all values of } n \geq 2. \qquad \text{(S2.3)}$$

For differing valuations of the rent $\{V_1 > V_2 > \cdots > V_n\}$, in discriminating contests, only the two highest valuation contenders take an active role in a contest and neither spends more than the valuation V_2 of the lower valuation contender (Hillman & Riley, 1989). The active contenders choose their rent-seeking outlays from a distribution over the range of $\{0, V_2\}$. The low-valuation contender makes a strictly positive outlay with probability V_2/V_1. The expected value of total rent-seeking expenditures is:

$$Ex_1 + Ex_2 = \left(\frac{V_2}{V_1}\right)\left(\frac{V_2 + V_1}{2}\right). \qquad \text{(S2.4)}$$

Rent dissipation is always, on average, incomplete with respect to the lower valuation V_2 because:

$$Ex_1 + Ex_2 = V_2\left(\frac{V_2 + V_1}{2}\right), \quad \text{where} \left(\frac{V_2 + V_1}{2V_1}\right) < 1. \tag{S2.5}$$

However, we see that $D \to 1$ as $V_2 \to V_1$. There may be asymmetric information and contenders may not know how other contenders value the rent-seeking prize. If contenders know that valuations are drawn independently from the uniform distribution with $V \in (0, V^*)$ and if contenders' spending levels are increasing in valuations of the prize, then total expected outlays are (Hillman & Riley, 1989):

$$E\left(\sum_{j=1}^{N} x_j\right) = \left(\frac{(n-1)}{(n+1)}\right) V^*. \tag{S2.6}$$

As the number of contenders for the rent increases, each contender judges that even if he or she has a high valuation, there now are increasing numbers of others who also have high valuations; therefore, more has to be spent to win and rent dissipation increases.

In Tullock probabilistic contests (Tullock, 1980), with r indicating returns to scale from rent-seeking expenditures, a contender spending x_i has a probability of winning a rent-seeking contest given by:

$$\rho_i(x_1, \ldots, x_n) = \frac{x_i^r}{\sum_{j=1}^{n} x_i^r}. \tag{S2.7}$$

If the highest bid wins, $r = \infty$. When $r = 1$, the Tullock contest is equivalent to a lottery, and the number of lottery tickets purchased relative to lottery tickets issued determines the likelihood of rent-seeking success. Expected utility of contender i with the Tullock contest-success function (S2.7) is:

$$EU_i = \frac{x_i^r}{\sum_{j=1}^{n} x_i^r} V - x_i. \tag{S2.8}$$

In a symmetric Nash equilibrium, the outlay x common to all rent seekers is:

$$x = \left(\frac{n-1}{n^2}\right) rV. \tag{S2.9}$$

The second-order condition requires:

$$r < \left(\frac{n}{n-2}\right). \tag{S2.10}$$

Expected utility from participation in the contest is strictly positive if:

$$r < \left(\frac{n}{n-1}\right). \tag{S2.11}$$

It follows that if the second-order condition (S2.10) is satisfied, it is worthwhile to participate in the Tullock contest. With $r = 1$, rent dissipation is:

$$D \equiv \frac{nx}{V} = \left(\frac{n-1}{n}\right). \tag{S2.12}$$

Therefore, $D \to 1$ as $n \to \infty$. For example, when $n = 2$, rent dissipation in the Nash equilibrium is 50 percent.

Supplement S2B: Institutions and natural monopoly

Natural monopoly arises because of fixed costs incurred in infrastructure investment. It is inefficient to duplicate the fixed costs. Hence, monopoly is cost-efficient, or "natural." Electricity supply (although not electricity production) is a natural monopoly. Delivery of water or gas through pipelines is a natural monopoly. Dumping of waste and garbage is a regional natural monopoly because of fixed costs incurred in setting up and using a dumping site. Railroad tracks may be a natural monopoly; however, transportation and freight services on the tracks are not a natural monopoly because different suppliers can competitively use the tracks.

Natural monopoly can be due to insufficient demand to warrant duplicative competitive supply. On routes where demand is sufficiently low, bus and air transportation can be a natural monopoly. Schools can be local natural monopolies. A doctor in a small town can likewise be a natural monopolist.

In a number of cases, technology has ended natural monopoly. When telephone communication was exclusively through wires, the telephone company was a natural monopoly that installed the infrastructure, maintained network conformity, and owned the communications infrastructure that physically connected users to one another. Competition was first introduced into long-distance communication by requiring regional telephone companies to act as conduits for competing long-distance companies. Cellular telephones introduced competition into local as well as long-distance communication. The Internet introduced voice communication through personal computers. Mail and parcels sent through the post office used to be regarded as a natural monopoly, but mail eventually came to be supplied competitively through private courier and express services. The advent of the facsimile machine provided competition for hand-delivered mail. E-mail became a substitute for letters written on paper. In many countries, government mail service was preserved as a monopoly by law until private-courier and express-service competition made it clear that the government mail service was not a natural monopoly but rather government monopolization.

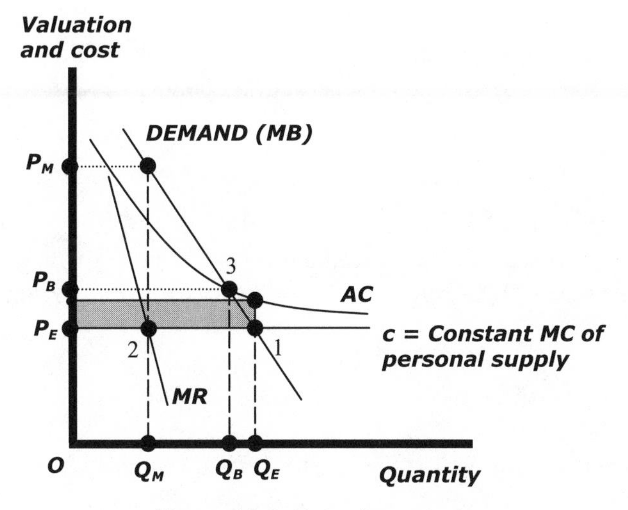

Figure S2.1. Natural monopoly.

Financing solutions for natural monopoly

Figure S2.1 shows the declining average cost that is characteristic of natural monopoly. The source of declining average cost AC is a fixed cost F divided among increasingly greater quantities supplied.[27]

In addition to average cost, figure S2.1 shows a constant cost c for each unit of output delivered to the buyer: c is the personal marginal cost associated with connection to the infrastructure that has a fixed cost F. Total cost of supply C is the sum of the fixed cost F and the additional per-unit cost c of supplying users. With the total quantity supplied equal to Q, total cost is:

$$C = F + cQ. \tag{S2.13}$$

Average cost is:

$$AC = \frac{F}{Q} + c, \tag{S2.14}$$

which is declining in the quantity supplied Q. The declining AC confirms that there is a natural monopoly. AC is always greater than marginal cost of personal supply c, and AC approaches the constant marginal cost c as the quantity supplied increases. Different public policies result in outcomes at points 1, 2, and 3.

[27] The source of natural monopoly can be a *sunk cost* rather than a *fixed cost*. A sunk cost is incurred once and for always (for example, communication cables, railway tracks, electricity lines, or natural gas pipelines). A fixed cost is a recurring per-period cost that is independent of the number of users or the extent of use (for example, maintenance of communication cables, railway tracks, electricity lines, or natural gas pipelines).

Efficient supply

Efficiency is achieved by maximizing $W = B - C$, which results in the outcome point 1, where market demand intersects MC. At point 1:

$$MB = P_E = MC\,(= c)\,, \tag{S2.15}$$

where P_E is price and Q_E is quantity supplied. A privately owned natural monopoly would make losses by charging price P_E and providing the efficient output Q_E because at Q_E average cost of supply exceeds price. Profits (or losses) are given by:

$$\pi = Q \cdot (P - AC). \tag{S2.16}$$

The shaded area in figure S2.1 is the loss to a private supplier from efficient supply. The losses need to be covered through subsidies if supply is to take place.

Efficient supply by a privately owned natural monopoly requires government to provide subsidies.

Maximum profits

Profits are maximized at point 2, where price is P_M and output is Q_M. The profit-maximizing outcome is inefficient because $Q_M < Q_E$.

The self-financing price

At point 3, price $P_B = AC$ and the quantity Q_B supplied. The price is self-financing and the natural monopoly does not make a loss. No subsidy is required. However, supply is inefficiently small because $Q_B < Q_E$.

The case against subsidies

There are a number of arguments against the subsidy solution at point 1.

Choice of effort

The amount in subsidies required for the efficient solution at point 1 depends on AC. Cost, in turn, depends on the effort of the natural monopolist. Because of the subsidies from the government, the natural monopolist faces a "soft budget" under which losses are automatically covered. There is no incentive, therefore, to exert effort to keep costs low. The task of determining the subsidy at point 1 in general is assigned to a government agency. Because of unobservable effort and the soft budget, the government agency confronts a principal–agent problem. The natural monopolist determines costs through unobservable effort and thereby can increase the magnitude of the subsidy, whereas the government agency – if the faithful agent of taxpayers – wants costs of supply and thereby also the amount of the subsidy to be minimized.

Misrepresentation of costs

For any choice of effort, the natural monopolist can report AC strategically and thereby misrepresent costs (within bounds of credibility). A natural monopolist, depending on circumstances, can gain by reporting higher or lower than true AC. The government agency therefore does not know in advance the direction of strategic cost misrepresentation.[28] This is a distinctly different problem from the principal–agent problem that is the result of unobservable effort. Here, the government regulatory agency does not know true costs. In the previous principal–agent problem, the government agency could observe and therefore knew costs but could not observe effort.

Capture

The case against subsidies includes *capture*, which occurs when the government regulatory agency does not pursue the public interest but rather accommodates public policy to the interest of the natural monopoly.[29] Being "captured" is here voluntary. The capture is ostensibly in the interest of the employees of the government agency because, otherwise, they would have no reason to agree to be captured. In its most explicit form, capture is achieved through bribery. There are more subtle means of capture than outright bribery. Employees of the government agency might be provided with jobs after they leave government employment – which is also a form of bribery. Capture can also be part of the political principal–agent problem. The government agency determining the subsidy to be provided to the natural monopolist may be accountable to political supervisors, who benefit from campaign contributions and other expressions of political gratitude of the natural monopolist.

Competitive bidding

Subsidies can be avoided by a public policy of competitive bidding for the price at which supply will take place. The outcome is then the solution at point 3 in figure S2.1 and the offer of the self-financing price P_B.

Revenue maximization

A government seeking maximal revenue from the winning bid would ask for bids for the right to be an unconstrained monopolist that can set price P_M and supply output Q_M. By inviting bids for the right to be the monopolist and leaving open the choice of the price that the winning bidder can set, the government transfers

[28] The subsidy in figure S2.1 depends on the claim regarding marginal cost of supply c. A lower than true value of c expands the quantity on which the subsidy is paid but reduces the value of the per-unit subsidy. A higher than true value for c reduces the quantity on which the subsidy is paid but increases the value of the per-unit subsidy. Therefore, the value of the total subsidy payment can sometimes be increased by higher claims of cost than true costs and sometimes by lower claims.

[29] The problem of capture was noted in 1971 by George Stigler (1911–91), who was a professor at the University of Chicago. Stigler received the Nobel Prize in economics in 1982.

the present value of monopoly profits to itself and leaves the public to confront the unregulated profit-maximizing monopolist.

Incomplete contracts

Competitive bidding for the price at which supply will take place avoids the problems associated with payment of subsidies to a natural monopolist but introduces new problems. The right to provide water, electricity, or cable television can be determined by competitive bidding, with the winning bidder having the right of supply for a designated number of years. During those years, technology and quality standards in all likelihood will change. The contract for supply, therefore, should include contingencies for such change, but the types of changes that will take place, in general, are not known before the changes actually occur. Because of the impossibility of including all contingencies in the contract designating conditions of supply, the supply contract is incomplete. There may then be legal disputes when the unforeseen contingencies arise.

Transfer of ownership of infrastructure

If an incumbent supplier loses in a round of bidding, ownership of infrastructure needs to be transferred to the winning bidder. A firm may have invested in infrastructure to provide cable-television services. After a designated number of years of natural monopoly, competitive bidding takes place to determine the future supplier, and the initial supplier loses the bid. The initial supplier owns the infrastructure but, after losing the bid, no longer has the right to use the infrastructure to provide cable services. It is inefficient for the new supplier to invest anew and duplicate the existing infrastructure. Duplication would defeat the purpose of competitive bidding, which is to allow supply under conditions of sharing of nonduplicated fixed costs. Reaching an agreement on price for the transfer of ownership of the infrastructure can involve complex bargaining and can delay the transfer of the right to supply.

Open access

An incumbent natural monopolist could be legally required to provide open access to use of infrastructure to all potential competitors. For example, cable companies might be obliged to allow other suppliers to offer Internet access through their cable system. The right of access can apply to use of electricity supply grids, rail lines, gas pipelines, and telephone lines. When open access is made compulsory, property rights are compromised. The initial natural monopolist, who made the investments and owns the infrastructure, did not envisage being compelled to allow competitors to use the infrastructure. Open-access requirements are retroactive and without compensation contradict the rule of law.

Waste management

A special case of natural monopoly is the storage of waste, particularly hazardous waste. The circumstances are special because waste is brought to the disposal site and a payment is made for *delivering the waste*. Usually, payment is made by a seller to a supplier. However, in the case of delivery of waste, the supplier makes the payment. The payment is not voluntary. There are incentives, therefore, for illegal disposal of waste to avoid the cost of transporting the waste and the compulsory payment to the operator of the waste-disposal site. The incentive to dump waste illegally is reduced if no payment is required when delivering waste to the disposal site.

If the monitoring of disposal of waste is imperfect, the socially preferred policy requires paying for waste delivered to the disposal site (although never paying enough to justify generating waste for delivery). Payments for waste delivered require government subsidies to the private owners of disposal sites. A private owner, of course, could never make a profit without a subsidy if obliged to pay when waste is delivered to the site. Competitive bidding could still establish a least-cost operator of the waste-disposal site. The bids are now for negative prices – that is, for how much the government will pay the waste-disposal operator.

Ownership by government and privatization

The principal–agent problems between a government regulatory agency and a privately owned natural monopolist are avoided when government is the owner of a natural monopoly. The government as natural monopolist knows the subsidies that accompany efficient supply, which can be directly financed through the government budget. Problems of incomplete contracts in competitive bidding solutions do not arise because there is no need for contracts when the government is itself the supplier. Problems of transfer of ownership or use of infrastructure do not arise because no transfer of ownership takes place.

Throughout most of the 20th century, the solution of government ownership and supply was prominent almost everywhere, with the exception of the United States.[30] A natural monopoly under government control was often referred to as a *state-owned firm*. The natural monopoly, however, was effectively a department of government, and appointments to senior management and to the board of directors were often political decisions.

In the latter part of the 20th century, governments in Europe and elsewhere embarked on a process of *privatization*, or conversion of natural monopolies to private ownership. Privatization reflected awareness of the bureaucratic principal–agent problem.

[30] Outside of the United States, natural monopolies tended to be government-owned. In the United States, electricity generation and supply were privately owned, as were the firms that shipped and marketed natural gas and producers of defense equipment. Among natural monopolies, only water supply in general has been provided in the United States by public entities. In the United States, the natural-monopoly telephone company, AT&T, was privately owned. When technology changed, AT&T local services were divided among regional firms, and AT&T became a long-distance carrier subject to competition from other firms.

Political will to implement privatization was required because of the political benefits of government ownership. Privatization was often resisted because of rents available to the administrating bureaucracy and employees of the state-owned firms. Often, compensation had to be paid for the rents lost. The magnitudes of the rents were reflected in the extent of opposition to privatization and in the value of the payments required to compensate employees for agreeing to privatization. After privatization, the magnitude of the rents enjoyed under government ownership was revealed in the profits of the firm under private ownership.

Privatization introduces the need for public-policy decisions toward privately owned natural monopoly, which returns us to the beginning of this supplement.

Supplement S2C: Labor self-management

The institutions of labor self-management are designed to achieve equality for workers. Workers are organized in labor cooperatives and are themselves the employers and therefore are freed from the decisions of employers. Employers view wage payments as a *cost,* but members of a labor cooperative view wage payments as a *benefit* to be maximized. A labor cooperative maximizes the wage that members pay to themselves by maximizing the value of the *average* product of cooperative members. Figure S2.2 shows the value of the marginal product of labor $p \cdot MP_L$ and the value of the average product of labor $p \cdot AP_L$. The maximal wage w^{max} is obtained where $p \cdot AP_L$ is maximized in a cooperative with L_0 members.

The wage paid in a competitive labor market that exists outside of the labor cooperative is w_1. A profit-maximizing firm would choose efficient labor employment L_1 at point D where $p \cdot MP_L = w_1$ (the value of the marginal product of labor equals the market-determined wage).

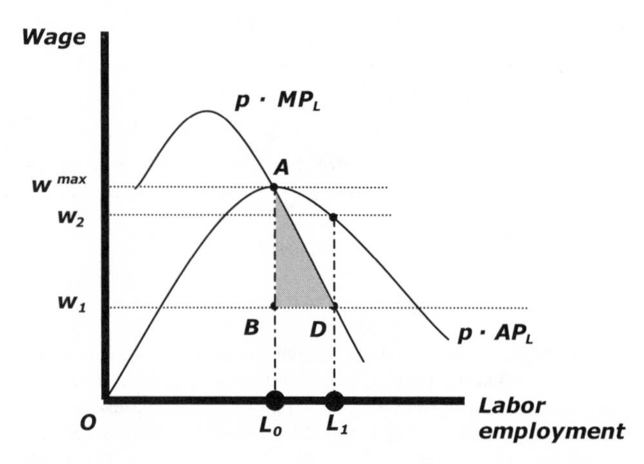

Figure S2.2. Employment with labor self-management.

Because $L_0 < L_1$, employment in the labor cooperative is inefficiently small. The loss in terms of both efficiency and profits from choosing L_0 workers rather than L_1 is the shaded area ABD in figure S2.2.[31]

The labor cooperative could achieve efficiency by employing an additional $(L_1 - L_0)$ workers at the market wage w_1. The gain of ABD could be shared among the cooperative's L_0 members.

The cooperative, however, has egalitarian principles. The principles are inconsistent with the inequality when there are two categories of workers: (1) hired workers who earn the wage w_1, and (2) members of the labor cooperative who receive $w^{max} > w_1$. The egalitarian principles prevent paying the market wage w_1 to the additional workers required for efficient employment.

If an additional $(L_1 - L_0)$ workers become equal members of the workers' cooperative, egalitarian principles are not compromised and efficient employment is achieved. However, everyone then receives the wage w_2, which is less than w^{max}. To achieve efficient employment while remaining loyal to their egalitarian objective, the preexisting members of the labor cooperative therefore have to give up income. Thus, if cooperative members are not prepared to forgo income:

> *The institution of self-managed labor cooperatives is an instance of inconsistency between objectives of efficiency and equality.*

Incentives and monitoring

A further question concerns incentives within the labor cooperative: Why should workers exert productive effort when they know that they will receive a wage that will be determined as the *average* value of everybody's contributions? Monitoring of work effort is required. The following story is told about a group of men pulling a barge of cargo on a river. A person oversees their efforts with a whip. A foreign observer on a riverboat remarks that the presence of the overseer with the whip is inhumane, to which the captain of the boat replies: "Who do you think hired the man with the whip in the first place?" The answer, of course, is that the workers pulling the barge hired the overseer with the whip.[32]

The kibbutz

The market wage in figure S2.2 indicates that labor markets coexist with the self-managed labor cooperative. Self-managed labor cooperatives have been uncommon in market economies. The most prominent case of successful labor self-management has been the kibbutz in Israel. *Kibbutz* means "collective" in the

[31] Adding $(L_1 - L_0)$ workers increases the total value of output by the area under the $p \cdot MP_L$ function between L_0 and L_1, whereas the cost of employing the additional workers is the area $w_1 \cdot (L_1 - L_0)$. The difference is the area ABD.

[32] The case is described by Cheung (1983) based on observations in pre-communist China.

Hebrew language.[33] The kibbutz as an organizational form offered advantages over the market and private property when Jews were reestablishing themselves in their ancestral home. The kibbutz preempted the need for job offers from employers, who might offer low wages – or the labor market might offer no work at all. Kibbutz members could also cooperate in providing personal security and defense.[34] Originally a collective farm, the kibbutz diversified over time to include light industry and tourism. Young people from other countries came to spend time on a kibbutz to experience the social solidarity of working and living together and contributing according to ability rather than personal reward. In the course of time, the outside economy developed to offer opportunities and although the kibbutz provided security from unemployment and also provided basic needs and beyond, young people began leaving. When asked why they had left the personal security of a kibbutz for the uncertainties of incomes provided through labor markets, a common reply was, "We wanted to see what we could achieve by ourselves." By the beginning of the 21st century, the kibbutz, in most cases, had undergone institutional change from the original collective beginnings. Often, privatization in some form had taken place. Meals were no longer necessarily communal, housing was often privatized, people had the right to own other private property, incomes paid within the kibbutz were based on the value of personal contributions, and kibbutz members were permitted to work in the outside labor market.[35]

Summary

This chapter has been concerned with institutions and governance. Institutions and governance are fundamental for studying public finance and public policy. When responsibilities are given to government to use public finance and public policy to achieve the objectives of efficiency and social justice, political decision makers can exercise political discretion in the decisions that are made, and the government bureaucracy likewise has discretion when implementing the decisions. The political and bureaucratic discretion is due to asymmetric information that limits transparency of government to taxpayers and voters. Because of lack of transparency, taxpayers and voters face lack of accountability regarding political and bureaucratic behavior. Our investigation of institutions and governance has suggested limitations on calling on government. The limitations were most

[33] The first kibbutz, Degania A, was founded in 1910 on the shore of Lake Galilee.

[34] In 1948, the State of Israel was reestablished and the government took responsibility for security and defense. Before then, under British rule, the Jewish population often had to provide its own defense.

[35] Degania A, the first kibbutz, voted for privatization in October 2007. Already at that time, egalitarian principles no longer applied in the kibbutz. Members of the kibbutz were receiving different incomes and housing, and property had been divided among kibbutz members.

evident in a description of a society in which all economic decisions are made by politicians and bureaucrats.

Section 1 described the political principal–agent problem:

1A. There is asymmetric information between taxpayers or voters and political decision makers. Taxpayers and voters do not have the means of perfectly observing political decisions because of the limited information provided in the government budget; with regard to information that is available, there is a free-rider problem; and incentives of rational ignorance limit voters' information.

1B. To win elections, politicians may require political contributions offered by interest groups seeking public-finance decisions and public policies that depart from the public interest. Principled political candidates face a prisoners' dilemma in deciding whether to accept political contributions from special-interest groups; in the Nash equilibrium, the contributions are accepted. Public finance for political expenses can substitute for private money; however, the rules for participatory public funding also affect political incentives when policies are decided. Voters are disadvantaged in disciplining political representatives by the awareness that one vote is not decisive; compulsory voting, however, resolves a voter-coordination problem. Voters are also disadvantaged because nonsalient policy issues are left to political discretion and because of smaller stakes than interest groups in the outcome of a political decision. There is a paradox because special-interest money is used to convince voters how to vote (if they vote). Objective media would assist voters in ameliorating the asymmetric-information problem. Regulation of political contributions is imperfect. Political endorsements from the media and from "celebrities" have monetary value. Term limits can ensure that political power does not become entrenched, but there is also an argument that term limits compel politicians to have short time horizons. Voters can have differing interests regarding term limits, depending on the seniority of their representatives.

1C. Personal outcomes obtained through rent seeking are in general socially unjust, but also rent seeking is a source of inefficiency because of socially unproductive uses of resources. The decision whether to participate in rent seeking can be another instance of the prisoners' dilemma. Rent seeking is often delegated to lobbyists, which allows political decision makers to avoid visible rent creation. When rent creation is accompanied by social loss, the complete social cost of political discretion includes efficiency losses due to both rent creation and rent seeking (we used as an example the case of monopoly). The social cost of rent seeking usually cannot be directly observed. Rent seekers and political decision makers will deny that rent seeking is taking place. The inability to observe and directly measure time and resources used in rent seeking underlies the focus of the theory of rent-seeking contests. We use the predictions of the theory of rent-seeking contests to infer rent dissipation. Complete rent dissipation permits the observed value of a contested rent to be used as the measure of the social loss due to rent seeking. Complete rent dissipation occurs in competitive rent-seeking contests and in all-pay auctions. Under conditions in which rents are completely dissipated at a point in time, complete rent dissipation also occurs when rents endure over time, whether or not rents will in the future be re-contested or disappear. Rent dissipation is incomplete in small-number probabilistic Tullock contests. Voter opposition limits but need not prevent rent creation. Rent creation and rent seeking can extend beyond political decisions; in a rent-seeking society, rent creation and rent seeking are pervasive in all aspects of life; in particular, jobs and professions are not determined according to personal ability and merit. Awareness of rent seeking introduces ambiguities in judging how people behave toward one another. In making a case for the market, Adam Smith was also decrying the mercantilist economic system in which rents and rent seeking are prevalent. There are two types of competition, one socially beneficial and the other – competition for rents – not socially beneficial. Rent seeking is facilitated when private property rights are imperfectly protected; it has been proposed that the prevalence of lawyers in a society is an indication of the propensity for rent seeking. Social losses from rent seeking do not occur when it is known that political decision makers make decisions about public finance and public policy in accord with predetermined normative principles of efficiency and social justice.

1D. Political decision makers can extract rents. The extracted rents can be exchanged for political support and may be contested in rent-seeking contests. Political rent extraction can take the form of declarations of intent to propose legislation that evokes political contributions to preempt the legislation being enacted. The rent creation and rent seeking – and rent extraction – that occur in high-income democratic societies can be unethical but, in general, the activities are not illegal. Illegality involves corruption. In low-income and authoritarian societies, politicians overtly use the authority of the state for personal self-enrichment. In high-income societies, the political principal–agent problem is expressed in the use of political discretion for *political* and not personal monetary gain, and personal corruption that provides personal benefit is an aberration. A society is not corrupt if corrupt politicians are exposed and brought before the courts. In a corrupt society, corrupt politicians and leaders stay in office.

Section 2 described the bureaucratic principal–agent problem that arises because of discretionary behavior in government bureaucracies.

2A. Max Weber set out normative precepts for how bureaucrats should behave to achieve outcomes consistent with the public interest. However, because behavior in bureaucracies is the private information of bureaucrats, asymmetric information allows bureaucrats to choose more extensive bureaucratic hierarchies and greater public spending than taxpayers want. Bureaucratic rents are possible because government bureaucracies are monopolies. Bureaucracies cannot become bankrupt and incomes are assured through tax revenue. Normative theories of bureaucracy differ from positive explanations and predictions regarding bureaucratic behavior.

2B. Bureaucrats can increase personal benefits by increasing demand for their services. Artificial scarcity of their time is created through internally assigned "paperwork" or computer equivalents. The scheduling of regular meetings among themselves allow bureaucrats to look busy.

2C. Asymmetric information is facilitated by the inability to measure bureaucratic output. Markets do not, in general, exist to measure the value of the output of a government department or agency.

2D. Because of the absence of markets to value output of bureaucrats, the means available for addressing the principal–agent problems in the private sector cannot be applied to government bureaucracies. Incentive-based contracts could provide rewards for cost-containment but benefits forgone because of reduced spending remain non-measurable. Information asymmetries limit prospects for monitoring of government bureaucrats by politicians or political appointees. Efficiency wages in government bureaucracies do not solve the problem of asymmetric information that confronts taxpayers and voters. The best (and perhaps only) prospect for solving the bureaucratic principal–agent problem is the Thomas-à-Becket effect; if present throughout the bureaucracy, the Thomas-à-Becket effect would result in Max Weber's socially beneficial bureaucratic culture.

Section 3 described maximal government. Political and bureaucratic principal–agent problems are then maximal. We used the communist system to describe maximal government.

3A. The ideology of communism (or socialism) is based on the primacy of achieving social equality. People are asked to contribute to society's output according to their abilities without regard for their own personal benefits or rewards. People were thus required to be altruistic. Friedrich von Hayek predicted that attempts to change human nature from behavior motivated by personal incentives would be unsuccessful. Hayek pointed out that markets and private property, through an evolutionary process, are the only institutions that consistently provide high income for the general population. Communism nonetheless won the hearts and minds of many people. Hayek was criticized for his prediction that the attempts at social re-engineering of human nature would be unsuccessful and that communism would fail.

3B. When governments make all economic decisions with markets absent, there are severe informational inefficiencies. There are no incentives for people to suggest improving change when the government owns production facilities and does not provide rewards according to the value of personal contributions.

3C. Communal property in theory achieves social equality. In communist societies, there was inequality through unequal opportunities for theft and for rent extraction in general. The theory was that women would be better off when property was communal than when they were themselves regarded as property in a market economy; however, women achieved rights in private-property market economies. The prediction was that communal property would end envy; however, envy persisted because people knew that inequality was due to successful rent seeking and privilege and not market reward determined according to personal ability and merit.

3D. Hayek observed that a person who aspires to and succeeds in becoming the ruler who controls all collective property is by nature a megalomaniac. Adam Smith had remarked on how the market limits the personal power of any one person. Aspects of the problems of maximal government are present when responsibilities are delegated to governments in market economies. However, the personal freedom of market economies with private property is the antithesis of the denial of personal freedom in a society with institutions of imposed order and collective property.

There were three supplements.

- Supplement S2A elaborated on rent dissipation predicted in theoretical models of rent-seeking contests. Conditions can be identified that would result in complete rent dissipation. In general, it is difficult to know whether such conditions are present in any particular instance. Nonetheless, the theory of rent-seeking contests provides indications of when the observed value of a contested rent might approximate the social cost of rent seeking.
- Supplement S2B described natural monopoly. Natural monopoly exists when there are benefits from sharing fixed costs and more than one supplier would inefficiently duplicate the fixed costs. Changes in technology have diminished the number of natural monopolies. There are three public-policy

solutions for privately-owned natural monopoly: (1) allowing the monopoly to set unregulated prices; (2) government subsidies to achieve efficient output; and (3) competitive bidding, which does not require subsidies from the government budget but results in smaller than efficient output. There are arguments against the subsidy solution because of principal–agent problems. The case for competitive bidding is avoidance of the principal–agent problems; competitive bidding requires means of transferring ownership of supply facilities. Outside of the United States, the approach to solving the principal–agent problems was to place the natural monopoly under government ownership. As a consequence, the bureaucratic principal–agent problem was introduced. Avoidance of the bureaucratic principal–agent problem was the motivation for privatization. After privatization, a society faces a privately owned natural monopoly and the question of the choice of appropriate public policy.

- Supplement S2C described the institution of labor self-management. In a labor cooperative committed to an egalitarian objective, if workers are not prepared to forgo income, labor employment is inefficiently small. The labor cooperative is then another example of conflict between objectives of ex-post equality and efficiency. The example of the workers who themselves hired an overseer with a whip demonstrated the incentive and monitoring problems in a labor cooperative. The case of the kibbutz demonstrated that the most successful implementation of labor self-management cooperatives succumbed eventually to incentives of reward according to personal contribution.

In the chapters that follow, the questions often will be normative. We shall ask how governments can best use public finance and public policy to achieve efficiency and social justice when markets have failed to do so. When the quest is for normative solutions, we shall keep in mind (if only perhaps in the background) the role of institutions, because institutions determine what can be expected from governments.

Literature notes

2.1 The political principal–agent problem

The role of institutions in determining efficiency was emphasized by North (1981; Nobel Prize in economics, 1993). On origins and determinants of political institutions, see La Porta, Lopez-de-Silanes, Shleifer, and Vishny (1999) and Acemoglu and Robinson (2005). On impediments to democratic institutions, see Borooah and Paldam (2007). For empirical studies showing how institutions affect economic outcomes in different countries, see Knack and Keefer (1995) and Hall and Jones (1999).

Acemoglu, D., and J. A. Robinson, 2005. *Economic Origins of Dictatorship and Democracy*. Cambridge University Press, New York.
Borooah, V. K., and M. Paldam, 2007. Why is the world short of democracy?: A cross-country analysis of barriers to representative government. *European Journal of Political Economy* 23:582–604.
Hall, R. E., and C. I. Jones, 1999. Why do some countries produce so much more output per worker than others? *Quarterly Journal of Economics* 114:83–116.
Knack, S., and P. Keefer, 1995. Institutions and economic performance: Cross-country tests using alternative institutional measures. *Economics and Politics* 7:207–27.
La Porta, R., F. Lopez-de-Silanes, A. Shleifer, and R. Vishny, 1999. The quality of government. *Journal of Law, Economics and Organization* 15:222–79.
North, D. C., 1981. *Structure and Change in Economic History*. W. W. Norton and Company, New York.

On rational ignorance, see:

Downs, A., 1957. *An Economic Theory of Democracy*. Harper and Row, New York.

On the political principal–agent problem, see:

Barro, R. J., 1973. The control of politicians: An economic model. *Public Choice* 14:19–42.
Ferejohn, J., 1986. Incumbent performance and electoral control. *Public Choice* 50:5–25.

Zupan (1990) described principled voting behavior of lame-duck political representatives in the U.S. Congress.

Zupan, M., 1990. The last period problem in politics: Do congressional representatives not subject to a reelection constraint alter their voting behavior? *Public Choice* 65: 167–80.

On the principal–agent problem and good government, see:

Besely, T., 2006. *Principled Agents?: The Political Economy of Good Government*. Oxford University Press, Oxford.

On the media, see:

Djankov S., C. McLiesh, T. Nenova, and A. Shleifer, 2003. Who owns the media? *The Journal of Law and Economics* 46:341–82.
Gentzkow, M., and J. M. Shapiro, 2008. Competition and truth in the market for news. *Journal of Economic Perspectives* 22:133–54.
Leeson, P. T., 2008. Media freedom, political knowledge, and participation. *Journal of Economic Perspectives* 22:155–69.

On term limits, see:

Dick, A. R., and J. R. Lott, 1993. Reconciling voters' behavior with legislative term limits. *Journal of Public Economics* 50:1–14.

The political trade-off between special-interest and voter support is described in Peltzman (1976) and Hillman (1982).

Hillman, A. L., 1982. Declining industries and political-support protectionist motives. *American Economic Review* 72:1180–7. Reprinted in R. D. Congleton, A. L. Hillman, and K. A. Konrad (Eds.), 2008. *Forty Years of Research on Rent Seeking 2: Applications: Rent Seeking in Practice*. Springer, Berlin, pp. 105–12.
Peltzman, S., 1976. Toward a more general theory of regulation. *Journal of Law and Economics* 19:171–240.

The efficiency losses due to rent seeking were pointed out by Tullock (1967). Krueger (1974) introduced the term *rent seeking*. Buchanan (1980) compared competition in markets and competition for rents. Congleton (1980) introduced institutions into the study of rent seeking. Hillman and Ursprung (2000) showed how changes in institutions affect rent seeking by political insiders and outsiders.

Buchanan, J. M., 1980. Rent seeking and profit seeking. In J. M. Buchanan, R. D. Tollison, and G. Tullock (Eds.), *Toward a Theory of the Rent-Seeking Society*. Texas A&M University Press, College Station, pp. 3–15.

Congleton, R. D., 1980. Competitive process, competitive waste, and institutions. In J. M. Buchanan, R. D. Tollison, and G. Tullock (Eds.), *Toward a Theory of the Rent Seeking Society*. Texas A&M University Press, College Station, pp. 153–79.

Hillman, A. L., and H. W. Ursprung, 2000. Political culture and economic decline. *European Journal of Political Economy* 16:189–212.

Krueger, A. O., 1974. The political economy of the rent-seeking society. *American Economic Review* 64:291–303.

Tullock, G., 1967. The welfare costs of monopoly, tariffs, and theft. *Western Economic Journal* 5:224–32.

The previously listed papers are reprinted in Congleton et al., 2008. The introduction to the volumes summarizes the rent-seeking literature.

Congleton, R. D., A. L. Hillman, and K. A. Konrad (Eds.), 2008. *Forty Years of Research on Rent Seeking 1: The Theory of Rent-Seeking*. Springer, Berlin.

Congleton, R. D., A. L. Hillman, and K. A. Konrad (Eds.), 2008. *Forty Years of Research on Rent Seeking 2: Applications: Rent Seeking in Practice*. Springer, Berlin.

Willis (1912) described political rent creation in the early 20th-century United States. Tullock (1988) indicated later examples. Park, Philippopoulos, and Vassilatos (2005) described rent seeking through public finance.

Park, H., A. Philippopoulos, and V. Vassilatos, 2005. Choosing the size of the public sector under rent seeking from state coffers. *European Journal of Political Economy* 21:830–50.

Tullock, G., 1988. *The Economics of Special Privilege and Rent Seeking*. Kluwer Academic Publishers, Boston.

Willis, H. P., 1912. Political obstacles to anti-trust legislation. *Journal of Political Economy* 20:588–98.

On political persuasion as rent seeking, see:

Congleton, R. D., 1986. Rent-seeking aspects of political advertising. *Public Choice* 49:249–65. Reprinted in Congleton et al., 2008.

On the law, lawyers, and rent seeking, see:

Baye, M. R., D. Kovenock, and C. G. de Vries, 2005. Comparative analysis of litigation systems: An auction-theoretic approach. *Economic Journal* 115:583–601.

Farmer, A., and P. Pecorino, 1999. Legal expenditure as a rent-seeking game. *Public Choice* 100:271–88.

Parisi, F., 2002. Rent seeking through litigation: Adversarial and inquisitorial systems compared. *International Review of Law and Economics* 22:193–216.

Tullock, G., 1975. On the efficient organization of trials. *Kyklos* 28:745–62.

The previously listed papers are reprinted in Congleton et al., 2008.

On rent extraction, see:

Appelbaum, E., and E. Katz, 1987. Seeking rents by setting rents: The political economy of rent seeking. *Economic Journal* 97:685–99. Reprinted in Congleton et al., 2008.
McChesney, F. S., 1997. *Money for Nothing: Politicians, Rent Extraction, and Political Extortion*. Harvard University Press, Cambridge MA.

On rent dissipation, see the literature guide to supplement S2A.

Baik and Kim (1997) described delegation of rent seeking.
Baik, K. H., and I. G. Kim, 1997. Delegation in contests. *European Journal of Political Economy* 13:281–98.

On the distinction between bribes and rents, and on the conversion of bribes to rents, see:

Hillman, A. L., and E. Katz, 1987. Hierarchical structure and the social costs of bribes and transfers. *Journal of Public Economics* 34:129–42. Reprinted in Congleton et al., 2008.

On rent seeking under mercantilism, see:

Baysinger, B., R. B. Ekelund, and R. D. Tollison, 1980. Mercantilism as a rent-seeking society. In J. M. Buchanan, R. D. Tollison, and G. Tullock (Eds.), *Toward a Theory of the Rent Seeking Society*. Texas A&M Press, College Station, pp. 235–68. Reprinted in Congleton et al., 2008.

2.2 Government bureaucracy

On the normative theory of bureaucracy, see Weber (1947). Niskanen (1971) described the self-interest model of bureaucracy. For a formalization of the principal–agent problem of bureaucracy, see Tirole (1994).

Niskanen, W., 1971. *Bureaucracy and Representative Government*. Aldine, Chicago.
Tirole, J., 1994. The internal organization of government. *Oxford Economic Papers* 46:1–29.
Weber, M., 1947. *The Theory of Social and Economic Organization*. W. Hodge, Edinburgh.

Rowley and Elgin (1988) proposed a bargaining approach to understanding the relationship between political decision makers and bureaucracy. On political representatives and government bureaucracies, see Ferejohn and Shipan (1990).

Ferejohn, J. A., and C. Shipan, 1990. Congressional influence on bureaucracy. *Journal of Law, Economics, and Organization* 6:1–20.
Rowley, C. K., and R. Elgin, 1988. Government and its bureaucracy: A bilateral bargaining versus principal–agent approach. In C. K. Rowley, R. D. Tollison, and G. Tullock (Eds.), *The Political Economy of Rent Seeking*. Kluwer Academic Publishers, Boston, pp. 267–90.

On the complexity of evaluating output of bureaucracies and report on a case study, see:

Heckman, J., C. Heinrich, and J. Smith, 1997. Assessing the performance of performance standards in public bureaucracies. *American Economic Review* 87:389–95.

2.3 Life without markets and private property

Principles and ideas of socialism were set out by Marx (1887/1994) and Engels (1884/1972). Lange (1938) proposed that a government agency could calculate market prices even if markets did not exist.

Engels, F., 1884/1972. *The Origin of the Family, Private Property and the State*. Pathfinder Press, New York.
Lange, O., 1938. *On the Economic Meaning of Socialism*. B. E. Lippincott (Ed.), University of Minnesota Press, Minneapolis.
Marx, K., 1887/1994. *Capital: A Critical Analysis of Capitalist Production*. F. Engels (Ed.), Progress Publishers, Moscow.

On critiques of the institutions of socialism, see von Mises (1951), Pejovich (1987), and Hayek (1944/1972, 1988). On ideological opposition to Hayek, see Caldwell (1998).

Caldwell, B., 1998. Hayek and socialism. *Journal of Economic Literature* 35:1856–90.
Hayek von, F. A., 1944/1972. *The Road to Serfdom*. University of Chicago Press, Chicago.
Hayek von, F. A., 1988. *The Fatal Conceit: The Errors of Socialism*. W. W. Bartley III (Ed.), Routledge, London.
Pejovich, S., 1987. Freedom, property rights, and innovation in socialism. *Kyklos* 40:461–75.
von Mises, L., 1951. *Socialism*. Yale University Press, New Haven CT.

Rent seeking under communism was described by Hillman and Schnytzer (1986) and Anderson and Boettke (1997). Levy (2007) described how goods were obtained for final consumption.

Anderson, G. M., and P. J. Boettke, 1997. Soviet venality: A rent-seeking model of the communist state. *Public Choice* 93:37–53.
Hillman, A. L., and A. Schnytzer, 1986. Illegal activities and purges in a Soviet-type economy: A rent-seeking perspective. *International Review of Law and Economics* 6:87–99. Reprinted in Congleton et al., 2008.
Levy, D., 2007. Price adjustment under the table: Evidence on efficiency-enhancing corruption. *European Journal of Political Economy* 23:423–47.

Supplement S2A: Rent seeking and rent dissipation

Probabilistic contests were introduced in Tullock (1980). Justifications for presuming complete rent dissipation were provided in Hillman and Katz (1984) for competitive rent seeking and by Hillman and Samet (1987) for strategic discriminating contests (or all-pay auctions). For an overview of rent dissipation, see Hillman and Riley (1989).

Hillman, A. L., and E. Katz, 1984. Risk-averse rent-seekers and the social cost of monopoly power. *Economic Journal* 94:104–10.
Hillman, A. L., and J. Riley, 1989. Politically contestable rents and transfers. *Economics and Politics* 1:17–39.
Hillman, A. L., and D. Samet, 1987. Dissipation of contestable rents by small numbers of contenders. *Public Choice* 54:63–82.
Tullock, G., 1980. Efficient rent-seeking. In J. M. Buchanan, R. D. Tollison, and G. Tullock (Eds.), *Toward a Theory of the Rent-Seeking Society*. Texas A&M University Press, College Station, pp. 97–112.

The previously listed papers are reprinted in Congleton et al. (2008).

On rent dissipation with enduring rents, see:

Aidt, T. S., and A. L. Hillman, 2008. Enduring rents. *European Journal of Political Economy* 24:454–3.

Supplement S2B: Institutions and natural monopoly

The case for self-financing user pricing was made by Demsetz (1968). On capture theory, see Stigler (1971).

Demsetz, H., 1968. Why regulate utilities? *Journal of Law and Economics* 11:55–65.
Stigler, G. J., 1971. The theory of economic regulation. *Bell Journal of Economics and Management Science* 2:3–21.

Supplement S2C: Labor self-management

The literature on the theory of labor self-management was reviewed by Bonin and Putterman (1987). The story of the workers who hired the overseer is from Cheung (1983).

Bonin, J. P., and L. Putterman, 1987. *Economics of Cooperation and the Labor-Managed Economy*. Harwood, Chur, Switzerland.
Cheung, S., 1983. The contractual nature of the firm. *Journal of Law and Economics* 26:1–21.

Kornai (1983) observed the contradictions that are present when markets exist but private ownership of capital is disallowed. De facto labor self-management arose after the end of communism when planning ceased and the introduction of markets preceded privatization: see Hinds (1992). Bogetiç (1982) considered privatization through employee ownership and described employee-ownership schemes.

Bogetiç, Ž., 1982. Is there a case for employee ownership? In A. L. Hillman and B. Milanovic (Eds.), *The Transition from Socialism in Eastern Europe: Domestic Restructuring and Foreign Trade*. The World Bank, Washington DC, pp. 83–104.
Hinds, M., 1992. Policy effectiveness in reforming socialist economies. In A. L. Hillman and B. Milanovic (Eds.), *The Transition from Socialism in Eastern Europe: Domestic Restructuring and Foreign Trade*. The World Bank, Washington DC, pp. 13–39.
Kornai, J., 1983. *Contradictions and Dilemmas: Studies on the Socialist Economy and Society*. Corvina, Budapest, and MIT Press, Cambridge MA.

On the kibbutz, see Barkai (1987) and Abramitzsky (2008).

Abramitzsky, R., 2008. The limits of equality: Insights into the Israeli kibbutz. *Quarterly Journal of Economics* 123:1111–59.
Barkai, H., 1987. Kibbutz efficiency and the incentive conundrum. In S. Hedlund (Ed.), *Incentives and Economic Systems*. New York University Press, New York, pp. 228–63.

3

PUBLIC GOODS

Chapter 1 showed how competitive markets achieve efficiency for private goods – or goods that benefit one person. We also noted that for public goods, which can benefit many people simultaneously, we do not expect markets to result in efficient supply of public goods because people can benefit when others pay. In chapter 1, we also encountered an example of a public good in the rule of law. In this chapter, we investigate public goods in detail.

Because many people benefit simultaneously, public goods could well be called *collective* goods. The collective benefit suggests a need for collective decisions. Public goods thereby provide a foundation for a "theory of the state," through the need for institutions of government that allow collective decisions to be made.

The need for government is, however, subject to the characteristics of institutions: we saw in chapter 2 that political and bureaucratic principal–agent problems impose limitations on delegating responsibilities to governments.

In this chapter, we shall for the most part set aside the limitations of political and bureaucratic principal–agent problems. We shall ask normative questions about the desirable role of government as if political decision makers and bureaucrats could always be assured to be the faithful agents of taxpayers and voters. The questions that we ask are, therefore, about what political and bureaucratic decision makers who faithfully seek the public interest *should do* – or *can do* – to ensure availability of public goods. Should we decide that there are limitations relying on government, the reasons will be other than political and bureaucratic principal–agent problems. We shall see that the main problem confronting governments is lack of required information – or asymmetric information.

At the onset in studying public goods, we need to distinguish between public supply and public finance. Public goods are not "public" because supply is necessarily by the public sector or by government; for example, education provides public-good or collective benefits because many people benefit from better educated fellow citizens, but education can be private rather than in government schools. Education in private schools can also be publicly financed through government subsidies. Thus, although public goods are often publicly supplied as well as publicly financed, there is a distinction between public supply and public finance:

> *Public supply describes delivery of a public good through government, as in the case of education in a government school; public finance describes public spending on a public good, which might be privately supplied.*

Section 1 of this chapter describes types of public goods and investigates possibilities for financing public goods through voluntary private payments, as in markets. In section 2, we seek solutions to the problem of asymmetric information. Section 3 describes cost-benefit analysis.

3.1 Types of Public Goods

We begin with the properties of public goods.

A. Properties of public goods

Benefits from private and public goods

For a private good, an amount that one person has is not available to others. If individual i has an amount $x_i \geq 0$ and X is the total available quantity of a private good, then:

$$X = \sum_{j=1}^{n} x_j. \tag{3.1}$$

Private goods are therefore divided or distributed among a population.[1] For public goods, no similar division or distribution takes place. A total quantity G of a public good is also the quantity g_i available to each of n individuals:

$$G = g_1 = g_2 = g_3 = \cdots\cdots = g_n. \tag{3.2}$$

That is:

> *The quantity of a public good available to one person is also the quantity available to everybody.*

Although the quantity is the same, in general, people differ in their valuations of public goods. When a Mozart symphony is played, some people will enjoy the music, whereas others may find the music unappealing and may prefer jazz or hard rock. The people who enjoy the Mozart symphony, in principle, are prepared to pay to listen to the music. People who find the music unappealing should be prepared to pay to have the music stopped or to be allowed to leave, or they could request compensation if they have no choice but to listen to the music.[2]

The transition from private to collective benefit

When there is only one person, goods that could potentially be public goods are private goods. A story by Daniel Defoe, first published in 1719, tells of Robinson Crusoe living in isolation on an island. For Crusoe alone on the island, all goods are private goods. Public goods are introduced, and a transition from private to

[1] Private goods, of course, are not necessarily perfectly divisible; the water in the desert and the baby in the judgment of Solomon were not divisible. Divisibility of private goods is an approximation. The characterizing properties of private goods are that amounts available to individuals can differ and what one person has, another person cannot have.

[2] Technology can change public goods to private goods: listening to music in the presence of other people was once a public good, but that is no longer the case.

collective benefit takes place, when others arrive on the island. Some goods that were previously private in exclusively benefiting Crusoe now become collective in also benefiting the new arrivals. With others benefiting, Crusoe is expected to seek sharing of costs. There are trails and paths to maintain. There may be pools where mosquitoes breed that cause malaria, dengue fever, and other diseases. A lighthouse or watchtower might be required. As the population increases, trails become roads and highways. Bridges may be required. The population may want local and national parks. Lifeguards will be required at the island's beaches. A meteorological service would provide collective benefit through weather forecasts. Education provides a public good through the benefits from having educated fellow citizens. A museum, library, and zoo would also provide collective benefit to the island's residents. Embassies and consulates may be established in faraway places. A tourism agency could advertise the attractions of the island. There will also be demand for public goods that provide *options* for use, such as a fire department, police, ambulance service, and defense force: many people simultaneously benefit from the *option* to use these services, although everybody prefers that actual use not be required. Crusoe and the population that has joined him face the normative questions:

(1) How much of the different public goods should be supplied?
(2) How should the public goods be financed?

Answers to these questions differ for pure and congestible public goods.

Characteristics of pure and congestible public goods

Figure 3.1a shows the characteristics of a *pure* public good.

> *Individual benefits from a pure public good are independent of the number of users.*

In figure 3.1a, individual benefit remains unchanged as the number of users increases.

Figure 3.1b shows a public good that is pure up to a number n_1 of users, after which congestion begins and individual benefit declines. With more than n_2 users, positive individual benefit ceases. For example, after more than n_2 cars are on a congested highway, people are prepared, in principle, to pay to avoid the highway. If using the highway, they are also prepared to pay to have others leave the highway. A person who pays other drivers to leave the highway is *privately financing* a public good in the form of reduced congestion for all other drivers remaining on the highway.

Congestible public goods can usually be duplicated. Whether duplicated or not, people can often be excluded from congestible public goods at low cost. The possibility of exclusion allows markets to be created in which people pay in order to benefit. Government, therefore, has no necessary responsibility in the supply

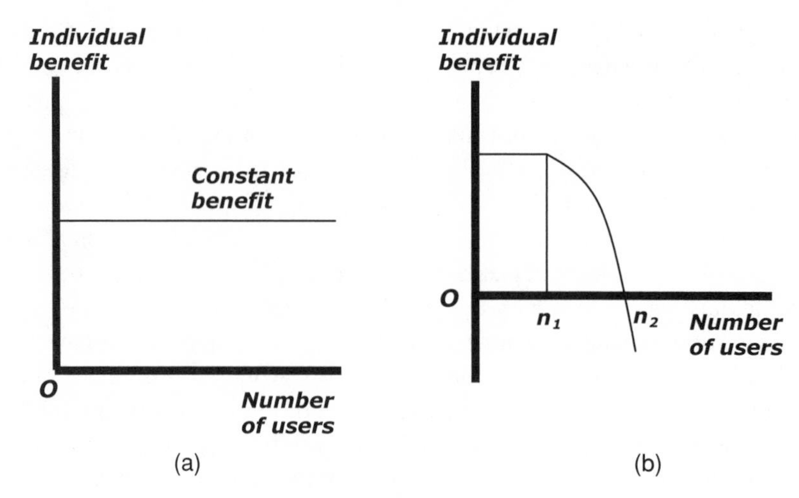

Figure 3.1. (a) A pure public good. (b) A congestible public good.

of congestible public goods. Supply can be private, as in the case of gyms; movie theaters; concerts; sports events; transportation; private schools; private hospitals; and toll roads, tunnels, and bridges. Supply can also be competitive if there are many private suppliers. Hence, in general:

Congestible public goods can be privately and competitively supplied.

In investigating the responsibility of governments, we can therefore focus our attention on pure public goods as in figure 3.1a or on congestible public goods that remain noncongested as in figure 3.1b when there are fewer than n_1 users.

If public roads are congested or where there is traffic congestion in an inner-city area, governments can levy taxes to reduce congestion. The taxes create incentives not to use a road or not to enter an inner-city area. Taxes, therefore, can have two distinct purposes: (1) to reduce congestion, and (2) to provide revenue for the government. When we study externalities, we shall consider taxes that have the objective of reducing congestion or changing personal behavior in various ways. In this chapter, when we consider taxes, the purpose of the taxes is to provide government revenue to pay for pure public goods.

Public goods and natural monopoly

Monopoly (or a single supplier) is "natural" or cost-efficient when there are fixed costs of supply; the single supplier avoids unnecessary duplication of fixed costs. For a private good, as shown in figure 3.2, natural monopoly arises when average cost, which is equal to fixed cost F divided by total quantity supplied, is declining.[3] For a public good, also shown in figure 3.2, declining average cost is equal to the fixed cost divided by the number of people to whom the public good is available.

[3] See supplement S2B on natural monopoly in the case of a private good.

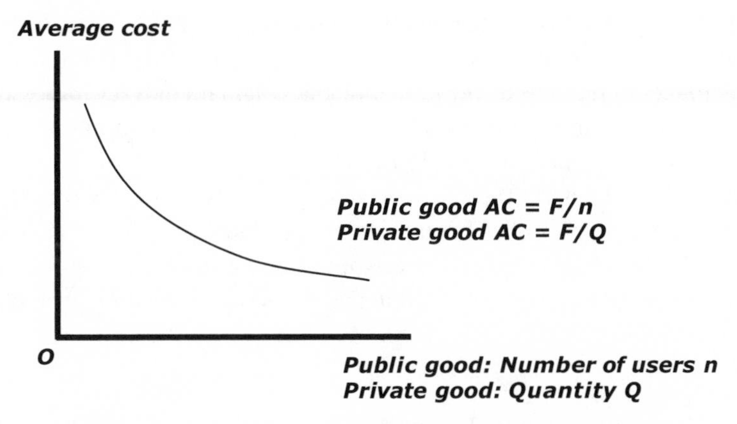

Figure 3.2. Natural monopoly for private and public goods.

A lighthouse is an often-used example of a pure public good. The benefit from a lighthouse is collective. There is a fixed cost of constructing a lighthouse; it is wasteful and unnecessary to incur the fixed cost of an identical lighthouse situated next to an existing one. A lighthouse is therefore at the same time a pure public good and a natural monopoly.

More generally, the example of the lighthouse illustrates that:

All pure public goods are natural monopolies.

Because public goods are natural monopolies, the question arises:

Who will be the monopoly supplier?

Often, the monopoly supplier is government – for example, for law enforcement and natural security.

Publicly financed private security firms could provide law-enforcement services. The monopoly of government on legal coercion would then be delegated to private persons, who would be given control over restriction of freedom of citizens. The private-profit motive of law enforcers could result in citizens facing fabricated crimes and infringements and confronting extortion when threatened with arrest.[4]

Private supply and holdup problems

A government that is a monopolist for a public good may also be a monopsonist in purchase of inputs required to supply the public good. When there are no buyers other than the government, a private supplier who has produced, for example, defense equipment, relies on the government to pay a pre-agreed contractually specified price. The private supplier then faces a potential holdup problem; a holdup occurs if, after equipment has been produced, a government reneges on

[4] Such extortion occurs in countries where police – although they are employees of the government – personally retain money paid in fines.

the contractually specified price and offers a lower price. A holdup can also occur in the opposite direction; a private supplier can proclaim that unanticipated cost overruns make adherence to the terms of the original contract impossible and insist on a higher than contractually specified price when supply is necessary and other producers have not made the investments that allow delivery of the equipment. Mutual trust is therefore necessary for private supply. In the United States, defense equipment has been privately produced, by competing suppliers; outside of the United States, producers of defense equipment were, in general, government-owned monopolies, until in many cases privatization took place.

Public inputs

Public goods are often inputs. The rule of law is, for example, a public input that allows productive activity to take place and markets to exist; defense equipment is an input into national security; roads and bridges are public inputs into transportation. Conclusions about public goods, in general, apply to public inputs.

Collective harm

Public goods and also public inputs can do collective harm; damage to the environment collectively harms everybody. We shall refer to *public goods* as encompassing both collective benefit and collective harm. A public good can also benefit some people and disadvantage others, as in the case of music that some people like and others do not. Unless otherwise indicated, we shall view people as benefiting from public goods.

Public goods and altruism

People who personally pay for public goods seek benefit for themselves and also inadvertently benefit others. When parents complain about an ineffective teacher, the parents are motivated by benefit for their own child but also provide a public-good benefit for all other parents with children in the class. Payment for public goods contrasts with altruistic behavior: the intent of payment for public goods is self-benefit, whereas altruistic behavior helps others without personal benefit for oneself.[5]

Exclusion

People cannot always exclude themselves from pure public goods, nor is it always possible to exclude people – for example, in the case of benefits from the rule of law, competitive markets, and national defense. However:

> *Where exclusion is possible, exclusion from a pure public good is inefficient.*

[5] There is also a view that because altruism benefits altruistic people who feel good about themselves as a consequence of their altruistic behavior, there is no pure altruism.

The total benefit to n people from a pure public good is:

$$W_n = \sum_{j=1}^{n} B_j - C. \tag{3.3}$$

When an additional person benefits, the fixed cost C of supplying the public good remains unchanged; however, with $(n+1)$ beneficiaries, total benefit from the public good increases to:

$$W_{n+1} = \sum_{j=1}^{n+1} B_j - C. \tag{3.4}$$

The increase in total benefit from the public good is the personal benefit to the additional person:

$$\Delta W = B_{n+1} > 0. \tag{3.5}$$

Allowing an additional person to benefit from an available public good is Pareto-improving: someone is better off and no one is worse off.

The MC of use of an existing public good by an additional person is zero:

$$MC^{use} = 0. \tag{3.6}$$

Efficient use requires that:

$$MB^{use} = MC^{use}. \tag{3.7}$$

Therefore, efficient use requires free use or free access to existing public goods:

$$P^{use} = 0. \tag{3.8}$$

The cost of supply of a public good differs from the cost of use. A bridge is costly to build. However, once the fixed costs of building the bridge have been incurred and the bridge exists, the *cost of use* of a noncongested bridge is zero. The efficient price of use of the bridge is therefore zero.

Efficient use requires that access to pure public goods be free.

The dilemma of exclusion

We return now to Robinson Crusoe and the new arrivals on the island. Crusoe may appeal to the new arrivals for cooperation in personally contributing to the fixed cost of building a lighthouse. Some of the newly arrived people might claim that they do not need a lighthouse. After the lighthouse has been built, efficiency requires that no one be excluded from its benefits. Exclusion, however, is possible: someone stationed in the lighthouse could turn off the light whenever the boat of someone who did not contribute (a free rider) is seen in the vicinity. Exclusion is inefficient for two reasons: there should be free access to use, and the person on watch in the lighthouse could be productively employed rather than spending time to exclude people from benefit of the lighthouse – even if people as free riders who refused to contribute to construction of the lighthouse deserve to be excluded.

Inhabitants of a neighboring island might be predators and raids may be taking place. When Crusoe asks for private contributions for voluntary spending on defense, an inhabitant on the island might refuse to contribute and declare to Crusoe: "I am a nice person. If everybody were like me, we would have no problems with the people on the neighboring island. Those people evidently have a problem with you, not with me." When predatory raiders from a neighboring island begin attacking a farm belonging to the person who refused to contribute to defense preparedness, Crusoe faces a dilemma. Without the free rider's contribution, the fixed costs of the defense equipment have been incurred and the means of resistance to the predators are available. It is inefficient to exclude the free rider from defense – it is also unethical not to save a life when saving a life is possible.

Early fire companies were private and sold private membership for assistance in case of fire. When there was a fire in a house whose owner had not paid the fire company, the firefighters might arrive but only to ensure the safety of houses owned by people in the vicinity who had paid for fire-protection services. Permitting houses of people who did not pay to burn down was inefficient. However, if the houses of those who had not paid were not allowed to burn down, *no one* would have an incentive to pay for having the fire company on call in case of fire.

Crusoe is not the government. Crusoe is making proposals and appealing for voluntary contributions to collective spending on public goods. He is imposing costs on himself in time and effort to make the proposals and appeal for voluntary payments. In appealing to people to make voluntary contributions, he is benevolently seeking efficient outcomes for *all* inhabitants of the island – although he personally also gains when costs of public goods are shared with others. Life would be easier for Crusoe if he had the authority of government and could impose compulsory taxes to finance public spending on public goods.

B. Voluntary personal payments for public goods

We now address the question:

> *How effective can a society be in supplying public goods without a government that has the authority to tax?*

Figure 3.3a shows demand for a private good. Total market demand is the *horizontal* sum of the individual demands MB_1 and MB_2 of two people. At the market equilibrium price P_E, person 1 purchases the quantity q_1^* and person 2 purchases the quantity q_2^*, and market demand at price P_E is $Q^* = (q_1^* + q_2^*)$.

Figure 3.3b shows total demand for a public good, defined either in terms of quantity or quality. For a public good, the quantity or standard available to

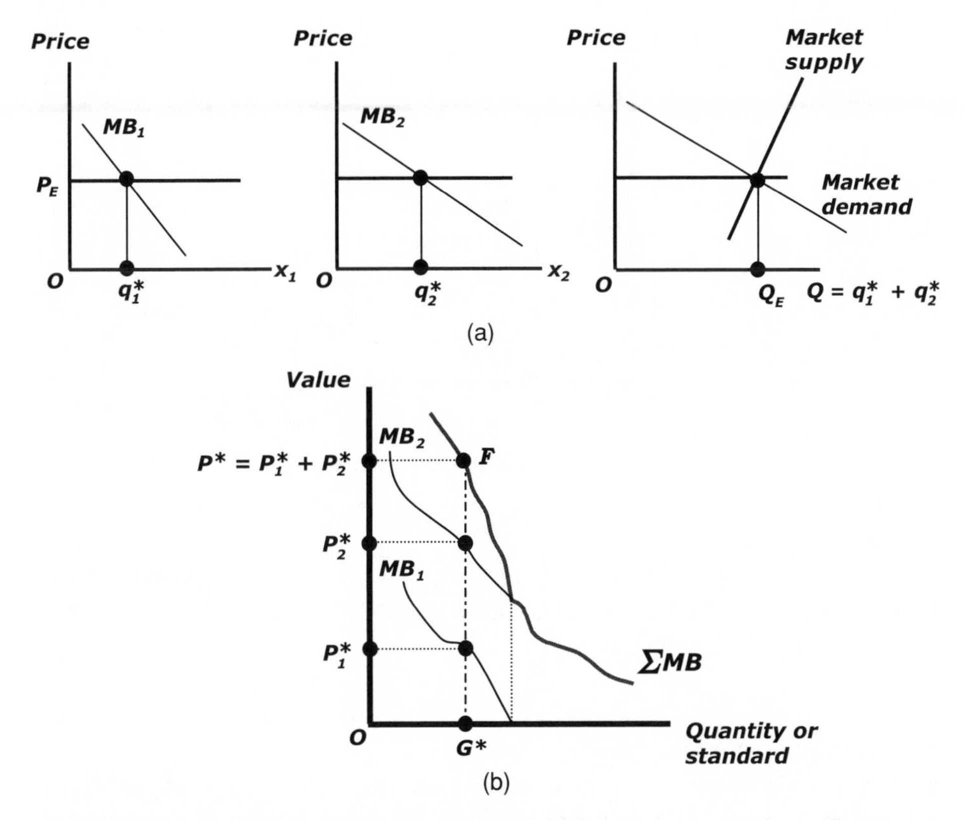

Figure 3.3. (a) Market demand for private goods. (b) Demand expressed as willingness to pay for different quantities or standards of public goods.

one person is also that available to everyone else. Therefore, collective (or total) demand for a public good is found by asking:

> *How much are all beneficiaries of a public good willing to pay in total for a given common quantity or standard?*

In figure 3.3b, person 1's marginal willingness to pay for the public good at the common quantity G^* is P_1^*. Person 2's marginal willingness to pay is P_2^*. Combined marginal willingness to pay at the quantity G^* is $(P_1^* + P_2^*) = P^*$. Point F in figure 3.3b is on the combined demand function $\sum MB$ of persons 1 and 2. The combined or collective demand function is found by *vertically* summing MB_1 and MB_2 at different quantities or standards of the public good.[6]

Private and public goods thus differ in the way in which individual demands are summed to obtain total demand. For private goods, the summation is horizontal; for public goods, the summation is vertical.

[6] In figure 3.3b, the market-demand function $\sum MB$ coincides with the demand MB_2 of high-valuation person 2 after demand MB_1 of the low-valuation person reaches zero (which is the lowest value of MB_1).

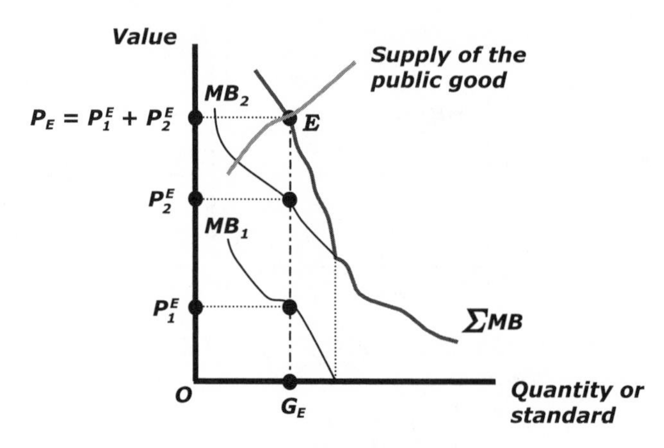

Figure 3.4. A market for public goods.

Supply

There is, in principle, no difference between *supply functions* for private and public goods. As for private goods, the inputs required for public goods are generally competitively supplied in markets.[7]

Efficient voluntary payments for public goods

Figure 3.4 combines a competitive supply function for a public good with total willingness to pay $\sum MB$. At point E, where quantities demanded and supplied are equal, payment of price P_E of the public good is shared, with person 1 paying the personal per-unit price P_1^E and person 2 paying the personal per-unit price P_2^E. The personal per-unit prices in figure 3.4 are determined by each person's marginal benefit at the equilibrium quantity G_E. We see that:

$$P_1^E = MB_1, \quad P_2^E = MB_2. \tag{3.9}$$

Summing the personal per-unit prices and personal marginal benefits in expression (3.9), we have:

$$P^E = P_1^E + P_2^E = \sum_i MB_i. \tag{3.10}$$

Because the inputs for public goods are competitively supplied:

$$P^E = MC. \tag{3.11}$$

[7] Although the *inputs* are competitively supplied, supply of the *benefits* of a pure public good remains a natural monopoly. For example, if the public good is security provided by police officers in a patrol car, the police officers are hired in labor markets and the police vehicle is purchased in a market. The marginal cost of supply of the inputs for the public good is the combined MC of the police car and the officers.

Combining expressions (3.10) and (3.11), we have at point E:

$$\sum_i MB_i = MC. \tag{3.12}$$

The condition (3.12) is satisfied when people voluntarily pay for public goods according to personal benefit. The condition (3.12) also ensures efficiency of public good supply. Total benefit from the public good is:

$$W = \sum_i MB_i - C. \tag{3.13}$$

Total benefit is therefore maximized when:

$$\sum_i MB_i = MC. \tag{3.14}$$

The condition (3.12) describing the outcome of voluntary payments at point E is therefore also the condition for maximum W.[8]

Hence, we conclude:

> *Voluntary payment for public goods according to personal benefit maximizes W and so is efficient.*

There has been no reason to anticipate otherwise. Personal payment in competitive markets is efficient for private goods; for public goods, the only change is that total demand is derived through vertical rather than horizontal summation of individual demands.

Supplement S3D: An efficient economy with public and private goods

Supplement S3D shows how the condition for efficient supply of a public good $\sum MB = MC$ is derived in general equilibrium.

Asymmetric information and under-supply of public goods

For private goods, individuals face the same market price and choose different personal quantities; for public goods, individuals have the same quantity or standard but are asked to pay different personal prices based on personal benefit. Personal benefit, however, is subjective private information. Personal payment for public goods, therefore, involves asymmetric information: only people themselves know their own personal benefits.

By taking advantage of asymmetric information and understating true personal benefit, people can reduce the personal price that they pay. Figure 3.5a shows the personal gain from understating true marginal benefit. By claiming

[8] The condition for efficient supply of a public good is known as the *Samuelson rule*, after Paul Samuelson of MIT (Nobel Prize in economics, 1970).

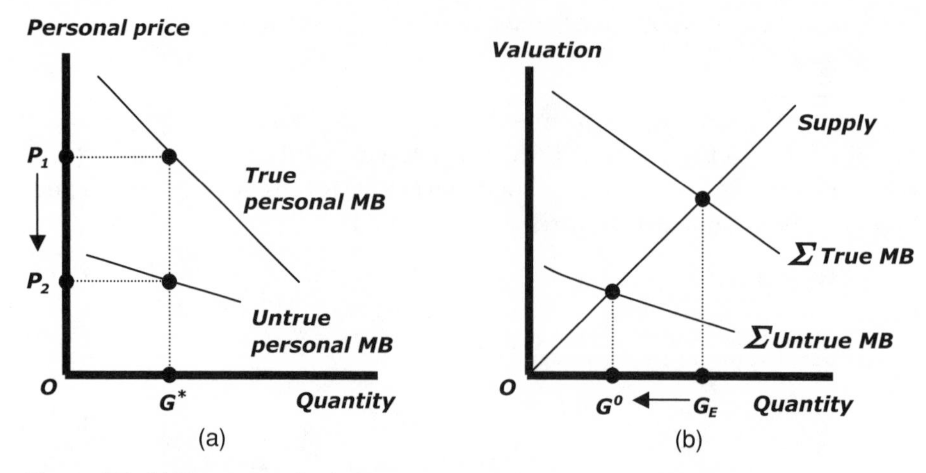

Figure 3.5. (a) The personal gain from understating benefit. (b) Inefficient supply due to misrepresented benefits.

lower than true *MB*, the person in figure 3.5a reduces the personal price when the quantity supplied is G^* from P_1 to P_2.

In a competitive market for private goods, there can be no personal benefit from misrepresenting personal preferences or willingness to pay. By misrepresenting preferences for private goods, people can only reduce their benefit.

Perhaps not everyone would be deceptive when asked to reveal personal benefit from a public good. Some people might answer honestly. However, because of asymmetric information, we could never know if people were being honest or were misrepresenting preferences to reduce their personal price.

The consequence of deception by only one person in a large population is negligible. Figure 3.5b shows the downward shift in the combined $\sum$untrue *MB* function of the population when many people deceptively claim low personal benefit. The quantity G^0 of the public good that is provided is less than the efficient quantity G_E.

For exposition, we are depicting people's *MB* functions for public goods as if we know the location of the functions. Because personal *MB* is subjective information, we do not know the location of these functions. The location is known only to the individuals themselves.

We conclude:

> *Personal incentives to understate benefit suggest that voluntarily financed public goods will be under-supplied relative to the efficient quantity or standard.*

The term *free riding* describes relying on others to pay.

> *Under-supply of voluntarily financed public goods arises because of free-riding incentives.*

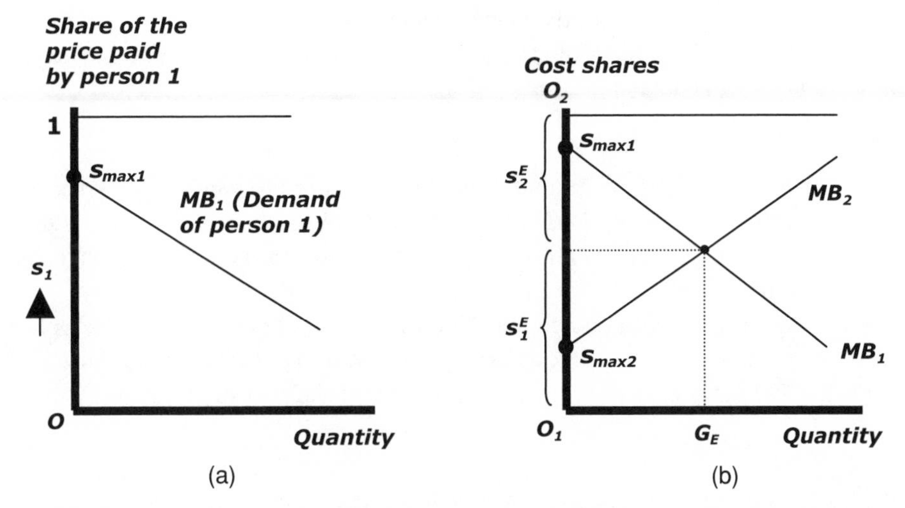

Figure 3.6. (a) Person 1's demand for a public good depends on the share s_1 that he or she pays. (b) There is consensus that the efficient quantity G^* should be supplied when cost shares are s_1^E and s_2^E.

The ideal Lindahl consensus

The ideal efficient outcome for voluntarily financed public goods is known as the *Lindahl solution*, achieved through the Lindahl mechanism.[9] In the Lindahl solution, people are described as paying a share of the cost of public goods according to their true preferences. No one free rides. The Lindahl solution emphasizes the need for consensus on the quantity or standard of a public good. Consensus is important.

> *Ideally, people should not be compelled to pay for a quantity or standard of a public good that they do not want; therefore, it is desirable that there be consensus about the quantity or standard.*

We previously described a market for a public good by expressing total demand as $\sum MB$ and supply in terms of the MC of inputs. To demonstrate the ideal Lindahl solution, we change how we look at demand and supply. In figure 3.6a, the horizontal axis measures the common quantity of a public good. No one is excluded from benefit so there is an efficient *price of use* of zero. Still, there is a need to pay for the public good. The Lindahl solution determines the efficient quantity (or standard) available to everyone and efficient sharing of payment by beneficiaries of the public good. MB_1 in figure 3.6a is person 1's demand, expressed as marginal willingness to pay for the public good. Demand depends on the personal per-unit price P_1 or cost share that person 1 pays.

[9] The Lindahl solution was proposed in 1919 by the Swedish economist, Erik Lindahl (1891–1960).

The public good is competitively supplied at a given market price P. Person 1 pays a share s_1 of the price P of the public good. Therefore, person 1's cost share or personal price is determined as:

$$P_1 = s_1 P. \tag{3.15}$$

The maximum cost share P_1 that person 1 is prepared to pay is s_{max1}. At a cost share in excess of s_{max1}, person 1's demand is zero. With the price P of the public good given, person 1's demand for the public good increases as the personal cost share s_1 declines from s_{max1}.

We again proceed with two people. The Lindahl solution, in principle, applies to any number of people who voluntarily contribute to paying for a public good.

Person 2's cost share is s_2 of price P. The sum of the cost shares is:

$$\sum_i s_i = 1. \tag{3.16}$$

Figure 3.6b shows marginal willingness-to-pay MB_2 of person 2 measured from origin O_2. At origin O_1 of person 1, the cost shares are $s_1 = 0$ and $s_2 = 1$. At origin O_2 of person 2, the cost shares are $s_2 = 0$ and $s_1 = 1$. At a cost share greater than s_{max2}, person 2 has zero demand. Demand of person 2 for the public good increases along MB_2 as the cost share s_2 declines from s_{max2}.

Figure 3.6b can be interpreted in terms of demand and supply. Demand of one person is supply for the other.

> *Because a public good provides collective benefit no matter who pays, payment by one person for the public good is free supply for the other.*

The Lindahl solution is shown in figure 3.6b, where there is consensus about demand for the public good; that is, where:

$$MB_1 = MB_2. \tag{3.17}$$

The Lindahl solution is therefore characterized by the consensus quantity demanded G_E and cost shares s_1^E and s_2^E.

We next show that the Lindahl-consensus solution results in supply of an efficient quantity or standard of the public good. The condition (3.17) indicates that when G_E is supplied, total net benefit $(B_1 + B_2)$ to the two persons from the public good is maximized. We can also confirm that supply of the consensus quantity G_E is efficient by showing that the Lindahl solution replicates the efficiency condition for public-good supply:

$$\sum_i MB_i = MC. \tag{3.18}$$

In figure 3.6b, at the quantity or standard G_E:

$$P_i = s_i^E P = MB_i(G_E) \quad i = 1, 2. \tag{3.19}$$

Summing for the two people, we have:

$$(P_1 + P_2) = (s_1^E + s_2^E)P = \sum MB. \tag{3.20}$$

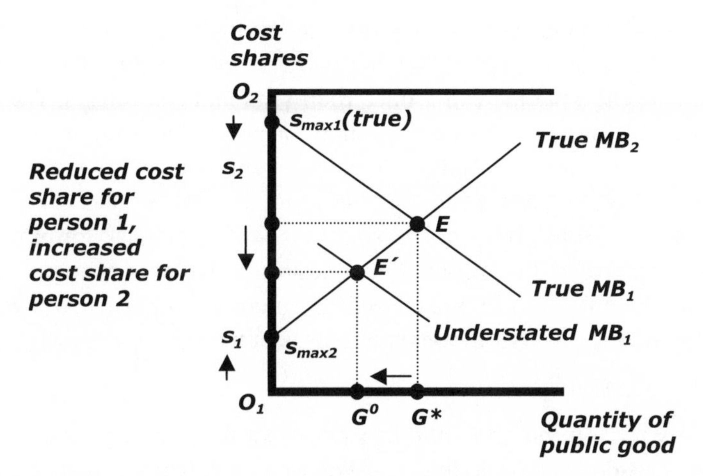

Figure 3.7. Lindahl cost sharing is not feasible because cost shares can be manipulated by misrepresenting personal benefit.

With $P = MC$ because of competitive supply of the public good and because $(s_1^E + s_2^E) = 1$, the efficiency condition (3.18) follows from the expression (3.20). Thus:

> *The Lindahl voluntary-payment consensus results in efficient supply of public goods through voluntary personal payments.*

However, the efficient Lindahl solution requires people to be truthful about their benefits expressed in willingness to pay for public goods. In figure 3.7, understatement of personal benefit by person 1 changes the determination of personal cost shares from point E to point E'. At point E', person 1 has a lower cost share than at point E and the cost share of person 2 has increased. The misrepresented preferences of person 1 change the consensus quantity from the efficient quantity G^* to the inefficient quantity G^0. Person 2 confronts the same incentive to misrepresent personal benefit. The mutual incentives to understate true benefit once more result in inefficient under-supply of the public good.

Strategic behavior

Understatement of personal benefit introduces strategic considerations. Person 1 would not want to understate benefit too much; understatement of benefit that increases person 2's cost share to s_{max2} or above would result in person 2 making no contribution at all to financing the public good. Likewise, if by misrepresenting preferences person 2 were to increase person 1's cost share to s_{max1} or above, person 1 would not contribute to financing the public good.

The Lindahl solution as a benchmark

The Lindahl solution is a normative portrayal of ideal truthful behavior of beneficiaries of public goods. People are thus viewed as trusting and trustworthy.

The Lindahl solution is, however, contrary to the premise that people maximize utility or do the best for themselves because misrepresenting their preferences when others do not, people can reduce their personal cost shares. We shall not propose that the Lindahl solution is feasible. Because of asymmetric information regarding personal benefits (only individuals themselves know their own benefits), we would indeed never know if the Lindahl solution had been achieved. We can nonetheless use the Lindahl solution as a benchmark for efficient payment and supply of public goods. Our question is whether there is some way of achieving the efficient Lindahl consensus outcome. In particular, can governments replicate the efficient Lindahl consensus outcome?

The prisoners' dilemma and voluntary payment for public goods

Before we consider responsibilities for governments, which would use compulsory taxes to finance public goods, we explore further possibilities of voluntary payments. The prisoners' dilemma and Nash equilibrium can be used to describe outcomes of voluntary payment for public goods. In table 3.1, two people face the *binary decision* (yes or no) of whether to contribute to paying for a public good. The first number is again the benefit to person 1 and the second number is the benefit to person 2; the numbers also indicate the rankings of outcomes. The personally best outcome at 4 is obtained by not paying when the other person pays; 3 is the common benefit when both people pay; 2 is the common benefit when nobody pays; and the lowest benefit 1 is obtained by contributing to the public good when the other person does not.

The efficient outcome that maximizes total benefit $(B_1 + B_2)$ is at (3, 3), where both people contribute to payment for the public good. The dominant strategy is not to contribute. The Nash equilibrium is at (2, 2), where nobody contributes and the public good is not provided.

With sequential decisions, the Nash equilibrium is also at (2, 2): the person choosing first does not contribute (which is the dominant strategy) and the person choosing second has a dominant strategy of not contributing.

Based on the prisoners' dilemma, we therefore reiterate our previous conclusions about the inefficiency of voluntary payments for public goods:

> *The outcome for voluntary payments for public goods is the inefficient Nash equilibrium.*

TABLE 3.1. THE PUBLIC-GOOD PRISONERS' DILEMMA

	Person 2 contributes	Person 2 does not contribute
Person 1 contributes	3, 3	1, 4
Person 1 does not contribute	4, 1	2, 2

Communication could take place; a promise that a person will cooperate by contributing is, in effect, an attempt to convince the other person of the intention to behave *irrationally* because it is rational self-interested behavior not to cooperate in a single-encounter prisoners' dilemma game. When considering the prisoners' dilemma of anarchy in chapter 1, we observed that there is also no incentive to cooperate when the number of rounds of interaction is finite and known in advance. There is, in particular, no incentive to cooperate in contributing to the public good when interaction is anonymous in large populations because there is then no value to having a personal reputation as a person who cooperates by contributing.[10]

The prisoners' dilemma and the Lindahl solution

The personal behavior underlying the prisoners' dilemma differs from that of the Lindahl solution. The Lindahl solution achieves efficiency because people truthfully pay for public goods according to personal benefit but also because people respond to supply by others by increasing their own supply; that is, people view payments for the public good by others as subsidizing their own payments through reduced personal cost shares.

In the Nash equilibrium of the prisoners' dilemma, on the contrary, when one person pays, the other person's best response is not to pay. Payments by others are not viewed as personal subsidies. This is because of the presumption (or conjecture) of Nash behavior that personal decisions are made taking other people's decisions as given; this means that behavior is based on others not responding to the decision that a person makes.

In the Lindahl case, a person conjectures that "if I contribute more to the public good, the other person will also contribute more, since I will have reduced the other person's cost share and therefore the other person's demand will increase." This behavioral conjecture internalizes the response of others to a person's public-good contribution.

Strategic behavior depends on such conjectures or presumptions about how people perceive that other people will respond to their decisions. The Nash equilibrium of the prisoners' dilemma is based on the *Nash behavioral conjecture* that, when making their decisions, people take the decisions of others to be given. Therefore, people do not take into account how their decision will affect the decisions of others. There is rationality in Nash behavior: in the Nash equilibrium, people look at the decisions of others and decide that they can do no better, given the decisions others have made.

Nash behavior however results in free riding through people decreasing their contributions in response to increased contributions by others (see the elaboration in supplement S3A), whereas because voluntary payments by others *subsidize* a person's own contribution to public goods, people might *increase* their

[10] The role of reputation was described in the repeated prisoners' dilemma of anarchy.

own voluntary spending in response to increased voluntary spending by others. Outcomes might then arise that approach efficient Lindahl voluntary payments.

Experimental evidence

Does experimental evidence on personal payment for public goods support the hypothesis of Nash behavior? A version of the public-good game proceeds as follows. Two people are each given $10 (or some other unit of currency). They have the binary choice of keeping the money for themselves for private benefit or contributing the entire amount to providing a public good. The contribution of 10 to the public good provides collective benefits of 7 to everyone (including the person contributing). The game is described in the prisoners' dilemma in table 3.1a.[11] When both people contribute to the public good, they each have $(7 + 7) = 14$. When one person contributes and the other does not, the person contributing has a benefit of 7 (from the public good) and the person not contributing has a benefit of 17 (the original 10 that he or she has kept plus the public-good benefit of 7 provided by the other person). When neither person contributes to the public good, both retain the 10 with which each began.

The prediction based on Nash equilibrium for a single-round game is that no one will contribute. Yet, in experiments, instances of cooperation are revealed in which the efficient outcome at (14, 14) is achieved.

TABLE 3.1a. THE PRISONERS' DILEMMA IN A PUBLIC-GOOD EXPERIMENT

	Person 2 contributes	Person 2 does not contribute
Person 1 contributes	14, 14	7, 17
Person 1 does not contribute	17, 7	10, 10

Cooperation also arises in repeated games that are played against the same person a preannounced number of times. In repeated games, few people cooperate in the last round; they apparently realize that, in the final round, reputation for cooperating has no value; but they have not computed backwards the disincentive for cooperation in any previous rounds of the game.

In another version of the public-good game, the decision is not binary (whether or not to contribute). Rather, people are given a sum of money – for example, $10 – and are asked *to divide the money* between private benefit (through keeping the money) and contributing to a public good. With x_i denoting the amount that

[11] The prisoners' dilemma is defined by the rankings of net benefits or payoffs in table 3.1. The actual values of the payoffs do not matter. In table 3.1a, the ranking of payoffs $\{17, 14, 10, 7\}$ is the same as $\{4, 3, 2, 1\}$ in table 3.1.

a person i keeps for private-good benefit and g_i denoting the amount contributed to the public good, each individual has a budget constraint:

$$10 = x_i + g_i \quad i = 1, 2. \tag{3.21}$$

People are informed that they are in a game against others who face the same decision.

When there are two players, the amount of the public good available is the sum of the two persons' contributions given as:

$$G = g_1 + g_2. \tag{3.22}$$

The two people are also told that they will be rewarded according to a formula that determines personal total benefits B_i – for example, the formula could be:

$$B_i = 3x_i + 2G = 3x_i + 2(g_1 + g_2) \quad i = 1, 2. \tag{3.23}$$

In the formula in expression (3.23), a dollar spent on the private good provides private benefit of 3 and a dollar spent on the public good provides simultaneous personal benefit of 2 to each person. Total benefit from a personal contribution of a dollar to the public good is therefore 4. Social benefit (total benefit for both people) is maximized by contributing all money to the public good, in which case each person individually has benefit of 20 and $(B_1 + B_2) = 40$, with all benefit coming from the public good.

TABLE 3.1b. THE PUBLIC-GOOD GAME WHEN MONEY CAN BE DIVIDED

	Person 2 contributes	Person 2 does not contribute
Person 1 contributes	40, 40	20, 50
Person 1 does not contribute	50, 20	30, 30

Table 3.1b shows outcomes determined by the formula in expression (3.23). The highest personal return of 50 is obtained by free riding and not contributing anything to the public good when the other person contributes the entire \$10. The lowest return of 20 is obtained by a person who contributes the entire \$10 to the public good when the other person contributes nothing.

The dominant strategy in table 3.1b is to contribute nothing to the public good, which results in the Nash equilibrium at (30, 30). The efficient outcome (40, 40) requires both people to contribute the entire \$10 to the public good. The prediction based on Nash behavior is that neither person will contribute any money to the public good and that the outcome will be the Nash equilibrium (30, 30).

In experiments in which the game in table 3.1b is repeated a known number of rounds against the *same person* (so that reputation matters), people tend to respond to the uncertainty about whether they are playing against a "cooperative-type" person or a rational maximizing person who follows Nash behavior by initially contributing approximately half of the money to the public good. Contributions then tend to decrease in subsequent rounds. Again, in the final round, players usually contribute nothing. The cooperation expressed in positive contributions to the public good in all but the final round is contrary to Nash predictions. Rationally, there should be no cooperation in the final round because of common knowledge of players that there is no incentive to cooperate in the final round. That is, a person may wish to cooperate in the final round but knows that the other person knows that it is not in his or her interest to cooperate because reputation has no value in the final round. If common knowledge about rational behavior deters cooperation in the final round, why does *backward induction* not preempt cooperation in previous rounds?[12]

Trust and norms of conduct

By initially cooperating and contributing to the public good, people begin by trusting others to choose the same reciprocating, collectively beneficial behavior. No communication takes place before the decision about contributing to the public good is made; nonetheless, people appear to anticipate cooperative behavior based on norms of conduct within the society.[13]

Evidence reveals that personal contact affects behavior. Instances of cooperation increase when people are introduced to one another before rounds of the public-good game are played. Cooperation also increases if people are merely permitted to see one another.

Behavior revealed in experiments thus transcends the self-interested rationality of choosing the dominant strategy in the prisoners' dilemma of not contributing to the public good. Perhaps the cooperative behavior is a reflection of instinct. The instinct to cooperate appears basic to human nature. Again, we can go back to the time of hunter–gatherer groups. Because hunter–gatherer groups had perhaps no more than 120 people, personal behavior could be witnessed and monitored by others in the group. Also, however, cooperation enhanced prospects for individual survival, and for survival of the group. Cooperation provided protection. Perhaps the instinct to cooperate has been retained in the form of a social norm or presumption of cooperation.

Experiments reveal that people become disenchanted when expectations of reciprocal cooperation by others are not realized. People are then willing to punish others who did not cooperate, even if in the act of punishment they themselves incur a loss. Once betrayed in a repeated game by not having had trust reciprocated, people may decide never to trust the other person again for the remaining rounds of the game. People who punish at a cost to themselves are providing a

[12] The method of backward induction indicates there is no incentive for cooperation in any round.

[13] The personal decisions are made simultaneously or without one person knowing the decision of the other. Cooperative behavior is therefore not a response to the behavior of the other person but rather can only be based on the anticipation of how other people will behave.

public good, through the incentives they provide for the people who are being punished to cooperate in the future when again playing the repeated prisoners' dilemma against others.

If people preannounce that they will never be trusting again if betrayed, and if the announcement is credible, the outcome could be ongoing cooperation – until the last interaction, in which a threat to never cooperate in the future if betrayed is irrelevant because there is no future. This is consistent with the evidence that large numbers of people cease cooperation in the final round of interactions. Apparently, they anticipate reciprocated cooperation if they cooperate, and punishment if they cease to cooperate earlier. They perceive that there is no benefit from cooperation in the final round because of the end of interaction.[14]

Economics students and cooperation

Economics students participating in public-good games tend to cooperate less than other students. Why is this so? Have the students self-selected themselves as types who tend not to cooperate by choosing to study economics? Or have economics students been influenced in their behavior by studying the prisoners' dilemma? Even students in introductory economics courses who have not yet been taught the logic of the prisoners' dilemma cooperate less than other students.

We do not expect students who know the logical foundations of the Nash equilibrium of the prisoners' dilemma to cooperate. The Nash equilibrium is based on common knowledge that "everybody behaves rationally," and that "everybody knows that everybody behaves rationally," and further that "everybody knows that everybody knows," and so on. Economics students may better understand the logical consequence of common knowledge that, when people expect *other* people to behave rationally, the best response is to behave rationally oneself – and the outcome is then the inefficient Nash equilibrium.[15]

Cooperation as expressive behavior

Cooperation can also be explained as expressive behavior. People cooperate to express their cooperative nature to themselves. Self-identity can be based on the feeling that people have about themselves as being pleasant and non-exploitative and as not being the sort of person who takes advantage of others. Some people may even continue cooperating when others do not so as to demonstrate how

[14] We previously observed that a necessary condition for choosing cooperation is a sufficiently low discount rate. A person who uses a sufficiently high discount rate to compare present and future benefits will choose the present benefit from not cooperating and forgo future benefits from ongoing cooperation. The discount rate is not an issue in the experiments on voluntary contributions to public goods. Time is condensed, with rounds of public-good games taking place in proximity in time to one another.

[15] If it is known that economists behave strictly rationally and therefore non-cooperatively, we would expect people who are not economists to cooperate when playing the public-good game among themselves but not to cooperate when they are told that they will be playing the public-good game against economists. Evidence from experiments suggests that this is the case.

much nicer they are than the non-cooperating types with whom they are matched in an experiment. The sums of money involved in the experiments (such as $10) are often sufficiently small for the self-affirmation of identity to be achievable at low cost.

Experimental evidence and public finance

Although public-good experiments show that people often cooperate, societies do not rely on voluntary contributions to finance spending on public goods. If reliance on voluntary payments to finance public goods were possible, there would be no need to impose taxes; with taxes imposed, there would be no tax evasion.

Supplement S3A: Group size and voluntary public-good contributions

The Nash equilibrium for voluntary financing of public goods depends on the number of people who benefit from a public good. Supplement S3A considers the consequences for free riding and total voluntary contributions to a public good when the size of a group increases. Effectiveness of voluntary provision of public goods is measured as the ratio between total voluntary contributions in the Nash equilibrium and total contributions as would be provided through the efficient Lindahl consensus. The effectiveness of voluntary collective action in providing public goods, in general, declines as group size increases.

Complexity in sequential and discrete public-good games

Public-good games can be quite complex when decisions about voluntary payment are made sequentially over time. For example, when valuations of public goods differ, a high-valuation person has an incentive to wait for a low-valuation person to contribute first. By contributing first, a high-valuation person may spend enough on the public good to satisfy the demand of the low-valuation person, and the low-valuation person would then contribute nothing. A high-valuation person may be prepared to contribute $5,000 for a neighborhood park for children if no one else contributes, whereas a low-valuation person is satisfied with spending $1,000 if no one else contributes. The two people know each other's valuation. The high-valuation person knows that if he or she contributes more than $1,000, the low-valuation person will contribute nothing and therefore waits for the low-valuation person to contribute first. The low-valuation person, however, waits for the high-valuation person to pay for the public good. Each person has an incentive to wait for the other to contribute first. However, utility is lost by waiting and deferring supply of the public good. The two people are engaged in a game in which the question is how costs will be shared (there is no asymmetric information). Such games involve bargaining. The person who is more patient has an advantage. A person who is pregnant has an advantage over a person who already has a child.

A discrete public good requires a minimal contribution before any benefit is provided. Donors may make pledges that become contributions only if total pledges reach the threshold at which benefits begin. When nearly enough money has been pledged, individuals have an incentive to add pledges to reach the threshold. However, everyone knows that everyone else has an incentive to provide the money that will allow the threshold to be reached. We can predict, nonetheless, that if a million dollars has been pledged for medical equipment for a children's hospital and only $100 more is required to reach the cost of the equipment, obtaining the additional $100 will not be difficult. Indeed, there may be a contest to provide the last payment because of utility from self-esteem or social approval.

C. Weakest-link and volunteer-type public goods

For a public good for which contributions are described by the prisoners' dilemma, the amount of the public good available is the sum of everyone's contributions. That is, when n people make contributions g_i $(i = 1, \ldots, n)$, the total quantity available is the sum:

$$G = \sum_{i=1}^{n} g_i. \tag{3.24}$$

For other types of public goods that are not characterized by the prisoners' dilemma, the summation of personal contributions in expression (3.24) to obtain total availability of a public good does not apply.

Weakest-link public goods

A weakest-link public good has the property that the amount of the public good available to everybody is the *least amount* that is provided by any member of a population. When person i provides g_i, the amount G available to everyone is therefore:

$$G = \min(g_1, g_2, g_3, \ldots, g_n) = G_1 = G_2 = G_3 = \cdots = G_n \tag{3.25}$$

For example, if three people provide 5, 7, and 12, the amount available to everyone is the smallest amount 5. The resources used in providing more than 5 will have been wasted. The amount 5 is available because each person has provided *at least* 5. An example is a seawall that protects homes against seawater on a circular island.[16] Homeowners construct individual segments of the protective wall along the shore facing their house. The public good is defense against encroaching seawater – which can enter anywhere along the shore of the island and then

[16] This is the example that was used by Jack Hirshleifer (1925–2005) when he introduced the concept of weakest-link public goods (Hirshleifer, 1983).

flow on and spread out to flood all houses on the island. The level of protection is determined by the lowest height of any one homeowner's wall.

For weakest-link public goods, the lowest standard therefore determines the overall standard. A neighborhood, for example, can be unsafe because of the behavior of one person. The quality of a road is determined by its most impassable section. The effectiveness of defense is determined at the weakest link in the defensive chain. The time taken for a group to complete a hike is determined by the fitness of the most unfit hiker.[17]

We return to the example of the seawall, with two homeowners on the island. The choice is binary, whether or not to spend on the seawall, and decisions are made simultaneously and without prior communication. The public good is provided only if both people contribute.

For example, the two people each have $10. Their binary choice is to spend $6 or nothing on the seawall. If they both spend $6, their total spending of $12 results in $B_1 = B_2 = 24$; that is, they each obtain benefit of 24 from the seawall that is provided. If one person alone spends $6, the payment for the seawall is wasted: the person who spent the money is left with $4 and the person who did not contribute remains with the original $10. When neither person contributes, both remain with their original $10.

The consequence is the structure of benefits (or payoffs) shown in table 3.2. There are Nash equilibria at both (24, 24) and (10, 10). The efficient outcome is (24, 24), in which total benefit $\sum B$ is 48. This is also the personally most advantageous outcome for each person (because 24 is the maximum that a person can achieve). This is evidently the outcome that both people want. There is, however, no dominant strategy to guide behavior. Whether one person's best decision is to build a section of wall depends on whether the other person builds a section of wall.

TABLE 3.2. WEAKEST-LINK PUBLIC GOODS

	Person 2 contributes	Person 2 does not contribute
Person 1 contributes	24, 24 $(0.3) \cdot (0.3) = 0.09$	4, 10 $(0.3) \cdot (0.7) = 0.21$
Person 1 does not contribute	10, 4 $(0.7) \cdot (0.3) = 0.21$	10, 10 $(0.7) \cdot (0.7) = 0.49$

[17] Choral singing or a musical performance by a symphony orchestra or band consists of collective inputs of singers and performers to provide the public good, which is the song or the music. The quality of the public good is determined by the lowest quality input because a poor-quality singer or performer can ruin the performance of everyone else. Likewise, a football team is a public good in terms of effectiveness and the team may be as good as its weakest link.

With no dominant strategy, we look for a mixed-strategy equilibrium, which describes probabilities of taking different actions. We denote by P the probability of one person contributing to the public good that makes the other person indifferent between contributing and not contributing. We can establish that the equilibrium value of P is *0.3*, which – because the game is symmetric – applies to both people.[18] Table 3.2 shows the probabilities of the four possible outcomes.[19]

For weakest-link public goods, a society faces a *coordination* problem. Everyone wants to contribute to provide the public good, but one person's contribution alone is not sufficient.[20]

Sequential decisions solve the coordination problem. The first person to decide contributes (builds a section of the seawall) and the best response of the second person is to do likewise. The outcome of sequential decisions is therefore the efficient Nash equilibrium at (24, 24). In figure 3.8 YES and NO refer to whether a person contributes. Person 1 arbitrarily decides first. Because this is a game with complete information, person 1 knows how person 2 will respond to his or her decision. Person 1 realizes that not contributing to the public good will lead person 2 to also not contribute and that the outcome will be at (10, 10). If person 1 decides to contribute, person 2's best response will be to contribute and the outcome will be at (24, 24). Person 1 therefore contributes (or chooses yes in figure 3.8). Person 2 then also chooses yes, and the public good is supplied at (24, 24).

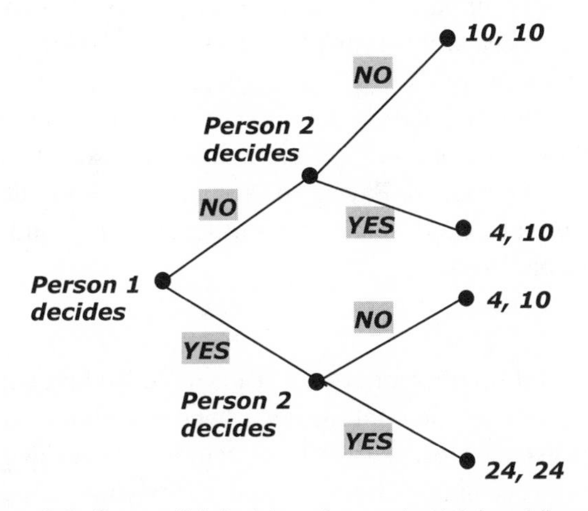

Figure 3.8. Sequential decisions for weakest-link public goods.

[18] The expected benefit of person 1 from providing the public good is $\{24P + 4(1 - P)\}$. Person 1 can obtain a return of 10 with certainty by not providing the public good. Person 1 is therefore indifferent between providing and not providing the public good when $\{24P + 4(1 - P)\} = 10$. Solving for P gives 0.3.

[19] The public good is provided with probability $(0.3) \cdot (0.3) = 9$ percent. With probability $(0.7) \cdot (0.7) = 49$ percent, neither person contributes to the public good. Each person contributes when the other does not with probability $(0.3) \cdot (0.7) = 21$ percent, so the probability that one person wastefully contributes is 42 percent.

[20] The weakest-link game in table 3.2 is an example of a coordination game.

When populations are large, the efficient outcome is likewise achieved through sequential decisions. The person deciding first contributes, as does the second person and all others in turn. With rational behavior, we expect everyone to contribute and the public good to be provided.

Cheap talk

Cheap talk is a term used to describe a declaration of intent on which it is costless to renege. In the prisoners' dilemma, someone might promise to cooperate by contributing to the public good, but not cooperating yields a better personal outcome. A promise of cooperation in the prisoners' dilemma is thus cheap talk. However, in coordination games such as supply of weakest-link public goods, cheap talk provides valuable communication. It is in the self-interest of people who declare that they will contribute to the public good to actually do so. Others also declare their intentions to contribute and it is in everyone's interest to follow through with their declared intentions. The coordination problem is solved and the public good is supplied.[21]

A role for government

A government can enforce and thereby coordinate individual decisions about weakest-link public goods. In the example of the protective seawall, a government could ensure that private decisions are coordinated by mandating minimum heights for compulsory, privately financed seawalls. Taxation and public spending are not necessary because everyone has an interest in participating to provide the efficient outcome. In cases in which strategic behavior is described by the prisoners' dilemma, the role of government is to avoid free riding; in the case of weakest-link public goods, free riding is impossible because unless everyone pays, the public good is not provided. Paying for a weakest-link public good is almost like paying for a private good. Every person needs to pay and wants to pay – provided everyone else pays.

Different standards

People might want different standards. For example, some people may want a seawall that covers reasonable contingencies, whereas others may want protection against tidal waves or storm surges that occur with very low probability. The people who want a very high wall might consider paying the people who want

[21] Harm is done if some people do not follow through with declared intentions. If a group of people promises to appear at a hearing to complain about high-speed traffic in their neighborhood or at a school to complain about an ineffective teacher, and if *everyone's presence* is required for credibility, there is a cost imposed on people who attend as they declared they would, if others renege on their promise and do not attend. Everyone would gain – the people who attended and the people who did not – if the public good, here in the form of public pressure for enforcement of traffic regulations or a better teacher, were provided. In the weakest-link case, the public good is, therefore, not provided if some people lack the self-discipline to follow through with their declarations; in not acting according to their declarations, such people harm others as well as themselves.

lower walls to increase the height of their part of the wall. However, such offers of payment provide incentives for free-riding behavior. People who, in fact, want a high wall benefit from declaring that they would be happy with a low wall.[22]

Volunteer-type public goods

Volunteer-type public goods are a second category of public goods that differs from the prisoners' dilemma. In this case, the quantity or standard of the public good is the *maximal* amount provided through someone's personal contribution. That is:

$$G = \max(g_1, g_2, g_3, \ldots, g_n) = G_1 = G_2 = G_3 = \cdots = G_n \tag{3.26}$$

If three people provide (4, 10, 15), the amount available is 15 and the resources used by the people providing the smaller amounts have been wasted. Such an outcome is not a Nash equilibrium because the people providing the lower amounts (4, 10) are better off providing zero, given that the third person is providing 15.

Help might be required to move a disabled car to the side of the road or to thwart an assault or a robbery. All bystanders may feel better when help is provided to a person in need: the awareness that people in need are being helped is the collective benefit or public good. The person being helped receives private benefit from the assistance that is given. Although many people are pleased that someone in need is helped, the person who actually provides the assistance incurs a personal cost. A person who stops to remove a rock from a road incurs a personal cost but provides benefits to other drivers. If a bottle has been broken on a path, there is a personal cost of picking up the broken glass, but everyone benefits. Who will ask people creating a disturbance in a movie theater to be quiet? When two exams are scheduled at unreasonably close times, who will ask for rescheduling of the exams, with benefit to everyone? If one person must be present at a meeting to represent a group of people, who will come to the meeting? A story from the Netherlands tells of a boy who placed his finger in a hole in a dike to stem the inflow of water that would have flooded the land. The boy is a hero in the story because he personally provided a public good to the rest of the population; however, in the nature of public goods, by his actions he personally benefited by saving himself. Passengers lining up to board a plane may notice that someone is acting suspiciously. However, they may not wish to voice their suspicion to security personnel because of the personal cost through embarrassment of being mistaken about the intentions of the suspicious-looking person. A passenger who brings the suspicious person to the attention of the security personnel incurs a personal cost. Everyone benefits when the suspicious person is found to be harmless – or not. Everyone in a neighborhood may know that a gang is

[22] When different people want different standards, the standard can be determined by voting. We shall study voting in chapter 6.

making the streets unsafe. Someone who reports the identity of gang members to the police and is willing to testify in court incurs a personal cost of possible retribution and provides a public-good benefit for other neighborhood residents. When a judge makes an incorrect decision, a person who appeals and overturns the decision provides a pure public good for everyone else who gains from the correct precedent being established.[23]

Supply of a volunteer public good may require contributions from more than one person. Two people may be required to push a disabled car to the side of the road or to overpower a mugger. A number of passengers on a plane may have to act to overcome terrorists. As long as not all beneficiaries are required to contribute to providing the public good, we have a good that is similar to a volunteer-type public good.

Who provides the public good?

Volunteer-type public goods are provided personally. Who will bear the personal cost of providing the volunteer public good? When individuals differ in valuation of *benefits* from the public good and everyone knows each other's valuation, a high-valuation person is expected to provide the public good. Everyone knows that the high-valuation person has the most to gain. If personal *costs* of providing the public good differ and are known to all, a low-cost person is expected to provide the public good. A group of hikers may have run out of water. The hikers decide that the group should rest under a tree and send one person to bring help and water. The fittest person might volunteer to go for help (the lowest cost person). Or, a hiker who needs special medication may volunteer to go for help to ensure that he or she receives the medication on time (the highest valuation person then goes). The maximum-valuation or minimum-cost person is maximizing personal benefit by "volunteering." The "volunteer" makes the calculation that he or she should go to find help rather than rely on others. Others gain because of the public-good nature of the benefit.

The game of "chicken"

If everyone prefers that the cost of volunteering be imposed on others, a game of "chicken" emerges. When nobody wants to go for help and everybody waits for others to go, it is possible that no one might go. Table 3.3 shows the relationship between a volunteer-type decision and the game of chicken. The game is symmetric, with two identical people confronting the same costs and benefits. The public good provides a common benefit of 12 and the personal cost to any person providing the public good is 2. It is sufficient for one person to incur the cost of 2 for the public good to be provided. Each person knows the benefits and costs of the other, so the two people know they have identical benefits and costs.

[23] Hirshleifer (1983) used the description "best-shot" to characterize such public goods. He was motivated by a situation in which people are being shot at and wish to defend themselves by shooting back. The public good of defense for the group under attack is provided by the "best shot."

TABLE 3.3. VOLUNTEER-TYPE PUBLIC GOODS AND THE GAME OF CHICKEN

	Person 2 contributes	Person 2 does not contribute
Person 1 contributes	10, 10 $(0.8) \cdot (0.8) = 0.64$	10, 12 $(0.8) \cdot (0.2) = 0.16$
Person 1 does not contribute	12, 10 $(0.2) \cdot (0.8) = 0.16$	2, 2 $(0.2) \cdot (0.2) = 0.04$

When neither person provides the public good, both people have a benefit of 2. A person who provides the public good has a benefit of $(12 - 2) = 10$. The best personal outcome of 12 is obtained when the other person incurs the cost of providing the public good.

The total benefit when both people provide the public good is $(10 + 10) = 20$. This is not a Nash equilibrium.[24] The minimum total benefit is $(2 + 2) = 4$ when neither person provides the public good. This also is not a Nash equilibrium.[25] There are Nash equilibria at (12, 10) and (10, 12), where one person provides the public good and the other does not. The two Nash equilibria are also efficient because total benefit is maximal $(12 + 10) = 22$.[26] Again, there is no dominant strategy.[27] In the mixed-strategy equilibrium, the probability that either person will provide the public good is 0.8.[28] Table 3.3 shows the probabilities of the four different possible outcomes.[29]

We have been describing simultaneous decisions, or decisions made by one person who does not know the decision made by the other person. Figure 3.9 shows the outcome when decisions are made sequentially.

[24] Given that one person is providing the public good, the other person can do better by not providing the public good, thereby obtaining a benefit of 12 rather than 10.

[25] A person can personally do better by providing the public good, given that the other person does not.

[26] For volunteer public goods, there are as many efficient Nash equilibria as there are people because an efficient equilibrium requires that one person alone contributes to provide the public good.

[27] If the other person provides the public good, the best response is not to provide the public good. If the other person does not provide the public good, the best response is to provide the public good. Neither person knows whether the other person will provide the public good.

[28] We denote by P_2 the probability that person 2 will provide the public good. Person 1's expected benefit from not providing the public good is $\{12P_2 + 2(1 - P_2)\}$. By providing the public good, person 1 obtains a benefit of 10 with certainty, independently of person 2's decision. Person 1 is indifferent between providing and not providing the public good when $\{12P_2 + 2(1 - P_2)\} = 10$. Solving reveals that person 1 is indifferent between providing and not providing the public good when $P_2 = 0.8$. Because behavior is symmetric, the solution for the probability P_1 that person 1 will act to provide the public good is also 0.8.

[29] The public good is not provided with a probability of 4 percent. In the other three cases, the public good is provided (because it is sufficient that one person provide the public good); therefore, the probability that the public good will be provided is $(64 + 32) = 96$ percent. Although the probability that the public good will be provided is here quite high, the probability of an *efficient* outcome is only $(0.16 + 0.16) = 32$ percent. A wasteful duplicative outcome occurs with the probability of 64 percent.

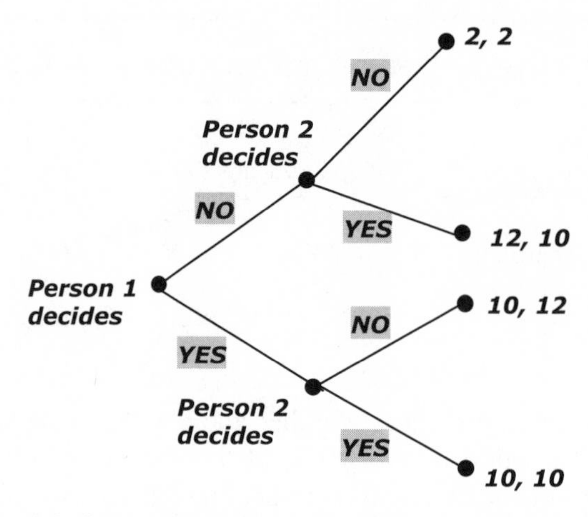

Figure 3.9. Sequential decisions for volunteer-type public goods.

In figure 3.9, YES and NO again refer to whether a person contributes and person 1 again arbitrarily decides first. Person 1 wants to achieve the outcome (12, 10), which gives maximum benefit (or payoff) of 12. Person 1 therefore chooses not to supply the public good, knowing that person 2 will be left with a choice between 2 if he or she does not supply the public good and 10 if he or she does. The outcome is then (12, 10), as person 1 wanted. The outcome of sequential decisions is efficient. One person (the second to decide) supplies the public good. Sequential decisions determine which of the two efficient Nash equilibria will be obtained. The first person to decide imposes the cost of supply on the second person.[30]

With larger populations and sequential decisions, each person can choose to rely on the next person, if there is a next person. If the number of people is a known finite number – for example, 20 – then the 20th person provides the public good. The last person has no one else on whom to rely. The situation is more complex when there is uncertainty about the number of people so that the 19th person, for example, is not sure whether there is a 20th person. People then have to weigh the personal benefit obtained with certainty through personal action against the uncertain outcome when they choose to rely on someone else providing the public good, when there may be no one else.[31]

[30] Or, people will seek ways of committing not to provide the public good, leaving the public good to be supplied by the last person who has not committed.

[31] We can also consider simultaneous decisions by many people. We might also want to consider that people, in general, do not know each other's benefits or costs, which introduces the additional uncertainty that people do not know each other's incentives to provide the public good. In such circumstances, does a larger population increase the likelihood that the public good will be provided? The larger the population, the greater is the likelihood that at least one person will provide the public good. At the same time, however, the greater is the number of other people on whom each individual can rely perhaps to provide the public good. Because the two effects counter one another, an increase in population can increase or decrease the probability of someone providing

Social norms and personal behavior

Collective benefits within a household often take the form of personally provided volunteer-type public goods. For example, it may be sufficient for one person to cook a meal, do the grocery shopping, clean the house, replace a lightbulb or fuse, or pay the bills. In such cases, supply of volunteer-type public goods is often based on convention. Within a household, conventions are established by repeated personal contact that may give rise to either specialization or taking turns in performing different tasks. Within broader society, we cannot rely on similar conventions. Social norms, however, influence personal behavior through our expectations about how we feel we should act in different situations. For example, people who stop to help a stranded driver even if they are on their way to a movie and will be late are responding to the social norm of helping others in distress and are not relying on the likelihood that others will provide help. Social norms affect behavior through stigma and social esteem (disapproval or approval by others) or conscience (self-disapproval of one's own behavior). A society in which the social norm is to take personal responsibility to provide volunteer-type public goods is more pleasant than a society in which the norm is to wait for others to act.[32]

The role for government

Because decisions are personal and voluntary, other than through education, there is no role for government for volunteer-type public goods.

Personal freedom as a voluntarily privately supplied public good

A contribution to personal freedom is a voluntarily privately supplied public good. The public good of personal freedom is provided by replacing autocratic rulers with democratic institutions. With the exception the deposed dictator and his inner circle of associates, everyone benefits from personal freedom.

The people who actively participate in attempting to displace autocratic rulers personally bear costs by exposing themselves to danger if the attempt at revolt or revolution fails. The circumstances are those of a volunteer-type public good because the participation of everyone is not required for an autocrat to be deposed. Indeed, we might ask why anyone would participate in a revolt or revolution rather than choose to free ride, for the benefits of freedom will be provided to everyone as a public good, whether or not people actively participate in the revolt or revolution.

Often, revolts and revolutions do not result in personal freedom for the population. The benefits are rather personal for the leaders of the revolution who

the public good. When a population becomes very large, the probability that the public good is supplied approaches a finite limit. For elaboration, see Xu (2001).

32 Can people free ride on social norms? If people know that it is the social norm to help others in distress, they might choose not to help because of the belief that others will help if they do not. Such behavior undermines the social norm.

become less-than-democratic rulers of the country.[33] In other cases, revolutions institutionalized democratic principles but the military leader of the revolutionary forces nonetheless became the ruler after the success of the revolution.[34]

D. National security

Natural security is perhaps the most important of public goods. History is replete with wars through which – as Nietzsche described – the strong imposed their will on the weak with no ethical restraint. Throughout history, rulers and peoples have attacked others to subjugate and to create empires and colonies. The object has been enrichment through conquest and predation rather than through productive activity. War is a limiting case of rent seeking.

> *War is inefficient because of unproductive use of resources in aggression and defense.*

The outcome of war can also be unjust.

> *The outcome of a war is socially unjust when predators win wars.*

It is rational for aggressors to initiate a war only if victory seems inevitable and the expected benefits from the war exceed the expected costs. Rulers and countries that initiated wars and lost miscalculated the ability and will to resist of the people they sought to subjugate – or they misjudged the alliances that would be formed against them.

We are interested in national security and defense because:

> *Deterrence and defense against foreign predators are pure public goods that require public spending.*

When deterrence is achieved, there is no war but resources nonetheless have been used in convincing potential foreign aggressors that war is not worthwhile.

[33] Communist revolutions have resulted in the leader of the revolution becoming the authoritarian post-revolutionary ruler. Lenin (1870–1924) led the communist October Revolution of 1917 in Russia and became the authoritarian ruler after the revolution. Mao Zedong (1893–1976) led the communist forces to victory in China and ruled communist China from 1949 to the end of his life. Fidel Castro led the Cuban revolution in 1959 and remained ruler of communist Cuba until his formal retirement for health reasons in 2008 (informally, his brother had ruled since 2006). The famed French Revolution of 1789, which proclaimed principles of "liberty, fraternity, and equality," was also followed by dictatorship.

[34] In England, parliament led a revolution against the king, Charles I, who was executed in 1649. In that revolution, members of a democratic institution (although not representative of all the people) acted against a king. The leader of the parliamentary military forces, Oliver Cromwell (1599–1658), became "Lord Protector" and oversaw institutionalization of principles that provided parliament with enduring fiscal responsibilities after the monarchy was restored. The American Revolution of 1776 institutionalized democratic principles in the U.S. Constitution (the democratic principles had already been present, to a large degree, in the laws of the individual American colonies). George Washington (1732–99), who had led the revolutionary army, was elected president of the United States in 1789.

Defense spending as a strategic decision

Defense as a pure public good has the special characteristic that benefits from public spending depend not only on one's *own* spending but also on the spending decisions of the potential adversary. Table 3.4 shows how spending on military preparedness is a prisoners' dilemma. The dominant strategy is to spend. The Nash equilibrium results in (2, 2), in which both countries spend on military preparedness and neutralize one another. The efficient outcome (3, 3) requires that neither country undertake military spending. If credible commitment not to spend is impossible, a promise to cooperate is cheap talk. If a promise to not arm or to develop weapons secretly cannot be monitored, the outcome is the inefficient Nash equilibrium (2, 2). This outcome is described as an "arms race."

Attempts at cooperation to escape the inefficient Nash equilibrium (2, 2) to arrive at (3, 3) can take the form of international treaties that limit the types of weapons and defensive systems that countries can have. Efforts then, however, can be redirected at finding new ways to expand military capabilities that are outside of the treaties. The treaties are also sometimes not honored: nuclear capability has been developed even though governments signed treaties declaring that they would not do so.

TABLE 3.4. SPENDING ON MILITARY PREPAREDNESS AS A PRISONERS' DILEMMA

	Country 2 does not spend on military preparedness	Country 2 spends on military preparedness
Country 1 does not spend on military preparedness	3, 3	1, 4
Country 1 spends on military preparedness	4, 1	2, 2

Defense coalitions

More resources provide more effective deterrence. There are, therefore, incentives for countries to form defense coalitions or military alliances. With national security a pure public good, the benefits from military spending by one country can be freely provided to people in other countries. Free-riding problems can, however, arise in defense coalitions, with governments of some participating countries attempting to underpay and still receive the benefits of being coalition members.

Free riding within a country

Free-riding problems affecting defense can also arise within a country. As in the case of the dilemma that confronted Robinson Crusoe, some people may claim that they object to participating in defense as a matter of principle. If the need for defense is not imagined but real, such people are free riding on the efforts of others.

Governments at times have used conscription (or compulsory participation of the population for defense) to avoid free riding that might take place. At the same time, rather than seeking to free ride, people have volunteered to participate in contributing to defense.

When the participation of everyone in national defense is not required, defense can be publicly financed through payments to people who choose a military career. There is a "volunteer" army because people voluntarily choose military careers. The volunteer army is not an example of a volunteer-type public good because the "volunteers" are being paid. There are, however, elements of volunteer-type public goods if people who choose to serve in the military take the view that defense is necessary (for themselves and their families as well as others) and if incomes in military service do not fully compensate for the personal dangers confronted.

Capabilities and technology

The Nash equilibrium in military spending at (2, 2) in table 3.4 is a symmetric outcome in which countries with equal capabilities spend to maintain a balance of power. Capabilities need not be symmetric. A larger, richer country can mobilize more resources for military capability than a smaller, poorer country. A smaller country may then be at the mercy of a larger, stronger country. There is peace if the strong country is not predatory and does not seek foreign conquests. Indeed:

> *A strong country acting ethically provides a pure public good by sustaining peace in an otherwise anarchic world.*

When there is conflict, wars have often been won by the side with the larger population and more resources available for mobilization. At other times, motivation and determination, as well as a sense of justice, have proven to be decisive rather than population and resources – in particular, when people are defending their country against an aggressor.

Technology has diminished advantages of country size and resources in determining military effectiveness. Nuclear, chemical, and biological weapons have made a country's population and the resources available less important and also have increased the vulnerability of civilian populations. Private markets in nuclear, chemical, and biological weapons – and sales for personal gain by government leaders and officials in some countries – increase the dangers.

Democracy

Democracies do not tend to wage war on one another, nor do democracies initiate conflict.[35] Democracies, however, often have been attacked by nondemocratic

[35] An exception was the U.S. Civil War.

countries. Historical precedent suggests that democracy in all countries would end international conflict and ultimately eliminate the need for defense spending. In autocracies, the ruler personifies the grandeur of the state. The wealth of the state may be the ruler's personal property. Gains from war are likewise personal for the autocratic ruler. The costs of war, on the other hand, are imposed on the population that provides the soldiers and suffers the consequences of retaliation of the countries that were attacked. In democracies, political decision makers and political representatives are accountable to the domestic population that would bear the costs of war. At the same time, political decision makers and political representatives in democracies obtain no personal benefits from aggressive war. We thereby have an economic explanation in terms of personal benefits and costs for why autocracies initiate wars and democracies do not.[36]

> *In autocracies, the ruler personally enjoys the benefits of conquest and imposes the costs on the people; in democracies, the benefits of conquest are not personal but the costs are, so voters oppose the initiation of war.*

Because of personal costs, some voters in democracies may oppose self-defense or may favor deferral of self-defense.

Supply of defense equipment

Because of the enormity of the loss that can be faced if defense is not possible, there are incentives not to rely on foreign suppliers for defense equipment. Reliance on foreign suppliers opens a country's population to the possibility that defense equipment will not be available when required. There is a saying that "countries have interests, not friends." That being the case, foreigners may not honor contracts to supply defense equipment. In general, if a foreign obligation to supply is not honored, it is impossible to organize immediate alternatives through self-supply or from other foreign sources. Governments may therefore prefer to rely on domestic suppliers or own production for defense equipment. Dependence on foreign supply is thereby avoided.

Asymmetric warfare and defense against terrorism

The aim of defense spending is deterrence by revealing means of imposing costs on aggressors through retaliation. Traditionally, the potential aggressor has been

[36] Does electoral uncertainty reduce defense spending in democracies? An incumbent government incurs the political costs of defense spending through reduced present consumption, but if the incumbent government loses the next election, the political benefits from defense spending will accrue to the new government. There are then political incentives to under-spend on defense. Garfinkel (1994) proposed such an argument based on political time horizons to explain data showing lower military spending in democracies than under nondemocratic regimes. Military spending is used by nondemocratic regimes to subjugate their own people, who might otherwise demand democratic institutions, which also explains why military spending is higher in autocratic than in democratic regimes.

the government of another country. Although governments in different countries have aided and abetted terrorism – and have given safe haven to terrorists – defense against terrorism differs from defense against foreign governments because warfare is asymmetric. Terrorists do not use traditional military means of aggression involving armies; rather, terrorists attempt to hide from view and emerge randomly to attack people going about their everyday lives. The aim of terrorists is randomly to kill and maim so as to spread fear, so that people become terrified and so that the will to resist the terrorists' demands is weakened.[37]

The personal costs of terrorism

Defense against terror is costly because of public spending on national security. There are as well personal costs of terrorism incurred through personal expenses and inconveniences. Security searches at airports increase the costs of travel and increase travel time. Travelers are subject to indignities of personal search. There are personal costs in the inconvenience that personal items cannot be taken onto a plane because terrorists in the past attempted to crash airliners using detonating liquids intended to resemble water or cosmetics. There is general anxiety in knowing that terrorists would kill us if they could and that they might have access to nerve gas, to the virus that causes smallpox, to chemical or biological weapons, or to bombs containing radioactive material that can be transported in suitcases. The greatest private cost of terrorism, of course, is incurred by people who lose their life or are maimed in a terrorist attack – or suffer the personal loss of family and friends.

Poverty and terrorism

Is terrorism the consequence of frustration due to poverty or low incomes in foreign countries? If this were so, there would be a ready economic solution to the problem of terrorism: terrorism could be stopped through economic development. Terrorism does not, however, usually originate among poor people. For example, the Islamic terrorists who attacked the United States on September 11, 2001, were not from the poorer segments of their society. Poor people in their home society cannot afford to send their children abroad to study. The terrorists were from the elite classes who have the means to send their sons to study abroad. Studies of the relationship between education and poverty and the propensity to engage in terrorism show that terrorists who engage in attacks in Western democracies overall tend to be neither uneducated nor poor.[38]

[37] On September 11, 2001, some 3,000 people were killed in the United States by 19 Islamic terrorists who did not use typical military weapons. The attackers were from different countries (however, 15 of the attackers were citizens of one country, the kingdom of Saudi Arabia). The attack on the United States demonstrated how harm could be done without advanced military technology. Asymmetric warfare through terrorist attacks has occurred in many other locations, before and after the act on September 11, 2001, on the United States.

[38] Krueger and Maleckova (2003) reviewed the evidence showing that Islamic terrorists are not uneducated and are not motivated by poverty or low incomes.

What do terrorists want?

Terrorists often have supreme-value objectives.

> *A supreme-value objective is an objective that is sought without the possibility of compromise.*

For example, radical Islam requires adherents to make every possible personal sacrifice, including giving up their life, to achieve the supreme-value objective of subjugating the non-Islamic world to Islam – the word *Islam* means submission. The supreme values require the pursuit of objectives to be ongoing, although lulls and truces are permitted if the nonbelievers are temporarily too strong to overcome.

Incentives and rewards

Incentives and rewards promote terrorism. In the case of radical Islam, male Muslims who die in the course of seeking the fulfillment of the supreme-value objectives are martyrs who, it is believed, will be provided with 72 virgins in heaven. The rewards promised in the next world lead radical Islamic terrorists to look forward to death. A favored slogan of radical Islam is: "We love death more than you love life." Parents of terrorists declare that they are proud of their children for being martyrs and that they look forward to their other children having the same opportunity. Before their actual death, Islamic terrorists participate in ceremonies in which they are honored; in the honor bestowed in the ceremonies, they "die before they die."[39]

Radical Islam has not been the source of all terrorism nor of all suicide terrorism; Tamils in Sri Lanka have, for example, also killed people by killing themselves. However, young men can be extremely dangerous when they fervently believe that after they die in the act of killing or maiming nonbelievers, 72 virgins will await them. Male-female contact is inhibited when a culture designates the death penalty, inflicted by parents or brothers, for a woman who was found to be in the unaccompanied presence of a male from outside her extended family.[40] Polygamy also leaves some men without women. When female company in this world is hard to come by, the attractions for men of the virgins promised in a next world can become compelling.[41]

[39] Bernholz (2004) described supreme values and Islamic terrorism. On the ceremonies where the suicide terrorists are honored and declared dead before they die, see Murawiec (2008).

[40] The penalty for a woman (or girl) who has been raped is death on the supposition that the rape was the consequence of immodest attire or behavior that attracted the man or men.

[41] There have been cases where the suicide killers were women. The women are not promised afterlife benefits parallel to the benefits of men. When women have been sent to commit suicide, the alternative has often been a death at the hands of family members for having "dishonored the family." The women are offered the alternative of dying for the cause of Islam by killing nonbelievers.

The public-policy question in defense against suicide terrorism is:

> *How can deterrence be effective when the adversary wants to die – or how is it possible to deter those who already regard themselves as dead?*

Deterring terrorism

The terrorists who attacked the United States on September 11, 2001, or the commuters in London on July 7, 2007, and the many victims in other cases in other countries, knew with certainty beforehand that they would die. Terrorists who seek death cannot be deterred by threats of death. Terrorists, however, may care about the assets and wealth of their parents and their families, who the evidence shows are in general not poor. Given that the terrorists are intent on dying, their possible concern for parents and families offers the only way to deter acts of terrorism. An announcement might, therefore, be made that the assets of families of terrorists will be appropriated. There is, however, a moral dilemma in a policy of punishing terrorists' families because the families did not themselves commit terrorist acts. Nonetheless, intending terrorists who have been warned beforehand of the financial cost that will be imposed on their families may be deterred from committing acts of terror. Deterrence will then have been effective and the assets of the terrorists' families will not be appropriated. This is the outcome sought by the societies that the terrorists seek to harm.

TABLE 3.5. PENALTIES ON FAMILY ASSETS

	Terrorists' decision	
Victims' decision	Commit terrorist acts	Do not commit terrorist acts
Penalties imposed on terrorists' families	2, 3	3, 1
No penalties imposed on terrorists' families	1, 4	4, 2

Table 3.5 shows the valuation and ranking of outcomes of victims of terrorism and terrorists when the instrument of public policy is a financial penalty imposed on terrorists' families. The first number is the benefit to the victims; the second number is the benefit to the terrorists.

In table 3.5, the terrorists' preferred outcome of 4 is obtained when they can kill nonbelievers without penalties to their families. The terrorists' least preferred outcome of 1 is when there are penalties imposed on their families and no acts of terrorism have been committed. The terrorists have a benefit of 3 when they commit acts of terrorism and their families incur a cost; they have a benefit of 2 if they do not commit acts of terrorism and no penalty is imposed on their families.

The terrorists' intended victims do not seek direct benefit from appropriation of the assets of terrorists' families. The terrorists' victims want only that the threat of the penalty be successful in deterring terrorism. The ranking of outcomes for victims of terrorism in table 3.5 shows that the intended victims place first priority

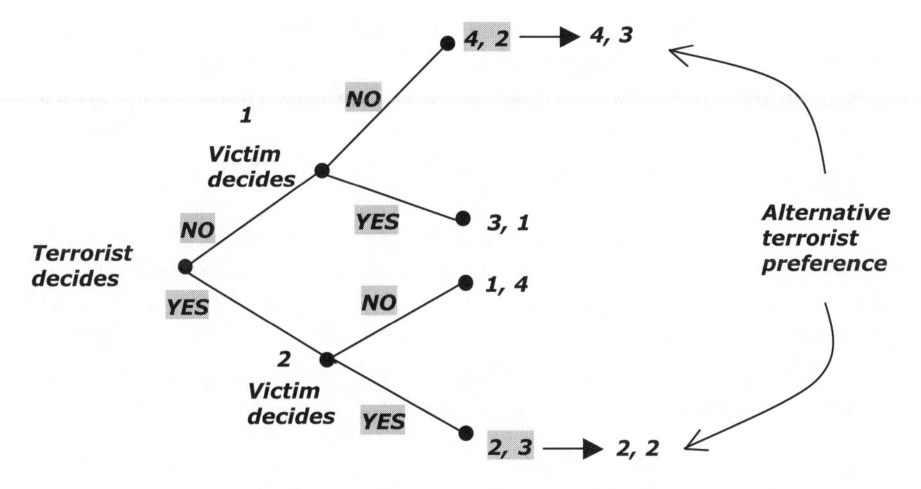

Figure 3.10. Penalties on family assets.

on avoiding terrorism. Their preferred outcome 4 occurs when there is no terrorism and no penalty is imposed on terrorists' families; 3 is the outcome when there is no terrorism and a penalty is imposed; terrorists' victims rank outcomes in which terrorist acts occur as least desirable at 2 and at 1.

Neither the victims of terrorism nor the terrorists want the terrorists' families to be penalized: for both terrorists' intended victims and terrorists themselves, the respective best outcomes of 4 occur with no penalties on terrorists' families. The difference is that terrorists' intended victims want no penalty on family assets with no terrorism; the terrorists want no penalty on their families with terrorism.

The victims of terrorism have no dominant strategy. The dominant strategy of the terrorists is to commit acts of terrorism. With the terrorists choosing terrorism, the Nash equilibrium is at (2, 3), where acts of terrorism are committed and penalties are imposed on terrorists' families.

Figure 3.10 shows sequential decisions. The terrorists decide first whether to commit acts of terror. The outcomes at (3, 1) and (1, 4) are not equilibrium possibilities.[42] Terrorists are better off at (2, 3) than at (4, 2). The terrorists, therefore, ensure that (2, 3) is the equilibrium by choosing to commit acts of terrorism. Deterrence has been ineffective because the terrorists choose terrorism, notwithstanding the penalty on their families.

However, terrorists may have alternative rankings of outcomes. In the alternative terrorists' preferences shown in figure 3.10, intending terrorists prefer the (no, no) outcome (no terrorism, no penalty) to the (yes, yes) outcome (terrorism and penalty on their family). Refraining from committing acts of terrorism results in the outcome (4, 3).

[42] If there is no terrorism, the intended victims will never choose to penalize the family. In figure 3.10, when the victims decide at node 1, they will always choose to obtain 4 by not penalizing the family; therefore, (3, 1) cannot be an equilibrium choice. When there is terrorism, the victims at node 2 penalize the family, in accordance with the public policy of attempting deterrence.

The terrorists determine the outcome by choosing first. The "games" between terrorists and their victims are repeated over time. Whether a policy of penalizing families through appropriation of family assets is effective in deterring terrorism depends of the terrorists' rankings of outcomes. Without the penalty, there is no credible deterrent for the intending terrorists who prefer the (no, no) solution in figure 3.10.

A penalty on terrorists' families may be unjust. Of course, it is also unjust to find oneself a passenger on a flight that is about to crash because of terrorists seeking martyrdom and virgins; or being at work and finding that a plane is crashing through the window; or commuting to work in a train or bus and finding ourselves in the presence of a terrorist whose push of a button will send him to his sought-after paradise and virgins, and us – if we are lucky – to a hospital.

Moral dilemmas

Terrorism poses moral dilemmas other than whether to impose financial penalties on terrorists' families. For example, there is a moral dilemma if terrorists use ambulances as transport to reach their victims. Ambulances should be used to transport people who are ill or injured; however, terrorists will have established the precedent that ambulances also may transport terrorists. There is a moral dilemma if the presumption is no longer that only injured or ill people are transported in ambulances. The terrorists who use the ambulances know that this moral dilemma will arise and hope to be able to continue to use ambulances for safe transportation. Another moral dilemma arises when terrorists use children as human shields; if self-defense by the terrorists' intended victims results in the deaths of the children, the terrorist leaders rely on the media to publicize the tragic outcome, hoping that blame will be placed on the intended victims.

Profiling

A civilized society does not discriminate based on color, creed, or beliefs. The theory of statistically based discrimination nonetheless indicates that there are efficiency gains from profiling when prior evidence indicates that people with identifiable visible attributes or beliefs are more likely to commit terrorist acts than others. Yet, using profiling to discriminate in the questioning and detaining of people contradicts civil liberties. Many people might be waiting to board a plane, and prior evidence may indicate that only people fitting particular profiles have ever hijacked and crashed planes. If only some people among the passengers waiting to board the plane have profiles associated with terrorists, should all passengers be searched and questioned, or should special attention be directed at the people that fit the profile of terrorists? Equal treatment of all passengers is costly in terms of passengers' time and deployment of security personnel. Discrimination through profiling, however, violates the principle that people should be treated equally and are innocent of wrongdoing unless proven otherwise. Terrorism introduces a moral dilemma because of the efficiency of profiling.

Collective punishment

Another moral dilemma arises because of collective punishment when it is impossible to distinguish between intending terrorists and well-meaning people. A group of people may wish to visit a university campus and only one of the visitors wishes to detonate himself as a human bomb in a student cafeteria. Refusing the entire group entry to the campus imposes collective punishment. People who regard human rights as more important than saving innocent lives will object to the collective punishment. We have defined *cheap talk* as proclamations that have no personal consequences. If people claiming that human rights are more important than saving lives will not be in the university cafeteria, the proclamation of the preeminence of human rights over saving lives is cheap talk. The proclamation is expressive behavior; people who make the proclamation can feel good because they can take a position that they view as morally meritorious and because they are not personally exposed to danger.

Dilemmas of human rights

Judges decide whether the constitution has been respected and the law has been obeyed, and lawyers defend clients. As citizens, we also want the rule of law. When deterrence is impossible and the only recourse in defense against terror is preemption, government agencies responsible for protecting a society against terrorism may seek information about impending terrorist attacks by means that depart from usual procedures in conditions of arrest and holding suspects. Societies again face dilemmas: the choice is between preempting terrorism and violating human rights. In this dilemma, the legal profession has self-interest in insisting on the strict application of legal procedures; adherence to these procedures is the source of the legal profession's personal incomes. The self-interest of the legal profession is not advanced when their prospective clients are covertly held for extended interrogation or are tried by military tribunals.

Social and political divisions

The moral dilemmas that arise because of terrorism can be socially and politically divisive. On one side of the debate is the position that attempts should be made to come to terms with and appease terrorists. On the other side of the debate, the evidence may be presented showing that in the course of history, policies of appeasement when adversaries have supreme-value objectives have never succeeded because supreme-value adversaries do not accept compromises.[43]

[43] For the evidence on different supreme-value systems throughout history, see Bernholz (1993). In a famous case of attempted appeasement, Neville Chamberlain, a prime minister of the United Kingdom, declared in 1938 that by making concessions to the supreme-value German government (Germany was allowed to annex a part of the neighboring country of Czechoslovakia, which was too weak to resist), he had brought "peace in our time." The United Kingdom was at war with Germany the following year. The German leader declared that the agreement with Chamberlain had the worth of a scrap of paper.

Supporters of a position of appeasement of terrorists might also be accused of seeking to justify the terrorists' behavior and of placing the blame for terrorism on the victims of terrorism. The social and political divisions due to the debate can be profound.[44]

3.2 Information and Public Goods

We now return to public goods more generally and consider the question:

> *Can governments solve the asymmetric-information and free-rider problems that prevent efficient financing of public goods through voluntary payments?*

We shall seek answers to this question only for public goods of the prisoners'-dilemma type. In the case of volunteer-type public goods, free riding is efficient; in the case of weakest-link public goods, no one wants to free ride; in the case of national security, the behavior of adversaries more so than domestic preferences determines spending on the public good of deterrence or defense. Only for public goods of the prisoners'-dilemma type is there a presumptive role for government to avoid free riding and to attempt to counter preference misrepresentation: when people seek to free ride, government has the advantage of legal coercion of payment for public goods through taxation.

A. Can governments solve the information problem?

The public-good prisoners' dilemma that was shown in table 3.1 makes calling on government to finance public goods appear easier than it is. People were regarded as having identical valuations of a public good, and total spending required for efficient supply of the public good was known. A government could therefore levy *equal taxes* to finance *known* efficient public spending. The more challenging assignment for government is to replicate the efficient Lindahl consensus solution when personal valuations of benefit from public goods differ among people and the personal valuations are private information, so there is asymmetric information.

[44] Battered-wife syndrome is behavior in which – in the course of continual beatings by violent, unstable men – women soul-search, attempting to understand what they have done to deserve the beatings. The women believe that they are to blame or may believe that they have no means of defense, and search for ways to appease the man. The behavior does not change over continual beatings. The analogy is to when ways are sought to appease supreme-value terrorists and to when terrorism is blamed on the victims.

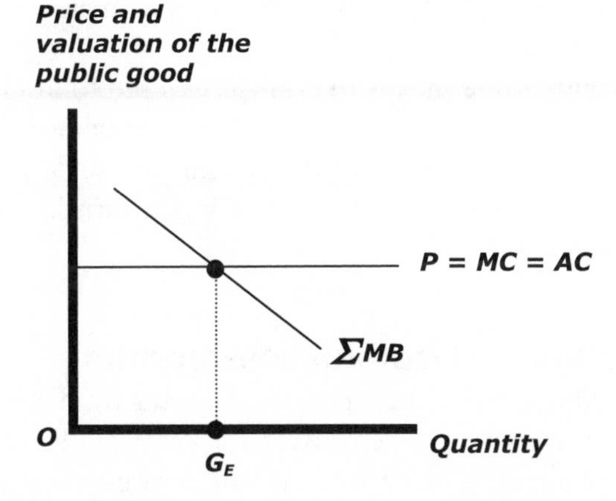

Figure 3.11. Government faces an asymmetric-information problem.

For a population of n people, a government would ideally seek to replace voluntary personal Lindahl prices with compulsory personal per-unit taxes T_i so that for each of the n people in the population in the government's jurisdiction:

$$T_i = MB_i, \quad i = 1, \ldots, n. \tag{3.27}$$

A government does not, however, know the personal benefits MB_i and so cannot set personal taxes to replicate the efficient personal Lindahl prices or cost shares.

People could be asked to state their personal marginal benefits from public goods; however, when people know that their declared marginal benefits determine their personal tax payments, the incentive to understate benefit reappears.

Lacking verifiably true information on personal marginal benefits, governments cannot determine efficient spending on the public good by using the condition for efficient public good supply:

$$\sum_i MB_i = MC. \tag{3.28}$$

In figure 3.11, the price P of a public good is competitively determined under conditions of constant cost ($P = MC = AC$). A government would require information on the sum $\sum MB$ to determine the efficient quantity G_E of the public good. The information, however, is not available because of asymmetric information.

We conclude:

> *Governments levying taxes to finance public goods confront the same asymmetric-information problem that impedes efficient supply through voluntary payments.*

If governments are to achieve efficient supply of public goods, the asymmetric-information problem therefore has to be solved. Incentives have to be provided for people to reveal their *MB* functions that express their valuations of public goods through their willingness to pay.

We shall investigate three means that might be used to attempt to solve the public-good information problem. The means are a mechanism designed to elicit truthful personal responses; a market for payment for use of a public good; and locational choice from among different government jurisdictions that provide public goods to residents.

B. The Clarke tax and truthful self-reporting

People can be asked to declare their personal benefits from a public good, after assurances that public goods will be provided through public spending and that reported personal valuations of benefit will *not* be used to determine personal payments for financing the public good. The government needs to know only the sum of marginal benefits $\sum MB$ to apply the efficiency condition (3.28) and so the reporting of benefits could be anonymous. People know their tax obligations. Because of their small contribution to financing public spending, people have incentives to declare high personal *MB*, which implies asking for high public spending on public goods. Benefits reported without an obligation to pay, and based on others paying, can therefore lead to overstatement of true benefit and thereby to over-provision of public goods. The over-provision of publicly financed public goods contrasts with the under-provision suggested when people are asked to make voluntary personal payments for public goods.

TABLE 3.6. THE CLARKE TAX

Person 1	Person 2	Person 3
100	70	−80
Tax = 10	Tax = 0	Tax = 0

There is a way, however, that incentives can be provided for people to report their benefits from public goods *voluntarily* and *truthfully*. Table 3.6 describes the benefits of two people from a publicly financed public good and the loss imposed by the public good on a third person. The public-good project, for example, might be a highway. Persons 1 and 2 benefit from the highway, although differently. Person 3 lives near the proposed highway and will lose as a consequence of noise and air pollution.

Public finance for the public good in table 3.6 is efficient by the cost-benefit criterion because $W = B - C > 0$. The total benefit is $\sum B = 170$ and the total loss is $C = 80$. Because of asymmetric information, the government does not know the personal benefits and costs. Only the three people know their own respective personal benefits or losses.

Rules for the Clarke tax

Incentives to reveal true personal benefits and costs can be provided through a process known as the *Clarke tax*, named after Edward Clarke, who proposed this tax in the early 1970s. To implement the Clarke tax, the following rules are imposed:

- A person pays a tax if the information about personal loss or benefit that the person declares changes the decision about whether the public good is to be supplied (that is, the information that a person provides changes whether $W = B - C$ is positive or negative). People therefore pay a tax for being decisive. The tax is therefore zero if the information that a person reveals does not change the public-spending decision.
- The amount of the tax payment is equal to the net loss imposed on all other people as a consequence of a person's participating in and changing the public-spending decision.
- The tax revenue is not used to finance the project, nor is the tax revenue distributed in any other way that benefits the people involved in providing information. The tax revenue is transferred to the government budget and is spent in a way such that benefits to the people involved in declaring their benefits or costs for the public good are zero or negligible.

To apply these rules, we start with person 1 in table 3.6.

Values of the Clarke tax

We see in table 3.6 that when person 1 does not participate in the cost-benefit valuation and persons 2 and 3 truthfully report their valuations, spending on the public good does not pass the cost-benefit test: the loss of 80 for person 3 exceeds the benefit of 70 for person 2.

In the next step of the procedure, we allow person 1 to participate. By participating and declaring true benefit of 100, person 1 changes the cost-benefit outcome because the total benefit to persons 1 and 2 of 170 exceeds the loss of 80 to person 3. Person 1 has been decisive in determining whether the project will be financed and therefore pays a tax. The tax is the value of the loss imposed on the rest of the population due to person 1's changing the decision. Person 1 has provided a benefit of 70 to person 2 and imposed a loss of 80 on person 3. Person 1 therefore pays a Clarke tax of $(80 - 70) = 10$.

Person 2 pays a Clarke tax of zero because – with or without person 2's participation in providing personal information – the project passes the cost-benefit test (because the benefit of 100 to person 1 is, in any event, greater than the loss of 80 incurred by person 3). Person 2's participation, therefore, does not affect whether the public good is provided. Person 3 also pays no tax because – with or without person 3's participation – total benefits exceed costs.

The impossibility of gain through misrepresentation of personal valuation

The value of the Clarke tax depends on information provided by *other people*. Nothing that people say about their own valuation of benefits or costs affects the value of the Clarke tax that a person pays. Therefore, there is no means of using misrepresentation of one's own benefits or costs to improve personal outcomes.

The Clarke tax and Nash equilibrium

The Clarke tax results in a Nash equilibrium. The dominant strategy of each person is to reveal truthfully personal benefit or loss from the public good and to pay the Clarke tax.

Person 1

Person 1 gains from paying a tax of 10 and switching the decision in favor of the project. The gain for person 1 from changing the public spending decision is 100, which exceeds the tax of 10 that person 1 pays. Person 1 cannot manipulate the amount of the tax paid by declaring other than true benefit. Person 1's tax is determined by the net cost imposed on persons 2 and 3 as a consequence of the change in the cost-benefit decision. Because the tax is determined by the valuations of the other two people and not by person 1's declaration of benefit, person 1 has no reason to misrepresent personal benefit by declaring a value other than the true 100.

Person 2

Person 2 also has no reason to misrepresent true valuation of benefit. Person 2 benefits from the public good and pays zero tax when revealing true benefit.

Person 3

Person 3 loses 80 when the public good is supplied. The combined benefit of persons 1 and 2 is 170, so person 3 could block the project by lying and declaring a personal loss of 171 from the public good. Such misrepresentation to block the project, however, is not in person 3's interest. By declaring a loss of 171 to block the project, person 3 faces a Clarke tax of 170 because this is the cost imposed on persons 1 and 2 if person 3 is decisive and the project is blocked. The Clarke tax of 170 that person 3 would pay to block the project exceeds person 3's loss of 80 if the project proceeds. Person 3, therefore, has no incentive to report an untruthful loss to block the project.[45]

[45] A claimed loss by person 3 of 171 is the minimum that blocks the project. By declaring a loss of 1,000, person 3 still pays the same Clarke tax of 170 because the Clarke tax is determined by the losses imposed on persons 1 and 2, not by person 3's declared loss.

The dominant strategy and the Nash equilibrium

No one, therefore, has an incentive to misrepresent true benefits or losses. The dominant strategy is to report true benefit, and the Nash equilibrium is that everyone reports true benefit – that is, given that everyone else truthfully reports personal benefits or losses, the best personal response that anyone can make is also to report truthfully personal benefit or loss.

Revenue from the Clarke tax

What is the role of condition (3) that the revenue from the Clarke tax not be used to finance the public good or to benefit the people involved in the cost-benefit decision in other ways? To see why condition (3) is required, we return to the tax paid by person 1, which is determined by the net loss that person 1 imposes on persons 2 and 3. Persons 2 and 3 would have an incentive to increase person 1's tax if they were to benefit from the tax paid by person 1. For example, if person 2 were deceptively to claim a benefit of zero rather than the true benefit of 70, the Clarke tax of person 1 would increase to 80. Or, person 3 could increase person 1's tax by claiming a greater loss than the true loss of 80. The requirement that people affected by the cost-benefit decision not benefit from the revenue from the Clarke tax eliminates the incentive for such misrepresentation of personal benefit or cost to increase other people's tax payments.[46]

The Clarke tax when no one is decisive

The Clarke tax is payment for being decisive. Table 3.7 shows a case in which no one is decisive.

TABLE 3.7. THE CLARKE TAX WHEN NO ONE IS DECISIVE

Person 1	Person 2	Person 3	Person 4
20	20	20	−30
Tax = 0	Tax = 0	Tax = 0	Tax = 0

[46] Also, no coalitions are allowed. Person 2 could decrease person 1's Clarke tax by claiming a higher than true benefit of 70. Person 1 would be prepared to pay person 2 for this deception, so persons 1 and 2 could form a coalition to gain at the expense of person 3. Person 2 might deceptively claim a benefit of 81. Then, the project satisfies the cost-benefit criterion without person 1 being decisive in determining whether the public good is provided, and person 1 no longer pays a tax; nor is person 2 decisive, so person 2 also pays no tax. Such deception eliminates payment of the Clarke tax but does not change the outcome that the project is revealed as justified by the cost-benefit criterion, based on declared valuations.

The project in table 3.7 is warranted by cost-benefit analysis because the total benefits of 60 to persons 1, 2, and 3 exceed the loss of 30 to person 4. The government does not know the values of personal benefits and losses and applies the Clarke tax. The Clarke tax for each person is zero because no one's participation in the evaluation of benefit and cost is decisive in changing the outcome. Persons 1, 2, and 3 pay no Clarke tax and are happy with the outcome that the project is to be publicly financed. Person 4 loses from the project and could change the cost-benefit decision to finance the project by declaring a loss of 61. Person 4 would then be decisive and would have to pay a Clarke tax of 60 (which is the loss imposed on persons 1, 2, and 3 due to person 4's changing the decision). Person 4 is, however, better off declaring the true loss of 30. Although the Clarke tax for everybody is zero, the presence of the Clarke tax deters an untruthful declaration of loss by person 4.

The Clarke tax with two projects

Table 3.8 shows an example in which a decision is required between public finance for one of two projects, A or B. In this example, three people each have a positive benefit from the two alternative projects.

The total benefit from project A is 170, which exceeds the total benefit of 160 from project B. Project A would therefore be chosen in preference to project B if the government knew the personal valuations in table 3.8. To obtain information to determine whether project A or project B should be publicly financed, the government applies the Clarke tax.

If person 1 does not participate in the cost-benefit calculation, project B is chosen in preference to project A (because without person 1, the total benefit from project A is 100 and the total benefit from project B is 130). When person 1 participates truthfully in the cost-benefit calculation, the decision changes to project A (because the total benefit from project A is then 170 compared to the total benefit of 160 from project B). Participation by person 1 changes the cost-benefit outcome, and so person 1 pays a Clarke tax; the value of the tax is 30, which is the net loss imposed on persons 2 and 3 due to the change (person 2 gains 30 and person 3 loses 60 from the change from financing project B to financing project A).

TABLE 3.8. THE CLARKE TAX WITH TWO PROJECTS

	Person 1	Person 2	Person 3
Project A	70	80	20
Project B	30	50	80
Clarke tax	Tax = 30	Tax = 20	Tax = 0

The participation of person 2 likewise changes the financing decision.[47] The Clarke tax for person 2 is 20.[48] The participation of person 3 does not change the financing decision, and the Clarke tax for person 3 is therefore zero.[49]

The dominant strategy again is to declare true personal benefit. In the Nash equilibrium, therefore, true personal benefits from the projects are revealed.

Use of the Clarke tax

Use of the Clarke tax requires interaction among the large numbers of people who might benefit from publicly financed public goods. A person who is aware that large numbers of other people are involved in providing information for computation of the Clarke tax also may perceive that the personal likelihood of being decisive and so having to pay the Clarke tax is low. Individuals might therefore conclude that the values of their declarations of personal benefit or cost are of no importance. If people do not take care to report their true valuations because they believe that their Clarke tax will be zero, the correct information required for the cost-benefit comparisons will not be provided.

Resistance would also be expected to the Clarke tax by taxpayers because of the uncertainty about personal taxes before values of the Clarke tax are determined. There might be complaints of unfairness – in particular, if high personal taxes are determined for low-income people. The taxes, moreover, do not finance the public good; in fact, revenue from the Clarke tax should *not* be used to finance the public goods for which information about costs and benefits is being sought. The Clarke tax is an incentive mechanism to lead people to reveal information truthfully, and people may regard as unjust the use of a tax only for revealing information. For political reasons, a government also might not like the uncertainty of not knowing beforehand how the Clarke mechanism will determine tax obligations for different people.

No government ever appears to have used the Clarke tax as a means of solving the public-good asymmetric-information problem.

C. User prices

A market in which people pay for access to – or use of – public goods reveals personal information about valuations of public goods. We shall refer to prices paid for access to public goods as *user prices*. User prices require low-cost means of exclusion of people who do not pay. In the case of private goods, exclusion is intrinsic in the nature of the good: only people who pay can benefit from private

[47] Without the participation of person 2, the benefit from project B is 110 and the benefit from project A is 90; with the participation of person 2, the benefit from project A is again 170 and the benefit from project B is 160.

[48] Person 1 gains 40 from person 2's participation and person 3 loses 60.

[49] Without the participation of person 3, the benefit from project A is 150 and the benefit from project B is 80. With person 3's participation, the benefit from project A is 170 and from project B is 160.

goods because the benefit is personal. Exclusion is impossible from various public goods, such as benefits from the rule of law, competitive markets, and national security or defense. There are also cases in which exclusion is possible but we do not want to exclude, such as the services provided by the police and court system. Exclusion from schooling and education as well as from health insurance and health care is feasible; therefore, private markets exist for education and health care. Exclusion from roads and highways and from bridges and tunnels is also possible; all transportation systems allow exclusion. Exclusion from museums, art galleries, and zoos – as well as from obtaining drivers' licenses and passports and other certification – is possible. Hence, user prices can be charged.

A user price is an application of the benefit principle of payment.

The benefit principle of payment is that people who benefit should pay.

The benefit principle applies to personal payments in any market because, in markets, people need to pay in order to benefit. The benefit principle is a normative proposition when stated as:

People who benefit should pay.

The converse of the normative statement of the benefit principle is:

People who do not benefit should not have to pay.

Lindahl prices and user prices

We applied the benefit principle when we considered voluntary payments for public goods, as in the case of the Lindahl solution. People pay for public goods in order to benefit. However, if there is no exclusion, they can also free ride and benefit without paying. The Lindahl solution showed how mutual free riding could be efficient: if people voluntarily pay their Lindahl prices based on their true benefits from a public good, the consensus quantity of the public good is the efficient quantity.

Once the efficient Lindahl quantity (or standard) of the public good is known, efficient use of the public good requires free access. The free access is Pareto-improving: people with access to use the public good are better off and no one is made worse off. Therefore, to ensure efficient access:

Lindahl prices do not exclude people from access to use of public goods.

If feasible, the personally paid Lindahl prices would, for example, finance the acquisition of art in an art museum or the purchase, feeding, and housing of animals in a zoo – and entry would be free. The Lindahl prices would similarly finance a highway or a bridge and – without congestion – efficient access requires no payment for use. Because of the information problem, Lindahl prices, however, are not feasible – which is why we are led to consider alternative means of financing public goods through user prices.

User prices differ from Lindahl prices.

By paying user prices, people reveal information about personal *MB* when they voluntarily pay, for example, for education and health care or a toll road, bridge, tunnel, national park, beach, museum, or zoo. If person *i* voluntarily pays the user price P_i^{use}, we know that:

$$MB_i \geq P_i^{use}. \tag{3.29}$$

That is, person *i*'s valuation of use exceeds (or is at least equal to) the user price paid.

People reveal their personal benefit by paying user prices.

The efficient user price is zero: because the *MC* of use of a pure public good is zero, it follows that the price of access to the public good should be zero. Children looking at an elephant in a zoo should pay a zero price because the *MC* of looking at the elephant is zero. However, a zero price provides no revenue to pay for the elephant's food and upkeep.

User prices provide revenue to pay for public goods.

Indirect user prices

User prices can be paid voluntarily and directly. Payment of user prices can also be voluntary but *indirect*. For example, a tax on gasoline is a tax on use of roads and a tax on automobiles is a tax on the option to use a road. The user prices can be avoided by not using or owning an automobile.

Subsidies and partial user prices

User prices are partial when governments subsidize part of the costs of public goods. Education is often subsidized from public revenue, with school fees covering only part of the cost of education. Similarly, health care may be subsidized, as may be entry to museums and art galleries. Public transportation is often subsidized.

Natural monopoly

User prices for public goods reintroduce natural monopoly and the question of whether the monopoly supplier should be the government or a private supplier. If supply is profitable, private supply is feasible. Private supply is also feasible if government subsidies cover losses incurred in supply.

Two-part user prices

Administration of a school district and teaching children in classrooms are distinct tasks. Teaching effectiveness declines as the number of children or students in a classroom increases beyond some size.[50] School administrators and curriculum developers, however, provide services that are a public good for larger numbers of children – through effectiveness of school organization, selection and monitoring of teachers and instructors, and updating of the curriculum to include new knowledge. User prices that finance schooling are therefore two-part payments. One user price would finance costs of school-district administration; the other would finance costs at the level of the school and classroom, including the salary of the teacher.[51]

User prices and fixed costs

When public goods are congested, the purpose of user prices is to limit access so as to avoid congestion. We shall now consider user prices paid when public goods are not congested. The purpose of the user prices is thus not to avoid congestion or crowding but rather to have users (those who benefit) pay for the public good.

We denote by F the fixed cost per unit of time of providing a public good. For example, in the classroom, the fixed costs F include the cost per hour or per day of the teacher or instructor. There are also other fixed costs that are attributable to the class. The cost of the class includes attributed parts of salaries of the school administrators as well as the past costs of education (or investment in human capital) of teachers and instructors and past costs of the physical investment that provided the school campus and buildings. Similarly, in the case of health care, the fixed costs F consist of salaries of medical staff and attributed costs of investment in equipment and hospitals; a public-good benefit is also provided through option demand (the public-good benefit is the option to use the facilities, if the need arises).

Payment of user prices spreads past fixed capital costs (or costs of investment) over time. The attribution of fixed costs over time is an exercise in accounting. We shall not study how accountants compute the attribution of fixed costs over time. Nor shall we study, for example, how accountants attribute parts of the fixed costs of school administrators over classrooms to compute the fixed cost F per semester of a course being taught. Our assignment is not to study accounting.

We therefore now consider a public good for which accountants have informed us of the fixed cost F per month, semester, or year.

> *With the cost known, what are the consequences of a public policy of seeking to finance the fixed cost F through user prices?*

[50] Returning to figure 3.1b, we have, for example, $n_1 = 25$. After $n_2 = 50$, there may no longer be positive benefit from children spending time in the classroom.

[51] Two-part user pricing has been studied for admission to an amusement park. To maximize profits, should admission to the amusement park be free with user prices charged for rides of the different types? Or should there be a price of admission, with rides free once the price of admission has been paid?

Self-financing user prices

The fixed cost F reflects the natural-monopoly characteristic of the public good.

A self-financing user price paid by all users covers the fixed cost F.

With n users, the *average cost* of use (per period of time) is:

$$AC = \frac{F}{n}. \tag{3.30}$$

Figure 3.12a shows an average cost function as in expression (3.30). All user prices equal to AC are self-financing. Average cost AC and, therefore, self-financing user prices decline with the number of users. For example, for $n_2 > n_1$, self-financing user prices are $P^2_{use} < P^1_{use}$.

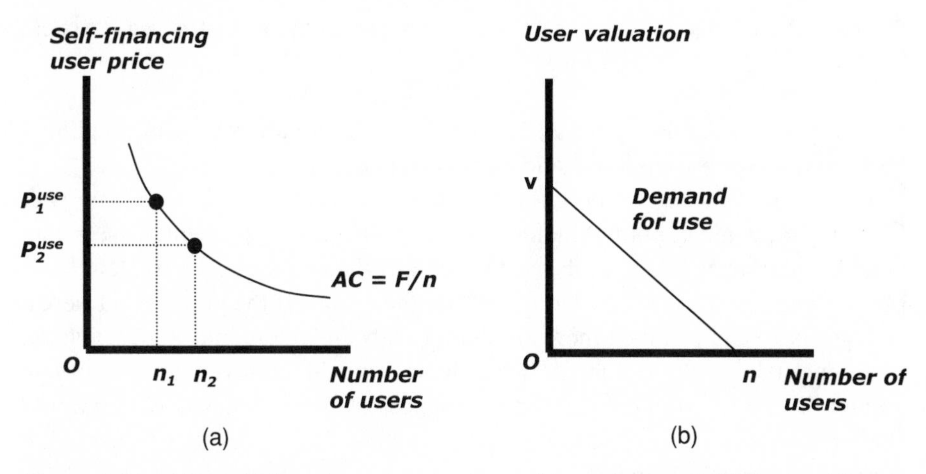

Figure 3.12. (a) The self-financing user price is equal to average cost. (b) Demand for use of a public facility.

Figure 3.12b shows demand for use. A population of n potential users is ranked along the demand function according to willingness to pay for use. The highest-valuation user has valuation v, and the lowest-valuation user has valuation zero (person n). Demand is not measured in terms of quantity but rather expresses whether a person is prepared to pay for use (or access), which is a dichotomous decision (yes or no).[52]

Figure 3.13a shows two self-financing user prices, P_1^{use} and P_2^{use}, at points 1 and 2, with:

$$n_1 P_1^{use} = n_2 P_2^{use} = F. \tag{3.31}$$

AC is a rectangular hyperbola defined by the fixed cost F. At point 1, n_1 people are willing to pay the user price P_1^{use}. At point 2, a greater number of people n_2

[52] The demand function is shown as continuous although people are measured in discrete terms. A large population provides an approximation to a continuous function. Linearity of the demand function is, as in previous instances, for exposition only.

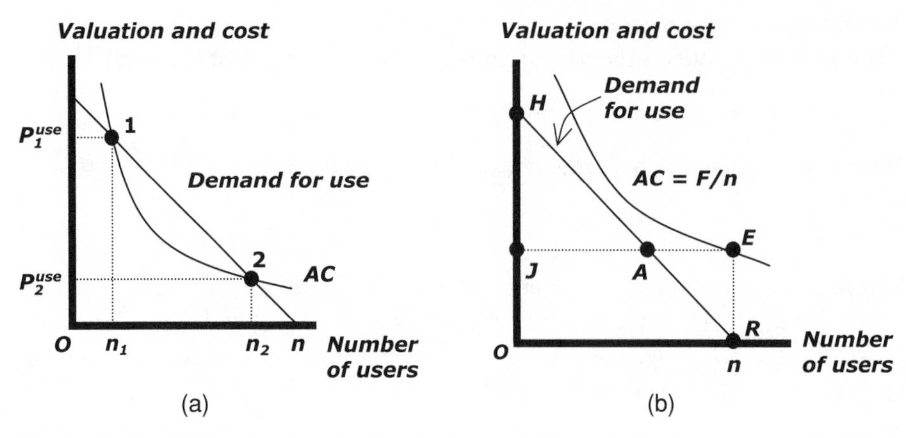

Figure 3.13. (a) Determination of self-financing user prices. (b) Demand for use of a public facility with no self-financing user price.

is willing to pay the user price P_2^{use}. Point 2 is a Pareto improvement on point 1 because the user price is lower and more people benefit.

Exclusion is inefficient because the marginal cost of use is zero. The self-financing outcome at point 2 inefficiently excludes $(n - n_2)$ potential users who would benefit from access to the public good. If the public good were, for example, a bridge, $(n - n_2)$ people would not use the bridge. If the public good were a college classroom in which there are empty seats and additional students would not reduce the benefit to students in the class (or would improve the class through greater diversity in background and experience), self-financing school fees would similarly inefficiently exclude $(n - n_2)$ potential students. Although exclusion is inefficient, a self-financing user price finances availability of public goods by requiring payment for benefit.

Do self-financing user prices necessarily exist?

Self-financing user prices may not necessarily exist. The population of potential users may be too small or the population may not sufficiently value the public good.

In figure 3.13a, a population smaller than n_1 cannot self-finance the public good through user prices. With fewer than n_1 users, average cost AC exceeds the user prices that people in the population are willing to pay (as expressed in demand for use). If there are fewer than n_1 users, a self-financing solution is therefore impossible because of an insufficient number of people sharing the fixed cost.

Figure 3.13b shows a case in which self-financing user prices do not exist because the public good is insufficiently valued. For any number of users in figure 3.13b:

$$AC > P^{use}. \tag{3.32}$$

In figure 3.13b, although there exists no self-financing user price, when the entire number of potential users is permitted free access, the cost-benefit criterion $W = (B - C) > 0$ is satisfied.[53]

A community therefore may not be able to support a self-financed public good (a school system, medical center, art gallery, archeological museum, or zoo) because the population is too small or because personal valuations of benefit of potential users are insufficiently high to cover average cost. In particular:

> *Self-financing user prices need not exist for socially worthwhile projects that satisfy the cost-benefit criterion* $W = (B - C) > 0$.

Who supplies the public good?

We return to the question, in the context now of user prices, of who supplies the public good. A community, for example, may require a bus service. In figure 3.14, a private natural-monopoly supplier would set $MR = MC$ to determine the profit-maximizing price P_M and would provide service to n_M users.[54] Figure 3.14 also shows the maximized profits of the private natural-monopoly supplier.

The private profit-maximizing supplier excludes $(n - n_M)$ potential users. The excluded users are the lowest-valuation users remaining, after n_M people pay the private supplier for use.

Supply by the private profit-maximizing supplier is inefficient, compared to the self-financing outcome in which n_2 users pay a user price of P^2_{use}. As do monopolies in general, the private natural monopoly charges an excessively high price and restricts supply – here, relative to the self-financing solution.[55]

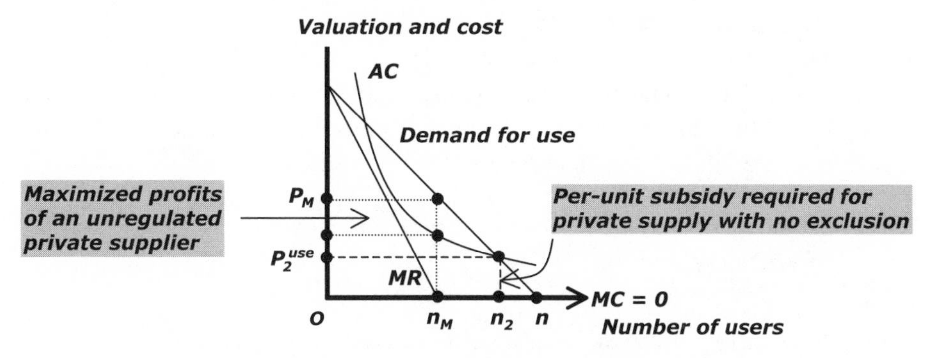

Figure 3.14. Private supply by a monopoly.

[53] The total benefit from the project in figure 3.13b when there is no exclusion is *OHR*. The total cost is *OJER*. Because *HJA* > *REA*, total benefit exceeds total cost based on valuations of use and, therefore, $W = B - C > 0$.

[54] Marginal revenue *MR* is derived from the demand function. Because all costs are fixed costs, marginal cost of use is zero and coincides with the horizontal axis.

[55] We are considering public goods and compare monopoly with a self-financing user price. For private goods, we compare monopoly with a competitive market solution.

For efficient use, all n potential users in figure 3.14 need to be given access to the public good at a zero price. Because no revenue would then be provided to finance the public good, efficient free access under private ownership requires that the private supplier receive a subsidy from government. Figure 3.14 shows the required per-unit subsidy when supply is private and there is no exclusion.

In supplement S2B, which describes natural monopoly and institutions, subsidies from government to private suppliers were shown to be subject to principal–agent problems. The effort decision of the private supplier determines AC of supply; however, effort in general is not observable. The private supplier can, therefore, obtain rents through low effort; low effort increases AC of supply, thereby increasing the per-unit subsidy received from the government.[56] The subsidy to the private supplier introduces a principal–agent problem if employees of the government agency are "captured" or come to identify with the private supplier in the course of repeated inspections and audits.

Rather than paying subsidies, governments can ask for competitive bids from private suppliers. The outcome of competitive bidding in figure 3.14 is the zero-profit user price P_2^{use}, at which there would be n_2 users and $(n - n_2)$ excluded potential users.[57]

Subsidies are also avoided if the government owns the natural monopoly. However, other principal–agent problems can then arise. There is a bureaucratic principal–agent problem because of incentives for budget maximization of the officials who administer the government bureaucracy. There is another type of problem if political appointments to the administering bureaucracy lack professional competence.[58]

Are user prices desirable?

We continue setting aside the issues of choice between public and private ownership. If all principal–agent problems could be avoided (due to behavior either of a private natural monopolist or behavior of political and bureaucratic decision makers), we are left seeking an answer to the normative question:

> *Are user prices desirable means of resolving the public-good asymmetric-information problem?*

[56] The private supplier's average cost AC may include joint costs due to other services or goods. For example, a privately subsidized bus company may also own a rental-car company. There are joint costs of managing the bus service and the rental-car company. The value of the subsidy for the bus service depends on how the joint costs are attributed and reported. Reported AC determines price. In turn, price determines demand. As noted in supplement S2B, misrepresentation of AC to maximize the total subsidy obtained from government can therefore lead a private supplier either to over- or under-report costs.

[57] Supplement S2B describes the competitive bidding process when there is natural monopoly for a private good.

[58] For more detail on natural monopoly, albeit in the case of private goods, see supplement S2B.

Social justice

Taxation is often based on the normative principle of ability to pay.

> *The ability-to-pay principle of taxation is that people should pay for public goods according to their means and without regard for personal benefit.*

The ability-to-pay principle results in people with higher incomes paying higher taxes for the financing of public goods. The benefit principle on which user prices are based might be regarded as unjust because people pay the same user prices independent of income.

Efficiency

We have been investigating user prices because of the objective of *efficiency*, not social justice. Ideally, we would want the Lindahl solution to be implemented, so providing efficiently financed public goods and efficient free access. We would then have efficiency in both dimensions – the efficient consensus quantity or standard of public goods and also efficient free access to use of (or benefit from) public goods. We have turned to user prices because the information problem prevents implementation of the Lindahl solution. User prices provide information about personal benefit through voluntary personal payment. Taxes determined according to ability-to-pay result in some people financing public goods that they do not use; the link between personal benefit and personal payment is broken, whereas user prices directly link voluntary personal spending to personal benefit.

Accountability

User prices provide accountability. When, for example, supplementary school fees are required for extracurricular activities or additional school equipment, school administrators are accountable to parents for how money is spent. When payment is through user prices, people are more attentive to whether appropriate benefits have been received.

User prices as an alternative to government supply

When government schools fail to provide quality education, households with the means to pay private-school fees are able to avoid the ineffective government schools. Even though government schools are "free," low-income parents may also pay user prices to escape low-quality government schools. Similarly, in cases where governments provide free-access tax-financed health care, user prices for private health care may be the only escape from the inadequacies of government supply.

The inefficiency of exclusion

The problem is that self-financing user prices inefficiently exclude. Children may be excluded from a zoo because parents refuse or are unable to pay the price of admission; no cost would be incurred by the children entering the zoo to look at the animals. In the case of a toll bridge, a person unable to pay might have to detour to a part of the river where the water is shallow enough to drive across – or may have to swim or wade across the river. A person without money cannot use a bus or train that has empty seats. A person who cannot pay school fees cannot occupy an empty seat in a classroom.

Prisons and police

Prisons and police are special cases of user prices that merit our attention. Prisons can be financed through user prices paid by inmates. The user prices are then, of course, involuntary. Should prisoners be obliged to pay user prices? An answer – perhaps expressive – is that convicted felons are themselves victims – of their upbringing and environment – and should not be further penalized by being made to pay user prices for time spent in prison. The counter answer is contained in the question why taxpayers and citizens, as victims of crime, should be obliged to pay, through taxes, for the upkeep of prisoners who committed the crimes. Prisoners may have personal assets and also, in most cases, are able to work. User prices paid by prisoners would oblige prison inmates to pay for their food and accommodation and other expenses. User prices would also deter crime.

Prisons can be privately owned. After sentencing within the judicial system, prisoners can be transferred to privately owned prisons for the duration of their sentence. Privately owned user-pay prisons can be profitable, just as is privately provided care for the aged. Through competitive bidding, providers of prison services can offer prices for keeping prisoners under different conditions ranging from low-security trusted prisoners to high-security conditions required for more serious offenders.

Police protection could be financed through user prices, with people paying whenever they call on the police for assistance. It would be unjust or, indeed, unethical to compel victims of crime to pay when government has been ineffective in enforcing the rule of law. User prices for calling on the police would also assist criminals by deterring the reporting of crimes.

Diversity in application of user prices

There is diversity among countries in application of user prices; in some countries, user prices are applied extensively to solve the public-good asymmetric-information problem; in other countries, user prices are uncommon. Some societies have thus decided that the benefit principle applied to payment for public goods through user prices is preferable to financing public goods through ability-to-pay taxation. Other societies have been influenced by the view that user prices are unjust or by the inefficiency of exclusion. In some low-income societies, voluntary user prices are paid to substitute for absent public spending. In both high- and low-income countries, people pay user prices to avoid the inadequacies of government schools and in some countries inadequacies of government-provided health care.

D. The Tiebout locational-choice mechanism

A close parallel to user prices is choice from among governments that levy different taxes to provide different public goods to taxpayers. Choosing a location in which to live and pay taxes is then like choosing user prices for public goods. The public goods come in bundles in different government jurisdictions.

Government jurisdictions are, in general, organized in hierarchies of government. A federal system of government has different levels ranging from central, state or provincial to county, district, or local government. The hierarchy of governments is a pyramid, with more local than state or regional governments and one national government.

When taxes in a local or regional government jurisdiction finance public goods, choice of location in the jurisdiction reveals people's private information about willingness to pay for the public goods; through location, people reveal their willingness to pay the taxes that finance the public goods. When public goods are chosen through location, there is a *locational market* for public goods. In the locational market, taxes are the equivalent of a user price. However, because all people who reside in a jurisdiction pay for and benefit from the public goods, there is no inefficient exclusion as can arise with user prices. Everyone lives and pays taxes somewhere.

Locational choice and efficient supply of public goods

Local governments within a federal system of government provide *local public goods*. The benefits from the public goods are local, to residents in the government jurisdiction. Of course, people may also choose location because of the weather, which is a public good independent of government. Locational choice of public goods can also occur at the national level. Our question about locational choice and public goods is:

> *Can choice of location among government jurisdictions replicate the efficiency of the Lindahl voluntary-payment solution for public goods?*

Preferences and differences among government jurisdictions

Locational options cater to people with different preferences for public goods. Some people may seek good schools and others may have no children (at all or living at home) and may feel no benefit from living in a jurisdiction or school district that levies high taxes to finance quality education. Location in a local-government jurisdiction determines quality of libraries and parks, availability of tennis and basketball courts, whether trees and flowers have been planted in public places, frequency and tidiness of collection of trash, and personal security. Jurisdictions also differ in the quality of politicians and in the culture of payment of taxes: the burden of public spending is more equally shared when all people pay taxes.

Tiebout and Samuelson on spontaneous and imposed order

Locational choice as a means of revealing preferences for public goods is called the *Tiebout mechanism*, after Charles Tiebout (1924–68), who proposed in 1956 that locational choice solves the public-good information problem. Tiebout's proposition can be interpreted as normative or positive. The normative proposition is an assertion that locational choice results in efficient supply of public goods. The positive proposition is the observation that people use locational choice to make decisions about public goods.

Charles Tiebout was replying, in particular, to the case for failure of markets to efficiently provide public goods that had been made by Paul Samuelson (1954, 1955). Samuelson had pointed out the condition $\sum MB = MC$ for efficient public-good supply and had concluded that efficiency could not be achieved through voluntary payment for public goods because people would not pay according to their true MB; imposed order was therefore required for public goods through taxation and centralized supply decisions of government agencies. Tiebout's reply was that there is spontaneous order in a locational market in which individuals make personal decisions about public goods in response to taxes (or prices) that they wish to pay. Tiebout's case was therefore that:

> *The locational mechanism for choosing public goods is equivalent to personal choice in a market: although taxes paid to governments are compulsory, the ability to choose governments to whom to pay taxes makes payment of taxes voluntary.*

The benefit principle

We have distinguished between benefit and ability to pay as principles of taxation. Locational choice is an application of the benefit principle of taxation. Payment of taxes is according to benefit revealed through locational choice. As with user prices, which are also based on the benefit principle, locational choice makes free riding impossible because locational choice is accompanied by the obligation to pay the taxes that finance public spending in the chosen jurisdiction.

Employment opportunities

If the locational-choice mechanism is to be effective in offering a wide scope of choice for public goods, employment or income-earning opportunities need to be available in – or within commuting distance of – the government jurisdiction that people choose.

The scope of choice

Locational choice provides an approximation to a competitive market for local public goods only if the scope of choice of public goods through location is sufficiently diverse to replicate the supply offers that, in principle, could be provided through markets. Because public goods come in bundles, large numbers of alternative jurisdictions may be required to offer the sought-after combinations of quality and quantity.

Norms and conventions as public goods
Norms and conventions are public goods. Public goods include conventions and norms about dress, whether studying is meritorious, and about how people entertain themselves. Locational choice allows people to choose a community in which they feel comfortable.

The Tiebout mechanism for choice of different types of public goods

The locational-choice mechanism allows people to choose from among different types of public goods. For example, parents want quality schools but people without families may not wish to pay taxes that finance local schools. Some people have a preference for public spending on tennis courts and parks where they can jog. Jurisdictions can offer the different types of public goods according to the benefit principle so that people do not have to pay for public goods that they do not want.

For the public goods provided in a jurisdiction, a government sets a *per-unit tax* T to finance public spending. The per-unit tax T is equal to the MC of supply of the public good (for example, salaries of teachers in the school system). People with the same preferences for types of public goods are attracted to and locate in the same government jurisdiction. The common MB of the people in the jurisdiction is thereby known, as is the size of the population n in the jurisdiction. The government determines efficient supply of a public good by applying the condition:

$$\sum_{i=1}^{n} MB_i = MC\,(= T). \tag{3.33}$$

In effect, the decision is not for one public good but for a bundle of public goods. The outcome is efficient supply of public goods.[59]

Choice of different quantities or qualities of the same public good

The Tiebout locational-choice mechanism is more complex when the choice is among quantities or qualities of the same public good. Figure 3.15 shows marginal willingness of two people to pay for a local public good provided in a government jurisdiction. One person has low marginal willingness to pay MB_L and the other has high marginal willingness to pay MB_H. We refer to the first person as low-benefit and to the second person as high-benefit.

[59] In chapter 4, we shall see that when public goods are financed through taxes, the efficiency condition for public-good supply requires amendment, to include social losses incurred in raising tax revenue. In this chapter, we portray the public-good efficiency condition as if there are no efficiency losses from governments' levying taxes.

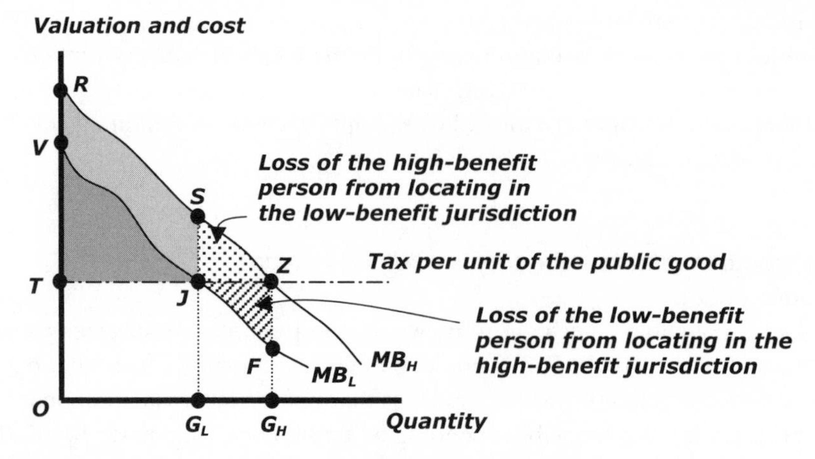

Figure 3.15. Separation of low- and high-benefit people by choice of jurisdiction.

Initially, both the low- and the high-benefit people are located in the same jurisdiction where they pay the same per-unit tax T to finance public spending on the public good. The per-unit tax T is like a price.

Given a per-unit tax T, the low-benefit person's preferred choice G_L is determined at point J, where:

$$T = MB_L. \tag{3.34}$$

The area VJT in figure 3.15 is the net benefit to the low-benefit person when supply of the public good is G_L.[60]

At the same per-unit tax T, the high-benefit person ideally wants the local government to supply the greater quantity of the public good G_H, which is determined at point Z in figure 3.15, where:

$$T = MB_H. \tag{3.35}$$

The net benefit to the high-benefit person from supply G_H is RZT.[61]

The jurisdiction may offer neither the quantity G_L nor the quantity G_H. Two other jurisdictions, however, may offer public spending on each person's desired quantities of the public good at the same per-unit tax T. By relocating to the jurisdiction that offers personally preferred public spending, each person achieves an outcome as if the public good were supplied in a market at a price equal to the per-unit tax T.

Incentives to reveal true benefits

The locational-choice mechanism provides incentives to reveal true benefits and thereby solves the public-good information and free-rider problems. The

[60] Area VJT is determined by deducting total personal taxes $OTJG_L$ from total personal benefit VJG_LO.

[61] Area RZT is determined by deducting total personal taxes $OTZG_H$ from total personal benefit $ORZG_H$.

high-benefit person cannot gain by claiming to be a low-benefit person. Declarations or claims are meaningless here. The high-benefit person could pretend to be a low-benefit person only by locating in the jurisdiction that offers the low quantity G_L of the public good. In figure 3.15, the high-benefit person would then lose *SJZ* by pretending to be a low-benefit person.[62]

The low-benefit person likewise loses by pretending to be a high-benefit person. By locating in the jurisdiction that provides G_H, the low-benefit person would be paying taxes for a greater supply of the public good than he or she wants. In figure 3.15, *JZF* is the loss to the low-benefit person from pretending to be a high-benefit person and locating in the high-benefit jurisdiction where the quantity (or quality) G_H is provided.[63]

All people have incentives to locate in a jurisdiction according to whether they are high- or low-benefit. It therefore follows that:

> *Locational choice among government jurisdictions solves the public-good preference-revelation problem.*

Natural monopoly and cost sharing

The solution to the information problem is the basis of the Tiebout case for the locational-choice mechanism. However, our account thus far of the Tiebout locational-choice mechanism is incomplete because we have not considered the consequences of the attribute of natural monopoly of public goods.

The natural-monopoly attribute of public-good supply is expressed in the efficient Lindahl voluntary-pricing consensus solution, for which all people who benefit from a public good are in the same government jurisdiction and all contribute to financing the public good. It is evident that:

> *Costs of supply per person are minimized by providing the public good in a single jurisdiction.*

Or:

> *Efficient cost sharing requires a single jurisdiction.*

However, in the Tiebout mechanism, people reveal information about their preferences by separating themselves into different jurisdictions.

> *The Tiebout separation into different jurisdictions contradicts the requirement of location in a single jurisdiction for efficient cost sharing of public goods.*

[62] By locating in the low-benefit jurisdiction, the high-benefit person reduces taxes from $OTZG_H$ to $OTJG_L$; that is, taxes decline by G_LJZG_H. However, total benefit declines by G_LSZG_H. The difference between the decline in benefit and the decline in taxes is the loss *SJZ*.

[63] By locating in the high-benefit jurisdiction, the low-benefit person pays additional taxes G_LJZG_H and receives additional benefit G_LJFG_H. The net loss is *JZF*.

Tiebout as a second-best outcome

The Lindahl solution, with everyone in the same jurisdiction, is the ideal or first-best outcome for financing supply of public goods. The Tiebout locational choice solution is a second-best outcome because the first-best Lindahl solution is not possible. The alternatives are (1) for preferences for public goods to be revealed by separation of people through locational choice; or (2) for costs per person of supply of public goods to be minimized by everyone sharing costs in the same jurisdiction.

> *Revelation of preferences through locational choice and cost minimization per person are not simultaneously possible.*

Cost sharing in a single jurisdiction

Governments do not know people's personal Lindahl prices. Because of asymmetric information, only individuals themselves have the information on personal benefits from public goods required to determine Lindahl prices. In the absence of information that would allow personalized Lindahl prices to be set, the government sets equal per-unit taxes for everyone. When the entire population is in the same jurisdiction, people face the common per-unit tax T in figure 3.15.

The per-unit tax T is a self-financing user price. With P indicating the price of a unit of the public good and with n people in a jurisdiction, the per-unit tax per person in figure 3.15 is determined by the n people equally sharing the payment of price P:

$$T = \frac{P}{n}. \tag{3.36}$$

This is the lowest possible price or tax per person because everyone is sharing the cost of the public good.

At the minimum price or per-unit tax T, there is disagreement regarding the quantity or standard of the public good that low- and high-benefit people want to have supplied. We do not have the *Lindahl consensus*. In figure 3.15, the absence of the Lindahl consensus is expressed in low-benefit people wanting G_L to be supplied and high-benefit people wanting supply of G_H.

Cost sharing in separate jurisdictions

We now divide the population of n people into two groups according to preferences. A number n_L of people have low marginal benefit MB_L and a number n_H have high marginal benefit MB_H, with:

$$n = n_L + n_H. \tag{3.37}$$

If the two groups separate, the per-unit taxes per person for financing supply of the public good in the two jurisdictions are:

$$T_L = \frac{P}{n_L}, \quad T_H = \frac{P}{n_H}. \tag{3.38}$$

These per-unit taxes in separate jurisdictions are, of course, greater than the per-unit tax T per person in expression (3.36) when the entire population of n people shares the cost of the public good.

The decision whether to leave a jurisdiction

We thus see that there are costs and benefits of separate jurisdictions.

> *The cost of separation is the need to pay the higher per-unit taxes.*
>
> *The benefit of separation is public spending on public goods according to personal preferences.*

The trade-off between cost sharing and catering to preferences determines whether a group leaves a heterogeneous jurisdiction to form its own homogeneous jurisdiction.

With all n people together in a single jurisdiction – and for example all having school-aged children – the high-benefit population wishes to hire professional but expensive school administrators for the school system. The low-benefit population sees no need for the additional taxation and public spending. Because of asymmetric information, the low-benefit population cannot be offered lower taxes as an incentive to remain in the jurisdiction after the expensive school administrators have been hired; the only credible way in which low-benefit people can identify themselves is to leave.

To illustrate the decision whether to stay or leave, we use an example where the numbers of low- and high-benefit people are equal so that $n_L = n_H$. In figure 3.16, T is the minimized per-unit tax (also called a *tax price*) when the entire population of n people is located in one jurisdiction. If the population divides into two equal, separate groups, tax prices are as indicated in expression (3.38).

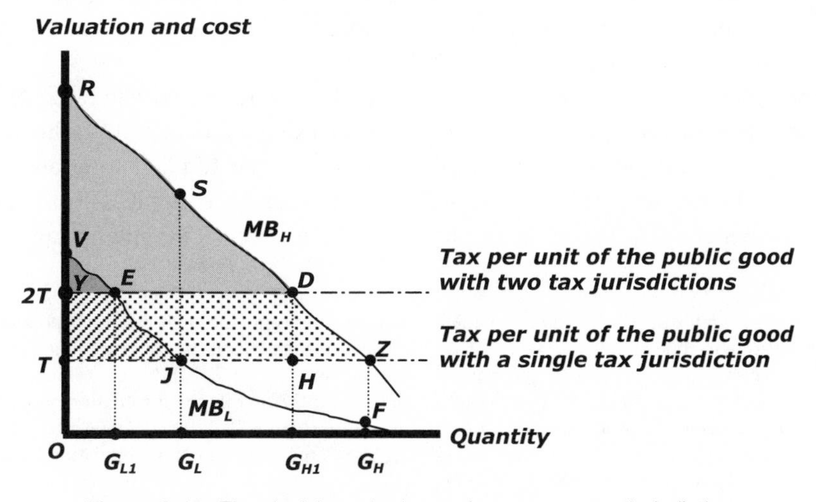

Figure 3.16. The decision whether to form a separate jurisdiction.

With only half the number of people sharing costs, the per-unit tax in the separate jurisdictions doubles in figure 3.16 to $2T$.

In the separate jurisdictions, with the per-unit tax equal to $2T$, the low-benefit population chooses G_{L1} of the public good at point E in figure 3.16 and the high-benefit jurisdiction chooses G_{H1} at point D. The separation into two jurisdictions solves the information problem but the costs per person of providing the public good have doubled.

In the single jurisdiction, the low-benefit population might control the government and decide on public-good supply. At the per-unit tax T (because costs are shared among all n people), in figure 3.16 the quantity G_L sought by the low-benefit population is then chosen. The *after-tax* benefit to a low-benefit person is then VJT.

The high-benefit people might decide to leave. After their departure, the per-unit cost facing the low-benefit population doubles to $2T$. At per-unit cost $2T$, the low-benefit population chooses G_{L1}. The departure of the high-benefit population reduces the after-tax benefit of a low-benefit person to VEY. The loss to a low-benefit person due to the departure of the high-benefit population is $EJTY$.

Alternatively, the high-benefit population may control choice of supply of the public good and the low-benefit population may leave the jurisdiction. In that case, the high-benefit population loses from the departure of the low-benefit population.[64]

A group that exits, gains – otherwise, it would not have left. With free voluntary decisions, it is, of course, sufficient for one group to wish to form its own jurisdiction for separation to occur.

Tiebout and Lindahl

Figure 3.17 shows the efficient Lindahl consensus in a single jurisdiction. G_{L1} and G_{H1} are efficient supplies to separated groups of low- and high-benefit users. For each separate group in its own jurisdiction, the public-good efficient-supply condition $\sum MB = MC(= P)$ is satisfied.

The efficient Lindahl-consensus quantity G_E is determined where $\sum MB = MC$ for the combined population of n people in a single jurisdiction. If the information problem did not prevent implementation of the Lindahl solution, costs would be shared among the entire population in the single combined jurisdiction, with low-benefit people paying T_L per unit and high-benefit people paying T_H.

[64] At the per-unit cost T with the low-benefit population present, the high-valuation population chooses public-good supply in figure 3.16 of G_H. The after-tax benefit per high-valuation person when the low-valuation population is present to share costs is then RZT. If the low-valuation population leaves the jurisdiction, the per-unit tax increases to $2T$ and the high-valuation population chooses public-good supply G_{H1}. The after-tax benefit to a high-valuation individual after the exit of the low-valuation population falls to RDY. The loss to the high-valuation population from the exit of the low-valuation population is $TYDZ$.

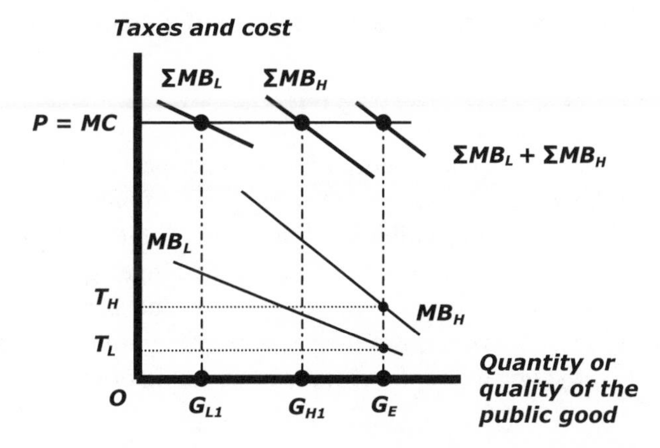

Figure 3.17. The efficient Lindahl consensus and the outcome of separation.

We see that in figure 3.17:

$$G_{L1} < G_{H1} < G_E. \tag{3.39}$$

That is, the efficient Lindahl-consensus quantity G_E in a single jurisdiction is greater than the quantities G_{L1} and G_{H1} provided in either of the separate jurisdictions. Thus, we confirm that:

> *The Lindahl-consensus solution with the population in a single jurisdiction is Pareto-improving compared to separate jurisdictions.*

Although people are better off with the Lindahl-consensus quantity G_E in a single jurisdiction than with G_{L1} and G_{L2} in separate jurisdictions, they are led by asymmetric information to choose the Tiebout outcome of separate jurisdictions.

It is sometimes observed that:

> *The first-best is the enemy of the second-best.*

This means that the efficiency of the unattainable first-best Lindahl-consensus solution, which requires no locational separation, should not be used to downplay the merit of the second-best Tiebout locational-choice mechanism. It is inappropriate to regard the Tiebout solution as inadequate because the Lindahl-consensus solution is preferable. The Tiebout solution is feasible (and is observed) whereas the Lindahl solution is not feasible (and is not observed). Indeed, the Tiebout locational-choice mechanism is a response to the infeasibility of the Lindahl-consensus solution.

Locational mobility

Whether we observe homogeneous Tiebout-type jurisdictions based on common preferences or mixed jurisdictions in which people have different preferences depends on locational mobility. The United States, for example, has been a mobile society. In other countries, people might be more reluctant to move away from family and friends.

Financing in mixed jurisdictions

In mixed jurisdictions, older and retired people may pay less in local taxes, in acknowledgment that they do not benefit from spending on schools in the manner of people with school-aged children. Age is a verifiable criterion that allows an approximation to Lindahl prices for older and younger people in the same jurisdiction. An alternative to the separate prices in the same jurisdiction is a "social contract" that everyone pays the same taxes regardless of age and that every generation of younger people is joined in financing of schools by the older generations.

Prices and politics in the Tiebout locational market

Because the Tiebout locational-choice mechanism for public goods is a substitute for a market, the payments paid in a locational market should be like the prices paid in any market. Price is a per-unit cost per person. Hence, the locational market requires *each person* to pay a price expressed as a per-unit tax, as in expressions (3.36) and (3.38). However, in practice, the per-person taxes that correspond to prices in markets are generally not levied. Rather, taxes are levied on the value of property or housing or on income, or a sales tax might be levied.

In practice, therefore, choice of public goods through location is not based on the benefit principle of markets. This is the consequence of politics.

The benefit principle of payment can be politically unpopular precisely because the people who benefit are required to pay. The benefit principle does not allow cross-subsidization; political decisions, however, often involve people who benefit by being subsidized by others.

What would we predict might happen if a government decided to apply the benefit principle of financing public goods, as the Tiebout locational mechanism and market principles require? We have evidence from a natural experiment that took place when the government of Prime Minister Margaret Thatcher in the United Kingdom introduced the benefit principle to local public finance; in 1988, a tax per person replaced property taxes as a means of financing local public services in the United Kingdom. The attempt at change was unsuccessful and, in 1991, the property tax was restored. The return to the property tax followed widespread noncompliance with the tax per beneficiary of public services. The benefit principle introduced through the tax per person increased tax obligations for people who lived in public housing and for people who lived in a house in which there were more than the average number of occupants. Taxes also increased for occupants of less expensive houses. Significant numbers of people refused to pay the per-person tax. The policy experiment came to an end because of successful popular (and political) resistance to the benefit principle for payment for local public goods.

Income and locational rents

The Tiebout locational-choice mechanism views people as having different preferences; however, income and wealth determine the public goods that people *can afford*. Jurisdictions, accordingly, often separate people by income and wealth and not necessarily by preferences for public goods. Zoning is the means of implementing separation by income and wealth; housing in a jurisdiction may be expensive because zoning regulations permit only expensive houses. The zoning regulations may be the consequence of the wealthy seeking exclusivity. Zoning regulations are also exclusion devices for local public goods. High-income people may wish to exclude low-income people, who would live in low-valued housing and would pay low property and income taxes but nonetheless would benefit from the jurisdiction's public goods.

Housing prices contain locational rents – which are like monopoly rents. As an example, Beverly Hills is a small, independent, local-government jurisdiction bordered by the city of Los Angeles. Housing in Beverly Hills is more expensive than in adjacent Los Angeles. Living in Beverly Hills provides access to the services that the local government provides, which are, in general, of a higher standard than the services provided in Los Angeles. Housing prices in Beverly Hills are higher than those in Los Angeles because more people want the services that are provided in Beverly Hills than Beverly Hills can accommodate. That is, there is *excess demand* to live and pay taxes in Beverly Hills. The excess demand makes the same house in Beverly Hills more expensive than it would be in Los Angeles.

The benefits of living in Beverly Hills are *capitalized* into the prices of houses or rentals. If not for the excess demand expressed in the locational rent, prices for identical houses would be the same in the two jurisdictions. Taxes would be higher in Beverly Hills, but the higher taxes would be precisely matched by the higher spending on local public goods.

If new jurisdictions were to offer the same types and standards of public goods (and perhaps prestige as a public good) as provided in Beverly Hills, the price of housing in Beverly Hills would fall. Without replication of benefits available from living in Beverly Hills, high-income people who can afford (and are willing) to pay the locational (or monopoly) rents live in Beverly Hills. Other people, whose incomes are not very high, would be prepared to pay for the same public goods as provided in Beverly Hills. However, they cannot afford the housing prices and rents because of excess demand for the public goods that Beverly Hills supplies.

We suggested that, unlike user prices, locational choice does not exclude because everyone has to live somewhere and pay the corresponding taxes and benefit from the public goods provided. However, a jurisdiction is "exclusive" when lower income people, who would be prepared to pay higher taxes in order to receive higher standard public goods, are excluded from the jurisdiction by locational rents that have increased housing prices. In all markets, demand depends on preferences, prices, and incomes or wealth. The locational market for public goods is, in this regard, no different from other markets. Exclusion takes place of those unwilling – or unable – to pay.

We therefore need to add a qualification to the Tiebout locational-choice mechanism:

> *The Tiebout mechanism of locational separation reflects differences in income and wealth as well as differences in preferences for public goods.*

This conclusion is an addition with overtones of questions about social justice: our focus has been on efficiency, through prospects for locational choice solving the information problem that impedes the efficient Lindahl supply of public goods.

Supplement S3B: Property taxes and incentives for zoning

Zoning incentives that restrict housing to attract high-income residents are described in supplement S3B.

Non-locational sharing through clubs

The Tiebout locational-choice mechanism is based on choice from among government jurisdictions. User prices reflect similar choice mechanisms without the requirement of choice of location in a government jurisdiction. More generally, the sharing of costs of public goods can be *non-locational* – and also not-for-profit. Non-locational cost sharing occurs when clubs provide public-good benefits to members – for example, country clubs, sports clubs, chess clubs, fan clubs, faith-based organizations, and campus societies. Willingness to pay membership fees reveals information about preferences and solves the asymmetric-information and free-rider problems. Non-profit clubs protect people from private natural monopoly: for example, a for-profit country club may take advantage of local monopoly to charge high prices, whereas a non-profit club can base membership on the equivalent of competitive prices.[65]

Cost sharing for public goods as a cooperation game

When personal benefits and costs are objective information, people cannot seek to free ride by misrepresenting preferences. All that is required is agreement on the sharing of costs. As an example, consider two groups of people who own

[65] A literature that studies the "theory of clubs" has similarities to the literature on the Tiebout locational-choice mechanism.

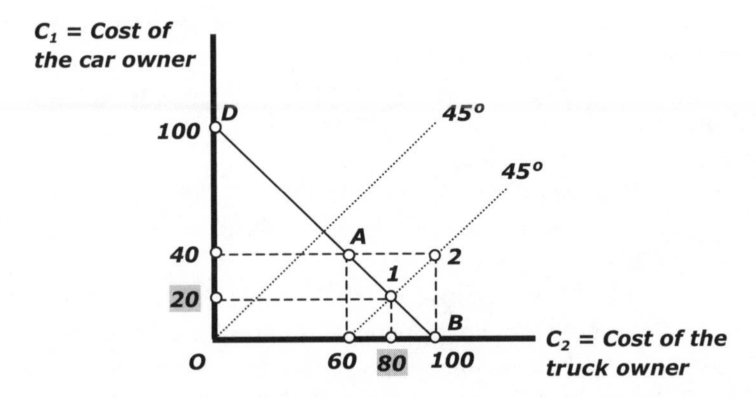

Figure 3.18. A bargaining outcome for cost sharing.

either cars or trucks and who would benefit from a road. The road will not become congested and is therefore a pure public good, but exclusion from use of a road is possible. Cars can use a road that is suitable for trucks, so it is wasteful for owners of cars and trucks to build separate roads. Owners of cars require an incentive to participate in financing the high-cost road suitable for trucks that they do not need. Owners of trucks might propose that car owners pay for the road that accommodates cars, while the truck owners pay for upgrading the road to accommodate trucks. Car owners might point out that truck owners are going to build the road anyway to accommodate trucks and that, because the *MC* of a car using the road is zero, cars should be allowed to use the road without payment. In these alternative proposals, the two groups are attempting to shift costs onto one another. If the truck owners attempt to place too great a share of the costs on the car owners, the car owners have an incentive to build their own road. If the car owners attempt to free ride and do not offer to contribute enough to the high-cost road, the truck owners may finance their own separate road and exclude cars. The owners of cars and trucks can mutually gain by coming to an agreement on sharing the cost of the one road that can accommodate cars and trucks. How might the costs of the single (natural-monopoly) public-good road be shared?

Figure 3.18 shows an example in which there is one car owner and one truck owner. On the axes, C_1 indicates the costs of the car owner and C_2 the costs of the truck owner. The cost of the road sufficient for the car owner is 40 and the cost of the road required by the truck owner is 100. If separate roads are financed and built, the outcome is at point 2. The line *DB* indicates possible sharing of the cost 100 of building a single road. All outcomes along *DB* are efficient in financing one road for both users.

The owner of the car will participate in the efficient coalition (of two) that finances the single road if $C_1 < 40$ (because 40 is the cost to the car owner of building a road for use of the car). The truck owner benefits from the coalition that builds the single road as long as $C_I > 0$ (that is, the car owner makes a positive contribution to paying for the road).

The two individuals now bargain over sharing of the cost of 100 of the single road. Feasible outcomes of bargaining are between points A and B on the line DB (these are the points for which $0 > C_I > 40$).

The two individuals know that if they fail to reach agreement on sharing costs along AB, the outcome will be separate roads at the *disagreement* point 2. Outcomes along AB are Pareto-superior to point 2.[66]

The individuals have an incentive to reach an agreement. Equal bargaining power (for example, both are equally patient) results in equal gains from cooperation. The outcome of bargaining is at point 1 on the 45° line through disagreement point 2. The cost of the public good (the road) is shared, with the truck owner paying 80 and the car owner paying 20.

Figure 3.18 shows the solution to a cooperative game. The prisoners' dilemma is, in contrast, a non-cooperative game and the Nash equilibrium correspondingly is a solution concept for non-cooperative games. The outcome shown in figure 3.18 is known as the *Nash bargaining solution for cooperative games*.[67] The disagreement point 2, which would be the outcome if no agreement on sharing the gains from cooperation were reached, is known as a *threat point* because this is the point to which a person can unilaterally threaten to retreat if no agreement is reached. A unilateral retreat from agreement by one person, of course, makes point 2 the outcome for both people.

The Nash bargaining solution takes the threat point as a reference point and divides the gains from sharing equally, as shown in figure 3.18. The gains from sharing are 40 – that is, the cost saved in not building the separate road for cars. Equal sharing of the gain of 40 gives a gain of 20 each. In the cooperative solution, the car owner therefore pays $(40 - 20) = 20$ and the truck owner pays $(100 - 20) = 80$, where 40 and 100 are, respectively, the costs that the car owner and truck owner would incur if there were no cooperation.[68]

[66] Costs are lower for both individuals along AB than at point 2. The gain to both people excludes the endpoints A and B, at which only one person gains in the move from point 2, which makes the change from point 2 still Pareto-improving (one person gains and the other does not lose).

[67] The Nash bargaining solution was set out by John Nash in 1950.

[68] The exclusion of cars by truck owners at threat point 2 is strategic because although $MC = 0$ for cars using the road that is suitable for trucks, truck owners are seeking to induce car owners to contribute to payment for the road. Another solution for cooperative games is known as the *Shapely value*, named after Lloyd Shapely, who proposed the solution in 1953. The Shapely value divides benefits from cooperation according to the expected value of the benefits that a person brings when joining a coalition. The coalition here consists of the car and truck owners. Neither requires the other to build a road, but both benefit when costs are shared. Although the Shapely value is a different solution concept from that of the Nash bargaining solution, the two solutions coincide in the example we have used. The Nash bargaining solution and the Shapely value for cooperative games coincide for all two-player, transferable-utility games (in our example, utility is transferable through money). Littlechild and Owen (1973) provided an example of an application of the Shapely value to sharing of costs by different types of aircraft using the same runway.

3.3 Cost-Benefit Analysis

Cost-benefit analysis is a last resort for obtaining information that might allow efficient decisions to be made about public spending on public goods. A proposal to construct a bridge requires evaluation of whether the future toll receipts will cover the costs of the bridge. The government will have information on costs that are revealed as market values (the construction cost of the bridge) but other costs are not expressed in markets, as for example potential harm to the environment. Benefits of savings of travel time also are not directly expressed in markets. Some costs and benefits, therefore, need to be computed. A decision is also required on how to compare costs and benefits over time.

The means of eliciting information about public goods that we have considered are, in principle, part of a cost-benefit analysis. If used, the Clarke tax would provide information about personal benefits and costs. However, although interesting, the Clarke tax is not used. In considering cost-benefit analysis, we shall therefore not include the Clarke tax as a means of eliciting information about valuations of public goods.

User prices provide information about benefit from public goods. If user prices cover costs, public spending was warranted (because total benefit expressed in willingness to pay the user prices exceeds the costs). Financing of public goods through user prices nonetheless requires cost-benefit analysis. For example, although costs of constructing a bridge may be covered over time through toll charges, costs and benefits of a bridge need to be evaluated before the bridge is built to determine whether building the bridge is socially warranted.

Cost-benefit analysis has a role in the locational-choice mechanism. When governments in jurisdictions choose taxation and public spending on public goods, cost-benefit analysis is required to evaluate the costs and benefits of public spending on the public goods that a jurisdiction offers.

A. Costs and benefits without market valuations

Cost-benefit analysis has two objectives:

(1) Costs and benefits are computed to determine if a project is worthwhile – that is, to establish whether $W = \sum B - C > 0$.
(2) The objective can be to find precise efficient spending on public goods.

Figure 3.19 shows a public-good project that is worthwhile for all quantities of the public good less than G_E. We see that for $G < G_E$:

$$W = \sum_{i=1}^{n} B_i - C > 0. \tag{3.40}$$

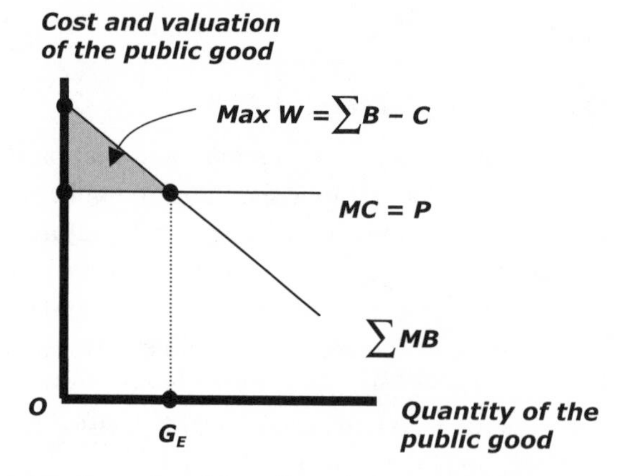

Figure 3.19. The objectives of cost-benefit analysis are to determine (1) if $W = B - C > 0$, and (2) efficient supply of a public good G_E when information on benefits or costs is not revealed in markets.

Social benefit in (3.40) is maximized at the efficient quantity G_E, where:

$$\sum_i MB_i = MC. \tag{3.41}$$

The shaded area indicates the maximal net benefit W obtainable when public spending on the public-good project provides precisely the efficient quantity G_E. Figure 3.19 looks like a market. Cost-benefit analysis, indeed, attempts to replicate the efficiency of a competitive market by seeking absent information about costs and benefits.

The public-good project could be a public zoo. The scale G of the zoo is defined by the number of animals and the types of facilities. The cost of the animals and providing them with shelter and food may be known (as $MC = P$ in figure 3.19); however, total benefit $\sum B$ to the population from the zoo is unknown. To measure total benefit, estimates are required of how many people would visit the zoo and how much they value seeing the animals. It may be decided to charge user prices to cover costs of the zoo; however, with the facility still not in existence, estimates are required of the prices that people will be prepared to pay, which requires estimates of people's benefits.

If a public-good project contributes to public health or public safety, estimates are required of the value of a life saved or of a reduction in the probability of someone being injured or becoming ill. If the project is a new building to expand a government department, estimates are required of the benefits to taxpayers from the activities of the additional government officials who would occupy the new building. For a crime-prevention program, estimates of benefits from the envisaged reduction in crime are required.

Markets do not exist that allow biodiversity to be valued. A dam may disturb the habitat of a rare toad. Valuations are then required of the cost of reduced biodiversity because of the adverse effect on the habitat of the toad.

Imprecision in cost-benefit analysis

There is imprecision in cost-benefit analysis. Often, the objective is to determine whether social benefit W can reasonably be expected to be positive. *Sensitivity analysis* is used in cost-benefit analysis to determine how conclusions depend on calculations and guesses that have been made of values of costs and benefits not expressed in markets.

The rhino

In some countries, there are people who believe that the ground-up horn of a rhino will overcome their sexual inadequacies or will act as an aphrodisiac on others. The demand for the horn of the rhino has threatened the viability of rhino populations. A program to save the rhinos requires a measure of the benefit of making rhinos safer. How do we measure the value of the life of a rhino? Should we value the benefits that people in another culture perceive from ingestion of the ground-up rhino horn? We may value saving the rhino from extinction more than catering to people's feelings about their sexual inadequacies.

Saving the rhinos also requires judgments about whether we want to place a positive value on the incomes of poachers. Poachers may require the protection of government officials, who can provide privileged access to nature reserves where, in principle, animals should be safe. The cost-benefit calculation therefore now takes us into the domain of governments in other countries. What do we do – or how do we respond – if to save rhinos and other threatened species of animals, we need to bribe foreign government officials to allow the animals to be saved? The bribes are part of our costs.

The value of human life

When cost-benefit analysis includes computations of the value of the life of a person, how do we place a precise value on human life? The value of human life could be regarded as infinite.

Approaches used to value life include asking people how much they are prepared to pay to avoid a designated probability of death. For example, by this procedure, a person who is prepared to pay \$100,000 to avoid a 1 percent probability of death values his or her own life at \$10 million. However, how much are people prepared to pay to avoid a 99 percent probability of death? They may be prepared to pay their entire wealth.

Also, how can values of different people's lives be compared? Can one person's life be worth more than the life of another? Decisions may have to be made between allocating public funds to support research to find cures for diseases that mainly affect children or other ailments that affect mainly adults and older people. An adult has made an investment in education and may have knowledge and experience that has high market value and provides high personal income. A child has not yet made an investment in education and has as yet no knowledge and experience that provides market income. A strict economic approach based on the value of income lost would place a lower value on the life of a child than on the life of an older person who has made investments in education. The value of a life, however, is more than income lost. Saving the lives of young people, on the contrary, may be judged more valuable than saving the life of an older person.

Brakes may fail on a car and the driver has no choice but to run over one of two pedestrians. One is known to be a student who has low income from a part-time job but is kindhearted and does volunteer work for charity. The other person is a high-income lawyer who cares only about himself and specializes in finding loopholes that allow firms to avoid regulations intended to protect the environment. The driver realizes that a court of law will compute the value of injuries according to a narrow economic criterion of lost personal income. Therefore, it is more costly to injure the high-income lawyer than the low-income charitable student.

B. Valuation over time

In general, the benefits and costs of public-good projects extend over time. For most types of public-good projects, costs are incurred today and benefits are in the future. When a bridge or a highway is built, or defense spending is undertaken, or a museum is established, the costs are, for example, mostly in the present and the benefits become available in the future. Sometimes the converse is the case: benefits are obtained today and the costs are imposed over time on future generations – for example, through environmental damage.

A project provides a net benefit of $(\sum B_0 - C_0)$ during the first year, $(\sum B_1 - C_1)$ during the following year, then $(\sum B_2 - C_2)$ in the next year, and so on for some ongoing period. Because the project provides public-good benefits, the benefits $\sum B_0$, $\sum B_1$, and $\sum B_2$ are summations over the population. A decision of how to compare benefits and costs at different periods requires the choice of a discount rate; that is, a rate is chosen at which to "discount" the future, or reduce benefits in the future compared to present benefits.

The usual presumption is that the discount rate is positive because of time preference. Benefits today are preferred to benefits tomorrow and costs tomorrow are preferred to costs today. Time preference is also reflected in a positive market interest rate: if we wish to transfer benefits from the future to the present, we need to borrow at the positive market interest rate. We avoid interest expenses if costs are tomorrow rather than today.

A zero discount rate gives the same weight to benefits and costs at any time in the future as to benefits and costs in the present. Future generations are then given the same weight in evaluation of benefits and costs as present generations – or we ourselves value our future benefits and costs no differently than our valuation of our present benefits and costs. Complete intergenerational altruism requires a zero discount rate; for example, the future existence of the rhino would be valued as we value the present existence of the rhino.

Choice of the discount rate can affect conclusions about whether a project merits public finance. The environment provides benefits that reach far into the future. A high discount rate increases the likelihood that a project that harms the environment will pass the test of cost-benefit analysis because of the lower weight given to environmental benefits for future generations.

A project with a one-time cost and a one-time benefit

We can consider as an example a project that requires a one-time public expenditure this year and provides a one-time benefit next year. The cost today is C_0 and benefits next year summed over the population are $\sum B_1$. With the rate of discount given as i, the cost-benefit criterion for justification of public finance for the project is:

$$W = \frac{\sum B_1}{(1+i)} - C_0 > 0. \tag{3.42}$$

If $\sum B_1 = 105$ and $C_0 = 100$, it follows from expression (3.42) that the project is justified if the rate of discount i is less than 5 percent. Choosing a discount rate in excess of 5 percent ensures a decision to reject the project. A discount rate of less than 5 percent, conversely, ensures a decision to provide public finance for the project.

A project with benefits for multiple years

A project may have a time horizon of N years. That is, the project may be expected to provide benefits or to incur costs over N years. If the discount rate has been chosen as zero so that all future benefits and costs are valued as if they were incurred today, and we measure benefits and costs at the end of each period, the net benefit over time from the project is the undiscounted sum:

$$W = \left(\sum B_0 - C_0\right) + \left(\sum B_1 - C_1\right) + \cdots + \left(\sum B_N - C_N\right). \tag{3.43}$$

To discount the future, we choose a positive discount rate, which discounts (or lowers) future costs and benefits. With a positive discount rate given by i, the cost-benefit criterion for a public investment is:

$$W = (B_0 - C_0) + \frac{\sum B_1 - C_1}{(1+i)} + \frac{\sum B_2 - C_2}{(1+i)^2} + \cdots + \frac{\sum B_N - C_N}{(1+i)^N} > 0. \tag{3.44}$$

Expression (3.44) shows the present value of the costs and benefits associated with the project. As we move out in time in expression (3.44) to include future benefits and costs, we reapply the discount rate again in every year that passes. The farther we go into the future, the smaller is our valuation today of the future years' benefits and costs. When the discount rate i is zero, expression (3.44) becomes the straight summation of net benefits over time, as shown in expression (3.43). When the discount placed on the future is infinity, all terms in (3.44) except today's values disappear, and we have the limiting case in which all that matters is today and now.

When $i > 0$, we can define a discount factor:

$$\delta \equiv \frac{1}{1+i} < 1. \tag{3.45}$$

This provides another way of expressing discounting. When we substitute the discount factor from expression (3.45) into the expression for present value (3.44), we have:

$$W = \left(\sum B_0 - C_0\right) + \delta\left(\sum B_1 - C_1\right) + \delta^2\left(\sum B_2 - C_2\right) + \cdots \tag{3.46}$$

where δ discounts the future.

In the special case in which benefits and costs are the same in each year and extend indefinitely into the future, the property of the sum of an infinite series can be used to express the present value of a project as:

$$W = \frac{\sum B_i - C_i}{i}. \tag{3.47}$$

What should the discount rate be?

If private-capital markets reflect the time preference of people in society, we might want to consider using the market rate of interest as the social rate of discount for valuing future costs and benefits of public investment. The market rate of interest indicates the compensation that has to be paid to people for deferring consumption to the future, and thereby reflects the market's valuation of time preference. If we wish to choose a social rate of discount that differs from the market interest rate, we need to make a case that private-capital markets are not efficient or that the market rate of interest does not accurately measure society's time preference.

We may regard the environment as a gift of nature that is not the possession of any generation to do with as it wishes and take the view that future generations should be treated equally with us in placing a value on environmental benefits and costs. We would then choose a discount rate of zero to apply to the preservation of the environment, even though the market interest rate is positive.

The difference between social and private risk might also lead us to choose a social rate of discount for evaluating costs and benefits of public projects lower than the market rate of interest. Private capital markets make allowance for private risk. Public-investment proposals spread risk over all the population and therefore should be evaluated at a lower risk-free discount rate.

The major problem is that decisions made today affect yet-unborn populations who are not present to express their preferences. Future generations may not find to their liking a high discount rate that was chosen in the past. We may also decide in the future that the discount rate we chose in the past was inappropriate; that is, we may regret that society did not choose a lower discount rate that places more weight on the future, when we ourselves arrive into the future. Looking back at decisions that were made in the past, we may wish that previous generations had been more attentive to the environment and that creatures that had become extinct had survived.[69]

C. The discount rate and choice between public projects

Often, cost-benefit analysis involves choosing between alternative public investments. A choice might be necessary between public investment in a subway system and in highway expansion. Table 3.9 shows a subway system that requires initial nonrepeated public spending of 1,400 and provides indefinite benefits of 60 per year. Expanding a highway system costs 400 (including environmental costs) and provides benefits of 50 per year for 10 years. After 10 years, the highway system needs to be expanded because of increased traffic.

TABLE 3.9. CHOICE BETWEEN TWO PROJECTS

	Subway	Highway
Cost C	1,400 once	400 every 10 years
Benefit each year B_i	60 per year	50 per year
A time horizon of 50 years		
Undiscounted total benefit $\sum B_i$	3,000	2,500
Undiscounted net benefit $\sum(B_i - C)$	1,600	500
Gain from choosing the subway	*1,100*	
A time horizon of 100 years		
Undiscounted total benefit $\sum B_i$	6,000	5,000
Undiscounted net benefit $\sum(B_i - C)$	4,600	1,000
Gain from choosing the subway	*3,600*	
Discounted at $i = 5\%$		
Total benefit $\sum B_i$	1,200	405 every 10 years
Total net benefit $\sum(B_i - C)$	−200	+5 every 10 years

A society that does not discount the future and that has a time horizon of 50 years will choose investment in the subway. The gain from choosing the subway is 1,100.[70] The subway is yet more worthwhile if, without discounting, the time horizon is 100 years. The gain from choosing the subway rather than the highway system is then 3,600.[71] When a discount rate of 5 percent is used, expanding the

[69] The dodo bird of Mauritius was declared extinct in 1681. The flightless bird was named a "dodo," or stupid, because of its gentle and trusting nature. In 1888, the parliament of the Australian state of Tasmania voted to place a bounty of one pound on the Tasmanian tiger; in 1936, the animal was listed as protected; in 1986, it was declared extinct.

[70] The benefits $\sum B_i$ from the subway over 50 years are 3,000, and the cost is 1,400, giving the net benefit of $\sum(B_i - C)$ of 1,600. The benefits $\sum B_i$ from the highway over 50 years are 2,500, and the cost is 2,000 (the cost is 400 every 10 years), giving the net benefit of $\sum(B_i - C)$ of 500.

[71] The benefits $\sum B_i$ from the subway are then 6,000, which – after subtracting the initial cost of 1,400 – gives total net benefit from the subway of $\sum(B_i - C)$ of 4,600. Over 100 years, the highway requires 10 repeated investments of 400, so the cost is 4,000. The benefit $\sum B_i$ from the highway over 100 years is 5,000, giving the net benefit of $\sum(B_i - C)$ of 1,000 from the highway.

highway system every 10 years is preferable to building the subway.[72] This example shows how the discount rate affects the choice between alternative public-investment projects when costs and benefits of projects are distributed differently over time.[73]

D. Income distribution and cost-benefit analysis

Cost-benefit analysis can be influenced by income-distribution consequences of public-spending decisions.

Changes in incomes because of public spending

Public spending often changes costs and benefits through people's incomes. Two alternative bridges may increase incomes of either low- or high-income people. Because of differences in the value of time, we expect a bridge to provide greater benefits for high-income people than for low-income people. Low-income people, however, might have low incomes because they are cut off by the absence of a bridge from high-income employment opportunities. When investigating which bridge should be constructed, cost-benefit analysis should then consider the future increase in incomes of present low-income people.

> *Determination of efficient public spending through cost-benefit analysis requires consideration of income consequences of alternative spending decisions.*

Social welfare functions

Cost-benefit analysis is directed at efficiency, including allowance for consequences for incomes of public investment. If social justice is also a concern (such as when we care how benefits and costs affect low-income people), an alternative social criterion is required that incorporates both efficiency and social justice. A social criterion that allows weight to be placed on efficiency and social justice is

[72] Because the subway provides benefits of 60 per year forever, we can use expression (3.47) to compute the present value of an indefinite flow of benefits of 60 discounted at 5 percent, which gives 1,200. Because the cost of building the subway is 1,400, the subway has a negative present value, equal to −200. Highway expansion costs 400 every 10 years and provides benefits of 50 per year. The present value of benefits of 50 per year for 10 years discounted at 5 percent is approximately 405, which exceeds the cost of 400.

[73] Our example comparing public investment in the subway with public investment in highway expansion has used constant benefits over time, whereas, in practice, we can expect benefits to increase over time – in particular, from the subway, which can be used to run trains with increasing frequency and with more carriages if demand increases over time. We could elaborate by changing benefits over time, as well as by allowing for different maintenance costs of the subway and the highway system and by including the different costs of mass-transit equipment and subway personnel compared with costs incurred in bus travel and travel in private cars and the costs of parking. We could also include the environmental cost of expanding the highway system and computations for projected loss of life and injury through highway accidents against the probability of a subway accident.

known as a *social welfare function*. We shall study social welfare functions when we come to the topic of social justice.

Cost-benefit analysis and political decisions

A political representative may succeed in obtaining public spending for a public-good project that benefits his or her constituency. If the public spending is not justified by cost-benefit analysis, the politician's constituents would be better off if they were given the public money directly rather than the public money being used to finance the proposed public spending. For example, the cost-benefit criterion is not satisfied if $100 of proposed present public spending provides benefits with a present value of $90. The constituents are better off receiving the $100 directly. The direct transfer of $100 will provide benefits of $100 (and more, because the benefit from personal spending in a market exceeds the value of the money spent). Politicians may not, however, not be able to give away public money, but they can provide publicly financed public-good projects. Politicians may be responding to requisites of political support or to rent-seeking activity. In either case:

Cost-benefit analysis can be compromised by political decisions.

Supplement S3

Supplement S3A: Group size and voluntary public-good contributions

How does group size affect voluntary public-good contributions? The answer determines how group size influences effectiveness of collective action. The objective of collective action can be to provide a public good for consumption or can be political – to influence policy decisions through campaign contributions or to provide resources for rent-seeking activities of a special-interest group.

Identical individuals

To compare the effectiveness in collective action of groups of different sizes, we treat individuals as identical. When we refer to the number of individuals in a group, we therefore have a common unit of measurement for specifying the size of the group.

Utility-maximizing choice of own contribution

As in the public-good experiments that were described, an individual i has predetermined income y_i, which can be allocated between personal private-good

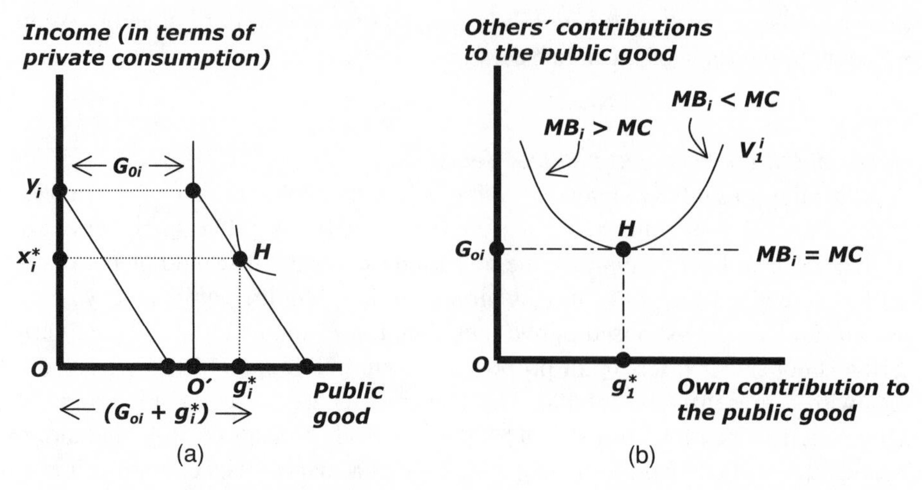

Figure S3.1. (a) The utility-maximizing choice, given the contributions of others to the public good. (b) The same utility-maximizing choice.

consumption x_i and a voluntary own-contribution g_i to a public good. The private good is competitively supplied, as are inputs for the public good. Therefore, price equals marginal cost for both the private and public goods. With P indicating the relative price of the public good, an individual's budget constraint is:

$$y_i = x_i + Pg_i. \tag{S3.1}$$

Total supply G of the public good available to individual i is his or her own-contribution g_i plus the amount G_i contributed by others:

$$G = g_i + G_i. \tag{S3.2}$$

An individual's utility function is:[74]

$$U^i = U^i(x_i, G). \tag{S3.3a}$$

Figure S3.1a shows the utility function in expression (S3.3a). Income y_i in figure S3.1a is measured in terms of private consumption. G_{oi} is the quantity of the public good provided by others. The availability of G_{oi} moves the origin for the individual's budget constraint from O to O'.

The Nash conjecture for strategic behavior is that others do not change their decisions in response to an individual's decision. The Nash choice, therefore, is made on the basis that G_{oi} will not change in response to the individual's own decision. The individual in figure S3.1a therefore maximizes utility given by expression (S3.3a) subject to the budget constraint in expression (S3.1) and subject to expression (S3.2) indicating total public-good supply.

With O' as the origin (because the contribution by others G_{oi} is taken as given), the utility-maximizing choice is at point H, where the individual has x_i^* of the

[74] Recall that we are using the terms *personal benefit* and *utility* interchangeably.

private good and makes the own-contribution to the public good g_i^* (measured from the origin at O'). Total availability of the public good to individual i (and to all others) is $(G_{oi} + g_i^*)$.

The utility-maximizing choice at point H is also shown in figure S3.1b. To arrive at figure S3.1b from figure S3.1a, we substitute the expressions (S3.1) and (S3.2) in the utility function (S3.3a) to express utility as:

$$U^i = U^i(y_i - Pg_i, G_i + g_i) = V^i(g_i, G_i : given\ P, y_i). \tag{S3.3b}$$

In the utility function in the form of expression (S3.3b), utility depends on the choice of the own-contribution g_i to the public good and on others' contributions G_i, given the relative price P of the public good and the individual's income y_i.

Utility is constant along V_1^i in figure S3.1b. Therefore:

$$dV^i = 0 = \frac{\partial V^i}{\partial g_i} \cdot dg_i + \frac{\partial V^i}{\partial G_i} \cdot dG_i. \tag{S3.4}$$

The slope of utility contours such as V_1^i is therefore:

$$\frac{dG_i}{dg_i} = -\left(\frac{\partial V^i}{\partial g_i}\right) \Big/ \left(\frac{\partial V^i}{\partial G_i}\right)\ for\ dV^i = 0. \tag{S3.5}$$

Expression (S3.5) is the ratio of two marginal benefits (or utilities) of the public good. The difference in marginal benefit is in *who* pays for the public good. The own-contribution g_i is personally financed at a marginal cost $P = MC$; therefore:

$$\frac{\partial V^i}{\partial g_i} = MB_i - MC. \tag{S3.6}$$

Others' contributions G_i provide marginal benefit at no personal cost; therefore:

$$\frac{\partial V^i}{\partial G_i} = MB_i. \tag{S3.7}$$

By substituting expressions (S3.6) and (S3.7) into expression (S3.5), we obtain the expression for the slope of utility contours such as the V_1^i curve in figure S3.1b as:

$$\frac{dG_i}{dg_i} = \frac{MB_i - MC}{MB_i}. \tag{S3.8}$$

The reaction function

The reaction function indicates how the own-contribution to the public good responds (or reacts) to changes in the contribution made by others. The reaction function is based on the Nash behavioral conjecture that when a decision is made about an own-contribution to the public good, the decisions of others about their contributions are taken as given.

> *The reaction function shows the individual's best or utility-maximizing response, given the contribution of others.*

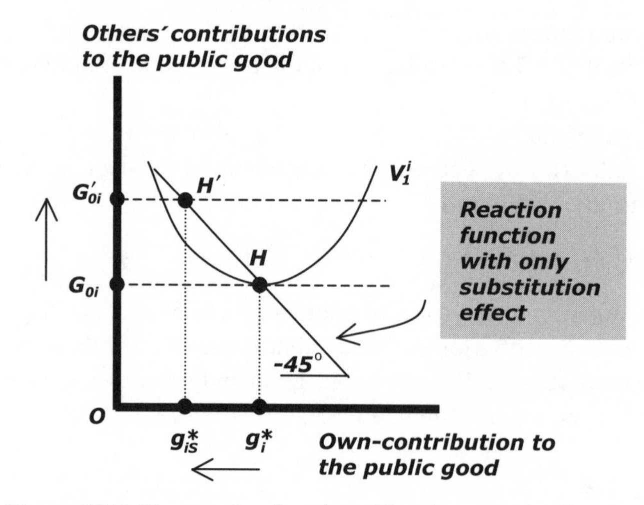

Figure S3.2. The reaction function with only a substitution effect.

Point H in figure S3.1b is on individual i's reaction function because the own-contribution g_i^* has been chosen to maximize individual i's utility, given the combined contributions G_{oi} of others. At points such as H, we have:

$$\frac{dV^i}{dg_i} = 0 = MB_i - MC.^{75} \tag{S3.9}$$

Figure S3.2 shows individual i's change in choice of own-contribution from g_i^* to g_{iS}^* when the contribution of others increases from G_{oi} to G'_{oi}. Point H' in figure S3.2 is another point on individual i's reaction function.

The substitution effect

The response in choice of own-contribution when the contribution of others changes is a combination of a substitution effect and an income effect. In the case shown in figure S3.2, there is only a substitution effect. Through the substitution effect, a person reduces own-contributions to a public good dollar-for-dollar in response to increased contributions by others. As indicated in figure S3.2, the slope of the reaction function with only a substitution effect is therefore −45°. That is, the substitution effect is −1.

When someone else pays for quantities of a public good from which we benefit, it is as if we have been given additional income. For example, if we contribute \$100 to a public good and then someone else contributes an additional \$40, when we reduce our spending on the public good by \$40, we have \$40 additional income and still have the benefit of \$100 spent on the public good. The

[75] We also see in figure S3.1b that given the contribution of others, G_{oi}, $MB_i < MC$ if the individual chooses an own-contribution less than g_i^* and $MB_i < MC$ if the individual chooses an own-contribution greater than g_i^*.

one-for-one substitution effect is that we can reduce our own voluntary contribution by the amount of increased spending by others and still have the same quantity of the public good.[76]

The income effect

We view the public good as a normal good for all individuals; therefore, individual demand increases with individual income. Also, an increase in income of one dollar does not increase personal spending on the public good by more than one dollar; only some share of increased income is spent on the public good. Because the contribution of others to a public good is equivalent to receiving additional income, through the income effect, an individual's demand for the public good increases when contributions by others increase. The income effect is therefore positive.

The reaction function with combined substitution and income effects

Figure S3.3 shows the reaction function with combined substitution and income effects. The substitution effect in response to the increase in contributions of others from G_{oi} to G'_{oi} is again shown as a change from point H to point H' and a one-for-one decrease in own provision from g_i^* to g_{iS}^*. The positive income effect increases own provision by $(g_{iT}^* - g_{iS}^*)$. The reaction function with combined income and substitution effects joins points H and H''. The combined substitution and income effects reduce the own-contribution from g_i^* to g_{iT}^*.

How large is the combined substitution and income effect?

The size of the income effect depends on the share of income spent on the public good. We denote by $0 > \mu > 1$ the share of an additional dollar of income spent on the public good. The slope of the reaction function is therefore $\{(-1 + \mu) > -1\}$. In general, we expect the income effect expressed in μ to be small because of the small share of any one good in total personal spending. Often, therefore, it

[76] From the individual's budget constraint (S3.1), we obtain:

$$G = \frac{(y_i - x_i)}{P} + G_i.$$

The utility function in expression (S3.3a) can be re-expressed as:

$$U^i(x_i, G) = U^i\left(x_i, \frac{y_i - x_i}{P} + G_i\right)$$

or:

$$U^i(x_i, G) = U^i\left(x_i, \left(\frac{y_i}{P} + G_i\right) - \frac{x_i}{P}\right).$$

Utility thus depends on the sum:

$$\left[\left(\frac{y_i}{P}\right) + G_i\right]$$

and not on the composition of own-income and public-good contributions by others.

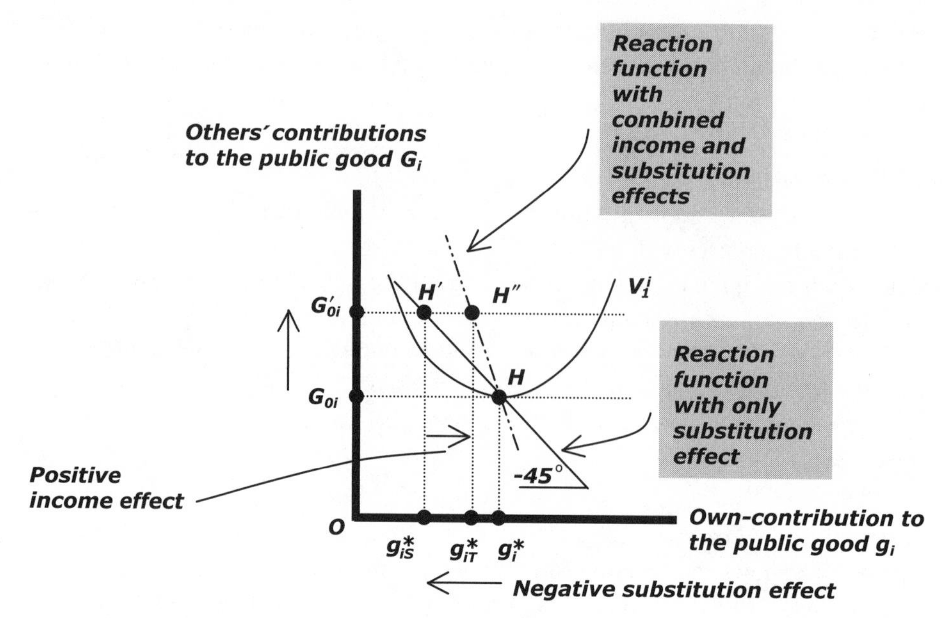

Figure S3.3. The reaction function with combined substitution and income effects.

is a reasonable approximation to omit income effects from consideration unless there are circumstances that suggest income effects are high.[77]

When others spend an additional dollar on a public good, through the substitution effect, personal own-spending on the public good falls by one dollar and income increases by one dollar. Because the public good is not the only good on which spending takes place, the entire dollar of additional income is not spent on the public good (that is, $0 > \mu > 1$), and the income effect is less than 1. Therefore:

The substitution effect is greater than the income effect.

Consequently, as in figure S3.3:

The slope of the reaction function combining substitution and income effects is negative.

Nash equilibrium for voluntary contributions

Figure S3.4a shows the reaction functions R_1 and R_2 of two people. The Nash equilibrium for the contributions to the public good is at point N, where the reaction functions intersect. At the point N, individual decisions are consistent in that both persons maximize utility given the contribution of the other. We denote the

[77] Income effects can be expected to be high when wages change.

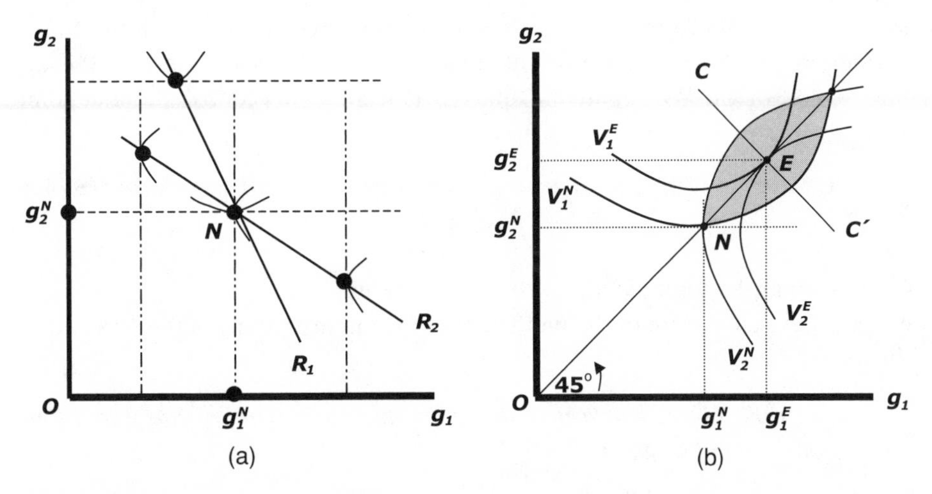

Figure S3.4. (a) The Nash equilibrium for voluntary contributions. (b) The Nash equilibrium and efficient contributions to the public good.

total quantity of the public good voluntarily supplied in the Nash equilibrium at N by G^N, where:

$$G^N = g_1^N + g_2^N. \tag{S3.10}$$

Efficient contributions

The indifference curves V_1^N and V_2^N in figure S3.4b show the two persons' utilities in the Nash equilibrium at N. The shaded area bounded by the indifference curves V_1^N and V_2^N indicates Pareto-improving outcomes relative to the Nash equilibrium at N (in the shaded area, both people are better off than at N). Pareto-efficient contributions to the public good are along the contract curve CC' – that is, no change can be made from points along CC' to make one person better off without making the other person worse off. Because indifference curves are tangential along the contract curve CC', it follows that:[78]

$$\frac{MB_1 - MC}{MB_1} = \frac{MB_2}{MB_2 - MC}. \tag{S3.11}$$

Efficiency of public-good supply on the contract curve is confirmed by rearranging expression (S3.11) to establish:

$$\sum_i MB_i = MC. \tag{S3.12}$$

The two individuals are identical; therefore, their Nash contributions at point N are equal. At point E on the contract curve where utilities are V_1^E and V_2^E,

[78] See expression (S3.8).

efficient contributions to the public good are also equal. That is, both the Nash-equilibrium point N and the efficient equal-contributions point E are on the 45° line from the origin. We denote the total efficient combined contributions at point E by G^E, where:

$$G^E = g_1^E + g_2^E. \quad \text{(S3.13)}$$

A measure of the inefficiency of the Nash equilibrium

We now have a measure of the inefficiency of voluntary supply in the Nash equilibrium.

> *The ratio G^N/G^E measures the inefficiency of voluntary Nash contributions to a public good.*

We wish to determine:

> *What happens to G^N/G^E as group size increases?*

Changes in the efficient quantity as group size increases

Figure S3.5a shows how the efficient quantity of the public good increases as group size increases. In the case in figure S3.5a, there are three individuals.[79] In the general case, for any group size n, social benefit from the public good is:

$$W = \sum_{i=1}^{n} B_i - C. \quad \text{(S3.14)}$$

The efficient quantity G^E is determined by:

$$\sum_{i=1}^{n} MB_i = MC. \quad \text{(S3.15)}$$

Therefore, as in figure S3.5a, the efficient quantity increases as n increases, from G_1^E when $n = 1$ to G_2^E when $n = 2$, and G_3^E when $n = 3$.[80]

Thus:

$$\frac{dG^E}{dn} > 0. \quad \text{(S3.16)}$$

[79] In figure S3.5a, each of three identical individuals has willingness to pay for the public good as given by MB_1. The vertical summation of the identical MB functions gives willingness to pay for groups of two and for three individuals. The increase in the efficient quantity of the public good when group size increases is independent, of course, of whether people have identical willingness to pay for public goods.

[80] In figure S3.5a, for any quantity of the public good, it is Pareto-efficient to allow additional potential beneficiaries access to the public good. However, when the number of beneficiaries increases, the efficient quantity also increases.

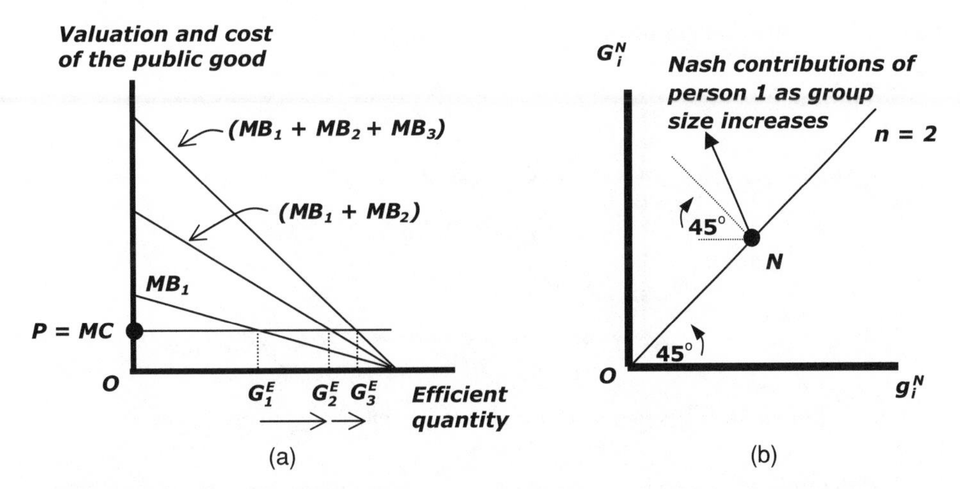

Figure S3.5. (a) The efficient quantity of a public good increases as group size increases. (b) Change in the Nash equilibrium contribution of person 1 as increased group size increases the combined contributions of all others.

The change in the Nash-equilibrium quantity as group size increases

With people identical and individual Nash contributions therefore equal, we have for person 1:

$$g_1^N = g^N = \frac{G_1^N + g^N}{n}. \tag{S3.17a}$$

Here, G_1^N denotes the total contributions of all people except person 1 in the Nash equilibrium.

Expression S3.17a can be solved to obtain the equal Nash contribution of each person i in the group as:

$$g^N = \frac{G_i^N}{(n-1)}. \tag{S3.17b}$$

When $n = 2$, expression (S3.17b) indicates that:

$$g^N = G_i^N. \tag{S3.17c}$$

That is, as we saw, the Nash equilibrium when $n = 2$ is on the 45° line from the origin.

In figure S3.5b, the Nash equilibrium for $n = 2$ is again shown on the 45° line at point N. With only a substitution effect, as n increases beyond 2, the Nash contribution decreases along the 45° line from point N. With a positive income

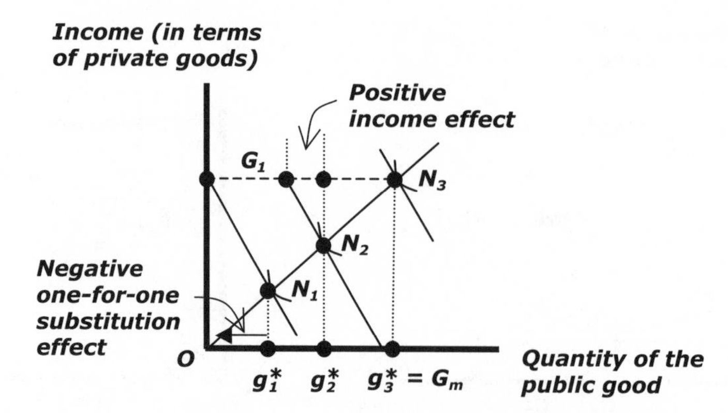

Figure S3.6. The tendency for voluntary contributions to go to zero.

effect, the individual Nash contribution decreases on the line with greater slope than 45°. In either case:

$$\frac{dg_i^N}{dn} < 0. \tag{S3.18}$$

The change in total Nash contributions with only a substitution effect

With only a substitution effect, the total Nash contribution G_N remains unchanged as group size increases:

$$\frac{dG^N}{dn} = 0. \tag{S3.19a}$$

Nash contributions with a positive income effect

What happens to total Nash contributions G^N when there is a positive income effect? To answer this question, we look at the effect of increases in group size on individual Nash contributions. Figure S3.6 shows the tendency for personal Nash contributions to go to zero as group size increases. We do not now need to regard people as identical. Person 1 chooses g_1^* at point N_1 when no one else is contributing to a public good and chooses g_2^* at point N_2 when others contribute G_1. The amount G_1 provided by others becomes the origin for measuring person 1's voluntary contributions after G_1 is provided. We see the one-to-one negative substitution response to provision by others of G_1 and the positive income effect. More people joining the group increases the quantity of the public good available to person 1. When others contribute the quantity G_m, person 1's demand g_3^* for the public good at point N_3 requires no personal spending; person 1 does not contribute to the public good because the contributions of others satisfy personal demand. N_1, N_2, and N_3 are points on person 1's reaction function. We see that contributions by others tend eventually to result in complete free riding.

Thus, with a positive income effect:

$$\frac{dG^N}{dn} \geq 0. \tag{S3.19b}$$

Group size and inefficiency in the Nash equilibrium

If there is only a substitution effect:

$$\frac{d(G^N/G^E)}{dn} < 0. \tag{S3.20}$$

There is only a substitution effect and no income effect if the utility function is of the form:

$$U(x, G) = x + B(G). \tag{S3.21}$$

For usual specifications of utility that include an income effect, the result remains as in expression (S3.20). In particular, the income effect can be expected to be small for any one public good, given the many goods on which income is spent.

We therefore conclude that, quite generally:

> *When group size increases, total Nash-equilibrium voluntary contributions to a public good become less efficient as measured by G^N/G^E.*

Group size and the benefits of enforced payment

If G^N/G^E decreases with group size:

> *Larger groups benefit more from payments enforced through taxation.*

Governments confront problems of asymmetric information in seeking to determine efficient spending on public goods; nonetheless, problems of asymmetric information aside, the larger the size of the group of beneficiaries from a public good, the greater are the benefits when the group delegates to government the responsibility for financing public goods through taxation. Still, setting the asymmetric-information problem aside does not mean that the asymmetric-information problem is not present to be resolved: we are returned to the Clarke tax, user prices, and the Tiebout locational-choice mechanism as means of eliciting personal information and to cost-benefit analysis as means of seeking to compute costs and benefits not revealed in markets.

Changes in income distribution

We can also ask:

> *How do changes in income distribution affect total Nash voluntary contributions to a public good?*

We ask this question without presuming that people necessarily have identical willingness to pay for public goods or identical incomes. Indeed, if incomes are originally identical, a change in income distribution makes incomes unequal. The following conclusion applies to changes in income distribution in a Nash equilibrium:

> *Total voluntary Nash-equilibrium contributions G^N to a public good are unaffected by changes in income distribution, as long as people make positive contributions in both the original and new Nash equilibrium.*[81]

If total efficient supply G^E of a public good were independent of income distribution, the measure G^N/G^E would also be independent of income distribution. Efficient supply G^E, however, does depend on income distribution. Whether G^E increases or declines depends on whether income is redistributed to people with greater or smaller demand for a public good.[82]

Public goods and rent seeking

When benefits sought are private goods (or private income), increases in the number of rent seekers tend to increase rent dissipation and thereby the social cost of rent seeking.[83] The rent-seeking prize, however, may be a public good that collectively benefits a group of individuals; each individual rent seeker then makes a private voluntary Nash contribution to the group's total resources available for rent seeking to obtain the benefits of the public good. Now, personal contributions are not personal payments that add to the total availability of a public good. The personal contribution to group rent seeking that an individual makes increases the probability that the group will be successful in obtaining the politically assigned rent. The principles that apply to personal contributions to public goods also apply to personal contributions to resources available for a group's rent-seeking activity. In particular, the one-to-one substitution effect limits total use of resources in rent seeking; because of the substitution effect, when group size increases, preexisting group members commensurately reduce their own contributions to the group's total rent-seeking resources that are used in contesting the public-good rent. With positive income effects, the tendency is (as shown in figure S3.6) for individuals to cease contributing as group size increases.

Supplement S3B: Property taxes and incentives for zoning

When property taxes finance public spending, the choice of the quality of housing determines the taxes that people pay. The choices of a location in a Tiebout

[81] The conclusion is based on the one-for-one substitution effect and on the equivalence of increases in income and increases in contributions by others to public goods. The requirement that people make positive contributions to the public good ensures that the latter equivalence holds. If individual i is not contributing to the public good when a quantity G^N of the public good is being provided in a Nash equilibrium, then $MB_i(G^N) < MC = P$ and the individual prefers additional income to someone else increasing contributions to the public good.

[82] If people differ in preferences and/or incomes, income redistribution changes the *MB*s that are summed to determine efficient supply according to $\sum MB = MC$.

[83] See chapter 2.

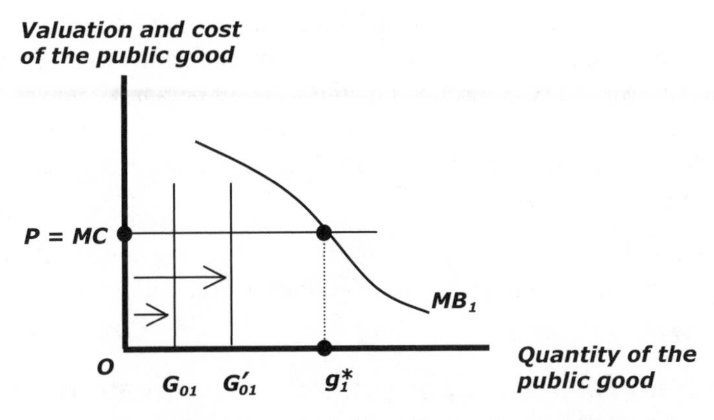

Figure S3.7. The substitution effect and zoning laws.

jurisdiction and of housing within the jurisdiction are voluntary. With property taxes financing payment for public goods, individual and family tax burdens depend on the quality of housing of others. People who live in a more modest house pay less for housing, which is personal consumption; through the property tax, they also contribute less to paying for public goods – or, if they live in government housing, they may not contribute at all.

Choice of the quality of housing – and of location in a particular jurisdiction – can be viewed as a Nash equilibrium. Figure S3.7 is another description of the one-to-one Nash-equilibrium substitution effect for public goods. The marginal willingness-to-pay function MB_1 of person 1 depicted in figure S3.7 is independent of income; there is no income effect. If no one else were to contribute to paying for the public good, person 1 would choose voluntarily to supply the quantity g_1^* (the public good then provides exclusive private benefit to person 1). The origin for measuring g_1^* is 0.

When others in the jurisdiction contribute to the public good by providing the quantity G_{01}, person 1 still wants the total quantity g_1^* (there is no income effect) and in the Nash equilibrium personally pays for the difference $(g_1^* - G_{01})$ as an own-contribution. The origin for person 1's own-contribution has moved to G_{01}. The one-to-one substitution effect is that person 1 has reduced his or her own contribution precisely by the quantity G_{01} that others have provided.

If the amount provided by others increases to G'_{01}, the origin for person 1's own contribution correspondingly moves to G'_{01}. In the Nash equilibrium, person 1 then provides the smaller amount $(g_1^* - G'_{01})$ as an own-contribution.

Modest or expensive houses can be built in the jurisdiction. If everyone benefits equally from the public good, people with a demand for modest housing gain through free riding because of the lower property taxes that they pay to finance the public good. Behavior can also be strategic: people may choose low-value housing to reduce their contributions through property taxes to financing public goods.

In figure S3.7, through the property tax, occupants of a modest house will provide person 1 with G_{01} of the public good in the Nash equilibrium; occupants of an expensive house will, however, provide person 1 with G'_{01}. At the same time, person 1 is reciprocally providing others with public goods through his or her property taxes, which are determined by the value of person 1's house.

To avoid free riding, residents of the jurisdiction who want high-value housing have an interest in zoning laws that ensure that fellow residents in the jurisdiction also live in expensive houses.

> *The one-to-one substitution effect for public goods explains the incentives for zoning laws when property taxes finance local public goods.*

Supplement S3C: Other approaches to private payment for public goods

We have viewed voluntary payment for public goods in terms of non-cooperative Nash equilibria and substitution and income effects. There are other approaches and suggestions.

Deviation from cooperation

We could begin from initial conditions where members of a group with a collective objective cooperate and do not free ride. If the group is sufficiently small, individual behavior may be observable and social pressures may deter free riding. The question about effectiveness of collective action of the group is then framed in terms of ability of the group to monitor behavior and to detect and penalize or ostracize free riding. The advantage of small over large groups is that free riding can be more readily detected; that is, the advantage of small groups is in the monitoring of individual behavior. Thus, in chapter 2, small interest groups were described as having organizational advantages over voters at large.

> *For a small group in which individual behavior is observable, initial cooperation can be presumed and the effectiveness of collective action depends on monitoring of contributions of members of the group.*

In large anonymous groups, such as voters, the Nash behavior that we have described is appropriate.

Joint supply of private and public goods

There have been proposals that the free-rider problem can be overcome when private and public goods are jointly supplied. For example, an interest group can provide private benefits such as magazines and personal advice for which people are required to pay. The profits from sale of the private good can then be used to finance a public good from which members of the group benefit, such as the collective action or lobbying of the interest group. Of course, for such financing of the public good to be possible, the interest group needs to be the monopolistic supplier of the private goods; otherwise, if there were competition in supply of the private good, sellers that provide only the private good and do not bundle the private and public goods would provide the private good at lower cost than a seller that bundles. Buyers who purchase the private good from the non-bundling seller would pay less and still benefit from the public good.

Voluntary financing public goods through lotteries

Spending on public goods is often financed through proceeds of lotteries. In this case as well, there is bundling or joint supply of a private and public good; the private good is the expected value of the prize in the lottery. Such lotteries provide greater total contributions to public goods than private voluntary Nash contributions. In providing voluntary contributions to a public good through purchase of lottery tickets, people also receive the private benefit of the chance of winning the lottery and therefore they spend more on lottery tickets than if they were contributing only to public goods. Part of the spending on lottery tickets finances the private-good prize to the winner of the lottery, but more is still available for spending on public goods.

Supplement S3D: An efficient economy with public and private goods

Supplement S1A provided a general-equilibrium picture of an economy with only private goods. General equilibrium can similarly be illustrated in an economy with private and public goods. The condition for efficient supply of public goods can thereby be derived in general equilibrium. For exposition, an economy is described with one private and one public good. Figure S3.8a shows an economy's production-possibilities frontier for a private good X and public good G. Competitive supply of factors of production ensures that production in the economy is efficient and therefore on the production-possibility frontier (see supplement S1A). The public good is simultaneously available to the entire population. The curve DE shows the feasible consumption possibilities available to person 2 when person 1 has utility maintained at U_1. The highest utility for person 2, U_2^{max}, is at point F, where public-good supply is G^*. The economy produces at point C on the production-possibility frontier, where total production of the private good in the economy is X^*, which is divided such that person 1 receives x_1^* and person 2 receives x_2^*. The outcome is Pareto-efficient because the outcome has been found by holding the utility of one person constant and maximizing the utility of the other; one person has been made as well off as possible, without reducing the utility of the other person. At points J and H on the production-possibility frontier, no quantity of private good is available for person 2. Between points J and H, maintaining person 1's utility at U_1 provides the positive quantities of private goods for consumption by person 2 that are given by the height of DE.

The slope of U_1 is the marginal rate of substitution MRS_1 for person 1 between the public and private good. The slope of the production-possibility frontier MRT

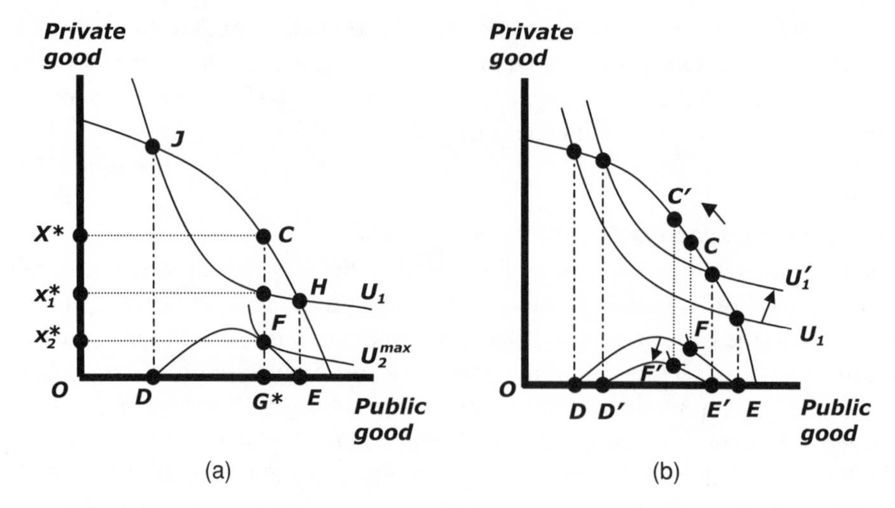

Figure S3.8. (a) Efficient choice of public and private goods. (b) Multiple efficient outcomes.

is the ratio of marginal costs of the public and private good. The derivation of the efficient frontier *DE* implies that at efficient point *F*, the slope of *DE* is:

$$MRS_2 = MRT - MRS_1. \tag{S3.22}$$

This implies:

$$MRT = \sum_i MRS_i, \tag{S3.23}$$

which is the general-equilibrium form of the Samuelson condition for efficient supply of public goods.

We have the definitions:

$$MRS_i \equiv \frac{MB_G^i}{MB_x^i}, \quad i = 1, 2 \tag{S3.24}$$

$$MRT \equiv \frac{MC_G}{MC_x}. \tag{S3.25}$$

In the competitive market for the private good:

$$MB_x^1 = MB_x^2 = P_X = MC_X. \tag{S3.26}$$

Substituting expression (S3.26) into expression (S3.23) returns us to the partial-equilibrium form of the Samuelson condition that we have used:

$$\sum_i MB_G^i = MC_G. \tag{S3.27}$$

In figure S3.8b , the level of utility held constant for person 1 when maximizing person 2's utility has been increased from U_1 to U_1'. The feasible-consumption frontier *DE* for person 2 contracts to the frontier *D′E′* and utility is maximized for person 2 at point *F′*. Person 2 has less of the private good at point *F′* than previously at point F. Both people have less of the public good at point C' than at point C.

Both points C and C' are efficient production points on the production-possibilities frontier. For different utility levels held constant for person 1 (or for person 2), we obtain different Pareto-efficient production combinations. In an economy with only private goods, there are likewise many Pareto-efficient outcomes (see supplement S1A).

What has been shown here? This demonstration, which is based on Samuelson (1955), re-expresses the partial-equilibrium efficiency condition for public-good supply $\sum MB = MC$ in the general-equilibrium form $\sum MRS = MRT$. However, all considerations about asymmetric information that we previously noted apply to the general-equilibrium portrayal. Personal marginal benefits are subjective information; therefore, the efficient Lindahl solution is infeasible and efficiency cannot be based on voluntary payments for public goods. Without information on personal marginal benefits, the points F or F' that determine the efficient quantity of the public good cannot be located.

Summary

This chapter has considered public goods, which provide collective benefit. Section 1 described types of public goods.

1A. We began with one person living alone and considered how increases in the population give rise to goods that provide collective benefit. Public goods can be pure or congested. Exclusion from the benefits of public goods may be possible, technically impossible, or impossible at reasonable cost. For pure public goods, exclusion is inefficient. We saw how dilemmas arise when people refuse to contribute to paying for public goods.

1B. The competitive market outcome for a public good is efficient, as for a private good, but the public-good market equilibrium cannot be implemented because of asymmetric information. The consensus Lindahl voluntary-payments equilibrium, which is the efficient solution for financing public goods, likewise cannot be implemented. Free-riding incentives can be described as a prisoners' dilemma, which is based on the Nash behavioral conjecture. In contrast, the Lindahl mechanism describes demand responses to cross-subsidization. Experimental evidence shows that contrary to the predictions of rational behavior under the conditions of the prisoners' dilemma, voluntary cooperation often takes place in payment for public goods. People may be acting on a presumption of a social norm of mutual trust. In the final round of public-good games, instances of cooperation decline. There is less cooperation among economics students.

Cooperation can reflect expressive behavior. Whatever the outcome of the experiments, societies do not rely on voluntary financing of public goods of the prisoners'-dilemma type. More complex public-good games were described in which contributions are sequential and for which benefits require achieving a threshold of spending.

1C. Weakest-link and volunteer public goods have a structure that differs from the prisoners' dilemma. Incentives for free riding are not present for weakest-link public goods; people do not want to free ride but rather want to pay contingent on everyone paying. Incentives for volunteer public goods are described by the game of chicken; supply for volunteer-type public goods depends on social conventions and inclinations of personal behavior.

1D. National security is another type of public good in which the benefits depend on own spending and the spending of adversaries. The objective of spending is deterrence. The Nash equilibrium of the prisoners' dilemma results in inefficient countervailing spending. Contributions to national security are also subject to an internal prisoners' dilemma. Because deterrence of aggressors can provide public-good benefits that can extend to residents of other countries, there are gains from forming defense coalitions; problems of free riding can then occur, with countries joining a defense alliance but relying on the spending of larger countries to provide the public good of deterring aggressors. War is an example of rent seeking; the rent-seeking prize for aggressors is benefits obtained through access to other societies' income and wealth. Democracies do not initiate wars. Countries with the most resources do not necessarily win wars. Technology has diminished the advantage of countries with large populations over countries with small populations. Terrorism involves asymmetric warfare. When terrorists have a supreme-value ideology, deterrence based on threats of harm to an adversary is ineffective; negotiating is also ineffective in stopping supreme-value terrorism in the long run because of the supreme-value objectives. Evidence indicates that supreme-value terrorists do not have low incomes. Defense against terrorism introduces moral dilemmas. Terrorism also imposes social costs through social divisions on the issue of whether appeasement is possible – or desirable.

Section 2 of this chapter considered the public-good information problem.

2A. The incentives to free ride in prisoners'-dilemma-type public goods underlie the case for delegating responsibility to governments to use legal coercion (or taxation) to compel payment for public goods. Governments then still face the asymmetric-information problem. We therefore considered means of solving the public-good asymmetric-information problem.

2B. The Clarke tax is a preference-revelation mechanism that, in principle, can solve the asymmetric-information problem. The Clarke tax, however, is not used. The objective of using the Clarke tax is to obtain information to allow efficient outcomes, but the outcomes of the Clarke tax could be socially unjust and politically inexpedient.

2C. User prices elicit information about valuation by applying the benefit principle to paying for public goods. The free-rider problem is solved because a market for use is created in which people need to pay in order to benefit. Means of exclusion are necessary. User prices are distinct from personal Lindahl prices, which would efficiently finance a public good and also permit efficient free access. User prices can be direct or indirect. Self-financing user prices may not exist, including in cases where the cost-benefit criterion is satisfied. User prices may allow private supply, thereby raising issues of public policy toward privately owned natural monopoly. User prices allow people to make personal decisions through the option not to pay; in contrast, financing through taxes based on the ability-to-pay principle can result in people paying for public goods from which they do not benefit. User prices, however, can inefficiently exclude and can be regarded as unjust because payment for public goods is independent of income; user prices are, in these regards, like all prices. User prices are a means of escaping cases of inadequate government supply of education and health care. We considered user prices in the context of prisons and police. Societies have made different choices regarding the scope of reliance on user prices.

2D. The Tiebout mechanism elicits information through locational choice. Free riding is impossible because of the requisites to locate and pay taxes in a jurisdiction in order to benefit from the public goods that the government of the jurisdiction finances (or provides). The Tiebout mechanism seeks to replicate a market and is a response to the proposal that public goods require centralized government provision. Although the Tiebout locational-choice mechanism solves the asymmetric-information problem, the Tiebout solution of separation by preferences into different jurisdictions is "second-best" because of natural monopoly and inefficient cost-sharing; the efficient Lindahl-consensus solution requires that people who value a public good differently share costs in a single jurisdiction. However, separation into separate jurisdictions may be inevitable when the only way for people to reveal their preferences credibly is to stay in or leave a jurisdiction. Location choice efficiently provides public goods when people want different *types* of public goods because then issues of sharing costs do not arise. Politics can prevent application of Tiebout prices; in general, taxes are not set as Tiebout prices but rather are influenced by income distribution and wealth, including the value of property. In practice, also, personal opportunities for locational choice depend on personal income and wealth, thereby reflecting ability to pay rather than only willingness to pay. Housing prices embody locational monopoly rents when a jurisdiction provides public goods that are not sufficiently replicated elsewhere; exclusion occurs because people who are prepared to pay for the public goods are unwilling or unable to pay the locational rents that make the "exclusive" housing expensive. Non-locational sharing of costs can take place through "clubs." Where there is no asymmetric information and personal costs and benefits are known, as in the example of sharing the costs of a road by owners of trucks and cars, beneficiaries of the public good are involved in a cooperative game of sharing costs. Cost sharing can be described as determined by bargaining; in particular, the Nash bargaining solution can be applied to determine cost sharing.

The last section of this chapter described cost-benefit analysis as a means of attempting to solve the public-good asymmetric-information problem by seeking information not revealed in markets.

3A. We considered the challenges of finding valuations not revealed in markets; cost-benefit analysis seeks values of life, time, health, reduced likelihood of accidents, quality of the environment, biodiversity, and other benefits or costs that are not revealed in markets.

3B. Cost-benefit analysis requires means of comparing benefits and costs over time. A discount rate needs to be chosen. Choice of the rate of discount can determine whether public-spending proposals are socially worthwhile. The market rate of interest is a candidate for an indicator of the rate of discount; however, a case can also be made that the market rate of discount is excessively high in not adequately representing preferences of future generations – and also in not accounting for risk-spreading in government spending. We also saw how "regret" can arise concerning past decisions about the discount rate.

3C. The example of the alternatives of a subway and highway expansion showed the consequences of using different discount rates to choose between public projects.

3D. Cost-benefit calculations include changes in incomes due to public spending. When income-distribution consequences are a concern, another criterion for decision making is required; we shall study social welfare functions when we consider the social objective of social justice. Political decisions can compromise cost-benefit analysis; governments do not extensively rely on cost-benefit analysis for making decisions on public spending. Often, political choices are simply made. Political choices are inefficient if people value money directly more than the benefits of spending the same amount of tax revenue on a public project. Rent seeking is a political distraction from cost-benefit analysis.

The supplements to this chapter extended the investigation of public goods.

S3A. In the Nash equilibrium, the effect of increases in group size on total voluntary private contributions to public goods depends on countervailing substitution and income effects. A measure of the effectiveness of collective action of a group is the proportion of efficient total voluntary spending achieved in the Nash equilibrium. In general, groups become less effective in collective action as group size increases. Larger groups benefit more, therefore, from payments enforced through taxation. Nash-equilibrium voluntary private contributions to public goods are independent of changes in the distribution of income, if positive personal contributions continue to be made before and after the redistribution of income. With rent seekers making Nash contributions, rent dissipation in group quests to obtain public-good rents is independent of the number of rent seekers in a group, if there are no income effects.

S3B. In the Tiebout locational-choice mechanism with public goods financed by property taxes, Nash-equilibrium payment of taxes through choice of location is determined by the value of houses on which the property taxes are levied. If all people derive equal benefit from public goods, the best-off people are those with the lowest-value houses, who free ride on payments by people who have chosen higher value housing. Because of the public-good substitution effect, people who want higher-value housing therefore have incentives for zoning laws that restrict or disallow low-income housing.

S3C. Other approaches to private payment for public goods do not rely on non-cooperative Nash equilibrium. The effectiveness of collective action can be viewed in terms of departures from an initial cooperative outcome; cooperation as the point of departure explains the effectiveness in collective action of small groups in which monitoring allows free riders to be readily detected. Public goods can be provided jointly with private goods, if private goods are not competitively supplied. Public goods financed through lotteries are also provided jointly with private benefit; more is provided for paying for public goods than total voluntary-payment Nash-equilibrium contributions to public goods.

S3D. The condition for efficient supply of a public good was re-expressed in general-equilibrium terms. The general-equilibrium representation changed none of our conclusions about public goods.

Literature notes

3.1 Types of public goods

For an exposition of public goods, see Buchanan (1968; Nobel Prize in economics, 1986). Wicksell (1896) proposed paying for public goods according to benefit; on the related ideal Lindahl-consensus solution, see Lindahl (1919). Samuelson (1954, 1955; Nobel Prize in 1970) derived the condition for efficient supply of public goods. The lighthouse is an often-used example of a pure public good; see, however, Coase (1974, Nobel Prize in 1991) on private ownership of lighthouses.

Buchanan, J. M., 1968. *The Demand and Supply of Public Goods.* Rand-McNalley, Chicago.

Coase, R. H., 1974. The lighthouse in economics. *Journal of Law and Economics* 17:357–76.

Lindahl, E., 1919. *Positive Lösung: Die Gerechtigkeit der Besteuerung.* Lund. Reprinted as: *Just taxation – A positive solution.* In R. A. Musgrave and A. T. Peacock (Eds.), 1967. *Classics in the Theory of Public Finance*, St. Martin's Press, New York, pp. 168–76.

Samuelson, P. A., 1954. The pure theory of public expenditure. *Review of Economics and Statistics* 36:387–9.

Samuelson, P. A., 1955. Diagrammatic exposition of a pure theory of public expenditure. *Review of Economics and Statistics* 37:350–6.

Wicksell, K., 1896. *A New Principle of Just Taxation.* Finanztheoretische Untersuchnung, Jena. Reprinted in R. A. Musgrave and A. T. Peacock (Eds.), 1967. *Classics in the Theory of Public Finance*, St. Martin's Press, New York, pp. 72–118.

On results of experiments on the public-good game and a review of literature on evolution of social conventions of cooperation, see:

Ostrom, E., 2000. Collective action and the evolution of social norms. *Journal of Economic Perspectives* 14:137–58.

On expressive behavior that confirms self-identity, which we suggested can influence decisions to cooperate in public-good games, see:

Akerlof, G. A., and R. E. Kranton, 2000. Economics and identity. *Quarterly Journal of Economics* 115:715–53.

On sequential voluntary financing of public goods, see:

Fershtman, C., and S. Nitzan, 1991. Dynamic voluntary provision of public goods. *European Economic Review* 35:1057–67.

Gradstein, M., 1994. Efficient provision of a discrete public good. *International Economic Review* 35:877–97.

Max, L. M., and S. A. Matthews, 2000. Dynamic voluntary provision to a public project. *Review of Economic Studies* 67:327–58.

Volunteer and weakest-link public goods were studied by Hirshleifer (1983); see also Harrison and Hirshleifer (1989), Cornes (1993), and Xu (2001). Hausken (2006) reviewed Hirshleifer's writings.

Cornes, R., 1993. Dyke maintenance and other stories: Some neglected types of public goods. *Quarterly Journal of Economics* 108:259–71.

Harrison, G., and J. Hirshleifer, 1989. An experimental evaluation of weakest-link/best-shot public goods. *Journal of Political Economy* 97:201–23.

Hausken, K., 2006. Jack Hirshleifer: A Nobel Prize left unbestowed. *European Journal of Political Economy* 22:251–76.
Hirshleifer, J., 1983. From weakest-link to best-shot: The voluntary provision of public goods. *Public Choice* 41:371–86 (and 1985, 46:221–3).
Xu, X., 2001. Group size and the private supply of a best-shot public good. *European Journal of Political Economy* 17:897–904.

On war and revolution, and the argument that revolutions are undertaken for private benefit of revolutionaries, see Tullock (1974). Schnytzer (1994) presented evidence on revolution as private voluntary supply of a public good.

Schnytzer, A., 1994. An economic model of regime change: Freedom as a public good. *Public Choice* 79:325–39.
Tullock, G., 1974. *The Social Dilemma: The Economics of War and Revolution*. University Publications, Blacksburg.

On the economics of defense, see:

Sandler, T., and K. Hartley, 1995. *The Economics of Defense*. Cambridge University Press, New York.

On self-reliance and defense, see:

Arad, R., and A. L. Hillman, 1979. Embargo threat, learning, and departure from comparative advantage. *Journal of International Economics* 9:265–75.
Mayer, W., 1977. The national defense tariff argument reconsidered. *Journal of International Economics* 7:363–77.

On defense spending and political competition and electoral uncertainty in democracies, see:

Garfinkel, M. R., 1994. Domestic politics and international conflict. *American Economic Review* 84:1294–309.

On defense spending in low-income countries, see:

Gupta, S. L., L. de Mello, and R. Sharan, 2001. Corruption and military spending. *European Journal of Political Economy* 17:749–77. Reprinted in G. T. Abed and S. Gupta (Eds.), 2002. *Governance, Corruption, and Economic Performance*. International Monetary Fund, Washington DC, pp. 300–32.

For an overview of terrorism, see Enders and Sandler (2006). On supreme values and terrorism, see Bernholz (2004). Murawiec (2008) described the impediments to deterrence when terrorists wish to die. For a view proposing accommodating terrorism, see Frey (2004); for a contrary view, see Inbar (2006). Bernholz (1993) described different supreme-value systems.

Bernholz, P., 1993. Necessary conditions for totalitarianism, supreme values, power, and personal interest. In G. Radnitzsky and H. Boullion (Eds.), Government: Servant or Master. Rodopi, Amsterdam and Atlanta, pp. 267–312.
Bernholz, P., 2004. Supreme values as the basis for terror. *European Journal of Political Economy* 20:291–516.
Enders, W., and T. Sandler, 2006. *The Political Economy of Terrorism*. Cambridge University Press, Cambridge U.K.
Frey, B. S., 2004. *Dealing with Terrorism: Stick or Carrot?* Edward Elgar, Cheltenham U.K.
Inbar, E., 2006. Review of B. S. Frey, *Dealing with Terrorism: Stick or Carrot? European Journal of Political Economy* 22:343–4.

Murawiec, L., 2008. Deterring those who are already dead? In H. Frisch and E. Inbar (Eds.), *Radical Islam and International Security*, Routledge, Abington, U.K., and New York, pp. 180–7.

On the moral dilemma that arises in defense against terrorism, see Franck, Hillman, and Krausz (2005). Yon (2008) described terrorists' use of ambulances for transportation.

Franck, R., A. L. Hillman, and M. Krausz, 2005. Public safety and the moral dilemma in the defense against terror. *Defense and Peace Economics* 16:347–64.
Yon, P., 2008. *Moment of Truth in Iraq*. Richard Vigilante Books, Minneapolis, MN.

Krueger and Maleckova (2003) presented evidence that terrorists, in general, are neither uneducated nor poor. Mueller (2004) considered civil rights and rights of terrorists. Papers in Brück and Wickström (2004) described economic consequences of terrorism.

Brück, T., and B.-A. Wickström (Eds.), 2004. Economic consequences of terror. *European Journal of Political Economy*. Special issue, June.
Krueger, A., and J. Maleckova, 2003. Education, poverty, and terrorism. *Journal of Economic Perspectives* 17:119–44.
Mueller, D. C., 2004. Rights and citizenship in a world of global terrorism. *European Journal of Political Economy* 20:335–48.

3.2 Information and public goods

On the Clarke tax, see Tideman and Tullock (1976) and Clarke (1980).

Clarke, E. H., 1980. *Demand Revelation and the Provision of Public Goods*. Ballinger, Cambridge MA.
Tideman, N., and G. Tullock, 1976. A new and superior process for making social choices. *Journal of Political Economy* 84:1145–59.

On user prices as an alternative to ineffective government supply in poor countries, see Jiminez (1987) and Hillman and Jenkner (2004).

Hillman, A. L., and E. Jenkner, 2004. User payments for basic education in low-income countries. In S. Gupta, B. Clements, and G. Inchauste (Eds.), *Helping Countries Develop: The Role of Fiscal Policy*. International Monetary Fund, Washington DC, pp. 233–64. Also: How to pay for basic education: Poor children in poor countries. *Economic Issues* 33, International Monetary Fund, Washington DC, 2004.
Jimenez, E., 1987. *Pricing Policy in the Social Sectors: Cost Recovery for Education and Health in Developing Countries*. Johns Hopkins University Press for the World Bank, Baltimore MD.

The locational-choice mechanism for public goods was proposed in:

Tiebout, C. M., 1956. A pure theory of local expenditures. *Journal of Political Economy* 64:416–24.

On non-locational sharing or the theory of clubs, see:

Buchanan, J. M., 1965. An economic theory of clubs. *Economica* 32:1–14.
Hillman, A. L., and P. L. Swan, 1983. Participation rules for Pareto-optimal clubs. *Journal of Public Economics* 20:55–76.

The Nash bargaining solution is from Nash (1950). Shapely (1953) derived the Shapely value; for an application of the Shapely value to cost sharing, see Littlechild and Owen (1973).

Littlechild, S. C., and G. Owen, 1973. A simple expression for the Shapely value in a special case. *Management Science* 20:370–2.
Nash, J. F., 1950. The bargaining problem. *Econometrica* 18:155–62.
Shapely, L. S., 1953. A value for n-person games. In H. W. Kuhn and A. W. Tucker (Eds.), Contributions to Game Theory II (*Annals of Mathematical Studies* 28), Princeton University Press, Princeton NJ, pp. 307–17.

3.3 Cost-benefit analysis

For an extensive review of aspects of cost-benefit analysis, see Mishan and Quah (2007). We did not consider topics relating to foreign resources; see, for example, Darvish-Lecker and Eckstein (1991).

Darvish-Lecker, T., and S. Eckstein, 1991. Optimizing foreign loan conditions for a public-sector project. *Journal of Policy Modeling* 13:529–50.
Mishan, E. J., and E. Quah, 2007. *Cost-Benefit Analysis*. Routledge, London.

On the case against a positive discount rate, see:

Price, C., 1993. *Time, Discounting, and Value*. Blackwell, Oxford.

On the valuation of safety and life, see Viscusi and Moore (1991). Usher (2001) described the dilemma confronting a driver who has to choose which pedestrian to injure. On offsetting savings of costs of early death, see Viscusi (1999).

Usher, D., 2001. Personal goods, efficiency, and the law. *European Journal of Political Economy* 17:673–703.
Viscusi, W. K., 1999. The government composition of the insurance costs of smoking. *Journal of Law and Economics* 42:575–609.
Viscusi, V. K., and M. J. Moore, 1991. Rates of time preference and valuations of the duration of life. *Journal of Public Economics* 38:297–317.

Supplement S3A: Group size and voluntary public-good contributions

For a detailed investigation of group size and spending on public goods, and on Nash and non-Nash conjectures, see Cornes and Sandler (1996). The original analysis of the effectiveness of collective action is by Olson (1965). On the tendency for own-contributions to go to zero, see Andreoni and McGuire (1993).

Andreoni, J., and M. McGuire, 1993. Identifying the free riders: A simple algorithm for determining who will contribute to a public good. *Journal of Public Economics* 51:447–54.
Cornes, R., and T. Sandler, 1996. *The Theory of Externalities, Public Goods, and Club Goods*. Cambridge University Press, New York.
Olson, M., 1965. *The Logic of Collective Action: Public Goods and the Theory of Groups*. Harvard University Press, Cambridge MA.

Warr (1983) and Bergstrom, Blume, and Varian (1986) showed that total Nash contributions to a public good are independent of the distribution of income, providing everyone makes positive contributions, before and after the income redistribution.

Bergstrom, T., L. Blume, and H. Varian, 1986. On the private provision of public goods. *Journal of Public Economics* 29:25–49.

Warr, P., 1983. The private provision of a public good is independent of the distribution of income. *Economics Letters* 13:207–11.

On collective action in rent seeking, see Ursprung (1990) and Riaz, Shogren, and Johnson (1995). Baik (1993) emphasized the tendencies for free riding. Gradstein (1993) compared the inefficiency of voluntary provision of public goods with the inefficiency of rent seeking.

Baik, K. B., 1993. Effort levels in contests: The public-good prize case. *Economics Letters* 41:363–7.
Gradstein, M., 1993. Rent seeking and the provision of public goods. *Economic Journal* 103:1236–43.
Riaz, K., Shogren, J. S., and Johnson, S. R., 1995. A general model of rent seeking for a public good. *Public Choice* 82:243–59.
Ursprung, H. W., 1990. Public goods, rent dissipation, and candidate competition. *Economics and Politics* 2:115–32.

The previously listed papers are reprinted in:

Congleton, R. D., A. L. Hillman, and K. A. Konrad (Eds.), 2008. *Forty Years of Research on Rent Seeking 1: The Theory of Rent-Seeking*. Springer, Berlin.

Supplement S3B: Property taxes and incentives for zoning

On asymmetries in contributions to public goods, see:

Konrad, K. A., 1994. The strategic advantage of being poor: Public and private provision of public goods. *Economica* 61:79–93.

Supplement S3C: Other approaches to private payment for public goods

Stigler (1964) proposed cooperation as the point of departure for evaluating the effectiveness of collective action. Olson (1965 – listed previously) observed that public goods could be supplied jointly with private goods. Stigler (1974) pointed out the consequences of competition in supply of the private good. On joint supply of private and public goods, see also Pecorino (2001) and Mayer (2002). On joint supply through lotteries, see Morgan (2000).

Mayer, W., 2002. On the efficiency of by-product lobbying. *Public Choice* 112:275–92.
Morgan, J., 2000. Financing public goods by means of lotteries. *Review of Economic Studies* 67:761–84.
Pecorino, P., 2001. Can by-product lobbying firms compete? *Journal of Public Economics* 82:377–97.
Stigler, G. J., 1964. A theory of oligopoly. *Journal of Political Economy* 72:44–61.
Stigler, G. J., 1974. Free riders and collective action: An appendix to theories of economic regulation. *Bell Journal of Economics and Management Science* 5:359–65.

Supplement S3D: An efficient economy with public and private goods

The exposition is based on:

Samuelson, P. A., 1955. Diagrammatic exposition of a pure theory of public expenditure. *Review of Economics and Statistics* 37:350–6.

4

PUBLIC FINANCE FOR PUBLIC GOODS

Societies assign responsibilities for financing public goods to governments because of the asymmetric-information problem and the associated incentives to misrepresent preferences (or free ride). In this chapter, we study the financing of public goods by governments. Our focus is on efficiency rather than social justice.

In investigating how efficient public finance for public goods might be achieved, we face practical impediments. Political and bureaucratic principal–agent problems can prevent efficient outcomes in the public interest. Our conclusion from chapter 3 is that governments remain subject to the asymmetric-information problem; governments cannot observe and so do not know the true subjective benefits $\sum MB$ that public goods provide to a population.

Without revelation of personal preferences through the Clarke tax, we could hope that governments have nonetheless been successful in using cost-benefit analysis to approximate $\sum MB$. That is, ideally we would want governments to have used cost-benefit analysis to attempt to identify the efficient public spending that the government's taxes will finance. Because of the principal–agent problems, we cannot predict that attempts at cost-benefit analysis will necessary have been made; indeed, in practice, decisions regarding public spending are political and are revealed when a government presents its budget.

The Tiebout locational-choice mechanism is based on choice among governments. The asymmetric-information problem is solved when people voluntarily group themselves into government jurisdictions according to their preferences for different public goods.[1] We cannot, however, necessarily rely on the locational-choice mechanism always to solve the preference revelation problem and so to provide governments with information on $\sum MB$. User prices also lead people to reveal information about their preferences; user prices where feasible are an alternative to the taxation that we now consider.

In this chapter, we shall not focus on the asymmetric-information impediments to financing public goods. We shall be concerned with the *consequences* of using public finance to provide public goods. We accept that a role for government through taxation and public finance is required because of the asymmetric-information problem that prevents efficient financing of public goods through voluntary payments. Our premise for this chapter is:

> *Governments can solve the free-rider problem by making payment for public goods compulsory through taxes.*

In practice, this premise leaves us with governments levying compulsory taxes to pay for public goods that they are not sure how people value. The public goods are, however, needed; we know that people have demands for public goods; and that reliance on voluntary payments will result in under-supply or perhaps no public goods at all. We have no recourse, therefore, but to turn to government.

[1] As we saw, the first-best Lindahl voluntary pricing outcome is not achieved when people want different quantities of public goods but nonetheless the outcome is a feasible second-best solution.

Although governments face asymmetric information, at least through compulsory taxation, governments solve free-rider problems. The resources for spending on public goods with be forthcoming through tax revenue, even if governments do not have the information required to spend the tax revenue efficiently.

We shall not in this chapter ask normative questions about the desirable *structure* of taxation. That is, we shall not ask whether different goods should be taxed at lower and higher rates; nor shall we ask about the desirable structure of income taxes and for example whether income taxes should be progressive (that is, whether people with a higher income should pay a greater share of their income in taxes). We leave these questions, which concern "optimal taxation" and which involve trade-offs between efficiency and social justice, to later.

Section 1 of this chapter describes the excess burden of taxation and consequences for public finance for public goods; section 2 looks at tax evasion; and section 3 describes government borrowing (or bond financing) as a means of financing public spending on public goods. Normative questions in this chapter are:

> *How should the condition for efficient public spending $\sum MB = MC$ be amended when spending on public goods is financed by compulsory taxation rather than by voluntary personal contributions?*
>
> *How should governments respond when tax evasion can take place?*
>
> *When should governments ideally use borrowing rather than taxes to finance public spending on public goods?*

4.1 Taxation

We now look at financing of public goods through taxation. The responsibility for financing public goods has therefore been delegated to governments.

> *What are the consequences of tax-financing of public goods if we pretend that there are no principal–agent problems and that governments do not confront asymmetric-information problems?*

A. Efficient tax-financed public spending

When taxes are used to finance public goods, an efficiency loss known as the *excess burden of taxation* is present. The excess burden arises for both direct and indirect taxes:

> *A direct tax is paid when income is earned.*
>
> *An indirect tax is paid when income is spent.*

We begin by describing the excess burden of a personal income tax, which is a direct tax.

The excess burden of an income tax

In figure 4.1, S_L is the labor-supply function of an individual who receives a given hourly wage determined in a competitive labor market as w. If there is no taxation, the person chooses to work L_2 hours. A proportional income tax at a rate of t percent reduces the net-of-tax wage per hour to $w(1 - t)$, and hours worked decline to L_1.[2]

The tax affects market behavior through the reduction in labor supply from L_2 to L_1. The change in market behavior is a *substitution response*. Free time or leisure is substituted for productive time.[3]

The tax leaves unchanged the individual's given competitively determined gross (before-tax) market wage w. Because of the change in labor supply, gross (before-tax) income in figure 4.1 has declined from $AEHO$ to $ABJO$. Net-of-tax income is $DCJO$. The difference between gross income and net-of-tax income is $ABCD$, which is paid as taxes to the government.

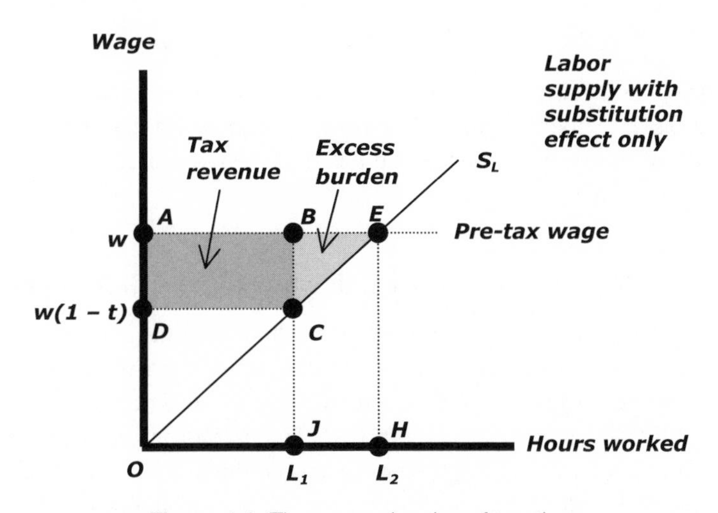

Figure 4.1. The excess burden of taxation.

[2] In general, income taxes are not proportional. For exposition of the idea of the excess burden of taxation, we now look at a tax imposed at a single rate.

[3] The labor-supply response to a tax consists of the substitution effect and also an income effect. The income effect is that lower real income because of increased taxation reduces demand for leisure (which is a normal good) and therefore increases labor supply. The substitution effect reduces labor supply. Therefore, in principle, a labor-supply function could have a negative slope. The labor-supply function in figure 4.1 and subsequent labor-supply functions are based on the substitution effect alone.

The excess burden of the income tax in figure 4.1 is revealed by asking the person being taxed one of the following two questions:

(1) How much are you prepared to pay to avoid the government levying the tax on you?
(2) If the tax is levied, how much does the government have to give you to compensate you for the tax?

The first question presumes that the tax is not levied and asks how much the person would have been willing to pay to avoid the tax. The second question presumes that the tax is in place and asks how much the person requires as compensation for the tax having been levied. The answers to both questions are, of course, subjective information.

In seeking answers to questions (1) and (2), we need to know whether the person in figure 4.1 feels that he or she is deriving benefit from the taxes paid to the government. If there is benefit, the taxes paid are not a personal loss but are the consequence of delegation to government of the responsibility to finance public goods. Indeed, the payment of taxes could happen to be the amount (of course, this is unlikely) that the person would pay voluntarily in the Lindahl consensus outcome for personal payments for public goods. Still:

The tax has imposed a personal loss.

The personal loss is the additional or excess burden of taxation shown in figure 4.1 as the area *BEC*: the person whose labor supply is shown in figure 4.1 is prepared to pay *BEC* to avoid paying the tax and has to be compensated by the amount of money *BEC* for paying the tax.[4]

Supplement S4A: The excess burden with substitution and income effects

The answer to question (1) about how much the individual is prepared to pay to avoid the tax is often called the *equivalent variation* because this is the *equivalent* amount of income that, if taken away when there is no tax, results in the same disutility as when the tax is imposed. The answer to question (2) about how much income the individual requires as compensation after the tax has been imposed is called the *compensating variation*. In figure 4.1, the excess burden of taxation *BEC* is the answer to both the questions. Figure 4.1 is based on the substitution effect alone (see footnote 3). Supplement S4A shows that when income effects are included, the answers to the two questions are no longer the same so that the equivalent and compensating variations give different values for the excess burden of taxation.

[4] Answers change if the person feels no benefit from paying taxes. The loss felt from paying a tax then includes the value of the tax.

Why is *BEC* a personal excess burden of taxation?

The excess burden of taxation is due to substitution: if there were no substitution response between leisure and work, there would be no excess burden of taxation. The personal cost of supplying labor is the leisure or free time that would otherwise have been available; the labor-supply function S_L is, therefore, a personal *MC* function expressing the marginal cost of labor supplied in terms of leisure. The area under the labor-supply function S_L at any number of hours worked is correspondingly the total personal cost of supplying labor.[5]

To confirm that the area *BEC* measures the excess burden of taxation, we proceed through the following steps:

- Before the tax is imposed, the individual's benefit from market participation in figure 4.1 is *OAE*, which consists of the benefit through income *AEHO* from supplying L_2 hours of labor minus the personal cost *OEH* of supplying L_2 hours of labor.
- After the tax is imposed, the individual's benefit from market participation is *OCD*, which is the difference between post-tax income *DCJO* and the personal cost *OCJ* in terms of free time forgone in supplying L_1 hours of labor.
- The effect of the tax, therefore, has been to reduce the gain from market participation by $(AEO - DCO) = AECD$.
- *AECD* has two components. One component is the tax revenue *ABCD* paid to the government, from which the individual derives benefit through the public finance for public goods. The other component is *BEC*, which is the additional personal loss or excess burden of taxation.

The excess burden of taxation is a personal loss borne by the taxpayer. The personal loss is not directly observed as any sum of money. It is something that a person had before the tax but that disappeared after the tax.

> *No sum of money equal to the excess burden of taxation changes hands. The excess burden of taxation is invisible.*

The elasticity of labor supply

Measurement of the excess burden of taxation in figure 4.1 requires knowing the elasticity of the labor-supply function S_L. We denote the elasticity of labor supply as ε_{SL}.[6] The elasticity can be constant or variable, depending on the form of the labor-supply function. Figure 4.1 shows a special case in which $\varepsilon_{SL} = 1$ (and ε_{SL}

[5] Summing the *MC* of supplying labor measured as leisure forgone gives the total cost of supplying a number of hours of labor.

[6] The elasticity ε_{SL} is the percentage increase in hours worked because of the substitution effect in response to a 1 percent increase in the net-of-tax wage. The elasticity based on the substitution effect is a positive number; that is, labor supply increases because of the substitution away from leisure to work as the net-of-tax wage increases. The elasticity is the slope when variables are expressed in logarithms. The slope depends on the units of measurement of the wage and time worked, whereas the elasticity, being a percentage change, is independent of units of measurement.

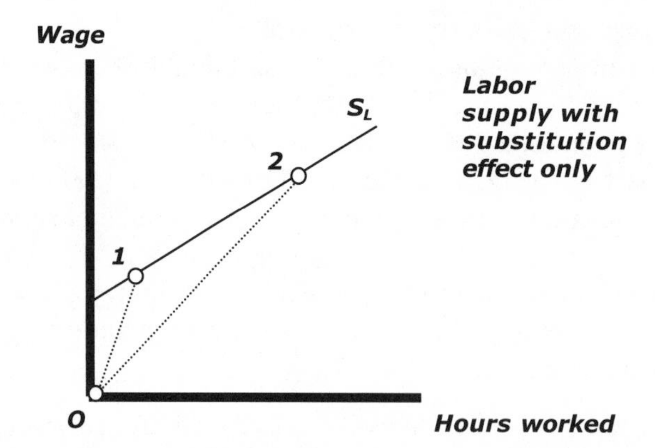

Figure 4.1a. A labor-supply function with an increasing elasticity of labor supply.

is therefore constant).[7] In figure 4.1a, the elasticity of labor supply ε_{SL} increases as the wage received (net of taxes) and hours worked increase.[8]

The formula for the excess burden of taxation

When the labor-supply function S_L is linear, as in figure 4.1, the area BEC is a triangle and the formula for the area of a triangle gives the value of the excess burden of taxation as:[9]

$$\frac{1}{2}(wL)\ \varepsilon_{SL}t^2. \tag{4.1}$$

The formula in expression (4.1) indicates that the excess burden of taxation increases with the *square* of the rate of taxation. We see in figure 4.2 that an

[7] In figure 4.1, the labor-supply function is of the form $L = \alpha \cdot w$, where α is constant. Therefore:

$$\frac{dL}{dw} = \alpha = \frac{L}{w}.$$

It follows that:

$$\left(\frac{dL/L}{dw/w}\right) \equiv \varepsilon_{SL} = 1.$$

The elasticity is 1 for any function that begins from the origin.

[8] In figure 4.1a, the slope dL/dw of the labor-supply function is constant and L/w increases for moves along the labor-supply function, as between points 1 and 2. The labor-supply elasticity, which can be expressed as:

$$\left(\frac{dL/dw}{L/w}\right) \equiv \varepsilon_{SL}$$

is therefore increasing along the labor-supply function.

[9] The formula in expression (4.1) follows from the area of a triangle as:

$$\frac{1}{2}\Delta w\Delta L = \frac{1}{2}tw\Delta L = \frac{1}{2}t^2(wL)\left(\frac{\Delta L}{\Delta w}\frac{w}{L}\right) = \frac{1}{2}(wL)\varepsilon_{SL}t^2.$$

In the special case in figure 4.1, in which labor-supply function is both linear and passes through the origin, the labor-supply elasticity ε_{SL} is constant and equal to 1. When ε_{SL} is not constant, the formula in expression (4.1) is appropriate for small changes in a tax for which the approximation can be made that ε_{SL} is constant.

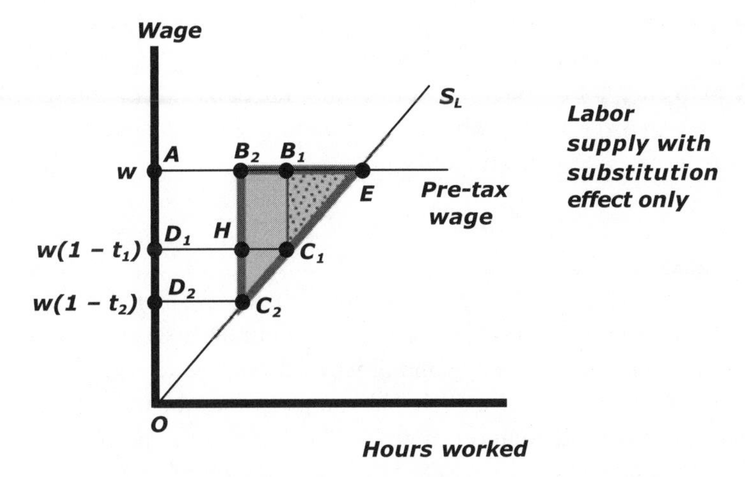

Figure 4.2. The excess burden and the rate of taxation.

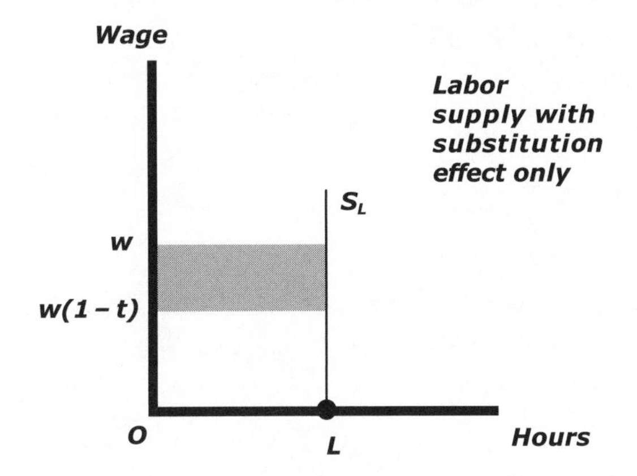

Figure 4.3. Taxation with no excess burden.

increase in the tax rate from t_1 to t_2 increases the excess burden of taxation from B_1EC_1 to B_2EC_2.

In figure 4.3, the person chooses to work the same number of hours L both before and after the introduction of the tax. There is no equivalent in figure 4.3 of the triangle BEC. Because $\varepsilon_{SL} = 0$, there is no substitution effect. Substituting $\varepsilon_{SL} = 0$ into the formula in expression (4.1) confirms the zero value of the excess burden of taxation.

The excess burden and intrusion into other markets

The excess burden of taxation arises because, through delegation of responsibility to government, payment for *public goods* is financed by taxes in the *labor market* – and not in a market for public goods. The taxes that finance public goods are an intrusion into the labor market, which has no direct connection with the market for public goods; there would be no excess burden if public goods were voluntarily financed in markets for public goods; payment would then be taking place in the same market in which the goods are supplied. Of course, taxes cannot be levied in the market for public goods because the market for public goods does not exist – which is the reason why the government is levying taxes on income to pay for the public good through public finance.

Indirect taxes

Direct taxes are levied in factor markets; indirect taxes are levied in product markets. Figure 4.4 shows a sales tax, which is an indirect tax, levied in a product market. MB_i is an individual's demand function for a private good. At a competitively determined market price P, the person purchases the quantity q_2. A sales tax at rate t increases the market price to $P(1+t)$ and the person responds by decreasing demand from q_2 to q_1. The revenue from the sales tax is $ABCD$.

The person being taxed can again be asked: (1) How much are you prepared to pay to avoid having the tax imposed? or (2) How much compensation would you require if the tax were imposed? In either case, with the person perceiving benefit from the public good financed by the payment of taxes, the answer in figure 4.4 is BEC. With ε_D indicating the person's elasticity of demand, the excess burden of the tax is the area of BEC, which is:

$$\frac{1}{2}(pq)\,\varepsilon_D t^2. \tag{4.2}$$

The demand elasticity ε_D appears in expression (4.2), just as the supply elasticity ε_{SL} appears in the similar expression (4.1).[10] In the labor market, the

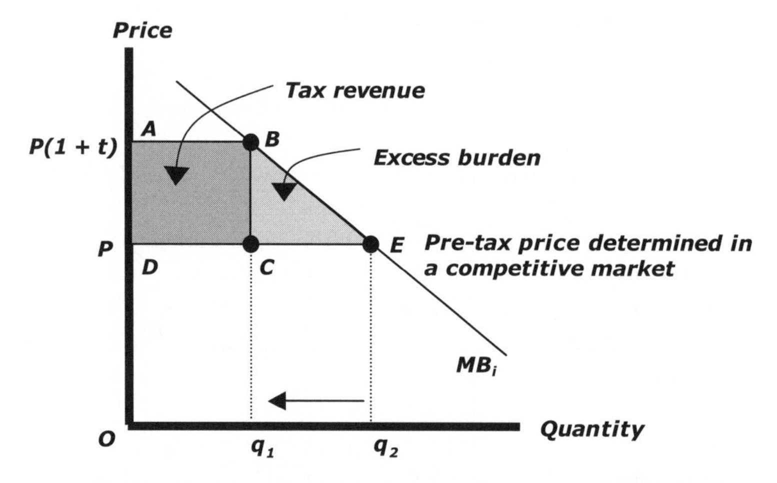

Figure 4.4. The excess burden of taxation when income is spent.

[10] The elasticity of demand is a negative number (quantity demanded declines as price increases), but we define the elasticity ε_D as a positive number and make the sign correction when deriving the expression (4.2).

individual is a seller (or supplier of labor services); therefore, the substitution response to a tax is expressed through the supply elasticity. In the case of a sales tax, the individual is the buyer; therefore, the substitution response is expressed through the demand elasticity.[11]

A value-added tax

A *value-added tax* is, like a sales tax, an indirect tax. The tax base for a sales tax is the value of goods sold (and therefore bought). A value-added tax is likewise paid when goods are sold but the tax base is value-added at different stages of production.

When the value-added tax payable is computed, a seller receives a tax credit for taxes paid on inputs that the seller purchased and used in the course of production. The tax paid is therefore only on the value added by the seller to the inputs that the seller bought.

The excess burden of a value-added tax is the same as for a sales tax, except that the "quantity" in figure 4.4 is replaced by "value added."[12]

Box 4.1 Example of a value-added tax

A person might buy a table from a carpenter for $300 plus payment of a 15 percent value-added tax; the price paid for the table is thus $345, of which $45 is the tax. The carpenter may have paid $100 for the wood used to produce the table. When buying the wood, the carpenter also paid a 15 percent tax on the wood, or $15. After the table is sold, the carpenter pays a tax of $30 = ($45 − $15) to the government; the carpenter provides proof, through receipts, of the payment of $15 in taxes when the wood was bought. The tax of $30 is levied on the value added to the wood by the carpenter's productive activity. In producing the table, the carpenter added $200 to the value of the wood (which was bought for $100). The tax is 15 percent of the value-added of $200.

An advantage of the value-added tax compared to a sales tax is that the value-added tax does not depend on the structure of ownership of productive activities. A sales tax would be paid every time a market transaction took place, with the tax levied *on the full value of the product.* By owning sawmills, carpenters could save the round of taxation in the sale of the wood. The carpenter may be skilled in making a table but may have no advantage in managing a

[11] In figure 4.4, again, demand is based only on the substitution effect. The demand function is called a *compensated demand function* because the substitution effect is measured when the individual has been compensated for income effects to keep utility constant (the substitution effect is a move along an indifference curve: see supplement S4A).

[12] A value-added tax can go by other names, such as for example a goods and services tax.

sawmill. The value-added tax provides no incentive for the carpenter to own a sawmill.

> *A value-added tax makes ownership at stages of production irrelevant in determining tax payments.*

A value-added tax makes income tax evasion difficult. Buyers of intermediate goods want receipts to verify purchase so that tax credits can be received. The receipts, at the same time, are evidence of income of the sellers from whom intermediate goods are bought. Thus:

> *With a value-added tax, buyers impose tax discipline on sellers.*

Indirect taxes and fiscal federalism

In federal systems of government, different levels of government may levy their own taxes. For example, the Tiebout locational-choice mechanism is based on decentralized governments levying taxes to finance public goods within their separate jurisdictions. Such "fiscal federalism" affects the administrative and compliance costs of different taxes that can be levied. Outside of the United States, a value-added tax is the common indirect tax. In the United States, state and local governments levy sales taxes. A value-added tax would require a complex administrative tracking procedure to determine in which states inputs had been purchased and in which states taxes had been paid at different stages of production. When producers in different states participate in intermediate stages of production of a particular good, a value-added tax at the state level would thus introduce complexities of tax administration that require communication and certification among different state and local governments. Final sales of goods would also need to be tracked if a value-added tax is to be collected on all final sales to consumers (sales taxes used by U.S. states are not levied on out-of-state sales).

The administrative and compliance costs arise when governments in a union such as the European Union levy their own value-added taxes: there cannot be unreported or free movement of goods across borders if tax payments require information on where inputs and goods were produced and purchased.

Value-added taxes levied by national governments make adjustments for intermediate and final goods that are imported and exported. The value-added tax is levied on imports; thereby foreign suppliers of intermediate goods are also taxed and have no advantage over domestic suppliers. The value-added tax can be rebated for exports. The value-added tax then does not have different effects depending on whether inputs are purchased abroad or sales are abroad.

Because of administrative complexity of a value-added tax through the need for the adjustments for domestic interstate trade, in general, states and localities in a federal system use a sales tax as an indirect tax. Value-added taxes are most easily levied by central governments.

In some countries, local governments levy value-added taxes. Institutions then may accommodate corruption. The taxes can be evaded by fictitious sales of final goods for consumption to people outside the tax jurisdiction who are not required to pay the tax – and so there is no tax to deliver to the government. Public money or tax revenue is converted to private income. Corruption also facilitates the documentation required for the fictitious sales.

Excise taxes

Sales and value-added taxes, in general, are levied at a uniform rate, although sometimes with exceptions – for example, for food or schoolbooks (the exemptions are implicit subsidies). Excise taxes are indirect taxes levied at higher than the general rates that apply for sales and value-added taxes, usually on goods for which demand is perceived to be quite inelastic, such as alcohol and tobacco.

Other costs of taxation

There are costs of taxation other than the excess burden.

Compliance costs of taxation

Compliance costs are incurred when taxpayers spend time in collecting and reporting the information required for tax-reporting obligations and when accountants, tax advisors, and lawyers spend time working on tax-related matters for clients. Taxpayers, of course, are entitled to seek professional advice to reduce legal tax obligations. We defined *rent seeking* as the unproductive use of time and resources in redistributive quests; rent seeking applies to compliance costs of taxation. Taxation is redistributive, in the transfer of income from taxpayers to governments. The time and abilities of accountants, tax advisors, and lawyers are used in attempting to avoid the redistribution.

Administrative costs of taxation

We noted the administrative costs of taxation in comparing indirect taxes in a federal system of government. Government employees processing taxpayers' files and auditing tax returns could use their time in productive rather than redistributive activities.

Rent seeking and costs of taxation

> *Rent-seeking losses are part of the compliance and administrative costs of taxation.*

Emotional costs of taxation

There is an emotional cost of taxation: in the course of tax audits, strangers with the backing of the law delve into the details of private lives. Some people fear confronting authority and suffer anxiety while waiting to hear whether their tax return has been accepted, even when to the best of their knowledge they have truthfully reported their income.

The different costs of taxation

Taxation is necessary if there is to be public spending. However:

> *There are efficiency losses due to the excess burden of taxation, and compliance and emotional costs of taxation.*

The costs of taxation thus consist of the excess burden of taxation, the compliance costs, and the emotional costs. Although the three types of costs of taxation are incurred, we proceed now to consider the consequences for efficient public spending of the excess burden of taxation.

Cost-benefit analysis and the excess burden of taxation

Efficient public spending is determined by cost-benefit analysis. To incorporate the excess burden of taxation into cost-benefit analysis, we denote by X the total excess burden incurred in collecting the tax revenue required to finance a project. The cost-benefit rule for justifying public spending then becomes:

$$W = \sum_{j=1}^{n} B_j - C - X > 0. \tag{4.3}$$

In expression (4.3), C is the cost of supply of a public good that benefits n people.

We denote by $MC_G = P$ the unit cost of competitively supplied inputs for the public good. MC_G is the marginal cost that we considered for voluntary payment for public goods when efficient supply of public goods through voluntary payments was described as requiring $\sum MB = MC$.

When taxes finance public goods, the additional cost X through the excess burden of taxation is present. We denote the additional marginal cost because of the excess burden of taxation by MC_X. From expression (4.3), efficient supply of public goods financed through taxation requires:

$$\sum_i MB_i = MC_G\ (\textit{inputs for the public good}) + MC_X\ (\textit{the excess burden}). \tag{4.4}$$

The marginal excess burden of tax-financed public spending

To establish the properties of the marginal excess burden of tax-financed public spending MC_X, we return to the direct tax on labor income in figure 4.1. Total tax revenue from a tax of t percent on labor income is:

$$R = t(wL). \tag{4.5}$$

From expression (4.5), the change in tax revenue when the rate of taxation marginally increases is:

$$\frac{dR}{dt} = wL \cdot (1 - \varepsilon_{SL}). \tag{4.6}$$

Therefore:

> *The change in tax revenue when a tax is marginally increased depends on the value of the elasticity of labor supply.*

Expression (4.6) indicates that an increase in the rate of taxation increases tax revenue if $\varepsilon_{SL} < 1$ (that is, if labor supply is inelastic). We now take $\varepsilon_{SL} < 1$ to be the case. We are viewing the objective when a government increases the tax rate as to increase tax revenue. A government would not, therefore, knowingly increase the tax rate if more tax revenue were not obtained.

To simplify exposition of the properties of MC_X, we now view the labor-supply elasticity $\varepsilon_{SL} < 1$ as constant.

For the value of the excess burden of taxation X, we return to expression (4.1). With total tax revenue expressed by (4.5), we observe that:

$$X = R \cdot \varepsilon_{SL} \cdot t. \tag{4.7}$$

The *average* excess burden per dollar of tax revenue is therefore:

$$\frac{X}{R} = \varepsilon_{SL} t. \tag{4.8}$$

Thus:

> *For any rate of taxation t, the average excess burden increases with the labor-supply elasticity ε_{SL}.*

The average excess burden per dollar of tax revenue increases because a higher labor-supply elasticity increases the substitution effect. Figure 4.5 shows the average excess burden of taxation for two elasticities of labor supply $\varepsilon'_{SL} > \varepsilon_{SL}$.

Expression (4.8) shows the *average* excess burden per dollar of government revenue. The amended efficiency condition in expression (4.4) for public-good supply contains the *marginal* excess burden MC_X when an additional dollar of

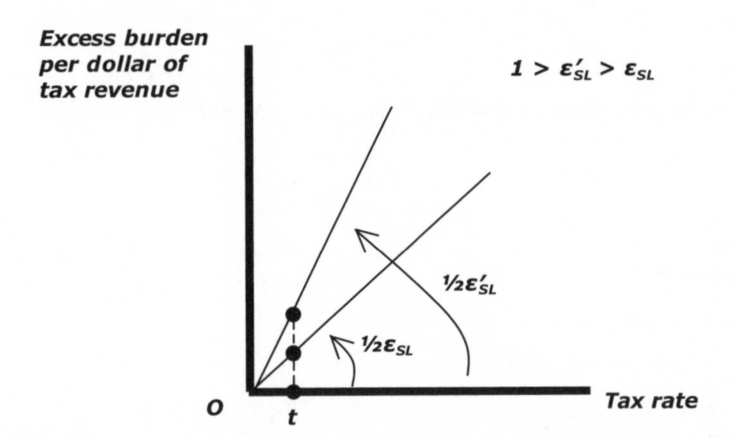

Figure 4.5. The average excess burden of taxation (per dollar of tax revenue).

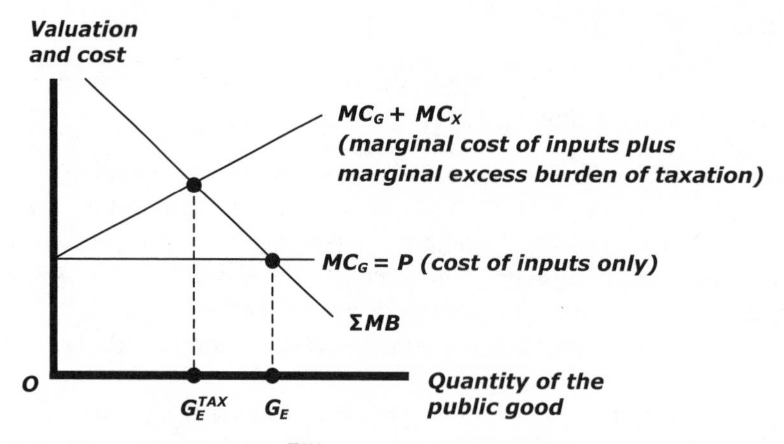

Figure 4.6. The efficient quantity G_E^{TAX} of a tax-financed public good is less than the efficient quantity G_E if payment were voluntary according to true benefit.

tax revenue is collected. The marginal excess burden is:

$$MC_X = \frac{t}{\left(\dfrac{1}{\varepsilon_{SL}} - 1\right)} > 0 \quad where\ \varepsilon_{SL} < 1.^{13} \tag{4.9}$$

Therefore, with the labor-supply elasticity $\varepsilon_{SL} < 1$ and constant:

The marginal excess burden MC_X is linear and is increasing the tax rate t.

Efficient tax-financed supply of a public good

Figure 4.6 shows the efficient quantity G_E^{TAX} of the tax-financed supply of a public good after accounting for the marginal excess burden of taxation MC_X. Efficient supply in figure 4.6, if spending were voluntary and truthful and there were no excess burden of taxation (as in the Lindahl solution), is G_E. We see that:

$$G_E^{TAX} < G_E. \tag{4.10}$$

Hence:

Because of the excess burden of taxation, efficient tax-financed spending on public goods is less than efficient voluntary spending.

[13] To derive expression (4.9), we note that from expression (4.1):

$$\frac{\partial X}{\partial t} = twL\varepsilon_{SL}.$$

From expression (4.5):

$$\frac{\partial R}{\partial t} = wL \cdot (1 - \varepsilon_{SL}).$$

Expression (4.10) for MC_X follows as:

$$\frac{dX}{dR} = \left(\frac{\frac{\partial X}{\partial t}}{\frac{\partial R}{\partial t}}\right) = \frac{t\varepsilon_{SL}}{1 - \varepsilon_{SL}} = \frac{t}{\left(\frac{1}{\varepsilon_{SL}} - 1\right)}.$$

The excess burden and accountability and transparency of public spending

Governments provide information in government budgets; through accountability, the information is intended to provide *transparency*. That is, the intent is to make government decisions visible to taxpayers and voters. Governments do not, in general, accompany statements of budgets with estimates (or ranges of estimates) of the excess burden of taxation. However:

> *Accountability and transparency require the government budget to include the excess burden of the taxes that finance public spending.*

Are taxes available that have no excess burden?

The excess burden of taxation is avoided if taxes do not cause substitution responses in market behavior. A tax with no substitution response is called a *lump-sum tax*. Figure 4.3 showed a market with no substitution responses and no excess burden of taxation; completely inelastic supply or demand in a market is, however, uncommon. If completely inelastic supply or demand were found, it is also unlikely that taxes in such markets would be recommended: for example, people requiring a life-preserving medication have completely inelastic demand, but it would be unethical to exploit people's distress by levying a tax on the medication. A tax on essential goods or services is also politically inexpedient – we are more likely to observe subsidies than taxes on essential goods or services.

Addiction and taxes

Governments that levy excise taxes on legal addictive goods such as tobacco and alcohol may declare that the intent of the taxes is to deter consumption; however, for people who are addicted, the taxes have low or no substitution effects. Because of addiction, the tax base is assured when taxes are levied and also the excess burdens of the taxes are low.

Tiebout locational choice and taxes

The Tiebout locational-choice mechanism for public goods is, in principle, an application of the benefit principle of taxation; that is, local public goods, in principle, should be financed by payment to governments of per-person, per-unit taxes such as would correspond to market prices. There would be no excess burden of taxation if the taxes paid to governments through voluntary locational choice were analogues of voluntarily paid market prices. We observed in chapter 3 that local public goods, in general, are not financed according to the benefit principle through taxes that are analogues of market prices; rather, property, income, and sales taxes finance public spending.

There are excess burdens of taxation from income and sales taxes. Often, the main tax for financing local public goods is a property tax on *improved* land, the value of which includes properties on the land (housing, commercial buildings, or factories). A tax on the value of improved land is a tax on adding to the value of a property through further investment. The substitution response to the tax is that investment is not undertaken or is undertaken elsewhere in lower tax jurisdictions. Substitution responses also occur through allowances in the tax code for depreciation.[14]

Henry George and taxes on unimproved value of land

Taxes on the *unimproved* value of land have no excess burden. The value of unimproved land is determined by the location of the land, which cannot be changed in response to a tax – unless secession can take place from the jurisdiction in which the government is levying the tax. Secession aside, land is trapped with no substitution response that allows "escape" from the tax.

Henry George (1839–97), writing in the 19th century in the United States, proposed that there should be only a single tax, levied on the tax base of the unimproved value of land. He did not base his case on the absence of an excess burden; rather, his case was based on social justice. He observed that people who owned land benefited when economic growth increased the value of their land, yet landowners had done nothing productive to merit the increase in their wealth.

A poll tax

A *poll tax* is a payment for the right to vote. If all citizens choose to exercise their right to vote, poll taxes are lump-sum taxes. However, poll taxes impose a cost of voting. Low-income people, in particular, might not pay the poll tax. By determining who votes, a poll tax can affect political decisions about taxation and public spending.[15]

A personal head tax

A *personal head tax* is a lump-sum tax with no substitution effect. The head tax is paid based on a person's existence and identity. The head tax cannot depend on any attribute or behavior that a person can change; that is, a head tax cannot depend on income, purchases, wealth, number of dependents, or marital status – nor can a head tax depend on personal ability, which people can hide. Because a head tax is personal and cannot be escaped, scope is introduced for unfairness in taxation; different people can be arbitrarily assigned different taxes. The only escape from a head tax is to leave the jurisdiction of the government levying the tax.[16]

[14] When investments in property are depreciated over time, investors receive tax-depreciation allowances and face the question if or where to reinvest. If taxes have become excessive, they can choose to reinvest elsewhere. The substitution effect occurs through the changed location of investment. Sometimes owners simply abandon properties; the owners have calculated that it is preferable to abandon the properties than to retain ownership and make necessary investments in renovations on the property because of the property taxes that would be incurred.

[15] In the United States, the last remaining poll taxes were abolished in 1963.

[16] If parents were responsible for paying head taxes levied on children, a head tax could deter some people from having children.

Head taxes would not be politically popular. In civil societies, taxes are levied on the market-determined value of a person's income or the market-determined value of property, not according to people's inalterable identities and attributes.

The benefit tax associated in principle with the Tiebout locational-choice mechanism is like a head tax; however, people who benefit from the public goods pay an equal tax-price and the option to leave and not pay the tax is present through relocation to the jurisdiction of another government.

The unavailability of taxes with no excess burden

We conclude that other than taxes on unimproved value of property, taxes without an excess burden are not feasible or not ethically or politically desirable. Hence:

> *Taxes without an excess burden are generally not used.*

Measurement of the excess burden of taxation

The information requirements of government for efficient tax-financed public spending include knowing the marginal excess burden of taxation. Invisibility of the excess burden of taxation makes measurement difficult. The excess burden cannot be simply observed but needs to be measured or computed.

Taxpayers could be asked in surveys how much they are prepared to pay to avoid the taxes that they pay or how much compensation they require for taxes having been levied. The questions, however, invite strategic responses (that is, not telling the truth) if payments are actually to take place; if payments are not to take place, people may feel that there is no point to departing from rational ignorance to compute the answers. They would also have to know what an excess burden is and how it is measured.

Rather than asking people, attempts can be made to estimate the excess burden of taxation from *aggregate* market data. Estimation of the excess burden could be approached systematically by listing government revenue from all taxes. With tax rates known, estimates of elasticities of demand and supply in each market could be used to compute the *average* excess burden of taxation (the total excess burden divided by tax revenue) and the *marginal* excess burden (the additional excess burden for an additional dollar of tax revenue). Two types of complexities are then encountered: (1) there are taxes with no tax revenue, and (2) taxes in one market result in excess burdens in other markets.

Taxes with no tax revenue

In figure 4.7a, a tax has reduced an individual's labor supply to zero so, with no tax base, there is no tax revenue. The excess burden of taxation is BEO. Hence:

> *The excess burden (which is invisible in the first place) may be invisible in a market that no longer exists.*

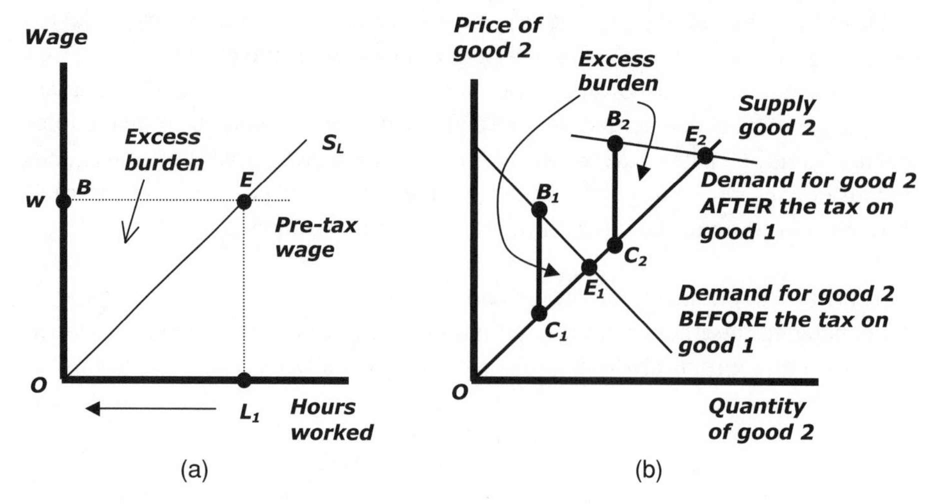

Figure 4.7. (a) A tax with an excess burden and no revenue. (b) The change in the excess burden in market 2 when the tax changes in market 1.

The nonexistence of the market in figure 4.7a compounds problems of estimation of the excess burden *BEO*.

Links between markets

Measurement of the excess burden of taxation requires accounting for links between markets. Substitution effects reduce demand in a market in which taxes are levied; at the same time, the substitution effect switches spending to other markets, where demand then increases. There are, therefore, affects on excess burdens of taxes in the other markets.

In figure 4.7b, an increase in the tax rate in the market for good 1 has increased demand for good 2 through the substitution effect. The level of the tax in market 2, which is shown as $B_1C_1 = B_2C_2$, remains unchanged when the tax on good 1 is increased. However, the increased tax in market 1 (which is not shown) increases the excess burden of taxation in market 2 from $B_1C_1E_1$ to $B_2C_2E_2$.[17]

Hence:

> *The excess burden of a tax in the market where the tax is levied understates the excess burden of taxation because of responses in other markets.*
>
> *The need to include consequences in other markets increases the complexity of measurement of the excess burden of taxation.*

The excess burden in labor markets

In labor markets, for people whose job description includes predetermined inflexible hours of work, little or no substitution is possible and excess burdens of

[17] In the case shown, the excess burden of taxation in market 2 has increased because of increased spending in that market and also a higher elasticity of demand.

taxation are small or nonexistent. People with more flexibility in choosing effort and hours worked have greater substitution responses (higher labor-supply elasticities) and therefore are subject to greater excess burdens of taxation.

The excess burden of taxation depends not only on *marginal adjustments* to labor supply but also on the decision whether to work at all for a living. When hours worked are not flexible, the choice is between having and not having a job.

The decision whether to have a job, in turn, depends on the values of payments provided by governments to people who do not work. If payments to people not working are sufficiently generous and taxes on income earned are sufficiently high (perhaps to finance the benefits for people not working), some people may decide that it is not worthwhile working for a living. The excess burden of taxation is then as shown in figure 4.7a; for the individual not working, market participation has ceased and it is as if the market does not exist.

> *The excess burden of taxation is affected by income that governments transfer to people not working.*

The diversity in empirical estimates of the excess burden

Empirical estimates of the excess burden of taxation have varied considerably. In the United States, for example, estimates of the marginal excess burden of taxation (the additional excess burden due to an additional dollar of tax revenue) have ranged from 7 to 39 cents. Tracing effects of taxes through other markets suggests higher values than this upper bound.

The estimates of the magnitude of the excess burden have consequences for the desirable scope of government. There are responsibilities that we might wish to assign to governments if we could be assured that the marginal excess burden is 7 cents on the dollar but not if it is 39 cents, or more.[18]

Why is there such diversity in estimates? The diversity may reflect the difficulties of accurate measurement; it is difficult to measure something that is invisible; that has consequences that require tracing through effects in the different markets in an economy; that includes changes in hours worked and the decision whether to have a job; and that also depends on the income received from the government when not working.

[18] The diversity in estimates reflects differences in values of labor-supply elasticities used for the calculations, as well as differences in the theoretical models that guide the computations. In studies for the United States in the 1980s, Stuart (1984) reported a 7 percent excess burden for the marginal dollar of tax revenue; Ballard, Shoven, and Whalley (1985) reported 12 percent; and Browning (1987) reported 21 percent. Fullerton (1991) proposed a common basis for comparing the estimates and revised the Ballard et al. number to 7 percent and the Browning number to 25 percent. Jorgensen and Yun (1993) reported a welfare loss through the excess burden of taxation of 18 percent of tax revenue as the *average* excess burden of taxation: for the marginal excess burden, they reported 39.1 percent. Allgood and Snow (1998) reported a range between 13 and 28 percent. Goulder and Williams (2003) used numerical simulations of a model of the U.S. economy to show that after substitution effects have been traced through other markets, measuring the excess burden of taxation only in the market where a tax is levied understates by multiples the true excess burden of the tax.

The ambiguities due to inadequate information – and the need for counterfactual information about what could have been – can leave scope for discretion and assumptions. Estimates of the excess burden can be influenced by personal predisposition regarding the desirable size of government. The lower the estimates of the marginal excess burden of taxation, the greater is the scope for assigning responsibilities to government through taxation and public spending; conversely, high marginal excess burdens of taxation imply greater efficiency losses if the size of government increases through increased taxation that expands public spending.

Evidence on the excess burden from social experiments

Are there other sources of evidence on the magnitudes of excess burdens? We can look to the evidence from the social experiments of socialism and communism. As we noted in chapter 2, in communist societies, the ideology implied the normative behavioral rule that:

> *People should contribute according to their ability and not according to personal reward.*

People were therefore asked (or compelled) to behave as if their personal elasticity of labor supply were zero.[19] A corollary was that:

> *Personal reward should reflect need and not the value of contribution to production.*

Personal needs were determined by government bureaucracies. There was no role for incentives. The evidence is that the natural experiment, which persisted over decades and generations, resulted in significant excess burdens.[20]

B. Tax revenue and the Laffer curve

What is the maximal revenue that a government can obtain? In the case of a tax on labor income, tax revenue is:

$$R = t(wL) = \{tax\ rate\} \cdot \{tax\ base\}. \qquad (4.11)$$

The gross market wage w that the individual receives in expression (4.11) is given and constant for any number of hours worked (see figure 4.1). When the tax rate increases, the net-of-tax wage $w(1 - t)$ declines and, through the substitution response, hours worked decline. Therefore:

> *Through the substitution effect, the tax base contracts when the rate of taxation increases.*

[19] With markets absent, taxation was not an explicit payment to the government but rather was implicit; the implicit tax was the difference between an individual's marginal contribution to production and the value of the reward that the individual received.

[20] People who lived through the experiments indicated the presence of the excess burden by reporting that "we pretended to work and they pretended to pay us."

Tax revenue

Although the tax base contracts, tax revenue increases if the increased tax rate more than compensates for the contraction of the tax base. We return to the change in tax revenue when the tax rate increases:

$$\frac{dR}{dt} = wL \cdot (1 - \varepsilon_{SL}). \tag{4.12}$$

When we considered the effect of the marginal excess burden MC_X on efficient public spending, we proposed $\varepsilon_{SL} < 1$. This ensured that tax revenue increased when the tax rate increased. We justified $\varepsilon_{SL} < 1$ on the grounds that a government could not increase the tax rate to finance additional public spending if the increase in the tax rate did not result in increased tax revenue.

The countervailing effects on tax revenue of an increased tax rate and smaller tax base, however, result in lower tax revenue if $\varepsilon_{SL} > 1$; if $\varepsilon_{SL} = 1$, tax revenue remains unchanged.[21]

Figure 4.8a shows an individual's labor-supply function with a *variable labor-supply elasticity*. The wage and hours worked have been converted to natural logarithms. The inverse slope of the labor-supply function therefore measures the value of the elasticity of labor supply ε_{SL}.

The labor-supply elasticity increases along the labor-supply function as the tax rate increases.[22] In figure 4.8a, tax revenue is maximized when $\varepsilon_{SL} = 1$. Along the labor-supply function beginning from the origin, tax revenue is first increasing (because $\varepsilon_{SL} < 1$) and then, after $\varepsilon_{SL} = 1$, tax revenue declines along the labor-supply function (because $\varepsilon_{SL} < 1$).

Figure 4.8b shows the relationship between tax revenue and the tax rate and follows directly from figure 4.8a. The relationship in figure 4.8b is known as the *Laffer curve.*

The Laffer curve is based on zero tax revenue when the rate of taxation is zero and also when the rate of taxation is 100 percent. We expect an individual to cease working before a tax rate of 100 percent. The 100 percent tax rate is shown for illustration in figure 4.8a as contracting the tax base to zero.[23]

[21] Returning to figure 4.2, when the tax rate is increased from t_1 to t_2, revenue of $B_2B_1C_1H$ is lost and revenue of $D_1HC_2D_2$ is gained. Tax revenue when the rate of taxation is t_1 is $AB_1C_1D_1$. When the rate of taxation is t_2, tax revenue is $AB_2C_2D_2$. Because in figure 4.2 $\varepsilon_{SL} = 1$, $D_1HC_2D_2 = B_2B_1C_1H$, and tax revenue remains constant.

[22] With the wage and labor supply expressed in natural logarithms, we obtain the labor-supply elasticity from the inverse slope of the labor-supply function as:

$$\frac{d\,lnL}{d\,lnw} = \frac{dL}{L} \cdot \frac{w}{dw} \equiv \varepsilon_{SL}.$$

[23] Arthur Laffer emphasized the relationship expressed in the Laffer curve. Figure 4.8a is the most convenient representation of a labor-supply function for showing the properties of a Laffer curve. Because the Laffer curve rests on the general observation that zero tax revenue is obtained both when the tax rate is zero and when the tax rate is 100 percent (or less), the foundations of the Laffer curve are quite general and do not require the form of the labor-supply function in figure 4.8a.

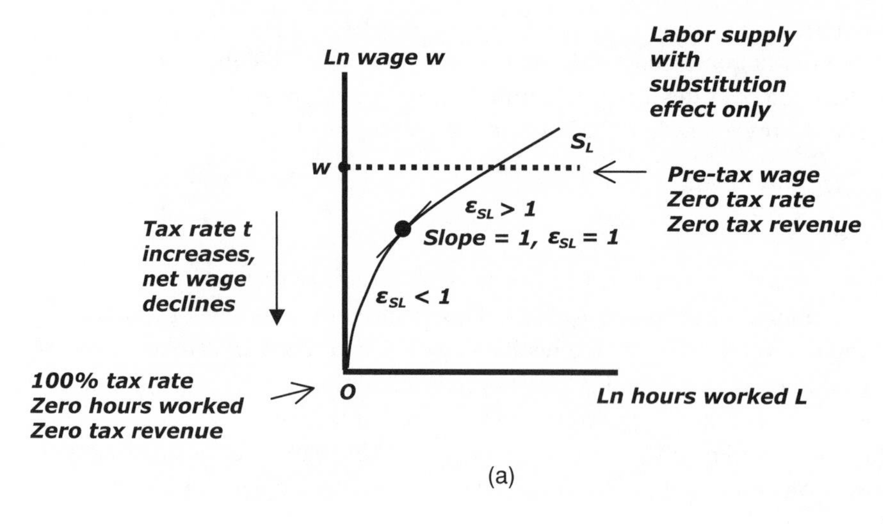

(a)

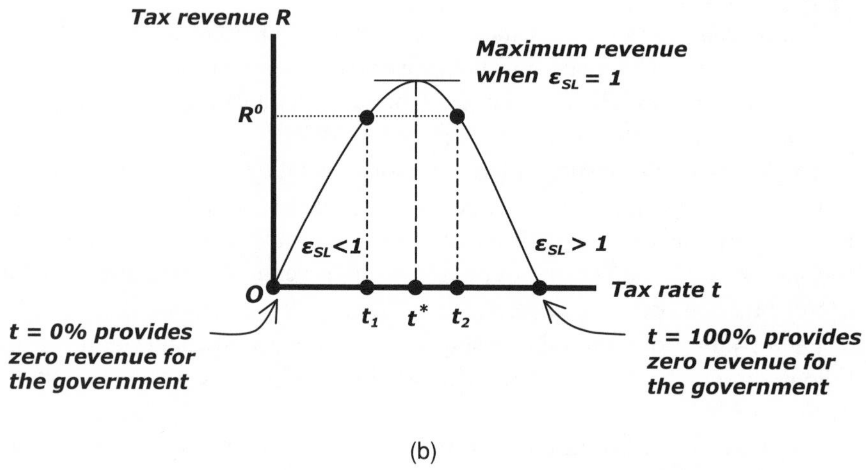

(b)

Figure 4.8. (a) The elasticity of labor supply and tax revenue. (b) The Laffer curve.

The tax revenue R^0 in figure 4.8b can be obtained by levying either the lower tax rate t_1 or the higher tax rate t_2. All tax rates in excess of t^*, *which maximizes revenue*, are on the "wrong" side of the Laffer curve.

> *On the "wrong" side of the Laffer curve, the same revenue can be obtained with a lower rate of taxation – and therefore also with a lower excess burden of taxation.*

Individual behavior and the aggregate Laffer curve

The labor-supply function and Laffer curve in figures 4.8a and 4.8b describe *individual behavior*. Estimation of a market labor-supply elasticity and a Laffer curve for an entire population requires aggregation of information in the labor market. With observations on labor-market available, econometric techniques allow the aggregate labor-supply elasticity and *aggregate Laffer curve* to be estimated. The aggregate Laffer curve would reveal the tax rate that maximizes total revenue from the tax on labor. Individuals, however, have their own personal labor-supply functions and labor-supply elasticities.

Values of the tax rate that drive individuals onto the wrong side of their personal Laffer curve differ for different people.

Investment and the Laffer curve

High taxes on returns from investment result in substitution effects; investment declines or capital moves elsewhere to other tax jurisdictions. There is, therefore, a Laffer curve for taxation of capital. A sufficiently high rate of taxation moves the government onto the wrong side of the Laffer curve for tax revenue from income from capital. When investment declines or capital leaves a tax jurisdiction, the marginal product of labor declines. The tax base for labor income therefore also contracts – along with the tax base for capital income. The Laffer curve for tax revenue from labor income is therefore affected by the tax rate on income from capital. Similarly, the Laffer curve for tax revenue from income from capital is affected by the tax rate on labor income.

A tax on one factor of production reduces the tax base of the other factor.[24]

Tax evasion and the Laffer curve

When tax rates increase, incentives are provided for people to not pay taxes. Another reason for the Laffer curve, therefore, is tax evasion when tax rates become too high. We shall presently study tax evasion in detail.

The political sensitivity of the Laffer curve

Information, in general, is imperfect and there can be debate as to where a government has located itself on the aggregate Laffer curve through choice of taxes. Location on the Laffer curve is revealed *empirically* by changing the rate of taxation and observing the revenue response. If tax revenue increases when the tax rate is reduced, the government is on the wrong side of the Laffer curve.

Ideology and beliefs about the effectiveness or need for government differ; some people have faith in benefits to a society of high government spending,

[24] Production functions usually have the property that the cross-derivative is positive. For a production function $F(L, K)$, the marginal products of labor L and capital K are the first derivatives:

$$\frac{\partial F}{\partial L} \equiv MP_L, \quad \frac{\partial F}{\partial K} \equiv MP_K.$$

The positive cross-derivative shows that marginal product of one factor of production increases with the quantities used of other factors of production:

$$\frac{\partial^2 F}{\partial K \partial L} \equiv \frac{\partial MP_L}{\partial K} = \frac{\partial MP_K}{\partial L} > 0.$$

The return to a factor of production is equal to the value of marginal product; that is, $w = P \cdot MP_L$ and $r = P \cdot MP_K$ (see supplement S1A). The positive cross-derivative implies that a decline in supply of one factor of production due to a tax increase also decreases the tax base of the other factor of production.

others favor more modest public spending and perhaps also reliance on user prices as an alternative to tax-financed public goods. The Laffer curve is politically sensitive for the people who prefer high government spending. In general, high government spending is associated with the need for high tax rates. The possibility implied by an aggregate Laffer curve that tax rates can be *reduced* to increase tax revenue therefore might be regarded by people favoring high government spending as a ploy, intended to decrease government spending by decreasing the tax rate.

Political sensitivity is compounded by the distinction between the short- and long-run Laffer curve, corresponding to short- and long-run elasticities of labor supply. A government on the wrong side of the Laffer curve may find that in the short run, lower tax rates may not significantly increase tax revenue. Substantial increases in tax revenue will require that tax rates be kept low for a sufficiently long period in order for taxpayers to believe that taxes will stay low. After being convinced that tax reductions are permanent (and not a ploy by the government), taxpayers will adjust their behavior and increase hours worked. They may also reveal income on which taxes were evaded when tax rates were higher.

A leviathan government and the Laffer curve

The term *leviathan government* describes a government that has the objective of setting the tax rate that yields maximum tax revenue on the Laffer curve. The leviathan government extracts rents through tax revenue that is used for government consumption. Government bureaucrats can benefit from increased salaries and from personal benefits from presiding over larger government budgets.[25]

C. Who pays a tax?

We expect governments to want to know who pays taxes. Otherwise, governments would be imposing taxes that randomly assign tax obligations. Random tax assignments would contradict two normative principles of just taxation, known as *horizontal equity* and *vertical equity*.

> *Horizontal equity requires that people who are identical in income and other attributes face the same tax obligations.*
>
> *Vertical equity requires that people who are not identical in income and other attributes face tax liabilities that are just in accounting for the sources of individual differences.*

To apply these principles, governments need to know who is paying a tax.

[25] The term *leviathan* comes from the book published in 1651 with the same name by Thomas Hobbes (1588–1679). Hobbes described and favored an absolute and complete monarch. He believed that absolute rule is necessary to save people from anarchy because, left to their own devices, people would take each other's property by force and the strong would be cruel to and kill the weak. Hobbes took the term *leviathan* from the Hebrew word for whale. We shall return to Hobbes.

Governments can legally specify who has the obligation to actually deliver tax revenue. We shall now see that people who are told by a government to "pay" a tax in the sense of having the responsibility to deliver tax revenue do not necessarily pay the tax. In other terminology:

The effective incidence of a tax describes who actually pays a tax.

The legal incidence of a tax describes who is legally obliged to deliver tax revenue to the government.

The effective incidence of a tax does not necessarily correspond to the legal incidence.

We previously identified two normative principles of taxation:

According to the benefit principle of taxation, those people who benefit from public spending should pay the taxes that finance the spending.

According to the ability-to-pay principle of taxation, people who can most afford to pay should pay taxes, without regard for personal benefit obtained from the taxes paid.

The benefit principle, requires that people who benefit pay. When taxes are levied according to the ability-to-pay principle, governments presumably want people with higher incomes to pay more in taxes. In either case:

If taxes are to be paid by intended taxpayers, governments need to be able to identify who is paying a tax.

A tax that sellers are obliged to deliver to the government

Figure 4.9 shows a market in which, with no tax, the competitive outcome is a price P_E and a quantity supplied Q_E at point E. The market could be for goods or for labor – or any market.

When sellers are required to deliver the tax revenue to the government (that is, the legal incidence is on sellers), the tax increases the cost of sellers. Without a tax, the price P_S in figure 4.9 received by sellers is equal to the equilibrium market price P_E. The tax establishes a new market-supply function $\{S + TAX\}$, which includes the cost imposed on sellers through the obligation to deliver the tax to the government. Point H at the intersection of the tax-inclusive supply function $\{S + TAX\}$ and demand D determines the post-tax price P'_B that buyers pay. Point J determines the post-tax price P'_S that sellers receive. The tax is the difference $(P'_B - P'_S)$ between the post-tax buying and selling prices.

Although sellers are obliged to deliver tax revenue to the government, sellers and buyers share the actual payment of the tax. The effective incidence of the tax is determined by the location of point G in figure 4.9. Sellers pay the part FA $(= GJ)$ of the tax, which is equal to the fall in price received by sellers from P_E to P'_S. Buyers pay the part of the tax $VF = HG$, which is equal to the increase in

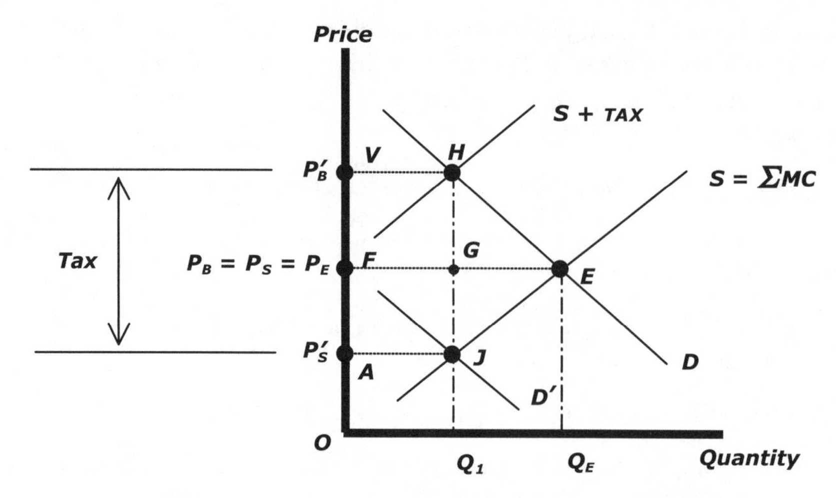

Figure 4.9. Payment of a tax depends on substitution possibilities.

the buying price from P_E before the tax to P'_B after the tax. Government revenue from the tax is *VHJA*, of which sellers pay *FGJA* and buyers pay *VFGH*.

A tax that buyers are obliged to deliver to the government

Precisely the same market outcome is obtained when it is buyers who are required to deliver the tax revenue to the government. In that case, buyers deduct the tax from their *MB's* expressed in market demand. The demand function after the tax, as viewed by buyers in figure 4.9, is then no longer *D* but *D′*. The demand function *D′* thus indicates the price that sellers receive after they have delivered the tax to the government. Supply of sellers is determined at point *J*, where the demand function *D′* intersects the supply function *S*. In the post-tax outcome at point *J*, buyers pay the same price P'_B and sellers receive the price P'_S as when the legal obligation to deliver tax revenue is placed on sellers.

Effective and legal tax incidence

In figure 4.9, buyers always pay the part of the tax $(P'_B - P_E)$ or *VF* (= *GH*) and sellers pay the part of the tax $(P_E - P'_S)$ or *FA* (= *GJ*). Therefore:

> *Effective tax incidence (who actually pays a tax) is independent of legal tax incidence (who is legally obliged to deliver the tax revenue to the government).*

Sharing of the excess burden

Just as payment of the tax is shared, so is the total excess burden of a tax. The total excess burden in figure 4.9 is *HEJ*, which is divided between buyers and sellers. *HGE* falls on buyers; *GEJ* falls on sellers.

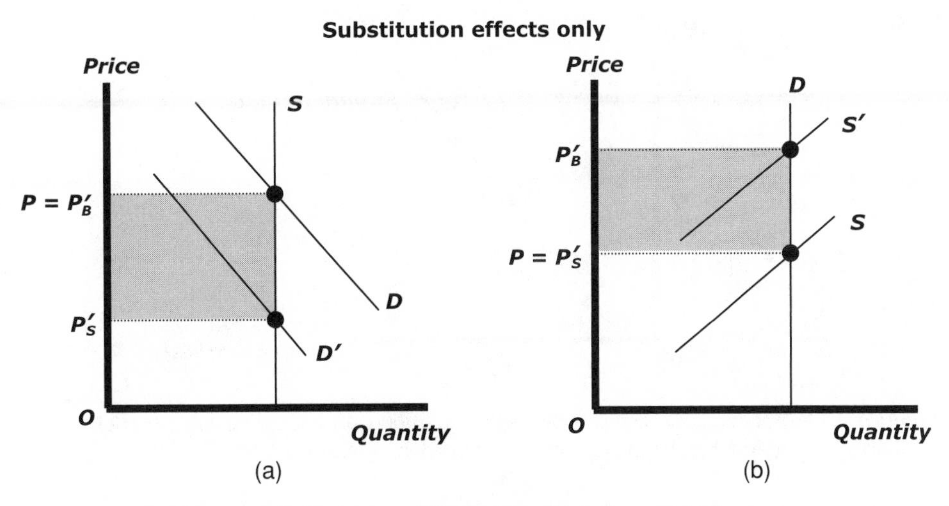

Figure 4.10. (a) A tax paid by sellers. (b) A tax paid by buyers.

Effective tax incidence when taxes have no excess burden

Substitution responses determine effective tax incidence and sharing of the excess burden, through demand and supply elasticities. In figure 4.10a, there is no substitution response on the supply side of the market (we are considering only possible substitution effects, with no income effects). Tax revenue is shown by the shaded area. Before and after the tax, the price paid by buyers is $P = P'_B$. When the tax is levied, the price P'_S received by suppliers falls by the full amount of the tax. Suppliers, therefore, pay the entire tax. Because there is no substitution response by sellers who pay the tax, there is no excess burden of taxation.

In figure 4.10b, buyers have no substitution response and therefore pay the entire tax. The tax increases the price paid by buyers to P'_B and leaves the price received by suppliers unchanged at $P = P'_S$. There is no excess burden of taxation because of no substitution response by the buyers who pay the tax.

The limiting cases in figures 4.10a and 4.10b show that:

> *The side of a market (buyers or sellers) with no substitution responses pays the entire tax.*
>
> *When one side of the market pays the entire tax, there is no excess burden of taxation.*

Political pronouncements and taxation

Figure 4.11 shows a labor market in which substitution possibilities are greater on the demand side of the market than on the supply side. The market equilibrium wage is w_E when there are no taxes. The tax increases the wage paid by employers (the buyers of labor) to w'_B and reduces the wage received by employees (the sellers of labor) to w'_S. Employees (or sellers) pay the greater part of the tax and bear the greater part of the excess burden. Thus, if policy makers place

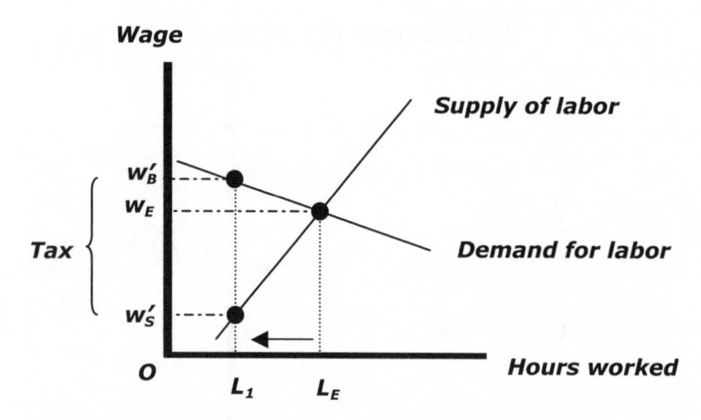

Figure 4.11. Substitution effects expressed in demand and supply elasticities determine who pays a tax and the sharing of the excess burden of taxation.

the legal obligation on employers to pay a payroll tax and if the labor market is described as in figure 4.11, employees, in effect, pay the greater part of the tax and bear the greater part of the excess burden. Or, when employers deliver payment for employees' health insurance to health-insurance companies, with the labor market as in figure 4.11, employees themselves, in effect, pay the greater part of the cost of health insurance and bear the greater part of the excess burden.[26]

Political pronouncements are made in terms of the legal incidence of taxation and not effective incidence. The pronouncements indicate either misinformation or disinformation about who actually pays a tax – and bears the excess burden.

> *Public policy pronouncements that associate effective tax incidence with legal tax incidence indicate misinformation (the political decision maker does not know economic principles) or disinformation (the political decision maker hopes that others do not know economic principles).*

Fiscal illusion and tax incidence

Misperceptions about taxation and public spending are known as *fiscal illusion*.

> *Fiscal illusion with regard to taxation occurs when taxpayers are not aware that they are paying taxes.*

Fiscal illusion and the effective incidence of taxes

People may not know that the legal incidence of a tax does not imply effective incidence; political benefits from disinformation about who pays a tax require the people who effectively pay the taxes to believe that others on whom legal incidence has been imposed are actually paying the taxes. To show political

[26] There is an excess burden of taxation because a tax in the labor market finances health insurance; market intrusion is therefore present. There is, of course, no excess burden of taxation if payment for health insurance is voluntary in a market for health insurance.

gratitude, the beneficiaries of disinformation about tax incidence need to know, however, that they are not actually effectively paying the taxes that they deliver to the government.

> *Political benefit from disinformation requires selective fiscal illusion about tax incidence.*

Fiscal illusion and the choice between direct and indirect taxes

Fiscal illusion affects the choice between direct and indirect taxes. Direct taxes such as income taxes are paid directly to the government by taxpayers. Indirect taxes are paid indirectly by buyers when sellers transfer tax revenue to the government. Taxpayers are generally aware of the direct taxes that they pay. They may not be aware of indirect taxes that are included in the price of goods and services.[27]

> *Because of fiscal illusion, political decision makers may prefer indirect taxes because people do not know they are being taxed.*

Fiscal illusion about indirect taxes is not present when – as is for example the usual case in the United States – prices are announced to buyers as the price "plus tax."

When there is fiscal illusion, people do not know that they are paying taxes but, nonetheless, the excess burden of taxation is still present. The substitution response that underlies the excess burden is a response to an increase in price and not a response to the believed *reason* for the price increase.

Fiscal illusion and bond financing

Fiscal illusion also arises when public spending is financed by government borrowing or from the sale of government bonds. We shall consider bond financing in the final section of this chapter.

Economy-wide effects on who pays taxes

We have seen that computing the *total excess burden* of a tax requires accounting for excess burdens in other markets when taxes in one market change. Economy-wide (or general-equilibrium) effects on taxes through links among markets similarly affect how the excess burden is shared and *who pays a tax*. As an example of economy-wide (or general-equilibrium) effects on who pays a tax, a tax on income from capital discourages investment and encourages people to move their capital elsewhere if they can. Income received by labor declines when accompanying capital that is used in production together with labor declines. A

[27] Fiscal illusion regarding payment of indirect taxes was noted by John Stuart Mill (1806–73) in his 1848 book, *Principles of Political Economy*. Mill observed that although direct taxes were unpopular, people appeared not to notice being "fleeced in the price of commodities." The reference to fleece here is to wool shorn from sheep.

tax on income from capital therefore decreases the future income of labor. A sales tax on toothbrushes benefits dentists. If dentists work longer hours and therefore play less golf, demand for golf clubs and for the services of caddies falls. Golf-club manufacturers and caddies thereby lose because of a sales tax on toothbrushes.[28] Rather than taxing toothbrushes, governments might subsidize toothbrushes. The same effects then arise in the opposite direction. Or, a government might limit imports of foreign sugar to allow domestic sugar producers to receive higher prices. The restrictions on sugar imports then affect the income of dentists and also golf-club manufacturers and caddies.

Tax burdens and economy-wide information: Conclusions

Governments require information in order to levy taxes according to either the benefit or the ability-to-pay principle of taxation. However, information in one market is not enough. Because of linkages among markets:

> *To know who in the final analysis pays a tax and who bears the excess burden of taxation, governments need to be able to trace the effect of the tax throughout all markets.*

With data available, the task of determining who pays taxes and who bears excess burdens is computational. We observed that computations of the excess burden of taxation result in diverse answers. Identifying who pays a tax and bears excess burdens is based on the same types of computations.

D. Taxes on international trade

Import duties or tariffs are a form of indirect taxation. Import duties merit our attention because of the motives that can underlie governments' decisions to tax international trade. Import duties provide governments with revenue; however, in high-income countries, the primary motive for levying import duties is not to obtain tax revenue.

> *In high-income countries, revenue from taxes on international trade is an incidental consequence of protectionist policies.*

Moreover:

> *A sales tax dominates an import duty as a revenue instrument; the sales tax collects more revenue with a lower excess burden than an import tax levied at the same rate as the sales tax.*

[28] Dentists play less golf because of a substitution effect. An income effect would lead dentists to play more golf. On substitution and income effects, see supplement S4A.

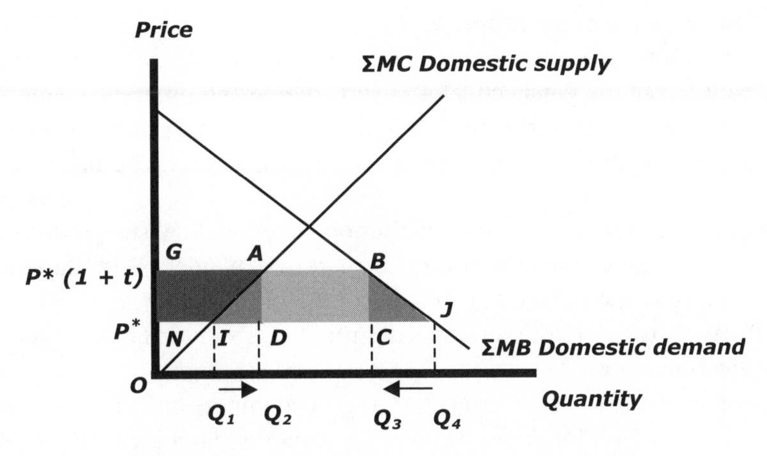

Figure 4.12. The excess burden of an import tariff.

The excess burden of an import tariff

Figure 4.12 shows the excess burden of an import tariff or tax on imports. The price of imports in the world market is given as P^*. At this price, under conditions of free trade in a competitive domestic market, the quantity Q_1 is supplied by local producers and domestic demand is Q_4. The quantity $(Q_4 - Q_1)$ of domestic sales consists of imports.

An import tariff of t percent increases the domestic price to $P^*(1 + t)$. Local producers respond by increasing output along the domestic supply function from Q_1 to Q_2. In response to a higher domestic price, domestic demand decreases from Q_4 to Q_3. Imports fall to $(Q_3 - Q_2)$. Revenue from the import tariff is $ABCD$. The import tariff benefits the domestic industry, in which profits increase by $GAIN$.[29]

The import tariff has resulted in two substitution responses: domestic demand has decreased Q_4 to Q_3, and domestic supply has increased from Q_1 to Q_2. Each substitution response is accompanied by an efficiency loss.

For domestic buyers, the excess burden of the import tax is JBC.[30] The efficiency loss because of the substitution response in production is DIA.[31]

[29] The increase in price to $P^*(1 + t)$ provides additional industry revenue $GADN$. However, of this, IAD is cost incurred in production (the area under the supply curve). Net benefit to the industry is $GAIN$.

[30] Before the import tax, total benefit for buyers from the quantity $(Q_4 - Q_3)$ is $BJ\,Q_4Q_3$ and the cost at the world price of the imports is $CJ\,Q_4Q_3$. JBC is the difference between the benefit and cost of the consumption $(Q_4 - Q_3)$ eliminated by the import tax and hence is the net loss due to the import tax.

[31] The cost of producing the output $(Q_2 - Q_1)$ domestically is the area under the supply function $IA\,Q_2Q_1$. The cost of obtaining this output as imports is IDQ_2Q_1. DIA is the additional cost of producing the output $(Q_2 - Q_1)$ locally rather than obtaining the goods as imports.

A sales tax in place of an import tariff

Rather than an import tax, a government could levy a sales tax at the same rate of *t* percent. From the perspective of buyers, there is no difference between the sales tax and the import tariff. In either case, the domestic price facing buyers is $P^*(1 + t)$. Consumption in either case is Q_3. There is an excess burden of taxation from the sales tax of *JBC*.

The sales tax, however, has no substitution effect on domestic producers. The efficiency loss *DIA* of the import tariff is therefore avoided. With the sales tax, domestic producers continue to confront competitive imports at the given world price P^*. With the domestic price facing producers remaining at P^*, domestic production remains at Q_1.

Imports after the sales tax are $(Q_3 - Q_1)$. The import tariff is levied only on imports. The *tax base* for the sales tax is all domestic purchases, without regard for whether goods are domestically produced or imported.

Revenue from the sales tax is *GBCN*, which exceeds the revenue from the import tax by *GADN*. The sales tax has converted both the industry profit from the tariff *GAIN* and the efficiency loss from the import tariff *DIA* to government revenue.

A sales tax is thus a more efficient means of raising revenue than an import tariff. A sales tax can provide the same tax revenue as an import tariff with a lower rate of taxation and a lower excess burden of taxation. Also, it is evident that because of the larger tax base of the sales tax, maximal revenue from a sales tax is greater than maximal revenue obtainable from an import tariff.

Costs of collecting revenue

Costs of collecting revenue from taxes on imports are low compared to a sales tax. A sales tax needs to be collected from many domestic sellers, whereas collection of an import duty requires stationing customs officials at limited locations where imports enter the country. Because of low collection costs and easy enforcement (although smuggling often took place), import duties were often historically the first taxes imposed by governments seeking tax revenue.

Protectionist rents

Governments in countries lacking domestic tax-collection capabilities might rely on import taxes for government revenue. However, when governments with domestic tax-collection capabilities impose import duties, we can infer that the purpose is to benefit domestic producers by providing *protectionist rents*. The presence of rents suggests rent seeking. The rents are expressed in the increased industry profits *GAIN* provided by an import tax. The protective import duty incidentally provides the tax revenue *ABCD*; if governments did not care about protectionist rents, they would replace all import duties with sales taxes. A sales tax would convert protectionist rents to tax revenue. Also, rather than two social losses from the two substitution effects of the import tariff, with a sales tax there would be only one substitution effect and one social loss, through the domestic substitution response in consumption. Therefore:

> *When tax administration allows domestic taxes to be collected, the purpose of a tax on imports cannot be to provide tax revenue because a sales tax is a superior revenue instrument.*
>
> *The purpose of a tax on imports is not revenue but rather to provide protectionist rents to domestic industry interests.*

Why use an import tariff?

If the objective is government revenue, a sales tax is preferable to an import tariff. If the objective is not government revenue but rather to provide protectionist rents, a production subsidy is more efficient. A subsidy to producers of $s = t$ percent increases the domestic price received by producers by the same percentage as the import tax:

$$P^*(1+s) = P^*(1+t). \tag{4.13}$$

The production subsidy provides the rents to producer interests by increasing the price received by producers. The import tariff likewise increases the price received by producers but results in the additional excess burden *BJC* because the import tariff also increases the price paid by consumers. Protectionist rents provided through a production subsidy thus avoid the excess burden *BJC* of an import duty.

Therefore, whether the objective is government revenue or to provide protectionist rents, there are more efficient means for implementing government policy than import tariffs.

With the purpose of import tariffs not to provide tax revenue but rather to provide protectionist rents to producer interests, the question is:

> *Given the smaller excess burden of a subsidy to domestic producers, why would governments choose to use import tariffs to provide the protectionist rents?*

One answer is that the taxes levied to finance the payment of a production subsidy also have excess burdens, which are matched against the additional excess burden *BJC* of using an import tariff. Also, an import duty *provides* government revenue, whereas a production subsidy requires *spending* government revenue. We can, however, turn for an answer to our question regarding use of import duties to asymmetric information and illusion. Industry rents, if provided through production subsidies, require information that is reported in the government budget; because of rational ignorance, many individual voters do not know the specific items in a government budget; nonetheless, with the government budget decided each year by voting in congress or parliament, visibility in the government budget opens production subsidies to the possibility of scrutiny and debate.

An import tax provides protectionist rents in a more subtle and hidden way. The rents do not appear in the government budget; rather buyers provide the rents directly to the domestic industry, through a higher domestic price directly paid to domestic producers.[32]

We noted in chapter 2 that when rent creation and rent seeking take place, both political decision makers and the successful rent seekers prefer that their activities be hidden from the public view.

> *Compared to production subsidies, import tariffs are a less efficient, but also less visible and, therefore, more politically feasible, way of providing, creating, assigning – and extracting – rents.*

Import quotas

Our final question about international trade concerns the choice between an *import duty* and an *import quota*. For a competitive domestic industry, an import duty and an import quota assigned to importers have precisely the same effects on demand, supply, and international trade – and, therefore, on prices and quantities. A quota that limits imports to $(Q_3 - Q_2)$ in figure 4.12 and an import tariff set at the rate t both result in the same imports $(Q_3 - Q_2)$ and the same domestic competitive domestic price $P^*(1 + t)$. The one difference between an import duty and an import quota is in who obtains revenue. The government obtains revenue *ABCD* from the import duty. The same revenue is divided as profit among importers who are privileged in having been assigned parts of the import quota. The privileged importers buy the imports in the world market at the price P^* to sell in the domestic market at the high price $P^*(1 + t)$. The privilege to engage in this trade is a gift of money – or a rent.

If rights to the import quota were competitively auctioned by the government, the government would obtain the same revenue *ABCD* from the auction as is provided by the import duty. Some governments have auctioned quotas. Usually, quota rights are not auctioned but are assigned and so governments do not obtain revenue from the quota. The purpose of the quota, then, cannot have been to provide the government with revenue. Indeed, by using an import quota rather than an import tariff, the government loses the revenue *ABCD*.

> *An import quota creates rents for private individuals at the expense of government revenue.*

The private profits from being assigned quota rents can set in place a rent-seeking contest. If rent dissipation can be presumed to be complete, the quota rents *ABCD* are an efficiency loss of rent creation to be added to excess burdens due to substitution effects.

[32] When a domestic buyer pays a domestic price $P^*(1 + t)$, the tariff component of the price is paid directly to the domestic producer, who benefits without money passing through the hands of government and being recorded in the government budget.

Producer interests, who are distinct from the privileged importers, seek the protectionist producer rent *GAIN*; they do not care whether the government creates the producer rent by using an import tariff or an import quota – unless they happen to be well positioned to compete for the privilege of also obtaining part of the rents from the import quota.

> *Why would a government forgo tariff revenue to create private rents through an import quota?*

This question was addressed in chapter 2 when we considered the political principal–agent problem, albeit in more general terms than the case of use of an import quota. Quota rents are an example of rent creation and rent seeking, and we would also suppose a source of political benefit through political support – and, if the political culture and institutions allow, political rent extraction.[33]

Conclusion regarding import taxes

Our conclusion is that taxes on imports are not levied for revenue reasons; import duties are rather protectionist tariffs. Import quotas transfer the revenue that the import taxes would have provided to privileged importers. However, the revenue from the import duty was incidental to the reason for the import duty in the first place. The protectionist rents and political benefits explain why is there is not always free trade, which we saw in chapter 1 is efficient in maximizing a population's total income.

4.2 Tax Evasion and the Shadow Economy

We turn now to tax evasion and the shadow economy. Our interest in tax evasion begins with the relationship to the prisoners' dilemma of public-good supply and the basic premise justifying public finance to replace voluntary payments – that

[33] An import tax and an assigned import quota are equivalent in all ways except for who benefits from revenue or rents if the domestic industry is competitive: if there is domestic monopoly, the equivalence no longer holds. A domestic industry may be competitive because a single domestic producer faces import competition; a tariff or quota can then create monopoly rents. Also, sometimes the rents from an import quota have been assigned to foreign producers: compensation is thereby given for the protectionism that has changed conditions of access of foreign exporters to the domestic market. The import quota is then known as a *voluntary export restraint*, suggesting that foreign exporters have voluntarily abided by an agreement to limit exports to the quantities allowed under the import quota.

although governments confront the asymmetric-information problem, nonetheless they can solve the free-rider problem.

A. Tax evasion as free riding

People who free ride in the case of the prisoners' dilemma refuse to voluntarily contribute to public goods according to their true valuations of benefit. The role of government in levying taxes is intended to solve the free-rider problem through compulsory payment. People, however, can still continue to free ride by refusing to pay taxes – although tax evasion is illegal.

Tax evasion is illegal free riding in contributions to public goods.

Consequently, tax evasion compromises the basic premise that governments have an advantage over voluntary payments for public goods in solving the free-rider problem. Because of tax evasion, some people still free ride.

Tax evasion and tax incidence

The difference between legal and effective tax incidence has consequences for tax evasion. People who are legally required to deliver tax revenue to the government but evade payment of taxes may be taking for themselves tax revenue that – for the most part, because of supply and demand elasticities – others effectively paid. Tax evasion is theft of government revenue. The theft goes, however, beyond free riding in refusing to pay own taxes; taxes that others effectively paid do not reach the government.

Public policies

When payment of taxes is based on self-assessment and self-reporting by taxpayers, tax compliance requires taxpayer honesty. If all taxpayers do not report and pay taxes that are due, governments confront an enforcement problem. Tax authorities could meticulously audit every tax return; however, the cost of all-inclusive auditing could exceed the benefits from additional tax revenue. Tax returns are therefore typically audited randomly, with penalties imposed on taxpayers who are detected to have under-reported income. Public policy consists of setting the likelihood of detection and the penalty. The expected penalty for tax evasion is:

$$\{\textit{probability of detection}\} \cdot \{\textit{penalty if detected}\}.$$

A government can increase the probability of detection; this is costly because of the additional personnel required to audit tax returns. Setting high penalties is not costly: additional resources are not required and revenue is provided from tax penalties and fines. To enforce tax compliance, penalties could, therefore, be set extremely high (such as confiscation of all assets). A principle of penalties commensurate with the offense deters extreme penalties for tax evasion. Tax evasion is theft from the government but, if a society wants the incentive to not commit armed robbery to be greater than the incentive to not evade taxes, the penalty for tax evasion cannot be the same as the penalty for armed robbery.

Public policy can also take the form of a tax amnesty. Governments can seek to take advantage of the guilt and anxiety of the people who have evaded taxes. The government can declare that people who voluntarily pay the taxes that they previously evaded will not be required to pay penalties. The amnesty provides past unpaid revenue and also opens a previously evading taxpayer's future income to taxation. Tax amnesties rely, however, on guilt and anxiety that may not be present.

Why do people evade taxes?

Tax evasion can reflect a feeling of injustice that taxes are too high, given the benefits received through public spending. People might feel that taxes take too much of their earned incomes and deliver too little in return. Tax evasion may also reflect distrust of government: because of asymmetric information (perhaps due to rational ignorance but also the inability to know), taxpayers do not know what governments are doing with the taxes they have paid. When there is a perception that taxes are not being used for social benefit, people feel less guilty about evading taxes – or they may not feel guilty at all.

Tax evasion depends on whether people feel guilt or shame. People who feel guilt do not evade taxes. People who feel shame are prepared to evade taxes if they know that they will not be detected but are concerned about the embarrassment and stigma if found out. There are also societies in which there is both guilt and shame (although guilt would usually preempt shame); in some societies there is neither guilt nor shame.

When enough people evade taxes, tax evasion becomes a social norm. When the social norm is *to not pay* taxes, being found to have evaded taxes does not embarrass or stigmatize. When it is the norm to not pay taxes, it is understood that punishment of someone for evading taxes is a political decision because the tax evader is behaving no differently than anyone else.

When honesty is the social norm in paying taxes and people feel shame (if not guilt), there is a cost of personal embarrassment or stigma in being found to have evaded taxes, in addition to the personal cost of penalties and fines.

We observed that when legality is not an issue and people are free to choose their behavior, cooperation takes the place of public-good prisoners' dilemma experiments, and that the cooperation can be due to social norms or expressive behavior that confirms personal identity. Similarly, social norms and expressive behavior can underlie truthful reporting of taxable incomes, even though the probability of a tax audit and detection may be low. The expressive behavior is that tax evasion would contradict a person's self-image as an honest person who does not cheat.

Tax evasion is also influenced by a person's aversion to risk of detection. People who are very averse to taking chances will not evade taxes. Also, people may not be good judges of objective probabilities and may overestimate the likelihood of detection.

Opportunities for tax evasion

Opportunities for tax evasion are not uniform. It is difficult to evade a property tax because the tax base, which is the property or house, is visible and ownership is well defined. There is little opportunity for employees to evade taxes when employers transfer employees' personal income, payroll, and social security taxes directly to the government. Sellers who sell to consumers who are final purchasers have the most extensive opportunities for tax evasion because final purchasers, in general, have no reason to ask for a receipt documenting the seller's revenue. Self-employed people and employers or owners of small businesses have opportunities to evade taxes by finding ways to understate revenues and overstate expenses. Estimates for the United States indicate that 1 percent of incomes from wages and salaries and 4 percent of income from taxable interest and dividends are under-reported; however, some 57 percent of nonfarm self-employed business income is estimated to be under-reported; for farm income, under-reporting has been estimated to be 74 percent.[34]

Tax evasion can take the form of exchange of services: a dentist may do "free" dental work for a lawyer who, in return, provides "free" legal services.

Indirect taxes (sales taxes, excise taxes, and import tariffs) can be evaded. Evasion of excise taxes and import duties through smuggling usually requires the complicity of corrupt, cooperating customs inspectors.

Multinational firms can attempt to use internal accounting prices to evade taxes. Internal accounting prices are used to value shipments between subsidiaries or branches in different countries; because the sales are within the same firm or conglomerate, the prices are known as *transfer prices*, for internal transfers. Through the appropriate setting of transfer prices, profits are moved from high- to low-tax jurisdictions. Within-firm transfer prices can also be used to evade indirect taxes. If there are import duties, low prices declared for intermediate goods shipped between subsidiaries reduce the duties paid. To counter transfer pricing, governments may not accept internal accounting prices as true prices.

In principle, everyone *should* pay the taxes that are due (this is, of course, a normative proposition). However, given that people evade taxes, unequal opportunities for tax evasion are a source of social injustice.

> *Unequal opportunities to evade taxes are a source of social injustice because of arbitrary sharing of the tax burden and of the excess burden of taxation.*

[34] For the source of these numbers and more information on past tax evasion in the United States, see Slemrod (2007).

Illegal immigrants

Even if they wanted to, illegal immigrants may not have the opportunity to pay taxes. Coming forward to declare their income for taxation exposes illegal immigrants to the threat of deportation.[35]

Tax avoidance and tax evasion

Tax evasion differs from *tax avoidance.* Tax evasion is illegal but tax avoidance is not.

> *Tax avoidance is the legal means of using tax laws to reduce tax payments.*

People engage in legal tax avoidance if they can substitute in consumption away from a taxed good to an untaxed good. However, more generally, tax avoidance requires the services of skilled tax accountants and tax lawyers who know how to take advantage of loopholes in tax laws that are often inordinately complex and sometimes almost ambiguous. Only high-income taxpayers may find it worthwhile or may be able to afford hiring the accountants and lawyers. People with lower incomes may only have tax evasion as a possibility for reducing tax payments. Again, there is inequality in opportunity or injustice.

> *There is injustice when some people can engage in tax avoidance and others only in tax evasion. Tax evasion does not incur the expenses of tax avoidance but is illegal and subject to penalties and stigma if detected.*

B. The behavior of the tax authorities

Benjamin Franklin wrote about the injunctions to tax-enforcement agents of the British Crown before the American Revolution of 1776:

> *If any revenue officers are suspected of the least tenderness for the people, discard them. If others are justly complained of, protect and reward them. If any of the under officers behave so as to provoke the people to drub them, promote those to better office.*

Benjamin Franklin viewed the injunctions of behavior of the tax-enforcement officials as part of the "rules by which a great empire may be reduced to a small one." He attributed the American Revolution in part to the behavior of English tax officials.[36]

[35] Children of illegal immigrants, of course, in general attend school. A policy of permitting children of illegal immigrants to attend government schools while maintaining the illegality of the parents is thus a burden to taxpayers that could be avoided or reduced if the parents could be placed within the tax system.

[36] A complaint underlying the Revolution was "no taxation without representation." Although the American colonies were required to pay excise taxes to the king of England, the colonies had no representation in the English parliament.

Presumptive taxation

Employees of the government tax authority are often paid a personal bonus for increasing tax revenue. To increase revenue, tax officials can apply *presumptive taxation*, according to which taxes are assessed based on a presumption of ability to earn income. For example, a tax inspector may know the average income of a category of taxpayers (for example, lawyers, plumbers, and taxi drivers). Presumptive tax assessments above the average of the distribution of true incomes increase the prospects of a bonus for the tax-administration employee. Taxpayers whose true tax obligations are below the average of their income-earning category can be expected to protest more strenuously about a presumptive tax assessment based on average income. Some taxpayers for whom the tax assessment is excessive compared to their true tax liability might, however, pay taxes that they do not owe; they may not be able to provide confirmatory evidence of lower than average income; they may also not be able to cope with the stress of ongoing communication with the tax administration; or they may pay the unjustified taxes to avoid expenses of tax lawyers and accountants.

Corrupt tax officials

In some countries, government tax inspectors can be corrupt. The corrupt officials accept bribes to under-report taxpayers' true incomes. The corrupt officials are then instrumental in facilitating tax evasion. Corrupt tax inspectors can also extort bribes from taxpayers by threatening to report that the taxpayers have earned higher than their true incomes. Corruption also affects the penalties that can be set for tax evasion; if tax officials can be bribed, high penalties increase the personal gains to a tax administration official from cooperating with a tax evader. High penalties thereby increase the incentive for corruption by increasing the gains to be shared from corruption between the tax inspector and the tax evader.

C. The shadow economy

The *shadow economy* consists of all unofficial or nonreported economic activity. Tax evasion and participation in the shadow economy are not necessarily the same. In the shadow economy, incomes are entirely outside the domain of taxation. Tax evasion therefore takes place in the shadow economy, but tax evasion also takes place in the official economy.

Welfare fraud

Welfare fraud occurs when people employed in the shadow economy declare themselves to be officially unemployed and receive unemployment benefits or welfare payments. Such people fraudulently take money from the government (that is, from taxpayers) while at the same time evading taxes on their income in the shadow economy.

Size of the shadow economy

Because the shadow economy is illegal, the size of the shadow economy cannot be directly observed and therefore has to be inferred – as is the case with rent seeking – or estimated. In the case of rent seeking, the observed rent is used to attempt to infer the value of resources used in rent seeking. In estimating the size of the shadow economy, researchers look for observed variables that are correlated with the size of the shadow economy – or that are correlated with the true size of national income including the shadow economy. The variables include the money supply, extent of cash payments, and use of electricity. Differences between total income and total spending provide indications of the size of the shadow economy, as do official statistics on differences between population size and people employed. More complex approaches base measurement on a variety of indicators and causes, treating the size of the shadow economy as an unknown variable to be estimated from a set of equations. Table 4.1 shows illustrative estimates based on such multi-indicator and multi-causal approaches.[37]

The table indicates substantial differences in the size of the shadow economy among countries. The largest shadow economies have been in the former Soviet Union (Georgia, Ukraine, and Russia). Turkey has had a large shadow economy, as has Greece; Mediterranean countries, in general, tend to have large shadow economies. Scandinavian countries also have large shadow economies. English-speaking countries tend to have smaller shadow economies; shadow economies have also been small in Japan, Austria, and Switzerland.[38]

Table 4.1 shows that there is a tendency for the size of the shadow economy to increase over time. Perhaps personal attitudes toward paying taxes change. Illegal migration affects the size of the shadow economy because illegal immigrants do not work in the formal economy. The size of the shadow economy is also affected by legal migration: immigrants may come from countries where governments are not trusted and where much economic activity takes place in the informal sector. The immigrants may take time to adapt to voluntary self-assessment and self-compliance in paying taxes.

Corruption and the shadow economy

When there is corruption in government and large sums of money pass hands in the form of bribes, the shadow economy is larger – because the illegal incomes are not reported and are not taxed. At the same time, the size of the shadow economy increases when people are reluctant to pay taxes because government is corrupt; the shadow economy may then be an escape from a corrupt tax administration.

[37] Schneider (2005) described different ways of estimating the size of the shadow economy.

[38] Belgium has had a larger shadow economy than its neighbors. Before the advent of the European common currency in 2002, Belgium used the same currency as Luxembourg, which may have facilitated transport of cash for deposit in banks across the border.

TABLE 4.1. THE SIZE OF THE SHADOW ECONOMY AS A PROPORTION OF REPORTED OFFICIAL GROSS NATIONAL PRODUCT

	1990	1995	2000	2005
Georgia	58	62	67	66
Ukraine	43	47	52	55
Russia	38	41	46	47
Turkey	26	29	32	33
Greece	23	29	29	26
India	–	–	23	25
Italy	23	26	27	23
Israel	16	19	22	23
Belgium	19	22	22	20
Portugal	16	22	23	20
Spain	16	22	23	20
Czech Republic	16	17	19	18
China	–	–	13	17
Norway	15	18	19	17
Denmark	11	18	18	16
Hong Kong SAR	12	13	17	16
Sweden	16	20	19	16
Germany	12	14	16	15
Canada	13	15	16	14
Ireland	11	16	16	14
Australia	10	13	13	13
France	9	15	15	13
Netherlands	12	14	13	13
New Zealand	9	11	13	11
United Kingdom	10	13	13	10
Austria	7	9	10	9
Japan	9	11	11	9
Switzerland	7	8	9	9
United States	7	9	9	8

Source: Schneider (2005, 2007). Numbers are rounded up.

Reliability of the estimates

How reliable are estimates such as those in table 4.1? After all, an attempt is being made to measure activity that is *purposely* hidden or kept invisible. Objections to estimates of the shadow economy can inevitably be expected. The methods used might be criticized and alternative methods of measurement might be proposed.

The incentive to claim exaggeration

Governments have an incentive to claim that estimates of their shadow economies are exaggerated. The governments may be embarrassed by the inadequacies of their tax enforcement capabilities. There may be embarrassment because of the inference that taxpayers do not trust political decision makers and do not believe that government bureaucrats use tax revenue in the public interest. The reason for a large indicated shadow economy may indeed be extensive bribes and other illegal income-earning activities, for example, drug-related and human-trafficking income, or illegal trade such as elephant tusks and rhino horns requiring complicity of people in government. Therefore:

> *Governments with a large shadow economy may be politically sensitive and may object that estimates overstate the true size of their shadow economy.*

Because a large shadow economy can be attributed to high taxation and high public spending, ideology can affect willingness to accept estimates that reveal a large shadow economy; there may thus be reluctance to accept as accurate evidence that appears to link high taxes and high public spending with refusal to pay taxes.

D. Inefficiency and illegality in a shadow economy

There is injustice when unequal opportunities for tax evasion result in discriminatory tax burdens; an ethical consideration is also that activity in the shadow economy provides a cost advantage for producers who do not pay taxes, so that honesty is penalized. Setting aside ethics and social justice, however, can tax evasion and the shadow economy be beneficial on efficiency grounds?

Inefficiency in the shadow economy

The case for efficiency of the shadow economy is that when taxes are not paid, the substitution effects that underlie the excess burden of taxation do not take place. However, tax evasion and the shadow economy create other inefficiencies. The scope for personal success is limited because excessive success of an economic activity in the shadow economy compromises the ability to remain invisible to tax authorities. People in the shadow economy are therefore limited in applying their abilities.

In the shadow economy, recourse to courts is not available for enforcing contracts and settling disputes. Dispute settlement in the shadow economy is personal and often violent.

The shadow economy invites corruption. Corrupt tax officials are provided with opportunities to seek bribes in return for allowing economic activity in the shadow economy to continue. As we have observed, corrupt tax officials can also fabricate infringements.

Conspicuous consumption and visible spending

Conspicuous consumption provides some people with utility through the house or apartment in which they live and the cars that they drive.[39] Conspicuous

[39] In some cases, the conspicuous consumption includes "trophy" wives or girlfriends. The male equivalent is sometimes called a "boy toy."

consumption also provides information to tax authorities about personal spending. Observable discrepancies between visible personal expenditures and reported income raise questions about the sources of the income being spent. The benefit of income is diminished if the income cannot be freely spent. The larger the shadow economy, the easier it is to spend income on which taxes have not been paid because both sellers and buyers have incentives to keep their transactions out of the view of tax authorities. However, the spending then cannot be on overly conspicuous consumption.

Money laundering

Large profits from illegal activity are difficult to spend or invest because tax authorities may ask about the sources of the money. Suppliers of drugs and others engaged in illegal activity therefore wish to find ways of converting illegally earned income to legal income, even if this involves payment of taxes. Thus, there is a demand for *money laundering*, which is the activity of transforming illegal profits to ostensibly legal income. In these cases, there is a wish to pay taxes in order to facilitate spending of the illegally earned profits.[40]

The Laffer curve and tax evasion

We observed that tax evasion can be a reason for a Laffer curve. High taxes decrease tax bases because of substitution effects away from productive activity. However, high taxes also provide incentives to move economic activity to the shadow economy. Low tax rates, in contrast, provide incentives to switch to the official economy.

4.3 Government Borrowing

We have been viewing public spending as financed through taxation. Public spending can also be financed through government borrowing or bond financing. A government can borrow by selling bonds to the public and using the proceeds for public spending. A government that borrows by selling bonds is making a commitment to pay interest over time to bondholders and to repay the value of

[40] Legal cash businesses are effective means of money-laundering; money-laundering is facilitated, for example, by ownership of gambling casinos because income can be attributed to profits of the casino. Corrupt bankers facilitate money-laundering by accepting cash deposits that are transferred to off-shore accounts, from where money is repatriated for legal spending and investment. If we see a business for which ongoing continuation does not appear warranted by the number of clients or customers, we might infer that the business is a conduit for money-laundering.

the bond at the end of the life of the bond.[41] To repay the bond, the government will require future taxes, or there will be a need to borrow again to refinance the bond, but eventually repayment will require future taxes. Therefore:

> *Bond financing of public spending is deferred taxation, including a deferred excess burden of taxation.*

A. Bond financing and the benefit principle of taxation

Bond financing is an application of the *benefit* principle of taxation over time. When the benefits from public spending extend over the life of future generations of taxpayers (including children or students who are not yet taxpayers and those as-yet unborn), through bond financing the future generations participate in the financing of public spending from which they benefit by paying future taxes. The normative rule based on the benefit principle of taxation is:

> *Current taxes should be used to finance current benefits from public spending; bond financing should be used to match future benefits with future tax payments.*

The costs of building a bridge, for example, are incurred at the time the public investment is made. The costs consist of the resources used in the project. The resources are withdrawn from other uses when the bridge is built. Bond financing compensates the generation of taxpayers that supplied the resources for building the bridge; the financing of the bridge is shared with future generations of beneficiaries.

A two-period example

Spreading the financing of a public project over time requires that generations overlap in time. A public project, for example, might benefit two generations X and Y that overlap in time. In the first period, generation X works, pays taxes T_X, and lends the government B_X (that is, generation X buys government bonds of value B_X). Together, the taxes T_X and the sale of bonds B_X finance the resource cost C of the project:

$$C = T_X + B_X. \tag{4.14}$$

Generation X has provided all of the resources and the financing C for the project, partly in payment of taxes T_X and partly by lending the government the value of the bonds B_X.

[41] Bond owners can receive money for their bonds before the repayment date of a bond by selling the bond in the bond market. When the bond is repaid, the owner receives the "face value," or nominal value, of the bond from the government. The amount received for a bond in the bond market depends on whether there have been changes in interest rates since the bond was issued by the government and the perceived risk of default.

TABLE 4.2. BOND FINANCING FOR PUBLIC SPENDING

Period 1	Period 2	Period 3
$T_X = 400$	$T_Y = 400$	$T_Z = 400$
$B_X = 800$	$B_Y = 400$	
	$B_X = 800 = T_Y + B_Y$	$B_Y = 400 = T_Z$
$D_1 = -800$	$D_2 = -400$	$D_3 = 0$
	Total cost: $C = 1{,}200 = T_X + T_Y + T_Z$	

In period 2, a new generation Y begins to work and pay taxes. Generation Y pays T_Y in taxes, which is its share of the cost of the project. The tax revenue T_Y is used to repay the bonds B_X to generation X.

If the interest rate is i, generation Y also pays taxes to finance the interest on the bond; therefore:

$$T_Y = B_X(1 + i). \tag{4.15}$$

Generation X thus receives back the face value of the bond plus interest. The interest paid is generation X's return for having deferred consumption to provide resources for the public-good project.

Through bond financing, the burden of financing has been spread over the two generations X and Y that benefit from the public project. Bond financing can similarly spread the burden of taxation (and the excess burden) over any number of generations. For example, table 4.2 shows a public project that provides benefits for three periods. There are three generations of beneficiaries. At each point in time, only two of the generations are simultaneously alive. Generation X is working and paying taxes when the project is undertaken and again bears the total initial cost of the project, through loss of alternative uses of the resources that the project used.

The total cost of the project in table 4.2 is 1,200 (dollars, euros, or other currency). For simplicity, we use an interest rate of zero. In the initial period when the project is undertaken, generation X pays $T_X = 400$ in taxes and lends the government $B_X = 800$. This provides the public finance of 1,200 for the project.

In the second period, generation Y pays taxes of $T_Y = 400$ and lends the government $B_Y = 400$. The sum of money $800 = T_Y + B_Y$ is paid by the government to generation X to redeem the bonds B_X. Generation X consumes this 800 and passes from the scene, to be replaced by generation Z.

In the third period, generation Z pays taxes of $T_Z = 400$. The taxes of 400 paid by generation Z are used to repay the bonds held by generation Y.

After completion of the three-period life of the project, each of the three generations has contributed equal tax shares of 400 to finance the project. The total taxes paid equal the total cost. That is, $C = 1{,}200 = T_X + T_Y + T_Z$.

After the transactions of period 1, the government has a debt of $D_1 = -800$. The debt is the excess of government spending over tax revenue. The debt is equal to the value of the bonds B_X sold to generation X. In period 2, the government repaid 800 and borrowed 400, giving an end-of-period-2 debt of $D_2 = -400$. In period 3, the government repaid the debt of 400 and did not borrow. The debt at the end of period 3 is therefore zero. Over the life of the project, the government budget for financing the project is balanced.

For simplicity, the example in table 4.2 has a zero interest rate. With a positive interest rate, taxes paid are greater than 400 for generations Y and Z to provide financing for the interest due on the government's bonds.

Default on government bonds

Generation Z could gain by reneging and refusing to transfer its share of the cost of the project to generation Y. Generation Z can do this by electing a government that declares it will not honor the bonds held by generation Y. Although there is government obligation to repay the loans, a government might declare that it does not recognize repayment obligations for debts of a previous government. In general, governments honor the sovereign debt obligations of previous governments. Yet, if a government did not pay the interest due and defaulted on bonds that had been issued in the past, the public project would continue to provide benefits. The project was completed in period 1 and the only change if a government reneges on honoring bond-redemption obligations is in intergenerational income distribution.

Sale of government bonds to foreigners

We have described government bonds as sold to citizens or taxpayers. The buyers of government bonds, however, can be foreigners who wish to diversify their asset portfolios. The purchase of government bonds by foreigners does not affect the distribution of payment for public goods over time by domestic taxpayers. In table 4.2, even if the bonds are sold to foreigners, the taxes to repay the bonds (and to pay interest on the bonds) continue to be levied on the different generations of domestic taxpayers.

B. Intergenerational tax sharing

Unintended intergenerational income redistribution can occur if the benefits from a project persist longer than originally envisaged. It may have been thought that the project in table 4.2 would provide benefits for three periods, but benefits continue for a fourth period. The project has been paid for and the generation earning income in the fourth period contributes nothing but nonetheless benefits.

Unequal intergenerational tax sharing can also arise by design. Generation X might altruistically pay the entire cost of the project, leaving future generations with a legacy of free benefits. Generation X could also fund the entire project by issuing bonds, thereby shifting the entire burden of taxation for financing the project onto future generations. In times of economic growth, later generations are better off than earlier generations. If a judgment is made that future generations should pay more than preceding generations, bond financing will be used disproportionately relative to taxation when the project is initially undertaken.

Bond financing for the benefit of a present generation

The initial generation X might also use the money received from the sale of bonds for its own benefit to finance its own present consumption. No benefit is then provided to future generations who nonetheless incur the cost through the taxes that finance the interest and repayment of the government borrowing.

Intergenerational income distribution

> *Bond financing can be manipulated to redistribute income among different generations.*

Ricardian equivalence

A person may be given the gift of a government bond of $1,000 that will be redeemed in 10 years. The bond pays interest (say, 5 percent annually). The person knows that after 10 years, he or she will be personally obliged to finance the repayment of the bond and, during the 10 years, must also personally finance the interest payments on the bond. That is, the gift of the bond is accompanied by future tax liabilities of the same value. Every year through the 10 years of the bond, the person pays to finance the interest that is received. In the 10th year, the person pays taxes of $1,000 to finance redemption of the bond. The gift of the bond therefore is worth precisely nothing. Hence:

> *A person who pays the taxes that finance interest and repayment of a government loan is indifferent between the government using the loan or taxation to finance public spending.*

This conclusion is known as the *Ricardian equivalence*, after David Ricardo (1772–1823).

Whether taxation or government borrowing is used to finance public spending *does* matter when payment of the interest and future repayment of the bond can be shifted to future generations, as in our examples with overlapping generations.

Nonetheless, equivalence between tax and bond financing is restored if older generations make compensating income or wealth transfers to younger generations or, in particular, their children; the voluntary transfers of income or wealth compensate younger generations for the future taxes they will need to pay because of government borrowing.

Generation Y might consist of the children of generation X. When a government finances public spending that benefits generation X through borrowing and transfers the burden of taxes in the future onto generation Y, parents in generation X can compensate their children in generation Y through gifts or bequests. The parents thereby return to their children the gift that they received from the government through bond financing.

Intergenerational altruism makes taxation and bond financing equivalent.

The equivalence requires parents to compute the value of their children's future tax liabilities that are due to government borrowing from which the parents have benefited. The parents can then provide precise compensation for the children's future tax obligations.

Ricardian equivalence requires that adequate transferable wealth be available to provide to future generations. Investments in education and experience (or human capital) are embodied in a person and cannot be transferred to other people. A desire by parents to return gifts from governments through bond financing to children can therefore affect forms of investment to ensure transferable wealth.

Governments sometimes tax gifts or bequests. The intergenerational altruistic behavior that restores Ricardian equivalence is thereby taxed.

The preferences of future taxpayers

When the intergenerational benefit principle is applied and public spending is financed through sale of bonds, the generation making the investment decision is presuming that future generations that will pay taxes to finance part of the cost will wish the public investment to have been made. Thus, if a highway is financed through government borrowing and taxes that are levied on three generations as in table 4.2, generation X making the investment is making a decision on behalf of generations Y and Z, whose future taxes will finance the repayment of the government bonds. Similarly, when we considered cost-benefit analysis for evaluating whether public spending on a project is warranted, there was a presumption that benefits of future generations were known – and also future generations' perceptions of costs; for example, the costs of environmental degradation. The preferences of future generations – and, therefore, of future taxpayers – are, of course, not known. There is asymmetric information: only each generation knows its own preferences for public spending, but also future generations are not present to be consulted about their preferences.

Even if, counterfactually, future generations could be present when the public investment is made, there is a free-riding problem. Future generations could declare that they will have little or no benefit from the public investment and could propose that the generation that is making the public investment decision, therefore, should finance the investment through taxes that it levies exclusively on itself. There would in that case be the reverse counterpart to the incentive for the generation deciding on the public investment to use bond financing to shift the burden of financing onto future generations, thereby benefiting without paying.

Issues involving future generations that are not present are difficult to resolve – precisely because the future generations are not present. However, even if the future generations were present (which they are not), the Clarke tax or some other way would be required of addressing the asymmetric-information problem between generations.

In practice, present generations have no choice but to make decisions on behalf of future generations. When a society is attacked by an aggressor, defense spending provides a public good that includes benefits for future generations; for, if the immediately threatened generation is effective in ending the threat, future generations that would have been subjugated by foreign invaders will also benefit. The public good of national security, therefore, extends over generations. It thus seems reasonable that future generations should pay part of the cost of ending the threat through the future taxes of bond financing.

C. Fiscal illusion in bond financing

Bond financing raises two questions about fiscal illusion:

- Are present taxpayers aware that bond financing implies future taxes?
- If so, do the taxpayers accurately perceive the values of future tax liabilities due to bond financing?

If the compensating transfers required for Ricardian equivalence are to take place, positive answers are required to both questions; people need to be aware of future tax liabilities because of bond financing. They also need to know the value of the future tax liabilities to be able to compute the intergenerational income transfers that compensate for future taxes on the next generation. Ricardo believed that "Ricardian equivalence" would fail because of fiscal illusion.

Elections allow taxpayers to vote to replace governments with whose policies they disagree. Asymmetric information because of fiscal illusion is the basis for a political principal–agent problem; through bond financing, government spending can exceed the spending that informed taxpayers would want.

D. Constitutional restraint on government borrowing

We have identified reasons why government borrowing through the sale of bonds can be socially undesirable: a government favoring contemporary taxpayers (who are the voters) might use bond financing to finance present consumption and impose tax obligations unjustified by the intergenerational benefit principle on future taxpayers (who are not present to vote); if there is fiscal illusion, present taxpayers may find that future tax payments (and excess burdens) are the consequence of greater government borrowing in the past than that to which they would have agreed, had they known.

A leviathan government that seeks to maximize tax revenue for self-interested spending can exploit fiscal illusion to circumvent obligations of accountability and transparency. There is a political principal–agent problem when political decision makers depart from the benefit principle to use bond financing for the benefit of a present generation; there is also a political principal–agent problem when a leviathan government takes advantage of fiscal illusion to increase revenue through government borrowing for its own contemporary benefit.

> *In the absence of assurances that the benefit principle of intergenerational financing will be strictly applied, future generations would want a legal or constitutional restraint that limits their obligations to pay taxes that finance past government borrowing.*

A budgetary surplus

We have been considering governments that require revenue to finance spending, but governments can also have surplus revenue. The question that then arises is what to do with the surplus. Alternatives are to use the surplus to (1) reduce present taxes, or (2) repay past government borrowing, by buying back previously issued government bonds. When the surplus is used to reduce taxation, the distribution of benefits corresponds to the distribution of the reduced burden of taxation (including the reduced excess burden of taxation). When the surplus is used to repay government borrowing, the beneficiaries are future taxpayers, who would have been required to pay future taxes and would have been subject to associated excess burdens of taxation.

Another possibility when a government budget surplus becomes available is that pressures arise for the government to spend the surplus revenue in ways that benefit particular groups rather than to take advantage of the surplus to reduce present or future taxes.

The decision about how to use a government budget surplus is therefore distributional and political. Constitutional restraint could also apply to what a government does when it has a budgetary surplus.

Supplement S4

Supplement S4A: The excess burden with substitution and income effects

We have based our analysis of the excess burden of taxation on the substitution effects that are the sources of excess burdens. Taxes also have income effects. In the case of labor supply, an increase in the rate of taxation reduces real income, which reduces demand for all normal goods, including leisure. Reduced leisure implies increased supply of labor. The income effect of an increase in the tax rate on labor supply is therefore positive. Thus, substitution and income effects of an increase in the tax rate have countervailing effects on labor supply.

With no income effect, we obtained the same measure of the excess burden of taxation when asking about willingness to pay to avoid a tax and compensation required because of a tax. With income effects, the answers to the questions and the measures of the excess burden of taxation differ.

To derive the excess burden of taxation, we shall now view the individual as deriving no benefit from a tax. With no benefit from taxes paid, if there were no excess burden, the willingness to pay to avoid the tax and the compensation required for imposition of the tax would precisely both equal the value of the tax revenue that the individual has provided to the government. The excess burden is willingness to pay to avoid the tax or compensation required in excess of the tax revenue.

The excess burden as payment to avoid the tax

We consider first the excess burden as payment to avoid the tax being levied. In figure S4A.1, the horizontal axis measures the quantity of a private good X, and the quantity of all other goods as a proxy for income is measured on the vertical axis. When X is leisure, we are describing labor supply. For illustration, we consider a tax on a good.

YO in figure S4A.1 is gross income earned before payment of a tax. The budget constraint at the pre-tax relative price is YA and the individual chooses to consume at point 1, which is on an *income-consumption curve* ICC_1 for the pre-tax relative price of good X. Pre-tax utility at point 1 is U_1.[42]

A tax on good X increases the relative price of good X and changes the budget constraint from YA to the post-tax budget constraint YB. The change in relative price also changes the income consumption curve to ICC_2.

Compared to the original income consumption curve ICC_1 before the tax, along ICC_2 proportionately less of good X is consumed. The move from ICC_1 to ICC_2 is the substitution response to the tax, which has increased the relative price of X. In particular, the substitution effect is expressed in a move along the indifference curve U_1 from point 1 on ICC_1 to point 5 on ICC_2.

Point 5 on ICC_2 is not a feasible consumption point. The income effect is a move along ICC_2 from point 5 to the post-tax consumption point 2, which is

[42] An income-consumption curve (ICC) shows how demand responds to increases in income when the relative price remains constant. The income effect is a move along the income-consumption curve. The ICCs in figure S4A.1 are shown as straight lines; in principle, any curve with a positive slope (indicating normal goods) is appropriate.

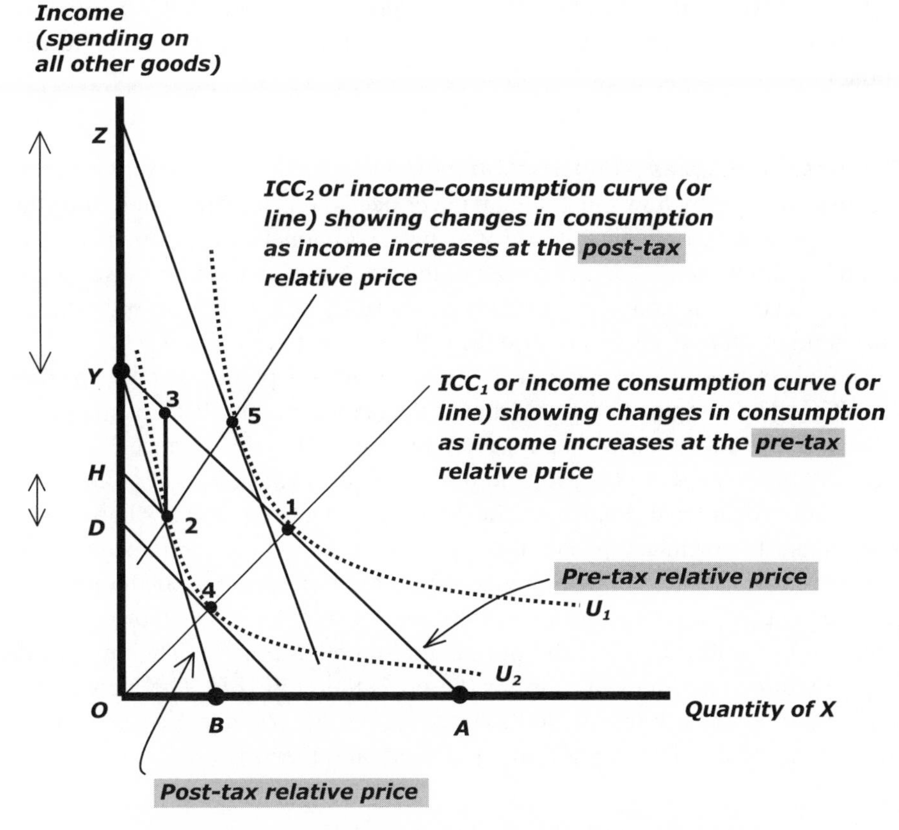

Figure S4A.1. The excess burden of a tax with income effects.

determined where the post-tax income consumption curve ICC_2 intersects the post-tax budget constraint *YB*. After the tax has been imposed, consumption at point 2 provides utility U_2.

After the tax, the individual's gross (tax-inclusive) income remains as given by the budget constraint *YA*. The difference between gross and net-of-tax income when the individual is consuming at point 2 is the distance 2-3. The individual is therefore paying the government the amount 2-3 in taxes.

We now ask the taxpayer who is consuming at point 2 how much he or she is prepared to pay *to avoid* paying the tax 2-3. We are therefore looking for a monetary value for the decline in utility from U_1 to U_2 because of the tax.

If the tax is not levied, the taxpayer remains on the *pre-tax* income consumption curve ICC_1. Remaining on ICC_1, the taxpayer has utility U_2 at point 4. Beginning from point 1 with utility U_1 and remaining on ICC_1, the taxpayer is maximally prepared to pay the amount of income that, if given up, would provide utility U_2 at point 4. The individual is therefore prepared to pay income *YD* to avoid the tax.

The tax revenue that the government collects if the tax is levied is *YH* (which is equal to 2-3). The difference *HD* is the personal loss due to the excess burden of the tax.

The excess burden as compensation for the tax

We now consider by how much the taxpayer needs to be compensated after the tax has been levied. Again, we are looking for a monetary equivalent for the decline in utility from U_1 to U_2 because of the tax. Now, however, because the tax has been levied (and compensation is being sought), we use the *post-tax* income-consumption curve ICC_2 to measure the difference between U_1 and U_2.

The substitution effect again moves the taxpayer from point 1 on ICC_1 to point 5 on ICC_2. The income effect again moves the taxpayer along ICC_2 from point 5 to point 2. The individual again pays as tax revenue *YH* or the distance 2-3, which is the difference between the pre- and post-tax budget constraints at point 2.

We now begin from point 2 on the post-tax budget constraint, where utility is U_2, and ask how much income the taxpayer needs to be given in order to be able to return to the level of utility U_1. With total income *ZO*, at the post-tax relative price, the taxpayer would maximize utility at point 5, which provides the same level of utility U_1 as at the pre-tax consumption point 1. The amount of income required as compensation for the tax is therefore *ZH*. The income *ZH* required as compensation for the tax exceeds the tax revenue *YH* paid to the government by *ZY*. The excess burden of taxation is therefore *ZY*.

The difference between the two measures of excess burden

We see in figure S4A.1 that the excess burden *ZY* after the tax has been imposed exceeds the excess burden *HD* based on willingness to pay to avoid the tax. This is a general conclusion. A question for discussion asks for an explanation of why this is so.

Summary

This chapter has investigated the consequences of assigning responsibilities to governments to finance public goods. We began by noting that governments can solve the public-good free-rider problem through compulsory taxation but, based on our conclusions in chapter 3, governments face an unresolved asymmetric-information problem – unless the Clarke tax has been used or locational choice is effective in revealing preferences, in which case there is, however, inefficient cost sharing if people wanting the same public goods are in separate jurisdictions. In order to proceed with an investigation of public finance for public goods, we had to presume that cost-benefit analysis had established a guide to efficient public spending. Setting asymmetric-information problems aside – and also initially political and bureaucratic principal–agent problems – section 1 reviewed the basic elements of using taxes to pay for public goods.

1A. The excess burden of taxation is a personal efficiency loss that taxpayers incur when taxes finance public spending. The excess burden arises because of intrusion into other markets of payments for public goods. The magnitude of the excess burden of taxation depends on the size of substitution effects expressed in demand and supply elasticities. Excess burdens are present for direct and indirect taxes. We compared a sales tax with a value-added tax, including consequences in a fiscal federal system. We noted that there are compliance, administrative, and emotional costs of taxation in addition to the excess burden. Average and marginal excess burdens were distinguished. We saw that the excess burden reduces the efficient quantity of a tax-financed public good below the efficient quantity that would be determined through voluntary payments. Accountability and transparency would require governments to report the excess burden of the taxes that are used. We considered whether taxes could be identified that have no excess burden. A tax on unimproved land, recommended by Henry George for social-justice reasons, has no excess burden. A head tax has no excess burden but can be arbitrarily levied. A poll tax affects who votes. A tax that finances public goods in Tiebout jurisdictions is a head tax, but people voluntarily chose a jurisdiction and can escape the tax by relocating. In general, the taxes that governments use have substitution effects and therefore excess burdens. Measurement of the excess burden requires accounting for cases where there is no tax revenue but an excess burden is present, so we cannot look for tax revenue as a necessary indication of the presence of an excess burden. The excess burden is increased by interdependencies among markets. In labor markets, the substitution effect and, therefore, the excess burden can be at the margin of choice between work and leisure or, alternatively, the choice influenced by taxation can be whether to have a job; the latter choice also depends on income available from the government if not working. Variation reported in measures of the excess burden may be due to data limitations and to the complexities of measurement; the magnitudes of excess burdens of taxation also have political connotations associated with the desired size of government as reflected in tax rates and public spending. Evidence from the experiment of communism indicates high excess burdens.

1B. The Laffer curve indicates the limits to tax revenue and shows the possibility of excessively high taxation. The Laffer curve is politically sensitive because of the conclusion that reducing taxes can increase government revenue. The Laffer curve shows the limits to leviathan government.

1C. To apply principles of horizontal and vertical equity for socially just taxation, governments need to know who pays a tax. The legal incidence of a tax does not indicate effective incidence or who actually pays a tax, which is determined by market substitution possibilities. The market substitution possibilities (or elasticities) also determine the sharing of excess burdens of taxation between buyers and sellers. As with the excess burden of taxation, links among markets (or general-equilibrium consequences of taxes) affect who pays a tax. Political pronouncements regarding who pays a tax based on legal incidence can reflect misinformation on the part of political decision makers or disinformation. Because legal tax incidence does not imply effective tax incidence and because the excess burden of taxation is invisible and generally not computed or reported, taxpayers and voters can be subject to fiscal illusion about who pays taxes and who bears excess burdens; taxpayers can also be subject to fiscal illusion by not being aware of indirect taxes. Governments require considerable information to identify who pays a tax. Without the information, neither the benefit nor ability-to-pay principle of taxation can be applied: governments cannot know whether people who have paid taxes have benefited, or whether taxes have been paid by people who have the ability to pay.

1D. A tax on imports is an indirect tax. Import taxes do not have a revenue justification when domestic sales taxes are feasible; sales taxes provide more revenue with lower excess burdens. The motives for governments levying taxes on imports are related to income distribution and rent creation through protectionist polices. A subsidy to producers could create the same protectionist rents as an import tax (or tariff) but with a lower excess burden; reduced transparency makes the import tariff the politically preferred instrument. Although an import duty provides revenue to the government, the revenue is incidental. Governments may choose to use import quotas to convert the tariff revenue to rents for privileged importers.

Section 2 considered tax evasion.

2A. Tax evasion is an expression of the free-riding incentives of the public-good prisoners' dilemma; if tax evasion occurs, governments do not have the consistent advantage over voluntary payments for public goods of ensuring no free riding through compulsory taxation. Tax evasion affects effective tax incidence because people may be evading taxes that others effectively have paid. We considered public policies toward tax evasion; public policies are combinations of probabilities of detection and penalties if detected. We also asked why people evade taxes; influences include whether there is trust of government, whether there is guilt or shame or both or neither, social norms, expressive behavior, and aversion to risk. People have different opportunities to evade taxes; we noted the low tax evasion by salary and wage earners and the high tax evasion by self-employed persons. Illegal immigrants may have no choice other than not to pay taxes. Multinational firms have means of evading taxes through transfer prices. We noted the distinction between tax avoidance and tax evasion and injustices associated with different people avoiding or evading taxes.

2B. We considered the behavior and the incentives of the tax authorities, including the use of presumptive taxation. We also noted the consequences of corrupt tax inspectors, although corruption is more characteristic of low-income countries than high-income democracies.

2C. A shadow economy is outside the domain of taxation. We observed that a shadow economy facilitates welfare fraud. Estimates of the size of a shadow economy show extensive differences in a government's abilities (or perhaps also willingness) to enforce payments of taxes. The data showed that the size of the shadow, in general, has been increasing over time. We also observed that a government can have motives to claim that estimates of the shadow economy are exaggerated. In countries where there is extensive corruption, a shadow economy can facilitate corruption or be an escape from corrupt tax officials.

2D. Because taxes are not paid, there is no excess burden of taxation in the shadow economy; however, there are limitations on growth of successful businesses and there is no rule of law. There are ethical problems: honest producers who pay taxes have cost disadvantages compared to competitors in the shadow economy who do not pay taxes. Personal benefits from income earned in the shadow economy are limited because of personal risks when conspicuous spending exceeds reported income. We described money laundering. The shadow economy and tax evasion are additional reasons for a Laffer curve, beyond work–leisure substitution.

Section 3 considered government borrowing or bond financing.

3A. Bond financing is deferred taxation. Ideally, the financing of public spending on public goods through government borrowing is an application of the benefit principle of taxation; beneficiaries from public spending in different generations can pay according to benefit.

3B. Bond financing may be used opportunistically to distribute income between generations. The principle of Ricardian equivalence proposes indifference between tax and bond financing when the same person who would pay present taxes also would pay future taxes that finance interest and repay the loan. An implication of Ricardian equivalence is that fully informed taxpayers can neutralize intergenerational redistribution. We considered future taxpayers who are not present when bond financing decisions are made.

3C. Fiscal illusion about bond financing can entail not being aware of future tax obligations or not knowing the value of the obligations. Fiscal illusion is an impediment to Ricardian equivalence (as Ricardo observed). Fiscal illusion regarding bond financing also allows a leviathan government to increase public spending beyond the spending that taxpayers ideally would have wanted.

3D. Because government borrowing can opportunistically impose unjustified intergenerational tax burdens, there is a case for legal or constitutional restraint on financing of public spending through government borrowing. The case for constitutional restraint similarly applies to decisions about how a government might act when faced with a revenue surplus.

There was one supplement to this chapter.

- Supplement S4A showed how the excess burden of taxation is affected by income effects. In that case, two measures of the excess burden – equivalent and compensating variation – differ.

Literature notes

4.1 Taxation

The excess burden of taxation was noted by Dupuit (1844/1969); see also Harberger (1964). A simplified presentation was used in this chapter to demonstrate that efficient tax-financing of public goods requires amending the cost-benefit criterion and the Samuelson rule for efficient public-good supply; for other formulations, see Usher (1984) and Wildasin (1984). Dahlby (1998) summarized the different formulae for the excess burden. On the excess burden and taxes that finance local public goods, see Zodrow (2007).

Dahlby, B., 1998. Progressive taxation and the social marginal cost of public finds. *Journal of Public Economics* 67:105–22.

Dupuit, J., 1844/1969. On the measurement of the utility of public works. In K. J. Arrow and T. Scitovsky (Eds.), *Readings in Welfare Economics*. Irwin, Homewood IL, pp. 255–83.

Harberger, A., 1964. The measurement of waste. *American Economic Review* 61:58–76.

Usher, D., 1984. An instructive derivation of the expression for the marginal cost of public funds. *Public Finance* 39:406–11.

Wildasin, D. E., 1984. On public provision with distortionary taxation. *Economic Enquiry* 22:227–43.

Zodrow, G. R., 2007. The property tax incidence debate and the mix of state and local finance of local public expenditures. *CESifo Economic Studies* 53:495–521.

For estimates and simulations of the efficiency loss of taxation, see Stuart (1984); Ballard, Shoven, and Whalley (1985); Browning (1987); Fullerton (1991); Jorgensen and Yun (1993); Allgood and Snow (1998); and Goulder and Williams (2003).

Allgood, S., and A. Snow, 1998. The marginal cost of raising tax revenue and redistributing income. *Journal of Political Economy* 106:1246–73.
Ballard, C. L., J. B. Shoven, and J. Whalley, 1985. General equilibrium computations of the marginal welfare costs of taxes in the United States. *American Economic Review* 75:128–38.
Browning, E. K., 1987. On the marginal welfare cost of taxation. *American Economic Review* 77:11–23.
Fullerton, D., 1991. Reconciling recent estimates of the marginal welfare cost of taxation. *American Economic Review* 81:302–08.
Goulder, L. H., and R. C. Williams III, 2003. The substantial bias from ignoring general equilibrium effects in estimating excess burden, and a practical solution. *Journal of Political Economy* 111:898–927.
Jorgensen, D. W., and K.-Y. Yun, 1993. The excess burden of taxation in the U.S. In A. Heimler and D. Meulders (Eds.), *Empirical Approaches to Economic Policy Modeling.* Chapman and Hall, New York, pp. 9–24.
Stuart, C., 1984. Welfare costs per additional dollar of tax revenue in the United States. *American Economic Review* 74:352–62.

Fideli and Forte (1999) described impediments to joint evasion of a value-added tax and income tax. On the different types of possible value-added taxes, see Tait (1988).

Fideli, S., and F. Forte, 1999. Joint income and VAT-chain evasion. *European Journal of Political Economy* 15:391–415.
Tait, A. A., 1988. *Value-Added Taxation: International Practice and Problems.* International Monetary Fund, Washington DC.

Hillman and Cassing (1985) described the political choice between import duties and quotas as means of protection. Hillman and Ursprung (1988) described political determination of import quotas assigned to foreign exporters, or voluntary export restraints. On quota rents, see Krueger (1974). For an overview of protectionist policies as means of rent creation, see Hillman (1989/2001).

Hillman, A. L., 1989/2001. *The Political Economy of Protection.* Harwood, Chur, Switzerland. Reprinted 2001, Routledge, London.
Hillman, A. L., and J. H. Cassing, 1985. Political influence motives and the choice between tariffs and quotas. *Journal of International Economics* 19:279–90.
Hillman, A. L., and H. W. Ursprung, 1988. Domestic politics, foreign interests and international trade policy. *American Economic Review* 78: 729–45. Reprinted in W. J. Ethier and A. L. Hillman (Eds.), 2008. *The WTO and the Political Economy of Trade Policy.* Edward Elgar, Cheltenham UK, pp. 99–115.
Krueger, A. O., 1974. The political economy of the rent-seeking society. *American Economic Review* 64:291–303.

See Ng (1987) for a proposal that taxes on goods that are valued for their value (such as diamonds) have no excess burden. Hillman and Katz (1984) described how taxation affects incentives for theft.

Hillman, A. L., and E. Katz, 1984. Excise taxes, import restrictions, and the allocation of time to illegal activity. *International Review of Law and Economics* 4:213–22.
Ng, Y.-K., 1987. Diamonds are a government's best friend: Burden-free taxes on goods valued for their value. *American Economic Review* 77:186–91.

On costs of tax administration, see:

Mayshar, J., 1991. Taxation with costly tax administration. *Scandinavian Journal of Economics* 93:75–88.
Slemrod, J., and S. Yitzhaki, 1987. The optimal size of a tax collection agency. *Scandinavian Journal of Economics* 80:25–34.

Fiscal illusion was introduced and studied by Puviani (1903/1973); see also Buchanan (1967).

Buchanan, J. M., 1967. *Public Finance in Democratic Process: Fiscal Institutions and Individual Choice*. The University of North Carolina Press, Chapel Hill.
Puviani, A., 1903/1973. Teoria dell' Ilusione Finanaziara. ISED, Milan.

Arthur Laffer informally proposed the Laffer curve. Fullerton (1982) suggested an alternative formulation of the Laffer curve based on tax rates and labor-supply elasticities.

Fullerton, D., 1982. On the possibility of an inverse relationship between tax rates and government revenues. *Journal of Public Economics* 19:3–22.

4.2 Tax evasion and the shadow economy

On tax evasion, see Cowell (1990). Slemrod (2007) described tax evasion in the United States. Graetz, Reinganum, and Wilde (1986) described a tax-compliance game. Tzur and Yaari (2000) compared methods of countering tax evasion. On conspicuous personal spending and tax evasion, see Yaniv (2003). On the difference between tax evasion and tax avoidance, see Brooks and Head (1997).

Brooks, M., and J. Head, 1997. Tax avoidance: In economics, law and public choice. In G. Cooper (Ed.), *Tax Avoidance and the Rule of Law*. International Bulletin of Fiscal Documentation, Amsterdam, pp. 53–91.
Cowell, F. A., 1990. *Cheating the Government: The Economics of Evasion*. MIT Press, Cambridge MA.
Graetz, M. J., J. F. Reinganum, and L. L. Wilde, 1986. The tax compliance game: Toward an interactive theory of law enforcement. *Journal of Law, Economics, and Organization* 2:1–32.
Slemrod, J., 2007. Cheating ourselves: The economics of tax evasion. *Journal of Economic Perspectives* 21:25–48.
Tzur, J., and V. Yaari, 2000. Tax evasion as the outcome of organizational design. *Journal of Accounting, Auditing, and Finance* 15:47–72.
Yaniv, G., 2003. Auditing ghosts by prosperity signals. *Economics Bulletin* 8:1–10.

Hindriks, Muthoo, and Keen (1999) described tax evasion with extortion by corrupt tax officials. On money laundering, see Masciandaro (1999). The quote from Benjamin Franklin was cited in Adams (1993). Hunter and Nelson (1995) and Young, Reksulak, and Shughart (2001) described political influence on tax inspections.

Adams, C., 1993. *For Good or Evil: The Impact of Taxes on the Course of Civilization*. Madison Books, London.
Hindriks, J., A. Muthoo, and M. Keen, 1999. Corruption, extortion and evasion. *Journal of Public Economics* 74:395–430.
Hunter, W. J., and M. A. Nelson, 1995. Tax enforcement: A public choice perspective. *Public Choice* 82:53–67.
Masciandaro, D., 1999. Money laundering: The economics of regulation. *European Journal of Law and Economics* 7:225–40.

Young, M., M. Reksulak, and W. F. Shughart II, 2001. The political economy of the IRS. *Economics and Politics* 13:201–20.

Schneider (2005) provided estimates of the shadow economy for 110 countries and reviewed the methods available for measurement.

Schneider, F., 2005. Shadow economies around the world: What do we really know? *European Journal of Political Economy* 21:598–642.

On the difficulties of measuring the informal economy, see:

Organisation for Economic Co-operation and Development, 2002. *Measuring the Non-Observed Economy: A Handbook*. Paris.

4.3 Government borrowing

Ricardian equivalence is from Ricardo (1817/1951): see Buchanan (1958), Barro (1974), and Buchanan (1976). On fiscal illusion and bond financing, see Buchanan and Wagner (1977).

Barro, R. J., 1974. Are government bonds net wealth? *Journal of Political Economy* 82:1095–117.
Buchanan, J. M., 1958. *Public Principles of Public Debt*. Irwin, Homewood IL.
Buchanan, J. M., 1976. Barro on the Ricardian equivalence theorem. *Journal of Political Economy* 84:337–42.
Buchanan, J. M., and R. Wagner, 1977. *Democracy in Deficit*. Academic Press, New York.
Ricardo, D., 1817/1951. *Principles of Political Economy and Taxation, Works and Correspondence*. P. Straffa (Ed.), Cambridge University Press, Cambridge UK.

Supplement S4A: The excess burden with substitution and income effects

The terms *equivalent* and *compensating variation* were introduced by Hicks (1939 and 1944). See also Mishan and Quah (2007).

Hicks, J. R., 1939 (2nd edition, 1944). *Value and Capital*. Clarendon Press, Oxford.
Hicks, J. R., 1944. The four consumers' surplus. *Review of Economic Studies* 11:31–41.
Mishan, E. J., and E. Quah, 2007. *Cost-Benefit Analysis*. Routledge, London.

5

MARKET CORRECTIONS

In this chapter we shall study market corrections due to externalities and paternalism. Section 1 describes prospects for private resolution of externalities. Section 2 considers resolution of externalities by government. Section 3 considers paternalistic public policies.

An externality is a cost or benefit not expressed in a market and therefore not internalized in buyers' or sellers' market decisions.

Whereas externalities arise when people's behavior or decisions affect *others*:

Paternalistic public policies are a response to the perception that people are making decisions that harm themselves or are failing to make decisions from which they would benefit.

We shall see, however, that paternalism can also arise with regard to what some people do to other people.

5.1 Externalities and Private Resolution

As we did with public goods, we first describe attributes of externalities and investigate outcomes through private voluntary action without government. We again begin using Robinson Crusoe for illustration.

A. Attributes of externalities

Robinson Crusoe alone on the island fishes in a stream. Crusoe has no formal property rights to the fish in the stream. Absence of property rights does not matter as long as Crusoe is alone on the island. When another person arrives and sets up a factory upstream that pollutes the water in the stream in which Crusoe fishes, the stream no longer supports the same number of fish and Crusoe incurs a loss. The owner of the factory has imposed a *negative externality* on Crusoe. There would be a *positive externality* if the factory were to discharge nutrients on which fish feed.

Whether imposing a negative or positive externality, the owner of the factory behaves – as the "invisible hand" requires – with the intent of maximizing personal utility or personal profits. The factory owner produces output for sale in a market. The factory owner, however, is not accounting for (or internalizing) the costs imposed on Crusoe (or is not accounting for any benefits provided). The market outcome based on the personal self-interested decisions of the factory owner, as a consequence, is inefficient. $W = B - C$ is not maximized because all

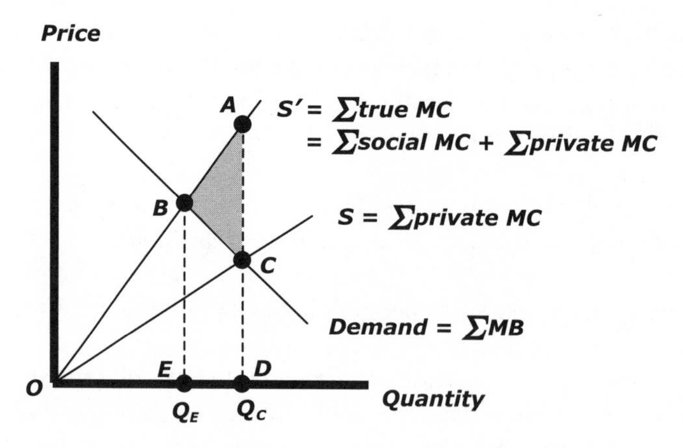

Figure 5.1. The gain from correction of a market externality.

benefits or costs have not been included in the factory owner's self-interested personal calculations.

Efficiency gains from resolution of an externality

Figure 5.1 illustrates inefficiency in a market when there is a negative externality. The market demand function $D = \sum MB$ accounts for all private benefits to buyers; there are no externalities associated with demand. Competitive market supply $S = \sum private\ MC$ is based on private MC of producers. The competitive market equilibrium (achieved through the competitive market-adjustment mechanism) is at point C. Point C is thus determined by private benefits and private costs.

There are additional costs not internalized by private producers; these are externalities. Producers do not pay these costs. For example, the costs might be incurred through degradation of the environment.

> *The true MC of supply consists of the private MC of supply that producers pay for labor, capital, and intermediate goods used in production plus the MC associated with externalities.*

We define MC associated with externalities as *social MC* because the MC is imposed on society; producers do not pay this cost; however, society incurs the cost. Thus:

$$True\ MC = private\ MC + social\ MC.$$

The supply function S' in figure 5.1 is based on the summation of producers' true MC of supply. Efficient output is determined at Q_E by S' and demand. In contrast, the competitive market output based on private costs alone is Q_C.

A reduction in output from Q_C to Q_E provides a social gain equal to the area ABC shown in figure 5.1. Equivalently, ABC is the efficiency loss to society when production is at Q_C rather than at Q_E.[1]

Externalities and public goods

The upstream factory adversely affecting Crusoe's fishing creates a one-to-one externality. If pollution of the stream affects many people, a public good, as well as an externality, is involved. Often, externalities and public goods occur together. To investigate externalities as distinct from public goods, we need to maintain a one-to-one relationship in which one person is affected by the decision or behavior of another person.

If a factory's output adversely affects numerous people (or at least two people) and if legal action against the factory is required, each affected person has an incentive to free ride by waiting for someone else to begin legal proceedings and to pay the costs of litigation. Therefore, when more than one person is affected, externalities involve problems of *collective action*.[2]

There is an externality problem between each person who fishes in the stream and the owner of the factory that pollutes the stream. There is a public-good relationship and a problem of collective action for two people who both fish in the stream and who both benefit from resolution of the externality problem with the factory.

The tragedy of the commons

There is an additional externality problem when two people fish in a stream: the two people impose negative externalities on one another because they are competing for the same fish. Together, they may overfish the stream, thereby not allowing a sustainable future stock of fish to persist. This type of externality is known as the *tragedy of the commons*. The *commons* refers to common ownership or absence of private ownership – in this case, absence of property rights to the fish in the stream. The *tragedy* is the depletion of the common resource – here, the fish.

Externalities involving consumers

The case of the factory affecting Crusoe's fishing and the depletion of the fish are externalities between producers. Often, producers' decisions affect not different producers but rather the public at large. Air quality or the quality of water in a

[1] The change from Q_C to Q_E reduces total benefit to buyers by the area $BCDE$. The true cost to society inclusive of environmental damage of the output reduction $(Q_C - Q_E)$ is $ABED$. The difference is ABC.

[2] Such collective action was considered in supplement S3A.

river or lake or at a beach deteriorates because of effluents. Or, people are disturbed by noise from trucks or airplanes. Emissions into the atmosphere may affect global warming, causing climate change. An adverse externality can be aesthetic: people may be disturbed by the unkempt garden of neighbors. Externalities can also be between different consumers: depletion of the ozone layer occurred because of gases that were used in people's refrigerators. Externalities between consumers include automobile pollution. Some people may dump trash on other people's property.

Beneficial externalities

These are examples of adverse externalities. In addition to the possibility of the factory emitting nutrients into the stream for the fish, instances of *beneficial* externalities include education and health. Better educated and healthier people provide benefits for others; however, people generally choose education and health based only on benefits to themselves without, therefore, internalizing the benefits for others.

The absence of intent

Just as the invisible hand provides *unintended* social benefit through self-interested market decisions, people who create externalities likewise intend neither to harm nor to benefit others.

> *There is no goodwill intended from a positive externality and no malice intended from a negative externality.*

Farmers who clear rain forests wish to expand the land that can be cultivated and do not internalize how their land-clearing activities affect the global climate.

Nonetheless, if people are aware of the adverse consequences of their decisions for others, negative externalities involve a lack of consideration. A person who acts with consideration for others does not impose negative externalities. Externalities can therefore be internalized by considerate personal behavior.

Social norms determine types of externalities that people can impose on one another without social disapproval. People may apologize for creating negative externalities, sometimes perfunctorily and sometimes with true intent.

Absence of intent applies when externalities are beneficial. People who inoculate themselves against diseases unintentionally protect others from contagion. People whose education has made them more thoughtful and pleasant companions provide unintentional external benefits.

Externalities for which corrections are not required

Not all externalities require correction. Externalities can be *inframarginal*, which means that the externalities are not marginally relevant. Let us consider a person

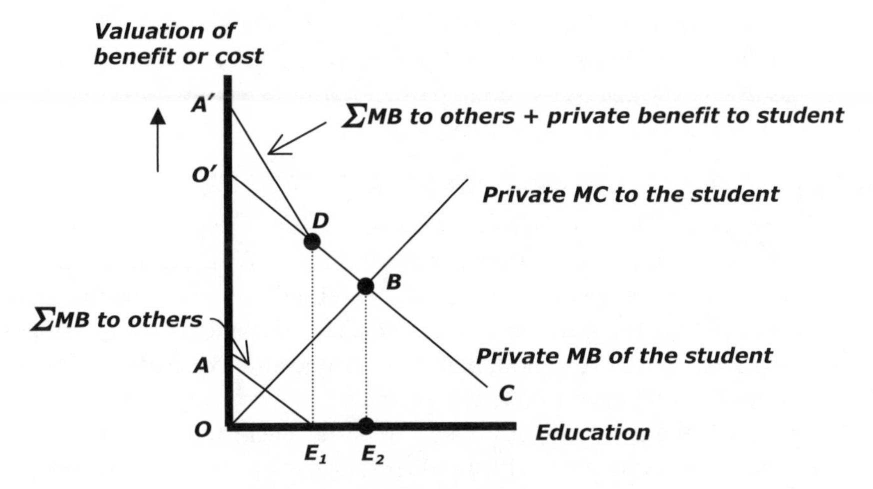

Figure 5.2. An inframarginal externality.

whose investment in higher education takes the form of writing a doctoral thesis on the inner meaning of life that can be discerned from the writings of William Shakespeare. The thesis sets out the student's insights, from which other people benefit; however, they may not benefit significantly. Figure 5.2 shows the personally optimal investment in education at point B, where the student's private MB is equal to the private MC. The student therefore chooses investment in education E_2.

Figure 5.2 shows the combined marginal benefits to others in society as AE_1. The combined benefits to others have the nature of a public good from which other people benefit simultaneously. Hence, the combined benefits are shown in the form of public-good benefits as $\{\sum MB\ to\ others\}$. When the student has made the investment in education at E_1, the MB for other people is zero. However, by investing in education up to E_1, the student has provided total positive externalities for others equal to the area AE_1O.[3]

That the externalities require no corrective response is confirmed by observing that the efficient outcome is also the personal utility-maximizing choice of the student. The combined true marginal benefit, which is the sum of the combined marginal benefit to others and the student's personal benefit, is $A'DBC$ shown in figure 5.2. The efficient outcome is at point B, which is also the personal choice of the student.[4]

[3] AE_1O is the area under the combined valuation function $\{\sum MB\ to\ others\}$.

[4] $A'DBC$ is the vertical summation of combined benefits to others $\{\sum MB\ to\ others\}$ given by AE_1 and the student's personal MB given by $O'DBC$ (that is, $OA = O'A'$). The summation of marginal benefits is vertical because the student's education is a public good that simultaneously provides personal benefit to the student and benefit to others through the positive externality. After point D, the combined total benefits and personal benefits of the student coincide because after E_1, there is no benefit to others from the student's investment in education.

Inframarginal externalities provide benefits (or impose costs) but do not require a corrective response because the externalities have no effect at the margin.

Personal interactions that are not externalities

Not all personal interactions involve externalities. When two people are in the desert and there is only enough water for one to survive, one person drinking the water does not create a negative externality. Externalities involve inefficiencies. One person drinking the water is a Pareto-efficient outcome: it is impossible to make one person better off without making someone else worse off by changing the behavior of the person drinking the water.

Two people in the desert might see a water bottle ahead and set off running to reach it. The person who reaches the bottle first drinks the water. There has been a contest that someone has won and another person has lost. We do not associate winning and losing a contest with externalities. In any assignment of a quantity of a good that provides private benefit, one person has less if another person has more, and there is no externality present that can be corrected to improve efficiency.

More people may come to the beach than an ice-cream vendor had expected. The vendor realizes that demand is higher than was anticipated and increases the price of ice cream. Through the increased price of the ice cream, people have now affected one another by their decision to come to the beach. Although the increase in price is directly due to the decision of people to come to the beach, the increased price of the ice cream is not a case of an externality. There is no externality because the market has *internalized* the increased demand through the increase in the market price.

If people compete for space at the beach or kick sand onto one another, however, there is an externality. Yet some people may prefer a crowded beach whereas others prefer personal space. Whether an externality is present, therefore, is subjective.

Missing markets and asymmetric information

A definition of an externality is a benefit or cost for which markets are missing. People may be willing to pay others to leave an overcrowded beach, stop smoking in their presence, or desist from unwelcome attention; however, no market exists in which the payments can be made. As in the case of public goods, markets in which externalities could be internalized may not exist because of asymmetric information. The sum of money that people are prepared to pay to not be bothered by others is private information. How much people who are bothering others are prepared to accept to change their behavior is also private information. As with public goods, there are incentives to misrepresent preferences. People bothering others have an incentive to claim higher than true personal losses from desisting and going elsewhere. People being harassed want to pay less than the personal subjective cost that the harassment imposes on them. Cost-benefit analysis is therefore required when externalities are present. A basic reason for the need for cost-benefit analysis is asymmetric information that has prevented the existence of markets that would reveal valuations of personal costs and benefits.

B. Private ownership solutions

We have now defined and characterized aspects of externalities. We therefore can direct our attention to resolutions for externality problems.

The tragedy of the commons

We noted when studying property rights that in hunter–gatherer societies, natural resources were abundant relative to demands of the population. In recent centuries as well, people would often graze their domesticated animals on land that had no private owners – or on land that was "common." Negative externalities arose when the common land could no longer efficiently accommodate everyone's animals. The inefficiency took the form of overgrazing. Too many animals grazing on the commons resulted in inadequate food and disturbed the natural balance that in the past had allowed replenishment of pasture grass.

When animals graze on the commons, each individual owner of animals internalizes the externalities among his or her own animals; however, the externalities that the person's animals impose on other people's animals are not internalized. If all animals on the commons belonged to one person, all externalities would be internalized. That is, single private ownership of all animals on the commons resolves the externality problem.[5]

A single owner of all the sheep on the commons could not legally prevent other people from arriving and placing their sheep on the commons unless the single owner of the sheep had legal ownership rights to the grazing land – which because of private property rights would then no longer be a common.

The circumstances on the commons are those of the prisoners' dilemma. Table 5.1 shows the prisoners' dilemma for two people who graze sheep on a

[5] Thus, with 100 sheep on the commons, each sheep imposes an externality on 99 other sheep. Ownership determines how externalities among sheep are internalized. A person who owns one sheep is not affected by externalities among sheep that he owns. However, if he buys an additional sheep from someone else, his two sheep impose externalities on one another; the sheep owner calculates the mutually disadvantageous externalities that his two sheep impose on one another and commensurately reduces his sheep's grazing time to internalize the externalities between the two sheep. If the sheep owner then buys another eight of the sheep, he internalizes the externalities that his 10 sheep impose on one another; he only cares about the effect of one of his sheep on the other nine and does not consider the externalities that any one of his 10 sheep impose on the other 90 sheep owned by others. A sheep owner who owns all of the 100 sheep on the commons internalizes the effect of each sheep on the other 99 sheep that he also owns and the internalization of the externalities is complete.

TABLE 5.1. THE TRAGEDY OF THE COMMONS AS A PRISONERS' DILEMMA

	Person 2 restricts the number of sheep	Person 2 has a large number of sheep
Person 1 restricts the number of sheep	3, 3	1, 4
Person 1 has a large number of sheep	4, 1	2, 2

common. The efficient outcome at (3, 3) is achieved when the two herders cooperate by each restricting the number of sheep on the field. A herder who voluntarily restricts the number of sheep when the other does not has benefit of 1, whereas the herder who does not restrict the number of sheep has benefit of 4. The Nash equilibrium is the inefficient outcome (2, 2) where there is inefficient overgrazing because of an excessive number of sheep on the field.

Private ownership

Private ownership allows the efficient outcome to be obtained. A private owner has an interest in maximizing the value of grazing land. The private owner, therefore, will take into account the reduction in the amount of feed grass available to all other animals when deciding whether to add another animal to the grazing flock.

When private ownership is introduced, access to the grazing ground requires payment to the owner of the field. If all people who used the field are given equal ownership shares, everyone is better off, after (1) paying the *user price* for access to the grazing ground, and (2) subsequently receiving dividends from the firm that owns the field and in which they have part ownership. In table 5.1, equally shared private ownership provides a benefit of 3 for each person, whereas free access to the commons provides a benefit of 2.

Overfishing is an example of the tragedy of the commons. A private owner restricts the number of fish caught in order to preserve the stock. Similarly, the private owners of a forest have an incentive to ensure that the forest is replenished rather than stripped bare; they know that a tree not cut down will still belong to them in the future.

Highway congestion is a case of the tragedy of the commons: drivers do not consider their effects on other drivers. A private owner of a highway maximizes profits by selling "noncongested travel." The private owner recognizes that drivers' willingness to pay to use the highway depends on the number of users and that crowding externalities are internalized by an appropriate user price for access to the road.[6]

[6] The purpose of user prices when there are no congestion externalities is to finance a public good. When there are congestion externalities, the purpose of the user price is to internalize externalities by deterring use by some people.

Conservation and the commons

A private owner of a field allows feed grass to be a sustainable resource over time. The incentive to conserve for the future is likewise present if a fishing area is privately owned; the private owner has an incentive not to overfish in order to allow the fish to reproduce so there will be fish in the future. When fishing areas in international waters are open to common access, there is often overfishing. In the case of a forest, free access creates a private incentive to strip the forest of trees today because any remaining trees in all likelihood will be felled by someone else.

Private ownership encourages conservation whereas common access encourages depletion.

Rent seeking and resolution of the tragedy of the commons

If there is a government that can designate legal ownership rights, people can set out to try to convince the government to give them private property rights to the commons. If the political decision makers are amenable to persuasion, the conditions are set in place for a rent-seeking contest in which resources are wastefully used in an attempt to obtain privileged benefits from political decisions.

The social benefit W from private ownership is the difference between profits under private ownership Π and the combined benefits A when there is open access to the common:

$$W = \Pi - A. \tag{5.1}$$

When rent seeking takes place, the profits Π from private ownership have become a rent to be sought. If rent seeking dissipates the entire rent obtained from private ownership, resources of value Π are used in contesting the rent.[7] We therefore subtract Π from the social benefit of private ownership in expression (5.1) to obtain the social benefit from private ownership after rent seeking. The outcome is:

$$W = (\Pi - A) - \Pi = -A. \tag{5.2}$$

Because of rent seeking, there is a social loss from private ownership rather than positive social benefit. The social loss is precisely equal to (minus) the value of benefits that would have been obtained with open access.

Only a proportion α of the rent Π might be dissipated in rent-seeking activities. We then deduct the part of the rent dissipated $\alpha\Pi$ from expression (5.1) to obtain the social gain from private ownership after rent seeking as:

$$W = (\Pi - A) - \alpha\Pi = (1 - \alpha)\Pi - A. \tag{5.3}$$

From expression (5.3), $W > 0$ requires that:

$$\alpha < \frac{\Pi - A}{\Pi}. \tag{5.4}$$

[7] As described in chapter 2, complete dissipation occurs when rent seeking is competitive and in a rent-seeking contest when the highest rent-seeking outlay wins the contest.

There thus remains positive social benefit when ownership of the commons is determined by rent seeking, if the rate of rent dissipation α is smaller than the rate of return from the assignment of property rights. It is important to ensure that property rights to the commons are designated without incentives for wasteful rent seeking because:

> *If the rate of rent dissipation exceeds the rate of return from assignment of property rights, resolution of the tragedy of the commons is not socially worthwhile.*

Dynasties and conquests of the commons

Rather than beginning with a government that can designate legal ownership rights, we can begin from anarchy, where there is no government and no formal rule of law. Without the formal rule of law, free access to a commons is a convention of behavior. Contests to control the commons take place when the convention of free access is no longer respected.

Dynastic hereditary monarchies might be established through conquests of the commons. Hereditary monarchy was intended to prevent rent-seeking contests from recurring. However, when land is the main productive asset, the monarch and the hereditary nobility as principal landowners are rich and the landless population is poor, and revolts and revolutions take place that monarchs and the nobility sometimes survive and sometimes do not.

The commons and the old and new worlds

In the English-speaking "new" world (the United States, Canada, Australia, and New Zealand), early European settlers arrived before indigenous peoples had established private property rights to land. The indigenous peoples lived in hunter–gatherer groups and had no system of legally protected property rights. They gathered food and hunted on the pre-privatized land. The pre-privatized land may have been informal common property. The indigenous peoples lost their free access to the land when the European arrivals declared the commons to be private property – of the new arrivals.

When the commons were privatized in the English-speaking new world, land in general was divided among small holders.[8] The division of land contrasted with the concentrated land holdings of the monarchs and nobility of the old world of Europe.

In the Spanish-speaking new world in South and Central America, concentrated ownership of land in a "hacienda" system replicated the unequally

[8] Individuals sometimes received large tracts of land from the English monarch – for example, William Penn, after whom the state of Pennsylvania is named. The land was subdivided and sold. In other cases, the people who had received land grants could not protect their property rights from families that had settled and worked the land. If a community elected its own judges, the judges might be expected to rule in favor of natural possession based on settlement and productive use of land rather than in favor of an absentee landlord.

distributed land in the old world of Europe. As in the English-speaking new world, property rights of the indigenous people were not respected; for example, in 1519, the Spanish conqueror, Cortes, simply killed the Aztec king, Montezuma.

Distributional consequences of ending the commons

Ending the commons has distributional consequences. If the commons have been privatized to give equal shares of ownership to all persons who previously used the commons (by issuing shares in a firm), all the previous users are – as we saw – better off. If, however, there has been a contest for ownership, people without ownership claims may lose. Previously, they grazed their sheep without payment; now, they must pay.

However, when there is private ownership, people benefit by paying for access to a field on which animals are provided with grass to eat; when access was free, there may have been little or no grass for animals because of overgrazing. Similarly, if a public highway is converted into a private toll road, people who pay the toll may gain compared to free access to a congested highway.

Distribution and efficiency

Not everyone may gain when the commons is privatized. Nonetheless, conversion to private ownership (or privatization) resolves the inefficiency of the externality of the tragedy of the commons.

Reciprocal beneficial externalities: The case of bees and apples

In the tragedy of the commons, people (or sheep) disadvantage one another: the disadvantage through the negative externalities is reciprocal.[9] In a case of reciprocal *beneficial* externalities, the owner of an apple orchard benefits from bees that pollinate apple trees, while a beekeeper benefits from the presence of the apple orchard because the trees in the orchard provide nectar for the bees' production of honey. The reciprocal benefits are not taken into account when the beekeeper decides how many bees to keep and when the owner of the apple orchard decides how many apple trees to plant.[10]

Figure 5.3 shows the circumstances of the beekeeper, who sells honey (the output) and can buy bees (the input) in competitive markets. The market price at which a bee can be bought is shown as P_{bees}. The combined marginal benefit from bees is:

$$\sum MB^{bees} = MB^{bh} + MB^{ba}, \tag{5.5}$$

[9] A sheep imposes negative externalities on other sheep and, at the same time, is disadvantaged by the negative externalities that other sheep impose on it.

[10] The reciprocal externalities of the bees and apples were described in 1952 by James Meade (1907–95), who was a professor at the London School of Economics and at the University of Cambridge. Meade received the Nobel Prize in economics in 1977.

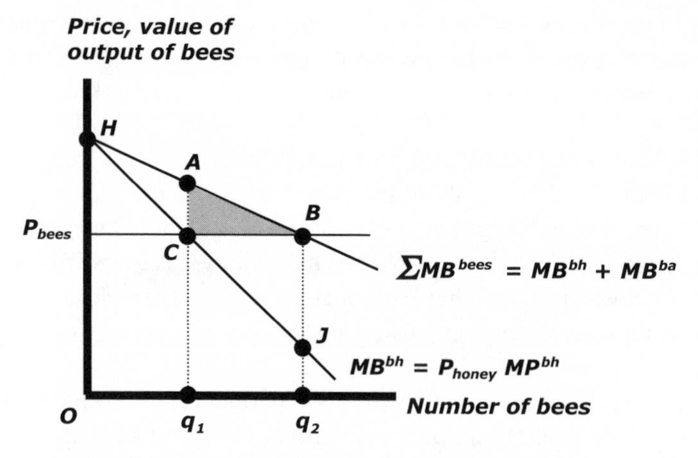

Figure 5.3. The gain from common private ownership.

where MB^{bh} is the value of the marginal product of bees to the beekeeper and MB^{ba} is the value of the marginal product of bees to the owner of the apple orchard. The profit-maximizing number of bees for the honey producer is q_1. At q_1, the beekeeper is providing a free benefit equal to the area HAC to the owner of the orchard.[11]

The beekeeper chooses q_1 bees because she values bees for their honey alone. The efficient number of bees is q_2, determined where the combined marginal benefit in expression (5.5) of bees in honey and apple production is equal to the price of a bee. The market price of a bee is also the marginal cost of a bee for the beekeeper. Thus the beekeeper chooses the number of bees q_1 such that:

$$\sum MB^{bees} = P^{bee}(= MC^{bee}). \tag{5.6}$$

The beekeeper would incur a personal loss equal to the area BCJ if she were independently to increase the number of bees to the efficient number q_2. If the beekeeper also owned the apple orchard, she would, however, gain area ABC by increasing the number of bees to q_2.[12]

Figure 5.3 tells half of the story of the reciprocal externalities. Because the beneficial externalities are reciprocal, ABC is *one part* of the efficiency gain from joint private ownership of the bees and the orchard. There is an additional corresponding gain when the apple orchard is expanded to take account of the benefit to the bees' honey production. Under separate ownership, the owner of

[11] The MC of a bee is the price P_{bees}. The MB from keeping bees is the value of the marginal product of bees in honey production, $MB^{bh} = P_{honey} MP^{bh}$, where P_{honey} is the price received for honey and MP^{bh} is the honey production of the marginal bee. The beekeeper maximizes profits by setting the MC of a bee equal to the MB from keeping a bee – that is, by setting $P_{bees} = MB^{bh} \equiv P_{honey} MP^{bh}$, which determines q_1 in figure 5.3.

[12] Increasing the number of bees from q_1 to q_2 yields a value of additional product of the bees given by ABq_2q_1, at a cost of the additional bees CBq_2q_1.

the orchard has too few apple trees. Under common ownership, the externality from the apple trees to honey production is internalized, and the number of apple trees is expanded to the efficient size.

When the bees and the apple orchard are separately owned, potential benefit is therefore lost because of the mutual neglect of positive externalities.

Under common private ownership, decisions are efficient because a common owner internalizes (or takes into account) the reciprocal benefits.

Public inputs and externalities

Expression (5.6) has the same general form as the condition $\sum MB = MC$ for efficient voluntary public-good supply. Indeed, the contribution of bees to production has public-input properties. Bees are a public input because they are simultaneously inputs for the beekeeper to produce honey and inputs for the owner of the apple orchard for whom they pollinate the apple trees.

Synergies and externalities

The term *synergies* rather than *externalities* is often used to describe benefits from common ownership. Firms' mergers and acquisitions are, however, not necessarily justified by mutually beneficial externalities or synergies; rather, managers have personal reasons to seek mergers and acquire other firms. Managers' incomes may increase with the size of the firm; mergers and acquisitions may be motivated by increased profits due to reduced competition; and also, managers have an interest in a diversified portfolio of income sources to reduce personal risk. Shareholders of a firm lose when the attention of managers is drawn away from the "core" activities in which the managers have expertise; shareholders tend to hold diversified portfolios of shares to spread risk and do not require the diversification that managers seek for personal benefit through mergers and acquisitions. Bankers acting as consultants also have incentives to encourage mergers and acquisitions in order to earn advisory fees.

Because of the personal incentives of management and bankers, when two firms merge or one firm acquires another, we cannot be certain that we are witnessing an efficiency-enhancing response to beneficial externalities.

A contractual alternative to common private ownership

The beekeeper and the owner of the apple orchard could stay under separate ownership and a contractual agreement could specify that the beekeeper will have the efficient number of bees and that the owner of the orchard will have the efficient number of apple trees. The contract would compensate the owner of the orchard for increasing the number of apple trees and the beekeeper for increasing the number of bees. The beekeeper and the owner of the orchard both gain, as in the case of common ownership.

Common ownership can be more costly than the contractual agreement. Under common ownership, more extensive coordination tasks confront management in the enlarged firm. There are few or no benefits from common management if the knowledge required for growing and selling apples has little to do with the knowledge required for keeping bees and selling honey.

Contractual solutions also can have disadvantages. Contracts may be incomplete. A complete contract specifies responsibilities and courses of action for all contingencies. An incomplete contract cannot and therefore does not include all contingencies. A rare, unanticipated disease might strike the apple trees, resulting in disagreement about whether the owner of the apple orchard had taken due precautions to avoid the disease. Or, the number of bees might decline for reasons that are unclear. Legal costs can be high when there is a dispute about contract compliance. The legal costs are avoided by common private ownership.

C. The Coase theorem

Common private ownership cannot resolve externality problems when externalities are the consequence of behavior of people because one person cannot buy and own another person. However, people can pay to change each other's behavior. A proposal known as the Coase theorem predicts that externalities between people will be voluntarily internalized by private negotiation, provided that legal rights have been specified and that costs of reaching agreement (also known as *transactions costs*) are not too high.[13]

To explain the reasoning behind the Coase theorem, we consider two people in a classroom. Person S (a smoker) benefits from cigarettes and person N (a nonsmoker) does not like cigarette smoke. In figure 5.4, MB_S is the declining *net* marginal benefit of smoker S from smoking cigarettes; the *net* marginal benefit is measured *after payment* of the price of cigarettes. MC_N is the increasing marginal cost imposed on nonsmoker N by the smoker's cigarettes.

The MB and MC functions in figure 5.4 describe marginal benefits and marginal costs of different people. Efficiency requires maximizing $W = B - C$, where the benefit B is that of the smoker and the cost C is that of the nonsmoker. In seeking efficiency, we again do not ask about the distribution of benefits and costs between the smoker and the nonsmoker.

> *The objective in seeking efficient resolution of an externality between two people is to maximize the difference between total benefit and total cost without regard for how the benefits and costs are distributed.*

[13] Ronald Coase, from the University of Chicago, received the Nobel Prize in economics in 1991.

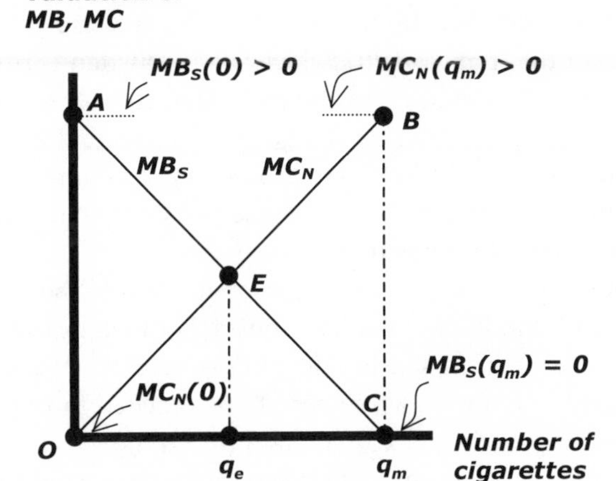

Figure 5.4. The Coase theorem.

Legal rights with the smoker

The smoker might have the legal right to smoke as he or she pleases. The smoker cares only to maximize personal utility and does not take into account (or internalize) the costs that smoking imposes on the nonsmoker. A smoker who can freely decide chooses q_m cigarettes, determined in figure 5.4 where $MB_S = 0$. Maximized total benefit for the smoker is the area ACO under the smoker's MB function.

When the smoker chooses q_m, the nonsmoker can compensate the smoker for not smoking the last cigarette and still gain from the reduction in the number of cigarettes smoked. That is, at q_m:

$$MC_N(q_m) > MB_S(q_m) = 0. \tag{5.7}$$

The nonsmoker has ample scope to pay the smoker not to smoke the last cigarette because the smoker receives zero marginal net benefit (after paying for the cigarette) from the last cigarette at q_m.

Pareto improvement takes place when person N (the nonsmoker) pays person S (the smoker) not to smoke the last cigarette. The process of compensation (or overcompensation) for not smoking a cigarette can continue until the number of cigarettes smoked declines to q_e, where the MB to the smoker is equal to the MC imposed on the nonsmoker.

For values smaller than q_e, the nonsmoker cannot compensate the smoker for not smoking and still be better off after paying the compensation. The equilibrium outcome of the process of compensation is therefore q_e, which is efficient because $W = B - C$ is maximized.

Point E in figure 5.4 has the characteristics of a market equilibrium – although the market for "not smoking a cigarette" has only one buyer and one seller and is therefore not a competitive market.

Sharing of the gains

The reduction in the number of cigarettes from q_m to q_e results in a total gain equal to the area of the triangle EBC, which can be divided between the smoker and the nonsmoker.[14] It would be irrational for the smoker and the nonsmoker not to come to an agreement on sharing the gain. How will the gain be shared?

One way of sharing the gain EBC is to proceed in the manner of cutting a cake, for which a solution is, "You cut and I choose the share that I want." This rule, of course, results in equal sharing of the cake.

More generally, we can consider the division of gains as the outcome of a bargaining process, with the smoker and the nonsmoker making offers and counteroffers until an agreement on sharing the gain is reached. We might think that it could take a long time for an agreement to be reached through such bargaining. The people involved in the bargaining process, however, can be expected to have positive time preference; that is, they can be expected to prefer to have their gains now rather than later. The longer they tie up each other in inconclusive bargaining, the less they have to share because the value of the total gain available declines over time due to the preference for present over future gains. The two people, therefore, each have an incentive to reach agreement as soon as possible.

The agreement that is reached will reflect the bargaining power of the two people. A way of measuring bargaining power is patience, or the discount rate that a person applies to the future. A more patient person has a lower discount rate (that is, discounts the future less) and has more bargaining power because he or she is prepared to wait longer for an agreement to be reached. That is, the more patient person has a smaller loss from deferring agreement to the future. When people have information about each other's discount rates, the more patient person can obtain a larger share of the benefit; there are still incentives for immediate agreement because both the patient and impatient person lose from delay, albeit differently.

Given the costs of delay, there is a mutual incentive to come to an agreement on sharing the gains as soon as possible.

Immediate agreement is an efficient bargaining outcome because no loss is incurred in waiting for an agreement to be reached.

Bargaining is more complex when people have incomplete information about each other's patience or time preference. Beliefs about the patience of the other person then matter. Bargaining under incomplete information about time preference of the other person can result in many possible outcomes and is inefficient when people defer reaching agreement.

[14] The total cost imposed on the nonsmoker from $(q_m - q_e)$ cigarettes is $q_e EBC$. The total benefit to the smoker from these cigarettes is $q_e EC$. The difference is the net gain EBC available to be shared.

Legal rights with the nonsmoker

The compensating payments that we have described are based on the legal right of smokers to smoke as they please. Person N (the nonsmoker), however, might have the legal right to determine air quality. If there is no smoking at all, the outcome in figure 5.4 is:

$$MB_S(0) > MC_N(0) = 0. \tag{5.8}$$

The MB of the smoker from the first cigarette exceeds the zero MC imposed on the nonsmoker. The smoker can therefore readily overcompensate the nonsmoker for being allowed to smoke a first cigarette. The smoking of one cigarette is a Pareto improvement compared to the prohibition of smoking. The smoker can continue to overcompensate the nonsmoker as long as $MB_S > MC_N$. The equilibrium number of cigarettes smoked is again q_e, where $MB_S = MC_N$. A market has been created for "the right to smoke a cigarette." The total gain available to be shared from the creation of the market is area AEO shown in figure 5.4.

The Coase theorem

We can now state the Coase theorem:

> *Externality problems are efficiently resolved by assignment of legal rights.*
>
> *The efficient resolution of an externality problem is independent of who has legal rights.*

After legal rights have been specified, two affected parties can create a market and use the market to achieve an efficient outcome. The efficient outcome does not depend on who has legal rights; we see in figure 5.4 that the efficient outcome is q_e, whether the smoker or the nonsmoker has legal rights.

Income effects

Although the Coase theorem states that legal rights do not affect the efficient outcome, the assignment of legal rights affects people's incomes by determining who makes and who receives payments. The payments are the source of an income effect. The consequences of income effects were excluded from the previous statement of the Coase theorem.

In figure 5.5a, the smoker has legal rights and the smoker's demand for cigarettes increases because of payments received from the nonsmoker. The increased demand moves the marginal benefit of the smoker to MB'_S and because of the income effect, the efficient outcome is at q'_e and not q_e.

In figure 5.5b, the nonsmoker has legal rights and therefore receives payments from the smoker. The increased income increases the nonsmoker's demand for clean air. The decline in the nonsmoker's willingness to suffer smoke is expressed in the new marginal cost function of the nonsmoker MC'_N. Because of the income

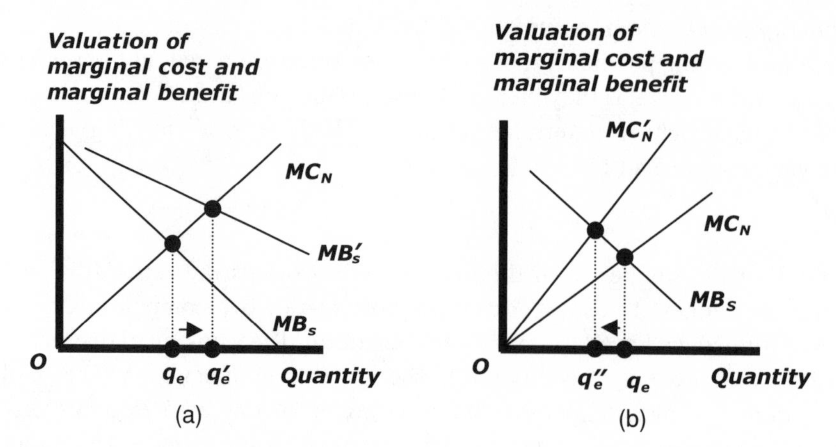

Figure 5.5. (a) An income effect when the polluter has legal rights. (b) An income effect when the victim has legal rights.

effect, the efficient number of cigarettes in the market for permission to smoke decreases to q''_e from q_e.

The Coase theorem is based on absence of significant income effects.

For goods or activities that are a small part of a person's budget, absence of income effects is a reasonable approximation.

Incentives and negligence

The Coase theorem states that the efficient outcome is independent of the assignment of legal rights. However, assignment of legal rights can be efficient or inefficient depending on the incentive not to be negligent. Whether pollution occurs may depend on the care taken by a producer to avoid accidental spills. A potential polluter who has legal rights to pollute has zero costs of negligence. The incentive to take care to avoid oil spills, for example, is greater when the cost of negligence is imposed on tanker owners.

The assignment of legal rights can determine the likelihood that a negative externality will arise.

Incentives for avoidance of negligence suggest a "polluter pays principle" – that is, that the public should have legal rights.

Failures of the predictions of the Coase theorem

If the predictions of the Coase theorem were correct, unresolved externalities would never be encountered because all externalities would have been resolved through private negotiation. Why, then, are unresolved externalities observed to exist? There are a number of reasons for the failure of the predictions of the Coase theorem.

Disputes over legal rights

There can be unresolved disputes about who has legal rights. If legal rights are not defined, the strong might exert their will on the weak – although, with the strong assigning legal rights to themselves, the Coase theorem still predicts voluntary negotiation to achieve an efficient outcome if the weak can pay the strong (which is possible if the strong have not appropriated the income of the weak).

Asymmetric information and disputes over the value of damage

There may be a dispute about the value of damage or whether damage was even incurred. Disputes particularly arise when damage is subjective. A smoker seeking compensation for not smoking can claim exaggerated benefit from a cigarette and a nonsmoker seeking compensation for cigarette smoke can claim exaggerated disutility from exposure to the smoke. There is asymmetric information because the location of the *MB* function is known only to the smoker and the location of the *MC* function is known only to the nonsmoker. Asymmetric information makes negotiation and bargaining time-consuming and possibly unpleasant. People will not begin to negotiate if the costs of negotiation and bargaining (or transactions costs) are expected to exceed the benefits that can be obtained from resolution of an externality. Because of transactions costs, markets between smokers and nonsmokers do not usually exist. Smokers once had legal rights to smoke where and as they wished. By the end of the 20th century, legal rights had changed to be with nonsmokers. When legal rights were with smokers, nonsmokers rarely attempted to pay smokers not to smoke; when nonsmokers have legal rights, smokers generally do not attempt to pay to be allowed to smoke. The transactions costs of creating the markets predicted by the Coase theorem are too high. If people fishing in a stream kept certified records of the number of fish they caught before a factory began polluting the stream, they could objectively verify the value of their losses and there would be no asymmetric information. If, however, the complaint is that the pollution is destroying the aesthetic quality of the stream or is preventing recreational enjoyment, there is a problem of asymmetric information because only the complainants know the true value of their losses.

Transactions costs without asymmetric information

Transactions costs can prevent the efficient outcome predicted by the Coase theorem without asymmetric information. At a crowded road intersection, high-value-of-time drivers in a hurry are willing to pay low-value-of-time drivers for priority access through the intersection. Markets allowing transactions between high- and low-value-of-time drivers at an intersection do not exist because the transactions costs of organizing such markets are excessive relative to the benefits. A driver will have passed through the intersection without the creation of a Coase market in less time than is required for the price of priority access to be paid. Rather than being resolved through the Coase theorem, the externality problem at the intersection is resolved by a traffic light or by a convention or rule that specifies who has priority.

Personal unwillingness to create markets

The Coase theorem often fails because of personal unwillingness to create markets. There is a line at the post office and you do not have time to wait. The externality is that other people who arrived first have priority in the line. You can create a market by offering the person at the front of the line money in return for his or her place (other people would not lose their relative place in the line). Yet people may not be prepared to accept payment for giving up their place in the line. They may feel insulted by the offer of money and may believe that a place in the line should not be for sale; although the view that a place in the line is not for sale can generally be changed by offering enough money. If a place in the line were sold, there might be complaints from other people whose positions in the line are unaffected by the transaction; although their place in the line does not change, they may regard the transaction as "unfair." The feeling of unfairness is expressed in the view, "I have been waiting in the line for my turn. It is unfair that you come along and use money to buy a place ahead of me." That is, there can be presumptions about what money should be allowed to buy.

People are often prepared to do things for free that they are not prepared to do for money. If people believe that there is justifiable reason, they may be prepared to give up their place in a line without payment. In the case of smoking, when a smoker has the legal right to smoke, the smoker might be offended by an offer of payment of money to stop smoking; the smoker might be prepared to stop smoking without payment, if asked nicely to do so.

Personal aversion to creating markets is an impediment to realizing the predictions of the Coase theorem.

Creating a market can change behavior. In one case, parents were arriving late to pick up children from kindergarten, thereby imposing an externality by keeping the kindergarten teachers waiting. A fine was therefore imposed on parents who arrived late. As a consequence of the fine, parents became less punctual and arrived even later. When there was no fine, the parents were *intrinsically motivated* to try to pick up the children on time. The fine created a market wherein parents could pay for coming late – and parents took advantage of the market to pay and be more flexible with their time.

Collective action and externalities

Externalities involving only two people (for example, the owner of an orchard and the owner of bees, a person fishing in a stream and a factory owner, a smoker and a nonsmoker) allow separation between externalities and public goods.

In general, when one individual is affected by an externality, others are also affected and the externality therefore also has public-good characteristics. A factory that pollutes the environment simultaneously harms a number of people. Similarly, there are effects on many people when aircraft noise disturbs residents, when people dump garbage in corridors or parks, or when a road becomes congested. When an externality has public-good characteristics, the free-rider problem of public goods arises. The free-rider problem is distinct from transactions costs of negotiation and bargaining that also impede realization of the predictions of the Coase theorem; transactions and bargaining costs are present when an externality involves only two people and there are no public-good aspects. When a factory emits harmful effluents in the vicinity of a school, parents have reason to be concerned; transactions costs of parents organizing for collective action are low because of the parents' common characteristic that their children attend the same school. Parents can identify and contact one other and call a meeting to devise a collective-action program against the factory. However, some parents might think strategically and conclude, "This issue is so important that nearly everybody will surely come to the meeting and so I do not have to attend." If enough parents think in this way, free riding prevails over effective collective action to solve externality problems.

Regulations that prohibit Coase bargaining

The outcome predicted by the Coase theorem cannot be achieved when regulations prevent private bargaining to internalize externalities. A professor may be prepared to allow a student who comes to office hours with questions to smoke cigarettes – at a price. However, a mutually beneficial trade is disallowed if the university administration has decided that no smoking is permitted in university buildings.[15]

Assignment of legal rights to minimize transactions costs

In the case of the smoker and the nonsmoker, the smoker pays for each cigarette smoked when the nonsmoker has legal rights, and the nonsmoker pays the smoker for each cigarette not smoked when it is the smoker who has legal rights. The number of cigarettes smoked is observable; the number of cigarettes not smoked is counterfactual and not observable. There can be disputes about the number of cigarettes the smoker would smoke if not paid to not smoke. Transactions costs are minimized when the nonsmoker has legal rights because the number of cigarettes smoked is directly observable.

> *Legal rights should be assigned to minimize transactions costs – that is, to minimize the likelihood of failure of the Coase theorem.*

[15] There would be a problem in allowing the student to pay the professor to smoke because of possible ambiguity in the additional benefits through grades that the student could expect from the professor after payment. Many years ago, before the negative externalities of smoking were well known, the professor would have been obliged to pay the student not to smoke.

Market capitalization and the Coase theorem

A decision may need to be made about the location of a facility that has negative externalities. The facility might be an airport, a waste-storage facility, a prison, a communications antenna, a drug-rehabilitation center, a halfway house, a police station, or a school. Residents often object to having these facilities in or near their neighborhood. The inconvenience, disturbance, or perceived health hazard reduces housing prices. The owners of the facilities could compensate residents for the decline in property values. The requirement of compensation for reduced housing prices is an application of the Coase theorem in which the residents have legal rights.

After compensation has been paid for the decline in market value of the houses because of the negative externality, the houses continue to have lower market values than similar houses in other locations not affected by negative externalities. People who buy a house from the original owner (who has received compensation) pay the lower price for the house. The lower housing price is the compensation to the new residents for the negative externality.

The same type of response as in refusal of people to accept compensating payments for giving up their place in a line can arise when offers of compensation are made for locating facilities with negative externalities in or near people's neighborhoods. People can express moral outrage or indignation at the suggestion that they should be compensated, for example, for having a nuclear-waste disposal site near their house. The indignation expresses the feeling that no amount of compensation justifies the reduction in quality of life from having the site near people's homes and that it is an insult even to be asked to accept compensation.

People can feel that it is unethical to accept money for agreeing to the location of sites with adverse externalities near their house. Indignation can also be self-interested. The acronym *NIMBY* stands for "not in my backyard." A disposal site, prison, drug-rehabilitation center, and other facilities must be located somewhere. NIMBYs prefer that the location be far from them, although they agree that the facility is necessary somewhere. Again, with enough money given in compensation and with assurances of safety, people may change their decision.

People may refuse to accept compensation to allow location of an undesirable facility near their homes because of uncertainty about future effects on health. Cigarette smoking was regarded for many years as elegant and not harmful. Asbestos was regarded as a safe construction material until a link was established to cancer. People may fear that a nuclear-waste disposal site will be harmful to health through a cumulative effect over a period of years. Because of the uncertainty, there can be a feeling of discomfort from having the suspect facility located nearby. There can also be a feeling of guilt when a house located near the suspect facility is sold to someone else.

Facilities with undesirable externalities are usually placed far from people's houses. Over time, as demand for housing grows, house construction can begin to encroach on the facility. The more adverse the externality associated with the facility, the lower is the price of the land around the facility and the lower are housing prices. People who move into the houses around the facility are therefore generally those with lower incomes who cannot afford higher priced housing. Correspondingly, if health problems occur, the people adversely affected tend to be lower income people.

D. Resolution of externalities through personal behavior

Externalities are internalized by means other than private ownership, Coase bargaining, and capitalization into market values. Personal behavior can internalize externalities.

Consideration for others

When externality problems arise, people do not intend to inconvenience others (or to provide benefits) but nonetheless externalities would not arise if people were considerate of others. Personally internalizing externalities is costly. The owner of the bees, for example, could increase the number of bees beyond the profit-maximizing number, but she incurs a loss if not compensated by the owner of the orchard. Or, people could exercise self-control in not playing loud music or being rowdy when they know that others are trying to sleep, but their behavior is not illegal and they would incur a personal loss in the exercise of self-control.

When externalities are resolved through consideration for others, the question arises of who will be considerate of whom. A nonsmoker who has legal rights can be considerate by allowing a smoker to smoke; if the cigarette smoke makes the nonsmoker feel unwell, being considerate means that the nonsmoker is willing to accept personal inconvenience. For the smoker, being considerate means not imposing on the nonsmoker's goodwill and deferring the cigarette or finding another place to smoke where no one is inconvenienced.

Self-esteem and social approval

People who make personal decisions to beneficially internalize externalities can derive utility from self-esteem and social approval. When environmentally friendly "green" cars are more expensive than cars with polluting gasoline engines, by driving an environmentally friendly car, a person makes a visible statement of having concern for the environment. Pollution is reduced and an example is set for others. Whether buying an environmentally friendly car is expressive behavior to confirm personal identity or is motivated by social approval, in either case, a personal, socially beneficial contribution has been made to internalizing an externality. People also create positive externalities by tending to beautiful gardens that others can see or by the choice of how they dress or by polite behavior. In these cases as well, personal decisions may be based on self-identity and social approval may be sought, but society benefits from the positive externalities.

Social norms and externalities

When the law is ambiguous, externalities can be internalized through social norms. A *social norm* is behavior that people adopt because everyone else is behaving in the same way and because people feel disutility or discomfort in deviating from the norm. Social norms are the basis for social conventions that can override personal preferences; that is, people may follow social norms because they wish to conform and do not wish to be socially ostracized.

Social norms determine permissible, socially acceptable personal behavior. The social norm may be to wait patiently in line and not to push or shove at a bus stop. Nonetheless, some people may deviate from the social norm and aggressively join a line near the front. Whether such people are permitted to have their way depends on whether there is a social norm of resistance to aggressive, inconsiderate behavior. Resistance is a volunteer-type public good: someone has to incur the personal cost of initiating resistance to inconsiderate and uncivil behavior. A further social norm determines whether others will help: Do other people who have been disadvantaged by the inconsiderate and uncivil behavior come to the assistance of the person who initiated resistance? Support through secondary resistance is less costly than initiating resistance. Whether there is a social norm of backing up the person who initiated resistance influences whether someone will resist inconsiderate and uncivil behavior in the first place.

When the social norm is not to litter, people may nonetheless litter a hiking trail in a nature preserve. They feel no guilt. However, they feel shame if observed by others. Because of the social norm, they therefore do not litter when their behavior is visible to others.

Personal dilemmas can arise because of threshold effects in externalities: a person may begin a hike fully intending to carry personal litter out of a nature preserve, but what does this person do when, because of a great amount of litter that others have left, the trail has gone beyond the threshold of being clean? Even considerate hikers may feel that they might just as well add to the extensive litter that already exists. Here, personal behavior is again determined by a social norm based on the behavior of others (who have littered).

Self-defense and crime

Crime is a source of negative externalities. We rely on government to protect us from crime through the rule of law. Externalities arise through crime because governments fail to enforce the rule of law perfectly. The externalities are expressed in people's willingness to pay to avoid being the victim of criminals.

A market sometimes exists for payment to avoid being harmed or having property damaged; the market results in extortion of money by criminals, who are engaged in rent extraction. Extortion indicates failure of governments to enforce the rule of law.

The public-policy question is:

> *If government is ineffective in providing protection against crime, should personal self-defense be legally permitted?*

Personal self-defense can take the form of carrying guns or mace or learning unarmed means of combat.

There can be disagreement about whether self-defense should be legal. Some people may object to a concealed gun as the means of self-defense by a potential victim. Related disagreement concerns whether markets in guns should be legal. Opponents to the right of self-defense by citizens carrying guns point to the externality that the legality of guns can result in innocent people being accidentally harmed when guns are not safely stored or handled; ready access to guns also results in impulsive behavior or crimes of passion.

The position of such opponents to the right of citizens to be armed in self-defense is based on the normative proposal that:

> *No one should have guns.*

All law-abiding citizens would agree with this normative proposition: in an ideal world, we would want no one to have guns. The case against guns can also be stated expressively. An opponent to the right of citizens to be armed may declare that "I am the sort of person who wants no guns in the world because I want only peace and tranquility and no one harming anyone else."

The counter-case of the proponents of the right to carry guns for self-defense is pragmatic. They do not disagree with the proposition that the world would be better off without guns. However, they point out that we do not live in an ideal world in which all guns can be eliminated. Rather, whether or not citizens have the legal right to carry guns, criminals will have guns. The counter-argument is, therefore, that forbidding citizens to have guns in self-defense facilitates crime and that victims needlessly die or are injured because criminals know that law-abiding citizens are easy prey who are not legally permitted to use guns to defend themselves.

Policy debates on different topics often take place with one side making expressive normative statements and the other side making positive predictive statements. The normative arguments are statements about the world as it should be. The positive statements are predictions about the world as it is. The debates can be ongoing, with one side continuing to repeat its expressive normative arguments and the other side repeating its observations and predictions.

A case against allowing citizens to carry guns is that if everyone carries a gun, everyone boarding a plane may, for example, be carrying a gun. Laws can prevent people taking a gun onto planes. However, it is also difficult to hijack a plane when all or many passengers are armed.[16]

Gun laws and locational externalities

The locational choice mechanism allows people to choose between living in government jurisdictions where citizens carrying guns is legal or illegal. Interjurisdictional externalities arise when neighboring communities or societies make different decisions about permitting the sale of guns and allowing people to carry guns. Criminals can then buy their guns where it is legal to do so and commit their crimes in neighboring communities where, because guns are illegal, they know that law-abiding citizens will not be armed.

Kidnapping and ransom

When ransom is paid to a kidnapper to release a hostage, an externality has been created. Incentives have been provided for yet more people to be kidnapped and held for ransom. If no one ever paid ransom, kidnapping would never occur.

Failure to report crime and externalities

In some cases, crimes are not reported because people believe that they will be subject to aggravation and perhaps humiliation through legal-system procedures. The externality in that case through personal behavior is that criminals continue to be free to commit crimes and harm more victims.

5.2 Public Policies and Externalities

We now turn from personal behavior to public policies. In calling on governments to take responsibility for resolving externality problems, we presume that costs and benefits associated with externalities have been identified and measured through cost-benefit analysis. Because externalities are costs or benefits not internalized in markets, governments, if they are to resolve externality problems efficiently, must have used cost-benefit to obtain the information that markets

[16] In the United States, the debate on the right of personal self-defense by carrying a gun centered on the interpretation of the Second Amendment to the U.S. Constitution, which states that "A well-regulated Militia, being necessary for the security of a free State, the right of the People to keep and bear Arms, should not be infringed." The perceived ambiguity was in whether the Amendment applied to the rights of citizens to organize militias or applied to the level of freedom of the individual to bear arms. A large component of the debate on interpretation came to an end when the U.S. Supreme Court ruled in 2008 that the Second Amendment gave people the right to keep guns in their own home for personal self-defense.

did not reveal. Cost-benefit analysis may have been required to estimate benefits from environmental policies or benefits through positive externalities associated with public spending on education or public health. Power stations burning coal or oil are sources of externalities through carbon emissions: nuclear power stations have no carbon emissions but require cost-benefit analysis to evaluate costs from future disposal of nuclear waste.[17]

> *Whatever the source of an externality, because market values are not available, governments seeking to resolve externality problems need to have found nonmarket valuations through cost-benefit analysis.*

Cost-benefit analysis is therefore an inseparable part of resolution of externality problems through public policies of governments; the questions about procedures for cost-benefit analysis raised when we considered absence of markets because of failures of voluntary payments for public goods reappear.

A. The case for government

The Coase theorem proposes that people will privately internalize externalities when possible. However, we have seen that there are various reasons why the Coase theorem might fail. When the Coase theorem fails and externalities are not internalized by private action, we turn to government.

Who decides when an externality merits public policy?

People can choose to personally take actions in response to personal externalities. However, who decides whether an externality exists that warrants public policy action by government? There is consensus about existence of externalities associated with the environment, public health (through preemption of infectious and contagious diseases), and education (through benefits to others from being more educated). The source of externalities, however, also can be a subjective feeling of personal like or dislike about which there is no consensus.

As a hypothetical example, someone who has an aversion to the color purple is willing to pay to not see the color purple and, in principle, is prepared to pay people to not wear purple clothes. It is impractical for a person with an aversion to the color purple to offer money to people to change their clothing to another color. The person with the aversion to the color purple, however, might seek out other people with the same dislike and form a collective-action group. The collective-action group could make the wearing of purple clothes an election issue or could lobby government to implement legislation that makes purple clothing illegal.

Public policy to make the color purple illegal would not be sensible. There have been times, nonetheless, when legal discrimination was based on the color

[17] Warren Young (1998) studied externalities and cost-benefit analysis for nuclear power stations.

Box 5.1 Externalities and discrimination

Anti-discrimination laws affect employer–employee and landlord–tenant relationships. A case has been made that markets internalize externalities associated with discrimination because an employer who discriminates on racial grounds may miss out on the best person for the job and a landlord may miss out on the most responsible tenant; the argument is that an employer or landlord then personally pays for any discrimination by forgoing profitable market decisions.[18] Nonetheless, a cost of discrimination falls on the victim when markets do not offer alternative identical employment or housing possibilities; that is, people lose from being the victims of discrimination when they do not have alternatives as good as the opportunities they were denied through discrimination. There is also disutility through indignity in being the victim of discrimination.

of a person's skin or ethnic background. A prohibition on wearing purple clothing is an annoyance, but compliance is possible. Changing one's skin color is not like changing one's clothing. Changing one's parents or ethnicity is impossible. Civil societies therefore limit the sources of externalities that can be declared as in the domain of public policy (see Box 5.1).

Personal freedom and externalities

Tuberculosis is an infectious disease of the lungs. The disease, which was once prevalent and still recurs, was often fatal but is generally curable through antibiotics. The antibiotics need to be taken over an extended period. An infected person who begins treatment and does not complete the required dosage of antibiotics creates a negative externality for society because partial treatment allows new strains of bacteria to develop that are resistant to the antibiotics. There are strains of tuberculosis that are extremely resistant to the usual antibiotics. The externality of antibiotic-resistant strains of tuberculosis is the basis of a case for a public policy of denial of personal freedom by requiring compulsory confinement of patients in order to supervise their intake of antibiotics. Compulsory confinement at the same time prevents the disease from spreading, thereby resolving another externality.

A prominent case study in public health is the story of "Typhoid Mary." Mary Mallon (which was her real name) was a carrier of typhoid but was herself immune to the disease. Working as a cook in New York City between 1900 and 1907, she infected (fatally, in one case) a number of people who ate her cakes and puddings. She was tracked down by the government and placed in confinement, where she spent the last 30 years of her life.

[18] The argument that markets internalize externalities associated with discrimination was made by Gary Becker (1971) of the University of Chicago (Nobel Prize in economics in 1992).

When awareness of AIDS became prominent in the 1980s, it was proposed that people identified as carriers of the HIV that eventually leads to AIDS (although there are rare exceptions of apparent natural immunity) should be marked (or tattooed) with indelible ink. The marking was intended as a warning to others and not as a sign of personal rebuke. The marking was thus proposed as a means of resolving an externality problem. The intention was to place the indelible mark on an inconspicuous part of the body (people walking in the street or wearing a swimsuit on a beach would not be identified). The proposal was rejected, although the identification mark would have saved lives. The mark was regarded as an infringement of personal rights of the people who tested HIV-positive and who did not want the stigma of being marked. Also rejected were proposals that people who were HIV-positive should be confined for the safety of the public. Laws differ among jurisdictions as to whether someone who is HIV-positive deliberately infecting other people constitutes murder. The public-policy response to AIDS differed, however, from the case of Typhoid Mary.

B. The means of public policy

If cost-benefit analysis has provided the required information, what are the public-policy means for correcting externalities?

Taxes and subsidies

Arthur Cecil Pigou (1877–1959), writing in *The Economics of Welfare* (1920/1962), proposed that taxes or subsidies be used to correct externalities. To see how Pigovian taxes and subsidies (named after Pigou) resolve externality problems, we look at figure 5.6, which shows a negative externality due to the output

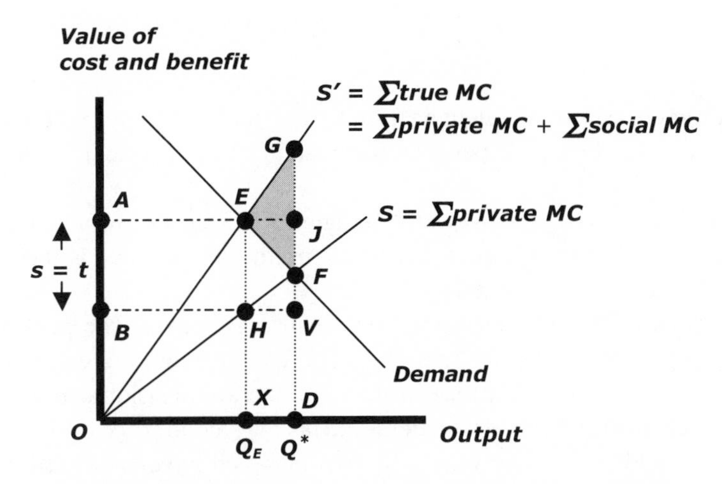

Figure 5.6. The use of a tax or subsidy to correct an externality.

of an industry. Figure 5.6 is based on the definitions that were used in figure 5.1. Again, there is a negative externality – for example, the harm to the environment. Market demand D reflects personal benefits of buyers. Competitive market supply S reflects *privately incurred* costs of producers or suppliers. The supply function S' is determined by the sum of privately incurred marginal costs of production plus the social marginal costs imposed on society and not internalized by suppliers. The social marginal costs have been determined by cost-benefit analysis.

The supply function S is thus $\{\sum private\ MC\}$. The supply function S' is $\sum true\ MC = \{\sum private\ MC + \sum social\ MC\}$.

As output increases, the gap between S and S' increases, indicating that social MC imposed on society is increasing as output of the industry expands.

The competitive market outcome based on the private-cost supply function S is at point F where output is Q^*. The efficient outcome for society is at point E based on the supply function S'.

Public policy to achieve efficiency requires decreasing output from Q^* to Q_E. The efficiency gain to society from this reduction in output is the shaded area GEF.

Private voluntary action through Coase-type negotiations, if feasible, would realize the gain GEF. When private voluntary Coase resolution of the externality is not feasible, a *tax* or a *subsidy* can correct the market outcome by moving the market outcome from point F to point E.

A corrective tax

The corrective per-unit tax in figure 5.6 is $AB = EH$. The tax is paid on each unit of output produced up to Q^*. The tax is determined as:

$$\begin{aligned} t &= \sum social\ MC(Q_E) \\ &= \sum true\ MC(Q_E) - \sum private\ MC(Q_E). \end{aligned} \tag{5.9}$$

The government uses cost-benefit analysis to find the efficient output Q_E and then sets the tax as the difference between social and private marginal cost evaluated at Q_E.

The revenue from the tax is $AEHB$ in figure 5.6. The tax revenue has no particular role in solving the externality problem; the tax revenue is incidental to using the tax to correct the externality.

The corrective tax internalizes the externality. By paying the per-unit tax t, producers are made to realize that there is a cost through the externality (for example, environmental damage) in their production decisions, in addition to their privately paid costs of production. The tax t is paid in place of the price that producers would pay if they were a market in which payments were made for environmental damage.

A corrective subsidy

The tax presupposes that society has the legal right to impose a price for environmental damage. Legal rights, however, could be with producers. Regulations might have changed after producers made their investments, and the rule of law requires that people cannot be made responsible for actions through retroactive changes in the law. If producers have legal rights, they should not be taxed.

A corrective subsidy provides producers with incentives to not produce beyond Q_E. The subsidy is paid on units of output $(Q^* - Q_E)$ that are *not* produced. The government again uses cost-benefit analysis to determine the efficient output Q_E and sets the per-unit subsidy as:

$$\begin{aligned} s &= \sum social\ MC(Q_E) \\ &= \sum true\ MC(Q_E) - \sum private\ MC(Q_E). \end{aligned} \tag{5.10}$$

The total subsidy paid to producers in the industry is the area *EJVH* in figure 5.6. Again, the value of the total subsidy is incidental to the objective of internalizing the externality. It is the per-unit subsidy s that affects behavior by providing the marginal inducement to not produce beyond Q_E.

The equivalence of the corrective tax and subsidy

The per-unit subsidy s is an amount of money *received* by producers. Still, the effect of the subsidy on producers' decisions is equivalent to a cost. The subsidy imposes an opportunity cost of producing output $(Q^* - Q_E)$ because the subsidy is lost if this output is produced.

The per-unit tax t is an explicit cost whereas the per-unit subsidy s is an equivalent opportunity cost. For a market price P, with the corrective tax, producers choose output so that:

$$P = private\ MC + t = private\ MC + social\ MC. \tag{5.11}$$

With the corrective subsidy, the choice of output is identically determined by:

$$P = MC + s = private\ MC + social\ MC. \tag{5.12}$$

Therefore:

The corrective Pigovian tax and subsidy equivalently affect producer incentives to achieve the efficient output Q_E.[19]

Whether a tax or subsidy should be used depends on whether society or producers have legal rights.[20]

[19] Both the per-unit tax and the per-unit subsidy equivalently move the industry supply function upward (not shown) because of the cost imposed by the tax and the opportunity cost due to the subsidy.

[20] Similarly, in the Coase theorem, the identities of who pays and who receives payment depend on legal rights.

Supplement S5A: Externalities and non-convexities

The Pigovian solution calls for the government to use taxes or subsidies to replicate the prices that are not revealed because of missing markets. Supplement S5A shows that because of particular attributes of externalities that result in "non-convexities," there may be no equilibrium price in a replicated market. There is no empirical evidence that the outcome ever happened. The circumstances are nonetheless theoretically interesting.

Tax revenue and externalities

When legal rights call for use of a corrective tax as the means of public policy, the tax revenue becomes part of general government revenue and is not paid to the victims of environmental damage. Corrective public policy requires only changing producer incentives, which is achieved by polluters paying the corrective tax in the same way that they would pay a price for "causing environmental damage" if such a market were to exist. Changing the behavior of producers does not require payments to people who are harmed by the adverse externality. Indeed, transferring the tax revenue to adversely affected people could have undesirable effects; it could become worthwhile for people to locate in a polluted area in order to become victims and thereby be eligible for compensating payments.

Under the conditions of private negotiation of the Coase theorem, victims *are* paid when they have legal rights. The payment to victims provides incentives for the victims to agree to compromise their legal rights to allow an adverse externality at the efficient level. A government that has taken responsibility for resolving the externality problem is the agent of the victims and acts on their behalf; in acting on behalf of the victims, the government uses the corrective tax to change producer incentives. As we noted previously, the tax revenue is an *incidental consequence* of using the tax to change producer behavior and is kept by the government.

Correspondingly, if the factory has legal rights, people harmed by pollution do not privately finance the corrective subsidy. Rather, the subsidy is publicly financed by government, which implements public policy as an agent of the public. The corrective subsidy is financed through the government budget by taxpayers in general and not by the particular taxpayers who happen to be victims of the factory's pollution.

Taxes and marginal damage

In figure 5.6, the area OEH is the total social cost of the environmental damage at efficient production Q_E.[21] A corrective tax based on payment according to

[21] The area OEH is the difference between the areas under the true and private MC functions, evaluated from output of zero to the efficient quantity of output Q_E.

marginal damage would provide revenue precisely equal to social cost OEH.[22] A tax based on marginal damage cannot be implemented in a competitive market: the level of the tax depends on the sequence in which output is produced and it is impractical to trace the order in which different producers produced units of output.[23]

Inputs that have adverse externalities

We have defined externalities in the product market where output is sold. The principles of Pigovian taxes and subsidies apply in markets for inputs. A tax on a polluting input makes producers personally aware that use of the input imposes a cost on society; a subsidy on inputs not used is an opportunity cost of using the inputs.

Who pays an environmental tax?

The legal requirement to pay a tax does not determine who effectively pays the tax: we have seen that legal tax incidence and effective tax incidence are not necessarily the same and in general differ, with the payment of a tax shared by buyers and sellers in accord with demand and supply elasticities. The objective of achieving efficiency by using a Pigovian tax to change behavior to internalize an externality has not included qualifications about who in the end might actually pay a tax. Nonetheless, we might care how payment of a tax is shared, and we might also care how incomes change throughout the economy because of the tax. In that case, more than cost-benefit analysis is required to evaluate the costs of externalities. As we observed when studying who pays taxes, determining the effects of a tax on income distribution requires a general-equilibrium evaluation that traces the effects in different markets of an economy.[24]

Sequencing of private resolution and public policy

A way of stating the Coase theorem is that public policy is not required to resolve externality problems when legal rights have been defined and efficient private voluntary resolution can take place. Stating the Coase theorem in this form allows emphasis on the sequencing of private resolution and public policy. Efficiency requires that attempts at private resolution take place first. The government then takes responsibility through public policy for resolving externality problems that remain after attempts have been made at private resolution.

In figure 5.7, Q_a is the profit-maximizing use of a polluting input. Efficient use of the input is determined at point E where use is Q_E. This would be the Coase

[22] The level of such a corrective tax varies with output and is equal to the difference between true and private marginal cost. With such a tax, producers would precisely pay, through the tax, the value of the marginal social damage for each unit of output.

[23] A tax equal to marginal damage, however, could be levied on a monopolist because the monopolist produces all output. Marginal additions to output of the single producer could be observed and taxed.

[24] Don Fullerton and Garth Heutel (2007) calculated general-equilibrium effects to show how environmental taxes change income distribution in the U.S. economy.

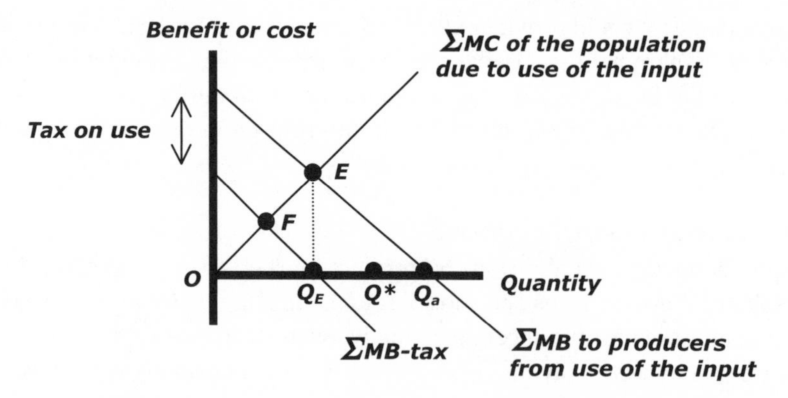

Figure 5.7. The sequencing of private resolution and public policy.

outcome if Coase bargaining were feasible. However, if private Coase negotiations are successful in reducing use from Q_a to only Q^*, the responsibility remains for government to complete the reduction in use to the efficient level Q_E through public policy.

If the government were to impose a tax on use *before* attempts at private resolution, the tax reduces the combined net marginal benefit to producers from use of the input to $\{\sum MB - tax\}$ and producers choose to use the efficient quantity Q_E. However, there now remain private incentives for Coase negotiation to move the outcome from efficient point E to point F. If successful, private negotiations reduce use of the input below efficient use Q_E.

Therefore:

> *In the sequencing of attempts at private resolution and public policy, efficiency requires that attempts at private resolution come first.*

Innovation as a response to a Pigovian tax or subsidy

A Pigovian tax provides an incentive for producers to innovate to avoid the tax. Similarly, a Pigovian subsidy provides an incentive to innovate in order to not lose the subsidy. The incentive to innovate to reduce pollution can result in technologies that provide a cleaner environment.

The case against subsidies

Although legal rights indicate whether a corrective tax or subsidy is appropriate for correcting an externality, there is a case against subsidies and, conversely, a case in favor of taxes – or, in favor of the principle that polluters should pay. Subsidies require taxes to finance the subsidies; therefore, there are excess burdens of taxation on taxpayers. We noted that the Coase theorem requires choosing assignment of legal rights to minimize transactions costs; the transactions costs similarly affect efficient choice of legal rights when externalities are internalized by public policy. To subsidize the activity of "not causing environmental damage," a government needs to know the counterfactual output that *would have been* produced if there were no subsidy. That is, in figure 5.6, to use the subsidy, the government needs to know the output Q^* that determines the base for payment of the subsidy. After corrective public policy has been introduced, the output Q^* is no longer observed. The amount produced Q_E, which is the tax base for levying the tax, is observable. The counterfactual output Q^* determines the total subsidy received by producers (but does not determine the per-unit subsidy s, which in figure 5.6 is determined by the observable difference between true and private MC at the efficient output Q_E). We might imagine producers who are paid subsidies to not produce looking for ways to increase the claimed counterfactual output Q^* (just as smokers who have legal rights could exaggerate their claims of the number of cigarettes that they intended to smoke in order to increase payments from nonsmokers). In increasing their claimed value of output produced without the subsidy, producers would be taking advantage of asymmetric information to engage in rent seeking from the government budget; the deception and rent-seeking behavior would be unethical but are consistent with profit-maximizing behavior.

The bureaucratic principal–agent problem is a source of reservations about use of subsidies. Public policy implemented through Pigovian subsidies requires an administrating bureaucracy that undertakes cost-benefit analysis to determine the corrective subsidy – or oversees the cost-benefit analysis of consultants – and disburses the subsidies. The subsidies paid can exceed the efficient subsidies required if an administering bureaucracy has been "captured" by industry interests.[25]

> *Asymmetric information and principal–agent problems justify a corrective tax rather than a subsidy.*

There is, of course, a problem if producers have legal rights.

A case against taxation

Figure 5.8 shows a positive externality associated with a person's education. In contrast to figure 5.2, in which education ceased at some point to benefit others, in this case the positive benefits from the externality persist and increase at the margin as the person invests in more education. The benefits for others in society given by $\{\sum social\ MB\}$ are expressed in the distance between $\{\sum true\ MB\}$ and $\{private\ MB\}$ of the student. The social MB may be the increasing likelihood as education continues that the student will be a successful researcher who, for example, will find a cure for ailments from which many people suffer.[26]

With no incentives other than personal benefit and cost, the person in figure 5.8 would choose E_1 but society wants the person to choose E_2. The increase from E_1 to E_2 provides a social gain of area FGH. A subsidy of GH resolves the

[25] The problem of capture similarly arises when subsidies are paid to provide incentives for a natural monopolist to choose efficient output. See supplement S2B.

[26] There have been proposals that there are positive externalities from keeping children at school and off the street because of reduced crime. By being at school, children avoid contact with those who would lead them into a life of crime.

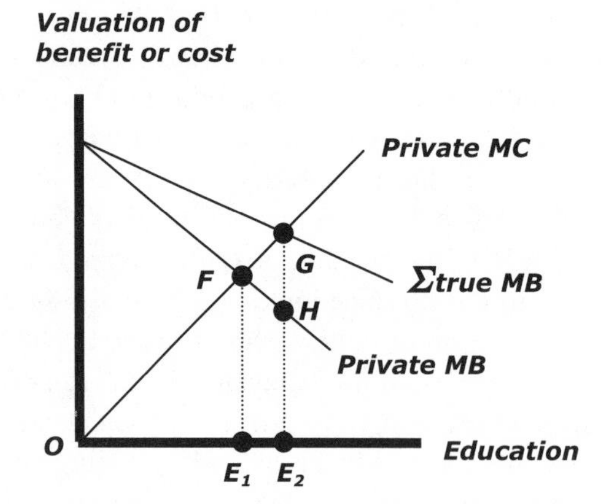

Figure 5.8. Education as a positive externality.

externality problem by ensuring that social benefits of education are internalized in the personal-education decision and results in a personal choice of E_2.

The Pigovian tax alternative to the subsidy is a tax on years of education between E_1 and E_2 that are not undertaken. Social justice suggests that in a choice between Pigovian taxes and subsidies to resolve education externalities, governments should subsidize education rather than tax "non-education." With the tax uniform for everybody, teenagers who are compelled to work because their parents are poor might pay the tax and continue working. Or, a teenager who lacks the temperament or ability for formal study might have to pay the tax.[27]

Regulation

An alternative to Pigovian taxes and subsidies is direct regulation of externalities. The same information is required for efficient direct regulation as for efficient use of Pigovian taxes and subsidies. The government needs to know the efficient output or input, which requires cost-benefit analysis.

In practice, regulation does not attempt to replicate the efficient outcome. On the contrary, direct regulation can impede the efficient outcome. It follows from the Coase theorem that regulation is an inefficient response to existence of externalities. When, for example, regulations specify that smoking in a classroom is not permitted, nonsmokers and smokers can no longer mutually gain through Coase negotiations that result in perhaps some limited smoking at a compensating price paid by smokers. Generally:

Direct regulation prevents efficient Coase bargaining.

For policy makers, regulation is, however, easy to implement. Legal restraint is imposed on allowable behavior and penalties are set for noncompliance.

[27] When governments subsidize education, discretion regarding attending school is not left to parents or children.

Environmental policy, for example, becomes part of law. In the case of externalities associated with education, children are compelled to attend school until a minimum age. Direct regulation sets requirements to use unleaded fuel and exhaust filters. In hot climates, direct regulation sometimes requires private vehicles to be air-conditioned to spare *other* drivers the negative externality of sharing the road with drivers who are impatient because of the summer heat. Emissions of pollutants can be directly regulated by designating the types of technologies and inputs that can be used. Direct regulation can limit permitted decibels of noise. Cigarette smoking is directly regulated through prohibition of smoking in public places.[28]

Legal rights and regulation

Changes in legal rights through regulation have distributional effects. Direct regulation that prohibits smoking makes nonsmokers better off. Similarly, a change in legal rights giving women the right of protection from sexual harassment in the workplace makes women better off – and harassers worse off. Direct regulation requires a clear, unambiguous definition of the type of behavior that is to be restricted. Medical studies led to the banning of smoking on airplanes when statistics revealed high rates of cancer for flight attendants, who were inhaling passengers' smoke. In the case of sexual harassment, defining disallowed behavior is more complex than the prohibition of smoking. Some societies allow people to compliment one another on their appearance, whereas the compliments in other societies might be viewed with suspicion and distrust and as a preamble to harassment. Therefore, different societies have adopted different interpretations of the sexual-harassment externality.

Regulation and reciprocal externalities

Direct regulation need not make some people better off at the expense of others; when there are *reciprocal externalities*, direct regulation can make everyone better off. Reciprocal externalities occur, for example, through pollution from automobiles. Individual drivers might prefer that all other drivers use more expensive but more environmentally friendly unleaded fuel, while they themselves continue to use cheaper, more polluting fuel, in the knowledge that one automobile using leaded fuel (their automobile) has a negligible adverse effect on the environment. These circumstances define a prisoners' dilemma. The dominant strategy is to use cheaper leaded fuel: if other people use leaded fuel, the best personal response is also to use the leaded fuel; if other people use the more expensive unleaded fuel, the best personal response is again to use leaded fuel. Independent personal decisions based on private self-interest therefore result in everyone choosing environmentally unfriendly leaded fuel, but everyone is better off when all drivers use only unleaded fuel, which can be achieved through direct regulation.

[28] Regulation can be more stringent than prohibiting smoking in public places. In the Australian state of Tasmania, for example, smoking is prohibited in a car in which children are present.

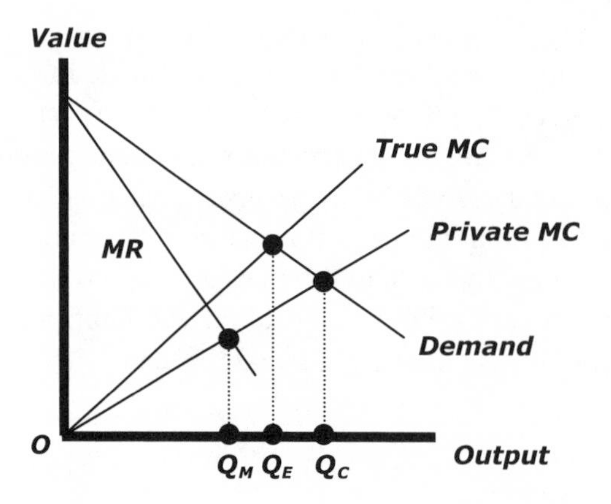

Figure 5.9. The use of a quota and monopoly.

Quotas

Emissions quotas are another public-policy means to correct externality problems. Use of quotas requires governments to make decisions about the magnitude of total allowable emissions and also how the quota is distributed among producers. Possibilities for distribution are (1) the quota rights are auctioned to a highest bidder, (2) they are sold through a competitive market, and (3) they are given away to incumbent producers without payment.

Auction of quotas

When quota rights are auctioned, the purchaser can intend to use the quota rights to produce output. However, the quota rights also can be used to preempt output by other producers. Securing an entire emissions quota makes a producer a monopoly through the exclusive right to environmentally harmful emissions. A government obtains maximum revenue from auction of a quota when one producer is permitted to buy the entire quota; in principle, the single buyer is prepared to pay the value of monopoly profits for the rights to the entire quota, resulting in the highest competitive bid for the entire quota equal to the value of monopoly profits.

Figure 5.9 shows an environmental externality with a unit of a quota defined as the right to produce a unit of a polluting output. Thus, a quantity of emissions rights provides the right to produce a corresponding quantity of output. Because of the externality, the true MC of production exceeds the private MC. Total production when competitive firms do not internalize the environmental externality is Q_C. The government uses cost-benefit analysis to determine efficient production Q_E and sets a limit on emissions consistent with production of Q_E. A firm that is successful in monopolizing the market through purchase of the Q_E quota rights produces the profit-maximizing output Q_M, determined where:

$$MR = private\ MC. \tag{5.13}$$

The objective of public policy is to use a quota to reduce industry output from Q_C to the efficient output Q_E. However, the firm that has monopolized the industry uses only Q_M units of the quota for production. The part $(Q_E - Q_M)$ of the quota has not been acquired for the purpose of production but rather to forestall production by competitors.

A monopolist as an environmentalist's ally

A monopolist can be an environmentalist's ally. Environmentalists may be dissatisfied with the government's choice of quota Q_E in figure 5.9 and may wish to have a more stringent environmental policy. The successful monopolist (who won the bidding for the entire quota of emissions rights) produces profit-maximizing output Q_M and so, in effect, imposes stricter environmental standards than were sought through public policy that set the output quota at Q_E. The monopoly outcome $Q_M < Q_E$ is more satisfying for the more stringent environmentalists.

When there is no public policy to correct an externality, a monopoly can be preferable to a competitive market. In figure 5.9, that monopoly output Q_M might more closely approximate the efficient output Q_E than the output Q_C of a competitive industry. If government is inactive through public policy, environmentalists would then prefer monopoly to competition. A monopoly for export of elephant tusks from Africa, for example, would be preferable to unregulated competitive supply; more elephants would live because of the higher monopoly price.[29]

Sale of quota rights in a competitive market

A government agency can supply quota rights in a market for emissions rights, in which producers can also trade rights among themselves. With many buyers and sellers, the market in emissions can be competitive. In figure 5.10, a government agency sets an emissions-rights quota of Q_E. The competitive market price of the polluting input is P_1. When no public policy restricts use of the polluting input, demand for the input is Q^*. With the quota Q_E determining efficient supply of emissions rights, the total price of the polluting input for users is $(P_1 + P_2)$. At

[29] We have encountered here a case of the *theory of the second best*, which indicates that if two sources of inefficiency are present, it may be better to leave both efficiency problems unresolved than to resolve just one of the problems. We have here monopoly and an environmental externality together. The first-best outcome for the society is achieved when both problems are resolved through public policy. There is no assurance of improvement if public policy addresses only one source of inefficiency. In figure 5.9, public policy to eliminate monopoly and implement competition while not addressing the externality problem results in inefficient output Q_C, whereas allowing the monopoly to persist results in the inefficient outcome Q_M. A computation is required to establish which of the two inefficient outcomes is preferred; the answer, in principle, can go either way. The computation requires comparing $W = B - C$ at Q_M and at Q_C. We face the question of whether to include monopoly profits in the benefits B; because the profits, in principle, could be taxed and transferred to consumers, the profits are part of social benefit; however, monopoly profits can be dissipated in inefficient rent seeking.

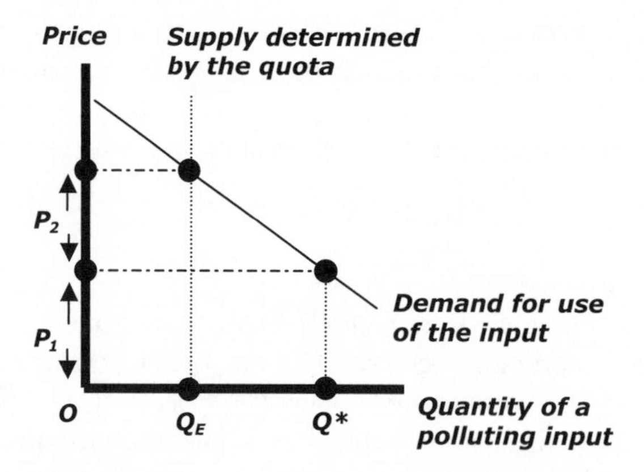

Figure 5.10. A competitive market for quota rights.

this price, demand for the input equals the supply Q_E determined by the quota. P_2 is the price of a unit of emissions rights.

The competitive market assigns the right to produce to producers who can most profitably use the polluting inputs and who pay the price P_2 for the right of use. Producers who can innovate or who take more care to reduce emissions are rewarded by being able to sell emissions rights they no longer need or by needing to purchase fewer emissions rights.

By selling quota rights at the price P_2 in a competitive market for emissions rights as in figure 5.10, a government duplicates the outcome of a corrective Pigovian tax or subsidy. The price P_2 in the competitive market for emissions rights is precisely equal to the efficient Pigovian tax or subsidy.

Distribution of the quota among existing producers

Rather than selling quota rights, a government can establish a market for emissions rights by initially giving rights away *free* to existing producers. The decision to give the emissions quota away could be based on a sense of justice. Producers may have made investments in productive capacity when there was no social awareness of harm to the environment. Now, through no fault of their own, the producers confront social awareness of environmental problems.

Figure 5.11 shows a competitive industry in which, before recognition of the social cost of environmental damage, competitive industry output is Q_C and the market price is P_C. An individual firm in the industry produces the average-cost-minimizing output q_C.

After environmental costs are acknowledged, the industry's true social market-supply function is recognized as $S' = \sum(\mathit{true\ MC})$, which determines the socially efficient output as Q_E and the corresponding efficient market price as P_E. The government thus sets Q_E as the quota on emissions.

In the second step of the public-policy decision, the quota Q_E is distributed free among the existing producers. The distribution of quota rights might be in proportion to producers' outputs before the quota was introduced.

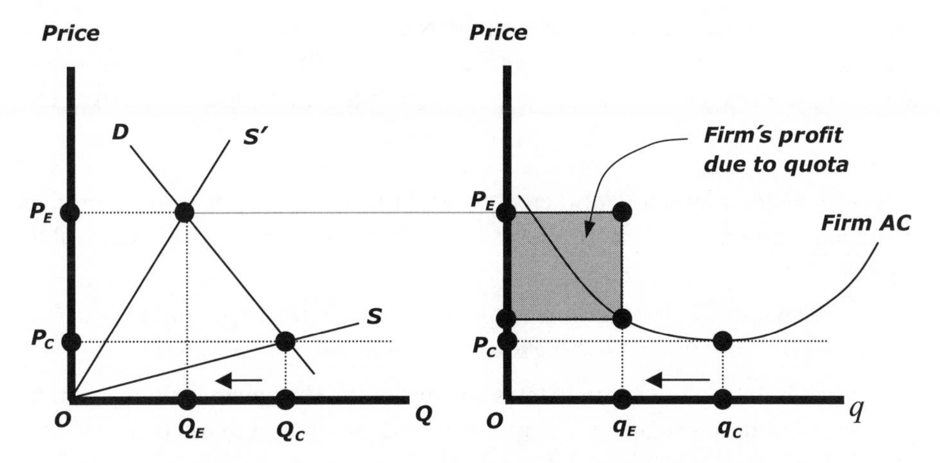

Figure 5.11. Assignment of quota rights to existing producers.

The quota of the individual producer in figure 5.11 allows production of q_E. After the free distribution of quota rights, individual firms are not producing at minimum average cost. The price market P_E is greater than average cost AC, and the firm earns excess profits shown by the shaded area.[30]

Owners of firms that were assigned free shares of the quota can capitalize their profits by selling quota rights in the emissions market. A new firm with a better product or a superior technology will want to buy emissions rights in order to be permitted to produce. A new firm with the *same* technology and costs of a preexisting firm can earn no more than competitive profits by buying quota rights because the asset (the right to emissions) that the new firm acquires yields no more than the rate of return equal to other risk-adjusted competitive returns available from other investments. Therefore:

> *The owners of the firms that receive free emissions rights when the rights are originally given out are the sole beneficiaries of the rents created by the introduction of the quota.*

C. Political decisions

To summarize, there are different means of implementing public policy to correct externalities: the alternatives are Pigovian tax-subsidy solutions, direct regulation, and quotas that can be sold to allow monopolization in competitive markets, or are given to producers without payment. Which of the different means of implementing public policy can we expect political decision makers to choose?

[30] Profits should attract entry of new firms into the industry, thereby increasing total supply and returning all firms to production at minimum average cost where non-competitive profits are not earned. Entry of new firms cannot take place and industry output cannot expand unless emissions rights are increased.

Producers as supporters of environmental policy

The different public-policy means can all achieve the efficient *total market output* at which externalities are internalized. The free distributed quota differs from the other outcomes, however, because production is not cost-efficient: average cost of producers in figure 5.11 is greater than minimum AC.

A free distributed quota also creates rents for incumbent producers through non-competitive profits. The producers, therefore, have reason to be thankful to political decision makers.

> *The rents from free distribution of emissions rights give producers an incentive to support socially beneficial pro-environmental policies.*[31]

Two cases, one in the United States and one in the European Union, illustrate assignment of quota rights by governments and creation of markets for trading of emissions rights (see Boxes 5.2 and 5.3).

Box 5.2 The U.S. market in SO_2 emissions

Coal-burning electricity power stations emit sulfur dioxide (SO_2), which harms plants and trees as well as aquatic life. In 1990, the U.S. government introduced a market for the right to emit SO_2. A maximum allowable quota on total emissions was set. The quota was decreased over time. Free rights to emit SO_2 were assigned to existing electricity utility companies. Each company was required to present sufficient quota rights to cover its emissions to the U.S. Environmental Protection Agency. Electricity utility companies without quota rights to match emissions faced financial penalties and further reductions in their allowable emissions levels. The quota rights were made tradable in the market for emissions rights. Incentives were thereby put in place to reduce emissions: the market rewarded companies for reducing emissions because unneeded quota rights could be sold in the market for emissions rights. The U.S. program establishing the market for SO_2 was based on distributing quota rights free to preexisting producers but could have been initiated through competitive sale of quota rights. A Pigovian tax on emissions of SO_2 could also have been used, or direct regulation could have set emissions standards and required investment in pollution abatement. By distributing the emissions-rights quota without charge to existing producers and establishing a market where emissions rights could be traded, the government made the emissions-reduction program attractive to producers.

[31] Producers oppose direct regulation because of costs of investment in pollution abatement. Producers also oppose Pigovian taxes because they pay the taxes. In figure 5.11, if a government uses a corrective Pigovian tax to achieve efficient output Q_E, producers incur losses in the short run. In the long run, after some producers have exited the industry, firms remaining will be producing at minimum average cost plus the tax and will be earning no more than the competitive level of profit for the industry. Free assignment of quota rights provides the rents indicated in figure 5.11.

Box 5.3 The European market in CO_2 emissions

A market for trading the right to emit carbon dioxide (CO_2) was introduced by the European Union (EU) in 2005. Governments of EU member countries were assigned national quotas for carbon emissions and the market determined the price of emissions rights. Immediately after introduction of the market, the price for the right to emit 1 ton of CO_2 was 30 euros. The prices then proceeded to fall as follows:

APRIL 2006	MAY 2006	MARCH 2007	SEPTEMBER 2007
30 Euros	10 Euros	1.2 Euros	10 Cents Euro

Hence, 18 months after the introduction of the market, the price of emissions rights was a mere 10 cents euro. The low price indicated little demand for emissions rights relative to the supply. The supply of emissions rights had been determined by governments. The decline in the price of emissions rights suggests that governments of European countries had accommodated industry interests by increasing emissions quotas. Indeed, in the European countries, little or no reduction in total emissions was achieved.

Political decisions and externalities

These two cases indicate political benefits for producers from environmental policy. In the U.S. case, the emissions rights, as predicted, were given to producers free of charge. In the European case, initial high market costs of producer compliance declined over time as governments increased the supply of emissions rights.

The political trade-off in environmental policy is revealed in other cases by failures of governments to respond spontaneously to environmental externality problems. Air quality at times has been allowed to deteriorate. Dumping of hazardous materials has been permitted. The quality of drinking water sometimes has been allowed to deteriorate through environmentally harmful runoffs from agriculture and industrial production. Recreational sites (beaches, rivers, and lakes) have become polluted. Emissions have been permitted to increase. Often, governments have not introduced remedial policies until there has been an environmental crisis.

When we considered the role of institutions in determining decisions about public finance and public policy, we noted the trade-off in political support that influences political decisions. Interest groups and voters differ in the means of providing political support. Interest groups provide money and voters provide votes – and, through political advertising, interest-group money influences how people vote. The trade-off between political support from interest groups and voters can explain political choice of environmental standards.

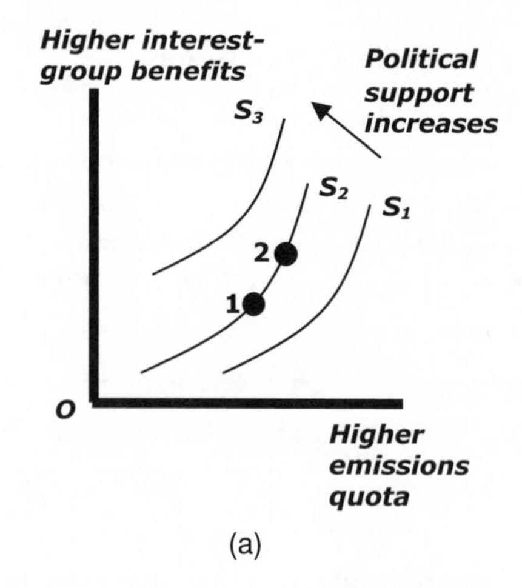

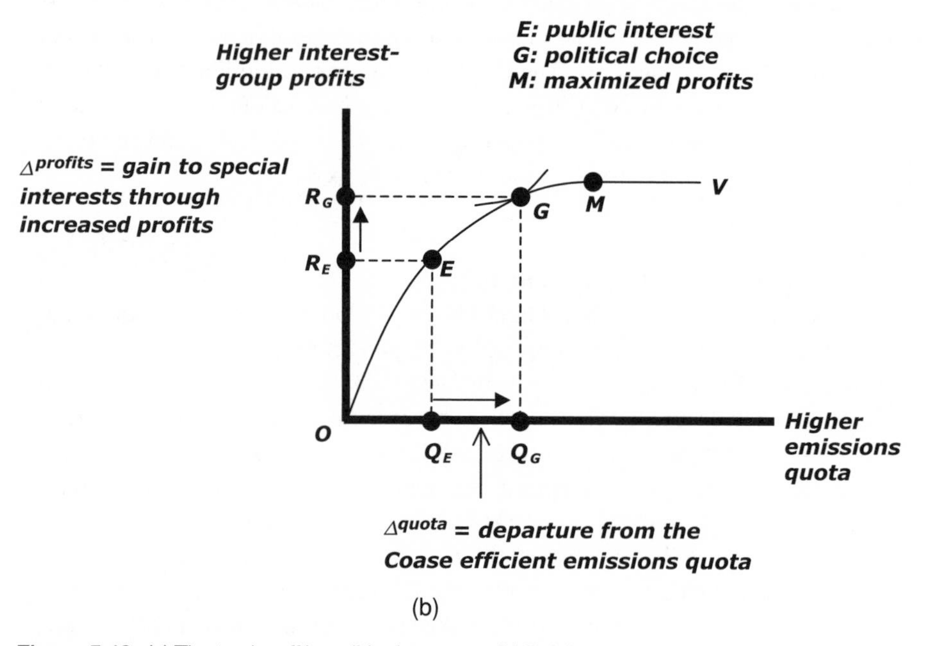

Figure 5.12. (a) The trade-off in political support. (b) Public policy based on political support from interest groups and voters.

Figure 5.12a shows the equal political-support contours for political decision makers described in chapter 2. Industry interests want the higher industry benefits obtainable from a laxer emissions quota. Voters, in contrast, want stringent emissions quotas.

In figure 5.12a, political support is constant along the contours S_1, S_2, and S_3. Political support S increases with a lower emissions quota because more stringent emissions quotas please voters. Political support also increases when interest-group benefits increase.[32]

Points 1 and 2 on the contour S_2 in figure 5.12a illustrate the political trade-off between political support from voters and the industry interest group; a move from point 1 to point 2 increases industry benefits because of the higher emissions quota. At the same time, political support from voters declines because of the higher emissions quota. Because points 1 and 2 indicate the same level of political support, the increase in political support from industry interests precisely matches the decline in political support from voters. The objective of the political decision makers is to choose the emissions quota that provides the highest level of political support.

Industry profits

The constraint on choice of public policy of political decision makers is OV in figure 5.12b. The function OV shows the increase in industry profits – or politically provided rents – as the emissions quota is increased. Maximum industry profits are at M on OV. An emissions quota greater than at M does not increase industry profits and would not be used by the industry.

The public interest

The efficient emissions quota that would result from the Coase theorem is Q_E at point E. Therefore, point E defines the public interest determined by replicating the efficient Coase outcome that would maximize $W = B - C$, taking into account the benefits of production and damage to the environment. At point E, the industry has profits R_E.

Maximum political support

Maximum political support is attained through the compromise between the public interest and producer interests at point G, where a political-support contour is tangential to the constraint OV. The politically determined emissions quota is Q_G. The political decision is a departure from the public interest. Permissible emissions Q_G higher than the Coase efficient public-interest emissions at Q_E are chosen. The higher emissions quota provides industry interests with the higher profits R_G.[33]

The origin for measuring political support

The origin for measuring political support in figure 5.12b is the efficient Coase public-interest point E. Political decision makers lose political support from voters when the emissions quota that is chosen exceeds the efficient quota Q_E at

[32] See also chapter 2.

[33] The gain to industry interests ($R_G - R_E$) is a politically created and politically assigned rent. If rent seeking occurs in the quest for industry profits, the rent is dissipated through resources and time used in rent seeking. The extent of rent dissipation determines the social loss due to rent seeking.

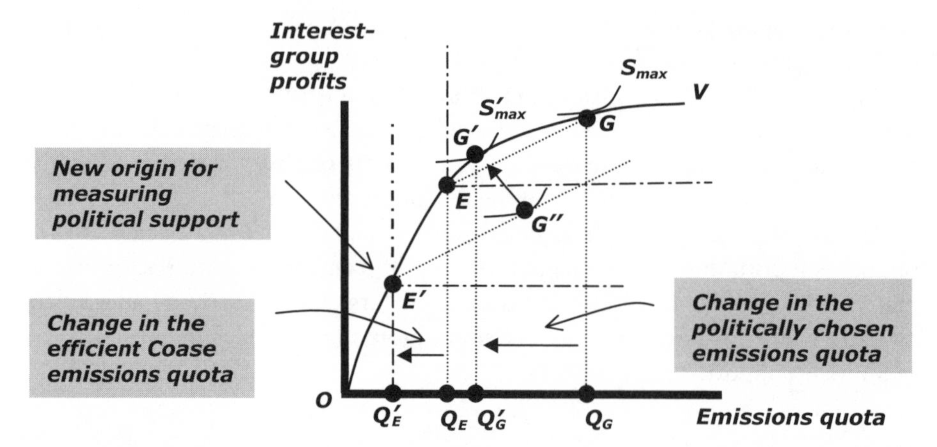

Figure 5.13. The change in public policy when public-interest environmental standards become more stringent.

point E. Industry interests are aware that they would have profits R_E if environmental policy were chosen in the public interest at point E and are appreciative of the higher profits R_G received at point G.

In determining their political support for political decision makers, voters and industry interests look at the change in their costs and benefits because of the political decision to depart from the public interest at point E. Based on whether they have lost or gained from the political decisions and on the extent of loss or gain, voters and industry interests make their political-support decisions.

Political support from industry interests and voters depends on the deviation of politically chosen public policy from the public interest.

Voters lose from the politically determined emissions quota at point G compared to the public-interest efficient outcome at point E. In figure 5.12b, the deviation of the politically chosen emissions quota from the efficient Coase quota is:

$$\Delta^{quota} = Q_G - Q_E. \tag{5.14}$$

The gain to producers from the deviation from the public interest is:

$$\Delta^{profits} = R_G - R_E. \tag{5.15}$$

A change in the public interest

We now look at the consequences when research reveals that the public interest requires a more stringent quota than Q_E at point E. Figure 5.13 shows such a change in the emissions quota that is in the public interest. The efficient quota on emissions that would be determined through the Coase theorem decreases from Q_E to Q'_E. The point E' becomes, therefore, the new origin for evaluation of political support.

After the change, voters and the industry reevaluate gains and losses from politically determined public policy: the contours indicating equal political support now have point E' as the origin.

Political decision makers now reevaluate their policy decision. They continue to choose policies along OV but now look for a new political compromise based on point E' as the public-interest origin for measurement of political support.

When point E was the public interest, maximum political support was S_{max} at point G. With point E' as the public interest, maximized political support is S'_{max}.[34]

In the new political compromise at point G', the emissions quota is lower than at point G. The emissions quota has decreased from Q_G to Q'_G. The deviation $\{\Delta^{quota}\}$ of the politically determined emissions quota from the efficient Coase quota has declined. The new public policy is closer, therefore, to the public interest, for which voters are appreciative.

Producers' profits decline in the move from point G to point G'. However, the additional industry benefits $\{\Delta^{profits}\}$ attributable to public policy have increased. The political response provides producers with a more advantageous outcome, through political willingness to allow greater additional profits compared to profits that would be earned, were public policy in the public interest.

Political optimization by political decision makers shares benefits to equate political support at the margin. If people were to discover oil in their backyard, political decision makers would maximize political support by taking (or taxing) the oil until the marginal political loss due to the dissatisfaction of the people who found the oil is equal to the marginal political gain from giving the oil to others. Voters did not find oil. However, the stricter, efficient environmental standards are a windfall gain for voters. The political response is to let voters have some of their windfall gain and to distribute some of the benefits to industry interests by greater departure from the public interest.[35]

Political institutions and the environment

Democratic institutions lead political decision makers to seek to maximize political support; hence, the trade-off in political support from voters and special interests when public policy decisions are made. With democratic institutions, political decision makers, in principle, are accountable to voters and taxpayers; however, the principal–agent problems confronting voters enable special interests to influence policy decisions, which results in deviation from the public interest. Nonetheless, with democratic institutions (and an informative, unbiased media), allowing environmental externalities to persist eventually becomes excessively

[34] Equal-political-support contours from the same origin do not intersect. The contours S'_{max} and S_{max} in figure 5.13 would intersect; however, S'_{max} and S_{max} belong to different sets of contours with respective origins at points E' and E.

[35] In figure 5.13, the distance $EG = E'G''$. Therefore, at points G and G'' values of $\{\Delta^{quota}\}$ and $\{\Delta^{profits}\}$ are the same. However, point G'' is not a politically efficient outcome. Voters and industry interests can both be made better off, and political support increases, if political decision makers move to point G' from point G''. In such a move, $\{\Delta^{quota}\}$ declines; voters benefit from the public policy more attuned to the public interest, and political support from voters increases. At the same time, $\{\Delta^{profits}\}$ increases, which increases political support from industry interests.

politically costly. Past failures are admitted and policies to protect the environment are enacted and implemented. When there is no democracy, public safety and environmental damage may be given little or no weight at all. Indeed, with few exceptions, the greatest environmental disasters have occurred when democratic institutions have been absent.[36]

D. Global externalities and international agreements

Global externalities affect the world at large. For example, emissions of CO_2, SO_2, methane, and nitrous oxide and the destruction of rain forests have been linked to global warming and climate change. Biodiversity is also a global externality.

Private resolution of global externalities

Private resolution of global externalities is possible. An example is the case of rain forests of Costa Rica. Although the continued presence of rain forests is globally beneficial (when forests are cut down, there is a negative global externality through the greenhouse effect), a nation has sovereignty over its rain forests. Rather than allowing rain forests to be cleared for private profit from timber, farming, and pasture, a country's government can sell rain forests to governments and to people who care about degradation of the global environment. Extensive free-rider problems can be expected because whoever pays to sustain a rain forest provides a public-good benefit to the global population. Yet, although we anticipate that free-rider problems would preempt the creation of a market in the sustaining of rain forests, the government of the Central American country of Costa Rica successfully established an international market for "not cutting down" rain forests in the 1990s. Parts of its rain forests have been sold to foreign governments. Few foreign governments participated in the market to buy and sustain the rain forests; the few that participated in the market created by Costa Rica provided a free public good to the populations (and governments) of the many other countries that chose not to participate. Private individuals have also used their personal wealth to buy and preserve part of the rain forests; these people have privately provided the world with a public good.

Biodiversity

Elephants are hunted for the ivory from their tusks. Rhinos are hunted because, as we have previously noted, people in some parts of the world believe that their horns, when ground up and ingested, are aphrodisiacs. Some species of

[36] Under totalitarian rule in the former Soviet Union, the most visible environmental disaster was a nuclear power station that melted down at Chernobyl. Another extreme environmental disaster has been the drying up of a substantial portion of the Aral Sea because of nonsustainable diversion of water for irrigation. The area around the Aral Sea also became contaminated from use of chemical fertilizers. People living in the area became chronically ill.

the world's largest mammals, the whales, have been hunted to near extinction. International agreements attempt to preserve wildlife and biodiversity, but not all governments have the same will or incentive to participate in the agreements or to comply.[37]

The ozone layer

Emissions of manmade chlorofluorocarbons and other substances (halons, carbon tetrachloride, and methyl chloroform) have been identified as the cause of a hole in the earth's ozone layer over the continent of Antarctica.[38] The ozone layer provides protection from ultraviolet radiation due to rays of the sun. A diminished ozone layer increases the incidence of skin cancer and is also harmful to agricultural crops. International agreement on eliminating emissions of chlorofluorocarbons was reached when the extent of the damage to the earth's ozone layer became known. Under the Montreal Protocol of 1987 on substances that deplete the ozone layer, governments agreed to the phasing out of emissions of ozone-depleting substances. Implementation of the Montreal Protocol by different countries was uneven. The World Bank assisted through its Global Environmental Facility by providing financing that resulted in governments of poorer countries complying with the Protocol.[39]

Climate change

Climate change has been described as a problem of monumental magnitude. Sir Nicolas Stern, who oversaw a comprehensive review of climate change,[40] proposed that:

> *Greenhouse gas emissions are externalities and represent the biggest market failure the world has seen.*[41]

Climate change is a case of the tragedy of the commons. The commons is the global atmosphere in which a stock of greenhouse gases accumulates. Every person on earth is involved in the tragedy of the commons because everyone leaves a "carbon footprint" through personal responsibility for emissions of CO_2 (minimally, we breathe, but we do more than that). The accumulation of the greenhouse gases is held responsible for global warming (hence, the name of the gases). As global warming proceeds, ice in Polar Regions and glaciers melt and sea

[37] There have been, in particular, controversies about the hunting of whales.

[38] Icy clouds in the stratospheric ozone layer result from stray chlorine atoms that emanate from chlorofluorocarbons and other substances. The ozone layer is destroyed when the stray chlorine atoms take oxygen atoms from ozone, which is a three-oxygen molecule.

[39] The World Bank is an international finance and development agency with headquarters in Washington, DC. The World Bank lends to poorer countries and also provides technical assistance and advice on economic policy.

[40] The study is *The Economics of Climate Change: The Stern Review*, published in 2007.

[41] Stern (2008, p. 1).

levels rise. The climate changes as ice is converted to water. The melting is compounded when ice frozen in the tundra melts after the upper layer has melted. The conversion of ice to water changes weather patterns, and some regions become more susceptible to drought.

Although the evidence indicates an increasing temperature, there is controversy about the contribution of humans to global warming. The earth has undergone severe climate change in the past, ranging from periods of high temperature to ice ages. Sir Nicolas Stern pointed out in the course of warning about climate change that if measures are not taken to change the trend of increasing temperatures, "over the next two centuries we are likely to see change at a rate that is fast forward in historical time and on a scale that the world has not seen for tens of millions of years." (Ibid. p. 2) That is, the earth has experienced heating in the past. The scientific question is:

> *At the margin, what is the human contribution to global warming?*

The economic question is:

> *Given the human contribution at the margin, what does cost-benefit analysis tell us about the desirability of public policies that would reduce greenhouse gas emissions?*

Merely asking these questions can be controversial among scientists and other people. The possible answers to the questions allow, in principle, for compromise in making every effort to apply public policies to reduce greenhouse gas emissions. The debate on the scope of the human contribution to climate change generally is formulated in two views. On the one side, the argument is that the earth is destined for doom if corrective public policies are not introduced. On the other side, the argument is that nature and not humanity is the principal cause of the climate change that has been observed and that high costs for abatement of emissions are not justified by the economic benefits.

We previously noted that choice of the discount rate matters for intergenerational welfare. A high discount rate would lead to the judgment that high costs of reducing emissions should not be imposed on present generations. A zero discount would give future generations as much weight in cost-benefit analysis as present generations and would justify greater costs imposed on present generations to preserve the environment for future generations. We should choose a zero discount rate in valuing the environment if we believe that future generations have as much right to quality of life (or life at all) as present generations.

The analogy of climate change to the tragedy of the commons is tempered by the dimension of time in the difference between stocks and flows. That is, a flow of sheep onto the commons creates a stock of sheep that readily can be reduced. The flow of greenhouse gas emissions creates a stock of gases in the atmosphere that cannot be readily reversed – hence, the urgency in the controversy. It is impossible to wait to see which side is correct and then, if environmental policy has been too lax, to take measures to reduce the stock of greenhouse gases. There is no analogy to simply removing excess sheep from the commons: the uncertainty about global warning involves harmful consequences that are – in the domain of length of human lives – irreversible. Risk aversion therefore favors the arguments pointing to dire consequences of climate change due to global warming, if human behavior does not change to substantially reduce emissions.

However, the debate remains with two sides. Often, the debate is not civil. Scientists engaged in climate-change research whose conclusions support a significant human contribution to climate change – and their supporters, including economists – often regard people who do not accept their conclusions as ignorant or uncaring about the future of humanity, or both. On the other side, those people suspicious of evidence that humanity and not nature is primarily responsible for climate change have accused scientists of purposefully and self-interestedly exaggerating the human contribution in order to receive grants for their research.

The prisoners' dilemma and impediments to international agreement

Because everyone in the world is involved in greenhouse-gas emissions through reciprocal externalities, agreements to reduce emissions involve all governments of the world. Agreements among governments, however, are subject to the prisoners' dilemma and free-riding incentives: emissions reductions are public goods that benefit everyone globally, whereas a government committing to a reduction in emissions imposes a cost on its own population through the need for adjustment to the stricter environmental standards.

The prisoners' dilemma that arises is shown in table 5.2. The dilemma applies to agreement among many countries, but we can look at governments of two countries. The efficient outcome is (30, 30) when the two governments agree to reduce emissions. The best outcome 40 for a government is achieved by free riding and not agreeing to reduce emissions when the government of the other country reduces emissions. The worst outcome 10 is when a country reduces emissions and the other country does not. The dominant strategy for each government

TABLE 5.2. THE PRISONERS' DILEMMA IN INTERNATIONAL ENVIRONMENTAL AGREEMENTS

	Government 2 agrees to reduce emissions	Government 2 refuses to reduce emissions
Government 1 agrees to reduce emissions	30, 30	10, 40
Government 1 refuses to reduce emissions	40, 10	20, 20

is not to reduce emissions, which results in the inefficient Nash equilibrium at (20, 20).[42] The prisoners' dilemma of international environmental externalities is thus a case of the tragedy of the commons, where the "commons" refers to the global environment. In the Nash equilibrium at (20, 20) in table 5.2, both countries' populations "overuse" the environment (as sheep in the case of the common field overused the common grazing ground in the Nash equilibrium). The "overuse" of the environment occurs because in the Nash equilibrium, each government adopts environmental policies that internalize only the externalities on the government's own population. Externalities from domestic production and consumption that adversely affect people in other countries are ignored (just as owners of sheep on the commons internalized only the externalities that their own sheep created for themselves and ignored the externalities that their sheep created for other sheep owners). In the case of the common field, the solution was privatization; the private owner maximized profits from selling access to the field by internalizing the externalities and allowing the efficient number of sheep onto the commons. Privatization is not a possible solution for the externality problems of the global environment. An escape from the prisoners' dilemma for environmental externalities requires cooperation among governments to agree to limit environmentally harmful emissions.

Cooperation to escape the Nash equilibrium at (20, 20) and to achieve the Pareto-superior outcome (30, 30) requires governments to reach agreement on:

(1) the magnitude of a *total reduction* in global emissions, and
(2) assignment of obligations to reduce emissions *among individual countries*

In a further step:

(3) Each country's emissions rights are assigned among local producers.

The decision about the desirable reduction in global emissions is based on technical information. The assignment of the global emissions quota among different countries affects the international distribution of income and wealth; as is characteristic of distributional questions, we expect disagreement about assignment of quotas for reductions in emissions among countries.

Two rules for international assignment of emissions quotas

Richer or more industrialized countries benefit from a rule for international assignment of emissions quotas that allocates the global emissions quota in proportion to contemporary emissions. Poorer, less industrialized countries benefit from a rule that assigns the global emissions quota on the basis of population; the case for assignment based on population is that each person on earth has

[42] In the symmetric prisoners' dilemma in table 5.2, the two countries' populations symmetrically affect the environment.

the same legal rights to the global environment, independent of contemporary contributions to greenhouse-gas emissions.[43]

The Coase theorem and assignment of legal rights among countries

After a decision has been made about the rule for assignment of the global emissions quota among countries, the emissions rights can be assigned. The Coase theorem then applies: income effects aside, efficient global use of emissions rights is independent of the assignment of legal rights to different countries.

Producers in a country do not necessarily use the country's assigned emissions quota. Rights to emissions can be traded in an international market, in which a country can be a net buyer or seller of emissions rights.

Tradability of emissions rights ensures global efficiency in the same way that a national market in emissions rights ensures domestic efficiency; producers who can more profitably take advantage of emissions rights can purchase rights from producers anywhere in the world who have lower demands for the rights to emit greenhouse gases. The market for emissions rights thus allows producers in the richer, more industrialized countries to use most of the quota of emissions rights, independent of how the global quota is distributed among richer or poorer countries, and the assignment of legal rights does not affect efficient use, in accord with the Coase theorem (when income effects are not significant).

> *The assignment of legal rights to an emissions quota is a distributional decision affecting incomes of different countries.*

National governments

A national government's choice of means of assigning the national quota among domestic producers affects domestic-producer profits and government revenue. If a government gives a country's assigned emissions quota away for free to national producers, producers benefit from free availability of the emissions quota and also from the sale of parts of emissions quotas not used. If a national government sells its emissions rights, the sale takes place at the market price to either domestic or foreign producers, and government revenue increases.

Free riding by governments

Free riding takes place when national governments refuse to participate in an international agreement that calls for all countries to reduce emissions: a government can decide to reject a share of the global emissions quota that it has been offered. In the prisoners' dilemma, the dominant strategy is to not cooperate in an

[43] Another topic of international negotiations is about the role of "sinks," which are forests and foliage that increase natural capacity to absorb greenhouse gases. Governments of countries with large absorption capacity wish to have the capacity of sinks included as a credit against their obligations to reduce emissions. Governments of countries that do not have substantial natural sinks tend to object.

agreement. In the Nash equilibrium at (20, 20) in table 5.2, each government independently pursues its own environmental policy and does not internalize externalities on populations in other countries.

Preconditions for international agreement among globally aware governments

Governments might act with responsibility and global awareness and have the intention to cooperate in international agreements with other governments. However, there are preconditions for cooperation among governments. The prisoners' dilemma in table 5.2 describes circumstances in which both countries have been assigned sufficient emissions rights to make participation in an international agreement worthwhile for each country. Both countries in table 5.2 prefer the globally efficient cooperative outcome (30, 30) to the non-cooperative Nash equilibrium outcome in which countries' benefits are (20, 20).

In table 5.3, the global quota has been assigned between countries so as to make benefits asymmetric. Government 1 is better off (with benefits of 20) without the agreement to reduce emissions than with the international cooperative agreement where government 1's benefits are 15.

The efficient global outcome remains an international agreement to reduce emissions, with maximal total global benefit of $(15 + 45) = 60$. The worst global outcome is with no agreement to reduce emissions, in which total global benefit is $(20 + 20) = 40$. Global benefit is $(40 + 10) = 50$ if one country unilaterally reduces emissions.

In table 5.3, government 1 has a dominant strategy of not agreeing to reduce emissions. After government 1 has chosen not to agree to reduce emissions, the best response of government 2 is also to not reduce emissions. The Nash equilibrium is at the outcome at (20, 20).

Beginning from the Nash equilibrium, government 1 has no incentive to enter into an agreement to reduce emissions. The international agreement is not Pareto-improving because government 1 loses in the move from (20, 20) to (15, 45).

TABLE 5.3. A QUOTA ASSIGNMENT DOES NOT PROVIDE THE GOVERNMENT OF COUNTRY 1 WITH AN INCENTIVE TO ENTER INTO AN INTERNATIONAL AGREEMENT TO REDUCE EMISSIONS

	Government 2 agrees to reduce emissions	Government 2 refuses to reduce emissions
Government 1 agrees to reduce emissions	15, 45	10, 40
Government 1 refuses to reduce emissions	40, 10	20, 20

In not cooperating in an international agreement, government 1 cannot be blamed or accused of intransigence or as not showing awareness of global environmental problems. Government 1 is being offered too small a share of the global emissions quota for cooperation in the international agreement to be attractive.

> *If not given sufficient emissions rights, a country may have no incentive to enter into an agreement to cooperate in restricting emissions.*

A more equal assignment of the global quota would give government 1 the required incentive to participate in an agreement to achieve the globally efficient outcome.

Why a global quota and not a tax on emissions?

We have described a global quota: a global tax on emissions (which is the Pigovian solution when society has legal rights and not producers), in principle, achieves the same outcome as a global emissions quota. The quota allows a target for total permissible global emissions to be set. The market then determines the price of emissions rights. A tax on emissions could precisely duplicate the quota if the global demand function expressing willingness to pay for emissions rights were known with certainty. However, because demand is not known with certainty, only the quota can ensure the predetermined limit on global emissions. Also, a tax on emissions provides revenue for the government and a quota can be assigned in ways that create and distribute rents domestically. Political decision makers, as we have seen, may prefer the latter option.

Environmentalists and producers as political allies

Environmental quality is a "luxury" good for which demand is highest in wealthiest countries; in poor societies, a large part of the population is concerned with satisfying basic needs. Differences in valuation of environmental damage can be a source of tension between richer and poorer countries. Environmentalists in richer countries can fear a "race to the bottom" in environmental standards: a race to the bottom occurs if environmental standards in richer countries decline so as to keep local costs near foreign production costs.

To avoid a race to the bottom, environmentalists in rich countries might support policies that restrict free international trade. The environmentalists reason that if foreign goods do not compete against domestically produced goods, there will be no political pressure from local producers to reduce domestic environmental standards for the purpose of competing with the foreign-produced imported goods. As we previously noted, stringent environmentalists might support monopolization of markets; because of the desire to preempt a race to the bottom in environmental standards, stringent environmentalists likewise might side with local import-competing producers in objecting to free trade or globalized markets. The environmentalists and producers have different motives: the environmentalists want to avoid a race to the bottom and thereby avoid degradation of the local environment; the local industry seeks protectionist policies because of protectionist rents and higher employment and job security when imports are restricted.

> *For different reasons, environmentalists and domestic industry interests can be political allies in seeking to persuade political decision makers to choose protectionist international-trade policies.*

The case of the dolphins

The case of protection of dolphins describes how environmentalists and producers can become successful allies. In tropical areas of the Pacific Ocean, dolphins swim over the top of schools of tuna. As a consequence, the dolphins become entangled in nets that are used to catch the tuna. In the 1980s, public awareness of the plight of the dolphins caught in tuna nets led U.S. consumers to boycott tuna. In 1988, the U.S. Congress amended the Marine Mammal Protection Act of 1972 to apply stringent pro-dolphin standards to imports. Imports of tuna that were caught with harm to dolphins were banned in 1990 – but only after the pro-environment Earth Island Institute took the U.S. government to court. The court action was against the U.S. Department of Commerce for failure to enforce the pro-dolphin policy for imports.

In 1990, the U.S. Congress passed a dolphin-protection consumer-information bill that prohibited canned tuna caught in the eastern tropical Pacific Ocean (principally by Mexican fishermen) from being labeled "dolphin-friendly." Protection of dolphins became a subject of international dispute when European governments rejected the right of the U.S. government to ban imports of Mexican-caught tuna canned in Europe and imported to the U.S. market. Despite European protests, the U.S. government maintained its pro-dolphin policy.

How did the pro-dolphin U.S. government policy come about? Domestic consumer sentiment always favored the dolphins. The change that took place was in the position of producer interests. Previously, suppliers of tuna to the U.S. market had used tuna caught in areas where dolphins were harmed. Suppliers to the U.S. market therefore opposed a ban on imports of tuna that had been caught through harm to dolphins. In the face of competition from low-cost foreign canned tuna, however, the U.S. canners had moved their canneries from the continental United States to off-shore U.S. territories, where they could benefit from lower labor costs and tax concessions. In the new locations, the U.S. suppliers did not use tuna that had been caught by harming dolphins. By now supporting a ban on imports of tuna caught with harm to dolphins, the U.S. suppliers were seeking to eliminate competitors from the domestic U.S. market. The U.S. pro-dolphin policy resulted in closure of smaller competing U.S. processing plants that relied on dolphin-unfriendly tuna. Environmentally concerned consumers found allies through the self-interest of the tuna processors who supplied the U.S. market. There was thus consensus among environmentalists and producers to protect the dolphins – and public policy changed to protect the dolphins.[44]

Global externalities and nondemocratic governments

Poor countries often are not democracies. There is a question of causality – does absence of democracy make people poor or is democracy absent because people are poor? Whichever is the case (and there could be simultaneity), nondemocratic institutions with rare exceptions result in self-serving government, with political decision makers using public finance and public policy for their own personal benefit. The evidence indicates that governments in autocratic countries show less regard for the environment than those in democratic countries. The personal-profit motives of nondemocratic rulers can be inconsistent with entering into and honoring international agreements to protect the environment.

In democratic countries, political decision makers might depart from the public interest in environmental policy – to the extent that is feasible given accountability to voters. There is a trade-off between political support from voters and industry interests. Nondemocratic rulers are in government in order to profit from being in business. Rulers, for example, may personally profit from the clearing of rain forests. They and their friends and families may own the factories that are the source of the environmentally degrading emissions. Because locally lax environmental standards allow lower cost local production than by producers elsewhere who confront higher environmental standards, nondemocratic political decision makers have incentives of personal profit to choose to not protect their home environment. Rulers in poor countries may subject their people to consequences of environmentally harmful production technologies that producers in richer countries do not use. Injustices in nondemocratic countries can therefore be compounded by the exposure of ordinary people, who may already have low life expectancies, to adverse environmental effects on their health.

Trade in hazardous waste

Governments in poor countries (the people controlling government are not poor) may agree to import hazardous waste. Generally, countries pay for goods they import. In the case of hazardous waste, governments receive payments to accept the imports. Rulers who are not democratically accountable to their people might not care about harm to the health of the people due to the imported waste, providing there is personal profit.[45]

[44] As was observed by Achim Körber (1998), everyone in the United States – consumers, producers, and government – had come to love Flipper.

[45] The international transportation of hazardous waste is regulated by an international agreement (the Basel Convention on transboundary movement of hazardous wastes and their disposal). The agreement requires that importing countries agree willingly to receive the hazardous waste and that exporting countries guarantee that the waste will not be disposed of or stored in a way that might be harmful to the environment.

The national discretion to choose environmental standards

Because countries are sovereign, a case might be made that there is national discretion to choose environmental policies. Therefore, the case might be made that if "poor countries" are voluntarily prepared to earn income by producing goods that locally degrade the environment and by accepting to live with hazardous waste, they should be allowed to do so, if that is what they want to do. However, environmental standards in poor countries are determined by the government, not the people. The governments generally offer little transparency and accountability to their people – and the governments (or the people controlling governments) may not care about the welfare of their people. There is an ethical case, therefore, for not accepting national sovereignty in decisions of nondemocratic governments to profit from importing hazardous waste.

Economic development and environmental awareness

If incomes in a country reach sufficiently high levels among the broad population, the newly emerged middle class becomes sensitive to the quality of the environment and seeks improvements in environmental quality from government. At the same time, the emerging middle class seeks a more transparent and accountable government. Economic development is therefore the path to solving problems of environmental externalities in poor countries, whether the externalities affect only the people in the country itself or the global environment. However, the rich governing elites in poor countries have an interest in resisting economic development, which would compromise their hold on political power and their personal profits from government, through the demands of greater transparency and accountability of the emerging middle class.

Are markets or governments to blame for environmental externalities?

Protests at times take place against free international trade or, equivalently, against globalization of markets. The protests are directed against the World Bank (which, we recall, funded the implementation in poorer countries of the Montreal Protocol to protect the ozone layer), the International Monetary Fund, and the World Trade Organization.[46] Environmental externalities persist in countries in which governments do not adopt public policies to internalize externalities through any of the possible corrective methods. Protests therefore should take place in the national capital in front of the presidential palace in countries where the national government does not protect the environment – or does not protect animals as required for sustained biodiversity.

[46] The International Monetary Fund (IMF) is an international agency that, like the World Bank, has a financial and advisory role in assisting governments. Like the World Bank, the IMF is located in Washington, DC. The World Bank focuses its assistance on poorer countries, whereas the IMF has a broader mandate. The World Trade Organization (WTO) has its headquarters in Geneva; the objectives of the WTO are to promote free international trade and to avoid discriminatory practices in international trade.

5.3 Paternalistic Public Policies

We now move from public policies based on the presence of externalities to paternalistic public policies. Public policies directed at resolving negative externalities are based on harm that people do *to others* through environmental degradation or in other ways. Paternalistic public policies are intended to prevent people from *harming themselves* – or not benefiting themselves. Paternalistic public policies contradict the basic premise of economic analysis that people are the best judges of their own welfare. Paternalistic policies are uncontroversial for children; there is general agreement that children should not participate in labor markets (that is, that child labor should be illegal) and should not be permitted to buy alcoholic beverages. However, paternalistic public policies for adults are controversial because of the claim that people should be permitted to do whatever they wish to themselves as long as they harm no one else – and that consenting adults should be allowed to do between themselves whatever they wish, provided that no one else is involved or affected. Nonetheless, societies generally choose to have paternalistic public policies.[47]

A. Cases of paternalism and hyperbolic discounting

In some cases, paternalistic public policies impose requirements of compulsory spending; in other cases, voluntary purchases are restricted. We now consider the various instances of paternalistic policies for which societies override personal preferences. We shall then consider a justification for paternalistic policies known as hyperbolic discounting.

Compulsory spending

Paternalism can involve compulsory spending. Governments impose taxes to finance compulsory spending on schooling and, in some countries, on health insurance or income for the elderly. Health insurance and pension schemes can also be compulsory personal purchases. Compulsory health insurance and compulsory savings for old age are also intended to prevent people from taking advantage of the goodwill of others by not providing for themselves and relying on others to pay if they need medical attention or become destitute. In that case, actions affect others and, in addition to paternalism, there are externalities present. Other examples of compulsory spending involve personal safety: seat belts in cars are legally required, as are often protective helmets when riding motorcycles, bicycles, or horses.

[47] The public policies are called *paternalistic*, based on the Latin word *pater*, meaning *father*. The term derives from domination understood to imply male domination.

Compulsory safety equipment

Government safety regulations can require protective clothing and eye or ear protection in various occupations. In such cases, the justification for a paternalistic public policy is that people cannot judge or do not know objective probabilities of being harmed; they may judge the future on the basis of past personal experience so that if nothing bad ever happened to them, nothing bad is ever expected to happen. Otherwise, with full information about probabilities and consequences, we would expect voluntary spending on personal safety; workers would spend their own money on safety equipment appropriate for their occupations.

Public policies might oblige employers to provide the safety equipment for employees. The effect, for employers, is then equivalent to a tax on employment equal to the value of the safety equipment. The legal incidence of the tax is on employers, who are legally required to pay for the safety equipment. As we know from our study of taxation, the effective incidence of the tax (that is, who actually pays the tax) depends on supply and demand elasticities in the labor market. If elasticity of the supply of labor is low and demand elasticity is high, the tax on employers is "shifted" to employees. The employees are then paternalistically being made to pay for their own safety equipment. Because the payment is not voluntary, there is an excess burden: we saw in chapter 4 that sharing of the excess burden of taxation also depends on supply and demand elasticities. If the cost of safety equipment that is legally imposed on employers is shifted to employees, there is an efficiency benefit if the employees were voluntarily to purchase the safety equipment: there would then be no excess burden of taxation.

Homeownership

Paternalistic public policies may encourage people to own their own homes. Perhaps homeownership is regarded as a basic right that governments should facilitate. Perhaps, also, there are perceived positive externalities when people own their own homes; homeownership may provide a personal sense of commitment that makes living in the neighborhood where most people own their houses more pleasant than in a neighborhood where most people rent. Governments can encourage homeownership by allowing tax deductions for payment on interest on home mortgages or by levying taxes on properties owned beyond personal housing (which discourages rental housing). Government agencies may be directly involved in providing or guaranteeing mortgages for homeownership. Or private firms, with the backing of implicit government assurances, may "buy" mortgages from the lending banks that are the point of contact with home buyers: in this case, governments support homeownership by underwriting the risk of default on mortgage repayments. The firms buying the mortgages from the banks that made the initial home loans are spreading risk through a large portfolio of mortgages. (See Box 5.4.)

Box 5.4 Housing markets and risk

When demand for houses is sufficient to keep housing prices increasing, there are incentives to borrow and to lend by providing mortgages because both the borrower and the lender expect that a house will be worth more in the future. People with low incomes can borrow expecting that if they cannot meet the obligations of their housing repayments, they will at least be able to sell their house at a profit. However, if housing prices begin to fall, the opposite incentives are set in place. People are discouraged from buying (they benefit from waiting for lower prices). People who have bought can find that the money owing on their mortgages exceeds the value of their house. They may then default on their repayments. After default, banks and mortgage companies own the houses, which they wish to sell, thus depressing housing prices further. With housing prices falling, banks do not wish to lend because they are aware that the falling prices will result in defaults on mortgage repayments. Government encouragement of homeownership can therefore create a housing boom by stimulating demand over time; but, if interest rates increase and borrowers are unable to continue their mortgage repayments, conditions can be created that result in a decline in demand for homeownership. Paternalistic encouragement of homeownership, particularly by people without the means of repayment when interest rates increase, can have extremely adverse economic consequences. The consequences affect the economy at large, and even the world, if the entire housing market – rather than specific regional markets in a country – is affected. Risk-spreading of mortgage and financial companies that was predicated on having a portfolio of mortgages from different regional housing markets will then be to no avail because the risk is systemic or involves the entire economic system and cannot be spread.

Undesirable markets

These cases involve paternalistic public policies that compel or encourage private purchases. In other instances, there are willing buyers and sellers who wish to engage in voluntary transactions but the markets that would allow the transactions to take place are disallowed; or, the markets are allowed to exist but consumption and supply are discouraged through taxes.

Addictions

The legality of markets in tobacco products persists despite incontrovertible evidence linking cigarette smoking to cancer, heart disease, and other health problems. Markets in tobacco products would be illegal if tobacco were a newly introduced product required to satisfy contemporary health-safety standards. A reason for persistence of markets in tobacco products is the political infeasibility of abolishing those markets when large numbers of voters smoke. Because nicotine is an addictive drug, purchases of tobacco are not entirely voluntary; there are substitutes for tobacco but demand is nonetheless quite inelastic. We noted in chapter 4 that taxation of addictive consumption provides governments with a secure tax base; new smokers, however, might be deterred by high taxes.[48]

Harmful drugs other than nicotine in tobacco result in addiction and debilitate and often eventually kill – for example, heroin. Markets in those drugs are illegal (but, in general, exist).

Alcohol can become an addiction and, in excess, also eventually kills, principally through cirrhosis of the liver. Gambling can become an addiction: prohibitions on gambling attempt to prevent people from impoverishing themselves and their dependents. Again, externalities and paternalism can coexist. The externality from addiction to drugs and gambling is that drug addicts may finance their habit through crime. Alcoholics, drug addicts, and addicted gamblers can also impose costs on society (including an excess burden of taxation) through the need to provide income for their destitute dependents.

Sale of alcohol is in some locations a government monopoly. The case for monopoly is the deterrence effect of high monopoly prices of consumption of alcohol. As the owner of the monopoly, the government obtains monopoly profits from sales to buyers who may be addicted. Sales taxes and taxation of profits of private sellers would likewise provide the government with revenue: Why then the need for a government monopoly? Monopoly by government provides bureaucratic rents because the monopoly seller of alcohol is a government agency; political appointments can also be made within the government agency.

Transplants and blood

There are cases in which markets are illegal but free supply is permitted or even encouraged. Markets for the supply of body organs to people awaiting transplants are generally illegal, whereas voluntary donation is legal and viewed as meritorious. Markets in blood similarly can be illegal whereas voluntary donation is regarded as meritorious. Markets would have undesirable consequences if unscrupulous people were to take organs and blood against people's will.

People who voluntarily donate blood do so out of intrinsically motivated altruism; they derive personal satisfaction from their behavior in helping others. When blood is a marketable commodity, the intrinsic motivation for supplying blood diminishes and can altogether disappear. People who supply blood for money may be using the market as a last resort for earning income and may impair their own health by selling too much of their blood. If low income is correlated with bad health, the people selling blood are providing blood that is more likely to be contaminated by disease than blood that is voluntarily supplied. Therefore, more

[48] Tobacco companies have been required to pay compensation to victims. In some cases, governments have sued tobacco companies for health-care costs incurred in treating victims. There have been counterclaims that governments save money when smokers do not survive to retirement age because social security or pensions then do not have to be paid. Smokers, however, can leave dependents who require public spending for income support.

blood may be available when markets in blood are illegal and the blood will be of higher quality.

Commercial sex

Sex is another case in which markets may be illegal, whereas subject to age restrictions voluntary activity is allowed. The case against markets in commercial sex is similar to the case against markets in blood. Supply can be a means of last resort for earning income and suppliers can harm themselves. The personal exploitation that is feared when there is a market for body organs or blood is present in markets for commercial sex: women can lose their freedom and become objects to be traded and transported against their will.

In general, people do not want their children to choose to earn income from commercial sex. Stigma is, therefore, also a reason for illegality of markets in sex. Even if enforcement is imperfect, through stigma, illegality of commercial sex limits choice of career options. Potential earnings for many people in the market for commercial sex are multiples of those available in alternative income-earning activities; stigma through illegality counterweighs the high incomes.[49]

Markets in babies for adoption

Markets in babies for adoption are illegal even though there are willing buyers and sellers. Markets are replaced by government mediation in adoption procedures. When babies are marketable commodities, having babies for supply to the adoption market can be a professional income-earning activity; however, whereas some people genuinely wish to adopt and provide children with good homes, other people may not have benevolent intentions. The absence of a market prevents unscrupulous people from buying babies and using the children as personal slaves and for nefarious purposes. When there is no legal market for babies, the incentive to steal babies is reduced.

Slavery and markets in people

Slavery and markets in people, of course, are illegal in contemporary Western societies; although slavery does exist in some other societies. There is a

[49] Why are earnings in the market for commercial sex so high? Lena Edlund and Evelyn Korn (2002) proposed that the high earnings reflect the opportunity cost of women forgoing marriage. They view marriage as procreational sex for which men are prepared to pay through resource transfers to the women who commit to exclusive sex within marriage to ensure paternity of children. Women as suppliers in the market for commercial recreational sex are compensated for the benefits that they would have received, had they chosen marital procreational commitment to one man. Women's marriage opportunities, however, are limited if men do not have the option of marriage because men cannot support a family. As incomes increase, more men choose marriage, reducing supply and increasing price in the market for commercial sex. For women whose opportunities for lasting commitment from men are limited, commercial sex, however, provides income: evidence provided by Kathryn Edin and Laura Lein (1997) showed that commercial sex has been the main supplemental income-earning activity of U.S. welfare mothers (supplemental because the government provides income).

fundamental and sufficient case against slavery based on the natural right to freedom. The absence of a market in people also reduces the incentive to kidnap or steal people.[50]

Cases of personal excess

There are cases in which markets are, in general, beneficial but some people harm themselves through personal excesses. Because people behave in different ways, the scope for paternalistic public policy in such cases is limited; self-harm is specific to the behavior of people who engage in personal excesses, but public policies cannot effectively target such people because policies cannot be selectively personalized.

Overeating and obesity

Everyone needs to eat but some people overeat. Overeating and consequent obesity make people more prone to disease and shorten life. The cause of weight gain is the imbalance between input of calories through food intake and calories expended. As societies have become richer, obesity has become more prevalent; however, obesity disproportionately affects low-income people. There is evidence that obesity reduces income, particularly for women, because of discrimination in employment and lower incomes of their spouse if they are married. The question for paternalistic public policy is: How can government control the quantity of a person's food intake and the amount of calorie-expending activity? Foods that are particularly conducive to weight gain could be highly taxed. However, some people simply want to eat such foods occasionally. Also, some people can eat considerable quantities of food and – because of their metabolism – not gain excessive weight.

Watching television

There is evidence that excessive television watching, particularly by children, reduces cognitive ability. It does not seem politically feasible to ban television, to regulate hours or set time quotas, or impose taxes on excessive television watching.

Exposure to the sun

Excessive exposure to the sun by people who do not have appropriate pigmentation can result in skin cancer. A government cannot regulate time spent exposed

[50] Institutions determine responses to destitution and debt. Biblical laws, for example, required debtors to sell themselves as slaves for the limited period of time required to be able to repay the debts. After the period for which they had sold themselves had passed, they were obliged to return to freedom. If they had become accustomed to the life of a slave and refused to accept freedom (perhaps because of personal attachments that had been formed while a slave), they were subjected to humiliation in order to increase the incentive to accept freedom. Slavery was, in these circumstances, a form of borrowing against future income. The debt may have been restitution that was due or a fine that had been imposed.

to the sun. Laws requiring the wearing of hats and protective covering when venturing out into the summer sun might be controversial because of possible disagreement over a person's susceptibility due to pigmentation, as well as disputes over the danger caused by the weather on a particular day.[51]

Alcohol

Alcohol can be consumed reasonably. In the case of alcohol, there are disadvantageous externalities to excessive consumption – particularly driving under the influence of alcohol, rowdy behavior, and molesting other people because of diminished inhibitions due to being intoxicated. Means are available to measure how much alcohol has been consumed and legal limitations can therefore be set on permissible alcohol intake when driving or when present in public places. However, there are no limitations on personal private consumption of alcohol; hence, people are free to kill themselves or become debilitated. Evidence also links alcohol consumption to teenage pregnancy.

Teenage pregnancy

Teenage pregnancy disrupts education and generally leaves the young mother without emotional and financial support from the father. If feasible, paternalistic public policies would set a lower limit on the age at which having a child is legally permissible. Societies often set lower limits on the age at which sex is permissible and make sex by an adult with a minor a crime (statutory rape).

Sexually transmitted disease

Sexually transmitted disease, including AIDS, is a case of externalities. Sexually transmitted disease is also, of course, a case of self-harm due to personal behavior.

Hyperbolic discounting

Paternalistic polices are intended to prevent people from making decisions that in the future they will regret. The regret introduces psychological aspects. People may feel anger at themselves today because of their actions yesterday. A person then distinguishes between different selves or personal identities in the present and the past.

Regret may be based on inadequate past information and the remorseful, "If only I had known, I would have acted otherwise." However, people often are well aware of future personal costs and nonetheless still choose to incur the future cost for a present benefit. They know that they will regret their decision tomorrow. Cigarette smokers benefit today knowing that their life may be cut short in the future. People may regret having become addicted to drugs or being

[51] Exposure to the sun is a source of vitamin D. Never being exposed to the sun can therefore result in another adverse effect on health.

HIV-positive. People may regret being pregnant (or causing other people to become pregnant). They may regret overeating. They may regret overexposure to the sun. They may regret not having studied, paid for health insurance, or saved for old age.

In these instances, information about future consequences of actions is available. If people were asked whether they will regret in the future the consequences of their present actions, their truthful answer would be yes. Yet, they go ahead and enjoy present benefits at the expense of predictable future personal costs. People thus confront *problems of self-control.*

Time horizons

Problems of self-control are associated with short time horizons; people place zero weight on the quality of life beyond a particular date. The short time horizon might be measured in months, days, hours – or, when decisions are impulsive, even minutes. Time horizons are affected by drugs and alcohol. However, without the influence of drugs and alcohol, people can still choose to live their life today as if there were no tomorrow – and regret their past decisions when tomorrow arrives.

Rational behavior and a constant discount rate

Different people can use different personal discount rates to compare personal benefits and costs over time. Whatever the discount rates that people choose:

> *Rational behavior requires that an individual use a constant rate of discount to compare personal costs and benefits over time.*

A decision that future costs do not justify a present benefit should be identical, when the valuation of benefits and costs is made today looking forward into the future or tomorrow looking back to today. This is assured by a constant discount rate. For example, with i an individual's personal discount rate, a decision to take a particular action may provide a personal benefit B_0 today and result in future costs $\{C_1, C_2, \ldots, C_N\}$ over N periods of time. The discounted benefit may be negative:

$$W = B_0 - \frac{C_1}{(1+i)} - \frac{C_2}{(1+i)^2} - \cdots - \frac{C_N}{(1+i)^N} < 0. \tag{5.16}$$

The discounted benefit is negative no matter the point in time at which the individual evaluates the consequences of taking the action that yields the benefit and the costs. The present benefit may be, for example, from smoking a cigarette and the future costs may be adverse health consequences.

Hyperbolic discounters

Hyperbolic discounters do not use a constant discount rate to evaluate benefits and costs over time. Rather, the discount rate changes over time. The change in the discount rate has two attributes: (1) for hyperbolic discounters, the change

For hyperbolic discounters, the discount rate for evaluating benefits and costs over time has the shape of a hyperbola, beginning from each point in time that is defined as the present.

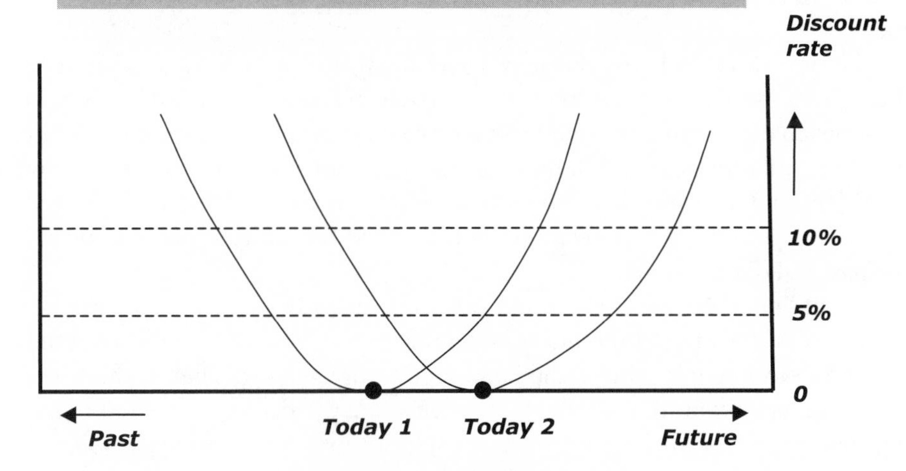

Figure 5.14. Hyperbolic discounting.

in the discount rate follows the shape of the hyperbolas in figure 5.14; and (2) as time moves, for example, from today 1 to today 2 in figure 5.14, the hyperbola moves with time.

In figure 5.14, today 1 and today 2 are two alternative present times. The discount rate increases hyperbolically away from each "today," where "today" is the point in time at which a decision is made. As figure 5.14 shows, "today" changes, with tomorrow becoming "today" when tomorrow arrives.

A benefit or cost on any "today" is assigned a zero discount rate. That is, on each day, the day's benefits and costs are valued fully. Benefits and costs in the future are discounted, at an increasing rate of discount as time moves away from the day on which benefits and costs are valued.

> *For hyperbolic discounters, the discount rate increases the farther away a benefit or cost is from the day on which a decision is made.*

A short time horizon is a special case of hyperbolic discounting. With a time horizon of one day, the rate of discount is zero for benefits and costs on the day a decision is made and is infinite looking into the future so that future benefits and costs have zero values.

People with the ability and opportunity to study may choose instead to enjoy the immediate benefit of earning income in an unskilled job while relaxing or enjoying themselves in the evenings with like-minded people (or with people who do not have their opportunities). In the meantime, other people are studying. The people not studying and having a good time may be disparaging about people who are studying.

A person having a good time when others are studying and who is a hyperbolic discounter fully enjoys present benefits and discounts future costs at an increasing rate. Every day, hyperbolic discounting provides the same perspective on the future – as in figure 5.14, where the hyperbola moves with time from today 1 and today 2.

The time distance between today 1 and today 2 may be a number of years. At today 1, the decision was made not to study because the immediate benefits outweighed the future discounted costs of not studying. Some years in the future, when today 2 arrives, the studious people have completed their studies and have good jobs and high incomes and can afford a quality of life that is beyond the reach of a person who chose to enjoy life to the full at each point in time in the past and did not study.

The utility of the person who did not study may depend on his or her personal income relative to the incomes of others. The person who did not study may now envy people who studied and regret not studying. That is, the hyperbolic discounter who did not study fully feels today 2's costs, expressed in having low relative income compared to people who studied. The hyperbolic discounter discounts past benefits at discount rates that increase the farther back in time that the past benefits occurred. The increasing high discount rates on past benefits make the benefits worth very little when viewed in retrospect from today 2. The low past discounted benefits (because of the increasingly high discount rates) do not justify the cost incurred at today 2 of having relatively low income; at time today 2, the hyperbolic discounter wishes that he or she had chosen to study at time today 1. The hyperbolic discounter thus now regrets the past decision not to study. He or she has feelings of regret because of feelings of envy.[52]

Hyperbolic discounters choose immediate gratification and in the future regret past decisions.

The decision whether to study is one example of behavior explained by hyperbolic discounting. There are many other examples – including smoking, drugs, excessive drinking, unprotected sex (and unprotected impulsive sex), overeating, and gambling. Evidence also reveals behavior described by hyperbolic discounting whereby people buy appliances or cars that have low prices but result in known high costs of use in the future. Behavior of buyers described by hyperbolic discounting can be exploited by sellers, who offer payment over time but no or low repayments until some time in the future. Homebuyers may be offered low interest rates in the initial years after purchase, with higher interest rates beginning in the future.

[52] High progressive income taxes will make the hyperbolic discounter feel better by reducing income disparities. We shall return to consider the structure of income taxation and reasons for progressive income taxes.

Procrastination

A form of behavior associated with hyperbolic discounting is procrastination, which occurs when costs are immediate and benefits are in the future. The decision or activity that is costly is deferred to the future: the cost is lower in the future than in the present because of the hyperbolic discount rates. At a constant rate of discount (or with rational behavior), today 1 in figure 5.14 may be the personally optimal time to begin preparing for an exam. However, the cost of studying is high at today 1 because the cost is not discounted, whereas the farther into the future the cost can be pushed, the lower is the cost from the perspective of today 1. Because hyperbolic discounting discounts or reduces the present value of the costs more the farther in the future that the costs can be pushed, a hyperbolic discounter procrastinates in preparing for the exam. The exam takes place at today 2. At today 2, the hyperbolic discounter feels the full cost of deferred preparing for the exam but discounts highly the past benefits. The person regrets his or her past procrastinating behavior. If the decision has been about when to start a diet, procrastination makes people put on more weight. Whatever the decision is about, hyperbolic discounters can procrastinate indefinitely. Every day they may declare that they will begin to study or to diet or to change their behavior in various beneficial ways tomorrow. When it is too late and further procrastination is impossible (the day of the exam has arrived), procrastinating hyperbolic discounters feel regret – and may blame their past selves for the past decisions that have resulted in their predicament.

> *Hyperbolic discounters procrastinate by choosing immediate gratification through deferral of costs into the future and regret past decisions when costs can no longer be shifted into the future.*

Obesity and the microwave oven

Trends of increasing obesity have been attributed to hyperbolic discounters having access to a microwave oven. A hyperbolic discounter who compares costs of food preparation before eating with future benefits when the food is ready may decide that incurring the cost of spending an hour preparing a meal does not justify the future benefits, which are highly discounted compared to low discount rate applied to costs of food preparation. Because the microwave oven reduces the time taken to prepare food to be eaten, the perceived discounted benefits from having the food available increase; the benefits are moved closer to the time at which the decision whether to prepare food for eating is made. The prediction is that if people are hyperbolic discounters, the microwave oven will make them fat or obese. They will come to regret the convenience of having a microwave oven.

Experiments

In experiments involving hyperbolic discounting, people are offered alternative sums of money at different times in the future. For example, they are given the choice between receiving $1,000 in 12 months and $1,100 in 13 months. The return for waiting an additional month is therefore 10 percent *for the month*. This return exceeds a reasonable personal discount rate. In general, people accept the 10 percent return for waiting the additional month by choosing the alternative of receiving $1,100 in 13 months. However, after they have made the decision, people are informed that they have the option to change their decision in the future to receive the $1,000 that will be available in 12 months. Hyperbolic discounters choose $1,100 in 13 months when the initial decision is made; when the day arrives 12 months in the future at which they can receive the $1,000, they change their prior decision to wait and take the money. They thereby forgo the 10 percent return available by waiting another month. Viewed from a year back, hyperbolic discounters compared the benefit from waiting a month to the cost of waiting and concluded that the 10 percent return for waiting an additional month was worthwhile. However, viewed from the day when the $1,000 is available, hyperbolic discounters choose immediate gratification. The dependence of the decision on the time at which the decision is made indicates that their discount rate is not constant. In making the switch to the more immediately available benefit, hyperbolic discounters are confirming that the value they place on benefits is higher the closer they are in time to realization of the benefits. The behavior in experiments, therefore, confirms the phenomenon of hyperbolic discounting. A general inference is that:

> *Hyperbolic discounters generally do not do well in life.*

Can hyperbolic discounting be rational behavior?

Uncertainty about future benefits and costs can increase when the benefits and costs are farther in the future; people might, therefore, rationally discount the uncertain future benefits and costs by adding a risk premium. A person may think, "I might die anyway from various causes so I might as well smoke and drink and take drugs, and overeat, and not invest in education." Such people may have information about their progenitors' genes. Or perhaps they cannot judge objective probabilities. Through self-determined realizations of predictions, they may belong to populations for which, objectively, life is short.

Hyperbolic discounting and public policy

The public-policy question regarding hyperbolic discounting is:

> *Should governments use paternalistic public policies to change behavior of hyperbolic discounters?*

Different people may give different answers to this question. There is an evident limitation on assigning to governments the responsibility to attempt to use public policy to correct for hyperbolic discounting: when a government has been given the legal right to compel personal self-control, personal freedom is subjugated to interpretation of desirable personal behavior by political representatives who decide on laws and officials in government bureaucracies who implement the laws. All personal freedom could be lost; moreover, people cannot, for example, be compelled to study. A government would, most basically, be subject to asymmetric information: the discount rate that people use for making intertemporal decisions is private information, as is whether the personal discount rate is constant as required for rational decisions over time, or whether people are hyperbolic discounters.

The paternalistic view justifying public policy is that, where feasible, people should be spared the future anger at themselves that they will feel because of their past behavior of immediate gratification or procrastination.

Will people be pleased that public policies have spared them from making personal decisions based on hyperbolic discounting? Paternalistic public policies are intended to prevent people from doing what they want to do; if prevented, people may never know the adverse outcomes of what they intended to do. Therefore, they may never be grateful for paternalistic public policies.

The libertarian view is that paternalistic public policies are an infringement on personal freedom and that people should be permitted to make their own decisions – and thereby their own mistakes – and should therefore be allowed to be angry at themselves if that is the consequence of their past actions. The libertarian view also recognizes the problem of specifying bounds on government interference in private lives. However, the libertarian view can also be a case of expressive behavior. The expressive behavior in this case is of people who, in principle, object to interference of government in personal lives; however, the same people might regret absence of paternalistic policies when hyperbolic discounting had led to unfortunate decisions by members of their family and by others for whom they personally care.[53]

Private resolution of problems of self-control

Problems of self-control due to hyperbolic discounting are often addressed through private resolution. Behavioral constraints that people impose on themselves suggest awareness of the problems of hyperbolic discounting and self-control. People choose to save in accounts that require payment of a penalty if money is withdrawn before a specified time. People also choose to pre-pay taxes although they could opt to pay when the taxes are due; by committing to pre-pay taxes, people forgo interest that could be earned until payment of taxes is required. When asked why they pre-pay taxes in installments, people reply that

[53] The libertarian view is expressed in a theory of "rational addiction," proposed by Kevin Murphy and Gary Becker (1988) of the University of Chicago. They described people as behaving rationally in being fully aware that consumption today of an addictive substance will cause addiction tomorrow. In their vision of how people behave, when people choose lifetime consumption, they perfectly internalize future addiction in present decisions and are not surprised in the future when they find themselves addicted to alcohol, drugs, or gambling. Their theory of rational addiction, therefore, views people as perfectly rational and aware of the future consequences of their present behavior.

they cannot trust themselves to not spend the money that they will need to pay their taxes. When people regard themselves as different selves over time, they face the problem that they need to be able to trust their different selves to cooperate. Cooperation entails a present self not spending the money that will be required by a future self to pay taxes that are due for the tax year. When people do not trust themselves, they prefer that each particular self on each payday pay the taxes that the self owes out of the paycheck that the self at the time receives.

Payday lending and hyperbolic discounting

The problems among people's different selves are expressed in a phenomenon known as "payday lending," whereby hyperbolic discounters take money from their future selves. There is "payday lending" because loans are repaid on payday; rather than waiting for their wages to be paid, hyperbolic discounters take short-term loans weeks or days before payday. In the United States, implicit interest rates of 15 percent have been reported as usual for a loan of two weeks.[54] The high interest rates that people are prepared to pay reflect the personal discount rates of hyperbolic discounting; people want immediate gratification and therefore are unwilling to wait until payday for their money. The behavior is precisely that of the experiments in which choices are made between alternative amounts of money available in the future.[55]

Paternalism and usury

A prohibition dating to biblical times disallows "usury" or the payment of interest on loans. The presumption underlying the biblical prohibition was that borrowers were poor people who required loans for consumption. The loans in the biblical context were thus a form of charity. It was regarded as unethical to take interest from people in need. If interest was charged, some people could become professional lenders benefiting from the misfortune of those who have fallen on hard times.[56]

In Western society, controversy regarding usury persisted to the time of Adam Smith, who took the perhaps uncharacteristic position of defending usury laws that set limits on market interest rates. The free-market position in a debate with Adam Smith was taken by Jeremy Bentham (1748–1832). Bentham (1787) declared that he could not comprehend why people who favored free markets nonetheless objected to market-determined interest rates. Adam Smith, as a professor of moral philosophy, was influenced by the moral aspects of the case

[54] The interest rate is 15 percent for the two weeks.

[55] The high interest rate is paid because the borrowers do not have alternative sources of credit and risk for the lender is high. Lenders face the risk that borrowers will take multiple loans from different lenders based on the one upcoming wage payment. The risk is reduced by the wish of borrowers to preserve reputation, to enable continued borrowing in the future.

[56] The loans on which interest was prohibited were thus not for productive investments. A "business dispensation" permitted interest in business transactions. Interest could be received from or paid to foreigners because business transactions of trade were involved and not charity.

against usury. Smith perceived a problem of hyperbolic discounting (he did not use the terminology): he viewed poor people as willing to pay high future interest for immediate gratification. Bentham's reply was that poor people should be permitted the same freedom as rich people to make personal decisions. He proposed that higher interest rates paid by the poor were due to the higher risks of lending to the poor and also the greater benefit of the poor from borrowing. Bentham declared that paternalistic public policy was not required because "nothing short of absolute idiotism can cause the individual to make a more groundless judgment than the legislator." Jeremy Bentham, therefore, took the position that freedom of personal choice should be assured, for everybody. Adam Smith judged paternalistic public policy to be justified because of hyperbolic discounting and problems of self-control.[57]

Illegal markets

Illegal markets invariably arise when public policies prohibit markets and there are willing buyers and sellers. If legal payday loans were not permitted, loans would be given illegally and the rule of law would not protect borrowers who default. Illegal markets exist for babies for adoption, narcotics, prostitution, gambling, and almost anything else that is illegal and for which people are willing to pay. Prices in illegal markets are higher than in legal markets because supply is limited by inhibitions due to stigma and because of penalties on suppliers. Supply is then by people who have no inhibitions about engaging in illegal activity and who are not deterred by the prospect of imprisonment. With the rule of law absent, relationships in illegal markets are as in Nietzschean anarchy, with the strong prevailing over the weak. Supplying drugs, for example, can be violently contested and innocent bystanders can be harmed. Because restricted illegal supply increases prices, drug users can be drawn into theft and robbery to find the means to sustain their habit.

People who have become wealthy through illegal markets can become role models who set the standards for aspirations of young people. The immediacy of large rewards relative to the delayed rewards from studying attracts young people into illegal supply and is another case of hyperbolic discounting.

Illegal markets pose dilemmas.

> *Markets that governments are attempting unsuccessfully to suppress continue to exist illegally and impose social costs that can be higher than the social benefits of allowing legal markets.*

[57] Jeremy Bentham, who was younger than Adam Smith, acknowledged Smith as his mentor. In a series of letters, Bentham sought to change Smith's mind on the issue of usury. Smith, however, remained steadfast. Smith sent Bentham a copy of the last revision of *The Wealth of Nations* (1789) in which the position against market-determined interest rates was maintained. For a summary of the debate between Jeremy Bentham and Adam Smith, see Joseph Persky (2007), who noted the declaration by Bentham.

If markets for drugs were legal, prices would be lower and there would be less theft and prostitution to finance drug habits. With lower prices due to legal supply, however, more people would experiment with and take drugs.

The dilemma of illegal markets is illustrated by experiences with prohibition of alcohol. Significant demand persisted in the illegal markets and the criminalization of supply introduced criminals into supply. Wherever it was introduced, the prohibition on alcohol was eventually rescinded.[58]

B. The limits of intuition: framing and bounded rationality

People often make decisions intuitively rather than closely evaluating available choices. Even if they try, they may not make rational or consistent decisions because information may not be presented in a way that accords with their intuition. A case in which people commonly make inconsistent choices is known as the *Allais paradox*.[59]

Table 5.4 shows two pairs of lotteries, {1 and 2} and {1A and 2A}. People are asked to choose between lotteries 1 and 2. Then they are asked to choose between lotteries 1A and 2A. The possible prizes in the lotteries, as indicated in table 5.4, are the low, intermediate, and high values $y_L = 0$, $y_M = 50$, and $y_H = 100$, respectively.

TABLE 5.4. CHOICE IN TWO SETS OF LOTTERIES

Lotteries		Probability of low income $y_L = 0$	Probability of medium income $y_M = 50$	Probability of high income $y_H = 100$
1	$Ey = 5.5$	0.89	0.11	0
2	$Ey = 10$	0.90	0	0.10
1A	$Ey = 50$	0	1.00	0
2A	$Ey = 54.5$	0.01	0.89	0.10

[58] Prohibition of alcohol persisted in the United States between 1920 and 1933 (the latter year saw the beginning of the Great Depression). Alcohol was also prohibited around the same time in other countries, particularly in cold climates (Finland 1919–32, Iceland 1915–22, Norway 1916–27, and Russia [subsequently the Soviet Union], 1914–25; Prince Edward Island in Canada prohibited alcohol between 1900 and 1948). In cold climates, alcohol increases the risk of death from hypothermia (freezing to death). Alcohol gives a feeling of warmth but actually increases body-heat loss. Alcohol was prohibited in the designated capital city of Australia, Canberra, in the Australian Federal Territory, between 1910 and 1928. Canberra was a new capital city built as a compromise and situated between the large cities of Sydney and Melbourne. When parliament and the accompanying politicians eventually moved to the new capital, the prohibition on alcohol was rescinded.

[59] The Allais paradox is named for Maurice Allais, whose paper was published in 1953 and who received the Nobel Prize in economics in 1988.

Lottery 2 provides higher expected income than lottery 1 (10 as compared to 5.5). Lottery 2A provides higher expected income than lottery 1A (54.5 as compared to 50). Because there is no cost of entry into choice of lotteries and no loss is possible, people opt to participate in choosing the lotteries.[60]

The lotteries are related. Lottery 1 is transformed into lottery 1A by shifting the probability of 0.89 from the zero prize to the prize of 50. The same shift in probability from the zero-income outcome to the medium-income outcome transforms lottery 2 into lottery 2A. However, the transformations of the lotteries may not be immediately evident to people. Experiments reveal that people do not perceive the transformations. If they did, they would realize that they are being asked to make two choices that are identical and they would consistently choose either lotteries 1 and 1 A or lotteries 2 and 2A.

> *In experiments, people usually choose lottery 2 in preference to lottery 1 and they choose lottery 1A in preference to lottery 2A.*[61]

This is the behavior known as the Allais paradox. There is a paradox because:

> *The choices offered are between equivalent lotteries and so generally observed behavior is inconsistent – yet consistently so among different people.*

Why are the choices between lotteries equivalent?

Let us consider the Allais paradox in more detail. Figure 5.15 is another way of showing the lotteries in table 5.4. The numbers at the end of the nodes are the values of the prizes. The numbers along the lines are the probabilities associated with having the prizes.

Lottery 1 can be viewed as follows. At node 1, lottery 1 gives a prize of zero with 0.89 probability and a further prize, which is itself a lottery, with 0.11 probability. The latter lottery is described at node 2: the second lottery consists of a prize of 50 with a probability of 1 (that is, with certainty) and zero chance of 100. At node 2, the probability is 1 of having medium income 50; therefore, the probability in lottery 1 of having 50 is 0.11, as indicated in table 5.4.

Lottery 2 can also be expressed as giving a prize of zero with 0.89 probability at node 1 and giving another lottery as the prize at node 2. The lottery at node 2 for lottery 2 gives prizes of (0, 50, 100) with respective probabilities of (1/11, 0/11, 10/11). At node 2, the probability of having zero income is 1/11 of 0.11, which is 0.01 and, which when added to 0.89 at node 1, gives 0.90 as in table 5.4 for the probability of having zero income. At node 2, the probability of having the

[60] Lottery 1A offers 50 with certainty and is therefore not strictly speaking a lottery. We can regard lottery 1A as a lottery with zero probabilities of all prizes except one.

[61] In choosing lottery 2 in preference to lottery 1, people are apparently focusing on the 10 percent chance of having high income of 100. In choosing lottery 1A in preference to lottery 2A, they appear to be influenced by the certainty of having 50 from lottery 2A.

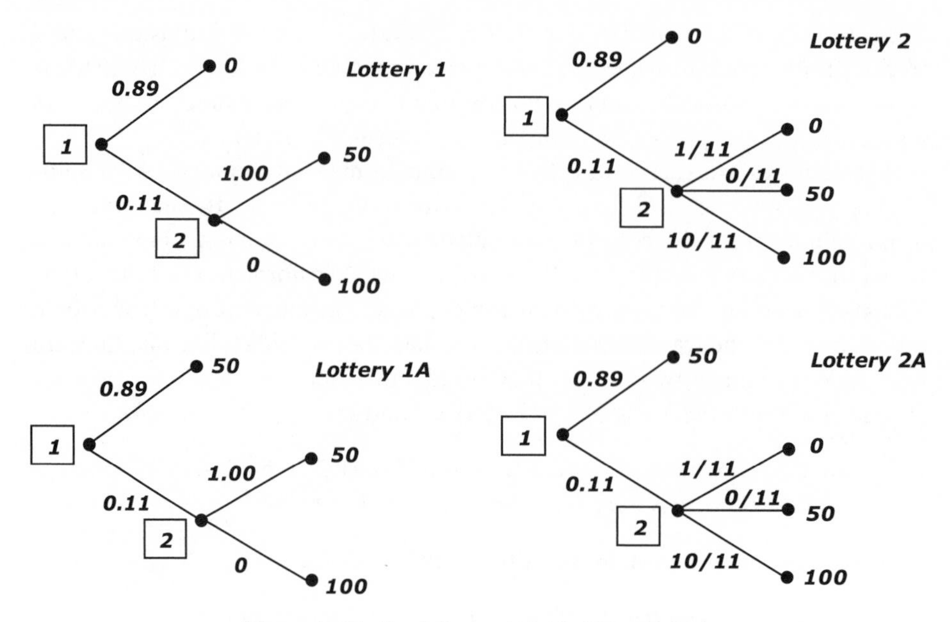

Figure 5.15. The lotteries in table 5.4 restated.

high income of 100 is 10/11. The probability of having the high income of 100 is therefore 0.11 – that is, the probability of reaching node 2 multiplied by 10/11, which is 0.10, as indicated for lottery 2 in table 5.4.

Evaluating the joint probabilities at the nodes similarly establishes that the probabilities for the compound lotteries 1A and 2A in figure 5.15 correspond to the probabilities in table 5.4.

Rational choices require people to compute these probabilities. Presenting the lotteries in the form of figure 5.15 makes clear that lotteries 1 and 2 have in common the 0.89 probability of a prize of zero at node 1, which indicates that:

> *The choice between lotteries 1 and 2 is effectively made at node 2 for each lottery.*

People who choose lottery 2 in preference to lottery 1 forgo the prize of 50 available with certainty at node 2 of lottery 1 for the further lottery at node 2 of lottery 2. The expected value of the lottery at node 2 of lottery 2 can be shown to be 95.45. People need to be very risk-averse to prefer 50 with certainty at node 2 of lottery 1 to the lottery at node 2 of lottery 2 that has an expected value of 95.45. Indeed, people generally choose lottery 2 as preferable to lottery 1.

When faced with the choice between lotteries 1A and 2A, people generally choose the certainty of 50 offered by lottery 1A. In figure 5.15, lotteries 1A and 2A have been re-expressed to show the common prize of 50 obtainable in each case with a probability of 0.89 at node 1. The choice between lotteries 1A and 2A is once more a choice at node 2 of each lottery. At node 2 of lottery 1A, the prize of 50 is offered with certainty. At node 2 of lottery 2A, a further lottery is offered that is precisely the lottery offered at node 2 of lottery 2.

The choices at node 2 are thus exactly the same whether the choice is between lotteries {1 and 2} or between lotteries {1A and 2A}. The choice between the pairs of lotteries should not be affected by the common probabilities in each pair at node 1; the relevant information for choosing between lotteries is at node 2 at which the choice between lotteries {1 and 2} and between lotteries {1A and 2A} is the same. Yet, people tend to choose differently in the two cases – which is the Allais paradox.[62]

What is happening in the actual behavior described as the Allais paradox? People are evidently not making the calculations that reveal that identical lotteries. Perhaps they do not know how to make the calculations. Perhaps they do not want to take the time; rather, they rely on intuition.

Framing effects

The pairs of lotteries look different in table 5.4. In looking different, the choice between lotteries is subject to a "framing" effect. That is, people are influenced by how the alternatives presented to them are framed.[63]

When the lotteries have been transformed as in figure 5.15 and the equivalence has been explained, people become aware that the lotteries are equivalent.

The Allais paradox is a subtle case of framing. The transformation from table 5.4 to figure 5.15 is not immediately evident and requires thought. Framing arises in more straightforward cases, where we would expect people to make consistent decisions, particularly people with advanced professional qualifications.

In one example, two groups of forensic psychologists and psychiatrists were given the same information about the likelihood that a psychiatric patient would harm someone within six months of being discharged. However, the information was framed in different ways. One group was told that "One out of ten patients who behave like this person is expected to be violent." A second group was told that "There is a 10 percent chance of this person being violent." The psychologists and psychiatrists were asked to assess the risk of someone being harmed by a released patient as high, medium, or low. The group that was given the information in percentage terms assigned a lower evaluation of risk than the first group, even though 10 percent is equivalent to 1 out of 10. A probability of 10 percent

[62] Formally, in behaving according to the Allais paradox, people are violating an axiom of rational choice called the *independence of irrelevant alternatives*.

[63] When facing the choice between lottery 1A and lottery 2A, people look at 50 as the certain alternative and avoid the perceived small risk of having nothing. Also, people often disregard the zero payoff altogether in figure 5.15. The probabilities of receiving the zero payoff look similar and they focus on the two positive returns of 50 and 100.

was regarded as an abstract concept, whereas the information that 1 in 10 people will do harm evoked images of actual outcomes to be avoided.[64]

Bounded rationality

Bounded rationality is the inability to absorb and utilize all information.[65] The Allais paradox demonstrates bounded rationality. An example of bounded rationality in a simpler context arises when financial advisors advertise that their firm has provided the highest return on investment in the last year. When financial advisors choose an investment portfolio, one advisor will necessarily be able to claim the highest return because of random outcomes. A financial advisor who consistently provides the highest returns over time in all likelihood will be arrested for obtaining information that enables insider trading, or will be eventually arrested for having used new investors' money to pay returns to prior investors.[66]

Public policy with framing and bounded rationality

What is the responsibility of government when people make mistakes because of framing and bounded rationality? In complex cases that correspond to the Allais paradox, the responsibility of government is to provide information that enables consistent rational choices to be made. However, a government cannot ensure that people will make the effort to understand information that it provides. In some cases, the information is provided in evident ways – as in the case of a health warning on a cigarette pack or a sign on a beach indicating dangerous swimming or surfing conditions – yet, people may ignore the information when making their decisions. According to the libertarian view, governments should – or can do – no more than provide information.

C. Community values and locational choice

The markets that a society prohibits are an expression of community values. In some communities, it is illegal to be seen drinking an alcoholic beverage in the streets; in other places, gambling is legal for visitors but not for local residents. Means of contraception have been illegal in some places. Just as locational choice through the Tiebout mechanism allows choice of public goods according to personal preferences for public goods, locational choice also allows people to choose locations where community values are consistent with their own personal values. With people sorting themselves by location into groups with similar preferences,

[64] The experiment was reported by Paul Slovic, John Monahan, and Donald G. Macgregor (2000).

[65] The term *bounded rationality* is associated with Herbert A. Simon (1916–2001), who received the Nobel Prize in economics in 1978. In another example, people may not understand the conditions and risks associated with variable rate mortgages on homes that they purchase.

[66] Such deception is known as a Ponzi scheme, after Charles Ponzi, who ran such a scheme in 1919–20 in Boston.

paternalistic public policies in a government jurisdiction do not restrain personal behavior in a community but rather reflect consensual community values chosen when people choose where to live.

Moral relativism

When different groups of people make different decisions about community values and norms of behavior, we confront the question whether we are – or should be – moral relativists.

> *Moral relativism is the position that precepts and customs of all societies should be judged relative to the standards of each society and that every society's standards have equal merit.*

It follows from the moral relativist position that people in one society or community should not judge the values and customs of other communities. A moral relativist therefore has a position similar to a libertarian who believes that people should be allowed to do whatever they want, provided others are not affected; a moral relativist believes that all societies likewise should be permitted to choose their own values and customs.

The contrary position to moral relativism views ethical principles as absolute and as applying in all circumstances at all times. People who take the position that ethical values are absolute are prepared to make judgments about customs and behavior in societies beyond their own.

> *Where are the limits of paternalism in judging benefits or harm in other societies?*

For moral relativists, paternalism ends at a society's borders, with foreign societies judged relative to the foreign society's own ethical standards.[67]

An example of the differences between moral relativism and absolute ethical standards is in willingness to criticize treatment of women; in some places, women are the property of men, have no personal rights to choose mates, and are reared for childbearing and work after sale to husbands. In the markets for women that exist in some of those locations, young girls have value only if they have had their sexual organs mutilated; the intention of the mutilation is that, after they have been sold as wives, the girls – and later as women – will be rendered incapable of sexual pleasure and so will not have reason to become involved with other men when, for example, the husbands have purchased and are preoccupied with new wives.[68]

[67] If moral relativists are also libertarians, they wish to see no paternalism in any community.

[68] Barbara Crossette observed regarding the sexual mutilation of young girls (2000, p. 184): "The practice has long served men by rendering the women they marry uninterested in sex or unappealing or inaccessible to any other man – a safe, albeit damaged, piece of property. Next comes the rationalization/belief that no girl or woman will be marriageable unless she has submitted to this process."

Moral relativists view behavior in foreign societies as reflecting the values of foreign culture that they are obliged to accept without making judgments based on the values of their own societies; that is, for moral relativists, political correctness based on respect for cultural diversity requires that foreign behavior be judged according to the norms of the foreign society. In contrast, people who judge according to absolute ethical standards reject the political correctness of moral relativism; they would, therefore, reject the need promulgated by moral relativists to be silent in face of foreign behavior that they regard as unjust or cruel and barbaric. Their paternalism would thus extend beyond the bounds of their own societies by their taking the position that cruel and unjust behavior is cruel and unjust everywhere.

D. Interdependent utilities and censorship

The resolution of externalities described by the Coase theorem allows legal rights, in principle, to be with anyone. Paternalistic policies, in contrast, express ethical societal presumptions about legal rights and permissible exchange. For example, pedophiles and drug dealers cannot have legal rights to their activities and societies do not need to compensate pedophiles and drug dealers for desisting from their activities. Thus:

> *Externalities allow, in principle, different assignments of legal rights. Paternalistic policies pre-specify legal rights.*
>
> *Externalities are resolved by creating markets. Paternalistic policies prohibit particular markets.*

There are similarities between externalities and paternalism because in both cases, there are *interdependent utilities.*

> *Externalities arise because the actions of others affect peoples' utilities; paternalism arises because people's utilities are affected by what others do to themselves – or, as the case of the treatment of girls and women in the foreign culture illustrated, by what other people do to others.*

We can consider an example of interdependent utilities associated with a mother and daughter's views on the reading of a book. The mother has heard that the book describes behavior to which she wishes her young (and, she believes, impressionable) daughter not be exposed. The mother's ranking of preferences regarding reading the book is:

(1) *No one reads the book.*
(2) ***The mother herself reads the book.***
(3) ***The daughter reads the book.***
(4) *The mother and the daughter both read the book.*

The mother regards reading the book as intrinsically undesirable. She is, however, prepared to incur the personal disutility of reading the book if the choice is between herself and her daughter reading the book. She prefers to have the book banned so that no one reads the book. The mother would have the same preferences, for example, about her young daughter smoking or experimenting with drugs. The mother's objective is to be maternalistic, to protect her daughter.

The daughter has different views than the mother. She regards the reading of the book favorably for both herself and her mother. She believes that she herself will enjoy reading the book but also that her mother will benefit from expanded horizons and new awareness from reading the book. The daughter's ranking of preferences is:

(1) *The mother and the daughter both read the book.*
(2) ***The mother herself reads the book.***
(3) ***The daughter reads the book.***
(4) *No one reads the book.*

For different reasons based on interdependent preferences, the mother and the daughter both prefer the mother reading the book to the daughter reading the book (as shown by the bold alternatives in both the mother's and daughter's rankings). We also see that:

The mother reading the book rather than the daughter is the consensus and Pareto-efficient outcome.

That is, both the mother and the daughter are better off (the outcome is Pareto-superior) if the mother rather than the daughter reads the book.

Yet:

With free choice, the daughter reads the book and the mother does not.

We now have a case for the imposed choice because:

Free choice can conflict with Pareto efficiency.

In the case of the reading of the book, Pareto efficiency is inconsistent with free choice. Pareto efficiency requires a public-policy decision that directs the mother to read the book.

The example of the decision about who reads the book was used by Amartya Sen (1970) to describe what he called "the impossibility of a Paretian liberal."[69] Sen did not refer to a mother and daughter but rather distinguished the two people as one being "prudish" and the other not.

The book that Sen used in his example was *Lady Chatterley's Lover* by the English writer, D. H. Lawrence (1885–1930). In the book, Lady Chatterley is an aristocrat whose husband is incapacitated. She has a relationship with the working-class gamekeeper. The book used explicit language that was not socially

[69] Amartya Sen received the Nobel Prize in economics in 1998.

acceptable at the time of its writing in 1928. As a consequence, the book was banned and could only initially be published privately in Italy. Publication of the book in the United States required a 1959 ruling of the Supreme Court based on the guarantee of free speech in the first amendment to the U.S. Constitution. Publication of the book in the United Kingdom in 1960 required the publishers to first win in an obscenity trial. The book subsequently became legally available elsewhere as standards of permissible written expression changed.

The paternalistic outcome is that the mother simply bans the book as inappropriate reading for the daughter and presumably other people's daughters as well. Censorship persisted in the first 30 years or so after Lawrence wrote the book. That is, there was neither a Pareto-efficient outcome in which the mother reads the book nor an outcome based on free choice in which the daughter reads the book; rather, there was an imposed outcome in which no one read the book.

At first, societies took the position of the mother; the book was defined as pornographic and disallowed for everybody (which is the mother's first preference). When the daughter's generation eventually had the legal right to decide, the book could be read by anyone who so wished (although the daughter would have wished to force reading of the book on her mother). Movies were made and the book became available online. By the 21st century, the contents of the book, by most community standards, were mild compared to other available material to which parents felt that their children should not be exposed.

Paternalism and eugenics

In England in 1877, Charles Bradlaugh and Annie Besant were tried for having published and circulated a pamphlet informing people about birth control. The government had declared the pamphlet to be obscene, and the authors were duly charged and appeared in court.[70]

The trial placed the ideas of the political economist, John Stuart Mill (who had died four years before the trial but whose writings were used as authoritative), against the position of the evolutionary theorist, Charles Darwin. John Stuart Mill had favored dissemination of information about contraception to allow people to control and plan births. Charles Darwin supported the government's case for censorship.

The trial took place at a time when *eugenics*, under the influence of the theory of natural selection, was an incipient science. The objective of the science of eugenics was to breed genetically perfect human beings.[71]

Formally, the trial was about obscenity; more basically, the issues concerned eugenics. The claim, supported by Charles Darwin, who was asked to be a witness

[70] The defendants had republished a 40-year-old text. For details of the trial, see Sandra Peart and David Levy (2008).

[71] The term *eugenics* was chosen by Sir Francis Galton. Galton proposed that the government should give prizes to couples from higher social classes who married. On Galton and eugenics, and the unscientific methods, see David Levy and Sandra Peart (2004).

at the trial, was that information about birth control would lead people to pursue recreational sex, thereby distracting people from having children. Wealthy people were regarded as genetically superior to poorer people. The distractions from breeding, it was feared by Darwin, would be disproportionately among the superior wealthier classes in society, who would use the information about birth control to not breed, whereas the lower classes, who were regarded as inferior and so should not breed, would continue to have high numbers of children. Natural selection, applied to humans, was thus used as the basis for the racist pseudoscience of eugenics.[72]

Charles Darwin was co-developer of the principle of natural selection. Alfred Russel Wallace (1823–1913) had independently arrived at the principle of natural selection. Wallace took a different view of the positive or predictive consequence of the relationship between natural selection and eugenics. He disagreed with Darwin on whether natural selection affected humans. Wallace pointed out that natural selection applied to animals because weak or unfit animals did not survive. He declared that sick or injured humans benefit from sympathy from other people and therefore, unlike unfit animals, survive. However, the prediction of who survived differed from the normative proposition of who should be allowed to survive, and with whose survival the society would be best off, which was the basis for Charles Darwin's involvement in the trial.

The jury found the defendants, Charles Bradlaugh and Annie Besant, guilty of obscenity – but the verdict was subsequently reversed on appeal. The defendants had sold their pamphlet for 6 pence. The same information had previously been available for 246 pence, which only wealthy people at the time could afford to pay. We might regard the jury's paternalistic thinking as puzzling, given the prominence of information in the debate. When only wealthy people could afford access to the information about birth control, it was the "genetically superior" wealthy classes who would know how to restrict their number of children. Unless the 6-pence pamphlet was available, the "genetically inferior" lower classes would continue breeding. Charles Darwin should have opposed censorship of the inexpensive pamphlet; he should have supported not only legal publication of the inexpensive pamphlet but also government subsidization and dissemination. Apparently, Darwin believed that the inferior lower classes would not bother to read the inexpensive pamphlet but that the wide dissemination of the pamphlet at 6 pence would increase information about birth control among the "genetically superior" wealthier classes.

Institutions mattered. The lower classes had no property and could have children without the problem of division of inheritance. The wealthier classes would be more influenced by information on birth control because they were conscious

[72] The consequences of eugenics continued into the 20th century. The ideology of the South African apartheid government viewed blacks as inferior to whites. Racism in the Americas was based on the same principle of the racial superiority of whites. The German government between 1933 and 1945 used eugenics to claim a perfect race could be bred and to justify mass murder of other peoples whom they claimed were genetically inferior.

of issues of inheritance of estates by their sons and were concerned with finding good matches in marriage for their daughters.

Darwin himself had 10 children, perhaps believing his own theories. Not all survived childhood.

Supplement S5

Supplement S5A: Externalities and non-convexities

Externalities have been associated with a "fundamental non-convexity" that can prevent the existence of an equilibrium market price. Because the equilibrium price does not exist, the price cannot be duplicated through public policy.

In figure S5A.1, the supply function is discontinuous, consisting of the segment OA, with a jump between points A and B, and then BC. The demand and supply functions do not intersect and there is, therefore, no equilibrium price. In such a case, even with full information about market supply and demand, a government cannot set a corrective tax or subsidy to duplicate the equilibrium price that internalizes an externality.

To show the circumstances underlying figure S5A.1, we consider again a factory that disrupts Robinson Crusoe's fishing by polluting a stream. In figure S5A.2, the vertical axis indicates the number of fish Crusoe catches and the horizontal axis indicates the output of the factory, which corresponds to the extent of environmental damage to the stream. The maximum number of fish that Crusoe can catch is Y_m when the factory does not produce and therefore does not pollute. As the factory begins to produce, Crusoe's catch of fish declines along the production-possibility frontier and falls to zero when the output (and corresponding environmental damage) of the factory is X_1. After Crusoe's fishing has

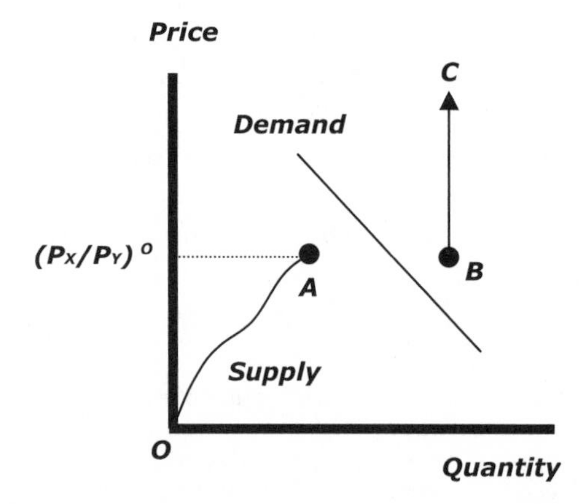

Figure S5A.1. A market with no equilibrium price.

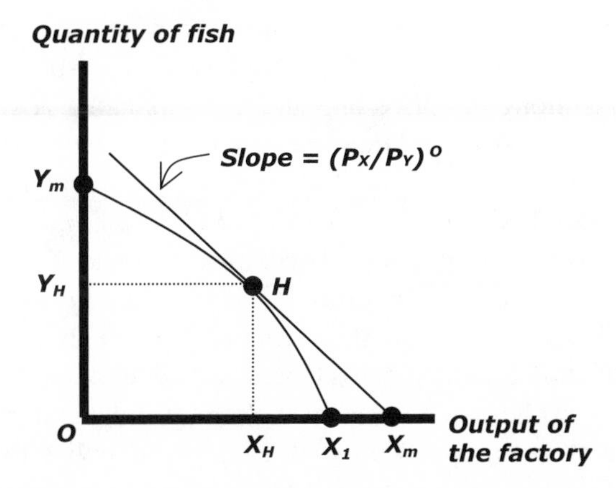

Figure S5A.2. The fundamental non-convexity due to externalities.

been reduced to zero, however, the factory can continue producing (and polluting). The maximum production and pollution of the factory is X_m. Therefore, the production-possibility frontier between fishing and output of the factory begins at Y_1 and ends at X_m. The production-possibility frontier is $Y_m X_1 X_m$ and so is non-convex.

We now introduce a "missing market" for the right to pollute and give legal rights in this market to Crusoe, who can sell units of the right to pollute to the factory. When he sells a unit of the right to pollute, Crusoe incurs a loss due to the adverse effect on his fishing. The opportunity cost of environmental damage, in terms of fish forgone, is measured by the slope of $Y_m X_1$.

Crusoe, however, can sell the right to pollute beyond X_1. He can continue selling the right to pollute after environmental damage has destroyed all his fishing prospects by selling a further $(X_m - X_1)$ units of the right to pollute. Without the right to pollute supplied by Crusoe, the factory cannot produce more output, even if Crusoe is no longer fishing.

Between points Y_m and H, Crusoe makes profit-maximizing decisions in response to the relative price between the right to pollute and output of fish.[73] At point H, the relative price of the right to pollute in terms of fish lost is $(P_X/P_Y)^o$. We see the same price in figure S5A.1 at the supply discontinuity.

In figure S5A.2, once Crusoe has reached point H, where he supplies X_H units of the right to pollute, his profit-maximizing response is not to continue to supply the right to pollute along the frontier $X_m X_1$ beyond point H but rather to jump to X^m. That is, after point H, Crusoe ceases fishing and only supplies rights to pollute. Crusoe's supply response is thus discontinuous between points H and X^m.

[73] The slope of the frontier $Y_m X_1$ is the relative supply price of the right to pollute.

Crusoe ignores points on the segment of the frontier HX_1 and jumps to X_m because points along HX_1 are Pareto-inferior (and correspondingly less profitable) than points along the price line HX_m. Points along HX_m lie outside of the feasible frontier $Y_m X_1 X_m$ and therefore are not feasible – with the exception of endpoints H and X_m. Hence, the discontinuous jump in supply between X_H and X^m in figure S5A.1 is at the relative price $(P_X/P_Y)^o$.

Crusoe incurs no loss in jumping between points H and X_m. All points along the line HX_m are of equal value in terms of fish and the right to pollute.

Replicating missing markets can thus be more complex than we might have at first thought. With cost-benefit analysis having provided the information on valuations necessary to replicate a missing market, the "fundamental non-convexity" in the theory of externalities can prevent using public policy to replicate equilibrium prices. However, there is no evidence of the circumstances that we have described having been observed.

Summary

This chapter has been concerned with responsibilities of governments to undertake market corrections due to externalities and paternalism. Section 1 described attributes of externalities and considered resolution of externalities through private action. The role of government was only to ensure the rule of law and thereby allow legal rights to be defined.

1A. Competitive markets fail to provide efficient outcomes when externalities are present; because of the externalities, private market decisions do not internalize all benefits or costs. Externality problems are most clearly demonstrated in one-to-one relationships; otherwise, with costs imposed on or benefits provided to many people simultaneously, externalities coexist with public goods. When externalities are present, there is no intent to impose costs or provide benefit. Inframarginal externalities provide benefits or impose costs but outcomes are efficient and no corrections for the existence of externalities are required. We distinguished externalities from instances where people affect one another but externalities are not present. We emphasized the role of asymmetric information in the "missing markets" that underlie externalities.

1B. Externality problems can be resolved through private ownership. The tragedy of the commons describes mutual disadvantageous externalities that are resolved through private property rights. The privatization required for efficiency can introduce the contestability of rent seeking and associated rent dissipation. There are effects on income distribution when the commons are privatized. We considered historical examples of conversion of the commons to private ownership. The case of the bees and the orchard demonstrated mutual beneficial externalities that could be internalized through private ownership; however, we observed that mergers of private productive activities are as well subject to other incentives and do not necessarily indicate gains through internalization of positive externalities. We noted that contractual alternatives to private ownership and considerations that determine whether contractual solutions are preferred to common ownership.

1C. The Coase theorem predicts efficient private resolution of externalities between people if legal private rights have been defined. The theorem states that the outcome of efficient private resolution of externalities is independent of who has legal rights; income effects qualify this prediction. Also, assignment of legal rights may matter because of incentives associated with liability rules. The predictions of the Coase theorem may not be realized for a number of reasons: transactions and bargaining costs limit applicability of the Coase theorem; regulation can prevent Coase bargaining; people may be unwilling to participate in the markets that are necessary for Coase payments to be made; when externalities coexist with public goods, costs of organizing collective action can prevent the efficient outcome predicted by the Coase theorem. As with public goods, location affects externalities: externalities are capitalized into market valuations. NIMBYs prefer, rationally, that sites with negative externalities be placed elsewhere, away from them. Just as individuals may refuse to consider accepting payment, communities may refuse to contemplate receiving compensation for location of hazardous and other sites near their neighborhoods. Distributional consequences are introduced (and, therefore, aspects of social justice) through the higher likelihood that lower income people seeking cheap housing will tend to be most disadvantaged by externalities.

1D. Externalities can be internalized through personal behavior. Consideration for others and self-esteem and social approval lead people voluntarily to internalize externalities. Social norms determine whether people impose – or are permitted to impose without resistance – adverse externalities on one another. We considered externalities through crime and encountered a controversy about the right of citizens to use weapons in personal self-defense.

Section 2 introduced public policy as means of resolution of externality problems.

2A. The impediments to realization of the predictions of the Coase theorem provide the grounds for assigning responsibility to governments, which then must be presumed to have used cost-benefit analysis to have information that allows efficient replication of missing markets. We considered the right to declare an externality that governments should resolve through public policy. We noted that when externalities affect public health, public-policy decisions can involve a conflict between personal rights and the public interest. The cases of Typhoid Mary and AIDS indicated different public-policy responses.

2B. The means of public policy available to governments are Pigovian taxes or subsidies, direct regulation, and quotas that set limits on permissible activities or emissions. As with the Coase theorem, Pigovian tax-subsidy solutions depend on legal rights that determine whether a tax or subsidy should be used; in sequencing, private Coase resolution should precede public policy; contrary to the private resolution of the Coase theorem, revenue from a Pigovian tax is not paid to victims of negative externalities nor are subsidies personally financed by the victims; feasibility and considerations of social justice affect choice of Pigovian tax-subsidy solutions. Regulation avoids the need for taxes or subsidies by directly specifying permissible behavior; this regulation resolves a prisoners' dilemma when externalities are reciprocal; regulation can also prevent efficient Coase outcomes. Use of quotas requires an accompanying decision about how emissions rights are distributed; a competitive market in quota rights replicates the efficient Pigovian tax solution; auctioning quota rights provides maximum government revenue but can create monopoly; because of second-best considerations, environmentalists might support monopoly. After a quota has been determined, emissions rights can also be distributed without payment to existing producers.

2C. Our next step was to investigate political decisions about choice of the means of resolution of externality problems. It is politically expedient to give free quota rights to existing producers. We looked at examples in the United States and the European Union of the creation of markets in emissions rights; both cases revealed political accommodation to producer interests. We observed more generally that governments have not always chosen environmental policies in the public interest; rather, governments in democracies have often had to be persuaded to adopt pro-environmental policies. We saw how the political principal–agent problem can result in choice of environmental policies as a political compromise. We noted evidence that the environment has been least protected in nondemocratic countries.

2D. The environment and biodiversity are cases of global externalities. There are rare instances of contributions to resolution of global environmental problems by private activity. However, generally, resolution of global environmental problems requires agreements among governments. Successful agreement was reached regarding the ozone layer. Climate change due to global warming has been described as the most significant externality that humanity has experienced; there are contrary interpretations of the extent of the human contribution to the problem. Global externality problems are difficult to resolve because of a prisoners' dilemma in which governments have incentives to attempt to shift the burden of reduction in emissions onto populations in other countries. As predicted by the Coase theorem, income effects aside, efficient usage of quota rights by producers in different countries does not depend on allocation of quotas across countries but the assignment of rights to a quota affects global income distribution. Governments in high- and low-income countries have different preferences about the rule for assigning a global emissions quota; those of high-income countries prefer assignment of a quota based on contemporary emissions, whereas those of low-income countries prefer assignment according to population. A precondition for achieving an efficient global cooperative solution is that national emissions quotas provide incentives for governments of individual countries to participate in the international agreement. Global quotas are preferred to taxes because technical information on limits to total emissions can be readily encompassed in a quota; also, taxes provide government revenue but quotas allow political discretion in determining private benefit from emissions rights. Environmentalists and domestic producers can have common cause in protectionist international trade policies; the example of the dolphins showed how such coalitions can arise. Global environmental problems are compounded by different sensitivities of governments and populations in richer and poorer countries to the quality of the environment. A country's institutions determine political sensitivities to exposure of local populations to pollution. Global markets are sometimes blamed for global externality problems due to the clearing of rain forests and destruction of animal habitats; however, the source of the externality problems is not existence of global markets, which allow gains from international trade; rather, the externalities are present if foreign governments and rulers do not perceive a need to adopt policies to protect the environment and their people in their own country.

The topic of section 3 was paternalistic public policies.

3A. Paternalistic policies take different forms. The policies can specify compulsory behavior. In various other cases, paternalistic policies are based on undesirable markets. We also noted cases of personal excess. A description of self-harming behavior is provided by hyperbolic discounting, which results in immediate gratification or procrastination. A special case of hyperbolic discounting is a short time horizon. Behavior consistent with hyperbolic discounting is confirmed in experiments. Hyperbolic discounting can reflect uncertainty concerning future costs and benefits. However, in general, hyperbolic discounting appears to involve irrational behavior in which people view themselves as different "selves" at different times. We considered whether hyperbolic discounting justified paternalistic public policies. People attempt to resolve problems of self-control through personal commitment even though financial losses are incurred, as in the case of prepayment of taxes. The phenomenon of "payday lending" confirms behavior described by hyperbolic discounting. We considered the biblical prohibition against usury and noted the differing positions taken on usury by Jeremy Bentham and Adam Smith. Social dilemmas arise when illegality of markets does not prevent the continued existence of the markets.

3B. The Allais paradox demonstrates the limits of intuition and shows how inconsistent decisions may be made because of framing and bounded rationality.

3C. Paternalistic public policies can be the consequence of locally chosen community norms. The norms are local public goods that people can choose, or choose to avoid, by locational choice. Different behavior in different locations introduces the normative question of whether we should be moral relativists and not judge norms and customs in other societies. The answer determines whether the scope of paternalistic concerns is expanded to what people do to others rather than being concerned only with what they do to themselves.

3D. The case of the mother's and the daughter's preferences about who should read a book showed how free choice can conflict with Pareto efficiency and illustrated issues of censorship. The 19th-century trial of Charles Bradlaugh and Annie Besant, in which Charles Darwin participated, provided an example of censorship being sought.

Supplement S5A showed externalities in general equilibrium.

- When cost-benefit analysis has provided all required information, because of non-convexities that are inherently associated with externalities, there can be an impediment to using public policy to duplicate prices in missing markets. However, no empirical evidence of the existence of the non-convexity appears to have been found.

Literature Notes

5.1 Externalities and private resolution

On the nature of externalities, see:

Scitovsky, T., 1955. Two concepts of external economies. *Journal of Political Economy* 17:143–51. Reprinted in K. J. Arrow and T. Scitovsky (Eds.), 1969. *Readings in Welfare Economics*. Richard D. Irwin, Homewood IL, pp. 242–55.

On externalities for which no corrections are required, see:

Buchanan, J. M., and C. Stubblebine, 1962. Externality. *Economica* 29:371–84.

On the tragedy of the commons, see:

Cornes, R., and T. Sandler, 1985. On commons and tragedies. *American Economic Review* 73:787–92.

de Meza, D., and J. R. Gould, 1987. Free access versus private property in a resource: Income distribution compared. *Journal of Political Economy* 100:1317–25.

For a view of externalities and rent seeking, see:

Buchanan, J. M., 1980. Rent seeking under external diseconomies. In J. M. Buchanan, R. D. Tollison, and G. Tullock (Eds.), *Toward a Theory of the Rent-Seeking Society*. Texas A&M Press, College Station, pp. 183–95.

On the reciprocal producer externalities described by Meade (1952), see also Cheung (1973).

Cheung, S. N. S., 1973. The fable of the bees: An economic investigation. *Journal of Law and Economics* 16:11–35.

Meade, J. E., 1952. External economies and diseconomies in a competitive situation. *Economic Journal* 62:54–67. Reprinted in K. J. Arrow and T. Scitovsky (Eds.), 1969. *Readings in Welfare Economics*. Richard D. Irwin, Homewood IL, pp. 185–98.

On the externality of reduced crime because of attendance at school, see:

Donohue, J. J., III, and P. Siegelman, 1998. Allocating resources among prisons and social programs in the battle against crime. *Journal of Legal Studies* 27:1–45.

Becker (1971) described discrimination as a response to an externality.

Becker, G., 1971. *The Economics of Discrimination*. University of Chicago Press, Chicago IL.

On externalities and guns, see:

Lott, J. R., 1998. *More Guns, Less Crime: Understanding Crime and Gun-Control Laws.* University of Chicago Press, Chicago, IL.

Health externalities were described by Avery, Heymann, and Zeckhauser (1995) and Geoffard and Philipson (1997). On AIDS, see Philipson and Posner (1993). On Typhoid Mary, see Leavitt (1995).

Avery, C., S. J. Heymann, and R. Zeckhauser, 1995. Risks to selves, risks to others. *American Economic Review, Papers and Proceedings* 85:61–6.

Geoffard, P.-Y., and T. Philipson, 1997. Disease eradication: Private versus public vaccination. *American Economic Review* 87:222–330.

Leavitt, J. W., 1995. Typhoid Mary strikes back: Bacteriological theory and practice in early 20th-century public health. *Isis* 86:617–18.
Philipson, T., and R. Posner, 1995. *Private Choices and Public Health: The AIDS Epidemic in an Economic Perspective.* Harvard University Press, Cambridge MA.

On the externalities due to the eventual need to dispose of waste from nuclear power stations, see:

Young, W., 1998. *Atomic Energy Costing.* Kluwer Academic Publishers, Boston and Dordrecht.

The Coase theorem is from:

Coase, R. C., 1960. The problem of social cost. *Journal of Law and Economics* 3:1–45.

On location and externalities, see Kunruether and Easterling (1990); Gerrard (1994); and Frey, Oberholzer-Gee, and Eichenberger (1996). On measurement of externalities through market capitalization, see Smith and Huang (1995).

Frey, B. S., F. Oberholzer-Gee, and R. Eichenberger, 1996. The old lady visits your backyard: A tale of morals and markets. *Journal of Political Economy* 104:1297–315.
Gerrard, M. B., 1994. *Whose Backyard, Whose Risk: Fear and Fairness in Toxic and Nuclear Waste Siting.* MIT Press, Cambridge MA.
Kunruether, H., and D. Easterling, 1990. Are risk-benefit trade-offs possible in siting hazardous facilities? *American Economic Review* 80:252–6.
Smith, V. K., and J.-C. Huang, 1995. Can markets value air quality? A meta-analysis of hedonic property value models. *Journal of Political Economy* 103:296–315.

5.2 Public policies and externalities

Tax-subsidy policies were proposed by Pigou (1920).

Pigou, A. C., 1962 (4th edition). *The Economics of Welfare.* Macmillan, London (1st edition, 1920).

For a general-equilibrium study of the effects of environmental taxes on incomes, see:

Fullerton, D., and G. Heutel, 2007. The general equilibrium incidence of environmental taxes. *Journal of Public Economics* 91:571–91.

Buchanan and Tullock (1975) pointed out the political preference for assigning quotas to incumbent producers.

Buchanan, J. M., and G. Tullock, 1975. Polluters' profits and political response: Direct controls versus taxes. *American Economic Review* 65:139–47.

On the U.S. market in emissions rights for SO_2, see Ellerman et al. (2000). On the European trading rights scheme for CO_2 emissions, see Ellerman et al. (2007).

Ellerman, A. D., P. L. Joskow, R. Schmalensee, J.-P. Montero, and E. M. Bailey, 2000. *Markets for Clean Air: The U.S. Acid Rain Program.* Cambridge University Press, New York.
Ellerman, A. D., B. K. Buchner, and C. Carraro (Eds.), 2007. *Allocation in the European Emissions Trading Scheme: Rights, Rents, and Fairness.* Cambridge University Press, Cambridge U.K.

Requate (1998) considered how taxes and tradeable permits influence incentives to innovate.

Requate, T., 1998. Incentives to innovate under emission taxes and tradeable permits. *European Journal of Political Economy* 14:139–65.

On international cartels and the environment, see:

Rauscher, M., 1990. Can cartelization solve the problem of tropical deforestation? *Weltwirtschaftliches Archiv* 126:378–87.

Peltzman (1976) described public policies chosen to maximize political support. The description of politically determined environmental policy is based on Hillman (1982). On the political economy of environmental policy, see also Aidt (1998) and Dijkstra (1999).

Aidt, T. S., 1998. Political internalization of economic externalities and environmental policy. *Journal of Public Economics* 69:1–16.
Dijkstra, B. R., 1999. *The Political Economy of Environmental Policy*. Edward Elgar, Cheltenham, U.K.
Hillman, A. L., 1982. Declining industries and political-support protectionist motives. *American Economic Review* 72:1180–7. Reprinted in W. J. Ethier and A. L. Hillman (Eds.), 2008. *The WTO and the Political Economy of Trade Policy*. Edward Elgar, Cheltenham U.K., pp. 43–50.
Peltzman, S., 1976. Toward a more general theory of regulation. *Journal of Law and Economics* 19:241–4.

Common interests of environmentalists and producers were described by Hillman and Ursprung (1992). On protection of the dolphins, see Körber (1998).

Hillman, A. L., and H. W. Ursprung. 1992. The influence of environmental concerns on the political determination of trade policy. In K. Anderson and R. Blackhurst (Eds.), *The Greening of World Trade Issues*. University of Michigan Press, Ann Arbor, pp. 195–220 .
Körber, A., 1998. Why everybody loves Flipper: The political economy of the U.S. dolphin-safe laws. *European Journal of Political Economy* 14:475–509.

On the Montreal Protocol, see:

Murdoch, J. C., and T. Sandler, 1997. The voluntary provision of a pure public good: The case of reduced CFC emissions and the Montreal Protocol. *Journal of Public Economics* 63:331–49.

On global warming and climate change, see:

Schelling, T. C., 1992. Some economics of global warming. *American Economic Review* 82:1–15.
Stern, N., 2007. *The Economics of Climate Change: The Stern Review*. Cambridge University Press, Cambridge U.K.
Stern, N., 2008. The economics of climate change. *American Economic Review* 98:1–37.

For the contrarian view on the scientific evidence, see:

Lomberg, B., 2001. *The Skeptical Environmentalist: Measuring the Real State of the World*. Cambridge University Press, Cambridge U.K.

On global environmental externalities and policy, see Petrakis and Xepapadeas (1996); Schultze and Ursprung (2001); and Marsiliani, Rauscher, and Withagen (2002).

Marsiliani, L., M. Rauscher, and C. Withagen (Eds.), 2002. *Environmental Policy and the International Economy*. Kluwer Academic Publishers, Boston and Dordrecht.

Petrakis, E., and A. Xepapadeas, 1996. Environmental consciousness and moral hazard in international agreements to protect the environment. *Journal of Public Economics* 60:95–110.
Schultze, G., and H. W. Ursprung (Eds.), 2001. *Globalization and the Environment.* Oxford University Press, Oxford.

On international trade in waste, see:

Cassing, J. H., and T. Kuhn, 2003. Trade in trash: Optimal environmental policy in the presence of international trade in waste. *Review of International Economics* 11:496–511.

On the personal self-interest of rulers in autocratic low-income countries, see Easterly (2001) and the summary in Hillman (2002). Congleton (1992) presented evidence on authoritarian regimes and the environment.

Congleton, R. D., 1992. Political institutions and pollution control. *Review of Economics and Statistics* 74:412–21.
Easterly, W., 2001. *The Elusive Quest for Growth: Economists' Adventures and Misadventures in the Tropics.* MIT Press, Cambridge MA.
Hillman, A. L., 2002. The World Bank and the persistence of poverty in poor countries. *European Journal of Political Economy* 18:783–97.

5.3 Paternalistic public policies

Musgrave (1959) and a subsequent literature, including Pazner (1972), Hillman (1978), and Besley (1988), discussed paternalistic public policy using the terminology of "merit wants." On goods or services that markets cannot or should not value, see Arrow (1997).

Arrow, K. J., 1997. Invaluable goods. *Journal of Economic Literature* 35:757–65.
Besley, T., 1988. A simple model of merit good arguments. *Journal of Public Economics* 35:371–83.
Hillman, A. L., 1978. Notions of merit want. *Public Finance* 35:213–26.
Musgrave, R., 1959. *The Theory of Public Finance.* McGraw Hill, New York.
Pazner, E. A., 1972. Merit wants and the theory of taxation. *Public Finance* 27:460–72.

On prohibition of child labor, see Landes and Solomon (1972), Horrell and Humphries (1995), and Moehling (1999).

Horrell, S., and J. Humphries, 1995. The exploitation of little children: Child labor and the family economy in the industrial revolution. *Explorations in Economic History* 32:485–516.
Landes, W. M., and L. C. Solomon, 1972. Compulsory schooling legislation: An economic analysis of law and social change in the nineteenth century. *Journal of Economic History* 22:54–91.
Moehling, C. M., 1999. State child labor laws and the decline of child labor. *Explorations in Economic History* 36:72–106.

On smoking, see Sloan et al. (2004). On objective probabilities and personal perceptions of risk, see Viscusi (1990).

Sloan, F. A., J. Ostermann, G. Picone, C. Conover, and D. H. Taylor, Jr., 2004. *The Price of Smoking.* MIT Press, Cambridge MA.
Viscusi, W. K., 1990. Do smokers underestimate risks? *Journal of Political Economy* 98:1253–69.

A theory of rational addiction was proposed by Becker and Murphy (1988).

Becker, G. J., and K. M. Murphy, 1988. A theory of rational addiction. *Journal of Political Economy* 96:675–700.

On the market in blood, see:

Hamish, S., 1992. Rationality and the market for human blood. *Journal of Economic Behavior and Organization* 19:125–45.
Titmuss, R. M., 1970. *The Gift Relationship: From Human Blood to Social Policy*. George Allen and Unwin, London.

On alcohol and sexually transmitted diseases, see:

Chesson, H., P. Harrison, and W. J. Kassler, 2000. Sex under the influence: The effects of alcohol policy on sexually transmitted disease rates in the U.S. *Journal of Law and Economics* 43:215–38.

Edlund and Korn (2002) proposed a general theory of markets for commercial sex. Edin and Lein (1997) described commercial sex when other income-earning opportunities are limited. On the regulation of activities involving sex, see Posner (1992).

Edin, K., and L. Lein, 1997. *Making Ends Meet: How Single Mothers Survive Welfare and Low-Wage Work*. Russell Sage Foundation, New York.
Edlund, L., and E. Korn, 2002. A theory of prostitution. *Journal of Political Economy* 110:181–214.
Posner, R., 1992. *Sex and Reason*. Harvard University Press, Cambridge MA.

On obesity, see Cutler, Glaeser, and Shapiro (2003). Rosin (2008) surveyed the issues that arise in the economic consequences of obesity.

Cutler, D. M., E. C. Glaeser, and J. M. Shapiro, 2003. Why have Americans become obese? *Journal of Economic Perspectives* 17:93–118.
Rosin, O., 2008. The economic causes of obesity: A survey. *Journal of Economic Surveys* 22:617–47.

On hyperbolic discounting, see:

Akerlof, G. A., 1991. Procrastination and obedience. *American Economic Review* 81:1–19.
Laibson, D., 1997. Golden eggs and hyperbolic discounting. *Quarterly Journal of Economics* 112:443–77.
Loewenstein, G., and J. Elster (Eds.), 1992. *Choice over Time*. The Russell Sage Foundation, New York.

On self-control in payment of taxes and other behavioral aspects of public finance, see:

McCaffery, E. J., and J. Slemrod (Eds.), 2006. *Behavioral Public Finance*. Russell Sage Foundation, New York.

Payday lending was described by Stegman (2007). Persky (2007) described Jeremy Bentham's case made to Adam Smith about control of interest rates. The biblical origins of prohibitions on taking interest were described by Gamoran (1971).

Gamoran, H., 1971. The biblical law against loans on interest. *Journal of Near Eastern Studies* 30:127–34.
Persky, J., 2007. From usury to interest. *Journal of Economic Perspectives* 21:227–36.
Stegman, A., 2007. Payday lending. *Journal of Economic Perspectives* 21:169–90.

The Allais paradox was noted in Allais (1953). The example of framing was from Slovic, Monahan, and Macgregor (2000). On bounded rationality, see Simon (1955).

Allais, M., 1953. Le comportement de l'homme rationnel devant le risque: critique des postulats et axiomes de l'école Américaine. *Econometrica* 21:503–46.
Simon, H. A., 1955. A behavioral model of rational choice. *Quarterly Journal of Economics* 68:99–118.
Slovic, P., J. Monahan, and D. G. Macgregor, 2000. Violent risk assessment and risk communication: The effect of using actual cases, providing instructions, and employing probability versus frequency formats. *Law and Human Behavior* 24:271–96.

On Ponzi schemes and other financial deceptions, see:

Matulich, S., and D. M. Currie (Eds.), 2009. *Handbook of Frauds, Scams, and Swindles.* CRC Press, Francis & Taylor Group, Boca Raton FL.

On behavior toward girls and women in some other countries, see:

Crossette, B., 2000. Culture, gender, and human rights. In L. E. Harrison and S. P. Huntington (Eds.), *Culture Matters: How Values Shape Human Progress*. Basic Books, New York, pp. 178–99.

Sen (1970) presented the example of the conflict between Pareto efficiency and free choice when there are interdependent paternalistic preferences.

Sen, A. K., 1970. The impossibility of a Paretian liberal. *Journal of Political Economy* 78:152–7.

Peart and Levy (2008) described the trial involving dissemination of information about contraception. On the role of Galton in eugenics and the absence of scientific standards, see Levy and Peart (2004).

Levy, D. A., and S. J. Peart, 2004. Statistical prejudice: From eugenics to immigrants. *European Journal of Political Economy* 20:5–22.
Peart, S. A., and D. M. Levy, 2008. Darwin's unpublished letter at the Bradlaugh–Besant trial: A question of divided expert judgment. *European Journal of Political Economy* 23:343–53.

On the case against paternalistic public policies, see:

Meadowcroft, J. (Ed.), 2008. *Prohibitions.* Institute of Economic Affairs, London.

Supplement S5A: Externalities and non-convexities

The non-convexities associated with externalities were pointed out by:

Baumol, W. J., and D. F. Bradford, 1972. Detrimental externalities and non-convexity of the production set. *Economica* 39:160–76.
Starrett, D. A., 1972. Fundamental non-convexities in the theory of externalities. *Journal of Economic Theory* 4:180–99.

6

VOTING

In our normative analysis, we have until now considered personal decisions in markets (or, in the case of externalities, personal behavior in the absence of markets or in creating markets). The personal decisions were accompanied – and influenced – by public finance and public-policy decisions. Governments made the decisions about public finance and public policy, whereas people made the personal decisions that determined their own personal outcomes. In this chapter, we study collective decisions about public finance and public finance made by voting. People do not, therefore, determine their own personal outcomes by making personal decisions. Personal outcomes are determined through the collective outcome of decisions of voting.

Because the probability of one person's vote being decisive in large voting populations is effectively zero, the reason why people vote may not be that they expect to influence the outcome of voting. Voting may be expressive: voters may express themselves by identifying with a policy or with a candidate, as they might, for example, cheer for and identify with a sports team and be happy or sad according to whether "their" team wins; or, by expressing support for a candidate or political party, a voter may be communicating with and seeking approval from other people. People may also vote as an act of civic duty: they have been taught that taking the time to vote is correct pro-social behavior. Their utility from voting may be from democratic participation. We shall return to the question of why people vote. We shall begin by studying voting in circumstances in which all people exercise their right to vote and they vote according to their self-interest.

We saw in chapter 2, when we considered institutions, that voters can be influenced in their voting decisions by money spent on political persuasion and that candidates therefore benefit from campaign contributions. Even if principled and not wishing to accept campaign contributions from special interests, candidates can be caught in a prisoners' dilemma and accept the campaign contributions. We now nonetheless investigate voting in the absence of political principal–agent problems. Nor shall we consider bureaucratic principal–agent problems that arise when public policies are implemented and public spending takes place. We wish to determine outcomes of voting when there are no impediments – other than the attributes of voting itself – to achieving the social objectives of efficiency and social justice. Our questions are:

> *If markets fail to achieve efficiency in the presence of public goods and externalities, can voting achieve efficiency?*
>
> *Can voting achieve social justice?*

Rather than a society making the collective decisions about public finance and public policy through voting, a person in the population could be randomly chosen to make collective decisions on behalf of everyone. Would the randomly chosen person make "better" decisions than the collective decision of voters? That is, before we proceed to consider the outcomes of voting, we need to justify using voting to make collective decisions. We do not wish to rely on a justification for voting simply based on the declaration that "democracy is desirable." Rather, we require an analytical justification for making collective decisions by voting. An analytical justification for collective decisions through voting was provided by the Marquis de Condorcet (1743–94) in 1785 and is known as the *Condorcet jury theorem*.

The Condorcet jury theorem presupposes that all voters have the same objectives; in our case, efficiency or social justice. The only question concerns how an agreed common objective can best be achieved. For example, there are two alternative proposed means, A and B, of seeking to achieve efficiency. One means is correct and the other incorrect. The correct choice is A. However, there is uncertainty or imperfect information among voters, who only know that A is the correct decision with some probability. Under the conditions of the Condorcet jury theorem, the probability is taken to be the same for everyone and exceeds 0.5. The commonly held probability that A is the correct choice might, for example, be 0.6. Voters then randomize (as in the case of mixed strategies) and vote for alternative A with 60 percent probability (and for alternative B with 40 percent probability). The collective decision is determined as the alternative with the majority (more than 50 percent) of votes.

The Marquis de Condorcet showed that if everyone votes without being influenced by how others vote, then – as the number of voters increases – the likelihood that the correct decision A will have majority support increases. As the number of voters becomes very large, the likelihood that the majority makes the correct decision approaches certainty.

The Condorcet jury theorem is part of a field of study known as *decision theory* in which there is consensus about the objective. For example, a team of doctors is consulted on the appropriate treatment for a patient and the objective sought by everyone is to return the patient to good health. However, the doctors do not know with certainty which of two alternative treatments is appropriate, although they view one of the alternatives as the correct choice with probability in excess of 50 percent. Each may believe that A is the correct treatment with 60 percent probability. The likelihood that the collective decision made by majority voting will be correct increases as more doctors are consulted (or vote).

The Condorcet jury theorem is not applicable to many of the questions that we generally confront in the study of economics. People differ, for example, in preferences regarding public spending on public goods and about who should pay taxes that finance the public spending. They may be affected differently by externalities – or may be the sources of externalities. If the vote is on income redistribution, voters are usually influenced by whether they personally gain or lose from an income-redistribution proposal. They may also be influenced by whether low-income people gain or lose. The Condorcet jury theorem, which is based on a single objective common to all voters, provides no answers about voting outcomes when people have different objectives.

In chapter 1, we noted the objections of Adam Smith and Friedrich von Hayek to centralized "imposed order" as an alternative to personal decisions in markets; such "imposed order" is subject to information limitations because the information required for efficient centralized decisions is revealed in the personal market decisions that no longer take place after centralized "imposed order" has replaced markets. Through the Condorcet jury theorem, the same objections to imposed order apply when the imposed order would replace individual participation in collective decisions. The Condorcet jury theorem shows that in the presence of information limitations, the collective decisions of democracy are preferable to dictatorship – and also to randomly selecting someone to make decisions on behalf of society – and this is so even if the dictator or randomly selected decision maker seeks an objective on which everyone agrees.

We shall, from here on, consider voting when individual voters have different personal objectives. We shall describe voting on public spending on public goods of the prisoners'-dilemma type, for which the total quantity or quality is determined by the sum of individual contributions and there are free-rider problems (in contrast to volunteer and weakest-link public goods for which this is not the case). Voters have different preferences for spending on public goods and, if possible, they also prefer that others pay (or that they free ride). Voting can involve externalities: the public good might be the quality of the environment and the question to be determined by voting might be how much to spend or how much income to forgo to maintain environmental quality. Voting can also involve income redistribution: the different preferences of voters are then about how, or whether, they want income to be redistributed. In section 1, we consider voting on public spending on public goods. Section 2 introduces the institutions of representative democracy in which, in the course of political competition, voters elect political representatives. Section 3 investigates voting on income redistribution.

6.1 The Median Voter and Majority Voting

A first step in investigating outcomes of voting is to decide on a voting rule that determines when a proposal has been accepted.

A. Voting and efficient public spending

A possible voting rule is consensus or unanimity. After a decision has been made by voting, everyone has the same quantity or quality of a public good. A consensus voting rule requires everyone to agree on the common quantity or quality.

Voting and the Lindahl consensus

Consensus regarding the quantity or quality of a public good to be supplied is a property of the efficient Lindahl voluntary payment solution for financing public

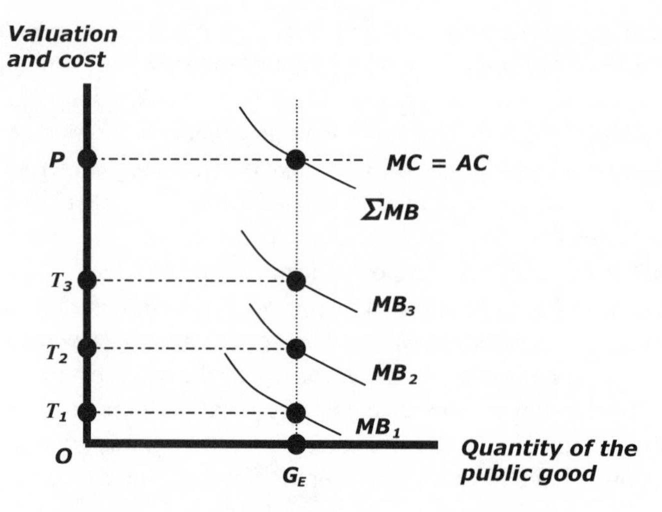

Figure 6.1. The Lindahl consensus through voting.

goods. The Lindahl voluntary payment solution is infeasible because of asymmetric information (or because of the incentive to free ride on the payments of others). Can the efficient Lindahl consensus be achieved through voting with a consensus rule for accepting voting outcomes?

When consensus is the voting rule, any individual voter has the ability to veto any proposal. A voter, by voting according to self-interest, can therefore block a proposal from which he or she would personally lose. If there is support for a proposal by consensus, all voters have compared personal benefit with personal cost and have decided to support the proposal. Therefore:

> *A consensus voting rule assures Pareto improvement for all proposals that are accepted.*

Pareto improvement is assured because of the ability of anyone who would lose from a taxation and public-spending proposal to veto the proposal.

In figure 6.1, MB_1, MB_2, and MB_3 are marginal benefits and so indicate marginal willingness to pay of three taxpayers for a public good. $\sum MB$ is the total marginal benefit (obtained as indicated in chapter 3 by summing the individual MB functions vertically, as is required for public goods). The price of the public good is given as P, which – due to competitive markets for supply – is equal to MC (and here also AC) of the public good. Efficient voluntary spending on the public good requires choice of the quantity G_E, determined by the condition for efficient supply $\sum MB = MC\ (= P)$.

In figure 6.1, the Lindahl tax payments, equal to Lindahl personal prices, are T_i $(i = 1, 2, 3)$, determined when the personal per-unit tax for each voter equals personal MB:

$$T_i = MB_i \quad i = 1, 2, 3. \tag{6.1}$$

The personal Lindahl per-unit tax payments are personal cost shares of the price of the unit of the public good, so that:

$$\sum_i T_i = P. \tag{6.2}$$

However, Lindahl prices are voluntary and are not taxes. Nonetheless, if beneficiaries of public goods paid their Lindahl prices as in expression (6.1) as compulsory taxes, the outcome would be efficient consensus supply of public goods. There would also be no excess burden of taxation, because payment for public goods would be made directly by the beneficiaries of public goods rather than through taxes levied in other markets. We saw in chapter 4 that it is the intrusion of taxes into other markets that is the source of the excess burden of taxation, through substitution effects. We also saw in chapter 4 that when taxes have an excess burden, the efficient quantity or quality of the public good is less than the quantity or quality that would be chosen through the voluntary payments of the ideal Lindahl mechanism. Lindahl prices paid as compulsory taxes would be efficient in financing efficient public spending on public goods and avoiding the substitution effects in other markets that underlie the excess burden of taxation.

Voting takes place after a government has announced voters' different personal tax shares. If the government were to announce the Lindahl cost shares T_i ($i = 1, 2, 3$) in figure 6.1, the three voters, by consensus, would vote for the efficient quantity G_E to be supplied. By voting for G_E, each voter maximizes personal utility, as indicated in expression (6.1), given a voter's *MB* function and preannounced tax share.

Taxpayers, of course, have no incentive to truthfully reveal their personal *MB* functions shown in figure 6.1 when they know that their declared personal benefits will be used to determine their personal tax payments. The public-good asymmetric-information problem has not been resolved and the incentive remains to understate personal benefit to reduce the total personal payment at the predetermined personal tax share that the government has announced.

However, voting does not rely on the ability of the government to observe personal *MB* functions. To determine the outcome of voting, all that needs to be observed is the personal voting decision regarding the choice of the quantity or quality of the public good. A government could therefore randomly choose and announce personal tax shares for different voters, and then voters vote. The outcome, entirely fortuitously, could be a consensus vote by taxpayers on the quantity of the public good. In that case, because a consensus vote results in the efficient choice, the government would know that the efficient quantity G_E of the public good had been chosen.

We therefore might propose that governments attempt to find the personal tax shares that are equal to efficient Lindahl prices through an iterative process. Different combinations of personal taxes could be announced until a consensus vote is obtained.

It is unlikely that governments will take heed of a suggestion to iteratively announce personal taxes in the quest for the Lindahl consensus. The costs in terms of time of seeking unanimity in large populations deter such a quest.[1]

Transactions costs and opportunism with a consensus voting rule

If a proposal to supply a tax-financed quantity of a public good satisfies the cost-benefit rule $\{W = B - C > 0\}$ (where cost includes the excess burden of taxation) and all individuals personally gain from a proposal, the efficient project should be supported by consensus. However, a proposal for public spending for which $\{W = B - C > 0\}$ may result in some people losing. The public spending proposal is then not Pareto-improving. Individuals who lose will vote against the proposal and if the voting rule is consensus the socially worthwhile project will not be accepted for public finance. For people who lose from a proposal, the efficient Lindahl price is negative; that is, the losers need to be paid or compensated if they are not to veto the proposal. People pay taxes rather than Lindahl prices: compensation is demanded because the taxes that losers from the proposal would pay through predetermined tax shares and the excess burden of taxation that they would incur exceed their total benefit from the public good. There is again asymmetric information if the losses of losers cannot be objectively verified. Thus, with willingness of the gainers to compensate the losers in order to achieve a consensus vote, determining values of payments required for compensation may not be straightforward. There are also free-rider problems among gainers from the proposal in making the compensatory transfers to losers. These impediments to applying a consensus voting rule are sometimes called "transactions costs"; here the transactions are among gainers and losers from an efficient proposal for public finance. There is a further problem: if information is private and so asymmetric, people who in fact gain from a proposal have an incentive to claim deceptively that they will lose. A proposal for taxation and public spending may truly entail a loss for the person demanding compensation, and so compensation may be just; however, a consensus voting rule also introduces scope for opportunistic extortion.

> *A consensus voting rule is subject to transactions costs and also presents maximal opportunities for opportunistic extortion because every voter can veto a proposal for taxation and public spending.*

One voter's threat to veto is, of course, of no consequence if other voters also opportunistically threaten to veto; the single voter is then no longer decisive in being able to allow the proposal to pass by being accepted by consensus. Voters who opportunistically threaten to veto need to be able to coordinate their behavior. Voting rules that require less than unanimity make opportunistic behavior

[1] Lindahl prices are based on a benefit principle of taxation, whereas the political preference may be to set taxes according to the ability-to-pay principle, in which case people with higher incomes pay more without regard for personal benefit from public spending. We are now looking for efficient spending. In section 3 of this chapter, we consider voting on income redistribution.

more difficult. If, for example, a 90 percent majority in favor is required for a proposal to be accepted, more than 10 percent of voters face the complex task of coordinating their attempt at opportunistic extortion. However, if they successfully coordinate their demands, free-rider problems among gainers will tend to prevent the income transfers to claimed losers being made.

Why consensus is not chosen

There are thus costs and benefits when choosing a voting decision rule. A unanimity or consensus voting rule ensures efficiency and Pareto improvement, if consensus is the revealed outcome of voting. However, finding the personal tax shares that result in a consensus decision is time consuming. Also, if a proposal satisfies the cost-benefit rule ($W = B - C > 0$) but some people lose, consensus requires compensation to losers but it may not be possible to make the payments – or making the compensating payments may require arduous prolonged negotiations (everyone has an incentive for an agreement to be reached because after compensation, everyone can gain). Beyond these transactions costs, even if proposals are in fact Pareto-improving, a consensus voting rule introduces opportunities for extortion through threat of opportunistic veto.

A majority-voting equilibrium

In general, because of these problems, the consensus voting rule is not used. The prevalent voting rule is majority-voting, under which a proposal is accepted if more than 50 percent of voters vote in favor – although when an issue is deemed particularly important, such as a change in a constitution, greater than 50 percent majorities are often required to change the status quo. We shall now apply the majority-voting rule to determine outcomes of voting on public goods.

Box 6.1 May's Theorem on majority voting

Is the 50 percent majority-voting rule arbitrary? Or can the rule be formally justified? The rule was justified axiomatically for choice between two alternatives by the U.S. mathematician Kenneth May (1915–77), who in 1952 derived a conclusion that has become known as May's theorem. May showed that if and only if specified axioms are satisfied does a collective decision rule have the property that collective decisions are made according to the 51 percent majority voting rule. Axiom 1 is decisiveness, meaning that a collective decision rule gives a decisive answer; axiom 2 is anonymity, requiring that outcomes depend on the number of votes and not on who casts a vote for or against; axiom 3 is neutrality, meaning that if people have the same preferences over two sets of alternatives, voting outcomes are consistent for the two sets of alternatives; and axiom 4 is positive responsiveness, which requires that a change in an individual's position from being against to being indifferent, or from indifferent to being in favor, does not result in a rejection of

(*continued*)

a proposal that had been previously accepted or had tied with the alternative proposal. May (1952) showed that the only voting rule that satisfies these axioms is the 50 percent majority voting rule. An explanation for not choosing a majority of less than 50 percent is quite straightforward: a 49 percent majority rule is not based on a majority and would result in indefinite formation of alternative 49 percent minority coalitions claiming to have won the vote. In section 3 of this chapter, where we shall consider voting on redistribution (here we are seeking efficient public spending on public goods), we shall encounter a justification for majority voting based on minimal personal exploitation through redistribution from a minority of voters to a majority.

When spending on public goods is to be decided through majority voting, if the Lindahl prices could be set as personal tax shares, the outcome would be – as we have seen – a consensus vote for the efficient quantity of a public good. However, with a government unable to set the efficient personal Lindahl prices as tax shares, how are tax shares to be determined?

Voters could be asked to vote jointly on tax shares and public spending. They would vote for low tax shares for themselves, high tax shares for others, and for high public spending. That is, such voting would be subject to free-riding incentives.

More usually, when voters vote on public spending (if they are given the opportunity to vote), personal tax obligations for increased public spending are predetermined. Voters could therefore compute the increase required in their taxes for different quantities of tax-financed public goods. Of course, voters may not have information about how different public-spending proposals affect their taxes. If they are rationally ignorant, they would vote without knowing how their personal taxes will change when public spending on a public good increases.

The absence of voter information on personal costs through taxes will not deter us from asking whether, under conditions in which voters know their personal tax shares for financing of public goods, majority voting on public goods results in efficient public spending. We need a cost-sharing rule for financing public spending to proceed: the rule that we choose is equal cost sharing among all taxpayers. Equal sharing of costs is arbitrary but we view taxpayers as paying the same tax shares because of the unattainable information (we shall not consider use of the Clarke tax) required to set the efficient Lindahl prices as tax shares. With the competitively determined price P of a public good given, each of n taxpayers therefore pays the equal share of the price (or cost):

$$T_i = \frac{P}{n}. \tag{6.3}$$

Figure 6.2 shows the equal-tax-share rule applied to three taxpayers, each of whom is obliged to pay, through taxes, a third of the price P of the public good.

Although voters pay the same tax shares, they benefit differently from the public good. Each MB function in figure 6.2 is a voter's private information. A voter knows the location of his or her own MB function and does not know the

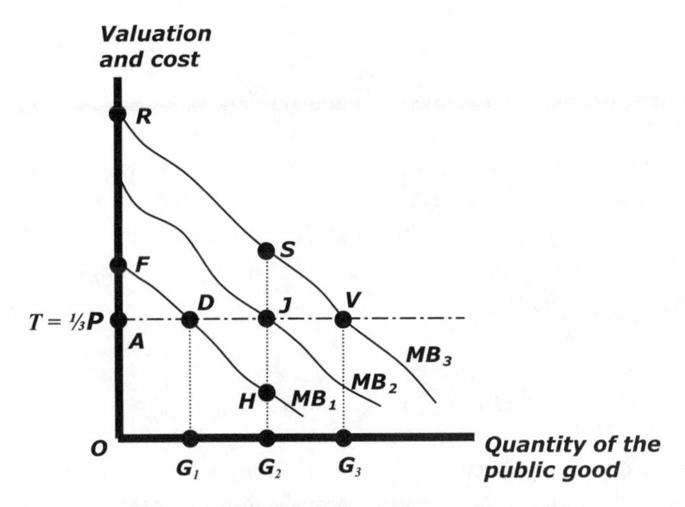

Figure 6.2. A majority-voting equilibrium.

location of other voters' MB functions. A government knows the location of no one's MB function. We as outside observers pretend that the locations of the personal MB functions are visible to us – although they are not.

Our objective is to find an outcome of majority voting subject to the asymmetric information that is present among taxpayers – and between taxpayers and the government. Voters know their tax shares and their own MB, which is sufficient information for each voter as taxpayer to determine the quantity of the public good that he or she ideally wants supplied. Each voter finds the ideally desired or utility-maximizing quantity of the public good by setting the personal tax share equal to personal marginal benefit:

$$T_i = MB_i, \quad i = 1, 2, 3. \tag{6.4}$$

With the equal tax share T in figure 6.2, taxpayer 1 ideally wants G_1 of the public good to be supplied, taxpayer 2 wants G_2, and taxpayer 3 wants G_3.

We can now ask the taxpayers to vote on the quantity of the public good. If the question placed before the taxpayers were, "How much of the public good do you want?," we would obtain the three different answers, G_1, G_2, and G_3, with no majority for any quantity.

We can, however, ask the taxpayers the different question, "Do you favor an increase in supply in the public good?" If a majority favors an increase, supply is increased. If a majority votes against increased supply, the quantity supplied does not change: in that case, the majority-voting equilibrium has been found. We could also frame the question as, "Do you favor a decrease in supply?" The majority-voting equilibrium is then obtained when there is no majority in favor of reducing supply. Either way:

> *In a majority-voting equilibrium, there is no majority support in favor of change.*

In figure 6.2, at quantity G_1:

$$MB_1(G_1) = T, \quad MB_2(G_1) > T, \quad MB_3(G_1) > T. \tag{6.5}$$

For voter 1, G_1 is the personally optimal supply; voter 1 therefore votes against increasing supply beyond G_1. For voters 2 and 3, utility or personal benefit increases when supply increases beyond G_1 and these two taxpayers vote to increase supply. There is majority support for increasing supply; therefore, the quantity supplied increases.

At G_2:

$$MB_1(G_2) < T, \quad MB_2(G_2) = T, \quad MB_3(G_2) > T. \tag{6.6}$$

Therefore, at G_2, voter 2 has attained personally optimal supply and so joins voter 1 in opposing further increased supply. Voter 3 wants to increase supply to G_3. However, with the majority (voters 1 and 2) voting against increasing supply beyond G_2, the quantity G_2 is the equilibrium supply determined by majority voting.[2]

The median voter

Taxpayer 2 is the median voter.

> *The median voter is decisive in determining the majority-voting equilibrium.*

Expression (6.6) shows that the collective choice G_2 determined by majority voting is the preferred choice of only the median voter.

The low-benefit (or low-demand) taxpayer 1 ideally wants G_1 but is required to pay the same taxes as the other voters to finance the collectively decided quantity G_2. Taxpayer 1 loses DJH from the increase in supply from G_1 to G_2. Taxpayer 1 incurs a net loss from the majority decision to supply G_2 if the loss of DJH from supply $(G_2 - G_1)$ exceeds the net benefit ADF from supply of G_1.[3]

Unlike taxpayer 1, taxpayer 3 can only have positive benefit from the majority-voting decision. However, when G_2 is supplied, taxpayer 3 forgoes the additional benefit SVJ that he or she would obtain if supply were G_3.[4]

[2] If we begin from quantity G_3 and ask the voters if they favor a decrease in supply, by two votes to one (voters 1 and 2 in favor and voter 3 against) there is a majority in favor of decreasing supply. This majority is maintained until supply is reduced to G_2. Voter 2 then joins voter 3 in voting against further decreases in supply and G_2 is again the majority voting equilibrium.

[3] Taxpayer 1's loss from the additional quantity $(G_2 - G_1)$ is DJH. Taxpayer 1 pays DJG_2G_1 for the quantity $(G_2 - G_1)$ but has total benefit of only DHG_2G_1. Taxpayer 1 therefore loses the difference DJH from the increase in supply from G_1 to G_2.

[4] Taxpayer 3's net benefit from supply of G_3 rather than G_2 is SJV. The increase in supply to G_3 would cost taxpayer 3 JVG_3G_2. Total benefit to taxpayer 3 from increasing supply to G_3 is SVG_3G_2. The difference is SJV.

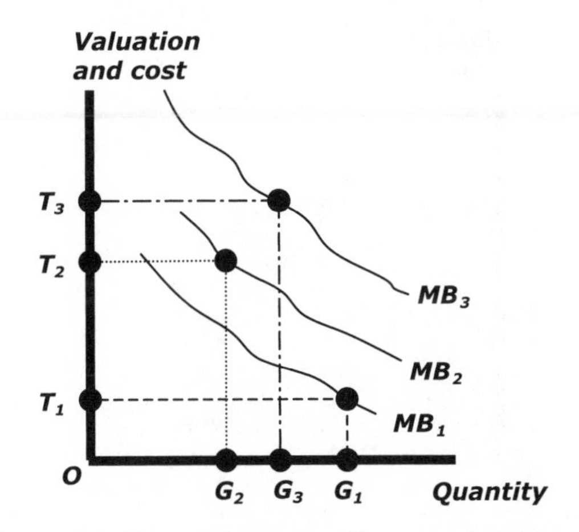

Figure 6.3. The median voter with unequal tax shares.

We conclude:

Only the median voter is completely happy with the outcome of majority voting.

Voters ideally wanting less of the public good than the median voter can lose in the majority-voting equilibrium.

Voters ideally wanting more of the public good than the median voter cannot lose in the majority-voting equilibrium but are derived of additional benefit.

The identity of the median voter

Taxpayers' different tax obligations could result in unequal tax shares, as in figure 6.3. For the indicated tax shares, taxpayer 3 is the median voter. As the median voter, taxpayer 3 is decisive in determining the majority-voting equilibrium as G_3. With the equal taxes in figure 6.2, taxpayer 2 was the median voter. Figure 6.3 shows that:

The identity of the median voter depends on the structure of taxes.

In figure 6.4, the *MB* functions of taxpayers 1 and 2 intersect. Two different market prices of the public good determine equal tax shares as $T_1 = P_1/n$ and $T_2 = P_2/n$. At the higher price P_2 of the public good, voter 1 is the median voter and the equilibrium quantity determined by majority voting is voter 1's preferred choice G_1'. At the lower price P_1, voter 2 is the median voter and the equilibrium quantity is voter 2's preferred choice G_2. Thus:

The identity of the median voter can change with the price of the public good.

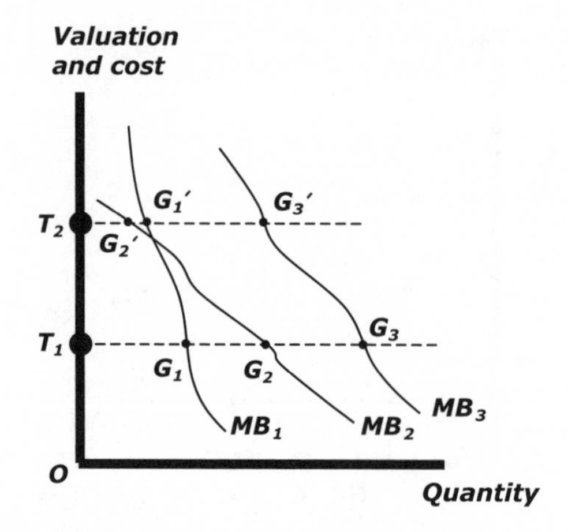

Figure 6.4. The identity of the median voter can change.

The outcome in the majority-voting equilibrium is sometimes referred to as the *dictatorship of the median voter*. However, compared to other dictators, the dictatorship of the median voter is innocuous. The identity of the median voter is not predetermined but rather depends on tax shares and the market price of public goods. In general, the median voter will not know that he or she is the median voter. The median voter is thus, in general, a dictator who does not know that he or she is a dictator.

Does majority voting result in efficient public spending?

Our focal normative question is:

> *Does majority voting result in efficient public spending on public goods?*

In figure 6.5, the efficient quantity G_E is determined by the public-good efficiency condition $\sum MB = MC$. The median voter's marginal benefit or marginal

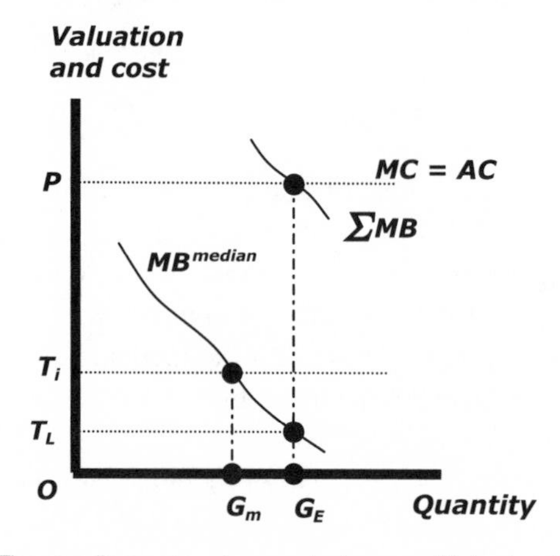

Figure 6.5. The median voter does not choose efficient public spending.

willingness to pay for the public good is MB^{median}. T_L is the median voter's Lindahl tax share. If paying the Lindahl tax share, the median voter would choose efficient supply G_E of the public good according to:

$$T_L = MB^{median}. \tag{6.7}$$

There is little likelihood of the tax system resulting in the median voter confronting his or her Lindahl tax share; this could happen only by luck. In figure 6.5, the median voter's tax share as determined by the tax system that is being used is shown as T_i and the median voter chooses G_m, which is less than efficient supply G_E. The median voter's choice could also exceed efficient supply G_E. Only if the median voter's tax share were fortuitously equal to the Lindahl cost share T_L would efficient supply be chosen through majority voting.

> *In general, the majority-voting equilibrium does not result in efficient supply of a public good.*

The distribution of benefits in the population

Nonetheless, there are special circumstances in which majority voting or choice by the median voter results in efficient public spending. Figure 6.6a shows a normal distribution of *net* valuations of public spending in a population after taxes have been paid. With the median and average valuations equal, and in the special case of equal tax shares, choice by the median voter results in efficient public spending on public goods.[5]

People with higher incomes may want more of a public good (that is, the public good is a normal good). As shown in figure 6.6b, the average valuation in the population in that case exceeds the median. In the majority-voting equilibrium, because the median voter is decisive, less-than-efficient public spending is then chosen. When financing of public goods is by voluntary payment, we predict under-supply of public goods because of free-riding incentives. In the circumstances that we are now considering, *compulsory* taxes finance public spending and therefore under-supply cannot be due to free riding. The under-supply is due to the median voter wanting ideally less public spending than the voter with the average valuation.

[5] To see why this is so, we consider a population with n voters. Average MB of the population is:

$$MB^{average} \equiv \frac{\sum_{j=1}^{n} MB_j}{n}.$$

With equal sharing of costs and $P = MC$ for the public good, the preferred supply of the voter in the population with the average valuation of the public good is determined by:

$$MB^{average} = \frac{P}{n} = \frac{MC}{n}$$

and therefore:

$$n \cdot MB^{average} = \sum MB = MC.$$

A median voter who happens to have the average MB of the population therefore chooses efficient public spending.

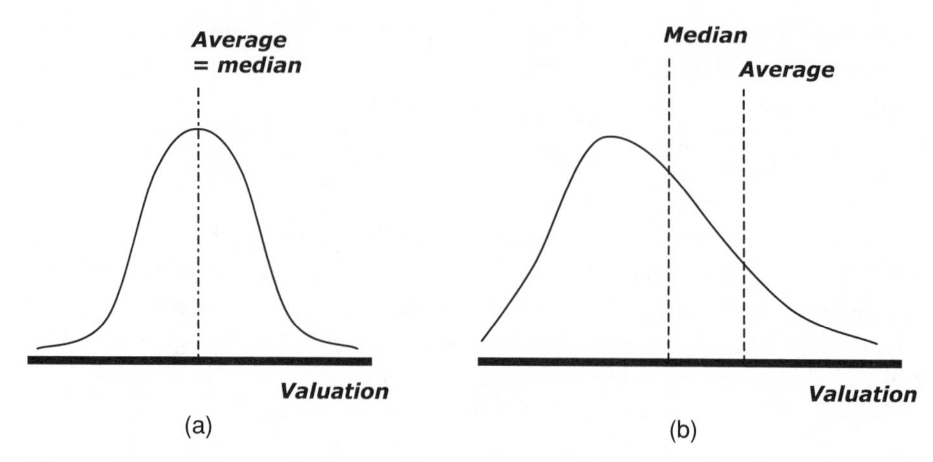

Figure 6.6. (a) Valuations are normally distributed. (b) Average valuation exceeds the median.

The alternative case is also possible in which the voters with high incomes have low valuations of public goods. Low-income voters may want publicly financed shared recreational amenities, good government schools, and personal security from the police, whereas high-income voters might use a private swimming pool, be a member of a private country club, send their children to a private school, and have private security guards. The valuation of public goods of the median voter then exceeds the average valuation, and majority voting (or choice by the median voter) results in over-supply of a public good relative to efficient supply.

> *There is little reason to believe that majority voting will result in efficient public spending on public goods; depending on whether low- or high-income voters value public goods more, the outcome of majority voting is under-supply or over-supply of public goods.*

Voting on externalities

Voting can be about externalities. When the issue is the stringency of environmental policy, a majority-voting equilibrium is sought by asking voters whether they favor increasing an emissions quota. The median voter's preferences again determine the majority-voting equilibrium, and we have no reason to expect that the median voter will choose the efficient internalization of externalities as would be determined by Coase theorem.

Voting versus markets

Our study of public finance and public policy began in chapter 1 with a presumption in favor of the efficiency of personal market decisions. We now observe the basis for a presumption against the efficiency of collective nonmarket decisions made by majority voting. We would predict, of course, that we use our incomes more efficiently and more effectively in terms of personal utility when we make personal spending decisions in markets than when we pool our incomes with others through taxes and the median voter decides how the pooled money is to be spent.

The Condorcet jury theorem indicates that collective decisions made in a democracy with many people voting are more likely to result in correct answers than decisions made by a dictator or a small elite. The collective decisions of broadly based democracy are therefore preferable to narrowly based authoritarian decisions. However:

> *All else equal, private spending in markets of our own income based on our own personal preferences is preferable to public spending determined through majority voting (or based on the median voter's preferences).*

B. The Condorcet winner and efficient public-spending proposals

We now diminish our expectations for outcomes of majority voting. Rather than seeking an efficient outcome for public spending, we ask whether majority voting ensures at least that the cost-benefit rule for publicly financed spending is satisfied:

> *Does majority voting select efficient public proposals for which $W = B - C > 0$ over inefficient proposals for which $W = B - C < 0$?*

The Condorcet winner

Table 6.1a shows the rankings by three taxpayers of three taxation and public-spending proposals, X, Y, and Z. The public-finance proposals are for different quantities of the same public good, with $X < Y < Z$. A choice from among the three alternative quantities is to be made through majority voting. Voters (or taxpayers) have determined their rankings of the proposals after knowing their own benefits from each proposal and their increased personal tax payment required to finance each proposal. Information about personal benefit is private; voters only know their own rankings of proposals and not the rankings of anyone else.

TABLE 6.1a. RANKINGS BY VOTERS OF ALTERNATIVE PUBLIC SPENDING PROPOSALS

Voter 1	Voter 2	Voter 3
X	Y	Z
Y	X	Y
Z	Z	X

The voters vote in accord with personal rankings. Once more, if we ask voters which proposal they prefer, each will give a different answer. Voter 1 will choose *X*, voter 2 will choose *Y*, and voter 3 will choose *Z*.

We therefore ask the voters to vote *on pairs* of proposals. We use the symbol P to denote "preferred to by majority voting." In table 6.1a, the outcome is:

- $\{Y \text{ P } X\}$ when the vote is between *X* and *Y*
- $\{Y \text{ P } Z\}$ when the vote is between *Y* and *Z*
- $\{X \text{ P } Z\}$ when the vote is between *X* and *Z*

We now define the *Condorcet winner* (also named after the Marquis de Condorcet):

> *The Condorcet winner defeats all other proposals in pair-wise majority voting.*

The Condorcet winner in table 6.1a is thus proposal *Y*. The outcome of the vote between *X* and *Z* does not matter for determining the Condorcet winner. Proposal *Y* has majority support (two votes to one) when matched against *X* and has majority support (two votes to one) when matched against *Z*.

Single-peaked preferences

Figure 6.2 demonstrated an equilibrium outcome of majority voting, with the equilibrium quantity of the public good determined by the preferences of the median voter. Figure 6.7a shows the utility of the median voter (or voter 2) from different quantities of the public good. The quantities of the public good in figure 6.7a are those in figure 6.2. The utility-maximizing quantity for the median voter is shown as G_m (equal in figure 6.2 to G_2). Because the quantity G_m maximizes the utility of the median voter, the median voter's utility function has a "peak" at G_m and because of the unique maximum, the utility function is "single-peaked." Other voters, whose utility functions are not shown in figure 6.7a, similarly have single-peaked preferences that identify their unique preferred or utility-maximizing quantity of the public good (G_1 for voter 1 and G_3 for voter 3). A stable equilibrium outcome of majority voting was obtained based on the preferences of voters in figure 6.2 because all voters have single-peaked preferences that give rise to single-peaked utility functions of the form in figure 6.7a.

Figure 6.7b shows again voters' rankings in table 6.1a. By joining the points indicating voters' rankings, we obtain an after-tax net benefit (or utility) function for each voter. All voters in figure 6.7b (and therefore in table 6.1a) have *single-peaked preferences*. That is, each voter's net-benefit function has a single local maximum, which is also the single global maximum. Voter 1 has a single peak for utility at *X*. For voter 2, the single peak is at *Y*. Voter 3 has a single peak at *Z*.

Cycling or instability of voting outcomes

Figure 6.7c shows a case in which one of the voters does not have single-peaked preferences. Voter 3's preferences are not single-peaked because the net-benefit

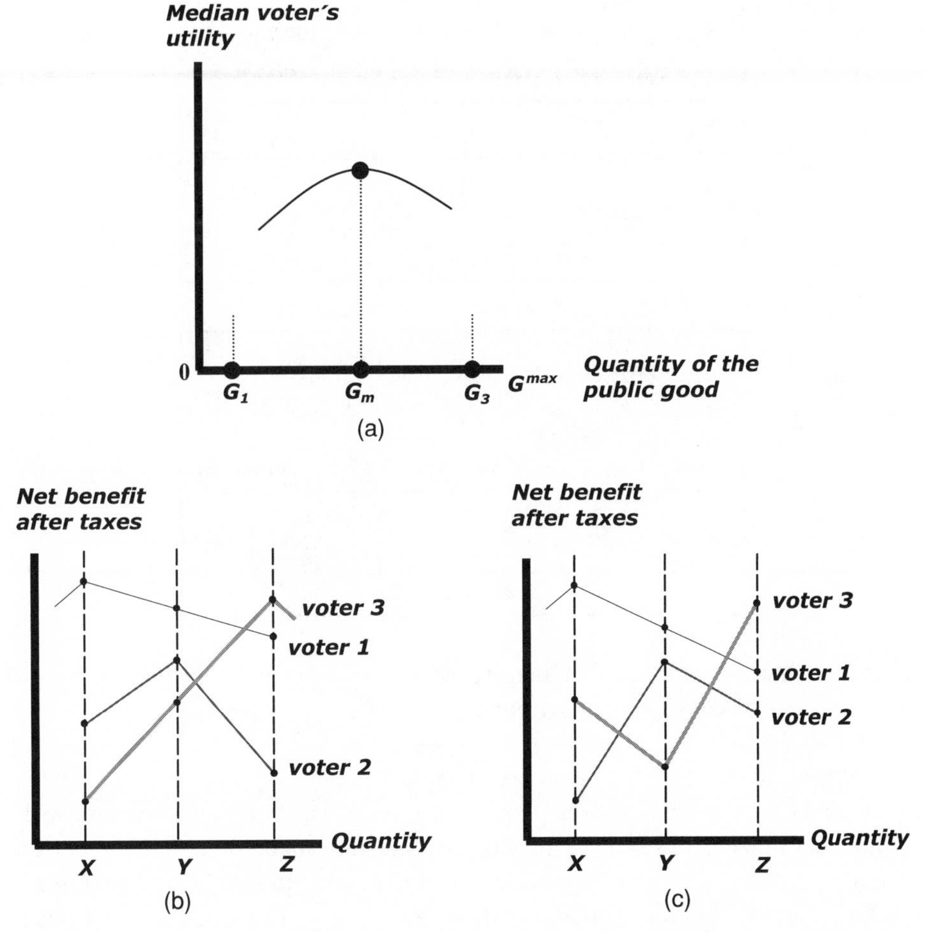

Figure 6.7. (a) The median voter has single-peaked preferences. (b) The single-peaked preferences of the voters of table 6.1a. (c) The preferences of the voters of table 6.1b with voter 3's preferences not single-peaked.

or utility function of voter 3 has two local maxima, at X and Z.[6] Table 6.1b shows voters' ranking in figure 6.7c. Now, with voter 3 not having single-peaked preferences, majority voting results in indefinite cycling among alternatives. We see that:

- $\{X \text{ P } Y\}$ when the vote is between X and Y
- $\{Y \text{ P } Z\}$ when the vote is between Y and Z
- $\{Z \text{ P } X\}$ when the vote is between Z and X.

Every proposal, therefore, can be defeated by another proposal and a stable outcome of majority voting does not exist. That is, indefinite cycling among voting

[6] The heights of the net-benefit functions (or levels of utility of the different voters) are arbitrary and do not matter in determining the outcome of voting. Each voter's decision about how to vote depends solely on the voter's own ranking of alternatives – and not on other voters' rankings nor on other voters' costs and benefits as a consequence of the voting decision that is made.

TABLE 6.1b. RANKINGS BY VOTERS OF ALTERNATIVE PUBLIC-SPENDING PROPOSALS

Voter 1	Voter 2	Voter 3
X	Y	Z
Y	Z	X
Z	X	Y

TABLE 6.1c. RANKINGS BY VOTERS OF ALTERNATIVE PUBLIC-SPENDING PROPOSALS

Voter 1	Voter 2	Voter 3
Z	X	Y
X	Z	Z
Y	Y	X

outcomes takes place without identifying a Condorcet winner. The indefinite cycling occurs because voter 3's preferences are not single-peaked.

The reason for non-single-peaked preferences

Why might a voter have non-single-peaked preferences? The question on which voting takes place, for example, may be how much to spend on national security. If enough cannot be spent to provide effective deterrence, voter 3 prefers minimal spending to the intermediate spending alternative. The result is that voter 3 has non-single-peaked preferences.

Choice over different types of public goods

We have described choice over different quantities or qualities of a public good but alternatives X, Y, and Z could also represent different types of public goods. For example, the choice may be among the alternatives of (X) increased spending on education, (Y) increased entertainment budgets for diplomatic personnel in embassies abroad, and (Z) increased funding for national parks. The placement of such different projects on the horizontal axis in figures 6.7b or 6.7c is arbitrary.[7] If the positioning of X, Y, and Z representing different projects (and not different spending alternatives for the same project) can be rearranged so that each voter has single-peaked preferences, cycling does not occur. For example, in table 6.1c, voters 1 and 2 do not have single-peaked preferences when the proposals are

[7] For different projects, we have no rule for positioning of the alternatives. Of course, when the alternatives are different quantities of the same public good, relative positions are determined by the ranking of proposed values of public spending.

TABLE 6.1d. RANKINGS OF VOTERS IN TABLE 6.1a AND FIGURE 6.2 COINCIDE

Voter 1	Voter 2	Voter 3
$X = G_1$	$Y = G_2$	$Z = G_3$
$Y = G_2$	$Z = G_3$	$Y = G_2$
$Z = G_3$	$X = G_1$	$X = G_1$

positioned as first X, then Y, and then Z. When the proposals are positioned as first X, then Z, and then Y, however, preferences are single-peaked. We see that in table 6.1c $\{Z \text{ P } X\}$ and $\{Z \text{ P } Y\}$; Z is therefore the stable determinate Condorcet winner.[8]

The relationship between the Condorcet winner and the majority-voting equilibrium

The Condorcet winner and the outcome in the majority-voting equilibrium are related; indeed, they are one and the same. When in figure 6.2 the majority-voting equilibrium G_2 was determined, voters chose from *continuous* quantities. The Condorcet winner was determined as the outcome of pair-wise majority voting over *discrete* choices. The quantities G_1, G_2, and G_3 in figure 6.2 can be associated with the discrete alternatives in table 6.1a X, Y, and Z. Table 6.1a can then be re-expressed in the form of table 6.1d. The voters in figure 6.2 have single-peaked preferences. Table 6.1d shows that voter 2, who was the median voter in figure 6.2, is also the median voter in table 6.1a.[9]

Control over the agenda

When cycling occurs, an additional rule can be imposed that losers in sequential pair-wise contests are eliminated. A voter who determines the order in which voting takes place – or sets the agenda – then also determines the outcome of voting. With taxpayers' rankings as in table 6.1b, the agenda may be set so that the first pair-wise vote is on the choice between X and Y. Then $\{X \text{ P } Y\}$ and Y is eliminated. The next round of voting sets Z against X. In this vote the outcome is $\{Z \text{ P } X\}$. Z is therefore the winner. The outcome, however, has been predetermined by the order of voting. If the first vote were between Y and Z, then Y

[8] That is, there is a Condorcet winner if there exists a positioning of alternatives that results in single-peaked preferences for all voters.

[9] As in figure 6.2, voter 1's net benefit declines as the quantity increases from voter 1's preferred quantity G_1 (=X). Voter 3's net benefit declines as the quantity declines from voter 3's preferred quantity G_3 (=Z). Voters 1 and 3 thus have single-peaked preferences. Voter 2 also has single-peaked preferences: the single peak is at voter 2's preferred quantity G_2 (=Y). In table 6.1a, G_2 (=Y) is the Condorcet winner, independent of voter 2's ranking of G_1 (=X) and G_3 (=Z) – that is, independent of whether voter 2 prefers G_1 (=X) to G_3 (=Z).

would eliminate Z; in the next vote, X would win over Y. Alternatively, if the first vote were between alternatives Z and X, Y would win. We conclude, therefore:

Unless preferences of all voters are single-peaked, majority voting cannot be relied on to result in a stable determinate collective decision – unless losers are eliminated, in which case the outcome is determined by control over the agenda.

We shall rely on voters with single-peaked preferences to answer our question of whether majority voting ensures that efficient proposals that pass the test of cost-benefit analysis are chosen over inefficient proposals.

The Condorcet winner and cost-benefit analysis

In table 6.1a, where preferences are single-peaked, the Condorcet winner was project Y. Table 6.2a shows an example of possible costs and benefits for the three voters from project Y. The total cost of proposal Y is 300, which is financed by equal cost-sharing among voters, with each voter paying 100. Each voter's benefit is private information, known only to the voter personally. Benefits for the three voters from proposal Y are 30, 130, and 110. A cost-benefit calculation of $W = B - C$ reveals a negative value $-30 = (270 - 300)$ for proposal Y. Nonetheless, proposal Y was chosen as the Condorcet winner under majority voting.

TABLE 6.2a. BENEFITS AND COSTS FOR THE CONDORCET WINNER PROPOSAL Y

	Cost to the voter of the proposal	Voter benefit from the proposal	Voter net benefit from the proposal
Voter 1	100	30	−70
Voter 2	100	130	30
Voter 3	100	110	10
Total	Total cost = 300	Total benefit = 270	Total net benefit = −30

Table 6.2b shows possible voter benefits and costs for proposal X, which in table 6.1a lost to proposal Y by majority voting. The total cost of proposal X is again 300, financed by equal cost shares of 100. Proposal X provides positive benefit of 400 to voter 1 and results in losses for voters 2 and 3 of 20 and 30, respectively; hence, voter 1 voted in favor of proposal X but not voters 2 and 3. The outcome of majority voting was, therefore, that proposal X lost to proposal Y. Proposal X has a positive net benefit of $350 = (650 - 300)$ and is therefore efficient in satisfying the cost-benefit rule $W = B - C > 0$.

We define a *Condorcet loser* as a proposal that is defeated in pair-wise voting by all other proposals. Proposal X is a Condorcet loser because in table 6.1a, X is defeated in majority voting by both proposals Y and Z.

TABLE 6.2b. BENEFITS AND COSTS FOR THE CONDORCET LOSER PROPOSAL X

	Cost to the voter of the proposal	Voter benefit from the proposal	Voter net benefit from the proposal
Voter 1	100	500	400
Voter 2	100	80	−20
Voter 3	100	70	−30
Total	Total cost = 300	Total benefit = 650	Total net benefit = 350

We therefore conclude:

An inefficient proposal can be a Condorcet winner.

An efficient proposal can be a Condorcet loser.

Voting externalities

There are externalities associated with voting. Proposal X with positive net benefit to society (of 350) was defeated by proposal Y with negative net benefit (of −30). In choosing proposal Y in preference to proposal X, voters 2 and 3 imposed negative externalities on voter 1, who would have had a net benefit of 400 from proposal X but lost 70 because proposal Y defeated X. Thus, majority voting resulted in the choice of an inefficient proposal, but also externalities were created because of the distributional consequences of voting.

Externalities through voting arise because voters base their voting decisions only on own personal *rankings* of the proposals. The values of gains and losses, for themselves and for others, do not influence their voting decisions.

In voting for proposal Y in preference to proposal X, voters 2 and 3 did not care about (or internalize) voter 1's loss of 70 from proposal X and the gain of 400 from proposal Y. However, voters' values of gains and losses determine whether public spending on a proposal is justified by the cost-benefit rule $W = B - C > 0$.

A proposal that is inefficient in not satisfying the cost-benefit rule can be the Condorcet winner because voting decisions are insensitive to how much losers lose and how much gainers gain.

Pareto improvement and compensatory payments

Compensatory payments prevent choice of inefficient proposals. Voter 1 gains 400 from proposal X, whereas voters 2 and 3 gain a total of 40 from proposal Y. Voter 1 can therefore readily compensate voters 2 and 3 for their agreeing to vote for proposal X rather than Y. Because compensation (and over-compensation) is possible, Pareto improvement can be ensured by switching to public finance for proposal X rather than the Condorcet winner Y.[10]

Markets in votes

In making compensatory payments, voter 1, in effect, would be buying the votes of voters 2 and 3. However, markets in votes are illegal. There are two reasons for the illegality.

One reason is the principle that personal income or wealth should not determine how many votes a person controls. The principle of democratic equality of "one person, one vote" is inconsistent with a market for votes, which would allow people to buy votes and vote more than once.

The second reason for not permitting a market in votes is based on the value of aggregated votes. In a large population of voters, a rational voter will correctly perceive that it is unlikely that a single vote will affect the outcome of majority voting: it is personally irrational, as we have noted, to take time to vote based on a personal benefit-cost calculation. When voting is not compulsory, people vote expressively to confirm self-identity or out of a sense of civic duty (or to confirm that they have a sense of civic duty). Nonetheless, if there were a market for votes, some people would be prepared to sell their vote for a small sum of money (other people would not sell their votes because they believe that selling votes is unethical). When a buyer of votes buys increasingly larger numbers of votes, the probability increases that the total votes that have been bought can be used decisively. There is value added through aggregation: the value of the bloc of votes exceeds the sum of the values of the single votes. A person or group that buys sufficient votes in a market for votes therefore can undermine democracy.

There are thus justifiable reasons for markets in votes being illegal. Nonetheless:

> *Absence of markets for votes prevents the payments that would prevent inefficient proposals being chosen by majority voting.*

C. Logrolling

Although markets in which people pay money for votes are illegal, vote-trading among elected political representatives can legally take place. Vote-trading takes the form of an agreement that "If you vote for my preferred proposal, I will vote for your preferred proposal." That is, coalitions are formed to support designated proposals. The formation of such voting coalitions is known as *logrolling* because, although one person can cut down a tree, it takes the cooperation of two people to roll the log.

> *Does logrolling result in efficient public spending?*

[10] Taxpayer 1 does not need to compensate both taxpayers 2 and 3 to obtain majority support for proposal X. Support from either taxpayer 2 or taxpayer 3 is sufficient for a new majority. Pareto improvement (no one losing) requires, of course, that taxpayer 1 compensate both taxpayers 2 and 3.

TABLE 6.3. LOGROLLING WITH SOCIALLY JUSTIFIED PROPOSALS

	Net benefit to Politician 1	Net benefit to Politician 2	Net benefit to Politician 3	Total net benefit
Proposal D	110	−20	−30	60
Proposal E	−20	100	−30	50
Proposal F	−30	−30	100	40

Logrolling with efficient proposals

In table 6.3, three political representatives (to whom we shall refer as "politicians") face a vote on three proposals: *D*, *E*, and *F*. Taxes will be collected and each proposal will be publicly financed through the government budget, if there is majority support for funding the proposal. The proposals now, therefore, are not alternatives as we previously considered; every proposal can be financed if a majority supports the proposal. The final column in table 6.3 shows the total net benefit from a proposal. Each proposal provides positive net benefit; therefore, public spending on each proposal is socially justified by the cost-benefit criterion.

The three proposals differ in distributional consequences. Each proposal provides positive net benefit to only one politician's constituency. In a vote on whether to finance each proposal separately, politician 1 supports only proposal *D*, politician 2 only proposal *E*, and politician 3 only proposal *F*. Although public spending on all three proposals satisfies the cost-benefit criterion, when put to a separate vote, each proposal is rejected by majority voting.

Two politicians can form a coalition to make a majority in favor of the proposals that each wants funded through public spending. The three possible coalitions between politicians are (1, 2), (2, 3), and (1, 3), which provide majority support for pairs of proposals (*D, E*), (*E, F*), and (*D, F*), respectively.

We denote a coalition between politicians *i* and *j* as $V(i, j)$ and the net benefits to politician *i*'s constituency from the two proposals supported by the voting coalition as B_i $(i = 1, 2, 3)$. If politicians 1 and 2 combine to form a coalition to support proposals *D* and *E*, we have:[11]

$$V(1,2) \rightarrow projects(D, E) \rightarrow B_1 = 90,\ \ B_2 = 80,\ \ B_3 = -60,\ \ \sum B_i = 110. \quad (6.8)$$

If politicians 1 and 3 form a coalition:

$$V(1,3) \rightarrow projects(D, F) \rightarrow B_1 = 80,\ \ B_2 = -50,\ \ B_3 = 70,\ \ \sum B_i = 100. \quad (6.9)$$

If politicians 2 and 3 form a coalition:

$$V(2,3) \rightarrow projects(E, F) \rightarrow B_1 = -50,\ \ B_2 = 70,\ \ B_3 = 70,\ \ \sum B_i = 90. \quad (6.10)$$

[11] The arrows signify "implies."

The coalition $V(1, 2)$ provides maximal *total* benefit and also greatest *individual* net benefit for politicians 1 and 2.[12] Politicians 1 and 2 therefore combine their votes to vote in favor of proposals D and E and both vote against proposal F. The constituency of politician 1 thereby obtains a net benefit of 90 and the constituency of politician 2 a net benefit of 80. A loss of 60 is imposed on the constituency of politician 3.

Proposal F, which is not financed, provides positive net benefit and, according to the cost-benefit rule, should also be financed. Logrolling has resulted in acceptance for public finance of two of three efficient proposals.

The two most valuable proposals are here accepted for public finance. The outcome is unfortunate for the constituency of politician 3, on whom negative externalities have been imposed. The constituency of politician 3 is obliged to pay taxes that finance two proposals from which it loses.[13]

Therefore, when all projects are efficient in satisfying the cost-benefit rule $W = B - C > 0$:

> *In the absence of logrolling, no proposal may be publicly financed; logrolling results in public finance for some efficient projects and can leave other efficient projects without public finance; and logrolling has arbitrary distributional effects through the externalities of collective decisions.*

Logrolling with inefficient proposals

Table 6.4 shows three public spending proposals that have negative net benefit and so are inefficient. Each politician's constituency again benefits from only one proposal. The three possible coalitions are:

$$V(1, 2) \rightarrow projects(D, E) \rightarrow B_1 = 10,\ B_2 = 10,\ B_3 = -60,\ \sum B_i = -40. \tag{6.11}$$

$$V(1, 3) \rightarrow projects(D, F) \rightarrow B_1 = 10,\ B_2 = -70,\ B_3 = -10,\ \sum B_i = -50. \tag{6.12}$$

$$V(2, 3) \rightarrow projects(E, F) \rightarrow B_1 = -80,\ B_2 = 20,\ B_3 = -10,\ \sum B_i = -70. \tag{6.13}$$

Because only the coalition $V(1, 2)$ provides positive net benefit for two coalition members, this is the coalition that will be formed. There will, therefore, be majority support for public finance for proposals D and E. Proposal F will not be financed.

[12] Politician 1 gains 90 from a coalition with politician 2 and gains 80 from a coalition with politician 3. Politician 1's preferred coalition partner is therefore politician 2. The gain to politician 2 from a coalition with politician 3 is 70, which is less than the gain of 80 from the coalition with politician 1. Politician 1 is therefore reciprocally politician 2's preferred coalition partner.

[13] The valuations of net benefits or losses of the politicians coincide with the valuations of their constituencies only if there is no political principal–agent problem – which, for our exposition of logrolling, we take to be the case.

TABLE 6.4. LOGROLLING WITH SOCIALLY UNJUSTIFIED PROPOSALS

	Net benefit to Politician 1	Net benefit to Politician 2	Net benefit to Politician 3	Total net benefit
Proposal D	50	−40	−30	−20
Proposal E	−40	50	−30	−20
Proposal F	−40	−30	20	−50

This case illustrates:

Logrolling can result in majority support for proposals for which public finance is not justified by cost-benefit analysis.

Fortuitous efficiency

Logrolling could be fortuitously efficient: we can readily formulate a case where a logrolling coalition of two voters supports two efficient projects and a third project not financed is inefficient. The general conclusion is that:

Logrolling does not ensure efficient public spending – and indeed only fortuitously (by luck) could public spending determined through logrolling be efficient.

Logrolling with money payments

When logrolling takes place, votes are exchanged for votes and are not traded for money. We expect money payments among politicians – and among the politicians' constituencies – to be illegal. Nonetheless, there might be ways in which money payments could be made. What happens to the outcomes of logrolling when money payments (also known as side payments) can take place to entice politicians – or political parties – to leave an existing coalition and join a new coalition?

To consider this question, we return to the efficient public-spending proposals in table 6.3. We saw that, for the projects and preferences in table 6.3, the coalition $V(1, 2)$ forms when no monetary transfers are possible. With money payments possible, politician 3, who is excluded from the coalition $V(1, 2)$, can entice either politician 1 or politician 2 to join him in a new coalition.

Table 6.3a shows the outcome of enticement of politician 1. Politician 3 makes a monetary transfer of 11 to politician 1. The transfer provides politician 1 with benefit of 91 from the new coalition $V(1, 3)$. Politician 1 is therefore better off than she was in the original coalition $V(1, 2)$, which provided her with a benefit of 90. After making the payment to politician 1 to form the coalition $V(1, 3)$, politician 3 has a benefit of 59, which is preferable to his loss of 60 when the coalition is $V(1, 2)$.

TABLE 6.3a. THE INSTABILITY OF LOGROLLING FOR THE PROJECTS IN TABLE 6.3 WHEN MONEY TRANSFERS TAKE PLACE

	Coalition $V(1, 2)$ proposals (D, E)	Coalition $V(1, 3)$ proposals (D, F)	Coalition $V(1, 3)$, proposals (D, F), with payment from politician 3 to 1
Voter 1	90	80	91
Voter 2	80	−50	−50
Voter 3	−60	70	59
Total net benefit	110	100	100

Politician 3 could have chosen to make the offer to politician 2 rather than to politician 1. He chose to make the offer to politician 1 because, with $V(1,3) = 100 > V(2,3) = 90$, the coalition $V(1,3)$ offers greater total benefit than $V(2,3)$, and therefore offers greater personal benefit through sharing of the benefits.

Just as the original logrolling coalition $V(1,2)$ is unstable, the new coalition $V(1,3)$ is also unstable. The now excluded politician 2, who loses 50 because of the coalition $V(1,3)$, can approach either politician 1 or politician 3 with an offer of payment for leaving the coalition $V(1,3)$ and forming a coalition with him. Because $V(1,2) = 110 > V(2,3) = 90$, the incentive is for politician 2 to pay politician 1 to return to him to re-form $V(1,2)$.[14]

The conclusion is that:

> *If money transfers can take place, any coalition formed through logrolling is unstable.*

All-inclusive logrolling coalitions

Monetary payments facilitate all-inclusive logrolling coalitions that provide public finance for all efficient proposals. In table 6.3, politician 3 could pay politicians 1 and 2 to support public finance for proposal F. All three efficient proposals would then be financed.

When money transfers cannot take place, the only gains possible through logrolling and coalition formation are the gains directly obtained from a public-spending proposal: the incentives for a logrolling coalition between politicians 1 and 2 in table 6.3 without money payments were thus based on the benefits to politician 1 from project D and the benefits to politician 2 from project E. Money transfers allow incentives to be introduced also to finance the efficient

[14] We might think that having been left by politician 1, politician 2 will turn to politician 3 rather than invite politician 1 back. However, perhaps emotions do not influence the coalitions that form, nor do principles of loyalty here hold coalitions together. There are no binding contracts and only personal benefits from coalition formation determine decisions to join or leave coalitions.

project *F*: politician 3 gains 100 from project *F*, while politicians 1 and 2 together lose 60, leaving a gain of 40 to be shared – through money transfers from politician 3 to politicians 1 and 2. The money transfers compensate politicians 1 and 2 – or compensate the constituencies of these politicians for their losses.

In sequential decisions, first the logrolling coalition of politicians 1 and 2 forms to finance projects *D* and *E*, and then politician 3 pays to provide incentives for politicians 1 and 2 also to vote in favor of project *F*. We can just as well focus on the unfinanced project *F* alone, which offers benefits to be shared because the project is efficient.

Quite generally, because of benefits to be shared, consensus can be found in favor of public finance of *any* efficient proposal justified by the cost-benefit rule $W = B - C > 0$. There is similarity to the Coase theorem, which predicts realization of all benefits from internalization of externalities. In the case of voting, as in the case of the Coase theorem, before the efficiency gains are available, a decision needs to be reached on how benefits are to be shared. Cooperative bargaining solutions, for example, can be applied to determining the sharing among politicians 1, 2, and 3 of the gains from project *F*.[15]

In table 6.4, no project satisfies the test of cost-benefit analysis but through logrolling between politicians 1 and 2 two inefficient projects are financed, at the expense of the constituency of politician 3. The latter constituency loses 60 from the formation of the logrolling coalition $V(1, 2)$, whereas the total gain to the constituencies of politicians 1 and 2 is 40. The constituency of politician 3 can therefore gain by paying politicians 1 and 2 (or their constituencies) *not* to form their coalition to support public finance for the inefficient proposals *D* and *E*. The opportunity to make the payments results in benefits for politician 3's constituency. Nonetheless, politician 3's constituency is paying to avoid losses from majority-supported socially unwarranted proposals for public finance. The constituency of politician 3, in effect, would be confronting extortion to reduce its losses from decisions by the majority.

Why is there stability in coalitions?

The instability predicted by the inclusion of monetary payments into logrolling is rarely observed. There are incentives of reputation to maintain coalitions that have been formed. Members of an existing majority coalition also know that if they defect by accepting an offer to join another coalition, the benefits of defection may be short term and outweighed by the future losses should they

[15] The agreement of politician 3 is unnecessary to allow the sharing of the gains between politicians 1 and 2 from joint funding of projects *D* and *E*. With monetary payments possible, politicians 1 and 2 are not confined to sharing of the gains as shown in table 6.3: other sharing outcomes are possible, again determined by cooperative bargaining solutions. We demonstrated the Nash-bargaining solution in the case of cost sharing by the owners of trucks and cars in chapter 3. The Shapely value solution to a cooperative game provides each person with the expected value of the person's contribution to total value of the benefits of forming the coalition.

be excluded from new majority coalitions formed in subsequent rounds of coalition instability. Discount rates therefore affect coalition stability: a politician with a low discount rate will not defect.

Stability can also indicate *lack of opportunity* to gain from switching coalitions. There are high transactions costs of payments among the constituencies of voters that benefit or lose from different proposals for public finance – even if political representatives act as coordinators (in collecting contributions from individual voters) and as facilitators (in voting in accord with the logrolling agreement). Problems of collection action arise because individual members of a constituency are required to make personal voluntary contributions to a public good, which is the advancement of the common objective of the constituency. Because of transactions costs and free-rider problems, monetary transfers among constituencies, therefore, do not take place. Most basically, however, the monetary transfers are presumptively illegal and would be viewed as "bribes."

The political benefit of logrolling

The political benefit of logrolling with no accompanying money transfers is precisely that no money changes hands. There can no accusation of bribery. The pure vote trading can be implicit through reciprocal support when different politicians' preferred projects are put to a vote.

D. Checks and balances

The term *tyranny of the majority* describes the ability of the majority under majority voting to dictate outcomes to the minority. The tyranny of the majority can be countered through checks and balances:

> *Checks and balances take the form of legal or constitutional rules that protect a minority of taxpayers from outcomes dictated by votes of the majority.*

Checks and balances are provided by an independent judiciary, duplicated legislative bodies (such as a house of representatives and a senate), and divisions of authority between executive and legislative branches of government.

Table 6.5 returns us to the public-good prisoners' dilemma and shows how checks and balances ensure efficiency and social justice. The outcome in table 6.5 is determined by majority voting by two groups of voters. At (2, 2), the group with

TABLE 6.5. VOTING AND THE PUBLIC-GOOD PRISONERS' DILEMMA

	Group 2 pays	Group 2 does not pay
Group 1 pays	3, 3	1, 4
Group 1 does not pay	4, 1	2, 2

a majority or both groups vote that no one pays taxes to finance the public good, which is then not provided. At (3, 3), the group with a majority or both groups vote that everyone pays taxes to provide the public good and there is Pareto improvement relative to (2, 2). In the asymmetric outcomes at (4, 1) and (1, 4), the majority votes that only members of the minority group will pay taxes to finance the public good: majority voting in these latter asymmetric cases therefore exhibits the tyranny of the majority.

A rule requiring non-discrimination through public finance rules out the asymmetric outcomes at (4, 1) and (1, 4) and restricts the choice to a vote on the symmetric outcomes at (2, 2) and (3, 3). When confronted with the choice between (2, 2) and (3, 3), both groups vote in favor of (3, 3) – although it is sufficient for (3, 3) to be the outcome if the majority votes in favor. At (3, 3), there is consensus favoring everyone paying. At (2, 2), there is also a consensus outcome where nobody pays. The outcome at (3, 3) is the efficient consensus. Hence:

> *A rule requiring a symmetric outcome of majority voting under the payoffs of the prisoners' dilemma is equivalent to a consensus voting rule.*

Bundling of public spending on public goods

Groups in the same population may have different demands for or want different types of public goods. For example, group 1 may want police patrols during the day and early evening, whereas group 2 wants the patrols to continue throughout the night. Because of differences in preferences in the population, the non-discriminatory symmetric outcome at (3, 3) in table 6.5 applies to total public spending through the government budget on the many public goods that are chosen simultaneously for public finance – or to *bundles* of public goods. At (3, 3), combinations of taxation and spending on public goods are chosen from which all taxpayers benefit.[16]

Checks and balances in fiscal federal systems

Under fiscal federalism, taxation and public spending take place in hierarchical or federal systems of government. The federal or highest level of government caters to the entire population; state and regional governments cater to smaller groups; and local governments cater to the smallest groups. Opportunities to choose public goods through the Tiebout locational choice mechanism result in greater homogeneity of populations in jurisdictions at lower levels of government; at higher levels of government, there is correspondingly greater variety of voter preferences and incomes. Therefore, at higher levels of government, there is also greater likelihood of disagreement between majority and minority groups of voters and thus greater need for checks and balances.

[16] More generally, the objectives are horizontal equity (equal treatment of equals) and also vertical equity (equal treatment of people who are "unequal" in having different preferences for public spending).

Secession and personal exit

If checks and balances are absent so that voting outcomes are persistently asymmetric at (4, 1) or (1, 4), a disadvantaged minority on which losses are consistently imposed by the majority can be expected to wish to secede from the jurisdiction of the collective decision-making body. We saw how incentives for secession or exit of groups arise when we studied the Tiebout locational choice mechanism as a solution to the public-good asymmetric-information problem: depending on the benefits from sharing costs in a combined jurisdiction, a minority group whose preferences for public goods differ from the majority's preferences might gain by leaving to form its own jurisdiction in which public goods are supplied according to its own preferences. We also observed that the majority has an interest in keeping the minority in the jurisdiction so that the minority will continue to contribute through taxation to the financing of the public spending that the majority wants; therefore, if rules enforcing the non-discriminatory outcome (3, 3) for taxation and public finance are not being applied and a minority wishes to leave, we expect the majority to oppose secession. There is, on the other hand, no fiscal incentive for secession if legal or constitutional rules are being applied that avoid discriminatory public-finance outcomes in which benefits are unequally provided or costs are unequally shared.

Exit can take the form of secession of a geographical area, which forms a new government jurisdiction. The equivalent of secession at the level of the individual (or family) is personal exit. By exiting, people create or join a population in which the majority has preferences similar to theirs for public spending:

> *Secession and personal exit are responses to absence of checks and balances.*

By creating homogeneous populations of voters, secession and personal locational choice avoid the tyranny of the majority in determination of taxes and public spending.[17]

Instability of voting outcomes as a form of checks and balances

We presented a view that instability of voting outcomes is undesirable because of inability to obtain a determinate collective choice through majority voting. However, instability becomes similar to a form of checks and balances when each unstable voting outcome prevails over some period of time. Through the cycling over outcomes that is the reason for "instability," all groups of voters benefit from having their preferred public spending financed for some periods. Allowing all voters to benefit some of the time is socially just – compared to a "stable" outcome that persists over time and maintains the preferred outcome of one group of voters. Also, when some public spending proposals satisfy the cost-benefit

[17] If locational sorting has solved the preference-revelation or asymmetric-information problem through creation of homogeneous populations of voters, the efficient Lindahl consensus outcome can be implemented, with equal Lindahl prices levied as equal taxes.

criterion and some do not, cycling among proposals ensures that – at least some of the time – efficient proposals are financed.[18]

Democracy is based on "cycling" – through one political party eventually replacing another in government. The cycling of political parties in government occurs because of changes in voter's perceptions of competence of politicians or voters' perceiving inadequacies in government policies. Or, perhaps, without reference to substance of competence or policies, voters may want change in order to see new faces in government after one party has been in office for a considerable period. "Stability," with one political party persisting in office, is not democracy but is rather the dictatorship of a single party. "Stable" government occurs when ethnic, tribal, or religious groups who form a majority only ever support the one political party. The tyranny of the majority under majority voting need not be the same as the tyranny of a dictator who rules without the rule of law; however, majority voting nonetheless becomes a form of dictatorship when, with stable majority-determined outcomes, the same political party and its supporters continue to control public spending and to decide how taxes are levied.

> *Instability through rotation in office is desirable, particularly if checks and balances are not present to counter the tyranny of the majority.*

6.2 Political Competition

Institutions of direct and representative democracy differ.

> *When voters directly vote on issues of public finance and public policy, the institutions are those of direct democracy; when voters elect representatives who in turn vote on their behalf, the institutions are those of representative democracy.*

Our conclusions about majority voting apply to direct democracy in which voters directly vote on policies and to representative democracy in which voters elect representatives who then vote on policies on their behalf.

[18] The distributional advantages of cycling compared to stable majority voting outcomes were observed by James Buchanan (1954; Nobel Prize in economics, 1986). Supplement S7B will describe an "impossibility theorem" set out by Kenneth Arrow (1950; Nobel Prize in economics, 1972) showing that under reasonable axioms and with ordinal utility, no determinate social (or collective) choice may be achievable. One of Arrow's axioms was that there be no dictatorship. Arrow proposed that removing this axiom and allowing dictatorship was a means of establishing stable collective choice. The dictatorship that provides stable collective choice could be by one person or by a group of people. In a response to Arrow, Buchanan (1954) observed that the instability of collective decisions that dictatorship avoided was not necessarily socially disadvantageous as Arrow proposed; on the contrary, instability was socially beneficial in allowing different groups to benefit in turn from collective decisions when there are no checks and balances to ensure equal benefits from collective decisions.

Under representative democracy, there is political competition among candidates in contests for political office. In the competition for elected office, the candidates announce their policies and the winning candidates are chosen as political representatives. We shall now study policy determination through the political competition of representative democracy. We shall view the policy announcements made by a political candidate as indicating the policies that the candidate will implement or support if successful in the election; we do not now, therefore, consider the credibility of politicians' and political candidates' policy pronouncements. Voters (unless, as we shall see, they are expressive) support candidates whose policy pronouncements, if implemented (if a candidate wins), provide highest personal utility relative to policy pronouncements of other candidates. In the circumstances we now describe, voters are forward-looking in making judgments based on announced future policies; they are not retroactive in judging politicians on past decisions and past performance.

A. Direct and representative democracy

Before investigating policy determination through political competition in representative democracy, we look at the differences between direct and representative democracy as institutions of collective decision making.

The prevalence of representative democracy reflects high costs of seeking individual voters' opinions on each issue. There may also have been a feeling in the past that taxation and public-spending decisions are better made by political representatives who can dedicate their time to studying the issues to be decided and therefore can be better informed than voters at large, who may be subject to rational ignorance. Over time, information technology diminished the costs of direct voting. Coded transmission through the Internet and e-mail can allow voters to express views on issues under conditions of confidentiality while allowing verification that people have had the right to vote and that they have only voted once on each issue. Communications technology has also provided means for voters to become better informed; the Internet provides information with an immediacy that was not possible when systems of representative democracy were first established.

In many jurisdictions, issues considered of substantive importance are not left to decisions of political representatives but rather are decided by direct democracy through a plebiscite or referendum.[19] Jurisdictions also differ in scope of opportunities for direct democracy; for example, in states of the United States, plebiscites or referenda are common in some states and are rare or do not at all occur in other states. Voters have, of course, more influence over policy decisions when they themselves vote to determine outcomes. Policy proposals that depart from the public interest can then be blocked. However, often the choice is not

[19] An example of an issue of substantive importance is the constitution or form of government; thus, in 1999, voters in Australia directly determined in a referendum whether to replace the constitutional monarchy whereby the English monarch is the nominal head of state with a republic. The majority voted against the proposed change to a republic.

between the public interest and benefit for special interests but rather between outcomes sought by groups of voters with different preferences regarding taxation and public spending.

In Switzerland, the regional government jurisdictions (called *cantons*) use direct and representative democracy to different degrees. Switzerland is therefore a natural location to study the different consequences of direct and representative democracy. Evidence from Switzerland indicates that – as we could expect – voters are better informed about issues when they personally vote through direct democracy than when political representatives vote on their behalf. There is less rational ignorance under direct democracy. Voters rationally acquire more information because, under direct democracy, voters need to make their own decisions about how to vote on issues that under representative democracy are decided by votes of elected politicians.

Direct democracy also appears to provide greater personal satisfaction. Under direct democracy, substantive issues of public finance and public policy become part of everyday discussion among voters. People are more inclined than under representative democracy to ask one other, "How are you going to vote and why?" Studies also show that people feel "happier" under direct democracy, by feeling more in control of their lives. Of course, it remains the case that one individual vote has effectively zero chance of being decisive. Nonetheless, people feel personally more in control of their lives when they can directly vote according to their own decision rather than relying on a politician to vote on their behalf. If voting is expressive, people are happy that they have given the opportunity to express themselves – although they may not identify with the majority voting outcome and would have been happier had the result been otherwise.

> *Under direct democracy, people are better informed and seemingly happier than representative democracy.*

Ostrogorski's paradox

Voting outcomes over the same issues with the same voter preferences can differ depending on whether voting takes place under direct or representative democracy. Table 6.6 shows *Ostrogorski's paradox* (named after Moise Ostrogorski, who set out the paradox in 1903). There are three public-spending proposals: *A*, *B*, and *C*. For example, project *A* is defense spending, project *B* is subsidies for

TABLE 6.6. OSTROGORSKI'S PARADOX

	A = Defense	B = Opera	C = Highways
Group 1 (20%)	No (candidate 1)	No (candidate 1)	Yes (candidate 2)
Group 2 (20%)	No (candidate 1)	Yes (candidate 2)	No (candidate 1)
Group 3 (20%)	Yes (candidate 2)	No (candidate 1)	No (candidate 1)
Group 4 (40%)	Yes (candidate 2)	Yes (candidate 2)	Yes (candidate 2)

the opera and other cultural performances and events, and project *C* is greater spending for highways. Taxes can be levied to finance any and all projects if there is majority support from voters.

The voters in table 6.6 are divided into four groups with different preferences for public spending. A "yes" indicates that a group favors a project; a "no" indicates that a group opposes a project. Voters in group 1 want only the highway spending; voters in group 2 want only cultural spending; and voters in group 3 want only defense spending. Voters in group 4 want public spending on all three projects. Groups 1, 2, and 3 each contain 20 percent of voters and group 4 contains the remaining 40 percent of voters.

Direct democracy

In voting under direct democracy, a decision is made on each issue separately. Separate votes, therefore, are taken on the three questions whether to levy taxes to finance projects *A*, *B*, and *C*. The outcome is determined by majority voting. Under direct democracy, a majority supports taxation and public spending on all three projects.[20]

Representative democracy

Under representative democracy, two political candidates compete for electoral office by seeking voter support from the single constituency composed of all four groups of voters. Candidate 1 opposes public spending on any project. Candidate 2 supports public spending on each project. In table 6.6, where "no" indicates a group's opposition to funding a project, voters in the group support candidate 1; where "yes" indicates a group's support for public spending on a project, there is support for candidate 2. Benefits for voters in groups 1, 2, and 3 from the one project that they want are smaller than the losses incurred in paying taxes to fund the other two projects that they do not want; therefore, these groups support candidate 1 who opposes public spending. Voters in group 4 support candidate 2, whose pro-spending position coincides precisely with their preference for spending on all projects. The outcome of political competition under representative democracy is therefore that candidate 1 wins with 60 percent of the vote versus 40 percent for candidate 2. Therefore, under representative democracy, no public spending takes place for any of the projects.

The paradox

Under direct democracy, there is majority support for public finance for each project. Under representative democracy, there is no support for public finance for any project. Ostrogorski's paradox shows that:

> *The outcome of majority voting under representative democracy can be the precise opposite of the outcome under direct democracy.*

[20] In each case, the majority consists of the 40 percent in group 4 plus the 20 percent in the group that favors the project.

The differences in voting outcomes are due to the way in which preferences of voters are aggregated. With direct democracy, voters' preferences over specific issues determine the outcome. With representative democracy, issues are bundled or aggregated in the policy declarations of political candidates.

Although aspects of social justice are present through voting externalities and the dictates of the majority over the minority, our objective here in considering voting is efficient public spending. The information in table 6.6 is insufficient to indicate whether the outcome of direct or representative democracy is socially preferred in terms of efficiency (we also have insufficient information, including absence of criteria, to make judgments about social justice). We have seen that majority voting does not ensure that efficient projects are financed or that inefficient projects are not financed. For example, if in table 6.6 all three projects are efficient by the test of cost-benefit analysis that $W = B - C > 0$, the outcome of direct democracy is preferred; if none of the projects is efficient, the outcome of representative democracy is preferred.

B. Political competition with a single issue

We now turn our attention to the political competition of representative democracy. We remain in circumstances where information is insufficient to make judgments about the efficiency of voting outcomes – nor is there information to allow judgments about social justice. We nonetheless study the political competition of representative democracy because of the widespread use of this means of making collective decisions. Our criterion now becomes, however, something other than the difference between benefits and costs that determines the efficiency of economic decisions. We ask whether political competition replicates the outcome that would be determined under majority voting by the median voter or the outcome that would be chosen as the Condorcet winner. The standard is political; normatively desirable properties are attributed to the median voter's preferences, which are made to epitomize the preferences of society, or to the Condorcet winner, which defeats all other proposals in pair-wise voting. However, we have seen that neither choice according to the preferences of the median voter nor the outcome that is the Condorcet winner ensures efficiency (or social justice).

Figure 6.8a shows the simplest possible setting for political competition. Two candidates for political office take policy positions regarding public spending on a single public good. Voters know their tax obligations for financing the public good. Given their tax obligations, they can determine their personally preferred or utility-maximizing supply of the public good along the horizontal axis in figure 6.8a. All voters have preferences that are single-peaked: that is, each voter has a unique preferred quantity for the public good. The utility of the median voter is maximized at G_m. Voters' utility-maximizing quantities are uniformly distributed between a minimum of zero and a maximum of G^{max}. Taxpayers achieve their best outcome by voting for a candidate who proposes supply of the public good that is closest to their utility-maximizing choice. All voters vote. Two

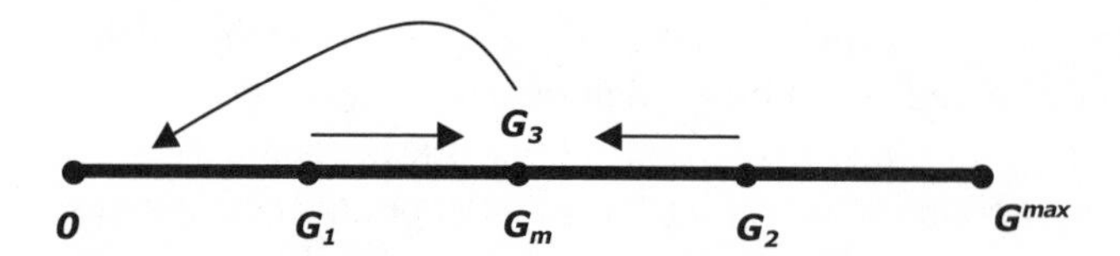

Figure 6.8a. Political competition with a single policy issue.

political candidates choose their policy positions with the objective of winning the election. Initially, candidate 1 announces:

$$G_1 < G_m \tag{6.14}$$

and candidate 2 announces:

$$G_m < G_2. \tag{6.15}$$

We are looking for equilibrium policy pronouncements. We apply the Nash-equilibrium concept to define equilibrium: therefore, in equilibrium, for given distribution of voters' preferences, no candidate wishes to change his or her announced policy, given the announced policy of the other candidate.

The candidates are assured of support from voters whose preferences are more extreme than their policy pronouncements. All taxpayers who ideally want G_1 or less vote for candidate 1 when candidate 1 announces the policy G_1; all taxpayers who ideally want G_2 or more vote for candidate 2 when candidate 2 announces the policy G_2. Taxpayers who want quantities between G_1 and G_2 make their voting decisions based on whether their personal utility-maximizing supply is closer to G_1 or G_2.

Under these conditions, policy announcements converge to the preferred policy of the median voter. In equilibrium, the candidates' policies are indistinguishable and the policy chosen is that of the median voter.[21]

The unique Nash equilibrium for political candidates on a single issue is that each candidate announces the preferred policy of the median voter.

Policy convergence in practice

Although competing candidates' policies often are observed to converge, the complete duplication of policy positions predicted by the two-candidate model of political competition is not usually observed in practice. Complete duplication of policies would eliminate the basis for a political contest based on policy differences; policies could then offer voters no guide for choosing between candidates. If there were complete policy duplication, voting could not be based on issues of policy substance but could only be expressive and based on self-identification of a voter with other attributes of a candidate, such as looks, ethnic background,

[21] Convergence through locational competition is associated with Harold Hotelling (1895–1973) and was described in Hotelling (1929). Downs (1957) studied convergence through political competition.

religion, the college or university that a candidate attended, or the candidate's rhetorical ability.[22]

When only policies determine voters' choices, the preferred policy of the median voter may not be known to the two candidates. The candidates may conduct opinion polls in an attempt to identify the position of the median voter but still may not know the policy preferences of the median voter with certainty. Candidates with different perceptions of the identity of the median voter then choose different policies. The candidate who wins the election is the one who has been more accurate in identifying the policy position of the median voter.

Expressive voters and abstention

When candidates converge to the preferred policy of the median voter, the candidates rely on continued support from "locked-in" voters. Thus in figure 6.8a, when converging to the median voter's choice, candidate 1 relies on continued support from voters ideally wanting less public spending than she proposes; similarly, in the course of converging to the median voter's position by announcing policies of reduced spending, candidate 2 relies on continued support from voters ideally wanting greater public spending.

Expressive voters at the respective ends of the policy spectrum, however, may be alienated by the perceived opportunism of a candidate who moves to the middle and may respond by abstaining from voting. We note that:

> *Voting can be expressive with regard to policies or expressive with regard to attributes of candidates.*

The expressive voters who abstain personally identify with policies near one end of the spectrum: when candidates converge to the position of the median voter, they feel that they "have no one to vote for" as representing the policy with which they identify.

On the other hand, voters who vote expressively based not on policies but on identification with candidates' attributes will not abstain from voting, even if, because of convergence, policies of candidates are more or less the same or even identical.

A voter who is not expressive does not abstain. The non-expressive voter (also known as "instrumental" because the voter views the vote as an instrument for implementing a desired policy) bases his or her voting decision on maximized utility from voting by measuring distances between his or her preferred position and the positions of the candidates. The non-expressive or instrumental voter thus votes for the candidate with the position relatively closer to his or her preferred position without regard for the absolute position taken by the candidate – whereas expressive voters care about the absolute position and abstain

[22] With complete convergence, political campaign contributions, which we are not considering here, could not be based on candidates' support for different policies.

if the absolute position of a candidate deviates sufficiently from their preferred position.

> *With voters not influenced by the time costs of voting, instrumental or non-expressive voters never abstain, nor do voters whose support for candidates is expressively based on candidates' attributes, whereas voters who vote expressively with regard to policies abstain if they cannot adequately express themselves through the policy positions that candidates propose.*

Candidates' responses to abstention

Systematic known abstention by particular groups of voters changes the identity of the median voter and thereby the policy to which the candidates converge. If, for example, voters on the political right of the spectrum do not vote instrumentally but rather expressively identify with the policies of the right and abstain, the median voter is located farther to the political left and abstention will have moved the equilibrium policy farther away from the abstainers' preferred policies.[23] When there are abstentions, the equilibrium policy is determined by the preferred policy of the median voter among people who actually vote. To determine the position of the median voter in the population of actual voters who remain after expressive abstentions, the political candidates need to know the distribution of abstainers. If abstentions are random and unknown to the candidates before the election, the candidates can do no better than to announce the policy of the median voter based on the median of the entire population of potential voters, if the identity of this median voter is known.

Convergence and primary systems of voting

When voting is in two stages, with parties choosing political candidates in primary elections, if only registered party members can vote in the primary elections, the electorate is segmented in the primary stage. Because the segmented populations of voters have different preferences, the announced policies that win primaries are generally more extreme in catering to the median voter among party members than the announced policy that caters to the median voter in the all-inclusive general election. Candidates who win primaries are therefore expected to moderate their positions and converge toward the center in the second-round, all-inclusive contest.[24]

[23] In figure 6.8a, the political right favoring small government and low public spending and the political left favoring large government and high public spending are respectively on the left and the right of the scale.

[24] If primaries are open so that members of other parties and independent voters can participate, voting decisions become strategic. Voters need to decide whether to vote for a primary candidate who they actually would like to see win the general election or whether to vote for a primary candidate who they believe will be defeated by the candidate of another party that they prefer to win the general election.

Reputation and commitment

Our formal framework looks at an election at a point in time, with voters making decisions based only on candidates' present policy pronouncements. Decisions of political candidates in the past, therefore, have no consequences for present electoral success; nor do present decisions of candidates affect future electoral success. Political candidates may understand, however, that they are involved in a repeated game that goes beyond a single election and that reputation therefore matters for future electoral success. Voters who vote expressively for honesty and consistency may feel particularly uneasy about supporting a candidate who was perceived as opportunistic in the past. Convergence of policy pronouncements does not take place if a political candidate adheres to a policy position because of reputational concerns. A candidate may also not converge toward the position of the median voter because of commitment to ideology or belief in what is best for society. By not converging, a candidate is assured of electoral defeat.[25]

In figure 6.8a, candidate 2 may maintain a policy of G_2. Candidate 2 then loses with certainty against candidate 1, who is flexible in adapting policy to voter support. To maximize votes, candidate 1 converges to G_2. Candidate 1 then has the support of the 75 percent of voters who ideally want less than G_2. However, candidate 1 has now chosen the policy sought by candidate 2. Indeed, by acting strategically, candidate 2 has led candidate 1 to choose candidate 2's preferred policy. Although choice of G_2 maximizes votes for candidate 1, it is not necessary for candidate 1 to maximize votes to win the election. Winning the election requires only in excess of 50 percent of the vote. This is achieved by candidate 1 choosing slightly in excess of G_1.

> *An inflexible candidate not only loses with certainty but, by not converging to the policy of the median voter, the inflexible candidate also allows the opponent to choose a more extreme policy.*

For example, by being inflexible at G_2 in figure 6.8a, candidate 2, who is the candidate of high taxation and high public spending, facilitates the majority-voting outcome of $(G_1 + \varepsilon)$, where taxation and public spending are low.

More than two candidates

We have viewed political competition as between two candidates. With three candidates, there is no Nash-equilibrium policy. In figure 6.8a, with all voters voting instrumentally (there are no abstentions) candidate 3 initially announces policy G_3 to duplicate the preferred policy G_m of the median voter, and candidates 1 and 2 initially announce policies G_1 and G_2. These policy announcements are not a Nash equilibrium. Candidates 1 and 2 can do better by converging to the median voter's position at G_m, where voter 3 is located with the announcement

[25] Gus Hall (1910–2000), for example, was the Communist Party candidate for U.S. president four times and did not change his policy position.

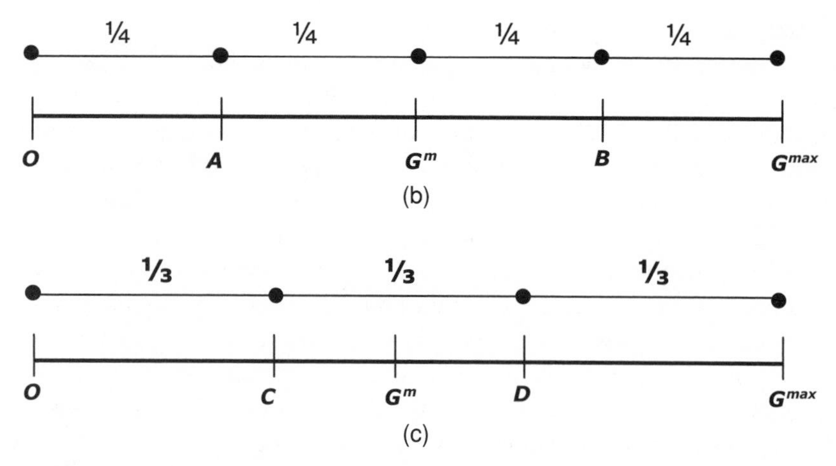

Figure 6.8. (b) Political competition with four candidates and a single policy issue. (c) Political competition with five candidates and a single policy issue.

G_3. As candidates 1 and 2 converge toward G_m, political support for candidate 3 declines; more voters find their personally preferred positions closer to the policies of candidates 1 and 2 who are converging toward the median voter's preferred policy. At some stage, in response to the declining voter support as candidates 1 and 2 converge toward G_m, candidate 3 can do better by jumping to either the left or the right. In figure 6.8a, the jump by candidate 3 places candidate 1 in the middle, who then will also, in turn, have an incentive to jump.

The jumps in policy announcement by the candidate in the middle take place because winning an election requires more than the support of only the median voter; to win, a candidate requires the support of an additional 50 percent of voters *in addition to* the median voter. Positioning of a candidate at the median voter's preferred policy G_m therefore cannot ensure a candidate's electoral success. Indeed, such positioning ensures defeat when other candidates are drawing away political support by converging toward the median voter's position.

Stability is restored when a fourth candidate enters the political contest. Figure 6.8b shows the Nash equilibrium for four candidates. G^{max} is once more the maximal quantity of a public good sought in the population and G^m is sought by the median voter in the uniform distribution over $(0, G^{max})$. Candidates 1 and 2 locate themselves at point A at 25 percent of the maximal quantity and candidates 3 and 4 locate themselves at point B at 75 percent of the maximal quantity. Neither policy A nor B is the policy sought by the median voter.

Figure 6.8c shows the outcome when a fifth candidate enters the political contest. In the Nash equilibrium, two candidates locate themselves at point C at one third of the maximal quantity and two candidates locate themselves at point D at two thirds of the maximal quantity. The fifth candidate chooses the position of the median voter. With a sixth candidate, three sets of candidates sharing one third of the vote is a Nash equilibrium. We stop with six candidates.[26]

[26] For more detail, see Reinhard Selten (1971; Nobel Prize in economics, 1994).

C. Political competition with multiple issues

We have been considering only one policy issue. We now turn our attention to political competition when there are multiple policy issues. It is sufficient to consider two policy issues. Figure 6.9a shows quantities of two public goods, *X* and *Y*, about which public-spending decisions are to be made. With the personal taxes required to finance the public spending known, the preferred choice for voter 1 is at point 1, where public spending is on the quantities X_1 and Y_1 of the two public goods.

Voter 1's utility declines as the distance from the preferred point 1 increases in any direction. The indifference curves that define different levels of utility for voter 1 are concentric circles around point 1. Point *E* on the inner circle provides more of both public goods than point 1. Point *B*, in turn, provides more of both public goods than point *E*. Nonetheless, voter 1 prefers point 1 – with less of both public goods – to either point *E* or point *B*.

Usually, more goods are preferred to fewer goods. However, figure 6.9a does not show all the goods from which voter 1 derives utility. In addition to the publicly financed public goods, voter 1 benefits from private market spending. We denote voter 1's private consumption by *Z*. Voter 1's utility is thus made up of the benefit from the public goods *X* and *Y*, as well as the benefit from private consumption *Z*.

Figure 6.9a separates the utility from the public goods from the utility derived from private consumption. Voter 1 has a limited demand for spending on the public goods because personal income left after payment of taxes to finance the supply of public goods is available to be spent on private consumption *Z*. Because of the benefit from private consumption *Z*, the voter ideally wants to be taxed no more than the personal taxes required to finance the quantities of public goods at point 1 (when others are also paying taxes determined by their tax obligations). A political candidate can be assured of voter 1's support by proposing to supply the combination of public goods at voter 1's ideal point 1.

Figure 6.9b introduces preferences for public spending of a second voter, whose preferred spending is at point 2. We see that voter 2 ideally wants more public spending on both public goods than voter 1.

The contract curve in figure 6.9b joins the preferred points 1 and 2 of voters 1 and 2.[27] All points on the contract curve are Pareto-efficient: therefore, once on the contract curve, no Pareto-improving change can take place.[28]

A political candidate whose policy proposal is on the contract curve defeats a candidate who proposes a policy off of the contract curve. For example, in

[27] The contract curve joins points of tangency of voters' indifference curves (see supplement S1A).

[28] For example, beginning from point *E* on the contract curve in figure 6.9b, moving toward point 1 along the contract curve makes voter 1 better off and makes voter 2 worse off. Moving toward point 2 along the contract curve conversely makes voter 2 better off and voter 1 worse off. Moving off the contract curve makes one or both of the voters worse off. Beginning from a point not on the contract curve such as point *D*, both voters are made better off by a move to a point inside the shaded area, and a move onto the contract curve such as point *J* ends possibilities for Pareto improvement.

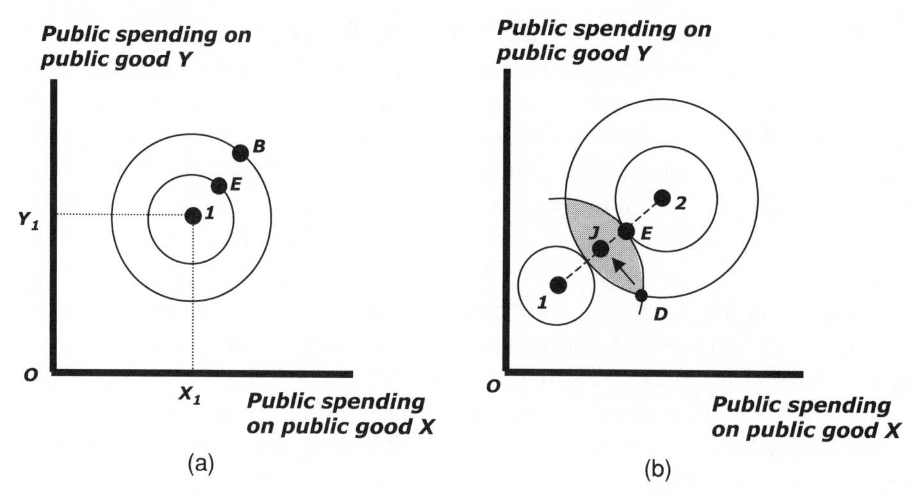

Figure 6.9. (a) A voter's preferred combination of public spending. (b) Pareto-efficient public-spending proposals.

figure 6.9b, if candidate 1 proposes supply of public goods at point *D* not on the contract curve, candidate 2 can win the support of voters 1 and 2 by proposing a policy such as *J* on the contract curve because point *J* provides both voters with higher utility than point *D*.

We therefore conclude:

Candidates will only announce policies that are on a contract curve.

Thus, in looking for Nash-equilibrium policy pronouncements, we confine our search to policies on a contract curve.

Three voters are needed to consider majority voting. Figure 6.10 introduces a third voter, whose preferred public-good supply is at point 3. There are now three contract curves joining the preferred points 1, 2, and 3 of the three voters. The three contract curves form the shaded triangle shown in the figure.

In looking for an equilibrium for candidates' policy pronouncements, we begin in figure 6.10 with the decision of candidate 1, who chooses a policy arbitrarily somewhere on a contract curve. The arbitrary choice of candidate 1 can be, for example, point *D* on the contract curve for voters 1 and 3. Because *D* is on the contract curve for voters 1 and 3, indifference curves (the circles) of these voters are tangential at point *D*.

An indifference curve of voter 2 passes through point *D*. The indifference curve of voter 2 can be used to define points on the other two contract curves that voters prefer to candidate 1's policy position at point *D*.

We see, for example, that voters 1 and 2 prefer point *E* to candidate 1's policy position at point *D*. Therefore, by announcing the policy at point *E*, candidate 2 defeats candidate 1 by majority voting. Voter 3 loses from a move from point *D*

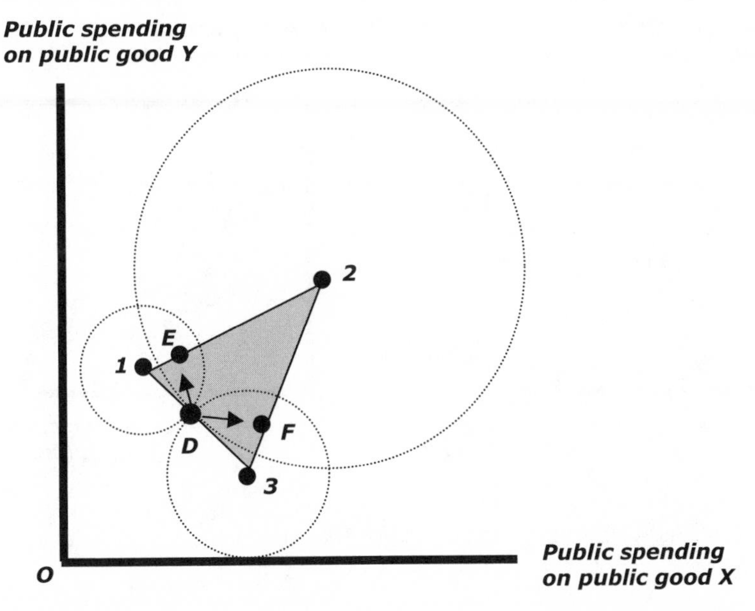

Figure 6.10. The instability of political competition when candidates announce policies on two issues.

to point E and supports candidate 1; however, voters 1 and 2 gain at point E relative to point D and support candidate 2, who wins the election.

Alternatively, candidate 2 could choose a policy at a point such as F. Voters 2 and 3 are better off at point F than at point D, so these voters provide majority support for candidate 2. Candidate 1 is supported only by voter 1, who loses from a move from point D to point F.

The process of political competition began with a choice by candidate 1 that was on one of the contract curves but otherwise arbitrary. It does not matter which policy on which contract curve candidate 1 chooses: there are always policies on the other two contract curves that provide majority support for candidate 2.

There is no Nash equilibrium. After candidate 2 has chosen the policy at point E or point F that defeats candidate 1, candidate 1 wins by changing from the original policy declaration at point D to a policy that defeats candidate 2.

Hence:

> *There is, in general, no Nash equilibrium when two political candidates take policy positions on two issues.*

When there are two candidates and more than two policies, the contract curves are in higher dimensions and there is also, in general, no Nash equilibrium.

The prediction is, therefore, instability of political candidates' policy pronouncements. We once more return to the question of why stability is observed.

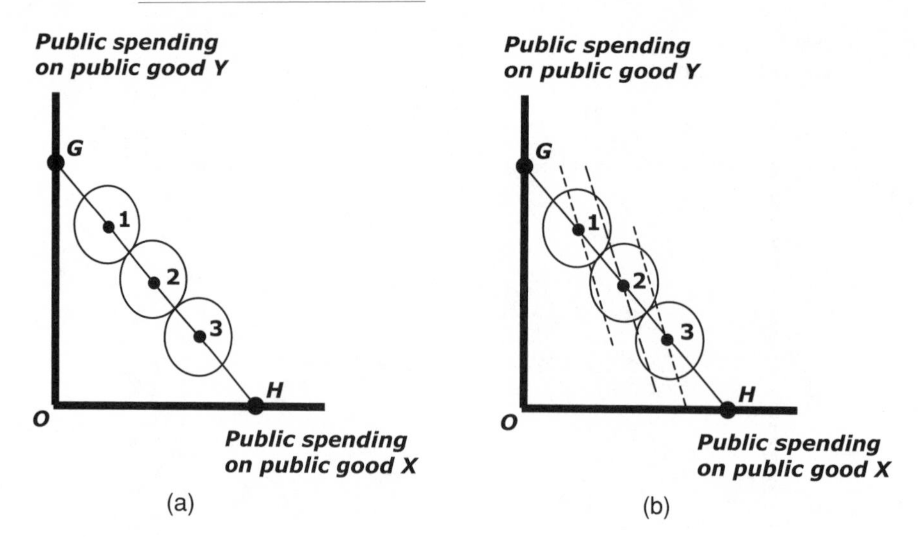

Figure 6.11. (a) A stable policy proposal. (b) The relative price of public goods and the contract curve.

A special case of a stable equilibrium

Figure 6.11a shows a special case in which a stable outcome of political competition exists. The preferred policies of all three voters lie along the same straight line *GH*, which combines all contract curves for the three voters.

In these circumstances, which could only occur incidentally, the issues of how much to spend on *X* and how much to spend on *Y* have been reduced to a single issue, which is where along the line *GH* public spending should be. Voter 2 is the median voter on this single issue, and the unique stable equilibrium outcome of majority voting is voter 2's preferred point 2. The majority-voting equilibrium is determined by asking the voters whether they wish to move farther along *GH* toward point 2. There is a majority in favor of change at every point except at point 2.

If the slope of the line *GH* happens to coincide with the relative price of the two public goods *X* and *Y*, then, in addition to indicating the all-inclusive contract curve, the line *GH* also indicates a level of public spending on the two public goods. The voters then agree on the level of public spending but disagree on the composition of public spending between the public goods *X* and *Y*.

In general, the relative price of the public goods is not equal to the slope of the contract curve.[29] Figure 6.11b shows the typical case in which the slope of the contract curve and the relative price of the public goods differ. The relative price of the public goods is indicated as the common slope of the dashed lines. Each voter now not only wants a different combination of public goods along the contract curve but also a different level of public spending, as determined

[29] The relative price of public goods and the slope of a contract curve, of course, are not related and need not be equal. In particular, the contract curve can have a positive slope, whereas the slope of the line indicating the relative price of public goods is always negative.

by the dashed budget lines. Voter 3 wants the most public spending and voter 1 the least. A stable majority-voting equilibrium in figure 6.11b again exists at the preferred outcome of median voter 2 at point 2, which determines both total public spending and the mix of spending.

Ideological or principled candidates

We observed – in the case of political competition between two candidates with a single issue – how candidates who ideologically adhere to a predetermined policy position lose with certainty. A candidate who takes an inflexible ideological position also loses with certainty when there are two issues. Whatever the ideological position taken, there is a policy position that another candidate can take to win with certainty.

Principled political coalitions

Voters may form coalitions based on principles about the size of government. The principles override personal benefit and result in stable outcomes of majority voting when there are multiple issues. Such coalitions are, in effect, political parties. In figure 6.12a, by construction in order to simplify, the slope of the contract curve between voters 1 and 3 preferred points also indicates the relative price of the two public goods: the contract curve for voters 1 and 3 coincides, therefore, with a budget line for total spending on public goods *X* and *Y*. Voters 1 and 3 have a common interest in lower public spending than the public spending ideally sought by voter 2 and form a coalition based on adherence to the principle that they will not support higher public spending than the spending indicated by the budget line between their preferred policy positions (which is also here their contract curve).

After candidate 1 has announced the policy at point *D*, voter 1 therefore will not switch to support candidate 2 after candidate 2 has announced the policy at point *E*, even though voter 1's utility is higher at point *E* than at point *D*. Voter 3 will similarly not support a candidate who proposes the policy at point *F*, even though similarly voter 3's utility is higher at point *F* than at point *D*.

Voters 1 and 3 thereby subordinate personal utility to the principle of limiting public spending and taxation. Voters 1 and 3 disagree, however, on the composition of public spending. Voter 1 wants point 1 and voter 3 wants point 3. Voter 2 is decisive in determining the majority-voting outcome at point *D* on the budget line between points 1 and 3.[30]

[30] More generally, the majority-voting equilibrium constrained by the agreement between voters 1 and 3 to limit public spending is at the point where an indifference curve of voter 2 is tangential to the line joining the preferred positions of voters 1 and 3, which need not be at the point *D*, which we designated as the policy pronouncement of candidate 1. In figure 6.12a, along the contract curve of voters 1 and 3, voter 2's utility is maximized at point *D*. The policy position at point *D* is a majority-voting equilibrium. Voters 1 and 3 oppose a movement away from point *D* toward

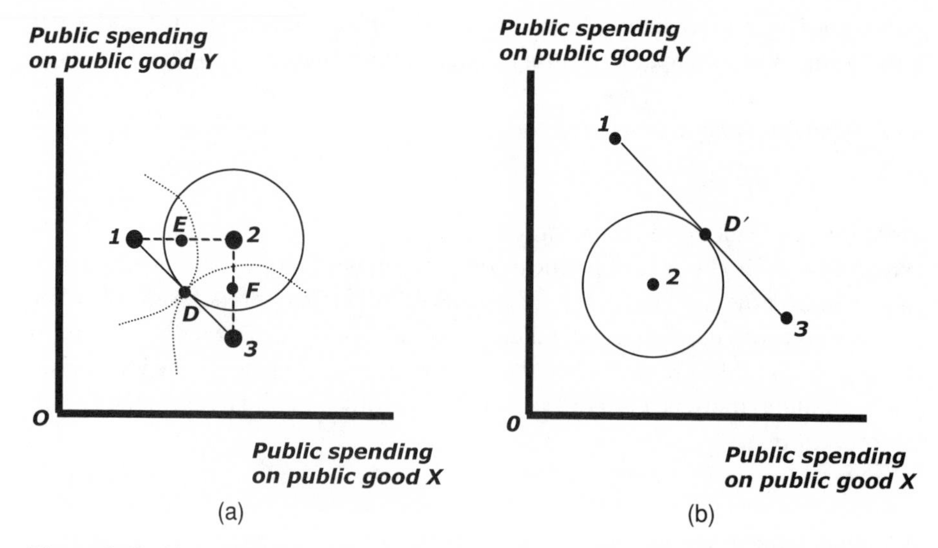

Figure 6.12. (a) A coalition between voters 1 and 3 based on adhering to a principle of low public spending. (b) A coalition between voters 1 and 3 based on adhering to a principle of high public spending.

Figure 6.12b shows a converse case in which voter 2 ideally wants less public spending on public goods and less taxation than voters 1 and 3. With voters 1 and 3 committed in principle to more public spending than that sought by voter 2, voter 2 is once more the decisive voter in determining the composition of public spending, and there is a stable majority-voting equilibrium at point D'.

Expressive voting and stable outcomes

For expressive voters, utility from voting is obtained through identification with either a candidate's attributes or policies. If expressive voting is based on attributes of candidates rather than policies, the predicted instability of policy pronouncements does not arise. Indeed, expressive voters who make their voting decisions on the basis of candidates' attributes may be rationally ignorant of a candidate's proposed policies. They do not need to know the policies to obtain the satisfaction of expressing themselves through their voting for the candidate that they "like."

If voters vote expressively with respect to policies, the distance of candidates' policies from expressive voters' preferred policies determines voter turnout. For example, returning to figure 6.10, the policy positions at points D and E may be sufficiently close to point 1 to allow voter 1 to vote expressively, and likewise the

point 2. Along the contract curve between voters 1 and 2, voter 2 joins with voter 1 in opposing a movement away from point D toward point 3 and voter 2 joins with voter 3 in opposing a move from point D toward point 1. There is therefore no majority support for a movement away from point D. Thus, point D is a majority-voting equilibrium.

policies at points D and F may be sufficiently close to point 3 to allow voter 3 to vote expressively. However, policy positions at points D, E, and F may all be too far from point 2 to allow voter 2 to vote expressively. Voter 2 then abstains. Now consider many voters of types 1, 2, and 3. With voters of type 2 expressively abstaining "because they have no one to vote for," the relative numbers of voters with preferences of voters 1 and 3 determines the majority voting outcome at point 1 or point 3.

Expressive voting changes conclusions about outcomes of majority voting and is a possible reason for stability.

D. Systems of voting and the Condorcet winner

Countries and jurisdictions differ in systems of voting that are used. We now compare systems of voting. Our question is:

Do the systems of voting that are used ensure choice of the Condorcet winner?

In comparing voting systems, we can attribute neither efficiency nor social justice to choice of the Condorcet winner. We have seen that the Condorcet winner does not ensure efficient collective decisions and that accompanying checks and balances are required if the "tyranny" of stable outcomes of majority voting is to be avoided.

We are therefore left with weak normative economic foundations for the desirability of choosing the Condorcet winner. However, there is little that we can do except proceed with the Condorcet winner as the normative principle of collective choice through majority voting. We do not know whether the Condorcet winner achieves the social objectives of efficiency and social justice. However, at least we know that the Condorcet winner is the alternative that defeats all other choices in pair-wise voting. That is, as we noted, the criterion is political, in consistency with principles of majority-determined democratic choice.

If democratic choice were all that mattered – and not the consequences for efficiency and social justice – we could assign normative significance to the Condorcet winner.

Using democratic merit (and not seeking merit through economic criteria), we now consider voting systems used in practice and ask whether the voting systems choose the Condorcet winner.

Two-round-elimination voting

A commonly used system of voting allows for a second-round of voting if (with more than two candidates) no candidate receives a majority (more than 50 percent) in the first round. The two candidates with the greatest number of votes

TABLE 6.7. TWO-ROUND-ELIMINATION VOTING

Ranking of group 1 (4 voters)	Ranking of group 2 (2 voters)	Ranking of group 3 (3 voters)
A	B	C
B	C	B
C	A	A

in the first round proceed to the second round, and all other candidates are eliminated.

Table 6.7 shows the ranking of three groups of taxpayers over three alternative projects: *A*, *B*, and *C*. Three political candidates compete for political office. Each candidate represents one of the three groups. In a first round of voting, the candidate representing group 1 receives four votes, the candidate representing group 2 receives two votes, and the candidate representing group 3 receives three votes. No candidate wins by majority voting (a majority of more than 50 percent) in the first round.

A second round of voting then takes place, with the candidate of group 2, who received the lowest number of votes in the first round, eliminated. In the second round, voters in group 2 vote for the candidate of group 3 because these voters prefer project *C* to project *A*. The candidate of group 3 therefore wins in the second round, and project *C* is financed through public spending. The Condorcet winner in table 6.7, however, is project *B*.[31]

The system of two-round-elimination voting does not ensure selection of the Condorcet winner.

Plurality

The system of elimination using two-round voting is based on majority voting. In an alternative to majority voting, a *plurality* (any majority, including less than 50 percent support) is sufficient to win a political contest. There is one round of voting in which voters vote for their preferred choice. When there are two candidates, plurality voting is equivalent to majority voting. When there are more than two candidates, the winning candidate does not need the support of more than 50 percent of the voters. The plurality rule is commonly used. The rule provides a determinate collective decision because it is immune to the instabilities of cycling.

In the example shown in table 6.8, seven voters are divided into three groups. When voting takes place under a plurality rule, the candidate of group 1 wins

[31] In table 6.7, project *B* defeats project *A* by five votes to four, and project *B* defeats project *C* by six votes to three.

TABLE 6.8. PLURALITY VOTING

Ranking of group 1 (3 voters)	Ranking of group 2 (2 voters)	Ranking of group 3 (2 voters)
A	B	C
B	C	B
C	A	A

(because that candidate has the support of three voters and the other two candidates each have the support of two voters). Project A is therefore financed through the government budget. Project B, however, is the Condorcet winner.[32]

Plurality voting does not ensure selection of the Condorcet winner.

Moreover, in the case shown in table 6.8, the winner under plurality voting is the Condorcet loser.[33]

Proportional representation

Under proportional representation, political parties have representatives in a parliament in proportion to the number of votes obtained.[34] Table 6.9 shows the rankings of projects A, B, and C for supporters of three parties. One representative is elected for each 10,000 votes received. Party 1 wins three seats and parties 2 and 3 each win two seats. Because no party has a majority, no project has majority support. Project B, however, is the Condorcet winner.[35]

Public spending and the tyranny of the majority

After voting has taken place, a coalition between at least two of the parties is required to establish a majority in the parliament. The two parties forming a coalition are able to ensure financing of their preferred projects. Of the three different coalitions that are possible, natural coalition partners seem to be parties 2 and 3 because both groups supporting these parties rank the preferred project A of party 1 in last place.[36]

32 By majority voting, project B is preferred to project A by four votes to three, and project B is preferred to project C by five votes to two.

33 Alternative A, which wins under plurality voting, is defeated by both projects B and C, in each case by four votes to three.

34 A minimum percentage of votes is usually required for representation.

35 Project B defeats project A by five votes to four and defeats project C by seven votes to two.

36 As we have seen when considering logrolling, the *rankings* alone in table 6.9 are insufficient for predicting which coalition will form. Additional information is required about the net benefits from the different projects to supporters of each party. If compensatory side payments can be made, problems of coalition instability are introduced because any coalition can be broken by an offer from the party excluded from the coalition. We set these issues aside here to compare public spending under proportional representation with public spending under other electoral systems.

TABLE 6.9. PROPORTIONAL REPRESENTATION

Ranking of supporters of party 1 (40,000 voters)	Ranking of supporters of party 2 (30,000 voters)	Ranking of supporters of party 3 (20,000 voters)
A	B	C
B	C	B
C	A	A

Under two-round-elimination voting in table 6.9 on the alternatives *A*, *B*, and *C*, the Condorcet winner project *B* is eliminated in the first round of voting and project *C* defeats project *A* in the second round by five votes to four. Under plurality voting in table 6.9, project *A* is publicly financed. In these cases, all voters pay taxes to finance the single project preferred by the winning party. Under proportional representation, if a coalition is required for a majority, as in our example in figure 6.9, satisfying coalition members requires that each coalition member's preferred project be publicly financed. Coalitions under proportional representation are therefore similar to those of logrolling.

We can conclude:

> *Compared to two-round-elimination voting and to plurality voting, public spending and taxation are expected to be greater under proportional representation because of the need to cater to public-spending preferences of coalition members.*

Coalition members under proportional representation benefit from public spending on their preferred projects. If the coalition consists of parties 2 and 3, projects *B* and *C* are therefore publicly financed. Supporters of party 1 excluded from the coalition pay taxes that finance public spending that excludes their preferred project *A*.

Of the three voting systems we have considered, supporters of a party whose favored project is not financed are most disadvantaged under proportional representation. The excluded voters' taxes finance two non-preferred projects under proportional representation and one nonpreferred project under two-round-elimination and plurality voting.

> *Proportional representation can reduce the tyranny of the majority by increasing the size of the majority that benefits from public spending but can also increase the tyranny of the majority through the greater burden of taxation without benefit imposed on the minority.*

The power of small groups

Under proportional representation, small parties or groups may have power beyond their representation because of the inability of a large party to form a coalition without support from a small party.

Fairness in representation

In the pure form of proportional representation, there are no electoral districts; the entire country is a single constituency. An advantage of proportional representation over an electoral system with multiple constituencies or contestable seats is fairness in representation. For example, 49 percent of voters who support a political party may be equally distributed over the 100 seats in a parliament. When elections take place, a second party supported by the remaining 51 percent of voters (who are also equally distributed) wins all the seats in parliament in a constituency-based system. Under proportional representation, there is one constituency – the entire country – and seats in parliament are divided 51 to 49. Therefore, under proportional representation, the location of voters in the country does not matter for determining political representation. Voters are not effectively disenfranchised because they happen to live in constituencies in which they form a minority of the electorate.

Personal accountability of politicians

A disadvantage of proportional representation is lack of personal accountability of politicians to voters. Elected representatives owe their electoral success under proportional representation to being placed sufficiently high on a party list of candidates. The representatives are thankful to the party operatives or primary voters who gave them a high place on the list of candidates. Accountability of politicians to voters is limited or nonexistent. Under proportional representation, voters do not directly vote for elected representatives but rather vote for a list of candidates. Therefore, voters cannot identify "their" representative – whereas, when there are individual contestable constituencies, voters know who their political representative is and political representatives know who the voters are to whom they are accountable.[37]

Preferential voting

A system of voting known as *preferential voting* is similar to two-round-elimination voting but voting takes place only once. Voters indicate their preferences among all candidates. The candidate with the lowest number of votes is eliminated. Then, votes are recounted of voters who ranked the eliminated candidate their first preference. The second-preference votes of these voters then become first-preference votes for the remaining candidates. The process of elimination of last-placed candidates and recounting continues until two candidates remain. The candidate with the higher number of votes among the two remaining candidates wins the election. The characteristic feature of this system of voting is that voters' preferences continue to matter until a winner is determined.[38]

[37] In some countries, there are hybrid systems that combine proportional representation with individual-representative constituencies. Also, sometimes constituencies elect more than a single representative.

[38] The preferential system of voting, for example, is used in Australia.

TABLE 6.10a. THE CONDORCET WINNER CHOSEN THROUGH PREFERENTIAL VOTING

Ranking of group 1 (party 1 = 6 voters)	Ranking of group 2 (party 2 = 4 voters)	Ranking of group 3 (party 3 = 3 voters)
A	B	C
B	C	B
C	A	A

TABLE 6.10b. PREFERENTIAL VOTING DOES NOT RESULT IN CHOICE OF THE CONDORCET WINNER

Ranking of group 1 (party 1 = 6 voters)	Ranking of group 2 (party 2 = 3 voters)	Ranking of group 3 (party 3 = 4 voters)
A	B	C
B	C	B
C	A	A

Table 6.10a provides an example with three political parties (or candidates). The thirteen voters in the three groups in table 6.10a support their respective three political parties: when they vote, they indicate their preferences or ranking of the other parties, as in the table. The party receiving the lowest number of first-preference votes is eliminated. This is the party of group 3 (which has three votes, as compared to four votes for the party of group 2 and six votes for the party of group 1).

Under a plurality system, the party of group 1 with the largest number of first-choice votes would have won. Under preferential voting, the second-preference votes of the eliminated party 3 become first-preference votes for party 2, which defeats party 1 by seven votes to six. The choice of project *B* of the winning party 2 is also the Condorcet winner.

In table 6.10b, the numbers of votes for groups 2 and 3 have switched. Group 2 has three voters and group 3 has four voters. Now, the party of group 2 is eliminated because it has the lowest number of first-preference votes. The supporters of the eliminated party prefer project *C* to project *A*, so their second preferences become votes for the party of group 3, which wins the election and finances project *C*. The Condorcet winner, however, is still project *B*.

Hence:

Preferential voting does not ensure choice of the Condorcet winner.

Therefore, the system of preferential voting fares no better in necessarily choosing the Condorcet winner than the other systems of voting that we have considered.

Increased popularity and electoral defeat

It is desirable that an electoral system reward a political party whose popularity increases. However:

> *Under the system of preferential voting, an increase in popularity can lead to electoral defeat.*

This can occur because the outcome of preferential voting is sensitive to the identity of the party that is eliminated – or, where there are more parties, to the order of the elimination of parties.

In table 6.11a, the party of group 2 is eliminated in the first round. The supporters of the eliminated party prefer project *C* to project *A*, and so give their second-preference votes to the party of group 3, which then defeats the party of group 1 by eleven votes to six and finances project *C*.

Table 6.11b shows a change in political popularity compared to table 6.11a. Two members of group 1 have transferred their voting allegiance to group 3. The popularity of the party of group 3 has therefore increased, compared to table 6.11a. When elections take place, the party of group 1 has the lowest number of first-preference votes and is eliminated. The supporters of party 1 prefer project

TABLE 6.11a. THE PARTY OF GROUP 3 WINS THROUGH SECOND-PREFERENCES OF THE PARTY OF GROUP 2

Ranking of group 1 (party 1 = 6 voters)	Ranking of group 2 (party 2 = 5 voters)	Ranking of group 3 (party 3 = 6 voters)
A	B	C
B	C	B
C	A	A

TABLE 6.11b. POPULARITY OF PARTY 3 OF GROUP 3 INCREASES AND PARTY 3 LOSES

Ranking of group 1 (party 1 = 4 voters)	Ranking of group 2 (party 2 = 5 voters)	Ranking of group 3 (party 3 = 8 voters)
A	B	C
B	C	B
C	A	A

B to project *C* and so give their second-preference votes to party 2. Party 2 therefore wins by nine votes to eight. The party of group 3 has lost the election because of a change that increased its popularity with voters.

Approval voting

Preferential voting allows voters to vote more than once by casting contingent votes on the principle that if a voter's first choice is eliminated, voters can vote for their second choice. Under a system of voting known as *approval voting*, voters can also vote more than once. Voters are permitted to vote for as many parties or candidates as they wish. That is, they can vote for whoever they approve. Like preferential voting, approval voting allows voters the personal satisfaction of voting for their true first choice, even if the likelihood of that choice winning is low.

In table 6.12a, seven voters are distributed over three parties. Voters in group 1 have an incentive to avoid the outcome *C*, and voters in groups 2 and 3 have an incentive to avoid the outcome *A*. Approval voting allows voters to vote for their preferred alternative while also voting for their intermediate choice as a form of insurance. With voters voting for their first and second choices, there are seven votes for *B*, four votes for *C*, and three votes for *A*. Alternative *B* wins under approval voting and is also the Condorcet winner. Alternative *A*, which wins under the plurality voting rule, is in last place.

Table 6.12b shows another example in which there are four proposals: *A*, *B*, *C*, and *D*. There are four voters in group 1, three voters in group 2, and two voters

TABLE 6.12a. APPROVAL VOTING

Ranking of group 1 (3 voters)	Ranking of group 2 (2 voters)	Ranking of group 3 (2 voters)
A	B	C
B	C	B
C	A	A

TABLE 6.12b. APPROVAL VOTING WITH FOUR ALTERNATIVES

Ranking of group 1 (4 voters)	Ranking of group 2 (3 voters)	Ranking of group 3 (2 voters)
A	B	C
D	D	B
B	C	D
C	A	A

TABLE 6.12c. UNCERTAINTY AND APPROVAL VOTING

Ranking of group 1 (5 voters)	Ranking of group 2 (2 voters)	Ranking of group 3 (2 voters)
A	B	C
B	C	B
C	A	A

in group 3. Alternative B is the Condorcet winner.[39] However, if all voters vote for their first two preferred alternatives, alternative D wins.[40] Therefore:

Approval voting does not ensure that the Condorcet winner is chosen.

In general, voters are imperfectly informed about each other's preferences. The uncertainty can prevent a collective decision in favor of the preferred choice of the majority. In table 6.12c, the five voters in group 1 form an absolute majority of voters and prefer project A. These voters may not know, however, that they form an absolute majority. To insure themselves (given the uncertainty) against the undesirable outcome of project C winning, the voters in group 1 might decide to vote for their second choice of project B in addition to their preferred choice of project A. Groups 2 and 3 may vote only for their respective preferred projects, or may vote for their two highest ranked projects. In either case, project B wins. Had group 1's voters known that they were in the majority, they could have voted only for project A and their preferred alternative would have won.

When comparing decisions made by approval voting with the outcome of other systems of voting, information about voters' preferences is not enough to determine the outcome of approval voting. We also need to know whether voters will choose to vote for one or both of the first and second (or further) ranked alternatives.

6.3 Voting on Income Redistribution

Voting on public spending has the potential to bring Pareto improvement: even if voting on public goods does not result in precise efficient supply, everyone can be better off as the consequence of availability of a publicly financed public

[39] Project B defeats project A by five votes to four, project B defeats project C by seven votes to two, and project B defeats project D by five votes to four.

[40] Project D receives seven votes, project B receives five votes, project A receives four votes, and project C receives two votes.

good. Voting on income redistribution, which we shall now study, contradicts Pareto improvement: when income is redistributed, some people are better off (the beneficiaries of income transfers) and some are worse off (the people whose taxes finance income transfers).

Through majority voting, any coalition of 51 percent of voters, in principle, can vote to redistribute income or wealth to themselves from the other 49 percent of voters. The redistribution of income or wealth need have no particular social-justice or ethical justification. The only criterion for benefiting is to be in the majority coalition, whereas people in the minority whose taxes finance the income transfers lose.

The tyranny of the majority thus provides the background for a consideration of voting and redistribution. A majority can be based on any attribute that 51 percent of voters have in common. Provided only that they have a majority, voters who are old can vote to distribute income to themselves from the young. A majority of 51 percent of voters could have brown eyes and could vote to distribute income to itself from the minority of voters whose eyes are a different color. In general, the majority and minority are based on income: low-income voters seek to redistribute income to themselves from high-income voters, but the opposite can also be the case.

A. Majority voting and income redistribution

The reason for voting on public finance for public goods is that public goods cannot be efficiently provided through voluntary payments: by voting to finance and supply public goods, all voters can benefit. That is, the voting can provide Pareto-improving change, through the benefits of public goods. Voting on income redistribution, however, is akin to redistributing private goods, or private incomes. If behavior is self-interested, by voting on private goods or income, people are simply seeking to benefit themselves, as they would do in markets (and as in markets Adam Smith would have had them do). Our question is:

Why use voting to decide on public finance for private goods?

An example showing why public finance might be used to finance private goods was provided by the public-choice scholar, Gordon Tullock, in 1959.[41] Tullock described a number of people, each with private access roads linking their home to a highway. The access roads provide strictly private benefit. The people meet and decide that maintenance of the access roads will be publicly financed by identical taxes that each will pay. Because each access road provides private benefit, a decision has been made to provide *public* finance for *private* goods. We might now be puzzled and ask why the private access roads are not privately financed through personal market decisions. The benefits, after all, are private

[41] The public-choice school of economics incorporated political and collective decisions into economic analysis.

and not collective. Private spending would avoid the excess burden of taxation and the costs to taxpayers of salaries of the administering government bureaucracy. Private spending would also avoid any political and bureaucratic principal–agent problems.

The inefficiency of cross-subsidized collective spending on private goods

Private spending would also avoid the inefficiency of the cross-subsidized collective spending. The cost of maintaining a private road is the competitively determined price P. For exposition, we treat everyone as having the same MB from road maintenance. If n people pay taxes to finance the maintenance of the private roads, taxpayers calculate that their personal cost is P/n because financing of all expenditures is shared with everyone else. Each taxpayer, therefore, votes for a level of publicly financed spending determined by:

$$\frac{P}{n} = MB \text{ or } P = MC = nMB. \tag{6.16}$$

We have thus arrived at the condition for efficient financing of a public good, but the good is private. Ten people who are at a professional conference go out to eat at a restaurant. Before ordering, an announcement is made that the bill will be split equally at the end of the evening. The menu includes some quite expensive dishes. Each person makes the calculation that whatever he or she orders, the personal cost will be 10 percent of each dollar spent because of the sharing rule for paying the total bill. Everyone therefore orders the most expensive dishes and everyone pays a large amount when the bill is presented at the end of the evening. If it were pre-agreed that all people will personally pay for what they personally ordered, spending a dollar costs a dollar. There is then no cross-subsidization. Each person chooses from the menu according to $P = MB$, which is efficient. Therefore:

> *Collective spending for private consumption results in inefficient overspending.*

Majority voting when benefits are private

We return to the example of maintenance of the roads. After it has been decided that maintenance of the roads will be publicly financed, a vote is taken on choosing a voting rule for future collective decisions. A coalition of 51 percent of voters proposes majority voting as the rule. The same coalition of 51 percent of voters then proposes that only their roads be maintained through public finance and that the 49 percent minority pay the taxes that finance the maintenance of the majority's roads. The members of the 51 percent majority coalition are thus proposing that taxation and public spending be used for their private benefit. Because they are a majority, the proposal has majority support. Hence, we have another instance of the tyranny of the majority.

A justification for the majority voting rule for redistribution

People who confront the uncertainty that they do not know beforehand whether they will be in a majority coalition that benefits from redistribution or a minority coalition that loses rationally choose the 51 percent majority-voting rule. If they will be members of the winning coalition, voters will want the size of the majority coalition to be as small as possible in order to maximize their personal share of benefits financed by the minority; conversely, voters who will be members of the losing coalition will want the size of the minority coalition to be as large as possible in order to minimize their personal share of the cost of the payment to the majority. When a vote on the voting rule is taken before people know whether they will be in the majority or minority coalition, everybody, therefore, votes for the 51 percent majority voting rule because:

> *When voting is about redistribution from one group to another, majority voting is the least exploitative voting rule.*

Alternatively stated, the majority voting rule maximizes expected utility when people do not know before a redistributive vote is taken whether they will be in the majority or minority.[42]

Coalition instability

Voting coalitions on income redistribution are unstable. The members of the 51 percent majority might each gain 100 and the members of the 49 percent minority might each lose 130 (the loss consists of taxes paid plus the excess burden of taxation). By offering more than 100 to each defector in return for switching coalitions, the 49 percent minority could bribe two members of the majority to join them to make a new majority coalition. The benefit to members of the minority from becoming the majority provide ample surplus for bribing the two defectors. We previously noted reasons why defection from majority coalitions does not take place. In particular, prospective defectors are aware that their benefits in the new coalition depend on the new coalition holding together. They will therefore seek guarantees that the new coalition will not break up to leave them stranded outside another new majority in the future. If binding guarantees cannot be provided, defection will not take place, and the initial majority coalition will be stable. We also observed that discount rates of prospective defectors matter. Furthermore, instability can be desirable: instability allows sharing of benefits from being in the majority coalition, whereas stability ensures that the same people persistently benefit from being in the majority coalition, and the same people also persistently lose from being in the minority coalition.

Income redistribution by majority voting

Abilities in a population usually have the normal distribution (although perhaps by construction of the measure of ability). Income before taxes and, more

[42] For formalizations of this idea, see Rae (1969) and Taylor (1969).

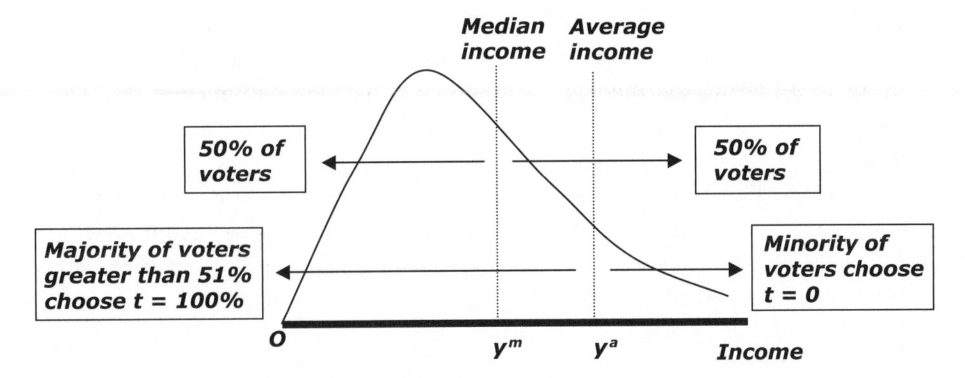

Figure 6.13. Voting and the distribution of income.

so, wealth is usually skewed, with the average exceeding the median: that is, as shown in figure 6.13, a majority of people have income or wealth that is less than the average of the population. Through majority voting, the low-income or low-wealth majority of voters can vote to redistribute income or wealth to themselves from the high-income or high-wealth minority.

We consider redistribution of income rather than wealth (although the question is the same) and ask:

> *How much redistribution will take place through majority voting if voters choose taxation and income redistribution to maximize their utility?*

Members of a 51 percent low-income majority could vote to redistribute all income to themselves by appropriating the income of the 49 percent high-income minority (they might leave subsistence income for the taxed minority). Such appropriation would turn the former high-income minority into a destitute minority population. The redistribution by the majority would be unethical: the circumstances would be those of the Nietzschean strong and weak, in which the strong are the voters in the majority group and the weak are the voters in the minority group.

We therefore consider an alternative scheme for taxation and redistribution that has the property of no discrimination: the tax rate that applies to one person applies to everyone else and all people receive the same tax-financed income transfer. The non-discrimination rule ensures that:

> *After income redistribution, the original high-income minority will be no worse off than the original low-income majority.*

That is, today's poor do not become tomorrow's rich and also, conversely, today's rich do not become tomorrow's poor.

To simplify matters and not because we believe that reality has this feature, we proceed *as if* there are no labor-leisure substitution effects and so no excess burden of taxation. Therefore, we are viewing taxation as having no effect on incentives to work and people as contributing (or working and exerting effort) according to their abilities and without regard for personal reward. Thus, when pre-tax income is taxed, people do not reduce hours worked: labor supply is inelastic and the pre-tax income earned is also the post-tax income. We shall presently reintroduce labor-leisure substitution effects and the excess burden of taxation.

To describe the income redistribution subject to the non-discrimination rule, we denote by t the equal rate of taxation applied to all pre-tax incomes (which are also post-tax incomes). With n persons earning different individual incomes y_i, a proportional tax rate t yields total tax revenue:

$$R = t \sum_{i=1}^{n} y_i. \tag{6.17}$$

We denote by y^a the average earned pre-tax income in the population. The tax revenue is redistributed so that each person receives the equal income transfer:

$$s = \frac{R}{n} = t \left(\frac{\sum_{i=1}^{n} y_i}{n} \right) = t y^a. \tag{6.18}$$

Each taxpayer thus receives a share of tax revenue equal to the rate of taxation multiplied by the average pre-tax income in the population.

With hours worked not affected by taxes, incomes y^i in expressions (6.17) and (6.18) are independent of the tax rate, as is the average income y^a of the population.

Figure 6.13 shows the income distribution of the population (which is the same before and after taxation and redistribution) and the average income of the population y^a and the median income y^m.

We now view people as voting (instrumentally and not expressively) according to their self-interest – and as having decided to vote. A person's decision on how to vote depends on whether he or she has income less than or greater than the average y^a. The vote on the tax rate is:

$$\begin{aligned} t &= 100\% \quad \text{if } y^i < y^a \\ t &= 0\% \quad \text{if } y^i > y^a. \end{aligned} \tag{6.19}$$

Because $y^a > y^m$, a majority in excess of 51 percent votes for a tax of 100 percent on income. The majority is shown in figure 6.13 as consisting of all voters with less than average income y^a. A minority of voters with incomes higher than the average y^a votes for zero taxation and no income redistribution.

The majority vote thus maximizes the tax revenue available for redistribution by converting all personal income in the society to tax revenue. Redistributing the tax revenue equally results in:

$$y_i = y^a, \quad i = 1, \ldots, n. \tag{6.20}$$

That is, everyone has a post-tax income equal to the average income y^a in the population.

> *With no excess burden of taxation and discrimination possible in neither the rate of income taxation nor distribution of tax revenue, the outcome of majority voting is maximally appropriative taxation and post-tax income equality.*[43]

Why is majority voting in practice not maximally appropriative?

We do not observe the maximally appropriative taxes and equal distribution of income predicted by majority voting. Apparently, it is not in the self-interest of the majority to vote for and implement such an outcome. A number of considerations deter the majority from imposing ex-post equality through complete redistribution.

The excess burden of taxation and the Laffer curve

By not accounting for substitution effects and the excess burden of taxation, we also did not account for incentives to work. A person who knows that his or her post-tax income is to be the average of the total income in the population has little or no incentive to work. Through the substitution to leisure, the tax base therefore will shrink and there will be little or no income to redistribute. Income available for redistribution through taxation is thus bounded by the Laffer curve because of substitution effects associated with the excess burden of taxation – and also because of incentives to move to the shadow economy when rates of taxation become excessively high. The majority would, therefore, not vote for a tax rate in excess of the rate that maximizes total revenue on the Laffer curve. There may also be awareness that high taxes will diminish incentives for new investment and will lead capital to move elsewhere, so in the future there will less capital income to tax; that is, there may be awareness of a Laffer curve that bounds tax revenue from taxation of income from capital. Thus:

> *The majority may understand that widespread income redistribution or "spreading the wealth" will result in little or no income to redistribute nor future wealth to spread.*

Self-interest preempts, therefore, the majority supporting an appropriative tax rate and equal redistribution. Nonetheless, we noted in chapter 2 that communism or socialism embarked on a policy of ex-post equality. Because of the awareness of substitution effects, excess burdens, and incentives, communism

[43] If compensatory side-payments could take place, coalition instability could arise; although the number of voters here is large and the transactions costs of negotiating and paying people to change their votes are high. We shall presently consider the possibility that high-income voters form a coalition together with low-income countries against the voters in the middle. There will then have been coalition instability if the initial coalition was based on 51 percent including the median voter.

sought to re-engineer and create a "new man" and "new woman" who would contribute to society altruistically without care for the incentives of personal rewards. Hayek's critique was that the idea that a "new man" and "new woman" could be socially re-engineered was a "fatal conceit" for communism and socialism. If a new man and woman devoid of need for incentives to be productive cannot be re-engineered, the substitution effects and inefficiencies of excess burdens are present when income is redistributed. The average income y^a is then low. Envy or an ideology in which social equality is a supreme value not to be compromised can nonetheless result in the decision to proceed with extensive redistribution, even though as a consequence everyone has low income.

Economic mobility and economic growth

Economic mobility refers to people moving within the income distribution. There is economic mobility when a present low-income person moves to the high-income part of the income distribution. Economic mobility can also be downward. If one person moves up in the income distribution, another person – of necessity – moves down. Through economic growth, however, the incomes of everyone in the income distribution can increase. Economic mobility and economic growth can lead people to anticipate being in the high income part of the income distribution in the future. Everyone cannot, of course, move up in the income distribution at the same time; however, equalizing change may be anticipated in the future income distribution because of, for example, more equal opportunities through education. If future pre-tax incomes will be more equal, less of a change in pre-tax personal income will be required for a person to move from having below-average to above-average income. Given the prospect of future upward mobility, present low-income people are reluctant to vote for high taxes and high redistribution because of the likelihood that in the future they will have above-average income and will therefore lose from income redistribution.[44]

Immigration

Immigration can be low- or high-skilled, depending on self-selection of immigrants and a country's immigration policy. Low-skilled immigration decreases the average income in a population and moves pre-immigration low-income inhabitants up in the income distribution. Low-income inhabitants of the host country may also upgrade their skills in response to low-skilled immigration. Low-income, low-skilled people in the population who anticipate an upward move in the future income distribution because of immigration realize that they will lose

[44] However, if optimistic expectations are disappointed, people can become impatient and intolerant of inequality. Albert Hirschman (1973) used the analogy of people waiting in two lanes of stalled traffic to describe disappointment due to lack of realization of optimistic expectations. When one lane of traffic begins to move but not the other, the first reaction of the people in the lane that remains blocked is optimism that soon they also will be able to advance. If the blocked lane is still not moving after some time passes, the feelings of people in the blocked lane change from optimism to envy, and they may begin to force their way into the lane in which traffic is moving.

from future high redistributive taxes and income transfers. Voters with pre-tax incomes around the average realize in particular that the change in the skill composition of the population will place them at above-average income in the future. When voters internalize the consequences of immigration, they therefore vote for moderate taxes and redistribution. Extensive benefits for people not at all working may attract immigrants who seek to benefit from the welfare payments that are provided. Voters may also internalize that voting for high taxes and extensive redistribution will attract such immigrants.

The number of issues

Under representative democracy, when a number of issues are bundled in the policy platforms of political candidates or parties, voters cannot vote selectively on each individual issue – as they can under direct democracy. There may be more salient issues for voters than extensive income redistribution – for example, societal institutions or national security.

The right of natural possession

The right of natural possession as a principle of social justice would lead voters to reject high taxation and extensive income redistribution. Low-income voters may believe that pre-tax earned personal incomes reflect personal effort and merit. All voters may regard high taxation as akin to theft.[45]

Are high incomes regarded as due to luck or effort?

Attitudes toward taxation and redistribution are influenced by whether people believe that high incomes and personal success are primarily due to personal effort and exertion or are basically the consequence of good or bad luck. People who believe in luck, as a matter of principle, are more prepared to vote for high taxes and high redistribution than people who believe in the primacy of personal effort and exertion as having determined personal outcomes.[46]

Conclusions on voting on income distribution

For the reasons indicated, appropriative taxation and equal redistribution are not observed in high-income Western democratic societies – and therefore indeed the societies are high-income. However, there are differences among high-income countries. In high-income welfare states tax rates are not completely appropriative but are nonetheless high, and income redistribution is extensive. We shall return to high-income welfare states.

[45] An alternative belief that "property is theft" and that therefore no one has a personal right to own anything is the basis for support for high or appropriative taxation. The claim that "property is theft" was expressed by Pierre-Joseph Proudhon (1809–65), in his 1840 book, *What Is Property?: Or, an Enquiry into the Principle of Right and Government.*

[46] Attitudes differ in different societies. For example, opinion polls generally show that people in the United States and some other societies are more inclined to believe that personal outcomes in life reflect mainly effort and exertion, whereas people in Europe are more inclined to believe that personal outcomes mainly reflect luck.

B. The franchise and voting on income redistribution

Historically, when democracy was first introduced, the franchise (or right to vote) was restricted to property owners. There was concern that the more numerous poor would vote to appropriate the property of the rich. As a middle class developed and society was no longer composed of just rich and poor, and as industries and businesses that were the sources of middle-class incomes began to replace land as the primary income source, the franchise was extended, first to men and then to women. The age at which the right to vote was given was also reduced in the course of time, often because of the principle that if people were old enough to fight for their country, they were old enough to vote.

Concerns similar to those of property owners in the past are expressed in contemporary proposals that the franchise should be restricted to people who are net contributors to government revenue. The argument is that net beneficiaries of income transfers from the government budget should not have the right to vote because they have incentives to vote for high taxes and large income transfers from which they personally benefit. In many countries, depending on the tax laws at the time, large proportions of the population do not pay taxes or are not net contributors to the government budget. Such proposals would therefore severely restrict the franchise. However, the motives for the proposals are to limit excess burdens of taxation and to maintain incentives for productive effort and investment – and to provide incentives for high-income earners in the population not to emigrate.

The case is also made that government bureaucrats should not have the right to vote. Government bureaucrats have incentives to vote for high taxes and high government spending, in order to finance the high salaries and enlarged bureaucracies associated with the bureaucratic principal–agent problem.

Women in the past benefited more than men from government income transfers. They consequently tended to vote more than men in favor of higher taxation and large government spending. Evidence indicates that increases in budgetary income transfers are correlated with extensions of the voting franchise to women. Women have been more vulnerable than men to adverse personal circumstances. In the traditional model in which the man earns the family income and the woman stays at home and raises the children, the woman and the children can be destitute if the man dies or leaves or if, in the event of a divorce, the woman cannot secure an adequate claim to the man's future income or if the man reneges on obligations to pay alimony and support his children. In circumstances in which the traditional family model no longer applies, marriage and commitment from men are not prerequisites for women having children; however, some single mothers nonetheless require publicly financed government income support.

Income vulnerability of women is influenced by the proportion of men and women of marriageable age in the population. The number of male children born is typically marginally greater than the number of female children. However, conditions can lead to substantial male–female imbalances. In the American West in the 19th century, men outnumbered women, and women were given great respect or placed "on a pedestal" by men. Western states in the United States were the first to give women the right to vote.[47]

When men are in the minority, not all women who seek a stable partner can find a man willing to enter into a long-term commitment. Available men may respond to the sexual imbalance by having short-term relationships with many women. Women, in turn, accept the short-term relationships because of the lack of alternatives. Women may also be better educated and more responsible than men and unwilling to accept lower quality men as long-term partners. Women who wish to have children may then forgo the commitment of support from the father (or fathers) of their children. The government may take the responsibility of being "father of last resort" for the support of mothers and children, so providing an incentive for women, in particular single mothers, to vote in favor of extensive welfare benefits.[48]

Conclusions on the franchise and voting on income redistribution

The franchise affects voting on income redistribution; hence, the franchise was initially given only for the wealthy classes or owners of property. There are sometimes calls for restriction of the franchise because of incentives of net beneficiaries of government income transfers and employees of government bureaucracies for vote for high taxes. The extension of the franchise to women increased voting in favor of taxation and redistribution of income.

C. The decision to vote

The decision about voting has two parts: whether to vote and how to vote. Income redistribution through voting is influenced by both decisions.

We previously considered why people might vote. There may be utility from participation in democratic processes or a feeling of obligation to act in accord with civic duty; people may experience guilt if they do not vote, even if they know that their individual vote cannot be decisive in affecting the outcome. They may

[47] Wyoming was the first U.S. state to give women the right to vote; by the beginning of the 20th century, women also had the right to vote in Utah, Colorado, and Idaho. The U.S. federal government did not give women the right to vote until 1920, although since 1788 women had the right to stand for election, if not themselves vote. New Zealand had given women the franchise in 1893. The colony of South Australia gave women the right to vote in 1895 and women voted in the 1902 election in the newly formed Commonwealth of Australia. Finland gave women the right to vote in 1907 (while under Russian rule). In the United Kingdom, women older than age 30 were allowed to vote in 1918 and, in 1928, women achieved voting rights equal to men. The franchise for women seems correlated with losing a war: women received the right to vote in Germany in 1918 and in Japan in 1945.

[48] Gender imbalance has, for example, in the past particularly affected African Americans in the United States. The sustained gender imbalance, particularly in the latter decades of the 20th century, has been attributed to a disproportionate number of young males in the armed services as well as in prison and to a higher death rate for young males for different reasons including street violence, drug overdoses, and alcohol. For more information, see Wilson (2002).

vote out of solidarity with their group. Such voting may be expressive. We have noted other instances of expressive voting, and the relation between expressive voting and abstention.

People may refrain from voting even if the issue is income redistribution in their favor because they realize that the probability of their one vote being decisive is effectively zero. Although voting seems irrational in terms of a personal cost-benefit calculation, if no one voted because everyone believed that one vote is irrelevant, there would be an incentive for one person to vote and therefore to be decisive: no one voting is not, therefore, a Nash equilibrium. If it were known that no one else intends to vote, each voter would have an incentive to vote. However, when there are large number of voters, such strategic considerations do not matter. In terms of the number of people who vote, the likelihood of one vote affecting the outcome is insignificant.

In chapter 2, when introducing institutions, we observed that compulsory voting solves a coordination problem among voters. Voters know that others with their same views will also vote. The mutual commitment to vote through compulsory voting promises a large and possibly decisive bloc of votes – even though each individual voter may still be aware that his or her individual vote is of no consequence. However, the decision to vote is now non-discretionary and everyone subject to the same qualms about whether to vote is nonetheless obliged to vote.

People may also be motivated to vote because of political positions observed in their personal reference group. They may vote to offset the vote of a particular person who they know will take a position contrary to theirs. In response to the question, "Why did you vote given the irrationality of voting?," the reply might be, "The only reason that I voted was to neutralize your vote."

An empirical regularity is that often high-income people vote in proportionately greater numbers than low-income people, even though the cost of voting is greater for high-income people, who have a higher value of time. Perhaps there is a common explanation for why people who have a high income also disproportionately vote: high-income people may be more attuned to personal obligation, which may also underlie their motivation to succeed and earn high incomes. High-income people may also gain more from voting expressively: their self-image is confirmed as a responsible successful person in society who cares about and participates in society's collective decisions.

In chapter 1, when comparing behavior in markets and voting, we observed that when voting expressively, people may vote against their own economic self-interest and support, for example, egalitarian principles calling for extensive redistribution of income and wealth. The cost of voting in favor of the egalitarian principles is effectively zero in terms of the expectation of being decisive in determining the voting outcome: the benefit is the feeling of solidarity with people who have less.

There is evidence that personal cost and expected benefit influence voter turnout. In general, fewer people vote when inclement weather increases the personal cost of voting. More people vote when opinion polls indicate a close political contest.[49]

In some elections, people are observed to spend hours in line waiting for their turn to vote. Such behavior is observed when people are introduced for the first time to democracy, or reintroduced: voting is expressive through the feeling of utility from democratic participation that was previously denied. People may also spend time in queues waiting to vote when the choices presented are stark alternatives that are particularly conducive to expressive voting. By revealed behavior, the cost of voting in terms of time is less than the personal utility obtained through expressive identification with a candidate. In addition to taking the time to vote, people also behave expressively in volunteering their time to assist candidates.

Our general conclusion is:

The propensity to vote or likelihood of different people voting affects redistribution of income through voting.

D. Who benefits from income redistribution?

The income redistribution that takes place in a society is revealed by a comparison between incomes before and after taxes and income redistribution. Evidence shows that in high-income democratic societies, income redistribution does not benefit the median voter (the person with the median income in the income distribution). Rather, income redistribution benefits poor or low-income people. The redistribution of income tends to be greater, the greater the initial inequality in market-determined pre-tax incomes.[50]

The evidence therefore does not support the prediction that a majority coalition including the median voter self-interestedly determines voting outcomes for personal advantage. We face the question:

Why does the median voter in a democratic society not benefit from majority voting on income redistribution?

Voter participation

Perhaps the median voter does not benefit from income redistribution because of voter participation – or because of who actually votes. If enough high-income people do not vote, the actual median voter could have a quite low income and

[49] Evidence on personal costs and benefits of voting is provided by the introduction of the secret ballot. Secret voting was first introduced in Australia and then the United States in the later part of the 19th century. Economic incentives to vote are suggested by the consequences of the introduction of secret voting for voter turnout: evidence from the United States suggests after voting became secret and therefore nonverifiable, voter participation declined because people could no longer be paid to vote for a particular candidate.

[50] Evidence is provided by Branko Milanovic (2000) of the World Bank, who investigated 24 democratic societies.

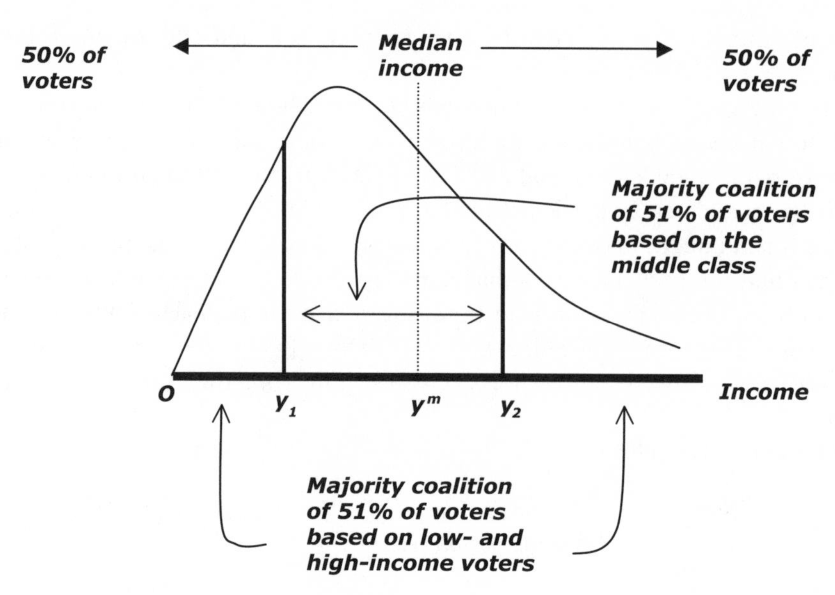

Figure 6.14. A majority based on low- and high-income voters.

benefit from income redistribution. It is, however, usually on the contrary people with low incomes who tend disproportionately not to vote. The median income among actual voters is, therefore, higher than the median income in the total population. If voting benefited the actual median voter, income redistribution would then benefit high-income voters, which is not the case. Because it is low-income people who benefit from income redistribution, we can conclude that the reason why the median voter does not gain from income redistribution is not voter participation.

A coalition of low- and high-income voters

We have viewed the coalition of the majority of voters as including the voter with median income. However, the median voter need not be in the majority coalition. High-income voters can form a majority coalition with the low-income voters. Figure 6.14 shows a majority coalition of 51 percent formed among voters with incomes smaller than y_1 and higher than y_2. The voter with median income y^m is then not a member of the majority coalition. This coalition of "the ends against the middle" is advantageous for the high-income population, which redistributes income only to the low-income population and not to the middle class.[51]

[51] The 30 percent of voters with the highest incomes, for example, might vote for income redistribution targeted to the 21 percent of voters with the lowest incomes. The income redistribution is financed by the taxes paid by the 30 percent of voters with the highest incomes, together with taxes paid by the middle 49 percent of the population who are outside the majority coalition. The income transfers to the lowest 21 percent of the population are then financed by the taxes of 79 percent of the population. This outcome is preferred by both the low-income 21 percent and the high-income 30 percent to the alternative majority division based on the median voter joined by all voters with less than median income. Through the coalition formed at the two tails of the income

Social justice

Another hypothesis is that in democratic societies, majority voting is not used for self-interested income redistribution. Rather, low-income people are helped because of conceptions of social justice.

A coalition of the middle class and Director's law

Yet, it might be surprising if the median voter or the middle class did not benefit in some way from voting. In figure 6.14, although a majority coalition of "the ends against the middle" is possible, a majority coalition can also be based on the "middle against the ends." That is, voters in the middle of the income distribution or the middle class could form a coalition against the poor and the rich who are in the tails of the income distribution. Although the median voter does not benefit from *income* redistribution, redistribution also takes place through public spending on public goods. A conclusion known as *Director's law* states that:

> *Median voters or the middle class disproportionately and systematically benefit from public spending on public goods.*[52]

In some countries or regions, wealthier people tend to send their children to private schools and private universities, whereas the children of middle-income people are more likely to attend publicly financed schools and universities. If few children of poorer or richer families attend a government-subsidized college or university, government subsidies to higher education disproportionately benefit the middle class.

The middle class benefits disproportionately from publicly financed police and security services. Very wealthy people often have their own private security guards. Lower income people may have little property to defend – but they are also disproportionately victims of crime if they may live in low-income Nietzschean neighborhoods where, akin to anarchy, outcomes are determined by who is strong and who is weak.

People who travel more extensively benefit more from publicly financed highways and airports. Lower income people tend to travel less. People who travel to other countries also benefit from embassies and consulates in foreign countries, which provide assistance to travelers if there is a need.

Public housing provides shelter for low-income people. Wealthy people might prefer and can afford housing in locations that provide privacy. Middle-income people benefit from public housing for low-income people because lower income people have a place to live. The public housing is a private good for people living in the housing. The middle class obtains a public-good benefit from lower income people having housing – and not living on the streets in their neighborhoods.

distribution, the 21 percent lowest income population can receive more and the 30 percent highest income population can pay less.

[52] Director's law is named after Aaron Director (1901–2004), who taught at the University of Chicago. Director's law was stated (1970) by George Stigler (1911–91). Stigler, who also taught at the University of Chicago, received the Nobel Prize in economics in 1982.

What is the basis for Director's law?

> *Why does the middle class benefit disproportionately from publicly financed public goods but not from redistribution of income?*

It would be blatantly and visibly ungenerous for the middle class to vote for itself income transfers at the expense of low-income people in the population. Such self-benefit would be inconsistent with middle-class voters' self-identity as being caring people with a social conscience. Because of expressive voting by voters, it would be politically inexpedient for a political party to propose income distribution in favor of the middle class, although thereby the middle class would materially benefit. Expressive voting, however, does not prevent voting in favor of benefit from public spending on public goods because, in principle, public goods can benefit anyone. In principle, anyone can attend a subsidized college or university or benefit from personal security provided by law enforcement, from public highways and airports, and foreign representation.

The middle class and tax deductions

Wealthy people may not need mortgages to buy homes and under sustainable conditions in housing markets, poor people may be unable to afford to borrow to become homeowners. Middle-class people, therefore, may be the main owners of homes financed by mortgages. When interest payments on mortgages are tax deductible, it is the middle class that systematically and disproportionately benefits. Similarly, if contributions to pension funds are tax deductions, the middle class – and also higher-income taxpayers – disproportionately benefit compared to low-income people.

> *The middle class benefits disproportionately from tax deductions: to benefit from tax deductions, people need to have the income that is required to make the payments that provide the tax deductions.*

Expressive voting and Director's law

Benefits from public goods and tax deductions are not targeted but rather in principle are available to everyone. The benefits thus are consistent with expressive voting based on social conscience and benevolence because the middle class does not vote benefits for itself at the expense of others in society. Income transfers targeted to the middle class are inconsistent with expressive voting based on social conscience and benevolence. The middle class consequently benefits from public spending on public goods – and disproportionately so – but not from publicly financed income transfers.

Conclusions on voting

In chapter 2, voters as a group seeking the public interest were described as confronting special interests that sought deviations from socially preferred policies. In this chapter, voters have not been juxtaposed against interest groups. Interest groups have been placed on the sidelines (they return through campaign contributions and political persuasion to participate in determining the final outcome of collective and political decisions). We have looked at voters with different interests. If special-interest groups remain on the sidelines and voters do not have conflicting interests but do not know with certainty the best policies (perhaps because of rational ignorance), we are back to the Condorcet jury theorem with which we began this chapter.

Self-sorting and voting

Self-sorting through Tiebout locational choice solves the problems of majority voting. It is undesirable for voters who have no children to block, by majority voting, public spending on public schools or preventive health-care facilities for children. Similarly, it is undesirable that people who do not like nature should vote to block the creation and maintenance of parks and open areas that benefit others. People who like opera should be able to vote for the subsidies that are often required to keep opera companies viable, and people who like football might want subsidies for the local football field and perhaps for the team. People who feel that crime is not a problem should be allowed to vote for low or no public spending on law enforcement. People who believe that guns create crime should be allowed to vote for and implement gun-control laws. People who believe that the threat of terrorism is exaggerated should be allowed to vote for and implement public policies that do not include public spending to preempt terrorism. People who are pacifists should be allowed to vote against military spending and to demonstrate their faith in their beliefs by living in jurisdictions without defense. People who favor particular dress codes should be able to vote to have their dress codes in their own jurisdictions. Both inefficiency and the social injustice of the tyranny of the majority are resolved by self-sorting into government jurisdictions.

> *When jurisdictions consist of people with the same objectives, majority voting becomes consensus; and outcomes of voting by consensus are efficient and socially just.*

The case for democracy when personal objectives differ

The Condorcet jury theorem is the basis for the case for democracy but requires voters to seek a common objective. When people's personal objectives differ, societies confront the tyranny of the majority. Checks and balances, however, can protect the minority; also, in democratic societies, representatives of different voting groups alternate in political office through election outcomes.

> *When jurisdictions consist of people with diverse objectives, democratic institutions with checks and balances and rotation in political office are superior to any other alternative for making collective decisions.*

The choice between market decisions and voting

Our conclusions about the merits of the institutions of democracy differ from conclusions about the choice between market decisions and voting. Chapter 1 showed how competitive markets achieve efficiency through aggregation of individual supply and demand decisions into market outcomes (through "the invisible hand"). Voting also aggregates personal decisions. Aggregation of personal decisions through voting provides, however, no assurance of efficiency – nor of social justice – because collective decisions determined by majority voting are imposed rather than voluntary.

> *Market decisions are voluntary and so do not involve coercion; voting involves coercion through the imposition of majority decisions.*

Because of the voluntary decisions in market and the coercion of voting, our conclusion is that:

> *Voting should be minimized and decisions should be made personally in markets – where possible.*

Our conclusion regarding the collective decisions of voting is a restatement of the presumption stated in chapter 1 in favor of personal voluntary market decisions.

Summary

This chapter investigated whether efficiency and social justice are ensured by voting. The Condorcet jury theorem showed the desirability of broad democracy. The theorem applies when there is a common objective and people differ over the means of achieving the objective; the theorem therefore does not apply when people have different preferences – about public spending on public goods or income redistribution. Section 1 considered voting on public spending on public goods.

1A. Investigating outcomes of voting requires first the choice of the voting rule. A decision by consensus ensures Pareto efficiency; Lindahl prices set as personal tax shares achieve efficiency with consensus in voting; however, people have no reason to reveal their true personal benefits when they know that they will be taxed according to benefit. Asymmetric information therefore persists when decisions about public goods are made by voting. The Lindahl personal taxes could be sought by iteratively proposing different personal taxes for people in a population and different public spending, and searching for a consensus response from voters. However, because the procedure is time consuming, governments do not engage in this practice. There are also problems in using a consensus rule because of transactions costs between gainers and losers in implementing efficient proposals and because of possibilities for opportunistic extortion. In a majority-voting equilibrium when taxes are predetermined, only the median voter achieves a personally preferred outcome. There is no reason to expect the median voter, who is decisive in majority voting, to choose efficient public spending – although if the median voter is fortuitously the voter with the average valuation of a public good, efficiency is achieved.

1B. Single-peaked preferences of voters ensure existence of a Condorcet winner. However, preferences may not be single-peaked and majority voting can therefore be subject to cycling; when cycling occurs, control of the agenda determines the outcome of majority voting. The Condorcet winner can be an inefficient spending proposal that defeats an efficient spending proposal. Voting imposes externalities of collective decision making that could be resolved through compensating payments; the compensation would result in efficient decisions through payment for changing how people vote. Although a market in votes would eliminate public financing of inefficient projects, there are justifiable reasons why markets in votes are illegal.

1C. Logrolling neither ensures that efficient projects are financed nor that inefficient projects are not financed. Logrolling is unstable if money payments can take place; reasons for observed stability are reputation, transactions costs of making transfers among constituencies, and inability to ensure that a new coalition will not be unstable. Monetary transfers with logrolling would ensure an all-inclusive coalition that finances all efficient projects and does not finance inefficient projects. Coalitions are reintroduced when benefits from the all-inclusive coalition are assigned. Payments would be a form of extortion if losers from an inefficient project were required to pay to forestall funding of the project. Because the money payments are presumptively illegal, in general, the relevant conclusions about logrolling do not involve payments among gainers and losers.

1D. Majority voting requires accompanying checks and balances. The checks and balances ensure non-discrimination in public finance in the prisoners' dilemma among majority and minority groups of voters. The checks and balances apply to total public spending and taxation. In a federal system, the greatest need for checks and balances is at the highest level of government, where there is in general greatest heterogeneity in the population. Where checks and balances are inadequate, there are incentives for secession and personal exit; locational choice is a solution to the problems of majority voting because jurisdictions in which voters have the same preferences avoid the tyranny of the majority. In the absence of checks and balances, instability or rotation among groups controlling government is preferable to stability; indeed, democracy requires rotation in office.

In section 2, we studied the political competition of representative democracy.

2A. Ostrogorski's paradox shows that outcomes of direct voting (or direct democracy) need not coincide with voting outcomes when collective decisions are determined through political competition in representative democracy. We cannot judge on efficiency grounds whether direct or representative democracy is preferable (the Condorcet winner does not ensure efficient choices). However, evidence indicates that people are better informed, have more substantive conversations, and are happier when collective decisions are made through direct democracy.

2B. When there are two political candidates and one policy issue, political competition duplicates the policy sought by the median voter. There is no stable outcome when there are three candidates; stability can return with more than two candidates. Expressive voters who identify with policies will tend to abstain as a candidate converges to the center, which can inhibit convergence. Expressive voters who identify with attributes of candidates do not abstain even if candidates' policies are identical. Non-expressive or instrumental voters maximize utility by never abstaining. Candidates who have won primary elections tend to converge to the policies of the median voter in the general electorate. Additionally, proceeding beyond a framework of a political contest at a point in time, candidates do not converge if reputation matters for success in future elections. Candidates also do not converge if committed by ideology or principle to a policy position. A candidate who does not converge to the policy of the median voter loses the election with certainty. A committed inflexible candidate also ensures an outcome personally inferior on the policy spectrum to the median-voter outcome obtained by convergence.

2C. When there are two candidates and two policy issues (or more), there is, in general, no equilibrium outcome of political competition. Again, a candidate who chooses policy ideologically loses with certainty and there is a determinate outcome. There is a determinate outcome when voters are ideological or principled and form coalitions on the basis of preferences about the size of public spending: such voter coalitions are the basis for political parties. Expressive voting is a possible reason for stability because of abstention when the decision whether to vote is expressive with regard to policy or because of sustained candidate support when voters vote expressively based on a candidate's attributes.

2D. Systems of voting used in practice do not, as a general principle, result in choice of the Condorcet winner. Preference for choosing the Condorcet winner has no normative economic basis; we saw that efficient projects can be rejected and inefficient projects chosen as

Condorcet winners. Nonetheless, the Condorcet winner satisfies the principle of democratic choice of being preferred by majority voting to all other alternatives. The relation of the Condorcet winner to voting outcomes was demonstrated for two-round elimination voting, plurality criteria, proportional representation, preferential voting, and approval voting.

In section 3, we studied voting on income redistribution. Our perspective was not normative in terms of what should happen. We were concerned with the positive question of what we can predict might happen when voters can redistribute income through majority voting.

3A. Voting on public spending on public goods can provide Pareto-improvement, but voting on income redistribution is, by nature, not Pareto-improving because one person provides income to another. The income redistribution is arbitrary if the only criterion for benefitting from redistribution is belonging to a majority. Voting on redistribution of income introduces public finance for private goods. Cross-subsidization of private goods through shared payments creates incentives for inefficient over-consumption. The example of the access roads demonstrated the incentives for a majority to finance private benefits through public finance. Majority voting is the least exploitative voting rule. There is prospective coalition instability when income is redistributed through majority voting. When voters can choose a nondiscriminatory rate of taxation that applies to all incomes in a population and tax revenue is redistributed equally as income, majority voting results in appropriative taxation – because the median voter in the income distribution has lower income than the average income. Appropriative taxation is inhibited by excess burdens of taxation and the tax revenue limits of the Laffer curve, by prospects for social mobility, and by incentives for and consequences of immigration. Other issues may be more salient to voters than income redistribution or voters may reject high taxes and extensive redistribution on grounds of the natural right of possession. Whether voters support high taxes and extensive redistribution also depends on whether they believe that luck or personal effort is the main determinant of personal incomes.

3B. The franchise affects voting on income redistribution because of who has the right to vote. Only wealthy classes who were owners of property initially voted. There are proposals for restricting the franchise to people who, through the taxes they pay, make net positive contributions to public spending – and excluding employees of government bureaucracies from voting on issues of taxation and government spending. Voting on income redistribution was influenced by extension of the franchise to women. Changes in the institution of the family can affect women's voting incentives.

3C. Redistribution through voting also depends on whether people vote – and the motivation for voting. We considered reasons for voting when people are aware that their single vote cannot be decisive.

3D. The evidence shows that median voter does not benefit from income redistribution in democratic high-income societies. The beneficiaries are rather low-income people. The extent of redistribution increases with pre-tax income inequality. A majority based on the median voter or middle class therefore does not take advantage of majority voting to redistribute income to itself. This outcome cannot be explained by the relationship between income and the likelihood of voting because high-income people are more likely to vote than low-income people. A possible explanation is a coalition consisting of high- and low-income voters. An explanation not based on self-interest is that the income redistribution to low-income people indicates an objective of social justice. However, for public goods, public spending is as predicted by self-interested majority voting; the middle class forms a coalition against the ends of the income distribution. Director's law points to voters in the middle class as the primary beneficiaries of public spending on public goods. Voters in the middle class also benefit from tax concessions. Expressive voting is inconsistent with middle-class voters voting to distribute income to themselves from people with low incomes but not with public spending on public goods and tax concessions, which can in principle benefit anybody.

Our conclusion was that majority voting assures neither efficiency nor social justice. However, the problems of majority voting are avoided when people have sorted themselves through locational choice in jurisdictions of populations with the same preferences. Problems of majority voting when people in a jurisdiction differ in preferences are ameliorated by checks and balances and rotation in political office. The problems associated with majority voting suggest that when possible, personal voluntary market decisions are preferred to the coerced (for the minority) collective decisions of majority voting.

Literature notes

6.1 The median voter and majority voting

Our focus has been on aspects of voting relevant to public finance and public policy. The theory of voting is the subject of a substantial literature: see, for example, Merrill and Grofman (1999).

Merrill, S., and B. Grofman, 1999. *A Unified Theory of Voting: Directional and Proximity Spatial Models*. Cambridge University Press, Cambridge U.K.

The Condorcet jury theorem and the Condorcet winner appeared in de Condorcet (1785). The theorem is the foundation for a field of study known as decision theory: see, for example, Nitzan and Paroush (1985).

de Condorcet, M., 1785. *Essai sur l'Application de l'Analyse à la Probabilité des Decisions Rendues á la Pluraliste des Voix*. Paris.
Nitzan S., and J. Paroush, 1985. *Collective Decision Making: An Economic Outlook*. Cambridge University Press, Cambridge U.K.

On voting rules, see Buchanan and Tullock (1962) and Guttman (1998). On proposals for departures for majority voting, see Wickström (1986). May's theorem axiomatically justifying the majority-voting rule was set out in May (1952): for a statement of the axioms, see also Mueller (2003, pp. 133–6).

Buchanan, J. M., and G. Tullock, 1962. *The Calculus of Consent: Logical Foundations of Constitutional Democracy*. University of Michigan Press, Ann Arbor MI.
Guttman, J. L., 1998. Unanimity and majority rule: The calculus of consent reconsidered. *European Journal of Political Economy* 14:189–207.
May, K. O., 1952. A set of independent, necessary and sufficient conditions for simple majority decision. *Econometrica* 20:680–4.
Mueller, D. C., 2003. Public Choice III. Cambridge University Press, Cambridge U.K.
Wickström, B.-A., 1986. Optimal majorities for decision rules of varying importance. *Public Choice* 48:273–90.

On the median voter, see:

Bergstrom, T. C., 1979. When does majority rule provide public goods efficiently? *Scandinavian Journal of Economics* 81:217–26.
Bowen, H. R., 1946. The interpretation of voting in the allocation of economic resources. *Quarterly Journal of Economics* 58:27–48. Reprinted in K. J. Arrow and T. Scitovsky (Eds.), 1969. *Readings in Welfare Economics*. Richard D. Irwin, Homewood IL, pp. 115–32.

Cycling and single-peaked preferences were described in:

Black, D., 1948. On the rationale of group decision making. *Journal of Political Economy* 56:23–36. Reprinted in K. J. Arrow and T. Scitovsky (Eds.), 1969. *Readings in Welfare Economics*. Richard D. Irwin, Homewood IL, pp. 133–46.

On political coalitions, see Riker (1962). On coalition stability, see Tullock (1981) and Congleton and Tollison (1999).

Congleton, R. D., and Tollison, R. D., 1999. The stability-inducing properties of very unstable coalitions: Avoiding the downward spiral of majoritarian rent seeking. *European Journal of Political Economy* 15:193–205.
Riker, W., 1962. *The Theory of Political Coalitions*. Yale University Press, New Haven CT.
Tullock, G., 1981. Why so much stability? *Public Choice* 37:189–202.

Buchanan (1954) pointed out the benefits of cycling when the alternative is persistent benefits for one group.

Buchanan, J. M., 1954. Social choice, democracy, and free markets. *Journal of Political Economy* 62:114–23.

On markets for votes, see:

Kochin, M. S., and L. A. Kochin, 1998. When is buying votes wrong? *Public Choice* 97:645–62.

On the theory of logrolling, see Bernholz (1977). For an empirical study, see Stratmann (1992).

Bernholz, P., 1977. Prisoners' dilemma, logrolling, and cyclical group preferences. *Public Choice* 29:73–86.
Stratmann, T., 1992. The effects of logrolling on Congressional voting. *American Economic Review* 82:1162–76.

On secession, see:

Buchanan, J. M., and R. L. Faith, 1987. Secession and the limits of taxation: Towards a theory of internal exit. *American Economic Review* 77:1023–31.

On locational choice and voting, see:

Kollman, K., J. H. Miller, and S. E. Page, 1997. Political institutions and sorting in a Tiebout model. *American Economic Review* 87:977–92.

For a view on checks and balances, see:

Persson, T., G. Roland, and G. Tabellini, 1997. Separation of powers and political accountability. *Quarterly Journal of Economics* 112:1163–202.

On issues decided by direct democracy, with elements of expressive voting, see:

Davidson, S., T. R. L. Fry, and K. Jarvis, 2006. Direct democracy in Australia: Voter behavior in the choice between a constitutional monarchy and a republic. *European Journal of Political Economy* 22:86–73.
Karahan, G. R., and W. F. Shughart II, 2004. Under two flags: Symbolic voting in the State of Mississippi. *Public Choice* 118:105–24.

Mayer (1984) and Weck-Hannemann (1990) described international trade policy determined in direct democracy:

Mayer, W., 1984. Endogenous tariff formation. *American Economic Review* 74:970–85.
Weck-Hannemann, H., 1990. Protectionism in direct democracy. *Journal of Institutional and Theoretical Economics* 146:389–418.

6.2 Political competition

For a comparison between direct and representative democracy describing the experience in Switzerland, see:

Feld, L. P., and G. Kirchgässner, 2000. Direct democracy, political culture, and the outcome of economic policy: A report on the Swiss experience. *European Journal of Political Economy* 16:287–306.

Ostrogorski's paradox is from Ostrogorski (1903); see also Nurmi (1999).

Nurmi, H., 1999. *Voting Paradoxes and How to Deal with Them*. Springer, Berlin.
Ostrogorski, M., 1903. *La démocratie et l'organisation des partis politiques*. Calmann-Levy, Paris (2 volumes).

Hotelling (1929) described locational competition. See Downs (1957) on political competition. Selten (1971) investigated the stability of political competition with different numbers of candidates. For an overview of policies determined through political competition, see Ursprung (1991) and Roemer (2001).

Downs, A., 1957. *An Economic Theory of Democracy*. Harper and Row, New York.

Hotelling, H., 1929. Stability in competition. *Economic Journal* 39:41–57.
Roemer, J., 2001. *Political Competition: Theory and Applications*. Harvard University Press, Cambridge MA.
Selten, R., 1971. Anwendungen der Spieltheorie auf die Politische Wissenschaft. In H. Maier (Ed.), *Politik und Wissenschaft*. C. H. Beck, München, pp. 287–320.
Ursprung, H. W., 1991. Economic policies and political competition. In A. L. Hillman (Ed.), *Markets and Politicians: Politicized Economic Choice*. Kluwer Academic Publishers, Boston and Dordrecht, pp. 1–26.

Expressive voting with one and two policy issues was described by Brennan and Hamlin (1998).

Brennan, G., and A. Hamlin, 1998. Expressive voting and electoral equilibrium. *Public Choice* 95:149–75.

Nurmi (1987) compared different voting systems. For a description of proportional representation, see Baron and Diermeier (2001). Bandyopadhyay and Oak (2008) described formation of coalition governments in the presence of rents and the influence of ideology. On approval voting, see Brams and Fishburn (1986).

Bandyopadhyay, S., and M. P. Oak, 2008. Coalition governments in a model of parliamentary democracy. *European Journal of Political Economy* 24:554–61.
Baron, D., and D. Diermeier, 2001. Elections, governments and parliaments under proportional representation. *Quarterly Journal of Economics* 116:933–67.
Brams, S., and P. C. Fishburn, 1986. *Approval Voting*. Birkhäuser, Boston.
Nurmi, H., 1987. *Comparing Voting Systems*. Kluwer Academic Publishers, Dordrecht.

6.3 Voting on income redistribution

Tullock (1959) described voting on public spending on private goods.

Tullock, G., 1959. Problems of majority voting. *Journal of Political Economy* 67:571–9. Reprinted in K. J. Arrow and T. Scitovsky (Eds.), 1969. *Readings in Welfare Economics*. Richard D. Irwin, Homewood IL, pp. 169–78.

On the majority-voting rule for redistributive decisions, see Rae (1969) and Taylor (1969). See also Mueller (2003, pp. 136–7) (see previous listing):

Rae, D. W., 1969. Decision rules and individual values in constitutional choice. *American Political Science Review* 63:40–56.
Taylor, M. J., 1969. Proof of a theorem on majority rule. *Behavioral Science* 14:228–31.

On income redistribution and voting, see Meltzer and Richard (1981). Bowles and Jones (1991) described income redistribution with differing incentives to vote.

Bowles, R., and P. Jones, 1991. Political participation and the limits to redistribution. *European Journal of Political Economy* 7:127–39.
Meltzer, A. H., and S. F. Richard, 1981. A rational theory of the size of government. *Journal of Political Economy* 89:914–27.

On the limits to redistribution, see:

Harms, P., and S. Zink, 2003. Limits to redistribution: A survey. *European Journal of Political Economy* 19:651–68.

On social mobility and voting, see Benabou and Ok (2001). The analogy between the traffic lane and patience for personal advancement is from Hirschman (1973).

Benabou, R., and E. A. Ok, 2001. Social mobility and the demand for redistribution: The POUM (prospect of upward mobility) hypothesis. *Quarterly Journal of Economics* 116:447–87.

Hirschman, A. O., 1973. The changing tolerance for income inequality in the course of economic development. *Quarterly Journal of Economics* 87:544–66.

Fuest and Thum (2001) described upward movement in the income distribution as a consequence of immigration. Hansen (2003) described how voters internalize immigration when voting on redistribution.

Fuest, C., and M. Thum, 2001. Immigration and skill formation in unionized markets. *European Journal of Political Economy* 17:557–73.

Hansen, J. D., 2003. Immigration and income redistribution in welfare states. *European Journal of Political Economy* 19:735–46.

On voting contrary to personal economic self-interest, see:

Roemer, J. E., 1998. Why the poor do not appropriate the rich: An old argument in new garb. *Journal of Public Economics* 70:399–426.

On strategic aspects of voting and the probability of being decisive, see:

Owen, G., and B. Grofman, 1984. To vote or not to vote: The paradox of nonvoting. *Public Choice* 42:311–25.

The reasons why people vote when they know they cannot influence the outcome of voting were considered by Glazer (1987). Empirical support for the hypothesis that voting is expressive was provided by Guttman, Hilger, and Shachmurove (1994). The theme of expressive voting was developed by Schuessler (2000).

Glazer, A., 1987. A new theory of voting: Why vote when millions of others do. *Decision and Theory* 22:257–70.

Guttman, J. L., N. Hilger, and Y. Shachmurove, 1994. Voting as investment vs. voting as consumption: New evidence. *Kyklos* 47:197–207.

Schuessler, A. A., 2000. *A Logic of Expressive Choice*. Princeton University Press, Princeton NJ.

Heckelman (1995) presented evidence showing that the introduction of the secret ballot reduced voter turnout rates. On voter turnout, see also Matsusaka and Palda (1999).

Heckelman, J. C., 1995. The effects of the secret ballot on voter turnout rates. *Public Choice* 82:107–24.

Matsusaka, J. G., and F. Palda, 1999. Voter turnout: How much can we explain? *Public Choice* 98:431–46.

Breyer and Ursprung (1998) described how a majority coalition can exclude the median voter.

Breyer, F., and H. W. Ursprung, 1998. Are the rich too rich to be appropriated? Economic power and the feasibility of constitutional limits to redistribution. *Public Choice* 94:135–56.

On gender and voting, see Husted and Kenny (1997), Lott and Kenny (1999), Abrams and Settle (1999), Edlund and Pande (2002), and Aidt and Dallal (2008).

Abrams, B. A., and R. F. Settle, 1999. Women's suffrage and the growth of the welfare state. *Public Choice* 100:289–300.

Aidt, T. S., and B. Dallal, 2008. Female voting power: The contribution of women's suffrage to the growth of social spending in Western Europe (1869–1960). *Public Choice* 134:391–417.

Edlund, L., and R. Pande, 2002. Why have women become left-wing? The political gender gap and the decline in marriage. *Quarterly Journal of Economics* 117:917–61.

Husted, T. A., and L. W. Kenny, 1997. The effect of the expansion of the franchise on the size of government. *Journal of Political Economy* 105:54–82.

Lott, J. R., and L. W. Kenny, 1999. Did women's suffrage change the size and scope of government? *Journal of Political Economy* 107:1163–98.

On gender imbalances, see:

Wilson, J. Q., 2002. *The Marriage Problem: How Our Culture Has Weakened Families.* Harper Collins, New York.

On the proposal that the franchise be restricted to voters who are net contributors to the government budget, see:

Mueller, D., 2003. Interest groups, redistribution and the size of government. In S. L. Winer and H. Shibata (Eds.), *Political Economy and Public Finance.* Edward Elgar, Cheltenham U.K., pp. 123–46.

On bureaucrats as voters, see:

Frey, B. S., and W. W. Pommerehne, 1982. How powerful are public bureaucrats as voters? *Public Choice* 38:253–62.

On the effect of income on the likelihood of voting, see:

Frey, B. S., 1971. Why do high-income people participate more in politics? *Public Choice* 11:101–5.

On the evidence that the median voter does not benefit from income redistribution, see:

Milanovic, B., 2000. The median-voter hypothesis, income inequality, and income distribution: An empirical test with the required data. *European Journal of Political Economy* 16:367–410.

Director's law was described by Stigler (1970).

Stigler, G., 1970. Director's law of public income distribution. *Journal of Law and Economics* 13:1–10.

7

SOCIAL JUSTICE

We shall now study social justice. We have seen that, unless the rich and the poor form a coalition against the middle, self-interested majority voting is predicted to result in income transfers that benefit the median voter. Director's law indicates that the middle class, of which we expect the median voter in high-income democracies to be part, disproportionately benefits from publicly financed public goods – and the middle class also benefits from tax deductions. Nonetheless, in high-income democracies, the beneficiaries of income redistribution are not the middle class but rather low-income people. The evidence, which was indicated in the previous chapter, therefore does not verify the prediction that the median voter or middle class will use majority voting for personal benefit through income transfers. Rather, in high-income democracies, redistribution of income is consistent with the conception of social justice that people who have not fared well in life should be helped.

However, the taxes paid to finance the income transfers to low-income people are compulsory. The taxes and income transfers contradict Pareto efficiency (taxpayers lose and recipients of income transfers gain) and are contrary to the principle of the natural right of possession of people to their own income. We confront, therefore, the normative question:

How are involuntary income transfers justified?

We shall address this question on the supposition that governments can identify who is effectively paying taxes and bears the burden of taxation, and who benefits from the redistribution of tax revenue, given (as we saw in chapter 4) that legal and effective incidence of taxes and subsidies generally differ. We shall now have to take for granted that governments know who is effectively paying taxes and who is benefiting from income transfer payments. If governments know who is paying and who is benefiting, we can also ask the further normative question:

How much income should be transferred among people?

We have seen that questions of efficiency cannot be separated from questions of income distribution or social justice. The quest for efficient financing of public goods could not be disassociated from who pays and who free rides. Resolution of externality problems has distributional consequences through who has legal rights and who therefore pays or receives payment. Majority voting on public goods has distributional consequences depending on whether a voter is in a majority or minority group (the tyranny of the majority has evident distributional consequences).

When the questions have been about efficiency, we therefore encountered social justice through effects on income distribution. Our focal questions will now be about social justice and once again we shall see that social justice cannot be separated from efficiency. Indeed, social justice and efficiency can be inconsistent or contradictory objectives – as we saw in our introductory chapter, for example, in the case of the water in the desert. We have noted different definitions of social justice – ex-post equality, ex-ante equality, and the natural right of possession – and, in the course of now seeking the objective of social justice, we shall have to take care to indicate the definition that is being used.

7.1 Social Justice and Insurance

Social justice can be viewed as related to insurance. We define social justice in terms of insurance:

> *Social justice is achieved when people are provided with complete insurance whereby people who fare well in life fully compensate those who do not fare well – because of the full compensation, after the income transfers predicated on insurance, all people have equal ex-post outcomes.*

The definition of social justice is therefore ex-post equality. Insurance is the ex-ante sharing of risk and also the ex-post sharing of incomes. Complete insurance means that people are completely compensated for having low incomes by people who have high incomes – and everyone thereby has equal ex-post income.

Our beginning is once more without government, now in circumstances where people not know their future income prospects. With future personal incomes uncertain, insurance protects against being destitute or having low income. To describe uncertain personal income, we divide future income into two parts, known and unknown. The known part of income is y^A. Actual future income, which we denote by y, is determined by the addition of a random component of income μ to known future income:

$$y = y^A + \mu. \tag{7.1}$$

The distribution of μ determines the pre-tax income distribution in a society.

We shall consider the case in which the random part of income μ can have only two values. A person experiences a favorable outcome in life $\mu^H > 0$, which results in high personal income:

$$y^H = y^A + \mu_H > 0, \tag{7.2}$$

or, alternatively, an unfavorable outcome $\mu^L < 0$ results in low personal income:

$$y^L = y^A + \mu_L > 0. \tag{7.3}$$

Expression (7.3) indicates that the adverse outcome μ_L cannot make low income y_L negative. The good and adverse outcomes are equally likely:

$$\textit{probability}\ \mu_H = \textit{probability}\ \mu_L = 0.5. \tag{7.4}$$

The random parts of income are symmetric:

$$\mu_H = -\mu_L. \tag{7.5}$$

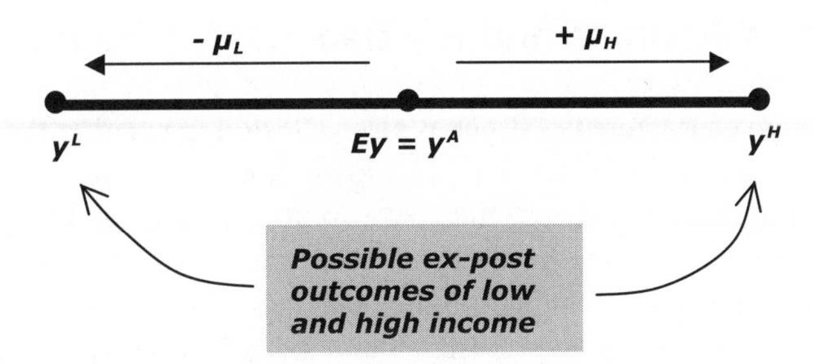

Figure 7.1. Random income.

Because of the symmetry, the expected or average value of future income Ey is equal to y^A:

$$Ey = \frac{y^H + y^L}{2} = \frac{(y^A + \mu_H) + (y^A - \mu_L)}{2} = y^A. \tag{7.6}$$

Figure 7.1 shows random income described by expressions (7.1)–(7.6). People know with certainty the income $Ey = y^A$ that they will have *on average*. They do not know if they will be lucky and actually have high income y^H or be unlucky and actually have low income y^L.

Supplement S7A: Measurement of income inequality

We are describing for illustration income distribution with two types of people: those who experience high income and those who experience low income. Supplement S7A describes measurement of income equality with more general distributions of income.

In section 1 of this chapter, the random components of income μ_H and μ_L are *exogenous* to personal actions, meaning that individuals' pre-tax incomes depend purely on fate or luck. In section 2, the random components of income μ_H and μ_L are *endogenous* to personal actions, meaning that individuals by their decisions and behavior influence whether they experience a good outcome μ_H or an adverse outcome μ_L. The influence on personal outcomes is through effort exerted in seeking to ensure a good outcome and to avoid an adverse outcome. Personal behavior is then subject to moral hazard.

> *Moral hazard occurs when the presence of insurance influences personal-effort decisions.*

We shall elaborate on moral hazard. There cannot be moral hazard when personal outcomes are purely a matter of luck or fate – which is the case that we now consider.

A. Uncertain incomes and the demand for insurance

Good or bad luck expressed in μ_H or μ_L can be due to innate ability that reflects inherited characteristics. Luck is also reflected in whether the family and peer environment encourage children to study to improve future income-earning prospects. Children cannot choose their own abilities or families. Obligations may also be present to care for small children without the assistance of a partner; people may be unemployed; or changes in financial markets may reduce market values of personal assets. Genetic predispositions in health affect income, or people can have good or bad luck with health. They can also have good or bad luck with partners and in marriage; divorce often reduces personal incomes.

A veil of ignorance

To express the uncertainties over which people have no control, we use the metaphor of a *veil of ignorance.*

> *The veil of ignorance is a metaphor for conditions under which people know nothing about their future selves.*

The metaphor of the veil of ignorance is counterfactual because people, in fact, do know who they are. However, we can nonetheless consider the decisions that people, in principle, would make under conditions of anonymity behind a veil of ignorance in which they know nothing about their future selves – or as if they have not yet been born.

People behind a veil of ignorance know the income distribution in the society into which they will be born. Based on our illustrative specification of the realizations of μ, the income distribution has half of a population with high pre-tax income and half with low pre-tax income. The people behind a veil of ignorance know to which society they will belong.[1]

Risk aversion and insurance

People are usually *risk averse.* The degree of risk aversion can be *behaviorally* inferred by asking people how much they are prepared to pay to avoid a fair gamble (when they stand to win or lose a sum of money with equal probability): the more a person is prepared to pay to avoid a fair gamble, the greater is the person's risk aversion. A person who is willing to pay nothing to avoid a fair gamble is *risk neutral.* We can, for example, ask someone, "How much are you prepared to pay to avoid a fair gamble where you will gain or lose $1,000 with equal likelihood?" The expected value of this gamble is zero. Risk-averse people are not indifferent between this fair gamble and having zero with certainty. They

[1] In section 3 of this chapter, we shall consider global social insurance when people behind a veil of ignorance do not have this information.

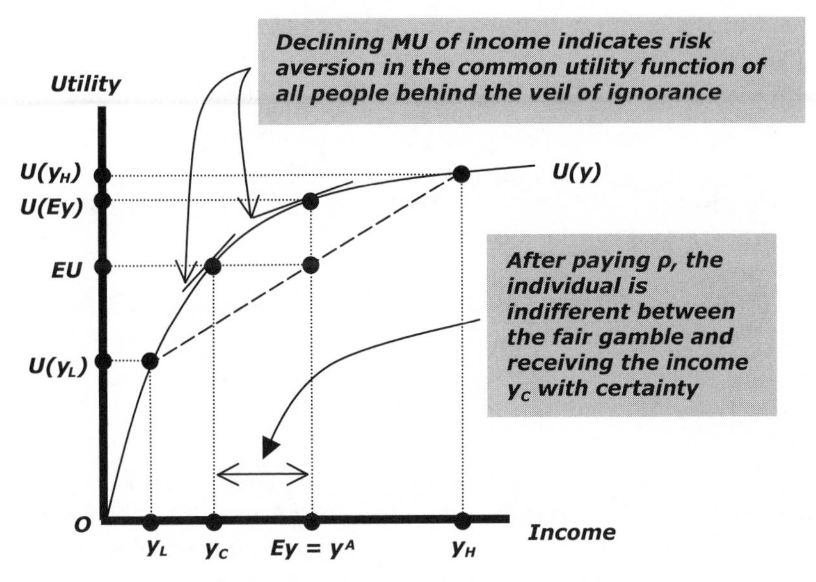

Figure 7.2. Risk aversion and insurance.

are prepared to pay a sum of money to avoid the fair gamble. The more they are prepared to pay, the more risk averse they are.

A person who is prepared to pay to avoid a fair gamble values additions to income less than income losses; therefore:

For risk-averse people, the marginal utility of income is declining.

In figure 7.2, individual utility $U(y)$ increases with personal income y. The slope of the utility function $U(y)$ is the marginal utility (MU) of income, which decreases as income y increases; hence, indicating risk aversion.[2]

We have previously referred to marginal utility MU as marginal benefit MB. We shall now use marginal utility MU and marginal benefit MB interchangeably.

The utility of having income Ey in figure 7.2 is $U(Ey)$. Low income y_L provides utility $U(y_L)$ and high income y_H provides utility $U(y_H)$. Expected utility EU is the average of the utilities $U(y_L)$ and $U(y_H)$.[3]

The fair gamble that is being offered is the chance of having low income y_L or high income y_H with equal probabilities of 50 percent. $Ey = y^A$ is the expected income provided by the fair gamble.

The fair gamble is also a gamble over utilities $U(y_H)$ and $U(y_L)$. Expected utility from participating in the fair gamble is EU, which is the utility obtained

[2] Risk aversion can be measured by the rate at which the MU of income (the slope of the utility function) declines as income increases. A measure of risk aversion is the elasticity of MU with respect to income, known as *relative risk aversion*.

[3] Expected (or average) utility EU is found by joining the points of utility from low and high income on the utility function and finding the midpoint of the straight line that joins these two points.

on average from a lottery that gives the utilities $U(y_H)$ and $U(y_L)$ with equal probabilities.[4]

EU is an average utility that is never attained. The income y_C in figure 7.2 gives the same utility as EU with certainty.

> *The income y_C is the certainty-equivalent income for the fair gamble that gives expected income Ey and expected utility EU.*

The certainty-equivalent income y_C gives the individual EU but *with no risk.*

A risk-averse person whose utility is shown in figure 7.2 is prepared to pay to avoid the fair gamble on future income and to receive instead the income y_C with certainty. How much is the individual prepared to pay to avoid the fair gamble?

With the same utility EU equivalently obtainable from either the fair gamble that has average or expected income $Ey = y^A$ or from having the income y_C with certainty, we see in figure 7.2 that the amount that the individual is prepared to pay to avoid the fair gamble is maximally:

$$\rho = Ey - y_c > 0. \tag{7.7}$$

The positive value of ρ, which is a payment to avoid risk, confirms risk aversion.

Ex-ante equality and ex-post inequality

People behind a veil of ignorance are equal ex-ante: everyone has same utility function and faces the same uncertainty about future income. People will not be equal ex-post after emerging from behind the veil of ignorance because some people will experience $\mu_L < 0$ and have low income y_L and others will experience $\mu_H > 0$ and have high income y_H. There is, therefore, ex-ante equality but people face ex-post inequality.

Inequality aversion

We can reframe the question "How much are you prepared to pay to avoid the fair gamble?" as "How much are you prepared to pay maximally to personally avoid ex-post inequality when you and someone else confront the fair gamble and one of you will have high income and the other low income?" The answer to this latter question is again the value of ρ in expression (7.7). The desire to avoid ex-post equality is not a matter of ideology or principle. The issue is personal. By paying ρ in expression (7.7) and obtaining in return the certainty-equivalent income y_C, the person avoids personal exposure to the risk of having low income – but also forgoes having high income.

[4] Because of risk aversion, in figure 7.1, $U(E_y) > EU$. For a person who is risk-neutral, the utility function $U(y)$ is linear and $U(Ey)$ equals EU.

Insurance markets

In return for a person paying ρ, an insurance company is prepared to bear the risk associated with income uncertainty. The insurance company provides everyone with the certain income y_C so that individuals' incomes no longer depend on whether a person experiences μ_L or μ_H. Behind the veil of ignorance and therefore before knowing whether they will be lucky or unlucky in life, people agree that in return for receiving y_C with certainty, they will transfer their future income, be it y_H or y_L as the case may be, to the insurance company. In bearing all risk and providing future income y_C to everyone with certainty, the insurance company provides *complete insurance*. The complete insurance spreads risk and results in ex-post income equality.

> *Complete insurance makes personal income independent of whether a person experiences a bad or good outcome.*

The insurance company receives a payment on average of $y^A = Ey$ from each person. Because the insurance company pays out y_C per person, the profit of the insurance company is $\rho = (Ey - y_C)$ per person. Profit for the insurance company is ensured by the law of large numbers, which states that sufficient repetitions make objective probabilities actual probabilities.[5]

The profits of the insurance company depend on risk aversion. A linear utility function would indicate risk neutrality and $\rho = 0$. That is, risk-neutral people are not prepared to pay to avoid risk. Risk-neutral people provide an insurance company with no profit.

The gain from competitive insurance markets

The risk-averse people whose common utility function is shown in figure 7.2 are indifferent between participating in the fair gamble and paying ρ to an insurance company to avoid the fair gamble. If they could pay less than ρ for insurance, they would gain from insurance. Competition in the insurance market reduces the price of insurance below ρ. When competition in the insurance market eliminates above-competitive profits, ρ is the personal gain from insurance for insured individuals.[6]

Mutual risk-sharing contracts

Rather than use an insurance market to "buy" insurance, risk-averse people could agree to a contract whereby they cooperate to mutually pool (or share) risk associated with personal future incomes. The agreement to share risk would

[5] That is, flip a coin 10 times and the result may not be half heads and half tails, but for 100 flips of the coin, the outcome will be close to half. This occurs although the outcome of each flip of the coin is independent of the outcome of the previous flip. Insurance companies confront no risk when objective probabilities of outcomes are known. For events that require large unpredictable payouts, insurance companies may reinsure; that is, they may spread risk among themselves.

[6] Administrative costs of insurance companies reduce the benefits from competitive insurance markets below ρ.

duplicate the outcome of a competitive insurance market. As in competitive insurance markets, ρ is the personal gain, from the mutual risk-pooling agreement.

Efficiency and social justice through insurance

The voluntary pooling of risk through either competitive insurance markets or mutual risk-sharing contracts is efficient. Pareto improvement takes place because all people gain ρ from the risk sharing. A rule for social justice is *equal treatment of equals*. Equals are treated equally through the insurance contract because people who are equal ex-ante behind the veil of ignorance are also equal ex-post: the complete insurance gives them y_C independently of whether they will experience the fortunate outcome μ_H or unfortunate outcome μ_L. Hence, with social justice defined as ex-post income equality after the realization of μ:

Insurance markets efficiently ensure social justice.

Revealed information

People seek insurance because of uncertainty or risk.

Revealed personal information is an impediment to insurance.

For example, the information provided through the human-genome project, which has identified human genes and allows people to be categorized in accord with risk of different diseases, impedes health insurance. If everyone's health risks could be perfectly identified, no health-insurance contract would be possible because there would be no risk to be pooled through insurance.

Social insurance

Behind a veil of ignorance, personal information is not revealed and insurance companies would be willing to provide insurance contracts. The insurance companies would enter into contracts to provide the certainty-equivalent income y_C after people know whether they have experienced good or bad outcomes. However, there are, of course, no insurance companies behind the veil of ignorance; we shall not extend the metaphor to include the presence of insurance companies behind the veil of ignorance. Behind the veil of ignorance, people would agree to a mutual risk-sharing contract whereby those people who will have experienced a good outcome pay people who will have experienced a bad outcome. However, enforceable contracts cannot be written behind the veil of ignorance. We therefore now introduce government. After μ is determined and people know whether they have high or low incomes, a government takes the responsibility of enforcing compulsory *social* insurance (for the society) *as if* the insurance contract had been determined when people were anonymous behind a veil of ignorance.

Insurance through government is social insurance because everyone in society is included in the social-insurance contract and participation is compulsory.

Therefore, through the legal monopoly on coercion and the ability thereby to compel payment of taxes, governments ensure that the people who experienced the good outcome μ_H make compensatory income transfers to people who experienced the unfortunate outcome μ_L. This is the contract to which risk-averse people behind the veil of ignorance would have agreed. The government is therefore enforcing the contract that risk-averse people would have wanted when they confronted risk about their future incomes.

B. Social welfare functions and social insurance contracts

Choice of a social-insurance contract behind the veil of ignorance – to be implemented through government when people will know who they are – is correspondingly choice of a social welfare function.

A social welfare function

The objective of maximizing $\{W = B - C\}$ can guide public-policy decisions when the social objective is efficiency. When the objective is social justice, the objective is to maximize a *social welfare function*, which includes judgments about the distribution of benefits and costs among the people in a population.

With n people in a society, a social welfare function measures total welfare W of the population as:

$$W = f(U_1, U_2, U_3, \ldots, U_n). \tag{7.8}$$

Total social welfare W thus depends on values of the individual utilities U_i of the people in the population. In expression (7.8), social welfare depends *only* on personal utilities of the population. The social welfare function is therefore described as *utilitarian*.

Social welfare and Pareto improvement

Pareto improvement increases social welfare. That is, if the utility U_i of any person i increases and everyone else's utility remains constant:

$$\frac{\partial W}{\partial U_i} = \omega_i > 0, \quad i = 1, \ldots, n. \tag{7.9}$$

In expression (7.9), ω_i is an individual's *social weight* in the measurement of social welfare. Expression (7.9) therefore states that every person has positive weight

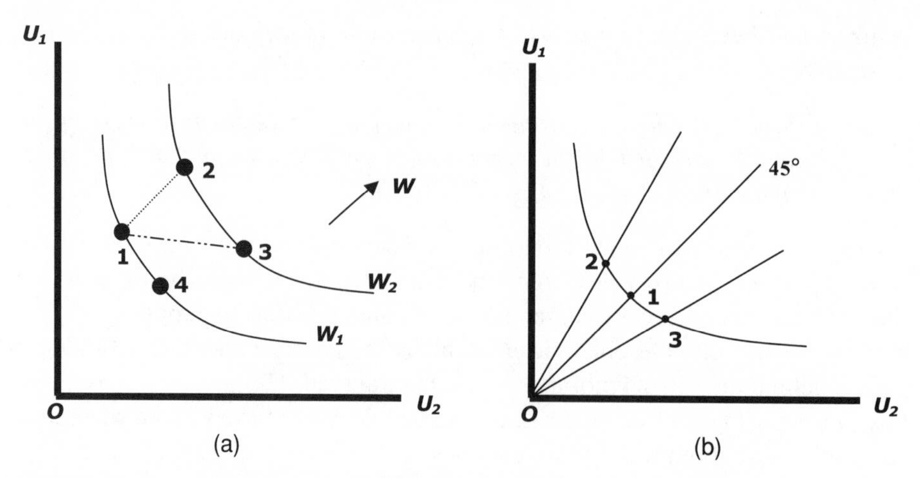

Figure 7.3. (a) Pareto improvement and social welfare. (b) Social welfare contours and anonymity.

in the measurement of society's total welfare. Thus, if any person is better off (and no one is worse off), society is better off. Figure 7.3a shows a social welfare function for a society composed of two people. Social welfare is constant along the contours W_1 and W_2, where W_2 indicates higher social welfare than W_1. Consistent with expression (7.9), Pareto-improving change from point 1 to point 2 increases social welfare. However, Pareto improvement is not *necessary* for social welfare to increase. In figure 7.3a, a move from point 1 to point 3 increases social welfare, even though person 1 has lost. Society is also indifferent between points 1 and 4, although person 1 is better off at point 1 and person 2 is better off at point 4.

Social welfare increases whenever there is Pareto-improving change.

Social welfare can increase without Pareto-improving change (that is, even though a person is made worse off).

Interpersonal comparisons of utility

In figure 7.3a, interpersonal comparisons of utilities are being made.

An interpersonal comparison of utilities is a judgment about comparative values of different people's utilities.

Interpersonal comparisons allow judgments about how changes in different people's utilities affect social welfare.

A common utility function for the population behind the veil of ignorance provides the means of interpersonal comparisons of utility through a cardinal measure of utility.[7] The common utility function rules out the possibility of a judgment that two people with the same income benefit differently – or have different utilities.

> *A common utility function preempts privilege or prejudice that would be present if some people were to be regarded as being capable of benefiting more from income than others.*

Anonymity

Privilege or prejudice is also preempted by anonymity in the social welfare function. Figure 7.3b shows a social welfare contour that is symmetric around the equal-utility 45° line. The symmetry ensures that the shape of the social welfare contour is independent of the identities of the people whose utilities are measured on the axes. It does not matter, then, from the viewpoint of treatment by the social welfare function whether someone is (or will be) person 1 or person 2.[8]

Supplement S7B: An impossibility theorem for social aggregation

Social welfare functions were introduced by Abram Bergson (1914–2003) in 1938 and were further developed by Paul Samuelson (1947; Noble Prize in economics, 1970). The social welfare function is often described in economic literature as maximized by a social planner (also called a benevolent dictator), who decides on production and determines consumption for the people in a population. Bergson had worked in the Soviet Union's government planning agency before arriving after World War II in the United States, where he taught at Columbia and Harvard universities. Supplement S7B describes a conclusion expressed in a theorem by Kenneth Arrow (1950; Nobel Prize in economics, 1972) that it is generally impossible to aggregate the preferences of people in a society to obtain a social welfare function that represents stable social preferences. Arrow proposed that a social welfare function would generally require a dictator to choose social preferences. When we studied voting, we saw that cycling over alternatives could occur indefinitely, unless a particular voter could determine the agenda for voting. Determining the agenda is equivalent to dictatorship because the person determining the agenda also determines the outcome of voting. Arrow called his conclusion an "impossibility theorem" because of the demonstration of the impossibility of a social

(*continued*)

[7] When the measurement of utility is ordinal, the utility function only *ranks* personal outcomes of the *same* individual. With ordinal utility, we could therefore not compare the consequences of distributing income in different ways among people – although, when Pareto improvement takes place, we could with ordinal utility conclude that social welfare has increased.

[8] The social welfare contour in figure 7.2b has the same symmetric shape whichever direction we move from point 1 on the 45° line. Points 2 and 3 are the same distance from point 1 and are the same distance from the origin.

Supplement S7B (*continued*)

welfare function. Arrow's impossibility theorem will not hinder us in asking questions about social justice. Arrow's theorem does not apply when, as in our case, utility is cardinal and interpersonal comparisons can be made. We shall also not require the Bergson–Samuelson social planner because we limit the scope of application of the social welfare function to choice behind the veil of ignorance, where all people are viewed as being identical in not knowing who they will be and in having the same utility function.

Distribution of predetermined income

The social welfare function can be used to describe a decision behind the veil of ignorance about how a predetermined amount of income Y will be divided, after people will have emerged from behind the veil of ignorance. Person 1 will receive income y_1 and person 2 will receive income y_2, with:

$$Y = y_1 + y_2. \tag{7.10}$$

Utilities of the two people from the distribution of income y_1 and y_2 evaluated by the common utility function are:

$$U_1 = U(y_1), \quad U_2 = U(y_2). \tag{7.11}$$

In figure 7.4a, the frontier SV shows the utilities possible for the two people from different possible distributions of income. SV is the utility-possibility frontier.

> *The utility-possibility frontier shows the distribution of utilities possible from distribution of a given amount of income.*

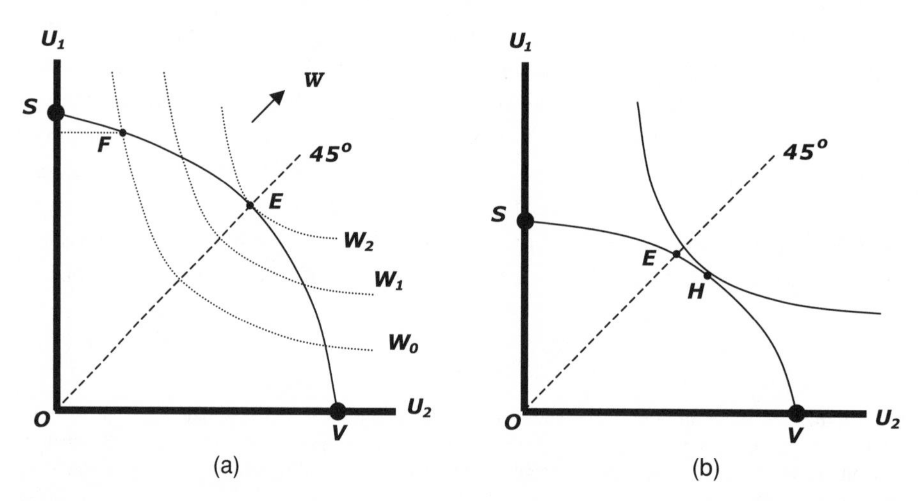

Figure 7.4. (a) Distribution of a predetermined amount of income. (b) Distribution of income with nonidentical utilities.

All distributions of the income Y along the utility-possibility frontier SV in figure 7.4a are Pareto-efficient.[9] Because of identical utility functions and diminishing marginal utility of income, the frontier SV is symmetrically concave around the equal-utility 45° line.[10] Maximal social welfare W_2 is achieved at point E on the 45° line by equal division of the income to achieve ex-post equality of income and utility.

Nonidentical utilities

How is social welfare maximized if people are not viewed as having identical utility functions? Figure 7.4b shows the utility-possibility frontier SV when person 2 is defined as having greater personal capability for enjoyment of income than person 1. Giving the entire income Y to person 2 gives that person utility OV, which exceeds the utility OS of person 1 from the entire income Y. Social welfare now is not maximized through equality at point E but rather at point H, where utility is higher for person 2 than for person 1. The outcome is *privilege* for person 2, through a claim of superior capacity of person 2 to benefit from income. We shall proceed with identical utility functions based on equal capacities of people to benefit from income.

Social insurance and private insurance

The outcome of the equality of incomes through income distribution to maximize social welfare is the same as the complete-insurance outcome that would be achieved through private-insurance markets. Private insurance is voluntary. Income transfers through government are involuntary, financed by compulsory taxes. The compulsory taxes introduce an excess burden of taxation. The income Y does not spontaneously become available for distribution but rather is earned through *productive activity* of people; the earned income is then redistributed through taxes and budgetary spending; the redistribution requires taxes for which there is an excess burden.

The leaky bucket of redistribution

The efficiency losses through the excess burden of taxation result in a "leaky bucket" of redistribution. The leaky bucket is not present when income is

[9] At any point along SV (for example, point F), one person cannot be made better off without the other person being made worse off.

[10] If all income is given to person 1, the outcome in figure 7.4a is at point S. If all income is given to person 2, the outcome is at point V. Because utility functions are identical, person 1's utility OS from the entire income Y is the same as the utility OV when person 2 is given the entire income Y. That is, $OS = OV$. Divisions in which each person receives some part of Y result in outcomes along the utility-possibility curve SV between points S and V. The concavity of SV is due to declining marginal utility from additional personal income. If the society, for example, is at point S where person 1 has the entire available income Y and person 2 has nothing, and some income is then given to person 2, because of diminishing marginal utility, person 1 loses less than person 2 gains. For example, the transfer of income to person 2 at S moves the society to point F, where person 2 has gained more than person 1 has lost.

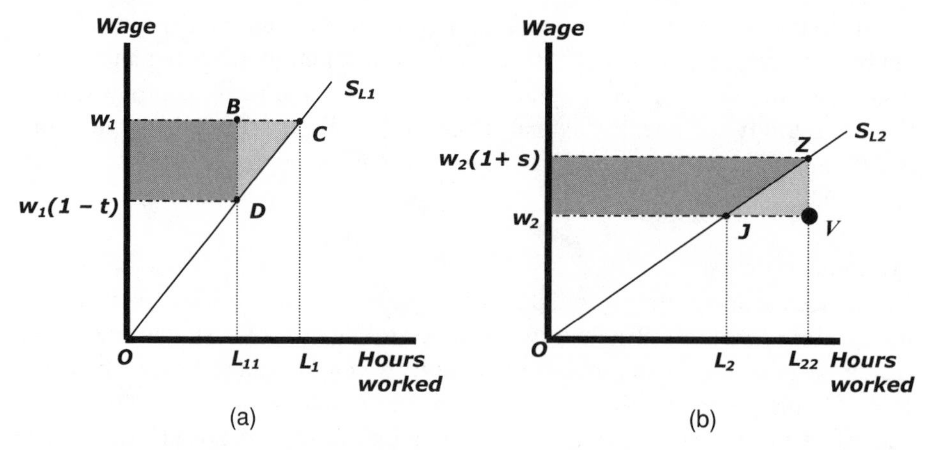

Figure 7.5. (a) The leaky bucket of redistribution and the taxpayer. (b) The transfer recipient and the leaky bucket of redistribution.

redistributed without taxation under the voluntary contracts of a private-insurance company.[11]

> *The efficiency losses due to the excess burden of taxation result in a leaky bucket of income redistribution.*

If income transfers are financed by government borrowing, the taxes and excess burdens – and the leaky bucket – are in the future.

The source of the leaky bucket of income redistribution

The source of the leaky bucket of income redistribution is shown in figures 7.5a and 7.5b. In figure 7.5a, person 1 is taxed. S_{L1} is person 1's labor-supply function. At a given market-determined hourly wage w_1, person 1 chooses to work L_1 hours. An income tax at rate t reduces the post-tax wage to $w_1(1 - t)$ and leisure is substituted for work. Hours worked decline to L_{11}. The tax revenue that person 1 pays to the government is shown by the shaded rectangle in figure 7.5a and the excess burden of taxation is area BCD.

The revenue from taxing person 1 is given to person 2. The income transfer may require person 2 not to work, which makes person 2 unproductive. Alternatively, the tax revenue can be used to subsidize person 2's market-determined wage. Figure 7.5b shows person 2's labor-supply function S_{L2} and market wage w_2. A subsidy of s for each hour worked increases person 2's post-transfer wage to $w_2(1 + s)$. Person 2 responds by increasing hours worked from L_2 to L_{22}. The income transfer received by person 2 is shown by the rectangle in figure 7.5b, which is equal to the rectangle showing tax revenue in figure 7.5a. The

[11] There is, of course, no excess burden of taxation from voluntary market transactions – in this case, in the insurance market.

wage-subsidy to person 2 results in an efficiency loss indicated in figure 7.5b by the area *JVZ*.[12]

Persons 1 and 2 are making substitution decisions between labor and leisure; therefore, the utility function now includes leisure as well as income. The substitution responses are the sources of the excess burden of taxation.

By adding the efficiency losses *BCD* in figure 7.5a and *JVZ* in figure 7.5b, we obtain the loss from the leak in the bucket of redistribution.[13] The loss is personal. Person 1 as taxpayer bears the loss *BCD*. Similarly, the efficiency loss *JVC* is a subtraction from the benefit to the recipient of the income transfer.

There are further leaks, or losses, because of costs of tax administration and costs of taxpayers' compliance with tax laws. An additional cost is public spending on the government bureaucracy that sends social workers to certify a recipient's eligibility for the income transfers and that administers the income transfers to the recipients.

When behind the veil of ignorance, people do not know whether they will be lucky and have a good outcome μ_H or unlucky and have a bad outcome μ_L; therefore, they do not know whether they will be taxpayers or beneficiaries of income transfers. However, because they personally bear the efficiency losses of the leaky bucket and other administrative costs of income redistribution, people behind the veil of ignorance take account of the efficiency losses when deciding on how income should be redistributed when they will have emerged from behind the veil of ignorance.

Feasible redistribution

The leaky bucket of income redistribution defines feasible redistribution. Although people are anonymous behind the veil of ignorance, we can label two people behind the veil of ignorance as person 1 and person 2. In figure 7.6, points F_1 and F_2 on the utility-possibility frontier *SV* show alternative utilities obtained through market pre-tax incomes after persons 1 and 2 have emerged from behind the veil of ignorance. Outcome F_1 is favorable for person 1 and outcome F_2 is favorable for person 2. The higher utility for person 1 at F_1 and the higher utility for person 2 at F_2 may reflect greater ability, more fortunate family circumstances, or better educational opportunities. Viewed from behind the veil of ignorance, F_1 and F_2 are equally likely and are symmetric. Behind the veil of ignorance, people are identical and there is ex-ante equality. At F_1 or F_2, people know who they are and there is inequality.[14]

[12] Person 2's valuation of the income transfer in terms of leisure or free time is given by the area under the supply of labor function between w_2 and $w_2(1 + s)$. This area is less than the income transfer by *JVZ* because of the opportunity cost in terms of free time or leisure of supplying labor.

[13] If the income transfer is \$10,000, if *BCD* is \$1,500, and if *JVZ* is \$1,000, the leak in the bucket is \$2,500. There has then been a 25 percent loss through the leaky bucket.

[14] F_1 is the same distance from point *S* as F_2 is from point *V*. F_1 and F_2 are therefore the same distance from the equal-utility point *E*.

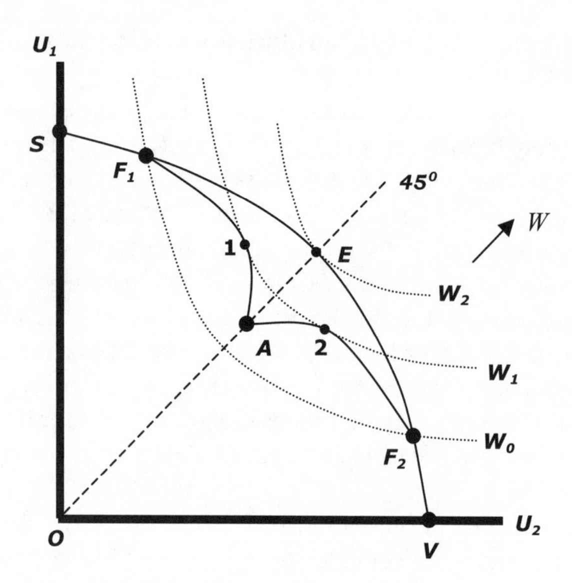

Figure 7.6. Incomplete insurance with a leaky bucket of redistribution.

Because of the leaky bucket, point E with social welfare W_2 now is not feasible. Redistribution along SV could only take place if people supplied labor without regard for reward or, equivalently, if incentives did not affect personal decisions to be productive.

The leaky bucket determines feasible income redistribution beginning from either F_1 or F_2. Feasible redistribution is along F_1A if the market outcome is at F_1 and along F_2A if the market outcome is at F_2.

The excess burden of taxation increases with the tax revenue collected.[15] Outcomes along F_1A and F_2A thus lie increasingly farther inside SV as we leave F_1 and F_2 because of the greater tax revenue required for greater income redistribution.

Social welfare is maximized in figure 7.6 subject to the leaky bucket of redistribution. If the outcome after emerging from behind the veil of ignorance has been point F_1, the society maximizes social welfare by redistribution of income to attain point 1. If the outcome after emerging from behind the veil of ignorance has been point F_2, the society maximizes social welfare by redistribution of income to attain point 2.

The income redistribution increases social welfare: the initial predistribution social welfare is W_0 and the postdistribution social welfare is W_1. Point A would result in ex-post equality through redistribution and is feasible. However, social welfare at point A is less than W_1.[16]

[15] See chapter 4.

[16] In figure 7.6, the changes in the utilities of the two people in the movement from F_1 or F_2 to point 1 or point 2 include the consequences of the changes in leisure. Although income is lost by the person who pays the taxes that finance income redistribution, the taxpayer gains leisure through

The leaky bucket and economic growth

We have described the leaky bucket as affecting levels of income and utility. The leaky bucket also affects growth of income. Disincentives of high taxes and extensive income redistribution deter not only labor supply but also investment, including investment in personal future ability to earn income (or human capital).

Through effects on economic growth, the efficiency costs of the leaky bucket are expressed in lower future as well as present incomes.

C. Choice of social insurance behind a veil of ignorance

Figure 7.6 describes a social insurance contract that redistributes income from F_1 to point 1 or from F_2 to point 2, depending on who has experienced the fortunate and unfortunate random outcomes μ_H and μ_L and thereby who has higher and lower market-determined income.

Maximizing a social welfare function behind the veil of ignorance specifies the properties of a social insurance contract to be implemented when people emerge from behind the veil of ignorance.

Choice of a social welfare function is thus important because of the corresponding choice of social insurance. Many possible social welfare functions and associated social insurance contracts can be chosen behind the veil of ignorance. The limiting cases are associated with Jeremy Bentham and John Rawls, who lived centuries apart. We have been using a social welfare function that is an intermediate case between the two limiting cases of Bentham and Rawls.

Bentham

The social welfare function associated with the English political economist Jeremy Bentham (1748–1832) is based on seeking "the greatest good for the greatest number."[17] Bentham's objective has been interpreted as implying that social welfare is defined by the sum of the utilities of the people in a population. For n people, the Bentham social welfare function is:

$$W = \sum_{i=1}^{n} U_i. \tag{7.12}$$

substitution that decreases hours worked. If income is transferred through a wage subsidy, the income recipient loses leisure. An explanation of the concavity of the utility-possibility frontier now cannot rest on diminishing marginal utility of income alone but needs to be supplemented by the presence of leisure in the utility function as well as income.

[17] Bentham believed that it would be possible one day to measure individual capacities for enjoyment, which would allow objectively comparable measurement of different utilities of different people.

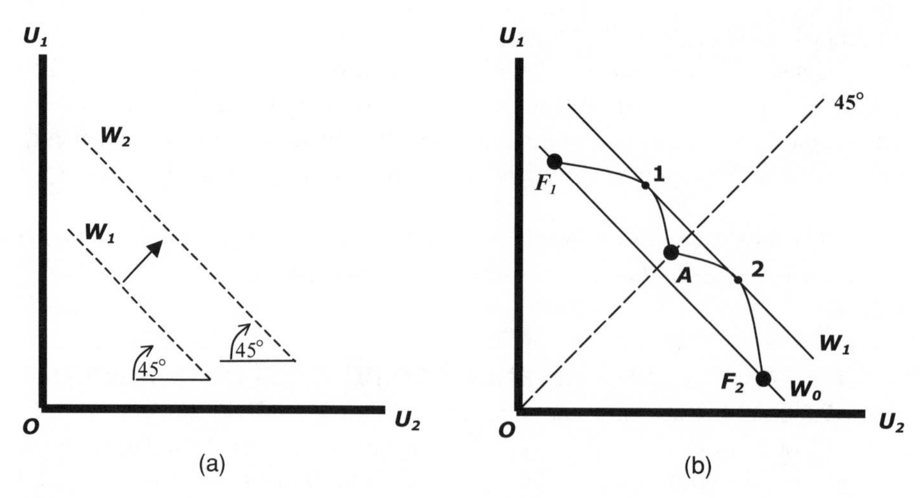

Figure 7.7. (a) Bentham's measure of social welfare. (b) The Bentham social insurance contract.

The Bentham social welfare function gives all people equal social weights (equal to 1). We see that only the *sum* of utilities matters for measurement of Bentham social welfare; the *distribution* of utilities does not matter. For two people, Bentham social welfare is:

$$W = U_1 + U_2. \tag{7.13}$$

The dashed lines with 45° slope in figure 7.7a show constant levels of Bentham social welfare.[18]

Figure 7.7b shows the social insurance contract associated with the Bentham social welfare function. Points F_1 and F_2 are the equally likely market-determined outcomes for persons 1 and 2 (the utility-possibility frontier SV if there were no leaky bucket is not shown in figure 7.7b). Feasible redistribution possibilities determined by the leaky bucket are along F_1A and F_2A. Beginning from either point F_1 or point F_2, income redistribution increases social welfare from W_0 to W_1.[19]

Because utilities are not equalized at points 1 and 2:

Bentham provides incomplete insurance.

Complete insurance would bring the society to the 45° line at point A. At point A, Bentham social welfare is lower than W_1.

[18] When Bentham social welfare is constant, $dW = 0 = dU_1 + dU_2$. The slope of a social welfare contour is therefore -1.

[19] If F_1 is the outcome after people's identities and market-determined incomes are known, social welfare is maximized by redistribution of income from person 1 to person 2 along F_1A to point 1. If the market outcome is at F_2, the redistribution is along F_2A to point 2.

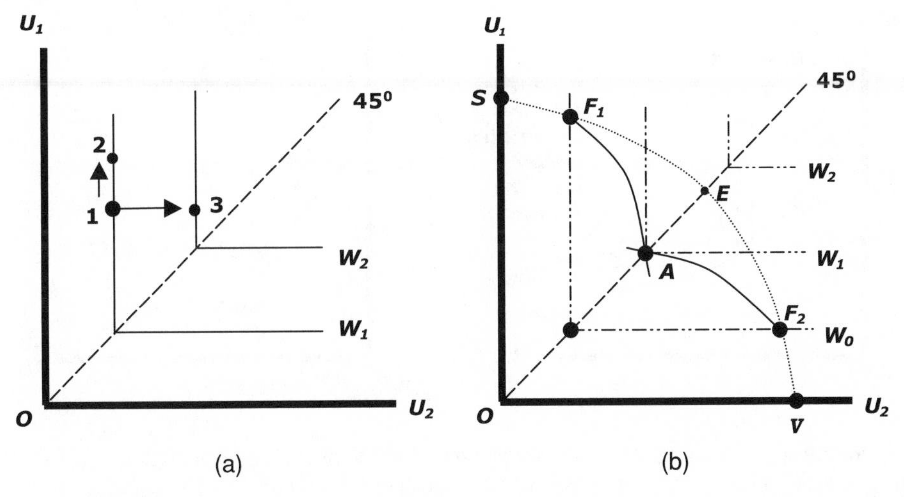

Figure 7.8. (a) Rawls' measure of social welfare. (b) Complete insurance with Rawls' social insurance contract.

Rawls and the weakest link

The philosopher, John Rawls (1921–2002), who taught at Harvard University, proposed that maximizing social welfare requires maximizing the utility of the worst-off person in society. If a society is as strong as its weakest link, the worst-off person in the society is the weakest link. Rawls proposed that people behind the veil of ignorance, not knowing who they will be, would wish all attention to be focused on improving the circumstances of the most unfortunate person – who perhaps they will be. After having done the best that is possible for the most unfortunate person, a society could then proceed to maximize the utility of the next most disadvantaged person, and so on. Throughout this procedure, only the utility of the worst-off person ever matters for defining social welfare.

The Rawls social welfare function is of the max–min form:

$$W = max\{min\, U\}. \tag{7.14}$$

That is, social welfare is maximized when the utility of the person who has minimum utility is maximized.

Figure 7.8a shows the Rawls measure of social welfare. Because only improvements in the well-being of the poorest person count as improving social welfare, the Rawls social welfare function does not satisfy the condition that a Pareto-improving change increases social welfare. The right angles at the 45° line indicate that there is no trade-off in social welfare between making richer and poorer people better off. Only the utility of the worst-off person counts in determining social welfare.[20]

[20] Above the 45° line in figure 7.8a, person 1 has higher utility than person 2, so social welfare cannot increase unless the low-utility person 2 becomes better off. A move from point 1 to point 2 does not change social welfare because, although the utility of better-off person 1 increases, there is no change in the utility of less-well-off person 2. There has been a Pareto improvement (person 1 is made better off and person 2 is no worse off). However, social welfare does not increase because

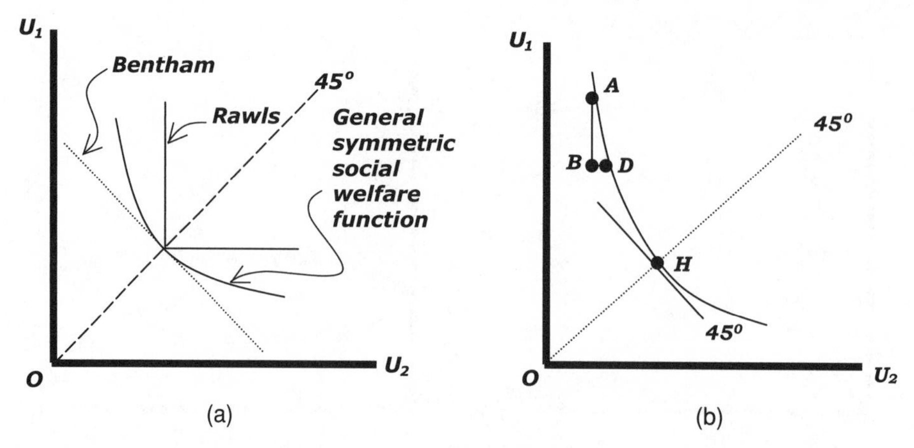

Figure 7.9. (a) Limiting cases of social welfare and social insurance contracts. (b) The slope of a social welfare contour expresses relative social weights.

Figure 7.8b shows social insurance through choice of the Rawls social welfare function. Beginning from market-determined utilities at either point F_1 or point F_2 where social welfare is W_0, social insurance calls for redistribution along F_1A or F_2A until ex-post equality is achieved at point A. Insurance at point A is complete because ex-post utilities after taxation and redistribution are equal. The social insurance contract increases social welfare from predistribution W_0 to postdistribution W_1.

The Rawls social welfare function provides complete insurance.

Although the Rawls social welfare function results in complete insurance and thereby in ex-post equality, the Rawls objective is not ex-post equality. Rather, ex-post equality is the consequence of the Rawls objective of maximization of the utility of the worst-off person. We shall presently see that because of the Laffer curve and limitations on tax revenue, complete insurance and ex-post equality are not necessary consequences of the Rawls definition of social welfare.

Bentham and Rawls as limiting cases

Figure 7.9a shows how Bentham and Rawls are limiting cases of social welfare functions. Also shown is a symmetric social welfare function that is intermediate between Bentham and Rawls.

Bentham and Rawls are limiting cases because Bentham cares only about the sum of utilities and not the distribution of utilities. Rawls cares only about distribution of utilities and, in particular, the utility of the worst-off person.

How do we interpret the social welfare function in figure 7.9a between Rawls and Bentham? Figure 7.9b shows a contour of the intermediate social welfare

the utility of the person who is the "weakest link" in the society has not increased. Rawls's measure of social welfare is increased by a move from point 1 to point 3 because this change increases the utility of worse-off person 2.

function. Along the contour, the two people's social weights change. The two people have equal social weights only at the 45° line at point H where their utilities are equal. Away from the 45° line, the person with lower utility has greater social weight. For example, at point A, where person 1 has higher utility than person 2, the slope of the social welfare contour indicates greater social weight for low-utility person 2 than for high-utility person 1.

If the social welfare function in figure 7.9b were chosen behind the veil of ignorance, the two people (not yet knowing their future outcomes in life) will have agreed that social welfare will be regarded as constant when high-utility person 1 at point A gives up utility AB to provide the smaller amount of utility BD to low-utility person 2. The agreement behind the veil of ignorance will have specified that whoever will be the lower utility person will have higher social weight. Through the slope of social-welfare contours, the agreement behind the veil of ignorance will also have specified social aversion to inequality. Social aversion to inequality is measured by the amount of utility that can be taken from a high-utility person and transferred to a low-utility person while keeping social welfare constant. In figure 7.9b, social aversion to inequality thus increases with departure (in either direction) from equality at point H.[21]

The slope of a welfare contour of a social welfare function expresses social aversion to inequality.

Bentham and Rawls are limiting cases of aversion to inequality.

Figure 7.10a compares Bentham and Rawls when there are no excess burdens of taxation and so no leaks in the bucket of redistribution, as would happen if people did not respond to labor-market incentives and worked and supplied labor without regard for personal reward. Beginning from market outcomes at either point F_1 or point F_2, Bentham and Rawls both provide complete insurance at point E – as does any symmetric social welfare function between that of Rawls and Bentham.

With no leaks in the bucket of redistribution, aversion to inequality does not affect social insurance based on a symmetric social welfare function: any symmetric social welfare function provides complete insurance and results in postdistributional ex-post equality.

[21] The same conclusion about the slope of the welfare contour applies when person 2 has high utility and person 1 has low utility. Constant social welfare along a social welfare contour implies:

$$dW = \omega_1 dU_1 + \omega_2 dU_2 = 0,$$

where ω_i is the weight of individual i in social welfare. The slope of a social welfare contour is:

$$\frac{dU_1}{dU_2} = -\frac{\omega_2}{\omega_1}.$$

At point H, the weights in figure 7.9b are equal and the slope of the social welfare contour is -1. The slope changes with departure from equality at point H, with the low-utility person being given increasingly greater relative social weight as inequality increases.

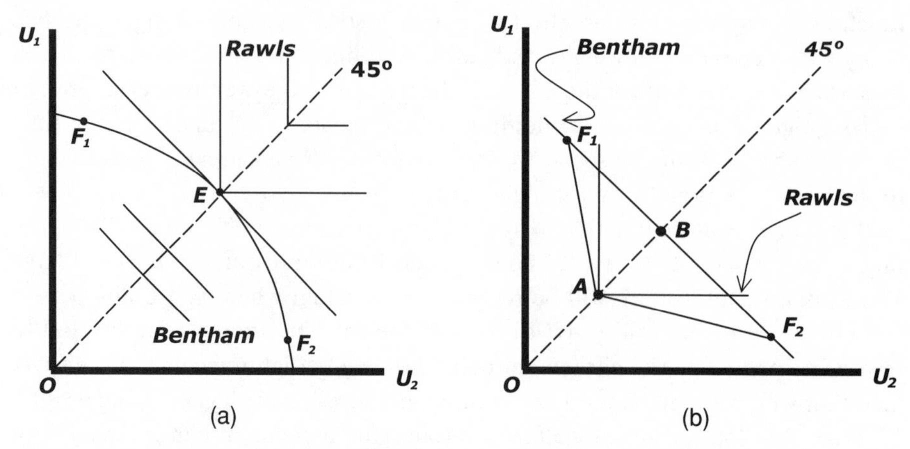

Figure 7.10. (a) With no leaky bucket, Bentham and Rawls provide complete insurance. (b) An extremely leaky bucket: Rawls continues to provide social insurance but Bentham provides no social insurance.

Figure 7.10b shows, in contrast to absence of a leaky bucket, choice of social insurance with an extremely leaky bucket. The feasible redistribution frontiers F_1A and F_2A fall away precipitously (linearity is for exposition) as redistribution takes place. For Bentham, no possible ex-post redistribution of income can improve on an agreement behind the veil of ignorance to remain at the market-determined outcomes at points F_1 or F_2.[22] A Bentham social welfare function now results in no social insurance because the efficiency costs of redistribution are too high to warrant any redistribution taking place. Rawls's measure of social welfare, however, is greater at the complete-insurance outcome at point A than at the market-determined outcomes at point F_1 or point F_2. Rawls therefore continues to provide complete insurance notwithstanding the very leaky bucket of redistribution.[23]

The comparisons in figures 7.10a and 7.10b show that:

> *Social insurance contracts associated with different social welfare functions differ because of different sensitivities of social welfare functions to the efficiency costs of redistribution through the leaky bucket.*

Bentham is the most sensitive to efficiency costs of redistribution through the leaky bucket. Rawls is not at all sensitive to efficiency losses as long as the worst-off person is not harmed.

[22] Bentham postdistribution points 1 and 2 in figure 7.7b coincide in figure 7.10b with the initial market income-distribution points F_1 and F_2.

[23] No redistribution, of course, will occur with either Rawls or Bentham (or any social welfare function) if society happens to emerge from behind the veil of ignorance to find itself on the 45° equal-utility line.

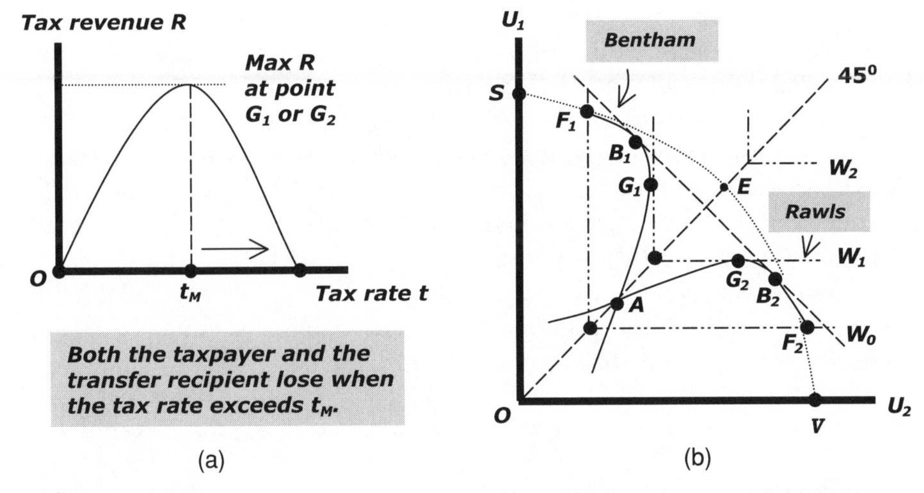

Figure 7.11. (a) The Laffer curve as a constraint on redistribution. (b) Social insurance with a revenue constraint.

The Laffer curve and income redistribution

We saw in chapter 4 that the Laffer curve limits the amount of tax revenue that is available for redistribution of income. Figure 7.11a shows the Laffer curve for a taxpayer who is financing income transfers. Tax revenue is maximized at the tax rate t_M. A rate of taxation in excess of t_M reduces utility of both the taxpayer and the recipient of an income transfer that the taxpayer's taxes finance. The taxpayer loses because, beyond the tax rate t_M, the rate of taxation and the excess burden increase. The recipient loses because, beyond the tax rate t_M, there is less revenue available to be redistributed.

After emerging from behind the veil of ignorance, person 1 may find that she has high income and therefore is the taxpayer. Income redistribution therefore begins from point F_1 in figure 7.11b. Departures from F_1 increase the tax rate and the excess burden of taxation, thereby decreasing utility U_1 of person 1, who is the taxpayer. The taxpayer's utility U_1 thus declines along the feasible utility-possibility frontier F_1G_1A.

Between points F_1 and G_1, the utility U_2 of person 2 – who is the transfer recipient – increases because increases in the rate of taxation along the Laffer curve increase tax revenue available for redistribution. At point G_1, the tax rate has reached t_M and tax revenue available for redistribution has been maximized. Increases in the tax rate beyond t_M reduce the tax revenue that person 1 provides for transfer to person 2, thereby decreasing the utility U_2 of the transfer recipient. Therefore, after point G_1, utility U_2 of the recipient of the income transfer declines.[24]

[24] The same symmetry occurs if, after emerging from behind the veil of ignorance, person 2 is revealed as the taxpayer and person 1 is revealed as the income recipient. The feasible utility-possibility frontier is then F_2G_2A. After point G_2, further increases in the tax rate reduce the utilities of both the taxpayer person 2 and the income recipient person 1.

Rawls subject to the Laffer curve

In figure 7.11b, because of the revenue constraint imposed by the Laffer curve, Rawls no longer provides complete insurance. Insurance through Rawls is incomplete at either point G_1 (if the initial market-determined outcome is at point F_1) or point G_2 (if the initial market-determined outcome is at point F_2). The incomplete insurance increases social welfare as measured by the Rawls social welfare function from W_0 to W_1. Increases in taxation beyond G_1 or G_2 reduce the utility of the worse-off person (who is person 2 if the initial market-determined income distribution was at point 1 or person 1 if the initial market-determined distribution was at point F_2). A Rawls social welfare function or social insurance contract therefore ceases redistributing income at point G_1 or point G_2.

The Laffer curve can prevent complete insurance when Rawls is chosen.

The Rawls social welfare function has a supreme-value objective in seeking maximum utility for the worst-off person: nothing other than the utility of the worst-off person matters.

A supreme-value objective is sought without compromise; there are no trade-offs allowed in the quest for the supreme-value objective.

Equality can be a supreme-value objective.[25] If the revenue constraint of the Laffer curve is not an impediment, choosing Rawls is consistent with equality as a supreme-value objective (as in figure 7.8b).

The difference between Rawls and equality as a supreme value is illustrated in figure 7.11b, where Rawls stops redistributing at point G_1 or point G_2 and does not continue to the ex-post income-equality point A. Although equality would be achieved at point A, the achievement of equality, by redistributing beyond point G_1 or point G_2, compromises the Rawls supreme value of not disadvantaging the worst-off person.

Bentham and the Laffer curve

Bentham provides incomplete insurance in figure 7.11b at point B_1 (if the initial market-determined outcome is at point F_1) or at point B_2 (if the initial market-determined outcome is at point F_2). In figure 7.11b, Rawls provides greater insurance (or moves closer to ex-post equality) than Bentham (the Rawls points G_1 and G_2 are closer to the 45° equality line than the Bentham points B_1 and B_2). Bentham's incomplete social insurance contract does not require reaching point G_1 or point G_2. Therefore:

Bentham social insurance is not hindered by the revenue constraint of the Laffer curve.

[25] Communism or socialism, in principle, imposes such a supreme value.

The choice of the social insurance contract

Our focal question is:

> *Behind the veil of ignorance, will people choose Bentham or Rawls, or a social welfare function and social insurance contract in between?*

We have seen that this question only has meaning when there is a leaky bucket of redistribution: when there are no leaks in the bucket of redistribution, all symmetric social welfare functions result in compete insurance. The choice of the social insurance contract (or social welfare function) takes place behind the veil of ignorance, with people aware that there is a leaky bucket of redistribution. Behind the veil of ignorance, people also know that they will have a common utility function as in figure 7.2 expressing risk aversion. The common utility function expressing risk aversion appears in any social welfare function that might be chosen, be it Bentham, Rawls, or a function in between.

> *Risk-aversion expressed in the utility function cannot be the reason for choice of a social insurance contract through choice of a social welfare function: the utility function is the same in all cases.*

The Bentham social welfare function is the sum of personal utilities that express personal risk aversion; the Rawls social welfare function maximizes the utility of the worst-off person, who is likewise risk-averse.

Social welfare functions are distinguished by the slopes of their contours, with Bentham exhibiting no social aversion to inequality and Rawls exhibiting complete aversion. We see that there is a distinction between personal risk aversion as expressed in the slope of the utility function in figure 7.2 and social aversion to inequality expressed in the slope of a social-welfare contour. Personal risk aversion is about personal income. Social aversion to inequality is about ex-post utilities.

Therefore, the question is:

> *Behind the veil of ignorance when people do not know how they will fare in life (although they know the utilities that they will have from different outcomes), with the same risk aversion expressed in the personal utility function, which of the different social welfare functions expressing social aversion to inequality is chosen?*

Let us look again at the Bentham social welfare function.[26] We shall now see that Bentham is the rational choice for a social welfare function because choice of Bentham maximizes expected utility behind the veil of ignorance.

[26] The Bentham social welfare function is linear in utilities, which indicates neutrality with regard to utilities that people have when social welfare is maximized.

Maximization of expected utility is rational because expected utility assigns objectively true probabilities to different uncertain outcomes.[27]

The case for choosing Bentham is that:

Only choice of the Bentham social welfare function is equivalent to maximizing expected utility behind the veil of ignorance.

To show the equivalence between choosing Bentham and maximizing expected utility, we consider n people behind a veil of ignorance who know that after emerging from behind the veil of ignorance, there will be n^H people who will have experienced the good outcome μ_H and n^L people who will have experienced the unfortunate outcome μ_L. The population therefore will be divided as:

$$n = n^H + n^L. \tag{7.15}$$

The social insurance contract requires that the n^H people who will experience good outcomes will pay taxes to finance transfers of income to the n^L unlucky people who will experience bad outcomes. After the Bentham social insurance contract has been implemented through taxation and income transfers, the n^H lucky people will have high utility U^H and the n^L unlucky people will have low utility U^L. We have seen that Bentham responds to the leaky bucket of redistribution by providing incomplete insurance; therefore:

$$U^H > U^L. \tag{7.16}$$

The Bentham social welfare function sums utilities of the two groups in the population as:

$$W = n^H U^H + n^L U^L. \tag{7.17}$$

Behind the veil of ignorance, people do not know whether they will have high or low utility, but they know that they confront the following objective probabilities of the two possible outcomes:[28]

$$\frac{n^H}{n} = p^H = \textit{probability of having high income} \tag{7.18}$$

$$\frac{n^L}{n} = p^L = \textit{probability of having low income}. \tag{7.19}$$

[27] The rationality of maximizing expected utility is based on axioms of rational behavior set out by John von Neumann and Oscar Morgenstern in 1944. For an exposition of the axioms, see, for example, David Kreps (1990, pp. 72–81).

[28] The probabilities are objective because the probabilities are known to indicate accurately the likelihood of the outcomes.

We obtain expected utility of any person in the population behind the veil of ignorance by dividing Bentham social welfare in expression (7.17) by the number of people n in the population:

$$\frac{W}{n} = p^H U^H + p^L U^L = EU. \tag{7.20}$$

Because n is a constant, maximizing social welfare W in expression (7.17) is equivalent to maximizing W/n in expression (7.20). Choosing Bentham as the social welfare function is therefore equivalent to maximizing expected utility of any person behind the veil of ignorance.

Now consider again Rawls. Rawls gives positive weight in social welfare to whoever will be the worst-off person and gives zero weight to everyone else. Rationality requires, however, accounting for the likelihood that after emerging from behind the veil of ignorance, a person will not be the worst-off person. Bentham accounts for the possibility that a person could be anyone and gives weights equal to the objective (true) probabilities of being different people who experience different incomes.

Bentham's lottery and the certainty in life offered by Rawls

We cannot compare levels of social welfare measured by Bentham and Rawls social welfare functions because each social welfare function is a distinct means of measuring social welfare. However, because we are using a common utility function to measure personal utility, personal utilities can be compared as outcomes of choice of different social welfare functions and social insurance contracts.

Figure 7.12 shows social insurance contracts when the Laffer curve does not restrain income redistribution.[29] Rawls eliminates uncertainty from life by providing complete insurance at point A. By choosing the social welfare function of Rawls, a population therefore knows with certainty, before emerging from behind the veil of ignorance, that everyone will have the future personal utility U_C.

Choosing the Bentham social welfare function results in a lottery with outcomes either at point B_1 or point B_2. The lottery "prizes" are utilities of either U_H or U_L. Expected utility EU from the Bentham lottery is at point B (EU is the average of the utilities at points B_1 and B_2).[30]

[29] We now also exclude the illustrative cases in which the efficiency costs of redistribution (the leaks in the bucket) are either zero or too high for Bentham to warrant redistribution through social insurance.

[30] In the Bentham lottery, the utilities U_H and U_L are obtained *after* redistribution of income as required by the Bentham social insurance contract. In figure 7.2, we described a lottery over high and low incomes y_H and y_L. These were incomes *before* the redistribution through an insurance contract. Incomes, of course, translate directly into utilities (see figure 7.2), so we can use utilities as prizes in lotteries.

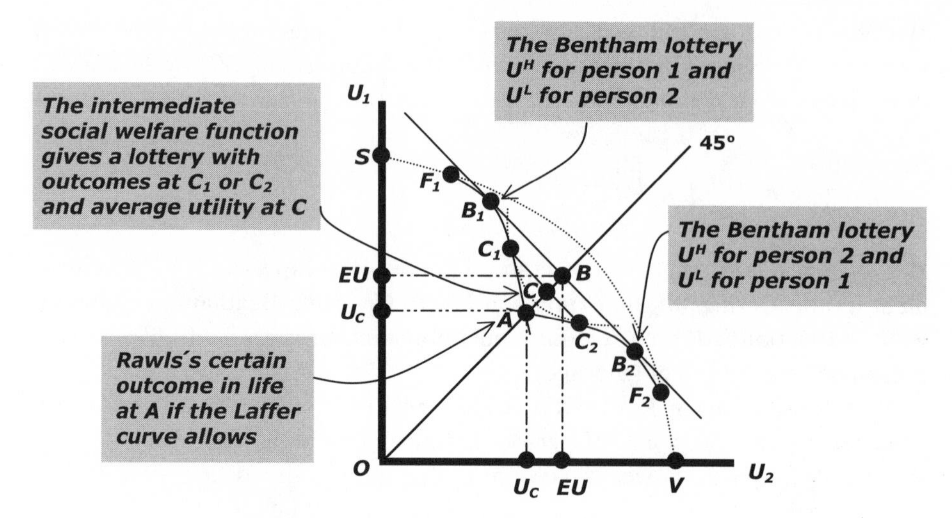

Figure 7.12. Possible social insurance contracts.

The lottery from a social welfare function between Bentham and Rawls

Figure 7.12 also shows a lottery based on a social welfare function between Bentham and Rawls. The prizes in this lottery are the high and low utilities symmetrically obtained at points C_1 and C_2. Average utility from this lottery at point C is less than expected utility at point B from the Bentham lottery.[31] The lower average utility at point C is accompanied by greater equality than provided by Bentham's lottery.[32] An example of a social welfare function between Bentham and Rawls is named after John Nash (for whom the Nash equilibrium is named). The Nash social welfare function takes the form:

$$W = (U_1 - U_{1O}) \cdot (U_2 - U_{2O}). \tag{7.21}$$

Here, U_{1O} and U_{2O} are the utilities that the two individuals have in the absence of a social insurance contract.[33]

[31] We refer to *average* utility obtainable from a lottery and *expected* utility obtainable from the Bentham lottery. Expected utility from Bentham is a particular case of average utility. However, expected utility has the particular connotation associated with rationality through objective weights equal to objective probabilities of outcomes.

[32] There is greater ex-post equality at points C_1 and C_2, which are closer to the 45° equality line than the Bentham points B_1 and B_2.

[33] U_{1O} and U_{2O} are the averages of the personal utilities obtainable in the market-determined outcomes at points F_1 and F_2, where people remain in the absence of a social insurance contract (at points F_1 and F_2, as shown in figure 7.6, social welfare is the same but personal utilities differ). More generally, U_{1O} and U_{2O} are the values at the disagreement or "threat" point (threat of withdrawing from cooperation) when the Nash bargaining solution is used to determine the distribution of benefits from cooperation. We applied the Nash bargaining solution in chapter 3 to sharing of costs of a public good (the owners of a car and a truck sharing the costs of a road).

Avoiding a lottery by choosing Rawls

Expected utility at point B from incomplete social insurance through the Bentham lottery and average utility at point C from incomplete insurance through the lottery provided by a Nash or other intermediate social welfare function both exceed the certain utility U_C provided by Rawls through complete insurance at equality point A. However, only Rawls avoids a lottery.

Lotteries in which prizes are lotteries

Reality is more complicated than people experiencing μ_H or μ_L after emerging from behind the veil of ignorance. Uncertainty during the course of life (as distinct from uncertainty behind the veil of ignorance) makes the "prizes" of the Bentham lottery other lotteries. The prizes in the lotteries behind the veil of ignorance are therefore, in effect, lottery tickets that give further probabilities of different outcomes during the course of life.[34]

The fundamental choice between social equality and efficiency

The fundamental choice is between social equality and efficiency. Societal choices through social insurance in figure 7.12 are in between (and including) the Bentham expected-utility point B and the Rawls complete insurance point A. The choice is thus between being more equal ex-post or being overall better off through higher average utility for the population. Therefore:

> *Choice of the social insurance contract through choice of a social welfare function is a choice between greater efficiency and greater ex-post (post-distributional) equality.*

Bentham is the rational choice, based on the rationality of maximization of expected utility. Nonetheless, Bentham has not always been chosen. In not choosing Bentham, societies indicate unwillingness to expose populations to the Bentham lottery; that is, societies indicate aversion to the social inequality that is the outcome of the Bentham lottery.

We note again that everyone has the utility function in figure 7.2 and is risk averse with respect to personal income, independently of the social welfare function that is chosen. The question in choosing a social welfare function and social insurance is: How sensitive is a society to the efficiency losses of the leaky bucket as an impediment to ex-post equality (or complete insurance)? For Bentham, the efficiency losses of the leaky bucket are an impediment to equality, but not for Rawls – unless the inefficiency of the leaky bucket were to harm the worst-off person. The choice in democracies is political.

> *Political parties take positions on the efficiency-equality spectrum.*

[34] For example, a good outcome may be a lottery ticket that gives an 80 percent chance of being in the top 10 percent of earned income and a 20 percent chance of being in the remaining 90 percent. A bad outcome may be a lottery ticket that gives an 80 percent chance of being in the bottom 10 percent of earned income and a 20 percent chance of having higher earned income.

Parties of the left prefer ex-post equality. Parties of the right prefer efficiency and are more prepared to accept the inequality that is the outcome of the Bentham lottery.

Subjective weights on efficiency and equality

The Nash social welfare function has the smooth contours between Bentham and Rawls. Another way of representing choices between Bentham and Rawls is to specify the social welfare function as:

$$W = p^L U^L + \alpha p^H U^H. \tag{7.22}$$

Here, as in the Bentham social welfare function, P^L and P^H are the objective (true) probabilities of unlucky and lucky outcomes μ_L and μ_H, and U^L and U^H are the low and high utilities that an individual obtains after social insurance (that is, after taxation and income redistribution have taken place, based on the social insurance contract). α is a constant, where $0 \leq \alpha \leq 1$.

The value of α determines the positioning of the social welfare function between Bentham and Rawls. If $\alpha = 0$, Rawls has been chosen (because maximizing social welfare is equivalent to maximizing low utility U^L). If $\alpha = 1$, Bentham has been chosen (because then expected utility is maximized). A social welfare function in between Bentham and Rawls has been chosen if $0 < \alpha < 1$.[35] Figure 7.13 shows Bentham, Rawls, and an in-between social welfare function. Whether person 1 or person 2 has high utility U^H or low utility U^L after taxation and income redistribution depends on whether an outcome is above or below the equal-utility 45° line.

In figure 7.13, we see again the Bentham lottery with equally likely outcomes at points B_1 and B_2 and expected utility at point B. The lottery of the in-between social welfare function gives equal likelihoods of being at points C_1 and C_2 with average utility C. Beginning from Bentham, change in choice of a social welfare function takes place as α declines (from $\alpha = 1$ for Bentham). The decline in α decreases high utility U^H and increases low utility U^L that will be obtained through social insurance. When α reaches zero, the Rawls outcome at point A is attained where $U^H = U^L$ and where utility of people in the society therefore does not depend on whether a person experienced a good outcome μ_H or a bad outcome μ_L.

[35] The Nash function is an example of an intermediate social welfare function with smooth contours. This is not the case with the general social welfare function in expression (7.22), in which the slope of the line indicating equal social welfare is:

$$\frac{dU^L}{dU^H} = \frac{-\alpha p^H}{p^L} = constant.$$

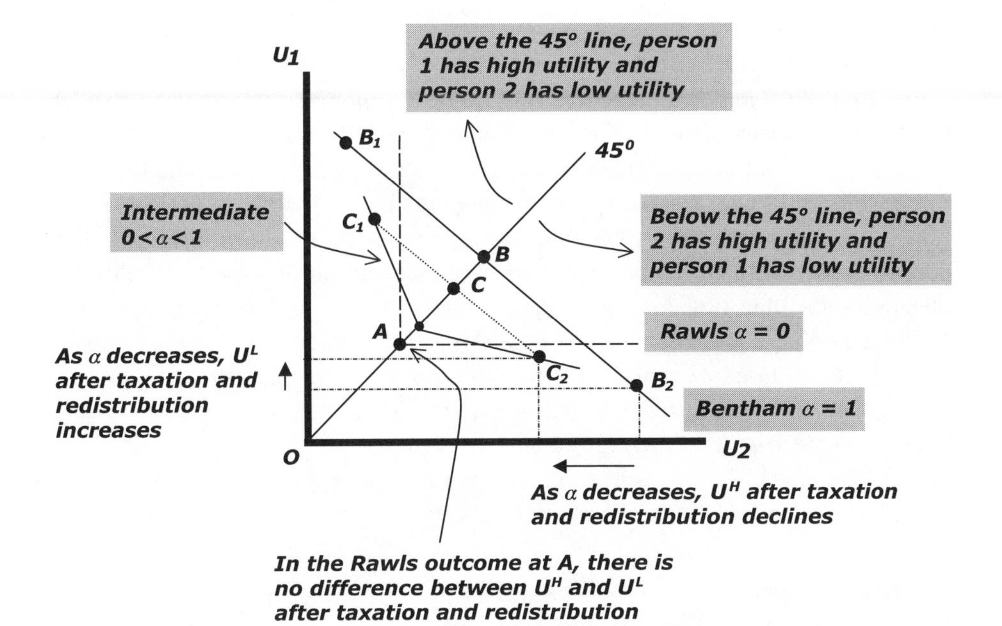

Figure 7.13. Social welfare functions obtained by varying α in the general social welfare function (7.22).

Choice according to true or objective probabilities of experiencing good and bad outcomes entails $\alpha = 1$ in expression (7.22) and results in choosing Bentham. The other choices for which $0 \leq \alpha < 1$ depart from Bentham by *subjectively* placing more weight than is objectively justified on avoiding bad outcomes. In the limiting case of Rawls, where $\alpha = 0$, the likelihood of a good outcome is altogether ignored; all weight is subjectively placed on having a bad outcome and being the worst-off person.

> *Departing from Bentham to choose a social welfare function with $\alpha < 1$ is a subjective decision to increase the weight on experiencing a bad outcome and, correspondingly, to discount subjectively the likelihood of experiencing a good outcome.*

Why deviate from the objective probabilities?

Why might people want to deviate from the objective probabilities of the Bentham social welfare function – and, correspondingly, from maximization of expected utility? The reason for deviating from Bentham cannot be risk aversion with respect to income. The utility function is the same in all cases. Because the personal utility function already accounts for risk aversion, why not apply objectively true probabilities to good and bad outcomes and so choose the Bentham social welfare function?

Prospect theory

An explanation for deviation from behavior predicted by maximization of expected utility – and therefore from choice of Bentham – was proposed in 1979 by the psychologists Daniel Kahneman and Amos Tversky (1937–96).[36] They described prospect theory, which perceives people as subjectively evaluating personal gains and losses from a specified reference point or status quo. An implication of prospect theory is behavior that exhibits *loss aversion*, meaning that people depart from behavior predicted by maximization of expected utility by placing larger than objectively justified weights on low-probability events that would bring large losses – which is precisely how people behave if they depart from Bentham in expression (7.22) to choose $\alpha < 1$. Prospect theory was suggested as an alternative to expected-utility theory in order to explain behavior in experiments that was observed to be inconsistent with the rationality of maximizing expected utility. Prospect theory was thus inferred by psychologists from observed human behavior under uncertainty.[37]

Avoidance of regret

Related to prospect theory is avoidance of regret. After the Bentham social welfare function has been chosen, a person may emerge from behind the veil of ignorance to find that he or she has experienced the adverse outcome μ_L. Such a person may then feel regret that Rawls was not chosen behind the veil of ignorance. If Rawls is chosen, there can be no regret about experiencing the adverse outcome μ_L because Rawls places all weight on being the worst-off person.

Choice of Rawls minimizes regret from experiencing an adverse outcome.

Behavioral economists sometimes describe people as seeking to maximize "happiness" rather than maximizing utility from consumption or material wealth. Being "happy" can have numerous aspects, including personal relationships, health, and feelings of adequacy in coping with self-control (and avoiding hyperbolic discounting and immediate gratification or procrastination), and other challenges of life. Regret affects happiness. People are unhappy when they have regrets about past decisions – including regret when, finding themselves with a bad outcome in life, people realize that they would have been better off with the Rawls social insurance contract.

[36] Kahneman was awarded the Nobel Prize in economics in 2002.

[37] An example of prospect theory was the reluctance of some people to travel by air for some time after terrorists used passenger planes as explosive devices in the attack on the United States on September 11, 2001. People instead traveled in cars. With security measures against further terrorist attacks using civilian aircraft in place, the objective probability of being killed in a car accident was higher than the probability of being killed by terrorists in the course of air travel.

The work ethic

The efficiency costs of attaining the social equality point A in figure 7.13 (and previous figures) increase with the leaks in the bucket of redistribution. There are fewer leaks in the bucket of redistribution, the more prevalent in a society is a work ethic:

> *People who behave according to a work ethic choose to work because of the intrinsic value of work and because of a feeling of disutility (or guilt) if they are not productive.*

A work ethic is part of communist ideology, which requires people to contribute according to personal ability and not to be influenced in work decisions by personal rewards. The work ethic that communism idealized was not achieved as a general rule for the behavior of the population. As Hayek predicted, it was impossible under communism to change human nature to make productive contributions independent of personal reward.[38]

A welfare state combines private property and markets with extensive social insurance. Taxes are high, as are tax-financed benefits to the population. A welfare state has chosen the Rawls social insurance contract. The prime examples of welfare states have been in Scandinavia. In democratic elections, voters in Scandinavian countries have tended persistently to support the high taxes and extensive income redistribution of Rawls-type social insurance. Yet, although there has been extensive social insurance, high average personal incomes were sustained. The high taxes did not, therefore, substantially diminish productive incentives through labor–leisure substitution effects. A work ethic was ostensibly prevalent.

> *Prevalence of a work ethic allows extensive social insurance while sustaining high average incomes.*

> *If a work ethic is not prevalent, the personal risk of experiencing an adverse outcome in Bentham's lottery is balanced against having equal but perhaps no meaningful income under the complete insurance of Rawls.*

The reason for a work ethic

The contrasting experiences under communism and in the Scandinavian welfare states suggest the question:

> *Why is a work ethic more prevalent in some societies than others?*

We observed in chapter 1 how Nietzschean behavior discourages a work ethic. If the rule of law is not present and the right of natural possession is not respected,

[38] We noted previously the saying among people that "we pretend to work and they pretend to pay us."

the ability of the strong to appropriate the output of the weak discourages the weak from working. We do not expect, therefore, a work ethic to be prevalent in Nietzschean societies. Indeed, Nietzschean societies, which are sometimes categorized as "developing countries," have low average incomes. People are unwilling to work when they know that the product of their work can be taken from them through the coercion of the strong. Because of appropriation, preference for leisure and, correspondingly, not having a work ethic can become an intergenerationally transmitted social norm. There is then also no social insurance. Other than an elite that controls government, people are generally poor. Luck in experiencing μ_H or μ_L is reflected in whether a person has or has not been born to a family of the elites.

The sociologist, Max Weber (1864–1920), whose writings we encountered when considering bureaucracy and who described exemplary bureaucratic behavior, studied the relationship between religion and economic outcomes. In his essay, *The Protestant Ethic and the Spirit of Capitalism*, first published in 1905, Weber linked the presence of a work ethic in a population to Protestantism. Correspondingly, the Protestant Scandinavian welfare states have had the high incomes and extensive social insurance contracts consistent with a work ethic. Extensive social insurance has also been present in Protestant Western European societies and in the United Kingdom and countries (Australia, Canada, New Zealand and the United States) initially founded as English and therefore Protestant colonies. A work ethic is also prevalent in the norms of behavior of cultures other than Protestant, including Jewish and Chinese.[39]

The work ethic and tax evasion

The leisure–work substitution that underlies the excess burden of taxation is not the sole reason for a leaky bucket of redistribution. We have seen that tax evasion and a shadow or informal economy are also sources of efficiency losses. Economic activity in the shadow economy is also not taxed and tax revenue therefore is not provided for redistribution. In chapter 4 (table 4.1, page 286) we noted evidence indicating large, informal economies in Scandinavian welfare states. The large, informal economies are consistent with the work ethic. Rather than responding to high taxes by substituting leisure and free time for work, people with a work ethic continue to work. They respond to high taxes not by working less but rather by not paying taxes.

[39] The Scandinavian welfare states are Lutheran. Martin Luther (1483–1546), who was instrumental in the Protestant Reformation, proposed that all work has intrinsic value independent of the type of work performed, so that people engaged in simple tasks had as much merit through their work as more skilled people and nobility or landowners. The merit of work was thus independent of the social order. Max Weber's inference from Protestantism to a work ethic and high incomes has been qualified by the observation that Protestants were encouraged to read the bible for themselves rather than to rely on the mediation of interpretation and explanation of cleries, in consequence of which the historically higher Protestant than Catholic incomes included a return to literacy.

Bentham and the rule of law

Our default for choice of a social welfare function is Bentham. We choose Bentham because of the rationality of expected utility maximization under the conditions of uncertainty that would confront people behind a veil of ignorance. Choosing Bentham does not imply unconstrained maximization of the sum of people's utilities. Rather:

> *Maximization of the Bentham summation of utilities is restrained by the rule of law.*

Without the qualification of the constraint of the rule of law, appropriation, extortion, rape, and enslavement would be permissible means of maximizing the Bentham summation of utilities. When the rule of law acts as a restraint, the limits on redistribution are through the Laffer curve, which indicates the value of the tax revenue that can be maximally collected for redistribution when taxes are compulsory but people can legally substitute leisure for work (although they may also illegally evade taxes and substitute to the informal sector). In our subsequent investigations, unless we indicate otherwise, the social insurance contract is that of Bentham.

D. Adverse selection and time inconsistency

After emerging from behind the veil of ignorance, people discover whether the Bentham lottery has given them μ_H or μ_L. There is asymmetric information if they know their own outcomes but not the outcomes of others. The people who know that they have experienced μ_H lose from remaining in an insurance pool that includes people who may have experienced μ_L. Insurance requires the presence of personal risk or uncertainty. However, after emerging from behind the veil of ignorance, everyone knows his or her personal outcome. People who know that their personal prospects are good have an incentive to leave the insurance pool and people who know that their personal prospects are poor "select themselves" as wanting to continue to participate in insurance. If participation in insurance is voluntary, a phenomenon known as adverse selection takes place. Adverse selection makes voluntary insurance nonsustainable.[40]

[40] Adverse selection was described by George Akerlof (1970; Nobel Prize in economics, 2001) using the example of a market for used cars. Information was asymmetric in that only owners of cars knew the true quality of a car and the price of used cars was determined by the average quality of cars for sale in the market. In these circumstances, a person who knows that his or her car is of better quality than average withdraws the car from the market. The average quality of cars remaining for sale in the market, therefore, falls, and the price falls. Other car owners now find that their cars are above the average quality of the market and that their cars are, therefore, worth more than the market price – therefore, they also withdraw their cars from the market. The process continues until only the worst quality cars remain for sale in the market. In the case of insurance, the process of averse selection is the same: the people who select themselves to remain in an insurance pool are those with the worst prospects for earning high income.

Adverse selection occurs when people with private information about themselves indicating that they can expect to lose from insurance exit an insurance pool, leaving behind only people who expected to benefit from the income sharing of insurance.

A government can prevent adverse selection by making participation in "insurance" compulsory. Income redistribution then takes place with certainty from people who experienced the good outcome μ_H to people who experienced the adverse outcome μ_L.

If governments make social insurance compulsory, the consequence is not the random payouts of insurance but rather systematic predictable income transfers.

The systematic income transfers are the reason why people who experienced the good outcome μ_H want to exit the insurance pool. However, the income redistribution that people who experienced good outcomes wish to avoid through exit from the insurance pool was agreed on behind the veil of ignorance when people lacked information about their future selves.

The case for compulsory social insurance enforced by government rests on a *time-inconsistency problem.*

A time-inconsistency problem arises when optimal present decisions about future behavior are no longer optimal when the future arrives.

Time inconsistency is expressed in people agreeing – when they are behind the veil of ignorance – to an insurance contract that will apply when they will have emerged from behind the veil of ignorance. However, those people who emerge to find that they have good prospects in life realize that it is no longer optimal (or worthwhile) for them to participate in the insurance to which they had agreed when behind the veil of ignorance and therefore seek to exit the insurance pool.

In enforcing compliance with the social insurance contract, governments respond to a time-inconsistency problem.

The veil of ignorance is a metaphor and is counterfactual. However, if people were presented with the opportunity to decide behind a veil of ignorance, they would have wanted there to be social insurance after their outcomes in life are revealed. By making participation in social insurance compulsory, governments therefore insist that the social insurance contract to which people would have agreed behind the veil of ignorance cannot be renegotiated or abrogated after information is revealed about people's personal circumstances. The government therefore acts as if a binding social insurance contract had been decided upon behind the veil of ignorance. People would have wanted the insurance when they confronted uncertainty behind the veil of ignorance. By making participation in insurance compulsory when people have emerged from behind the veil of ignorance (although at this juncture, this is no longer insurance but systematic income redistribution), the government ensures that the social insurance contract is honored. Without the role of government in enforcing the contract, the contract could not have entered into – or described – when people were still behind the veil of ignorance.

7.2 Moral Hazard

We have thus far viewed social insurance as a response to outcomes in life determined solely by exogenous luck or fate. The luck has been in whether people experience the exogenous good outcome μ_H or the adverse outcome μ_L.

We now extend our investigation of social insurance to include the recognition that personal outcomes also depend on personal behavior. In particular, the likelihood that a person will have high or low income depends on whether the effort has been made to be self-reliant through investing in income-earning skills and education and through looking for a job. Through effort at self-reliance, the personal outcomes μ_H and μ_L are no longer exogenously determined by pure luck but rather become the endogenous consequences of personal decisions. Personal incentives to be self-reliant introduce the effects of moral hazard on social insurance.

A. Moral hazard and insurance

An insurance contract is based on exogenous probabilities of events that affect income. When there is moral hazard, probabilities of events are endogenously determined by actions that people take.

> *Moral hazard occurs when the presence of insurance affects personal decisions in ways that make personal benefit from insurance more likely.*

There is moral hazard when people make low effort to be self-reliant because of anticipation of benefit from insurance. The hazard is *moral* because people exploit the presence of insurance for their own advantage through types of personal behavior that are not intended when the insurance is provided.

When personal income is guaranteed by insurance, a person might prefer to spend the day with friends in a bar or on the beach rather than working for a living, or might not look for a job, or might behave in a way that leads to dismissal from any job. Insurance that compensates for income losses from not successfully completing studies might lead some people to decide not to continue to study.

Moral hazard and personal effort

We can consider two alternative personal-effort choices:

$$e_H = \textit{high effort to avoid the bad outcome } \mu_L$$
$$e_L = \textit{low effort to avoid the bad outcome } \mu_L.$$

We now include effort in the personal utility function. Effort has disutility. Because of the disutility of effort (or anxiety or stress), for the same amount of personal income earned y_I, utility is lower with high effort than with low effort:

$$U(y_I, e_H) < U(y_I, e_L). \tag{7.23}$$

We distinguish between two types of effort decisions:

- *Taxpayers* may reduce work effort in response to taxes by substituting leisure or free time for work. This substitution is the source of the excess burden of taxation and thereby of the leaky bucket of redistribution. There is no uncertainty when taxpayers make this effort decision. Taxpayers know that they are taxpayers.
- *Prospective recipients of income transfers* make effort decisions that affect the likelihood that they will be self-reliant and will not require income transfers (or welfare payments). This effort decision is associated with moral hazard and is made under conditions of uncertainty about future personal outcomes.

Thus, the two types of effort decisions differ in whose behavior is being described. Reduced work effort in response to taxation occurs because a taxpayer is being taxed and there is no uncertainty: this type of reduced work effort is the source of the leaky bucket of redistribution. Reduced effort due to moral hazard occurs under conditions of uncertainty when people know that they will receive tax-financed benefits through insurance if they will have low or no income.

The work–leisure substitution that underlies the inefficiency of the leaky bucket was not influenced by the presence of insurance. However, insurance affects productive effort through moral hazard when people who anticipate being recipients of tax-financed income transfers reduce effort at being self-reliant.

As is the case with adverse selection, moral hazard involves asymmetric information. People have private information about whether they have chosen high or low effort to be self-reliant. Others (including a private insurance company or the government) can observe an outcome of high personal income y_H or low personal income y_L but cannot observe whether a person chose high effort e_H or low effort e_L.

The effort decision influences the probabilities of experiencing either the good outcome μ_H that provides high income or the adverse outcome μ_L that provides low income. Probabilities of personal outcomes contingent on the effort decision sum to 1:

$$\Pr(\mu_H \mid e_i) + \Pr(\mu_L \mid e_i) = 1, \quad i = H, L. \tag{7.24}$$

The probability of a good personal outcome μ_H is greater with high effort than with low effort:

$$\Pr(\mu_H \mid e_H) > \Pr(\mu_H \mid e_L). \tag{7.25}$$

Correspondingly, the probability of an adverse personal outcome μ_L is greater with low effort than with high effort:

$$\Pr(\mu_L \mid e_L) > \Pr(\mu_L \mid e_H). \tag{7.26}$$

People who choose high effort e_H can be unlucky and experience the adverse outcome μ_L: they may conscientiously look for a job or study or seek to improve their labor-market skills, yet still find themselves with low income. Because of the element of luck, two people can therefore make different unobservable effort decisions and be observed to have the same income. The two people are indistinguishable to outside observers because of asymmetric information about the personal-effort decision.

Hence:

Whether a person has high or low income depends on both luck and effort.

Because of asymmetric information, other people do not know whether low income is due solely to bad luck or also to low effort.

The prisoners' dilemma and moral hazard

Because of moral hazard, there is a prisoners' dilemma in choice of effort. Table 7.1 shows the prisoners' dilemma for two people. Each person can choose high or low effort to be self-reliant. Choice of effort affects the probabilities of having good or bad outcomes in the manner shown in expressions (7.25) and (7.26).

The prisoners' dilemma arises in a voluntary insurance contract. When choosing personal effort, a person knows that a voluntary insurance contract that

TABLE 7.1. THE PRISONERS' DILEMMA AND MORAL HAZARD

	Person 2 chooses high effort	Person 2 chooses low effort
Person 1 chooses high effort	3, 3	1, 4
Person 1 chooses low effort	4, 1	2, 2

provides complete insurance is in place. Because insurance is voluntary, there are no taxes and no excess burdens of taxation. Government is present in no way other than to provide the legal framework of the rule of law that is the basis for the voluntary insurance contract.

The private voluntary insurance contract stipulates that when two people have different incomes, the person with higher income will transfer income to the person with lower income. Because of the complete insurance, incomes after the income transfer are equal.

Incomes are thus shared through private voluntary insurance. The possible personal outcomes are:

- When both people choose high effort e_H, the likelihood is maximized that after income sharing, each person will have high income y_H.
- When both people choose low effort e_L, the likelihood is maximized that after income sharing, each person will have low income y_L.
- If one person chooses high effort e_H and the other chooses low effort e_L, the likelihood is maximized that the two people will share $(y_H + y_L)$. In that case, each person will have the average y_A of high and low income, where:

$$y_H > y_A = \frac{y_H + y_L}{2} > y_L. \tag{7.27}$$

However:

Although personal incomes are shared through insurance, the cost of exerting high effort is personal and is not shared.

The sharing of incomes and the personal non-shared cost of effort give rise to the prisoners' dilemma in table 7.1.

- The highest likelihood of obtaining the personally best outcome 4 occurs when a person chooses low effort and the other person chooses high effort. The maximal benefit 4 is obtained by free riding on the high effort of others while personally exerting low effort.
- Both people choosing high effort results in the greatest likelihood that both will have benefit of 3.
- Both people choosing low effort results in the greatest likelihood that both will have benefit of 2.
- The highest likelihood of obtaining the personally worst outcome of benefit 1 occurs when a person chooses high effort and the other person chooses low effort.

There is therefore a prisoners' dilemma.[41] The dominant strategy is to choose low effort. In the Nash equilibrium, both people therefore choose low effort and the outcome is (2, 2). Thus:

> *In the Nash equilibrium with moral hazard, the likelihood is maximized that everyone will have low income.*

The prisoners' dilemma here is similar to when decisions are about voluntary personal payment for public goods. In the case of the public-good prisoners' dilemma, the lowest personal utility is obtained by contributing to paying for the public good when others free ride. In the case of the moral-hazard prisoners' dilemma, lowest personal utility is attained when a person chooses high effort and the other person free rides by choosing low effort.[42]

Income as a common pool

High effort increases the likelihood of earning high income, but the income earned is shared through the pooling of incomes because of complete insurance. When the population is large because of income sharing, the personal return from high effort is insignificant, whereas the benefit from *not* exerting high effort is personal and is not shared with others. Earned income is a *common pool* and there is a common-pool problem, similar to the case of the sharing in the tragedy of the commons when we considered externalities. When n people share a common pool of income, they know that they will receive the average of everyone's incomes:

$$y_A = \frac{\sum_{i=1}^{n} y_i}{n}. \tag{7.28}$$

Average income in expression (7.28) can be divided into the personal contribution to the pool of shared income of person 1 and the contribution of all others:

$$y_A = \left(\frac{y_1}{n} + \frac{\sum_{i=2}^{n} y_i}{n} \right). \tag{7.29}$$

[41] The payoffs establishing the prisoners' dilemma are, in terms of the expected utility of person 1:

$$4 = EU^1(y_A^1, e_L^1 \mid e_H^2) > 3 = EU^1(y_H^1, e_H^1 \mid e_H^2) > 2 = EU^1(y_L^1, e_L^1 \mid e_L^2) > 1 = EU^1(y_A^1, e_H^1 \mid e_L^2).$$

[42] Risk aversion also suggests choice of low effort. The return from low effort is certain through increased personal utility. The return from high effort is uncertain because, despite high effort, the personal outcome may be low income because of bad luck. Risk aversion therefore biases the choice toward low effort. The Nash equilibrium in table 7.1 is low effort without appeal to risk aversion.

Person 1 keeps y_I/n of own-earned income: the income y_A that person 1 will have in the end is therefore little affected by the personal-effort decision. All people make the calculation that they will receive only the share $1/n$ of the income that they personally earn. In the prisoners' dilemma, low effort is therefore the dominant strategy.

Self-deprivation and moral hazard

The Nash equilibrium of the prisoners' dilemma has resulted in *self-deprivation.* The incentives are for people, through choice of effort, to *choose* to place themselves in personal circumstances in which there is a high likelihood of personally earning low income.

Moral hazard and the failure of voluntary insurance

If insurance can be avoided, the adverse incentives to exert high effort because of the common-pool problem of incomes disappear. In the absence of the income-sharing through insurance, a person's expected utility depends on the personal choice of effort (and also on luck) and not on the combined consequences of effort choices of others. Without pooling of incomes, although there is the same disutility of effort, there is, therefore, high expected utility from exerting personal effort because high income will not have to be shared. Therefore, because of moral hazard, given the choice, people choose no insurance and high effort.[43]

Thus:

Moral hazard results in the failure of voluntary insurance.

Everyone is better off without the disincentives of the common-pool problem. In terms of the tragedy of the commons, incomes are privatized.

In the absence of insurance, the income distribution is unequal. The incentives are present for all people to exert high effort. However, some people will be unlucky and nonetheless experience unfortunate outcomes that result in low personal incomes. Hence the unequal incomes.

B. Behavior without moral hazard

There are circumstances in which there is no moral-hazard problem.

If there is no random component of income, effort alone determines personal income. A person's effort decision can then be inferred from observed personal income and information about effort is therefore no longer asymmetric. That is,

[43] That is, without insurance, expected utility from choosing high effort exceeds expected utility from choosing low effort, where:

$$EU^{high\ effort} > EU^{low\ effort}$$

$$EU^{high\ effort} = \Pr(\mu_H \mid e_H)U(y_H) + \Pr(\mu_L \mid e_H)U(y_L)$$

$$EU^{low\ effort} = \Pr(\mu_H \mid e_L)U(y_H) + \Pr(\mu_L \mid e_L)U(y_L).$$

with no randomness in income, we have $\mu_H = \mu_L = 0$; an outcome of high income y_H indicates that high effort e_H was chosen, whereas an outcome of low income y_L indicates that low effort e_L was chosen. There is no role for insurance because there is no uncertainty about why income is low.

There is also, of course, no asymmetric information and no moral-hazard problem if personal-effort choices are observable. The insurance contract then specifies the necessity of having been observed to have chosen high effort in order to receive payouts from insurance in the event of low income.

However:

With personal incomes affected by random components μ_L and μ_H and with effort at self-reliance unobservable, can a society escape the moral-hazard prisoners' dilemma and provide insurance against low incomes?

A work ethic and moral hazard

We have distinguished two types of effort: (1) the productive effort of taxpayers, and (2) the effort of prospective income-transfer recipients at being self-reliant. When considering the first type of effort and the choice between social insurance according to Bentham and Rawls, we saw that the more prevalent is a work ethic in a population, the lower is the efficiency loss of redistribution through the leaky bucket. We used the definition of a work ethic that:

A person who behaves according to a work ethic contributes according to ability with little regard for the level of taxation.

We now define a work ethic a second time – in this case, with respect to the decision to be self-reliant.

A person who behaves according to a work ethic systematically chooses high effort to be self-reliant even though insurance is available.

It is evident that in societies in which the entire population has a work ethic, insurance is not subject to income losses from moral hazard. In table 7.1, there is no prisoners' dilemma when all people have a work ethic. Everyone chooses high effort, notwithstanding the pooling of incomes through insurance. However, in realistic circumstances, populations are mixed: some people have a work ethic and some do not. We now consider what happens in such diverse populations.

C. Moral hazard and adverse selection in diverse populations

When the population is diverse, information about who has a work ethic may be private and therefore asymmetric. That is, outside observers may be unable to distinguish people according to type as having a work ethic or not – because unlucky people who exerted effort to be self-reliant may be indistinguishable from people who did not attempt to be self-reliant.

TABLE 7.2. TWO NORMS OF BEHAVIOR IN THE POPULATION

	Person 2 has no work ethic and chooses high effort	Person 2 has no work ethic and chooses low effort
Person 1 with a work ethic chooses high effort	4,3	3,4
Person 1 with a work ethic chooses low effort	1,1	2,2

Table 7.2 shows the payoffs to the two types of people who differ in whether they behave according to a work ethic. Person 2 is subject to moral hazard and behaves strategically in choosing effort at self-reliance. This person has the same ranking of payoffs as in the moral-hazard prisoners' dilemma in table 7.1. Person 1 in table 7.2 has a work ethic and has payoffs or benefits as follows:

- Person 1 has the highest payoff 4 when both people choose high effort. The probability that both people will have high income is then the greatest. Person 1 is happy because she is personally exerting high effort and is matching the high effort of the other person.
- The payoff of 3 for person 1 occurs when she chooses high effort and the other person chooses low effort. Person 1 is happy to be choosing high effort but would be happier (through a payoff of 4) if the other person also chose high effort.
- Person 1 has a payoff of 2 from choosing low effort when the other person is also choosing low effort. Under these circumstances, the likelihood that both people will have low income is maximal.
- Person 1 has the lowest possible personal payoff of 1 when she chooses low effort but the other person chooses high effort. She feels personally inadequate in not matching the high effort of the other person and also feels guilt about exploiting the effort (or goodwill) of the other person. The guilt feeling is not reciprocal: the highest payoff for person 2 occurs through exploiting person 1's work ethic.

The dominant strategy of person 1 with a work ethic is to choose high effort. Person 2's best response to person 1's choice of high effort is to choose low effort. The Nash equilibrium is at (3,4), where person 1 exerts high effort and person 2 chooses low effort. The most likely outcomes are that person 1 has high earned income and person 2 has low earned income. Therefore:

In a diverse population, people with a work ethic systematically make income transfers to people whose behavior is subject to moral hazard.

The desire of person 1 with a work ethic to be self-reliant allows person 2 to maximize utility by choosing to not be self-reliant.

If person 1 were compelled to choose low effort (person 1 might become ill or be unable to work because of the need to care for a small child), person 2 would still choose low effort. The outcome would then be at (2,2).

A work ethic and diverse populations

In considering social insurance when only exogenous luck determines incomes, we compared societies' choices of social welfare functions and asked why the work ethic might be more prevalent in some societies than others. Table 7.2 extended beyond the two representative people to large populations suggests the parallel question:

> *Why is there diversity with regard to a work ethic in being self-reliant?*

A work ethic may be expressive: people with a work ethic may exert high effort to be self-reliant due to self-image and self-respect to confirm that they are capable and productive members of society. They would feel uncomfortable or personally inadequate if they were to take advantage of insurance as a source of income. Their sense of self-worth may be reflected in a pre-tax income that they earn. Consciously or through demonstration, they transmit the work ethic to their children. A work ethic also may be due to stigma – that is, because of otherwise adverse perceptions by family and peers who are able to observe a person's effort decision. Individual ability and human capital also affect whether a work ethic is present: people who are rewarded highly in labor markets have more to lose if they do not exert effort to be self-reliant. Being highly skilled or having high human capital (or being educated) is also the consequence of a work ethic applied to studying. Is the work ethic related to religion? We have noted the linkage proposed by Max Weber between a work ethic and Protestantism and that other cultures as well have a work ethic.[44]

Whatever the source of the work ethic, a question underlying table 7.2 is:

> *How do societies that begin with a work ethic as a norm of behavior come to confront moral hazard?*

The question is important because moral hazard can threaten the sustainability of the social insurance contract. As we saw, if no one has a work ethic and therefore everyone is subject to moral hazard, all individuals prefer that there be no insurance – because of the adverse effects of insurance through the common-pool

[44] Martin Luther proclaimed the merit of all work. The French Protestant theologian John Calvin (1509–64) (who lived in Geneva) proposed that salvation in the next world was indicated by success in this world. The predetermination of salvation provided incentives to be productive and successful in this world as a prelude to success in the next. A focus on the endeavors of this world is the basis for a work ethic in Jewish, Chinese, and Japanese cultures. Rachel McCleary and Robert Barro (2006) have reviewed economic research on the contemporary relationship between religion and economic success.

problem of incomes on the incentive to exert high effort. If only some people have a work ethic and the population is diverse, as in table 7.2, the people with a work ethic may decide that they are no longer willing to finance the incomes of people subject to moral hazard. Voluntary insurance then ends. If the insurance is not voluntary but has been imposed by government, the people with a work ethic will seek to end the social insurance contract by political means – or they may emigrate, in which case, adverse selection takes place according to who remains in and who exits from the society.

Moral hazard due to change in norms in a society

A norm of a work ethic was part of the traditional model of the family in which the man takes responsibility for earning income to provide for a woman and children. Income transfers from government, if available, are asked for only if there has been misfortune. When marriage becomes less prevalent and formal commitments of marriage are replaced by relationships that, if people want, can be transient, a woman may decide to have children without commitment from a man to support the children. As with some animals, some men may impregnate and disappear to take no responsibility for rearing the young. Perhaps because of the sense of adventure in variety and new beginnings, the women may not want the company of the same men all the time. Men without responsibilities for providing incomes for children can choose to make do with a high leisure component in personal utility. Single mothers do the best they can depending on their individual circumstances and may have the independent means to support their children, and some fathers may contribute. However, some women without the financial support of men require welfare payments for themselves and the children. When people with a work ethic (and previous study ethic) pay taxes that finance income transfers to the women and children who, in the traditional family model, would be dependents of the fathers of the children, the work ethic is no longer the unique social norm. The government has taken the role of an insurance company providing income to people who, consequently, need make no effort to be self-reliant. At the same time, welfare payments are also made to people who exerted high effort to be self-reliant but were genuinely unlucky in personal outcomes. There also may be people without a work ethic who did not exert high effort at self-reliance but were nonetheless lucky and do not require income support from the government.

> *Changes in norms of behavior within populations create societies with diverse social norms regarding a work ethic.*

Moral hazard due to norms from outside a society

The source of change in norms of behavior can also be from outside a society, through immigration. When people decide to emigrate from their home country, a process of self-selection occurs. People with a work ethic wish to emigrate to a country where the personal return to having a work ethic is high. They therefore seek a society without the high taxation required to finance an extensive social insurance contract. They also seek a society with high economic mobility. The immigrants with a work ethic contribute to their new society by earning incomes and paying taxes, thereby sharing in the payments for public goods and the financing of other public spending, such as pensions and health care for the elderly. Illegal immigrants also, in general, seek out societies with a work ethic and without a welfare state: because they are illegal, the immigrants cannot benefit from welfare payments. The illegal immigrants look for locations where productive effort and effort at self-reliance are rewarded – and perhaps where immigration authorities do not care all that much about illegal immigrants, as long as the immigrants are law abiding and productive.

However, there is adverse selection when people without a work ethic, and who are therefore susceptible to moral hazard, choose to emigrate to a welfare state. Residents in a welfare state to which immigrants relocate may only ever have known exogenous bad luck as the reason for low incomes, and therefore may view immigrants as also necessarily victims of exogenous bad luck. The residents of the host welfare state may anticipate that a work ethic among the immigrants will provide the basis for self-reliance, after initial help has been provided.

Whereas some immigrants take advantage of the new opportunities to become productive members of their new society, because of the adverse selection in choosing location, others may not, thereby disappointing expectations of eventual self-reliance of immigrants. There may be further disappointment if some immigrants do not integrate into the local society by learning the language and if children of immigrants do not take advantage of educational opportunities that the host society offers.

Adverse selection through immigration can make the social insurance contract of the host country unsustainable, particularly if immigrants have significantly more children than the original host population and if immigrants' children do not become productive members of society. Cultural transmission may take place from parents to children: the children observe that their immigrant parents are supported by income transfers from the government and may conclude that likewise they do not need to become self-reliant.

Why do host populations allow adverse selection through immigration? If the residents of the host country believe that unfortunate people are, of necessity, victims of exogenous bad luck (like the good or bad luck of people who emerge from behind a veil of ignorance), bad luck can be interpreted to be repeated in the domestic outcomes of the self-selected immigrants. Because the host society of the welfare state is high-income (due to the work ethic), immigrants who do not become self-reliant can continue to be regarded as victims who deserve ongoing help.

Immigrants' decisions about where to relocate are subject to adverse selection. The adverse selection results in populations that are diverse in susceptibility to moral hazard.

Sources of attitudes to a work ethic

Immigrants may not have a tradition of a work ethic because of cultural transmission from circumstances in their home countries. In some of their home societies, having a work ethic could have been dangerous: in various low-income countries, relationships are Nietzschean, with the strong prevailing over the weak, and personal property rights are often not protected. The strong are the autocratic rulers, who fear that they will be forcefully overthrown – losing their wealth and their life as well. The rulers fear that accumulated private wealth will be used to challenge their control of government and are therefore cautious and suspicious when people accumulate private wealth. Because the private wealth is viewed as a threat by the rulers, there is personal danger from having a work ethic. As in the Nietzschean anarchy that we considered without the rule of law, people learn to appear – and out of absence of choice to be – lazy and unproductive so as not to attract the attention and suspicion of the local ruler. The local ruler's fears arise because for a citizen who has resources, the best personal investment may be to contest the rents of the ruler. The ruler's objective in disallowing private wealth is to preempt the contesting of the rents from the ruler's control of government. Because people are not permitted to accumulate private wealth, the ruler may distribute charity to preempt or quell unpopularity and unrest. The charity may also be required by local beliefs and customs because the culture is predicated on a very unequal distribution of wealth and income.

People's perceptions and priors sometimes change slowly. When relocating to Western countries, immigrants may bring with them the model of the relationship between the ruler and the population in their home society. In their former home, there have been no personal benefits possible from a work ethic – and, indeed, a work ethic may have been dangerous because of the threat perceived by the ruler. It may therefore take time for immigrants to recognize the personal benefits of a work ethic in their new location. The model brought with them by the immigrants may also associate the power of government with charity through noblesse oblige. In the eyes of the immigrants, the income transfers from a government in their new location replace the charity that may have been provided by the rich rulers in their former home country. A culture of dependence is thereby sustained.

Institutions can affect attitudes to a work ethic in other ways. For example, past slavery can be the reason why a work ethic takes time to develop. Slaves are compelled to work for the benefit of their owners. The slaveowners deny slaves personal freedom and may dehumanize the slaves. Family and other lasting personal relationships among slaves may be impossible because individual slaves are property to be sold at the whim of the master. We might, therefore, expect generations that have experienced slavery to have a collective memory of work as forced labor. When the people of Israel were liberated from slavery in Egypt some 3,500 years ago, the former slaves wandered the desert for 40 years during which time they were sustained by "manna from heaven" for which they did not have to work. Only after the generation that had experienced slavery had passed from the scene did self-reliance begin.

In a culture in which property is communal and people live in hunter–gatherer societies, private property and personal wealth cannot be accumulated. People take from nature what they need at the time. A culture may impart contentment with what people have. The stresses of contact with outside societies, however, may destroy the equanimity of contentment with basic needs. Responses to the contact with (or impositions of) outside cultures can differ. In some cases, because of the persistence of past preconceptions based on communal property and sharing, adaptation to new institutions of private property and to associated incentives for personal wealth accumulation may be difficult and long lasting.

Discrimination can stifle a work ethic. When people look for jobs but find themselves discriminated against, the motivation to look for work declines. In the end, motivation to look for jobs may be absent altogether: people may cease looking for jobs because of a prediction of discrimination in the labor market.

There may be a presumption that people do not have a work ethic because they have not in the past been self-reliant but have been supported by income transfers from the government. However, when welfare reform takes place and income transfers cease or become conditional on work, people look for and find work. Not working is then revealed to have been due to incentives of social insurance that created moral hazard.

D. Public-policy responses to moral hazard

Public policy is required because of the failures of voluntary insurance. In the game with a diverse population in table 7.2, if the insurance contract and income-pooling are voluntary, people with a work ethic can exit the insurance pool. If all people with a work ethic exit, the people who behave strategically in choosing low effort have no one from whom to systematically receive income transfers. The circumstances revert, therefore, to the symmetric prisoners' dilemma shown in table 7.1, in which the behavior of everyone in the insurance pool is subject to moral hazard: if insurance is voluntary, everyone then leaves the insurance pool because of moral hazard. Voluntary insurance has then failed, first because of adverse selection and second because of moral hazard.

In the absence of voluntary insurance (or insurance markets), people can self-insure for future contingencies through personal precautionary savings. However, precautionary saving is not the optimal response to uncertain future income; the optimal personal response to uncertainty is risk-pooling through insurance. Nonetheless, if adverse selection and moral hazard prevent voluntary insurance – and government does not provide insurance – saving as self-insurance is the sole means of protection against adverse personal future outcomes.

Adverse selection and moral hazard are two reasons why asymmetric information results in failures of voluntary insurance. A third reason arises when because of asymmetric information, objective verification of outcomes is impossible. People may have private information about what has happened to them. However, insurance requires means of objective verification of outcomes against which insurance is sought. For example, someone may declare, "I cannot emotionally cope with the stress of going to work." Verifying emotional impediments to working for a living is difficult or impossible. Social workers can try to verify claims that a primary income earner has left the household and no longer takes responsibility for children, or that people who claim to be unemployed are truly unemployed and are not working informally (and so are not receiving money from the government under the false pretense of unemployment and also evading taxes on income earned).

Governments and moral hazard

If private voluntary insurance has failed and governments take the responsibility to provide social insurance, the asymmetric information that underlies the moral-hazard problem nonetheless remains. How can public policy address moral hazard?

A solution to the moral-hazard problem is incomplete social insurance that makes exerting low effort at self-reliance an unattractive personal choice. That is, welfare benefits are set so low that exerting low effort and facing the prospect of having low income and receiving the welfare benefits is unattractive compared to exerting high effort at self-reliance.

> *The moral-hazard problem is solved through incomplete social insurance that makes earning high pre-tax income and being a taxpayer preferable to earning low income and receiving an income transfer.*[45]

Solving the moral-hazard problem also solves the adverse-selection problem. If incomplete insurance has made choosing high effort everyone's best choice, everyone has an incentive to participate in the insurance pool.

> *With everyone choosing high effort because low income transfers of incomplete insurance have made low effort not worthwhile, any person observed to have low income has been genuinely unlucky and therefore is a victim of fate who deserves help through social insurance.*

[45] The moral-hazard problem is solved if:

$$EU(y, e_H) = \Pr(\mu_H \mid e_H)U(y_H - tax) + \Pr(\mu_L \mid e_H)U(y_L + income\ transfer)$$
$$> EU(y, e_L) = \Pr(\mu_H \mid e_L)U(y_H - tax) + \Pr(\mu_L \mid e_L)U(y_L + income\ transfer).$$

A social dilemma

People who are observed to experience bad outcomes could be helped more than the incomplete insurance designed to prevent moral hazard allows, if society were involved in a one-time game. If help could be given as a "surprise" after a person has experienced an adverse personal outcome, there would be no moral hazard because the surprise could not affect past incentives to exert effort to be self-reliant. However, societies cannot provide help as unanticipated surprises. People make repeated decisions over time regarding effort at self-reliance. In the repeated game, moral hazard is reintroduced when people take advantage of asymmetric information to choose low effort in response to the high social insurance benefits that are anticipated and so are no longer a surprise.

There is, therefore, a social dilemma in resolving the moral-hazard problem. Because of the low income transfers when people experience bad outcomes, everyone chooses high effort. However, some people nonetheless experience random unfortunate outcomes through no fault of their own. Yet, high income transfers to the people who experienced the genuinely random unfortunate outcomes cannot be made without reintroducing moral hazard. Because of the social dilemma, societies might decide to live with rather than attempt to eliminate moral hazard.

We now need to designate which social welfare function a society has chosen behind the veil of ignorance based on the leaky bucket of redistribution and exogenous luck as the determinant of personal outcomes. We proceed to consider a society that has chosen Bentham.

The two cases for incomplete insurance

With Bentham chosen behind the veil of ignorance because of the rationality of maximizing expected utility, social insurance is incomplete. A government implements the Bentham social insurance contract after the society has emerged from behind the veil of ignorance. When still behind the veil of ignorance, people will have agreed that adverse selection will be preempted by compulsory social insurance to solve the time-inconsistency problem. In providing and enforcing compulsory social insurance, the government resolves the time-inconsistency problem and avoids adverse selection after people have been able to observe their personal outcome. Exit from social insurance is not possible (unless through emigration) and everyone is part of the social insurance contract.[46]

After having emerged from behind the veil of ignorance, if all people do not have a work ethic, the society confronts moral hazard as a response to the existence of the Bentham social insurance contract. Because Bentham social insurance is incomplete, moral hazard is alleviated. Nonetheless, Bentham social

[46] Behind the veil of ignorance, some people may not want Bentham. We could extend the metaphor to people presorting themselves into groups and emerging from behind the veil of ignorance with their risk-sharing group.

insurance was chosen behind the veil of ignorance based on the labor–leisure substitution decisions associated with the leaky bucket of redistribution and without accounting for the moral-hazard problem that arises when, after emergence from behind the veil of ignorance, good and adverse personal outcomes in life are not exogenous but rather are influenced by personal-effort decisions at self-reliance.

We see that there are two cases for incomplete social insurance. One case is based on social insurance chosen behind a veil of ignorance, where people have no information about their future self. The second case is based on moral hazard when, after emergence from behind the veil of ignorance, information is asymmetric because people have private information about whether they choose high or low effort to be self-reliant.

How incomplete will social insurance be when the no-information veil-of-ignorance and asymmetric-information moral-hazard cases for incomplete insurance are combined?

We have no definitive answer to this question. The public-policy decision depends on sensitivity to two types of errors that arise because of moral hazard.

A type-1 error arises when people in genuine need through no fault of their own are insufficiently helped by social insurance. A type-2 error arises when people who could be self-reliant choose low effort at self-reliance and benefit from the income transfers of social insurance.

Sensitivity to type-1 errors can expand social insurance beyond Bentham's incomplete insurance. Sensitivity to type-2 errors, conversely, can make choice of social insurance less complete than Bentham.

How the incomplete insurance of Bentham is amended to take account of moral hazard depends on sensitivities to type-1 and type-2 errors.

Political sensitivities to the two types of error differ. The left of the political spectrum is generally less willing to make the mistake of a type-1 error. The right, on the contrary, may be less willing to make type-2 errors.

The distinction that has been made between exogenous luck and personal outcomes that are endogenous through effort at self-reliance would not be present if effort at self-reliance were also the consequence of luck. Parents and the surroundings into which people are born influence personal decisions about whether to study and affect attitudes to achieving personal success through personal effort. People with limited education and low skills may lack incentives to exert high effort at self-reliance because of the low income that they would earn even from a favorable outcome μ_H: as we have observed, having a work ethic can depend on the personal return from work. Thus, political sensitivities with regard to making type-1 and type-2 errors differ but there can also be disagreement about whether type-2 errors exist at all (and therefore about whether moral hazard exists).

> *If people are victims of exogenous fate and have no choice about not being self-reliant, there are no type-2 errors and therefore there is no moral hazard.*

The left on the ideological spectrum is sympathetic to the view that type-2 errors are not relevant for public policy because people with a low personal income are victims of fate and that the low income is the consequence of the unfairness of unequal opportunities in life. The right is more inclined to interpret low incomes *in the presence of insurance* as the consequence of moral hazard; the right might indeed perceive overly generous social insurance as *creating* low incomes through moral hazard.

There are people, including economists, whose views accord with those of the left and also those whose views accord with those of the right. In general, economists place store in the role of incentives in influencing personal choices; but, there are economists who take the view that incentives do not affect the choice to be self-reliant because people who are not self-reliant have been the victim of circumstance and have had no choice.

The extent of moral hazard is, therefore, controversial. Recourse to empirical evidence on the prevalence of moral hazard is limited because moral hazard is based on unobservable effort. However, there is evidence from the consequences of welfare reforms that reduce welfare benefits. We shall look at this evidence in the following chapter. First we consider the prospects for social justice without government.

7.3 Social Justice without Government

In investigating the social objective of efficiency when public goods and externalities are present, we began with private voluntary decisions and came in the end to roles for government because of inadequacies or failures of markets. In investigating social justice, our focus has been on government and social insurance because of the failures of private insurance markets in providing the insurance that risk-averse people seek. In the final section of this chapter on social justice, we ask: If private insurance markets fail, can social justice nonetheless be achieved without government? If altruism and charity could be relied on to provide income for people in need, income transfers would be voluntary and the efficiency losses through the leaks in the bucket of redistribution because of the excess burden of taxation would not arise.

A. Altruism and charity

Charity is, by nature, private. We do not describe governments as acting "charitably." Charity is also quite consistent with self-interested personal behavior.

Although Adam Smith emphasized the virtue of self-interest in the market, in his book, *Theory of Moral Sentiments* (1759), he observed that human nature leads people to be altruistically concerned about the well-being of others:

> However selfish soever man may be supposed, there are evidently some principles in his nature, which interest him in the fortune of others, and render their happiness necessary to him, though he derives nothing from it, except the pleasure of seeing it.

Adam Smith thus observed that people feel sympathy (or empathy) for one another.

Interdependent utilities

Charitable inclinations are expressed in interdependent utilities whereby personal utility is determined not only by a person's own circumstances but also by the circumstances of others. We can consider again a given amount of income Y to be distributed between two people, where y_i is the amount of income received by individual i, so that:

$$Y = y_1 + y_2. \tag{7.30}$$

If the two people cared only about themselves, their utility functions would be:

$$U_1 = U_1(y_1), \quad U_2 = U_2(y_2). \tag{7.31}$$

Each would then ideally want to have the entire income Y. When the two people care about one other, their utility functions are:

$$U_1 = U_1(y_1, y_2), \quad U_2 = U_2(y_2, y_1). \tag{7.32}$$

Each person's well-being now depends not only on how much he or she has but also on how much is available to the other person. Altruism is expressed in each person's utility as increasing when the other person has more income:

$$\frac{\partial U_1}{\partial y_2} > 0, \quad \frac{\partial U_2}{\partial y_1} > 0. \tag{7.33}$$

The personal benefit expressed here is due to the other person having more and not to satisfaction from giving. The increase in utility is, for example, from seeing that the other person is not destitute or hungry.[47]

Figure 7.14 shows the utilities of two people with the interdependent utilities in expression (7.32). At point A, person 1 has all available income ($Y = y_1$); at point D, person 2 has all available income ($Y = y_2$).

Beginning from point A, person 1 can increase his or her own utility by voluntarily transferring income to person 2 but only until point B is reached. After

[47] The interdependence between utilities in expression (7.32) can also describe envy. In that case, a person's feeling of well-being decreases when the other person has more.

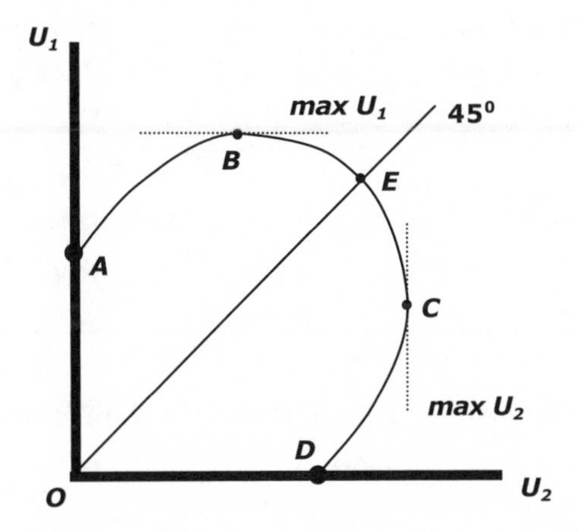

Figure 7.14. Interdependent utilities and Pareto-improving voluntary income transfers.

point *B*, the personal loss from giving exceeds the personal gain from seeing that person 2 is better off. After point *B*, person 1's utility begins to fall. The utility of person 2, who is the recipient, continues to increase along *BC* because of the income transfers received. Beginning from point *A*, person 1 makes voluntary income transfers to person 2 up to point *B*, where person 1's utility U_1 is maximized.

The same process of voluntary transfers can begin from point *D*, where person 2 has everything and person 1 has nothing. Person 2 will make voluntary income transfers up to point *C*, where person 2's utility U_2 is maximized.

Depending on whether the initial position is *A* or *D*, the society ends up at either *B* or *C*. In either case, income redistribution takes place through voluntary transfers without government. The income transfers are Pareto-improving because the donor and the recipient are both better off after the transfers have been made.

A three-person society

Figure 7.14 and the interdependent utilities in expression (7.32) show a population of two people. Often, looking at two people is sufficient to establish a general principle for a society that consists of many people. In the case of voluntary income transfers, however, the situation changes substantially when we add a third person.

We can consider person 1 and person 2 who are well off and person 3 who is poor or unfortunate. Person 1 and person 2 are aware that person 3 will suffer hunger and deprivation if not assisted. The utilities of person 1 and person 2 depend on their own income and also on the income of disadvantaged person 3, so that:

$$U_1 = U_1(y_1, y_3), \quad U_2 = U_2(y_2, y_3). \tag{7.34}$$

TABLE 7.3. THE PRISONERS' DILEMMA OF PRIVATE INCOME TRANSFERS WHEN EACH PERSON PREFERS THAT THE OTHER GIVE

	Person 2 gives	Person 2 does not give
Person 1 gives	3,3	1,4
Person 1 does not give	4,1	2,2

Person 3 is so unfortunate that he has in mind no one other than himself, and his utility is:

$$U_3 = U_3(y_3). \tag{7.35}$$

Although person 1 and person 2 feel better when person 3 is better off, they nonetheless each prefer that the other provide the income that helps person 3.

The income of the unfortunate person y_3 appears in the utility functions of both persons 1 and 2 and has the characteristics of a public good. That is, person 1 and person 2 provide benefits to one another when either makes voluntary contributions that increase the income of person 3.

The public-good nature of the income transfers to person 3 introduces a free-riding problem. Person 1 and person 2 both have an incentive to act strategically to attempt to place the burden of helping the unfortunate person on the other. When the issue is not how much to give unfortunate person 3 but whether to give, we have the prisoners' dilemma between the two potential donors in table 7.3. The dominant strategy is not to give and the Nash equilibrium is that neither person gives. Both people are better off if they can move from the Nash equilibrium to the efficient outcome at (3,3), where they share the burden of providing income for person 3. Government can enforce the efficient outcome by compelling person 1 and person 2 to pay taxes that finance income transfers to person 3.

We have therefore identified a justification based on the prisoners' dilemma for taxes to finance income redistribution. Higher income people want to see income transfers made to unfortunate people but, because of the public-good nature of the income transfers and the prisoners' dilemma, they cannot achieve the transfers voluntarily and independently. Government resolves the prisoners' dilemma and the free-rider problem through taxation and publicly financed income transfers to the unfortunate people in a society.

Table 7.3 describes a symmetric prisoners' dilemma. When preferences of donors differ, we are returned to the problem of asymmetric information as impeding resolution by government of the public-good prisoners' dilemma. Governments do not know donors' benefits from assistance given to unfortunate people. In the absence of this information, a government can only make a best estimate about the taxes to levy on the two donors to finance an income transfer.

Expressive voting for redistribution

Through expressive voting, people derive utility from how they vote. In chapter 1, when comparing markets and voting, we noted that, for some people, it may be sufficient to vote in favor of income transfers to obtain utility through feeling generous. At the same time, actually giving money to other people may result in disutility.

A two-person example

We can consider an example of two taxpayers, both of whose votes in favor are required for a transfer of income to take place to others. Either voter can therefore veto income transfers by voting against or also by abstaining from voting. For both people:

$$U(\textit{voting in favor of transfers}) = 1.$$
$$U(\textit{paying for income transfers}) = -2.$$
$$U(\textit{not voting for and therefore not paying taxes for income transfers}) = 0.$$

The payoffs from the different combinations of decisions are shown in table 7.4.

Each person is best off with a benefit of 1 obtained from voting for income transfers that do not have to be made because the other person has voted against (and has thereby vetoed) the transfers.

A decision to vote against the income transfers (which then do not have to be made) provides utility of zero, whatever the decision of the other voter.

If both people vote in favor of the income transfers, they have utility of 1 from their expressive voting but disutility of −2 because they actually have to make the income transfers. They are left with utility of −1.

There is no dominant strategy. There are two Nash equilibria in pure strategies at (1,0) and (0,1) in which one person votes in favor of the transfers and the other does not. The Nash equilibrium in mixed strategies is to vote in favor of or against income transfers with a probability of 0.5. The likelihood of each of the four outcomes in table 7.4 is 0.25. The expected utility from participation in the

TABLE 7.4. VOTING FOR INCOME TRANSFERS INCREASES UTILITY BUT PERSONALLY PAYING TO FINANCE TRANSFERS DECREASES UTILITY

	Person 2 votes against income transfers	Person 2 votes in favor of income transfers
Person 1 votes against income transfers	0,0	0,1
Person 1 votes in favor of income transfers	1,0	−1,−1

game is positive and equal to 0.5. The probability of the outcome for the voters in which they both vote in favor of the income transfers is thus 0.25.[48]

If decisions are sequential, the first person to vote chooses to vote in favor of the income transfers and the second person votes against, thus vetoing the income transfers. A person who can credibly commit to vote in favor of the income transfers therefore gains from expressive voting. The second person vetoes, which is what the first person knows the second person will do – and wants the second person to do. Indeed, the decision of the person deciding first to vote in favor of the income transfers is predicated on knowing that the second person will veto.

Large numbers of voters

The example in table 7.4 describes two voters who behave strategically knowing that one vote against (or an abstention) vetoes the income transfers. In general, because of large numbers of voters, individual voters know that their vote will not be decisive under majority voting. They therefore take the positive utility that is available from voting expressively in favor of the income transfers. The dominant strategy is to vote in favor of the income transfers because of the utility from expressive voting when voters know that they will not be decisive in influencing the voting outcome. The income transfers take place if a majority votes expressively (or in other circumstances genuinely) in favor. No person regrets having voted as he or she did because voting against the income transfers would not have influenced the outcome, given how other people voted. The Nash equilibrium is that people vote in favor of the transfers, although each voter has utility of −1, derived from utility of 1 from voting for the transfers, and utility of −2 from having to finance the transfers.

Expressive voting is conducive to income transfers.

Utility from giving

We have described people as deriving utility from seeing that others have been helped or from voting to help others. In contrast to these cases, people may derive pleasure from actually giving. Table 7.5 shows two charitable people who derive utility from giving. The best personal outcome 10 is achieved when a person has the satisfaction of being the sole donor. The next best outcome 8 is obtained when both donors give. The donors in table 7.5 do not like to free ride: their benefit when they free ride on the charitable contributions of the other is 5. The worst

[48] Each person can obtain zero with certainty by voting against the income transfers. The benefit from voting in favor depends on the decision of the other person. Denoting the probability that the other person votes against by P_A, the expected utility from voting in favor of the transfers is $\{1 \cdot P_A + (-1)(1 - P_A)\}$. Setting this expression equal to the certain utility of zero from voting against the income transfers and solving yields $P_A = 0.5$.

TABLE 7.5. CHARITY WHEN THE ACT OF GIVING INCREASES UTILITY AND HIGHEST UTILITY IS ACHIEVED BY BEING THE SOLE DONOR

	Person 2 gives	Person 2 does not give
Person 1 gives	8, 8	10, 5
Person 1 does not give	5, 10	0, 0

TABLE 7.6. CHARITY WHEN THE ACT OF GIVING INCREASES UTILITY AND HIGHEST UTILITY IS OBTAINED BY GIVING TOGETHER WITH OTHERS

	Person 2 gives	Person 2 does not give
Person 1 gives	10, 10	8, 5
Person 1 does not give	5, 8	0, 0

outcome for both donors is (0,0), when neither gives. The dominant strategy in table 7.5 is to give.[49] The Nash equilibrium is at (8,8), where both voluntarily give. The Nash equilibrium is efficient: $(8 + 8) = 16$ is the maximum combined benefit for both donors.[50] The donors have no reason to invite taxation by government. They both voluntarily give as their best personal strategies. Accordingly, they both save the excess burden of taxation.[51]

The two donors may experience pleasure from giving and may prefer that they give together. In table 7.6, the best outcome for both donors is that both give, at (10,10).[52] The dominant strategy is again to give.

The exploitation of charitable intentions

We now turn from interactions among donors to the interaction between a donor who has utility from giving and an income recipient who does not have a work ethic. There is no moral hazard because there is no asymmetric information: the donor can observe whether the recipient is making an effort to be self-reliant.

[49] If person 2 does not give, person 1 obtains 10 by giving. If person 2 does give, person 1 obtains 8 by giving – and symmetrically for person 2.

[50] We are looking at the desirability of outcomes from the perspective of the donors, not the recipient.

[51] Rather than deciding simultaneously, the two people in table 7.5 could make their decision sequentially. Because the dominant strategy is to give, the same efficient Nash equilibrium is achieved through sequential decisions.

[52] The next best outcome 8 occurs when one donor gives and the other does not. The donors again do not like to free ride (which gives a donor a benefit of 5), and the worst outcome is that neither gives.

TABLE 7.7. THE EXPLOITATION OF CHARITABLE FEELINGS

	The recipient exerts effort to be self-reliant	The recipient does not exert effort to be self-reliant
The donor does not give	2, 2	1, 1
The donor gives	4, 3	3, 4

Table 7.7 shows the outcomes of strategic interaction between the donor and the recipient: the donor decides whether to give money to the recipient and the recipient decides whether to exert effort to be self-reliant. The game is not symmetric. The first number in table 7.7 is the ranking (or benefit) of the donor and the second number is the ranking (or benefit) of the recipient of the charity.[53]

The donor and the recipient both consider the worst outcome to be (1,1), in which the donor does not provide income support and the recipient does not make an effort to be self-reliant. The recipient then has no means of support and could starve to death, which is an outcome neither the donor nor the recipient wants.

The donor and the recipient agree that (2,2) is the next-worse outcome. This outcome, in which the donor does not provide income support and the recipient makes an effort to be self-reliant, is contrary to the nature of both people. The donor likes to give but in this case does not give. The recipient does not like to work but here exerts effort to be self-reliant. For their own different reasons, neither the donor nor the recipient likes this outcome.

The outcome preferred by the donor is (4,3), in which the donor provides income support and the recipient makes the effort to be self-reliant. The outcome preferred by the recipient is (3,4), in which the donor provides income support and the recipient makes no effort at self-reliance.

The recipient does not have a dominant strategy. If the donor does not give, the recipient's best response is to exert effort to be self-reliant. If the donor gives, the recipient's best response is to not make an effort to be self-reliant.

The donor, however, does have a dominant strategy. Whatever the recipient does, the best response of the donor is to give. The decision to give assures either 3 or 4 for the donor.

The recipient knows that the dominant strategy of the donor is to give and therefore chooses not to make the effort to be self-reliant, resulting in the outcome at (3,4). This outcome is a Nash equilibrium – neither the donor nor the recipient can do better by independently changing the decision that each has made.

[53] The game was first described in 1975 by James Buchanan (Nobel Prize in economics, 1986). For reasons that the behavior of the recipient will make clear, Buchanan described the recipient as a "parasite."

At (3,4), the recipient achieves the best personal outcome but not the donor. The donor would like the recipient to make an effort at finding a job, which would move the outcome to (4,3). The recipient may be low-skilled and would not earn a high income if working, but the donor wants the recipient to make an effort in any event to earn whatever personal income that is possible while the recipient is provided with supplementary income support.

The donor is unhappy with the outcome in which the recipient makes no effort to be self-reliant. What can the donor do?

Misrepresented preferences by the donor

To change the outcome, the donor could declare the preferences set out in table 7.8 – although the donor's true preferences, in fact, are as shown in table 7.7. In table 7.8, the donor misrepresents preferences in an attempt to change the recipient's behavior. The donor declares that she has highest utility 4 when the recipient makes no effort to be self-reliant and the donor does not give. The donor is now indicating that if the recipient makes no effort to be self-reliant when the offer of supplementary assistance is available for choosing to work, then the recipient deserves to die of hunger. The donor's new preferences give her utility 3 when the recipient makes the effort to be self-reliant and she gives the recipient money. The donor has utility 2 from not giving when the recipient is trying to be self-reliant. The donor's declared lowest utility 1 is now when she gives and the recipient makes no effort to be self-reliant. The preferences or ranking of outcomes of the recipient in table 7.8 remain unchanged from table 7.7.

Under the declared new preferences for the donor in table 7.8, neither the donor nor the recipient has a dominant strategy and there is no Nash equilibrium in pure strategies.[54] In looking for an equilibrium, we note that the recipient does not want to die of starvation and therefore is not prepared to gamble on ending up at (4,1), where he starves.

TABLE 7.8. THE CHARITABLE PERSON SEEKS TO MISREPRESENT PREFERENCES

	The recipient exerts effort to be self-reliant	The recipient does not exert effort to be self-reliant
The donor does not give	2,2	4,1
The donor gives	3,3	1,4

[54] The outcome at (3,3) is not a Nash equilibrium because the recipient can do better at (1,4), which is also not a Nash equilibrium because the donor can do better at (4,1). Neither is (4,1) a Nash equilibrium because the recipient can do better at (2,2). The outcome at (2,2) is not a Nash equilibrium because the donor does better at (3,3) (as also does the recipient).

The recipient adopts a max–min strategy. That is, the recipient makes the decision that results in the least potential self-harm, thereby avoiding the possibility of the outcome (4,1). The recipient makes the following calculation:

- If I fail to make the effort to be self-reliant, the donor will give me no money and I shall starve at (4,1).
- If I do make the effort to be self-reliant, the donor will give me money, and I shall then certainly live at (3,3).

The recipient therefore makes the effort to be self-reliant and the outcome in table 7.8 is at (3,3), which, based on the donor's true preferences in table 7.7, is the outcome that the donor wants.

For the change in the recipient's behavior to take place, the recipient must believe that the donor will indeed allow him to starve. Because table 7.8 does not represent the donor's true preferences, if the recipient chose not to work, the donor would not let the recipient starve. The outcome would again be the Nash equilibrium based on the donor's true preferences at (3,4) in table 7.7, in which the recipient exploits the charitable nature of the donor and makes no effort to be self-reliant and receives income from the donor.

Rules, not discretion

Because of lack of credibility, the donor declaring not to care if the recipient starves may not be effective in changing the recipient's behavior. A government bureaucracy, however, can credibly mediate between the donor and the recipient. The bureaucracy follows "rules, not discretion." That is, the bureaucracy is given the responsibility of disbursing income support according to strict rules. The bureaucracy has no discretion about the conditions under which income transfers are provided. The government bureaucracy informs the recipient that income support will not be provided unless the recipient makes an effort to be self-reliant and earn income and that this is a rule with no exceptions. The government bureaucracy thereby enforces the outcome that is desired by the donor. The recipient chooses to make the effort to be self-reliant and receives income support from government (no longer directly from the donor). The government, by mediating between the donor and the recipient, thereby saves charitable people from the consequences of their own kind nature. In applying this solution, which may the only solution, donors are subject to the bureaucratic principal–agent problem and, because taxes are required, there is an excess burden of taxation.

Degrees of charity

Private charitable contributions are often made anonymously by giving to a charitable organization. In that case, neither the donor nor the recipient is aware of the identity of the other. Degrees of charity have been proposed according to whether the donor knows the identity of the recipient or the recipient knows the identity of the donor.[55]

Social status

Rather than donors giving anonymously to charity, donations can be intentionally conspicuous. Charitable donations are part of the quest for social status that attracts people to charity balls and dinners. Charitable causes then gain from the self-interest of the donors, whose conspicuous and publicized charitable donations serve the purpose of displaying personal wealth to others. Thorstein Veblen (1857–1929), in his book *The Theory of the Leisure Class* (1899), described how people display their wealth through conspicuous consumption. Conspicuous giving to charity is also a means of displaying wealth. The contest for status is similar to a rent-seeking contest. Status is sought relative to the status of others. There is, therefore, a prisoners' dilemma similar to the rent-seeking prisoners' dilemma. The contest for status may use resources in socially unproductive ways through visible displays of wealth, as Veblen observed. However, the contest for status has social benefits when status is achieved by visible charitable activities.

Can the quest for social status also be an impediment to voluntary charitable transfers? If wealth and high income are the sources of social status, charitable giving reduces social status. If the rich like to be in the presence of other rich people, voluntary income redistribution that sufficiently reduces income and wealth inequality would not allow the rich to identify themselves through their wealth. For example, they could not take vacations at expensive resorts that the middle class cannot afford, air travel could not be first class, and they could not send their children to expensive private colleges where social contacts can be made with children from other wealthy families.[56]

Wealth and high income are not necessary for social status. In many societies, status is conferred by education, by profession, and by volunteering to help people in need. In some countries, incomes of university professors have been low, reflecting the view that high incomes are unnecessary because of the compensation of the social status of being a professor. In the prestigious English universities, Cambridge and Oxford, there was a presumption – following on from prior monastic traditions – that scholars would not marry but rather would dedicate their life to learning without the encumbrance of a spouse and children. The

[55] Maimonides (1135–1204), also known as the Rambam, distinguished eight levels of charity. The highest degree is charity that will make a person self-reliant and end the need for future charity. The second highest degree of charity is mutual anonymity. The degree of charity is greater when the donor knows the identity of the recipient and the recipient does not know the identity of the donor than when the converse is the case. The degree of charity also depends on whether charity is given before the person in need asks and whether the charity is given willingly or under a feeling of duress.

[56] Giacomo Corneo and Hans Peter Grüner (2000) proposed that charitable transfers were limited by the quest to maintain social status.

colleges in which scholars resided provided basic life needs in the form of accommodation, meals, and social life based on social interaction within a community of scholars. Social status depended on scholastic or research achievements and also on the ability to be erudite and witty and thereby please one's colleagues.[57]

Private charity and public assistance

When governments provide income transfers, people may not see the need to contribute twice – once through the taxes that finance government income transfers and again voluntarily through private charity. There may, therefore, be a belief that when government has taken responsibility for helping people in need, private charity is not necessary. A person seeking charity might then be directed to a social worker who can offer guidance on how to obtain income transfers from government. The amount of private charity in that case depends on the extent to which people view government income transfers as substitutes for private giving. If people have utility from personally giving, they will, of course, continue to give personally. The amount of private charity also depends on how many people are prepared to actually give rather than expressively declaring that "something should be done to help the needy." That is, private charity depends on the scope of the free-rider problem in voluntary private charitable transfers. The behavior of the beneficiaries of private charity also determines the amount of private charity. People are unwilling to give if they perceive moral hazard. If recipients are observed to be taking advantage of charitable inclinations, private donors can become disenchanted and their preferences can truly change from those of table 7.7 to those of table 7.8.

B. Experimental evidence on norms of fairness

Conceptions of fairness and generosity that influence voluntary giving are revealed by behavior in two experimental situations known as the *ultimatum game* and the *dictatorship game.*

The ultimatum game

In the ultimatum game, a sum of money is made available for division between two people. One person is chosen to act as the donor and the second as the

[57] The tradition that scholars not marry has origins in the monastic celibacy requirement of the Catholic Church. The requirement that monks (and nuns) and priests not marry has been linked to preservation of property rights of the church. If monks and priests were to have a family, their wife and children could claim the monastery or house in which they lived as their personal property. In the absence of a family, when the priest died, property reverted to the church without contest. Motives for the monastic tradition have also been linked to hereditary monarchs' and the nobility's fears of children of scholars. The minds of scholars become attuned to thinking and studying. The fear was that scholars might have children who would be led to question rules that assured the power and wealth of the hereditary monarchs and the nobility. The hereditary monarchs and nobility married and generally also intermarried.

recipient. The identities of the two people are hidden from one another. The sum of money to be divided might be, for example, $100. The donor is asked to propose a division of the $100. The recipient can respond by accepting or rejecting the division proposed by the donor. If the recipient accepts the proposal, the money is divided according to the donor's proposal. If the recipient rejects the proposal, no one receives anything. The donor and the recipient play the game once only.

Rational behavior in these circumstances is for the recipient to accept any positive sum of money offered by the donor. If the donor offers the recipient $1 out of the $100, the recipient should take the $1. The offer is a take-it-or-leave-it ultimatum and $1 is better than nothing for the recipient. By rejecting the offer, however, the recipient ensures that the donor also receives nothing. Therefore, by rejecting an offer, the recipient can punish "unfair" offers.

Because the game is not repeated with the same people, rejection of an offer does not personally benefit the recipient through disciplining of the donor in future games. By rejecting an offer, the recipient is inflicting self-punishment as the cost of punishing perceived unfair behavior by an anonymous person with whom no further interaction will knowingly take place. The punishment is irrational by economic criteria for efficiency: the principle of Pareto efficiency is that "more is better than less."

A donor who believes that the recipient will reject an unfair offer has reason to make "fair" offers. The ultimatum game involves the following questions:

- How will the recipient behave? Will the recipient act rationally (by economic criteria) and accept any sum of money that the donor offers, or will the recipient reject an offer that he or she feels is unfair?
- What does the donor believe? Which offers does the donor believe that the recipient will accept? Does the donor believe that the recipient will reject a low offer?

It is sufficient for the donor to believe that the recipient will reject a low offer for a low offer not to be made. If the donor believes that the recipient will react to violation of an idea of fairness by not accepting a very unequal offer, we can expect offers of division to be reasonably equal.

If a donor makes an equal offer, we do not know if this is because the donor is a generous person who believes in equal sharing or if the donor fears the recipient's rejection of an unequal offer. Surveys of results from experiments indicate that, in general, donors propose that they keep 60 percent and offer 40 percent to the recipient and that such offers are, in general, accepted.[58] We thus have a "norm of behavior" for ultimatum games.

Table 7.9 shows outcomes of ultimatum games in different locations around the world. In three states of the United States, in Japan, in Israel, and also in Indonesia when the sum to be divided was high, the mode for the proportion offered was one half (the means are less than the mode because some people

[58] Oosterbeek, Sloof, and Van De Kuilen (2004).

TABLE 7.9. OUTCOMES OF THE ULTIMATUM GAME IN DIFFERENT LOCATIONS

	United States			Japan	Israel	Indonesia		Amazon tribe
	CA	PA	AZ			High sum	Low sum	
Numbers (pairs)	15	27	24	29	30	37	94	21
Value	$160	$10	$10	$10	$10	$80–120	$10–15	$160
Mean	0.48	0.45	0.44	0.45	0.36	0.44	0.44	0.26
Mode	0.50	0.50	0.50	0.50	0.50	0.50	0.40	0.15
Rate of rejection	0	0.22	0.083	0.24	0.33	0.081	0.19	0.048
Rejected if >20% offered	0/0	0/1	–	2/4 = 50%	5/7 = 71%	0/0	9/15 = 60%	1/10 = 10%

Source: Summary by Joseph Henrich (2000).

offered less than half).[59] In Indonesia, when the amount divided was a low sum, the modal offer was 40 percent, but some donors offered a greater share, resulting in a higher mean (44 percent).

Rejection rates are also shown, as well as rejections when offers were less than 20 percent. In the Indonesian case, rejections were high when the amount to be divided was small but not when the amount to be divided was high. In Japan and Israel, there were high rejection rates when less than 20 percent was offered. In Israel, although the modal offer was 50 percent, the mean was only 36 percent; just under a quarter of the offers were under 20 percent, on the apparent expectation that the recipients would behave rationally and accept the low offer as better than nothing; however, the rejection rate of the low offer was 71 percent.

The general conclusion is that the prediction of rationality whereby low offers are made and accepted is not borne out; rather, donors make offers based on donors' perceptions of what recipients will regard as fair – or just.

The standard of fairness as near-equal division appears universal. An interpretation is that recipients believe that donors should understand that luck in being chosen as the donor could have gone the other way and that the money should therefore be more or less shared. There is a relationship to the veil of ignorance: behind a veil of ignorance, people do not know whether they will be donors or recipients – and personal outcomes should not depend on which is the case.

Aberrant rational behavior

The aberration in table 7.9 is a tribe in the Peruvian Amazon, for whom the modal offer was only 15 percent and the mean 26 percent. The tribe lived a near-subsistence life in small family and tribal units and had little social contact with other people. The quite small offers that were made were often not rejected. Overall, members of the tribe exhibited a smaller than usual feeling of being obliged to share. Unequal payoffs seemed to be viewed fatalistically as the result of luck: the belief appeared to be that the people who had been chosen as donors had been lucky and the people chosen as recipients had been unlucky, without the equalizing role of a veil of ignorance. The aberration from the norm of fairness as near-equal sharing therefore comes from a nonmarket near-subsistence society. A few participants from the tribe had, however, been exposed to Western culture: when chosen as donors, they made equal sharing offers. We might presume that the people exposed to Western culture knew how their fellow tribe members would behave and that low offers could, therefore, be made and would in all likelihood be accepted. The equal offers therefore reflected a conception of fairness that differed from other members of the tribe who had not been exposed to Western influences. The members of the tribe acted rationally in accepting low offers and also rationally in proposing low offers that they apparently anticipated would be accepted. We anticipate that hunter–gatherer societies will share

[59] The mode is the number that has the highest frequency or the number that the greatest number of people offered.

equally, because of insurance, should any member of a group not succeed in finding sufficient food at any one time. Why did the members of the Amazon tribe not share equally in the ultimatum game? The Amazon Indians were not primarily hunters but rather used the conditions of the rain forest to gather food and also to plant crops, principally manioc, a starch root crop.

Rejections of generous offers

In the ultimatum game, generous offers exceeding half of the money are generally accepted. The complexity of the dependence of societal relationships on culture is illustrated by cases in which generous offers of more than half the money are rejected because the generous offers are regarded as insulting. In an experiment in China, a university student rejected a generous offer with the observation that the person offering the money was "using the mind of a petty man to measure the heart of a gentleman." Chinese middle-school students offered more than half were concerned that they were being offered money that they had done nothing to deserve. The usual response among the students was to divide the money equally because no one deserved the money and certainly no one deserved more money than anyone else.[60]

The dictatorship game

In the dictatorship game, a person who is given a sum of money can dictate how the money is to be shared with another person. The decision of the prospective donor is not strategic because the recipient has no decision to make. The recipient simply keeps any money that he or she is given. By giving away money, donors act expressively in confirming to themselves their self-image as generous and caring persons; or donors may truly belief in sharing, in which case, the question is: What else do they share in other circumstances? In general, less is given in dictatorship games than in ultimatum games. The larger sums given in ultimatum games reflect the additional motive for giving, which is to preempt rejection of the offer.

Punishment of unfair behavior

People tend to punish behavior that is perceived as unfair. In one type of experiment, people who receive money could choose an even division with an anonymous person or keep nearly the entire amount. In a subsequent second round, people deciding on division of the money were told whether the anonymous person with whom they could share the money had shared equally where this person

[60] The study was undertaken by Chen Kang and Fang-Fang Tang (2009), who also reported on cultural differences between Buddhist Tibetans and Han Chinese. Generous offers are also rejected in cultures where "gift exchange" occurs. The generous offers are rejected because of a mindset that a generous offer is a gift that will need to be reciprocated. The mindset is reported as present even though a one-time anonymous interaction is taking place. See Henrich et al. (2001).

decided on a division of money in the first round or kept most of the money. The tendency was to punish the people who were not generous in the first round by not sharing with them in the second round. Moreover, people were prepared to incur a personal cost in order to punish perceived selfish behavior: they were prepared to have less for themselves to ensure less for people who did not share; that is, they were prepared to pay to punish unfairness at a cost to themselves.

Collective decisions

A collective decision by a group usually results in more generous sharing than an individual decision. People care about how others in the group view them and make more generous proposals than if they were anonymously deciding alone. By tending to act more charitably in groups than as individuals, people indicate that they care more about how others perceive them than about how they perceive themselves: they apparently do not feel guilty about being ungenerous but feel shame if others observe them not to be generous.

Norms of reciprocating behavior

By giving money in the dictatorship game, people might be behaving in the way that they would have wanted others to behave with regard to them, had the roles been reversed: that is, they may be following norms of reciprocating behavior. Reciprocal sharing occurred in hunter–gatherer societies: when a successful hunter brought back an animal too big to be eaten alone, the animal was shared with the group; the next time, another hunter might be successful and that hunter would also share his animal with the group. A consistently successful hunter might also be rewarded by finding himself more valued by the women of the group as a progenitor of children who would be expected to be successful hunters.

Anonymous behavior and social approval

People tend to not share when no one observes their behavior. The dictatorship game requires that the donor and recipient be mutually anonymous, so that donors will not be intimidated, embarrassed, or otherwise personally influenced by the recipient when making the sharing decision.[61] The donor or person proposing a division of the money, however, is usually observed by the researcher who is conducting the experiment. When anonymity in the dictatorship game includes the experimenter not being able to know the decision of the donor, amounts given decline, as do the number of people who give at all.[62] The evidence from behavior under complete anonymity confirms that not only self-image (if at all) is involved in the sharing decision but also the desire for social approval. This

[61] A problem with the dictatorship game is that because of the anonymity, the person deciding on division of the money may not believe that the recipient exists.

[62] Elizabeth Hoffman et al. (1994) reported that under conditions of complete anonymity, 64 percent of people kept all the money and only 8 percent gave more than $4 out of $10.

evidence is consistent with the motive of social approval when people propose generous sharing in group decisions.[63]

Dividing earned and unearned money

In some ultimatum and dictatorship experiments, a distinction is made between the sharing of earned and unearned money. Unearned money is a gift. Earned money is "won" in a preliminary contest, with reinforcement that the donor has "earned" and deserves the money. Perhaps predictably, people are less generous in giving away money that they feel they have earned than money they have received as a gift. The natural right of possession comes into play when money has been earned through personal effort.

Differences in behavior between ultimatum and dictatorship games

In the ultimatum game, people give in order to feel good or because they feel that giving is the correct decision, but they also give because they fear retribution. In the dictatorship game, there is no fear of retribution and donors give less to recipients. Indeed, in the dictatorship game, as we observed, little tends to be given at all under conditions of complete anonymity.

> *Comparisons of outcomes of dictatorship and ultimatum games reveal how the role of conceptions of social justice changes under the different circumstances of nonstrategic and strategic behavior.*

In one experiment, donors first observed recipients performing a task that required effort. In dictatorship games, in which behavior is not strategic, donors rewarded recipients on the basis of merit according to the tasks performed; non-deserving recipients who were perceived to have not exerted much effort in their tasks were mildly punished.

When conditions change from the dictatorship game to the ultimatum game, behavior becomes strategic because donors need to consider the responses of recipients, without whose agreement there is nothing to share. As we might predict, with the donor thinking strategically in the ultimatum game and concerned about the response of the donor, conceptions of what the recipient will regard as a "fair" division of the money replace donors' decisions about reward and punishment based on the recipient's effort in assigned tasks. In the change to the ultimatum game, rewards for effort are diminished and punishment for not exerting effort is altogether eliminated.[64]

The role of social justice therefore changes between the two games. In the dictatorship game, donors apply principles of social justice, as expressed in rewards

[63] Kristen Hawkes (1993) reported evidence of the role of social approval as underlying sharing in a hunter–gatherer society.

[64] The experiment was described by Bradley J. Ruffle (1998).

given according to effort or merit: the conception of reward according to merit is related to the natural right of possession. In the ultimatum game, the ability of the recipient to refuse an offer and thereby create circumstances in which the donor has nothing changes the outcome to equality (or the usual 60–40 division because of an advantage given to the donor). However, the equality is not due to a conception of social justice on the part of the donor but rather the threat of reprisal by the recipient.

Gender differences in ultimatum games

Evidence on gender differences in ultimatum games is mixed. Some studies find that men offer more to women than to men. Women also tend to offer more to women than men. Because the income transfers are anonymous other than gender, we can only speculate why men offer more to women to whom they will never be able to communicate their generous behavior. Women offering more to women is explained by solidarity. Other studies show that in ultimatum games, both men and women make lower offers when the recipient is known to be a woman. Women, moreover, are more inclined than men to accept a low offer; in taking the money that is offered, women thus behave rationally.

Gender differences in dictatorship games

Systematic gender differences have been reported in behavior in dictatorship games. A cost of giving can be introduced into dictatorship games: for example, for every $3 given to the recipient, the donor might lose $1 (which is equivalent to an excess burden of taxation and thereby efficiency loss through the leaky bucket of redistribution). Men are more sensitive to the cost of generosity (the value of the loss or price of making the transfer) than women. Whether men or women are more generous therefore depends on the price paid for giving (or the efficiency loss). Men are more generous than women when the cost of giving or efficiency loss is low, and women are more generous than men when the cost of giving (or efficiency loss) is high because women tend to give independently of the price of giving.

These experiments suggest different personal choice of social welfare functions. In the experiments, tokens are transferred from donors to recipients. The tokens have different redemption values for recipients. A loss in value of a token when a donor gives a token to a recipient is the price of giving or efficiency loss from giving. A donor who chooses to maximize the sum of the donor's own income and the income of the recipient is choosing behavior suggestive of the Bentham social welfare function: more men than women maximized the sum of benefits. Women more than men indicated a preference for equality, expressed in the Rawls social welfare function by choosing an equal division of own income and the donor's income: more than half of the women revealed Rawls-type egalitarian preferences compared to a quarter of the men.

However, in the same experiments, half of the men and 40 percent of the women behaved in a self-interested selfish way, keeping all or most of the money for themselves.[65]

C. Intergenerational economic mobility

Social justice without income transfers from government includes opportunities for personal advancement through intergenerational economic mobility. Economic mobility (also sometimes called social mobility) measures how people fare in life relative to their parents. High economic mobility generally requires equal opportunities for personal improvement – and is therefore related to ex-ante equality as the definition of social justice.

Estimates of intergenerational economic mobility

Studies of intergenerational economic mobility estimate the relationship between data on children's incomes Y^{child} and the incomes of their parents Y^{parent} when the parents were at the same stage of life as the children. An equation is estimated for:

$$Y^{child} = a + bY^{parent} + \mu, \tag{7.36}$$

where μ is a random-error term. The constant term a expresses growth (or, if negative, decline) of incomes over time between generations. When incomes are in logarithms, the coefficient b is an elasticity. If the variances of the distributions of Y^{child} and Y^{parent} are equal, b is the correlation coefficient between children's and parents' incomes.

If the data reveals $b = 0$, there is complete economic mobility.[66] If $b = 1$, there is complete immobility.

If $0 < b < 1$, regression to the mean in income inequality is taking place (parents with high incomes do not necessarily have children who will have high incomes and, similarly, parents with low incomes do not necessarily have children who will have low incomes). Francis Galton (1822–1911), who studied inherited human characteristics (Galton, 1889), predicted an equalizing process through regression to the mean of the population because, with the characteristics of a child on average those of the parents, the child is closer to the population mean than at least one of the parents. The averaging process increases equality.[67]

[65] The evidence, based on behavior of students in economics courses at Iowa State University and the University of Wisconsin, was reported by James Andeoni and Lise Vesterlund (2001).

[66] If $b < 0$, higher parental income is associated with lower income of children (that is, children of wealthy parents may decide to live off parental wealth and children of poor parents are motivated to try harder and persistently earn more than their parents).

[67] For example, suppose that we could accurately measure innate ability and that the average measure in a society is 100. Two parents who have respective measures of 120 and 140 have a child who (on average) has a measure of 130, which is closer to the mean than one of the parents.

TABLE 7.10. COMPARISONS OF ECONOMIC MOBILITY, FATHERS AND SONS, b IN EXPRESSION (7.40)

United Kingdom[a]	0.42, 0.57
United States[b]	0.40
Canada[a]	0.23
Sweden[a]	0.13, 0.14, 0.28
Norway[c]	0.155, 0.13
Germany[a]	0.11, 0.34
Finland[a]	0.13, 0.22

Sources: [a]Solon (2002); [b]Solon (1992); Zimmerman (1992); [c]Bratberg, Nilsen, and Vaage (2005).

Although Galton focused on inherited characteristics, peer and neighborhood effects and attitudes within families to encouraging education affect incomes – as well as luck and susceptibility to moral hazard.

Studies for different countries suggest convergence of incomes to the mean over a small number of generations.[68] The estimated value for b in expression (7.35), of course, depends on the sample of people who provide the data for the estimation. Table 7.10 shows measures of economic mobility for males for a sample of high-income countries. With the exception of the United States and the United Kingdom, the countries in table 7.10 have welfare states of different degrees in which the combination of high taxes and high social spending results in high economic mobility.

Characteristics other than income

Table 7.11 shows the range of correlations and the average correlation across generations in the United States in the 20th century for a number of personal economic characteristics other than income. The lowest correlation is for years of schooling and the highest correlation is for consumption. Table 7.11 indicates that the identity of parents matters more in determining personal consumption than personal income, wealth, or wages. It seems that people tend to run down family wealth to maintain consumption at the standards to which they have become accustomed. The intergenerational correlation is higher for income than for wages because income includes the non-wage returns from family assets and wealth. The intergenerational correlation is, in turn, higher for wealth than for wages or income. Wealth is run down across generations, as indicated by the higher correlation across generations of consumption than wealth.

[68] Becker and Tomes (1986) reviewed results of studies for a number of countries. They suggested reversion to the mean as a general rule by the third generation.

TABLE 7.11. U.S. INTERGENERATIONAL ECONOMIC CHARACTERISTICS

Economic characteristic	Range of estimates	Average
Years of schooling	0.14–0.45	0.29
Earnings, wages	0.11–0.59	0.34
Family income	0.14–0.65	0.43
Family wealth	0.27–0.76	0.50
Family consumption	0.59–0.77	0.68

Source: Mulligan (1999).

Should economic mobility be maximized?

There is virtue to economic mobility. The virtue of economic mobility does not imply that ex-post mobility should be maximized but rather that governments should provide conditions of ex-ante equality that allow people to advance themselves on merit. To maximize economic mobility, income consequences of inherited traits would have to be neutralized and inheritances would have to be taxed completely. Alternatively, all wealth and income would need to be collectivized and incomes made independent of abilities. The result is socialism, and we are returned to the adverse consequences of absence of incentives of markets and private property rights, and problems of maximal government.

Assortative mating

Assortative mating occurs when there are systematic rather than random tendencies when males and females sort themselves into couples. High-ability, high-income women may disproportionately tend to have children with high-ability, high-income men – and, conversely, low-ability, low-income women may disproportionately tend to have children with low-ability, low-income men. If people tend to mate with someone in their own group, and abilities are inherited or culturally transmitted from parents, there is reversion to the mean only *within subgroups* of the different sorted groups. Hence:

> *Assortative mating decreases economic mobility.*

There are also consequences of differences in fertility within groups:

> *Social immobility increases if high-ability, high-income women have fewer children than low-ability, low-income women.*

In the limiting case where high-ability, high-income women have no children at all, in the following generation, children of other women replace their missing children in the higher ends of the income distribution.[69]

Economic mobility of women

The studies of economic mobility have focused more on incomes of fathers and sons because of data from eras in which the mother tended to look after children and the family relied on the father's income. For the United States, the available data indicate lower economic mobility for women than men, with consequences for women of associative sorting.[70] In the United Kingdom, the data also indicate lower economic mobility for women than for men.[71] Whether women work is important, and the generation of women that provides the data therefore matters: women born and educated (and who married) when the traditional model of the family was in place exhibit lower economic mobility because of absence of market earnings than women born and educated when women expected to have careers no differently than men.[72]

Meritocracy in labor markets

Economic mobility requires meritocracy in labor markets. There is no point in investing in education and, indeed, being one of the most successful students if jobs are obtained on the basis of privileged family connections. When privilege matters, economic mobility is low because children of privileged families, over time, continue to have the best jobs.[73]

[69] High-ability women who have mated with high-ability men may choose not to work or not to work full-time. Evidence of assortative mating then comes from correlations between income-earning abilities of partners. The correlation between earned incomes of spouses is smaller than the correlation between their hourly wages (which measure the ability to earn income).

[70] Chadwick and Solon (2002) studied the economic mobility of women in the United States and suggested an elasticity for 0.43 of the relationship between women's incomes and parents, below the measure for men of 0.54 (the measure is higher than the 0.4 or so usually reported for men in the United States because of use of family income rather than the father's earnings). They suggested that the difference between men and women revealed by the data may not be statistically significant. Assortative mating is reflected in similarities between the elasticity of women's incomes and husbands' incomes, with respect to women's parents' income.

[71] Dearden, Machin, and Reed (1997) reported values of between 0.4 and 0.6 for men and between 0.45 and 0.7 for women, in each case relative to the income of the father and also years of schooling.

[72] A study in Norway (Bratberg, Nilsen, and Vaage, 2005), for example, compared economic mobility in a welfare state for people born in 1950 and 1960. The results for men in table 7.8 are 0.155 and 0.13, respectively. For women, the corresponding values are 0.221 for 1950 and 0.126 for 1960, indicating increased economic mobility for women, whereas for men, economic mobility changed little.

[73] The privileged families will also be best placed through personal wealth to educate their children. In societies with privilege rather than meritocracy, high returns may be observed to education; however, the observed high returns do not reflect educational attainment but rather the absence of meritocracy in the labor market. If jobs were assigned by merit and not by privileged family

Income distribution and economic mobility

Two people might have respective incomes of 100 and 200. Each has a child, and when the children earn incomes, the child of the low-income parent has the income of 200 and the child of the high-income parent has 100. There has been no change in income distribution but there has been perfect high economic mobility. For economic mobility, it matters whose incomes changed but the income distribution is independent of the identities of the people who have the different incomes. In particular, as the example here shows:

> *High economic mobility does not necessarily imply a more equal income distribution.*

If $b > 1$ in equation (7.36), income inequality increases between generations.[74] However, the data indicate that $b < 1$ and so children of high-income parents have lower incomes on average than their parents, and children of low-income parents have higher incomes on average than their parents. Through reversion to the mean, inequality therefore declines. Thus:

> *For indicated values of b economic mobility reduces income equality without the need for taxation and public spending on income transfers.*

Social instability

Social immobility has often given rise to social instability. The wealth of the hereditary rich has often been appropriated when there has been limited economic mobility.

Economic mobility and social insurance

Economic mobility does not end the demand for social insurance. The time dimensions for social insurance and economic mobility differ. Social insurance is provided for needs that are immediate. Economic mobility involves change over generations.

Moral hazard and economic mobility

As with social insurance, there are moral-hazard problems associated with economic mobility. It may be impossible to observe whether the reason why people

background, observed returns to education would be lower because the return to education would reflect only education and not the hidden influence of privileged family background. Lam and Schoeni (1993) studied privileged family backgrounds and the returns to education in Brazil, where income and wealth distribution were very unequal and observed returns to education were very high, and found that taking family background into account reduced the return to education.

[74] b is an elasticity. If $b > 1$, children persistently earn more than their parents (for example, by 20 percent) but children with higher income parents begin from a larger base.

have not fared well is limited economic mobility or lack of effort to take advantage of available favorable opportunities for economic mobility.

D. Global social justice

There is no global government. Global social justice therefore requires achieving social justice without government.

In some countries, the social insurance contract is nonexistent. Social ties and family relationships substitute for the absent social insurance. People want children, with the hope that the children will look after them in advanced years. They know that they cannot rely on government for help in old age, although life expectancy may be so low that the likelihood of reaching advanced years is also low. In poor countries where there is no social insurance, family relationships often are not sufficient to stave off hunger and deprivation. People who cannot provide for themselves are destitute or starve if not given private charity or not helped through foreign aid.

A global insurance contract behind the veil of ignorance

Being born into a poor family in the poor countries of the world is an event against which we would all seek insurance when designing an insurance contract behind the veil of ignorance. The global social insurance would provide compensating payments for adversity wherever in the world we happen to be born and wherever we happen to find ourselves.

We would want the global social insurance contract, for example, to provide protection against being born into a Nietzschean society in which there is no rule of law and groups of men use their superior physical strength to rape and pillage at will. We would want protection against living in a country run for the benefit of one man, one family, or one tribe, where our home is a hovel with a dirt floor and we have no electricity or running water, and where we do not have access to basic health services or education. The country in which we live might have extensive natural resources but, if we are not members of a privileged family, we would still be very poor. If we live on land where oil is discovered, we may find that not only do we have no benefits from the discovery, but also we are displaced and hounded to distance ourselves from the location where the oil is found. The government may send armed men to rape and pillage – and kill – to force us to move.

When behind the veil of ignorance, we would want protection against being born in a country where a large part of the population is HIV-positive. We would want to avoid being part of the population in countries where men believe that sex with a virgin (of any age) cures them of AIDS. Where the HIV-virus is prevalent, education is lost when children do not go to school and instead stay home to attend to parents and other family members with AIDS. In countries that are poor to begin with, people die of AIDS during what should be their productive years, leaving children as orphans to cope alone.

Women in some societies are exploited and traded and, as we previously noted, subject to inhumane practices to make them subservient to men. There is a bias against educating girls in some cultures. When women are not permitted to leave the home except in the presence of a family member, the limitations on women's activities outside the household restrict employment opportunities and disallow diversities of life available outside the confinement of the home.

Faced with possibilities of adversity in other countries, behind the veil of ignorance we would want a global insurance contract that applies wherever we would be born.

The World Bank and global insurance

Global social insurance is expressed in bilateral aid programs of governments of richer countries and the aid resources provided by international aid agencies. The International Monetary Fund and regional development banks provide resources intended to maintain economic stability and to stimulate economic growth; however, the major international agency concerned with helping poor people in poor countries is the World Bank.

Insurance, in principle, compensates for random adverse events. The foreign assistance provided because of adversity in poor countries has not been random. Rather, aid has been given systematically to the same countries over the course of time. The evidence indicates, moreover, that the aid provided to governments of poor countries has been ineffective in helping the large parts of populations that are poor to escape from poverty. Aid resources are provided but the poor in poor countries stay poor.[75]

The distinction between "poor people in poor countries" and "poor countries" is important. There are rich people in poor countries. The rich generally are connected to government or seek to ensure that they have family members among government officials. The purpose of the family members in government is to provide opportunities for other members of the family to enrich themselves through government-provided privilege; family members in government also protect family assets from the government. Poor countries (or countries with low per capita incomes) tend to have more unequal distributions of income (or more

[75] The empirical evidence on the ineffectiveness of aid was reviewed by Hristos Doucouliagos and Martin Paldam (2008). The data for their study consisted of the results of prior empirical studies. Initial empirical studies were optimistic in the results reported about the effectiveness of aid. As the database expanded over time, the results in the studies converged to zero effectiveness. Doucouliagos and Paldam's review of the empirical studies suggests that the optimistic results were often reported by people in the "aid industry" who had an interest in showing that the aid provided by the agencies for which they worked was effective.

social inequality) than richer countries, before and after social insurance (if there is any social insurance in the poor countries).

Moral hazard

Aid donors, acting as if under the terms of a global insurance contract, appear to have confronted moral-hazard problems. Resources have been provided to governments in poor countries with the intention that the governments would improve the conditions of the poor by public spending on health care, education, and infrastructure. Yet, after resources have been provided, additional resources have been required – and still more – in a process that yielded little or no improvement in the lives of the poor. The phenomenon of continued aid with little or no benefit (or deterioration of living standards) for poor people in poor countries was described by William Easterly (2001), who recounted his experiences as an economist seeking at the World Bank to improve the lives of the poor in poor countries. The World Bank, over the decades since its founding in 1944, made concessional loans and provided aid resources to governments of poor countries on condition that governments choose public policies that improve the lives of the poor. Easterly pointed out that the aid continued to the governments even if the governments did not fulfill their obligation of using the resources to help the poor:

> ...even if the conditions are not met, the donors want to alleviate the lot of the poor, and so they give the aid anyway. The recipients can anticipate this behavior of donors and thus sit tight without doing reforms or helping the poor.[76]

Easterly described the poor in poor countries as hostages held by their own governments:

> The poor are held hostage to extract aid from the donors.[77]

The governments that receive the aid do not wish the conditions of the poor in their countries to improve because the World Bank and other donors would then no longer provide aid that the local rulers can appropriate for themselves.

There is asymmetric information and so moral hazard if the World Bank cannot observe the efforts of the governments in using aid resources to help the poor. However, the circumstances are often not those of asymmetric information; the appropriation of resources intended for the poor by government officials in poor countries is common knowledge. The World Bank knows the appropriation takes place and the government officials who appropriate the aid resources know that the World Bank knows.

[76] Easterly (2001), p. 116.
[77] Ibid.

The World Bank confronts the problem of how to respond to appropriation of aid for personal benefit by government officials. One response is to view the theft of resources intended for poor as an inevitable tax that needs to be paid to help the poor. The rate of taxation is the proportion of aid resources taken by government officials and elites in poor countries. In Indonesia, after a change of government, the new government requested that the World Bank deduct from the country's debts the part of past foreign aid that had not benefited the population but had rather been appropriated by the family of the previous president. The case for refusing the request is that without permitting the theft by the ruling family, the World Bank would have been unable to provide the loans for development assistance. The theft provided the incentive for the government to allow the assistance.

Debt forgiveness

Although some extremely poor countries received direct grants, World Bank assistance has been provided in the form of concessionary loans (loans at low interest rates). Some governments cannot repay the loans, although by defaulting on World Bank loans, governments in poor countries in general lose access to borrowing possibilities in world capital markets. When debts cannot be repaid, pressures arise to cancel the debts, on the grounds that the debts impede ongoing development assistance through new loans. Moral hazard arises through cancellation of debts. Canceling debts is intended to provide the opportunity for a fresh start. Yet, after the debt has been canceled, new debt soon reaches levels at which the only solution is again cancellation of the debt. Commenting on this cycle of indebtedness and debt cancellation, William Easterly observed that:

> The same mismanagement of funds that caused the high debt will prevent the aid sent through debt relief from reaching the truly poor.[78]

The principal–agent problem

Aid resources in poor countries thus enrich local political leaders and government officials and their families, and avarice and corruption in government underlie the empirical findings that aid has been ineffective in improving the lives of the poor in poor countries. There is a principal–agent problem. Donors such as the World Bank that provide the aid resources should be the principals. Governments in poor countries should be agents who dispense the resources to help the poor as intended by the principals. However, governments in poor countries become the principals and the aid resources intended to help the poor are diverted.

Table 7.12 shows the dilemma confronting an aid agency such as the World Bank. The first number is the utility of the donor (the World Bank) and the

[78] Ibid., p. 136.

TABLE 7.12. THE DILEMMA OF FOREIGN AID

	Government in the poor country helps the poor	Government in the poor country does not help the poor
Donor gives aid	4, 1	3, 4
Donor does not give aid	2, 2	1, 3

second number is the utility of the government receiving the aid (not the utility of the poor whom the aid is intended to benefit). The decision facing the donor is whether to provide aid. The decision facing the government in the poor country is whether to use the aid for the intended objective of helping the poor.

The donor's first preference, 4, is that the aid is given and reaches the poor. The donor's second preference, 3, is that the aid is given and does not reach the poor. The donor has benefit 2 if the aid is not given and the government wishes to help the poor and has the lowest benefit 1 when the aid is not given and the government does not wish to help the poor.

The best outcome, 4, for the government is to receive the aid and not help the poor. Next best is 3 if the aid is not given. The outcome at 2 for the government occurs if there is no aid and the government tries ineffectually to help the poor. The worst outcome 1 for the government is that aid is given and reaches the poor.

The dominant strategy of the donor is to give and the dominant strategy of the government is not helping the poor. The Nash equilibrium is at (3,4). The aid is given and is appropriated.

The benefits to the recipient government from theft of aid resources

If aid resources reach the poor, the circumstances of the poor will improve; however, if the poor do not remain poor, there will be no more aid for the government in the aid-receiving country to appropriate because the donor's aid program will have been successful. The government in the poor country also does not want the aid to reach the poor because a middle class that would emerge through economic development will seek democracy and accountability from rulers. Appropriation of aid resources, therefore, provides the government with two benefits: there is a direct benefit through the resources stolen and a further benefit in that calls for democracy and accountability that would accompany successful economic development are preempted.

The incentives of the donor

Why does the donor persist in giving the aid given that the dominant strategy of the government is to not use aid resources to help the poor? The donor and the recipient government are in a repeated game in which beliefs and reputation can matter. The government is the gatekeeper for delivering the aid and perhaps the donor believes (or wants to believe) that the government will change for the better. As Easterly pointed out, the donor feels obligated to be a donor and to give. The donor therefore continues to give, hoping that a new government will arise that cares about the poor; therefore, aid can persist even if ineffective in helping the poor.

We noted that the donor can view appropriation by the aid-receiving government as a tax that allows some of the aid to reach the poor in poor countries. Consistently, the recipient government wishes to keep collecting the tax. However, the recipient government must ensure that the poor stay sufficiently poor for the aid resources that are taxed to continue to be forthcoming. Ineffective aid then persists.

Our explanation for the continuation of ineffective aid rests on the dominant strategy of the donor, which is to give. However, the donor may cease giving when the behavior of a recipient government oversteps bounds of reasonableness. Aid can then always continue to other governments. A donor would be in a difficult position if there were no one to try to help. The World Bank and its highly professional staff exist to help people in need in poor countries.

Global representative government

Global government could implement the global insurance contract that we would all seek behind the veil of ignorance. We do not have global government. Do we want global government? To see what global representative government might look like, we move from the professional agencies of the World Bank as well as the International Monetary Fund to the United Nations (UN). The UN is the closest institution to global representative government. The UN reflects the attributes of governments of the individual member countries. The whole is the sum of the parts. The governments that appropriate the aid resources intended to help the poor are represented at the UN. The corruption that is institutionalized in many UN member countries and norms of personal behavior are retained and transposed to the new organizational setting when government officials leave their home-government bureaucracies for positions in the UN bureaucracy.[79]

Would the global social insurance contract that we would choose behind the veil of ignorance be implemented by a global government? The same political

[79] Studies contained in the volume edited by George Abed and Sanjeev Gupta (2002) describe and document corruption in governments in poor countries. A study by Emanuele Baldacci et al. (2004) found that economic growth in poor countries increased when government spending fell, indicating that the marginal effect of government spending on growth was negative. Two researchers at the World Bank had access to detailed data that allowed them to trace public spending on schooling for children in Uganda. The researchers, Ritva Reinikka and Jakob Svensson found, in a study published in 2004, that only 13 percent of the money assigned by government for the schools actually reached the schools and the children. The remaining 87 percent of the money was appropriated by government officials.

leaders and government officials who interfere with and prevent global social insurance when the World Bank and other donors attempt to help the poor in poor countries would be part of the global government that would be responsible for the global social insurance program. Were there to be global government, we would risk losing the social insurance contracts that we have in our own societies.[80]

Supplement S7

Supplement S7A: Measurement of income inequality

If social justice is related to income inequality, we require means of measuring the extent of inequality. There are a number of possible measures; here, we consider two.

An often-used measure of inequality is known as the *Gini coefficient*. Figure S7.1a shows how the Gini coefficient is computed. With a given population and a given distribution of income among the members of the population, the horizontal axis measures the proportion of income and the vertical axis measures the proportion of the population. Along the 45° line, there is complete equality of incomes: 25 percent of the population has 25 percent of the income, 50 percent of the population has 50 percent of the income, and so on. The curved line, which is known as a *Lorenz curve*, shows the actual income distribution. At point 1, 50 percent of the population has 50 percent of the income, but point 2 on the Lorenz curve indicates that, in fact, for the society that the Lorenz curve represents, 50 percent of the population has more than 50 percent of the income. The Gini coefficient is the shaded area divided by the area on one side of the diagonal (half the box). The smaller the shaded area, the more equal is the income distribution. When the Lorenz curve and the 45° line coincide, the shaded area disappears and the Gini coefficient reaches its minimum value of zero, at which there is complete income equality.[81]

[80] Corruption occurs in the World Bank and the International Monetary Fund but is an aberration. Why is there such a difference between these organizations and the United Nations? Whereas the United Nations General Assembly gives one country one vote, at the World Bank and the International Monetary Fund, voting is through accountability predicated on the resources that countries provide. Indeed, important decisions at the United Nations are made by the Security Council, where permanent members can exercise the right of veto.

[81] When there are n people in the population with incomes $\{y_1, \ldots, y_n\}$ and with average income y_a, the Gini coefficient is computed as:

$$\frac{1}{N^2 y_a} \sum_{i=1}^{N} \sum_{j=1}^{N} \frac{|y_i - y_j|}{2}.$$

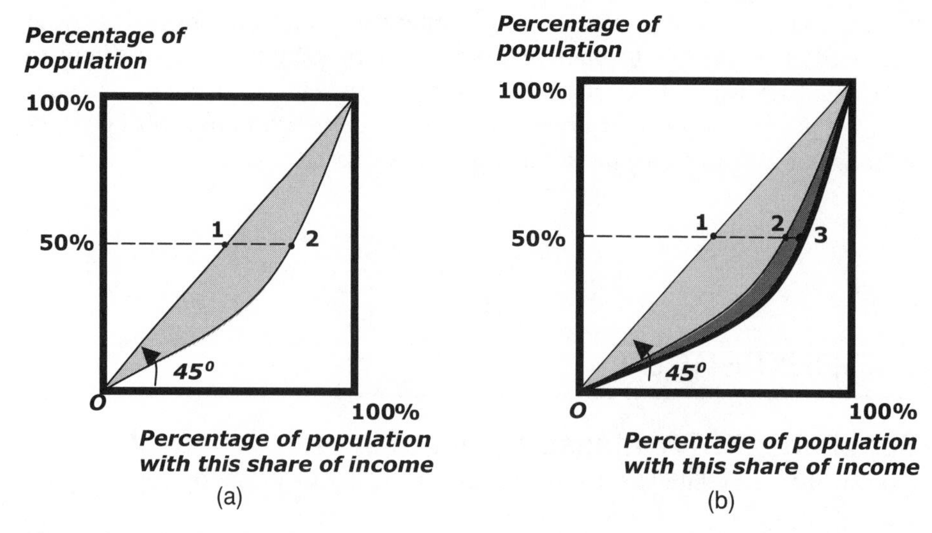

Figure S7.1. (a) The Gini coefficient as a measure of economic inequality. (b) A comparison between two income distributions.

Figure S7.1b shows a comparison between income distributions in two societies. We see that one society has a more unequal distribution of income than the other. At point 1, 50 percent of the population would have 50 percent of the income. Comparing points 2 and 3, we see that at point 2, 50 percent of the population has a smaller share of income than at point 3. For any percentage of the population, the society with the larger Gini coefficient (whose Lorenz curve is farther to the right) has a more unequal income distribution.

When two people together earn \$100 of income, the value of the Gini coefficient is defined by the percentage of income above 50 percent earned by the higher income person. For example, if one person earns \$70 and the other \$30, the Gini coefficient is 0.2. If one person earns \$90 and the other \$10, the Gini coefficient is 0.4. When each person earns \$50, the Gini coefficient is zero, confirming complete equality.

Without the leaky bucket of income distribution and with identical utility for all people, all symmetric social welfare functions are maximized when post-tax incomes are equal. Any income inequality therefore reduces social welfare. A measure of inequality therefore can be based on the welfare loss from deviation from full-equality maximum social welfare if there were no leaky bucket – that is, if all people contributed according to their abilities so that there are no efficiency losses through the excess burden of taxation when income is transferred. Such a measure was proposed by Anthony Atkinson in 1970. When y_a is the average income of the population and everyone has the same utility function (so Arrow's impossibility theorem is not a problem, see the next supplement), the Bentham social welfare function is maximized by giving everyone the average income (see also chapter 6 on the outcome of majority voting on redistribution when there are no excess burdens of taxation). Maximal social welfare is greater than (or not less than) the social welfare attained with the actual distribution of income; that is:

$$\max W = \sum_{i=1}^{N} u(y_a) \geq \sum_{i=1}^{N} u(y_i). \tag{S7.1}$$

Let the certainty-equivalent income that provides the same utility as the mean income y_a be y_c. The risk premium is $(y_a - y_c)$. The measure of inequality is:

$$A \equiv \frac{\textit{risk premium}}{\textit{mean income}} = \frac{y_a - y_c}{y_a}. \tag{S7.2}$$

This measure is invariant to the scale on which income is measured if and only if relative risk aversion R is constant, in which case:

$$\begin{aligned} A &\equiv 1 - \frac{1}{y_a}\left[\frac{1}{N}\sum_{i=1}^{N} y_i^{1-r}\right]^{\frac{1}{1-r}} \qquad R > 0, r \neq 1 \\ A &\equiv 1 - \frac{1}{y_a}(y_1 y_2 y_3 \ldots y_N)^{\frac{1}{N}} \qquad \text{for } R = 1 \end{aligned} \tag{S7.3}$$

Inequality reduces social welfare. Take two distributions of income:

$$\begin{aligned} &y_1, y_2, y_3, \ldots, y_N \\ &y_1^*, y_2^*, y_3^*, \ldots, y_N^* \end{aligned} \tag{S7.4}$$

with the same mean. The first gives higher (or not lower) social welfare if:

$$\sum_{i=1}^{N} u(y_i) \geq \sum_{i=1}^{N} u(y_i^*). \tag{S7.5}$$

This is so if and only if the Lorenz curve for the y distribution dominates the Lorenz curve for the y^* distribution.[82]

Supplement S7B: An impossibility theorem for social aggregation

A social welfare function is an aggregate measure of the total welfare of the members of a society. The members of a society have preferences over their own consumption, the consumption of others, the different public goods in society, and externalities for which markets do not exist, all of which should be acknowledged in a social welfare function. Kenneth Arrow (1950) proposed axioms that

[82] Income distributions can result in Lorenz curves that cross, in which case another way of comparing inequality is required. See Anthony Shorrocks (1983).

preferences expressed in the social welfare function should satisfy, including that there be no dictator whose personal preferences dictate the outcome for the rest of the society.[83] Arrow derived an "impossibility theorem" and concluded:

> If we exclude the possibility of interpersonal comparisons of utility, then the only methods of passing from individual tastes to social preferences which will be satisfactory and which will be defined for a wide range of individual orderings are either imposed or dictatorial.[84]

Arrow reached his conclusion about his impossibility theorem by excluding "the possibility of interpersonal comparisons of utility." We, however, have adopted interpersonal comparisons of utility in viewing all people as identical when choosing the social welfare function behind the veil of ignorance. We viewed people as identical or equal because we acknowledged that we had no way of measuring and thereby comparing utilities of people, but also we did not want to give people privilege or penalize people through different personal capacities to benefit from income. Arrow's impossibility theorem tells us that a social welfare function that aggregates over preferences of individuals whom we acknowledge are different and have different visions of how society ought to distribute income and provide public goods requires allowing a dictator to choose on behalf of society – or the range of outcomes over which social choices are made needs to be restricted. The field of social choice is concerned with consequences of the relaxation of the conditions that underlie Arrow's impossibility theorem.

Summary

A first view of social justice is in terms of the natural right of possession protected by the rule of law. In chapter 1, when we considered outcomes in which the rule of law is absent and the strong take what they wish from the weak, we saw that social justice was absent and efficiency was not achieved because institutions were missing that would protect the natural right of possession of people to the output they had produced or to the value they had created. The natural right of possession of people to the income they have earned is likewise compromised when people are compelled through taxes to give part of their income

[83] The conditions include that a social choice can always be made between alternatives. If social state A is preferred to B and B is preferred to C, then A is preferred to C – that is, transitivity. Another condition is "independence of irrelevant alternatives" (for example, a person who has decided to vote for a political candidate in preference to rival candidates does not change his or her vote when one of the rival candidates drops out of the political contest). Arrow also required "citizens' sovereignty," which is that individuals in a society "be free to choose, by varying their values, among the alternatives available. That is, alternatives are not externally excluded from the possibilities of citizens' choices by some outside rule."

[84] Arrow and Scitovsky (1969, p. 64).

to others. Compulsory income transfers through taxation are inconsistent with Pareto improvement. In this chapter, we have investigated how, nevertheless, tax-financed income transfers might be normatively justified, even though the taxpayer is made worse off and the income recipient gains. The normative justification for involuntary income redistribution is in terms of insurance.

1A. Risk-averse people confronting uncertainty about income have a demand for insurance. The demand is expressed in the difference between certainty-equivalent income and the value of the fair gamble given by uncertain outcomes for income. A competitive insurance market or mutual risk pooling efficiently provides the complete insurance that people want. Complete insurance results in ex-post equality of incomes, which is socially just if people are identical before uncertainty about personal incomes is resolved. There can be no insurance after personal outcomes have been revealed. The insurance contract, therefore, is entered into behind a veil of ignorance.

1B. The metaphor of the veil of ignorance allowed us to consider people as if they know nothing about themselves or others. Behind the veil of ignorance, people can only be identical, so we assigned a common utility function to the population. To preserve anonymity and to avoid privilege, we also considered only symmetric social welfare functions. The insurance decided behind a veil of ignorance is social, through government, because the government implements the insurance contract after people emerge from behind the veil of ignorance and so know whether they have high or low market-earned income. Because the insurance contract is implemented through government, there is a leaky bucket of redistribution, due to the efficiency losses through the excess burden of taxation.

1C. A social welfare function defines a social insurance contract and expresses social aversion to inequality. Bentham and Rawls are limiting cases, with Bentham maximizing the sum of utilities and so expressing no social aversion to inequality and Rawls expressing complete aversion to inequality by focusing on the worst-off person; a Nash social welfare function is a case between Bentham and Rawls. If not subject to the constraint of the Laffer curve, Rawls provides complete insurance. If there is no leak in the bucket of redistribution, all symmetric social welfare functions, including Bentham and Rawls, provide complete insurance. Social welfare functions therefore differ in social insurance and aversion to inequality only when there is a trade-off between equality and efficiency (where efficiency is expressed as higher expected or average utility). Choice of Bentham is justified by the rationality of maximizing expected utility. Prospect theory describes people departing from maximization of expected utility in a way consistent with choosing Rawls. Or people may choose Rawls to avoid regret. The extent of the leak in the bucket of redistribution determines the social loss from providing more insurance than the incomplete insurance of Bentham. A work ethic reduces a society's costs of choosing Rawls. Some welfare states chose Rawls-type social insurance but maintained high average incomes. The evidence of tax evasion and a significant informal economy in the welfare states is consistent with a work ethic because people do not respond to high taxes by substituting leisure for work. Departure from Bentham entails subjectively placing higher weights on adverse outcomes than warranted by objective probabilities. Although Bentham is justified by the rationality of maximizing expected utility, maximization of the Bentham sum of utilities of the population is, however, subject to the restrictions of the rule of law.

1D. When the population has emerged from behind the veil of ignorance, the government avoids adverse selection and a time-inconsistency problem by making participation in social insurance compulsory. This is what people choosing a social welfare function and a social insurance contract behind the veil of ignorance would have wanted.

In section 2, we studied social insurance in the presence of moral hazard. Personal outcomes then were no longer predetermined solely by fate but rather depended on personal efforts to be self-reliant.

2A. We distinguished two effort decisions: the effort decision of taxpayers when confronting work–leisure choices that underlie the leaky bucket of redistribution and the decision to exert effort to be self-reliant and so avoid the need for tax-financed income transfers. People whose personal behavior is not guided by a work ethic and who therefore do not exert effort to be self-reliant are susceptible to moral hazard. When the entire population is susceptible to moral hazard, the income pooling of complete insurance combined with the personal cost of effort give rise to a prisoners' dilemma. In the Nash equilibrium, everyone exerts low effort at self-reliance. Voluntary insurance then fails because of moral hazard: people can do better by exerting high effort and avoiding the common-pool problem of shared incomes.

2B. Behavior is not subject to moral hazard if there is no random component of income or effort is observable. There is also no moral hazard if the entire population has a work ethic.

2C. More generally, populations consist of both people who have a work ethic and people susceptible to moral hazard. With voluntary insurance, in the Nash equilibrium, people with a work ethic systematically pay parts of their income to people susceptible to moral hazard. There is adverse selection when the people with a work ethic exit the voluntary insurance pool. A society that begins with a population that has a work ethic can become diverse with moral hazard present because of changes in norms of behavior of part of the population. Through adverse selection, immigrant populations can introduce moral hazard. Adverse selection can also take place through emigration. Slavery is inconsistent with a work ethic. Experience with and presumption of discrimination can inhibit a work ethic, as can cultural retention of norms of behavior from when common property prevented personal wealth accumulation.

2D. Adverse selection, moral hazard, and also inability to verify the outcomes against which insurance is sought result in failure of private markets to provide insurance. Suitably incomplete insurance preempts moral hazard; and if everyone is exerting high effort to be reliant, there is also no adverse selection. The Bentham social insurance contract provides incomplete insurance based on the leaky bucket of redistribution; the question is whether a public policy to preempt moral hazard requires insurance that is more incomplete than Bentham. There is a social dilemma in using incomplete insurance to resolve the moral-hazard problem because people who have experienced unfortunate outcomes through no fault of their own may be insufficiently helped. Choice of public policy depends on sensitivity to type-1 and type-2 errors: an increased likelihood of a type-1 error disadvantages people who are victims of exogenous misfortune; an increased likelihood of a type-2 error benefits people who take advantage of society's benevolence and do not make an effort to be self-reliant. The public policy decision is political or ideological. A position associated with the left of the political spectrum is that type-2 errors do not exist: this view regards all people with low incomes as victims of misfortune with outcomes predetermined and so beyond their personal control. In that case, moral hazard is not recognized to exist. The right of the political spectrum emphasizes that personal actions have personal consequences and views personal outcomes in life as foremost reflecting the personal decision whether to choose effort at self-reliance. Unobservable effort allows the views of left and right to coexist. We cannot resolve the disagreements regarding moral hazard. We can but make our own judgments in our own communities and societies.

The final section of this chapter considered social justice without government.

3A. Prospects for voluntary income redistribution without government depend on how charitable feelings are expressed. There is a prisoners' dilemma and taxes are required if charitable feelings are expressed as caring about the unfortunate but with a preference that others give. People may not directly give money to others but may vote on income redistribution: when voting is expressive, outcomes can be contrary to the income redistribution that would occur if people knew that their votes were decisive. We also considered voluntary income transfers when people experience utility from giving. We observed that benevolence of donors can be exploited: we investigated a case in which a donor who derives utility from personally helping others confronts a recipient without a work ethic. The donor prefers to help the recipient with supplemental income support when the recipient at the same time makes an effort to be self-reliant. In the Nash equilibrium, the recipient does not attempt to be self-reliant. The donor can attempt to misrepresent preferences to induce the recipient to work, but because of questions of credibility a role for government emerges through a bureaucracy that disburses entitlements according to rules, not discretion. Degrees of charity can be ranked according to whether the donor knows the identity of the recipient and the recipient knows the identity of the donor, and other criteria. The quest for status leads people to give conspicuously to charity; the desire to maintain status, however, can impede charitable donations.

3B. We considered attitudes to fairness and charitable behavior expressed through behavior in ultimatum and dictatorship games. In both cases, people in general behave contrary to the prediction of self-interested rational behavior. In the ultimatum game, donors in general divide the money more or less equally, either because they favor equality or fear retribution. In dictatorship games, donors are also often generous: however, when the decision is entirely anonymous with the experimenter also not knowing the division, behavior of donors is not generous. Behavior varies among cultures. Members of an Amazon tribe provided an aberration of the ultimatum game by proposing and accepting low offers, which is rational although perhaps fatalistic behavior. In experiments where donors earn the money to be redistributed by performing tasks that require effort, the donors are more inclined to keep money rather than give money away. Behavior changes between dictatorship and ultimatum games: donors reward effort when making transfers to recipients in the dictatorship game, which is consistent with a rule for social justice of natural right of possession; in ultimatum games, the donor does not correspondingly reward effort of the recipient. Evidence on gender differences in behavior in ultimatum games is mixed. In dictatorship games, men are influenced more than women by the efficiency losses of income transfers; women tend to give independently of the cost of giving. Evidence indicates that men behave more in accord with a Bentham social welfare function and women more in accord with a Rawls social welfare function. Still, in these experiments, half of men and 40 percent of women kept all or most of the money for themselves. People behave more generously when the donor decision is made collectively.

3C. Economic mobility offers social justice without income transfers from governments – although economic mobility requires that governments provide equal educational opportunities and thereby ex-ante equality. Social justice through economic mobility is expressed in reward according to ability or merit, with personal incomes of children not determined by incomes of parents. Societies differ in social or economic mobility. Associative sorting is an impediment to economic mobility, unless high-ability women have low fertility. Economic mobility can take place without changes in income redistribution: for income distribution, it does not matter who receives income so with the same income distribution, people can trade places through economic mobility. The data in Western democracies indicate increasing equality in income distribution as a consequence of economic mobility because of reversion toward the mean of the income distribution. Women in the past experienced less economic mobility than men. Economic mobility is not a substitute for social insurance because of different time dimensions. There can be moral hazard through effort choices to take advantage of opportunities through economic mobility.

3D. Behind a veil of ignorance, we would want insurance to include the possibility of being born into a poor family in a poor country. There is, however, no global government to provide global social justice. The World Bank and other donors attempt to provide global insurance through aid to governments in poor countries. Global representative government cannot be expected to achieve global social justice. A global government, if representative, would include representatives of the many governments in the world that have impeded attempts by the World Bank and other donors to implement a global insurance contract.

Supplement S7A described measures of inequality. Supplement S7B described the Arrow impossibility theorem.

S7A. The Gini coefficient is a measure of income inequality. Other measures include a measure based on deviations from the equality that is obtained by maximizing a symmetric social welfare function when there are no leaks in the bucket of redistribution.

S7B. The Arrow impossibility theorem states that in general a social welfare function that encompasses the preferences of all people in a society cannot be found and that social decisions therefore require dictatorship. The theorem rests on absence of interpersonal comparisons of utility. We allowed for interpersonal comparisons of utility and regarded all people as having identical utility functions, to prevent privilege or adverse discrimination through different utility functions attributed to different people.

Literature notes

7.1 Social justice and insurance

For evidence on exogenous luck or fate in life, see:

Black, S., P. Devereux, and K. Salvanes, 2005. Why the apple doesn't fall far: Understanding intergenerational transmission of human capital. *American Economic Review* 95:437–49.

Currie, J., and E. Moretti, 2003. Mother's education and the intergenerational transmission of human capital: Evidence from college openings. *Quarterly Journal of Economics* 118:1495–532.

Duncan, G. J., and J. Brooks-Gunn (Eds.), 1997. *Consequences of Growing Up Poor.* Russell Sage Foundation, New York.

A controversial study is Herrnstein and Murray (1994). For a commentary, see Goldberger and Manski (1995).

Goldberger, A. S., and C. F. Manski, 1995. The Bell Curve: Intelligence and Class Structure in American Life by Richard J. Herrnstein and Charles Murray. *Journal of Economic Literature* 33:762–76.

Herrnstein, R. J., and C. Murray, 1995. *The Bell Curve: Intelligence and Class Structure in American Life.* The Free Press, New York.

Original writings of Bentham and Rawls are:

Bentham, J., 1879. *An Introduction to the Principles of Morals and Legislation.* The Clarendon Press, Oxford.

Rawls, J. A., 1971. *A Theory of Justice.* Belknap Press, Cambridge MA.

On interpersonal comparisons of utility, see:

Ng, Y.-K., 1997. A case for happiness, cardinalism, and interpersonal comparability. *Economic Journal* 107:1848–58.

Social welfare functions to be maximized by social planners were described by Bergson (1938) and Samuelson (1947).

Bergson, A., 1938. A reformulation of certain aspects of welfare economics. *Quarterly Journal of Economics* 52:310–34. Reprinted in K. J. Arrow and T. Scitovsky (Eds.), 1969. *Readings in Welfare Economics.* Irwin, Homewood IL, pp. 7–25.

Samuelson, P. A., 1947. *Foundations of Economic Analysis.* Harvard University Press, Cambridge MA.

On the foundations for expected utility, see Von Neumann and Morgenstern (1944). On Bentham and expected utility, see Harsanyi (1955).

Harsanyi, J. C., 1955. Cardinal welfare, individualistic ethics, and interpersonal comparisons of utility. *Journal of Political Economy* 63:209–321. Reprinted in K. J. Arrow and T. Scitovsky (Eds.), 1969. *Readings in Welfare Economics.* Irwin, Homewood IL, pp. 46–60.

Von Neumann, J., and O. Morgenstern, 1944. *Theory of Games and Economic Behavior.* Princeton University Press, Princeton NJ.

Varian (1980) and Sinn (1995) presented views of income redistribution as insurance provided through government.

Sinn, H.-W., 1995. A theory of the welfare state. *Scandinavian Journal of Economics* 97: 495–526.
Varian, H. R., 1980. Redistributive taxation as social insurance. *Journal of Public Economics* 14:49–68.

The term *leaky bucket* is from Okun (1975). See also Browning and Johnson (1984) and Ballard (1988).

Ballard, C. L., 1988. The marginal efficiency cost of redistribution. *American Economic Review* 78:1019–33.
Browning, E. K., and W. R. Johnson, 1984. The trade-off between equality and efficiency. *Journal of Political Economy* 92:175–203.
Okun, A. M., 1975. *Equality and Efficiency: The Big Tradeoff*. Brookings Institution Press, Washington DC.

On the work ethic, see Weber (1905/1920/1958) and Congleton (1991). For evidence on the relationship between religion and income, see McCleary and Barro (2006).

Congleton, R. D., 1991. The economic role of a work ethic. *Journal of Economic Behavior and Organization* 15:365–85.
McCleary, R. M., and R. J. Barro, 2006. Religion and the economy. *Journal of Economic Perspectives* 20:49–72.
Weber, M., 1905/1920/1958. *The Protestant Ethic and the Spirit of Capitalism*. Scribner, New York.

Akerlof (1970) described adverse selection.

Akerlof, G., 1970. The market for "lemons": Quality uncertainty and the market mechanism. *Quarterly Journal of Economics* 84:488–500.

On prospect theory, see Kahneman and Tversky (1979). See also Quiggin (1982) and Yaari (1987).

Kahneman, D., and A. Tversky, 1979. Prospect theory: An analysis of decision under risk. *Econometrica* 47:313–27.
Quiggin, J., 1982. A theory of anticipated utility. *Journal of Economic Behavior and Organization* 3:323–43.
Yaari, M., 1987. The dual theory of choice under risk. *Econometrica* 55:95–117.

7.2 Moral hazard

On hunter–gatherers, see Hawkes (1993).

Hawkes, K., 1993. Why do hunter–gatherers work? An ancient version of the problem of public goods. *Current Anthropology* 34:314–61.

On migration and welfare payments, see Borjas (1999), Dodson (2001), and Nannestad (2004). See Huntington (1996) on cultural differences.

Borjas, G., 1999. *Heaven's Door*. Princeton University Press, Princeton NJ.
Dodson, M. E., 2001. Welfare generosity and locational choices among U.*S*. immigrants. *International Review of Law and Economics* 21:47–68.
Huntington, S. P., 1996. *The Clash of Civilizations and the Making of World Order*. Simon and Schuster, New York.

Nannestad, P., 2004. Immigration as a challenge to the Danish welfare state? *European Journal of Political Economy* 20:755–67.

7.3 Social justice without government

On interdependent utilities and voluntary income transfers, see Hochman and Rogers (1969). Sugden (1982) pointed out limitations of using Nash behavior to describe voluntary giving.

Hochman, H. M., and J. D. Rogers, 1969. Pareto optimal redistribution. *American Economic Review* 59:542–57.
Sugden, R., 1982. On the economics of philanthropy. *Economic Journal* 92:341–50.

On the effect of government income transfers on private charity, see:

Abrams, B. A., and M. S. Schmitz, 1978. The crowding-out effect of government transfers on private charitable contributions. *Public Choice* 33:29–40.
Roberts, R. D., 1984. A positive model of private charity and public transfers. *Journal of Political Economy* 92:136–48.

The donor's dilemma was set out in:

Buchanan, J. M., 1975. The Samaritan's dilemma. In E. Phelps (Ed.), *Altruism, Morality and Economic Theory*. Russell Sage Foundation, New York, pp. 71–87.

On social status and giving, see Veblen (1899/1934). Harbaugh (1998) distinguished between the utility of giving and the utility of being seen to give and presented evidence showing that visibility in giving increases voluntary giving. Glazer and Konrad (1996) described social status as an incentive for charitable giving. Corneo and Grüner (2000) proposed that preservation of social status is an impediment to charitable transfers. Congleton (1989) pointed out that status seeking is a contest similar to rent seeking but with potential beneficial externalities.

Congleton, R. D., 1989. Efficient status seeking: Externalities and the evolution of status games. *Journal of Economic Behavior and Organization* 11:175–90.
Corneo, G., and H.-P. Grüner, 2000. Social limits to redistribution. *American Economic Review* 90:1491–507.
Glazer, A., and K. A. Konrad, 1996. A signaling explanation for charity. *American Economic Review* 86:1019–28.
Harbaugh, W. T., 1998. The prestige motive for making charitable transfers. *American Economic Review* 88:277–82.
Veblen, T., 1899/1934. *The Theory of the Leisure Class*. Modern Library, New York.

On ultimatum and dictatorship games, see Hoffman, McCabe, Shachat, and Smith (1994); Eckel and Grossman (1996); Henrich (2000); Henrich et al. (2001); and Chen and Fang-Fang (2009). Oosterbeek, Sloof, and Van De Kuilen (2004) reviewed the evidence on cultural differences. On group decisions, see Cason and Mui (1997). Ruffle (1998) described differences between outcomes of dictatorship and ultimatum games when donors observe recipients' effort. Andreoni and Vesterlund (2001) reported gender differences in altruism in dictatorship games.

Andreoni, J., and L. Vesterlund, 2001. Which is the fairer sex? Gender differences in altruism. *Quarterly Journal of Economics* 116:293–312.
Cason, T. N., and V.-L. Mui, 1997. A laboratory study of group polarization in the team dictator game. *Economic Journal* 107:1465–83.

Chen, Kang, and Tang Fang-Fang, 2009. Cultural differences between Tibetans and ethnic Han Chinese in ultimatum bargaining experiments. *European Journal of Political Economy* 25:78–84.
Eckel, C. C., and P. J. Grossman, 1996. The relative price of fairness: Gender differences in a punishment game. *Journal of Economic Behavior and Organization* 30:143–58.
Henrich, J., 2000. Does culture matter in economic behavior? Ultimatum game bargaining among the Machiguenga in the Peruvian Amazon. *American Economic Review* 90: 973–9.
Henrich, J., R. Boyd, S. Bowles, C. Camerer, E. Fehr, H. Gintis, and R. McElreath, 2001. In search of *homo economicus*: Behavioral experiments in 15 small-scale societies. *American Economic Review, Papers and Proceedings* 91:73–8.
Hoffman, E., K. McCabe, K. Shachat, and V. Smith, 1994. Preferences, property rights, and anonymity in bargaining games. *Games and Economic Behavior* 7:346–80.
Oosterbeek, H., R. Sloof, and G. Van De Kuilen, 2004. Cultural differences in ultimatum game experiments: Evidence from a meta-analysis. *Experimental Economics* 7:171–88.
Ruffle, B. S., 1998. More is better, but fair is fair: Tipping in dictator and ultimatum games. *Games and Economic Behavior* 23:247–65.

Galton (1889) described reversion to the mean.

Galton, F., 1889. *Natural Inheritance*. Macmillan, London.

On economic mobility, see:

Becker, G., and N. Tomes, 1986. Human capital and the rise and fall of families (The family and the distribution of economic rewards). *Journal of Labor Economics* part 2, 4:S1–S39.
Bratberg, E., Ø. A. Nilsen, and K. Vaage, 2007. Intergenerational earnings mobility in Norway: Levels and trends. *Scandinavian Journal of Economics* 107:419–37.
Chadwick, L., and G. Solon, 2002. Intergenerational income mobility among daughters. *American Economic Review* 92:335–44.
Dearden, L., S. Machin, and H. Reed, 1997. Intergenerational mobility in Britain. *Economic Journal* 107:47–66.
Lam, D., and R. F. Schoeni, 1993. Effects of family background on earnings and returns to schooling: Evidence from Brazil. *Journal of Political Economy* 101:710–40.
Mulligan, C. B., 1999. Galton versus the human capital approach to inheritance. *Journal of Political Economy* 107:S184–S224.
Solon, G., 1992. Intergenerational income mobility in the U.S. *American Economic Review* 82:393–408.
Solon, G., 2002. Cross-country differences in intergenerational earnings mobility. *Journal of Economic Perspectives* 16:59–66.
Zimmerman, D. J., 1992. Regression toward mediocrity in economic stature. *American Economic Review* 82:409–29.

On the ineffectiveness of aid as a means of global social insurance, see Easterly (2001), Hillman (2002), and Doucouliagos and Paldam (2008). On corruption in governments in low-income countries, see Abed and Gupta (2002). Reinikka and Svensson (2004) provided a case study of corruption in which all but a small part of intended public funding for schools failed to reach the schools. Evidence on the disadvantageous consequences of government spending in low-income countries was reported by Baldacci, Hillman, and Kojo (2004).

Abed, G. T., and S. Gupta (Eds.), 2002. *Governance, Corruption, and Economic Performance*. International Monetary Fund, Washington DC.

Baldacci, E., A. L. Hillman, and N. Kojo, 2004. Growth, governance, and fiscal-policy transmission channels in low-income countries. *European Journal of Political Economy* 20:517–49. Reprinted in S. Gupta, B. Clements, and G. Inchauste (Eds.), 2004. *Helping Countries Develop: The Role of Fiscal Policy*. International Monetary Fund, Washington DC, pp. 67–104.

Doucouliagos, H., and M. Paldam, 2008. Aid effectiveness on growth: A meta-study. *European Journal of Political Economy* 24:1–24.

Easterly, W., 2001. *The Elusive Quest for Growth: Economists' Adventures and Misadventures in the Tropics*. The MIT Press, Cambridge MA.

Hillman, A. L., 2002. The World Bank and the persistence of poverty in poor countries. *European Journal of Political Economy* 18:783–97.

Reinikka, R., and J. Svensson, 2004. Local capture: Evidence from a central government transfer program in Uganda. *Quarterly Journal of Economics* 119:679–705.

Supplement S7A: Measurement of income inequality

There is a substantial literature on measurement of economic inequality. For an introduction, see:

Fields, G. R., and E. A. Ok, 1999. The measurement of income mobility: An introduction to the literature. In J. Silver (Ed.), *Handbook on Income Inequality*. Kluwer Academic Publishers, Dordrecht, pp. 557–98.

On Atkinson's measure, see:

Atkinson, A. B., 1970. On the measurement of economic inequality. *Journal of Economic Theory* 2:244–63.

On resolving measurement ambiguities, see:

Shorrocks, A. F., 1983. Ranking income distributions. *Economica* 50:1–17.

Supplement S7B: An impossibility theorem for social aggregation

Arrow's theorem was set out in:

Arrow, K. J., 1950. A difficulty in the concept of social welfare. *Journal of Political Economy* 58:328–46. Reprinted in K. J. Arrow and T. Scitovsky (Eds.), 1969. *Readings in Welfare Economics*. Irwin, Homewood IL, pp. 147–68.

8

ENTITLEMENTS

A social insurance contract provides entitlements. Entitlements are of two types: (1) universal and therefore intended for all as a means of seeking ex-ante equality; or (2) targeted to designated groups, who are given the entitlements because of designated needs. Section 1 of this chapter considers whether or how entitlements can achieve equality of opportunity (or ex-ante equality) and investigates the consequences of entitlements for incentives. Section 2 is about the entitlement to income during retirement or old age. The topic of section 3 is the entitlement to health care and health insurance.

8.1 The Attributes and Consequences of Entitlements

The entitlements that are part of a social insurance contract can be provided in the form of income transfers (money) or as in-kind transfers. In the previous chapter, we viewed the entitlements as income or money paid by people who had experienced good outcomes to people who had experienced adverse outcomes. Often, however, entitlements are in-kind, in the form of education, housing, food vouchers, and health care, as well as advice from social workers about how to obtain access to entitlements. In-kind transfers provide designated goods and services: money can be transferred to anyone for any purpose.[1]

A. Money and in-kind transfers

Our first questions concern the choice between money and in-kind transfers as means of delivery of entitlements.

The choice between money and in-kind transfers

Our normative question is:

> *Should the entitlements of a social insurance contract be provided as income or as in-kind transfers?*

Our positive question is:

> *In which form do we predict entitlements will be provided?*

[1] When a passerby on the street is asked for money by a person who declares that he is hungry, the passerby might offer to buy the hungry person a meal but the offer of the meal is turned down. The rejection of the offer of the in-kind transfer indicates that the money was not sought for food.

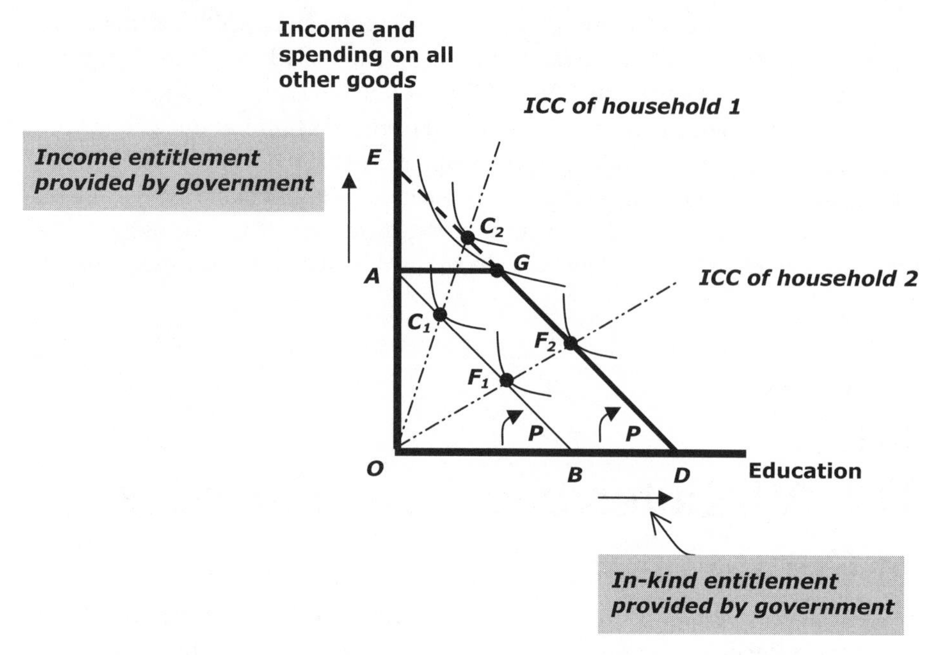

Figure 8.1. In-kind transfers and income from the recipient's perspective.

Figure 8.1 shows the difference from the perspective of beneficiaries of entitlements between an in-kind transfer and money or income. The example for the in-kind transfer, which we shall generally retain, is education; however, conclusions apply to all in-kind transfers.

The initial pre-transfer budget constraint in figure 8.1 is *AB*. An income entitlement of *AE* moves the budget constraint to *ED*. The slope of the budget lines *AB* and *ED* is determined by a market-determined relative price of education *P* that remains constant. Two households have the same pre- and post-transfer incomes indicated by the budget constraints. Household 1 chooses market spending at point C_1 when the budget constraint is *AB* and point C_2 after the income entitlement has moved the budget constraint to *ED*. In response to the income entitlement, household 2 moves from market spending at point F_1 to point F_2.

Each household has moved along its income-consumption curve, ICC. The income-consumption curves are shown as linear for exposition.

> *An income-consumption curve (or line) ICC shows increases in demand when income increases and the relative price remains constant.*[2]

[2] An income-consumption curve or line joins utility-maximizing points on each budget line. The slope of the budget lines is fixed because, along an income-consumption curve, relative price (which is the slope of a budget constraint) remains unchanged. The income-consumption curve shows the change in demand due to a change in income, or an income effect. The substitution effect is a move along an indifference curve. In our case, there is no substitution effect because we are considering only increases in income through the entitlement with no change in relative price.

The positive slope of an income-consumption curve indicates that both goods are "normal"; that is, demand for both goods increases with income.

The utilities of both households in figure 8.1 have increased because of the income entitlement. Moreover, both households are optimizing and cannot do better than respond as they have to the income entitlement.

As an alternative to the income entitlement EA, the government may decide to provide the two households with an in-kind transfer of free education. The duration or quality of education is increased by BD. Because BD is equal to AG, the budget constraint after the in-kind transfer is AGD. Compared to the income entitlement, the in-kind entitlement has eliminated the segment EG from the post-entitlement budget constraint.

The elimination of the segment EG does not affect household 2, which still moves from F_1 to F_2 in response to the now in-kind entitlement. However, the in-kind entitlement reduces the utility of household 1, for whom choice of point C_2 is no longer feasible. The best that household 1 can do when the entitlement is provided as in-kind is to choose point G, where utility is lower than at point C_2. The relative positions of the income-consumption curves (or lines) show that household 2, which is indifferent between an income transfer and the in-kind entitlement, has a greater preference for spending on education than household 1, which loses when the in-kind transfer replaces an income transfer.[3]

The cost of providing the entitlement whether in terms of income or in-kind is the same; that is, the cost to taxpayers including the excess burden of taxation is the same.

We see that recipients may be indifferent between income and in-kind entitlements. However:

> *If not indifferent, recipients prefer that entitlements be provided in terms of income rather in-kind, because of the greater freedom of choice when entitlements are provided in terms of income.*

We have asked about the preference of the beneficiaries of entitlements. What of the preference of taxpayers? Do taxpayers prefer income or in-kind transfers? We shall now see that taxpayers prefer in-kind transfers.

Figure 8.2 shows two households with different incomes and the same preferences for educating children. A high-income household has pre-tax income Y_H and a low-income household has pre-tax income Y_L. Each household has a school-aged child. The two households have common preferences regarding spending on schooling, which are expressed in the common income-consumption curve (or line) ICC. With the relative price of education given, all voluntary spending choices on schooling for both households are on the ICC line. When there are no government schools, the households choose spending on schooling in private markets at points H and L, respectively.[4]

[3] For a choice from any budget constraint, household 1 spends less on education than household 2.

[4] The positive slope of the ICC in figure 8.2 indicates that education is again a normal good.

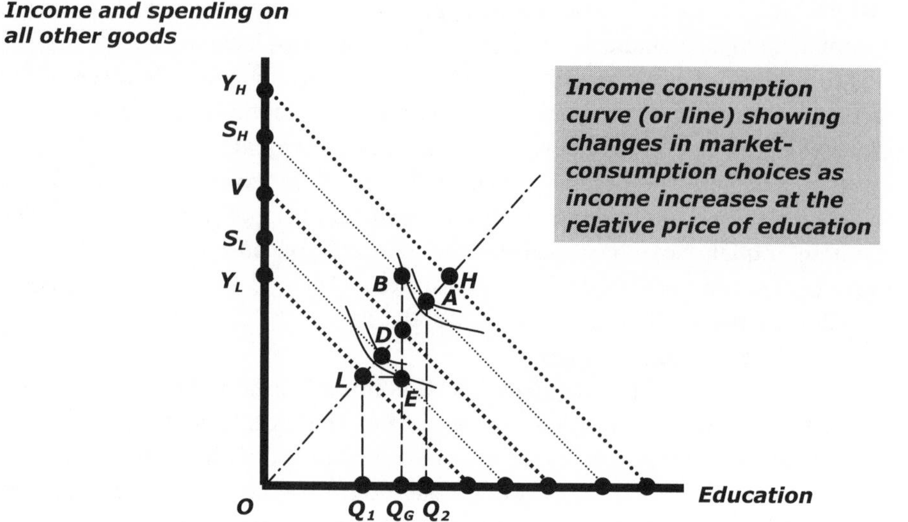

Figure 8.2. The choice between in-kind and income transfers.

Private spending outcomes at points H and L are not equal because of the different incomes of the parents. In a public policy decision, a government sets $Q_G > Q_I$ as a compulsory schooling entitlement for children. The entitlement exceeds the market choice of the low-income household at point L. The high-income household's voluntary market spending at point H exceeds the entitlement Q_G set by the government. The entitlement Q_G equalizes schooling for the children of the two households when both households send the children to the same government school. The objective is thereby achieved of ex-ante equality in education.

When the government provides free-access compulsory government schools of educational quality Q_G, the low-income household is provided with an in-kind transfer of schooling equal to $(Q_G - Q_I)$ and moves in figure 8.2 from point L to point E. The low-income household continues to pay for Q_I, but now the payment is through taxes to the government (with an excess burden) and not through private spending for schooling. The additional schooling $(Q_G - Q_I)$ provided through the in-kind transfer is financed by a tax on the high-income household.

The cost of providing the in-kind transfer $(Q_G - Q_I)$ to the low-income household is $(S_L - Y_L)$. The high-income household therefore pays a tax $(Y_H - S_H)$ equal to $(S_L - Y_L)$ to finance the in-kind transfer and bears an excess burden.

There are excess burdens of taxation because government schools are financed through taxation. In figure 8.2, we omit the effects on utilities of the excess burdens of taxation – but the excess burdens are present.

After paying the tax, the high-income household's remaining post-tax income is S_H. With this post-tax income, the high-income household would like to choose point A on the ICC line and provide schooling at Q_2, which exceeds the entitlement chosen by the government. The high-income household, however, is compelled to be at lower-utility point *B* and, through taxation, to pay for the compulsory government-provided in-kind entitlement Q_G.

Rather than being given the in-kind transfer $(Q_G - Q_I)$ through the compulsory government school, the low-income household could alternatively be given the money that finances the in-kind transfer. The low-income household would then receive $(S_L - Y_L)$ as additional income. With this additional income to spend as it wishes through private market spending (the market replaces the compulsory government school that provides the in-kind transfer), the low-income household would choose point *D* on the ICC line.

At point *D*, the low-income household is not voluntarily spending enough on schooling to achieve the entitlement Q_G. To voluntarily spend enough on schooling to reach Q_G, the low-income household requires income *V*. The income *V* can be provided to the low-income household by taxing the high-income household to give the low-income household a direct income transfer of $(Y_H - V) = (V - Y_L)$.

After taxation and the income transfer that result in the low-income household voluntarily choosing private spending at the level of entitlement Q_G, in the example in figure 8.2, the two households have the same income *V*.[5] With after-tax income *V*, the (previously) high-income household also voluntarily spends to provide education at the level of the entitlement Q_G.

Which form of delivery of entitlement do taxpayers prefer?

The objective of public policy is to provide the entitlement Q_G for the low-income household. To finance the entitlement as an in-kind transfer, the high-income household pays a tax of $(Y_H - S_H)$ and incurs the associated excess burden of taxation. To finance the income transfer that ensures the entitlement, the high-income family pays the higher tax of $(Y_H - V)$ and incurs the associated higher excess burden of taxation. Hence:

> *The household whose taxes finance the entitlement is better off with the in-kind transfer than with the money transfer.*

Money transfers allow the recipients of transfers to make their own self-interested spending decisions. However, change from in-kind to money transfers is not Pareto-improving.

> *Although a beneficiary of an entitlement gains when the entitlement is provided through money transfers rather than in-kind, taxpayers lose.*

The social objective is not to maximize the utility of the beneficiary at the expense of the taxpayer. The objective is rather to ensure that the entitlement Q_G is provided.

[5] The equal post-tax income is part of our exposition. It is not a general requirement of a post-tax outcome.

Reasons for compulsory in-kind transfers

There are reasons other than the tax burden for taxpayers' preferring in-kind transfers. There is, first, the paternalistic motive when education has been judged as beneficial for children. If money rather than in-kind transfers were provided, a society would have to rely on parents choosing to spend to educate children. In figure 8.2 parents who receive a sufficient income transfer spend to achieve the entitlement. Extortion would, however, be attempted if parents were to declare, "Pay me enough and I shall send my children to school." In-kind transfers eliminate parental discretion and avoid extortion. Second, entitlements through compulsory schooling are in taxpayers' interest because education increases children's future incomes and so increases the likelihood that children, when grown, will be self-reliant and not require tax-financed transfers through social insurance. High-income households therefore have an interest in financing entitlements to education for children from low-income households. Compulsory entitlements ensure that children actually attend school and that society therefore obtains the beneficial externalities of a more educated population.

Entitlements other than education

Parents could be given money to pay for inoculations and vaccinations of their children against childhood diseases. In-kind transfers ensure that the inoculations and vaccinations take place. The social objective of protecting the children (and people who might come into contact with them) is thereby assured. There are paternalistic reasons for ensuring delivery of entitlements to housing because societies do not want people to be homeless, deprived of shelter, and living on the streets – and there are also beneficial externalities.

Market responses and the value of entitlements

We saw in chapter 4 that the legal incidence of a tax does not indicate effective incidence. Just as the legal obligation to pay a tax does not determine who effectively pays the tax, likewise:

> *The identity of the beneficiary of a subsidy (paid in money) is not determined by the legal right to receive the entitlement.*

Governments might, for example, perceive homeownership as an entitlement and subsidize homeownership through tax deductibility of interest payments and through implicit or explicit guarantees for mortgages. The subsidy increases demand for homeownership. If demand increases in an area where the supply of housing is inelastic or fixed, the beneficiaries of the subsidy are the sellers of houses, not the buyers.

If colleges and universities can admit only limited numbers of students and can set tuition fees, subsidies to students through conditions of loans or scholarships increase tuition without increasing the number of students.

When employers are required to provide maternity benefits, from the perspective of employers, the need to pay the benefits is a tax on employing people who are entitled to the benefits. Women are potentially eligible for the benefits, and so market wages of women fall. Women then finance the entitlements through reduced wages. If the subsidy is designated as in-kind (a number of days after birth that a woman is paid a salary without working), the monetary value of the days lost is internalized in the market wage. All women receive a lower wage unless they can credibly commit to not being future beneficiaries of the entitlement.

Vouchers as means of delivering in-kind entitlements

In-kind entitlements can be delivered through vouchers.[6] Vouchers can deliver entitlements to schooling, food, housing, health insurance and health care, and vocational training (or retraining). Vouchers can also be used to convert unemployment benefits into employment subsidies.

Vouchers introduce competition into supply of publicly financed services. Vouchers that finance costs of schooling allow all schools, public and private, to compete for students. Parents can seek the best educational standards for children without limitations imposed by location in a school district or parents' ability or willingness to pay for education.

Through vouchers, public finance is separated from government supply in the delivery of entitlements. When people receive vouchers for food entitlements, governments do not supply the food but rather the vouchers finance market purchases of food. Vouchers for schooling finance personal spending on the education of children without the need for government involvement in supply through government schools. Delivery of housing entitlements through vouchers allows personal choice in private housing markets. Vouchers for health insurance and health care similarly permit personal choices and supply through markets.

Vouchers eliminate government procurement.

In government schools, for example, procurement ranges from purchase of pencils to the construction of school buildings. Government procurement requires government officials to make decisions about public spending. A dedicated government bureaucracy as described by Max Weber would always choose least-cost private suppliers subject to requisite quality standards and would never accept personal benefits in exchange for choosing inflated bids from suppliers. However, principal–agent problems can also arise, with bureaucracies expanding public spending to benefit from larger budgets and expanding the size of administrative hierarchies. In some cultures but also in high-income democracies, bribes might be given to government officials in return for favors in choosing private

[6] The vouchers are money that can be used only for the designated entitlement and for the sum indicated by the voucher. Vouchers are also sometimes called stamps, as in the case of food stamps.

suppliers who may or may not be the least-cost suppliers.[7] When entitlements are delivered through vouchers, the government bureaucracy determines eligibility for vouchers, but the government bureaucracy is not required to make decisions about spending of tax revenue.

An objection might be raised that, through vouchers for schooling, sorting occurs whereby schools admit students according to ability and motivation, with the consequence that good and inferior students are in different schools. The alternative to selection of students in good schools according to ability and motivation is selection according to ability of parents to pay for superior schooling.

Teachers in government schools and administrators have reason to object to school vouchers. When schooling is a government monopoly so that children are obliged to attend government schools, teachers and administrators benefit from monopoly rents due to the absence of competition. The rents are expressed in the reduced effort of teachers and administrators. Teachers whose competence and patience have been diminished and who should retire can remain in the school system while exerting less effort at communicating with students and imparting knowledge. The competition in choice of schools, including private schools, introduced by vouchers could reduce budgets and salaries in government school systems. Teachers and administrators in government schools are also concerned that the exit of better students from the government school system facilitated by vouchers will confirm the attraction of superior education in private schools.

> *Teachers and administrators in government schools can be expected to resist a voucher system for delivery of schooling entitlements.*[8]

Whereas teachers and school administrators have reasons to oppose competition from private schools, health-care practitioners generally oppose government monopoly over health care. A market in which health-care practitioners directly cater to demand for health care provides higher incomes than when the sole provider of health services – and therefore the sole employer of health-care practitioners – is the government.

B. Education and other rejected entitlements

The entitlement to schooling or education is not targeted but is rather intended to be universal, or for every child in the society. The objective of the universal

[7] Chapter 2 described incentives in bureaucratic hierarchies, and also the possibility of corruption.

[8] Publicly financed vouchers for private schools were validated by the U.S. Supreme Court in 2002. In *Zelman v. Simmons–Harris*, the Court ruled that the vouchers do not contradict the First Amendment to the U.S. Constitution. However, the Court imposed stipulations. Schools that participate in a voucher program are not permitted to discriminate in acceptance of students based on ethnicity or religion. Schools are not permitted to teach an ideology of hatred and teach children to be demeaning of or to seek to diminish the rights of anyone in society.

entitlement to education is equality of opportunity or ex-ante equality.[9] An entitlement can be rejected by choosing market alternatives. If an entitlement intended to be universal is rejected for a superior market alternative, the objective of ex-ante equality is not achieved. Private schools are, in general, superior market alternatives to the entitlement to schooling in government schools.[10]

Government and private schools

Good schools have better administrators and better qualified and motivated teachers. Teachers in good schools generally enjoy teaching more because they teach better motivated students. The teachers are less prone to the fatigue and indifference that can arise from repetition over the years of more or less the same basic material. In good schools, teachers also benefit from interaction with more concerned parents. In some locations, government schools are excellent. In other locations, government schools are decidedly inferior to private schools. The reason can be simply sorting: because friends and fellow students are important in determining motivation for educational achievement, parents may prefer to send their children to private schools where, for extra payment, the children can be with other children whose parents are also willing to pay for a better education.[11]

Private schools need not have more resources per child than government schools; the contrary may be the case.[12] Additional resources do not necessarily improve the quality of education. Objective measures of inputs into education include the size of the education budget, number of computers per child, class size, and formal qualifications of the teachers. Although the relationship between educational quality and these variables is expected to be positive, there are adverse influences on the quality of education that money alone cannot rectify. Increased salaries for an overstaffed school-district administration or for inadequate and indifferent teachers increase spending but do not improve the quality of schooling. Although teachers can become apathetic and indifferent if they feel that society rewards them inadequately, higher incomes for teachers may not overcome inadequate teacher motivation. The satisfaction from teaching in classrooms in which norms encourage learning and respect for the teacher can attract

[9] Health care (see section 3) can also be a universal entitlement. In the societies with maximal government described in chapter 2, everything in life was an intended universal equal entitlement, including housing and jobs.

[10] We focus on education but other entitlements may be rejected. Health-care entitlements from governments may be rejected because of long waiting times and inadequate or impersonal treatment. People may not be able to rely on government entitlements for personal security and may hire personal bodyguards, or neighborhoods may hire private security services.

[11] Teachers in government schools in the United States have disproportionately sent their children to private schools (Schansberg, 1996, p. 82).

[12] In New York City, for example, government schools have had 10 times more employees per student and more than 60 times the number of administrators per student than Catholic schools (ibid., p. 85).

and keep good teachers when private schools pay lower salaries than government schools.

The quality of teaching is determined by who chooses to become a teacher. If salaries of teachers are low compared to alternatives and if being a teacher has low social status, the people who choose to be teachers are those who are unable to succeed in other professions. Young minds, consequently, are exposed to teachers who may not be the wisest or the most broadly knowledgeable and who may be cynical because teaching is their default income-earning option. Administrators may be drawn from the same people. Motivated good teachers will not want cynical colleagues and administrators, and they will move to private schools where they have the satisfaction of the company of likewise motivated good teachers. As noted, better students may also be in the private schools.

Government schools and market choices

We now consider the decision whether to reject a government's schooling entitlement. We shall consider households with the same incomes but that differ in preferences regarding spending on schooling.[13]

In figure 8.3, the quality of education is measured uniformly for private and government schools on the horizontal axis. The cost (or price) of schooling, denoted by the relative price P (which is the slope of the budget line), is shown as the same for government and private schools. Therefore, we here abstract from quality and cost differences between private and government schools.

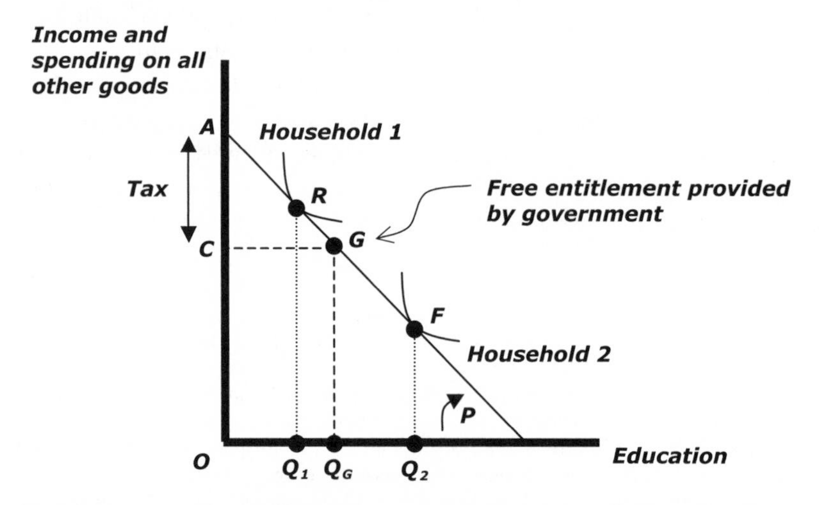

Figure 8.3. An in-kind entitlement when households have different preferences.

[13] In contrast, when we considered the choice of means of delivering entitlements, we compared households with the same preferences but different incomes.

The two households in figure 8.3 have the same pre-tax income OA. For household 1, the preferred choice of schooling, or education (we use the terms interchangeably), is at point R where the quality of education is Q_1. For household 2, the preferred choice is at point F, where the quality of education is Q_2. These are the respective private choices in a private market without government schools.

Then, a government introduces a compulsory in-kind entitlement of Q_G through government schools at point G and choice in the private market is no longer permitted. To finance the compulsory entitlement, both households pay income taxes AC. The taxes have excess burdens (not shown in figure 8.3). The entitlement Q_G can be either lower or higher than a household's preferred choice.[14] We observe in figure 8.3 that:

> *Each household was better off, by its own valuation of its own well-being, without the government entitlement.*

Our next step is to introduce the option to forgo the government entitlement by choosing private spending. The government requires that the quality Q_G be minimally provided – but not necessarily through government schools. Given the opportunity, some households reject the government entitlement and choose a market alternative, although there is no rebate of taxes when rejecting the government entitlement. That is, by rejecting the government entitlement, a household pays twice: once through taxes and again through market expenditure for the private alternative.

Households that reject the entitlement

Figure 8.4a shows a household that rejects the entitlement. OC is disposable after-tax income after the household has paid the tax AC (which is the average cost of schooling for a student). The choices after paying the tax are between (1) accepting the (after-tax) free government entitlement at point G, and (2) forgoing the government entitlement by choosing a point along HD through private spending.[15] Point J along HD provides higher utility than obtained from the government entitlement at point G. The household therefore spends privately in the market to provide quality Q_3 at point J. Without the presence of the tax-financed entitlement, the household is at point F.

> *The entitlement reduces utility for a household that rejects the entitlement.*

[14] Whereas figure 8.3 is based on the same cost of education in government as private schools, this is generally not the case. Private schools typically have lower quality-adjusted costs than government schools. See, for example, footnote 12.

[15] The effective post-tax budget constraint is $CGHD$ shown in figure 8.4a, which allows for the alternatives of choosing or rejecting the entitlement at point G. The entitlement at point G is Pareto-superior to any point along CH. Therefore, CH is not part of the effective (or relevant) post-tax budget constraint. The choice is between the entitlement at point G and private spending along HD.

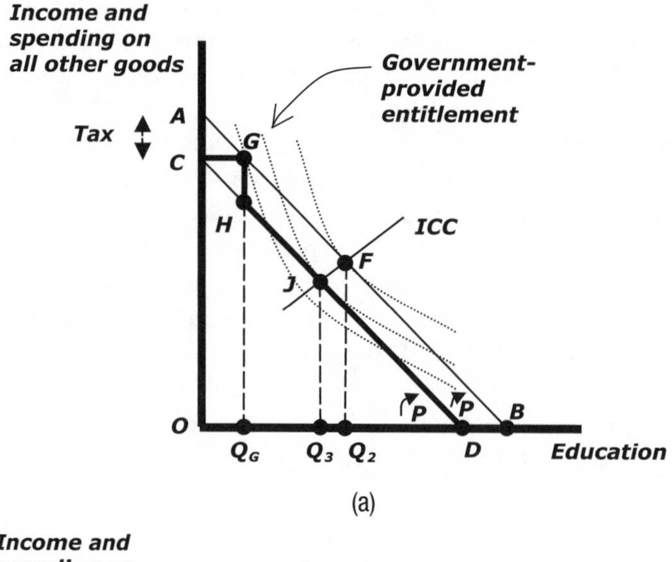

(a)

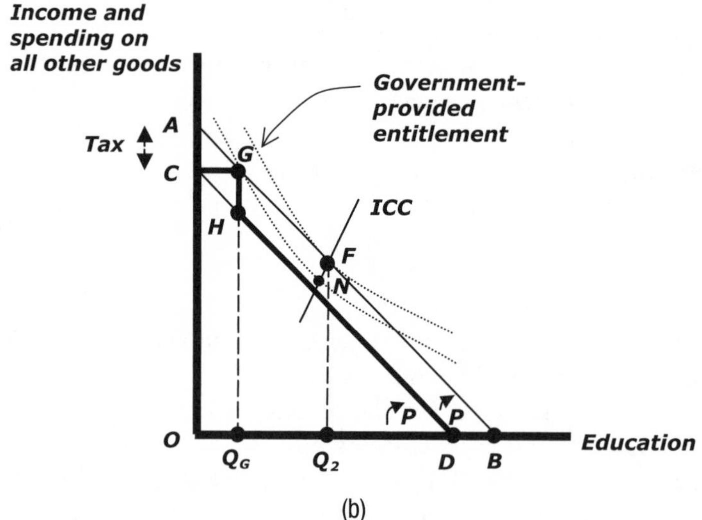

(b)

Figure 8.4. (a) The household rejects the entitlement. (b) The household accepts the entitlement.

A household that rejects the entitlement pays a tax *AC* to finance an entitlement from which it does not benefit. The loss from the entitlement is the tax payment *AC* plus the excess burden of taxation. The entitlement has moved the household in figure 8.4a from point *F* on the income-consumption curve (or line) ICC to point *J*. The household is prepared maximally to pay *FJ* (plus the not-shown excess burden of taxation) to end the government entitlement program or would require payment of *FJ* (plus the excess burden of taxation) as compensation for the government having provided the entitlement – where *FJ* is equal to the tax that is paid, *AC*.

Households that accept the entitlement

Households that accept the entitlement are nonetheless also prepared to pay to end the entitlement. In figure 8.4b, the household accepts the entitlement: utility for this household at entitlement point G exceeds the utility attainable through after-tax private spending at any point along HD. If we were to ask this household how much it is prepared to pay to end the government entitlement, the answer is an amount of income equal to FN plus the excess burden of taxation for the tax AC that the household paid. In the absence of the government entitlement and the tax AC, the household in figure 8.4b would choose to spend to obtain Q_2 at point F on the budget line AB. The entitlement and the accompanying tax result in the household choosing point G, where the entitlement has been accepted. Utility at point G is the same as utility at point N. The effect of the entitlement is therefore as if income FN had been taken from the household.

The entitlement reduces utility for a household that accepts the entitlement.

Who loses more?

The two households in figures 8.4a and 8.4b have equal pre-tax incomes and, when the entitlement is provided, pay equal taxes AC (and have the same excess burden of taxation). The households both choose Q_2 without the entitlement. The two households are, therefore, equal in utility before the entitlement is introduced but they are not equal after the entitlement is present: because of differences in preferences for spending on education, one household has rejected and the other has accepted the entitlement. We see from the different willingness to pay to avoid the presence of the entitlement (or the different compensating payment required) that:

Both households lose from the entitlement but the household that more highly values education loses more.

Preferences and incomes

Households with a higher income can, of course, better afford to send children to private schools than households with lower income. We have, however, compared households that differ in preferences but not in income.

Externalities and entitlements

The government entitlement exists because of household 1 in figure 8.3. Household 1 would choose point R if spending on schooling were private and therefore would not attain the minimum requirement Q_G. The government entitlement at point G increases schooling of a child in household 1. Because household 1 pays more in taxes to finance the entitlement than it wishes to spend on schooling, this household also loses from the entitlement. The reason for the government entitlement and compulsory schooling is household 1's low priority for schooling for children. Therefore:

> *Through the need for the government entitlement, households with low valuations of schooling impose adverse externalities on households that value schooling highly.*

That is, if there were no government entitlement, children in the households shown in figures 8.4a and 8.4b would benefit from higher quality education.[16]

Markets

The objective of the entitlement is ex-ante equality: rejected entitlements compromise the objective. Markets allow the entitlements to be rejected. Markets also allow the entitlement to be accepted but supplemented by private spending. In figures 8.4a and 8.4b, the opportunity for supplemental private spending creates the budget constraint *CGB*. Households then accept the government entitlement Q_G and add to the entitlement through private spending to attain Q_2.

> *Private spending, whether substituting for or supplementing an entitlement, creates ex-ante inequality by allowing departure from the intended equal entitlement.*

Private voluntary spending in markets, however, is Pareto-improving.[17] The case of the water in the desert in chapter 1 demonstrated how ex-post equality could conflict with Pareto improvement. We now see that also:

> *Because of inequality created through private spending in markets, the objective of ex-ante equality can conflict with Pareto improvement.*

Should governments disallow private spending?

In the attempt to maintain ex-ante equality through entitlements, governments could make private schools illegal. The same applies to ex-ante equality sought in private health care – or, indeed, housing or personal security. The reason for

[16] In the absence of the entitlement, with choices made in markets, a child in household 2 in figure 8.3 receives Q_2. If household 2 rejects the entitlement as in figure 8.4a, private spending on education Q_3 is less than Q_2. If household 2 accepts the entitlement as in figure 8.4b, the entitlement Q_G is also less than Q_2 that the household would have chosen without the entitlement.

[17] In figure 8.2, which showed households with unequal initial incomes and the same preferences for spending, the high-income household has post-tax income S_H after paying the taxes that finance the in-kind transfer to the low-income household. The entitlement Q_G places the high-income household at point *B*. With available post-tax income S_H, the high-income household prefers point *A* where the quality is Q_2. Supplemental private spending allows Q_2 at point *A* to be chosen through market addition to the entitlement Q_G. The low-income household remains with the entitlement Q_G. With $Q_G < Q_2$, there is, therefore, not ex-ante equality between the high- and low-income households – because of the supplemental market purchase.

disallowing markets would now differ from the case for paternalistic policies when markets result in self-harm. Here, the government would be making the judgment that spending on education or health care or personal security is meritorious – indeed, so much so as to merit a government entitlement – but the judgment will also have been made that markets should be disallowed so as to allow ex-ante equality to be achieved through the government entitlement.

Illegal supply

We observed how, in the case of paternalistic prohibitions, illegality of private spending invites illegal supply. For schooling and health care, the illegal supply is not provided, as with drugs, by professional criminals. Rather, the illegal supply is by teachers and medical practitioners.

Rent creation and rent seeking in health care

When there are long waiting times in a government health-care system that provides health care as an entitlement, rent seeking occurs, through the quest for favors and privileges. The personnel of a government medical system create rents by allowing people to avoid waiting times for medical treatment and by providing superior treatment for private payment. The inequality is then accompanied by rent creation and rent seeking. We return to health care in section 3.

Problems with private schools

Private schools usually provide better education than government schools – if only because private schools are financed by user prices according to the benefit principle of payment and the beneficiaries personally paying have an incentive to monitor and evaluate the benefits from their private spending. Nevertheless, there are a number of possible problems associated with private schools.

Signaling rather than learning

There are two theories about why people seek education (or parents seek education for children). One theory is that education enhances future productive contributions (that is, education increases human capital). The other theory is that education is no more than a signaling device that allows students to show their ability and thereby to distinguish themselves from people of lesser ability. If the purpose of education is to signal superior personal ability, schooling is privately useful. However, schooling is not socially beneficial because the externality of a more educated, knowledgeable population is not provided. Education or schooling is in that event a form of rent seeking.

> *If schooling serves only a signaling purpose, the purpose of investment in education is to provide personal credentials that certify ability to be admitted to good schools and to pass exams.*

A private school may provide a better signal even if the quality of education is the same as in government schools – or inferior. The expense of private schools signals wealth of parents. Colleges and universities may choose applicants from expensive private high schools because admitted students can pay full tuition and so do not require scholarships, and because wealthy graduates may add to university endowments.

Adverse selection and private schools

Private schools introduce adverse selection into schooling. Adverse selection takes place when exit from government schools to private schools reduces monitoring and involvement of parents and adversely affects children who remain in government schools. Adverse selection occurs through successive exit to private schools that continually reduces quality of government schools. Only children whose parents cannot afford to pay for private schools or children whose parents are satisfied with inferior-quality education remain in government schools. The objective of equalizing educational opportunities by entitlements, then, has not been achieved because of adverse selection.

Voting and resources for government schools

When adverse selection results in exit from government schools, fewer voters benefit from government schools. If government schools no longer serve middle-income parents because they have moved their children to private schools, the median voter may not favor more than minimal spending on government schools. Through voting and political decisions on public spending, adverse selection can, therefore, result in reduced public spending on government schools. Voting is thus another path of adverse selection: as more children exit government schools, resources through public spending for government schools decline – and more children are then taken out of government schools, and public spending and resources decline further.

The content of education

The content of education is a potentially serious problem when private schools offer not superior general education but exist to inculcate ideology than is inimical to participation in broad society. The entitlement to education is predicated on ensuring that children are provided with the information and skills required for future self-reliance and advancement in life. However, through discretion in the curriculum, private schools might, for example, not teach democratic principles. Children could be taught that because of their special privilege, all wealth in the due course of time will be theirs. The children then have no incentive to invest in skills and human capital that will allow them to become self-reliant members of society. In effect, the children are taught to be rent seekers where the rent-seeking prize is other people's property. Or, an ideology or belief system may have its own private schools in which girls are denied educational opportunities or are given no incentive to learn because they are told that they are destined for marriage at a very young age and will not be allowed to have a job. In such cases, private schools will not have provided the requisites of personal success in a market-based civil society.[18]

C. Is equal opportunity achievable?

Equal opportunity is not achieved when market choices allow rejection of or supplements to government entitlements. Failure of equal opportunity can also be due to the content of education in ideological private schools. In some locations, failure of equal opportunity occurs because students emerge from government schools functionally illiterate. Equal opportunity may also not be achievable for reasons other than attributes of government and private schools.

Entitlements and locational choice

Households have incentives to locate in jurisdictions where government-provided entitlements precisely match the personal spending that would maximize their utilities. Therefore, just as with public finance for public goods, public finance for free-access entitlements introduces locational incentives.[19]

The Tiebout locational mechanism applies to choice of entitlements.

Households differ in incomes and therefore in ability to pay – and so not just in willingness to pay as expressed in preferences. When entitlements are financed by local taxes, location results in unequal opportunities based on incomes. Ex-ante equality then cannot be achieved because a child in a low-income jurisdiction does not have the same entitlements as a child in a high-income jurisdiction.

Ex-ante equality when incomes differ can be achieved through a fiscal-federal structure of government. A central government can levy taxes on inhabitants of all subjurisdictions and redistribute the tax revenue among local jurisdictions according to the principle of equal opportunity for all children in the different school systems.

Another response to locational inequality is to change locational rules for school assignment. Children can be re-sorted within a school district or school districts can be merged. Re-sorting children among government schools through changes in locational rules redistributes wealth among homeowners. The quality of schools is capitalized into housing values. Changing school-district boundaries, therefore, imposes a cost on homeowners where government schools were good and benefits homeowners where government schools were inferior. A wealth transfer therefore takes place. Counterclaims of social justice can be expected

[18] The case can therefore be made for governments to regulate the content of education.

[19] Household 1 in figure 8.3 has an incentive to find a jurisdiction where the entitlement is Q_1. Household 2 has an incentive to find a jurisdiction where the entitlement is Q_2. Only a household that ideally wants Q_G has an incentive to stay.

in response to the wealth transfer. Parents in school districts where schools were good can make the case that "I worked hard and paid a lot of money to buy a house in a neighborhood where government schools are good: because of the change in locational criteria for school assignment, my child is no longer permitted to attend the local school, and besides which the injustice is compounded because the value of my house has fallen." Parents in a neighborhood or school district where schools were bad can make the case based on ex-ante equality that "All children should receive equal educational opportunities, and our children deserve the same opportunities as children elsewhere."

When entitlements are locally financed, low-income households might seek to locate in high-income jurisdictions while paying low shares of the taxes that finance the entitlements. Property taxes may be low for inexpensive housing that low-income households can afford, or public housing may be available that requires no payment of property taxes. High-income communities may use zoning laws to exclude low-income households by disallowing low-cost housing (see supplement S3B).

When people locate in a jurisdiction to benefit from a jurisdiction's tax-financed entitlements, there is greater political sensitivity than when the incentive for location is to benefit from but not pay for public goods (that is, to free ride on public goods).

> *The arrival of a non-taxpaying beneficiary of a public good does not require an increase in taxes; however, the arrival of a non-taxpaying beneficiary of a private-good entitlement imposes an increased tax burden on taxpayers.*

Unequal wages: discrimination or failure of equal opportunity?

In the United States, civil rights policies in the 1960s and 1970s made racial discrimination in schooling and labor markets illegal. However, decades after the introduction of the public policies aimed at ending discrimination, males in the group against whom there had been discrimination were still systematically earning low market wages.[20]

The explanation for the wage differences can be discrimination in the labor market or failure of equal opportunity (or both). Evidence in support of the labor-market-discrimination hypothesis would be that groups with the same skills and education are observed to be paid different wages. Labor-market discrimination is not indicated if income differences among groups coexist with systematic differences in groups' educational attainments.

[20] A study by Derek Neal and William Johnson (1996) revealed substantial racial differences in incomes in 1990–91: earnings of black males were 25 percent less and Hispanic males 18.4 percent less than for white males. The difference between black and white women was smaller, and was insignificant between white and Hispanic women. Pedro Carneiro, James J. Heckman, and Dimtriv V. Masterov (2005) confirmed the persistence of the trends after 1990–91. (Heckman received the Nobel Prize in economics in 2000.)

The empirical evidence suggests that income differences between racial groups in the United States have been due to systematic differences in educational attainment. The evidence therefore indicates that equality of opportunity through education was not provided – or, if provided, equal advantage was not taken of the opportunities.[21]

Norms of behavior and unequal beginnings

Low incomes in life are correlated with deficiencies in prenatal nutrition and low birth weight. Birth weight, in turn, is associated with the mother's nutrition and whether she smoked or used other self-abusing drugs during pregnancy.[22] After a child has been born, the home environment affects prospects for future personal and economic success in life. Family norms influence individual self-discipline and reliability, and affect personal motivation to succeed through self-improvement and self-reliance. Personal success is affected by response to disappointment and by patience as expressed in time horizons for allowing personal endeavors to come to fruition. Outside of the family, peer effects from the social and school environment influence attitudes toward study and scholastic success. Adverse stereotyped expectations diminish motivation and inhibit full achievement of personal potential. If family, peer, and group norms are the sources of ex-ante inequality, achieving ex-ante equality requires not public spending but rather changes in the norms and perceptions of families and groups. The challenges are expressed in a mother asking for advice about educating her about-to-be-born child. She asks, "When should I begin my child's education?" The answer is, "About 25 years ago." The investment in education of the child began with her parents' investment in education in her.

> *Prospects for ex-ante equality are affected by behavioral norms that reflect cultural transmission of values.*

Gender differences

The evidence shows substantial gender differences in taking advantage of opportunities that are offered. Controlling for ability, although black men earn less than white men, black women earn higher wages than white women. If there is discrimination, there is thus reverse discrimination for women.[23]

[21] Carneiro, Heckman, and Masterov (2005) reported that accounting for differences in skills and abilities reduced the male black–white wage difference by 76 percent and that the Hispanic male wage difference disappeared. They concluded that "the endowments that people bring to the labor market play a substantial role in accounting for minority wage gaps" (p. 3). Educational "endowments," of course, reflect past educational investments.

[22] Jere R. Behrman and Mark R. Rozenzweig (2004) provided evidence that future earnings are positively related to weight at birth. There are significant returns from increases in birth weight when the comparison begins from low birth weights. There are no returns from increased birth weight when birth weight is initially high.

[23] Carneiro, Heckman, and Masterov (2005).

A U.S. government program named "Moving to Opportunity" randomly chose single black mothers by lottery. The mothers could relocate with their families from low-income neighborhoods with inferior schools to neighborhoods where schools were better and where there was greater personal safety. The mothers were given housing vouchers to allow the relocation to the better neighborhood. After four to seven years of living in the better neighborhood, educational performance improved for female students. Criminal behavior also declined for female students. For males, the consequences were the contrary: the educational attainments declined and criminal behavior increased. Mental health of the mothers and daughters improved but not for young males.

In another experiment, students were randomly assigned to superior magnet schools and effects on students were studied by gender and race. The students who took the greatest advantage of the superior educational opportunities were white girls, who chose to attend schools with more rigorous academic programs and showed distinct gains in educational attainment. White girls were the only group in the study that showed significant increases in hours of homework as a consequence of winning the lottery that allowed choice of the academically more rigorous schools. Gender differences in response to educational opportunities are revealed to exist from early childhood. A study of assignment children from low-income households to preschool opportunities found benefits that persisted over time for girls and not for boys.[24]

> *The evidence indicates gender differences in willingness to take advantage of opportunities that are offered. Girls overall out-achieve boys when both are offered the same opportunities.*

Social identity and ex-ante equality

Evidence shows that social identity can be an impediment to ex-ante equality. Children who have been stereotyped as belonging to groups that are not expected to succeed in life may make no effort to change their personal outcomes from the predicted outcome.

Experimental evidence suggests that the reason for inferior performance is not people's beliefs about their own capabilities but a belief that the judges of performance are prejudiced because of the stereotype. If the judges are biased, there is no point in making an effort to succeed.

India has a caste system that places people in a social hierarchy. From birth, people are categorized according to family status, with accompanying expectations of personal achievement. In experiments, the performance of low-caste children competing against high-caste children in solving puzzles depended on whether social identity was private knowledge of the children (who only knew about themselves) or public knowledge (everyone knew the caste of everyone

[24] These outcomes were respectively reported by Jeffrey R. Kling, Jeffrey B. Liebman, and Lawrence F. Katz (2007); Justine S. Hastings, Thomas J. Kane, and Douglas O. Staiger (2006); and Michael Anderson (2005).

else). When private information made children anonymous with respect to social status, performance of the low- and high-caste children was more or less the same. Public knowledge of social status significantly reduced the performance of the low-caste children.[25]

Higher education

Evidence shows under-representation in higher education of high-ability individuals from poorer households. When scholarships and student loans are available, the under-representation is not due to financial restraints on tuition.[26]

Women are systematically over-represented in higher education. In the past, it was men who were over-represented. When the norm was that women would marry, raise children, and forgo careers, the systematic over-representation of men in higher education reflected the sharing of men's income inside the family. When norms changed and women could choose careers, the availability of higher-education opportunities resulted in more women than men, in general, attending college and university. The greater representation of women in higher education is consistent with the evidence showing that women take better advantage of educational opportunities.

High-ability students from poor households may obtain scholarships.[27] Prospective students from households in which parents do not or cannot provide financial support for higher education and who do not obtain scholarships might want to borrow against the future earnings that will be available after they complete their studies. Private lenders are unwilling to provide student loans if students lack collateral. Often, the only possible collateral could be through a contract that gives the lender the legal right to future earnings of a student, *whether or not* the student successfully completes the college or university degree. Such contracts are difficult for private lenders to enforce. Private lenders do not wish to be involved in such contracts. The private lenders would also confront adverse selection and moral hazard. There is adverse selection due to asymmetric information because a lender can only imperfectly observe the "type" of student seeking a loan: students have private information about their prospects of completing their studies and repaying the loans, and people taking out the loans may

[25] There was a 20 percent decline in the puzzles solved by the low-caste children. The experiment was conducted by Karla Hoff and Priyanka Pandey (2006).

[26] That is, the explanation cannot be that investment in education is "credit-constrained." Evidence that low-income households are under-represented in higher education is consistent across countries and is reported, for example, by James Heckman (2000) for the United States, David Greenaway and Michelle Haynes (2003) for the United Kingdom, and Buly A. Cardak and Chris Ryan (2006) for Australia.

[27] Often, scholarships are not financed by government but rather by the college or university. The criteria for receiving scholarships can then involve nonscholastic aptitudes including athletic ability. Good sports teams can be a major part of the prestige of a college or university. University and college administrators may feel that success in sports enhances student pride and also increases demand for admissions. Successful sports teams are also sources of profit through payments for attendance at games and through fees from media coverage.

systematically not expect to repay the loans. Data on high school academic performance could help banks and other private lenders distinguish students by prospects for loan repayment. There then is nonetheless moral hazard because students have private information about their personal effort in studying and also about their personal effort in earning income to repay loans should they cease studying. If students do not successfully complete their studies, the future high income from which it was intended that the loan be repaid may not be available. Because the conditions are generally not present under which private lenders are prepared to lend, governments are usually involved in student loans. Governments can provide guarantees of repayment of student loans to banks and other private lenders. Governments are then acting as insurance companies for the private providers of student loans.

Government might also provide loans directly through a government agency. Governments still face the problems of adverse selection and moral hazard but have an advantage in legal capabilities of enforcement of loan repayment.

Through government loan guarantees and government loans, taxpayers participate in the risks associated with students' not completing their studies, not earning incomes that allow the loans to be repaid, and then not repaying the loans. Higher interest rates compensate for the risk that loans will not be repaid.

Governments also confront questions of conditions of obligation to repay. If a person withdraws from the labor force after completing studies, should the loan be forgiven or should the loan become an obligation of family members? If a woman withdraws from the labor force to raise a family, should her husband be responsible for repaying his wife's student loans? Should she be responsible for repaying her husband's loans? What happens to the responsibility to repay the loan if the couple subsequently separates?

Also, the risk of default increases when banks are aware that the government has guaranteed student loans. There is in that case another type of moral hazard, in the nonobservable effort of the bank to secure loan repayment if default on a loan occurs.

Repayment of student loans can be made contingent on income. Income-contingent loan schemes require repayment of a loan only when personal income is sufficiently high. Income-contingent loans reduce uncertainty for the students taking the loans because the students know that they will only need to repay the loan if they will earn sufficient income to make the payments. Students, therefore, do not risk deprivation from having to make loan repayments and so are more willing to take the loans.[28]

[28] The first national income-contingent student loan scheme was introduced in Australia in 1989. Variants of income-contingent loans were introduced in New Zealand in 1992, the United States in 1993, Chile in 1994, and the United Kingdom in 1997. A limited scheme had been introduced in the 1980s in Sweden. Do the loans increase ex-ante equality, expressed in greater representation of low-income families in the student population? Evidence shows no significant change in participation in higher education across households of different income groups: again, not unavailability of equal opportunity but rather not taking advantage of opportunities is indicated to be the impediment to ex-ante equality. See Bruce Chapman and Chris Ryan (2005).

Box 8.1 An experiment with pooled risk

An income-contingent loan scheme was introduced at Yale University in the 1970s. The scheme was based on risk-pooling among students who accepted offers of admission. The students participated in a mutual insurance contract whereby those who in the future would experience good outcomes would cover the losses to the scheme from inability of other students to repay loans. Risk-pooling is subject to moral hazard through the effort to study and later to earn income after graduation. Adverse selection takes place through systematic participation in the loan program of students who believe, through private information, that they are less likely to succeed in repaying the loans. At the same time, students who believe that they will be successful and know that students with inferior prospects of success are in the insurance pool will not participate. The student loan scheme was not sustainable. Indeed, a problem for Yale was that students who expected to be successful in their studies preferred to accept offers of admission to other universities where student loans did not require participating in pooled risk.[29]

Should entitlements be provided through affirmative action?

If ex-ante equality cannot be otherwise assured, should entitlements to education be provided through *affirmative action*, which allows preferential access to colleges and universities of people who have been judged not to have had equal opportunities? Affirmative action is controversial. There is injustice when the criterion for preferential admission is belonging to a particular racial or ethnic group or having a particular type of name, because the beneficiaries may be people who satisfy the criteria but personally were not denied access to opportunities. People from outside the groups targeted for affirmative action can claim that there has been unfair discrimination when they discover that they have been denied admission to a college or university while others with inferior academic records have been admitted in their place. Students from the preferentially targeted groups who satisfy criteria for admission to a college or university on their own merit can feel that affirmative action is disparaging because of the presumption by others that they have benefited from discriminatory privilege when, in fact, their successes are the result of their own efforts and achievements.

Differences in abilities

How is equal opportunity to be provided when abilities differ? At school, faster learning and slower learning children both benefit from specialized attention. Should children who have learning disabilities receive special attention but not those who are fast learners and who become bored with the normal progress of

[29] The Yale student loan scheme was studied by Marc Nerlove (1975).

class learning? If children or students are not "equal" in aptitudes and abilities, does equality in educational opportunity imply the same educational means and pace of teaching for everyone? To address individual differences in ability, children can be screened at young ages, with higher ability children placed in special classes that advance at a faster pace than regular classes. However, separating better students into special classes lowers classroom standards.

Privilege and meritocracy

Ex-ante equality is intended to prevent privilege. Through ex-ante equality, the intention is that society becomes a meritocracy in which people succeed according to personal merit. A meritocracy based on ex-ante equality is socially just. A meritocracy is also efficient because through comparative advantage personal abilities can be matched with competencies required for different tasks. In a meritocracy based on ex-ante equality, a medical researcher, a professor, architect, builder, dentist, and others are not necessarily the children of privileged families but rather are the best in their field or profession that a society can have. Meritocracy underlies the social and economic mobility that is a means of seeking social justice without income redistribution through government.

D. Targeted entitlements and incentives

Universal entitlements such as education are intended to be accepted by everyone to facilitate achieving the social objective of ex-ante equality. Targeted entitlements are, in contrast, directed at people in need. Societies prefer that targeted entitlements, which include unemployment insurance and welfare payments, not be utilized. Other entitlements that societies prefer to not be utilized are in-kind transfers of housing and food. Self-reliance is preferred to accepting the need-based targeted entitlements. Incentives therefore are important. John Stuart Mill (1848, p. 334) stated the incentive problem in terms of the objective:

> ...to give the greatest amount of helpful need with the smallest encouragement to undue reliance on it.

Because entitlements affect incentives, we return, therefore, to the question:

> *How can public policy resolve the moral-hazard and adverse-selection principal–agent problems that arise because of the benevolence of the state?*

We addressed this question in somewhat abstract ways in the previous chapter when considering the objective of social justice. With respect to moral hazard, we identified the inevitability of making type-1 or type-2 errors. We now address the incentive problem more pragmatically in terms of design of public policy.

Unemployment insurance

We begin with public policy regarding unemployment insurance. The entitlements of unemployment insurance provide income conditional on having had a job.[30] The entitlements apply when unemployment is considered involuntary and is predicted to be temporary.

Why is there involuntary unemployment?

A number of explanations have been proposed for involuntary unemployment.

- A minimum wage: For low-skilled people, an explanation for unemployment is a minimum wage. Figure 8.5 shows a person who cannot earn a legally determined minimum wage. No employer will give this person a job. For example, by employing the person at the minimum wage for L_1 hours, an employer would lose an amount of money equal to the shaded area shown in the figure. When unemployment is due to a minimum wage, unemployment insurance may not be relevant because the requirements of having been previously employed and temporary unemployment may not be satisfied.[31]
- Deficient demand: The Keynesian explanation for unemployment, named after John Maynard Keynes (1883–1946), is based on insufficient demand

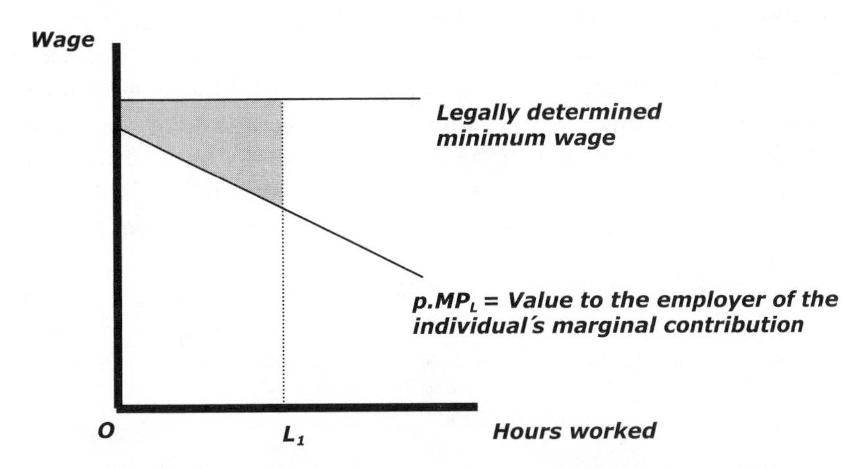

Figure 8.5. An individual unemployed because of a minimum wage.

[30] The entitlements are generally financed by payroll taxes paid by employers on behalf of employees, although employees may also contribute. We saw in chapter 4 that the true shares of payments of taxes and also shares of the excess burden of taxation depend on elasticities of supply and demand, not on the legal liability to pay a tax; if supply of labor is quite inelastic, the true share of the cost of unemployment insurance paid by the employee is high, even if nominally the employer is required to pay all or the greater part of the tax that finances the insurance.

[31] Prohibition of working at less than a legally determined minimum wage is a case of prohibited markets. A justification proposed for a legal minimum wage is to protect low-skilled workers from the monopsony of employers. Minimum wages are generally set to provide socially (or politically) acceptable minimal returns from working.

for workers and a real wage that does not fall to equate supply and demand in the labor market.

- Insider-outsider theory: Another explanation for unemployment views insiders in a firm as creating rents for themselves through high salaries and wages; the high wages and salaries restrict demand for labor inside firms and leave outsiders unemployed. Unemployment is, according to this explanation, the consequence of rent creation by people who have jobs and can determine wages.
- Efficiency wages: We considered efficiency wages as a possible solution to the bureaucratic principal–agent problem. Efficiency wages are also associated with rent creation, however, by employers. According to the *efficiency-wage hypothesis*, employers pay high wages in order to create rents for employees. Because of the rents, employees have incentives not to be caught exerting low effort (or shirking) because being dismissed will result in loss of the rents. The high wages that deter shirking create unemployment because the wages paid are in excess of the wages that would equate supply and demand in the labor market. The efficiency imparted by the high wages is that, although their effort is imperfectly observable by employers, workers choose to exert high effort. The efficiency-wage explanation for unemployment is similar to the explanation for unemployment proposed by Karl Marx (1818–83), whom we encountered as a founding father of communism. Marx explained unemployment to be a conspiracy of employers. In Marx's explanation, a "reserve army" of labor waits outside the factory gates for jobs to become available. Workers with jobs pass the unemployed workers at the factory gates and are thereby made aware that if they were to press for higher wages or better working conditions, or were to be found shirking, someone else would take their job – and it is they who will be outside the factory gates.
- Unemployment as a social custom: Unemployment has also been explained to be the consequence of a social custom whereby employers prefer to dismiss workers rather than to leave all workers employed but decrease wages.

Each of these explanations for unemployment can have validity.[32] Whatever the reason for a worker having become unemployed, we view unemployed workers as engaged in a search process whereby they seek to match their abilities and experience with job vacancies to obtain the highest possible income or job satisfaction. The duration of unemployment depends on the time taken to find a suitable match between the attributes of the person who is unemployed and the

[32] John Maynard Keynes, who is regarded as the founder of macroeconomics, set out his theory in 1936. The insider–outsider view of unemployment based on rent creation within firms was set out by Dennis Snower and Assar Lindbeck (1988). On the efficiency-wage hypothesis, see Carl Shapiro and Joseph Stiglitz (1984). Karl Marx set out his explanation in his book *Capital* published in 1887. Unemployment as a social custom was described by George Akerlof (1980).

attributes sought by an employer. That is, we view the quest to find a job in terms of *search theory*.[33]

The private benefit of unemployment insurance

Unemployment insurance is beneficial privately and socially. The *private benefit* is that people avoid being in need or destitute when they are temporarily not earning income. Unemployment insurance also allows averaging or smoothing of consumption over time. In the absence of unemployment insurance, unemployment might require people to mortgage their houses to provide collateral for loans for consumption. They could end up without both a job and a house if they are very unlucky. Unemployment insurance avoids the personal additional risks of having to mortgage assets for loans when people are already in adverse personal circumstances because of unemployment.

The social benefit of unemployment insurance

The *social benefit* of unemployment insurance is efficient job search, by increasing the length of time during which people can look for a suitable job. Without unemployment insurance, job choices might be made too quickly. By providing extended time to search for a job, unemployment insurance increases the likelihood that jobseekers will find jobs for which they are well suited rather than having to accept an unsuitable job. Other jobseekers benefit when jobseekers do not take jobs that are more suitable for other people. Unemployment insurance therefore is socially beneficial in improving matching between jobseekers and jobs – or in facilitating employment according to comparative advantage.

Asymmetric information and unemployment insurance

We noted three reasons associated with asymmetric information for failure of private insurance markets to provide insurance. The three reasons are present in the case of unemployment insurance. *Adverse selection* arises because of asymmetric information when people have private information about their likelihood of losing their job and the likelihood of finding a new one: some people tend to lose their job more often than others, perhaps because they are unlucky, but also perhaps because they lack qualities that employers value (for example, timeliness in arriving at work, consistency in coming to work, initiative, diligence); some people (perhaps the same people) also find it more difficult than others to receive a job offer. Governments can respond to failure of private insurance markets due to adverse selection by making unemployment insurance compulsory. However, with all people compelled to be in the same insurance pool, income is systematically redistributed from people less likely to be unemployed to people with a greater likelihood of losing their job and with greater likelihood of being unemployed for considerable periods. Private insurance markets also fail because of asymmetric information that results in *moral hazard*. The presence of

[33] The view of unemployment as a process of search was proposed in 1962 by George Stigler (1911–91). He received the Nobel Prize in 1982.

unemployment insurance can affect the unobservable effort that people put into keeping and finding jobs. Private insurance markets can fail to provide unemployment insurance for the third reason of asymmetric information about whether the outcome against which insurance is sought has arisen; a person who claims to be unemployed may actually have a job in the informal sector of the economy.

Asymmetric information and private lenders

In the absence of unemployment insurance, an unemployed person could attempt to borrow to finance living expenses with the intention of repaying the loan after finding a job. Private lenders, however, face the same deterrents of asymmetric information through adverse selection, moral hazard, and inability to verify unemployment. Private lenders have no assurance that jobseekers will find jobs and that they will ever be repaid.

The role of government in unemployment insurance

When private-insurance markets fail to provide unemployment insurance, government becomes the insurer of last resort. Compulsory taxes are levied to finance unemployment benefits (and there are excess burdens of taxation). Governments then confront the asymmetric-information problems. Governments can attempt to address the asymmetric-information problems by maintaining personal histories of unemployment: the likelihood and expected duration of future unemployment could be inferred from an individual's past unemployment record and judgments made about how the type or attributes of the person affect prospects for employment (adverse selection) and about the person's choice of personal effort to find or willingness to accept a job offer (moral hazard). Social workers and detectives might be used in an attempt to ascertain whether people are truly unemployed. However, collection of such information is costly and not all problems of asymmetric information will necessarily be resolved. Governments nonetheless oversee or provide unemployment insurance, which raises public-policy questions about the design of a government's unemployment-insurance program.

The schedule for payment of benefits over time

In response to asymmetric information, governments limit unemployment insurance to a specified period. Figure 8.6 shows a time limit for the duration of unemployment benefits and an individual's market wage if a job offer is accepted. Policies *A* and *B* provide alternative schedules for payment of unemployment benefits over time. Policy *A* pays constant unemployment benefits for the duration of the limited time that benefits are provided. Policy *B* pays unemployment benefits that decline over time. When not working, the individual has additional leisure, the value of which per unit of time is also shown in figure 8.6.[34] When

[34] Diminishing returns to leisure for a labor–leisure decision occur in figure 8.6 at a point in time but not over time. When not working, the number of hours of leisure at each point in time is constant. At a point in time, the total utility from leisure is, therefore, also constant. In figure 8.6 the constant value of leisure at each point in time is added to the value of unemployment benefits.

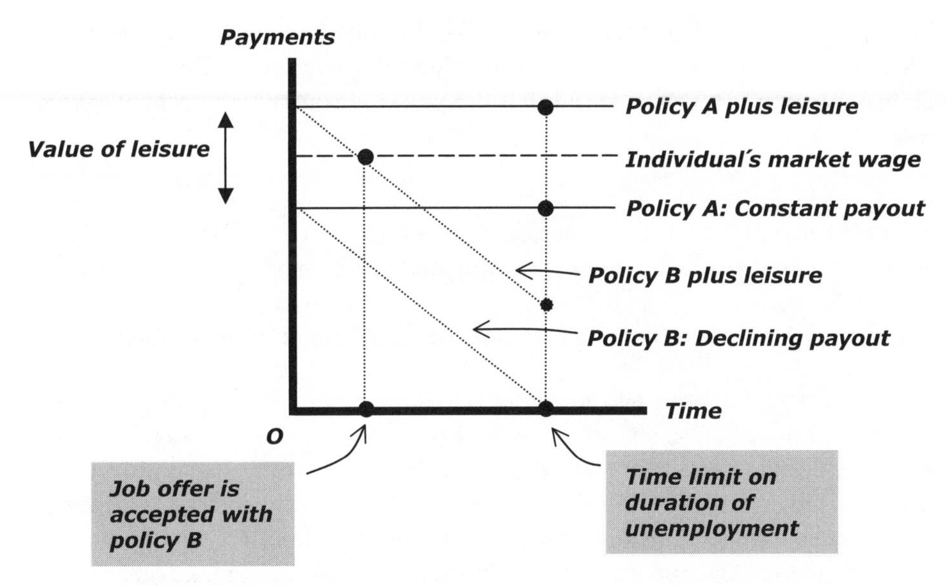

Figure 8.6. Unemployment insurance payouts.

the value of leisure is added to the constant payments of policy *A*, a job offer is not accepted until the time at which unemployment benefits cease – because the payments from policy *A* plus the value of leisure exceed the wage if a job offer is accepted. Adding the value of leisure to the benefits paid through policy *B*, however, provides an incentive to be willing to accept a job offer before the time limit for cessation of benefit payments is reached: the time at which the individual is willing to accept a job offer is determined where the wage if employed equals the payment from policy *B* plus the value of leisure. Of course, willingness to accept a job offer does not ensure that a job offer will have been received. Policy *B* addresses the moral-hazard problem but governments generally provide the constant payouts of policy *A*.

Compulsory self-financed unemployment benefits

Compulsory unemployment benefits can be self-financed. After a person who has been unemployed accepts a job offer, the income received during the period of unemployment could be repaid through compulsory payments to the government. The advantage of this scheme is that people are spending their own money when making use of unemployment benefits because they themselves will need to repay the money that they received. They have an incentive, therefore, to minimize time unemployed. The moral-hazard problem is resolved through personal internalization of the costs of paying unemployment benefits. In this design of unemployment insurance, people have their own personal compulsory unemployment-insurance account, into which they pay when employed and from which they withdraw money if unemployed. The moral-hazard problem is resolved because people are aware that they are spending their own money when drawing on the unemployment-insurance account. The purpose of insurance, however, is to spread risk over many people. Personal unemployment-insurance accounts do not spread risk because individuals have their own account. It is, of course, because risk is not spread that the personal compulsory accounts avoid moral hazard.

A work ethic and emotional stress of unemployment

People with a work ethic are not susceptible to moral hazard and suffer emotional stress if unemployed because of a feeling of inadequacy in being unable to be self-reliant. Because for people with a work ethic unemployment is demeaning and stressful, such people are willing to accept a suitable job offer immediately.

Unemployment insurance and job-protection laws

Because of the emotional costs of unemployment through loss of dignity, some countries have job-protection laws that make dismissing workers administratively complex and costly for employers, if even possible. If laws protect jobs, there is limited need for unemployment insurance for those workers who have jobs. Job-protection laws, however, make the decision of an employer to take on an additional worker risky because, if market conditions change, it will be impossible to fire the worker. It will also be difficult to fire a worker who is revealed in the course of time to be unsuitable, and it will not be possible to replace an inferior worker with an available superior and more qualified worker. Job-protection laws therefore create and sustain inefficient job-market matching. Because employers' expected benefits from hiring are reduced, job creation and economic growth also decline. For young people entering the labor market, unemployment insurance is preferable to job-protection laws. The beneficiaries of job-protection laws are incumbent workers and the politicians who benefited from political support in advocating for and implementing the policies. Societies with job-protection laws tend to have persistently higher unemployment than societies that protect workers through unemployment insurance.

Persistent welfare dependence

Payments received through unemployment insurance are intended for periods of temporary unemployment. There is welfare dependence when people are persistently not self-reliant because they do not work for a living.

Some people are incapable of working for a living because of physical or emotional impairment. There are also people for whom impairment is a limitation on the type of job that can be accepted (and that can be offered) but they actively seek productive employment in order to have a feeling of self-esteem and not be a financial burden on others. Special work conditions are often created to allow people with impairments to work.[35]

[35] In a number of cities, there are restaurants in which darkness brings patrons into equality with impaired waiters and waitresses who have limited or no vision. In other circumstances as well, people seek jobs within their capabilities.

Nonetheless, some people are incapable of working because of impairment. Whether or not we are behind the veil of ignorance, we would all agree that people for whom fate has resulted in impairment that prevents them from working should be helped through tax-financed income payments.

When people are capable of working and entitlements are provided contingent on not working, the possibility of moral hazard is present. The moral hazard can be the basis for persistence of welfare dependency.

In the previous chapter, we considered reasons why societies might be composed of people with diverse susceptibilities to moral hazard. We noted that in a society in which a work ethic was previously prevalent, susceptibility to moral hazard is created when norms of behavior change and stigma is no longer an impediment to receiving welfare payments. For individuals, norms are reflected in peer behavior: if peer behavior is to not work for a living, there is no stigma from not exerting effort to find a job.

Changed norms that eliminate stigma, therefore, can create welfare dependence through reliance on entitlements. However, norms could not change if entitlements were not present to allow behavior to change. That is, the presence of entitlements defines the scope of feasible personal behavior.

Norms and attitudes regarding single motherhood, for example, changed in the latter half of the 20th century. Women who in previous generations would have been deterred by stigma from being a single mother could choose to have children without stigma, but also knowing that the entitlement to income support is available.[36]

Before the entitlements were available, households traditionally relied on men for income. Men have fewer qualms about leaving families when they know that the government will replace them as providers. Welfare payments thus make men more willing to abrogate traditional responsibilities for providing income for mothers and children.[37]

The presence of entitlements thus facilitates welfare dependence. However, how entitlements affect behavior is also affected by the conditions for benefiting from entitlements – particularly whether income transfers from governments are contingent on working or not working.

Income support contingent on work

When welfare payments provide incomes contingent on not working, people may be capable of working, but labor-market incomes that can be earned are too low

[36] In the United States, for example, families with children headed by a female who had never been married increased from 3 percent of households in 1976 to 10 percent in 2000 (Blank, 2002). The change in norms occurred at the same time as benefits to single mothers from social security were declining. Evidence indicates that changed social norms influenced behavior more so than changes in government-provided benefits. For elaboration and evidence, see Margaret Brinig and F. H. Buckley (1999).

[37] Among homeless people, there tend to be more males than females. Often, the homeless are marginally functional and cannot cope with the responsibilities of having a home and a job.

to permit complete self-reliance. To allow a personal choice to work, governments can provide supplementary income transfers.

In chapter 7, in considering possibilities for social justice without government, we encountered a private donor who wanted to provide income support contingent on the recipient contributing to income by working. A proposed response to a Nash equilibrium in which the recipient did not work was to delegate responsibility for providing income assistance to a government bureaucracy that would follow "rules not discretion" and would enforce work as a condition for supplementary income transfers. However, when the government has replaced the private donor, the outcome can also be that the income recipient takes advantage of benevolence and does not work. The question that was asked when the charity of the private donor was the source of income transfers can be asked again with reference to the public-policy decisions of government:

> *How can public policy encourage people who are capable of working to choose to work?*

Choose is important here. We are seeking to identify public policies that result in *voluntary* choice of work in response to incentives that make work worthwhile.

Marginal and binary work decisions

The decision of whether to work is binary. In contrast, marginal work decisions are made when the decision has already been made to work. Marginal work decisions underlie the substitution effect between work and leisure that is the reason for excess burdens of taxation. Elasticities of labor supply determine the marginal adjustments that are made in hours worked when net-of-tax wages change. The leaky bucket of redistribution of income was described as due to such marginal work–leisure adjustments that result in efficiency losses because of the excess burden of taxation. We make the following distinction:

> *People who are working face marginal adjustment decisions in choosing between work and leisure.*
>
> *People who are not working but are capable of work face the binary decision of whether or not to work.*

We consider now the binary decision of whether or not to work.

Welfare payments

When tax-financed income support is provided through welfare payments to people who do not work, the activity of "not earning income" is subsidized. An alternative public policy is to make income support contingent on work. Figure 8.7 shows an individual's supply-of-labor function S_L. The individual's market-determined wage if he or she works is w. The market wage w can be a legal minimum wage but need not be. At the wage w, the individual would choose, if possible, not to work (the marginal disutility of productive effort expressed

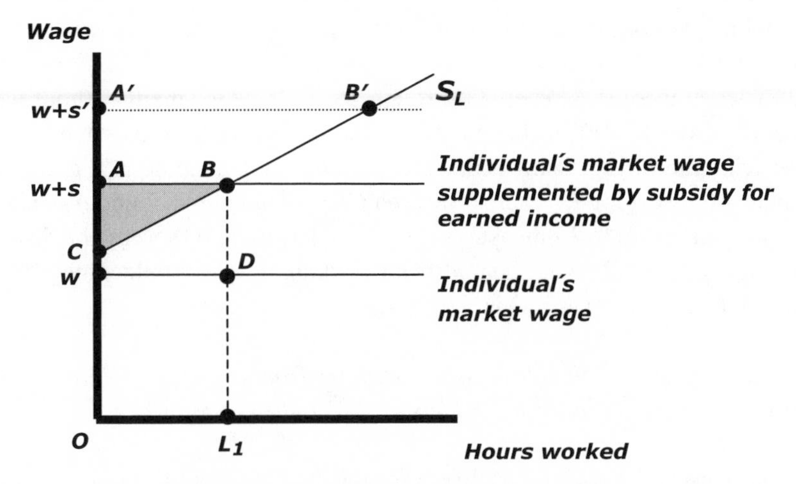

Figure 8.7. Payment conditional on work.

in the supply-of-labor function always exceeds the wage w that the individual can earn).

Welfare policy might provide the individual with an income transfer of y^{min} dollars. The excess burden of taxation increases the cost to taxpayers of the income transfer to more than y^{min} dollars.

If the welfare payment y^{min} were not provided and having no other source of income, the individual would be *biologically constrained* to work to avoid destitution and starvation. If asked, the individual would declare a dislike of work or the job that he or she has.

A wage subsidy

Public policy can be changed from welfare payments to a wage subsidy that also ensures that the income y^{min} is available. The transfer recipient continues to receive an income transfer but in a different way. The income transfer is now contingent on working.

In figure 8.7, a subsidy of s dollars for every hour worked increases the wage received to $(w + s)$ per hour. At this wage, the individual chooses to work L_1 hours.

The wage subsidy s is set to provide the same minimum income y^{min} that was previously provided in the form of welfare payments that were contingent on not working. In figure 8.7, the wage income received inclusive of the wage subsidy is equal to the area ABL_1O, which is equal to y^{min}. That is:

$$y^{min} = (w + s)L_1. \tag{8.1}$$

Loss to the transfer recipient because of the wage subsidy

Although the transfer recipient's income remains y^{min} after the change in policy to a wage subsidy, the transfer recipient, however, is worse off. Welfare payments provided the entitlement y^{min} without the need to exert work effort and without the discipline of a commitment to go to work. The wage subsidy imposes disutility of effort and work discipline.

Utility when income is received through the welfare payment without working is derived from y^{min} of income and maximal leisure. Utility when working and receiving the wage subsidy is derived from the same income y^{min} and leisure remaining after working L_1 hours. The area CBL_1O in figure 8.7 under the labor-supply function S_L up to L_1 measures the loss of leisure and thereby the disutility of working L_1 hours. The net benefit from working to earn the income y^{min} at a subsidized hourly wage $(w + s)$ is ABC.

The transfer recipient loses from a change from a welfare policy to a wage subsidy because of the loss of leisure due to the need to work.

To compensate the transfer recipient for the change in public policy, the wage subsidy would have to be greater than s dollars per hour. The area $A'B'C$ in figure 8.7 is the net benefit from participation in the labor market when the subsidy for earning income is s'. A subsidy of s' dollars per hour provides precise compensation for the change in public policy if the area $A'B'C$ is exactly equal to the income recipient's utility when obtaining maximal leisure by not working and receiving y^{min} as a welfare payment.

Gain to taxpayers from the wage subsidy

Taxpayers gain from the change to the wage subsidy. When the income y^{min} is provided without the need to work, taxes of ABL_1O are required to finance the income transfer. There is also a loss due to the excess burden of taxation. The wage subsidy lowers taxes to $ABDw$. The excess burden of taxation is also correspondingly smaller.

When the income transfer is provided without the need to work, the area DL_1Ow is a tax paid by taxpayers. The wage subsidy converts DL_1Ow to output produced by the transfer recipient who is receiving income through the wage subsidy. The value of this output is the transfer recipient's own contribution to his or her personal income.

Society's welfare

The change to the wage subsidy is not Pareto-improving because the transfer recipient has lost. We now designate the transfer recipient as person 1 and represent taxpayers by person 2. Social welfare can be measured as the *weighted* sum of utilities of the transfer recipient and the taxpayer:

$$W = \omega_1 U_1(y_1, \mathit{leisure}_1) + \omega_2 U_2(y_2, \mathit{leisure}_2). \tag{8.2}$$

With a policy of a wage subsidy, the transfer recipient loses leisure and the burden on taxpayers of ensuring that the transfer recipient has the minimum required income is reduced. If the social weight ω_1 of the transfer recipient is sufficiently high compared to the social weight of the taxpayer ω_2, in measuring social welfare, the loss in utility of the transfer recipient can outweigh the gains to the taxpayer from the change to the wage subsidy.

How should society value the leisure lost by the transfer recipient because of the change to the wage subsidy? The taxpayer and the beneficiary of the tax-financed income transfer are involved in a principal–agent relationship, with the taxpayer whose income finances the wage subsidy being the principal and the beneficiary the agent. The objective is to choose a public policy that maximizes the utility of the principal. Social weights are thus:

$$\omega_1 = 0, \quad \omega_2 = 1. \tag{8.3}$$

The wage subsidy is then preferred to the welfare payment.

In choosing the social weights in expression (8.3), society or the taxpayer as principal is not making a judgment that prevents people from choosing not to work for a living. Any person with adequate personal means can choose not to work, just as by choosing how many hours to work, people voluntarily divide their day between leisure and working. The weights in expression (8.3) reflect a judgment that:

> *Taxpayers are not obliged to provide income for people who are capable of working for a living but choose not to work – and taxpayers have the right to minimize their costs of ensuring that a minimum guaranteed income is provided.*

How would followers of Rawls value the leisure of the recipient? Followers of Rawls maximize the utility of the worst-off person in society. The worst-off person is the transfer recipient and not the taxpayer. The Rawls social welfare function, therefore, is obtained by choosing the social weights:

$$\omega_1 = 1, \quad \omega_2 = 0. \tag{8.4}$$

Based on these social weights, the transfer recipient would not need to work. Followers of Rawls, however, will choose the weights in expression (8.3) if they perceive virtue in a work ethic. A position that people should contribute according to their ability implies disregard for the transfer recipient's disutility from work.

Other benefits of wage subsidies

Wage subsidies as an alternative to welfare payments, therefore, benefit taxpayers, who pay lower taxes and who incur lower excess burdens of taxation in providing minimum-income entitlements. Society gains through increased output and, correspondingly, from the transfer recipient's own contribution to income through self-reliance. Other benefits of wage subsidies can also be identified.

The wage subsidy leads to entry into the labor market. Over time, incomes increase over the work-entry wage as job experience increases. The wage subsidy is then temporary. In changing personal behavior through labor-market participation, the wage subsidy thus changes norms to self-reliance. The self-reliance also provides self-esteem from personal contributions to own-income.

Wage subsidies provide social benefit by distracting people from a life of crime. Edmund Phelps (1994; Nobel Prize in economics, 2006) proposed that: "The relatively low wages and shortfall of jobs availability to the more disadvantaged workers push the more susceptible of them into intermittent criminal opportunities, which are plentiful and vastly better paying." If wage subsidies reduce the number of people in jail, there is a benefit to taxpayers who finance prisons – as well as the benefit of reduced crime.

Implementing a wage subsidy

In practice, a wage subsidy is not constant as shown in figure 8.7 but rather applies only at low levels of income.

How is a policy of providing a wage subsidy implemented?

A wage subsidy can be provided in the form of earned-income tax credits that make initial marginal tax rates negative. Earning income is then subsidized at low levels of income through the income tax.[38] As earned income increases, eventually – at high enough levels of income – the subsidy for earned income ends and marginal tax rates become positive.[39]

Alternatively, a wage subsidy can be paid by government to employers, who pass the subsidy on to subsidized employees when the employees are paid their wage. Employers, however, can appropriate part of the wage subsidy by reducing wages paid to a subsidized employee. Evidence confirms such behavior by employers.[40] The information that a particular worker is subsidized is made available when employers receive the employee's designated subsidy from the government. A wage subsidy paid through the income tax does not reveal to employers that a particular employee's wage is being subsidized, because although the wage is low, the employee may have other sources of taxable income.

[38] For example, the marginal tax rate might be –25 percent for the first $1,000 of income earned, in which case earning an income of $1,000 provides a total income of $1,250.

[39] In the United States, an earned-income tax credit that subsidizes earned income at low levels of income through the personal income tax was introduced in 1978. In the United Kingdom, a working family's tax credit introduced in 1999 replaced a previous less generous program; the new program was predicated on the recognition that the poorest households consisted of single mothers and couples with low incomes and not, as previously, elderly people or pensioners. There are cost savings for taxpayers if new government bureaucracies are not required when new government programs are introduced. When subsidies for earned income are part of income taxes, entitlements to subsidies are determined through personal reporting of earned income and a new government bureaucracy is not required to administer the entitlements. A problem with the earned-income tax credit arises when the credit applies to joint incomes. A couple jointly filing income-tax returns may have joint income that exceeds the income at which the tax credit applies, whereas individually, one or both individuals may qualify for the tax credit. The earned-income tax credit is then a tax on marriage or on a more informal but legally recognized joint living arrangement.

[40] Ghazala Yasmeen Azmat (2006) reported that in the United Kingdom, when the subsidy was provided through employers, employers paid subsidized employees less than nonsubsidized employees.

A wage subsidy reduces the cost to employers of subsidized workers relative to nonsubsidized workers. Employers therefore have an incentive to substitute subsidized for nonsubsidized workers. The substitution converts the entire wage subsidy to a benefit to the employer.[41] A wage subsidy therefore requires provisions for job protection of incumbent nonsubsidized workers. There is moral hazard because employers can fabricate excuses to fire a nonsubsidized employee. The opposite problem can also be present: the nonsubsidized employee may deserve to be fired, but firing would give the impression of opportunistic behavior by the employer.

Parallel policies

We have compared income entitlements that are contingent on not working with entitlements that require people to work. When the two means of providing entitlements are maintained as simultaneous parallel policies, people can choose how they wish to benefit from publicly financed income transfers. The person described in figure 8.7 would choose to receive the minimum-income entitlement as an income transfer that does not require work. A wage subsidy is generally not effective in encouraging labor-force participation if income from working with the wage subsidy is more or less the same as the income obtainable by not working – just as jobs at low, nonsubsidized wages may not be accepted when welfare payments provide more or less the same income without the need to work.

Welfare reform

A change in public policy from an income transfer contingent on not working to an income transfer that requires work for people capable of working is a *welfare reform*. A welfare reform reduces the tax burden (including the excess burden) on taxpayers. Taxpayers become more productive because of the reduced taxes. The wage subsidy also makes recipients of the income transfers more productive.

Whether a welfare reform succeeds depends on changes in behavior. Do people who were receiving welfare payments choose to work when policies attempt to change incentives to encourage work? The feasibility of welfare reform depends particularly on the credibility of government when a policy announcement is made that people who are capable of working will receive income support only if they work.

A comprehensive welfare reform took place in the United States in 1998. A program of federal government cash entitlements to families with dependent children was replaced by programs that gave state governments control over welfare payments. Entitlements to income transfers were made conditional on having a

[41] In figure 8.7, the wage paid by the employer is w, whereas the employee receives the subsidized wage $w(1+s)$. Another employee may be receiving a wage of $w(1+s)$ without being subsidized by the government. Because a subsidized worker costs the employer only w, the employer gains the entire subsidy by substituting a subsidized worker for a nonsubsidized worker.

job, and limitations were placed on the time that a person could, over the course of life, benefit from welfare payments. Greater scrutiny was applied to investigating personal circumstances of people on the welfare rolls. A social objective of the welfare reform was to discourage single motherhood and to encourage two-parent families. Because of discretion allowed by the federal government to local administering governments, conditions and responses differed among localities. Subject to regional differences, the welfare reform substantially reduced welfare dependency in the United States.[42] Governments in other countries have recognized the need for encouraging self-reliance for people capable of working.[43]

> *Welfare reforms that succeed in encouraging self-reliance are the highest form of charity (people are not given fish but rather learn how to fish).*

Yet, changed incentives alone can be insufficient to induce people to choose to take a job. Jobs, of course, need to be available that are suitable for people who are low-skilled and have limited job experience. A policy of subsidizing earned income to bring unskilled single mothers into the labor market also requires affordable child care or availability of child care through the extended family.

Also, economic incentives to accept jobs are ineffective if personal values are retained from circumstances of life in which working for a living was unnecessary to receive income transfers. Self-discipline of arriving at the workplace at a designated time and attending to assigned tasks initially may be difficult for people who have not been accustomed to organizing their time according to predetermined schedules or who have been used to deferring tasks to the future (or have been hyperbolic discounters).[44] If personal behavior does not change, credibility is tested of the policy announcement that no income support will be provided without visible effort at self-reliance. Moral hazard can persist because in a civil

[42] Rebecca Blank (2002) described the U.S. welfare reform. Between 1994 and 2000, welfare caseloads declined by 58.5 percent. Workforce participation by unmarried mothers increased by 10 percent between 1994 and 1999. The share of women who had been receiving public assistance the previous year and reported themselves as employed increased from 19.8 percent in 1990 to 44.3 percent in 2000. The share of all families in poverty declined from 11.9 percent in 1992 to 8.6 percent in 2000. Food-stamp caseloads fell by 38.5 percent between 1994 and 2000. Overall, wages for less skilled women rose in the 1990s. However, labor-force participation of unskilled men continued a falling trend in the 1990s. Blank described previous programs that had been less successful, including mandatory training for people who were capable of working. The mandatory training appeared to be not valued in markets and was less beneficial in leading to employment than work experience.

[43] On welfare reform in Australia, see Peter Saunders (2002). Charles Michalopoulos, Philip K. Robins, and David Card (2005) described programs designed to change incentives to work in Canada. A welfare reform introduced in the United Kingdom increased incentives to work but did not substantially increase labor-force participation of targeted welfare recipients: there was debate about whether labor-force participation increased at all. On disincentives to work in Germany, see Alfred Boss and Thomas Elender (2005). Herwig Immervoll, Hendrik Jacobsen Kleuven, Claus Thrustrup Kreiner, and Emmanuel Saez (2007) used simulations to study how welfare reform might affect work incentives in European countries.

[44] See Glenn Loury (1996) on personal values and social norms as countering intended work incentives of public policy.

society, welfare payments will likely be provided to people in need who do not work, even if official policy is to provide income support only as a subsidy for work.[45]

8.2 The Entitlement to Income during Old Age

Entitlements provided after retirement and during old age are not important only for older people. The financing of the entitlements may place a burden on younger people.

A. An intergenerational social contract

We begin from circumstances in which private savings are not available as means of providing for old-age consumption. This occurs when food cannot be stored and when there are no financial or real assets that can be owned and sold in the future to finance consumption during years of retirement. The conditions, therefore, are those of a hunter–gatherer society.

A hunter–gatherer society

In a hunter–gatherer society, food is obtained by hunting animals and by gathering fruit and vegetables that grow in the wild. Under these conditions, the old can survive only if the young give them food. There is no money in this society: if there were money, people could store money and use the money to finance consumption during old age. The young might be willing to provide the old with food only if the old provide something in return. The old, however, have nothing with which they can pay the young because the old no longer work and have been unable to store food or assets during their productive years.

Now let us introduce money as certificates of entitlement to consumption. The old can trade the certificates for food with the young. The young generation will

[45] The U.S. welfare reform set, in principle, a lifetime limit on time receiving welfare. The time limit was intended to provide incentives to use welfare payments only in times of true need. The time limit became a soft rather than a hard or binding constraint. For example, in the state of Connecticut, a woman could receive an indefinite exemption from the need to work if she were "deemed unemployable due to limited work history and human capital." Exemptions were granted if family income was low and it was judged that a good-faith effort had been made to find and retain employment. If no good-faith determination was made, an extension of time on welfare was possible if there were "circumstances beyond the recipient's control that prevent(ed) her from working" (Bitler, Gelbach, and Hoynes, 2006, p. 996).

be prepared to accept the certificates of entitlement in exchange for food if the certificates can later be exchanged for food when the young have themselves become old and have retired from productive activity.

The transferable certificates of entitlement to old-age consumption allow a social contract whereby the productive generation always provides food for the retired generation. Under the social contract, no two generations engage in bilateral exchange with one another. The transfers of consumption are unilateral from productive young people at any point in time to the retired generation.

The social contract involves generations as yet unborn, who in the future will accept certificates of entitlement and provide old people with food. The unborn generations, of course, are not present when the social contract is set out. The social contract may specify the amount of food that the old will receive. Generations as yet unborn are obliged under the contract to make the designated future transfers of food, even though they did not participate in the formulation of the conditions of the social contract. However, everyone in each generation gains from the social contract by having food and being cared for in their old age:

The intergenerational contract is Pareto-improving.

If the social contract whereby the young provide for the old cannot be implemented, a society is in an unfortunate situation. The old starve and, because everyone eventually becomes old, everyone's life span is shortened.

If a generation of productive people were to renege on the social contract by refusing to provide food for the old, the reneging generation would have more to consume during its productive years. The reneging generation, when old, would have to rely on the next younger generation to feed them. They would have to hope that the next generation of young workers did not copy their own behavior in refusing to feed the old. It is clearly not in the self-interest of any productive generation to break the chain of intergenerational transfers. The continuation of intergenerational transfers is the source of a working generation's own future survival. Abrogating the contract of intergenerational transfers would make every generation worse off.

There have been hunter–gatherer societies without a social contract of intergenerational transfers. In those societies, by not providing for the old, the younger productive generations set the precedent for their own early demise.

Demonstration effects

The intergenerational contract is based on a continued precedent of caring for and feeding the old. Can the precedent be based on a demonstration effect?

A demonstration effect occurs when people set examples that they intend others to follow.

A demonstration effect would thus explain income transfers from the young to the old if the young productive generation provides income for the old with the intention of setting an example for children and students not yet working. The generation setting the example hopes to benefit when it is old and cannot fend for itself.

Intergenerational transfers would break down if a demonstration effect were the reason for the income transfers. Members of a young productive generation would reason: "We do not need to provide for the old in order that our children will provide for us when we are old. Our children will provide for us in any event. Our children will want to provide for us because, by providing for us, they demonstrate the act of making the transfers to their young, so that their young will provide for them in the future." With each productive generation rationally reasoning this way, no intergenerational transfers take place.

> *A demonstration effect does not provide a rational basis for intergenerational transfers from the young to the old.*

Ethical norms

An alternative to a demonstration effect as the basis for ongoing transfers from the young to the old is an ethical norm that the young should support the old.[46] The ethical norm ensures continuation of the efficient contract whereby the young will be cared for when they are themselves old. Therefore:

> *A norm of ethical behavior of providing for the old is efficient.*

The social contract and pay-as-you-go transfers

The injunction of children caring for parents places the ethical norm of support for the old within the family. A government collectivizes the intergenerational income transfers by taxing young people and transferring income to retired people. Such publicly financed intergenerational transfers are known as *pay-as-you-go schemes.*

> *Under a pay-as-you-go scheme, taxes paid by working generations are used to finance the consumption of retired generations.*

Under a pay-as-you-go scheme, there is no accumulated fund that finances old-age consumption.

A free-rider problem and taxation

In a pay-as-you-go scheme of intergenerational transfers, collective payments are made by a working generation to finance private consumption for an older generation. The collective transfer from the young productive population to retired

[46] Such an ethical norm is expressed in the injunction: "Honor your father and mother so that your days on earth may be long."

people introduces free-riding incentives. Without the compulsory payments of taxation, some members of the young working population might choose not to make transfers to the old, while relying on a "social safety net" of tax-financed consumption to provide for them when they are old and have retired. Compulsory taxes during productive years preempt such free-rider behavior.

B. Sustainability of intergenerational income transfers

Pay-as-you-go schemes of intergenerational income transfers become unsustainable if there is an excessive decline in the dependency ratio. We define the dependency ratio excluding children:

> *The dependency ratio for adults is the number of people receiving income transfers relative to the number of people financing the income transfers.*

That is, if the number of people in the retired generation is n_R and the number of people in the generation that is working is n_W, the dependency ratio is:

$$\alpha = \left(\frac{n_R}{n_W}\right). \tag{8.5}$$

The dependency ratio α increases when:

- People take earlier retirement (an increase in n_R).
- Improvements in health standards result in people living longer after retirement (also an increase in n_R).
- Demographic change takes place whereby birth rates decline and so a younger generation has fewer people (a decrease in n_W).

We retain for now the framework of a society where old people can only survive if the young provide them with income. Pay-as-you-go schemes can designate the contributions that people make when working or designate the benefits that people receive when retired.

Designated contributions

For simplicity, we shall consider all members of the same generation as earning the same income. A rate of tax t is levied on the lifetime income y of each member of a productive generation for the purpose of financing transfers to retired people. In practice, the tax can be specifically for providing the income transfers (a social security tax), or can be part of the general collection of tax revenue and pensions can be financed through the government budget. Each working person has an income during his or her working life of $y(1-t)$ after paying the tax.

The total value of the taxes collected from the working generation is $n_W ty$. Each member of the retired generation receives:

$$\tau = \left(\frac{n_W}{n_R}\right) ty = \frac{ty}{\alpha}. \tag{8.6}$$

Therefore:

> *As the dependency ratio increases, each retired person receives a smaller income transfer.*

We denote the rate of population increase between generations by g. That is:

$$n_W = n_R(1+g). \tag{8.7}$$

Substituting the expression (8.7) into (8.6) gives the transfer received by an individual in the retired generation as:

$$\tau = (1+g)ty. \tag{8.8}$$

A retired person will have paid ty in taxes when working and receives the amount given by expression (8.8) when retired. Therefore:

> *The rate of population growth g is the rate of return from the intergenerational pay-as-you-go income-transfer scheme.*

If population size does not change between generations so that $g = 0$, the rate of return from the intergenerational transfer scheme is zero. Or, if g is negative, the return from the pay-as-you-go scheme is negative.

Even with g zero or negative, the intergenerational transfer scheme is beneficial. The transfers allow consumption to be transferred from the productive period of a person's life to the period when the person is not working.

If population is growing so that $g > 0$, the pay-as-you-go scheme of intergenerational transfers yields a positive rate of return. Retired people not only are provided with old-age consumption but also receive back more than they originally contributed.

Designated benefits for retired people

An alternative to designated payments is an intergenerational transfer scheme with designated benefits for retired people. For example, all retired people may be entitled to post-retirement income, or pension Z. The tax payment per member of the working population required to finance the designated benefit Z is:

$$T = \frac{n_R}{n_W} \cdot Z = \alpha Z. \tag{8.9}$$

Therefore:

> *The tax per member of a working generation required to finance the designated benefit increases with the dependency ratio.*

The tax payment T depends on the relative size of the two generations, or on demographics. If the population is increasing, the dependency ratio is declining and therefore the tax burden (and excess burden) on members of the working generation is declining. The tax burden (and excess burden) conversely increases over time if the dependency ratio is increasing over time.

The benefit of being the first generation of beneficiaries

High designated benefits for retired people benefit initial participants in a pay-as-you-go intergenerational income-transfer scheme. The first beneficiaries will have paid nothing (the scheme did not exist when they were working) and when retired they benefited from the contributions made by the working generation.

A Ponzi scheme

Pay-as-you-go social security and pension schemes that provide high designated benefits to retired people can be like a Ponzi scheme.[47] Initial participants gain whereas later participants lose. However, participation in a Ponzi scheme is voluntary (and foolish). Participation in a tax-financed intergenerational transfer scheme of social security is compulsory.

Solutions to the problem of increasing tax burdens

With designated benefits, when in expression (8.9) tax burdens on working generations increase because of increases in the dependency ratio, the tax-paying working population might propose a downward revision of retirement benefits Z. The retired population, and people close to retirement, would have reason to object. From their perspective, the proposal is a violation of the intergenerational social contract. The retired population financed retirement benefits at the specified level of benefits Z in the past when working and paying taxes. When retired and no longer working, the older population expects to receive the same benefits that it provided when paying for retirement benefits for others.

To decrease their tax burden, members of the young working population might propose an increase in the age at which retirement benefits become available. Because n_W would increase and n_R would decline, the dependency ratio α would decline, thereby lowering the tax T on the working population. People nearing retirement might object to this proposal.

The tax burden for financing the designated benefits of pay-as-you-go retirement benefits falls if the productivity of the working population increases. Productivity growth increases the pre-tax per capita income y of the working population. Even if population is declining, sufficient growth in productivity can provide a positive return from an intergenerational transfer scheme.

[47] In a Ponzi scheme (named for Charles Ponzi, the first well-known perpetrator), high returns to initial investors are financed by borrowing at high interest rates from other investors. The scheme breaks down when no more investors can be found to finance the high interest rates for previous investors. In the chain-letter version, people receive a letter or e-mail with a list of people to whom they are asked to send money. The new participants in the scheme are invited to add their names to the list of future recipients of money and to forward the letter to other people who are invited to join by sending money to the new participant in the scheme and to the others on the original list. No investment takes place by the initial investors in a Ponzi scheme. Unidirectional transfers take place as in pay-as-you-go intergenerational transfer schemes. Initial investors receive high returns, whereas later investors lose their money when the Ponzi scheme ultimately breaks down (as it must because the population of participants is finite).

Demographic problems can therefore be solved or moderated by increased investment in education that increases a working generation's productivity. A working generation that will benefit in the future at retirement consequently has an incentive to increase spending on education of the young.[48]

Immigration of productive people can expand the tax base for intergenerational transfers. However, larger numbers of immigrants that are feasible may be required to sustain the defined benefits of an intergenerational transfer scheme.[49] Eventually, the immigrants themselves will retire and become eligible for intergenerational transfers. Increasing immigration may be required over time to sustain the benefits to which the old have become accustomed.

Whereas immigration can be part of the solution, emigration can be part of the problem. Faced with high taxes because of demographic imbalance, young productive people can choose to emigrate to tax jurisdictions where taxes to finance intergenerational transfers are lower. Such emigration further deteriorates the demographic imbalance. The society from which the productive young are emigrating confronts the problem of adverse selection: as more young productive people leave, the tax burden on those productive people remaining increases, so they too might be inclined to emigrate – and their emigration further increases the tax burden on those who have so far remained.

The demographic prisoners' dilemma

Suppose, only hypothetically, that children provide no intrinsic personal benefit to parents and that the cost of having and raising children falls exclusively on parents. When grown and working, however, the children pay taxes that finance income transfers to all members of the older population. The conditions of a prisoners' dilemma are then present. Each person will wish personally to have no children and will wish to impose the burden of having children on others. The dominant strategy is to attempt to free ride in receiving income support in old age. In the Nash equilibrium of the prisoners' dilemma, there will be no children and therefore no future tax base for intergenerational income transfers.[50]

An escape from the demographic prisoners' dilemma takes place if the pay-as-you-go intergenerational transfers are canceled and incomes of children become a personal and not a collective means of providing intergenerational transfers. Grown working children then care only for their own aged parents. People who do not have children then condemn themselves to an early death because they will receive no support in their old age.

[48] For example, if people are twice as productive, the tax burden per taxpayer is halved because it is as if twice as many taxpayers were financing the designated benefits to the retired population.

[49] Immigration is possible as a solution when net-of-tax wages and tax-financed benefits in a country are higher than in foreign locations so that productive people can be attracted to immigrate.

[50] Each person makes the calculation: "If others have children, my best response is not to have children, and if others do not have children, again my best response is not to have children."

In poorer countries of the world, governments have not provided social security and children have been a form of personal insurance within the extended family. The output of the extended family is shared among all family members.[51] Yet, when the extended family is the means of providing social security, some uncaring children might not provide for their parents, thereby leaving their parents destitute in old age. Some people may simply not have children.[52] Requiring reliance on one's own children for survival during advanced years can be capricious and unjust.

Insurance against not having children is provided through a collective scheme of intergenerational transfers that pools all children's contributions to provide consumption for all old people. The government is then providing social insurance against the risk that people find themselves without children. However, a society then confronts the demographic prisoners' dilemma because of the collectivization of benefits from having children. There is moral hazard: a government providing old-age social insurance cannot precisely identify reasons why people have not had children and therefore cannot penalize free riding.

Compensation for people who have productive children

Privatized social security through the family is a response to the demographic prisoners' dilemma but, as we have seen, is not a satisfactory response because of people who cannot rely on a family for old-age support. People who do not have children, however, can compensate those who do through tax credits and deductions and direct transfer payments based on the number of children. Schooling and child health services are often subsidized. Childless people then contribute to the cost of other people's children through taxes that finance education and health care for children – and benefit when old from the then-grown children's intergenerational transfers.

The Tiebout mechanism and fiscal federalism

If, through the Tiebout locational-choice mechanism, people without children locate in areas where they are not required to finance schools but they receive retirement benefits through a national or federal level of government, childless people are free riding for old-age provision on people who have children. The multiple governments of fiscal federalism allow people to choose public goods, community values, and private-good tax-financed entitlements according to their preferences. Free riding with regard to intergenerational transfers is avoided if investment in education that provides future productive children is financed by taxes levied at the federal or central level of government.

[51] The older retired generation often contributes by caring for the young children when the parents who are the productive generation are at work.

[52] They may not have been able or the opportunities for having children may not have presented themselves.

Free riding and personal costs of parents

With fiscal federalism, free riding is present nonetheless if many of the costs of having and rearing children are private, non-monetized, uncompensated, and fall on the parents.[53]

Unequal benefits from intergenerational income redistribution

The income redistribution through intergenerational transfers need not be equal, either between or within generations. Between generations, in particular, we noted that the first generation of beneficiaries of a pay-as-you-go scheme necessarily gains from the scheme because this generation made no payments and only receives benefits. Also, the last working generation before a scheme becomes bankrupt necessarily loses because it pays into the scheme but receives no payout. Within generations, women tend to gain relative to men by retiring earlier and living longer. People in bad health lose because they have a lower chance of reaching the age at which retirement benefits begin. If the dependency ratio is increasing, older people gain more than younger people.

Generational accounting

The viability of a pay-as-you-go intergenerational transfer scheme can be determined through generational accounting. For example, with designated benefits for people reaching retirement age, a government knows with some accuracy the present value of future obligations to pay pensions and social security over the next 50 years because these are obligations based on people who are alive today who will reach retirement age in the future. The obligations are the designated benefits for the next 50 years:

$$\{B_1, B_2, B_3, \ldots, B_{50}\}. \tag{8.10}$$

Based on prevailing tax rates, the government also knows its future revenue for financing retirement obligations:

$$\{R_1, R_2, R_3, \ldots, R_{50}\}. \tag{8.11}$$

With δ indicating the discount rate (see chapter 3), a pension or social security scheme based on designated benefits is viable if the present value of the net revenue stream is positive. That is, viability requires:

$$PV = (R_0 - B_0) + \delta(R_1 - B_1) + \delta^2(R_2 - B_2) + \cdots + \delta^{50}(R_{50} - B_{50}) > 0. \tag{8.12}$$

[53] Personal non-monetized costs arise when people feel that children limit entertainment and lifestyle opportunities. A child may increase the cost of switching partners and can interfere with personal career advancement.

If this condition is not satisfied, the pay-as-you-go scheme of intergenerational income transfers is technically bankrupt.

In many or, indeed, most high-income countries that have intergenerational pay-as-you-go transfer schemes, because of increasing dependency ratios, generational accounting indicates impending bankruptcy. What can stave off bankruptcy?

Willingness to have more children is one answer. Another answer is higher productivity growth. Government may be unable, however, to influence fertility or productivity sufficiently to avoid the bankruptcy of the intergenerational transfer scheme.

In terms of policy that can be directly implemented by governments, higher retirement ages and lower designated benefits combined with higher tax rates would defer bankruptcy. However, as we have noted, people will have spent their life financing other retired people's consumption through pay-as-you-go transfers according to the terms of the implicit social contract that they envisaged would also apply to them. They therefore regard as unjust changes in eligibility and benefits that leave them worse off. Having fulfilled their obligations in providing income for older generations, they wish to receive their entitlements when they are the ones who are old and not working. Their argument is that social justice requires obligations to be honored. However, if condition (8.12) is not satisfied, the pay-as-you-go intergenerational transfer scheme is actuarially bankrupt. Actual bankruptcy will occur at a point in time in the future when revenue received in taxes from people working will be insufficient to match the government's payout obligations to retired people.

The sustained continuation of an intergenerational transfer scheme under threat of bankruptcy requires reducing benefits or increasing taxes – or both. The default policy option otherwise will be that governments will print money to pay for retirement benefits through inflationary financing.

Political procrastination

Imbalances in an intergenerational transfer scheme are reduced if benefits are decreased or taxes are increased in the present rather than the future. The timing determines the generations that bear the costs of adjustment. A generation about to retire may not care much that deferring adjustments to the future may make future viability beyond their time horizon for obtaining transfers impossible.

The adjustments required to attempt to make an intergenerational transfer viable are politically unpopular. Tax increases on generations that are working and financing the pay-as-you-go transfers are politically unpopular. Reducing benefits is politically unpopular with those people who are about to retire and would be unpopular with retirees if the reduced benefits are retroactive. Contemporary politicians can therefore be expected to defer introducing the policy changes required that might allow a pay-as-you-go intergenerational transfer scheme to be sustained longer into the future. Politicians who point out longer-term consequences and suggest change are expected to face protests and may lose elections to political rivals who continue with the politically expedient policy of procrastination in addressing problems of sustainability of intergenerational transfers.

C. Personal voluntary provision for retirement

If we truly lived in a hunter–gatherer society, intergenerational pay-as-you-go transfers would be the only means of providing for the old. Obviously, we do not live in hunter–gatherer societies. Rather, we live in societies with financial markets. Through financial markets, people can make personal voluntary provision for retirement.

A store of value

We take a first step beyond a hunter–gatherer society when money or gold or silver is introduced as a store of value over time and there are markets in food and shelter. During their working years, people voluntarily save for their old age, and when they are old they can use their savings to buy food and shelter. A store of value and markets thereby allow people personally to transfer consumption from working to retired years.

Government bonds

In a further step, we introduce financial assets. A government can sell bonds. People buy the bonds during the working period of their life and sell the bonds during their retirement years to finance their old-age consumption. When income is required, the bonds might be sold back to the government (the government might redeem the bonds), but the bonds can also be sold to people who are working and who wish to provide for their own old age. Therefore, bond markets facilitate consumption during retired years. Bonds thus perform the same function as a pay-as-you-go intergenerational transfer scheme. Intertemporal transfers from young to old, however, are now voluntary through markets. The old sell their bonds for money in the bond market and use the money to buy food and shelter. Later, the bonds will be sold again to finance old-age consumption by the working generation that bought the bonds.

The means through money as a store of value and government bonds to allow self-provision for old age do not solve the demographic problems of increasing dependency ratios. Although the old have means of paying for their own consumption, the young still have to produce for both themselves and the old. If there are fewer young people relative to old people over time, less is available for consumption per person in the society.

In a society in which population is declining, consider people who are 50 years old and who wish to finance consumption beginning 20 years in the future at age 70. They buy a bond for $100 that can be redeemed for $100 in 20 years, (there has been no inflation and the interest rate on the bond is zero). The reason for having bought the bond is to transfer consumption over time. In the absence of the bond, there is no way of providing for future consumption. People require a means of deferring consumption to the future; because they have no choice, they accept the zero interest rate on the bond.

A loaf of bread costs $1 when the bond is purchased but $2 in 20 years when the bond is sold to finance consumption. The increase in price has not occurred because of inflation but rather because of demographic change. With people having had fewer children than the generation before them, there will be fewer young productive people in the future whose output feeds the entire population of working and retired people. The real rate of interest over the period of the bond, therefore, is negative, at minus 50 percent. The negative real rate of interest is known in advance. Nonetheless, people will still wish to buy the bond when they are 50 years old and sell the bond when they are 70 years old because this is the only way they can assure their survival at age 70 (when they will not be working and not earning income).

The returns to voluntary intertemporal transfers can be negative for the same demographic reasons that compulsory pay-as-you-go schemes can yield negative returns. In both cases, people are provided with future consumption, but how much is available for consumption depends on how many people are working relative to how many people are consuming – when only the young work and both the young and the old consume.

Durable productive assets

In addition to financial assets such as bonds, privately owned durable real productive assets also allow the old to release themselves from dependence on the young for old-age consumption – because the old can receive income from ownership of the productive assets. The first change from a hunter–gatherer society is generally to an agrarian society. With private ownership of agricultural land, the old can pay the young to work the land and can live from the surplus returns from the land. In modern society, although asset values can vary over time, housing and stock markets similarly permit old-age consumption through asset ownership.

Durable productive assets result in positive rates of interest: the rate of interest is equal to the marginal benefit provided by capital over time (or the value of the marginal product of capital), which is positive. Still, if population is in decline, there are fewer and fewer people of working age over time. The decrease in available labor relative to capital or productive land increases the real income of labor and reduces the real incomes of people (the elderly and retired) who live from interest income. The demographic problems are still present: fewer people are working to sustain the total population of young and old. Also, however, market returns to durable productive assets change to redistribute income from the old to the young.

Should saving be voluntary or compulsory?

Financial markets and private-asset ownership allow private voluntary savings for old age but do not ensure that everyone will have adequate means of support during retirement. Some people may have been unable to save in the course of their working life because they did not earn enough income. Some people may have made a decision not to save for retirement. The reason for not saving may be hyperbolic discounting: people at age 20 may fail to envisage their needs at age 30 or 40, much less at age 70 or 80. Beyond hyperbolic discounting, people may simply not like to think of themselves as being old one day. By the time recognition of the need to provide for old-age consumption takes hold, it may be too late to accumulate adequate personal savings to allow a reasonable living standard during retirement. Moral hazard can also be present. People may decide not to save but rather to rely on the conscience of society to save them from destitution when old.

People who fail voluntarily to provide for old age will have to be provided with food and shelter when they are old, through either private charity or the public finance of government. Public finance will require taxation. The taxpayers will be the working generation and also other retired people who were prudent and voluntarily saved for their old age.

To preempt the need for tax-financed payments to people who did not make provision for their old age, a society can decide that personal saving for old age should be compulsory. That is, people can be legally required to invest in personal pension funds that will provide them with income during retirement.

Compulsory personal pension funds do not solve the problem of people who lack the means to save for their old age. Such people will likely have received income transfers from government during their younger years and will continue to receive tax-financed income transfers in their later years.

Individual or pooled personal savings?

When personal saving to provide for old age is compulsory, a society confronts the further question of whether the compulsory savings should be individual or pooled. Pooled savings spread risk. With individual savings, there is a risk that savings may be lost in unwise investment decisions or because of bad fortune.

In the long run, risk can generally be avoided by diversification through mutual funds and private pension schemes or through linkage to broad stock indexes. Stock markets can be volatile, with upturns and downturns. In the long run, a diversified portfolio of stocks tends to provide a return that reflects the fundamentals of the growth of the economy.

A personal scheme protects against *biometric risk* – which is the risk that an individual or dependent family members will live long enough to reach an age at which income is no longer earned. This is a personal risk.

Pooled savings protect against an unstable family life, lack of investment in human capital (or education), and unemployment or illness during working years.

Pooled savings return us to the problems of asymmetric information through moral hazard and adverse selection.

When savings are pooled, income redistribution takes place when people die and leave a dependent spouse and children. People who die after marrying a number of times can have multiple previous spouses with dependent children.

All people pay into the pooled fund when they earn income, but not all people survive to reach the age when payouts begin. Therefore, income redistribution takes place from people who have a shorter life to people who live longer. When richer people tend to live longer than poorer people, the income redistribution is from poor to rich because the poor are less likely to reach retirement age to obtain the benefits.

In some countries, income for old age is subject to a means test, which determines payments according to "need." The need is defined by other income that retired people have available to them and by their wealth. Loss of benefits through a means test can be avoided by relinquishing ownership of property and other assets, which can be passed to children and other beneficiaries while still alive. When assets are not relinquished and no benefits during retirement are obtained, high-income people will have paid into the savings pool but receive nothing in return. An individual that has not been financially successful will have paid in little and, when retired, receives a pension from the government.

Personal contributions and political decisions

Whether individual or pooled, a scheme of personal savings for old age and personal payments into a social security fund are personal property accumulated through personal contributions. Political decisions cannot be readily made to appropriate or redistribute this private property. Public pension payments funded through taxation are not based on personal contributions. A government-funded collective pension scheme is more susceptible to change and vulnerable to appropriation through political decisions than a scheme that identifies and records personal contributions.

Effects on savings and growth

When intergenerational transfers take place through a pay-as-you-go scheme, people may think that their taxes have been "invested" to create a fund that will be the source of payouts when they retire. Their future retirement payments, however, are based on an "unfunded" scheme of transfers because their taxes in the past directly financed income transfers to the old. Because of the anticipated future income entitlements when old, people may also feel that they do not need to save and accumulate personal assets. When personal savings finance old-age consumption, the savings are invested to create productive assets. Economic growth is higher when personal savings are transformed to productive assets than when pay-as-you-go intergenerational transfers are used to provide for old-age consumption.

D. Transition from intergenerational dependence

People who are working can compare the returns provided from continuation of old-age entitlements financed by an "unfunded" pay-as-you-go intergenerational transfer scheme (which has no asset-backed fund) and alternative investments through financial markets. The rate of return to the pay-as-you-go scheme is g in expression (8.7). If the rate of return in financial markets is r, young working people benefit by exiting the pay-as-you-go scheme if:

$$r > g. \tag{8.13}$$

In particular, if changes in the dependency ratio have made g negative, and if r is positive (as is the case as long as there is productive capital), condition (8.13) is satisfied. Young people then lose from the continuation of the pay-as-you-go scheme, whereas they gain from a "funded" scheme that has asset backing through personal savings.

The benefit to the young from termination of the pay-as-you-go scheme places the young in distributional conflict with the old. Both a young working generation and a retired generation can appeal to social justice. The case for social justice made by the people in the retired generation is that they honored the intergenerational contract when they were working and earning income. The case for social justice made by the young generation is that they too want a reasonable standard of living in the future when they retire and that continuation of the pay-as-you-go system will not provide them such reasonable future living standards. The young generation can also make the claim that they did not participate in the decisions about the value of designated benefits to the retired generation and that they feel under no obligation to honor an arrangement to which they did not agree, especially if defined benefits for retired people seem inordinately high.

The young can also claim that the retired generation deserves its predicament through having failed to have enough children to provide a future working-age generation that could provide adequate support through intergenerational income transfers. Moreover, knowing that their generation did not have enough children, the retired people should have supplemented their social security taxes with private savings. The means of private savings were available because members of the retired generation did not have the high personal expenses incurred in rearing children.

Terminating the pay-as-you-go intergenerational contract would violate Pareto efficiency. The young generation would be made better off and the retired generation would be made worse off. With a low or negative rate of population growth g, the change from intergenerational transfers to a funded scheme with accumulated assets would benefit all future generations, who would receive the rate of return r from their personal investments rather than the low or negative return g that is determined by the rate of population growth.

The excess burden of taxation

Ending the pay-as-you-go scheme would end the social security taxes or other taxes that finance entitlements to the old. There is an efficiency gain because ending the taxes also ends the excess burden of taxation. The young benefit from replacement of compulsory taxes with savings and also by avoiding the excess burden of taxation. The old lose because they no longer receive the pay-as-you-go transfers. Compensation of the old by the young would require taxation and therefore would bring back the excess burden of taxation.[54]

Bond financing to spread the cost of the change

The change from tax-financed intergenerational transfers to an individual saving scheme is efficient for society in aggregate. The young, however, obtain the entire benefits from the change and all losses fall on the old. The cost of ending pay-as-you-go intergenerational entitlements can be spread more evenly over generations if bond financing is used to maintain the consumption of the old. Future taxpayers then share the costs of change in the same way as bond financing spreads the cost of a durable public good over future generations. A government can issue bonds and use the revenue from the sale of the bonds to finance consumption of the retired generation. The bonds are bought by the working generation, which will redeem the bonds when it retires, at which time a new working generation can be taxed to provide revenue for the bond redemption.

Voting for change

The decision whether to end pay-as-you-go transfers could be made by voting, with the majority deciding. With everyone voting according to self-interest, retired persons would vote to retain pay-as-you-go entitlements. People beginning their working careers would vote to end the entitlements. What of people in between?

Because past personal contributions to the pay-as-you-go transfer system have been consumed by the retired generation and cannot be restored, a middle-aged person has nothing to show for past personal social security taxes that have been paid, other than the obligation to be repaid in the future through the pay-as-you-go scheme. For example, with $r > g$ (the market rate of return from investment exceeds the rate of population growth), let us consider a person who begins to work at the age of 24. This person would vote to end the pay-as-you-go scheme

[54] For example, under a pay-as-you-go scheme, the young may be paying taxes of 1,000. The tax revenue is transferred to the old for consumption. The excess burden of the taxation on the young may, for example, be 300. Ending the pay-as-you-go intergenerational transfers provides the young with a benefit of 1,300 and the old lose their previous transfers of 1,000. Compensating the old requires giving them 1,000, which requires taxes on the young of 1,000 and an excess burden of 300.

because of the higher market rate of return from investment in assets. A person aged 44 is still some years from retirement but might vote to continue the pay-as-you-go intergenerational transfers. At age 44, the present value of future retirement payments through future pay-as-you-go transfer entitlements could exceed the benefits from switching to private-asset accumulation to obtain the higher market return because all past "investments" through payment of pay-as-you-go social security taxes have been lost.

Outcomes of voting are affected by demographic trends that determine the number of voters in different age groups. With population declining and older people living longer, the older population has a political advantage in determining outcomes by majority voting.

Under conditions of representative democracy, political decisions on particular issues need not be decided by majority voting. Rather, political influence through campaign contributions and other forms of political support (for example, helping to mobilize voters on Election Day) can also influence political decisions. The retired and near-retired population can have an advantage in acting as a single-issue interest group to influence public-policy decisions.

Therefore:

> *Pay-as-you-go transfer intergenerational entitlements can persist even though the schemes provide returns that are inferior to the returns from investments in real and financial assets.*

The incentive for deferral of solving problems

We noted the problem of political procrastination in solving problems of intergenerational transfers. The political incentive is to defer solving the problem of unviable intergenerational income transfer schemes and so to leave the problem for future politicians. The young at any time do not want the double burden of paying taxes to finance intergenerational transfers while also saving personally for their own old age. The old do not want reduced benefits that would be required to ease the burden of the double financing of the young.[55]

[55] A parable indicates the incentives. A king once offered to pay a large reward to anyone who would accept the assignment of teaching his dog to talk within 10 years. The penalty for failure after accepting the obligation and the reward, however, was severe (death). For a long time, no one dared to accept the challenge of teaching the king's dog to talk. Then, finally, one person (a politician) came forward and declared to the king that he would teach the dog to talk. The king gave the politician his reward for accepting the assignment, and the politician took the dog and left the palace. Outside the palace, a crowd of people that had gathered asked the politician, "How could you agree to such an impossible assignment?" The politician replied: "In the course of 10 years, the dog might die, the king could die, or I might die. Or the dog might learn to talk." Teaching the dog to talk is the challenge of sustaining the social contract of pay-as-you-go intergenerational transfers in the face of imbalance in generational accounts. The death of the dog or of the king is spontaneous resolution of the problem from a source not explained (or is wishful thinking). The immediate reward for the politician is in the next election, by declaring the feasibility of the prospect that the dog can be taught to talk. If the king lives and if the dog lives and does not learn to talk, there will be a problem. If the politician does not live, the obligation to teach the dog to talk will have been passed on to future politicians or a future government.

Box 8.2 Intergenerational risk sharing and catastrophe insurance

An entire generation can suffer from an adverse shock to its income. Such an adverse shock occurred, for example, during the Great Depression of the 1930s when, because of stock-market declines in asset values and persisting high unemployment, large numbers of people would have reached old age without any means of support. The U.S. pay-as-you-go social security scheme was introduced during this time, providing retired people with free retirement benefits financed by pay-as-you-go taxes levied on people earning income. In 2008 the stock market declined and unemployment increased because of a financial crisis initiated by mortgages for home loans given to people who in due course could not make the repayments: there were significant declines in values of people's assets that were intended to be used for retirement consumption, but the crisis was not of the scale as the Great Depression and social security was in place. A society can also confront an adverse shock from a natural disaster such as an earthquake, a flood, or a war. Through pay-as-you-go income transfers, the living standards (or lives) of the population whose assets are wiped out are sustained when those people reach retirement age. When a generation A has been subject to the adverse shock that has wiped out its assets, a younger generation B that is working could, through a pay-as-you-go scheme, transfer income to generation A when that generation ceases working. There is, however, no gain through the risk sharing of generation B with generation A. The younger working generation B has already witnessed the adverse outcome for generation A. Members of generation B would maximize their personal lifetime income by not making the income transfers to generation A. Without governments to enforce compulsory income transfers through taxation, intergenerational risk sharing breaks downs – unless the younger generation voluntarily acts as if it adheres to an intergenerational social contract. For localized catastrophic events, governments provide catastrophe insurance. People may not purchase insurance against events that have low probabilities because of the belief that the event will never happen. As long as the probability of the event is positive, insurance should be purchased. However, the insurance premium for protection may be regarded as inordinately high, given the perceived probability of the event. For example, a hurricane may never have wiped out a city and so people have no experience with the event ever happening. When the event occurs, assets and sources of livelihood are lost. In general, governments offer disaster relief. Moral hazard arises if, after a catastrophe has occurred, people view the disaster relief as an indication that government will always provide insurance. People may build houses in an area that is prone to hurricanes, knowing that the government is acting as insurer in the event that a severe hurricane recurs.

8.3

The Entitlement to Health Care and Health Insurance

We have used schooling or education as the primary example of a universal entitlement. Health care is also an entitlement, although sometimes the entitlement is limited to the poor and the elderly. A person who is sick or injured cannot be expected to have the state of mind to make health-care decisions under market conditions. Sick or injured people do not usually have the time and composure, or mindset, to evaluate alternative market-supply offers for treatment. The stress of circumstances of ill health or injury may not allow a reasoned consideration of alternative supply offers. It would be disconcerting to negotiate the costs of treatment in a hospital emergency room. A person who requires medical care might be prepared to pay large sums of money for treatment. A market transaction also exposes a person seeking immediate medical treatment to the potential for extortion.

There is asymmetric information in markets for health care. People decide that they need advice or treatment when they discern symptoms that suggest to them that they require medical care, but they may not know how to identify the reasons for their medical problems or the most effective treatment. Therefore, they rely on the advice of medical-service providers. Asymmetric information introduces the scope for opportunistic behavior by medical practitioners. Treatment may be offered that is ineffective or detrimental. Because of asymmetric information, health care is regulated by government through certification of those permitted to provide medical treatment as well as the effectiveness of drugs and medicines. Self-regulation also takes place by medical practitioners through professional associations. Regulation is complicated by medical treatment often not being an exact science. There can be disagreements about appropriate treatment. Symptoms can be consistent with many different ailments. Mistakes can be made in diagnosis and laboratory testing. The challenge in regulation and self-regulation is to define reasonable error.

A. The problem of containing health costs

A major problem in health care is containment of costs. The special attributes of health care make cost containment difficult and can lead to cost escalation over time. Medical research produces new medicines, new devices, and new procedures that require costly investments. Over time, the new costly procedures become commonplace and more familiar to medical practitioners, and new medical equipment is introduced into hospitals and clinics. The population that can benefit from the new procedures and equipment expands, and medical costs increase correspondingly. Attempts to contain costs by limiting the use of new procedures or by limiting access to new medicines encounter ethical objections.

There are also impediments to containing the costs of a health-administration bureaucracy. Attempts at reducing the administrative expenses of providing health care can be deflected to reduced care for patients. When proposals for reductions in an administrative health-care budget are made, the cost reductions can be presented as for example necessitating taking away life-preserving medications from children rather than as imparting efficiency to bureaucratic hierarchies or reducing unjustifiably high bureaucratic salaries.

Medical practitioners purchase insurance against the financial consequences of their mistakes. Health-care costs increase because of high insurance costs for medical practitioners.

Demographic change increases health-care costs when elderly people come to comprise a larger part of the population. Economic and moral dilemmas of health-care costs tend to arise particularly toward the end of life. A large part of lifetime health costs tends to be incurred in the last months of life. Denying the chronically and incurably ill the last months of their life could substantially reduce health-care costs but is unethical and unexpected recoveries occur. Some societies allow euthanasia when suffering has become intolerable by reasonable conditions of what a person might be expected to endure, despite ethical objections based on the sanctity of life.

Increased health-care spending does not always result in increased benefits. Asymmetric information can make unclear what people are buying (or what the government is paying for). Studies have found that greater spending on health care does not necessarily improve the quality of health care.[56]

B. The market for health insurance

To allow a separation between medical treatment and the immediacy of market transactions, health care usually involves the purchase of health insurance. When people have insurance, monetary considerations of a market are not primary when health care is required. Sick and injured people do not have to worry about whether they can afford treatment, and the health-care system that supplies medical treatment can focus on providing the necessary care rather than waiting before treatment is given to ensure that the patient has the means to pay.

[56] David Cutler (2000, p. 52) observed that in the United States, although publicly financed spending for elderly persons (through medicare) is twice as high in some regions of the country than others, reflecting different access to expensive procedures, nonetheless the difference in spending is not reflected in differences in health. He noted that international comparisons similarly indicate that living closer to a sophisticated hospital is more likely to result in more complex or advanced treatments but personal outcomes do not much differ for patients who live farther away from such a hospital. Evidence also suggests that up to one-third of the use of many common procedures is either inappropriate or of equivocal value, whereas in other circumstances, particularly outpatient use of prescription drugs, many people can receive too little care.

Insurance also spreads risk by providing protection against large, unforeseen medical expenses.

Private-insurance markets, however, may fail to provide insurance. Some medical ailments are difficult to verify (for example, a backache or hallucinations). There are recorded cases of people who are hypochondriacs and of people who have a compulsive need to undergo surgery. Such people artificially increase the costs imposed on health-insurance companies. Moral hazard affects health insurance if people respond by taking health-related risks. For example, there is moral hazard if health insurance increases the likelihood that a skier will attempt a particularly dangerous downhill run.

However, people do not normally increase their exposure to injury or illness because they have health insurance. The more important problem for health-insurance markets is adverse selection: people who have private information that they have a higher than average likelihood of requiring medical care have greater incentives to seek insurance and they systematically impose costs on others who know that they have a lower than average likelihood of requiring medical care. The people who expect to be healthier than average wish to avoid being in the same insurance group as the people who expect to be in need of medical care. Adverse selection can be avoided by offering different health-insurance contracts catering to low- and high-risk people. High-risk people will choose high-premium, high-benefit policies, whereas low-risk people will choose low-premium, low-benefit policies. Everyone will want insurance against low-probability unfortunate events.

The scope for adverse selection increased when in 2000 a mapping of the human genetic structure was basically completed. Information about the human genome can allow predictions of future personal health. The purpose of insurance is to pool risk due to events that affect people randomly. However, with genetic dispositions known, randomness is eliminated for many health problems. People can be tested for genetic predispositions. If the results indicate the likelihood of good health, they will make the information known to private health insurance companies, and they will seek lower health insurance premiums because of their lower health risk. Or, they will seek to form insurance groups with people who have similar low genetically predetermined probabilities of need for particular types of health care. An insurance company can infer that people who do not make the results of their personal tests known have reason to keep the results to themselves because of revealed genetic predisposition that will result in high future health-care costs. Private-insurance companies would then not offer to insure people who do not disclose their genetic health predisposition. Availability of information about personal genetic characteristics thus limits the scope of private-insurance markets.

Market alternatives

Market alternatives for health care take different forms, depending on whether the insurer and the health provider are the same or different private entities.

When different private firms provide health insurance and health care separately, the providers of health care and the patient know that the insurance company is obliged to pay for costs of treatment. The effective cost to the physician or hospital and the cost to the patient of additional procedures or medicines are therefore zero. In that case, the insurance company is exposed to the risk of excessive health outlays because the true marginal cost is not zero. To avoid excessive costs, the insurance company issues general directives about how much can be charged for different procedures and which medications can be prescribed.

In setting guidelines for physician behavior and patient treatment, the private-insurance company is attempting to solve a principal–agent problem. If monitoring by the insurance company is to take place and directives are to be set to control costs, the insurance company might wish to address the principal–agent problem by being the health-care provider, employing the physician, and owning the hospital.

When the insurance company is also the health-care provider, another type of incentive problem arises. To maximize profits, the combined private health-insurance and health-care company (HMO, or health-management organization) has an incentive to provide minimal service. The public then relies on competition among HMOs to provide health care that is not focused on maximal profits through cost containment. Imperfect information by the public can make personal evaluation of comparative offers of health care difficult. A patient is informed only of permitted treatments and medications and may not know about alternatives disallowed because of cost-containment measures.

The possibilities are either that the private insurance company and the private health provider are one and the same or are separate. Whichever is the case, adverse incentives are present. If the insurance provider and the health-care provider are separate commercial entities, the insurance company confronts problems of cost containment because the people making the decisions about health-care expenses are not the people paying the costs. A joint insurance health-care provider can specify allowable treatments and has an incentive to limit allowable procedures and medications. Yet, these are the alternatives: insurance and health care are provided separately or they are provided by one private firm.

Universal health entitlements through markets

A private market for health insurance can leave people without health coverage. What is to be done about the uninsured and the uninsurable?

We can look at a failed attempt in the United States in the 1990s to introduce entitlements to nationwide universal health insurance through private provision of health care. Universal compulsory health insurance would have involved government in the provision of health care in specifying payments to health-care providers. Physicians and other medical practitioners would have lost income from the regulation by government. Medical practitioners made past personal investments in education based on the anticipation of earning market-determined incomes, and they could claim that government regulation of their income was equivalent to retroactive taxation for which there was no offer to provide compensation. The government would also need to become involved in the pharmaceutical market. Containing health-care costs requires designating permissible medicines and setting maximum prices at which pharmaceutical companies are permitted to sell their products. A consequence, however, is that pharmaceutical companies face diminished incentives to develop new medications. At the same time, the regulation of the pharmaceutical industry imposes financial losses on people who own stock in pharmaceutical companies because lower profits (or the expectation of lower profits) depress stock prices. Owners of stock in pharmaceutical companies would not be compensated for those losses. The owners of stock are not necessarily the wealthier people in society who can "afford the loss." People own stock in pharmaceutical companies directly, or indirectly through either ownership of mutual funds or personal retirement savings programs.

Compulsory universal health coverage redistributes income to people who cannot afford private health insurance or who do not have health coverage provided by their employer. Universal mandatory health insurance requires a source of financing. If some people cannot pay for their coverage, others pay for them.

Mandatory universal health coverage also introduces personal loss through the restricted choice of quality of health care. The reduced choice of quality falls on those people who lack the financial means to seek health care outside of the allowable procedures and treatments covered by the universal mandatory insurance.

A broad coalition can thus be expected to oppose government-mandated universal compulsory health insurance. The people who benefit from universal compulsory health coverage are those who are too poor to afford health insurance in a private market and would be provided with free or highly subsidized medical services under universal coverage. The consent of a majority of voters, or of representatives of the voters, is required to introduce a mandatory universal program of health care. In the Unites States in the 1990s, the majority was not found, despite the support of the prestige and political patronage of the office of the president.[57]

Private competition with universal compulsory coverage

Although the U.S. attempt failed, we can nonetheless consider the consequences of universal entitlements to mandatory health insurance in the private market for health care. The government determines a list of health-care services and

[57] Self-interest need not be the sole consideration in a person's position on entitlements to government-mandated universal health coverage. People may support a basic entitlement to health care through universal coverage as a matter of principle even if the entitlement is not in their personal interest.

medications that are the entitlement of each citizen, sets allowable prices and treatments, and allows market competition among private providers in offering the designated health-care services. The health-care providers, for their part, cannot refuse insurance to people with chronic illnesses, old people, or people with lifestyles that have higher than average expected health costs. Market elements have thus become minimal. Insurance companies do not decide on the services that are covered by insurance and do not decide who their clients are because they are obliged to accept everyone who applies. Health-care providers do not decide on the price for coverage because insurance payments are regulated. For the population, participation is compulsory through regulated health-insurance payments.

Even when participation in health insurance is compulsory and coverage in principle is universal, there is nonetheless no assurance that everyone will take advantage of entitlements. Evidence shows that when universal free-access health care is available, lower income people can be less aware of their health needs and be less inclined to seek medical advice.[58]

When health insurance is compulsory, health-insurance companies and health-care providers can make a case that because they are compelled to accept all applicants for health care, government has a responsibility to finance any losses that might arise. With government assigned the role of financier of last resort, moral hazard enters. There is a principal–agent problem: health-insurance companies and health-care providers confront a soft-budget constraint. Because losses will be covered, incentives are reduced to contain costs. Incentives, on the contrary, are present for opportunistic cost enhancement through increased spending on staff and administrative salaries. If government attempts to enforce cost containment by refusing to finance the providers' deficits, the providers can initiate a health-care crisis by not providing treatment, claiming insufficient resources.

C. Socialized medicine

If a government socializes health insurance and health care, people receive tax-financed free treatment directly from the government. The health-care system is run by government and medical-care providers become government employees. The government is again financier of last resort, now directly through the government budget. There can again be a soft-budget constraint because of the imperative to save lives and return people to good health. Because of the direct responsibility of government to provide health care, all failures of the health-care system become directly attributable to government, so politicians become directly involved in health care. The administration of health-care spending becomes part of the government bureaucracy; therefore, spending on health care becomes subject to the bureaucratic principal–agent problem. The soft budget of health-care spending is compounded by the soft budget of government bureaucracy.

[58] See Katz and Hofer (1994).

Attempts to contain costs of socialized medicine generally result in either low-quality health care or long waiting times for treatment. The objective of socialized medicine is to provide an entitlement of equal health care for everyone. In principle, an accompanying private market should be unnecessary. Long waiting times for consultations and treatment and impersonal medical attention, however, can lead people to forgo free-access, publicly financed entitlements for private markets. The result is two levels of medical care: an inferior level for those who use government health care and a superior level for those who can afford or are willing to pay for private treatment.

Socialized medicine has adverse incentives if the medical practitioners who are employed in the government system also have private practices. In that case, low quality and long waiting times for free treatment within the socialized system of health care can be an opportunistic response of the medical practitioners, who gain from the demand that is created for the better quality and more immediate attention provided through their own parallel private practices. If patients do not seek treatment in parallel private practices, there are incentives for corruption in the bureaucracy that administers the socialized government health system: people can pay for queue-jumping when waiting for treatment. Personal contacts in the administering bureaucracy can also help in reducing waiting times. As previously noted, rent creation and rent seeking can occur when governments provide free-access health-care entitlements.

D. Health-care choices

Expense is not the primary concern when a person is trying to regain good health. Yet, health care involves resources and money. A contradiction thus arises between the principle of doing everything possible to save a life or return people to good health and the limitations of available resources. Nonetheless, health-care choices have to be made and resources allocated. A case against choosing private supply of health care through markets is based on the principle that all people should have a basic entitlement to health care. The private market for health insurance is also limited in providing health coverage because of adverse selection and because of exclusion of some people who cannot afford health insurance. Private markets also have adverse incentives that differ depending on whether the insurance company and the health-care provider are one and the same entity.

Because of the problems of private supply of health care and private insurance, a decision may be made to socialize health care, which is then provided directly by government-paid medical practitioners and administrative staff as a free, tax-financed entitlement. Then, problems of low-quality health care and extended waiting times for treatment can be encountered and opportunistically manipulated offers of immediate private medical attention. Yet, reliance on private markets alone leaves some people without health insurance.

Choosing socially desirable health-care provision therefore presents dilemmas. The failures of private-market provision, particularly exclusion of parts of the population, point in the direction of forgoing markets and turning to government to take responsibility for ensuring universal health-care coverage. The introduction of government into health insurance and health care leads to soft-budget problems because of the compounded difficulty of containing health-care costs when the public finance of government is the source of finance of last resort.

Some societies choose to rely principally on the voluntary decisions of the market, whereas others choose considerable involvement of government. Where health care is provided through government, the criticisms are about inefficiencies, waiting times and quality of treatment, and insufficient individual choice; low salaries when health care is part of government bureaucracy also provide incentives for medical practitioners to emigrate. When health care is through private markets, the criticisms are about social injustices because of exclusion of people from health insurance and about profit-motivated procedures that increase costs but do not necessarily benefit patients. The dilemmas of the choice between market decisions and government entitlements are perhaps nowhere so revealed as in health insurance and health care.

Summary

In chapter 7, entitlements appeared abstractly as part of a social insurance contract associated with a social welfare function. This chapter viewed entitlements in a less abstract way. Section 1 described universal and targeted entitlements. With equality of opportunity as the social objective, societies want universal entitlements such as schooling and education to be accepted. Societies prefer, on the other hand, that targeted entitlements (unemployment benefits, welfare payments, and in-kind transfers of housing and food) not be accepted or that the circumstances required for eligibility for the entitlements not be present.

1A. Section 1 began with the choice between money and in-kind transfers as means of delivering entitlements. Recipients prefer transfers of money. Taxpayers prefer in-kind transfers. In-kind transfers also provide increased assurance that schooling entitlements will make children future self-reliant adults; in-kind transfers allow the objective of ex-ante equality to be sought without the intermediating need to rely on decisions of parents; therefore, in-kind transfers facilitate paternalistic policies. Because of market-substitution responses, money transfers or subsidies need not benefit intended beneficiaries. We considered the benefits of vouchers as a means of delivering in-kind entitlements and the sources of opposition to vouchers.

1B. We examined the quest for ex-ante equality through intended universal entitlements, using the example of schooling for children.

We considered why households might reject government entitlements even if rejection of the entitlements entails paying twice: once through taxes that provide no benefit and again in the private market. We saw that, whether the entitlements are accepted or rejected, the presence of entitlements impose losses on households: the entitlements increase ex-ante equality but reduce quality of education for households that more highly value education. The losses from the entitlement are externalities from the existence of households that place low values on education and because of whom the government entitlement has been introduced. Markets disrupt the quest for ex-ante equality through entitlements; we concluded that disallowing markets is undesirable and is generally not feasible (which was also the conclusion when we considered paternalism). We noted problems associated with private schools: benefits of schooling depend on whether choice of schools is for the purpose of signaling or education; private schools are the source of adverse selection, including consequences through voting on resources for government schools; and ideological content of education in private schools can prevent ex-ante equality.

1C. Inequality of opportunity or ex-ante inequality also occurs for reasons other than qualities of government and private schools. A source of inequality is differences in local-government financing of schools. In a manner similar to public goods, locational choice can be used to choose entitlements and ex-ante inequality through unequal opportunity can emerge and be sustained. We also noted injustices than can occur because of market capitalization when public policies change locational school attendance criteria. Failure of ex-ante equality and labor-market discrimination are two hypotheses for explaining persistent labor-market inequality; the U.S. evidence points to failure of ex-ante inequality; failures of ex-ante equality are also indicated by evidence indicating that in different countries, high-ability students from low-income households are under-represented in higher education. Failure of ex-ante inequality can be due to differences in family environments and peer groups that affect the propensity to take advantage of educational opportunities. There are also cultural impediments to ex-ante equality through social identity and stereotyping. The evidence shows that there are gender differences in propensities to take advantage of educational and other opportunities; the gender differences favor girls, beginning from a young age. Finance for higher education can also be an impediment to ex-ante equality; government loan guarantees and income-contingent loan repayments are intended to promote ex-ante equality by providing access to higher education. We also considered the case for "affirmative action" to correct for past unequal opportunities. We asked how equality of opportunity is to be interpreted when children and students have different abilities. We noted that equality of opportunity or ex-ante equality is fundamental to meritocracy that allows efficient matching of personal competencies to tasks.

1D. We considered targeted entitlements that governments prefer not be accepted and investigated the links between targeted entitlements and incentives. Unemployment insurance has private and social benefits but is subject to problems of asymmetric information that deter insurance through private insurance markets. We considered the design of unemployment insurance provided by governments, including proposals concerning the value of benefits over time and for private accounts. Emotional stress from unemployment for people who feel inadequate when unemployed is a personal cost of unemployment. We compared unemployment insurance with job-protection laws. We distinguished between unemployment and persistent welfare dependence. People who are persistently unemployed face the binary decision of whether or not to work. Incentives of welfare payments contingent on not working were compared with wage subsidies that are contingent on working; change from welfare payments to wage subsidies is not Pareto-improving because the transfer recipient loses through the need to exert effort in the labor market; however, taxpayers gain. We therefore considered the choice of weights on utilities of taxpayers and transfer recipients in the measurement of social welfare. Wage subsidies introduce people to self-reliance and the prospects of higher future incomes. We also noted consequences regarding distraction from crime. Wage subsidies can be implemented as earned-income tax credits or direct payment through employers; there are incentives for opportunistic behavior by employers in the latter case. We noted the incentives that are present when parallel public polices allow choice between income support contingent on not working and working. Experience with welfare reform was described. We noted the credibility problem when in a civil society a time limit is set on lifetime eligibility for welfare payments.

Section 2 described the entitlement to income during old age. The ex-ante equality in this case is the equal opportunity to benefit from life after retirement and in old age.

2A. Pay-as-you-go intergenerational transfers are consistent with the conditions of a hunter–gatherer society in which the sole means of the old staying alive is to be sustained by the young. A social contract stipulating intergenerational transfers in a hunter–gatherer society is Pareto-improving. The contract is not based on a demonstration effect but rather requires "respecting the old" as an ethical principle. A free-rider problem in intergenerational transfers is solved through taxation.

2B. We compared designated contributions with designated benefits. In either case, the viability of pay-as-you-go income transfers is undermined by an increasing dependency ratio. There is a demographic free-rider problem when people seek to use other people's children as the tax base for future income transfers. The first generation in a designated benefit scheme always gains. However, more generally, pay-as-you-go income transfers can be Ponzi schemes: demographic change – expressed in declining fertility, earlier retirement, and longer lives – has made pay-as-you-go income-transfer schemes in many countries actuarially bankrupt. A solution requires higher taxes, lower benefits, or higher retirement ages, which are politically unpopular – and so there is often political procrastination. Other solutions are increased economic growth and immigration of productive people, both of which expand the tax base; growth is not entirely discretionary and immigration, in the course of time, could increase the dependency ratio. A fiscal federal system prevents free riding by people who do not have children. A default response to imbalances in intergenerational transfers is inflationary financing. We noted reasons for unequal benefits from income redistribution through intergenerational income transfers, including gender and the relationship between incomes and whether people reach an age at which benefits are provided.

2C. We do not live in hunter–gatherer societies. Money as a store of value, markets for food and shelter, and financial and real assets allow people to survive during old age without an intergenerational contract with younger working generations. Replacing pay-as-you-go intergenerational transfers with asset-backed schemes thus ends reliance of older people on transfers from the younger working generation. Questions then arise about whether personal asset-backed retirement schemes should be compulsory or voluntary and whether the schemes should be individual or pooled. Personal property rights to funded schemes inhibit political decisions, which can change intergenerational transfers financed out of general tax revenue. A funded scheme with asset backing increases economic growth compared to unfunded schemes in which contributions of working generations are consumed by retired generations. Even with negative returns because of demographic consequences, people want intergenerational transfers to continue if the transfers are the only means of being sustained in old age.

2D. Retired and older people who contributed to a pay-as-you-go intergenerational transfer scheme during their working life confront the risk that the pay-as-you-go transfers will be discontinued because higher returns are available to younger people from investments in asset markets. Ending the unfunded intergenerational transfers also eliminates the excess burden of taxation. Change to a funded scheme is unjust for generations working during the time of transition that are required to pay taxes to finance the entitlement obligations to older generations while also being required to save personally for their own retirement. Abrogating the implicit social contract by ceasing payments to retired generations is also unjust. Bond financing would spread the burden of transition over future generations. Although an asset-backed (or funded) retirement scheme may provide a greater rate of return than a pay-as-you-go scheme for which the return may be negative, a majority of voters nonetheless may favor retaining the pay-as-you-go system. However, with pay-as-you-go schemes not viable in the long term, adjustments through reduced benefits for retired generations, increased retirement age, or higher taxes on working generations are inevitable. The politically expedient policy response is deferral of change to the future.

Section 3 examined entitlements to health care and health insurance.

3A. We noted the problems of cost containment because of the special nature of health care and also asymmetric information between the medical practitioner and the patient. Demographic change increases health care costs when the elderly become a larger part of the population. Evidence indicates that effectiveness of treatment does not necessarily increase with spending on health care.

3B. Because of attributes that make markets inappropriate means of providing health care, markets for health insurance replace markets for health care. Adverse selection and moral hazard are problems in health-insurance markets. We noted the dilemmas of choice in organization form in health-insurance markets. Also, private health-insurance markets leave some people insured or uninsurable. We examined consequences of attempting to introduce compulsory health insurance as a universal entitlement through markets.

3C. We described outcomes of socialized medicine.

3D. Health-insurance and health-care choices demonstrate the advantages and disadvantages of relying on markets and governments.

Literature notes

8.1 The attributes and consequences of entitlements

Nichols and Zeckhauser (1982) proposed in-kind transfers as means of targeting and thereby limiting benefits of welfare programs. Moffit (1983) observed that stigma deters people from applying for welfare benefits to which they have entitlements.

Moffit, R. A., 1983. An economic model of welfare stigma. *American Economic Review* 73:1023–38.
Nichols, A., and R. Zeckhauser, 1982. Targeting transfers through restrictions on recipients. *American Economic Review, Papers and Proceedings* 72:372–8.

On vouchers and schools, see:

Epple, D., and R. E. Romano, 1998. Competition between private and public schools, vouchers, and peer-group pressures. *American Economic Review* 88:33–63.

Sonstelie (1982) estimated the welfare cost of free government schools. On government and private schools, see Schansberg (1996) and Toma (1996). Peltzman (1993, 1996) attributed the decline in the quality of government schools in the United States to centralization of funding and unionization of teachers.

Peltzman, S., 1993. The political economy of the decline of American public education. *Journal of Law and Economics* 36:331–70.
Peltzman, S., 1996. Political economy of public education: Non-college-bound students. *Journal of Law and Economics* 39:73–120.
Schansberg, D. E., 1996. *Poor Policy: How Government Harms the Poor.* Westview Press, Boulder CO.
Sonstelie, J., 1982. The welfare cost of free public schools. *Journal of Political Economy* 90:794–808.
Toma, E. F., 1996. Public funding and private schooling across countries. *Journal of Law and Economics* 39:121–48.

On adverse selection in school choice and voting, see:

Glomm, G., and B. Ravikumar, 1998. Opting out of publicly provided services: A majority voting result. *Social Choice and Welfare* 15:187–99.

Inman (1978) studied alternatives to local financing of schools.

Inman, R. P., 1978. Optimal fiscal reform of metropolitan schools. *American Economic Review* 68:107–22.

For evidence on the effects of locational competition on government schools, see:

Hoxby, C. M., 2000. Does competition among public schools benefit students and taxpayers? *American Economic Review* 90:1209–38.

Evidence on under-representation of low-income families in higher education is provided by Heckman (2000), Greenaway and Haynes (2003), and Cardak and Ryan (2006).

Cardak, B. A., and C. Ryan, 2006. *Why are high-ability individuals from poor backgrounds under-represented at university?* Available at SSRN: http://ssrn.com/abstract=914025.
Greenaway, D., and M. Haynes, 2003. Funding higher education in the UK: The role of fees and loans. *Economic Journal* 113:F150–F166.
Heckman, J. J., 2000. Policies to foster human capital. *Research in Economics* 54:3–56.

Neal and Johnson (1996) and Carneiro, Heckman, and Masterov (2005) studied reasons for market income differences by race. On neighborhoods and ex-ante inequality in the United States, see Borjas (1995), who found benefits; and Cutler and Glaeser (1997), who found disadvantages. Edin, Fredriksson, and Åslund (2003) concluded based on evidence from Sweden that immigrants benefit from living in segregated enclaves. On cultural impediments to ex-ante equality, see Austen-Smith and Fryer (2006).

Austen-Smith, D., and R. G. Fryer, Jr., 2006. An economic analysis of "acting white." *Quarterly Journal of Economics* 120:551–83.

Borjas, G., 1995. Ethnicity, neighborhoods, and human capital externalities. *American Economic Review* 85:365–90.
Carneiro, P., J. J. Heckman, and D. V. Masterov, 2005. Labor market discrimination and racial differences in prefactor markets. *Journal of Law and Economics* 48:1–39.
Cutler, D. M., and E. L. Glaeser, 1997. Are ghettos good or bad? *Quarterly Journal of Economics* 112:827–72.
Edin, P.-A., P. Fredriksson, and O. Åslund, 2003. Ethnic enclaves and the economic success of immigrants: Evidence from a natural experiment. *Quarterly Journal of Economics* 118:329–57.
Neal, D., and W. Johnson, 1996. The role of prefactor markets in black–white wage differences. *Journal of Political Economy* 104:869–95.

Kling, Liebman, and Katz (2007); Hastings, Kane, and Staiger (2006); and Anderson (2005) reported evidence on how gender affects response to educational opportunity. Hoff and Pandey (2006) reported the experiment on social identity and stereotyping.

Anderson, M., 2005. Uncovering gender differences in the effects of early intervention: A reevaluation of the Abecedarian Perry Pre-school and early training programs. Available at SSRN: http://ssrn.com/abstract=812426.
Hastings, J. S., T. J. Kane, and D. O. Staiger, 2006. Gender and performance: Evidence from school assignment by randomized lottery. *American Economic Review, Papers and Proceedings* 96:232–6.
Hoff, K., and P. Pandey, 2006. Discrimination, social identity and durable inequalities. *American Economic Review, Papers and Proceedings* 96:206–11.
Kling, J. R., J. B. Liebman, and L. F. Katz, 2007. Experimental analysis of neighborhood effects. *Econometrica* 75:83–119.

On government schools and the content of education, see:

Lott, J. L., 1990. An explanation for public provision of schooling: The importance of indoctrination. *Journal of Law and Economics* 33:199–231.

On income-contingent loans for financing higher education, see Chapman (2006). Chapman and Ryan (2005) reported the change in university enrollment after the introduction of an income-contingent loan repayment scheme. Nerlove (1975) described adverse selection and moral hazard when student loans pool risk.

Chapman, B., 2006. Income-contingent loans for higher education: International reform. In E. Hanushek and F. Welch (Eds.), *Economics of Education Handbook*. North-Holland, Amsterdam, pp. 1435–503.
Chapman, B., and C. Ryan, 2005. The access implications of income-related charges for higher education: Lessons from Australia. *Economics of Education Review* 24:491–512.
Nerlove, M., 1975. Some problems in the use of income-contingent loans for the finance of higher education. *Journal of Political Economy* 83:157–83.

On affirmative action, see:

Coate, S., and G. L. Loury, 1993. Will affirmative-action policies eliminate negative stereotypes? *American Economic Review* 83:1220–40.

On entitlements to maternity benefits and intended beneficiaries, see:

Gruber, J., 1994. The incidence of mandated maternity benefits. *American Economic Review* 84:622–41.

Garatt and Marshall (1994) proposed that public finance for higher education is the consequence of a social contract based on not everyone being able to attend college or university.

Garatt, R., and J. M. Marshall, 1994. Public finance for private goods: The case of college education. *Journal of Political Economy* 102:566–82.

The quote regarding entitlements and incentives is from Mill (1948).

Mill, J. S., 1848. *Principles of Political Economy. Books IV and V*. Penguin, Harmonsworth U.K.

Theories of unemployment were proposed by Akerlof (1980), Marx (1887), Keynes (1936), Shapiro and Stiglitz (1984), and Lindbeck and Snower (1988). Search theory was introduced by Stigler (1962).

Akerlof, G. A., 1980. A theory of social custom, of which unemployment may be one consequence. *Quarterly Journal of Economics* 94:749–75.
Keynes, J. M., 1936. *The General Theory of Interest, Employment, and Money*. Macmillan, London.
Lindbeck, A., and D. Snower, 1988. *The Insider-Outsider Theory of Employment and Unemployment*. MIT Press, Cambridge MA.
Marx, K., 1887. *Capital: A Critical Analysis of Capitalist Production*. F. Engels (Ed.). Progress Publishers, Moscow.
Shapiro, C., and J. Stiglitz, 1984. Equilibrium unemployment as a worker discipline device. *American Economic Review* 74:433–44.
Stigler, G. J., 1962. Information in the labor market. *Journal of Political Economy* 70:94–105.

On unemployment insurance and incentives, see Shavell and Weiss (1979) and Marimon and Zilibotti (1999). Snower (1994) proposed converting unemployment benefits to vouchers for wage subsidies.

Marimon, R., and Z. Zilibotti, 1999. Unemployment vs. mismatch of talents: Reconsidering unemployment benefits. *Economic Journal* 109:266–91.
Shavell, S., and L. Weiss, 1979. The optimal payment of unemployment insurance over time. *Journal of Political Economy* 87:1347–62.
Snower, D., 1994. Converting unemployment benefits into employment subsidies. *American Economic Review, Papers and Proceedings* 84:65–70.

Neugart (2005) studied political determination of the attributes of unemployment insurance.

Neugart, M., 2005. Unemployment insurance: The role of electoral systems and regional labour markets. *European Journal of Political Economy* 21:815–29.

On the determinants of political support for employment protection, see Saint-Paul (2002). On the political choice between unemployment insurance and employment protection, see Neugart (2008).

Neugart, M., 2008. The choice of insurance in the labor market. *Public Choice* 134:445–62.
Saint-Paul, G., 2002. The political economy of unemployment protection. *Journal of Political Economy* 110:672–704.

Besley and Coate (1992) studied targeted income transfers when high-ability people could pretend to have low ability in order to qualify for welfare payments. Phelps (1994) proposed subsidizing work. For a study that includes the binary decision of whether to work and marginal labor-supply adjustments, see Saez (2002).

Besley, T., and S. Coate, 1992. Workfare vs. welfare: Incentive arguments for work requirements in poverty alleviation programs. *American Economic Review* 82:249–61.

Phelps, E .S., 1994. Low-wage employment subsidies versus the welfare state. *American Economic Review, Papers and Proceedings* 84:54–8.
Saez, E., 2002. Optimal income transfer programs: Intensive versus extensive labor supply responses. *Quarterly Journal of Economics* 117:1039–73.

The history of the U.S. earned-income tax credit is described by Holz and Scholz (2003). Azmat (2008) described the U.K. case. Eissa and Hoynes (2004) showed that in the United States, because the earned-income tax credit is based on family income, married women withdrew from the labor force.

Azmat, G. Y., 2008. The incidence of an earned-income tax credit: Impact of wages in the U.K. CEP Discussion Paper 0724, London.
Eissa, N., and H. Hoynes, 2004. Taxes and the labor-market participation of married couples: The earned income-tax credit. *Journal of Public Economics* 88:1931–58.
Holz, V. J., and J. K. Scholz, 2003. The earned income tax credit. In R. A. Moffit (Ed.), *Means-Tested Transfer Programs in the U.S.* University of Chicago Press, Chicago IL, pp. 141–98.

Moffit (1999) and Rosenzweig (1999) investigated the effects of welfare payments on martial and fertility incentives. On the relationship between social norms and welfare payments, see Lindbeck, Nyberg, and Weibull (1999). On the need to change social norms for successful welfare reform, see Loury (1996). Brinig and Buckley (1999) described the interface between changes in norms regarding single-motherhood and welfare payments. Antel (1992) provided evidence showing persistence of welfare dependency across generations before the U.S. welfare reform of the 1990s. Eissa, Kleven, and Kreiner (2008) provided evidence showing that for single mothers, the effect of taxes on labor-market participation is more significant than substitution at the margin between hours worked and leisure.

Antel, J. J., 1992. The intergenerational transfer of welfare dependency: Some statistical evidence. *Review of Economics and Statistics* 74:467–73.
Brinig, M. F., and F. H. Buckley, 1999. The price of virtue. *Public Choice* 98:111–29.
Eissa, N., H. J. Kleven, and C. T. Kreiner, 2008. Evaluation of four tax reforms in the United States: Labor supply and welfare effects for single mothers. *Journal of Public Economics* 92:795–816.
Lindbeck, A., S. Nyberg, and J. W. Weibull, 1999. Social norms and economic incentives in the welfare state. *Quarterly Journal of Economics* 114:1–38.
Loury, G. L., 1996. A dissent from the incentive approach to reducing poverty. In M. R. Darby (Ed.), *Reducing Poverty in America: Views and Approaches.* Sage Publications, Thousand Oaks CA, pp. 111–20.
Moffit, R. A., 1998. The effect of welfare on marriage and fertility. In R. A. Moffit (Ed.), *Welfare, the Family, and Reproductive Behavior.* National Academy Press, Washington DC, pp. 50–98.
Rosenzweig, M. R., 1999. Welfare, marital prospects, and non-marital childbearing. *Journal of Political Economy* 107:S3–S32.

On the consequences of welfare reform in the United States, see Blank (2002) and Bitler, Gelbach, and Hoynes (2006). On Australia, see Saunders (2002); on Canada, see Michalopoulos, Robins, and Card (2005); and on Germany, see Boss and Elender (2005). For a simulation study of European countries, see Immervoll, Kleuven, Kreiner, and Saez (2007).

Bitler, M. P., J. B. Gelbach, and H. W. Hoynes, 2006. What mean aspects miss: Distributional effects of welfare reform experiments. *American Economic Review* 96:988–1012.

Blank, R., 2002. Evaluating welfare reform in the United States. *Journal of Economic Literature* 40:1105–66.
Boss, A., and T. Elender, 2008. Incentives to work: The case of Germany. Kiel Working Paper 1238. Kiel Institute for World Economics, Kiel, Germany.
Immervoll, H., H. J. Kleuven, C. T. Kreiner, and E. Saez, 2007. Welfare reform in European countries: A microsimulation analysis. *Economic Journal* 117:1–44.
Michalopoulos, C., P. K. Robins, and D. Card, 2008. When financial work incentives pay for themselves: Evidence from a randomized social experiment for welfare recipients. *Journal of Public Economics* 89:5–29.
Saunders, P., 2002. *The Ends and Means of Welfare: Coping with Economic and Social Change.* Cambridge University Press, Cambridge U.K.

8.2 The entitlement to income during old age

On the history of social security, see Verbon (1988). On approaches to providing for old age, see Fenge, de Menil and Pestieau (2008).

Fenge, R., de Menil, G., and P. Pestieau, 2008. *Pension Strategies in Europe and the United States.* MIT Press, Cambridge MA.
Verbon, H. A. A., 1988. *The Evolution of Public Pension Systems.* Springer-Verlag, Berlin.

On interest rates and inter-temporal consumption, see:

Samuelson, P. A., 1958. An exact consumption-loan model of interest with and without the social contrivance of money. *Journal of Political Economy* 66:467–82.

On the role of the extended family in self-interested intergenerational redistribution, see:

Cigno, A., 1993. Intergenerational transfers without altruism. *European Journal of Political Economy* 9:505–18.

On the viability of income transfer schemes, see:

Disney, R., 1998. *Can We Afford to Grow Older: A Perspective on Aging.* MIT Press, Cambridge MA.

On education and growth as a solution to demographic problems, see:

Kaganovich, M., and I. Zilcha, 1999. Education, social security, and growth. *Journal of Public Economics* 40:37–58.
Zhang, J., 1998. Social security and endogenous growth. *Journal of Public Economics* 58:185–213.

On migration and intergenerational redistribution, see Storesletten (2000) and Hillman (2002). On emigration, see von Hagen and Waltz (1995).

Hillman, A. L., 2002. Immigration and intergenerational transfers. In H. Siebert (Ed.), *Economic Policy for Aging Societies*, Springer, Berlin, pp. 213–26.
Storesletten, K., 2000. Sustaining fiscal policy through immigration. *Journal of Political Economy* 108:300–23.
von Hagen, J., and U. Waltz, 1998. Social security and migration in an aging Europe. In B. Eichengreen, J. Frieden, and J. von Hagen (Eds.), *Politics and Institutions in an Integrated Europe.* Springer, Berlin, pp. 177–92.

On generational accounting, see:

Auerbach, A., L. J. Kotlikoff, and W. Liebfritz, 1999. *Generational Accounting around the World.* University of Chicago Press, Chicago IL.

For a survey of political economy models of social security, see:

Galasso, V., and P. Profeta, 2002. Political economy models of social security: A survey. *European Journal of Political Economy* 18:1–29.

On change from pay-as-you-go transfers, see Brunner (1996), Feldstein (1998), Disney (2000), and Sinn (2000).

Brunner, J. K., 1996. Transition from a pay-as-you-go to a fully funded pension system: The case of differing individuals and intergenerational fairness. *Journal of Public Economics* 60:131–48.
Disney, R., 2000. Crises in public pension programmes in OECD: What are the reform options? *Economic Journal* 110:F1–F23.
Feldstein, M. (Ed.), 1998. *Privatizing Social Security*. Chicago University Press, Chicago IL.
Sinn, H.-W., 2000. Why a funded pension system is useful and why it is not. *International Tax and Finance Journal* 7:389–410.

On intergenerational risk sharing, see Gordon and Varian (1988). For a case study of government response to catastrophe, see Congleton (2006).

Congleton, R. D., 2006. The story of Katrina: New Orleans and the political economy of catastrophe. *Public Choice* 127:5–30.
Gordon, R., and H. R. Varian, 1988. Intergenerational risk sharing. *Journal of Public Economics* 37:185–202.

8.3 The entitlement to health care and health insurance

Many colleges and universities offer courses or complete programs on the economics of health care. The *Journal of Health Economics*, *Health Affairs*, *Health Care Financing Review*, and other journals provide specialized investigations of health-care issues. On the demand for health, see Grossman (1972). On uncertainty and health care, see Arrow (1963) and Cutler and Reber (1998).

Arrow, K. J., 1963. Uncertainty and the welfare economics of medical care. *American Economic Review* 53:941–69.
Cutler, D. M., and S. Reber, 1998. Paying for health insurance: The trade-off between competition and adverse selection. *Quarterly Journal of Economics* 113:433–66.
Grossman, M., 1972. On the concept of health capital and the demand for health. *Journal of Political Economy* 80:223–55.

On managed health care and competition, see:

Newhouse, J. P., 1996. Reimbursing health plans and health providers: Efficiency in production versus selection. *Journal of Economic Literature* 34:1236–63.
van de Ven, M., 1995. Regulated competition in health care: With or without a global budget. *European Economic Review* 39:786–94.

On spending and the quality of health care, see:

Cutler, D. M., 2000. Walking the tightrope of Medicare reform. *Journal of Economic Perspectives* 14:45–56.
Skinner, J., and J. Wennberg, 2000. How much is enough? Efficiency and Medicare spending in the last six months of life. In D. Cutler (Ed.), *The Changing Hospital Industry*, University of Chicago Press, Chicago IL, pp. 169–93.

On the benefits of privileged health care, see:

Smith, J. P., 1999. Healthy bodies and thick wallets: The dual relation between health and economic status. *Journal of Economic Perspectives* 13:145–166.

On impediments to effective universal coverage, see Katz and Hofer (1994).

Katz, S., and T. Hofer, 1994. Socioeconomic disparities in preventive care persist despite universal coverage. *Journal of the American Medical Association* 27:530–4.

On government-administered health care and markets, see:

Olivella, P., 2002. Shifting public-health-sector waiting lists to the private sector. *European Journal of Political Economy* 19:103–32.

On the relation between health expressed in weight at birth and future income, see:

Behrman, J. R., and M. R. Rozenzweig, 2004. Returns to birthweight. *The Review of Economics and Statistics* 86:586–601.

9

CHOICE OF TAXATION

Taxation has been present in our investigation of public goods, externalities, paternalism, social justice, and entitlements: public spending requires that governments have tax revenue to spend, and taxes affect incentives and are the sources of efficiency losses through the excess burden of taxation. We also studied tax evasion as an application of the prisoners' dilemma of voluntary payment for public goods (people who evade payment of taxes are free riding on tax payments of honest taxpayers). We observed how the Laffer curve constrains the amount of tax revenue that governments can collect and that a leviathan government would seek to maximize tax revenue without regard for benefit for taxpayers (in which case, we might want to rethink judgments about tax evasion). In the different instances where we considered taxation, (1) there was a single tax rate, (2) there was a designated tax base, and (3) one government was involved in taxation and public spending. In section 1 of this chapter, we depart from a single tax to look at the structure of tax rates. Section 2 considers choice of the tax base – or choice of what to tax. On a number of occasions, beginning with the Tiebout locational-choice mechanism, we encountered fiscal federalism, that is, taxation and public spending in the context of intergovernmental fiscal relations. Section 3 brings together our prior observations on fiscal federalism and adds further perspectives and questions.

9.1 Optimal Taxation

Optimal taxation is "optimal" in achieving either the social objectives of efficiency or social justice. Because efficiency and social justice conflict when social justice is defined as ex-post equality (recall the leaky bucket of redistribution when the objective is to maximize a social welfare function and choose a social insurance contract), optimal taxation can also be "optimal" in achieving an appropriate balance or trade-off between efficient and socially just taxation.

A. The Ramsey rule for efficient taxation

Efficient taxation is defined as taxation that minimizes the efficiency losses incurred through the excess burden of taxation – for a given amount of tax revenue. The solution for efficient taxation is known as the Ramsey rule, named for the British scholar, Frank Ramsey (1903–30), who derived the rule in 1929.

Sales taxes are to be levied on two goods, A and B. The fact that legal and effective incidence of taxes differ does not now matter because we are not concerned with the distribution of the burden and excess burden of taxation. The objective is to minimize the *total* excess burden of taxes on the two goods when seeking a given amount of tax revenue R.

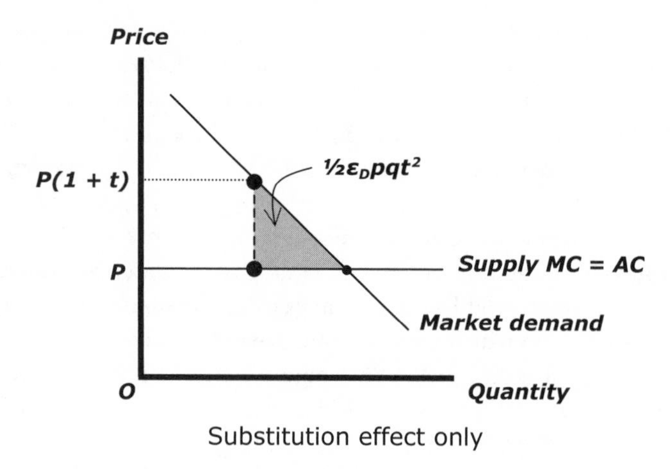

Figure 9.1. The Ramsey rule minimizes the excess burden of taxation across markets.

Tax rates are t_A for good A and t_B for good B.[1] Markets for goods A and B are competitive. Figure 9.1 shows supply at constant costs ($MC = AC$). We consider once more only substitution effects. With ε_{Di} denoting the market demand elasticity of good i and viewing the elasticity as a positive number (or absolute value):

> *The Ramsey rule for efficient taxation is that tax rates should be inversely related to demand elasticities:*

$$\frac{t_A}{t_B} = \frac{\varepsilon_{DB}}{\varepsilon_{DA}}. \tag{9.1}$$

The tax rate should therefore be higher on the good that has the lower price elasticity of demand. If there exists a market in which the demand elasticity is zero, taxes should be imposed only in that market.

The Ramsey rule extends to any number of taxes on different goods. The Ramsey rule applies to taxes levied on different components or sources of income that a person might have and also applies to different people earning incomes from the same source.[2]

[1] The taxes are in percentage terms or are set as *ad valorem* taxes. The taxes could also be specific or set in value terms. Whether taxes are set in *ad valorem* or specific terms has consequences when there is inflation (inflation erodes the value of specific taxes) and when there is uncertainty about market prices (a lower market price increases the rate of a specific tax, whereas an *ad valorem* tax by definition always maintains the same rate of taxation).

[2] The Ramsey rule in expression (9.1) is based on (1) constant costs of supply for the two goods A and B (as shown in figure 9.1), and (2) a tax in one market not affecting tax revenue in other markets (that is, cross-price elasticities are zero). The expression for the Ramsey rule is more complex when these conditions are not satisfied, but the basic principle is retained that efficient taxation requires tax rates to be lower when market elasticities are higher.

How is the Ramsey rule derived?

The excess burden of the tax in figure 9.1 is:[3]

$$\frac{1}{2}\varepsilon_D pqt^2. \tag{9.2}$$

With markets for two goods, A and B, there are two figures like figure 9.1, one for each market. Taxation is efficient when the two tax rates t_A and t_B minimize the combined excess burden in the two markets of raising target revenue R. The sum of the excess burdens of taxation in the markets for goods A and B is:

$$\frac{1}{2}\varepsilon_{DA} p_A q_A t_A^2 + \frac{1}{2}\varepsilon_{DB} p_B q_B t_B^2. \tag{9.3}$$

The revenue target is:

$$R = t_A P_A Q_A + t_B P_B Q_B, \tag{9.4}$$

where Q_i $(i = A, B)$ are the quantities sold in the market. The solution to minimizing the sum of excess burdens (9.3) subject to the revenue target (9.4) is the Ramsey rule in expression (9.1).[4]

Expression (9.1) indicates the ratio between the tax rates t_A and t_B. When we know the ratio between the tax rates, substitution into expression (9.4) provides the absolute values of the tax rates t_A and t_B that minimize the excess burden of taxation *and* provide sufficient combined revenue to meet the government's revenue target R.

Efficient taxation of personal incomes

The Ramsey rule applies to taxation of goods as well as taxation of income. With the revenue target given, we could envisage different constant proportional income-tax rates t_1 and t_2 levied on two people's incomes.[5] With ε_{S1} and ε_{S2} denoting the two people's individual labor-supply elasticities (the elasticities

[3] The formula for the excess burden of taxation was derived in chapter 4.

[4] The Ramsey rule follows from forming the Lagrangean function from expressions (9.3) and (9.4):

$$L = \frac{1}{2}\varepsilon_{DA} p_A q_A t_A^2 + \frac{1}{2}\varepsilon_{DB} p_B q_B t_B^2 - \lambda\left(R - t_A P_A Q_A - t_B P_B Q_B\right),$$

where λ is the Lagrangean multiplier, the value of which is the shadow price of tax revenue in terms of the efficiency loss due to the excess burden of taxation. Differentiating with respect to the tax rates t_A and t_B establishes that $t_A \varepsilon_{DA} = t_B \varepsilon_{DB}$, which implies the Ramsey rule in expression (9.1). If, for some reason, with many goods, a particular good cannot be taxed or a tax on a good cannot be changed, the Lagrangean function includes an additional constraint. In this second-best framework, the first-best efficient outcome is not attainable and the Ramsey rule accommodates the inability to adjust one of the taxes.

[5] We are here not looking at the structure of an income-tax schedule. One tax rate characterizes the income tax for each person.

indicate substitution responses between work and leisure), the Ramsey rule for efficient proportional income taxes levied on the two people is:

$$\frac{t_1}{t_2} = \frac{\varepsilon_{S2}}{\varepsilon_{S1}}. \tag{9.5}$$

The income-tax rates should therefore be inversely related to personal labor-market-supply elasticities.

> *The Ramsey rule ensures that public goods and entitlements are financed by efficient taxation; therefore, when the Ramsey rule is applied, the leaks in the bucket of redistribution are minimal.*

The logic of the Ramsey rule for efficient taxation

The logic of the Ramsey rule for efficient taxation follows from the relationship between substitution effects and the excess burden of taxation. A marginal increase in a tax rate marginally increases the excess burden of taxation through a substitution effect in market behavior, through either spending or earning income. For efficient taxation, the marginal losses due to the excess burdens of increases in different taxes should be equal. In expressions (9.1) and (9.5), the greater the elasticity, the greater is the substitution response to the tax; therefore, to keep the combined excess burden of taxation low, low taxes should be levied in markets where elasticities and therefore, substitution effects, are high.

Social justice and the Ramsey rule

In principle, everyone should favor efficient financing of public spending. Yet, efficiency is not the sole social objective. We also seek social justice. The Ramsey rule does not necessarily result in social justice. Indeed, the Ramsey rule can contradict social justice.

Social injustice in taxes on goods

Efficient taxation according to the Ramsey rule requires tax rates to be high for goods that have no close substitutes because demand elasticities for such goods are low. The Ramsey rule thus calls for high tax rates on necessities such as food and housing, medication, toothbrushes, soap, wheelchairs, and baby cereal. Tax rates should be low on designer clothes, dining in luxury restaurants, jewelry, yachts, and private planes because demand elasticities (and substitution opportunities) for these goods are high. Efficiency requires keeping substitution responses to a minimum; therefore, the Ramsey rule proposes high tax rates for goods and services that people continue to purchase (or still need to buy) after taxation has increased the price to buyers. Yet, tax rates that are selectively high on goods and services that are necessities and are large components of low-income people's spending contradict social justice.

Social injustice in taxation of personal incomes

The recommendations of the Ramsey rule also contradict social justice in recommendations for taxation of personal incomes. Person 1 may be independently wealthy but is prepared to work if paid enough. Person 2 has no sources of income other than from work and has no choice but to work for a living. Person 1's labor-supply elasticity is high because of the alternative of not working, whereas the poorer person's labor-supply elasticity is low because of the need to earn income from work to survive. Hence, in expression (9.5), we have $\varepsilon_{S1} > \varepsilon_{S2}$. The Ramsey rule requires the wealthier person to be taxed at a lower rate than the poorer person who has less flexibility when making labor-supply decisions.

Conflict between efficiency and social justice

The Ramsey rule indicates how to achieve efficient taxation. However:

The Ramsey rule introduces conflict between efficiency and social justice.

Box 9.1 A leviathan government and the Ramsey rule

A leviathan government can use the Ramsey rule to maximize tax revenue subject to a limit on the excess burden of taxation. The leviathan government would solve:

$$Max\ R = t_A P_A Q_A + t_B P_B Q_B$$

subject to:

$$\overline{D} \leq \frac{1}{2}\varepsilon_{DA} p_A q_A t_A^2 + \frac{1}{2}\varepsilon_{DB} p_B q_B t_B^2,$$

where $\overline{D}$ is the upper limit to the excess burden of taxation and Q_i $(i = A, B)$ are the quantities sold in the market. The solution is again the Ramsey rule in expression (9.5).[6] Political impediments due to the conflict between efficiency and social justice may not deter a leviathan government from applying the Ramsey rule. A leviathan government may not be sensitive to political support from taxpayers.

Efficient taxation and gender differences

In the traditional model of the family, a man and a woman live together in a monogamous relationship and have children. When the children are young, the woman might reduce labor-market participation and forgo career-advancement opportunities. Family income – and cultural transmission of values – determine when or if the woman reenters the labor market and how much she works. In the traditional model of the family, the woman's labor-supply elasticity is, therefore, greater than that of the man. The Ramsey rule therefore requires higher tax

[6] The leviathan government solves the dual problem of that used to determine the Ramsey rule.

rates on the income of men than on the income earned by women – on efficiency grounds, because women's substitution possibilities include caring for their young children at home. Women's greater substitution possibilities also increase labor-supply elasticities through discretion in the decision of whether to have another child. The conclusions from the Ramsey rule thus depend on whether men and women differ in labor-market behavior and in home and income responsibilities. When women have decided on a career unencumbered by family responsibilities or when (subject to biological limitations) the man shares all responsibilities, the Ramsey rule calls for equal personal tax treatment of men and women.

Asymmetric information and the Ramsey rule

Because the Ramsey rule calls for taxing everyone according to individual labor-supply elasticities, applying the rule is subject to asymmetric information: a person's labor-market intentions and opportunities are private information that a government could not be expected to have. Nor can the Ramsey rule be readily applied to determine different tax rates for different groups of people. For example, some women have low labor-market elasticities because of career commitments whereas other women are prepared to contemplate withdrawing from the labor market, at least temporarily, to have a family. Efficient Ramsey taxes require governments to be able to distinguish between the two types of women. Quite generally:

> *Applying the Ramsey rule is subject to asymmetric information because only people themselves know their labor-market supply elasticities – and their demand elasticities for different goods and services.*

Thus, because of individual differences and asymmetric information about elasticities (for example, an evening at the opera is a necessity for some people and not for others), personal Ramsey taxes or Ramsey taxes for groups of people are impossible or difficult to determine.

Taxation of innate ability

If innate personal abilities could be taxed, there would be no substitution responses and no excess burden of taxation. Taxes based on personal innate abilities are therefore efficient according to the Ramsey rule. Innate ability is difficult to measure. If measurement were nonetheless possible, would we want people to be taxed according to their ability to earn income – and not according to the income they actually earn?

High-ability people can differ in their preferences regarding combining a traditional family with a career. When taxation is based on innate ability to earn income, choosing a lifestyle that includes a family results in the same personal obligation to pay taxes as choosing a life focused on career goals.

Taxation according to ability is a tax on preferences of people who voluntarily wish to forgo high income to seek other sources of personal satisfaction in life.

Taxing ability as proposed by the Ramsey rule would be an intrusion in people's personal lives and their personal choices – and thereby their personal freedom.

If taxation were based on innate ability, people would have incentives to hide their true abilities from the government. They would pretend to have low ability. Parents might train their children to avoid revealing true high ability.

Taxes based on ability have high excess burdens because of the acts undertaken on the pretense of displaying low ability.

Taxation of beauty

There have been studies of the role of beauty in determining personal incomes. "Better looking" people were found to choose the types of jobs where beauty yields a higher return (where beauty is the basis for comparative advantage), but the evidence also shows that beauty increases personal income within occupations.[7] If beauty were innate, a market return to beauty would be similar to a market return to innate ability. The Ramsey rule would then propose that people be taxed according to their beauty on the grounds that substitution away from beauty is impossible and therefore beauty can be taxed without an excess burden. If beauty can be manipulated or hidden, there are substitution effects and excess burdens. Thus, like the pretense of low ability, parents would train their children to appear personally unattractive to avoid being taxed or parents would hide good-looking children from the government. Or, people judged to be beautiful would emigrate.

The impracticality of the Ramsey rule

The practicality of the Ramsey rule is limited by asymmetric information about personal substitution possibilities and intentions (as we noted, women committed to careers cannot be distinguished from those who are not). Taxation in accord with ability is unjust as well as impractical. Political decision makers in democracies are also reluctant to use the Ramsey rule because high taxes on necessities are unpopular with voters. Economists nonetheless study the Ramsey rule because of the importance of the social objective of efficiency.

B. The equal-sacrifice principle for socially just taxation

We now leave the quest for efficient taxes through the Ramsey rule to look for social justice in taxation.

[7] A study was undertaken by Daniel Hamermesh and Jeff Biddle (1994).

Progressive taxes

Social justice in taxation is often associated with a progressive income tax schedule. Progressivity of taxation is defined in terms of the average tax rate. With R indicating the total amount a person pays in taxes and Y indicating the person's total pre-tax income, the average rate of taxation is:

$$t_A \equiv \frac{\text{Total taxes paid}}{\text{Total income earned}} = \frac{R}{Y}. \tag{9.6}$$

A tax schedule is locally progressive if the average rate of taxation increases with income.

Conversely, a tax schedule is locally regressive when the average rate of taxation declines with income. With proportional taxation, the average rate of taxation remains constant. Some few countries have a proportional income tax (as we used when demonstrating the excess burden of taxation). Most countries have progressive income tax rates.

The average rate of taxation is defined for *total* taxes that an individual pays and *total* income that the individual earns. The marginal tax rate is the change in total taxes paid when income marginally increases:

$$t_M \equiv \frac{\partial R}{\partial Y}. \tag{9.7}$$

The marginal tax can also be used to define progressive taxes:

An income tax schedule is locally progressive if the marginal tax rate increases with pre-tax income.

To study the structure of taxes in an income-tax schedule, we now temporarily set aside the objective of efficiency and therefore also the Ramsey rule. We eliminate substitution responses to taxation; hence, people will not be viewed as substituting leisure for productive income-earning activity when tax rates increase. This implies also that there is no Laffer curve. In fact, substitution effects, of course, are present and are indicated by changes in people's willingness to work when taxes change. However, to seek only social justice without having to be concerned about efficiency effects of taxation, we now ask the question:

If there were no inefficiency because there is no substitution response to taxation, what would be the grounds for proposing progressive taxation as socially just?

The ability-to-pay principle of taxation

The ability-to-pay principle of taxation contrasts with the benefit principle of taxation. The benefit principle is applied when user prices are paid and when taxes are chosen through location in Tiebout jurisdictions. The benefit principle is accompanied by accountability because people know what they are paying for and judge whether the payment is justified by what is received. In contrast, the principle of "ability to pay" requires people to pay taxes according to their income, independent of personal benefit from the spending of tax revenue.

The ability-to-pay principle is related to two other principles of social justice in taxation. The principle of horizontally equitable taxation requires that people with the same income pay the same taxes ("equal treatment of equals"). The principle of vertical equity requires equal tax treatment of people who have different incomes (with adjustments, for example, for numbers of dependents).

Vertical equity in taxation is a more complex objective than horizontal equity because of the need to define the meaning of equal treatment in taxation when people's incomes are unequal. Vertical equity is the criterion that is applied when a progressive income tax has been chosen: when income taxes are progressive, judgments have been made about taxes paid by people who have unequal incomes.

Diminishing marginal utility of income

We are looking for a justification of the social justice of progressive income taxes. We begin our search with the consequences of diminishing marginal utility of income. Figure 9.2 shows a utility function with diminishing *MU* of income, which is indicated by the declining slope of the utility function at the different levels of income $Y_1 < Y_2 < Y_3$. Diminishing *MU* of income implies that people value additions to income less at higher levels of income. We previously saw that diminishing *MU* indicates risk aversion.

> *Because of diminishing MU of income, people lose less utility from paying a dollar of taxation, the higher are their incomes.*

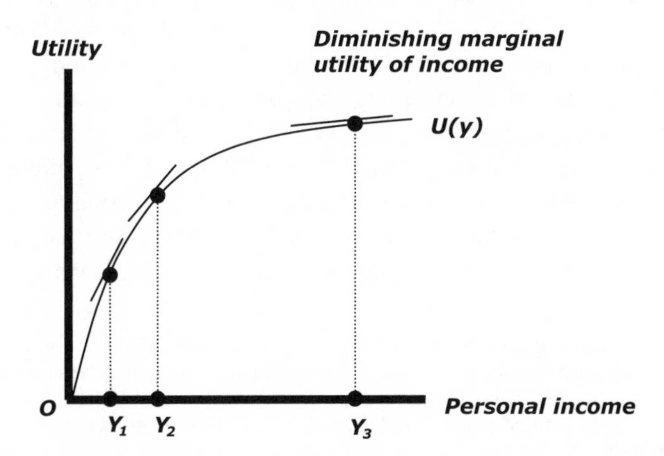

Figure 9.2. Diminishing marginal utility of income indicates declining marginal loss of utility from taxation.

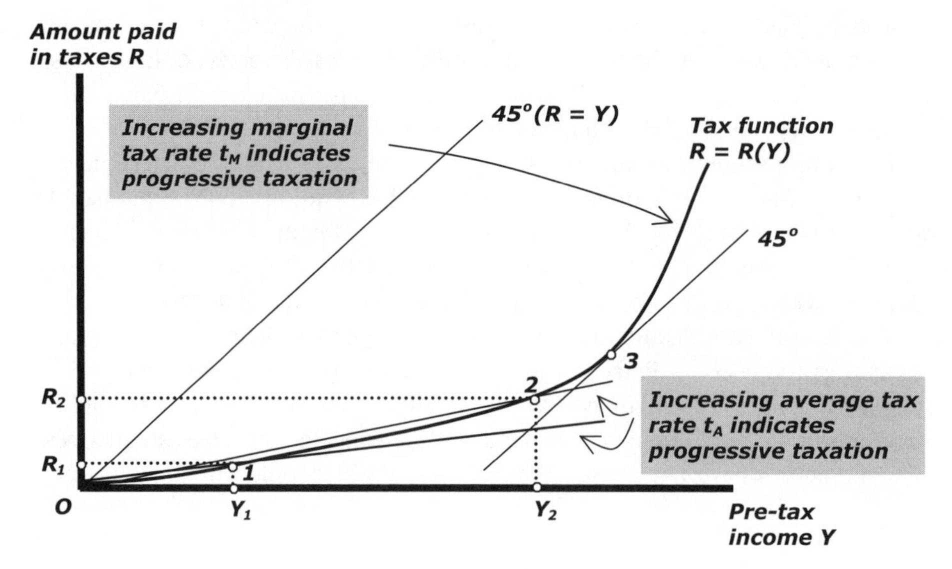

Figure 9.3. A progressive tax function.

An income-tax schedule

An income-tax schedule shows the relationship between total taxes paid R and total pre-tax income Y. Figure 9.3 shows an income-tax schedule for personal income earned by an individual. The tax function is:

$$R = R(Y). \tag{9.8}$$

In figure 9.3, the marginal tax rate t_M is given by the slope of the income-tax function. The marginal tax rate is everywhere increasing; therefore, taxation is progressive for all levels of pre-tax income Y.

The average tax rate t_A also everywhere increases with pre-tax income. For example, t_A increases when pre-tax income increases in figure 9.3 from Y_1 to Y_2.[8]

The changes in the average and marginal rates are related. Because the marginal tax rate increases, the average rate of taxation $t_A = R(Y)/Y$ increases. The increasing marginal and average rates indicate progressive taxation.[9]

Along the 45° line from the origin in figure 9.3, total taxes paid are equal to total pre-tax income (that is, $R = Y$). As long as the tax function $R(Y)$ lies below the 45° line, the constraint is satisfied that $R \leq Y$; that is, the total taxes that an individual pays do not exceed the individual's total pre-tax income.

[8] When pre-tax income is Y_1, the amount paid in taxes is determined at point 1 on the tax function as R_1; when pre-tax income is higher at Y_2, the amount paid in taxes is determined at point 2 on the tax function as R_2. The slopes of the straight lines from the origin to points 1 and 2 indicate the average tax paid. We see that $R_1/Y_1 < R_2/Y_2$; therefore, taxation is progressive for an increase in income from Y_1 to Y_2.

[9] We shall presently look at linear income-tax schedules and see that an income-tax schedule can be progressive, defined by t_A increasing, without an increasing marginal tax rate t_M. An increasing marginal tax rate is sufficient but not necessary for progressivity in the income-tax schedule.

At point 3 in figure 9.3, the slope of the tax schedule $R(Y)$ is 45° and the marginal tax rate t_M is therefore 100 percent.[10] Beyond point 3, the marginal tax rate exceeds 100 percent: the taxpayer would then be paying more taxation on additions to pre-tax income than the additional income that has been earned.

We expect, of course, that high marginal tax rates, particularly marginal tax rates in excess of 100 percent, would have severe adverse effects on efficiency through the substitution between work effort and leisure and through attempts to hide income from the government. We might also want to ask why a government would want to impose such high tax rates given the severe disincentives for productive activity (or legal productive activity).

A government imposing high marginal tax rates must be aware of the disincentives for people to be productive because of the high taxes. Does the government perhaps not want people with high incomes to keep working? We shall return to this question. However, for the time being, we are omitting from consideration efficiency losses from substitution responses to taxes.

An income-tax schedule with tax brackets

Income-tax schedules in practice do not have the smooth continuous form of figure 9.3 but rather are piecewise linear functions with tax rates that change in steps or "brackets," as shown in figure 9.4. The tax function in figure 9.4 has tax brackets for ranges of income ending at points 1, 2, and 3. The tax brackets therefore end at incomes Y_1, Y_2, and Y_3, where total taxes paid are correspondingly R_1,

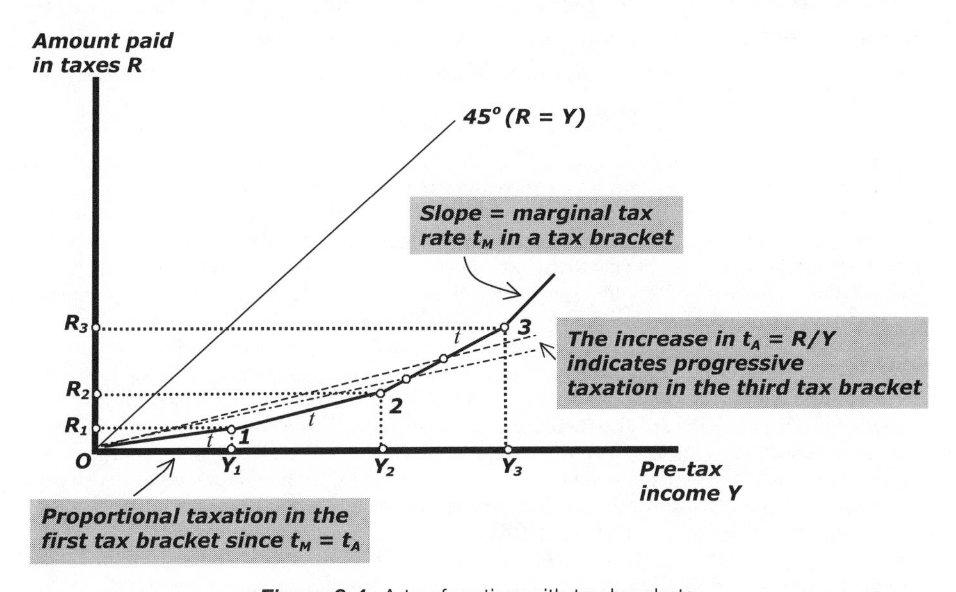

Figure 9.4. A tax function with tax brackets.

[10] At point 3, $dR/dY = 1$ and so $dR = dY$, indicating that the increase in the tax paid dR when pre-tax income increases by dY is equal to the increase in income.

R_2, and R_3. Figure 9.4 is illustrative. There can, of course, be any number of tax brackets in an income-tax schedule.

A tax bracket is defined by a within-bracket constant marginal rate of taxation t_M. The marginal tax rates in figure 9.4 increase across successive tax brackets. In the first tax bracket, the marginal rate of taxation t_M is equal to the average rate of taxation t_A. Taxation in the first tax bracket is therefore proportional. For increases in income beyond the highest income Y_1 in the first tax bracket, taxation is progressive because the average rate of taxation $t_A = R/Y$ increases.

The average rate of taxation increases after the first tax bracket for all subsequent increases in pre-tax income, whether the increase in pre-tax income is within the same tax bracket or between tax brackets. For illustration, figure 9.4 shows an increase in the average tax rate $t_A = R/Y$ in the third tax bracket.[11]

The normative question about progressive taxation

Our normative question is:

> *To be socially just, does an income-tax structure necessarily have to be progressive?*

Recall that in asking this question, we have neutralized efficiency considerations that affect a tax structure. That is, we are temporarily viewing income taxes as lump-sum taxes with no excess burden of taxation.[12]

When we ask whether progressive taxation is socially just, we require a definition of social justice. If people were confronting uncertainty behind a veil of ignorance, we could use the insurance definition of social justice. However, we do not now use this definition.

[11] Figure 9.4 shows the marginal tax rate as increasing in the fourth tax bracket. If the marginal rate of taxation were to decline in the fourth tax bracket, we could not necessarily infer that taxation in the fourth tax bracket is regressive by the definition of the change in the average tax rate $t_A = R/Y$. Taxation would be regressive in the fourth tax bracket (t_A would decline with increases in income) only if the marginal rate of taxation t_M in the fourth tax bracket were less than the average rate of taxation t_A paid on combined income $(Y_1 + Y_2 + Y_3)$ in the previous three tax brackets. Taxation is regressive at the margin if the marginal rate of taxation declines between two tax brackets. As an example, consider tax brackets defined in terms of sequential additions to annual income of $10,000, with *marginal* tax rates of 5 and 10 percent in the first two tax brackets and a marginal tax rate of 5 percent in the third tax bracket. The *average* rate of taxation paid on income up to $10,000 is 5 percent, which is the marginal rate in the first tax bracket; therefore, taxation is proportional in the first tax bracket. Within the second tax bracket, the marginal tax rate is constant at 10 percent but taxation is progressive because t_A is increasing. For example, the amount paid in taxes on an income of $12,000 is $700 ($500 + 10 percent of $2,000) and the amount paid in taxes on an income of $15,000 is $1,000 ($500 + 10 percent of $5,000); t_A has therefore increased from 5.8 to 6.7 percent. In the third tax bracket, taxation is regressive because the marginal tax rate of 5 percent is less than the average tax rate of 7.5 percent in the first two brackets. For example, between incomes of $24,000 and $28,000, t_A declines from 7.1 to 6.8 percent.

[12] On lump-sum taxes, see chapter 4.

The ability-to-pay principle and socially just taxation

We could consider using the ability-to-pay principle as a guide to the choice of a socially just tax schedule. However:

> *The ability-to-pay principle requires only that people with higher incomes pay more in taxes.*

The ability-to-pay principle, therefore, does not imply progressive income taxation. The ability-to-pay principle requires only that the marginal rate of taxation be positive, which is the case whether taxation is progressive or regressive or proportional.

The equal-sacrifice principle of taxation

What, then, is the definition of social justice that we can apply to justify progressive taxation? We cannot simply base a case for progressive incomes taxes on an intuition of fairness.

Progressive taxation has been studied against the background of the equal-sacrifice principle of taxation.

> *The equal-sacrifice principle of taxation requires that the total utility loss from payment of taxes should be the same for everyone, no matter what a person's pre-tax income happens to be.*

The equal-sacrifice principle dates at least to John Stuart Mill, who in 1848 associated "equality of taxation" with "equality of sacrifice."

The equal-sacrifice principle is defined in terms of *total taxes* paid and *total personal utility* lost by taxpayers from paying the taxes. The principle requires that for all taxpayers, the total loss in utility from paying total taxes be equal. We use the utility function in figure 9.2 (or a utility function with the same properties) as the common basis for measurement of the total loss in taxpayers' utilities from paying taxes. That is, the *MU* of income is declining and therefore the personal *marginal sacrifice* (or utility loss) from paying taxes declines as income increases.

> *The equal-sacrifice principle takes into account the diminishing MU of income whereby constant marginal tax rates impose smaller marginal "sacrifices" in utility lost on people with higher incomes.*

With the utility function exhibiting declining *MU* of income, we approach social justice in taxation by asking the questions:

> *Does equal total personal sacrifice in paying taxes imply that income taxes are necessarily progressive?*
>
> *Do all progressive income taxes result in equal sacrifice?*

The answers to these questions are:

> *The equal-sacrifice principle does not imply that taxation is necessarily progressive.*
>
> *Progressive taxes need not satisfy the equal-sacrifice principle.*

Derivation of an equal-sacrifice income-tax schedule

To demonstrate these conclusions, we denote the common utility of all taxpayers by $U(Y)$. Here, Y is pre-tax earned income, which is the tax base. Because substitution effects of taxation are absent, the income Y does not depend on taxation. The total tax paid by a taxpayer earning pre-tax income Y is $R(Y)$. The utility from after-tax income is therefore $U[Y - R(Y)]$.

We define sacrifice from paying taxes as S. Equal sacrifice for all taxpayers through utility lost in paying taxes requires that for any pre-tax income Y:

$$S = U[Y] - U[Y - R(Y)] = c = constant.^{13} \tag{9.9}$$

That is, whatever the pre-tax income Y that a person has, the loss S in utility from paying taxes R (which depends on income Y through the tax schedule) should be equal for everyone.[14] Equation (9.9) can be solved to obtain the equal-sacrifice tax schedule $R^E(Y)$. The average tax rate when a person is taxed according the equal-sacrifice tax schedule is:

$$t_A \equiv \frac{R^E(Y)}{Y} = 1 - \frac{U^{-1}[U(Y) - c]}{Y}. \tag{9.10}$$

Expression (9.10) contains the information to indicate whether the equal-sacrifice income tax schedule $R^E(Y)$ is necessarily progressive. The tax schedule would be necessarily progressive if the average tax rate were everywhere increasing with pre-tax income; that is, if:

$$\frac{\partial t_A}{\partial Y} \equiv \frac{\partial R^E(Y)/Y}{\partial Y} > 0. \tag{9.11}$$

Whether the expression (9.11) is positive as required for progressive taxation depends on the properties of the common utility function $U(Y)$ that was chosen

[13] The expression (9.9) defines equal sacrifice in absolute terms as the difference between pre- and post-tax income. Equal *proportional* sacrifice has also been proposed as a measure of equal sacrifice. In that case, we would have

$$S = \frac{U(Y)}{U(Y - R(Y))} = constant.$$

From the properties of utility functions, this is equivalent to expression (9.9). Taking logarithms gives the expression for absolute equal sacrifice (9.9); a logarithmic transformation preserves the utility function.

[14] A person earning \$100,000 a year and a person earning \$50,000 a year should pay taxes so that their respective utility losses from paying the taxes are equal. If the high-income person loses as much utility from paying \$30,000 in taxes as the low-income person loses from paying \$10,000 in taxes, the equal-sacrifice principle is satisfied – in this case, with progressive taxation.

to measure the utility loss of all taxpayers from paying taxes. We imposed the constraint on choice of $U(Y)$ of diminishing MU of income. However, diminishing MU of income is not sufficient to ensure that expression (9.11) is positive and therefore is not sufficient to ensure that equal sacrifice necessarily requires progressive taxation. It is rather the case that:

> *Utility functions that exhibit diminishing MU of income are consistent with equal-sacrifice tax functions that can be progressive, proportional, or regressive.*

What is the condition that needs to be satisfied for an equal-sacrifice tax function to be progressive? Progressivity follows only if the MU of income (or the slope of the utility function) declines sufficiently with income so that the elasticity of $MU(Y)$ exceeds unity (in absolute value).[15] Although we are not now concerned with risk, this condition can be expressed in terms of *relative risk aversion* defined as the positive number:[16]

$$RRA \equiv \frac{dMU}{MU} \bigg/ \frac{dy}{y} = \frac{\%\ change\ in\ MU}{\%\ change\ in\ y}. \tag{9.12}$$

If relative risk aversion is constant, the utility function $U(Y)$ is of the form:

$$U^i = \frac{y_i^{1-RRA} - 1}{1 - RRA} \qquad for\ RRA \neq 1$$

$$U^i = \log y_i \qquad for\ RRA = 1. \tag{9.13}$$

If two people have pre-tax incomes $y_1 > y_2$, then, with the utility function in expression (9.13):

$$\frac{MU_1}{MU_2} = \left(\frac{y_1}{y_2}\right)^{RRA}. \tag{9.14}$$

If $RRA = 1$, levels of income and the MUs of income are inversely proportional.

We need a utility function to measure the "sacrifice" of taxpayers from paying taxes: choosing the utility function of the form in expression (9.13) has the advantage that the value of relative risk aversion RRA is a constant parameter. Then:

> *If $RRA > 1$, an equal-sacrifice income-tax schedule is progressive.*
>
> *If $RRA < 1$, an equal-sacrifice income-tax schedule is regressive.*

Examples confirm that utility functions with diminishing MU of income can result in a regressive equal-sacrifice tax function.[17]

[15] This was observed by Paul Samuelson (1947). The proof follows from expanding expression (9.11) by differentiating expression (9.10).

[16] Because marginal utility is declining with income, the number is negative. However, we relate to the number as positive or an absolute value.

[17] The following is an example of a utility function (from H. Peyton Young, 1987) with diminishing marginal utility of income for which equal sacrifice implies regressive taxation: $U(Y) = aY^{1/2} + b$,

The reverse process is to begin with an arbitrarily chosen progressive income-tax schedule, as might be used by a government. We then look for a utility function that, when substituted into the expression for equal sacrifice (9.9), will yield the chosen progressive income-tax schedule. However, for a chosen progressive income tax schedule, a utility function cannot necessarily be found that yields equal sacrifice in utility lost from payment of total taxes.

> *An income-tax schedule can be progressive without equal sacrifice from taxes paid.*[18]

When the utility function is of the form (9.13), the value of *RRA* determines whether the equal-sacrifice principle implies progressive taxation. We could thus approach equal-sacrifice in taxation by determining the value of *RRA* in a society. Of course, now we are relying on a single utility function to represent everyone in a society. Although people no doubt differ, it is generally proposed that relative risk aversion is around unity.[19]

> *With $RRA = 1$, equal sacrifice from paying taxes requires proportional income taxation.*

C. Optimal income taxation

The equal-sacrifice principle is based on people supplying labor without regard for reward (labor supply is inelastic and taxes are lump-sum with no work–leisure substitution effects). In the realistic circumstances in which people's effort and work decisions depend on the incentives of rewards, there are efficiency losses because of excess burdens of taxation. We now restore excess burdens of taxation and also return to the definition of social justice as achieved by maximizing a social welfare function.

where $a > 0$. For this utility function, equal sacrifice over all ranges of pre-tax incomes implies $(aY^{1/2} + b) - (a(Y - R)^{1/2} + b) = c$, where c is constant for all $Y \geq 0$. For pre-tax income sufficiently high (where $Y \geq c^2/a^2$), the equal-sacrifice tax function $R(Y) = (c/a)2Y^{1/2} - c/a)$ is strictly regressive. For lower levels of pre-tax income (where $0 < Y < c^2/a^2$), there is no real-valued solution for a tax function.

[18] Young (1987) derived the class of utility functions for which equal sacrifice is scale-invariant, in the sense that re-indexing of tax brackets can take place while preserving equal sacrifice (this can be the case if and only if the utility function exhibits constant relative risk aversion) and derived tax functions that can represent equal sacrifice at all levels of income (a proportional tax and a tax function with a constant elasticity of substitution). Tapan Mitra and Efe A. Ok (1997) categorized the class of progressive taxes that are inconsistent with equal sacrifice, in the sense that there does not exist a utility function that can be used to measure the sacrifice from taxation that is consistent with the equal-sacrifice condition in expression (9.9). A tax schedule for which there is no utility function that gives equal sacrifice is necessarily inequitable by the equal-sacrifice principle.

[19] Greater values of R have also been suggested. Accuracy in measurement is an issue. Layard, Nickell, and Mayraz (2008) suggested the number 1.26, with a high range of 1.34 and a low range of 1.19. The numbers are averages derived from studies in which people are asked to evaluate their subjective happiness and combined with other data from 50 countries. The number 1.26 is an average that provides no guidance for any one society.

We know from our investigation of social justice that if there are no efficiency losses through the excess burden of taxation (if there are no leaks in the bucket of redistribution), maximizing a symmetric social welfare function from Bentham to Rawls and all social welfare functions in between results in post-tax ex-post equality. As was the case when we considered voting on taxation with no efficiency losses, the tax rate would be 100 percent and all income would be equally redistributed to achieve equal post-tax incomes. However, given that there are leaks in the bucket of redistribution because taxes affect labor-supply decisions, we can ask:

What is the structure of an income tax that maximizes social welfare when there are efficiency losses from taxation?

The answer to this question is an "optimal income-tax schedule."

The optimal income-tax schedule takes into account the trade-off between efficiency and social justice.

Through sensitivity to efficiency losses from taxation, an optimal income-tax structure depends on the social welfare function that is chosen. We saw that a Bentham social function exhibits greatest sensitivity to inefficiency, whereas a Rawls social welfare function focuses on the well-being of the worst-off person in society and exhibits no sensitivity at all to inefficiency (except insofar as inefficiency reduces the utility of the worst-off person).

A linear income tax

Figure 9.3 showed a progressive income-tax function with increasing marginal tax rates (and therefore also increasing average tax rates). Figure 9.5 shows the special case of a linear personal income tax. The individual's market-determined income is Y. The total tax revenue that the individual pays to the government is R. *Everyone* in the population receives an income transfer G from the government.

Earned income Y is taxed at a constant flat or proportional rate t. The total taxes that an individual i pays are, accordingly:

$$R_i = -G + tY_i. \tag{9.15}$$

The slope of the linear income-tax schedule indicates the proportional tax rate t. All people in the population receive the same sum G as an income transfer from the government, and everyone also faces the same constant marginal income tax rate t. However, as indicated by the index i in expression (9.15), people have different pre-tax earned incomes and pay different personal taxes.

In figure 9.5, a person earning the pre-tax income Y_0 pays zero net taxes. The taxes tY_0 that this person pays to the government are exactly equal to the income transfer G received from the government.

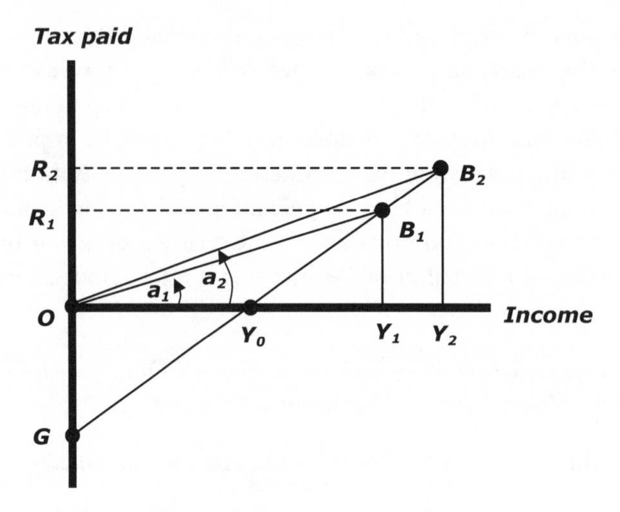

Figure 9.5. A linear income tax.

People with pre-tax incomes in excess of Y_0 pay positive taxes. People with pre-tax market incomes below Y_0 receive net income transfers from the government (they pay negative income taxes).

If personal incomes are random, the income tax provides social insurance. People with pre-tax earned incomes less than Y_0 receive income support through the tax system, and those with pre-tax incomes higher than Y_0 pay taxes to finance the income-support payments to the low-income population. The pre-tax market income Y_0 is the dividing income between people who receive income support and people who pay taxes to finance income support for others.[20]

Taxation is progressive if people with higher pre-tax incomes pay higher shares of their income as taxes. We see in figure 9.5 that a person with market income Y_1 pays total taxes R_1 and has the average tax rate:

$$t_A \equiv a_1 = \frac{R_1}{Y_1}. \tag{9.16}$$

The average tax rate a_1 is the slope of the line OB_1. A person with higher pre-tax income Y_2 pays higher total taxes R_2 and has the higher average tax rate a_2 given by the slope of the line OB_2. Therefore:

> *A linear income tax is progressive, although the marginal tax rate is constant.*

Although the tax structure is progressive, the flat rate of income taxation provides favorable incentives to work.

Choosing an optimal linear income tax has the simplicity of needing to choose only one rate of taxation. The rate of taxation t determines the income transfer G

[20] For example, if the government provides a basic income support of $1,000 a month and the tax rate is 20 percent, the break-even income Y_0 is $5,000 a month.

paid to everyone in the population by determining the tax revenue that is available for redistribution.

The value of the income support G indicates the extent of social insurance in the tax structure. A higher value of G provides more social insurance by providing more income support for the low-income population. At the same time, higher tax revenue is required to finance the more generous income support. More tax revenue, in turn, results in a greater excess burden of taxation (more leaks in the bucket of redistribution).

Choice of the income subsidy G is linked to the choice of the tax rate t through the government's budget constraint, which requires that total tax revenue be equal to total transfer payments. With a population of n people, the government's budget constraint is:

$$t \sum_{i=1}^{n} Y_i = nG. \tag{9.17}$$

All n people in the population receive the same transfer G. The tax rate t is levied on the tax base of income of the n people in the population.

A complexity

A complexity in the solution for the optimal linear income tax is that an individual's pre-tax market income Y_i depends on the tax rate t and also on the income subsidy G that is provided. In turn, G is linked to the tax rate t through the government budget constraint (9.17). Hence, the budget constraint of the government becomes:

$$nG = t \sum_{i=1}^{n} Y_i(t, G), \tag{9.18}$$

where:

$$Y_i = Y_i(t, G) \tag{9.19}$$

expresses the dependence of taxable earned income Y_i on the tax rate and on the income transfer received from government. It follows that:

> *The optimal solution for the tax and income transfer needs to be consistent with the incentives of people to supply the labor that provides the tax base on which the income tax is levied.*

Choice of the social welfare function for deriving the optimal tax rate

A society that chooses the optimal linear income tax by maximizing Rawls's social welfare function requires more tax revenue for income redistribution than a society that chooses Bentham's social welfare function. Because the Rawls social welfare function focuses on the well-being of the people who are worst off in having lowest pre-tax incomes, a higher value of the income transfer G is required for income support at low-income levels. A higher value of the tax rate t is correspondingly required to finance the larger income transfers. Because of the higher tax rate, there is then also a greater efficiency loss through the higher excess burden of taxation.

Value of the optimal tax rate

Simulation studies suggest that progressive systems of income taxation can generally be replaced with a "flat" or proportional rate of income taxation of 20 to 25 percent to yield the same revenue as the progressive tax system in place. The replacement linear income tax would have limited or no exemptions from taxable income. The income subsidy G can be determined by requisite living standards and can consist of money and in-kind transfers. Because the marginal tax rate is constant and low, incentives are provided to work rather than substitute leisure for work. Tax evasion and an informal economy are discouraged by the low tax rate. Because of the social insurance through the tax system, moral hazard remains present.

The Laffer curve and the structure of income taxation

If the same tax revenue as provided by progressive taxation can be obtained with greater efficiency by a flat or proportional tax rate, we have evidence for the Laffer curve. A progressive tax structure places the government on the wrong (or inefficient side) of the Laffer curve. Why do governments then retain progressive taxes? It appears that there is something intrinsically appealing about progressive taxation for political decision makers – although we have seen that there is no necessary link between the fairness of equal sacrifice and progressive taxation.

The general optimal income-tax problem

The general optimal income-tax problem looks for the optimal income-tax schedule $R(Y)$ in figure 9.3 in which tax rates can vary with income – although also income transfers can be provided to people with low incomes, which is not shown as a possibility in figure 9.3. The solution for the general optimal income-tax problem could be a linear tax function as shown in figure 9.5.

Finding a general structure of optimal income taxation is considerably more complicated than finding the parameters of the optimal linear income tax. The solution to the general optimal income-tax problem is a tax function or tax schedule $R(Y)$, whereas the optimal linear income-tax problem requires solving for the single tax rate t.

The general optimal income-tax problem is associated with the Scottish economist, James A. Mirrlees (Nobel Prize in economics, 1996), who set out the problem in 1971. Ideally, from the vantage of the Mirrlees problem, there are no leaks in the bucket of redistribution. For example, if personal abilities are innate and cannot be manipulated, taxes on abilities have no excess burden, so there would be no leaky bucket and no efficiency losses from taxation. As we saw in chapter 7, maximizing any symmetric social welfare function – for example, Bentham – would result in ex-post equality; we saw in chapter 6 that the equality of income could be attained through appropriative taxation and equal redistribution.

We have concluded that taxing people's abilities is unjust. However, the problem facing Mirrlees was asymmetric information. Individuals' abilities are private information and therefore are not observable. Governments thus confront an asymmetric-information problem when seeking to tax ability. A government can observe personal incomes earned through the application of personal ability but not ability itself. Because only personal incomes are observable, only personal incomes can be taxed.

Mirrlees therefore confronted a second-best problem. He wanted ideally to tax innate ability so that there would be no efficiency impediments to post-tax income equality. However, only earned incomes are observable and taxation of income introduces work–leisure substitution effects and a leaky bucket of redistribution. Choosing and maximizing for example a Bentham social welfare function therefore introduces an efficiency-equality trade-off, because of which social insurance is incomplete and so complete income equality is not achieved.

Mirrlees derived the optimal income-tax structure by maximizing social welfare when all people have the same utility function but differ in their unobserved abilities to earn income. The government in the Mirrlees optimal income-tax problem could not observe how many hours a person worked or how much effort a person put into work. The government, however, did know the distribution of abilities in the population. An additional constraint in the formal analysis ensured that individual decisions to work maximized personal utility for the structure of taxes that a government chooses. As in the linear income-tax problem, the optimal income-tax schedule includes negative rates of taxation or income transfers for people with low pre-tax incomes. The government therefore has the budget constraint that tax revenue collected is equal to the value of income transfers.

The trade-off between progressive and regressive taxation

The optimal income tax finds the optimal (social-welfare maximizing) trade-off between progressive and regressive taxation. Progressive taxation is desirable because of the objective – implicit in the social welfare function – of ex-post (post-tax) equality.[21] The Ramsey rule suggests that the efficient structure of an income-tax schedule is regressive.[22] Another case for a regressive tax schedule follows from the effects of taxation on the tax base. Because of effects on the

[21] High-income people with low marginal utilities of income pay taxes that finance income transfers for low-income people with higher marginal utilities of income. If there were no impediments of work–leisure substitution responses (if people contributed according to their ability), social welfare would be maximized when everyone has the same post-tax income and when, therefore, marginal utilities of income are equal for all people (whose equal marginal utilities are identified through the common utility function that people have been assigned).

[22] High-income people at the margin have larger labor-supply elasticities because they can substitute leisure for labor and still have sufficient net-of-tax income; low-income people do not have the same leisure substitution possibilities because they need the income that they earn at the margin and so have smaller labor-supply elasticities.

tax base, the beneficiaries of income transfers have reason to prefer that regressive income taxes be levied on taxpayers whose taxes finance income transfers. Progressive taxes provide incentives for people to choose leisure rather than work when income increases; leisure cannot be transferred to others. Regressive taxes provide incentives to choose work rather than leisure as income increases; the income from work can be taxed and transferred.[23]

> *Revenue available for redistribution is greater with regressive than progressive income taxes.*[24]

Incentives for people to reveal ability through income

The solution to the Mirrlees optimal income tax is that:

> *The tax system should provide incentives for higher ability people to reveal their ability by earning at least as much income as lower ability people.*
>
> *The tax structure therefore should not discourage more able people from working more than less able people.*

A higher ability person can always copy the work behavior of a lower ability person. The higher ability person then earns the same (observable) income as the lower ability person but works fewer (nonobservable) hours or exerts less (nonobservable) effort. To induce higher ability people to exert more effort, the optimal income tax should provide a higher ability person with a higher level of post-tax utility than a person who has less ability.

Zero marginal tax rates at the bottom and top of income distribution

The Mirrlees optimal income-tax structure has zero marginal tax rates at the bottom and top of the income distribution. Regressive marginal tax rates approaching zero for the highest income earners encourage high-income people

[23] To illustrate the case for regressive taxation through the tax base, we consider a dentist who likes to play golf. If the tax structure is progressive, the dentist is taxed at 10 percent for the first hour's income, at 20 percent for the second hour's income, and so on. After eight hours of work, the dentist may be paying taxes that are 80 percent on the last hour's income. At this point or before, the dentist may decide to stop taking patients and to head for the golf course. With a regressive tax, incentives are reversed. The dentist pays 80 percent tax on the first hour's income, and the tax rate falls on income earned in subsequent hours. The dentist might then confront a 10 percent tax rate on income earned in the eighth hour of the day. The regressive tax structure gives the dentist an incentive to keep working longer in the course of the day by encouraging substitution of hours worked for benefit from playing golf. The tax revenue paid by the dentist to the government finances an income transfer to a low-income person. The dentist's utility from playing golf cannot be transferred to another person, but income earned from work can be transferred through taxation. The regressive tax provides greater tax revenue that can be transferred to a low-income person through the greater incentive to keep working and to keep earning taxable income during the course of the day.

[24] There is a disincentive for low-income people to work under regressive taxation. If work incentives were the sole determinants of the structure of the income-tax schedule, the choice would be between the disincentives for low-income people to work at low levels of income under regressive taxation and the disincentives for high-income people to work at high levels of income under progressive taxation.

to keep working and to provide income that expands the tax base. A zero marginal tax rate at the highest income is optimal because the highest income person is thereby not discouraged from working more. If the highest income person is deterred from working because of a positive marginal tax rate, the income-tax structure cannot be efficient because when the highest ability person works more (by free choice), he or she is better off. At the same time, no tax revenue is lost to the government by the decision to work more. If everyone is working, the marginal tax rate is also zero for the lowest ability person in the population. The disincentives to work suggest that the income-tax schedule should begin with zero tax rates. The initial zero marginal rate of income taxation provides incentives to enter the labor force. Such incentives are provided by an earned-income tax credit at low levels of income or wage subsidies that counteract taxes in the tax schedule at low levels of income.

The choice of the utility function

We have not answered the question of whether the optimal income tax is basically progressive or regressive. In the solution to the Mirrlees optimal income-tax problem, much hinges on the choice of the common utility function that is used to describe the labor-supply behavior of the population. The utility function indicates substitution between work and leisure and determines the excess burden of taxation through the elasticity of labor supply. Choice of the utility function therefore influences the extent of departure of the optimal income tax from a choice of taxation and redistribution that results in post-tax equality. Therefore, the answers are in the assumptions. If a utility function is chosen whereby labor supply is quite inelastic, taxes do not much affect efficiency, and the optimal income tax can focus on achieving equality in post-tax income distribution and can be quite progressive. If a utility function is chosen for which people respond to high marginal taxes by significantly reducing work hours or work effort, the optimal income tax is not very progressive and may be regressive.

The conclusions

Mirrlees was inconclusive about the general properties of the optimal income-tax structure. The Mirrlees optimal income-tax problem is one of the most technically complex exercises justifiably undertaken in economic analysis. We shall not replicate his formal analysis (see, however, Mirrlees, 1971). Mirrlees expressed his sentiments after he completed his investigation of the properties of the optimal income tax.

> Being aware that many of the arguments used in favour of low marginal tax rates for the rich are, at best, premised on the odd assumption that any means of raising the national income is good, even if it diverts part of that income from rich to poor, I must confess that I had expected the rigorous analysis of income taxation in the utilitarian manner to provide an argument for high tax rates. It has not done so.[25]

[25] Mirrlees (1971, p. 207).

That is, Mirrlees began with the presumption that high progressive tax rates are socially beneficial and that the social benefit would be confirmed by the properties of an income-tax schedule that maximized a Bentham (utilitarian) social welfare function. His analysis did not confirm his presumption. Mirrlees continued:

> I had also expected to be able to show that there was no great need to strive for low marginal tax rates on low incomes when constructing negative-income-tax proposals. The feeling has been to some extent confirmed. But my expectation that the minimum consumption level would be high has not been confirmed. Instead, virtually everybody is brought into the work force.[26]

That is, high marginal tax rates on low incomes were found consistent with an optimal tax structure. The optimal income-tax schedule also required nearly everyone to be working rather than some part of the population living off only income transfers and not being productively employed.[27] Using computations and simulations, Mirrlees suggested that the optimal income-tax structure is not very progressive and that the highest marginal rate should not exceed 30 to 35 percent.[28]

D. Political and social objectives

We now ask why tax structures are complex, and why cycles of tax reform occur that reduce the complexity of taxes, with the complexity, however, subsequently reappearing. We shall conclude this section with the basic question: Why do governments, in general, choose income tax structures that are progressive?

Complex tax structures and tax reform

Desirable income-tax structures are simple, with few marginal tax rates and with limited progressivity, limited exemptions from payment of taxes, and limited tax deductions.[29] Yet, in practice, tax structures are, on the contrary, often complex, with numerous exemptions and deductions. The exemptions and deductions are often selectively targeted to people in the population. The selectiveness in targeting has been interpreted as suggesting politically determined discrimination

[26] Ibid.

[27] Mirrlees' exposition was based on everyone who wanted to work having a job. He pointed out that involuntary employment was not part of his analysis (ibid.).

[28] When we looked at results of measures of the excess burden of taxation, we found a wide diversity of reported values, which suggested that beliefs or priors can matter through the assumptions that researchers have made. Similarly, in simulations to determine the optimal income tax, parameter choices can reflect beliefs or priors. For an example, see Emmanuel Saez (2001) for a suggestion that top marginal tax rates of an optimal income tax are between 50 and 80 percent.

[29] A *tax exemption* refers to an entity that is exempt from payment of income tax. A *tax deduction* refers to expenses that can be deducted from taxable income.

among different categories of taxpayers.[30] Also, complex tax codes promote rational ignorance on the part of taxpayers and citizens; accountants and tax lawyers who earn their income by providing professional advice on tax matters benefit from the complexity of tax codes.

Changes or tax reforms to simplify complex tax codes and progressive income-tax schedules sometimes take place. The tax code is simplified to remove inefficiencies and undue complexities of deductions and exemptions, and marginal tax rates are reduced. The number of tax brackets is also often reduced. By eliminating inefficiencies, a tax reform might result in Pareto-improving change – leaving aside losses to tax lawyers and accountants.

A criterion for tax reform is that a reform be Dalton-improving. Hugh Dalton (1887–1962) proposed in 1920 that a tax reform be limited to redistributing income from high- to low-income households with no change in the ranking of households in the income distribution. That is, the reform should not result in higher income households being displaced in the income distribution by lower income households. Otherwise, lower income households benefit from the tax reform while new lower income households are created. It then becomes difficult to judge whether the tax reform has increased social welfare.

After a simplifying tax reform has taken place, complexity in the tax laws generally returns. A clean slate on tax exemptions and deductions after a substantive simplifying reform opens new opportunities for political responses that once more result in selective changes in tax laws. Rent seeking occurs and tax deductions and exemptions for different groups of taxpayers are legislated. Tax revenue falls because of the exemptions and deductions. Other taxes increase in the attempt to compensate for the fall in tax revenue. When the inefficiencies and injustice of the complex tax structure again become overwhelmingly evident, another tax reform takes place.

Why are income taxes progressive?

We now return to a question that has arisen a number of times: Why do governments in general choose income taxes that are progressive? We sought a normative justification for progressive taxes through the equal-sacrifice principle. Studies show that it is sometimes possible to work backwards from the observed progressive tax schedule $R(Y)$ to find a utility function $U(Y)$, which – when used to measure loss of utility from payment of taxes – provides a close approximation to equal sacrifice in observed progressive tax schedules.[31] An outcome in which

[30] Walter Hettich and Stanley Winer (1999) proposed that complex tax structures reflect political objectives and suggested a framework of political decision making to explain the different tax treatment of different classes of taxpayers.

[31] H. Peyton Young (1990) undertook the exercise of working back from the observed progressive income-tax schedules of the United States, West Germany, Italy, Japan, and the United Kingdom to determine whether the progressive taxes were consistent with the equal-sacrifice principle. He statistically estimated what the underlying utility functions in each country would have to be in

a progressive tax structure is consistent with equal sacrifice, however, can only be fortuitous. Governments do not design income-tax schedules using the equal-sacrifice principle. The equal-sacrifice principle opens governments to the possibility, in principle, that tax rates will be regressive. Regressive income taxes would, however, be politically unpopular. Given that regressive taxation is consistent with equal sacrifice, political decision makers would not want to use the equal-sacrifice principle as the basis for designing an income tax.

The Laffer-curve comparison shows that governments can obtain the same tax revenue from simple low-rate linear income taxes as from complex, less efficient progressive income-tax schedules. Nonetheless, governments generally prefer progressive income taxes. One reason for the political preference for a complex progressive tax system is the political benefit from the political discretion to choose who benefits from the deductions and exemptions of the tax code. However, the structure of the income tax is a salient issue for voters at large who do not necessarily benefit from the politically assigned deductions and exemptions. Progressive taxation seems "fair" to voters. Moreover, the feeling of fairness of progressive taxes does not depend on how tax revenue is spent.

Progressive taxes and post-tax incomes

When taxes are progressive, the post-tax income distribution is made more equal.[32]

Progressive taxes make post-tax incomes more equal.

order for the tax schedules to imply equal sacrifice. The equal-sacrifice principle would be confirmed to apply to the observed progressive income-tax schedule if (1) the estimated common utility function was consistent with usual properties of utility functions, and (2) the equal-sacrifice income-tax schedule derived from the utility function were consistent with the observed tax schedules that governments had chosen. He found that his estimated utility functions of the different countries had similar values of constant relative risk aversion with $R > 1$, which is consistent with the requirement for equal sacrifice to imply progressive taxation. Consistency was also found between the equal-sacrifice principle and observed marginal tax rates of the brackets of the income-tax schedules – with exceptions. A study by Mitra and Ok (1996) investigated taxation in a number of countries and concluded that only in the U.S. and Turkey did income-tax schedules violate the equal-sacrifice principle with certainty. The study was for the years 1988–91. The U.S. Tax Reform Act of 1986 (for tax rates that became effective in 1988) reduced the degree of progression in the U.S. federal personal income tax.

[32] Consider three people earning pre-tax incomes y_A, y_B, and y_C. The incomes are in three tax brackets such that:

$$y_A = y_1 > y_B = y_1 + y_2 > y_C = y_1 + y_2 + y_3.$$

Marginal tax rates in the three tax brackets are:

$$t_{M1} < t_{M2} < t_{M3}.$$

After-tax incomes in each tax bracket are:

$$y_1(1 - t_{M1}),\ y_2(1 - t_{M2}),\ y_3(1 - t_{M3}).$$

Progressive taxation has diminished the differences between the individuals' post-tax incomes: $y_A(1 - t_{AA})$, $y_B(1 - t_{AB})$, $y_C(1 - t_{AC})$, where t_{Ai} $(i = A,B,C)$ is a taxpayer's average tax rate.

Progressive taxes and pre-tax incomes

Increasing marginal tax rates in progressive taxation, combined with declining marginal income of income, leads high-income people to substitute leisure for work as income increases. Consequently:

> *Progressive taxes make pre-tax incomes more equal.*

Inequality aversion or envy

Because high-income people substitute leisure for work in response to progressive taxes:

> *Progressive taxation is consistent with inequality aversion in incomes or envy, if someone who has more time for leisure is envied less than someone who has more income.*

That is, envy declines when high-income people, who could have higher incomes if they worked, respond to high marginal tax rates by choosing more leisure.

The double effectiveness of progressive taxation

When there is envy (or people are averse to inequality), progressive taxation is doubly effective:

- Progressive taxes reduce *pre-tax income inequality* before the taxes are paid, through the discouragement of work effort of people whose marginal additions to income would be highly taxed if they worked more.
- Progressive taxes reduce *post-tax inequality* after taxes have been paid on earned income.

Origins of envy in human behavior

To find origins for envy, we look as we have done in other instances to a hunter–gatherer society. Norms of behavior in a hunter–gatherer society require sharing, particularly food. A person who has more than others has not fulfilled the obligation of sharing – the inequality could only have resulted from not sharing. Someone who has more than others has not only failed to share: such a person has also taken from nature more than a fair share of nature's bounty. A means of having more than others is also predatory behavior, through the strong taking from the weak. Hunter–gatherer norms therefore associate having more than others with greed and predation.

Social mobility and taxation

A final question concerning social consequences of taxation is: Do high tax rates and high progressivity obstruct social mobility? Wealthy families may have income from endowed wealth. People beginning from humble origins need to accumulate assets to achieve wealth. High tax rates and high progressivity in the income-tax structure favor preservation of the status of the traditional wealthy families by inhibiting wealth creation by people beginning from a low personal asset base.

9.2 Capital and Other Tax Bases

We have been focusing on direct taxes on personal income and indirect taxes. However, various types of other taxes are available to governments. The different possible taxes raise questions about what to tax and how.

A. Taxation of income from capital

The Ramsey rule for efficient taxation justifies taxing income from capital differently than income from labor. With ε_{SK} and ε_{SL} indicating supply elasticities and t_L and t_K indicating the rates of taxation of labor income and income from capital, the Ramsey rule proposes that tax rates be set so that:

$$\frac{t_L}{t_K} = \frac{\varepsilon_{SK}}{\varepsilon_{SL}}. \qquad (9.20)$$

The supply elasticities include opportunities to leave a tax jurisdiction. If capital can readily leave, the elasticity of supply of capital ε_{SK} is high. Conversely, if labor cannot leave, the elasticity of supply of labor ε_{SL} is low. The Ramsey rule therefore implies that the rate of taxation on income from capital should be lower than the rate of taxation on income from labor. If capital in a tax jurisdiction is part of a broader capital market and can simply leave in response to a tax on income from capital, the tax rate on capital indicated by the Ramsey rule is zero.[33]

The home bias in investment

Possibilities for taxing capital depend on the willingness of investors to hold assets outside their tax jurisdiction. Investors often seem reluctant to hold foreign assets, which results in a "home bias" in asset holdings. The home bias may be due to investors' believing that they are better informed about investments in their home markets. Investors may also trust their own government more than foreign governments to protect their ownership rights. The home bias reduces the supply elasticity of capital and, through the Ramsey rule, increases the efficient tax on income from capital relative to income from labor.

Social justice and taxation of capital

A government may believe that social justice requires taxing income from capital at a higher rate than income from labor. The presence of capital markets that

[33] If the broader market, for example, offers a return of 5 percent, any attempt to tax capital to reduce the local return below 5 percent will lead investors to move their capital outside the jurisdiction where they can obtain the 5 percent return.

extend beyond the government's tax jurisdiction, however, limits the scope for taxing income from capital. If capital can leave the jurisdiction to escape the tax, a government has no choice but to set low taxes on income from capital and high taxes on income from labor because, by attempting to tax income from capital too highly, the government ends up with little or no capital in its jurisdiction to tax.

Portfolio investment and real assets

When people choose to save rather than consume, resources can be invested to create capital. The capital can be human capital invested in the skills, ability, and knowledge of a person or can take the form of physical capital. When we refer to movement of capital out of a tax jurisdiction, we mean physical capital as well as human capital. Machinery and equipment move as firms relocate their operations to other tax jurisdictions, and high human-capital people might also move to escape taxes.

People are also described as "investing" when they buy stocks or shares in a company or when they buy government or corporate bonds. Such portfolio investment changes the ownership of assets but does not create new assets. Where people hold their personal investment portfolios affects their tax obligations through the different taxes that different governments levy.

Where people "hold" their asset portfolios is a legal fiction. For example, a portfolio of shares in U.S., European, and Japanese companies can be "held" in a Caribbean island where low taxes (or no taxes) are levied on income from portfolio investments of nonresidents. The government of the Caribbean island gains tax revenue by attracting offices of "off-share" portfolio-management companies and through legal fees.

Locations with low or no taxes on nonresidents' income from portfolio investment are known as *tax havens*. The presence of tax havens limits other governments' abilities to tax income from ownership of capital. When taxes on income from capital increase, no actual capital may leave the tax jurisdiction; however, an asset "portfolio" may leave by transfer of the location of ownership of the asset portfolio to a tax haven.

We distinguish between investment as financial capital and as physical capital. In both cases, capital can be mobile. However, portfolio investment is more mobile than physical investment.

Residence-based taxation

To avoid loss of tax revenue by transfer of assets to foreign locations, governments may define tax liability based on the location of the taxpayer's residence and not on the location of the investment company's office that holds assets in the name of the taxpayer. However, even with residence-based taxation, assets can be held abroad beyond the reach of the taxation authorities if foreign banks maintain a policy of confidentiality regarding identities of account holders.

Taxpayers are then engaging in tax evasion by holding asset portfolios in foreign tax havens.

Time inconsistency

Taxation of income from capital is subject to the problem of time inconsistency. Financial capital is mobile but not physical capital in place after an investment has been made because the capital cannot then readily move elsewhere. The supply elasticity of capital after the investment has been made is zero. The supply elasticity of capital before the investment is made is high because of alternative locations where the investment can be made and also because of the option not to make the investment at all. The supply elasticity of capital before the investment decision has been made is therefore greater than after the investment has been made. A government that wishes to apply the Ramsey rule for efficient taxation could announce a low rate of taxation of income from capital before an investment is made because of the high supply elasticity of capital. However, after the investment has been made, the Ramsey rule calls for a high rate of taxation on income from the investment because of the subsequent low (or zero) supply elasticity of capital. Announcement by a government of a low rate of taxation on income from capital is therefore time-inconsistent. The low tax announced today will not be the tax rate that the government will wish to apply tomorrow. The announcement of a low tax rate before the investment has been made will therefore not be credible to investors; they know that it is in the interest of the government to increase the tax rate after an investment has been made. If the announcement of a low tax rate is not credible, investments will not be made because of the anticipation by investors of high taxes in the future.

There is a saying that "the best tax is an old tax." That is, it is wise for government not to change taxes. Stable taxes allow investment decisions to be made without the uncertainty in having to predict future government tax policy. Investment, by nature, is subject to uncertainty. Uncertainty about taxes increases the uncertainty that firms face when deciding whether to invest. A reputation for stable taxes is a way of establishing and confirming a commitment not to take advantage through high taxation of capital that becomes immobile after an investment has been made.

Similar considerations affect taxation of natural resources. After an exploration company has discovered an oil deposit, the income earned from the oil is a rent because there is no way to use the asset other than to extract oil. The Ramsey rule calls for appropriative taxes on rents because rents are returns from investments for which supply elasticities are zero. There is again a time-inconsistency problem. The elasticity of supply of capital for oil exploration is high, which – by the Ramsey rule – calls for low tax rates on future income from successful exploration. However, after oil is found, the Ramsey rule calls for high taxes.

B. Corporate or company taxation

The corporate or company tax is a tax on the profits of firms. After wages and salaries of employees and other expenses and interest have been paid, the residual, or profit, is a return to the owners of equity or shares in the company.

The corporate tax allows governments to discriminate in their tax treatment of profits (and losses) of corporations and personal incomes. Tax structures, as well as tax rates, generally differ between individuals and corporations. Whereas personal income taxes tend to be progressive, corporate taxes tend to have flat rates.

Income earned by a corporation belongs, in principle, to the corporation's individual shareholders. If adjustments are not made for the taxes paid by individuals through personal taxation, the corporate income tax results in individuals' incomes from ownership of shares in corporations being taxed twice. An individual's income from ownership of a share in a corporation is taxed through the corporate income tax. Then, when the income is distributed as a dividend to shareholders, the same income from capital ownership is taxed again at the rate of personal income taxation applicable when the individual receives the dividends.[34]

Because the profits earned by corporations ultimately belong to individuals, it should be sufficient to have only a personal income tax. There should be no need, therefore, for a separate corporate income tax. Or, if there is to be a corporate profits tax, individuals should receive tax credits for taxes paid on corporate profits.[35]

The corporation as an independent legal entity

The corporation is an independent legal entity that retains its identity when ownership changes (through the buying and selling of shares) and when management changes. Also, under the principle of limited liability, owners of the capital of the corporation are liable for losses only up to the level of their investments (or, in some cases, also not yet contributed investments). That is, limited liability ensures that the bankruptcy of a firm does not bring with it the bankruptcy of shareholders, who are limited in their personal obligations to cover losses by the corporation.

The corporation, therefore, facilitates individual participation in risky investments by permitting people to avoid losing their other personal assets if the corporation incurs high losses or becomes bankrupt. The corporation or firm, however, can be a separate legal entity without necessarily having a separate tax

[34] Identifying the individuals who ultimately pay a corporate income tax necessitates tracing the effects of the tax through the entire economy (or, in a global world economy, through the entire world). Here, we are identifying tax liability with ownership of stock in the corporation.

[35] Personal tax rates can differ for income earned from labor and capital according to the source of the income.

liability. The tax liability of the corporation can be computed and distributed among the individuals who own the firm. In the event of losses or bankruptcy, the liability of taxpayers to participate in the losses remains limited to the personal investment made in the firm.[36]

Selective policies

Perhaps the corporate tax is justified as a means for facilitating government policies that encourage or discourage the economic activity undertaken by a firm. We saw, for example, when considering externalities in chapter 4, that corrective taxes or subsidies on production activities might be required to achieve efficiency. However, we did not identify the corporate profits tax as having a role in achieving efficiency.[37]

The corporate profits tax and risk

Income from wages and salaries is, in general, risk-free because individuals receive predetermined wages and salaries (although they may receive bonuses). Risk generally falls on the owners of the capital. The corporate profits tax affects investment behavior in the face of risk.

If there are losses, the losses can be offset against tax liabilities from future profits. Even if future profits are never made and the capital provided by investors is all lost, the accumulated losses have value as tax offsets for profitable firms. A profitable firm can generally buy the firm that has accumulated losses and use the losses to reduce its own tax liabilities. Risk is therefore shared with the government through a firm's use of losses to reduce tax liability.

The provisions of the corporate profits tax permit special accommodations to risk to be made. For example, oil and natural-gas exploration companies can be given special allowances in writing off exploration costs. Research and development expenses reduce taxes for pharmaceutical and other knowledge-based industries. Depreciation allowances that reduce taxes can also be selectively determined to reflect risks of investment in plants and machinery in different industries. The special industry accommodations of the tax system to risk, however, do not require a separate corporate profits tax. After the tax concessions and allowances have been taken into account, profits can be distributed to shareholders and personal tax obligations can be determined according to the personal incomes of the individual owners of the firm.

[36] We are using the terms *corporation*, *company*, and *firm* interchangeably.

[37] For example, the profits of tobacco companies could be taxed to discourage the production and sale of cigarettes. Returns to investments in cigarette production and sales could be taxed, but the cigarette-externality problem is solved by imposing taxes on consumption or production in the market for cigarettes. Policies in the market for cigarettes solve externality problems without the need to impose taxes on the supply of investment capital to the cigarette industry.

Capital gains

A means of avoiding double taxation of corporate profits is to provide individual tax credits for taxes that corporations have paid. In the absence of such personal tax credits for corporate profit payments, there are incentives to not distribute corporate profits as dividends but rather to keep the profits within the company for further investment in order to avoid personal taxes. The profits not distributed to shareholders are added to the capital value of the firm and are available as a means of financing investment that is tax-free from the perspective of the individual shareholder. If the profits passed through the hands of individual shareholders before being reinvested, the government would take a further part of the profits through the personal income tax paid by individuals.

Therefore, by retaining rather than paying out profits to shareholders, the corporation provides individual shareholders with the benefit of a capital gain because the value of shareholdings in the firm increases. A capital-gains tax, however, imposes tax obligations when an individual sells the assets or shares of the firm. The capital-gains tax is often applied at a flat rate that is lower than the highest marginal personal income-tax rate. Individual taxpayers with high incomes then benefit when corporate profits are converted to increased share values, although they do not benefit as much as they might if there were no capital-gains tax.[38] There is no such gain if personal liability to pay a capital-gains tax is based on the personal marginal income-tax rate.

Why are dividends ever paid?

If there is no individual tax credit for the taxes paid through the corporate profits tax, and there is a tax advantage to shareholders from conversion of corporate profits to capital gains, why are corporate profits ever distributed as dividends? The reason for dividend payments appears to be related to information and signaling to investors.

A dividend demonstrates the ability of management to provide a cash payout from the firm's activities. Not paying dividends and instead retaining profits is beneficial for management of a firm because capital financing is made available internally without the need to persuade investors to contribute new capital. Paying dividends can oblige the corporation to raise new capital for its investment activities. The willingness of new investors to provide new capital to the firm provides investors with information about the confidence of the market in the firm's future prospects. Managers then can signal or provide information about the confidence that the capital market has in their abilities. The cost of providing this

[38] Capital-gains taxes can have different characteristics. Tax liability may depend on how long assets have been held. There can be (or should be) provision for portfolio realignment (that is, for sales of assets for the purpose of changing the asset composition of an investment portfolio). There should be an allowance made in taxation for increases in value due to inflation.

information is the more costly means of raising revenue through external market financing.

Payment of dividends also sets a lower bound to share prices. If the share price falls and the dividend is kept constant, the return from purchasing and holding the stock increases. When the yield reaches the approximate level of the market rate of interest, investors will purchase the stock for the return provided by the dividend payout. Therefore, the dividend payout (if sustainable) acts as insurance for the stock price.

External financing

The corporate-profits tax imparts a bias toward bond financing (that is, borrowing) for new external financing rather than issuing new equity because the interest that the firm pays to bondholders is a tax-deductible expense. For example, a firm might issue bonds for $1 million and pay annual interest of 7 percent. The $70,000 interest payment on the bonds is an expense deducted from the firm's profits. The firm could increase its capital by selling $1 million of new capital equity to shareholders. A $70,000 return received by the firm on this capital investment is taxable income. By using bond financing rather than equity financing as much as possible, the firm minimizes corporate taxes.

However, bond financing exposes the firm to increased risk. The $70,000 interest on bonds is due every year, even when the cash flow to finance the bond payment is not available. In the choice between bond and equity financing, there is a trade-off between tax advantages of bond financing and the risk resulting from the need to pay the interest on the bonds independently of corporate earnings.[39]

Why is there a corporate-profits tax?

We are still left looking for a justification for a separate corporate-profits tax. We have identified no efficiency reason for a corporate-profits tax, nor have we identified a social-justice reason for the tax. Considerations regarding tax deductions and exemptions, effects of risk, withholding of profits within the firm, and incentives regarding bond and equity financing also do not suggest a justification for a corporate-profits tax.

We conclude that with a corporate-profits tax in existence, individual taxpayers who are shareholders in a firm should receive a tax credit for the personal taxes that have been paid on their behalf through the corporate-profits tax. When individual shareholders in the company are not provided with such tax credits, the corporate-profits tax taxes the same income twice. There is then a simple revenue

[39] Without taxes, and under some further conditions, it can be shown that shareholders should be indifferent regarding the choice between equity and bond financing. This result is known as the *Modigliani–Miller theorem* (1958). Franco Modigliani received the Nobel Prize in economics in 1985.

motive for the corporate-profits tax: the tax allows a government to tax income earned by corporations twice.

C. An expenditure tax

An expenditure tax is an alternative to a direct tax on personal income. A personal expenditure tax is not a sales tax that is levied on separate purchases of goods or services. The personal expenditure tax is similar to a personal income tax. Individuals report the value of their total spending to the government and pay taxes on an annual basis. The tax structure can be progressive, just as with a personal income tax.[40]

To comply with a personal expenditure tax, a taxpayer reports (1) personal wealth at the beginning of the year, (2) personal wealth at the end of the year, and (3) personal income during the year. Personal income consists of income from all sources, including returns from investment of capital, income from ownership of stock or shares in companies, capital gains, and income from ownership of property.

A taxpayer, for example, might report personal wealth of $100,000 at the beginning of the year and $120,000 at the end of the year, with personal income of $50,000 during the year. The taxpayer therefore spent $30,000 during the year and is taxed on this $30,000. No taxes are paid on the $20,000 that was added to savings.

As another example, a person who has no income from a wage or salary may live off a family inheritance and reports having $500,000 at the beginning of the year, $450,000 at the end of the year, and income from interest during the year of $30,000. Personal expenditure during the year is therefore $80,000, which is the tax base on which the expenditure tax is levied. If income were taxed, the first person with income of $50,000 would pay more tax than the second person, who would pay tax on income of $30,000.

The expenditure tax determines tax liability based on money spent. The sources of a person's income are of no importance for the expenditure tax.

The money spent may have been earned as income as in the case of person 1 or may be the return from an investment as in the case of person 2; alternatively, the money spent may have been provided as a gift or the source of the money spent may be capital gains or corporate dividends. The personal expenditure tax thus eliminates separate taxes for different sources of income.

Tax rates

For the same tax revenue to be provided at any point in time, tax rates need to be higher for an expenditure tax than an income tax. The tax base for an income tax is broader, by including savings. A broader tax base, of course, allows lower

[40] An expenditure tax was proposed in 1955 by Nicholas Kaldor (1908–86) of Cambridge University.

rates of taxation for the same tax revenue. The social objective is not to choose the broadest tax base but rather to achieve social justice and efficiency.

Social justice

Is an expenditure tax socially just compared to an income tax? The case for social justice of the expenditure tax is that people are taxed according to their consumption and not according to the value of their contribution to production. Frugal people are taxed less than people who are extravagant in their spending.

Taxation of personal spending rather than personal income is consistent with taxing the source of personal utility, which is consumption.

Efficiency

An expenditure tax does not tax personal savings, whereas income is taxed whether spent or saved. Therefore:

Expenditure and income taxes have different substitution responses.

The substitution response to an income tax affects the work–leisure decision: the excess burden of the income tax is through substitution from productive income-earning effort and time. The substitution response to the income tax contracts the present tax base because of the substitution of leisure for time spent earning income.

The substitution response to an increase in the expenditure tax is to reduce personal spending. A person who decides to spend less may also decide to increase leisure and to earn less, which results in the same substitution response as to the income tax. However, a substitution response to an increase in an expenditure tax is also to increase savings and investment. The substitution response to the expenditure tax contracts the present tax base because of reduced personal spending; however, the future tax base expands through the future taxable personal spending that will take place out of the increased future income due to the increased saving and investment. The higher future taxes from an expenditure tax are the consequence of the higher economic growth with an expenditure tax.

The difference between the income tax and the expenditure tax is also in the timing of taxation. With the income tax, taxation occurs when income is earned; with the expenditure tax, taxation takes place when income is spent. A lifetime budget constraint limits the present value of lifetime personal spending to the present value of lifetime personal income (with amendments for bequests received and bequests given). Lifetime income is greater with the expenditure tax because the income tax encourages substitution from income-earning activity to leisure, whereas the expenditure tax encourages substitution from spending to investment.

> *Compared to an income tax at the same rate, an expenditure tax increases economic growth and provides greater lifetime tax revenue from taxpayers.*

Problems with an expenditure tax

There are a number of problems with an expenditure tax.

Concentrated spending

Spending is often more concentrated in time than income. The personal largest expenditure that most people make is buying a house. A progressive tax structure for the expenditure tax would make buying a house unattractive because of the high tax liability incurred in the year that the house is bought.[41] Similar considerations apply to cars and other consumer durables for which expenditure is at a point in time and the benefits are over time. An expenditure tax needs to accommodate the timing of spending by allowing taxes to be spread over time to match the benefits over time.

Tax evasion

Tax evasion can take place with an expenditure tax, as with an income tax. High-expenditure people (who would, in general, also be high-income people) could give tax-free gifts to low-expenditure people and send them shopping on their behalf. Gifts would therefore need to be taxable. If gifts within the family are to be tax-free, the "family" would have to be defined: we can imagine disagreement on who is or is not part of the same family or the same household.

Shared spending

Expenditures often provide shared benefits (for example, a number of people might use the same refrigerator). A personal expenditure tax would need to make allowance for shared spending.

Impediments to change

A problem arises in the change from an income tax to an expenditure tax. If an expenditure tax were to replace an income tax, people who have paid taxes all their working life according to the income they earned would be asked to pay taxes in later years in life according to what they spend. Change to an expenditure

[41] The incentive would be to rent to spread housing expenditures over time. A person or firm that bought the house for rental, however, would face the same problem of large expenditures in a single year. A mortgage allows the cost of buying a house to be spread over time.

tax from an income tax would therefore be unjust for older people who have paid income taxes over the years and are approaching the stage of their life in which they will spend but not earn income. Compensation could be provided through exemptions to the expenditure tax based on age. Care would then have to be taken to avoid transfers of money to people exempt from the expenditure tax, who could spend on behalf of nonexempt people.

Use of an expenditure tax

No government has replaced an income tax with an expenditure tax. The impediment could be the transition from the income tax to an expenditure tax, but governments initiating tax systems in new jurisdictions have also not chosen expenditure taxes. We infer that the expenditure tax is feared because of perceived uncertainty about the consequences. Or, the expenditure tax would be politically unpopular – the expenditure tax is, in particular, more personally intrusive than an income tax because people are obliged to divulge information to governments about all personal assets and wealth. With an income tax, the government only asks for information about the income that people have earned.

D. Other taxes

We conclude our consideration of what to tax – or what can be taxed – with some other taxes.

Taxes on wealth

Wealth is past earned income that has been saved or invested. A wealth tax is therefore a retroactive tax on income. Introducing a wealth tax is thus inconsistent with the principle of the rule of law that laws not be retroactive. Nonetheless, governments might introduce wealth taxes. If a wealth tax comes as a surprise and if taxpayers could believe that wealth will never be taxed again, a tax on personal wealth would have no excess burden because there would be no associated substitution effect.

A recurring wealth tax is not a surprise. If a wealth tax were imposed once and a promise were made never to tax wealth again, the promise may not be believed because the government's declared policy of never taxing wealth is not time-consistent. We recall that a time-inconsistent policy is a policy that will be optimal for the government to implement in the future even if the government declares today that it will not implement the policy. That is, in the future, the government can obtain tax revenue from again taxing wealth, even though the government declared that it will never tax wealth again. Knowing that the government's declaration is time-inconsistent, people will base their decisions on the presumption that taxation of wealth will again take place. People therefore have incentives to consume to avoid accumulating wealth. There are also incentives to hide wealth.

Wealth can be inherited. When wealth is taxed at death, there is similarly a substitution effect through incentives to consume rather than accumulate wealth. Taxes at death are usually accompanied by gift taxes, to prevent tax avoidance by giving gifts while still alive.

An estate or inheritance tax is a tax on intergenerational altruism: parents may wish to bequeath wealth to children but the substitution effect of an estate or inheritance tax leads parents to increase consumption during their lifetime. It is sometimes said that estate and inheritance taxes are taxes on ignorance – of the ways that wealth and estates can be protected from wealth and estate taxes.[42]

Lotteries

Lotteries are a means for governments to obtain revenue. We observed in chapter 3 how a lottery can in principle finance public goods through voluntary payments. Revenue might be collected by a government agency that directly manages a lottery or might be provided by selling the right to operate legal lotteries to private firms. A lottery is an unfair gamble because, through the taxation component, the government takes a share of the lottery revenue. The implicit tax in the lottery reduces the value of prizes below the value of the revenue from the sale of lottery tickets. The unfair gamble can only be sustained when the lottery is a monopoly. If there were competition, competitors would announce increased percentage payouts from lotteries until, through competition, the value of the payout in prizes would approach the value of the net revenue from sale of lottery tickets.

Adam Smith made the following observations about lotteries (in the *Wealth of Nations*, 1776, chapter 10):

> In state lotteries, the tickets are not really worth the price. There is not a more certain proposition in mathematics than the more tickets you adventure upon, the more likely you are to be a loser. Adventure on all the tickets in the lottery and you lose for certain; and the greater the number of your tickets, the nearer you approach this certainty.

Adam Smith also noted that the sole source of demand for lottery tickets is the "vain hope of gaining some of the great prizes." Low-income people tend to spend more on lottery tickets; consequently, taxation through a lottery tends to be regressive.

Taxation through inflation and financial repression

Governments have resorted to satisfying revenue needs by printing money. Financial repression has also been used to provide governments with revenue. In both cases, a government obtains revenue by being a monopoly.

[42] Depending on tax laws, estate and inheritance taxes can be avoided through trusts or by incorporation of family companies that have no finite life.

Government has a monopoly on printing the domestic currency. Printing money without accompanying increases in availability of goods or assets increases nominal prices. The government pays the increased nominal prices when spending the money that it is printing. The government gains, however, from the reduced real value of nominal assets in the economy. For example, if there has been overnight inflation of 20 percent, a $100 bill placed under a pillow before going to sleep is worth only $80 in the morning. The $100 bill now buys only $80 worth of goods or assets, and a tax of 20 percent has therefore been imposed overnight. This is the inflation tax.

For inflation to be a tax, people must be surprised by the inflation. Otherwise, domestic financial markets will account for inflation by including the expected rate of inflation in the nominal interest rate. For example, suppose that the rate of interest is 3 percent per year when there is no inflation. That is, the real (inflation-free) rate of interest is 3 percent. Then, suppose that inflation of 4 percent per year is anticipated. The nominal rate of interest now increases to 7 percent because people who lend money will want the 3 percent real return plus an additional 4 percent compensation for the expected inflation.[43]

Unanticipated inflation also reduces the real value of government debt, thereby reducing the real value of the payments that a government makes to redeem its bonds. When unanticipated inflation reduces the future value of government bonds, the beneficiaries are future taxpayers for whom taxes for redeeming the bonds are reduced. Therefore, unanticipated inflation causes an intergenerational transfer of income from present holders of government bonds to future taxpayers.

Financial repression provides government revenue by restricting the rights of people to invest abroad. For example, the interest rate available to investors in the global capital market might be 5 percent, but a government may not allow its citizens to invest abroad and may set a domestic interest rate of 2 percent. By borrowing from its citizens at 2 percent, the government then gains compared to the 5 percent interest that the government would be obliged to pay for its borrowing if people had access to the global capital market.[44] Revenue from repression of domestic financial markets requires a government to legislate for itself a monopoly position in domestic financial markets and to make investment by the population outside the country illegal.

Inflation and financial repression as means of providing government revenue have been primarily used by governments in poorer countries.

[43] If inflation turns out to be higher than the anticipated 4 percent, lenders will have lost. Lenders gain if inflation is lower than the anticipated 4 percent.

[44] The government could also gain by borrowing from its citizens at 2 percent and lending the same funds at 5 percent in the global capital market. Another means of gain for a government through financial repression is to require that the country's financial institutions hold some part of their assets in its low-yielding bonds.

Should indirect taxes accompany the optimal income tax?

If a government has successfully designed an optimal income tax that maximizes social welfare, the question arises:

When an optimal income tax is in place, are indirect taxes required at all?

Our reasoning might be that there is no need for indirect taxes if the optimal balance between efficiency and social justice has been achieved through direct taxation of personal income. Anthony Atkinson and Joseph Stiglitz[45] confirmed that indirect taxes are not required, provided that some conditions were satisfied. The conditions are that all taxpayers have the same utility function and differ only in abilities to earn income (these are the conditions that Mirrlees imposed when setting out the optimal income-tax problem). Also, the common preferences of the population need to be separable between labor supply and utility from consumption of goods.[46]

When consumption preferences differ, indirect taxes affect people in different ways.[47] Indirect taxes can then be used to target people who have particular preferences. For example, indirect taxes on tobacco products target smokers, in addition to the personal income taxes that smokers pay. If a government has identified cigarette smokers as a group that it wishes to tax, this group of people can be taxed through a tax on tobacco because only these people spend on tobacco products. Thus, the income tax taxes incomes but indirect taxes also allow goods to be selectively taxed.

Let us now consider two people who have the same utility function (the same preferences) and different abilities. Although they have the same preferences, the

[45] Stiglitz received the Nobel Prize in economics in 2001.

[46] Identical separable utility and different income-earning abilities allow the Bentham social welfare function for a population of n persons to be expressed as:

$$W = \sum_{i=1}^{n} v(\ell^i) + \sum_{i=1}^{n} u(c_1^i, c_2^i, \ldots, c_m^i),$$

where ℓ^i is leisure and c^i is consumption of individual i. The income of individual i after the leisure/labor-supply decision is $y^i = w^i \gamma^i L^i$, where w is a market wage, L^i is labor supply, and γ^i is the individual's ability. The larger γ^i is, the more income a person earns from any given number of hours worked. The optimal income tax maximizes the sum of utilities based on the different leisure choices, which have determined different incomes from different individual labor-supply decisions and different personal abilities. The second part of social welfare is the sum of utilities from consumption of goods. With the optimal income tax already trading-off efficiency and social justice, indirect taxes would impose excess burdens of taxation with no gain from social justice. Much depends on the structure of preferences. Common homothetic consumption preferences ensure that expenditure shares are the same for all people independent of their incomes and that indirect taxes therefore symmetrically affect all people in terms of relative excess burdens.

[47] James Mirrlees (1976) considered the broader class of consumption preferences consistent with a personal income tax that required no additional indirect taxes.

different incomes of the low- and high-ability people can lead them to consume different goods. As a limiting case, the high-ability person might only consume good A (dining in gourmet restaurants), whereas the low-ability person might only consume good B (groceries used for cooking at home). An indirect tax on good A imposes a utility loss on the high-ability person through taxes paid and the excess burden of taxation.

Can we, however, necessarily associate income levels with particular spending patterns? Some people whose pre-tax incomes are not very high may be prepared to live without owning a car or without going to football games in order to afford gourmet meals because good food is important for the quality of their life. Similarly, people with low-income earning ability may wish to attend operas rather than go to the movies, although tickets to the opera generally cost many times more than movie tickets. High indirect taxes on gourmet meals and opera tickets change the spending pattern of lower income people, who – because of indirect taxes – may not be able to afford gourmet meals or going to the opera. An excess burden of taxation is imposed on low-income lovers of gourmet meals and the opera because of the substitution effect on their spending.

A case for indirect taxes to accompany optimal income taxes stereotypes people. In a population with a broad range of spending preferences, selective indirect taxes become unwarranted intrusions into personal choices.

Tax evasion and choice of direct and indirect taxes

A case for indirect taxes has been based on tax evasion. Direct taxes on income can be more readily evaded than indirect taxes. If evasion of income taxes increases with the marginal tax rates of a progressive income, tax evasion is reduced when at the margin indirect taxation substitutes for direct taxation.[48]

Choice of taxes and a leviathan government

A leviathan government maximizing tax revenue from taxation will wish to use both direct and indirect taxes and, indeed, any tax that increases revenue. When we see a government levying a personal income tax accompanied by a plethora of different indirect and other taxes, we may well be observing a leviathan government.[49]

[48] This case for a combination of direct and indirect taxes was made by Antonio de Viti de Marco (1936, reprinted 1959).

[49] A government observed to be selecting different rates of indirect taxation may also be setting taxes with the objective of providing political favors. Uniform taxes limit political discretion in choice of indirect taxes. Agnar Sandmo (1974) showed how under special conditions on individual preferences, uniform taxes could be efficient in satisfying the Ramsey rule.

9.3 Fiscal Federalism

A theme that has been reoccurring as we have studied responsibilities of government is personal benefit from choice among governments. When there have been multiple governments, we have encountered fiscal federalism.

Fiscal federalism describes a structure of multiple governments with designated taxation and spending responsibilities.

Choice among governments takes place through choice of location. There are no legal impediments to migration within a fiscal federal system of government. People can move freely between government jurisdictions – subject to having sufficient income or wealth to afford housing prices or rental costs.

There is, in general, more limited choice through location of the central or federal government. Such choice requires international migration, which is subject to the restrictions of governments' immigration policies. However, because of the choice available from among lower level governments, no government in a fiscal federal system other than the federal government has a legal monopoly on public finance and public policy. Therefore:

In a fiscal federal system, the personal freedom of markets is replicated through locational choice.

There are thus two ways to change governments in a fiscal federal system. One way is through elections. The other way is by leaving the jurisdiction of one government for the jurisdiction of another government. Such choice has been described in terms of "exit, voice, and loyalty." Voting is "voice" – we have noted the impediments to efficiency and social justice that arise when voting is used to determine collective decisions about public policy, but voting decisions can also be about competence of people in government and can be in response to evidence of leviathan self-serving government. "Exit" is choosing another government. "Loyalty" determines the effort exerted or patience in attempting to use voice before resorting to exit.[50]

We shall proceed by first bringing together our previous conclusions about how multiple governments affect achievement of the social objectives of efficiency and social justice. Then, tax competition will be described, in which governments strategically choose tax rates on capital that is mobile in being moveable between tax jurisdictions. We shall look at political behavior and then consider voting in fiscal federal systems.

[50] The framework for choice was described by Albert Hirschman in his book *Exit, Voice, and Loyalty*, published in 1970.

A. Efficiency, social justice, and fiscal federalism

Our first question about fiscal federalism is normative:

> *Is decentralized government within a fiscal federal system beneficial in facilitating achievement of the social objectives of efficiency and social justice?*

Public goods

To answer this question in the context of public goods, we need only review our past conclusions. We saw that the multiple governments of a fiscal federal system allow choice to pay for and benefit from public goods through the Tiebout locational-choice mechanism. Locational choice does not replicate the ideal efficient Lindahl consensus solution for voluntary payments for pure public goods, which because of the natural monopoly attribute of pure public goods would be efficiently supplied in a single jurisdiction. Tiebout locational sorting according to preferences is nonetheless a second-best solution when the Lindahl first-best voluntary-payments outcome is unattainable: the asymmetric-information problem of public goods is resolved because people reveal willingness to pay for public goods through location. Locational choice is efficiently first-best when people want different types of public goods and when local public goods provide local benefits; then people do not pay for types of public goods that they do not want, and local replicated supply is efficient because benefit from local public goods declines with distance from the facilities providing the public goods. Locational choice converts taxes into voluntary payments based on the benefit principle, because choosing taxes to pay in a jurisdiction is similar to choosing prices to pay in markets. We observed that taxes on property and on income and the use of indirect taxes to finance public goods differ from the per-person (or per-family) prices that would replicate the price in a market. Nonetheless, competition among governments offers choice, and the need to pay in order to benefit solves the public-good free-rider problem. There are informational advantages to supply of public goods by decentralized governments, which can be expected to know more about people's preferences for public goods (because people have located according to preferences) than centralized government.

> *Fiscal federalism by offering choice among governments solves (or ameliorates) the public-good problems of asymmetric information and free riding.*

An ideal fiscal federal structure for public goods

An ideal fiscal federal structure for public goods includes both hierarchical levels of government and horizontally replicated government. The vertical structure of government allows public goods to be provided to cost-efficient sharing groups of different sizes by central, state, and local governments. The central or highest level of government has the responsibility for pure public goods such as a national road system, national security, and diplomatic representation. Downward in the hierarchy of governments, smaller tax jurisdictions provide public goods for which desired numbers of beneficiaries are smaller. At the base of the pyramid of governments, local jurisdictions provide local public goods that benefit local communities. At each level of the pyramid, a horizontal structure of government ideally provides sufficient locational choice to approximate supply in a competitive market. Ideally, choice is provided among the different bundles of public goods that people might want.

Community values as public goods

We have observed that community values are public goods. Locational choice thereby also allows people to choose the community values with which they feel comfortable. Public goods can also involve conflict because of different personal preferences – as we noted, a public good that provides benefit for someone (a Beethoven symphony) can be something that someone else is prepared to pay to avoid. Differences in the community values that people want are likewise sources of potential conflict. Locational choice can therefore resolve disagreements on whether, for example, commercial sex should be openly available on street corners (because parents may not wish to have to explain to young children the nature of the services that are being commercially offered and why such services should not be given priority as a prospective career opportunity).

Locational choice allows community choice of norms.[51]

Externalities

In a fiscal-federal structure, externalities among communities can be internalized by higher levels of government. For example, if one community has strict gun-control laws and a neighboring community does not, criminals can buy their guns in one community and commit their crimes in the community where with high likelihood their victims will not be armed. Or, if a community has lax environmental standards and a neighboring community has strict standards, the community with strict environmental laws can be harmed environmentally by effluent and deterioration in air quality that originates in the neighboring community. Externalities that cross jurisdictional boundaries are therefore the basis for a case for higher-level government jurisdictions that can use public policy to internalize and resolve the externality problems. We saw that problems of the global environment can remain unresolved because of reciprocal externalities of the

[51] However, questions of choice between moral relativism and absolute ethical principles remain. See chapter 5. Moral relativists accept as equally meritorious all cultures and value systems because they judge morality relative to the norms of each particular group. People who define morality in terms of absolute ethical principles will object, for example, to forced marriages of pubescent girls to older men and to forced marriage in general. Our culture may be the object of criticism by others who object to democratic principles and to the freedom that our society gives to women. A clash of cultures – see Samuel Huntington (1996) – then persists even if locational sorting according to cultural values has taken place.

tragedy-of-the-commons type that involve people in different national jurisdictions. A case for global government is based on internalization of global externalities. However, global government can be expected to be the source of profound political and bureaucratic principal–agent problems. We shall return in this chapter to globally centralized government.[52]

> *Externalities among jurisdictions underlie a case for higher-level government.*

Natural monopoly for private goods

Fiscal federalism facilitates efficient supply when there is natural monopoly for a private good. We can consider the following illustrative example. Three communities – 1, 2, and 3 – can share fixed costs of a project that provides private benefits to the communities' populations. For example, each community has a given demand for water supply (we shall not consider the responsiveness of demand to price). The cost of supply for a community depends on whether it chooses to make the infrastructure investment itself or joins with another community, or other communities, in sharing the cost. If a community chooses to provide its own infrastructure, the cost for each of the three single communities is:

$$C(1) = C(2) = C(3) = 150.$$

For coalitions of two communities, the cost is:

$$C(1, 2) = C(2, 3) = C(3, 1) = 180.$$

If all three communities join to share the costs, the total cost is:

$$C(1, 2, 3) = 300.$$

Therefore:

- The cost of supply for a community supplying alone is 150.
- The cost of supply for a community in a coalition of two is 90.
- The cost of supply for a community when all three communities combine is 100.

Costs for any individual community are thus minimized by a coalition of two communities.

Two communities therefore have an incentive to form a coalition and to provide water supply to their residents at a cost per community of 90. Communities

[52] Because externalities usually affect many people simultaneously, externalities are also public goods that either provide positive collective benefit or result in negative collective harm. The case for fiscal federalism to resolve problems of externalities is therefore a case of public goods that transcend jurisdictional boundaries.

1 and 2 might form a coalition. The total cost of providing water for all three communities is then:

$$C(1,2) + C(3) = 180 + 150 = 330 > 300 = C(1,2,3).$$

That is, when two communities form a coalition, the combined or total cost of 330 for all three communities is greater than the combined or total cost of 300 for the all-inclusive supply coalition of the three communities. Because the supply coalition of all three communities minimizes total costs of supply, supply of water is a natural monopoly. The natural monopoly, however, is not sustainable by voluntary decisions of the individual communities because a coalition of two communities can achieve a lower cost per community than when all communities join to provide the service together.[53]

The excluded community 3 can approach the coalition of communities 1 and 2 and offer to pay 120 for supply through all-inclusive coalition. By paying 120 instead of the 150 that it is obliged to pay as a lone supplier, the excluded community saves 30, whereas the communities in the coalition of two are no worse off.

If the previously excluded community pays 120 in the all-inclusive coalition, this community secures all the gains from the Pareto-improving change. The other two communities, however, might negotiate a share of the gains. As a limiting case, they could ask the excluded community to pay 149, which gives the excluded community a gain of 1 from an all-inclusive coalition and leaves the two communities in the original coalition with 29 to share. As previously discussed, in such situations, there is a bargaining problem. When there is a possibility of Pareto-improving change, we expect the change to be implemented voluntarily as the outcome of bargaining.

Again, there are issues of coalition stability. A coalition of two communities is unstable because the excluded third community can offer a payment that will make worthwhile defection of one of the coalition members to form a new two-community coalition.[54] The new two-community coalition formed after the breakup of the previous coalition is also unstable.

The problems of bargaining over sharing of benefits among the three jurisdictions and instability of two-jurisdiction coalitions are avoided when a higher level of government takes responsibility for supply to all three communities. The

[53] We previously defined natural monopoly as occurring when average cost is continually declining in output provided to users. Average cost in the preceding three-community example does not continually decline with the number of users. Average cost is minimized by two users. Continuous declining average cost indicates the presence of conditions of natural monopoly. However, all cases of natural monopoly need not involve continuously declining average cost.

[54] For example, the excluded community can offer to reduce the cost of one of the included communities to below 90, in return for joining it in a new coalition. If the excluded community offers to pay 100 of the two-community shared cost of 180, it is better off than being excluded and paying 150. The new coalition partner that it has enticed pays 80 in the new two-community coalition and gains 10.

higher level of government minimizes the total cost of supply by enforcing a stable cost-minimizing, all-inclusive coalition.

> *Natural monopoly for goods that provide private benefit is the basis for a case for higher-level government.*

Conclusion: Fiscal federalism and efficiency

Fiscal federalism enhances efficiency.

- A locational market is provided for choice of public goods. Decentralized government allows choice among governments; hierarchies of government provide public goods for different sized populations.
- Externalities among lower level decentralized governments are internalized by centralized government.
- Fiscal federalism is efficient because of private-good natural monopoly.

The benefit principle and locational choice

Locational choice is based on the benefit principle. The total taxes that individuals and families pay to governments in a fiscal federal system should correspond precisely to the total costs of the types of public goods that are provided. Taxes, therefore, should be paid to the central or federal government to finance the pure public goods that central government provides, such as national defense and the rule of law, perhaps social security and pensions (because of demographic free riding by people who do not have children and so do not contribute to the intergenerational tax base), and international representation. Taxes paid to state governments should finance the public goods provided at the state level, such as highway systems, bridges, rule of law and police, and perhaps higher education and health care. At the local level, taxes should finance schools, roads, parks, playgrounds, collection of litter and trash, and personal protection from unsafe, unleashed dogs. Notwithstanding the benefit principle that underlies locational choice, fiscal federal systems in general redistribute income among jurisdictions.

Fiscal federalism and insurance through regional income-pooling

Fiscal federalism provides insurance through income-pooling in the face of region-specific uncertainty. Regions of a country may differ in production specialization and therefore have different incomes and different government tax revenue depending on market prices of the goods and services that a region produces. Regional catastrophes also occur because of extreme weather. Private-insurance markets may not provide insurance against region-specific income risk; in particular, regional insurance markets will be unwilling to provide insurance if correlated (or systemic) risk makes risk-spreading within the region impossible. The central or federal government acts, however, as insurer of last resort through income redistribution and disaster relief. The component states or regions of federal government are a "portfolio" for risk-pooling, given each region's specific risks.

A benefit of fiscal federalism is insurance through tax-pooling at higher levels of government.

Entitlements and social insurance

People can move within a fiscal federal system to take advantage of entitlements. The possibility of free movement prevents jurisdictions from choosing entitlements that residents want because of incentives of low-income people to relocate in order to benefit from the entitlements without commensurately contributing to costs. Communities may therefore use zoning and consequent high housing prices to prevent location in response to entitlements. There is then unequal opportunity, for example, for children in different jurisdictions. Centralized government is a means of attempting to avoid the ex-ante inequality or unequal opportunity. Equal entitlements financed by a central government end incentives to move in order to benefit from welfare payments and other entitlements: the central or federal government can levy taxes on all taxpayers and redistribute the tax revenue among all subjurisdictions. Local public spending is then subsidized in low-income jurisdictions by taxpayers in high-income jurisdictions. The income redistribution is consistent with the provisions of a social insurance contract decided behind a veil of ignorance when inhabitants (and their children) did not know the jurisdiction or neighborhood into which they would be born.

A benefit of fiscal federalism is equal opportunity provided through taxation and public spending at higher levels of government.

B. Tax competition

When we considered choice of tax bases, we noted that the Ramsey rule for efficient taxation proposes that taxes on mobile capital should be lower than taxes on immobile labor because of different opportunities to escape taxation by leaving the jurisdiction. Low tax rates on mobile capital is a normative recommendation, based on the objective of efficient taxation. As a positive proposition, we *predict* low rates of taxation on mobile capital because of tax competition among jurisdictions.

Post-tax returns to mobile capital are equalized among different tax jurisdictions (after adjustment for risk). Mobile capital responds to a tax by leaving the jurisdiction where the tax has been levied. In the new equilibrium, after-tax returns are again equalized across tax jurisdictions. Figure 9.6 shows this process.

In figure 9.6, a fixed amount of mobile capital K indicated by the distance O_1O_2 is allocated through a competitive capital market between two tax jurisdictions. O_1 is the origin for measurement of capital in jurisdiction 1 and O_2 is the origin

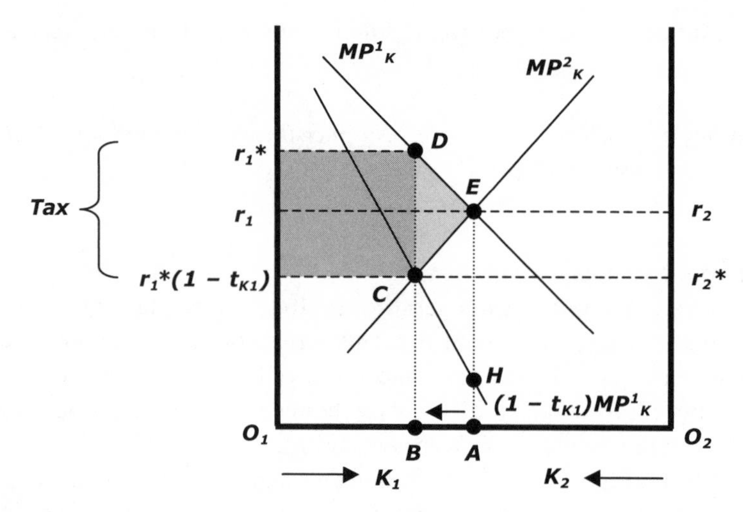

Figure 9.6. The change in the tax base due to a tax on income from mobile capital in jurisdiction 1.

for jurisdiction 2.[55] A quantity of capital K_1 is located in jurisdiction 1 and a quantity K_2 is located in jurisdiction 2, so that:

$$K = K_1 + K_2. \tag{9.21}$$

When there are no taxes on income from capital in either jurisdiction, the competitive market allocation of capital between the two jurisdictions is at point A, determined by equality at point E between the value of the marginal product of capital MP^i_K $(i = 1, 2)$ in the two jurisdictions.[56] In a competitive market, the value of the marginal product of capital equals the return to capital r_i $(i = 1, 2)$ and so the two jurisdictions have the same return to capital:

$$r_1 = r_2. \tag{9.22}$$

The government in jurisdiction 1 then levies a tax at the rate t_{K1} on income earned from capital in its jurisdiction. The tax is levied on income from capital in the jurisdiction of the government, independently of the residence or citizenship of the owner of capital.

In figure 9.6, the tax changes the function indicating the now net return to capital in jurisdiction 1 to $(1 - t_{K1})MP_K$. With no movement of capital, at point A, the return to capital in jurisdiction 1 falls from the value at point E to that at point H. Because of the tax, the equality of returns from capital in expression (9.22) therefore no longer holds for the allocation of capital between the jurisdictions at point A.

In response to the inequality of post-tax returns at point A, capital leaves jurisdiction 1 for jurisdiction 2, where there is no tax. The new post-tax market

[55] Some capital will be immobile. Owners of immobile capital will have lost because of the time-inconsistency problem of taxation of income from capital.

[56] The value of the marginal product of capital is $P \cdot MP_K$, where P is the price of the output produced using the capital. We set $P = 1$.

allocation of capital between the two jurisdictions is at point C, where the *post-tax* rates of return from capital in the two jurisdictions are equalized. The new post-tax allocation of capital is at point B.

Thus, as a consequence of the tax imposed by the government in jurisdiction 1:

$$(1 - t_{K1})MP_K^1 = MP_K^2 \tag{9.23}$$

and:

$$(1 - t_{K1})r_1^* = r_2^*. \tag{9.24}$$

The tax in jurisdiction 1 has resulted in the quantity of capital AB moving from jurisdiction 1 to jurisdiction 2. Therefore:

The tax base has contracted in the jurisdiction where the tax was imposed and has expanded in the jurisdiction without a tax.

The tax on capital income in jurisdiction 1 has reduced the private return to capital in both jurisdictions, from the return given by expression (9.22) to the return given by expression (9.24). The excess burden of the tax on income from capital levied by the government of jurisdiction 1 is the area DEC shown in figure 9.6.[57]

When we studied public finance for public goods in chapter 4, we observed that the excess burden of a tax reduces efficient public spending on public goods below efficient voluntary private spending. There is a similar consequence when mobile capital is taxed to finance public goods:

When the tax base is mobile capital, efficient public spending on public goods is less than efficient Lindahl voluntary spending.

In chapter 4, efficient public spending was reduced by tax financing because of the contraction of the tax base due to the substitution between leisure and work. In the case of taxes levied on mobile capital, an increase in taxation likewise contracts the tax base because of exit of capital from the jurisdiction.

When we studied social justice and income redistribution in chapter 7, the leaky bucket was similarly due to the substitution effect between leisure and work. If income from mobile capital is taxed for redistribution to labor, the leaky bucket is expressed in the contraction of the tax base as mobile capital leaves in response to the tax. We can view a good or adverse outcome after emerging from behind the veil of ignorance as determined according to ownership of capital. The income redistribution through the social insurance contract is then impeded by the leaky bucket of exit of mobile capital. In figure 9.6, the government in

[57] Before the tax was imposed, the quantity of capital AB was producing a quantity of output $BAED$ (the area under the marginal product of capital function for region 1). After the tax is imposed, the relocated capital produces the smaller output $ECBA$ (the area under the marginal product of capital function for region 2). The loss in output because of the relocation of capital in response to the tax is the difference between those areas, which is the area DEC.

jurisdiction 1 obtains tax revenue from the tax on the return to capital equal to the shaded rectangle. The value of the tax revenue is:

$$R = tr_I^* K_I. \tag{9.25}$$

As with the change in tax revenue when taxes affect leisure-work choices, tax revenue from the tax on mobile capital can decline when the tax rate is increased. The change in tax revenue depends on the elasticity of supply of capital to the jurisdiction. The quantity of capital K_I that remains in the jurisdiction declines in response to the tax. The decline in revenue can be precipitous if, because of a high supply elasticity, a large quantity of capital exits the jurisdiction. Figure 9.7 shows the rate of return to capital in a competitive capital market within the jurisdiction of the national or federal government. Alternatively, the return to capital could be determined in a competitive global capital market. Taxes do not affect the competitively determined market rate of return that an investor can always obtain. In figure 9.7, a tax imposed by the government in jurisdiction 1 results in exit of capital AB from the government's jurisdiction. Further increases in the tax rate result in exit of capital BF. A sufficiently high rate of taxation results in the disappearance of the domestic tax base for mobile capital.

A mobile tax base thus limits public spending. A government may be left with little choice other than to tax the immobile people in its jurisdiction because mobile factors will respond to the announcement of a tax by simply moving away.

> *When the tax base is mobile capital, the leaky bucket that indicates efficiency losses from redistribution includes the contraction of the tax base because of exit of mobile capital.*

Moreover, when capital exits a jurisdiction, the value of the marginal product of labor – and therefore the wage – falls.

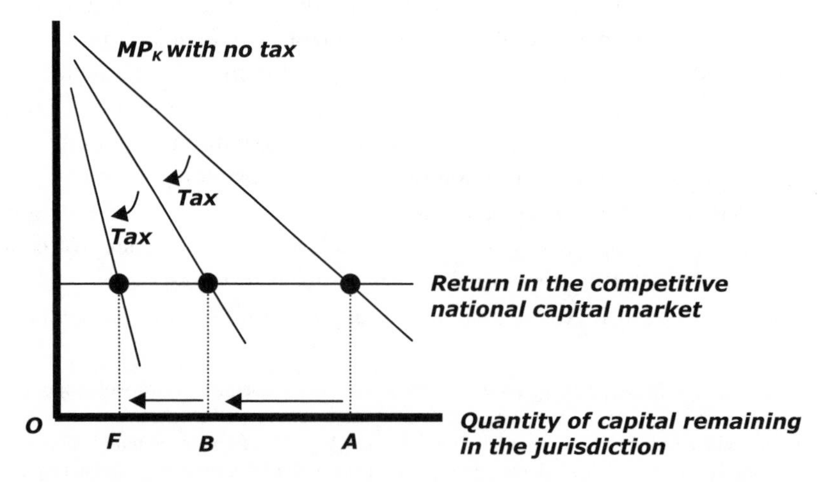

Figure 9.7. Successive tax increases with a competitive global capital market.

Source and residence principles of taxation

Under the *source* principle of taxation, the owner of capital pays taxes to the government in the location where the income from capital is earned; decisions about where to locate capital are made, therefore, by comparing post-tax returns in different locations and the investment decision is sensitive to taxes in different jurisdictions. This is the case we have been considering. Under the *residence* principle of taxation, a recipient of income from capital pays taxes to his or her home government no matter where the capital is located. Because the same tax is paid independently of where capital is invested, owners of capital seek the highest return available in any jurisdiction. If taxes are levied on a residence basis, a tax on capital imposed by the government of the investor's home jurisdiction cannot be escaped by moving capital to another jurisdiction. To escape a tax, the investor needs to move along with the capital.

> *When taxes on mobile capital are levied according to residence of the owners of capital, issues of tax competition do not arise because taxes cannot be escaped by changing the location of capital.*

Double tax agreements

If both residence- and source-based taxes are levied, income from capital is taxed twice: investors pay taxes on income earned from capital to the government of the outside tax jurisdiction, and they pay taxes again on the same income to the home government of their tax jurisdiction. Agreements between governments can avoid this double burden of taxation: a double-tax agreement allows taxes paid in one tax jurisdiction to be deducted from tax obligations in another. Double-tax agreements thus provide compensating tax offsets for taxes paid to another government.

Tax competition and tax coordination

When taxation is on a source basis (taxes are levied and paid where the capital is located and income earned), governments can perceive, correctly, that they are in competition for tax bases and that by reducing taxes, they can hope to attract new capital to add to their tax base. The end result of competition among governments to attract mobile capital can be that capital is not taxed and perhaps is subsidized.

Table 9.1 shows the prisoners' dilemma of tax competition. A government is best off when it has a low tax and the government in another jurisdiction has a high tax. The dominant strategy is to choose a low tax. The Nash equilibrium is therefore where each government has a low tax. Tax coordination whereby each government sets a high tax is a Pareto improvement for the governments in moving the outcome from the Nash equilibrium at (2,2) to (3,3).

The Nash equilibrium at (2,2) is sometimes described as a "race to the bottom" in taxes on mobile capital. The race to the bottom is avoided if taxation is

TABLE 9.1. TAX COMPETITION AS A PRISONERS' DILEMMA

	Government 2 chooses a high tax	Government 2 chooses a low tax
Government 1 chooses a high tax	3, 3	1, 4
Government 1 chooses a low tax	4, 1	2, 2

centralized, rather than decentralized at the level of state or local governments. The central or federal government can levy taxes and distribute the tax revenue to the lower-level governments.[58]

Indirect taxes

Tax competition can occur with respect to indirect taxes. There is then also a tax-coordination problem among governments for indirect taxes. When governments do not enforce border controls, people respond to different rates of sales tax by shopping in low-tax jurisdictions. When a neighboring jurisdiction has a lower sales tax on liquor, some people might drive to the neighboring jurisdiction to drink. They might then drive home intoxicated.

C. Political behavior

Because fiscal federalism involves decisions made by governments, we expect decisions and behavior based on political objectives to be present. How governments behave affects the social desirability of tax competition.

Is tax competition desirable?

The benefits in table 9.1 refer to governments, not to taxpayers. The interests of governments and taxpayers coincide when there are no political or bureaucratic principal–agent problems; in this case, tax competition is harmful to residents of a tax jurisdiction. However, when political and bureaucratic principal–agent problems are present and, therefore, public spending is not assured to be in the public interest, the low taxes of the Nash equilibrium are advantageous for taxpayers, by providing a discipline on the level of the taxes that governments can levy.

> *Whether tax competition is advantageous or disadvantageous to taxpayers and citizens depends on whether there are political and bureaucratic principle–agent problems.*

[58] If a federal government does not exist, then it can be created, as in the case of the European Union.

Locational mobility and escape from the leviathan

There is a principal–agent problem when a leviathan government seeks to maximize tax revenue without regard for benefit of taxpayers. When taxes are levied on personal income or sales taxes are used, locational mobility in a fiscal federal system restrains taxation of a leviathan revenue-maximizing government because the tax base contracts when people and capital leave. Escape from leviathan government is impossible, however, when taxes are levied on immobile tax bases. Local government jurisdictions often use property taxes to raise revenue; property is an immobile tax base that cannot leave a tax jurisdiction. After a leviathan government has announced increases in property taxes, homeowners cannot escape the higher taxes by selling their house and moving to another government jurisdiction. The higher taxes with no benefit to taxpayers are capitalized into the value of houses and therefore property values fall. The decline in a property value is equal to the present value of the obligation of the homeowner to pay the increased taxes that will provide no benefit. Homeowners who sell their house after the tax increase has been announced pay the present value of the entire future tax increase through the reduced price received for their house. The homebuyers to whom houses are sold after the tax increase is announced correspondingly do not pay the tax. The buyers of houses after the tax increase has been announced transfer money to the government in the future when they pay property taxes; however, they have been compensated for the future taxes by the reduced price that they paid for the house.

> *A tax on property with no accompanying benefits cannot be escaped by selling the house or property.*

To avoid losses, owners of property need to change the government that has decided on the tax policy that has decreased property values.

Local-government principal–agent problems and yardstick competition

Do taxpayers know that they are paying taxes to a leviathan government? Taxpayers are subject to rational ignorance; they face a free-rider problem in acquiring and acting on information about behavior of political and bureaucratic decision makers; and they face lack of transparency when local governments do not reveal costs of supply of local public goods. A process known as *yardstick competition* assists taxpayers in overcoming local-government principal–agent problems. By observing taxes and supply of public goods in neighboring jurisdictions, taxpayers can make comparisons that allow judgments to be made about the decisions and behavior of their own local government officials. The comparative judgments are made by the "yardstick" of the behavior and decisions of neighboring local governments. Yardstick competition requires, of course, the means of comparing a government serving its citizens and taxpayers with a leviathan government. That is, a government without political and bureaucratic principal–agent problems needs to be present to provide the yardstick for comparison between governments. The presence of such a government is revealed when a jurisdiction provides superior quality local public goods for the same taxes as paid in other jurisdictions or provides the same quality of services for lower taxes.

The presence of multiple governments that include a government not subject to political and bureaucratic principal–agent problems is a source of information for voters on the performance of their own local government.

Voters can use the information from comparisons of governments to decide whether to support political incumbents or challengers in local-government elections. When better political and bureaucratic performance is observed in other jurisdictions, voters and taxpayers can conclude that better local government is possible. At the same time, incumbent local politicians who are aware that voters are judging their performance against the performance of their counterparts in other jurisdictions have an incentive to exert effort to ensure that their performance compares favorably with outcomes in other jurisdictions. Indeed, governments are involved in a game: they decide whether to serve the public interest or to take advantage of asymmetric information to serve themselves. There is a prisoners' dilemma. Two governments would be best off if they acted as leviathan governments and maximized tax revenue for their own benefit. However, a government that does not act in the public interest loses because of the electoral consequences of information revealed through yardstick competition when the other government does act in the public interest. The government that has acted in the public interest when the other has chosen to act as a leviathan gains through voters' comparisons. As in the other cases of the prisoners' dilemma that we considered, there is a dominant strategy, here to act in the public interest, which is the Nash equilibrium, although both governments would be better off if they could coordinate not to act in the public interest – which would not be revealed to voters because both governments would be acting in the same way.

Because of governments' inability to coordinate leviathan behavior, yardstick competition contributes to solving local-government political and bureaucratic principal–agent problems.

Empirical evidence supports the effectiveness of yardstick competition as a means whereby voters obtain information and discipline local-government officials.[59]

Yardstick competition is based on political competition. Yardstick competition is ineffective, of course, as a means of disciplining local government officials

[59] A study by Timothy Besley and Anne Case (1995) confirmed, for example, the presence of yardstick competition in U.S. local government.

who are appointed by higher levels of government rather than being elected by the local population.

Political income redistribution

A central government has the advantage in collecting tax revenue that tax competition among subjurisdictions is avoided. However, once the central government has the authority to tax and spend – and to redistribute tax revenue among jurisdictions – political discretion can replace normatively guided rules for taxation and public spending. That is:

Fiscal federalism can be used for politically motivated redistribution.

Moral hazard

In a fiscal federal system, the moral-hazard problem arises when a lower level of government spends the allocation of tax revenue that has been assigned by the central government. The state or local governments, for example, may be given public funds for schools, based on a formula of the number of children and needs of children, given parents' incomes. The local government spending the tax revenue is not accountable to all taxpayers who have paid the taxes that are being spent. Indeed, rather than seeking efficient, transparent, and accountable public spending, taxpayers in the local jurisdiction may want as much centrally provided tax revenue to be spent as possible – because the taxes being spent are paid in part by taxpayers in other jurisdictions. We encounter here another case of the inefficiency of shared private spending: we recall the example of the final bill at a restaurant when people compute their personal price as a shared cost.

There is moral hazard when a local government does not make an effort to use the tax revenue provided by the central government effectively and requests further funding when the assigned tax revenue has been spent. For example, local governments may spend the tax revenue on salaries and benefits of public-school administrators rather than on improving conditions for children in the classrooms. Tax revenue may be used to increase salaries of public health-care administrators, who might then complain that not enough money is available for vital projects such as inoculation of young children or convincing high school students of the personal disadvantages of cigarette smoking or other behavior with personally disadvantageous long-term consequences.

When a lower-level government claims to the central government that tax revenue has been spent, the central government confronts a "holdup problem." The holdup is that the lower-level government can extract additional revenue from the central government by threatening to reduce spending on public health, threatening to close schools, or reducing the size of the police force. The central government may have no choice but to respond to the holdup by increasing the lower-level government's budgetary funding. There is then no fiscal discipline on lower level government, which confronts a "soft budget."

> *Moral hazard and holdups are disadvantages of centralized taxation and redistribution of tax revenue among lower-level governments.*

Proximity to political decision makers

Decentralized government offers advantages for taxpayers through proximity to political decision makers and to the administrating bureaucracy. Asymmetric information and rational ignorance are reduced by lower personal costs of being informed about taxation and public spending. The local press, if not politically captured, can provide accurate local information. Proximity allows greater ease of access to people in government. Fewer participating citizens and voters are required at the local level of government for effective expressions of dissatisfaction with the behavior of politicians and officials in the bureaucracy. Direct democracy through a referendum might be more readily possible at the local-government level. Therefore:

> *Transparency of government and political accountability are greater with decentralized than centralized government.*

Rent seeking and fiscal federalism

In our investigation of rent seeking, we compared socially beneficial competition in markets in which output is supplied with socially unproductive rent-seeking contests. Ideally, we would want no rent seeking. However, if rent seeking is unavoidable, multiple smaller contests in a system of decentralized government are socially preferable to an all-inclusive contest to influence centralized government. Splitting up contests so that rents are sought from multiple governments reduces the competitiveness of rent seeking and thereby reduces the total resources wastefully used in rent seeking.

Incentives for rent seeking also differ according to whether government is centralized or decentralized. Rent seeking requires opportunities for furtive activities that are unobservable by taxpayers and voters. Such opportunities are found more at the federal government in the national capital, far from the prying eyes of taxpayers and voters dispersed throughout the regions and states of the country. In the national capital, rent seekers further benefit from the availability of specialized lobbyists.

In the national capital, the central government has pooled tax revenue collected from people in subjurisdictions of the country. Rent seeking takes place to influence the spending of the pooled or collectivized tax revenue. In smaller decentralized jurisdictions, taxpayers are more sensitive to political decisions about spending "their" tax money. That is, taxpayers have greater feeling of personal property rights to tax revenue collected at decentralized levels of government.

As we observed, proximity to political decision makers reduces rational ignorance. A consequence of the reduced rational ignorance is that rent creation and rent seeking are restrained at decentralized levels of government by the greater visibility of beneficiaries of politically provided rents.

We can conclude that:

> *Decentralized government is less conducive to rent creation and rent seeking than centralized government.*

Capture

Capture results in opportunities for use of government for self-advantage. The benefits of decentralized government are not enjoyed if government is captured by local elites. In low-income societies, capture by elites can take place at both centralized and decentralized levels of government; however, local elites have greater advantages at local levels of government, where they may face less opposition to capture. There is, in general, more competition for capture of central government.

> *In low-income countries, local governments are more easily captured than central governments.*

Conclusions about choice between decentralized and centralized government thus, as we expect, depend on the institutions that determine accountability and transparency of government and that establish the extent to which political decision makers and government bureaucrats are able or permitted to benefit themselves, and in low-income countries to provide benefits for controlling elites.

D. Voting and fiscal federalism

When we studied voting, we noted how choice from among multiple governments avoids the tyranny of the majority: when people choose location according to preferences, communities of voters have similar preferences and there is no minority to be exploited through majority voting. This theme of avoiding undesirable consequences of majority voting can be developed further by comparing outcomes of majority voting under alternative centralized and decentralized governmental structures. In now making such a comparison, we shall consider financing of a pure public good. Because a pure public good is a natural monopoly, the advantage is with centralized government in avoiding replication of payment for public goods. Nonetheless, decentralized government may be preferred by a majority of voters.

The common-pool problem of centralized tax revenue

Taxes provide a common pool of revenue. There is a common-pool problem when people contribute equally to the pool of tax revenue, but some groups benefit disproportionately. We shall use an example to demonstrate the tax-revenue

TABLE 9.2. INDIVIDUAL PRE-TAX BENEFITS FROM PUBLIC GOODS

Public good Total cost = 900	Pre-tax benefits of group 1 (3 voters)	Pre-tax benefits of group 2 (3 voters)	Pre-tax benefits group 3 (3 voters)
X	1,000	500	100
Y	500	1,000	500
Z	100	100	1,000

TABLE 9.2a. INDIVIDUAL POST-TAX BENEFITS IN A CENTRALIZED JURISDICTION

Deduction of cost of 100 per person	Post-tax benefits of group 1 (3 voters)	Post-tax benefits of group 2 (3 voters)	Post-tax benefits of group 3 (3 voters)
X	900	400	0
Y	400	900	400
Z	0	0	900

common-pool problem and to compare voting on centralized and decentralized supply of public goods.

Table 9.2 shows the pre-tax benefits of three groups of people from spending on three public-good projects *X*, *Y*, and *Z*. Each group consists of three people, who are also together as voters in three subjurisdictions of a larger jurisdiction.

The total cost of each of the public-good projects *X*, *Y*, and *Z* is 900. Only one of the projects is chosen in a jurisdiction, with the decision made by majority voting. Costs of the chosen project are shared equally among all voters in a jurisdiction. In table 9.2, we see that each group has a different preferred public-good project.

Table 9.2a shows individual post-tax benefits from supply in a centralized jurisdiction. Each voter pays a cost share of 100 to finance the public good that is chosen by majority voting. The Condorcet winner in table 9.2a is *Y*. In a centralized jurisdiction, voters in group 2 therefore obtain their first preference, financed by equal taxes paid by all nine voters. The voters in group 2 have benefited in the centralized jurisdiction. The taxes of voters in groups 1 and 3 contribute to financing *Y*, which is group 2's preferred choice.[60]

Table 9.2b shows post-tax benefits when voters are in three separate decentralized jurisdictions. There are three taxpayers in each jurisdiction and the cost of the public good is again equal to 900, so each taxpayer now pays a tax of 300

[60] *Y* defeats both *X* and *Z* by six votes to three.

TABLE 9.2b. INDIVIDUAL POST-TAX BENEFITS IN DECENTRALIZED JURISDICTIONS

Deduction of cost of 300 per person	Post-tax benefits of group 1 (3 voters)	Post-tax benefits of group 2 (3 voters)	Post-tax benefits of group 3 (3 voters)
X	700	200	−200
Y	200	700	200
Z	−200	−200	700

to finance the public good chosen in the jurisdiction. The values in table 9.2b are obtained by deducting 300 from individual pre-tax benefits in table 9.2. In each decentralized jurisdiction, voters in table 9.2b by consensus choose their preferred public good. All voters have a post-tax benefit of 700 (given by the individual benefit in table 9.2 of 1,000 from the preferred public good, minus the 300 cost per person).

Comparing tables 9.2a and 9.2b, we see that taxpayers in groups 1 and 3 are better off with decentralized government, whereas taxpayers in group 2 are better off under centralized government. Decentralized government is also efficient or equivalently maximizes Bentham social welfare.[61]

If group 2 is decisive in determining the structure of government, government will be centralized. Through centralized government, group 2 benefits from the common pool of tax revenue provided by the addition of tax payments of groups 1 and 3, who contribute to paying for group 2's preferred project.

Centralized government allows the group that determines collective choice through majority voting in the centralized jurisdiction to benefit from the common pool of taxes.

It follows that:

The beneficiaries of majority voting under the centralized government have incentives to resist decentralized government.

Thus we return to the majority's incentives noted in chapter 3. In the case here, a minority group is unambiguously better off in its own separate jurisdiction although taxes per voter are higher.

[61] In the centralized jurisdiction in table 9.2a, Y provides each individual in groups 1 and 3 with net benefit of 400 and each individual in group 2 with net benefit of 900. There are three individuals in each group; therefore, $W = \sum W_i = 5{,}100$. With decentralized government in table 9.2b, each person has net benefit of 700, so $W = \sum W_i = 6{,}300$.

A demand function

In the example that we have used, demand for the public goods *X*, *Y*, and *Z* does not change when costs per taxpayer change. That is, demand for public goods is inelastic, or fixed. However, we expect demand for public goods to increase when costs per taxpayer decline. Thus, in the centralized jurisdiction, because of the larger number of taxpayers sharing costs, demand of each group is greater. If good *Y* remains the Condorcet winner after demand has increased, the common pool of revenue finances the greater quantity of good *Y* sought by group 2.

Conclusion about fiscal federalism and voting

We add, therefore, to our conclusion that decentralized jurisdictions avoid the tyranny of the majority:

> *Decentralized jurisdictions avoid the common-pool problem of centralized tax revenue.*

Other voting rules

We have used the Condorcet winner and majority voting to illustrate the common-pool problem of centralized tax revenue. The pair-wise majority voting on alternatives that determines the Condorcet winner generally does not take place. The conclusions about the common-pool problem, however, do not depend on voting procedures. For example, there may be four voters in group 2 and three voters in each of groups 1 and 3 and the voting rule may be plurality – in which case, group 2 is again the beneficiary of the common pool of tax revenue in the centralized jurisdiction.

Fiscal federalism and global government

The highest level of a fiscal federal structure would be global government, which would be given responsibility for resolving global externality problems and overseeing the pursuit of global social justice. We previously observed grounds for reservations about the desirability of global government. The representatives of national governments that would be represented in global government include those that appropriate resources intended for the world's poor. Behavior of the rich elites that control governments in many poor countries is often as predicted by Nietzsche, with the strong behaving unethically toward the weak. We do not want such governments to have the means to influence our life. Because of such governments, people leave their home countries to seek better government elsewhere. A global government would leave no means of escape from bad government.[62]

[62] The closest approximation to a world parliament is the United Nations General Assembly, which often has given positions of prominence to representatives of governments that repress their people.

Summary

In previous chapters, taxation was considered in conjunction with public spending. In this chapter, we have looked at taxation without the necessary accompaniment of how revenue from taxation is to be spent. Section 1 considered the optimal structure of taxation (a normative question) and also sought an answer for why progressive taxes are used (a positive question).

1A. The Ramsey rule indicates the efficient structure of taxes for different goods or for different people. The Ramsey rule seeks efficiency and is often inconsistent with social justice. Applying the Ramsey rule is also subject to problems of asymmetric information. Taxing innate ability or beauty as the Ramsey rule proposes would be an intrusion into personal lifestyle decisions. The Ramsey rule would be politically unpopular. A leviathan government could apply the Ramsey rule to maximize tax revenue subject to a restraint on efficiency losses from taxation.

1B. The equal-sacrifice principle defines taxation as socially just when an equal loss of utility is imposed on all taxpayers. When we investigated the equal-sacrifice principle, we set aside effects of taxation on efficiency; with no efficiency losses through the excess burden of taxation, a case for progressive taxes could be sought under the most favorable conditions. The equal-sacrifice principle requires specifying a common utility function that measures utility lost through taxation. Although we chose a utility function that exhibits diminishing marginal utility of income, the equal-sacrifice principle nonetheless does not imply and is not implied by progressive taxes. If the common utility function has constant relative risk aversion of unity, the equal-sacrifice tax schedule has a constant proportional tax rate.

1C. The theory of optimal income taxation looks for a trade-off between the efficiency costs of taxation and ex-post, post-tax equality of incomes. A simple and perhaps sufficient formulation of optimal income taxation is the linear income tax, which has a constant marginal tax rate but is progressive. We noted the computational advantages of a linear income tax and also the beneficial work incentives and the social insurance that are provided. Estimates indicate that a simple linear income tax with limited or no deductions and exemptions could provide the same tax revenue as complex progressive tax schedules; there is, therefore, a Laffer curve in choice of the structure of taxation. The more general form of the optimal income-tax problem does not constrain the tax schedule to be linear. Ideally, in the optimal income-tax problem, people would be taxed on nonsubstitutable innate ability. Because personal ability is not observable, personal income is taxed. Optimal income taxation is a second-best problem of asymmetric information. A characteristic of the Mirrlees solution for optimal taxation is that the income-tax structure should not give people incentives to hide their abilities, in the sense of choosing to work and earn less income than someone of lesser ability. The analysis of optimal income-tax theory indicates that the income-tax schedule should begin and end with a zero marginal tax rate. Little of generality about the desired structure of an income-tax schedule emerges from the solution to the Mirrlees general optimal income-tax problem. The social welfare function pushes in the direction of greater progressivity in the tax schedule. Efficiency losses and tax-base effects counter the progressivity. Mirrlees used simulations to conclude that the income-tax structure should be moderately progressive and the top rate of taxation not too high. Solutions to the optimal income-tax problem depend on the utility function that is used to represent labor-supply incentives, and also on the choice of the social welfare function.

1D. Political objectives can affect choice of income-tax schedules. Complexity in an income-tax structure encourages rational ignorance and benefits accountants and tax lawyers. Simplifying tax reform takes place when inefficiencies and injustices visibly abound. After tax reform, the tax code generally reverts to complexity. Progressive taxes increase equality in both pre- and post-tax incomes. High progressive taxes suggest a social preference that people who could earn higher incomes choose leisure at the margin rather than income-providing work. Progressive taxes are consistent with inequality aversion and with envy. The origins of inequality aversion and envy can be traced to behavior in hunter–gatherer societies.

In section 2, the questions changed from personal taxation of income to other tax bases.

2A. We considered taxation of income from capital. The Ramsey rule suggests lower taxes on income from mobile capital that can leave a tax jurisdiction than on labor income, which raises concerns of social justice in disproportionately placing the burden of taxation on immobile labor. We noted the time-inconsistency problem of taxation of capital and the advantages of stable predictable taxes on income from capital.

2B. We sought to understand the reason for a separate tax (and tax rate) for corporate profits (or a company tax) because corporate profits are part of the incomes of the owners of firms and can be taxed as part of personal taxation. We looked at capital-gains taxation and asked why firms pay dividends and how taxation affects decisions about corporate finance through choice between debt and equity.

2C. A personal expenditure tax can be designed in a manner similar to a personal income tax. The expenditure tax has the ethical justification of being consistent with taxing utility, which depends on personal consumption rather than on income. The expenditure tax simplifies taxation because taxation of expenditure is independent of the source of the income (or wealth) that finances personal spending. An expenditure and income tax have different substitution effects. Economic growth is greater with an expenditure tax because savings and, therefore, investment are not taxed. There are problems of transition in moving from a personal income tax to a personal expenditure tax. Governments do not use expenditure taxes. An expenditure tax is more personally intrusive than an income tax.

2D. We considered other tax bases. Although wealth taxes and estate and inheritance taxes can provide governments with revenue, our conclusions did not suggest a case for such taxes. The taxes are on frugality and modest consumption, on intergenerational altruism, and on lack of sophistication in tax avoidance. Lotteries, inflation, and financial repression are forms of taxation. Lotteries are taxes on objectively unjustified optimism or exuberance. Inflation and financial repression have been observed principally in low-income, nondemocratic countries. If characteristics of an optimal income tax could be identified, a government would not need indirect taxes because the optimal trade-off between efficiency and social justice will have been achieved through the income tax. A case for indirect taxes based on targeting goods that high-income people buy stereotypes people by income when people differ in preferences. A case for indirect taxes is based on evasion of income taxes. A leviathan government uses every tax base possible.

Fiscal federalism has been discussed in previous chapters. Section 3 of this chapter collected previous conclusions about fiscal federalism and added further observations on how multiple-government structures affect taxation and public spending. Our normative conclusion was that, overall, decentralized government through fiscal federalism is socially beneficial.

3A. We considered fiscal federalism from a normative vantage point and noted the advantages and disadvantages of centralized and decentralized government. Fiscal federalism promotes personal freedom through choice among governments. The benefits of a fiscal federal structure of government include decentralized Tiebout supply of public goods, centralized correction of externalities, and centralized cost sharing when there is natural monopoly. The multiple governments of a fiscal federal structure also allow choice of community values as public goods. Fiscal federalism is beneficial in allowing risk-pooling. A fiscal-federal structure of government facilitates ex-ante equality in entitlements through centralized taxation and public spending decisions – entitlements can be independent of location within subjurisdictions. However, holdup problems associated with moral hazard arise when central governments levy taxes and redistribute tax revenue to lower level governments.

3B. When taxation is source- and not residence-based, tax competition can occur, expressed in a prisoners' dilemma in the setting of tax rates. In the Nash equilibrium, governments set low taxes. Assigning responsibility for taxation to a centralized government avoids tax competition. The centralized government redistributes the tax revenue to the subjurisdictions that would have confronted tax competition, had taxes been decentralized. To facilitate investment across tax jurisdictions, national governments enter into double-tax agreements. Tax competition also affects indirect taxes.

3C. We considered political aspects of fiscal federalism. The low taxes through tax competition are socially beneficial if voters and taxpayers confront political and bureaucratic principle–agent problems. The multiple governments of fiscal federalism allow voters to use yardstick competition to compare and judge the competence and honesty of political decision makers. Decentralization of government under fiscal federalism allows taxpayers to escape from an income tax and an indirect tax of a leviathan government; property taxes of a leviathan government cannot be escaped by relocation because of capitalization of property taxes into housing prices. Centralization of taxation and public spending in fiscal-federal systems introduces the scope for political discretion in redistribution of tax revenue among lower levels of government – unless there are strict guidelines for taxation and spending of tax revenue to which political decision makers in the federal or central government adhere. The benefits of decentralized government include greater transparency of government and political accountability due to personal proximity to government. Centralization of government increases rational ignorance and reduces political accountability. Centralization affects incentives for rent creation and rent seeking; rent seekers benefit from greater anonymity in a centralized jurisdiction. Institutions, including possibilities of capture, affect the relative merits of centralized and decentralized government.

3D. We had previously noted that decentralized government solves problems of majority voting on spending on public goods because when people have sorted themselves by preferences, no minority is present to be disadvantaged by majority voting. We supplemented this conclusion by showing how under centralized government, a problem arises due to majority control over the common pool of tax revenue. We also considered whether we want to add a global government to existing fiscal-federal structures.

Literature notes

9.1 Optimal taxation

The Ramsey rule is from:

Ramsey, F. P., 1929. A contribution to the theory of taxation. *Economic Journal* 37:47–61.

On beauty and the labor market, see:

Hamermesh, D. S., and J. E. Biddle, 1994. Beauty and the labor market. *American Economic Review* 84:1174–94.

There is a substantial literature on influences on female labor participation. For example, see:

Fernández, R., A. Fogli, and C. Olivetti, 2004. Mothers and sons: Preference formation and female labor-force participation. *Quarterly Journal of Economics* 119:1249–99.

Grossbard-Shechtman, S., and S. Neuman, 2003. Marriage and work for pay. In S. Grossbard-Shechtman (Ed.), *Marriage and the Economy: Theory and Evidence from Advanced Industrial Societies*. Cambridge University Press, New York, pp. 222–49.

On the equal-sacrifice principle, see:

D'Antoni, M., 1999. Piecewise linear tax functions, progressivity, and the principle of equal sacrifice. *Economic Letters* 65:191–7.

Mill, J. S., 1848. *Principles of Political Economy*. Longmans Green, London.

Mitra, T., and E. A. Ok, 1996. Personal income taxation and the principle of equal sacrifice revisited. *International Economic Review* 37:925–48.

Mitra, T., and E. A. Ok, 1997. On the equitability of progressive taxation. *Journal of Economic Theory* 73:316–34.

Ok, E. A., 1995. On the principle of equal sacrifice in income taxation. *Journal of Public Economics* 58:453–68.

Samuelson, P., 1947. *Foundations of Economic Analysis*. Harvard University Press, Cambridge MA.

Young, H. P., 1987. Progressive taxation and the equal-sacrifice principle. *Journal of Public Economics* 32:203–14.

Young, H. P., 1990. Progressive taxation and equal sacrifice. *American Economic Review* 80:253–66.

On proposed values for relative risk aversion, see:

Layard, R., S. Nickell, and G. Mayraz, 2008. The marginal utility of income. *Journal of Public Economics* 92:1846–57.

On the optimal linear income tax, see:

Ihori, T., 1987. The optimal linear income tax: A diagrammatic analysis. *Journal of Public Economics* 34:379–90.

Sheshinski, E., 1972. The optimal linear income tax. *Review of Economic Studies* 39:297–302.

On the general optimal income-taxation problem, see:

Mirrlees, J. A., 1971. An exploration in the theory of optimal income taxation. *Review of Economic Studies* 38:175–208.

Mirrlees, J. A., 1976. Optimal tax theory: A synthesis. *Journal of Public Economics* 6:327–58.

Mirrlees, J. A., 1999. Information and incentives: The economics of carrots and sticks. Nobel Prize Lecture. *Economic Journal* 107:1311–29.

Ferguson (2001) described instances of high marginal tax rates. Diamond (1998) and Saez (2001) proposed high marginal tax rates.

Diamond, P. A., 1998. Optimal income taxation: An example with a U-shaped pattern of optimal marginal tax rates. *American Economic Review* 88:83–95.
Ferguson, N., 2001. *The Cash Nexus*. Penguin Books, London.
Saez, E., 2001. Using elasticities to derive optimal income tax rates. *Review of Economic Studies* 68:205–29.

On the case for simple low-tax structures, see:

Boskin, M. J. (Ed.), 1996. *Frontiers of Tax Reform*. Hoover Institution Press, Stanford CA.
Hall, R. E., and A. Rabushka, 1995. *The Flat Tax* (2nd Edition). Hoover Institution Press, Stanford CA.

Boskin and Sheshinski (1978) derived an optimal income when envy is present (utility depends on own after-tax consumption and average after-tax consumption in a group) and showed how the consequence of making allowance for envy is greater progressivity expressed in higher marginal tax rates.

Boskin, M. J., and E. Sheshinski, 1978. Optimal redistributive taxation when individual welfare depends upon relative income. *Quarterly Journal of Economics* 92:589–601.

Rubin (2002) observed the relationship between progressive taxes and the human emotion of envy:

Rubin, P. H., 2002. *Darwinian Politics: The Evolutionary Origins of Freedom*. Rutgers University Press, New Brunswick NJ.

On taxes as the outcome of political processes, see:

Hettich, W., and S. L. Winer, 1999. *Democratic Choice and Taxation: A Theoretical and Empirical Analysis*. Cambridge University Press, New York.

On the theory of Pareto-improving tax reform, see Guesnerie (1995). On the Dalton criterion for tax reform, see Dalton (1920).

Dalton, H., 1920. The measurement of the inequality of income. *Economic Journal* 30:348–61.
Guesnerie, R., 1995. *A Contribution to the Pure Theory of Taxation*. Cambridge University Press, Cambridge U.K.

9.2 Capital and other tax bases

On time inconsistency and taxation, see Kydland and Prescott (1980). Finn E. Kydland and Edward E. Prescott received the Nobel Prize in economics in 2004.

Kydland, F., and E. Prescott, 1980. Dynamic optimal taxation, rational expectations, and optimal control. *Journal of Economic Dynamics and Control* 2:79–91.

On who pays the corporate income tax, see:

Harberger, A. C., 1962. The incidence of the corporation income tax. *Journal of Political Economy* 70:215–40.

On the excess burden of taxation and the corporate income tax, see Gordon (1985); on the relationship between personal taxation and corporate financing decisions, see Graham (1999); on dividends as a signal, see Bernheim and Wantz (1995); and on means of financing, see Modigliani and Miller (1958). Franco Modigliani received the Nobel Prize in economics in 1985.

Bernheim, D. B., and A. Wantz, 1995. A tax-based test of the dividend signaling hypothesis. *American Economic Review* 85:532–51.
Graham, J. R., 1999. Do personal taxes affect corporate financing decisions? *Journal of Public Economics* 73:147–85.
Gordon, R. H., 1985. Taxation of corporate capital income: Tax revenues versus tax distortions. *Quarterly Journal of Economics* 100:1–29.
Modigliani, F., and M. Miller, 1958. The cost of capital, corporation finance, and the theory of investment. *American Economic Review* 48:261–99.

On the bias toward home investment, see Feldstein and Horiaka (1980).

Feldstein, M. S., and C. Horiaka, 1980. Domestic savings and international capital flows. *Economic Journal* 90:314–29.

The theory of taxation of consumption and capital is set out in:

Batina, R. G., and T. Ihori, 2000. *Consumption Tax Policy and the Taxation of Capital.* Oxford University Press, Oxford.

On the basis for the income tax, see:

Haig, R. M., 1921. *The Federal Income Tax*. Columbia University Press, New York.
Simons, H. C., 1938. *Personal Income Taxation*. University of Chicago Press, Chicago IL.

For a proposal for an expenditure tax, see Kaldor (1955). On the income tax and expenditure taxes, see Pechman (1990). Fullerton, Shoven, and Whalley (1983) simulated replacement of the U.S. income tax with an expenditure tax.

Fullerton, D., J. B. Shoven, and J. Whalley, 1983. Replacing the U.S. income tax with a progressive consumption tax: A sequenced general equilibrium approach. *Journal of Public Economics* 20:3–23.
Kaldor, N., 1955. *An Expenditure Tax*. George Allen & Unwin Ltd., London.
Pechman, J. E., 1990. The future of the income tax. *American Economic Review* 80: 1–20.

On the ethics of estate and gift taxes, see Erreygers and Vandevelde (1997); on how people respond to those taxes, see Poterba (2001).

Erreygers, G., and T. Vandevelde, 1997. *Is Inheritance Legitimate? Ethical and Economic Aspects of Wealth Transfers*. Springer, Heidelberg.
Poterba, J. M., 2001. Estate and gift taxes and inter vivos giving in the U.S. *Journal of Public Economics* 79:237–64.

On inflation as a tax, see:

Barro, R. J., 1972. Inflationary finance and the welfare cost of inflation. *Journal of Political Economy* 80:978–1001.
Phelps, E. S., 1973. Inflation in the theory of public finance. *Swedish Journal of Economics* 75:67–82.

On lotteries as taxation, see Gully and Scott (1993), Walker (1998), and Beenstock, Goldin, and Haitovsky (2000).

Beenstock, M., E. Goldin, and Y. Haitovsky, 2000. What jackpot? The optimal lottery tax. *European Journal of Political Economy* 16:655–71.
Gully, O. D., and F. A. Scott, 1993. The demand for wagering on state-operated lotto games. *National Tax Journal* 46:13–22.
Walker, I., 1998. The economic analysis of lotteries. *Economic Policy* 27:357–402.

On taxation through financial repression, see Fry (1982) and Giovannini and de Melo (1993).

Fry, M., 1982. Models of financially repressed developing economies. *World Development* 10:731–50.
Giovannini, A., and M. de Melo, 1993. Government revenue from financial repression. *American Economic Review* 83:953–63.

On indirect taxes as an accompaniment of direct taxation, see Atkinson and Stiglitz (1976), Christiansen (1984), and Saez (2002).

Atkinson, A. B., and J. Stiglitz, 1976. The design of tax structure: Direct versus indirect taxation. *Journal of Public Economics* 6:55–75.
Christiansen, V. A., 1984. Which commodity taxes should supplement the income tax? *Journal of Public Economics* 24:195–220.
Saez, E., 2002. The desirability of commodity taxation under non-linear income taxation and heterogeneous tastes. *Journal of Public Economics* 83:217–30.

On tax evasion as a reason for using both direct and indirect taxes, see:

Boadway, R., M. Marchand, and P. Pestieau, 1994. Towards a theory of direct-indirect tax mix. *Journal of Public Economics* 55:71–88.
De Marco, Antonio deViti, 1936/1950. *First Principles of Public Finance*. Jonathan Cape, London.

On differences in tax systems, see:

Sandford, C., 2000. *Why Tax Systems Differ: A Comparative Study of the Political Economy of Taxation*. Fiscal Publications, Bath.

9.3 Fiscal federalism

A standard reference on fiscal federalism is:

Oates, W. E., 1972. *Fiscal Federalism*. Harcourt Brace Jovanovich, New York.

For a review of fiscal-federal institutional structures, see:

Inman, R. P., and D. L. Rubinfeld, 1997. Rethinking federalism. *Journal of Economic Perpsectives* 11:43–64.

The framework of exit, voice, and loyalty was described in:

Hirschman, A., 1970. *Exit, Voice, and Loyalty*. Harvard University Press, Cambridge MA.

On fiscal federalism and risk sharing, see Asdrubali, Sørensen, and Yosha (1996) on the United States and Goldberg and Levi (2000) on Europe.

Asdrubali, P., B. E. Sørensen, and O. Yosha, 1996. Channels of interstate risk sharing: United States 1963–90. *Quarterly Journal of Economics* 111, 1081–110.
Goldberg, M. A., and M. D. Levi, 2000. The European Union as a country portfolio. *European Journal of Political Economy* 16:411–27.

On source and residence-based taxation, see:

Ihori, T., 1991. Capital income taxation in a world economy: A territorial system versus a residence system. *Economic Journal* 101:958–65.

On equality in a federal system, see Buchanan (1950). The normative case for assigning to a federal government the responsibility to finance entitlements was made by Brown and Oates (1987).

Brown, C. C., and W. E. Oates, 1987. Assistance to the poor in a federal system. *Journal of Public Economics* 32:307–30.
Buchanan, J. M., 1950. Federalism and fiscal equity. *American Economic Review* 40:583–99.

On tax competition and coordination, see:

Genser, B., 1992. Tax competition and harmonization in federal economies. In H.-J. Viscera (Ed.), *European Integration in the World Economy*. Springer, Heidelberg, pp. 184–205.
Sørensen, P. B., 2000. Tax coordination: Its desirability and redistribution implications. *Economic Policy* 31:431–72.

On tax competition as a discipline on governments, see:

Edwards, J., and M. Keen, 1996. Tax competition and Leviathan. *European Economic Review* 40:113–34.
Eggert, W., 2001. Capital tax competition with socially wasteful government consumption. *European Journal of Political Economy* 17:517–29.
Rauscher, M., 1998. Leviathan and competition among jurisdictions: The case of benefit taxation. *Journal of Urban Economics* 44:59–67.
Wilson, J. D., 1986. A theory of interregional tax competition. *Journal of Urban Economics* 19:296–315.

On capitalization of taxes in property values as an impediment to avoiding leviathan government, see:

Caplan, B., 2001. Standing Tiebout on his head: Tax capitalization and the monopoly power of local governments. *Public Choice* 108:101–22.

On information and disciplining through comparative performance of governments, see:

Besley, T., and A. Case, 1995. Incumbent behavior: Vote-seeking, tax-setting and yardstick competition. *American Economic Review* 85:25–45.
Salmon, P., 1987. Decentralization as an incentive scheme. *Oxford Review of Economic Policy* 3:24–34.

On soft budgets and the holdup problem of fiscal federalism, see:

Goodspeed, T., 2002. Bailouts in a federation. *International Tax and Public Finance* 9:409–21.

On accountability and decentralization, see Seabright (1996). On decentralized government and corruption, see Fisman and Gatti (2002) and Arikan (2004). On fiscal federalism and rent seeking, see Wärneryd (1998).

Arikan, G. G., 2004. Fiscal decentralization: A remedy for corruption. *International Tax and Public Finance* 11:175–95.
Fisman, R., and R. Gatti, 2002. Decentralization and corruption: Evidence across countries. *Journal of Public Economics* 83:325–45.

Seabright, P., 1996. Accountability and decentralization in government: An incomplete contracts model. *European Economic Review* 40:61–89.
Wärneryd, K., 1998. Distributional conflict and jurisdictional organization. *Journal of Public Economics* 69:435–50.

Baqir (2002) presented evidence showing that public spending increases with the size of jurisdictions.

Baqir, R., 2002. Districting and government overspending. *Journal of Political Economy* 110:1318–54.

On constitutional constraints in fiscal-federal systems, see:

Vaubel, R., 1996. Constitutional safeguards against centralization in federal states: An international cross-section analysis. *Constitutional Political Economy* 7:79–102.

On the decomposition of states, see:

Bolton, P., and G. Roland, 1997. The break-up of countries: A political economy analysis. *Quarterly Journal of Economics* 112:1057–90.
Hillman, A. L., 2005. Political institutions, jurisdictional boundaries, and rent creation. *Keio Economic Studies* 42:25–37. W. J. Ethier and M. Yano (Eds.), special issue in honor of Professor Michihiro Ohyama.

For views on the need for global government, see:

Tanzi, V., 2008. The future of fiscal federalism. *European Journal of Political Economy* 24:705–12.
Vaubel, R., 2009. The future of fiscal federalism and the need for global government: A response to Vito Tanzi. *European Journal of Political Economy* 25.

10

THE NEED FOR GOVERNMENT

This final chapter is about the need for government. In section 1, we consider the growth of government from the time of Adam Smith and ask whether the growth of government has been consistently socially beneficial. In section 2, we investigate the role in a society of trust, also known as social capital. We conclude in section 3 with an overview of why economists' views on the need for government can differ.

10.1 Growth of Government and the Need for Government

A measure of the size of government is by fiscal criteria of taxation and public spending. Measurement of the size of government includes, however, also regulation by governments of economic activity and ownership of firms by governments. Hence, the scope of taxation and public spending, or public finance, is only a partial measure of the size of government. We include public policy as an indication of involvement of government when we consider resolution of externality problems and the seeking of paternalistic objectives through regulation and when we consider, for example, the role of international trade policy in social insurance and income redistribution.

A. How and why did government grow?

The questions of how and why government grew take us to economic history. A course in economic history provides a comprehensive background for answering our questions. We shall make do with a more limited perspective.

Table 10.1 shows social spending by government from the time of publication of Adam Smith's *Wealth of Nations* in 1776 up to the mid-19th century. Only in the countries shown in the table did public spending take place for public education and to assist the poor. We see that the public spending, where it existed, was small or miniscule. Adding private charity would not significantly change the picture in table 10.1.

Incomes and the quality of life

In the pre-industrial agrarian societies, income derived primarily from agriculture. The royal family and noble families owned the land through inheritance, and the masses of the people worked the land as serfs, often subject to restrictions on moving elsewhere to another "master." Artisans and others providing services could congregate in villages or urban areas. Being poor was generally viewed as fate or divine providence, as was being of the nobility and thereby being wealthy,

TABLE 10.1. GOVERNMENT SOCIAL SPENDING UP TO THE MID-19TH CENTURY

Country	Year	Government relief for the poor (proportion of GNP)	Public education, primary through university (proportion of GNP)
England and Wales	1776	1.59%	Zero
	1820/21	2.66%	Zero
	1850	1.07%	0.07%
United States	1850	0.13%	0.33%
Netherlands	1790	1.70%	
	1850	1.38%	
Belgium	1820	1.03%	
	1850	0.28%	0.38%
Sweden	1829	0.02%	
Other Countries	1776–1815	Zero or negligible	Zero or negligible

Source: Lindert (2004).

or being king or queen. Social mobility was negligible. The nobility intermarried among themselves, did not necessarily work, and employed servants. With ownership of the principal productive resource – land – unequally distributed, income distribution was also unequal. A good job for people from families of modest means was often to be "in service," to serve the hereditary landed rich.

Public health was not well understood. Water supply and sewage often intermixed. People walking in city streets might have to avoid sewerage being thrown on their heads when chamber pots were emptied through windows. With water supply insufficiently pure, people drank wine or beer as substitutes and persistent inebriation was common. Life spans were often short, with people succumbing to ailments that not-yet-discovered antibiotics would have readily cured. Medical practitioners could hasten death by their "cures," which included treatment such as bleeding by use of leaches to "purge" the body of its ills. Women were at substantial risk in childbirth because the role of bacteria in causing infections was not understood.[1] The role of the housefly in transmitting disease was misunderstood: the disease-carrying fly was labeled "friendly" because in distinction to other insects, it does not bite. Dental hygiene was not understood and teeth did not last long, on average. With mortality high, cities often grew in population only because poor arrivals from the countryside exceeded the number of poor people dying in the squalor of the city.

At the time of publication of Adam Smith's *Wealth of Nations*, in England the authority of the monarchy had been diminished by limitations on royal

[1] Bacteria had been observed in 1683 by the Dutch lens maker Anthonie van Leeuwenhoek (1632–1723) but the link to disease only came to be understood much later. The first antibiotic, penicillin, although discovered in 1928, did not become widely used until the 1940s.

prerogatives that had been instituted over the course of time in return for parliament providing tax revenue. Parliament had ruled for a while without a king, under Oliver Cromwell. When votes in parliament took place on taxes, the landowning classes were voting on how to tax themselves. The right to vote and to be a political representative was based on privilege conferred by ownership of land. In England, a person who owned land in more than one electorate had the legal right to vote more than once. Democracy was not "one man, one vote" – rather, a man might have no vote or another man might be eligible to vote more than once. It was only privileged *men* who voted. Outside of the United Kingdom, with few exceptions, government was autocratic. English rule over Ireland was also autocratic.

Sources of government revenue

The main sources of tax revenue were excise taxes and import duties. These taxes could be collected with relative administrative ease. Duties were levied on tea, sugar, salt, and other spices. The American Revolution against colonial rule began with the dumping into Boston Harbor of tea that the English king had sought to tax. In different countries, smuggling became a source of private income as people attempted to evade the excise taxes and to sell at the high domestic prices. Smuggling introduced corruption as government officials responsible for preventing smuggling shared in the profits.

Rulers could also obtain revenue by selling the right to be a domestic – or foreign-trade monopolist. The ideology of mercantilism, which Adam Smith criticized, saw the objective as being to sell to other countries and not to buy, and to use gold and silver received in payment for exports to finance an army that could conquer or defend as required. With rulers not wishing to provide gold and silver by buying (or importing) from a rival who could use the wealth against them, a colonial empire was a way of avoiding payments to foreigners as well as expanding tax bases through control over resources and people. Monarchs were often preoccupied with predation, either through their own predatory intent or the designs of other rulers seeking to take lands and colonies away from them.

Private bankers might lend to finance the monarchs' wars of conquest or their defense needs. The lenders were often people not bound by usury laws. If a ruler lost a war, the lenders could experience difficulty in obtaining repayment of the debt. There was also the risk that because the ruler was sovereign, the ruler might simply decide not to repay whether a war was won or lost.

The Industrial Revolution and the middle class

The Industrial Revolution ended the role of land as the primary source of wealth. Energy from steam replaced the energy of animals and humans as well as the energy of wind in windmills and sails of ships. At the onset of industrialization, investment in infrastructure was generally private. Private toll roads, canals, and railroads were built. Long-distance travel took place in privately owned ships.

We observed when considering public goods that lighthouses were privately constructed. The main concern of government was national defense and internal security, including the protection of the monarchy from insurrection. As we saw in chapter 5 in considering paternalism with regard to information about contraception, there was a presumption that the landed rich were genetically superior to the poor. However, the profits from private investments created private wealth and a nouveau-riche population that eventually received the right to vote and intermarried with the nobility. Intermarriage provided the nouveau riche with titles and status, and members of the nobility who had became impoverished relative to the requisites of their lifestyles were provided with money. For some landed nobility, marrying for money thus became a substitute for ongoing marrying among themselves. The Industrial Revolution and the development of a middle class began a process of growth of government through broadly based taxation and public spending.[2]

Wagner's law

As incomes in the 19th century grew, the German economist, Adolph Wagner (1835–1917), noticed that the size of government grew more than commensurately. He formulated a proposition that has become known as *Wagner's law.*

> *Wagner's law states that the size of government as measured by public spending increases proportionately more than the growth of national income (Wagner, 1893).*

By the beginning of the 21st century, social spending of governments in high-income countries had grown substantially compared to the absent or small social spending indicated in table 10.1. Growth of social spending particularly occurred in the course of the 20th century. Table 10.2 shows combined changes in public spending during the 20th century on welfare payments, unemployment benefits, retirement or pension benefits, and housing subsidies in high-income countries. Social spending grew considerably in all countries. The highest share of social spending to gross national product (GNP) was found in the four Scandinavian "welfare states" where extensive social insurance was provided. As a general tendency, the data in table 10.2 confirm Wagner's law for social spending. In Germany, social spending grew after reunification resulted in transfers of income

[2] An income tax was introduced in England in 1798 to pay for a war against Napoleon. Expenses of the U.S. Civil War led the Northern government to introduce an income tax in 1862. In both cases, the tax rates and tax revenue were small. Income taxes including taxes on corporate profits did not become prominent tax bases until administrative tax-collection capabilities were established in the 20th century. An income tax had been levied in the Han dynasty in China 2,000 years ago: tax revenue was also collected in China during the Han dynasty by a property owner being asked to declare a value as the base for a property tax, with the government having the right, however, to buy the property at the declared price.

TABLE 10.2. THE SHARE OF SOCIAL SPENDING TO GNP IN THE 20TH CENTURY

Country	1910	1930	1980	1990	1995
Japan	0.18%	0.21%	10%	12%	12%
United States	0.56%	0.56%	11%	12%	14%
Australia	1.12%	2.11%	11%	14%	15%
Greece	0	0.07%	9%	14%	14%
Portugal	0	0	10%	13%	15%
Canada	0	0.31%	13%	17%	18%
New Zealand	1.35%	2.43%	16%	22%	18%
Ireland	*	3.74%	16%	18%	18%
Spain	0.02%	0.07%	13%	17%	19%
Austria	0	1.20%	23%	25%	21%
United Kingdom	1.38%	2.24%	17%	18%	23%
Italy	0	0.08%	17%	21%	24%
Netherlands	0.39%	1.03%	27%	28%	26%
Germany	0.59%	4.82%	20%	20%	25%
France	0.81%	1.05%	23%	24%	27%
Belgium	0.43%	0.56%	22%	23%	27%
Norway	1.18%	2.39%	19%	26%	28%
Demark	1.75%	3.11%	26%	27%	31%
Finland	0.90%	2.97%	18%	25%	32%
Sweden	1.03%	2.59%	30%	32%	33%

* Did not exist as an independent state.

through social spending to the population living in the former Communist eastern part of the country. Low social spending in Japan reflects a work ethic and a culture of self-reliance and, therefore, absence of a need for social spending; Japan also did not allow immigration. The United States and Australia are immigrant countries that sought to attract productive immigrants by incomplete social insurance, thereby providing incentives for immigration of self-reliant people. Canada has been a country of immigration but with more extensive social insurance and with wealth criteria for immigration.

Contradictions of Wagner's law

Wagner's law is not uniformly verified: exceptions occur in table 10.2 for New Zealand, Austria, and marginally in the Netherlands. Returning to table 10.1, we see a rejection of Wagner's law in the first half of the 19th century for spending on relief for the poor, most pronouncedly in England and Wales and Belgium, and also in the Netherlands. Why did social spending decline? The English political economist, Thomas Malthus (1766–1834), proposed that societies were caught in poverty traps because reproduction was limited only by people not having the means to feed themselves and their offspring. Malthus's idea that higher incomes of the poor leads to population growth that eventually restores incomes to subsistence levels made assistance to the poor self-defeating, because assistance to the poor over the course of time could not be effective in raising living standards.

Explanations for Wagner's law

The exceptions aside, what underlies the general tendency expressed in Wagner's law for the size of government to grow? There are explanations that focus on (1) increased demand for public spending, (2) increases in the supply of tax revenue, and (3) political-economy reasons, including extension of the voting franchise and the arise of interest groups with common sources of income and thereby common self-interested public-policy objectives.

Demand-side influences on the growth of government

Demand for public spending increases when governments are assigned responsibilities to achieve social objectives.

Public goods

If public goods are normal goods, demand by voters and taxpayers increases with income (with prices given). Wagner's law implies that the income elasticity of demand for public goods exceeds 1. The prisoners' dilemma, information asymmetries, and free-rider incentives that prevent efficient Lindahl supply result in governments being given responsibility for financing and usually also supplying public goods. Governments remain subject to asymmetric information about citizens' preferences concerning public goods (we do not expect governments to use the Clarke tax to elicit information); however, compulsory taxes and government borrowing allow governments to supply public goods where no supply may be possible if reliance were on voluntary payment. Demand for public goods increases the size of government when growth of the middle class transforms previous private goods to public goods. For the wealthy landed classes, roads were private on their estates and recreation was private on their personal croquet and tennis courts, polo fields, and private hunting grounds. The sons of the wealthy (more so than daughters) attended private (also called public) schools and thereafter exclusive colleges and universities financed by user prices. As the middle class grew, services that had provided private benefit and had been privately supplied for the rich became public goods collectively sought by the middle classes through public finance. We recall the empirical observation known as Director's law, which is that public spending on public goods principally benefits the middle class.

Externalities

As incomes increase, people become more bothered by and attentive to adverse externalities. Clean water and, eventually, clean air become important. Resolving externalities associated with public health comes to be understood as important for the quality of life. People also seek protection from the externalities of crime and personal harassment – and from cigarette smoke of others when research revealed that inhaling smoke from others' cigarettes reduces the length and quality of life.

Social insurance and entitlements

The entitlements of social insurance increase public spending. There is more to insure against when people have higher incomes and wealth because of the greater relative personal loss of having little or nothing in a wealthy society. We saw that income transfers to the poor and disadvantaged can be viewed as a public good; government grows when people want more social equality (a public good).[3]

Demographics, health, and income transfers to the old

Demographics and health affect the size of government. Improvements in health care result in people living longer. The increasing numbers of people who survive to reach retirement age place demands on government to ensure that old people live with dignity. When people live longer, demand increases for public financed health-care entitlements for older people.

Paternalism and regulation

Demand for paternalistic policies and regulation increases with income. People become less gullible and want protection from charlatans. For example, for considerable periods, gullible people could be sold "snake oil" and other "medications" as a cure for various ailments. As income grew and education advanced, people became more conscious of fraud and product safety. There was a demand for government to regulate pharmaceuticals and drugs. Where decentralized government provided the opportunities, communities chose various other paternalistic policies consistent with sought-after standards of life.

Supply of revenue and the growth of government

These are demand-side influences on the growth of government. When government grows because of influences from the demand side and government responds benevolently (there are no political or bureaucratic principal–agent problems), benefit can be inferred from a government's response to the demand for increased public spending. People would express their demand through markets if possible: with markets failing to provide efficient outcomes because of asymmetric information that impedes private payment for public goods and

[3] For example, as incomes increased, child labor declined as parents sent children to school. After significant numbers of parents had sent children to school, schooling was made compulsory and government schools were introduced or expanded to accommodate the needs of compulsory schooling.

private resolution of externality problems – and if markets cater to demands that societies paternalistically find unpleasant or regard as harmful – people turn to government. However, governments then need the requisite revenue to fulfill the designated responsibilities. Unavailability of tax bases and the Laffer curve limit supply of tax revenue and thereby constrain growth of government – as does tax evasion.

Yet, also, because of political and bureaucratic principal–agent problems and fiscal illusion, governments can spend more than voters and taxpayers wish and can choose spending from which taxpayers and voters do not benefit: when government grows because of increased supply of tax revenue, there is more ambivalence about social benefits than when government grows because of increased demand by voters and taxpayers for public spending.

How does the access of government to tax revenue increase? There are a number of ways.

Growth of the tax base

Tax revenue grows when taxation opportunities expand. In the course of economic growth, people come to have above-subsistence incomes that can be taxed. Tax bases also expand when people who previously lived a self-sufficient life provide for themselves and their families through taxable market transactions.

Women in the labor market

The entry of women into the labor market expanded revenue opportunities for governments. Women in the labor market earn taxable incomes, as do (in principle) child minders and household domestic help that take over past traditional household activities from the women who are working. Entry of women into the workforce was, in particular, a response to men leaving the labor market for military service during World War II in the mid-20th century. When the war ended, the precedent for women working rather than staying at home had been established. The availability of effective contraception beginning in the 1960s further freed women to participate in the labor market. Because marriage no longer implied the necessity of children – or an unpredictable number of children – women could be relied on for stable labor-force participation. Further change occurred to expand the tax base when women chose careers and deferred marriage or chose not to marry, as well as when social norms changed so that marriage and children and financial dependence on men were no longer necessary attributes of a relationship.

Amenability of people to taxation

Advances in transportation and communication expanded tax revenue for governments by allowing people to be taxed who had previously been out of reach of government tax collectors. The growth of the corporate sector reduced self-employment and increased the proportion of workers for whom employers deducted taxation at source for delivery to government. The transactions costs of collecting taxes declined for governments and opportunities for tax evasion declined for taxpayers.

Fiscal illusion

Fiscal illusion increases supply of tax revenue for governments because taxpayers do not know that they are paying taxes and therefore do not seek to lower taxes through political means. We observed in chapter 4 how taxpayers can be subject to fiscal illusion regarding payment of indirect taxes and government borrowing.[4]

Political influences on growth of government

The third category of influence on growth of government is political.

Majority voting

Majority voting can increase growth of government. When a minority pays a substantial part of taxes, the majority has an incentive to vote for more public finance, and taxation and public spending increase.

Extension of the franchise

The franchise was originally based on ownership of property because the propertied classes feared appropriation of their property through majority voting. The franchise was extended when property was no longer the principal determinant of incomes. After the franchise was extended, the majority still had an incentive to vote to transfer to itself income from the minority. Nonetheless, we have seen that the beneficiaries of government income transfers are generally the poor and not the median voter. Conversely, Director's law reflects the extension of the franchise to the middle class. We also observed that coalitions can form between the rich and the poor to tax the middle class: the rich thereby can have an incentive to support the political party that favors extensive redistribution.

Voting by women

We also saw that women tend to vote in favor of expansion of the social insurance role of government because of their vulnerability in the traditional family to the loss of their husband who was the primary income earner. We noted the evidence indicating that the extension of the franchise to women increased the size of government.

Voting by government bureaucrats

Growth of government increases the size of the administering government bureaucracy. The government bureaucracy wants growth of government for

[4] Another source of fiscal illusion occurs through payment of property taxes. If people who rent do not pay property taxes directly but rather the property taxes are included in the rent paid, renters may not be aware that part of their rent payment is a tax to the government.

self-interested reasons. Reflecting voting by government bureaucrats, voter support in constituencies in or around capital cities is generally greater for political parties that favor growth of government. We can envisage the consequences for growth of government if a majority of voters were government employees whose salaries are paid for through tax-financed public spending. Growth of government feeds back on itself. Larger governments require larger bureaucracies, which have more bureaucrats who vote for a political party that favors high taxation and larger government budgets. We noted proposals to limit voting rights of employees of government bureaucracies on fiscal issues.

Fiscal federalism and centralized government

Fiscal federalism facilitates growth of government when centralization of taxation reduces competition among governments through choice of location. Tax competition does not restrain tax increases. There is less demand for accountability and transparency when governments in subjurisdictions spend revenue provided by the federal government. Public spending can increase through "holdups" and moral hazard. It is also the case that with centralized government, public spending can increase when the common pool of tax revenue is controlled through majority voting.[5]

Interest groups and the size of government

Interests groups, particularly often associated with international trade, have influenced the size of government.

Market specialization and interest groups

Markets allow specialization in production – which, as we have noted, was called by Adam Smith *division of labor*. The specialization provides incentives to form special-interest groups whose members have a common interest in rent seeking. Outcomes of rent seeking are influenced by asymmetries between political effectiveness of voters and interest groups. The collective-action issues that we were addressed in chapter 3 arise: because of income effects, larger groups contribute more to the collective objective of influencing policy decisions; however, smaller groups have advantages in monitoring deviations from cooperation and members of income-based interest groups are motivated by larger stakes in the outcome of political persuasion than individual voters, who have smaller stakes in each policy issue and who confront multiple interest groups, each focused on influencing political decisions on their particular issue. The organizational advantage of

[5] In the United States, the growth of government in the 20th century was accompanied by change in the fiscal federal structure of taxation. At the beginning of the 20th century, spending by the federal government was half of the spending of state and local governments; at the end of the 20th century, the proportions had reversed, with the federal government spending twice as much as state and local governments.

interest groups in collective action results in public policy and public spending that increases the size of government. A source of the growth of government is therefore the specialization in production associated with markets, through interest group activities.

Protectionist policies

Income-based interest groups have had particular advantages when the common source of income has been in an industry that competes with imports. Rents were often created through protectionist international-trade policies. The protectionist policies increased the incomes of people with capital or skills specific to employment in import-competing industries. In general, more voters lose from protection of an industry than gain. Protectionist policies, however, were rarely the focal issue of an election, leaving protectionist decisions to political discretion. The protectionist policies were assisted by framing because the policies could be explained as required to prevent foreign competition "decreasing our own people's incomes" or "depriving our own people of jobs."[6]

Liberalization of international trade

As they become wealthier, people diversify their income sources, through asset diversification by buying stocks and bonds. The asset diversification spreads risk and so provides insurance against declines in income from any one source. A person whose diversified sources of income match the components of national income wants national income to be maximized, which is achieved by the efficient policy of free international trade. Special-interest groups with narrowly based income sources thus decline in prominence as asset diversification increases, as then does the demand for special-interest policies. Although calls for protectionist policies do not cease, by the beginning of the 21st century, governments in high-income countries had withdrawn considerably from restricting

[6] The U.S. Civil War is a case where common interest in trade policy was geographically concentrated. Although usually predominantly associated with the issue of slavery, the U.S. Civil War also involved differing positions of North and South on international trade policy. The comparative advantage in international trade of the United States and also, in particular, the comparative advantage of the South with regard to the North, was in agriculture (tobacco and cotton) for which slaves were specifically used. The industrial North benefited from protectionist policies for its manufactured-goods industries, in which the United States had a comparative disadvantage in world markets but in which the North had a comparative advantage relative to the South. The South benefited from free trade, which enabled its agricultural exports to be sold abroad at higher relative prices in foreign markets than could be obtained if, because of protectionist policies, international trade did not take place and trade was restricted to within the United States, with the South's agricultural goods being traded domestically for the North's industrial manufactured goods. However, also, before the Civil War, the tariff was the principal source of revenue for the federal government (an income tax was introduced by the North in the course of the war; see footnote 2). Before the Civil War, the tariff was thus used for revenue purposes. The debate over the tariff was therefore not only about protectionism but also about the size of government through the revenue that would be available to the federal government.

international trade. Trade liberalization had taken place through a process of "exchange of market access," whereby in multilateral agreements governments had reduced protectionist barriers and had allowed each others' exporters to sell in their respective domestic markets. Domestic import-competing industries were exposed to foreign competition, which entailed a political cost through loss of political support, but at the political gain of increased incomes in export industries. "Exchange of market access" resulted, therefore, in liberalization of international trade. Domestic-asset markets had at the same time expanded and become integrated into an international capital market: the further asset diversification opportunities additionally diminished the incentives to call on governments to choose protectionist policies that increase narrowly based special-interest incomes.[7]

International trade policy and size of government

Does openness of an economy – or the value of international trade relative to national income – increase the size of government? That is, is greater social insurance sought and provided when a country relies more on international trade – that is, when reliance on transactions with foreigners increases. Our view of social insurance has been in terms of the uncertainty confronting people behind a veil of ignorance before they know who they will be and before they therefore know their income-earning opportunities. After people have emerged from behind the veil of ignorance, they confront uncertainty about their incomes because of the possibility of changes in relative prices. In particular, people earning incomes from industry-specific skills and capital gain when the relative price of the industry's output increases and conversely lose when the relative price of the industry's output falls.

In principle, uncertainty about personal incomes due to changes in domestic relative prices should affect the demand for social insurance and public spending

[7] Multilateral trade liberalization was facilitated by the Most-Favored–Nation Clause of international trade agreements, which requires that reductions in import duties (or tariffs) provided to imports from one country automatically apply to imports from all countries with which a country has an international trade agreement. A concern of governments was that if they entered into a bilateral agreement to liberalize trade, the "concessions" that they receive from the foreign government that is the partner in the bilateral agreement would be rendered valueless by the foreign government offering superior "concessions" to another governments in another bilateral agreement. For example, in a bilateral agreement for exchange of market access, a government could receive a concession of a 20 percent reduction in a foreign government's import duties. Then, in a new bilateral agreement with another country's government, the same foreign government could proceed to provide a 30 percent reduction in import duties. The 30 percent reduction in import duties devalues the worth of the original agreement with the first country, whose exporters are disadvantaged by only having a 20 percent reduction in import duties. The Most-Favored–Nation Clause of international trade agreements ensures that trade "concessions" received in the process of exchange of market access are not devalued because a reduction in duties that applies to one country also applies to other countries. Because of the Most-Favored–Nation clause, international trade agreements have been multilateral rather than bilateral. Broadly based liberalization of international trade in consequence took place.

no differently than uncertainty due to changes in world relative prices. Nonetheless, there are differences in public-policy responses.

Protectionist policies close an economy from international trade and thereby also from foreign-originating changes in relative prices of traded goods. People earning incomes in import-competing industries gain at the expense, however, of income losses for the economy at large (because of the inefficiency of the protectionist policies shown in chapter 4).

Protection can also be described as a social-insurance contract: the contract stipulates that an industry disadvantaged by changes in foreign prices will receive compensation through import duties that protect the industry against the cheaper imports. Consumers at large, of course, would gain from the cheaper imports: the social-insurance contract is restricted to income redistribution to benefit people earning income in import-competing industries.

As an alternative to protection, governments can directly provide social insurance based on changes in world prices (or the terms of trade). Import competition is an arbitrary reason for a reduction in income or losing a job: nonetheless, framing creates opportunities for social insurance to be provided because of changes in world prices. When events that change incomes have origins outside the country, people whose incomes decline can be perceived – and portrayed – as meriting compensation because foreigners are to blame. A case is then made for income protection against income or job losses due to change originating abroad, in addition to the social insurance that exists.[8]

The empirical evidence suggests that more open economies tend to have larger governments expressed in greater social spending relative to national income. The reason can be additional social insurance when incomes are exposed to change through international trade. Another explanation is that whereas personal incomes in traded-goods industries are subject to risk, public spending can be regarded as risk-free: risk-aversion is therefore proposed as a reason for larger government when an economy is more open.[9]

The size of government depends on the various different influences that we have noted. The Scandinavian welfare states, which have the largest size government because of their extensive social insurance contracts, are open economies: however, there is no necessary link between their being open and the decision to adopt a comprehensive social insurance contract.

[8] For example, in 1974, the U.S. government implemented Trade Adjustment Assistance, which provides an entitlement to an income transfer contingent on workers having lost their job because of import competition. There have been similar programs elsewhere. The number of beneficiaries of such programs is generally small relative to beneficiaries of more general unemployment benefits because of the need to certify that a job loss occurred specifically because of import competition and not for another reason.

[9] If government size is defined to include interventionist policies, governments that are large in being interventionist can also be expected to be interventionist in international trade, which results in a negative relationship between size of government and openness to international trade.

B. Social benefit and the growth of government

We have identified different reasons for the growth of government that occurred in the 20th century. All the various reasons matter. Empirical determination of the significance of the different reasons is hindered by simultaneity in the occurrence of the different effects. Demand for public spending as well as public policy grew, tax bases expanded to supply increased revenue for governments, and growth of government was influenced politically by changes through voting and the rent seeking of special interests. We now ask the question:

Has growth of government been socially beneficial?

The answer depends on the time dimension; we shall consider two. First, we look at the growth of government beginning in the 18th century when Adam Smith lived. Then, we shall look at data on the growth of government in the latter half of the 20th century.

Benefits of growth of government since Adam Smith

As noted in chapter 1, Adam Smith described virtue and social benefit through markets. Markets have indeed provided social benefit since the time of Adam Smith, and those societies that sought to progress without markets were unsuccessful (hence, Hayek's case for the market). However, not only markets but also the public finance and public policy of government have brought substantial social benefit. The growth of government in high-income societies since the time of Adam Smith has facilitated the high incomes by providing the rule of law, allowing supply of public goods, and resolving externality problems. Paternalistic public policies have addressed hyperbolic discounting, bounded rationality, and framing (such as arise in the Allais paradox), and there has been resolution of issues of censorship and associated inconsistencies between Pareto efficiency and free choice (in ways in which not everyone may agree). Absence of private insurance for personal incomes has been addressed through social insurance, which has reduced insecurities of life through the government-provided entitlements. For ordinary people at the time of Adam Smith, life was lived under harsh material conditions. The only people who might hark back with nostalgia to the time of Adam Smith when the role of government was miniscule are the descendants of those who would not have been ordinary people but rather would have enjoyed lives of hereditary privilege.[10]

[10] The benefits of the growth of government between the 18th and 20th centuries for high-income societies were documented by Peter H. Lindert in his 2004 book, *Growing Public*, which also provided the data in tables 10.1 and 10.2. Benefits from growth of government through colonization depended on the identity of the colonizer. In many cases, colonization was extremely disadvantageous for the local peoples. For example, on the case of the Belgian Congo, which was the personal domain of King Léopard II of the Belgians, see Adam Hochschild (1998).

TABLE 10.3. INCREASE IN PUBLIC SPENDING 1960–90

	Large governments[a]		Medium governments[b]		Small governments[c]	
	1960	1990	1960	1990	1960	1990
Government spending	31.0	55.1	29.3	44.9	23.0	34.6
Consumption	13.2	18.9	12.2	17.4	12.2	17.4
Transfers and subsidies	11.9	30.6	10.4	21.5	6.9	14.0
Interest	1.5	6.4	1.3	4.2	1.3	2.9
Investment	3.1	2.4	3.2	2.0	2.2	2.2

[a] Large governments had public spending more than 50 percent of GNP in 1990 (Belgium, Italy, the Netherlands, Norway, Sweden).
[b] Medium-sized governments had public spending between 40 and 50 percent of GNP in 1990 (Austria, Canada, France, Germany, Ireland, New Zealand, Spain).
[c] Small governments had public spending less than 40 percent of GNP in 1990 (Australia, Switzerland, United Kingdom, United States).
Source: Tanzi and Schuknecht (2000).

Growth of government in the latter half of the 20th century

We now turn to the growth of government in the latter half of the 20th century. Table 10.3 shows the growth of government through public spending between 1960 and 1990. Growth of government through public spending, of course, excludes the growth of government through regulation and paternalistic policies.[11]

In table 10.3, high-income countries are categorized according to whether government spending was large, medium, or small relative to the countries' GNP. Between 1960 and 1990, public spending increased for each group of countries. For the countries with large governments, public spending increased from 31 to 55.1 percent of GNP. In the medium-sized government category, government spending increased from 29.3 to 44.9 percent. In the small-sized government group, government spending also grew, from 23 to 34.6 percent.

The increases in the size of government relative to GNP for the categories of countries are:

Large governments	Medium governments	Small governments
67%	53%	50%

[11] The data in table 10.3 are from a study by Vito Tanzi and Ludger Schuknecht, *Public Spending in the 20th Century* (2000). The study was undertaken when both researchers were with the International Monetary Fund in Washington DC. Tanzi was the longstanding head in the International Monetary Fund of the Fiscal Affairs Department, which has the responsibility of evaluating taxation and public-spending policies in countries worldwide.

Table 10.3 shows the composition of the growth of public spending. In all three categories of countries:

- Government consumption expanded. Government consumption consists of government spending on itself. Included is the financing of the government bureaucracy and the general expenses of government.
- Transfers and subsidies expanded. The publicly financed payments made by governments to redistribute income are subject to the inefficiencies of the leaky bucket of redistribution and moral hazard, to the problems of voting and political decisions, and to adverse selection if immigration decisions can be made in response to social benefits.
- Interest payments expanded. The increased interest payments are the consequence of increased bond financing of government spending. Deferred tax payments because of government borrowing are subject to fiscal illusion and intergenerational opportunism.
- Public investment, which includes public goods, was a relatively small part of public spending and did not expand.

The time dimension for evaluation

The social benefit of the growth of government therefore depends on the time dimension for evaluation. Growth of government was beneficial from the beginning when social responsibilities of government were initially minuscule and revenue, in any event, was lacking. However, it appears that substantial parts of the growth of government in the second half of the 20th century cannot be identified as socially beneficial.

C. Hobbes and Locke on the desired nature of government

The English philosophers, Thomas Hobbes (1588–1679) and John Locke (1632–1704), expressed diametrically opposed views on the nature of desirable government. The source of their differing views on desirable government was their opposing views of the nature of people.

Hobbes on the nature of people and government

In his book, *Leviathan*, which was published in 1651, Thomas Hobbes made a case for a ruler with absolute authority over all people. All people should realize, claimed Hobbes, that it was in their personal interest to be subservient to a leviathan ruler. For Hobbes, the leviathan was required because of the nature of people, whom he regarded as cruel and disrespectful to one another. The absolute control of a leviathan ruler was necessary to control people's base instincts. Without the order imposed by the leviathan, there would be anarchy. Life would be "brutish" and "short," the rule of law would be absent, property rights would not be respected, and all people would contest all things. Neither life nor property would be safe. Hobbes viewed humanity as divided into people who were greedy or lazy. He viewed all people, regardless of whether they are greedy or lazy, as seeking power over others. Times of peace arose only because people feared retaliation from those whom they might harm or whose property they might take. Therefore, peace could not be based on goodwill among people but rather relied on defense and security for protection from the evil designs of others. Hobbes's absolute ruler or leviathan would ensure the rule of law, thereby allowing a civilized society to exist. The power of the leviathan would be absolute, permanent, and hereditary. The leviathan would own all property. The property would not be contestable because hereditary power is not contestable. Untrustworthy human nature thus made surrender to the leviathan the sole rational response if individuals were to live in a secure, civil society. Hobbes wrote centuries before the prisoners' dilemma was formally set out. Yet, he was stating the idea that people left to their own independent decisions would not beneficially cooperate, whereas voluntarily imposed coercive authority (we recall the paradox of gain through coercion) would improve the quality of everyone's life. Although Hobbes was justifying government by absolute hereditary monarchy, his position also applies when people are called on to be subservient to decisions made by majority voting; just as people would be subject to the leviathan as absolute ruler, so under majority voting the minority is subjugated to the decisions of the majority.

Locke on the nature of people and government

John Locke, also like Hobbes an English philosopher, provides us with a view of government that is the exact opposite of that of Hobbes. In his book, *Two Treatises of Government*, published in 1690, Locke made the case for a government that is accountable to the people. Locke viewed the natural state of men and women as being personal freedom. Every individual was entitled by natural law to be free of the imposed order of others, including being free of Hobbes's leviathan. As did Hobbes, Locke also appealed to human reason to justify his position. Locke proposed that the exercise of reason led men and women to understand that the state of nature was civilized rather than anarchic and murderous as Hobbes proposed. Through their abilities to reason, men and women would understand the natural right of possession. Lives and property thus would be respected without a need for the leviathan. People would naturally understand that if they failed to respect the life and property of others, they could not expect others to respect their own life and property. Locke thus proposed that the inefficient outcome of the Nash equilibrium of the prisoners' dilemma of anarchy would be avoided by mutual consent based on reason – although, like Hobbes, he did not formally set out the prisoners' dilemma. For Locke, the natural right of a man and a woman to freedom superseded the authority of any government. Government was the creation of the people and should be subservient to the people, not the other way around as Hobbes proposed. The authority of government rests in the people. Locke declared that "no government can have a right to obedience from a people that have not freely consented to it" (Locke, 1690/1960, II, paragraph 192). Political decision makers are accountable to the people, and the people have the natural right to remove and change their political decision makers at will if the politicians "be so foolish, or so wicked, as to lay and carry on decisions against the liberties and the properties of the subject."

Box 10.1 Hobbes and Samuel

Hobbes referred extensively in his book to biblical writings. The centerpiece of his case for the leviathan was from the Book of Samuel I, which recounts how, some 2,500 years before Hobbes, representatives of the tribes of Israel had come to the prophet Samuel requesting a king "as other peoples had." The 12 tribes of Israel were united by common ancestry and common history but had had no king. They had not needed a king (another person) to make laws and to rule over them because predetermined principles of the rule of law governed their behavior. In voluntarily asking for a king, the tribes were exemplary for Hobbes' case for the leviathan. Samuel's response to the tribes' request for a king was, therefore, extensively quoted by Hobbes (1651/1962, pp. 155–6). Samuel declared to the tribes that a king would take their sons and use them as personal charioteers and would take their daughters as perfumers, cooks, and bakers; he would take their fields, their vineyards, and their best olive trees, which he would give to those close to him; he would take 10 percent of their animals and other wealth; and they would be the king's servants. Hobbes quoted Samuel's response under the heading, *The Rights of the Monarch from Scripture*. Samuel's response was presented by Hobbes, therefore, as defining the rights of the leviathan. Hobbes presented Samuel's reply as normative, in indicating how people *should* behave toward the leviathan. Had Hobbes continued his quote from Samuel for one additional sentence, he would have reached Samuel's warning: "You will regret the day that you chose a king to rule over you." Samuel had not been normatively setting out the rights of the leviathan but rather had been predicting the dire consequences for personal freedom of appointing a king.[12]

Hobbes on liberty

Did Hobbes not care about the liberty of people? In his book, *Leviathan*, Hobbes devoted a chapter to "the liberty of subjects." He observed that much store is

[12] The representatives of the tribes came to Samuel asking for a king *to be appointed*. They were not anarchically contesting from which tribe the king would come. They wanted a king so that there would be cooperation in defense. The purpose of the king was efficiency in supply of the public good of national security. Samuel's focus in his reply was on *social justice*. Samuel predicted that the king would appropriate wealth for himself and would take and redistribute to his sycophants the people's property (the animals, fields, vineyards, and olive trees that are the wealth of an agrarian society).

put in personal liberty but that "the liberty which writers praise, is the liberty of sovereigns, not of private men." He declared that fear and liberty are "consistent" because fear of the leviathan was the only means of civilizing people to free them of the evil inclinations of each other. Hobbes used the analogy of a ship that would sink if possessions were not thrown overboard. People were free to not throw their possessions overboard (or to not give ownership to the leviathan), but the ship would then sink and possessions as well as life would be lost.[13]

D. Restraint on government

We have seen that growth of government can be excessive. Hobbes and Locke (and Samuel) gave us views of government. Do the different views of government imply a case for restraint on government?

The encompassing interest of the leviathan

Hobbes made the case for imposed order of government through the leviathan. Yet, we may well ask, from where does the leviathan come? Ostensibly, the leviathan is someone from the same population of people who Hobbes believed are in need of protection from one another because of their "base and evil instincts." Do we require the Thomas-à-Becket effect to ensure a benevolent leviathan? As did Thomas-à-Becket on taking the role of authority, the leviathan could leave his or her previous debased personality behind – for otherwise social justice under the rule of the leviathan would not be assured. Hobbes's hope was that the leviathan would seek efficiency because of an encompassing interest in owning everything and controlling everyone. The leviathan requires information to achieve efficiency. Markets would provide the information. Without markets, the recourse of the leviathan is to cost-benefit analysis and centralized ordinances and directives. Because of the impediments to efficiency through centralized imposed order, the leviathan might be led to introduce markets. The spontaneous order of the market would then replace the leviathan's imposed order and the leviathan would lose his or her hold over society. Indeed, the leviathan would be expected to fall because economic freedom in general is the precursor of political freedom.[14]

[13] Hobbes was evidently influenced by the Book of Jonah. He mentioned Jonah. When asked to go to the city of Nineveh and call on the inhabitants of the city to repent from evil, Jonah refused and instead went to the port of Jaffa and embarked on a ship with the intention to flee. A storm threatened the ship and everyone threw their possessions overboard, hoping to raise the ship in the water. Only when Jonah allowed himself to be thrown overboard did the storm subside. The analogy proposed by Hobbes is not complete because throwing possessions overboard was not sufficient to save the ship and, indeed, was unnecessary.

[14] The private ownership required for exchange in markets is inconsistent with the leviathan owning everything. The leviathan's last resort might be to tell the people, "You manage the collective property and go ahead and trade in markets but I shall continue to own everything and, in giving you economic freedom, be aware that I am not giving you political freedom." This is consistent with

Predicting demise if the economic freedom of markets were introduced, the leviathan may persist with centralized imposed order. The social objective of efficiency is not then achieved, nor is social justice. A society cannot place all hope in the Thomas-à-Becket effect if, as Hobbes proposed, all people are by nature either greedy or lazy: a greedy person and not a lazy person will have succeeded in becoming the leviathan. We therefore conclude that:

Society needs protection against Hobbes's leviathan.

Locke's accountable government

Locke's government is accountable to the people and can be recalled by the will of the people.[15]

Although accountable, Locke's government can avoid transparency. Transparency is limited by rational ignorance, fiscal illusion, and free-riding incentives in acquisition of information. Taxpayers and voters can then confront the political and bureaucratic principal–agent problems of representative government that allow growth of government without social benefit: governments can spend tax revenue on themselves; income redistribution can expand against the background of leaky buckets and moral hazard as well as political influence, rent seeking, and majority voting; and, against the background of fiscal illusion, interest payments increase because of government borrowing. We might therefore conclude:

Society needs protection against Locke's government.

Constitutional restraint

Whether the concept of government emanates from Hobbes or Locke, the question is:

How can society protect itself from growth of government that taxpayers and voters do not want?

the organization model of workers' management, in which workers choose employment but do not own capital. The governments of communism succumbed when they attempted to restrain political freedom by keeping the monopoly on power but began to allow economic freedom through markets. The successful examples of workers' management in the kibbutz in Israel were voluntary forms of collective organization.

[15] Locke did not propose one-person, one-vote democracy. He viewed property owners as electing the government. In a society with concentrated wealth (and where wealth was, for the most part, land), one-person, one-vote democracy could result in appropriation of the property of the landed rich by the landless poor (see chapter 6). Locke viewed the limitation of the right to vote to the landed classes as a means of protecting property rights. Locke believed that the landed rich would, by reason, ensure a benign and enlightened government that did not abuse individual freedom and that protected all people's rights of ownership.

Restraint on growth of government can be sought through a constitution. A constitution overrides the authority of government by subjecting people in government to designated rules of behavior. A constitution also overrides the will of the majority when majority voting takes place by protecting the rights of the minority. A constitution is part of a two-stage collective-decision-making process. The rules that restrain the actions and decisions of government are set out in the constitutional first stage of collective decision making. After the constitution has specified the scope of permissible behavior of government or the allowable behavior of the majority, political and collective decisions are made from alternatives in the second stage. Requirements for changing a constitution are more stringent than for changing the second-stage government decisions and laws. There is greater permanence and thereby stability in the first-stage constitutional phase of decision making.

> *The constitution protects people from government and the constitution is itself protected from government.*

Time-distancing of constitutional choice

A constitution should be free of personal self-interest. Yet, because a constitution is designed by people, the dilemma arises that would confront Hobbes regarding the honesty and integrity of his absolute leviathan ruler. How can a society ensure that the designers of the constitution will be forthright and honest and place the public interest before their personal self-interest? A solution is time-distancing of constitutional choice. The constitution should not come into effect until some distant time in the future. The distancing in time before implementation of a constitution ensures that present self-interest of the designers of the constitution does not enter into the contents of the constitution. The expectation is that people who self-interestedly control present government will recognize the benefits to future generations from the limitations on political discretion imposed by the constitution and will agree to the introduction of the constitution to restrain future political decision makers. The present designers of the constitution may be unwilling to support implementation of the constitution during any period when they might conceivably be in office. Separation between design and implementation thus protects the constitution by delaying implementation to a time beyond the time horizon of present-day political interests. The constitution will bind on future generations for whom the constitution is predetermined (including rules for making amendments to the constitution). Ideally, a constitution should have the characteristic that if unborn generations could have participated in the design of the constitution, they would have agreed to its provisions. The virtue of the constitution is precisely that it comes bequeathed from a point of time in the past so that contemporary special interests, who may wish to make changes for their own advantage, are unable to manipulate the constitution. A formal constitution is not required if past laws and precedents provide the rule of law and impose limitations on the decisions that governments can make.

Ulysses and the sirens

In chapter 2, we saw that principled politicians who are caught in a prisoners' dilemma benefit from a restraint placed on their own behavior. Or, for reasons of lack of self-control or hyperbolic discounting, politicians may not agree to the tying of their hands but they may nonetheless wish that the provisions of a constitution designed in the past were present and tied their hands. In Greek mythology, the legend of Ulysses describes the sirens who live on an island and whose songs charm to the extent that mariners feel compelled to throw themselves into the sea. Knowing the fatal attraction of the sirens, Ulysses had his sailors tie him to the mast of the ship. The sailors placed wax in their ears. The story of Ulysses and the sirens is a metaphor for government imposing voluntary restraint on itself. In voluntarily constraining himself and seeing to it that the sailors were likewise constrained and thereby protected from their own lack of self-control, Ulysses saved his own life and the lives of the sailors. Ulysses resolved a time-inconsistency problem. He knew that if the songs of the sirens were heard, he and the sailors would be drawn to collective misfortune. By constraining himself, Ulysses avoided behavior that would provide present benefit but which he knew he would ultimately regret. Ulysses avoided the impulsive behavior of hyperbolic discounting. In other circumstances, Ulysses and the sailors may not be in the same boat and the sirens may have special gifts for Ulysses. Even though Ulysses then may not agree to bind himself, he may agree to a constitution that binds a future ruler.

Zero-based budgeting

We conclude our consideration of restraint on government by noting the concept of zero-based budgeting. Under zero-based budgeting, cost-benefit analysis applies not only to increases in public spending but also the costs and benefits of government spending are evaluated beginning with the first dollar. Zero-based budgeting thus asks for evaluation of the costs and benefits of an entire preexisting government department and not merely justification for additional spending. For example, if the government budget provides for three preexisting deputy directors in a government department, zero-based budgeting allows discussion of whether the costs of salaries and amenities for the preexisting deputy directors are justified by the benefits to taxpayers. A justifying statement of the benefits to taxpayers is thereby required, even if no market exists to value the benefits. Governments do not generally use zero-based procedures. However:

> *Zero-based budgeting would provide transparency for taxpayers and voters wishing to judge whether public spending is desirable and would thereby act a prospective constraint on the size of government.*

10.2 Cooperation, Trust, and the Need for Government

Cooperation and trust in a society determine the extent of the need for government. To consider the roles of cooperation and trust, we return to the views on government of Hobbes and Locke. Hobbes viewed a society as positioned on a scale from anarchy to order. Anarchy was undesirable; therefore, because of the contentious nature of people, the leviathan was required to impose order. For Locke, the spectrum of choice was different. Locke viewed a society as positioned on a scale from individual freedom to repression. The objective was individual freedom, which is the natural right of men and women. Therefore, Locke's government does not tell the people what to do. Rather, in principle, the people tell Locke's government what to do – there are principal–agent problems but acknowledging principal–agent problems acknowledges that citizens and taxpayers are the principals and that government is the agent.

Hobbes and Locke presented contrary views of human nature. Hobbes viewed people as greedy or lazy and in need of the restraint of the imposed order of the leviathan. Locke's vision requires voluntary cooperation and trust among people. Otherwise – indeed, as Hobbes proposed – a government is required that limits the freedom of individuals. The freedom that the government would limit is the option not to cooperate in the prisoners' dilemma and if possible the freedom not to act in untrustworthy ways.

Is the voluntary cooperation and trust required by Locke for freedom from government attainable or feasible? Or, as Hobbes proposed, does the absence of cooperation and trust among people entail a need for the restraining hand of government – or, in Hobbes' terminology, a need for the leviathan?

A. Prospects for voluntary cooperation

Locke's view of personal freedom requires that people escape the prisoners' dilemma voluntarily by "natural reason." An appeal to rational behavior as "natural reason" does not solve the problem of the prisoners' dilemma: the inefficient Nash equilibrium of the prisoners' dilemma is the *consequence* of rational behavior. To voluntarily escape the prisoners' dilemma, people have to convince other people that they will behave irrationally by not choosing the dominant strategy of not cooperating – and they need to be convinced that other people will also *not* behave rationally.[16]

[16] Recall that the Nash equilibrium is attained through rational behavior whereby people maximize their expected utility subject to other people's anticipated rational behavior, under conditions of complete information where everyone can predict the rational behavior of everyone else.

Commitment to cooperate

Voluntary cooperation can be achieved in the prisoners' dilemma if people can make a credible commitment to cooperate. It is not enough to promise to cooperate. Merely promising to cooperate is "cheap talk." Rational behavior in the one-time prisoners' dilemma is to promise to cooperate and to behave rationally to maximize utility by not cooperating.

A promise to cooperate is made credible by introducing an additional benefit or cost that makes cooperation the best personal choice. An example is a penalty for not cooperating imposed by government, as we considered for solving the problem of anarchy. Now, however, we are not looking to government to enforce a solution to the prisoners' dilemma; we are looking for voluntary cooperation.

A credible commitment to cooperate can take the form of individuals depositing a sum of money with an outside party. Any person who subsequently fails to keep the promise to cooperate loses the deposit. The amount of money deposited with the outside party needs to be greater than the gain from not cooperating. In former times, cooperative outcomes were sustained along these lines by exchange of hostages or by strategic marriages. The hostages were generally never harmed. The purpose of the hostages was to change incentives so that cooperation is rational behavior.

"Exchange of hostages" or the holding of money by outside parties is not a practical means of enforcing voluntary cooperation among individuals in a modern society. Social interactions are too anonymous to be resolved in this way: too many anonymous people are interacting with too many other anonymous people. Every person in a society would have to find a way of making a credible commitment to cooperate with every other person. Spurious claims of non-cooperative behavior could arise. An outside party required for this complex arrangement (for example, to resolve disputed claims of non-cooperative behavior) is suggestive of a government and we are looking for cooperation without government.

A repeated prisoners' dilemma

When introducing the prisoners' dilemma, we observed that cooperation can be rational behavior if interactions are repeated over time. Two people may be required every day to make a decision whether to make a contribution to financing the supply of a public good. In this repeated game, the prisoners' dilemma game is played over and over again. People will cooperate and not free ride if the following conditions are satisfied:

- The interaction is indefinitely repeated into the future.
- Individuals do not discount the future too much; that is, the future is relatively important for both people.
- The identity of the people who are involved in the interaction will forever remain the same, and the people interacting under the conditions of the prisoners' dilemma know this.

Under these circumstances, rational individuals will cooperate. The escape from the prisoners' dilemma occurs because it is in the self-interest of both individuals to have a reputation for cooperating. If each person knows that the other is a person who always cooperates, and if each person knows that the other person knows of the reputation for cooperating, then the reputation of each individual as cooperating leads the other to likewise cooperate.[17]

The simultaneous presence of these three conditions is required to provide a rational escape from the prisoners' dilemma. If these conditions are not simultaneously satisfied, in the quest to achieve a cooperative equilibrium, each person is setting out to convince the other that he or she is irrational. The principal impediment to cooperation is the anonymity of a large society, which diminishes the value of personal reputation. We also saw that in the dictatorship game when decisions are completely anonymous, people tend to keep all or large parts of the money. They are generous when their behavior is not completely anonymous and they are generous in the ultimatum game because they fear retribution.

Rational people who know one another and who care about the future should cooperate in an infinitely repeated prisoners' dilemma; however, in interaction between two people, one person nevertheless might choose to behave opportunistically and not cooperate. The other person then needs to decide how to respond to the opportunistic behavior. One possible response is a strategy known as *tit-for-tat*. The strategy is to preannounce reciprocity. The response to cooperation is thereby declared to be further cooperation and the response to failure to cooperate is declared to be retaliatory non-cooperation. The retaliation of non-cooperation may continue for a preannounced number of future interactions. With future benefits sufficiently valued, the losses from opportunistic non-cooperation imposed by tit-for-tat make sustained cooperation a personally rational response. Again, anonymity is the problem. If tit-for-tat is to be an effective deterrent to non-cooperation, individuals must know with whom they will be interacting in the future. Otherwise, the threat of future punishment through tit-for-tat has no value. That is, the threat of retaliation has to be personal to be effective. Enforcement of voluntary cooperation through tit-for-tat is thus appropriate for personal interactions but not for interactions in a population of anonymous people. At the level of society, tit-for-tat cannot solve the prisoners' dilemma.

People may cooperate to seek social approval. The cooperation needs to be visible to others. Cooperation then has a similar role to reputation. If the quest

[17] We noted in chapter 1 that if the number of interactions is finite, there is no value to reputation in the last interaction and, by backward induction, there is then no value at all to cooperation in any round of interaction. If people do not know the number of times interactions will be repeated, reputation has value because of the prospect of continued interaction. The second condition for cooperation, that people sufficiently value benefits in the future relative to the present, is required to ensure that reputation has value. The third condition for cooperation that people know with whom they are interacting is required because if interactions are anonymous, there is no value to reputation from cooperating.

for social approval is to be the basis for cooperative behavior, people cannot live in anonymous societies in which no one knows who they are.

We have observed that people cooperate in public-good experiments. Contrary to the predictions of the prisoners' dilemma, anonymous people also cooperate in real life. They contribute to charity, do not litter, and join collective-action groups with objectives such as protection of the environment. When choosing to cooperate in large anonymous populations, people are not attempting to acquire personal reputations, nor are they seeking social approval by impressing others. Rather, cooperative behavior can only be due to self-esteem or ethical self-restraint. Cooperative behavior is then expressive in confirming self-identity or is the consequence of life lived according to ethical bounds on personal behavior. The structure of personal rewards has changed so that maximal personal benefit is no longer obtained from exploiting others but rather by cooperating with others. Such a changed personal reward structure was present when we described ethical people confronting opportunistically rational people in the prisoners' dilemma and when people derive utility from giving charity.[18]

B. Social norms and trust

People in a society may voluntarily cooperate because of a social norm of cooperation. The social norm leads people to expect that trust will be reciprocated. Thus, in the prisoners' dilemma, even if people are anonymous, social norms may lead people to make the judgment that the other person will cooperate.

> *Social norms of reciprocal trust can replace personal reputation as the basis for cooperation.*

Can trust be measured?

To consider measurement of trust in terms of behavioral responses, we leave the prisoners' dilemma to describe another form of interaction known as the *trust game*. The trust game is shown in figure 10.1. Two mutually anonymous people are placed in two separate rooms. Neither person knows who the other is, nor will personal identities of participants ever be revealed to one another. Person 1 is given $100 at node 1 in table 10.1. Person 1 can keep the entire $100 or transfer the $100 to person 2. In another version of the game, person 1 can decide how much of the $100 to transfer. In table 10.1, the decision of person 1 is binary, whether to keep or transfer the $100. If transferred, the $100 becomes $300 in the hands of person 2. Person 2, who has received the money, can keep the entire

[18] Nash behavior, which underlies the Nash equilibrium of the prisoners' dilemma, is based on people taking each other's decisions as given when maximizing their own utilities. In chapter 3, we considered non-Nash conjectures about how other people behave. For example, behavior can be reciprocating in that, rather than responding to voluntary payments of others by contributing less, a person may view a contribution by others as a subsidy and contribute more, as in the case of the behavioral responses described by the Lindahl mechanism for voluntary payment for public goods.

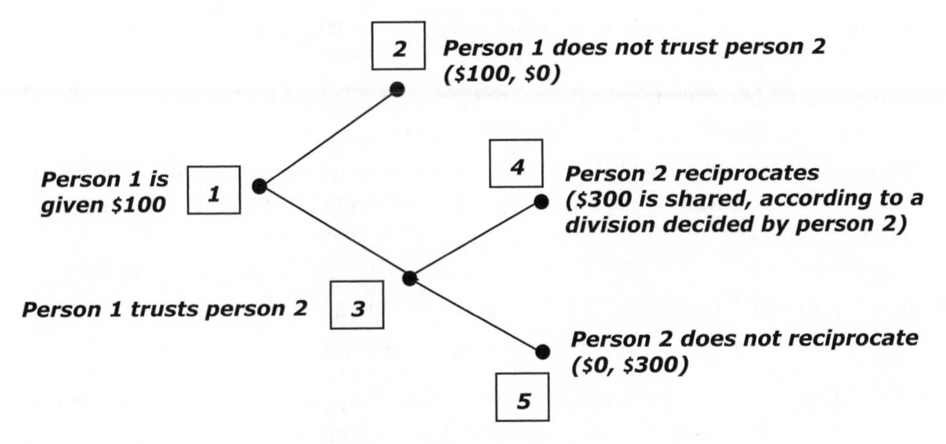

Figure 10.1. The trust game.

$300 or can reciprocate trust by giving a sum of money back to person 1. Both people know the rules of the game.

The equilibrium for this game based on rational maximizing behavior is for person 1 to keep the $100 because the best response of person 2 if the $100 is transferred is to keep the $300. There is no rational reason for person 2 to reciprocate and give money back to person 1. This is an anonymous one-time game in which reputation for reciprocating has no value.

Whether person 1 decides to go ahead with the initial wealth-increasing transfer will reflect whether social norms justify an expectation of reciprocating behavior. If person 1 believes that person 2 is not to be trusted, person 1 moves to node 2 in figure 10.1. The game then ends, with person 1 having $100 and person 2 having nothing, and with a wealth-creating and Pareto-improving opportunity having been lost. If person 1 believes that it is reasonable that person 2 will reciprocate trust and return more than $100, person 1 will make the wealth-increasing transfer by moving to node 3. Person 2 then decides whether to share the gains from person 1's trusting behavior with person 1. Because it is irrational to return money to person 1, a decision by person 2 to return money can only be based on self-esteem or ethics – or on personal behavior that has been subjugated to a social norm of reciprocity.

Person 1 has to decide whether to trust an anonymous stranger. Person 1's decision whether to trust person 2 will reflect expectations based on personal experience in the society where both people live.[19]

Person 2 has no strategic decision to make. Person 2's decision evokes no response and concludes the game. Nonetheless, if the transfer has been made,

[19] Person 1 makes a decision by comparing the utility of $100, which is obtained with certainty by not making the transfer to person 2, with the expected utility from transferring the $100 to person 2. Expected utility depends on the amount R that person 1 believes that person 2 will return, where R is a value between zero and $300. Person 1's decision will also depend on aversion to risk. The more risk averse he or she is, the greater the expected value of R that will be required for person 1 to decide in favor of making the transfer to person 2.

person 2 faces an ethical decision in whether to reciprocate trust and return money to person 1.

If person 1 has transferred the money, person 2 would be led by a conception of fairness to return at least the original $100 to person 1. Person 2 could decide to equally share the $300 and so give person 1 $150. Or, person 2 could decide to equally share the gain of $200 from the decision of person 1 to make the transfer, in which case person 2 keeps $100 and gives $200 to person 1.

Person 2 can also decide to take the entire $300 and leave the scene (anonymously), in which case the game ends at node 5 in figure 10.1.

Quite evidently:

> *People living in a society in which there is sufficient trust for the wealth-increasing transfer to be made will be better off than in a society in which the initial transfer is not made.*

There is evidence of gender differences in the trust game. Men and women are equally likely to make the transfer in the first place, so men and women are equally trusting (or distrusting). After the transfer has been made, women are, on average, more generous than men in rewarding or reciprocating trust. Still, neither men nor women seem particularly generous in sharing when reciprocating trust. In reported experiments, women returned on average 37.4 percent of the money, whereas men returned on average 28.6 percent. After the experiments, 57 percent of women compared to only 24 percent of men reported that they had felt "extremely obligated" to reciprocate trust – by returning money.[20]

C. Distrust and social segmentation

People do not like to feel that they have been exploited or made to look like a fool. A person who cooperates because of a belief that social norms will result in reciprocal cooperation can be expected to cease behaving cooperatively if the behavior of too many others is opportunistic and exploitative.

Societies with anonymous cooperative and opportunistic types of people

A person who has moved from a society in which the social norm is to cooperate to a society in which the social norm is to be opportunistic is nonetheless accustomed to cooperating. Trust can be expected quickly to cease when it becomes clear from the interactions with anonymous strangers that the person is in a location where non-cooperation and intent of exploitation are the behavioral norms. Alternatively, an individual from the society in which non-cooperation

[20] Evidence was reported by Rachel Croson and Nancy Buchan (1999) from experiments conducted in China, Japan, Korea, and the United States. Subjects in each country were beginning or junior business or economics students.

and deception are norms of behavior can arrive in a society in which cooperation based on mutual trust is the social norm. The new arrival may adapt personal behavior to the new benevolent social norm, thereby benefiting from mutual cooperation that was not possible in the former location where the norm of distrust and non-cooperation prevailed. The new arrival could also retain personal non-cooperative opportunistic behavior. With a sufficiently large number of new arrivals acting in this way, the population becomes divided between opportunistic people who do not cooperate and do not reciprocate trust and the original residents for whom cooperation and reciprocated trust have been the social norm. What can we expect to be the outcome when the two different types of people meet and randomly interact with one another in the prisoners' dilemma or trust game when people have no means of identifying one another as cooperative or opportunistic?

Opportunistic people benefit whenever they encounter a trusting person – they are able to exploit the trusting person. As long as the number of opportunistic people in the population remains small, the social norm of benevolent cooperation may still persist, with disappointments for those trusting people who are unlucky enough to encounter opportunistic people. After a sufficient number of personal experiences in which goodwill and trust have not been reciprocated, trusting people reevaluate their expectations and cease to be trusting. They no longer believe promises or accept personal checks in payment or give credit card numbers to suppliers that they do not personally know.

In a society with reciprocated trust, people thus benefit from the cooperative outcomes in the prisoners' dilemma and the trust game. However, in a society with social norms of distrust and opportunism, people live in a milieu of cynicism and mutual suspicion.

> *Trust is a public good that facilitates beneficial voluntary cooperation. Transaction costs in economic activity increase when the public good of trust dissipates and distrust displaces trust.*

Trust in anonymous market transactions

Table 10.4 shows two people who face a decision whether to trust one another in a market transaction. There are Nash equilibria at (10,10) and (0,0). In the first Nash equilibrium, there is mutual trust; in the second, there is mutual distrust. When there is mutual trust, the transaction takes place and the efficient outcome is achieved with a benefit of 10 for each person. With mutual distrust, the transaction does not take place and each person has zero.

If one person trusts the other but the trust is misplaced and the other person does not reciprocate trust, the trusting person loses 15, whereas the dishonest person gains 15. The interaction is then zero-sum because one person's gain is the other person's loss. When there is mutual trust, the interaction is positive-sum (there is a positive equally shared total benefit of 20).

TABLE 10.4. TRUST AND TRUSTWORTHINESS IN ANONYMOUS POPULATIONS

	Person 2 trusts person 1	Person 2 does not trust person 1 (or does not reciprocate trust)
Person 1 trusts person 2	10, 10	−15, 15
Person 1 does not trust person 2 (or does not reciprocate trust)	15, −15	0, 0

Trust in small groups

In small groups, trust can be sustained through reputation. Trust may then not extend beyond the immediate or extended family. The form of social organization may be clans or tribes, with trust limited to clan or tribe members. A small group with substantiated norms of trust among its members will become wealthier than the general population because of the lower transactions costs of doing business. The word of members of the group will suffice to allow business transactions to be completed without costly precautions and contracts to protect against opportunistic behavior. For others outside the group, absence of reputation may make transactions costs too high to permit participation in some markets in which trust is important because the personal costs of misjudging trustworthiness are high.

The interaction in table 10.4 was described as taking place once and as between anonymous people. Person 1 and person 2, however, may know each other's group identity. If they are from the same group, they may mutually trust one another; if they are from different groups, they may mutually distrust one another. When the two people are from the same group, the outcome is the mutually beneficial Nash equilibrium (10,10). When the two people are from different groups, the outcome is the Nash equilibrium with zero benefit to both.

Evidently:

There are efficiency gains from establishing trust.

D. Social capital

Benefits from trust require trust to have been established. It may be impossible to establish trust without a history of interactions – and as long as people choose not to interact, there will be no history of interactions on which to base trust. Without trust, the equilibrium in table 10.4 is that of zero benefit to both.

Because of the benefits from trust, trust has been described as social capital. The social capital, like all capital, is the consequence of investment. The investment is made through experience that justifies belief that trust will be reciprocated.

The concept of social capital was popularized by Robert D. Putnam in a book published in 2000 titled *Bowling Alone*. Putnam documented how activities that had traditionally been undertaken in social groups had, by the end of the 20th century, come to be more likely undertaken alone. People who "bowl alone" are islands unto themselves. They do not have social links to others and as a consequence are not trusting of others. Before television, and certainly before radio, people were more inclined to talk to one another and to be part of a social group. Entertainment was self-made. One or more of a group would bring a musical instrument and people might dance and sing – and talk. Trust was built through socializing interaction. In contemporary societies, technology has personalized entertainment: listening to music can be a personal experience through earphones that block social contact. Societal institutions affect whether people have the social contact that builds mutual trust. Older people are more likely to be lonely and to "bowl alone" if sex has been solely recreational and not procreational. Women are often more socially attuned and more communicative than men, although through gender equality career and lifestyle decisions can also, in the end, result in women "bowling alone." Social capital affects personal happiness. Governments cannot, however, readily implement public policies to increase social capital.

10.3 Views on the Need for Government

We have now completed our study of public finance and public policy. We are left, however, to summarize the answer to a final question:

> *Why do views on the need for public finance and public policy – or the need for government – differ?*

A. Political economy

We began our study in chapter 1 with Adam Smith's observation that because of the "invisible hand," guilt feelings are unnecessary when people do the best for themselves in markets. As a professor of moral philosophy, Adam Smith was seeking an ethical basis for the self-interested behavior that was revealed in human nature. Adam Smith and subsequent 19th-century authors, including David Ricardo and David Hume, to whose writings we have referred, provided the foundations for the development of political economy as a broad social science that recognized the interface between politics and economics. In the 20th century, however, economics separated from political economy. Through the separation, an attempt was made to establish economics as a scientific discipline independent of politics. The intention was to make economics like physics: mathematical formalism would reveal truth and there would be equilibria of different types. The role of economics in public policy was to describe efficient outcomes. After having been presented by economists with possible efficient outcomes, governments or political decision makers would choose an outcome to their liking based on distributional consequences. That is, the economists would show how to maximize the size of the cake (or national income) and governments or political decision makers would decide how to cut and distribute the cake. Economists would thereby be scientific about efficiency, which everyone could agree upon, and would not enter into the divisive decisions about the distribution of benefits (or costs).[21]

The view required a definition of economics whereby strict separation is maintained between efficiency and social justice. How was such a separation to be maintained? After all, we have seen that separation between questions of efficiency and social justice is, in general, impossible and that decisions about public finance and public policy therefore, in general, involve a trade-off between efficiency and social justice. We began our study in chapter 1 by making the trade-off between efficiency and social justice expressed as ex-post equality explicit through the example of the water–in–the–desert.

Nonetheless, economics in the 20th century separated decisions about efficiency from decisions about distribution: the means that enabled the separation was the artifact of lump-sum taxes as allowing the financing of public spending. If governments could use lump-sum taxes, people would not substitute leisure for work – because, by definition, lump-sum taxes have no substitution effects. The description of governments as using lump-sum taxes, which have no excess burden of taxation, for example, allowed the condition $\sum MB = MC$ for efficient voluntary supply of public goods to be applied when payment for public goods is not voluntary but rather governments levy taxes to finance public goods: through the artifact of the lump-sum taxes, publicly financed public goods could be described as efficiently financed by governments. The description of governments as using lump-sum taxes also eliminated the need to refer to leaks in the bucket of redistribution: when we studied social justice, we saw that in the absence of leaks in the bucket of income redistribution, all symmetric social welfare functions provide complete insurance and result in ex-post income equality. Lump-sum taxes also eliminate the Laffer curve from the study of public finance: the Laffer curve cannot be an impediment to governments collecting tax revenue if people do not substitute leisure for work. Incidentally, or perhaps not so in all cases, the separation between efficiency and social justice based on lump-sum taxes described people as behaving as the fathers of communism ideally wished them to behave. If lump-sum taxes could

[21] The case for the separation between economics and politics – or for economics without political economy – was made by the English economist, Lionel Robbins (1898–1984), in his *Essay on the Nature and Significance of Economic Science* (1932).

be used, people would not make work–leisure substitution decisions in response to changed incentives but would contribute altruistically to society according to ability.

The reality, of course, is that people respond to incentives and that governments do not use lump-sum taxes. Efficient government spending on public goods is less, therefore, than the ideal voluntary Lindahl spending. The bucket of redistribution has leaks and it therefore matters whether a Bentham or Rawls social welfare function – or a social welfare function in between – is chosen. Without lump-sum taxes, the Laffer curve constrains governments' revenue collection.

A political-economy view, as adopted in this book, recognizes that lump-sum taxes are not available to governments. Then, whether choices are required between efficiency and social justice depends on the definition of social justice. We have seen that there need be no conflict between efficiency and social justice when the definition of social justice is equality of opportunity, nor when the definition is the natural right of possession. However, if the definition of social justice is ex-post equality, societies face the trade-off between social justice and efficiency. We have observed how in various instances the choice when confronting the trade-off is made through ideology.

B. Fate and moral hazard

Ideology is involved in the view of human nature. Adam Smith, the father of the right in economics, accommodated self-interested human nature in his theory of the invisible hand. Karl Marx, the father of the left, and his followers proposed a view of the world that required changing human nature from people being self-interested and responding to incentives to their being altruistic and contributing according to ability to the common good. The supposition of this latter view is that people are fundamentally caring and do not take advantage of others. Therefore, in particular, human behavior is not subject to moral hazard. If moral hazard is absent, people do not take advantage of a benevolence state and people who do not fare well in life are necessarily victims of fate. A criticism from the right is that then also people can be regarded as incapable of doing better for themselves because their circumstances are not due to their own decisions but to exogenous bad luck. In a view taken from the left of a world without moral hazard, people who have fared well might regard themselves as destined for advantage through their good luck as compared to the bad luck of people who have not fared well. If unfortunate people can only be exogenous victims, those who fortune has made them superior in their outcomes and capabilities are obliged to help those who are unfortunate. In this view, which we associate with the left of the ideological spectrum, there is no place for the suggestion that people may have contributed to their unfortunate circumstances through responses to incentives (through moral hazard) and that, with appropriate incentives, they are capable of productive, self-reliant lives. With moral hazard excluded, there is no place for informing people, before effort decisions are made, that personal decisions and actions will have consequences because fate has not predetermined outcomes of life.

C. Why reliance on government is controversial

Reliance on governments is, therefore, controversial because of different views of human nature and the different consequences that follow for self-responsibility and for the responsibilities of government. Views from the left and from the right differ in various other ways that we have encountered.

A view from the left

A view from the left is expressed in the following propositions:

- *Principal–agent problems:* Political and bureaucratic principal–agent problems are minimal so that governments can be broadly trusted to make – and bureaucracies to implement – socially benevolent decisions about public finance and public policy. Rational ignorance and other reasons for asymmetric information of voters and taxpayers are not significant limitations to assigning responsibilities to government. Fiscal illusion is not important. Incentive effects of taxation and the Laffer curve are not significant constraints on collection of tax revenue. Moral hazard is not a significant problem because people, in general, do not take advantage of benevolence or insurance.
- *Voting and locational choice:* A representative individual is a good approximation for much economic analysis because people have similar preferences. Because preferences are similar, the tyranny of the majority in majority voting is not a significant problem. The view that people do not differ much in personal preferences for public spending diminishes the scope for benefit from locational choice as a means of matching public spending with personal preferences through decentralized government. Competitive discipline of governments through choice among governments is not required if there is no political principal–agent problem. Centralized government is favored over multiple government in a fiscal federal system: centralized government allows income to be redistributed through centralized taxation; tax competition that is harmful to benevolent governments is avoided; and centralized government eliminates opportunities for mobile capital and for people to escape taxes by relocating in low-tax jurisdictions.
- *The choice between efficiency and social justice:* A view from the left assigns priority to the objective of social and economic equality. Because equality requires income redistribution that only governments can legally impose, there is a preference for the imposed order of government. There is a sympathy for a Rawls social insurance contract or at least for a departure from the lottery in life and incomplete insurance of Bentham.

A view from the right

A view from the right stresses the merit of the social objective of efficiency. Social justice is defined more so as natural right of possession and ex-ante equality than ex-post equality. The view from the right is more circumspect about assigning responsibilities to governments. Because of asymmetric information and the excess burden of taxation, governments are less adept at achieving efficiency than at redistribution. The advantage of governments of being able to compel redistribution is not required when the primary social objective is regarded as efficiency. More particularly, the view from the right takes the following perspectives.

- *Principal–agent problems:* The political principal–agent problem is regarded as a limitation to assigning responsibilities to government. Politicians and bureaucrats are recognized to be *people* with self-interests and personal objectives. Information asymmetries including the consequences of rational ignorance allow principal–agent problems to exist. The Thomas-à-Becket effect may apply initially when people take political office or enter government employment but is not a long-term solution to the principal–agent problems. Because of fiscal illusion, rational ignorance, rent seeking, and requisites of electoral success that underlie the political principal–agent problems, the authority that government can exercise over citizens should be limited by constitutional restraint.
- *Asymmetric information and public policy:* Asymmetric information prevents a well-intentioned government from efficiently using public finance and public policy: thus, the asymmetric information that prevents efficient voluntary payment for public goods is also present when governments choose public spending on public goods. The excess burden of taxation makes public spending on public goods more costly for societies than voluntary payments. The Laffer curve limits the taxes that government can impose. There are two asymmetric-information problems: citizens and taxpayers do not know what governments are doing; and governments, even if well-intentioned, do not have the information to choose efficient policies, while there are efficiency losses through excess burdens when taxes are levied. Cost-benefit analysis is useful; however, because the information sought through cost-benefit analysis is not revealed in markets, the procedures of cost-benefit analysis are subject to informational impediments. The procedures can be arbitrary because decisions about costs and benefits are made without guidance from market values. Nonetheless, problems of the environment and biodiversity require accurate cost-benefit analysis, as do, more generally, all circumstances where there are "missing markets" due to externalities and public goods.
- *Voting:* Collective decisions made by voting should be limited and personal market decisions are preferred because majority voting ensures neither efficient nor socially just outcomes. Voting decisions may not be based on the substance of alternative policies; rather, people may vote expressively.

Ostrogorski's paradox shows how direct and representative democracy can give different outcomes. The problems of voting, in particular the tyranny of the majority, therefore suggest reliance on markets wherever possible. When voting is used, there are needs for checks and balances and people should have opportunities to choose locations in jurisdictions where there are like-minded voters.

- *Incentives and income redistribution:* The metaphor of the veil of ignorance allows a case to be made for a social insurance contract. The social insurance contract is chosen subject to the leaky bucket of redistribution. Just as are private insurance markets, social insurance is subject to adverse selection and moral hazard. If social insurance is justified by the veil of ignorance, there is also a justification for compulsory participation in social insurance to resolve the adverse section and time inconsistency problems. However, moral hazard introduces type-1 and type-2 errors that are impediments to social insurance. Although people may have bad luck, personal effort is more important than luck in determining personal outcomes in life. People receiving income transfers from government are not fatalistically victims but rather are responsive to incentives and capable of self-reliance – and self-esteem. However, if paid money not to work, people may choose to take the money. People incapable of self-reliance need to helped – but people who are impaired generally want the opportunity to make productive contributions subject to their limitations. It is paradoxical if impaired people work and able-bodied people do not.
- *Fiscal federalism and competition among governments:* A fiscal-federal structure of governments is beneficial because of choice among governments. Multiple governments are advantageous in providing choice of public goods and in providing information on comparative political performance that allows voters to judge the competence and honesty of political representatives. The decentralized governments of fiscal federalism avoid outcomes whereby, through majority voting in a centralized government jurisdiction, a majority captures the common pool of tax revenue.
- *Envy and altruism:* Interdependent utilities can be expressed in altruism but also envy is a basic human emotion. There is a link between progressive taxation and envy. Income redistribution appears to be influenced by envy when efficiency losses due to redistribution are subjugated to the objective of greater ex-post equality.
- *Private resolution and personal choices:* Means can be explored of voluntary finance for public goods through user prices and locational sorting and of private resolution of externality problems by specifying legal rights; and for private voluntary charitable giving to assist people in need. Equality of opportunity and social mobility allow a meritocracy and permit people to choose employment and professions according to personal comparative advantage. Vouchers allow personal choice of schools in conjunction with public finance and foster competition and equal opportunity in access through merit to better schools. If some people, including girls and young

women, take better advantage of educational entitlements, the consequent inequalities are consistent with social justice when entitlements provided equality of opportunity.

- *Global social justice and global government:* A global social insurance contract is justified by the choice that would be made behind the veil of ignorance, and foreign aid can be viewed as the global equivalent of social-insurance entitlements. However, foreign aid is unsuccessful in improving living conditions in poor countries because of the behavior of foreign governments and ruling elites. Poor people in poor countries remain poor because of the corruption and self-interest of people who control the governments in poor countries. Global representative government, which would of necessity include representatives of all the world's governments, is undesirable.
- *Efficiency and social justice:* Efficient change increases national income even though there are injustices through inability to compensate people who lose. Bentham is preferred to Rawls because Bentham is a rational objective but also because high expected utilities are preferred to assured equal but low incomes.
- *Competitive markets are preferred to government decisions* – or spontaneous order is preferred to imposed order – because of efficiency and also because of personal freedom.

There are agreements and also ambiguities:

- *Entitlements and equality:* The views from both the left and the right favor entitlements to provide equality of opportunity. The right is more concerned about how the entitlements affect incentives. For the left, a problem is that, generally, equality of opportunity results in ex-post inequality. The view from the left therefore confronts a need to reconcile the equality of equal opportunity with the inequality of ex-post outcomes.
- *Immigration:* Views from both the left and the right acknowledge that migration beneficially allows free movement of people who have a work ethic and a personal objective of self-reliance – and who wish to escape repressive and appropriative governments. A view from the left generally recognizes that, because of adverse selection, a generous social insurance contract is inconsistent with a policy of permitting unimpeded immigration – even though the principle of equal opportunity should apply to all people.
- *Paternalistic policies:* The view from the left can be sympathetic to paternalistic policies because of the preference for assigning responsibilities to governments rather than relying on markets. Because of the emphasis on personal freedom, a view from the right might be less receptive to paternalistic policies. However, a view from the right can be conservative rather than libertarian and thereby can support, for example, public-policy responses to hyperbolic discounting and problems of framing and bounded rationality. Neither the left nor the right might have a distinct view on whether the social costs of illegal markets justify retained illegality.

In summary, a view from the right focuses on the efficiency and freedom of market decisions and does not deny but rather is circumspect about improvements that political decision makers and government bureaucracies can achieve. A view from the left is more optimistic about what governments can achieve and more pessimistic that adequate social organization can be based on market decisions. There is common ground in the recognition of the social justice of equal opportunity – and the need for entitlements to provide equal opportunity. However, there may be disagreement about whether unequal personal outcomes reflect unwillingness to take advantage of opportunities provided or absence of opportunities in the first place.

D. Human nature

There would be no disagreement about the need for government if human nature did not require government. However, the same self-interested behavior that Adam Smith justified in markets through the invisible hand is also the reason for the need for government.

- There would be no need for government to maintain competitive markets if self-interested profit-maximizing behavior were not present and therefore no one took advantage of monopoly power.
- If all people respected the natural right of possession and the right to freedom and life of others, the rule of law through government would not be required.
- If all people were to reveal their true benefits from public goods and were voluntarily to pay efficient Lindahl prices, asymmetric information would not impede efficient supply of public goods; taxation would not be required to finance public goods; and the excess burden and administrative costs of government would not be incurred.
- There would be no tax evasion if people did not seek to free ride on tax payments of others.
- Public policy and public finance would not be required to resolve externality problems if people were considerate in taking into account how their behavior affects others.
- Paternalistic policies would be unnecessary if personal decisions were not subject to hyperbolic discounting, framing, and bounded rationality.
- The responsibility of government to provide social insurance would be unnecessary if the time-inconsistency problem and adverse selection were not present; that is, if people accepted and behaved according to the metaphor of the social insurance contract chosen behind the veil of ignorance when they do not yet know who they will be.
- There would be neither type-1 nor type-2 errors associated with social insurance, if behavior were not subject to moral hazard.
- Adverse selection would not undermine social insurance if people from outside the society respected that the entitlements of a society's social insurance

contract are intended as a response to the random personal insecurities of people within the society.

- There would be no political principal–agent problems if political decision makers and bureaucrats did not have personal objectives that deviate from the public interest.

Because the personal behavior required for an efficient and socially just society is in these ways inconsistent with self-interested human behavior, achievement of the objectives of efficiency and social justice generally requires more than voluntary decisions based on personal self-interest. There is, therefore, a need for government. The question is: "How much government is required?" Societies face the decision about how much government; this book has been about making that decision.

Writing in 1912 in the United States, H. Parker Willis declared:

> In a country with our type of government, far-reaching changes of law are obtained only through clear and strong presentation of distinct points of view. Refinements and subtleties twisting and turning "in many a backward streaming curve" have no place in political discussion, and when they are the staple of the argument, they will be disregarded.[22]

Distinct points of view have been presented as we proceeded through the topics of public finance and public policy. However, we have often looked at "refinements and subtleties" because, after all, we are not political decision makers – or perhaps not yet for some of us. We are students – and perhaps lifelong students – seeking to determine what we want from government and how we want government to treat us, and what can reasonably be expected of government.

Summary

The topic of this final chapter has been the need for government. Section 1 considered the growth of government.

1A. The size of government expressed in taxation and public spending as a share of national income has grown extensively since the time of Adam Smith. Societies have changed to become high-income countries through the predominance of a middle class. Wagner's law predicts growth of government relative to GNP or national income. Wagner's law is, in general, substantiated by data – although there are exceptions, with the views of Thomas Malthus perhaps influencing social spending in the 19th century. Explanations for Wagner's law are categorized into increased demand for public spending, increased

[22] Willis (1874–1937), in the *Journal of Political Economy* (1912, volume 20, page 590).

opportunities for public spending because of supply of government revenue, and consequences of voting and political decisions, including the common basis for formation of interests as people became more specialized in their market sources of personal income. Interest groups based on a common source of income in import-competing industries were particularly successful in seeking protectionist policies. Because of diversification of personal income sources as personal wealth increased and also the Most-Favored–Nation clause of international trade agreements, protectionism declined in the later years of the 20th century. There is evidence indicating that government spending is greater in more open economies, suggesting selective additional social insurance for people whose incomes are influenced by world-market prices. Framing facilitated protectionist policies and selective insurance. Risk aversion has also been proposed as a reason why more open economies have larger government spending.

1B. Growth of government since the 18th century provided substantial benefit. The quality of life has substantially improved. Evidence about growth of government in the second half of the 20th century is more circumspect because of increased spending of government on itself, increased income transfers from one part of the population to another, and increased interest payments on government borrowing.

1C. We compared views of the nature of desirable government set out by Hobbes and Locke. The views of government are related to views about the nature of men and women.

1D. Both the leviathan of Hobbes and the representative government of Locke require restraint. Ulysses and the sirens provided a metaphor for constitutional restraint. A constitution requires time-distancing between design and implementation in order to be effective. Zero-based budgeting would be a restraint on unwarranted growth of government.

Section 2 considered the relationship between the need for government and trust and cooperation in a society.

2A. We asked whether the cooperation and mutual trust sought by Locke could be achieved without government restraining personal behavior. Voluntary cooperation in the repeated prisoners' dilemma is particularly limited by anonymity in interactions. Self-esteem can be a reason for cooperation in large anonymous populations.

2B. Social norms of reciprocated trust allow people to cooperate. The trust game is a way to observe the degree of trust in a society.

2C. Trust determines whether benefits from market exchange are realized. Distrust undermines market transactions and results in social segmentation. We considered consequences of the presence in a society of both people who are trustworthy and trusting and people who are neither. Small groups of people who can identify with one another and are trustworthy and trusting have transactions-cost advantages over large anonymous populations.

2D. Trust has been interpreted as social capital. There is capital because the trust has been built up through investment in social relationships. Social capital, in turn, has been related to happiness. Evidence suggests that social relationships have become less important as incomes have increased. The analogy of "bowling alone" was used. More income has therefore not necessarily brought more happiness. Public finance and public policy of governments can seek efficiency and social justice but cannot compel social relationships that build trust and foster happiness.

Section 3 described why views on the need for government differ. We noted how political economy was transformed to efficiency-focused economics through the artifact of lump-sum taxes that were used to describe quests for efficiency and social justice as based on independent decisions. Without recourse to the artifact of lump-sum taxes, effects of public finance and public policy on efficiency and social justice are often inseparable. When choices between efficiency and social justice have to be made, we are returned to political economy. We noted how views on the need for government differ according to whether a perspective is adopted from the left and or the right of the economic spectrum. Adam Smith proposed that self-interest can be beneficially sought in competitive markets; however, we observed that the need for government also stems from self-interested human nature.

Literature notes

10.1 Growth of government and the need for government

On transition from autocracy and government revenue, see:

Congleton, R. D., 2001. On the durability of king and council: The continuum between dictatorship and democracy. *Constitutional Political Economy* 12:193–215.

Congleton, R. D., 2007. From royal to parliamentary rule without revolution: The economics of constitutional exchange within divided governments. *European Journal of Political Economy* 23:261–84.

On colonization in which local people did not benefit, see:

Hochschild, A., 1998. *King Leopard's Ghost.* Pan Macmillan, London.

The growth of government since the 18th century was described by Lindert (2004). On growth of government in the 20th century, see Tanzi and Schuknecht (2000).

Lindert, P. H., 2004. *Growing Public: Social Spending and Economic Growth since the Eighteenth Century*. Cambridge University Press, Cambridge U.K.
Tanzi, V., and L. Schuknecht, 2000. *Public Spending in the 20th Century*. Cambridge University Press, New York.

The growth of government in the United States was described by North (1985).

North, D. C., 1985. The growth of government in the United States: An economic historian's perspective. *Journal of Public Economics* 28:383–99.

Wagner's law appeared in Wagner (1893); see also Wagner (1958).

Wagner, A., 1893. *Grunglegung der Politischen Oekonomie* (3rd Edition). C. F. Winter, Leipzig.
Wagner, A., 1958 (reprinted). Three extracts on public finance. In R. A. Musgrave and R. Peacock (Eds.), *Classics in the Theory of Public Finance*. Macmillan, London, pp. 1–16.

Peltzman (1980) set out a political economy view of the growth of government that includes group formation, differences in incomes, and political responses to income-based voter coalitions. Demsetz (1982) explained growth of government with reference to specialization in production and interest groups.

Demsetz, H., 1982. The growth of government. In *Economic, Legal, and Political Dimensions of Competition*. North-Holland, Amsterdam, pp. 99–125.
Peltzman, S., 1980. The growth of government. *Journal of Law and Economics* 23:209–87.

Gemmell (1990) described government employees and the growth of government. Kau and Rubin (2002) pointed to the consequences of increased government revenue from labor-force participation of women. Sanz and Velázquez (2007) presented evidence showing that aging was the principal reason for the growth of government in high-income countries in the late 20th century.

Gemmell, N., 1990. Public employees' preferences and the size of the public sector. *Journal of Economic Behavior and Organization* 14:393–402.
Kau, J. B., and P. H. Rubin, 2002. The growth of government: Sources and limits. *Public Choice* 113:389–402.
Sanz, I., and F. J. Velázquez, 2007. The role of ageing in the growth of government and social welfare spending in the OECD. *European Journal of Political Economy* 23:917–31.

On fiscal federalism as facilitating the growth of government, see:

Brennan, G., and J. M. Buchanan, 1980. *The Power to Tax: Analytical Foundations of a Fiscal Constitution*. Cambridge University Press, Cambridge U.K.

For a view of growth of government combining demand for public spending, supply of revenue, and political aspects, see:

Tridimas, G., and S. L. Winer, 2005. The political economy of government size. *European Journal of Political Economy* 21:643–66.

The use of protectionist policies to provide social insurance to people earning income in import-competing and export (or traded-goods) industries was described by Cassing, Hillman, and Long (1986). On the more direct means of providing social insurance specifically to people earning income in traded-goods industries, see Cassing (1980). For an analysis of the U.S. Trade Adjustment Assistance program, see Brander and Spencer.

Brander, J. A., and B. Spencer, 1994. Trade adjustment assistance: Welfare and incentive effects of payments to displaced workers. *Journal of International Economics* 36:239–61.
Cassing, J. H., 1980. Alternatives to protectionism. In I. Leveson and J. W., Wheeler (Eds.), *Western Economies in Transition: Structural Change and Adjustment Policies in Industrial Countries*. Westview Press, Boulder CO, pp. 391–424.
Cassing, J. H., A. L. Hillman, and N. V. Long, 1986. Risk aversion, terms of trade variability, and social consensus trade policy. *Oxford Economic Papers* 38:234–42.

Trade liberalization as exchange of market access was described in Hillman and Moser (1996). On the transition from industry-specific self-interest to public interest through asset diversification, see Feeney and Hillman (2004). Schonhardt-Bailey (1991) attributed repeal of the Corn Laws in 19th-century England to political support for trade liberalization obtained through asset diversification. On trade liberalization through the nondiscrimination of the Most–Favored–Nation clause, see Ethier (2004).

Ethier, W. J., 2004. Political externalities, nondiscrimination and a multilateral world. *Review of International Economics* 12:303–20. Reprinted in W. J. Ethier and A. L. Hillman (Eds.), 2008. *The Political Economy of International Trade Policy and the World Trade Organization*. Edward Elgar, Cheltenham U.K., pp. 370–87.
Feeney, J., and A. L. Hillman, 2004. Trade liberalization through asset markets. *Journal of International Economics* 64:151–67. Reprinted in W. J. Ethier and A. L. Hillman (Eds.), 2008. *The Political Economy of International Trade Policy and the World Trade Organization*. Edward Elgar, Cheltenham U.K., pp. 173–89.
Hillman, A. L., and P. Moser, 1996. Trade liberalization as politically optimal exchange of market access. In M. Canzoneri, W. J. Ethier, and V. Grilli (Eds.), *The New Transatlantic Economy*, Cambridge University Press, New York, pp. 295–312. Reprinted in W. J. Ethier and A. L. Hillman (Eds.), *The WTO and the Political Economy of Trade Policy*, Edward Elgar, Cheltenham UK, 2008, pp. 290–307.
Schonhardt-Bailey, C., 1991. Specific factors, capital markets, portfolio diversification, and free trade: Determinants of repeal of the Corn Laws. *World Politics* 43:545–69.

On openness and government size, see:

Garen, J., and K. Trask, 2005. Do more open economies have bigger governments?: Another look. *Journal of Development Economics* 77:533–51.
Rodrik, R., 1998. Why do more open economies have bigger governments? *Journal of Political Economy* 106:997–1032.

On Hobbes and Locke (Hobbes [1651/1962], Locke [1690/1960]), see Rowley (2001). Grossman (2002) showed how a predatory king might benefit a society by preempting anarchy.

Grossman, H. I., 2002. Make us a king: Anarchy, predation, and the state. *European Journal of Political Economy* 18:31–46.
Hobbes, T., 1651/1962. *Leviathan (or the Matter, Forme and Power of a Commonwealth Ecclesiastical and Civil)*. Collier Books, New York.
Locke, J., 1960/1690. *Two Treatises of Government*. P. Lazlett (Ed.), Cambridge University Press, Cambridge U.K.
Rowley, C. K., 2001. Constitutional political economy and civil society. In R. Mudambi, P. Navarra, and G. Sobbrio (Eds.), *Rules and Reason: Perspectives on Constitutional Political Economy*, Cambridge University Press, New York, pp. 69–96.

On constitutional restraint, see Buchanan (1975) and Brennan and Buchanan (1985). The example of Ulysses and the sirens is from Elster (1984). On lagged implementation of a constitution, see Buchanan (1994).

Buchanan, J. M., 1975. *The Limits of Liberty: Between Anarchy and Leviathan*. University of Chicago Press, Chicago IL.
Buchanan, J. M., 1994. Lagged implementation as an element in constitutional strategy. *European Journal of Political Economy* 10:11–26.
Brennan, G., and J. M. Buchanan, 1985. *The Reason of Rules*. Cambridge University Press, Cambridge U.K.
Elster, J. 1984. *Ulysses and the Sirens*. Cambridge University Press, Cambridge U.K.

10.2 Cooperation, trust, and the need for government

On cooperation, see:

Axelrod, R., 1984. *The Evolution of Cooperation*. Basic Books, New York.
Fehr, E., and S. Gächter, 2000. Fairness and retaliation: The economics of reciprocity. *Journal of Economic Perspectives* 14:159–81.
Kreps, D., P. Milgrom, J. Roberts, and R. Wilson, 1982. Rational cooperation in the finitely repeated prisoners' dilemma. *Journal of Economic Theory* 27:245–52.
Shilony, Y., 2000. Diversity and ingenuity in voluntary collective action. *European Journal of Political Economy* 16:429–43.
Guttman, J. M., 2000. On the evolutionary stability of preferences for reciprocity. *European Journal of Political Economy* 16:31–50.

On reputation and social norms, see:

Guttman, J. M., 2001. Self-enforcing reciprocity norms and intergenerational transfers: Theory and evidence. *Journal of Public Economics* 81:17–51.

On esteem, see:

Brennan, G., and P. Pettit, 2004. *The Economy of Esteem: An Essay on Civil and Political Society*. Oxford University Press, Oxford.

On cooperation and common identity, see:

Grief, A., 1994. Cultural beliefs and the organization of society: A historical and theoretical reflection on collectivist and individualistic societies. *Journal of Political Economy* 102:912–50.
Rapoport, H., and A. Weiss, 2003. The optimal size for a minority. *Journal of Economic Behavior and Organization* 52:27–45.

On the trust game, see Berg, Dickhaut, and McCabe (1995). The evidence on gender and the trust game was from Croson and Buchan (1999).

Berg, J., J. Dickhaut, and K. McCabe, 1995. Trust, reciprocity, and social history. *Games and Economic Behavior* 10:122–42.
Croson, R., and N. Buchan, 1999. Gender and culture: International experimental evidence from trust games. *American Economic Review* 89:386–92.

On social capital, see:

Knack, S., and P. Keefer, 1997. Does social capital have an economic payoff? A cross-country investigation. *Quarterly Journal of Economics* 112:1251–88.
Putnam, R. D., 2000. *Bowling Alone: The Collapse and Revival of American Community*. Simon & Schuster, New York.

On income and happiness, see:

Easterlin, R. A., 1974. Does economic growth improve the human lot? Some empirical evidence. In P. A. David and M. W. Reder (Eds.), *Nations and Households in Economic*

Growth: Essays in Honor of Moses Abramovitz. Academic Press, New York, pp. 89–125.
Easterlin, R. A., 2002. *Happiness in Economics*. Edward Elgar, Cheltenham U.K.

10.3 Views on the need for government

On the view that limits the subject matter of economics to efficiency, see Robbins (1932). Musgrave (1910–2007), in a 1959 book that became a classic exposition on public finance, described efficiency and social justice as independently achievable objectives. On political correctness and views of government, see Hillman (1998). The final quote is from Willis (1912).

Hillman, A. L., 1998. Political economy and political correctness. *Public Choice* 96:219–39. Reprinted in R. D. Congleton, A. L. Hillman, and K. A. Konrad, 2008. *40 Years of Research on Rent Seeking 2 – Applications: Rent Seeking in Practice*. Springer, Berlin, pp. 791–811.
Musgrave, R., 1959. *The Theory of Public Finance*. McGraw Hill, New York.
Robbins, L., 1932 (2nd Edition 1935). *An Essay on the Nature and Significance of Economic Science*. Macmillan, London.
Willis, H. P., 1912. Political obstacles to anti-trust legislation. *Journal of Political Economy* 20:588–98.

TOPICS FOR DISCUSSION

The following questions are intended to confirm understanding of the topics of the book. The references are to articles cited in the literature survey at the end of the corresponding chapter.

1. Markets and Governments

1.1 The prima facie case for the market

1. Adam Smith took human nature to be self-serving but based the case for the market on ethical behavior: How was the conjunction between self-serving and ethical behavior achieved? Why is this conjunction regarded as an important contribution to moral philosophy and economics? Is the case for the market based on consistency between self-interested and ethical behavior distinct from the case for the market based on personal freedom? Adam Smith reached his conclusion unaided by a conception of a market that has supply and demand functions: Can you trace through his logical train of thought that without supply and demand functions resulted in the metaphor of the invisible hand? Although Adam Smith was not the originator of the idea of a market characterized by supply and demand, he is nonetheless regarded as the father of modern economics: Do you agree that this acclamation is justified?
2. Although our description of the three required conditions for efficiency of a competitive market is sequential (we describe one condition at a time), the conditions are achieved simultaneously in markets. Why is there simultaneity in the achievement of the conditions?
3. Explain the competitive-adjustment mechanism. How can the metaphor of the invisible hand be extended to the outcomes achieved through the competitive-adjustment mechanism when there are stable and unstable market equilibria?
4. Explain the informational advantages of "spontaneous order" compared to "imposed order." Why might people who have not studied economics prefer imposed to spontaneous order? Why might political decision makers prefer imposed order?

1.2 Efficiency and social justice

1. "Compensation is part of the definition of Pareto-efficiency but whether compensation is actually paid is a question of social justice." Elaborate on this statement.
2. Find information on the Luddite rebellions of the early 19th century. The Luddites protested uncompensated introduction of new technologies that deprived workers

of their jobs. The rebellions were violent and the leaders were hanged or deported to Australia. Was the Luddites' case justified? If you had been a worker at the time, would you have joined the Luddites' rebellion? If compensation cannot be implemented, would you recommend that public policy be based on allowing efficient change to proceed without compensation?

3. In the circumstances of the water in the desert, sharing the water benefits no one because neither person survives. Why might the person without the water nevertheless want the water to be shared?
4. What do the circumstances of the water in the desert and the judgment of Solomon have in common and what are the basic differences? If not everyone can go to college or university, should no one go? How does "owning the water" correspond to ability to succeed in higher education?
5. In consistency with the outcomes of the experiments that were described, people who are not economists often describe a policy or situation as "unfair" but complaints are rarely heard about inefficiency. Why do you believe this is so? How do political parties that emphasize efficiency over fairness (or social justice) ever win elections?
6. People who vote expressively obtain utility from the support they express through the act of voting but do not anticipate being decisive in affecting outcomes through their voting decisions. They may vote in favor of outcomes that they prefer not occur. Why can voting be expressive but not personal market behavior?
7. A story is told about a couple who leave home in the morning wearing frayed clothing and driving a modest car when their business is profitable. When their business is not doing well, they wear designer clothing and drive an expensive car. The reason that they behave in this way is so that their neighbors will be happy when they are happy and their neighbors will be unhappy when they are unhappy.* Does envy explain choice of ex-post equality as the criterion for social justice?
8. Three people who each have incomes of $1,000 are told that their future incomes will be, respectively, $1,500, $1,600, and $1,800. Alternatively, they are told that future incomes will $1,100, $1,700, and $1,800. In both cases, Pareto-improving change will thus take place. If you were one of the three people and you knew that your vote will be decisive, would you vote for accepting the Pareto-improving change in both cases? Would it matter which of the three people you were? If you knew that your vote would not be decisive, would you nonetheless vote expressively?
9. Compare the natural right of possession, equality of opportunity, and ex-post equality as criteria for social justice. Indicate the relationship between each criterion and Pareto efficiency. In terms of this relationship, how do the cases of the water in the desert and the judgment of Solomon differ?
10. If we were to accept the natural right of possession as the criterion for social justice, why would a competitive market equilibrium be both efficient and socially just? What are objections to the criterion of natural right of possession? What are objections to a rule for social justice that gives no role to the natural right of possession?

1.3 The rule of law

1. Prisoners were once private property protected by the rule of law. Bruno Frey and Heinz Buhofer (1988) described a case (from the battle of Poitiers in 1356) in which a prisoner was claimed as personal property, but the captor – after seeing someone

* With thanks to my colleague, Joseph Zur.

else who he could also take prisoner – went off to stake a claim to the new prisoner, leaving the first prisoner unattended. A new captor then appeared and claimed the first prisoner as his own. Prisoners at the time were privately valuable for ransom or for servitude. Private-property rights to the first prisoner were contested in court. The court ruled that the claim to legal possession had been forfeited when the first prisoner had been abandoned. When private-property rights to prisoners ceased, prisoners became the collective property of the state. The "state" had no personal incentive to keep prisoners alive and mass slaughter in warfare began. Would you recommend once more making prisoners private property?

2. Hernando de Soto (2000) made the case for giving squatters who had built on public land legal property rights, to allow their houses to be insured, and to allow property to be used as collateral in loans. Evaluate this public-policy proposal.
3. Adam Smith's "invisible hand" describes personal and social benefit from voluntary personal market decisions. In the Nash equilibrium of the prisoners' dilemma, there are both personal and social benefits from coercion. What is the reason for the differences?
4. English folktales describe a figure named Robin Hood who robbed the rich and gave the proceeds to the poor. In the folktales, the rich use the authority of government to appropriate the property of the poor and Robin Hood rectifies the initial theft through further appropriation. How does the case of Robin Hood correspond to anarchy? Were Robin Hood and the legal authority (the Sheriff of Nottingham) caught in a prisoners' dilemma? In original early versions of the story, Robin Hood was a predator who kept what he stole for himself; would this view of Robin Hood change any of your answers?
5. In the movie, "A Beautiful Mind," about the life of John Nash, Nash proposes a strategy for how he and two fellow male students should approach four women in a bar. One woman is the first preference of all three men and the other three women are the equal second preference. Nash proposes to his two colleagues that they all ignore their first preference and choose instead, between them, the three women who are their equal second preference – which is what they proceed to do. If the scene in the movie is intended to demonstrate Nash equilibrium, did the producers of the movie understand the concept of Nash equilibrium?
6. Change tables 1.3a and 1.3b to show a society in which the weak are less productive. What effect does this have on efficiency, defined as the ratio between total output produced (on average) by the strong and the weak and potential maximal output? What happens if the strong are less productive? What happens when the cost of appropriation increases?
7. There are many possible outcomes of stationary-bandit behavior with different distributions of benefits for the strong and the weak. Why is this so?
8. Why would you expect people who are not protected by the rule of law to emphasize investment in education rather than in land or other physical property? Which social norms would you expect the weak to transmit culturally to their children?
9. When the strong can have their way with the weak, why might we expect the unkempt, disheveled exterior of houses to hide beautiful interior rooms and courtyards? What behavior would you expect from women – or to be culturally imposed on women – in a Nietzschean society?
10. Begin with a society without the rule of law in which all people behave according to ethical rules of conduct, as in table 1.4a. Then, still without the rule of law, introduce some people who behave according to the payoffs of the prisoners' dilemma. The population now consists of different types of people as in table 1.4d. Why is the introduction of the rule of law not Pareto-improving? Should the non-Pareto-improving change to introduce the rule of law be permitted to take place? Should the losers from the introduction of the rule of law be compensated?

11. When a driver parking a car in a public parking lot gives money to a person who approaches the driver, is the payment being made to a stationary or roving bandit? With the parking lot public property, why might the government have failed to protect its property rights?
12. Should governments be legally liable for imperfect enforcement of the rule of law?
13. In what sense is insurance against theft a response to the inability of government to ensure the rule of law? Is insurance appeasement?
14. Would you prefer that a jury of citizens or a panel of appointed judges decide a case in which you are involved? Judges might claim professional knowledge of the law and that members of a jury are "amateurs." Would such a claim affect your decision?

Supplement S1A: Market efficiency in general equilibrium

1. Describe the objectives required to be achieved for efficiency in a competitive economy and how competitive markets ensure that the objectives are achieved.
2. How would you expect the complexity of a general-equilibrium model of a competitive economy to affect attitudes toward the choice between spontaneous and imposed order?

Supplement S1B: The competitive market-adjustment mechanism

1. Compare the market-adjustment mechanisms associated with Marshall and Walras.
2. Is one mechanism more plausible than the other? Does the idea of the invisible hand suggest that the Marshallian mechanism is more appropriate?

Supplement S1C: Monopoly profits and social justice

1. When monopoly is replaced by competition, should shareholders who owned stock in a former monopoly be compensated?
2. Would you recommend compensation for someone who bought a taxicab license and who then lost when a public-policy decision made the local taxi market more competitive?
3. Are your answers for owners of shares purchased in stock markets the same as for the owner of the taxi? Explain why your answers differ or are the same.

2. Institutions and Governance

2.1 The political principal–agent problem

1. Evidence presented by Knack and Keefer (1995), Hall and Jones (1999), and others showed that when there are good institutions, people are more productive and social indicators such as school attendance, health, and life expectancy are higher.

Borooah and Paldam (2007) concluded that high incomes are the cause of (or result in) democratic institutions rather than democratic institutions being the cause of high incomes: What are reasons for this direction of causality? Are there reasons that would justify the opposite direction of causality?

2. Do you perceive that "rational ignorance" about public finance and public policy is prevalent in the society in which you live? Attitudes toward whether voters should be described as "rationally ignorant" appear to be influenced by ideology: What are the beliefs that you expect people to have who object to the suggestion that voters are rationally ignorant about behavior and decisions of politicians? If voters are rationally ignorant, why do they vote?
3. Do the media contribute to solving the political principal–agent problem? Can you predict the position regarding support for particular politicians or parties taken by different newspapers or television channels? How does media bias affect rational ignorance and special-interest privileges?
4. If you wished to contest political office, what are the main obstacles that you would encounter and what would you need to overcome the obstacles? Are you sympathetic to a claim by political candidates and parties that because of the prisoners' dilemma, they have no choice but to accept political contributions from special interests?
5. Should political expenses be publicly financed? If so, which criteria would you propose for public financing of political expenses? In the jurisdictions in which you vote (or could vote), do candidates for political office receive publicly financed payments for campaign expenses? If so, what are the rules for receiving public money? Would you change public policy regarding the financing of political expenses?
6. What are your views on regulation of personal political contributions that excludes the value of political endorsements from owners of newspapers and entertainers? Why are voters influenced by the political endorsements of film stars, singers, and sports celebrities – and journalists?
7. Outline the cases for and against term limits. Do you support term limits for political representatives? Does your preference apply to all levels of government, from federal or central government to local government?
8. If compulsory voting solves a voter-coordination problem, why do we not observe more instances of compulsory voting? Is compulsory voting in the interest of political decision makers?
9. What is a "rent"? Distinguish rent creation, rent seeking, and rent extraction, and indicate the sources of associated social loss. Rent creation is often observable but rent seeking and rent extraction are not. Can the magnitude of social losses from rent seeking be inferred when rent seeking itself is not observable?
10. Are resources used in political advertising a case of rent seeking? Are resources used in advertising by firms a case of rent seeking?
11. Does rent seeking influence your personal life? Describe instances of rent seeking that you encounter.
12. A proposed measure of the prevalence of rent seeking is the number of lawyers in a society. Why has this measure been proposed?
13. "The prisoners' dilemma of rent seeking and the prisoners' dilemma of principled politicians are similar in that otherwise honest people feel compelled to behave in unethical ways." Do you agree?
14. Lobbyists often have an important intermediating role in rent seeking. Why is this so?
15. In Hillman and Ursprung (2000), a society is described in which two groups of people are seeking rents. A group of insiders has privileged direct access to contesting rents through influence on political decisions. Outsiders engage in rent-seeking

contests with the intent of becoming insiders. After political liberalization, insiders lose their privileged access to rent seeking because previous outsiders can now also directly compete for rents. Is there greater social justice because of the end of privilege in access to rent seeking? Can a society be worse off after open access to rent seeking makes rent seeking more competitive? How can increased social losses from more open access to rent seeking be avoided without restoring privileged access to the rent-seeking opportunities of political decisions?

16. In terms of social losses, how does payment of bribes differ from rent seeking?
17. Is a society corrupt if the activities of corrupt politicians are systematically revealed in the press?

2.2 Government bureaucracy

1. Why do the dedicated civil servants described by Max Weber exist more in some societies than in others? Do you believe that career government bureaucrats indeed seek to increase the size of the budgets that they control? Or, are government bureaucrats generally dedicated to serving the public as described by Max Weber? Do you have evidence? If you have no evidence, is that an indication of a principal–agent problem? Is it plausible to attribute self-interested behavior to buyers and sellers in markets and to political candidates contesting political office while maintaining that government bureaucrats do not have self-interested objectives?
2. How can public policy address the incentive for self-creation of demand by government bureaucracies or self-creation of tasks through memos and meetings?
3. If excess paperwork is a means whereby government bureaucrats provide signals for measurable output, how would you expect e-mail to change the behavior of government bureaucrats?
4. In the private sector, incentive schemes allow principals (for example, shareholders) to align the interests of agents (management) with their own objectives. Can similar schemes be used for solving the principal–agent problem between taxpayers and government bureaucracy? Is payment of high incomes as efficiency wages to government bureaucrats a means of overcoming the principal–agent problem of bureaucracy?
5. Do you believe that the Thomas-à-Becket effect is a credible basis for change in behavior when a person takes a position inside a government bureaucracy?
6. How does the political system affect the incentives and the ability of political representatives to monitor government bureaucracy? What are the sources of information asymmetries between political representatives and bureaucracy? How do the information asymmetries affect the ability of political representatives to monitor government bureaucracy?
7. Corruption is defined as the use of the authority of government for personal benefit – for example, to obtain bribes. A government bureaucracy oversees collection and spending of government revenue: What do you expect to be the consequence in corrupt societies? In high-income countries, corruption in government bureaucracy is uncommon: Is there a difference between corruption and self-interested budgetary expansion in government bureaucracies?

2.3 Life without markets and private property

1. Communism was motivated by the objective to end the inequality under institutions of markets and private property. View the movie "East-West" and provide

your impressions of life without markets and private property. Relate your impressions to the circumstances of the water in the desert and to the claim that "Unless everybody cannot have something, no one should have it." Could life without markets and private property in principle have been consistent with personal freedom?

2. Caldwell (1998) described how Hayek was viewed by contemporaries because of his prediction that communism would not succeed in re-engineering human nature to make people contribute according to ability and so without regard for personal reward. Why was Hayek's prediction unpopular with some professors of economics in high-income Western societies with institutions of markets and private property? People unhappy under communism sought to leave communist countries. Why did the professors who were critical of Hayek not emigrate to communist societies?
3. The co-founder of communism, Engels (1884), proposed that communal property liberates women from "ownership" by specific men. There seem to be more women at college or university than men (check the statistics). What are the consequences for the validity of Engel's argument?
4. What are the personal characteristics of the people who you would expect to succeed in controlling communal property? Why is the quest to succeed in controlling communal property a rent-seeking contest?
5. How would you expect to fare in life if all property were communal (except your basic possessions, such as clothing and shoes) and there were no markets? In markets, payment is with money. What are the requisites of personal success in obtaining goods and services when there are no markets and private property?

Supplement S2A: Rent seeking and rent dissipation

1. A declaration that governments ought faithfully to serve the public interest and should not be responsive to rent seeking is normative. Rent seeking is a positive concept that describes or predicts behavior. Why might people's claims or beliefs about the prevalence of rent seeking differ?
2. What is "rent dissipation"? How does rent dissipation measure social loss?
3. Use the example of monopoly to compare the social loss due to rent creation with the social loss due to rent seeking. Provide examples of how rent creation and rent seeking could, in principle, take place through the government budget.
4. Because rent seeking usually takes place in hidden contests, models of rent-seeking contests use the value of an observed rent to infer the value of the resources attracted into rent seeking. What are the principal conclusions from models of rent-seeking contests about the relationship between resources used in rent seeking and the values of observed rents?
5. What are the consequences for rent seeking when political decision makers are required "to follow rules" rather than being allowed "to exercise discretion"? Are there advantages of allowing political discretion, rather than requiring political decision makers and government officials to follow designated rules about public finance and public policy?

Supplement S2B: Institutions and natural monopoly

1. Compare regulation and competitive bidding as public-policy solutions to existence of natural monopoly. Outline the advantages and disadvantages of both public policies.

2. Competitive bidding for the right to be a natural monopolist can take place in terms of the price that buyers will be required pay for a good or service, or the amount of money that a bidder is prepared to pay to be the monopolist. How do outcomes for efficiency and social justice differ under the two types of competitive bidding?
3. A solution to natural monopoly is for government to own the natural monopoly. Yet, many countries that adopted the state-ownership solution to natural monopoly subsequently privatized government-owned natural monopolies. Why were the decisions made to privatize? Does the responsibility of government end when a natural monopoly has been privatized?

Supplement S2C: Labor self-management

1. Would you feel more comfortable or happier working in a labor cooperative where there are no employers and bosses telling you what to do than as an employee in a firm with private owners or shareholders?
2. Why are egalitarian objectives of a labor-managed cooperative inconsistent with efficient labor employment?
3. "Management buyouts" in which managers borrow to buy the assets of a firm are common whereas few "worker buyouts" occur. Why do we not observe more instances of institutions of labor management? What is the relevance of the story of the man with the whip to your answer?

3. Public Goods

3.1 Types of public goods

1. How does asymmetric information affect voluntary payment for public goods? What should Robinson Crusoe have done when he was quite certain that people were being untruthful about their benefits from public goods in order to avoid contributing to payment, after the public goods were already in existence?
2. Thinking about your life in the course of a day, classify the public goods from which you benefit, according to whether the type is prisoners' dilemma, volunteer-type public good, or weakest link. If people were asked voluntarily to finance the prisoners'-dilemma-type public goods in your list through anonymous voluntary contributions, which public goods do you believe would receive sufficient voluntary financing to approximate efficient spending? Could a professor or instructor be anticipated to receive a reasonable salary based on private voluntary contributions of students who anonymously place money in an envelope after each class, even when classes are interesting and lucidly presented?
3. Place yourself in the position of playing the public-good game in which you are asked to choose a division of money (that has been given to you for purposes of the experiment) between private spending and contribution to a public good. How would you choose to divide the money? Would your choice of division depend on whether you were interacting with economics students or students who intended to be social workers?

4. People living together in the same household face repeated prisoners'-dilemma public-good interactions. How are the problems resolved?
5. If a market could be established for voluntary payment for public goods, how would demand and supply in markets in private and public goods differ? How would personal freedom to choose (or a lack thereof) be expressed in the two types of markets? Why is consensus the critical attribute identifying efficiency in the Lindahl voluntary financing solution?
6. In one society, a driver stops and moves a rock to the side of the road. In another society, drivers swerve around the rock and continue on their way, even though the same drivers will be passing along the same stretch of road the next day. What are the reasons why behavior might differ in the two societies? What affects the probability that a volunteer-type public good will be provided, either efficiently or inefficiently?
7. What is "cheap talk?" Coordination problems are present in both the volunteer and weakest-link cases of public goods. Does cheap talk have the same role in both types of coordination problems? Why does no one wish to free ride in the case of weakest-link type public goods?
8. What are the special characteristics of national defense as a public good? A communist regime in the Soviet Union that ended in the early 1990s viewed societies with democratic institutions as enemies. "Pro-peace" demonstrations took place in Western democracies by people who proclaimed the need for unilateral disarmament in Western democracies. Describe the behavior of the protestors in the context of the prisoners' dilemma of national security.
9. In general, democracies do not initiate war; rather, wars usually begin with an attack on a democracy by a nondemocratic country. What do you believe are the reasons?
10. If the campus were threatened by terrorists, an ethical dilemma would arise in preempting terrorism by not allowing anyone identified with a group that had committed acts of terrorism in the past onto campus. Human-rights activists would point out that the decision compromised principles of human rights by imposing collective punishment. How could "cheap talk" about human rights be distinguished from a true principled position? Is the following statement necessarily cheap talk? "I would never agree to mistreatment of a captured terrorist, even if the life that might be saved by information that the terrorist could provide might be my own." If there is cheap talk, what is its purpose in this case? Is there a relationship between "expressive behavior" (people confirming their identity to themselves or others) and cheap talk?
11. Deterrence is impossible when terrorists declare that "we love death more than you love life" and look forward to death. To change suicide terrorists' incentives, would you support a policy of announcing financial penalties on families of terrorists who kill themselves in order to kill and maim innocent civilians? If incentives are changed and deterrence is effective, why is imposing the penalties unnecessary? Read Bernholz (2004) on supreme values and terrorism. Evaluate the feasibility of the solutions that are proposed in the paper to the problem of defense against terrorism.
12. A plane has been hijacked by two terrorists who, with high probability, wish to crash the plane. There are 150 passengers and crew on the plane. A group of 10 passengers acting together could with high probability overpower the terrorists but at risk of personal harm to themselves. Explain the circumstances and predictions about outcomes in terms of the theory of public goods. Which types of public goods are involved in this example?

3.2 Information and public goods

1. Government can solve the free-rider problem by legally compelling payment for public goods through taxes. Why is the ability of government to enforce payment through taxation insufficient for solving the problem of efficient public-good supply?
2. How does the Clarke tax overcome the incentive to misrepresent preferences regarding public goods? Provide another example of the use of the Clarke tax in which a government faces a choice between the financing of two projects. Why are governments reluctant to use the Clarke tax?
3. All cars could be equipped with measuring devices that calculate user prices for all road travel: Do you support such a proposal? Is it fair for people who have no children to pay taxes to finance schools? Could or should user prices be applied to police protection? Should convicted felons in jail pay user prices to finance the costs of prisons? Return to question 1 in section 3.1; for which public goods in your list is user pricing feasible and in which cases would you recommend user prices? Is a case in favor of user prices for public goods precisely the same as a case for private goods supplied through paying market prices? Evaluate user prices from the perspectives of efficiency and social justice. Would you like to live in a society in which taxation is minimized by applying user prices wherever possible?
4. Describe the circumstances under which self-financing user prices are feasible. If self-financing user prices are not feasible, should governments subsidize payment of user prices? Relate your answer to the case for subsidizing natural monopoly for private goods.
5. In Hillman and Jenkner (2004), cases are described in which low-income households in poor countries voluntarily choose to pay user prices for schooling of children, either because government schools are inadequate or do not exist. Nongovernment agencies and some governments in rich countries objected to the voluntary user prices on the grounds that governments in the poor countries have the responsibility to and therefore *should* provide good schools. At the same time, there were no objections to rich households in poor countries paying user prices to have their children attend private schools (often, the rich parents sent the children to schools outside the country). Identify the normative and positive propositions involved here. Is the normative declaration about what governments in poor countries ought to do (but do not do) expressive? Do you believe that poor parents in poor countries should be permitted to choose to pay user prices for schooling of their children in nongovernment schools? Do you believe that rich parents in poor countries should be permitted to choose to pay user prices for schooling of their children in private schools?
6. The Lindahl solution proposes (normatively) that people with different preferences for spending on the same public goods should reside and pay taxes in the same jurisdiction. Compare the Lindahl solution and the Tiebout locational-choice mechanism for public goods. Why is the Tiebout mechanism "second-best" compared to the ideal Lindahl solution? Is the locational-choice mechanism normative (a recommendation) or positive (a description), or both?
7. Tiebout was responding to the claim that centralized government supply of public goods was necessary because asymmetric information makes efficient supply through private voluntary payments impossible. How does the Tiebout locational-choice mechanism introduce choice for public goods akin to market decisions? The locational-choice mechanism is based on the benefit principle of payment, whereas centralized government supply is, in general, based on public spending financed according to the ability-to-pay principle. How might this difference affect political

decisions about the choice between the locational-choice mechanism and centralized government supply?

8. The Tiebout case for locational-choice as means of revealing information about benefits from public goods is based on differences in people's preferences for public goods. How do differences in *incomes* as the basis for locational choice affect the normative conclusions about desirability of outcomes of the locational-choice mechanism?
9. What is "locational rent"? What is the role of locational rents in the Tiebout locational-choice mechanism?
10. In the case of owners of cars and trucks sharing a road, why is there a cooperative game, in contrast to the non-cooperative game of the prisoners'-dilemma public good? What is the Nash bargaining solution to a cooperative game? Provide other examples in which financing of public goods involves a cooperative game. What is the common attribute of these examples?
11. Why is locational choice in separate government jurisdictions a desirable (not second-best) solution when people want completely different types of public goods?
12. Is there a difference in principle between user prices as means of financing public goods and the Tiebout locational mechanism? What does "the theory of clubs" describe? What is the relationship between the theory of clubs and the Tiebout locational-choice mechanism? Give examples of phenomena to which the theory of clubs applies. In all three cases – user prices, locational choice, and the theory of clubs – what is the common role of exclusion?

3.3 Cost-benefit analysis

1. Why does transparent and accountable government require governments to provide accompanying cost-benefit analysis for all public spending? Why is cost-benefit analysis not provided for all items in government budgets?
2. How does choice of the discount rate affect public-spending decisions based on cost-benefit analysis? When the environment or biodiversity is involved, should positive rates of discount be applied for evaluating public projects? Is there a general case for a zero discount rate for evaluating costs and benefits over time of public spending? That is, should future generations have the same weight in the computation of costs and benefits from public spending as present generations? Are there reasons for proposing that the market rate of interest indicates the discount rate that should be used in cost-benefit analysis for public spending?
3. Publicly financed projects can increase the probability that people will live longer or will avoid injury, as when governments finance highway improvement, provide subsidies for medical research, provide security personnel at airports, or finance police or national defense. If you were asked to do a cost-benefit analysis of public spending in such cases, how would you value an increase in the likelihood that a person's life will be saved?
4. When choices are required, should public investment be aimed at protecting the lives of the skilled educated population rather than the unskilled poor on the grounds of past investment in human capital and future income?
5. Cost-benefit analysis is intended to ensure efficient public spending, but political considerations influence spending of public money. If a political representative has the means to allocate public funds for an inefficient project (for which costs exceed benefits in his or her electoral district), the constituents would be better

off receiving the money directly. What do you expect to happen if the alternative of an efficiency-enhancing policy of direct income payments were proposed? Does rational ignorance have a role in your answer?

Supplement S3A: Group size and voluntary public-good contributions

1. Explain how income effects influence Nash voluntary contributions to public goods. How are total Nash contributions affected by the combination of substitution and income effects when the size of the group voluntarily contributing to public goods increases? Does "free riding" necessarily increase as the group size increases? How is free-riding defined in the case of this question?
2. When rent seeking takes place by members of a group who seek to benefit from a public good, how do outcomes differ from a case in which members of a group are seeking private benefits in the form of income to be shared?
3. Why, for total Nash group spending on a public good to be independent of the distribution of income in a group, is the qualification required that the same members of a group make positive voluntary contributions to financing the public good in the Nash equilibria before and after the redistribution of income?
4. Describe how the collective-action problem for public goods applies to both economics and politics.

Supplement S3B: Property taxes and incentives for zoning

1. Why can the payment for public goods through property taxes be regarded as voluntary?
2. When property taxes finance public goods, why are there incentives for zoning? Why does the substitution effect for voluntary provision of public goods provide incentives for residents of a jurisdiction to vote for zoning?

Supplement S3C: Other approaches to private payment for public goods

1. Compare the Nash-equilibrium approach to collective action to an approach that begins with the presumption of cooperation. Do implications about group size and the effectiveness of collective action differ in the two cases?
2. Is joint supply of public and private goods an effective means, in some cases, of avoiding the free-rider problem?
3. Describe how lotteries can be used to finance public goods.

Supplement S3D: An efficient economy with public and private goods

1. Compare the general-equilibrium outcome with public goods to the general-equilibrium outcome in supplement S1A in which only private goods are present.

2. The supplement shows the derivation of the Samuelson condition for efficient public-good supply in general equilibrium. Asymmetric information is missing from this derivation. What are the consequences for derivation of the Samuelson condition of acknowledging the presence of asymmetric information, that is, that people's *MB* from public goods is their own private information unknown to governments?

4. Public Finance for Public Goods

4.1 Taxation

1. What is the relationship between substitution effects and the excess burden of taxation?
2. The excess burden of taxation is invisible: how would you convince a political decision maker of the existence of the excess burden of taxation?
3. Is there any difference in principle between the excess burden of direct and indirect taxes?
4. How is the excess burden of taxation affected by substitution responses in other markets?
5. Are taxes with no excess burdens possible? Are such taxes politically feasible?
6. Ng (1987) proposed that taxes on goods such as diamonds do not have an excess burden of taxation because diamonds are valued intrinsically for their value and taxes increase their value. Evaluate this proposal. If a sales tax is imposed on diamonds (or an existing sales tax is increased), what are the consequences for people who already own diamonds?
7. In Hillman and Katz (1984) it was proposed that taxes on goods that are easy to steal are undesirable because the attractiveness of theft of the goods is increased. Why does this proposal indicate a reason for an efficiency loss of taxation related to rent seeking?
8. The administrative costs of taxation include the costs of the government taxation bureaucracy and the time people need to prepare tax returns or the cost of delegating tax preparation to accountants and tax lawyers. How are the administrative costs related to the social losses from rent seeking?
9. Emotional costs of taxation are difficult to measure. Can you suggest ways in which estimates of emotional costs might nonetheless be approached?
10. Does the absence of tax revenue in a market indicate no excess burden of taxation?
11. Empirical estimates of the excess burden of taxation vary. Are the high or low ranges of the estimates more likely to be true? What are the reasons for your conclusion?
12. What is the role of the excess burden of taxation in the derivation of the Laffer curve? Why is the concept of a Laffer curve sometimes controversial? What are the ideological beliefs or political preferences that you would expect to underlie resistance to the concept of the Laffer curve?
13. How would you contribute to a debate about whether employers should pay for health insurance for employees or whether employees should pay for their own health insurance? Why have laws, as for example in the United States, required employers to provide health insurance for employees?
14. Why is there no excess burden of a tax when one side of the market (buyers or sellers) pays the entire tax?

15. What is fiscal illusion? How does fiscal illusion affect awareness of tax incidence (or who pays taxes) and the political choice between direct and indirect taxes?
16. If there is fiscal illusion, are there consequences for utility when it is explained to buyers that part of the price that they are paying is a tax? In some locations, the seller announces the price and adds "plus tax" as separate information for the buyers. In other locations, the seller announces the price inclusive of tax. There can be no fiscal illusion in the first case, but fiscal illusion is possible in the second case. What are the consequences for buyers of the different ways of announcing price?
17. Compare a value-added tax with a sales tax. How do fiscal-federal systems of government affect the choice between the two types of taxes?
18. Compare a sales tax and import duty as means of collecting government revenue. Why can we presume that taxes on imports are not motivated by revenue? Why are imports taxed? Why have governments sometimes forgone tax revenue by choosing an import quota rather than an import duty (or a tariff) to limit imports? What is the role of rent creation and rent seeking in your answer?

4.2 Tax evasion and the shadow economy

1. How are the public-good prisoners' dilemma and tax evasion related? What are the influences on personal compliance with tax-payment obligations? Which policies can governments use against tax evasion?
2. Is it unfair that people in different professions have different opportunities for tax evasion? "Efficiency and social justice are both compromised by tax evasion and a shadow economy." Do you agree with this evaluation?
3. What is the difference between tax evasion and tax avoidance?
4. What is "presumptive taxation"? Do you believe that governments should be permitted to determine tax payments based on presumptive taxation?
5. How does a value-added tax affect opportunities for income-tax evasion?
6. What is "money laundering"? How is money laundering related to tax evasion?
7. The web site of Transparency International provides data on countries' corruption rankings. Schneider (2005) provided data on the size of the shadow economy including countries not included in table 4.1. Would you expect to see a systematic relationship when you compare the corruption data with the size of the shadow economy? What are the reasons for a relationship between corruption and a shadow economy?
8. The data indicate that the size of the shadow economy has increased over time in high-income countries. What reasons might underlie this phenomenon?
9. Summarize ways in which tax evasion and the size of the shadow economy are measured. Why might governments and others object to estimates of high values for tax evasion and the size of the shadow economy? Who might the "others" be in this case?
10. A person hired as housekeeper is obliged to pay income tax. Someone who stays at home to look after children and tend to the household does not pay taxes on the value of the services provided to his or her partner and family. Is the nonpayment of taxes tax evasion, tax avoidance, or neither?

4.3 Government borrowing

1. Why is public finance through government borrowing deferred taxation? Why is government borrowing – or bond financing – an application of the benefit principle of taxation?
2. A public project will provide benefits for three periods of time. The total cost of the project is 3,000, and benefits are divided over time such that the generation working in period 1 has 50 percent of the benefits, the generation working in period 2 has 30 percent of the benefits, and the generation working in period 3 has the remaining 20 percent of the benefits. With an interest rate of 5 percent, show how bond financing can distribute financing of the project commensurate with the distribution of benefits (each generation lives for two periods, the period when it is working and another period when it is retired). Interest payments are financed by the generation working when interest payments are due.
3. What is Ricardian equivalence?
4. What is the relationship between Ricardian equivalence and fiscal illusion in bond financing? What is the relationship between fiscal illusion in bond financing and rational ignorance? Why might fiscal illusion affect governments' use of bond financing? Do you believe that taxpayers know the value of their future tax obligations that are the consequence of past government borrowing? Does fiscal illusion justify constitutional restraint on government borrowing?
5. Why is fiscal illusion an ideologically sensitive topic? Who can be expected to downplay the role of fiscal illusion and for which reasons?
6. Although bond financing is justified by the benefit principle of taxation, how can bond financing be used opportunistically to assign taxes without regard for benefit?
7. Are the considerations that arise when a government has a budgetary surplus symmetric to the considerations when revenue is required to finance additional public spending? Would you propose constitutional or legal restraint on what governments are permitted to do with surplus revenue?

Supplement S4A: The excess burden with substitution and income effects

1. How do income effects affect the measurement of the excess burden of taxation?
2. Explain the differences between and the relative magnitudes of the measures known as compensating and equivalent variations.

5. Market Corrections

5.1 Externalities and private resolution

1. What is an externality? How can externalities exist that require no market corrections?
2. List the major negative externalities that you encounter in the course of a day, including the sources of the externalities. Can you judge further negative

externalities that you would encounter in the absence of legal rights that preempt negative externalities being imposed on you? List the positive externalities that you encounter. Why have the externalities that you encounter not been resolved in the manner predicted by the Coase theorem? Does your personal list of externalities include cases for which the large size of the affected group prevents voluntary resolution of the externalities? Can you identify externalities (positive or negative) that you would confront if behavior were not influenced by social norms and conventions?

3. How do private-property rights avoid the tragedy of the commons and thereby facilitate sustainable conservation of renewable natural resources such as forests and fishing stocks? Would private-property rights help preserve endangered species of animals?
4. Why are the social costs of rent seeking related to the way in which the commons are converted to private ownership? How do consequences for social justice arise when commons are privatized?
5. "Green" political parties and environmental groups have the primary objective of protecting the environment and saving societies from the tragedy of the commons. Often, they identify with an ideology that is suspicious of private-property rights and markets. Yet, we have proposed that private-property rights and markets allow externalities to be internalized. Why do green political parties and environmental groups generally focus on the need for government to resolve environmental problems rather than private resolution through the incentives of private ownership?
6. Are there times when you would like to create a market for "someone to stop bothering you"? Or, perhaps you would like more attention from a particular person. Is one of the reasons why you do not attempt to create a Coase-type market that you think offering money will be counterproductive? What are the general circumstances in which an offer of money in an attempt to create a market might be counterproductive?
7. What is the relationship between externalities and public goods? That is, when do externalities also become public goods? How do the various aspects of public goods associated with asymmetric information affect private resolution of externalities through the Coase theorem?
8. The neighbors are having a loud party and the noise bothers you. You go to the neighbor's house and conduct a poll asking everyone present how much they need to be paid for the party to stop. You find that the sum of money you would have to pay exceeds your benefit from stopping the party. What do you conclude about efficiency and fairness of the outcome? If there were no party but the neighbor was alone at home listening to loud music, would you expect the outcome of an attempt to resolve the externality problem to change?
9. Explain how market capitalization of externalities affects the Coase theorem. Why, because of capitalization, are low-income people generally more subject to adverse externalities than high-income people?
10. Summarize the reasons why the predictions of the Coase theorem can fail to be realized.
11. How are externalities internalized by personal behavior when self-esteem and social approval matter?
12. Review both sides of the case for citizens' right of self-defense by being armed. Distinguish between the normative and positive aspects of the arguments. Are there, in your view, expressive aspects of the debate (people taking positions to express their nature to themselves and others)?

5.2 Public policies and externalities

1. There are many possible externalities based on subjective likes and dislikes. How can a society determine the externalities that should be the target of resolution through public policy? Would you agree to a proposal that everyone should be obliged to shower or bathe once a day using soap and to change their clothes, and that verified complaints about people in public places who have failed to do so should be punishable by law? Are there externalities that you would like to see corrected that the government does not attempt to correct?
2. A person who has a contagious or infectious disease can be a source of a severe externality for others. What are the obstacles to seeking private resolution of such externalities through the Coase theorem? What is your opinion on the use of an indelible but inconspicuously placed marker that enables identification of people who are HIV-positive?
3. What are the similarities and dissimilarities between the Coase private-resolution solution for externalities and the Pigovian tax-subsidy solution through government? Do limitations on the Coase solution apply to Pigovian taxes and subsidies?
4. Why does the order of private resolution of externalities and public policy matter? In practice, which do you expect to come first?
5. Externality problems associated with education, smoking, and sexual harassment are generally addressed through public policies of direct regulation rather than through Pigovian taxes and subsidies. Why is this so?
6. Does the theory of the second-best justify a monopoly or a cartel when there are negative externalities?
7. Summarize the public-policy means available to governments to resolve externality problems and the influences affecting the choice by government from among the alternatives.
8. Find information on the environmental problems that occurred at Love Canal, New York, and in Woburn, Massachusetts, in the United States.* How did the harmful externalities arise and why were the externalities allowed to persist?
9. Environmental policies affect profits of firms. The political principal–agent problem suggests that political decision makers sensitive to political support may not use public policy to perfectly internalize externalities. Describe how environmental policy might be chosen as a trade-off between the interests of producers and the public interest. How are gains distributed or costs imposed when political decision makers respond to a change in public-interest standards? Why did the U.S. government protect the dolphins?
10. Governments can set national emissions quotas and choose the method of assignment of the emission rights to producers. The rights to emissions can then be traded in markets. What conclusions can be drawn from the experiences from the U.S. market in SO_2 and the European market in CO_2? Investigate the functioning of a market in emissions rights. Does the market that you have chosen to investigate appear competitive? Does government have an ongoing role in the market?
11. What conclusions do you draw from the successful international agreement on protection of the ozone layer known as the Montreal Protocol? What is the relationship between free-riding incentives and the need that was present for the World Bank to provide inducements for some governments to accept the provisions of the Montreal Protocol?

* On the latter case, see the book by Jonathan Harr (1996), *A Civil Action*, Vintage Books, New York.

12. Compare the cases for and against a significant human impact on global warming. Can a scientifically objective conclusion be reached, in your view, that the primary cause of global warming is human activity and not natural cycles of global warming and cooling such as have been observed in the past?
13. When global targets for emissions reductions are sought, should obligations to reduce emissions be assigned among countries based on contemporary emissions or on population? Does the assignment rule affect efficiency? Why is the Coase theorem relevant in your answer? How does assignment of the global quota for emissions among countries affect incentives of governments to participate in international agreements?
14. Evidence shows that autocratic governments do not protect the environment. When a government owns everything, would you expect the environment to be well protected? Find information on the Aral Sea. What is the relationship between government ownership and the tragedy of the commons?
15. "Foreign governments failing to adopt protective environmental policies are the source of externalities and not the World Bank and the International Monetary Fund, which promote free markets." If this is so, why are protests directed at the World Bank and the International Monetary Fund and not at the foreign governments? Would you expect representative global government to resolve benevolently global externality problems in the public interest?
16. Should foreign governments be permitted to use lax environmental standards as a source of their country's comparative advantage in international trade? Should foreign governments be permitted to import hazardous waste?

5.3 Paternalistic public policies

1. Is your position on paternalism that of the libertarians? Set out your views on whether government should be permitted to choose paternalistic public policies. Is the libertarian position "expressive"?
2. Blood, organ donations, and sex are cases in which voluntary giving is permitted but markets are often illegal. Review the case for illegality of markets in each case. Do the considerations that apply to blood also apply to organ donations and sex? Investigate legal prostitution in the U.S. state of Nevada. After your investigation, provide a conclusion whether in your view the legal market should be retained in Nevada or disallowed.
3. Give examples of different illegal markets and describe the consequences of illegality, as well as the outcomes that you would expect if markets were legalized. Do you believe that markets for sale of babies for adoption should be legal? Should purchase of foreign babies be legal?
4. What is hyperbolic discounting? Is hyperbolic discounting necessarily irrational behavior? Is hyperbolic discounting a justification for public policy? Conduct a survey and ask smokers if they are aware of the long-term consequences for their health from tars and nicotine in tobacco. Can you discover from their answers whether they are hyperbolic discounters?
5. Evidence links alcohol to sexually transmitted disease (see Chesson et al., 2000). Does this evidence suggest that excessive alcohol temporarily makes people hyperbolic discounters? Are there implications for public policy? More generally, is there a role for public policy when the problems stem from excesses but moderation does not result in self-harm?
6. Outline public policies that you would propose as the response to obesity. Or, would you propose that weight is a personal matter in which governments should

not intervene? Data show that low-income people are more likely to be obese than high-income people. Why do you believe that is so? Is hyperbolic discounting involved in obesity? For air travel, should obese people be required to pay for two side-by-side airline seats or be required to buy more expensive business-class tickets in order to have wider seats?

7. Compare the theory of "rational addiction" with hyperbolic discounting. Which theory do you find more convincing as the explanation for observed behavior?
8. Explain why the phenomenon of "payday lending" is an example of hyperbolic discounting. What, if anything, should governments do about payday lending? Do you agree with Jeremy Bentham or Adam Smith regarding interest rates and borrowing?
9. The Allais paradox illustrates "framing" and "bounded rationality"? Describe these latter concepts. Does the Allais paradox have consequences for paternalistic public policy?
10. Should all forms of gambling be illegal? What do you believe governments should do, if anything, if people make mistakes because they do not understand the concept of objective probability? How is your position on gambling related to personal and occupational safety? Why not rely on personal judgment to determine whether people wear seat belts or use appropriate protective means to protect against job hazards?
11. If you visit a legal casino during the day in mid-week in a non-holiday period (when most people are working), you may find that the population of patrons appears poorer on average than the general population. What do you conclude from this observation? Are there consequences for public policy?
12. Governments act paternalistically in only allowing certified investment advisors to give financial advice. Yet, by following the suggestions of certified investment advisors, people can incur financial losses. Is allowing only certified investment advisors to give investment advice justified? Would you approve of allowing anyone to be an investment advisor but obliging all past investment recommendations (not only the recommendations that were successful) to be publicly available on the Internet? Do you believe that medical surgeons should be legally obliged to publish their successes and failures on the Internet? In some places, advertising by lawyers and medical practitioners is prohibited and in other places such advertising is allowed. What do you believe underlies the different public policies toward prohibiting or allowing advertising by lawyers and medical practitioners?
13. Investigate where in the world slavery (and therefore a market in people) exists. Investigate also in which countries girls are systematically denied schooling relative to boys. Crossette (2000) described practices against girls that cause lifelong disabilities. Should paternalism extend to people in other societies? What is the basis for a position of moral relativism? Are you a moral relativist?
14. Set out your views on the different preferences of the mother and daughter regarding reading of the book that the mother feels is pornographic and that the daughter feels will expand her mother's horizons. At which age of the daughter could you accept the daughter's making her own decision about the book? How is public policy with regard to censorship involved in this example? How is Pareto efficiency involved?
15. Set out your views on the issues in the trial of Charles Bradlaugh and Annie Besant. What are your views on Charles Darwin's position in the trial?

6. Voting

6.1 The median voter and majority voting

1. What is the Condorcet jury theorem? How does the theorem provide a foundation for democratic decision-making processes?
2. If choice by the median voter cannot ensure efficiency in public-spending decisions, why is majority voting used rather than a consensus voting rule, which does ensure that an accepted proposal is Pareto-improving? What is the justification for majority voting as a collective decision-making rule? What is the intuitive explanation for May's theorem?
3. Why are single-peaked preferences important in the determination of outcomes of majority voting? Why is there often so much attention given to determining who will be the chairperson of a meeting and thereby will be able to choose the order of voting?
4. Why can majority voting through determination of the Condorcet winner result in choice of public finance for inefficient projects (for which $W = B - C < 0$)?
5. Markets for votes ensure that outcomes are always Pareto-improving because, as proposed by the Coase theorem, payments can take place to ensure that all efficiency gains are realized. Do you agree that markets for votes should nonetheless be illegal, even if the markets would result in efficient choice for public finance?
6. Even if markets for votes were allowed, information about net benefits from voting outcomes can be expected to be private, so the market for payment for votes would be subject to asymmetric information. How would this affect a market for votes, if a market for votes were allowed?
7. Does majority voting based on logrolling or vote trading (rather than sale of votes for money) ensure efficient public finance? Why are majority voting logrolling coalitions intrinsically unstable when money payments are allowed?
8. When a majority-voting logrolling coalition chooses public finance for inefficient projects that imposes costs on a constituency of voters, should the disadvantaged voters be permitted to pay the members of the majority coalition not to vote to provide public finance for the inefficient projects? Are such payments extortion?
9. More generally, when logrolling takes place and monetary payments are allowed, what are the impediments to efficient outcomes through all-inconclusive coalitions?
10. Is instability of voting coalitions necessarily undesirable?
11. What is the "tyranny of the majority"? Is it an exaggeration to use the term *tyranny* in the context of majority voting? That is, is there a difference between the tyranny of a dictator who imposes his will on people (why have dictators usually been men?) and the tyranny of a majority that imposes its will on a minority?
12. Does a group of voters who are systematically disadvantaged by the tyranny of the majority have the "natural right" to secede from the collective-decision-making body? What is meant by "natural right" in this context? The U.S. Civil War was a case of successfully resisted secession in which the issue was slavery, but also there was disagreement on whether international trade policy should be free trade or protectionist (we elaborate in chapter 10). Is your view of the attempt at secession by the South influenced by whether the issue was slavery or free trade? Investigate why slavery was abolished in other locations without civil war. In 1933, voters in the Australian state of Western Australia voted with a two-thirds majority to secede from the federal government Commonwealth of Australia, but the secession was

disallowed as unconstitutional. The province of Québec has also voted on the issue of secession from Canada. In Italy, a political party based in the north has had as its policy platform succession from the rest of Italy to create a new state of Padania. Investigate whether issues of public finance were involved in these cases. In Switzerland, the new canton (or regional government jurisdiction) of Jura was created in 1979; investigate the reason for secession and whether secession to create the new canton was resisted.

13. How can the tyranny of the majority be prevented when group decisions are made under the payoffs of the prisoners' dilemma? In a federal system of government, why would we expect checks and balances to be more prominent at high levels of government?
14. Does locational choice in a fiscal-federal system ameliorate or solve the problems of majority voting? How is solving the problem of the tyranny of the majority related to achieving efficient spending on public goods?
15. In 1999 Australian voters were asked whether they supported retaining the queen of England as head of state or change to become a republic with no ties to the British crown (see Davidson, Fry, and Jarvis, 2006). Although public opinion polls indicated majority support for a republic, the majority in the actual vote favored retaining the status quo. Can you conjecture why the opinion polls gave different results from the actual outcome? Why might expressive behavior be involved – in the answers given in the opinion polls or in the actual vote? Investigate the 2001 referendum in the U.S. state of Mississippi on retaining the state flag: Why was voting in the referendum expressive (see Karahan and Shughart, 2004)?

6.2 Political competition

1. With the availability of information technology that allows individual voters to express their opinions on different questions at low cost, do you believe that representative democracy should be replaced by direct democracy? Is your answer influenced by Ostrogorski's paradox? There is evidence that people feel happier under direct democracy. Yet, whether under direct or representative democracy, people would be rationally aware that the likelihood of their single vote being decisive is negligible. When then do they feel happier under direct democracy?
2. When political competition takes place between two candidates on a single policy issue (such as public spending on a public good), the prediction is that the two candidates converge to the policy position of the median voter. Have you observed convergence that makes political candidates barely distinguishable from one other on the major issues of an election? What do we infer from people bothering to vote after policy convergence has taken place?
3. When there are primary elections, how are policy positions of political candidates predicted to change between the positions taken in the primary elections and the general election? Have you observed such change?
4. Before a U.S. presidential election, voters who were interviewed indicated that they intended to vote for one of the candidates but nonetheless expressed agreement with the policy positions of the opposing candidate, when the views of the opposing candidate were deceptively presented to them as the views of the candidate whom they supported. Why does rational ignorance about candidates' policy positions not deter voters from deciding to vote?
5. When voters vote based on utilities personally derived from candidates' policy positions and there is a single issue, and two political candidates perceive that a

third candidate intends to enter the political contest, can the two candidates take policy positions that block the entry of the third candidate, because the third candidate is assured of electoral defeat if he or she enters the political contest.
6. In the case of two candidates and two policy issues, the theory predicts instability of policy pronouncements. Yet, substantial stability appears to be observed. What are reasons for the observed stability?
7. When there is a single issue or whether there are two issues, what is the relationship between expressive voting and abstention? How does the relationship depend on whether voters vote expressively based on policy positions or attributes of candidates?
8. What are the advantages and disadvantages of proportional representation compared to single-constituency seats?
9. In light of the attributes of voting systems, do you favor the voting system that is used where you vote? Or is there an alternative system of voting that you would like to see used? What are your views on approval voting?
10. Normative conclusions about efficiency and social justice suggest that personal decisions made in markets are preferable to collective decisions made through majority voting. Nonetheless, there are decisions that necessarily need to be made collectively. What are the requisites of socially desirable democratic systems of collective choice?

6.3 Voting on income redistribution

1. Voting on public spending on public goods can result in Pareto improvement but not voting on public spending on private goods. Why does voting nevertheless take place on public financing of private goods? Describe the conclusion about majority voting and public finance that follows from the example of voting on maintenance of the roads. Often, voters who like opera are able to pass proposals that provide public finance for subsidies to opera companies and voters who like football are able to pass proposals that provide public finance for subsidies for the local football field and the team. Why is the price of opera or football tickets not simply increased to establish a self-financing user price?
2. Political candidates may campaign on a slogan of "spreading the wealth" but, if elected, in general do not engage in extensive redistribution of income through high taxation. Why does the extensive redistribution not take place?
3. Societies in which people believe that high personal incomes are the consequence of luck are more inclined to have high taxation and extensive redistribution than societies in which the belief is that high personal incomes are due to personal effort and initiative. Why might different societies take these different views?
4. Societies in which a majority of voters believes in the natural right of possession do not vote for extensive redistribution. Why might people in a society define social justice as the natural right of possession? Is your answer related to the answer to the previous question?
5. Voters are disinclined to vote for extensive redistribution if they believe that they may have above-average income in the future, even if presently their incomes are below-average. What are the influences that can lead people with present below-average incomes to believe that voting for high taxation and extensive redistribution is against their future interests?
6. The franchise or who is permitted to vote affects redistribution through voting. Why historically did voting not begin with the principle of one person, one vote?

7. It has been proposed that when voting takes place to redistribute income, only those people whose taxes finance income transfers and not beneficiaries of the transfers should have the right to vote (see Mueller, 2003). Do you have reservations about allowing beneficiaries of income transfers to vote on income redistribution?
8. Evidence from voting outcomes in capital cities and surrounding suburbs where large numbers of government bureaucrats live indicates consistent voter support for a political party that favors high taxation and public spending. Do you believe that it is justified to separate issues of public finance from other issues and to not allow government employees to vote on fiscal issues that include the taxes that finance their salaries?
9. Why do you believe that women were, in general, given the right to vote after men were already entitled to vote? Why do you suppose that in the United States western states were the first to extend the franchise to women?
10. Evidence shows that income redistribution through taxation and public spending increased after the franchise was extended to women. Why do you believe this was the case?
11. Summarize the explanations for why people vote and indicate the consequences for income redistribution.
12. How would a majority-voting equilibrium on income distribution be established? What is the similarity to determination of the majority-voting equilibrium for public spending on public goods? Evidence reveals that the median voter in high-income democracies does not benefit from redistribution of income. Why would we not expect the median voter in a high-income democracy to vote self-interestedly for personal benefit from income distribution?
13. What are the incentives for voting coalitions composed of the ends of the income distribution against the middle? Could such coalitions reflect expressive voting?
14. What is Director's law? Why might we predict Director's law, even though the middle class or the median voter does not benefit from redistribution of income?
15. What is your general conclusion about the comparison between personal decisions made in markets and collective decisions made through majority voting?

7. Social Justice

7.1 Social justice and insurance

1. Can you judge how risk averse you are? How much would you pay to avoid a fair gamble of winning or losing $10, or $100, or $10,000? In figure 7.1, how is risk aversion reflected in the difference between certainty-equivalent income and the expected value of income obtained from the fair gamble? In chapter 1, we concluded that outcomes of competitive markets for goods and services were efficient but not necessarily socially just. What are the conditions under which the claim is be made that competitive insurance markets result in both efficiency and social justice?
2. Identical utility functions and symmetric social welfare functions were proposed as necessary beginnings for an investigation of social justice achieved through social insurance. Why is this so?

3. In which ways are Bentham and Rawls limiting cases of a social welfare function and social insurance contract?
4. How does the Laffer curve affect social insurance through Bentham and Rawls?
5. Why is Bentham the rational choice for a social welfare function? What is the meaning of "rational" in this case? Why might a social welfare function that departs from Bentham nonetheless be chosen? Why, in particular, might Rawls be chosen? Can you infer whether the social insurance contract in your society is closer to that of Bentham or Rawls?
6. Whichever social welfare function is chosen, individual utility is indicated by the same common-to-all utility function expressing personal risk aversion. Distinguish between personal risk aversion as expressed in the utility function and the aversion to inequality expressed in choice of a social welfare function.
7. How does presence or absence of a work ethic affect choice of the social welfare function behind the veil of ignorance? If you had to speculate on why a work ethic is more predominant in some countries' populations than others, are there possible answers that you might propose?
8. Is the choice of Rawls expressive? Is the choice of Bentham expressive?
9. In considering income redistribution, we have limited governments to taxation as the source of revenue and used the Laffer curve as a constraint on redistribution. Although payment of taxes is compulsory, why are taxes as a source of government revenue consistent with a free society? How might the Bentham sum of utilities be maximized if there are no constraints on what people can do?
10. What is adverse selection? How does adverse selection undermine voluntary insurance? Explain how adverse selection and a time-inconsistency problem underlie a case for governments enforcing compulsory participation in social insurance.

7.2 Moral hazard

1. After the social insurance contract has been chosen and people emerge from behind the veil of ignorance, how does the problem of moral hazard arise? What change in the nature of information, compared to absence of information behind the veil of ignorance, underlies moral hazard? How does effort associated with moral hazard differ from effort associated with the leaky bucket of redistribution?
2. When insurance is voluntary and everyone in the population is susceptible to moral hazard, why does the Nash equilibrium resemble the circumstances of the public-good free-rider problem – and how do the circumstances differ?
3. When only some people in a population have a work ethic, what is the outcome of choice of effort at self-reliance? Given the outcome, why can we expect adverse selection to be present to impede voluntary insurance?
4. Beginning from a society where a work ethic is the social norm, how might a heterogeneous society arise? Do you expect successful persisting welfare states necessarily to be homogeneous closed societies – homogeneous in that the society is like an extended family and closed in that people from outside the community cannot ask for income transfers?
5. We identified two distinct adverse-selection problems. What is the difference between the adverse-selection problem that arises when people know whether they have exogenously experienced good or bad luck and when personal outcomes depend on both luck and the decision whether to exert effort to be self-reliant? Are conclusions on whether government is justified in enforcing compulsory social insurance because of adverse selection the same in both cases?

6. How is adverse selection involved when immigrants choose to locate in a welfare state? Is there adverse selection when people leave a welfare state? Read Nannestad (2004) and set out your views on the dilemma of helping people in need from other countries through immigration.
7. Someone tells you that it was predetermined that after emerging from behind a veil of ignorance, some people would have a work ethic whereas others would be subject to moral hazard. This person also tells you that he, by fate, does not have a work ethic. Would you accept that having or not having a work ethic is a consequence of fate that is included in being lucky or unlucky as determined behind a veil of ignorance? Would you accept the argument that the social welfare function chosen behind the veil of ignorance should take into account, therefore, that some people will not have a work ethic – through no fault of their own because this was determined by fate?
8. How does incomplete insurance solve the moral-hazard problem? If Bentham were the social welfare function chosen behind the veil of ignorance, how do we reconcile the need for incomplete insurance under two different circumstances of information? What are the reasons in each case for incomplete insurance?
9. What are type-1 and type-2 errors associated with incomplete insurance directed at moral hazard? What is your position on the claim that luck and effort are not separate, independent effects on outcomes in life but rather that people who do not fare well in life are necessarily victims who should be helped? How does this claim affect willingness to recognize existence of type-1 and type-2 errors?
10. In your society, is moral hazard is a problem when people are provided with income transfers through social insurance? Do overly generous income transfers create moral hazard?

7.3 Social justice without government

1. Explain how altruism expressed in interdependent utilities gives rise to a prisoners' dilemma of private charity that requires resolution by government.
2. In circumstances where people obtain utility from voting in favor of income transfers but lose utility if actually required to make the transfers, why is it beneficial to be able to credibly commit to vote in favor of income transfers? Are there means of making such a credible commitment? If one voter declares the intention of voting in favor of income transfers, is this "cheap talk"? How do outcomes of voting differ between cases in which there are two voters, and in which there are many voters?
3. We observe much private charitable activity. What are the reasons that can explain private charity? Do you expect it to matter whether the giving of private charity is visible to others? Is "pleasure from giving" a more accurate description of how people commonly feel about helping others than the payoffs expressed in the prisoners' dilemma of interdependent utilities (where people feel better if unfortunate people are helped but prefer that others give)? Do experiments with the dictatorship game suggest the presence of substantial "pleasure from giving"? Students are, in general, the subjects in dictatorship-game experiments – and students have often not begun earning incomes. Do you believe that this affects behavior in dictatorship games?
4. Why might tax-financed welfare transfers reduce private charity? Would you give money to people who declare that they have no income, or would you direct them to social workers who can help them to obtain benefits through publicly financed

assistance programs? When programs of publicly financed assistance are available, why might a person still give money to a stranger? Consider the following circumstances: you visit a foreign country and see children of school age selling chewing gum at a time of day when they would be expected to be in school. Would you feel sorry for the children and buy gum from them? Is the behavior of someone who buys gum expressive?

5. In the Nash equilibrium of the game between the charitable person and the recipient who does not like to work, why does the charitable person wish to delegate the income transfers to a government bureaucracy? Does the bureaucratic principal–agent problem inhibit charitable transfers when people experience utility from giving?
6. How, if at all, do ultimatum and dictatorship games allow a judgment of whether societies can rely on voluntary charity to redistribute income? In ultimatum and dictatorship games, what proportion of $10 would you offer the other person? What proportion of $1,000 would you offer? What is the minimum offer that you would accept in the ultimatum game for the above two sums of money given to the donor? Describe the considerations that enter into your decision.
7. In the dictatorship game, people in one society may make generous divisions of the money, whereas in a second society, people choose to give nothing. In the ultimatum game, the people in the first society do not change their behavior but the people in the second society now make generous offers. What can we infer about conceptions of fairness and attitudes toward luck and effort as determinants of personal outcomes in the two societies?
8. Summarize and give your views about gender differences in outcomes of the dictatorship game. Gender differences in the ultimatum game appear to be more ambiguous. Is the ambiguity consistent with your expectations?
9. How does behavior in ultimatum and dictatorship games differ when individuals openly take part in discussions on how much to give collectively compared to personal anonymous decisions? Are you surprised by the difference in behavior? Are you surprised by the differences in amounts given when donors have "earned" the money that they can choose to divide? What do your answers imply about human nature?
10. Economic mobility requires educational opportunities and meritocracy in the job market (so that jobs are allocated not according to personal and family connections but rather according to individual merit). When economic mobility is low because of absence of either requisite, can public policy increase economic mobility?
11. When assortative mating takes place, the abilities or traits of the man and woman are correlated. Lam and Schoen (1993) found that in Brazil, incomes of men were more closely correlated with incomes of their wife's father than with incomes of their own father. In the United States, incomes of men are more highly correlated with incomes of their own father than their wife's father. What do you conclude about differences in economic mobility between the two countries? How can men systematically choose women with a father who has a higher income than their own father? Or is it perhaps not the men who are doing the choosing?
12. Do you perceive much economic mobility, expressed in the backgrounds of fellow students? In a class, what proportion of students are the first in their families to attend university or college?
13. Would you favor a global compulsory social insurance program that includes everyone in the world no matter where they were born or live? Explain your reasons.
14. In what sense do international agencies that provide aid as if there were a global social insurance contract confront a moral-hazard problem when the money is

given to governments in low-income countries to redistribute to the poor? How do institutions in different countries affect the feasibility of an effective global social insurance contract? What is the "hostage problem"? How does the hostage problem deter effective global social insurance?

15. Interdependent utilities are a way of formally expressing the idea of altruism – that is, that people care about the well-being of others. Yet, people appear to care unequally about the well-being of others. People make different charitable contributions to help the poor in their own region or country than the poor in faraway countries. Do you believe that these differences reflect empathy based on donors viewing themselves as having been behind a veil of ignorance with people in their local communities or countries? Conversely, why do people sometimes give money to help poor people in poor countries but not poor people in their own country?
16. People who donate to help the poor in poor countries do not always follow up their donations with requests for details on how their money helped the poor, or indeed ever reached the poor. Why do all donors not seek this information?
17. Why have donor agencies such as the World Bank continued to provide aid to governments in poor countries despite the evidence that the aid is ineffective in helping the poor?

Supplement S7A: Measurement of income inequality

1. How does the Gini coefficient measure inequality? We can compare two societies, one with a precisely equal distribution of income, and the other with an unequal distribution of income that Pareto dominates the equal incomes. The first society consists of five people who have incomes of 1,000 each, and the second society consists of five people with incomes of 1,200, 1,500, 2,000, 5,000, and 10,000. Is there merit in the "better" Gini coefficient of the first society?
2. How is the Atkinson measure of inequality related to the outcome of maximization of a symmetric social welfare function with no leaky bucket of redistribution? What would happen to the Atkinson measure if the measure were to acknowledge that seeking equality is subject to a leaky bucket?

Supplement S7B: An impossibility theorem for social aggregation

1. What does the Arrow "impossibility theorem" show to be impossible?
2. Explain why cardinal utility resolves the problem. Read Ng (1997) and present an evaluation of his case for cardinal utility.

8. Entitlements

8.1 The attributes and consequences of entitlements

1. When people are given entitlements as income, they can proceed to maximize utility by spending the income as they wish. Why, then, are entitlements often provided in-kind?

2. Investigate the entitlements that governments provide in the place where you live. Which entitlements are targeted and which are intended to be universal? Which are in-kind?
3. What are the social benefits and costs of using vouchers to deliver in-kind entitlements? Why might resistance to vouchers be expected and from whom?
4. Universal entitlements such as schooling for children are intended to achieve ex-ante equality or equality of opportunity. Why do entitlements to education in government schools affect households differently and impose more costs on some households than others, when compared to private decisions in markets without the entitlements and the accompanying taxes?
5. Do you believe that equal educational opportunities should be enforced through government schools or that the education that children receive should be allowed to vary with parents' income and willingness to spend on educating children? What are the consequences when entitlements can be rejected for market alternatives? Equality of opportunity would require illegalizing markets that facilitate personal spending on schooling on education: Should that be done, or can that be done?
6. Should households that reject entitlements for market alternatives receive tax credits as compensation for paying taxes but not benefiting from tax-financed entitlements? What are your views on vouchers as a means of avoiding double payment by detaching public finance for schooling from the need to attend government schools?
7. How do problems of adverse selection arise when government and private schools coexist? Can public policy address the problems of adverse selection?
8. How can it be determined whether persisting differences in market incomes of members of identifiable groups are the consequence of labor-market discrimination or failures of ex-ante equality? Can you propose an explanation for why, corrected for educational attainment, African-American men in the United States earn less than white men but African-American women earn higher wages than white women? Could the answer be discrimination?
9. What do you believe underlies the gender differences revealed in the different propensities to take advantage of educational opportunities? Do you believe that hyperbolic discounting is involved, with associated behavior of immediate gratification and procrastination? If so, why are men hyperbolic discounters and not women, or more so than women?
10. What are the future consequences for society – or for a group in society – if women are overall better educated than men? What happens to marriage and to fertility? Women have tended disproportionately to support political parties that favor high taxes and extensive income redistribution. Are the gender-based voting tendencies of the past expected to change?
11. Can public policy offer solutions if ex-ante equality – and therefore also ex-post equality – is hindered by self-fulfilling expectations based on personal identity or is impeded by the stereotyping of others?
12. Is choosing a jurisdiction according to entitlements of social insurance identical in consequences to locational choice of public goods? Outline the consequences for efficiency and social justice of locational choice of entitlements. Recall the zoning restrictions of supplement S3B: How does zoning affect prospects for ex-ante equality through locational choice? What are the consequences for public policy?
13. The beneficiaries of selective entitlements to higher education financed by public spending tend to be disproportionately students from middle-class households and also women more so than men. Are changes in public policy called for because of

the identity of the beneficiaries? What is the relevance of Director's law to your answer?

14. Do full, free, tax-financed benefits necessarily reach intended beneficiaries when governments specify entitlements but require employers to pay for entitlements of employees – for example, in the form of health insurance and maternity benefits? What is the relevance for your answer of the distinction between effective and legal tax incidence? What is the relevance of fiscal illusion?
15. Public housing that concentrates low-income beneficiaries in the one location is often an unsuccessful social policy. Why do you believe that this is so? Is there an alternative public policy to provide entitlements to housing that you would recommend? Should governments provide in-kind entitlements to housing?
16. What would you expect would be the consequences if the government were to announce an entitlement to a job for everyone?
17. How do adverse selection and moral hazard affect a student-loan program? How would you propose ideally to provide equal opportunity in higher education? Is the ideal means of financing higher education an income-contingent loan? Or would you propose free tax-financed higher education through scholarships assigned according to individual scholastic merit? How could you compensate – if at all – for absence of equal opportunity, as indicated by evidence indicating substantial consequences throughout later life of the quality of preschool opportunities? What are your views on "affirmative action" as a compensation for failure of ex-ante equality? Should children from immigrant families benefit from preferential college admission on the grounds that they may speak a foreign language at home, which may limit their skills of expression?
18. Because of the objective of equal opportunity, should public policy provide additional resources for scholastically superior children? That is, does equal opportunity include the opportunity for children to use their abilities to the full? Should public policy make additional resources available to children with learning problems? Is your answer to the latter two questions the same? Indicate why your answers are the same or differ?
19. An explanation for the phenomenon of public finance for higher education (proposed by Garatt and Marshall, 1994) is that there is a social contract, as if decided behind a veil of ignorance, based on the principles that (1) a society cannot afford or does not require everyone to have a college education, and (2) a lottery will determine who will benefit from a publicly financed or subsidized college education. According to this theory, people with the required abilities "win the lottery" and benefit from the free publicly financed higher education. How is this explanation for public finance for higher education related to the circumstances of the water in the desert? Evaluate this proposed normative explanation for why governments subsidize higher education against the background of the evidence supporting Director's law and evidence showing that low-income households are under-represented in higher education.
20. What is a meritocracy? What is the relationship between meritocracy and equality of opportunity (or ex-ante equality)? What is the relationship between meritocracy and economic or social mobility? If while visiting a foreign country someone accompanying you required medical treatment, what would you do if you observed that the country were not a meritocracy?
21. Targeted entitlements differ from intended universal entitlements because governments prefer that the targeted entitlements not be used. Give examples of such targeted entitlements. What is the relationship between incentives and the preference that targeted entitlements be rejected? If at one time it was possible to rely

on stigma, how should public policy change – if at all – when social norms change and stigma is no longer an impediment to accepting entitlements?

22. Summarize the different explanations for involuntary unemployment. If you were asked to design an unemployment insurance program, what attributes would the program have? Are the attributes that you propose influenced by the explanation for unemployment?
23. Dennis Snower (1994) proposed allowing people to convert their unemployment benefits to vouchers for wage subsidies that they can offer employers. Evaluate the proposal.
24. Edmund Phelps (1994) made a case for wage subsidies as alternatives to welfare payments. Evaluate his public-policy proposal. How do employer incentives affect the feasibility of a wage subsidy?
25. Brinig and Buckley (1999) concluded that entitlements changed social norms regarding single motherhood. Should a society be concerned if targeted entitlements change incentives of low-income people, whereas personal decisions of higher income people who are ineligible for entitlements are not affected?
26. Is a public policy of limitations on entitlements to welfare payments for any one person over the course of a lifetime desirable? Is the policy feasible; that is, can limitations on time on welfare be credibly imposed?
27. What are the requisites of successful welfare reform? Why do governments continue sometimes without welfare reform when it is evident that incentives of welfare policies are inappropriate for an efficiently functioning society?
28. Illegal immigrants generally are productive and do not pay taxes and are not eligible for the entitlements of the social insurance contract. Should children of illegal immigrants have free entitlements to tax-financed education? Should children of illegal immigrants have free entitlements for publicly financed immunization programs? If entitlements are provided to illegal immigrants or their children, how are incentives affected for illegal immigration? Is there a social dilemma regarding public policy?

8.2 The entitlement to income during old age

1. In a hunter–gatherer society, the old who can no longer fend for themselves can only stay alive through food and shelter provided by the young who gather food and hunt. A social contract allows intergenerational transfers so that the old in every generation can continue living. Why are the intergenerational transfers Pareto-improving? Why is a demonstration effect not a rational basis for the intergenerational transfers from the young to the old? If not a demonstration effect, what is the principle that allows the intergenerational transfers to be sustained? Why are the intergenerational transfers in a hunter–gatherer society precisely like a pay-as-you-go (unfunded) social security or pension scheme?
2. What are the sources of change in the dependency ratio? What are your views of a public policy of encouraging immigration as a means of solving problems associated with the dependency ratio? What other solutions would you propose to resolve problems of nonviability of an intergenerational transfer scheme that stem from changes in the dependency ratio?
3. What implications follow for intergenerational transfers from the fact that some people have more children than others, or that some people have children when others have none? Is there a free-riding problem? Is the existence of a government-implemented pay-as-you-go compulsory scheme of intergenerational transfers itself a reason why people choose to have fewer children?

4. Why have intergenerational transfers in which initial generations assign to themselves high retirement entitlements been compared to a Ponzi scheme?
5. How does generational accounting reveal whether a pay-as-you-go scheme is actuarially bankrupt? How viable are intergenerational transfers in your country? Why is there an incentive for political decision makers to shift a solution to a problem of nonsustainable intergenerational transfers to future decision makers? Are the political decision makers who defer solutions hyperbolic discounters?
6. Rather than receive transfers through a pay-as-you-go intergenerational scheme, people could save for their old age by buying government bonds. How does a bond market differ from a pay-as-you-go intergenerational transfer scheme? Does a bond market solve demographic problems? Could the interest rate on bonds be negative?
7. When a retirement scheme is funded (the money people save is used to invest in financial or real assets), people can make their own personal voluntary decisions about investments to provide for their old age. The government can also make the investments compulsory and compel people to pool their savings through mandatory mutual funds. Should government make savings for old age compulsory? Should the government insist on pooling?
8. When taxes are used to finance intergenerational income transfers, there is an excess burden of taxation, just as when taxes finance income redistribution within a generation. Elimination of the excess burden of taxation is the source of an efficiency gain when a change occurs from a pay-as-you-go scheme to an asset-backed scheme. Does this efficiency gain allow Pareto improvement for the working and retired generations?
9. Explain how bond financing can alleviate problems of social injustice when a decision is made to change from an unfunded (not-asset-backed) pay-as-you-go scheme to a funded (asset-backed) scheme? What are the problems of social injustice?
10. What should be the response of government when young generations complain that continued compulsory participation in compulsory pay-as-you-go social security yields inferior returns to investment in bonds or the stock market? If the question of whether to change from a pay-as-you-go scheme to a funded scheme is put before voters and the decision is made by majority voting, what do you expect the outcome to be? How are the policy preferences of the median voter influenced by changes in the dependency ratio?
11. Pay-as-you-go intergenerational transfers were introduced against the background of the Great Depression: Why was this so? Without the considerations introduced by the Great Depression, would governments have chosen compulsory savings for retirement in a funded asset-backed scheme rather than intergenerational transfers? Is there a role for public policy when circumstances similar to the Great Depression recur and, due to macroeconomic problems people near retirement find the value of the assets in their pension funds substantially reduced?
12. Read Congleton (2006) and provide your impressions of the effectiveness of public policy in the case described.

8.3 The entitlement to health care and health Insurance

1. What are the special characteristics of personal demand for health care? How do these characteristics influence markets for health care (as contrasted with markets for health insurance)? How do the special characteristics of health care make cost containment difficult? Evidence shows that increased spending on health care

does not necessarily ensure improved health care. Why do you believe that this is so?

2. How do the reasons for problems with private-insurance markets (adverse selection, moral hazard, inability to verify the circumstances against which insurance is sought) affect the private market for health insurance? How does the mapping of the human genome affect health insurance?
3. What are the advantages and disadvantages of "health-management organizations" compared to health-care providers and health-insurance companies as separate providers?
4. From whom would you expect opposition to a compulsory universal insurance scheme based on private insurance and private health care? If such a scheme were introduced, would you expect the scheme to solve problems of cost escalation?
5. Some countries have systems of socialized medicine that provide equal access to health care. The medical personnel are employees of government. Evaluate this solution for health care. How does socialized medicine differ in terms of consequences from compulsory, universal, privately provided, health insurance?
6. In a country that provides socialized medical care, the government is the primary employer of medical practitioners and nursing staff, and salaries are generally lower than when health care is provided through private markets. The costs of medical school in a country with socialized medicine also tend to be lower to match the lower salaries available locally after graduation. What do you expect to be the consequence when emigration can freely take place?
7. What do you believe is the ideal means of providing health insurance and health care?
8. On the scale of complete reliance on private markets and complete government control, how are personal health care and health insurance provided where you live or study? Do you believe that there should be more government involvement or less? Indicate the changes that you would propose.

9. Choice of Taxation

9.1 Optimal taxation

1. Explain the Ramsey rule for efficient taxation, how the rule is derived, and the logic underlying the rule. What is the role of the Ramsey rule in the determination of efficient public spending on public goods – and in the determination of efficient tax-financed income redistribution subject to the leaky bucket? Would you propose applying the Ramsey rule to choice of income-tax rates – or to choice of rates of indirect taxes for different goods? Would you agree to use of the Ramsey rule to determine income-tax rates based on gender and family circumstances? Explain why the Ramsey rule might be interpreted as requiring the taxation of ability or of "beauty": Would following the implications of this interpretation of the Ramsey rule be socially desirable?
2. Would a leviathan government have use for the Ramsey rule?
3. How is progressive, regressive, and proportional taxation defined? Is an indirect tax or a user price necessarily regressive?
4. Can regressive personal income taxes be desirable? Why would you envisage difficulty of candidates for political office making a case for a policy of regressive

taxes, even if it were demonstrated that there can be advantages of regressive taxes for income-transfer recipients because of effects on work incentives of taxpayers? Why might voters regard a proposal for regressive income taxation as disqualifying a political candidate as deserving of their political support?

5. What is the equal-sacrifice principle of socially just taxation? What are your views on the equal-sacrifice principle? Do you agree with the judgment of John Stuart Mill that equitable taxation requires equal sacrifice from paying taxes for all taxpayers? How is an equal-sacrifice tax schedule derived? Why does the derivation require choice of a common utility function for taxpayers? Why do governments not announce that they are hiring economists to seek to identify an income-tax schedule that will result in equal sacrifice from payment of taxes?
6. If a common utility function with constant relative risk aversion is chosen for taxpayers, how does the value of the parameter expressing risk aversion determine whether the equal-sacrifice income-tax schedule is progressive, proportional, or regressive? If indications are that relative risk aversion is close to one, what are the implications for the equal-sacrifice income-tax schedule?
7. With the equal-sacrifice principle of socially just taxation not necessarily implying progressive taxes and with progressive tax schedules not necessarily implying equal sacrifice from taxation, why are income-tax schedules nevertheless generally progressive?
8. Describe the optimal linear income tax. Which attribute of the linear income tax makes the tax progressive? What is the relationship between the policy variables of the linear tax system, and what are the trade-offs that enter into choice of the parameters? If the linear income tax is efficient and socially just (the optimal tax is obtained by maximizing a social welfare function), why do governments generally use more complex income taxes than the linear income tax?
9. The recommendations about the optimal structure of an income-tax schedule that follow from the general Mirrlees tax problem are inconclusive regarding whether taxation should be progressive or regressive: Why is this so? What was Mirrlees seeking or what were his expectations (or hopes) when he formulated the general optimal income-tax problem?
10. The solution to the general Mirrlees optimal income tax problem offers definitive recommendations of zero marginal tax rates at the beginning and at the end of the income distribution. Explain the reasons for these recommendations.
11. Does the structure of an income-tax schedule affect social mobility?
12. Why are income-tax structures often so inordinately complex such that specialized knowledge and training is required to understand the tax code? Explain the phenomenon of cycles of tax reform.
13. Investigate the structure of the personal income tax in the place where you live – including if applicable income taxes levied at lower levels of government than the federal government. If it were up to you, would you change the existing minimum income at which taxes become payable? Would you change the structure of marginal tax rates? What are the main tax deductions and tax exemptions in the principal personal income tax? In your view, are all the deductions and exemptions justified? What are the deductions and exemptions subsidizing? Would you add deductions or exemptions that are not present? Does the tax code subsidize or penalize couples filing together – or neither?
14. Does the personal income-tax structure tend to change with electoral results that favor one political party over another? Do the constituencies of the main political parties have different views of the ideal personal income-tax structure?
15. Investigate the proportion of the population that pays income taxes, and correspondingly the proportion of the population on whom the tax burden falls. Find

information if available on the proportion of income taxes paid by the people with the top one percent, five percent and ten percent of pretax incomes. What implications do you draw from the data about the efficiency and social justice of the personal income tax?

9.2 Capital and other tax bases

1. Would you accept the Ramsey rule as the basis for taxing income from capital at different rates from income earned from labor? If the decision were yours, which form of income would you tax at a higher rate? Does the Ramsey rule support or contradict your preference? How is income from capital (interest and dividends from ownership of stocks and shares, and capital gains) taxed in the place where you live? Are tax rates consistent with the Ramsey rule?
2. How does a home bias in asset portfolios affect taxation indicated by the Ramsey rule?
3. How does a time-inconsistency problem affect taxation of income from capital? What, if anything, can be done to solve the time-inconsistency problem?
4. In your view, is there a justification for a separate tax on corporate profits? Should taxes paid by a firm be tax credits deducted from the personal taxes paid by individual shareholders? What is the rate of taxation on profits of corporations or companies in the place where you live? Is the rate of corporate taxation higher or lower than the highest marginal tax rate on personal income? How does the relationship between the corporate-tax rate and the highest marginal personal income-tax rate affect economic incentives? Use the logic of the distinction between effective and legal tax incidence to offer a prediction about who effectively pays a corporate income tax. Why does your answer depend on whether an industry is competitive?
5. How does a corporate-profits tax affect firms' decisions regarding use of equity and bond financing? Why do firms pay dividends? Do you believe that a tax on capital gains is justified?
6. What are the main differences between direct taxes levied on personal income and on personal spending? Which tax is more justified and on what grounds? If a change were proposed from a personal income tax to a personal expenditure tax, what would be the impediments to implementing the change? Do you believe that the impediments to change explain why governments tax personal income and not personal expenditure? Or are there other consequences of the two tax bases that influence the choice of the tax base for direct taxation?
7. Do you support a wealth tax or a tax on inheritance? Is there an ethical or economic case for such taxes?
8. Lotteries provide tax revenue through voluntary decisions to buy lottery tickets. What are your views on Adam Smith's observations about lotteries? Does taxation through revenue from lotteries tend to be regressive? What is the relationship between use of lotteries for government revenue and the use of lotteries to finance public goods described in supplement S3C?
9. What is the tax base for inflation as a tax? Why, if inflation is to be a tax, does the inflation have to be unanticipated by the public? Why would governments use inflation as a tax?
10. How can financial repression be used as a form of taxation? Why would a government ever wish to raise revenue in this way?
11. If it were possible to determine an optimal income-tax schedule, why might proposals nonetheless be made for additional use of indirect taxes for tax-revenue purposes? Evaluate the case for the additional indirect taxes.

12. Consider the statement: "Because of the different tax bases for taxation, the same personal income is taxed over and over again in different ways when the income is earned, when the income is spent, and also if the income is saved. This is both inefficient and unfair." Do you agree with this statement? Why do different governments use different tax bases to raise revenue rather than simply taxing personal incomes? How would a leviathan government make use of different tax bases?

9.3 Fiscal federalism

1. How does the presence of public goods, externalities, and natural monopoly affect the case for centralized vs. decentralized government? How does insurance affect the case for fiscal federalism?
2. List public goods that governments provide and identify the levels of government that should appropriately levy taxes to finance the public goods according to the benefit principle of taxation. Are the public goods that you have identified, in fact, financed by the level of government that you have identified as appropriate? Why are taxes for financing public goods not necessarily levied at the level of government at which benefits are provided? What is the relationship between the benefit and ability-to-pay principles of taxation and the choice of a fiscal-federal structure of government?
3. Describe the issues that arise regarding entitlements in a fiscal-federal system of government.
4. Who bears the excess burden of taxation when a tax is levied on capital that is mobile between jurisdictions?
5. Why do the issues that arise concerning tax competition depend on whether taxation of income from capital is source-based or residence-based?
6. Is the presence of a prisoners' dilemma in tax competition among governments beneficial or disadvantageous for taxpayers?
7. Why do governments enter into double-tax agreements?
8. In a fiscal-federal system, lower-level governments are spending taxes paid by taxpayers and voters in other jurisdictions. What are the consequences of "spending other people's money" in a fiscal-federal structure of government?
9. What is the "holdup" problem in a fiscal-federal system? Why is the hold-up problem a case of moral hazard?
10. How does adverse selection arise in a fiscal-federal system? Can the adverse-selection problem be solved?
11. "The lower the level of government, the greater the transparency and accountability of government to taxpayers." Evaluate this claim.
12. How are the social losses due to rent seeking affected by a fiscal federal structure of government?
13. What is "yardstick competition"? What is the role of yardstick competition in fiscal federalism? Why is yardstick competition required?
14. "The monopoly power of a leviathan government to tax in its own jurisdiction can be escaped by locational mobility." To what extent, or in what circumstances, is this so?
15. Explain the relationship between majority voting and the common-pool problem for tax revenue in centralized government. How does decentralized government solve the common-pool problem of majority voting? How is the common-pool problem related to the choice between the ability-to-pay and benefit principles of taxation?

16. Provide an overall evaluation of fiscal federalism compared to centralized government in terms of the social objective of efficiency. Make the same comparison in terms of social justice and for the presence and resolution of political and bureaucratic principal–agent problems.

10. The Need for Government

10.1 Growth of government and the need for government

1. Table 10.1 shows little evidence of concern about educating the children of the poor from the time of Adam Smith to the mid-19th century. Table 10.2 shows low social transfers in the earlier 20th century, with little difference among countries; however, there was substantial diversity in social spending by the end of the 20th century. How might the change from uniformity to diversity among countries in social spending be explained?
2. What is Wagner's law? Summarize the arguments that have been proposed to explain Wagner's law. Although all explanations have a contributing role, which of the proposed explanations do you judge to be the most important? Rank the explanations by your view of importance and explain the reasons for your ranking.
3. Outline the benefits of the growth of government since the time of Adam Smith.
4. Tanzi and Schuknecht (2000) make a case that the growth of government in the second half of the 20th century was not socially beneficial. Outline the basis for their case against the background of the data in table 10.3. Could you make a counter case?
5. Summarize the views of Hobbes and Locke on how the nature of people determines the desirable nature of government. Do you sympathize more with the view of Hobbes or Locke as descriptive of the world in which we live? If asked normatively to describe the world as it should be, would your choice between Hobbes and Locke remain the same?
6. Where does majority voting fall in the categorization of the alternative views of government presented by Hobbes and Locke?
7. The case made by Hobbes was that the "encompassing interest" of the leviathan, who would own everything and control everyone, would ensure socially beneficial outcomes. Compare Hobbes' normative case for the leviathan with the maximal-government regimes described in chapter 2.
8. The Laffer curve constrains a leviathan government in the tax revenue that can be collected. What constrains a leviathan government from access to revenue from government borrowing?
9. Is time-distancing of decisions about a constitution an effective solution to constraining growth of government?
10. How is the concept of time-inconsistency relevant to the story of Ulysses and the sirens? What is the relevance of the relationship for the design of constitutions?
11. How is zero-based budgeting a constraint on growth of government? Why do governments not use zero-based budgeting?

10.2 Cooperation, trust, and the need for government

1. Why are cooperation and trust issues that arise when we consider the need for government?
2. Can cooperation emerge without government in repeated interactions of the prisoners' dilemma? What are the limitations on voluntary cooperation in a large society of anonymous people? Evaluate the prospects more generally for voluntary cooperation without government.
3. What are the social benefits of a presumption of trustworthiness among a population?
4. When a population that consists of people who are trusting and trustworthy begins to encounter people in the prisoners' dilemma who behave rationally and opportunistically for personal gain, what do you expect to be the outcome?
5. In the trust game, under conditions of compete anonymity, how much of $100 would you transfer to a recipient when the money is multiplied by 3? What would you do in the trust game if, as a recipient, you received the entire $300? Knowing that the initial sum that could have been transferred was $100, what would you do if you had received only $30? Would your answers change if all above sums of money were multiplied by 10?
6. In the trust game, would your behavior as either the person deciding to transfer $100 or the person deciding whether to return part of the $300 change, depending on whether the other anonymous student was of the opposite or same sex? Can you offer an explanation for different outcomes in the trust game according to gender?
7. In table 10.4, there are two Nash equilibria, one in which people trust one another and another in which neither trusts the other. What is the difference between this game and the prisoners' dilemma in terms of incentives for cooperation? If decisions were made sequentially in table 10.4. and person 1 decided first, what would you expect the outcome to be?
8. How does distrust among groups result in economic segmentation? Why do groups whose members trust one another have advantages in market transactions? What do you expect to be the response of people who are not members of a trusting group?
9. Why is trust also called social capital? How would you propose measuring social capital?
10. How does social capital affect "happiness"? Can public policy (or public finance) change unhappiness due to insufficient social capital?

10.3 Views on the need for government

1. In the final chapter, we began with economic history and ended with observations on the history of economic thought. Beginning with Adam Smith, whose entry into economics was through moral philosophy, the field of investigation called political economy developed in the course of the 19th century and into the 20th century. Then, however, a separation was made that so that efficiency and questions of income distribution or social justice could be depicted as separate issues, with economics defined as a field of investigation that focuses on efficiency. Why was the separation of economics from political economy sought? Why, correspondingly, was separation sought between achievement of the objectives of efficiency and social justice? Why was the lump-sum tax used as the means to implement the

separation between achieving efficiency and social justice, even though, in reality, lump-sum taxes are not used?

2. Our analysis of the issues of public finance and public policy has been based on the taxes that are used by governments. In which respects would our analysis of issues have been simpler if we had pretended that governments use lump-sum taxes?
3. Because lump-sum taxes have no substitution effects, people can be described as not responding to market incentives and as contributing according to ability – and growth of government can be described without the efficiency losses of the excess burden of taxation. Could the artifact of a lump-sum tax reflect a preference for an ideology?
4. When inseparability of questions of efficiency and social justice is acknowledged, the perspective is – as has been the case in this book – that of political economy. Ideology then matters. When we consider the views from the left and right, how much of the difference is due to ideology expressed in the definition of social justice and in priorities placed on achieving the social objectives of efficiency and social justice? How much of the difference is due to different perceptions of the importance of political and bureaucratic principal–agent problems? How much is due to different views of human nature (including whether moral hazard is prevalent)?
5. Adam Smith reconciled human nature and the social benefit of markets. Does human nature nonetheless underlie need for government?

Author Index

Subject Index